BIG TEN FOOTBALL

ALMANAC

VOLUME 1

---

an
Alpine College Conference Book
GORDON M. SAKS
Publisher

ALPINE BOOK COMPANY, INC.

527 Madison Avenue
New York, New York 10022

This annual publication is published by
Alpine Book Company, Inc. New York,
and Prentice-Hall, Inc., Englewood Cliffs, New Jersey
Copyright © by Alpine Book Company, Inc. All rights reserved.
No part of this book may be reproduced
without the written permission of the publisher.
Printed and bound in the United States of America.

ISBN: 0-13-076224-5

―――――――――

This book is dedicated to:

Sylvia Sakoloff, the publisher's mother, who prayed for the successful conclusion of this project, but passed away before seeing it's completion... may she rest in peace...

and

Ray Marquette, a member of the Big Ten Skywriters Hall of Fame, who lent a helping hand in the development of the idea for such an almanac...

―――――――――

Special thanks to:

Frank B. Jones, Alumni Secretary of The Indiana University Alumni Association who relentlessly pursued this publication for four years and helped solve the countless problems which arose before this volume went to press...

The co-authors for this publication are:

Tab Bennett, Sports Information Director, The University of Illinois

Tom Miller, Sports Information Director and **Kit Klingelhoffer,** Assistant Sports Information Director, Indiana University

Bob Denney, The University of Iowa

Will Perry, Sports Information Director, The University of Michigan

Fred Stabley, Sports Information Director, Michigan State University

Tom Greenhoe, Assistant Sports Information Director, The University of Minnesota

Jim Vruggink, Sports Information Director and **Don MacLachlan,** Assistant Sports Information Director, Northwestern University

Marv Homan, Sports Information Director, The Ohio State University

Tom Shupe, Sports Information Director, Purdue University

Jim Mott, Sports Information Director, The University of Wisconsin

Jeff Elliott, Sports Information Director, The Big Ten Conference

This almanac was published with the cooperation of The Big Ten Conference, Wayne Duke, Commissioner of Athletics, and with the support of The Big Ten Alumni Associations.

This book was designed by Ruth Baumann.

TABLE OF CONTENTS

Foreword by Commissioner Wayne Duke	5
Big Ten Historical Information	7
About the Member Universities	11
1978 in Retrospect	31
Illinois	40
Indiana	47
Iowa	54
Michigan	61
Michigan State	68
Minnesota	75
Northwestern	82
Ohio State	89
Purdue	96
Wisconsin	103
Final Official 1978 Complete Team Rosters	110
1978 Schedule	139
1978 Season: Play-by-Play	141
The Bowl Games: Peach-Gator-Rose	428
1979 Outlook	451
Illinois	459
Indiana	465
Iowa	479
Michigan	489
Michigan State	501
Minnesota	510
Northwestern	526
Ohio State	543
Purdue	554
Wisconsin	567
Official 1979 Complete Team Rosters	573
Official Big Ten Statistics	594
1979 Schedule	608

FOREWORD BY *BIG TEN* COMMISSIONER WAYNE DUKE

It's with a great deal of pride and pleasure that I welcome you to the first printing of the *BIG TEN FOOTBALL ALMANAC*. We're pleased to have this publication available to the great football fans throughout the country and especially here in the Midwest, where the support for Big Ten football over the years has been fantastic. Year in and year out Big Ten football draws the largest crowds each Saturday, and by season's end, will have attracted more people and will possess a larger per game average than any other collegiate or professional conference.

There is no question in my mind that the collegiate game is at an all-time peak, not only in fan interest and involvement, but in overall balance as well. I define balance as "competitive equality". It is a leveling off of competition that we have seen in recent years, not only in the Big Ten, but in college athletics across the country.

In the Big Ten last year, Michigan had to defeat an outstanding Purdue team and Ohio State the last two weeks of the season in order to stake a claim of the Conference championship. Even then, they had to share the title with Michigan State, the only team to defeat the Wolverines during the regular season. It was a great four-way race for the Conference championship, and was just another indication of the balance we are finding in the Big Ten.

I feel the Big Ten is certainly competitive with any other conference in the country. There is more competitive equality in the Big Ten now than at any other time in my eight years as commissioner. It's true not only in football, but in basketball and the other sports as well.

I've felt for some time now the foundation for achieving competitive balance lies in legislative equality. By that I mean everybody is operating under the same general set of rules and regulations so that nobody is placed at a disadvantage in the recruiting arena or on the playing field. Of course, adherence and compliance to those rules is equally as important and the Big Ten is committed to this policy. The limiting of athletic grants represents to me one of the most important pieces of athletic legislation ever adopted at the national level, particularly in football. With schools now limited to 30 new grants each year and a maximum of 95 at any one time, it will help assure better balance throughout the country.

In the Big Ten we feel we have reached competitive equality both within the conference and with other conferences. But more importantly, it has been achieved without sacrificing deep-rooted principles of what intercollegiate athletics ought to be all about. That is most gratifying of all.

I truly hope that you'll enjoy this premier edition of the *BIG TEN FOOTBALL ALMANAC*, and that it will provide you with an insight of what to expect for the 1979 season, as well as offering a thorough description of the 1978 season. Big Ten football in 1979 promises to be more exciting, more competitive and more balanced than it's been in the last decade. We will have several of our teams appearing on regional and national television; we stand a good chance of surpassing the all-time national attendance record that we established last year and could have as many as four teams participating in post-season bowl games. I invite you to become part of all the color, glamor and excitement of college football and join us on Saturday afternoons this fall for the Nation's No. 1 spectator sport—Big Ten Football.

Wayne Duke

BIG TEN CONFERENCE

James H. Smart

The Intercollegiate Conference of Faculty Representatives grew out of a meeting of the presidents of seven universities of the Middle West. This meeting, called by President James Smart of Purdue University, was held in Chicago on January 11, 1895, for the purpose of considering the regulation and control of intercollegiate athletics. At that meeting of the presidents, rules covering certain phases of intercollegiate activities were formulated, and an organization for regulation and control of athletic activities, consisting of appointed faculty representatives, one from each institution, was set up. The appointed faculty representatives held their first meeting on February 8, 1896. The minutes of that meeting refer to the "Intercollegiate Conference of Faculty Representatives". It is from that reference that the organization commonly known as the "Western Conference", "Big Ten", or "Intercollegiate Conference" derives its official title. The Conference thus is an association, the primary purpose of which is to insure faculty control and the regulation of intercollegiate athletics as institutional activities, and harmonious intercollegiate relationships among member institutions.

At the time of its organization, the Conference was composed of seven members, as follows:

University of Chicago
University of Illinois
University of Michigan
University of Minnesota
Northwestern University
Purdue University
University of Wisconsin

On December 1, 1899, Indiana University and the State University of Iowa were admitted to membership. The Ohio State University was admitted on April 6, 1912. The University of Michigan, which withdrew from the Conference on January 14, 1908, was, on June 9, 1917, invited to return, and resumed membership on November 20, 1917. The University of Chicago withdrew from the Conference as of June 30, 1946. Michigan State College (now Michigan State University) was admitted to membership May 20, 1949.

A significant step in the regulation of intercollegiate athletics was taken by two special conferences, which, at the call of President Angell of the University of Michigan, met in Chicago on January 19 and 20 and March 9, 1906. As a result of these conferences the Faculty Representatives on March 10, 1906, officially adopted the following rules which were remarkably novel for that time.

1. Eligible players must have met all entrance requirements, completed a full year's work and one year of residence.
2. Graduate students are not eligible, and the competition of an individual student is limited to three years.
3. No freshman intercollegiate competition allowed.
4. No training tables or training quarters permitted.
5. A drastic reduction in football schedules (five games).
6. Coaches to be appointed only by university bodies, in regular ways, and at moderate salaries.

Until 1912 there was no restriction upon the member institutions as to the eligibility of faculty members for appointment as representatives to the Conference. Two institutions, in that year, were represented by men who were devoting their full time to the work in physical education and athletics. At the Conference meeting on April 6, 1912, a recommendation from the Presidents of the Conference members was presented, proposing that the Conference should consist of two representatives from each institution, "one of whom at least should not be connected with the Department of Physical Training". This proposal was defeated by a vote of six to two. By a similar vote, however, it was provided that "the Faculty Representative of each University in the Conference must be a person who receives no pay for any services connected with Athletics or the Department of Physical Culture".

At a special meeting on September 26, 1918, the Conference suspended "its activities as a controlling body", at the same time tendering to the War Department "its services in carrying on athletic activities, both intramural and intercollegiate, in and among its members". It declared its former authority again in effect on December 7, 1918.

Another significant development in the control and management of intercollegiate athletic affairs in the Conference is found in the growth of responsibility of the Directors of Athletics. By 1922, the administration of intercollegiate athletic activities in the member institutions had become vested largely in Directors of

Athletics—men of professional rank devoting their full time to the task. By that time it had become customary for these officers of the member institutions to hold regular meetings, usually at the same time and place as the sessions of the Faculty Representatives. These meetings gave opportunity for better schedule making and for the drawing up of "Agreements" governing the conduct of athletics.

A significant step was taken in 1922 in the creation of the office of Commissioner of Athletics, the incumbent of which was not only "to study athletic problems of the various Western Conference universities and assist in enforcing the eligibility rules which govern Big Ten athletics", but also to conduct "an educational campaign looking toward the development of better sportsmanship, belief in the amateur law, and understanding of the values of competitive athletics". In July of that year, Major John L. Griffith was appointed to the office and served continuously until his death, which occurred on December 7, 1944. Kenneth L. Wilson, formerly Director of Athletics at Northwestern University, served as Commissioner from that date to July 1, 1961, when he retired. William R. Reed, who had been Assistant Commissioner since 1951, became the third Conference Commissioner, and served until his death on May 20, 1971. Wayne Duke became Commissioner on September 1, 1971.

The Big Ten Conference office is located in one of the fastest growing suburbs in the country, Schaumburg, Illinois. Located adjacent to the Woodfield Shopping Center, the largest of its kind in the world, Schaumburg is 25 miles northwest of the downtown Chicago area, and just a quick 15 minutes away from the world's busiest airport, O'Hare International. The office operation became a permanent fixture in Schaumburg in October of 1974, after having been located in the Sheraton-Chicago Hotel since 1962. Prior to that, the Conference office also held residencies in the LaSalle Hotel as well as the Sherman House in the Chicago loop.

Commissioner Wayne Duke and his staff of five men and six women oversee a number of operations essential to the existence of a strong conference. Duke is the chief administrative officer and is responsible for establishing specific Conference policies, systems and procedures, and to put into effect the general Conference policies, systems and procedures established by the Faculty Representatives, Joint Group and Directors of Athletics. He is the principal enforcement officer, serves as an ex officio member of all committees and meets periodically with athletic boards, athletic department staff members and athletes of the member schools. He reports to the Council of Ten, which consists of the chief administrative officer of each member university. Duke is a native of Burlington, Iowa and is a graduate of the University of Iowa.

There are two Assistant Commissioners in the Conference,

John Dewey and Dr. Charles D. Henry. Dewey joined the Conference staff in 1957 to fill the new position of Examiner. His current responsibilities include interpretations of Conference and NCAA rules, compliance and general administrative responsibilities, including the grant-in-aid program. He also oversees student-athlete eligibility, Conference finances and the Inter-Conference Letter of Intent program. Dewey is a native of Joliet, Illinois and received a B.S. degree in Business Administration at Northwestern University.

Henry joined the Big Ten staff in 1974 after serving as head of the Health, Physical Education and Recreation Department at Grambling for 17 years. Henry is the Conference liaison for the various coaching groups in the Conference, oversees the operation of the Big Ten Meets and represents the Big Ten with various related groups such as the Advisory Commission, AIAW (Association of Intercollegiate Athletics for Women) and academic and athletic counselors. Henry, who hails from Conway, Arkansas, was graduated from Philander Smith College (Little Rock) and received his master's and doctoral degrees from the University of Iowa.

Serving in the role as Supervisor of Officials is Herman Rohrig who joined the Big Ten as the Conference's first full-time supervisor of football and basketball officials in 1968. He is in charge of the recruitment of new officials, the assignment of officials and their evaluation in both football and basketball. Rohrig is a native of Lincoln, Nebraska, where he graduated from the University of Nebraska, gaining recognition as an All-Conference halfback during his junior year.

The Conference Service Bureau, which encompasses promotion, marketing, releases and dealings with members of the media, is headed by Director Jeff Elliott and his assistant Mark Rudner. The Service Bureau coordinates all activities for various special projects during the year, i.e. Football Kickoff Luncheon, Skywriter's Tour, Basketball Press Conference and various writer's luncheons. In addition, several Conference publications such as the Records Book, football and basketball previews and recruiting brochures are handled by the Service Bureau. Elliott also serves as the TV Coordinator on the Big Ten basketball Game-of-the-Week with TVS-NBC. Rudner's other specific responsibilities include the selection of All-Academic teams in football, basketball and baseball as well as coverage of the winter and spring non-revenue sports. Elliott joined the Big Ten in 1971 and is a graduate of Michigan State University, while Rudner is a 1978 graduate of Ohio State and has been with the Big Ten since January 1, 1979.

UNIVERSITY OF ILLINOIS

More than a century ago the University of Illinois opened in Urbana-Champaign, and it has been a leader in developing the tradition of education, research and public service characteristic of state universities.

The Urbana-Champaign campus is known around the world. A public university in India is patterned after it. Its findings are applied in the development of new countries in Africa. Its graduates are on every continent and in every country.

But it is in Illinois, whose citizens have built and supported the University and sent their sons and daughters to its campus, that the University has returned the greatest benefits.

U of I graduates are doctors and teachers, engineers and farmers, lawyers and executives, men and women whose leadership and service have benefited their communities, state and nation. The University's research, seeking out new information and its application, has brought better homes and buildings, health and highways, railways and airways, agriculture and industry, government and business, and has affected almost every field of human interest and activity. Through its extension and service activities, the University has brought information to the people, not only in the campus classrooms but in hundreds of conferences and meetings on the campus and off, through correspondence, and through radio and television.

The University opened March 2, 1868, with three faculty members and 77 students. Today the U of I, with a Board of Trustees responsible directly to the people of the state, has three campuses—at Urbana-Champaign, the Medical Center in Chicago, and Chicago Circle. The chief executive officer of the Urbana-Champaign campus is William P. Gerberding, Chancellor.

The University is one of sixty-nine land grant colleges and universities established under provisions of the Land Grant College Act signed by President Abraham Lincoln in 1862. The building in which the University opened was located on the site of present Illinois Field, south of University Avenue on the north end of the campus. The school had five departments. Today the Urbana-Champaign campus has 20 colleges and schools offering undergraduate, professional and graduate work. The University also includes numerous institutes, bureaus, experiment stations, the Office of Continuing Education and Public Service, and other statewide services.

The campus at Urbana-Champaign encompasses 705 acres, with an additional 1,900 acres of agricultural experiment fields in

Champaign County and a total of about 2,930 acres in the state. Nearby are timber reservations of 385 acres, the 1,492-acre University of Illinois-Willard Airport, 1,768-acre Robert Allerton Park, and other areas including those occupied by antenna and radio direction-finding research installations, and radio and optical telescope observatories. On the main campus there are 179 major buildings.

Many of the buildings are of particular interest to visitors. The "front door" to the campus is the Illini Union. Built and furnished without cost to the state, it includes lounges; guest rooms; food services; guest, meeting and recreation rooms; a paperback book center and browsing library; ticket sales; information desks, and other services.

The Assembly Hall is a multi-purpose structure for events such as convocations, concerts, stage productions, ice shows, basketball, exhibits and other activities. Various arrangements provide seating for up to 17,000 persons. The circular building has the world's largest edge-supported dome, 400 feet in diameter, arching 128 feet above the activity floor.

The University Library, with more than 11 million items in its collections, is the largest of any state university, third among all American colleges and universities, and fifth among all libraries of the nation.

The University's athletic program was conceived in 1892 to provide the opportunity for student-athletes to compete on an intercollegiate basis. Additionally it was looked on as a means of recreation and entertainment for other students, alumni and citizens in the form of spectator sports.

Currently the Athletic Association supports 11 inter-collegiate teams for men and eight for women.

INDIANA UNIVERSITY

One of the oldest state universities, Indiana University is a pioneer in higher education in the Midwest. Founded in 1820 as Indiana State Seminary, designated Indiana College in 1828, it became Indiana University in 1838.

It is chartered by the General Assembly of Indiana as *The University of the State* and, as such, is head of the public school system of the state.

From this small beginning I. U. has grown from a single building and ten students to a Bloomington campus of more than 1,850 wooded acres and a 1978 total of 31,884 full-time students, plus more than 42,000 students at the Indianapolis and regional campuses. They are contained within three major divisions: Indiana University at Bloomington, Indiana University-Purdue University at Indianapolis (IUPUI), and regional campuses at South Bend, Fort Wayne, Gary, Kokomo, Southeast (Jeffersonville-New Albany) and East (Richmond).

The University offers degrees in more than 60 fields, such as business, medicine, dentistry, education, law, music, optometry and the like. Since 1971 the University has been under the guidance of Dr. John W. Ryan, only the 14th president in more than 150 years.

Indiana has more than 216,000 living alumni and so many of them—almost 150—have headed institutions of higher learning; the University is known as "Mother of College Presidents."

The University has been a leader in many fields. It was among the first (1867) to admit women as students on an equal basis with men, among the first to introduce the elective course of study (1887), and military training (1840). A renowned faculty gives the University high ranking in scholastic and research achievement and national surveys rank its schools among the nation's leaders. Currently the School of Medicine graduates more physicans each year than any other medical college.

A well developed system of residence halls provides living quarters for more than 12,500 students and more than 1,400 units are provided for married students. Twenty sororities and 34 fraternities add more housing facilities.

The library system contains more than 4,500,000 items. It consists of the main library, the Lilly Library regional campuses, various schools and collections at housing units.

Athletically, I. U. has been a member of the Big Ten since 1899, less than four years after its founding. Since then the Hoosiers have been an honored and worthy member of this pioneering association of great Midwestern universities.

Indiana has won Big Ten championships in all but one of the sports in which it competes on a Conference level and ranks third among all members in the number. Only Michigan and Illinois surpass it in grand total.

Hoosier teams have ranked high in the national scene, winning 14 National Collegiate championships, plus 98 individual NCAA champions. Among them, three NCAA basketball titles and a record six-in-a-row swimming crowns.

Indiana is dedicated to the idea that it must pursue excellence in all fields of athletics and, as a consequence, it regularly ranks near the top in total sports' standings. To support this stand, IU has created an entirely new athletic plant in the last 30 years, offering facilities to both participant and spectator of unsurpassed quality.

"This University," said President Ryan, "has a commitment to excellence in all areas. Athletics, as an integral part of the University, is no exception."

UNIVERSITY OF IOWA

From its founding in 1847, The University of Iowa has been an educational pioneer. In 1860 the U of I became the first state university to admit women on an equal basis with men. In 1868 it established the first law school west of the Mississippi and in 1870 began to develop one of the first university-based medical centers in the Midwest. Today, the University ranks among the Midwest's leading centers of liberal arts, graduate and professional education.

Located in the heart of Iowa City, the University now has an enrollment of more than 22,000 students, over 1,500 faculty members and a 1,900-acre campus—a considerable expansion from 1855, when the school had a student body of 19, with three faculty members situated on a 10-acre campus. The University libraries now house more than 2,000,000 volumes, including a Health Sciences Library, which features a collection of rare books on the history of medicine.

The University is comprised of ten colleges—Liberal Arts, Graduate, Business Administration, Medicine, Engineering, Law, Nursing, Pharmacy, Dentistry and Education—as well as seven schools: Art and Art History, Journalism, Letters, Library Science, Music, Religion and Social Work.

The University has maintained its tradition as an innovator, originating the interdisciplinary science of speech pathology and pioneering in the acceptance of creative work—painting, sculpture, musical composition, poetry, drama and fiction writing—for thesis and dissertation credit. It's Writers Workshop has gained a world reputation in the teaching of creative writing. Under the leadership of Dr. James Van Allen, Iowa has also played a major role in the U.S. space programs, such as the current Voyager space probes.

The U of I hospitals and clinics serve as the apex of a major tertiary health care center, the largest university-owned teaching hospital in the country, with approximately 300,000 clinical visits and some 39,000 patients admitted annually.

The University's Hancher Auditorium, now in its seventh season, offering concerts, ballet and theatrical productions featuring such renowned artists and groups as Nathan Milstein, Alvin Ailey American Dance Theatre, and the Vienna Boys Choir.

UNIVERSITY OF MICHIGAN

Universities are judged by many standards, but The University of Michigan is particularly proud of her excellence in the three "A's"—Academics, Athletics and Alumni.

A few years ago on a day in October when Michigan's football team was ranked No.1 in the nation, one of its graduates, Samuel C.C. Ting, a native of Ann Arbor, was a Nobel Prize recipient in physics. It is not uncommon for a student, like James Earl Jones, to become an accomplished Broadway actor, while other students, like Cazzie Russell or Rudy Tomjanovich, become professional basketball stars.

Gerald R. Ford played football at Michigan, but also majored in economics and was accepted by the Yale Law School, where he graduated in the top third of his class and later entered politics.

While Michigan's basketball team was battling its way to the 1976 NCAA Championship Finals, a survey of 36 graduate programs by the American Council on Education reported Michigan had 12 academic departments among the top five in the nation and 23 among the top ten.

Meanwhile, the deans of professional schools across the nation ranked Michigan's College of Dentistry (now over 100 years old) and the College of Public Health as the best in the country. In fact, Michigan was ranked in the top ten in 15 of the 18 areas surveyed, the best overall record of any university.

Standard and Poor's recent survey of 53,000 top executives reveals that Michigan is the only non-eastern school ranked in the *top five* that send their graduates to executive positions.

So it has gone for the University, gaining a high ranking educationally while maintaining an excellent intercollegiate athletic program and a vast, participating alumni body.

It all began in 1817 when the Territory of Michigan chartered the ancestor of The University of Michigan, the Catholepistemiad of Michigania, located in the frontier town known as Detroit. The Rev. John Monteith was the first president. A new charter was issued by the state of Michigan in 1837, and the University of Michigan was reorganized and relocated in Ann Arbor where the orginal 40-acre campus site had been proffered as a gift. Buildings were completed in 1841 and the first college class was admitted.

Michigan's total enrollment in 1978 was over 46,000 students, which includes the Ann Arbor (35,824), Flint (3,821) and Dearborn (5,957) campuses. In 1977-78, a total of 10,625 degrees was awarded. There are more than 250,000 Michigan alumni throughout the world, the largest alumni body of any school in the nation.

Michigan faculty members are very active nationally. In recent years such groups as the American Historical Association, American Psychological Association, American Association of University Professors, and the American Association for Higher Education have chosen members of Michigan faculty as their presidents.

The University's library system—which holds more than 5 million volumes—includes the Graduate Library, Undergraduate Library, 21 divisional libraries, 7 departmental and area collections, and 4 special libraries. Six new library buildings have been authorized or built in the past decade including the Gerald R. Ford Presidential Library.

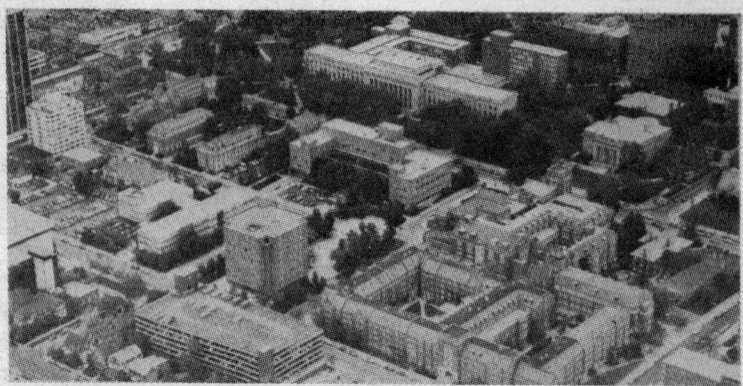

The University of Michigan received more than $83 million in Federal Research Grants in 1977 in such diversified areas as computer development, mental health and retardation, human genetics, ship design, business administration, highway safety, gerontology, and East Asian studies.

It offers students research facilities like the Phoenix Laboratory's 2-million-watt nuclear reactor, the internationally-known Institute for Social Research, observatories, museums, and centers for research on learning, language, economics, and social organization.

The University has 19 individual schools and colleges and two regional campuses. Related research and educational units include 31 centers, 19 institutes, 3 bureaus and 9 hospital units.

As a member of the Big Ten conference, Michigan has established an outstanding intercollegiate athletic record, with a total of 205 championships, including more football titles (29) than any other Big Ten school. The University also supports an extensive intramural and recreational sports program. Some 225 acres of land are devoted to athletics, including the Michigan Stadium, the nation's largest collegiate football stadium, which in 1978 set a record for an average attendance of over 104,000 people per game.

MICHIGAN STATE UNIVERSITY

At its founding in 1855, Michigan State University established a whole new concept of higher education, combining education with research and public service. This concept set the pattern for the nation's land-grant institutions.

A major academic and research center, Michigan State continues to pursue innovative approaches to meet the needs of an increasingly complex society.

More than 44,000 attend MSU. In terms of excellence, as well as size, its proportions are impressive: it leads all public universities in attracting national merit scholars and consistently ranks within the top 10 universities in the number of doctoral degrees granted. Five times in a six-year period, MSU students were selected for Rhodes Scholarships, the best record of any public university.

MSU's students—from 86 foreign nations, every state in the union, and every county in Michigan—pursue a wealth of academic programs in 17 colleges, a graduate school and an honors college. Michigan State is the nation's only university with three schools of medicine: human, veterinary and osteopathic. Other curricula range from fine arts to business, engineering, food science and high-energy physics. Michigan State also offers programs in innovative fields designed to meet problems in the inner city, developing nations and a highly urbanized society. It is at the forefront in helping to solve the nation's food and energy problems.

MSU's faculty, with broad competencies, is conducting some 2,800 research projects using such facilities as the cyclotron, the pesticide research center, a nuclear reactor, the MSU/Energy Research and Development Administration's plant research laboratory and the four lakes at the Water Quality Management Project. The university also utilizes nearby communities for social research and conducts research at experimental stations throughout the state.

The property holdings of MSU at East Lansing are in excess of five thousand acres. Of this total, some two thousand acres are in existing or planned campus development. The campus plantings act as a vast collection for research, teaching and observation in the allied fields of landscape architecture, horticulture, botany, forestry, etc. The W.J. Beal Botanical Garden is an outstanding campus garden with more than 5,000 herbaceous plant species and varieties. Woody components on campus number some 7,800 species and varieties, with more than 16,000 individual plantings. Buildings and structures number 383 on campus: 113 in the academic area, 27 residence halls, 219 apartment buildings, and 24 multi-purpose temporary buildings. There are 33 miles of roadways, 98 miles of walkways, and 12 miles of bicycle paths. Total parking spaces number 20,741.

MSU libraries have a rapidly growing collection of some 2,500,000 volumes which are grouped into three basic collections: the Research Library, the Undergraduate Library and the Science Library. All Government and United Nations publications plus selected Canadian documents are kept in the Documents Collection. The Special Collections Division houses approximately 75,000 volumes, including the Library's collection of rare books. Specialized libraries are located in several classroom buildings.

The Museum offers anthropological, biological, geological and historical displays for MSU classes, students, faculty, staff, and the public. It also houses research collections in Anthropology, History, Paleontology and Zoology which are used for scholarly studies and are features in the Museum's educational publications series.

Abrams Planetarium is one of the most active planetariums in the world. Instructional programs are offered for University classes and for area elementary and secondary school classes. A variety of public programs is offered throughout the year. The facility includes a 254-seat sky theater housing the planetarium's projector, a black light gallery, an exhibit hall and a gift shop.

A gift of the Kresge Foundation, the Kresge Art Gallery contains study areas, studios, classrooms and offices. The Center has spacious, well-appointed galleries where significant art exhibitions of the permanent collection and traveling collections are on display on weekdays as well as weekends.

Kellogg Center is MSU's conference center and guest house. The seven-story building is headquarters for the Continuing Education Service and Lifelong Education Programs, and annually hosts nearly 50,000 persons attending more than 600 conferences and meetings. It contains 193 air-conditioned guest rooms and complete dining and banquet facilities.

UNIVERSITY OF MINNESOTA

The University of Minnesota was founded in 1851, seven years before the territory achieved statehood. The U of M is now enjoying its 128th year of serving the higher educational needs of the great upper Midwest. The University ranks 8th in total enrollment (including evening classes) with some 75,000. The Twin Cities campus alone totals more than 45,000 students.

The University is dedicated to the task of training the youth of Minnesota and the region, and its success is measured in part by the success of its many graduates and faculty. Seven former Minnesota students have received the cherished Nobel Prize, including Dr. Norman C. Borlaug (peace prize 1970), Melvin Calvin (chemistry 1961), John Bradeen (physics 1956, 1972), Walter K. Brattain (medicine 1950), and Ernest O. Lawrence (physics 1939). Two others have been named recipients of the Pulitzer Prize, including John Berryman (1965) and Dominick Argento (1975).

Additional noted graduates who have gone on to extremely successful careers include the late former U.S. Senator and U.S. Vice-President Hubert H. Humphrey, pioneers in heart transplant surgery Dr. Christian Barnard and Dr. Norman E. Shumway, journalists Eric Severeid and Harry Reasoner, TIME magazine's Hedly Donovan, physicist Lawrence Hafsted, and actors Peter Graves and James Arness.

University scientists are constantly working on projects of vital importance to the future welfare of the state and nation in the school's diverse research laboratories on each of the campuses and agricultural experimental stations scattered throughout Minnesota.

The institution is a cultural as well as educational hub of the Upper Mississippi Valley area and the home of several cultural groups including the University Artists Course, University Theatre, the Mississippi River Showboat, the Minnesota Orchestra and area performances of the Metropolitan Opera.

Dr. C. Peter Magrath (as in Magraw) became the eleventh President of the University in October, 1974, at age 41. He is the youngest man to ever hold that post. Under his direction the University continues solid growth patterns. Prior to joining the U of M administrative staff, Dr. Magrath had served as vice chancellor for Academic Affairs at the University of Nebraska, and was also president of the State University of New York at Binghamton. He also holds the title of Professor of Political Science at Minnesota.

Minnesota's athletic history and traditions cover more than a century of competition. The first recorded athletic event took place

in 1876 when Minnesota lost its inaugural baseball game 91-39 to the St. Paul Saxons. Football came along in 1882 and basketball in 1896, while most other sports began in the early 1900's.

From 1951 through 1954, a legend was launched at the University of Minnesota when Paul Giel became a two-sport all-American in football and baseball. After professional careers in baseball and radio, Paul returned to his alma mater in 1971 and today serves as Director of Men's Intercollegiate Athletics. His drive was then, and remains today, to insure that Minnesota conducted a full, well-rounded athletic program in every sport it sponsors. Looking at Minnesota's "across the board" record in the Big Ten, Mr. Giel has been more than just successful in maintaining his goals.

Winning records have long been a tradition at Minnesota in all sports, and the present staff has done little to erode that statement. Today the University remains competitive in all men's intercollegiate athletic fields where it produces teams. The Golden Gopher is still the winning symbol in the Midwest.

NORTHWESTERN UNIVERSITY

Northwestern University was chartered as an independent institution of higher education in 1851, and its growth has paralleled the dynamic rise of Chicago, the metropolitan focus of the old Northwest Territory. Northwestern's development has fulfilled the expectation of its founders whose purpose was to establish a "university of the highest order of excellence."

Today Northwestern is one of the largest privately controlled universities in the United States. It has a total annual enrollment of about 22,000 men and women on its Evanston and Chicago campuses, including evening and summer students. Full-time undergraduate enrollment in Evanston, however, is held to approximately 6,600. Full-time graduate students in Evanston number about 2,600, and full-time enrollment in the professional schools on the Chicago campus is approximately 2,500.

To maintain Northwestern as a major center of learning, the University has completed the first phase of a long-range development program and has undertaken the second phase, toward the eighties, a five-year, $177 million fund-raising campaign.

Northwestern has two separate campuses fronting on Lake Michigan.

On the 170-acre Evanston campus are the College of Arts and Sciences, the Graduate School, the Technological Institute, the Schools of Education, Journalism, Music, and Speech, and the Graduate School of Management.

Twelve miles south is the Chicago campus. On this 14-acre site are the School of Law, the Medical School, the Dental School, and the Evening Divisions.

The Chicago campus is the heart of The McGraw Medical Center of Northwestern University, which coordinates the educational, research, and service facilities of the Medical School, the Dental School, and several member hospitals.

Robert H. Strotz, PhD is Northwestern University's 13th president. He earned his doctorate in economics at the University of Chicago in 1951. Mr. Strotz joined the Northwestern faculty in 1947 as an instructor in economics. In 1958, he was named professor; and in 1966, he was appointed Dean of the College of Arts and Sciences, the largest undergraduate college within the University. He held that post until his election to the presidency in July, 1970. Mr. Strotz is a member of Phi Beta Kappa, and holds an honorary Doctor of Laws degree from Illinois Wesleyan University. Active in various international and local organizations, Mr. Strotz is a member of the American Economics Association, the Royal

Economic Society, the American Statistical Association, and is a fellow of the Econometric Society. He currently is serving as Chairman of the Board of Directors of the Federal Reserve Bank of Chicago. The essential focus of Mr. Strotz's many publications has been on welfare economics, statistical estimation procedures in economics, and the theory of consumer behavior.

Northwestern's intercollegiate athletic program has 19 varsity teams (nine women's and ten men's) vying for championships in Big Ten, NCAA and AIAW competition.

In addition, two teams compete as varsity-club sports and 16 others enter conference and national competition as club sports.

The women's teams, in their fourth year of varsity existence, have made tremendous strides. Northwestern women play field hockey, volleyball, cross country and tennis in the fall, basketball, swimming and indoor track in the winter, and softball, outdoor track and tennis again in the spring.

The men's teams, who have been competing on a varsity level in some sports beginning in 1871 with baseball, now field a total of 10 varsity squads for championship competition in the Big Ten, the conference which Northwestern helped found in 1896. The Wildcats play football and cross country in the fall, basketball, swimming, wrestling and indoor track in the winter, and baseball, tennis, golf and outdoor track in the spring.

OHIO STATE UNIVERSITY

It all began in 1870, when the Ohio Legislature chose a site for a new college. A tract of land from the Neil Farm was chosen, because it was "far enough removed from the City of Columbus that the study habits of the students could not be interfered with by contacts with city life."

With little fanfare the new college opened September 17, 1873. There were 24 students and one building. The school was called Ohio Agricultural and Mechanical College. In 1878, the legislature changed the name to The Ohio State University.

In a relatively short period of time Ohio State has enjoyed remarkable growth in stature and in size. The University has become a nationally recognized center for research and graduate work.

In the fall quarter of 1978, a record 51,434 students took courses at Ohio State. This includes 30,980 full-time undergraduates, 9,744 in Graduate School, 2,782 in professional colleges and 7,837 part-time students. Of the total enrollment, 25,356 were women.

The Columbus campus consists of 381 buildings on 3,251 acres. Additional acreage is owned in other portions of the state. The replacement value of the land, buildings and equipment on the Columbus campus is $1,121,675,000.

Ohio State University is made up of 17 colleges and a Graduate School. There are nine special schools within the colleges.

The University has a teaching faculty of 3,342. In addition, Ohio State employs 13,300 non-teaching personnel.

Ohio State students may select from 210 undergraduate majors and 8,800 courses. A master's degree can be taken in 113 study areas and the doctoral degree in 85.

The Ohio State University operates regional campuses at Lima, Mansfield, Marion and Newark. There is an Agriculture Experiment Station in Wooster as well as a Technical Institute. The University conducts a Graduate Center at the Wright-Patterson Air Force Base near Dayton.

The Ohio State University Medical Center is one of the best-equipped and most comprehensive college-owned centers in the nation.

Harold L. Enarson has been President of The Ohio State University since 1972. Prior to this he served as Academic Vice President of the University of New Mexico for six years and as President of Cleveland State University for six years.

Dr. Enarson is a native of Iowa. He holds a B.A. degree from the

University of New Mexico, an M.A. from Stanford and a Ph.D. from The American University.

His professional background falls into four areas; labor relations, the health sciences, international education and in higher education.

President Enarson foresees The Ohio State University as entering an "age of refinement." The impressive physical plant is undergoing constant renovation and modernization. The enrollment has been stabilized by legislative decree. The University is opening its vast resources of people, knowledge and laboratories to research. A greatly expanded medical center with numerous research projects emphasizes its concern for mankind.

Dr. Enarson is encouraging the expansion of evening programs and of continuing education that now serve over 7,800 Ohio State students.

Ohio State University conducts one of the largest and most comprehensive athletic programs in the nation. There are 30 intercollegiate sports, 18 for men and 12 for women, with approximately 950 student-athletes participating each school year.

The athletic facilities at Ohio State University are excellent. The 83,112-seat football stadium has enjoyed 63 consecutive home sellouts and the basketball arena seats 13,489. With the completion of the new Mike Peppe Aquatic Center and the Paul G. Benedum Recreation Center in May, 1977, Ohio State's athletic facilities took another giant stride forward. These buildings add an additional 265,000 square feet of space for recreation and intramural sports.

Ohio State's athletic philosophy is based upon a broad intercollegiate program that emphasizes quality performances in all sports. Intercollegiate athletics at Ohio State have a rich tradition. Notable achievements from great individuals and teams have long been a Buckeye trademark. The impressive list of Ohio State All-Americans is a tribute to the quality of athletes to represent the University down through the years.

PURDUE UNIVERSITY

Despite its reputation for excellence in engineering, agriculture and science, people are Purdue's greatest strength. In just more than a century, Purdue has grown from a staff of six and a student body of 39 to a faculty in excess of 2,600 serving a student population of over 40,000 on four campuses.

A corps of astronauts, three U.S. Secretaries of Agriculture, college and corporation presidents, a U.S. Senator and two Nobel Prize winners claim Purdue as their alma mater, a mere few of nearly 215,000 alumni.

This fall, Purdue entered its 110th year under the guidance of its eighth president, Dr. Arthur Gene Hansen. Since its founding in 1869 as the Indiana link to the nation's land-grant system established by President Lincoln in the Morrill Act, Purdue has built solid reputations in a variety of academic disciplines. Some of its distinctions include:

- Annually ranks first in the number B.S. degrees granted in engineering.
- Enrolls more students in science courses than any other American university.
- Has the largest graduate student enrollment in pharmacy in the country.
- Has ranked 13th or higher in Ph.D. degrees awarded in the nation since 1953.
- Ranks ninth in the nation in the number of doctorates awarded in biology, sixth in chemistry, fifth in engineering, third in agriculture, third in psychology, and first in pharmacy.
- A chapter of Phi Beta Kappa, oldest Greek-letter society and honorary fraternity for liberal arts and sciences, was established at Purdue in 1971. Fewer than 200 U.S. colleges and universities have such chapters.

From those academic programs comes an alumni body that has made its impact in widely diversified fields throughout the nation and world. Some of Purdue's most distinguished alumni include:

- A roster of astronauts that lists Neil Armstrong, first man on the moon, Eugene A. Cernan, the last man to explore the moon's surface, and the late Virgil "Gus" Grissom and Roger B. Chafee who died in a tragic capsule fire at Cape Kennedy. Purdue takes pride in the unofficial title, "Mother of Astronauts," because of these men.
- Indiana senior U.S. Senator Birch Bayh, a graduate of Purdue's Agriculture School and president of the student body in 1952.
- Ben Roy Mottelson, Science '47, and Edward M. Purcell, Electrical Engineering '33, Nobel Prize recipients in physics.
- Chris Schenkel, Science '45, longtime sportscaster for ABC-TV.

- Donald B. Rice, president, the Rand Corporation.
- John R. Wooden, retired UCLA basketball coach and member of the Basketball Hall of Fame.

The mission of the University is not limited to the classrooms of the graduate and undergraduate programs, but reaches out actively to serve in many other ways. More than 90,000 are annually enrolled in more than 800 continuing education programs.

More subtle changes are occuring in curricula as the University remains highly sensitive to the needs and problems of modern society and of its students. An example is the four-year-old interdisciplinary engineering program which is "people-oriented" rather than "thing-oriented."

But that just proves once more that despite its size—the University is the nation's 20th largest university—Purdue's greatest foundation is its people.

UNIVERSITY OF WISCONSIN

An internationally-known photographer visiting the University of Wisconsin at Madison described it as "the most beautiful campus in the country, perhaps in the world."

Completing a six-month tour of college campuses in North America, he praised the nearness of Lake Mendota, the heavily-wooded hills, the all-round beauty of the setting.

Wisconsin residents and alumni are proud of their high-ranking institution of learning, visit it often, and take special interest in activities at the University.

Since its founding in 1849, the campus has become one of the great world centers of higher education. It is the oldest, largest, and most diversified of the 27 campuses which comprise the UW system, fourth largest in the United States.

It all began with a class of 17 students, meeting in a borrowed classroom in downtown Madison, then a little community of several thousand residents. Now it boasts an enrollment of almost 38,000 students taking some 4,600 courses in 128 departments. And Madison has a population of over 170,000.

One of the nation's first Land-Grant colleges, the Madison campus has colleges of agricultural and life sciences, engineering, and letters and science, and schools of allied health professions, business, education, family resources and consumer sciences, library, law, journalism and mass communication, medicine, natural resources, music, nursing, pharmacy, and social work.

There is much for visitors and students, too, to see. One of the finest of its kind, the Elvehjem Art Center attracts hundreds daily to view its many rare collections. Two union buildings serve as cultural and fun centers, one with a rathskeller that has been copied by other universities.

Chimes ring out from the Carillon Tower in the heart of the campus. Geology, history and physics museums, among others, are popular places. The University's Biotron, capable of simulating the diverse climates of the world, brings researchers and scientists to Madison.

Much praised, too, is the varied architectural style of campus buildings, with the old, including the venerable North, South, Bascom and Science halls, blending with the new high-rise Van Vleck and Van Hise Halls, contemporary Vilas Hall, and the Humanities Building.

Consider these dimensions:

—The Madison campus has 355 academic buildings with a book value of $314 million.

—Campus acreage in the city is 900 with an additional 1,244 acres of nature study area in a nearby arboretum.

—A total of 1,700 foreign students from 101 nations attend UW, giving the campus a rich international culture.

—An oft-cited faculty, the heart of the University, includes approximately 4,600 teachers, administrators, and other professional staff personnel.

The rich heritage and resources of the campus are dedicated to the *Wisconsin Idea,* which holds that it is the mission of the University to serve the public which supports it. That educational theme is mirrored in the slogan, "The boundaries of the campus are the boundaries of the state," a statement born in 1905.

It is also a university deeply committed to the concept of academic freedom. UW regents in 1894 proclaimed Wisconsin's dedication to "that continual and fearless sifting and winnowing by which alone truth can be found." Consequently, UW-Madison is concerned with progress and innovation. New ideas continue to take root and there is a constant, lively debate of issues.

1978 BIG TEN FOOTBALL REVIEW

Big Ten football in 1978 could be labeled a year of the "breakthrough". Or how about the year in which the Big Ten re-emphasized "competitive balance"? How about the year in which the so-called "Big Two-Little Eight" myth was finally put to rest?

Whatever phrase or description one chooses to select in reviewing the '78 Big Ten grid season, there is little doubt of the occurrence of several significant points, i.e.

*Michigan State tied Michigan for the Conference title, the first MSU championship since the glory days of 1965-66, and the first time a team other than Michigan or Ohio State had reached the No. 1 spot in the final standing since 1967. Several teams had been close—Purdue twice finished a game out, Northwestern was just one game behind Michigan in 1970, and twice before (1974 & 1977), Michigan State was denied a share of the title by just a half a game.

*For the first time since 1969, three Big Ten teams won eight games or more. Michigan had done so every year since 1968 and Ohio State had in all but one season, but a third Conference team hadn't managed to hit the eight win figure since Purdue joined the Wolverines and Buckeyes in the '68 season. Now, here in 1978, Michigan kept its streak intact and was joined by Purdue with nine wins and Michigan State with eight, including seven straight after opening with three losses in its first four games.

*For the first time in 11 years, dating back to 1967, four teams had finished within one game of first place. Purdue trailed the co-champions from the state of Michigan by just half a game and Ohio State was only one game out. Not since Purdue, Minnesota and Indiana tied with 6-1 marks in 1967 to edge out the Buckeyes' 5-2 record has there been such hot pursuit for the Conference title.

With two weeks left in the Big Ten season, Purdue still held solid possession of first place, a spot the Boilermakers had owned since October 14. That was the Saturday which saw the Boilermakers topple Ohio State 27-16, and Michigan State beat Michigan on its home field, 24-15 (two happenings that could be grouped together and included in the previous list, as not since 1967 had these two perennial Conference powers lost a league game on the same day). Now, three victories and a tie later, the Boilermakers were ready to take on their stiffest challenge of the year with a visit to Michigan Stadium. Only a 24-24 tie with Wisconsin the previous week prevented Purdue from entering the game with a perfect 6-0 mark. Instead, their 5-0-1 league status was just barely ahead of Michigan, Michigan State and Ohio State at 5-1.

It was another sellout throng of 105,000-plus that filled the huge Michigan stadium that November 18 day to watch two defensive-minded coaches match wits. Purdue's Jim Young had served as Michigan's defensive coordinator under Bo Schembechler for several glorious years in the early 70's before opting for the head coaching duties at Arizona. The game was Young's first return to Michigan since those days, though the two teams did battle a year ago in West Lafayette, with Michigan winning easily, 40-7. Predictions this year called for a much closer game.

Midway in the first quarter however, any predictions on this game might just as well have been tossed aside. There was a little over five minutes remaining of a scoreless first period when Purdue's sophomore sensation Mark Herrmann was brought down on a jarring hit by Michigan tackle Curtis Greer. The Boilermaker leader staggered to his feet and had to be helped from the field—diagnosis was a concussion and pinched nerve with no more playing time the rest of the day. Herrmann's loss was of major concern to Purdue's Jim Young who now had to call on untested backup QB Chuck Oliver.

"There are things with Oliver in there that we just weren't prepared to do," explained a somber Young afterwards. Oliver is an option quarterback and Purdue wasn't at all prepared to go against Michigan with an option attack.

As a result, the Boilermaker offense was limited to just 50 yards on the ground and just 54 more yards in the air after Herrmann's departure. Michigan, on the other hand, unleashed fullback Russell Davis for 134 of the team's 343 rushing yards, and while UM quarterback Rick Leach hit on only 5 of 11 passes for 54 yards, two were for touchdowns as the Wolverines prevailed by a 24-6 score.

The same Saturday, Michigan State once again turned out an awesome offensive show which produced more than 600 yards in total offense as the Spartans moved into a share of the league lead with an easy 52-3 conquest of Northwestern. Ohio State made it a threesome at the top by rallying for a pair of second half touchdowns to down Indiana, 21-18. Thus another epic battle between the Wolverines and Buckeyes was in the making, with the winner going to the Rose Bowl and the loser guaranteed a berth opposite Clemson in the Gator Bowl.

For Michigan State, its season finale would be in Spartan Stadium against Iowa the following Saturday. And while there was no bowl game awaiting the Spartans despite a fine 7-3 record to date, the Iowa contest held significance for other reasons. First, a win over the Hawkeyes would give the Spartans at least a share of the Big Ten Championship, the school's first since 1969. Second, the game would be the final contest in which State would have a three-year NCAA & Big Ten probation hanging over its head, as come Jan. 19 the Spartans would be free of the NCAA ruling, while this coming Sept. 1, the Big Ten would also lift its probationary status on the East Lansing residents, providing Spartan officials have kept a clean house the past three years (and all indications are they have).

That final Saturday, Michigan State played its "bowl game" and played to near perfection, coasting to a 35-0 halftime lead, and, with the reserves seeing much second half action, kept the score to a respectable 42-7. Amid cries of "Wait 'till next year!" and bumper stickers reading "Rose Bowl in '80", MSU third year coach Darryl Rogers couldn't hide his obvious satisfaction of the season just completed.

"I'd love to go to the Rose Bowl," he said afterwards. "but we knew we couldn't. Our goal was to win the Big Ten championship and we accomplished what we set out to do."

As so many of the OSU-MICH battles have been in recent years, the '78 contest turned out to be a low scoring, defensive battle. It was, however, the Blue defense that held the upper hand, a defense that was to hold the Ohio State offense (fifth in the nation scoring at 35 points a game) to just 11 first downs—only one of which came in the second half. Even more noteworthy, for the third straight game in this historic series, the Buckeyes were not able to produce a touchdown.

Michigan quarterback Rick Leach, looking for a strong individual game which might boost his stock in the Heisman Trophy voting, produced such an effort with 11 of 21 passing for 166 yards and two touchdowns.

Those stats, along with Leach's all-around play despite a painful hamstring injury, convinced Schembechler as to who should receive the most coveted collegiate football award.

"He (Leach) is the best football player in the United States of America. If he doesn't win the Heisman Award, I will be very much surprised," Schernbechler stated. "He is the greatest football player I have ever been associated with." Leach didn't win the Heisman Trophy, instead finishing third in the balloting, but you'll never convince Schembechler that the best college player in the country last year didn't wear a maize and blue #7 uniform.

All ten Conference teams experienced their ups and downs during the season. For a couple of schools, like Northwestern and Illinois, it was a season of frustration, starting from the 0-0 tie that the two teams battled to in the season opener. For the Wildcats, there was individual improvement and bright spots each week for rookie coach Rick Venturi, but alas, it never showed on the scoreboard. The 'Cats failed to win in their next ten outings as a rash of injuries crippled what had been tabbed a veteran defensive team and turned it into a group of untested, though improving, freshmen and sophomores.

The Illini didn't experience much success either, though a 28-14 win at Syracuse and a thrilling 20-20 tie with Wisconsin took some of the disappointment and sting out of Coach Gary Moeller's second year at Illinois. It was QB Rich Weiss' first collegiate action after missing the entire '77 season with a back injury, and his presence alone is cause for optimism in the Illini camp this fall. At times, it appeared linebacker John Sullivan was a one-man show, continually rolling up tackle figures in the 20's. It's little surprise he finished his career as the all-time Illini tackler with 501 total stops.

The youth of Illinois showed on more than one occasion. In the season finale at Minnesota 32 of the 54-man traveling squad were freshmen or sophomores, 12 of whom were starters. The team's final stats also indicate a promising future, as underclassmen led the team in rushing, passing, total offense, scoring, kickoff returns, and tackling.

Inconsistent play at quarterback proved to be the reason for Iowa's 2-9 year and 2-6 mark in the Conference. The Hawkeyes started four different quarterbacks during the season, and none of the four stood out above the rest, as the team's 41 percent passing mark might indicate. Sophomore Jeff Green, who played less than half of the year, was the top passer with 556 yards and three touchdowns, but had just a 40 percent completion mark.

The Hawkeyes main concern was not getting the ball enough to their main threat, Brad Reid. The junior split end scored six touchdowns, five on end-around plays including an 80 yarder against Wisconsin. Reid caught just 14 passes, but gained 322 yards for a 23 yard average per reception. Highlight of the dismal showing of the Hawkeyes had to be a 38-24 win over Wisconsin in which the Hawks' offense came alive for a total of over 400 yards.

It boiled down to that type of year for the Badgers: some weeks surprising success, others sputtering disappointment. For the second year in a row, the Badgers were undefeated after five games, though the fifth contest did end in a 20-20 tie with the Illini. But, like the 1977 schedule, which found Wisconsin tackling Michigan, Michigan State and Ohio State in succession (losing the three games by a combined 107-7 margin), the Badgers again had to face the three challengers and follow that with a game against vastly improved Purdue. It proved fatal for Coach Dave McClain's first UW squad, as the young defense allowed 42, 55, and 49 points on successive Saturdays. Despite three straight lop-sided scores, Wisconsin was ready for the Boilermakers and with the aid of an incredible fourth quarter rally, managed a 24-all tie.

A week later all was forgotten as lowly Iowa, losers of eight straight games since its opening win over Northwestern, stunned the Badgers by a 38-24 count. Only a convincing 48-10 win over Minnesota in the finale, giving McClain a 5-4-2 record in his rookie year at Madison, helped offset the loss at Iowa City. It was a day of the big play for the Badgers as Ira Matthews and Tom Stauss broke free for runs of 82 and 73 yards respectively. Matthews also returned a punt 64 yards for a touchdown to highlight a 500 yard total offensive production by Wisconsin.

Indiana and Minnesota were two other teams who had higher expectations in '78 than what proved to be true. The Hoosiers had more starters returning than any other team and optimism was high after a close opening loss at highly-touted LSU and a 14-7 win over defending Rose Bowl champions Washington. But in the third game of the season, Coach Lee Corso must have known it was going to be one of those years, as Nebraska came to Bloomington and promptly pasted the Hoosiers 69-17 before a regional TV audience. The Hoosier offense did come to life two weeks later, scoring over 30 points in four of the next five games, but a pair of close setbacks to Ohio State and Purdue in the final two weeks spelled a 4-7 season ending mark.

There was little question where the Hoosiers' might have been without linebacker Joe Norman, who set an all-time IU record with 199 tackles, over twice as many as any other player on the team. He had Corso's support as the top defensive player in the Big Ten last year.

"He was the best player on the field in every game we played," the ever popular Hoosier coach proclaimed. "His value to this team can not be overstated, as a competitor with tremendous ability and desire, as a leader of his teammates, and as a human being."

The team with the most irregular season had to be Minnesota which alternated wins & losses the final six weeks of play. Unfortunately, two early season, non-conference losses to Pac Ten teams prevented the Gophers from posting a fourth straight winning season, finishing at 5-6. But in the gloom of a disappointing season, came a ray of sunshine in tailback Marion Barber. The sophomore speedster finished as the Big Ten's top rusher in 1978 with a 121.0 per game average, well ahead of his nearest pursuer, Mike Harkrader of Indiana who wound up at 97.7. Barber also established a single season rushing record at Minnesota, gaining 1,210 yards in the 11 Gopher Games. UM passers connected on a school record .556 percent of their pass attempts with Mark Carlson's .566 and six TD passes ranking on top.

Michigan State proved to have one of the most prolific offensive attacks in the history of the Big Ten in 1978. The Spartans established two Conference marks with a total offense average of 523.1 yards a game (over 40 yards per game higher than the old record), while their 41.0 scoring average was just ahead of the previous best of 40.0 by the 1969 Ohio State team. QB Ed Smith had much to do with State's potent attack, as he himself moved to the top of the list of the Big Ten's all-time passing leaders in total yards. Smith finished with 5,706 passing yards and also set single season Conference records for passing yards (1,779), total offense yards (1,808) and TD passes (16). So devastating was the Michigan State offense that in the last six games of the year, MSU scored 280 points, an average of 45.0 per game!

The Spartans had three receivers with 33 receptions or more, quite a feat considering that only one other player in the Big Ten last year (David Charles of Wisconsin) had more than 33 catches during the entire season. It wasn't just a passing attack however, as State boasted four tailbacks with a combined total of just under 2,000 yards. Three of the four had a 6.0 average per carry or higher and three of the four return!

Ohio State QB Art Schlichter will well remember his collegiate debut, that coming against Penn State before a national TV audience, in which he had five passes intercepted. But Schlichter steadily improved during the year, and had only 16 other passes swiped in the remaining 10 games, while throwing for over 1,200 yards. His combined rush-pass figure of 1,840 yards set a single-season Buckeye record, and he will become the all-time OSU leader during his junior season if he maintains this pace.

Linebacker Tom Cousineau was selected as the team's MVP, which isn't surprising when looking at his 125 solo tackles in 1978 and 102 assists. That raised his career total to 628, and prompted Coach Woody Hayes to describe him as the "best college football player in the country this year, and the most complete and intense player I have ever seen." Quite some praise considering all the players who wore a Buckeye uniform during Hayes' 28 year tenure at Ohio State.

Purdue's 1978 season can best be summed up as "one in which the Boilers won a 'bucket' to put 'peaches' in." Translated, that would mean Purdue recaptured the Old Oaken Bucket from Indiana after a two year Hoosier hold on one of the country's most symbolic football traditions. The peaches were from Christmas Day's Peach Bowl win over Georgia Tech, the first post season bowl game for the Boilermakers since 1967's Rose Bowl game. The Bucket and Peach Bowl were the two biggest elements of a successful season for Coach Jim Young's second Purdue team, and more than made up for the disappointment of finishing third in the league race, a half game behind co-champions Michigan and Michigan State.

The defense, or better yet, the "junk defense" was the talk of West Lafayette in '78. Led by such stalwarts as Keena Turner, Kelvin Motts, and Ken Loushin, Purdue held five of its 12 opponents to less than 100 yards rushing in a game, including a season low of just 12 net yards rushing by Georgia Tech. Six times the opposition scored fewer than 10 points, including shutouts against Ohio U.,

Illinois & Northwestern. What's most incredible is that all but three players who started on defense in the Peach Bowl return this fall. With that type of defense and the passing of Mark Herrmann, it's little wonder the Boilers are having title aspirations and Pasadena fever.

One of the all-time great Big Ten backfields closed out a great career at Michigan last fall, as QB Rick Leach, TB Harlan Huckleby and FB Russell Davis all completed their fourth and final year for the Wolverines. Leach received the most recognition, and rightfully so, as the southpaw from Flint, Michigan established an all-time career record for total offense. Leach finished with 6,460 yards making him the only player in Conference history to exceed the 6,000 yard figure. Huckleby and Davis made their presence felt also as both runners joined Leach in gaining spots among Michigan's all-time top ten leading rushers. Huckleby was the top ground gainer last year with 741 yards with Davis adding 683 and Leach 611. Yet their combined total of just over 2,000 yards wasn't even half of the 4,512 net rushing yards Michigan accumulated as a team.

The defense was once again Michigan's strength much as it has been a Wolverine trademark during the 70s. Six opponents scored 6 points or less including four teams that didn't score at all. Twelve opponent passes were swiped by the secondary while the men up front allowed a meager 112.7 yards per game. Linebacker Ron Simpkins was the leader here, coming up with 156 tackles, 110 of them by himself. Dropping enemy runners behind the line of scrimmage became the rule rather than the exception for the defense, with Simpkins, Mike Trgovac and Tom Keitz all coming up with nine such stops while the team totals in this category showed 64 tackles for 348 yards in losses.

With the exciting four-way battle for the Big Ten championship, attendance at Conference stadiums was never better. It was a record-setting year for college football attendance and the Big Ten was the national leader for an unprecedented 21st consecutive season. A total of 3,668,926 fans filled Big Ten stadiums to watch 60 games last fall, an average of 61,149 per contest, the first time in the history of college football that any Conference has maintained a 60,000-plus average for an entire season. The Big Ten had flirted with the 60,000 figure on several occasions, but until last year's record-setting had never quite reached it.

For a sixth straight year, Michigan and Ohio State finished one-two in the school attendance derby. The Wolverines actually RAISED their all-time national record average of 104,203 of a year ago to 104,948 for the six games in UM Stadium in 1978. A crowd of 104,102 was on hand for Michigan's opener with Illinois last year, and that turned out to be the *smallest* of the six home crowds. Each week the total increased over the previous game count, until the

37

finale with Purdue when 105,410, the third largest crowd in Michigan history, watched the home-town favorites knock the Boilermakers out of first place with a 24-6 victory.

Ohio State, which won 14 straight national attendance crowns before Michigan started on its 100,000 average spurt, showed a 1978 average of 87,840, second highest ever in Buckeye history and just 17 fans per game behind the all-time mark set three years ago. Wisconsin and Michigan State were also among the top ten leaders in per game average last fall. The Badgers attracted over 500,000 fans for seven games and a 71,443 per game count, seventh best in the nation, while Michigan State showed the biggest increase in the Big Ten last year, jumping 9,556 over its 1977 mark, to post a 71,140 average and No. 10 ranking nationally.

Purdue also raised its season average over 1,700 fans per game and finished in the No. 14 spot with a 62,250 average. Iowa dropped off somewhat, but still had an impressive 53,214 per game mark to rank 21st among the national leaders.

Not only was it a record-setting year on a Conference level, but several schools established new single-game totals. They included Ohio State with an 88,358 total against Michigan in the season finale, Purdue's 69,900 crowd against Indiana the same week and Wisconsin's all-time best of 80,024 last fall for its game with Michigan. In addition, a pair of weekly Conference totals were set when 299,556 fans for four games on September 30 produced an average of 74,889, and on October 7 in the last week of non-conference play, a total of 502,611 Big Ten enthusiasts filled eight Conference stadiums for a 62,826 average. Indeed it was a record setting year in 1978, but with the budding enthusiasm and optimism growing for the '79 campaign, many of those newly-set records may already be in jeopardy.

BIG TEN
CONFERENCE
ILLINOIS
INDIANA
IOWA
MICHIGAN
MICH. STATE
MINNESOTA
NORTHWESTERN
OHIO STATE
PURDUE
WISCONSIN

ILLINOIS

Coach Gary Moeller's youthful *Fighting Illini* footballers paid their dues last season to a 1-8-2 record with hopes of better dividends in 1979. Of the final starting 22 players, 13 were either a sophomore or freshman who carry the same strong confidence of their coach that progress has been made and success will be accomplished.

"Last season was disappointing only from a record standpoint. We have made some great strides and I tell you—we are going to get there. We have kids in our program who are winners and know what it takes to turn things around. Our heads are still high and our confidence is great; a little more work and we'll be allright," remarked Moeller.

The disappointing record Moeller alluded to started with a 0-0 tie against Northwestern University in early September at the University of Illinois' Memorial Stadium. A stiff defense and missed opportunities on offense summed up the Illini effort during a blistering 93 degree heat wave. The game marked the first double shutout for an Illinois team since 1951 when a Rose Bowl bound Illini unit tied Ohio State 0-0 and was the eleventh such score in their grid iron history.

The defensive unit never allowed Northwestern to drive inside the Illini 30-yard line and gave up a mere rushing yardage of 83 in 36 attempts. On offense the Illinois eleven moved inside the Northwestern 30-yard line on six occasions and were beyond the 20 on four other surges, but never reached pay dirt.

In the following two weeks the Illini fell to two nationally ranked teams, visiting the University of Michigan and then hosting Stanford University.

Through three quarters the Illinois defense held the explosive Michigan offense to just 10 points; but Illinois' offense never got on track, then the defensive unit tired and began making mistakes enabling the Wolverines to register a 31-0 shutout.

Stanford's vaunted passing assault, combined with an effective running attack, sent the Californians back west celebrating a 35-10 win. Once again the Illini errors helped pave the victory lane. A bad snap on a punt and a fumble set up two Stanford touchdown drives of less than 30 yards and consecutive "roughing the kicker" penalties in a punting situation kept a third Cardinal touchdown drive alive.

The Illini then turned eastward for its lone victory of the year. Syracuse was the victim in a 28-14 strong display of Illinois offense. Six newcomers to the offense's starting lineup helped rack up 425

Defensive back Lloyd Levitt gets an early season interception versus Northwestern.

Lawrence McCullough, back-up QB, prepares for a snap from center.

41

Outside linebacker Earnest Adams (37) intercepts Purdue's pass intended for Dave Young.

yards, 324 of that yardage came on the ground. Two of the Illini scoring drives covered 80 yards while a third started 70 yards away.

Next stop on the Illini traveling itinerary was the University of Missouri. The Tigers had suffered losses the past two years to Illinois, but revenge was rejoiced as they enjoyed an easy 45-3 triumph.

The Illini offense was hampered in the first half as Missouri's defense forced four consecutive turnovers which eventually led to scores for the host. Four additional fourth quarter turnovers and 98 yards in total penalties, helped issue the Illini its worst point-spread loss of the season.

Better performances were offered the following Saturday afternoon by the Illini versus the University of Wisconsin, but it spelled yet another frustrated tie—this time 20-20.

Illinois dominated the game gaining 25 first downs to 14 by the Badgers, running 83 plays to Wisconsin's 59 and controlling the ball for nearly 17 minutes more than their opponent. The Illini offense grossed more than 220 yards on the ground against a team that had given up just 100 per game against the rush.

Once again, however, Illinois was its own worst enemy, fumbling five times and losing the ball on four of those incidents. Two fumbles set up Wisconsin scores while another bobble and an interception killed Illinois drives in Badger territory.

Figuring better days were ahead, disappointment was again served to the Illini by Purdue University (13-0).

Purdue ran twice as many plays as the Illini, and in the second half had possession for 19:54 compared to Illinois' 10:06. Illinois gained possession of the ball only three times in the final 30 minutes.

In its controlled offense and staunch defense, Purdue kept the Illini from any respectable field position. Of Illinois' nine possessions in the game, eight started on their own 20-yard line or inside.

Things didn't get any better the following week in taking on the Hoosiers of Indiana University as victory slipped away from the Illini, 31-10.

After scoring on its first drive to take a 7-0 lead, Illinois went into the locker room at halftime with a 10-10 tie. However, in the second half Indiana scored 21 unanswered points. Like the week before, the Illini only saw the ball once in the third period as the Hoosiers consumed time with two sustained scoring drives.

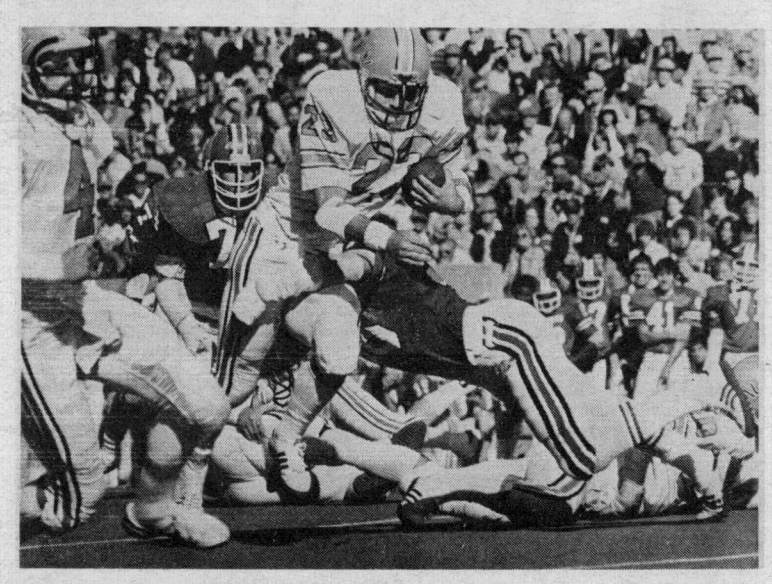

Durable Wayne Strader displays his strong running ability breaking tackle against Indiana.

The Illini were whistled for their highest total of penalty yardage of the year having 106 yards walked off in eight infractions. The loss broke a five game Illinois win streak over Indiana.

The last home game of the year was not a good farewell season closing for Memorial Stadium fans as they witnessed the Orange and Blue succumb 59-19 to Michigan State University.

Getting off on a good note with a 12-0 lead in the first five minutes of the game, Illinois saw the Spartans storm back to take a 14-12 halftime lead. In the second half, common problems plagued the Illini again. With Michigan State holding a slim 24-19 lead late in the third quarter, Illinois fumbled at its own 28-yard line to set up a

43

Quarterback Rich Weiss starts the option attack against the Hoosier defenders.

Tough defensive tackle Dennis Flynn.

44

Mark Dismuke enroute to a 13 yard TD scant against Stanford.

Spartan touchdown. That opened the floodgates as the visitors scored the first seven times they got the ball in the second half.

The next scheduled game was to be a reunion for Garry Moeller, returning to his alma mater as head coach for the first time, but the occasion wasn't a happy one—Ohio State clinched it 45-7.

A closely played first half (the Illini trailed 14-7 at halftime) was just the opposite during the second half as Illinois' offense committed costly turnovers that the Buckeyes graciously capitalized on in route to victory. Ohio State scored 38 of its points on drives that began at their own 49 or in Illinois territory.

Closing out the 1978 football campaign at Minnesota in a snowy 24-6 loss, the Illini fought a tough first half battle and reduced the margin to 14-6 late in the third quarter, but Minnesota took to the ground and chewed away 13 minutes in the final stanza, scoring 10 points. The Gophers strong running attack was just a bit too much for the thirty-four (of 54 team members) freshmen and sophomores to control.

Six of the Illini eight losses came to teams ranked in the wire services' top twenty during the season, and five of those opponents traveled to post season bowl games.

So although the strong opposition rendered Moeller's youthful gridders a frustrating year, a better prospectus is in light for Illinois. Strong game experience and a good nucleus will fashion the 1979 squad along with the indomitable spirit of the coach and the *Fighting Illini,* which should surface them to better rewards.

Tight end Lee Boeke gathers speed after a reception.

INDIANA

Indiana's rebuilding program, which under coach Lee Corso had progressed to a 5-6 and third-place Big Ten finish in 1976 and a 5-5-1 and fourth-place in 1977, looked ready to continue the advance—or, at very least, suffer little backsliding, in 1978.

But the Hoosiers got caught in an old and familiar bind, a lack of depth to protect against key losses due to injuries, and 1978 hopes were predicated on keeping a healthy squad—at least, healthy in the key places.

And when veteran fullback Tony D'Orazio injured a knee, to retire to the side for knee surgery, and tight end Dave Harangody, whom coaches rated as one of the nation's best, went the same route, it changed the complexion of things radically.

If one were asked to pick indispensable players, chances are he would have picked these two. D'Orazio, in addition to being a strong, quick runner, was an excellent pass receiver and without doubt the best blocking back on the squad. Harangody, 6-5, and 234, in addition to blocking ability was such a fine receiver that the spring practices had been devoted to revamping the passing game to one for tight ends.

That, as much as anything, placed the Hoosiers, before the first kickoff, in line for their 4-7 season.

There were highlights, to be sure. The 14-7 upset of defending Rose bowl champion Washington was one, victories in four of six home games softened the blow for Bloomington fans, and the 21-18 fright handed to Ohio State indicated Indiana was not as far off the pace as the record might imply.

And there were standouts: linebacker Joe Norman, so talented and playing with such enthusiasm that he was selected the outstanding defensive player of the game in a 69-17 loss to Nebraska; little Mike Harkrader, coming off knee surgery to rank second in the Big Ten in rushing; kicker David Freud, setting new conversion records with a 63-straight mark that ranked fifth all-time in the nation; freshman Tim Wilbur, tying a Big Ten record for interception returns; safety Dale Keneipp, establishing a new league record with a 92-yard fumble return; Norman and center Mark Heidel winning All Big-Ten selections and places on post-season all-star teams.

But there weren't enough, and replacements were hard to find, and the *robbing Peter to pay Paul* routine, which Corso had felt was over, forced a changing situation through most of the year.

Most Hoosier backers feared the worst in opening the season in the rabid surroundings at Baton Rouge against a team rankled by a 24-21 loss to Indiana the year before. As it turned out, it was an excellently played football game from the 83-yard drive that gave the Hoosiers a 7-0 lead in the first quarter to the closing minutes when Indiana found itself on the Tiger 12 on first down.

A blocked pitch, careening back to the 32, followed by an interception on a pass ended a final threat and a second-half comeback that brought IU from a 21-10 halftime deficit to a final 24-17 loss to one of the nation's ranking teams.

Indiana's superlative linebacker Joe Norman (35) puts the brakes on Iowa's Dennis Mosley in the Hoosiers' 34-14 victory in Bloomington.

LSU went into the game ranked as high as 11th in the nation and ultimately ended up among the bowlers. Darrick Burnett paced Indiana with 98 yards in 25 carries; All-American Charley Alexander gained 144 in 32. "We beat a real solid team and a physical one," said LSU coach Charlie McClendon afterwards.

Probably the Hoosiers' best game of the year and one of their best against this caliber of opposition, was next against the University of Washington, the defending Rose Bowl champion and 12th ranking in the nation. Three interceptions—two by Dave Abrams in his Big Ten Defensive Player of the Week game - and a fumble recovery took some of the steam from the offense powered by 155 yards from Joe Steele, and Indiana rambled to a 14-0 lead by the fourth quarter on a first-half 53-yard drive and an 80-yard march in the final period. Burnett's 117 yards, backed up by 52 from Mike Harkrader, who was being phased back into the offense after his lost season to surgery, and Jerry Bowers chipped in with 57. The Hoosiers did it on the ground, failing to complete one of their three

Mike Harkrader, Indiana U. running against Purdue.

pass attempts. Washington finally scored with 4:47 left as it went to the air, and Indiana came home with a 14-7 victory.

Joe Norman was picked the nation's No. 1 defensive player on the basis of 16 tackles, three of them for losses.

There is no way to explain some turns of events in sports. The Nebraska game on September 30 was one of them. Conceding that the Cornhuskers, ranked No. 10, were a better team, there is no rationale for what happened, other than that there are days when one team can do no wrong and the other nothing right.

A large regional television audience compounded the embarrassment as Nebraska scored the first four times it had the ball to jump out, 28-0, in less than 13 minutes. And when Indiana revived enough to close it to 28-10 and plant a faint notion of a comeback, the Cornhuskers were back at it again. It got to 69-10 before the Hoosiers could score again in the final seconds.

It was just as devastating on paper. Nebraska logged a stadium record 32 first downs and a staggering 613 yards of offense. "I felt like I was in a nightmare and would wake up any moment," said a stunned Lee Corso.

A measure of Norman's greatness: In a 69-17 loss his 17 tackles and overall play led ABC-TV to pick him the defensive player of the game.

After the debacle with Nebraska, Hoosier fans were confident their team would bounce back and vent its frustrations on the Badgers at Madison the following Saturday.

It never happened. A 71-yard punt return by Ira Matthews in the

Darrick Burnett, a senior in 1978, in action against Minnesota.

first quarter and the Badgers were off to a 21-0 halftime lead, booming to 28-0 before Indiana, now forced to the air, could score its lone marker well into the final period.

Indiana's once-vaulted ground game could produce but 37 yards as they lost 34-7.

The Hoosiers needed a laugher and they got it against outmanned Northwestern on Homecoming Day, Oct. 14, at Bloomington, defeating the Wildcats 38-10. Jumping on a pair of fumbles and an interception, the Hoosiers were out in front, 21-0, less than seven minutes into the first quarter. Coach Corso let his frontliners run it to 38-10 early in the third period, then went to his bench for the last 23 minutes of play.

Six turnovers, five lost fumbles and an interception, helped the Hoosiers on their way to a 412-yard day. Harkrader, back in the starting slot with Burnett on the shelf, had his first big day of the year with 162 yards rushing.

The following week IU travelled to East Lansing to encounter one of the strongest teams in the conference losing 49-14.

Spartan quarterback Eddie Smith was throwing bombs and the Big Ten's 1978 passing leader got the co-champions off to a 14-0 lead on just three plays, one an 86-yard pass play to Kirk Gibson, the other a 55-yarder to Samson Howard.

The Hoosiers, who had driven 60 yards from kickoff, only to have a field goal try blocked, got on the board with an 80-yard march in the second quarter but trailed, 35-7, at the half.

Freshman Tim Wilbur, who led the league in interceptions, tied a Big Ten record in the fourth period when he picked off one of Smith's passes and returned it 98 yards for a touchdown. But the issue had long been removed from doubt.

Smith wound up with 369 yards in the air, a new league mark, and the Spartans' 644 yards in offense broke the opponents' record of 613 set three weeks earlier by Nebraska.

Sticking to the ground, Indiana broke out of a 10-10 halftime tie in Bloomington against Illinois to score on long drives in its two third-quarter possessions and again with a reserve lineup in the fourth period to win 31-10 on October 28.

Harkrader ran for 164, his best day of the year, while Lonnie Johnson added 89 and Burnett came back from an injury to gain 31.

The victory was all the more satisfying in that it snapped a five-game Illini winning string in the series.

In a heartbreaking 32-31 loss to Minnesota in Minneapolis the following week, Indiana fans will long remember this as one of their most galling defeats; a game the Hoosiers had won time and again, yet surrendered with two seconds left on a field goal by Paul Rogind of the Gophers.

The Hoosiers had jumped out to a commanding 24-0 lead, play-

Scott Arnett.

ing alert, opportunistic football, with long pass plays—62 from Tim Clifford to Mike Friede, an 82-yarder by the same pair—a record-breaking 92-yard fumble return by Dale Keneipp....

It all seemed so easy, and when the Gophers closed to 24-14, a quick Hoosier TD seemed to have locked it up with just 12:51 left to play. But scrambling Wendell Avery, hitting on eight of 14 passes, turned it around, throwing for two quick scores, then, with 2:30 remaining, moving his club to the 14 for Rogind's winning field goal. The Gophers amassed 577 yards, 177 by 1978 rushing leader Marion Barber. Harkrader, No. 2 for the year, had 113.

On November 11, the Hoosiers combined Harkrader's 129-yard running and Scott Arnett's two-touchdown passing for a convincing 34-14 victory over Iowa at home. By halftime they were in front, 21-0 with a 253-48 yardage advantage, moving 197 on the ground against a team noted for its defense against the run.

Reserves played most of the second half. Even so, Norman

was brilliant, as always, registering 21 tackles, four of them for a total loss of 25 yards.

The Hoosiers were on the verge of springing the biggest upset of the 1978 Conference race against Ohio State at Bloomington on November 18, and the 10-7 lead at halftime had imaginations tingling in stadiums around the league. The Buckeyes had driven 83 yards early in the game to score but Indiana tied it up when the Bucks uncharacteristically gambled—and lost—on 4th and 1 on their 32 and the Hoosiers turned it into a TD. David Freud's field goal set up the 10-7 lead.

Fullback Tony D'Orazio, here taking a handoff from quarterback Scott Arnett in a 1977 game, is counted upon to come back from injury for 1979.

Ohio State took back the lead in the third, driving 98 yards and added a field goal in the fourth. But Indiana wasn't yet through. Tim Clifford passed his team down to a score, then threw for a two-point conversion and, with 5:01 left, the Hoosiers were within three points. Indiana then held and got the ball back with 2:15 remaining. They moved to midfield but here they went for it all, throwing from the split-end for an interception to come out on the short end of a 21-18 final tally.

Defensive star Norman, in his head-to-head meeting with Tom Cousineau, the Bucks' All-American, came up with 26 tackles.

The old Oaken Bucket went back to Purdue for the first time in the last three years in a game typical of the hardfought intra-state classic. The Boilermakers went up, 10-0, in the second period and when the Hoosiers retaliated with a 13 play, 83-yard score, came back with a field goal to take a 13-7 lead at the half.

Indiana didn't lack for opportunities. The Crimson was in Purdue territory nine times, all told, but could maintain the drive to score only once. And when the Boilermakers added a third-quarter score, set up by a lost fumble at the 36, Purdue had all it needed to safeguard its 20-7 victory.

The Purdue triumph came from the ground. Little-used Mike Augustyniak with 135 yards and Wally Jones with 103 augmented Mark Herrmann's passing, while Indiana, losing the battle in the trenches, had to go to the air more than it really wanted to do.

IOWA

On a balmy evening last August, Iowa football coach Bob Commings stepped to a podium at the University Athletic Club and gave over 500 state "I-Club" members some words of hope for the 1978 season.

Beginning his fifth year at the Hawkeyes" helm, Commings reminisced on the progress his staff had made since arriving in 1973. "Let me tell you all tonight that we are afloat at Iowa," he said. "We have come a long way, made steady improvement, and are ready to do some winning. Can we be a winner? Hell, yes. A bowl bid? Why not?"

The cheers Commings heard that night turned to catcalls and boos three months later. The Hawkeyes, the first senior-dominated team under Commings' guidance, finished the season at 2-9. Afloat? The Iowa football program, the critics would say, was sinking fast.

In an all-out effort to curb any further deterioration, Iowa Athletic Director Bump Elliott announced on Dec. 9, 1978 that North Texas State coach, Hayden Fry, would succeed Commings. The 46-year old Commings, a former Hawkeye lineman on the famed 1956 Rose Bowl championship squad, had inherited a program that suffered an 0-11 campaign in 1973. Commings' best year, a 5-6 mark in 1976, was also Iowa's best record since 1969. But the former Massillon, Ohio, prep coach ended his reign with a 17-38 record. "We committed the unpardonable sin this year," he was to say later. "We had a bad record during a rebuilding year."

Unlike Commings and four previous Iowa coaches, the 50-year old Fry comes to Iowa with no prior connections with the Big Ten. The hapless offense Iowa presented in 1978 may find a resurrection in the plans of Fry, a disciple of the Dallas Cowboy playbook. Fry says he also trades notes with Big Ten Coach of the Year, Darryl Rogers of Michigan State.

Fry said he was "amazed at the fan support" for the Hawkeyes during the past season. "Where I come from, 50,000 people just don't show up to watch a team that isn't winning. It's obvious you have a lot of crazy people around here."

The "crazy" Iowa fans turned out in large numbers in 1978, hoping the Hawkeyes would snap a national record losing streak of 16 consecutive non-winning seasons.

After a sluggish 20-3 victory over Northwestern in the season opener, Iowa was to drop its next eight games. Iowa was outscored 291-125, and was dominated 133-10 by foes in the second quarter. Of 16 touchdowns scored, six were by one player (junior split end

Brad Reid). Four of Reid's TD's came via the end-around play. Iowa managed only four scoring passes, three by sophomore quarterback Jeff Green and one by senior wingback Rod Morton.

The Hawkeyes were equally disjointed in running the ball, with 18 players rushing for a combined total of 1,366 yards and 11 touchdowns. Senior fullback Jon Lazar led all ball carriers with 423 yards for a 3.9 yard average. Reid enjoyed the longest play from scrimmage, galloping 80 yards on a broken option pass play in Iowa's only other win, a 38-24 conquest of Wisconsin.

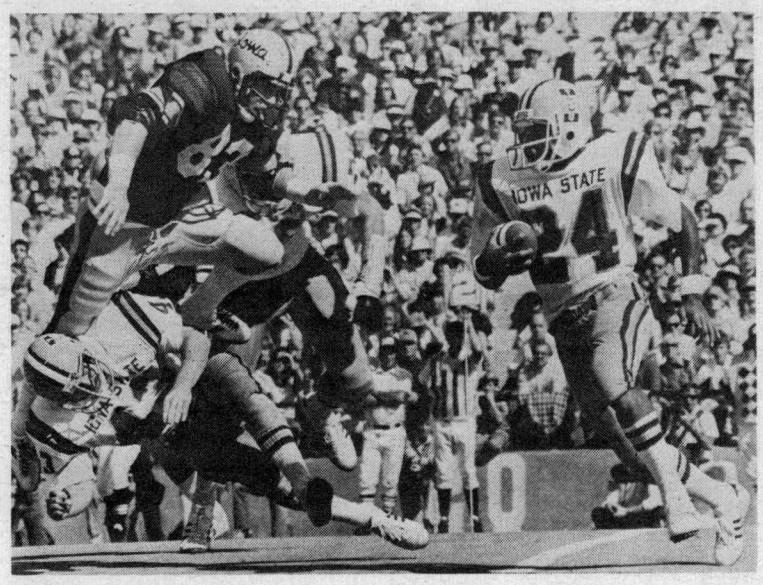

Jim Molini (83)-LB-Iowa, leaps over an Iowa State blocker to make a tackle.

During its eight-game losing skein, Iowa was out of the end zone for 15 consecutive quarters. From the third quarter of the Northwestern contest to the third quarter of the Minnesota clash (the season's fifth game), the Hawkeyes repeatedly failed to mount a sustained drive.

Why was Iowa's offense continually misfiring? Commings could not put his finger on the answer, saying, "we just seem to fail to execute properly on second and third down." The fan uproar seemed to reach a crescendo after the fourth week of the season, when Iowa fell 13-9 to Utah at Iowa City. It was the first victory ever by the Utes over a Big Ten team.

Despite the disappointment, Iowa never completely collapsed. Trailing Minnesota 22-0 in the third period, the Hawkeyes rallied before falling 22-20 at Minneapolis.

The Hawkeyes made Commings' finale at home a memorable one, exploding on Nov. 19 for 401 yards total offense to turn back

Kenny Burke (15), gains some tough yardage.

Wisconsin. Before the clock ran out, Iowa fans swarmed the field and tore down both goal posts.

A week later, after a 42-7 drubbing at Michigan State, Commings was to tell reporters that he wished the "Board (in Control of Athletics) would look at the situation (his tenure) objectively. I hope they look at more than the '78 season. I hope they base their decision on the total five years."

Two days later, with cameras whirring in the background, the Board concluded a three and a half hour meeting by voting in favor of firing Commings.

"I'm abdicating," said Commings. "I'm giving up my throne."

Briefly summarizing the season, Iowa began 1978 with a 20-3 victory over Northwestern.

Iowa startled a crowd of 56,840 in its opener with some razzle dazzle. Senior wingback Rod Morton fired a 55-yard halfback pass to split end Brad Reid to give Iowa a 7-0 lead in the first quarter. Hawkeye freshman linebacker, Todd Simonsen, followed two minutes later by recovering a fumble and racing into the end zone from four yards out. Reid added a 10-yard end around play, hurdling a tackler and somersaulting into score in the third quarter. Northwestern managed a 44-yard field goal by Nick Mirkopoulos. The game was a myriad of turnovers with five lost fumbles and two interceptions.

In the next game, Iowa State reserve quarterback Walter Grant came off the bench to throw for touchdowns of 47, 6, and 20 yards to lead the Cyclones to a surprisingly easy 31-0 win over the Hawkeyes. The Cyclones, ranked No. 20 in the Associated Press poll, took revenge on an Iowa team that won the initial encounter in the renewed intra-state rivalry in 1977, 12-10. The Cyclones shut down the Iowa running game, allowing 113 yards. When the passing game netted only 27 yards it was apparent that the Cyclones had scouted Iowa well. Iowa committed the only turnovers of the game, fumbling twice. The Cyclones took advantage of the first miscue to mount a 14-0 lead, then added a field goal of 34 yards by Steve Johnson for a 17-0 halftime lead. Victor Mack added a seven yard scoring run to Grant's third scoring strike of the day to wind up the Cyclone celebration.

Iowa lost to Arizona 23-3 as Iowa freshman Phil Blatches took the opening kickoff and raced 69 yards to the Arizona 30 to set up the Hawkeyes' only score, a 21-yard field goal by Scott Schilling. After that, it was all Arizona, as the Wildcats held the Hawkeyes to 151 yards total offense. Iowa didn't reach Arizona territory again until Dave Holsclaw's punt bounced off Dwayne Horton at the 25 early in the fourth quarter with the Hawkeyes recovering. However, Iowa gained only four yards in four plays. Arizona quarterback Jim Krohn took charge by throwing for TD's of 25 and 28 yards, and running three yards for another.

The following week Iowa stretched its string of touchdownless quarters to 13, managing only field goals of 25, 27 and 31 yards by Scott Schilling in a 13-9 loss to Utah. Utah's 5-foot-8 quarterback, Randy Gomez hit on 13 of 28 passes for 148 yards and a game-winning five-yard toss to Tony Lindsay with 10 minutes left to play. Tony Huko provided field goals of 25 and 46 yards to give the Utes their first win ever over a Big Ten team.

A brilliant comeback failed against Minnesota the next Saturday in a game in which, Iowa sophomore quarterback Jeff Green came off the bench to throw 12 of 23 passes for 205 yards and ran for two TD's, to spark Iowa in the second half. Minnesota opened a 22-0 lead in the third quarter before Green scored Iowa's first touchdown in 15 quarters with a one-yard sneak. Green handed the ball to Brad Reid for an 11-yard scoring run, then ran one yard for the final score. A two-point conversion failed, as the Hawkeye's suffered a 22-20 defeat.

Iowa played a lackluster first half against Gator Bowl bound Ohio State at Columbus on October 21, surrendering three touchdowns in 2 minutes, 10 seconds of the second quarter resulting in a 31-0 deficit. Iowa's only score came in the third

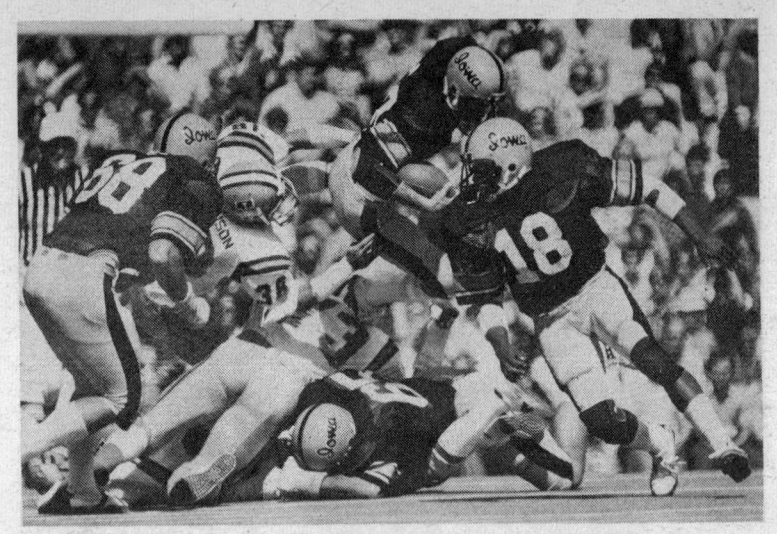

Don Willey (68) gains short yardage against intra-state rival, Iowa State University.

quarter on a five-yard run by fullback Jon Lazar: Starting quarterback Jeff Green, who won the job with a sparkling performance against Minnesota, injured his back in the third series of downs in the first quarter. Fourth-stringer Bill Dolan took over from there. The Buckeyes went to win 31-7.

Purdue, ranked No. 17 in the country and leading the Big Ten with a 4-0 record, came to Iowa city to rout the Hawkeyes 34-7 as the Boilermakers used two scoring passes by Mark Herrmann to race to a 17-7 lead and hold off a stubborn Iowa team. Iowa managed its only score on a dazzling 57-yard end-around run by split end Brad Reid in the third period. Iowa outgained Purdue 205-116 on the ground against a team that was the conference's leading rushing defense. It was the Boilermakers' 18th straight win over Iowa.

In the next to last home game, All-American quarterback Rick Leach passed for touchdowns of 36 and 14 yards and held Iowa in a daze by mastering third down situations to lead the Wolverines to an easy 34-0 win. Iowa, suffering its seventh straight loss, netted only 69 yards total offense, four by rushing. Michigan coach Bo Schembechler said, "Iowa's defense was underrated because their offense doesn't move the ball."

On November 11 at Bloomington, Indiana built a 24-0 lead in the first half, while Iowa totaled just three first downs and had 48 yards in offense. Iowa installed the I-formation for the first time this season. The Hawkeyes got on the scoreboard in the second half, but too late, on a five-yard scoring pass from Jeff Green to Rod Morton, and a one-yard run by reserve quarterback Bobby Commings, Jr. The Hoosiers won 34-14.

In Coach Comming's last home game, Iowa awoke on offense, startling a crowd of 44,444 and 22 Wisconsin Badgers, to explode for 401 yards total offense in sailing past Wisconsin 38-24. Brad Reid, twice named United Press International Offensive Player of the Week, ran for touchdowns of 10 and 80 yards and caught four passes for 96 yards. Iowa never trailed and led 38-17 with 1:09 to go when Wisconsin scored its final touchdown. Reid, scoring his first TD on his fourth end-around run of the season, added a dazzling 80-yard scoring run in the third period. Iowa's Jim Swift caught a 12-yard scoring pass from Jeff Green and teammate Phil Blatches added scoring runs of six and five yards to round out the offensive show.

Bill Dolan, fading back for a pass.

On November 25, Big Ten co-champion Michigan State showed why it had the best offense in the conference, blitzing Iowa early for a 35-0 halftime lead, then coasting to its eighth win in 11 outings totaling 42 points to Iowa's 7. Iowa scored its only touchdown, a 10-yard pass from Jeff Green to Jon Lazar in the third quarter, when Michigan State's Steve Smith fumbled an Iowa punt after signalling for a fair catch. Freshman Bill Bradley recovered at the 50.

Milton Turner, TB, charges with the ball.

MICHIGAN

The Wolverines of Michigan completed a successful season losing only one Big Ten game to a strong Michigan State team, and again tasting defeat in the Rose Bowl to the University of Southern California in a contest in which the outcome was seriously affected by an official's call that was reviewed long after the game as possibly being wrong.

In the opening game at Ann Arbor, a strong Wolverine defense held Illinois scoreless in a 31-0 win. Michigan broke open a 10-0 game with 21 points in the fourth period as Rick Leach scored two touchdowns, ran for 96 yards and passed for 75 yards. Michigan's defense held Illinois to just 177 yards in total offense. The victory was a costly one for Michigan as offensive tackle Bill Dufek broke a bone in his foot and would be on the sidelines until the Minnesota game. Leach was the Offensive Champion, while linebacker Ron Simpkins was the Defensive Champion and also the UPI's Defensive Player of the Week.

On September 23, at South Bend, Indiana, in a nationally televised game, the Wolverines defeated a highly rated Notre Dame team 28-14 as Michigan rallied for three touchdowns in the second half in the first game played between these teams since 1943. Rick Leach again was outstanding as he ran for Michigan's first touchdown to tie the game at 7-7, then fired touchdown passes of 5 yards, 17 yards and 40 yards in the second half. His three TD passes tied a Michigan record. Leach passed for 110 yards to lead the Michigan attack.

Jerry Meter had a pass interception and a dozen tackles to earn Defensive Champion and ABC-TV's Defensive Player of the game. Leach was ABC's Offensive Player and both the AP and UPI's Offensive Player of the Week. The coaches voted center Steve Nauta the top offensive award. Linebacker Mel Owens suffered a pinched nerve and was lost for the season, while tight end Gene Johnson injured his knee and missed the next two games.

Back in Ann Arbor on September 30, Michigan's second shutout of the season was achieved by holding Duke to 76 net yards in total offense in an impressive 52-0 victory. Nine Wolverines carried the ball for 388 yards as Harlan Huckleby led the way with 84. Michigan scored the first two times it had the ball, then recovered a Duke fumble and scored immediately for a 21-0 lead. Mike Jolly, who had two pass interceptions, was named Defensive Champion, while offensive guard John Arbeznik was the Offensive Champion.

Again at home the following week, in a surprisingly tight 21-17 win over the University of Arizona, Michigan scored late in the first

Roosevelt Smith (26) helping to fill in for the injured Harlan Huckleby, skirts end for short yardage against Minnesota.

period, but Arizona, coached by former Wolverine assistant coach Tony Mason, shocked another 100,000-plus crowd in Michigan Stadium by scoring the next 17 points. It took a 30-yard touchdown pass from Rick Leach to Doug Marsh with just 3:58 left in the first half to get the Wolverines back in the game. Michigan launched a 68-yard, fourth quarter drive and finally on fourth down Russell Davis punched it in for the winning TD with just 5:25 left to play. Harlan Huckleby, who gained 104 yards in just 18 carries, was the Offensive Champion, while middle guard Dale Keitz with 13 tackles and a blocked punt was the Defensive Champion.

On October 14, at Ann Arbor, Michigan State took a 17-point lead at halftime and went on to post its first victory over the Wolverines since 1969. The Spartans ran for 148 yards and passed for 248 in their 24-15 win, the most total offense ever produced against a Bo Schembechler defense at Michigan. Michigan tried to get back into the game in the third period as Rick Leach scored to make it 17-7, but Ed Smith tossed his second TD pass and Michigan could never catch up. Harlan Huckleby, who gained 98 yards, and Russell Davis with 85 shared the Offensive Champion Award while linebacker Ron Simpkins was named Defensive Champion. Leach, who went through the entire season with just four interceptions, had three of them in this game.

Michigan tight end Doug Marsh grabs this 17-yard scoring pass from Rick Leach to break a 14-14 tie with Notre Dame. Leach tossed two TD passes to Marsh and one to Ralph Clayton and scored a fourth touchdown himself to lead Michigan to a 28-14 victory.

    Michigan rebounded from its first defeat of the season the following week as Rick Leach scored two touchdowns and passed for a third to lead the Wolverines to their fifth victory of the season and their 600th in 99 years of intercollegiate football as they defeated the University of Wisconsin at Madison 42-0. Michigan gained 360 yards rushing and Leach passed for 101 of the 117 yards in the air, including a 65-yard strike to wingback Ralph Clayton, who was named Offensive Champion. Harlan Huckleby rushed for

98 yards before he was injured and freshman track sprinter Butch Woolfolk made his varsity debut by gaining 32 yards in six carries. Leach, who gained 44 yards rushing, was named the AP's Offensive Player of the Week, while defensive back Mike Harden was named the Defensive Champion by Bo's staff.

Minnesota became a 'red letter' game for the Wolverines immediately after the Gophers upset the Wolverines 16-0 in Minneapolis in 1977. Rick Leach took charge of the 1978 Homecoming

Lawrence Reid (23) uses a block from John Arbeznik (64) to gain four yards against Minnesota.

Game by accounting for five touchdowns, three on passes and two by running in a 42-10 rout over the visitors. His 26-yard pass to Ralph Clayton and his eight-yard run gave Michigan a 14-3 halftime

Michigan's Rodney Feaster (18) slips by Ohio State's Mike Guess (12) to score the Wolverines first touchdown on a 30-yard pass from Leach.

Michigan's Mike Jolly (16) blocks Joe Unis' field goal attempt. Mike Trgovac (77) also moves in for Michigan.

lead. Leach personally accounted for three touchdowns in the third period to cement the victory and return the Little Brown Jug to Ann Arbor. Freshman Butch Woolfolk make his first start at tailback and gained 131 yards in 22 carries. Leach added 62 on the ground and 143 in the air as the senior quarterback was named AP's Offensive Back of the Week and Michigan's Offensive Champion. Ron Simpkins was named Defensive Champion.

On November 4, at Iowa City, the Wolverines shut out the Hawkeyes 34-0. Rick Leach fired a pair of TD passes and moved Michigan 191 yards in the air despite playing less than three periods as the Wolverines rolled to their seventh victory of the season. Roosevelt Smith gained 70 yards in place of the injured Harlan Huckleby and Butch Woolfolk added 41. Ralph Clayton continued his excellent play as a pass receiver, catching three for 81 yards. Guard Greg Bartnick was named Offensive Champion, while linebacker Ron Simpkins with 11 tackles, two for losses, and a fumble recovery was named Defensive Champion for the fourth time this season and was named the AP's Defensive Player of the Week.

Rick Leach, playing just five minutes more than two periods, accounted for five touchdowns, as Michigan continued to push

Rick Leach pitches to tailback Harlan Huckleby (25) as fullback Russell Davis (33) blocks.

toward its eighth championship in last 10 years crushing Northwestern 59-14 at Evanston on November 11. Leach scored on a yard run, passed 9 yards to Ralph Clayton, passed 41 yards to Ralph Clayton, ran 12 yards for a touchdown and five yards for another before retiring to the bench with more than 10 minutes left in the third period. Michigan tied a Big Ten record with 37 first downs and the 28 first downs by rushing was one short of the 'M' team record. Leach gained 43 yards rushing and 131 yards passing to break the Big Ten's total offense record, while Harlan Huckleby had 138 yards on the ground in his first action in three weeks.

Rick Leach fired two touchdown passes to help Michigan to a 17-0 halftime lead and the Wolverines rolled to a 24-6 win over previously undefeated Purdue, which had allowed Wisconsin to gain a 24-24 tie the previous week. The victory was Michigan's fifth straight and set up a championship and Rose Bowl showdown in Columbus with Ohio State. Fullback Russell Davis, who was to become the only unanimous All-Big Ten offensive selection by the coach, broke loose for 134 yards rushing while Leach had 90 on the ground and 54 passing. Davis was the Offensive Champion while linebacker Jerry Meter was the Defensive Champion. Simpkins and middle guard Mike Trgovac shared the AP's Defensive Player of the Week Award.

Michigan won its eighth Big Ten title in 10 years and third straight trip to the Rose Bowl by defeating Ohio State 14-3 before a record crowd at Columbus. It was the second time Rick Leach was named Player of the Game on offense as he fired two touchdown passes, completed 11 of 21 for 166 yards and rushed for 23 yards. Michigan played without the services of tight end Mark Schmerge, tailback Harlan Huckleby, outside linebacker Tom Seabron and offensive guard John Arbeznik. Leach was named Michigan's Offensive Champion as well as ABC's offensive Player of the Game. Curtis Greer, a quick tackle, was the Defensive Champion for the second time in three games, Ron Simpkins, one of the finest linebackers ever at Michigan, accounted for 15 tackles, while his counterpart at OSU, Tom Cousineau, had 21 tackles.

MICHIGAN STATE

Michigan State's 1978 football season started in frustration and ended in jubilation. It was a saga to rival anything imagined by Horatio Alger.

Coach Darryl Rogers' third Michigan State team opened at Purdue. It was primed and ready as a loaded cannon and promptly exploded into a 14-0 first period lead. There was just one problem. For the second TD, veteran quarterback Eddie Smith, irreplaceable key to the Spartan offense, carried the ball into the end zone from three yards out. In hitting the ground, he fractured a bone in the back of his passing hand. His replacement was Bert Vaughn, a completely inexperienced sophomore. The offense stalled, Purdue rallied and won 21-14.

State, without Smith, defeated outmanned Syracuse 49-21 at East Lansing. A little old lady from Pasadena could have directed the Spartans in that one.

Eddie returned for the Southern California game at Los Angeles but every snap of the ball sent searing pain through his healing hand. His passing was way off and the Trojans won handily, 30-9.

He was much better against Notre Dame, but the Spartans still were down 22-6 at the half. The second half proved to be the turnaround for Eddie and the team. He threw three scoring passes as the Spartans closed the gap to 29-25 at game's end.

But at this point State's record was 1-3 and the rugged set of seven straight Big Ten games were coming up, starting with Michigan at Ann Arbor. No one knew for sure whether that spurt against Notre Dame meant the Spartans were back in the winning groove. It could have been part, at least, the result of an Irish letdown after building that convincing first half lead.

Fans, players and coaches had good reason to wonder whether a really dismal record was in the offing for a team whose preseason prospects had appeared to be so good. With players like Smith, Kirk Gibson, Mark Brammer, Eugene Byrd, Steve Smith, Mel Land, Jim Hinesly, Dan Bass, Tom Graves and other excellent athletes in uniform those early results seemed unreal.

The Michigan game dispelled all doubts. It proved conclusively that the Spartans were for real and that they would have to be counted as a Big Ten championship factor the rest of the way.

This is precisely what Coach Rogers had hoped for from the beginning. The official prospects piece in MSU's pre-season media guide had led off with these words:

"Michigan State anticipates having a football team this fall which, in the words of head coach Darryl Rogers, 'will be a major Big Ten factor.'"

"'We are continuing our building process and still lack depth at certain key positions,' he said. 'It is very important that we stay healthy through our difficult schedule.'"

Quarterback Eddie Smith hands ball to fast moving Leroy McGee who slashed for a good gain in Indiana game.

Spartan's All-Big Ten quarterback Eddie Smith (7) throws under pressure from an Irish attacker.

That last sentence applied most urgently to the quarterback position where there was just Eddie Smith with experience and know how in handling the complex pass-oriented Michigan State attack. And that was exactly where hard luck had struck early.

Against Michigan everything finally fell into place. Smith threw 36 times, completed 20 for 248 yards and two touchdowns and permitted no interceptions. State ran off and hid by 17-0 at the half. Three pass interceptions, two by Mike Marshall and the other by Mark Anderson, set up the three scores. Michigan stormed back with two touchdowns in the second half but MSU got one also and the final count was 24-15. It was the first Spartan victory since 1969 over the Wolverines, when that prior win came in the opening game of the first season that Bo Schembechler coached at Michigan. MSU rolled up 496 yards on offense, the highest total defense-proud Michigan had permitted since an Ohio State game in 1960.

The defense generally was excellent. It bent but didn't break under Michigan's assault. The offense was perfectly balanced. MSU gained 248 yards each via rushing and passing. Nine Spartans carried the ball, topped by Steve Smith's net of 87 yards. Eight of them caught passes, topped by Mark Brammers's seven for 79 yards and a score.

But the superb individual, the person who dominated the game, was Smith. For his efforts he was named Offensive Player of the Week nationally by SPORTS ILLUSTRATED magazine.

Despite this brilliant showing against its No. 1 rival, State still had no valid reason to anticipate rolling on undefeated to the end of the season and then claiming a share of the Big Ten crown. But that is what happened—victories over Indiana 49-14, Wisconsin 55-2, Illinois 59-19, Minnesota 33-9, Northwestern 52-3 and Iowa 42-7.

The only disappointment was the fact that because of its NCAA probation, which is now ended, MSU could not go to the Rose Bowl. Because of its Big Ten tie with Michigan at 7-1 records, plus the fact it beat the Wolverines in the big one, State would have been the Rose Bowl representative for the Big Ten.

En route through the season there occurred perhaps the biggest avalanche of record smashing in Big Ten history. Certainly it was so with the Michigan State team record book.

These record assaults included the following:

INDIVIDUAL RECORDS (Big Ten)
Career (Includes all games):
> *ED SMITH:* Established Big Ten career records for yards gained passing with 5,706; passes attempted with 789; and passes completed with 418.
>
> *KIRK GIBSON:* Established Big Ten career record for yards gained receiving with 2,347.

Season (Conference games only):
> *ED SMITH:* Established season records for yards gained passing with 1,779; yards gained rushing-passing with 1,808; and touchdown passes thrown with 16.
>
> *MORTEN ANDERSEN:* Established season record for P.A.T.'s scored with 44.

Game:
> *ED SMITH:* Established single game records for yards gained passing and total offense with 369 against Indiana.
>
> *DAN BASS:* Established record for longest scoring play with pass interception at 99 yards against Wisconsin.

INDIVIDUAL RECORDS (School)
Career:
> *ED SMITH:* Increased his career records for yards gained pass-

ing to 5,706; passes attempted to 789; passes completed to 418; and touchdown passes thrown to 43. Established career marks for yards gained rushing-passing with 5,556 and passes intercepted with 32.

KIRK GIBSON: Increased his career record for touchdown passes caught to 24. Established career marks for passes caught with 112 and yards gained receiving with 2,347.

Season:

ED SMITH: Established season marks for yards gained passing with 2,226; yards gained rushing-passing with 2,247; passes attempted with 292; passes completed with 169; and touchdown passes thrown with 20.

Crunch! Wisconsin fullback Tom Stauss (26) gets it from three sides at once in game with Michigan State. Identifiable Spartans are Angelo Fields (53) and Larry Savage (57).

KIRK GIBSON: Established season record for yards gained receiving with 806.

MORTEN ANDERSEN: Established season record for P.A.T.'s scored with 52.

RAY STACHOWICZ: Established season mark for punting average at 43.1.

Game:

ED SMITH: Set single game marks for yards gained passing and yards gained rushing-passing against Indiana with 369; passes attempted with 42 against Minnesota; and passes completed with 27 against Notre Dame. Tied the single game record for touchdown passes thrown with 4 against Wisconsin.

MORTEN ANDERSEN: Tied the single game mark for P.A.T's scored with 8 against Illinois.

Play:
DAN BASS: Established record for yards gained on an interception return with 99 against Wisconsin.

RAY STACHOWICZ: Established record for longest punt at 75 yards against Notre Dame.

TEAM RECORDS (School)
Season (all games): Michigan State established season records for points scored with 411; average yards gained rushing-passing per game with 481.0; average yards gained passing per game with 239.0; total first downs with 265; and first downs by passing with 124.

Game:
Michigan State established single game records for total first downs with 34 against Northwestern and first downs by passing with 19 against Minnesota; Smith's 369 yards passing against Indiana is a team offensive mark while his four touchdown passes thrown against Wisconsin and Andersen's eight P.A.T.'S scored against Illinois tied team offensive records.

TEAM RECORDS (Big Ten)
Season (Conference games only): Michigan State established single season Big Ten records for average yards gained rushing-passing per game with 523.1 and average points scored per game with 41.0.

Game:
Smith's 369 yards passing against Indiana is a team offensive record in the Big Ten.

Honors poured in thick and fast. Two Spartans—wide receiver Kirk Gibson and tight end Mark Brammer—were major first team All-American selections. Gibson was named by UPI, NEA, THE SPORTING NEWS and FOOTBALL NEWS. Brammer was tabbed by the Football Writers. Four others, quarterback Eddie Smith, offensive tackle Jim Hinesly, defensive tackle Mel Land and punter Ray Stachowicz, received All-America notices but not first team. These six plus linebacker Dan Bass, defensive back Tom Graves and split end Eugene Byrd made first team All-Big Ten on one or more of the units selected by the two wire services and the Chicago Tribune. Gibson, Brammer, Hinesly and Land were unanimous choices.

Spartan defensive tackle Tanya Webb (98) makes heroic leap attempt to block a punt by Iowa's Dave Holsclaw (3) but missed.

We've got a convoy! Bruce Reeves (30) escorts Steve Smith with kickoff in Indiana game. Smith led Spartan rushers against Hoosiers and scored two TD's.

Smith was named the team's most valuable player by teammates. Six seniors completed their careers by participating in All-Star bowl games. They were Gibson, who was named MVP of the North team in the Senior Bowl game; Smith, MVP in the Blue-Grey game, Hinsely, Land, Graves and defensive back Jerome Stanton.

Coach Rogers got into the action by being named Coach of the Year by THE SPORTING NEWS.

In its announcement of Rogers' selection to the nation's press, THE SPORTING NEWS stated:

> "Rogers has brought a new dimension to Big Ten football. In a conference dominated by coaches who place their main reliance on a running attack and employ the forward pass only as a last resort, Rogers has opened up the game, making it exciting with copius use of the pass."

It seemed a fitting postscript to a season which began like a disaster and wound up as a rousing success story.

MINNESOTA

The 1978 University of Minnesota football season was, in many respects, somewhat like a ride on a roller coaster.

The ups and downs, highs and lows were magnified into moments of extreme giddyness, or deep, deep despair.

Some say there is nothing wrong with a regular season record of five wins and six losses, or a Big Ten record of 4-4 good for fifth place. But those figures combined with high pre-season hopes simply did not add up in the minds of many locals.

In the end, following Minnesota's disastrous 48-10 loss to Wisconsin at Madison, it was decided to replace head coach Cal Stoll after he had completed seven seasons at Minnesota ending with a 39-39 record.

The search was begun immediately and in mid-December, "Smokey" Joe Salem, a Minnesota graduate, was named the new head coach for Gopher football.

The whole thing began in last August when a squad of 117 candidates assembled for pre-fall drills. Among those candidates were a healthy mixture of solid veterans, several men who had seen just enough duty to qualify them as ready reserves, and a good looking crop of rookies. The scene was set and hopes were high.

The opening game of 1978 saw the Toledo Rockets of the Mid-American Conference invade Memorial Stadium on the Gopher campus. Naturally, Minnesota was a heavy favorite.

The Gophers backed up that confidence by taking the opening kickoff and marched 57 yards in 12 plays from where ace kicker Paul Rogind booted a 27-yard field goal.

On the first play of the second quarter sophomore tailback Marion Barber, who was to set a new single season Minnesota rushing record before the year ended, broke over from three yards out to put UM ahead 10-0.

Three minutes later another soph tailback, Roy Artis, scored from one yard out, his first Gopher TD, and came back in another three minutes to score on a 5-yard run as the Gophers owned a comfortable 24-0 halftime buldge.

Minnesota relaxed somewhat in the second half and several reserves saw their first taste of action. Although Toledo, which had been held to 47 yards total offense in the first half, scored two touchdowns on passes, the Gophers added 14 points of their own on a 41-yard dash down the right sidelines by Barber, and a 36-yard pass play from QB Mark Tonn to SE Chester Cooper for the 38-12 final.

Then came the battle all Minnesota fans awaited...the mighty

Ohio State Buckeyes on Memorial Stadium turf. This time the Gophers really believed down deep they would finally dethrone the Bucks. But it was not to be.

Minnesota put itself in a giant hole right at the start giving up a fumble and a pass theft in their own end which the methodical Buckeyes turned into a quick 14 points.

Minnesota tight end Glen Bourquin holds on for dear life as he grabs one of two passes he caught against Ohio State. But it wasn't enough for the Gophers as OSU won 27-10 in the Twin Cities.

Ohio State scored again late in the first half as freshman QB Art Schlichter worked the option series to perfection befuddling the Gopher defense on the flanks.

But on the final play of the first half, Rogind put Minnesota on the board with a 39-yard field goal to make it 21-3, OSU.

Minnesota played a vastly improved second half, but still made the key mistakes that stopped several drives. After the Buckeyes

Minnesota tailback Marion Barber (41) swings outside behind the blocking of guard Jim Anderson (62) to gain good yardage on a sweep against Oregon State. Barber gained 60 yards for the day, but in a losing cause.

scored again following a 47-yard runback of a Gopher punt, reserve QB Mark Carlson passed Minnesota 75 yards in six plays with his final heave going to SB Ray Dilulo for a 15-yard TD. The final, Ohio 27, error prone Minnesota 10.

A trip to the west coast followed as Minnesota took on another national power, the UCLA Bruins. The year before, 1977, Minnesota upset the Uclans 27-13 in the Twin Cities. But this time the home team prevailed 17-3.

Led by fullback Kent Kitzmann, Minnesota drove all over the Los Angeles Coliseum field only to be denied any touchdowns because of that same old bug, key mistakes.

UCLA's first score came on fourth and one to cap a 14-yard drive following a blocked punt. They scored again on a broken play that resulted in a 32-yard TD pass from Rick Bashore to halfback Freeman McNeil to make it 14-0.

The Gophers moved smartly downfield in the third quarter only to again be denied continuity by several key penalties. So Rogind put his talented instep to work and booted a 36-yard field goal.

UCLA got its final score the same way, a 38-yard boot, and that was it. But there wasn't a man on the Gopher squad that didn't believe Minnesota, with the elimination of so many mistakes, could have defeated UCLA.

Kitzmann led the day with 84 yards on 21 carries while Barber

"No, No, Steve. You're supposed to strip the ball from him, not undress him." Nevertheless, Minnesota defensive end Steve Cunningham (70) took any route available to bring down Oregon State QB Steve Smith (15) last fall at Minneapolis.

picked up 60 in 18 tries.

Minnesota then returned home for possibly its biggest disappointment of the season. Oregon State invaded Memorial Stadium and walked away with a 17-14 upset. Again it was mistakes that cost the Gophers dearly...three interceptions and two lost fumbles.

But the heartbreaker came after Minnesota had taken a 7-3 lead in the first quarter. On the kickoff following UM's touchdown, a 9-yard pass from Carlson to TE Glenn Bouriquin, Oregon State's Tim Smith returned the boot 90 yards to score standing up and OSU had a lead it would never lose.

State scored on a short pass in the third period and Carlson threw 50 yards to SE Elmer Bailey in the final stanza to complete the scoring. The Gophers reached midfield and the OSU 35 in the final period but couldn't punch any further and suffered their third straight loss.

But the Gophers got back on the winning side the next week, handing Iowa a 22-20 loss again at home. It appeared after the first half that the Gophers had a laughter going their way. Not so.

Kitzmann went over from one yard out in the first quarter before Carlson and Bailey hooked up on a pair of identical 17-yard TD pass plays to give UM a 19-0 halftime lead. Then Rogind added a 27-yard field goal early in the third period and an apparent rout was on. Not so.

Iowa then unleashed a torrid passing attack with reserve QB Jeff Green leading the way. Green scored from one yard out, set up another running tally after connecting on some long bombs, and then scored again himself on another 1-yard plunge with 7:07 left to play. However, a run for the conversion failed when Green, attempting to pass, was smothered for a huge loss by nose guard Doug Friberg and Minnesota's 22-20 lead was safe.

The Gophers ran out the clock and had their first Big Ten win.

Minnesota made it two in row the following weekend traveling to Northwestern where the Gophers defeated the Wildcats 38-14. Kitzmann scored two on short runs, Barber took an 8-yard pass from Carlson for another score and later ran in from seven yards out. But the play of the day was a 72-yard dash to score by Artis which turned out to be Minnesota's longest gain of the season. Rogind added another field goal, this one from 30-yards out.

The next weekend saw the 61st renewal of the famed *"Little Brown Jug"* series against Michigan at Ann Arbor. To say that Michigan was "up" for this match would be a gross understatement. The year previous, Minnesota had upset the then Number One ranked Wolverines 16-0 for the first Gopher possession of the "Jug" in nine years. Ownership changed quickly.

All-American QB Rick Leach passed for three touchdowns and scored two more running to lead the Wolverines 42-10 over the Gophers. For Minnesota, only Barber's 75 yards rushing, a 20-yard field goal by Rogind, and Kitzmann's late 2-yard TD plunge averted a shutout.

With a 2-2 league record, the Gophers returned home to play one of the most improbable contests ever seen in Minneapolis.

The opponent was Indiana, long a thorn in Minnesota's hopes. And it appeared by halftime the Hoosiers were about to shove the thorn in deeper by taking a 24-7 lead. Two long Indiana bombs and a 92-yard return of an intercepted fumble caused most of the Gopher first half woes. Only a 1-yard plunge by Barber put UM on the board in the first 30 minutes.

Barber scored again in the third period to make it 24-14 only to see the Hoosiers up their lead to 31-14 early in the final stanza.

Then came the improbable comeback. Quarterback Wendell Avery came off the bench to spark a pair of wild drives with accurate passes and scrambling runs. He put the Gophers over the goal line twice on a 14-yard screen pass to Artis, and a 19-yard screen to Barber. Rogind booted the first conversion, but Avery passed for a 2-pointer to Bailey on the second. The score read Minnesota 29, Indiana 31.

Minnesota finally regained possession with 2:34 remaining when FS Keith Edwards made his third interception of the game at the Gopher 41. Indiana had tried a miracle bomb on third down from their own 23 after a holding penalty set them back.

Avery went to work again hitting short passes and running himself for gains of 5 and 7 yards. He helped move the ball to the Hoosier 14 where with 5 seconds left Minnesota called time out.

Enter the ice man—kicker Rogind—and, well, you know the rest. Rogind booted a perfect 31-yard placement and the Gophers had what NCAA historians later called the third largest comeback from deficit win in the game's history, 32-31.

Besides the heroics of Avery and Rogind, Barber chipped in with 177 yards rushing and three scores. For the day, Minnesota amassed 577 yards total offense.

Then it was back on the road to eventual Big Ten co-Champion Michigan State where the airborn Spartans put on another awesome pass display, their trademark all season, to whip the Gophers 33-9. MSU quarterback Eddie Smith enjoyed another terrific afternoon completing 26 of 42 aerials for 296 yards and a pair of scores. For the Gophers, Barber gained 75 yards and Avery passed 15 yards to Bailey for the Gopher TD. Rogind hit another field goal from 25 yards out in the second quarter after suffering his first miss in Big Ten play earlier.

The next Saturday afternoon belonged to Marion Barber and the Gopher offensive line. Minnesota returned home to host Illinois in hopes of running its season record to an even 5-5. Barber and his mates turned the trick.

After gaining 143 first half yards and scoring twice on runs of 1 and 15 yards (plus having a 44-yarder called back), Barber continued his personal assault on the Illini ending with a career high 233 yards rushing on 36 carries in Minnesota's 24-6 victory. Sophomore fullback Gary White enjoyed his first day over the century mark gaining 102 yards and scored his first collegiate TD to boot. Minnesota totaled 409 yards total offense.

And then came the day everyone in Gopherland would just as soon forget. A win at Wisconsin would mark a fourth consecutive winning season. But it was not to be. The teams hacked away at each other pretty evenly with UW holding a slim 14-10 halftime lead.

But the Badgers, mainly on the flying feet of running back and ace kick returner Ira Matthews, roared home with 34 second half points to crush Minnesota's hopes, 48-10. The only bright spots for Minnesota were a 4-yard TD run by Barber, his 10th score rushing that fall, and Rogind's 10th field goal of the campaign.

For the day Barber gained 111 yards giving him the all-time Minnesota single season rushing mark of 1,210 yards. For those and other efforts he was named first team All-Big Ten by AP, UPI, and the Chicago Tribune. And he has two more years remaining.

Captain and DE Stan Sytsma, SS Keith Brown and Rogind were also named to the Big Ten first honor teams. Barber ended it all by being named team MVP by his fellow players while Sytsma was voted the outstanding Gopher defensive player.

One fullback, Gary White (9), helps the officials signal a touchdown for Minnesota while the other fullback, Kent Kitzmann (44) cradles the ball in the Iowa end zone last fall. It was Minnesota's first score that afternoon as the Gophers won 22-20.

81

NORTHWESTERN

The 1978 football season was an investment year for Northwestern. Injuries plagued the Wildcats and forced rookie coach Rick Venturi to use several freshmen in pressure situations. After compiling and 0-10-1 mark in 1978, Venturi plans on using the freshmen along with his 1979 recruiting class as the nucleus of the future at Northwestern.

"I think out staff has proven that we can recruit," Venturi said. "We had between 19 and 22 freshman that played a lot last year. The 1978 season was actually an investment year for us. I've said all along that we get our junior varsity experience on Saturday afternoon out on the field."

It was a tough first year for Venturi as 11 players were lost for the season with injuries, and ten of those were knee casualties.

"The majority of our injuries have come on defense," Venturi said. "I lost flanker Todd Sheets and linebacker Scott Duncan before the season even started. However, Sheets will be coming back on offense next year with the *"Kitty Core"* and we should really be able to throw the rock a year from now."

The Wildcats, behind the arm of junior Kevin Strasser, developed a respected passing attack in 1978 and Venturi plans to build on that foundation next year.

"I really wanted to teach our players to throw and catch," Venturi said. "We have a super group of receivers and Strasser really did a fine job for us. When teams begin to defend against the pass more, then our running game can open up."

Venturi's passing plans were previewed in the season opener at Illinois. the optimistic Wildcats were searching for their second consecutive victory over the *Fighting Illini*, after winning 21-7, in the 1977 season finale. The game was particularly significant to Venturi because he served as an assistant coach at Illinois during the 1977 season.

"I've approached this season with one thing in mind—total improvement of the program," Venturi said at the time. "We're in a positive frame of mind heading into the season. Our overall objective is to be a better football team after eleven weeks than we are today."

In the game, Northwestern and Illinois battled to a 0-0 tie, marking the first shutout for Northwestern since a 30-0 whitewashing of Indiana in 1975.

Quarterback Kevin Strasser put on quite an aerial display in his first varsity start at Northwestern. He connected on 17 of 33 pass-

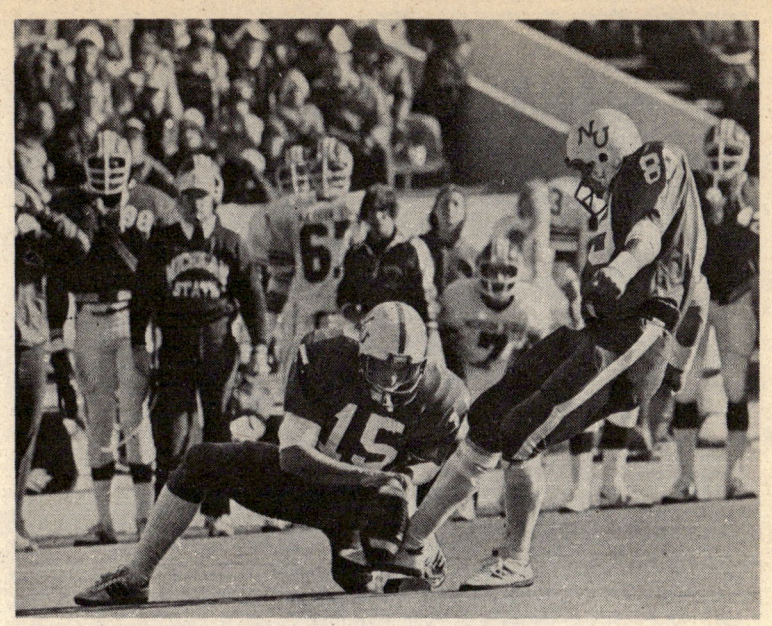

Senior Sam Poulos (89) puts his foot to a 36-yard field goal for Northwestern's only three points of the afternoon in the Big Ten finale against Michigan State.

Northwestern's Jim Dunlea (53), defensive tackle, prepares to apply the finishing hit to Michigan State fullback Alonzo Middleton. Dunlea had four tackles and three assists as a rare starter in his final Northwestern appearance.

83

Northwestern Head Coach Rick Venturi shows a little tender-loving concern for quarterback Kevin Strasser (13) during the game against Michigan. Togetherness and enthusiasm kept the team going in what was the "Investment Season" of Venturi's new program at NU.

ing attempts for 137 yards, including eight passes to sophomore split end Mike McGee.

The Wildcat defense also rose to the occasion several times paced by Pat Geegan and Jim Miller. However, during the course of the game, Miller and starting tackle Norm Wells suffered knee injuries which finished their respective seasons.

"I was very proud of our defense at Illinois," Venturi commented. "We played with a lot of class for a very young football team. We gave our best effort. We just hope to keep getting better tomorrow and the next day."

The next assignment for Northwestern was another road contest, at Iowa. The Hawkeyes are always one of the Big Ten's strongest defensive teams and they proved it again on September 18, holding the Wildcats to only three points in a 20-3 victory.

Crucial turnovers put the Wildcats in a quick hole but the young visitors continued to claw back. Midway through the second quarter, Dave Mishler was stopped on a fourth down-and-one situation at the Iowa five-yard line. The only points the frustrated Wildcats could put on the board was a 44-yard field goal by Nick Mirkopulos.

"We showed progress against Iowa and I was proud of the way we played," Venturi said. "We came back strong after a slow start and had a chance to get back in the game. We played four quarters of rock 'em, sock 'em football."

Venturi and his troops headed back to Evanston for their initial home contest of the season against Wisconsin. The Wildcats were exciting and promised a thrilling afternoon for the home fans.

Sure enough, Northwestern came out passing and had some favorable results. Strasser fired a 79-yard touchdown strike to McGee and the Wildcats pulled into a 7-7 tie late in the first quarter. The touchdown pass was the fourth longest in Northwestern history but unfortunately the Wildcats failed to put any more points on the board and suffered a 28-7 defeat at the hands of the then unbeaten Badgers.

Split end Tim Rooney (34) rushes on the field to congratulate quarterback Kevin Strasser (13) after a second-quarter touchdown pass to Steve Bogan against Michigan.

In addition to the loss, Northwestern was struck with serious injuries once again. Starting defensive tackle Mike Weitzman and defensive end Curt Grelle were knocked out of action for the remainder of the year with knee injuries.

"We did a few things better against Wisconsin," Venturi said. "We executed better offense and played tough despite some more injuries. Win, lose or draw, I want us to be a better team at the end of the game than we were at the beginning."

Another unbeaten team, 13th-ranked Colorado was the next challenge for Northwestern. A road contest with one of the best teams in the country was no easy chore for the Wildcats but the guests battled to a 7-7 tie with 3:29 remaining in the first half. Then the roof fell in. Colorado scored six points with only ten seconds left in the half and then registered two touchdowns in the span of three seconds after the intermission as the Buffs rolled to a 55-7 victory.

"For the first half, I though we were a pretty good football team," Venturi said. "The defense hung in there and the offense was able to move the ball. In the third quarter, we blew ourselves out of the game."

The enthusiastic Venturi and his Wildcats returned home the following Saturday to conclude the non-conference portion of the schedule against Arizona State. The Northwestern defense did a good job in the first ten minutes but finally surrendered three-first quarter touchdowns and Arizona State prevailed, 56-14.

One of the bright spots for the Wildcats was freshman split end Steve Bogan. The speedster from Weston, CT, snared two touchdown passes. For the afternoon, Bogan caught four passes for a total of 128 yards.

"Some of our freshmen played very well against Arizona State," Venturi said. "That was the first time we got a lot of our young kids into the game. I think this team has made a transition and in some respects, this is a new team."

The Wildcats headed into the halfway mark of their season with a 0-4-1 record but Venturi was confident things might be different in the 'second season', starting with a road game at Indiana.

"I'm very excited about the next six games and in essence, this is our second season," Venturi said. "All remaining games are Big Ten contests and I can see little things developing for our team along the way. Some young kids, including Bogan, are playing with enthusiasm."

Unfortunately, the Indiana game, or the Italian Bowl, as Venturi called it (matching Rick Venturi against Hoosier coach Lee Corso) didn't go according to Venturi's plans. Once again, a lost fumble deep in Northwestern territory put the Wildcats behind in the early stages of the game. Immediately following the Indiana touchdown, a Strasser aerial was picked off and returned to the Wildcat 24-yard line.

Two minutes later, Indiana hit paydirt again and went on to post a 38-10 conquest of Northwestern.

"Every game has a critical period and in this one it was early," Venturi said. "We were fired up and this was a big game for us. We have to learn to play in pressure situations."

The Strasser-to-Bogan combination went to work again the next week in a home clash with Minnesota. Strasser scooted 18 yards for a touchdown and had a hand in a 19-yard option pass from tailback Lou Tiberi to Bogan which resulted in a touchdown. Strasser completed 13 passes for 153 yards on the day and connected with Bogan three times for 42 yards in Minnesota's 38-14 victory.

"As long as we continue moving forward and progressing, I won't become discouraged about our program," Venturi said afterwards. "Every week we find a new player who steps in and gives us a good performance. We have made progressive changes that will help us build for the future."

The final four games on the Wildcat schedule would be tough one's for the young and inexperienced Wildcats. The four top teams in the Big Ten: Ohio State, Purdue, Michigan and Michigan State provided the opposition.

Winning at Columbus, OH, doesn't come easy. Northwestern lost 63-20 to Ohio State but gained some valuable experience. An option pass from Tiberi to Strasser for 11 yards fooled Woody Hayes and all the Buckeyes as Northwestern pulled into a 7-7 tie midway through the first quarter. As the game progressed, Ohio State's depth proved to be too much for the injury-plagued Wildcats.

"That was my longest afternoon of the season," Venturi admitted. "Defensively, we just couldn't hold the line and offensively we've got to play a perfect game to stay with some of the teams we are playing now."

Northwestern's final road game of the season was at Purdue and the Boilermakers were the hottest team in the conference at that point in time. Purdue didn't let down one bit against Northwestern and blanked the Wildcats 31-0 in Ross-Ade Stadium.

"We played as good a game on defense as we had to play to hope to pull the upset," Venturi commented. "But our offense just couldn't get anything going."

The Wildcats closed their season with home engagements against Michigan and Michigan State. The Wolverines, hungry for another conference championship, downed the Wildcats 59-14 and one week later Michigan State prevailed 52-3.

Despite the 0-10-1 record in his rookie season, Venturi remained optimistic and not discouraged.

"I haven't lost any enthusiasm nor the belief that we can get the job done at Northwestern," Venturi said. "Offensively, we have improved a mile from the beginning of the season. Also, we've had two different teams playing defense this year due to our injury situation. We must play great defense week in and week out in order to win consistently."

Strasser broke two school records in 1978. The junior signalcaller set a new Northwestern mark with 307 passing attempts in a season and another record with 151 completions on the year.

Sophomore tailback Tim Hill, Northwestern's leading receiver with 24 receptions, led the Big Ten in kickoff returns with a 25.1 average. Hill returned a kickoff 68 yards against Wisconsin in his best effort of the season.

Freshman Bogan also set a record in 1978. His six touchdown

Frustration was as great an opponent as any of the 11 teams on the schedule for Northwestern Coach Rick Venturi in 1978.

receptions are the most in Big Ten history by a freshman.

All in all, Venturi is confident his alma mater can turn the corner. He saw a few bright spots in 1978 and his continual enthusiasm for the job and dedication to construct a winning program remains.

"I honestly think we can have a winning program here," Venturi says. "That's what our staff works around the clock for. I won't sleep until we become a winner."

OHIO STATE

Ohio State began the 1978 season with an unprecedented string of six consecutive Big Ten football titles, either won outright or shared, and six straight bowl appearances, also a Big Ten record.

The number of consecutive conference championships ended at six, but the bowl appearances were extended to seven. Generally, the 1978 football season had to be considered sub-par by lofty Ohio State standards. Prospects were optimistic when the season began, for the Buckeyes had 14 returning regulars back from the championship team of 1977, equally divided between offense and defense. There was good speed at key positions, the size was adequate and the general team depth was above average. Only in the defensive secondary was depth a matter of concern.

The schedule was demanding, especially in the early season. The Buckeyes were to open with Penn State, a solid, experienced team that was rated high in the top ten in virtually every pre-season poll. The situation was further complicated for Ohio State since Penn State would play two games prior to the Ohio State game and therefore, would be in position to work out any problem areas that might develop before meeting the Buckeyes. Ohio State did not enjoy this luxury.

The result was a decisive 19-0 victory over Ohio State. Buckeye Coach Woody Hayes hoped to surprise the Nittany Lions by starting freshman quarterback Art Schlichter and by moving 1977 quarterback Rod Gerald to wide receiver. The Buckeyes came out throwing. They passed and passed but couldn't sustain a consistent offense against the rugged Penn State defense. In all Ohio State attempted an uncharacteristic 34 passes while trying only 43 running plays. And while Ohio State outgained Penn State 336 yards to 287, five interceptions and three lost fumbles were too much to overcome as Penn State turned over the ball only once.

What effect the opening loss to Penn State had upon the Ohio State season is open to speculation. Some believe the Buckeyes never recovered.

Game two against Minnesota was a total contrast to the opener. Ohio State virtually abandoned the passing game and turned to its familiar running game. The Buckeyes ran on 73 of 81 occasions and piled up 300 yards on the ground to only 57 in the air to overwhelm an unsuspecting Minnesota team that didn't believe the Buckeyes would change their tactics so radically in one short week.

Rod Gerald played mostly wide receiver in 1978. Here he plays quarterback vs. Penn State.

Art Schlichter sets up to pass vs. Penn State.

All Big Ten guard Fritz (56) leads the blocking for a Buckeye back.

Ohio State's next two opponents were Baylor and Southern Methodist, from the opportunistic, pass-minded Southwest Conference. Baylor was a surprisingly stubborn opponent. The Buckeyes plotted a ground assault while Baylor was determined to strike through the air. The result was a wild offensive show that saw 62 points scored and the lead change hands five times before Ohio State prevailed, 34-28. If the game proved anything, it was that Ohio State had an impressive, strong running attack but the Buckeye defense was vulnerable to the pass.

Unfortunately, Southern Methodist proved this beyond all doubt. While Ohio State was churning up the yardage by ground bursts, Southern Methodist was displaying a bewildering aerial game that connected on 36 of 57 passes for 341 yards. Neither defense could contain the opponent as each team scored 35 points.

Buckeye hopes of a seventh straight Big Ten championship were dealt a rude jolt in game five against Purdue. The fired up Boilermakers made effective use of a short passing game coupled with well-executed bursts from tackle to tackle to defeat the Buckeyes 27 to 16 at West Lafayette. Once again it was the pass that did in Ohio State, as Purdue hit on 22 of 34 tosses to sustain an offense that kept the Buckeye defense on the field much too long. The Buckeyes displayed a potent offense with 507 yards, well balanced with 259 on the ground and a surprising 289 in the air. Quarterbacks Mark Herrmann of Purdue and Art Schlichter staged a brilliant passing duel. The difference was in turnovers, as Ohio State fumbled six times losing the ball on four occasions, while Purdue had no fumbles.

With Ohio State's record two wins, two losses and one tie after five games and one and one in Big Ten play, the Buckeyes could not afford to lose again in conference play.

Game six found Ohio State hosting Iowa. The Buckeyes won handily 31-7 after building up a 31-0 lead at halftime. Ohio State ran for 321 yards and passed for 102 and had no turnovers, a dramatic turn-around from the previous week. The highlight of the game was a picture scoring pass from Schlichter to flanker Doug Donley that covered 78 yards.

Struggling Northwestern was Ohio State's next opponent and the scrappy but overmatched Wildcats were easy victims 63-20. Coach Woody Hayes used 66 players to keep the score respectable as ten different backs carried the ball. The Buckeye offense am-

Ohio State's swarming defense stops a Wisconsin ball carrier for short yardage.

massed 546 yards and 33 first downs against the Wildcats.

Ohio's next opponent was Wisconsin at Madison. Again the Buckeye offense was dominant, as Ohio State raced to a 21-7 halftime lead. Fullbacks Paul Campbell and Ric Volley ran with authority as the Ohio State offensive line had a decided edge over the Badger defensive front. The second half was more of the same as Ohio State scored two times in both the third and fourth quarters. When the game was over, Ohio State had a convincing 49-14 margin over the Badgers.

With three straight Big Ten victories and an overall conference mark of 4-1, Ohio State returned to Columbus for a game with Illinois. It was another solid win for the Buckeyes, 45-7. The margin could have been much greater had Coach Hayes so chosen. Ohio State substituted freely, using 62 players, including 11 different ball carriers. Even more significant was a strong showing of the Ohio State defense. The defensive unit, that had been pushed around on several previous occasions, played aggressive, hard-hitting football. Tackling was crisp and the Buckeye line shut down the Illinois offense convincingly. Linebacker Tom Cousineau was brilliant on defense as he had been all season, but against Illinois, other defenders asserted themselves. Linebacker Al Washington, middle guard Mark Sullivan, tackles Luther Henson and Byron Cato and halfback Vince Skillings played extremely well. Many observers believed that the Buckeyes had put it together and were about to emerge again as one of the nation's top teams. Not to be overlooked in the impressive win over Illinois, was an injury to tailback Cal Murray, who had played his way into prominence with consistently great efforts week after week. Little did Buckeye fans or coaches realize that Murray would not carry the ball in either of the two remaining regular season games and would make only a token appearance in the bowl game that was to follow.

Ohio's tenth opponent was Indiana. The game was played at Bloomington and, as usual, it brought out the best in Coach Lee Corso's scrappy Hoosiers. Ohio State marched 83 yards to score on its first possession, but Indiana tied it in the first period and kicked a field goal in the second quarter to take a 10-7 halftime lead. The Buckeyes came back in the third period with a awesome 98-yard, 20-play drive to regain the lead 14-10. When tailback Ricky Johnson raced 46 yards for a third Buckeye touchdown and a 21-10 lead, Ohio State fans breathed easier. Not for long though, as Indiana put together a 72-yard drive in 14 plays, along with a two-point conversion, to cut the Buckeye margin to 21-18. This proved to be the final score, but not before Buckeye fans endured more uncomfortable moments. Although Ohio State was able to defeat Indiana, many of the original doubts about the Buckeye's strength were rekindled.

Thus the stage was set for the annual showdown game with Michigan. Once again the Big Ten championship and a trip to the Rose Bowl was at stake, although for the first time in many years, the 1978 Big Ten race did not involve only Michigan and Ohio State, for Michigan State and Purdue were championship contenders. Michigan State could not go to a bowl because of probation, while Purdue had a loss to Michigan and a tie to Wisconsin on its record.

OSU MG Mark Sullivan scores his first career TD on a pass int. return vs. Iowa.

Michigan, Ohio State and Michigan State each had one Big Ten loss going into the final game.

As in recent years, the Michigan-Ohio State game was a defensive battle. Although both teams had high scoring, potent offenses, it was the defense that prevailed. Ohio State opened the scoring with a 29-yard field goal by Bob Atha, but Michigan took the lead by going 70 yards in four plays, including passes of 26, 14 and 30 yards. The half ended 7-3 in favor of Michigan. The second half was a nightmare for Ohio State's offense, as the Buckeyes neither scored nor registered a first down. Michigan managed one score, again on a pass, to win 14-3. The victory gave the Wolverines a share of the Big Ten crown with Michigan State and the right to play in the Rose Bowl. The loss dropped the Buckeyes to fourth in the Big Ten standings, the lowest since 1967, when Ohio State also finished fourth.

Thus, Ohio State finished the regular season with a 7-3-1 mark. The season began with a loss to Penn State and ended with a defeat to Michigan. In between were seven victories, one tie and a loss to Purdue. Ohio State had some standout football players but none greater than linebacker Tom Cousineau, who was a consensus All-American for the second straight year. His regular season total of 227 tackles far surpassed the school record. Coach Woody Hayes called Cousineau, "the best conditioned athlete I have ever coached", and few who saw him will disagree.

Guard Ken Fritz, tackle Joe Robinson and punter Tom Orosz were named to the All-Big Ten first team on offense, while tackle Keith Ferguson and tight end Jimmy Moore were named on the second team. On defense, Cousineau was an overwhelming choice on the first team along with teammates Kelton Dansler, Vince Skillings and Mike Guess. Byron Cato was named on the second unit.

PURDUE

Purdue's history-steeped and nationally-known football tradition, laced with legendary players and their *individual* accomplishments, returned to national prominence in 1978 *as a team*!

Great college players like Len Dawson, Bob Griese, Mike Phipps, Otis Armstrong, Darryl Stingley, Larry Burton, Mike Pruitt, Ken Novak, Dave Butz, Tim Foley, Gregg Bingham, and Leroy Keyes have graced Purdue's past and long ago put the school's name on the college football map.

But only once before—following the 1966 season—did a Boilermaker team compete in a bowl game when Purdue defeated Southern California 14-13 in the 1967 Rose Bowl.

Thus, Purdue's appearance in the 11th annual Peach Bowl marked only the second time in 92 years of Purdue football that the Boilermakers have appeared in a bowl game of any kind!

Two years ago, Purdue head coach Jim Young took over a program that hadn't enjoyed a winning season since 1972 and but one since '69. He guided his inexperienced first Boiler squad to a 5-6 finish.

In 1978, his still-young-but-maturing second Boilermaker team accomplished the following to the surprise of many but the delight of all:

*First winning season since 1972
*First bowl appearance since 1967 and only the second in 92 years of Purdue football
*First to win five straight games in one season since 1945.
*Most victories since 1969 equaling the school's only nine-win season (1966) with a Peach Bowl victory
*Regained the Old Oaken Bucket from intrastate rival Indiana
*Shut out three foes for the first time since 1966
*Held sole possession of first place in the Big Ten (for four weeks), the first Purdue team to do that since the final week of the 1967 season
*Defeated Ohio State (27-16) for the first time since 1967
*First team to go without a penalty in one game since 1948
*First team to avoid a shutout since 1973
*First team to limit the opposition to just six touchdowns via the rush for the entire season
*First team to go unbeaten at home since 1969
*Set Purdue's single-season home attendance record of 373,504

Purdue linebacker Kevin Motts.

*Stamped Purdue a "comer" in college football

Purdue's Cinderella Story fell together primarily due to a marvelous defense, a new-found ability to run, and a golden-armed sophomore quarterback named Mark Herrmann.

While Herrmann, already the Big Ten's No. 5 all-time career passer (4191 yards) just 22 games into his college career, draws most of the publicity because of the American sporting public's enchantment with outstanding passers, the Purdue defense and running game were the major reasons for the Boilers' resurgence. Just ask the head coach.

Purdue quarterback   Mark Hermann.

"The improvement in our defense and running game were the keys to our success this season," Young offers freely. "The defense was the best I've had in my six years as a head coach (four at Arizona and two at Purdue), and it also was very gratifying to watch our running game come along. Last year we couldn't run the ball across the field. But our ability to run the football this year gave us the threat to both run or pass, which you have to have in order to have a successful offense."

Young's defenders earned the moniker "Junk Defense" because of the many unusual formations or "looks" it threw at the

Purdue quarterback Mark Hermann fires a Boilermaker pass.

Wide receiver Raymond Smith catches a sideline pass against Notre Dame.

Purdue defensive tackle Marcus Johnson decks the Northwestern quarterback.

opposition. More often than not it successfully deceived the offensive blocking schemes. Wake Forest head coach John Mackovic, himself a former Young assistant coach, coined his own name for the unit—"The Crunch Bunch."

Whatever name it merited, the defense was spectacular! Four times last fall Boilermaker opponents rushed for less than 100 yards (Ohio, 98; Wake Forest, 43; Illinois, 70; and Northwestern, 38). Six times they passed for less than the century mark (Ohio, 91; Notre Dame, 95; Wake Forest, 89; Illinois, 52; Iowa, 92; and Michigan, 54). Six times the opposition scored fewer than 10 points; three of those were shutouts (Ohio, Illinois, and Northwestern). Only Wisconsin and Michigan hit the 20-point barrier. Only six touchdowns were scored against Purdue via the rush, a school record. And at season's end, the bottom line bordered on the amazing: Opponent net yards rushing per game, 138.1; opponent net yards passing per game, 127.5!

And in what may be the greatest accomplishment of them all, Young's "Junk Defense" was exciting to watch!

Purdue quarterback Mark Hermann prepares to unleash an aerial against Iowa.

Three juniors must be singled out as the heart of the defense: Cat-quick defensive end and Purdue's top all-planet candidate Keena Turner, who contributed a staggering 24 tackles for loss (for minus 189 yards); middle linebacker Kevin Motts, already Purdue's all-time career tackler who added 143 this fall; and nose guard Ken Loushin, whose 400-pound bench pressing strength demanded double and triple teaming.

As the season began, the diversity of Purdue's offense remained a huge question mark. Returning was Herrmann, the young man who threw for a sensational 2453 yards as a freshman to finish second nationally in passing, a solid corps of receivers considered second to none in the Big Ten, and a group of running backs who gained only 556 of the team's 1426 yards the year before.

A running complement to Herrmann's staggering passing threat had to be found or the gifted 6-5 slinger would be throwing into pass-prevent defenses for 11 straight Saturdays.

Enter unsung sophomore fullback John Macon and senior tailback Russell Pope. They, together with the late-season emergence of junior fullback Mike Augustyniak, the Indiana-game showcasing of freshman tailback Wally Jones, and an offensive line one year better and blessed with a season of relative health, brought the Boilers the offensive balance the doctor ordered.

Macon contributed four 100-yard afternoons. Pope added three. Better, yet, three times they did it the same day. And when sprained ankles slowed the two who handled the ball for 366 of the Boilers' 564 rushes in 1978, Augustyniak and Jones surfaced for 135 and 103 yards, respectively, in the satisfying season finale against archrival Indiana.

As for Herrmann, words hardly can describe the quiet young man's abilities. Only four players—Ed Smith (Michigan State), Mike Phipps (Purdue), Bob Griese (Purdue), and Maurie Daigneau (Northwestern)—in the history of the Big Ten have thrown for more yar-

Purdue defensive tackle Calvin Clark moves in on Ohio State quarterback Rod Gerald (7).

dage in their careers than Herrmann. But "Herm" still has half of his career ahead of him.

His talented right arm has lofted 569 passes in the 22 games he's played and 315 have found the waiting hands of Boiler receivers, an imposing completion percentage of 54 percent. Of those 315 completions, 30 have gone for touchdowns, spelling well over one TD pass per game.

It all added up to one of the finest seasons in the history of Boilermaker football, and the head coach summed it up before the Peach Bowl by saying: "We put a sign up in the players' locker room before last season that reads 'Reserved For The Next Purdue Bowl Team.' We have a picture to put in it now. The players deserve the bowl; they've worked hard all year. I hope they look upon it as a reward for a winning season. The players really have contributed to our football program and to Purdue University this year."

WISCONSIN

Wisconsin's 1978 football season produced a winning 5-4-2 record in the first year for Dave McClain as the Badgers' head football coach.

McClain had taken the Wisconsin job in December, 1977 following the resignation of John Jardine who, in his eighth year as Wisconsin football coach, had seen his team win the season's first five games, then lose the final six. Jardine had resigned after the ninth game—a 22-0 defeat by Purdue.

The 39-year-old McClain came to Wisconsin from Ball State University where he had compiled an overall 46-25-3 record in seven previous seasons including the Mid-American Conference championship in 1976, and Mid-American Conference "Coach-of the Year" honors in 1975.

In guiding Wisconsin to a winning season in 1978, McClain accomplished a feat last turned in by Ivan Williamson when he came to the Madison campus as successor to Harry Stuhldreher in 1949. Williamson's first team had a 5-3-1 record and he had the Badgers in Big Ten championship and Rose Bowl contention for six straight seasons before moving up to the athletic directorship following the 1955 season (4-5-0).

Wisconsin's winning season was the school's first since a 7-4-0 record in 1974 and its second since an overall 5-4-0 record in 1963.

The Badgers played a seven game home schedule in 1978—winning 4, losing 2, tying one—with over one-half million fans sitting in on the action (500,102) or an average of 71,443 per game and a ranking of seventh nationally in major college home attendance.

Wisconsin's home football attendance ranks fourth nationally during the 1970's decade with a total of 3,795,247 fans seeing the Badgers' 55 games in Camp Randall Stadium 1970 through 1978. That's an average attendance of 69,004 during that time and the Badgers have ranked in the top ten in attendance each year during the '70's.

Wisconsin started the 1978 football season with four consecutive victories before being tied at Illinois.

The wins came over Richmond 7-6, at Northwestern 28-7, over Oregon 22-19, and over Indiana 34-7.

Wisconsin won the Richmond game on an 80 yard pass play from freshman quarterback John Josten to Tri-Captain David Charles in the second period which overcame a pair of field goals

Wisconsin started a freshman quarterback John Josten (13) against the Spiders in the 1978 opener in Camp Randall Stadium won by Wisconsin 7-6.

by the losers.

Sparkling defensive play, especially by senior middle guard Dan Relich held the Spiders at bay when they threatened to overtake the Badgers late in the game.

The win at Northwestern was achieved by a solid running attack with senior tailback Ira Matthews and Junior fullback Tom Stauss each rushing for more than 100 yards, and Josten was perfect in the air—seven of seven for 79 yards—to complement the ground game. Ira Matthews contributed a 78 yard punt return for a touchdown as he set out to lead the nation's punt returners with a 16.9 yards per return average.

Junior quarterback Mike Kalasmiki rallied the Badgers gallantly in the waning moments to pull out a 22-19 win over Oregon in an intersectional clash in Camp Randall in the season's third game.

Injuries early in the game sidelined fullback Tom Stauss, quarterback John Josten, and tailback Ira Matthews, and when the Badgers failed to move the ball on the ground, Coach Dave McClain turned to Kalasmiki.

The junior, from Addison, Illinois, who came back from a late season knee injury in 1977, completed 16 of 35 passes for 232 yards and a pair of touchdowns in leading the Badgers to victory.

Wisconsin won its fourth game in a row, and its second in the Big Ten, a week later 34-7 over Indiana as Ira Matthews tallied three first half touchdowns to stun the Hoosiers.

His 71 yard punt return for TD started the Hoosiers' demise and he also tallied on runs of six and 26 from scrimmage as the Badgers built a 21-0 halftime lead.

The tie game at Illinois (20-20) in the fifth week of the season blunted the Wisconsin winning streak.

The Badgers led 20-12 midway through the final period when the Illini put together a 69 yard, 15 play march to make the score 20-18 with 2:56 to play. Quarterback Rich Weiss was the Illinois hero as he tallied the tying touchdown on an eight yard run, then tossed a pass—it was underthrown and tipped by Wisconsin outside linebacker Guy Boliaux, yet caught by tight end Lee Boeke—for two extra points that netted the tie.

Wisconsin defensive tackle Tom Schremp (76) congratulates teammate and linebacker Dennis Christenson (48) following Christenson's recovery of an Oregon fumble by Vince Williams early in the third period of game won by Badgers 22-19.

The Badgers returned home to play the top four teams in the conference back-to-back starting with Michigan's co-champions.

Michigan dominated the Badgers 42-0 on the scoreboard and won the statistical battle, too. The Wolverines ran 73 plays to gain 360 yards rushing and 117 in the air, while 60 plays for the Badgers netted 133 yards rushing and 94 via the aerial route.

The Badgers played at Michigan State—the other Big Ten co-champion— the following week and the Spartans did everything right after yielding an early safety to hand the Badgers a 55-2 setback.

State's 70 offensive plays netted 645 yards with quarterback Ed Smith dazzling the Badgers with 334 yards passing and four touchdowns as he completed 19 of 29 passes.

Wisconsin's Ira Matthews opens the game's scoring as he sets off on a 71 yard punt return with 6:50 left to play in first period.

Wisconsin amassed 378 yards total offense but could not convert the yardage into points on the scoreboard.

Wisconsin returned to Camp Randall Stadium to host Ohio State and the Buckeyes used the big play and Wisconsin miscues to gain a 49-14 verdict.

Big plays by the Buckeyes included a blocked punt for a touchdown early in the second period; a 96 yard kickoff return for a score by Tyrone Hicks just seconds after the Badgers had scored to make it a 14-7 contest late in the second period; and a 61 yard pass interception return for a score by Vince Skillings—he had registered the blocked punt that Otha Watson had fallen on for a score—early in the third period that put the game out of Wisconsin's reach.

Later, Ohio State took advantage of recovered Wisconsin fumbles at the Badgers' 29 and 13 yard lines for a pair of fourth period scores.

Wisconsin outgained Ohio State 327 yards to 316 in running 79 plays to 67 for the Buckeyes with senior Charles Green pacing the game's rushers with 101 yards on 23 carries and the game's final touchdown on a one yard plunge.

The season's ninth game found the Badgers hosting Purdue, the Big Ten's third place team, and the outcome was a stunning 24-24 tie. Wisconsin battled back from adversity to tally eighteen fourth period points—all in the final 11½ minutes of play thrilling the Homecoming crowd of 78,986.

Wisconsin held a 6-3 halftime lead, then saw Purdue dominate the third period and the early fourth period going on the passing arm of their sophomore quarterback Mark Herrmann to take a 24-6 lead.

Again it was the passing arm of Mike Kalasmiki that keyed the comeback with receivers Ray Sydnor, Wayne Souza and David Charles making the big plays. Kalasmiki tossed scoring passes of 31 yards to Souza and of three yards to Charles in the rally—a Steve Veith field goal of 32 yards was sandwiched in between the touchdown passes—and Kalasmiki concluded the rally with a two point pass play to Souza.

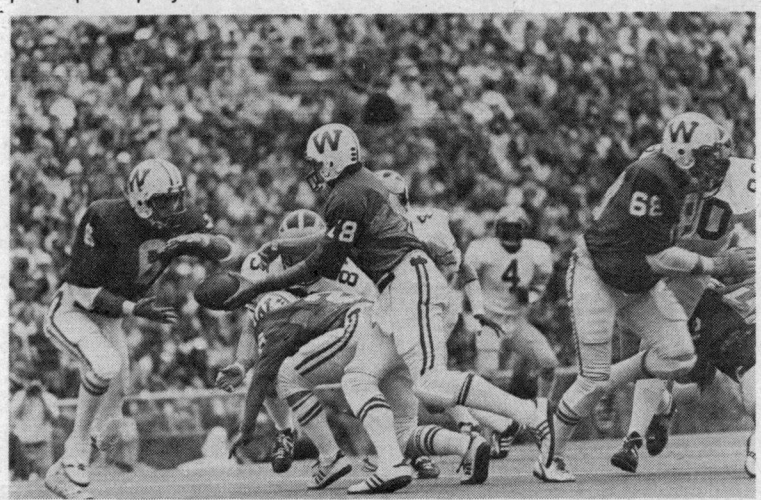

Wisconsin quarterback Mike Kalasmiki (18) prepares to hand-off to Wayne Souza on a play that gained five yards as Dave Krall (68), Badgers offensive tackle, leads the blocking...

Coach McClain pointed out, "It was just a tremendous comeback. I'm sure Purdue will be disappointed but for us it was a heck of a job by a heck of a bunch of guys. I don't know if it's almost a victory, but it's a darn good comeback."

The tie did relegate Purdue, which had entered the game with an unblemished conference mark of 5-0—to third place in the final standings with a 6-1-1 record as Michigan and Michigan State tied with 7-1 records for the Big Ten title.

A week later at Iowa City, it was Iowa's turn to surprise the football world as the Hawkeyes ended an eight game losing streak by outhustling, outfoxing, outhitting, and outscoring Wisconsin 38-24 before 44,444 fans in Kinnick Stadium.

Dave McClain noted, "It was the most disappointing loss I've ever been associated with."

Ten Iowa points within sixteen seconds late in the first period gave the Hawkeyes momentum and the Badgers never caught up

Wisconsin wide-receiver David Charles (10) is set to catch a Mike Kalasmiki (not shown) forward pass as Badgers fullback Tom Stauss (26) blocks Minnesota linebacker Ed Burns (36).

though the score was 17-14 at halftime and 24-17 entering the final period of play.

Two quick Iowa thrusts early in the final period resulted in scoring runs of six and five yards by freshman Phil Blatcher and a 38-17 lead with eight minutes to play.

The final Saturday saw Wisconsin gain its first winning season since 1974 and second since 1963 with a 48-10 rout of Minnesota in Camp Randall Stadium.

Ira Matthews capped his Wisconsin career with his second three touchdown afternoon of the campaign on a 31 yard scoring run from scrimmage, a 34 yard pass reception from Mike Kalasmiki for a second, and a 64 yard punt return for a third, and set up a fourth tally with an 82 yard run.

Mike Kalasmiki, named the team's most valuable player at the post-season banquet, completed 13 of 26 passes for 173 yards and three touchdowns—the aforementioned 34 yarder to Matthews which triggered a 34-0 second half Wisconsin surge—and nine yarders to Tom Stauss and Joe Ruetz.

Stauss' 73-yard scoring run and a one yard end-around by Tom Braker concluded the day's scoring in the latter stages of the game.

Wisconsin's running and passing attack amassed 500 yards on 74 plays, while Minnesota's 74 scrimmage plays netted just 288 yards.

Wisconsin defensive end Don Lorenz (43) wraps up Ohio State quarterback Art Schlichter for a twelve yard loss as Dennis Christenson (48) moves in to lend assistance.

Coach Dave McClain summed up the game's outcome succinctly, "It's the first step in the rebuilding of our tradition."

McClain added, "Pride was a factor. They believed they were going to win for their own personal dignity and prove to people we can win at Wisconsin."

Excitement along Wisconsin sideline as Badgers score in second period to trail Ohio State 14-7...

1978
ILLINOIS ALPHABETICAL TEAM ROSTER

(* Denotes letters won)

37	*	**Adams, Earnest**, OLB, 6-3, 200, So., Ft. Lauderdale, Fla.
84		**Atkins, Kelvin**, OLB, 6-4, 216, Fr., Orlando, Fla.
4		**Barnes, Jeff**, SE, 6-2, 192, Sr., Delta, Ohio
51		**Barry, Joe**, LB, 6-1, 204, Fr., Chicago
71		**Belmont, Lou**, OT, 6-4, 260, Fr., Northfield
83		**Blalock, Harold**, LB, 6-3, 197, Fr., Chicago
63		**Boeke, Greg**, C, 6-4, 227, So., Winnebago
80	*	**Boeke, Lee**, TE, 6-4, 219, So., Winnebago
15		**Bonner, Bonji**, DHB, 6-3, 196, Fr., St. Louis, Mo.
75	*	**Brzuskiewicz, Mike**, OG, 6-2, 227, Sr., Wheeling
89		**Burlingame, Keith**, DT, 6-2, 233, Sr., Wheaton
58		**Carmien, Tab**, OLB, 6-2, 204, So., St. Joseph
60		**Carrington, Mike**, OG, 6-2, 236, Fr., Chicago
74		**Coady, Tom**, OT, 6-2, 266, So., Greendale, Wis.
98		**Cozen, Doug**, TE, 6-3, 213, Jr., Oak Lawn
25		**Curtis, Joe**, TB, 6-0, 175, Fr., Chicago
28		**Dismuke, Mark**, TB, 5-8, 173, Fr., Peoria
95		**Doney, Scott**, MG, 5-11 205, Jr., Mt. Prospect
66		**Durrell, Kenny**, MG, 6-4, 230, Fr., Chicago
49		**Dwyer, Dave**, LB, 6-2, 229, So., Hillside
41		**Ekstrom, Rich**, LB, 6-3, 206, Fr., Urbana
1	*	**Finzer, David**, P-K, 6-0, 188, So., Chicago
52	*	**Flynn, Dennis**, DT, 6-3, 233, So., Munster, Ind.
36		**Foster, Greg**, TB, 6-2, 205, So., St. Louis
6		**George, Rick**, DHB, 6-1, 180, Fr., Collinsville
38	*	**Gillen, John**, LB, 6-3, 215, So., Arlington Hts.
87		**Gillen, Ken**, DT, 6-4, 217, Fr., Arlington Hts.
18	**	**Hardy, Dale**, S, 6-1, 183, Sr., Miami, Fla.
54		**Helle, Mark**, C, 6-2, 228, Fr., Edwardsville
48		**Holm, Tim**, DHB, 6-2, 187, Jr., Ellsworth, KS
3	*	**Jones, Cliff**, K, 5-11, 185, So., Tuscola
27	**	**Kelly, Dave**, DHB, 6-0, 194, Jr., LaGrange
68	*	**Kolloff, Tom**, OT, 6-4, 249, Jr., Chicago
21		**Levitt, Lloyd**, DHB, 6-2, 185, Sr., Chicago
15		**Lopez, John**, SE, 6-3, 180, Fr., Elk Grove Village
9		**McAvoy, Tim**, QB, 6-4, 201, Chicago
76		**McClure, Bob**, OG, 6-1, 228, Sr., Ladue, Mo.
11		**McCullough, Lawrence**, QB, 6-2, 186, Jr., Jacksonville, Fla.
62		**McMillin, Troy**, OG-T, 6-3, 226, So., DeKalb
29		**Mitchell, Eddie**, DHB, 6-3, 195, Fr., Memphis, Tenn.
30		**Moton, Jay**, S, 6-0, 186, Fr., Peoria
79		**Moton, Joe**, DT, 6-4, 224, Fr., Peoria
57		**Mulchrone, Pete**, LB, 6-2, 217, Fr., Chicago
72	*	**Norman, Tim**, OT, 6-6, 264, So., Winfield
78	*	**Pavesic, Ray**, OG, 6-1, 225, Jr., Harvey
20		**Perez, Dave**, TB, 5-8, 190, Fr., Carol Stream
26		**Powell, Larry**, TB, 5-11, 176, Jr., Newport News, Va.
59		**Priebe, Mike**, OT, 6-4, 243, Sr., Normal
86	**	**Ralph, Stanley**, MG, 6-3, 238, Sr., Hempstead, NY

No.		Name	Pos.	Ht.	Wt.	Class	Hometown
94	*	Ramshaw, Jerry	OLB	6-4	217	Jr.	Champaign
82	**	Rouse, Eric	FL	6-0	188	Sr.	Chicago
22		Schluter, Dave	SE	6-0	165	Fr.	Springfield
92	*	Scott, John	OLB	6-3	212	So.	Lockport
12		Shaw, Kenny	QB	6-1	174	Fr.	Orlando, Fla.
81		Sherrod, Mike	TE	6-6	225	Jr.	Robbins
34		Squirek, Jack	OLB	6-4	218	Fr.	Cuyahoga Hts., Ohio
23	*	Strader, Wayne	FB	6-3	210	So.	Geneseo
97	***	Sullivan, John	LB	6-3	221	Sr.	Massapequa Park, NY
65	**	Taylor, Randy	C	6-3	240	Sr.	LaSalle
67	*	Thiede, John	DT	6-4	225	Jr.	Janesville, Wisc.
42		Thomas, Calvin	FB	5-11	220	Fr.	St. Louis, Mo.
69	***	Thornton, Bruce	DT	6-6	262	Sr.	Detroit, Mich.
14	***	Tucker, Derwin	DHB	6-2	188	Sr.	Hampton, Va.
7		Venegoni, John	W	6-1	200	So.	Peoria
32		Watson, Shawn	TB	6-1	192	Fr.	Carterville
33	*	Weber, Charlie	FB	6-2	205	Sr.	Elgin
17		Weiss, Rich	QB	6-1	205	So.	Winnetka
64		Westerlind, Dan	OG	6-2	220	So.	Rockford
93		Wilson, Darryl	OLB	6-4	238	Fr.	University City, Mo.
16		Worthy, Tyrone	DB	6-0	186	Fr.	Detroit, Mich.

1978
INDIANA ALPHABETICAL TEAM ROSTER

(* Denotes letters won)

No.		Name	Pos.	Ht.	Wt.	Age	Class	Hometown-High School
2	***	Abrams, Dave	SS	6-1	185	21	Sr.	Troy, O.
73		Ahting, Gerhard	T	6-5	248	20	So.	Cincinnati, O. (Sycamore)
46		Alexander, Chuck	CB	5-10	182	20	Jr.	Mishawaka
21		Andrews, Brett	CB	5-8	165	20	Jr.	Indianapolis (Manual)
36	*	Arbuckle, Aaron	LB	6-3	220	20	Jr.	Greenwood (Center Grove)
16	**	Arnett, Scott	QB	6-3	202	21	Sr.	Columbus, O. (Walnut Ridge)
45	*	Barnes, Nick	CB	5-11	180	23	Sr.	South Bend (Mishawaka Marian)
29		Bowers, Jerry	FB	5-11	190	20	So.	Chapin, S. C.
43		Brooks, Glenn	TB	5-8	170	18	Fr.	Louisville, Ky. (Valley)
22		Burke, Kevin	TB	6-0	194	18	Fr.	Silver Springs, Md. (Northwood)
28	***	Burnett, Darrick	TB	5-11	184	22	Sr.	Gary (Roosevelt)
		Burnett, Ulysses	FL	5-9	160	23	Sr.	Gary (West)
99		Burtis, Christ	DE	6-0	218	18	Fr.	Hamilton, O. (Taft)
19		Clausen, Chris	CB	5-8	175	20	Jr.	Hinsdale, Ill.
14		Clifford, Tim	QB	6-1	204	19	So.	Cincinnati, O. (Colerain)
65	***	Colby, Terry	G	6-1	234	22	Sr.	Danville, Ill.
7		Corso, Steve	SE	5-11	160	19	Jr.	Bloomington (North)
96		Cross, Mike	G	6-0	228	20	Jr.	Cincinnati, O. (LaSalle)
40		Darring, Al	TB	6-0	185	20	So.	Indianapolis (North Central)
47		Davis, Corby	CB	5-11	160	19	So.	Northbrook, Ill. (Glenbrook North)
53		Deal, Mark	C	6-3	205	21	Sr.	Hobart
95	*	DeBord, Eric	DE	5-11	205	19	So.	Gatson (Wes Dal)
15		DeVault, Brett	QB	6-2	194	20	Jr.	Evansville (Mater Dei)
94	***	Doehla, George	DE	6-3	220	22	Sr.	Fort Wayne (Harding)

111

12	Evans, Greg	K	5-7	148	20	So.	Bloomington (South)
17	Evans, Marlin	LB	6-2	194	18	Fr.	Cincinnati, O. (Aiken)
80	*Fishel, Mark	FL	6-0	174	21	Jr.	Martinsville
5	**Freud, David	K	5-6	152	27	Sr.	Jerusalem, Israel
88	Friede, Mike	SE	6-4	194	21	Jr.	Goodland, Kan.
41	Frye, Kevin	FB	6-1	211	20	So.	Elwood
63	Goldin, Jeff	G	6-2	223	21	Jr.	Los Angeles, Calif. (Eagle Rock)
87	Gray, Stoner	SE	6-2	170	18	Fr.	Evansville (North)
24	*Harkrader, Mike	TB	5-7	175	20	So.	Middletown, O. (Fenwick)
50	**Heidel, Mark	C	6-0	230	21	Sr.	Cincinnati, O. (Moeller)
23	*Hodge, Ron	CB	5-11	190	22	Sr.	Gary (Emerson)
25	*Hopkins, Rodney	FB	5-7	195	21	Sr.	Bloomington (North)
10	Huck, Chad	QB	6-1	184	19	So.	Indianapolis (Roncalli)
38	Hunter, Jimmy	DE	6-2	209	18	Fr.	Tampa, Fla. (Hillsborough)
78	Iatarola, Bob	DT	6-2	240	21	Jr.	Gary (Andrean)
44	Johnson, Lonnie	FB	6-1	194	19	So.	Akron, O. (North)
64	Johnson, Mark	G	6-3	248	20	Jr.	Cincinnati, O. (Anderson)
69	Kaiser, Mark	DT	6-6	229	18	Fr.	Trafford, Pa. (Penn-Trafford)
31	Kalil, Fred	LB	5-10	185	19	So.	Mishawaka
37	**Keneipp, Dale	FS	5-9	162	21	Sr.	Hialeah, Fla. (Miami Lakes)
82	Kirwan, James	DT	6-4	238	23	Jr.	Worthington, O. (Rocky River)
92	**Leake, Al	DT	6-3	228	20	Jr.	St. Louis, Mo. (Sumner)
49	Longshore, Marc	CB	6-0	186	18	Fr.	Massillon, O.
6	Lovett, Larry	P	6-2	169	21	Jr.	Pointblank, Tex. (Coldspring)
33	Lundy, Nate	SE	6-0	160	19	So.	Chicago, Ill. (Community)
93	Madlung, Jerry	DT	6-0	235	21	Jr.	Lafayette
86	*McCord, Mike	TE	6-4	225	22	Sr.	Birmingham, Mich. (Brother Rice)
27	***McIntosh, Greg	DE	6-3	199	22	Sr.	Middletown, O. (Monroe)
30	Michalek, Tony	DE	6-1	214	18	Fr.	Midlothian, Ill. (Brother Rice)
71	Michko, Gerald	T	6-3	257	19	Jr.	Chicago, Ill. (DeSales)
1	Mitchell, Stephen	FL	6-0	169	18	Fr.	Washington, D. C. (Dunbar)
35	***Norman, Joe	LB	6-1	220	22	Sr.	Millersburg, O. (West Holmes)
98	Oakley, Darrell	MG	6-3	205	20	Jr.	Witchita, Kan.
58	*O'Keefe, Bob	C	6-1	230	21	Sr.	Louisville, Ky (Xavier)
79	Otto, Mike	T	6-4	273	20	So.	Indianapolis (Franklin Central)
56	*Patton, Mel	MG	5-9	216	21	Jr.	Milwaukee, Wis. (Tech)
72	**Peacock, Doug	T	6-4	255	21	Sr.	Greenfield (Eastern Hancock)
4	Pennick, Ron	FL	5-9	165	19	So.	Chicago, Ill. (Vocational)
66	**Phipps, Jeff	G	6-2	225	20	Jr.	Evansville (Central)
83	*Powers, Dan	TE	6-4	243	21	Sr.	Vince Grove, Ky. (Meade County)
48	Ramsey, Dart	FS	6-2	190	18	Fr.	Dayton, O. (Alter)
54	Ramsey, Mark	LB	6-3	222	19	So.	Dayton, O. (Alter)
57	Rodriguez, Mark	G	6-0	261	18	Fr.	Indianapolis (Lawrence North)
85	Rohan, Matt	TE	6-4	223	20	Jr.	Chicago, Ill. (Leo)
55	***Smith, Carl	DE	5-11	222	22	Sr.	Opa-Locka, Fla. (Coral City)
68	Smith, Denver	MG	6-0	234	19	Fr.	Dayton, O. (Meadowdale)
90	Sparks, Ozie	DE	6-0	194	19	Fr.	Duquesne, Pa.
59	Speer, Kevin	T	6-4	227	19	So.	Evansville (Harrison)

No	Name	Pos	Ht	Wt	Yr.	Hometown (High School)
84	Stephenson, Bob	TE	6-3	220	19 Fr.	Evansville (Reitz)
39	*Stewart, Dave	DE	5-10	220	20 Jr.	Terre Haute (North)
9	Straub, Steve	K	5-10	182	21 Sr.	Indianapolis (North Central)
20	*Swinehart, John	CB	6-0	171	21 Sr.	Fort Wayne (Leurs)
32	**Sybert, Doug	LB	6-2	217	21 Sr.	Lockport, Ill. (Central)
62	Tallen, Terry	DT	6-0	218	19 So.	Hamilton, O. (Badin)
61	Taylor, John	G	6-1	212	19 So.	Fort Wayne (Homestead)
52	Tillery, Bob	DT	6-2	231	21 Sr.	Indianapolis (Ben Davis)
67	Tillery, Brian	T	6-2	237	20 So.	Indianapolis (Ben Davis)
51	Tillery, Steve	LB	6-1	214	20 So.	Indianapolis (Ben Davis)
97	*Tisdale, Brent	DT	6-4	229	19 So.	Cleveland, O. (Shaw)
70	Wallace, Lucky	G	6-2	225	19 So.	Cincinnati, O. (Glen Este)
60	Walls, Craig	LB	6-1	200	18 Fr.	Pittsburgh, Pa. (Peabody)
11	Weir, Dave	SS	6-0	180	18 Fr.	West Homesteak, Pa. (Steel Valley)
63	*Weissert, Steve	MG	6-0	215	21 Sr.	Fort Wayne (Dwenger)
8	Wilbur, Tim	CB	6-0	182	18 Fr.	Indianapolis (Ben Davis)
74	Willhite, Randy	MG	6-1	227	20 Jr.	Lebanon
18	Zeoli, Dave	CB	6-2	180	18 Fr.	Jeannette, Pa. (Penn-Trafford)
77	Zilkowski, Ron	T	6-5	254	21 Sr.	Barrington, Ill.

1978

IOWA NUMERICAL TEAM ROSTER

(* Denotes letters won)

No	Name	Pos	Ht	Wt	Yr.	Hometown (High School)
1	Sean O'Hanlon	K	5-7	154	So.	Washington, Ia. (Washington)
2	**Mario Pace	DB	5-11	180	Jr.	Stow, O. (Stow)
3	*Dave Holsclaw	P-K	6-1	197	Jr.	Clinton, Ia. (Clinton)
4	George Person	DB	6-0	189	So.	Newark, N.J. (Barrington)
5	**Tim Gutshall	LB	6-0	205	Sr.	Massillon, O. (Washington)
6	Greg Schlickman	DB	6-0	200	Fr.	Dubuque, Ia. (Wahlert)
7	Steve Allison	TE	6-5	209	So.	Fairfield, Ia. (Perkin-Packwood)
8	Scott Schilling	K	6-1	206	Jr.	Wauwatosa, Wis. (Wauwatosa)
9	**Dave Becker	DB	6-2	190	Sr.	Atlantic, Ia. (Atlantic)
10	*Bobby Commings, Jr.	QB	6-1	200	So.	Iowa City, Ia. (City)
11	Bobby Stoops	DB	5-11	174	Fr.	Youngstown, O. (Cardinal Mooney)
12	Pete Gales	QB	6-3	170	So.	Paterson, N.J. (Kennedy)
13	*Bill Dolan	QB	6-0	200	Jr.	Winthrop, Ia. (E. Buchanan)
14	Darin Erickson	QB	6-5	195	Fr.	Northridge, Cal. (Cleveland)
15	Ken Burke	TB	6-1	194	Fr.	Chicago, Ill. (Morgan Park)
16	Mike Steverson	DB	5-10	169	Sr.	Davenport, Ia. (Central)
17	Jeff Green	QB	5-11	185	So.	Newhall, Cal. (Hart)
18	**Dennis Mosley	TB	5-10	176	Jr.	Youngstown, O. (Rayen)
19	Dorcus Patterson	WB	5-9	167	So.	Omaha, Neb. (South)
20	**Cedric Shaw	DB	6-0	192	Jr.	Newark, N.J. (Barrington)
21	Vic Holloway	FB	6-0	198	Fr.	Somerville, N.J. (Somerville)
22	Mike Lamson	DB	6-1	201	Fr.	Evergreen, Colo. (Evergreen)
23	*Kevin Ellis	DB	6-2	184	So.	DeWitt, Ia. (DeWitt-Clinton)
25	*Rod Morton	WB	5-11	187	Sr.	Neptune, N.J. (Neptune)
26	Tracy Crocker	WB	5-10	178	Fr.	Cedar Rapids, Ia. (Kennedy)
27	Phil Suess	QB	6-5	177	Jr.	Des Moines, Ia. (Dowling)
28	Phil Blatcher	FB	5-8	175	Fr.	New Orleans, La. (St. Augustine)

No.	Name	Pos	Ht	Wt	Yr	Hometown
29	*Jim Frazier	WB	5-9	174	So.	Waterloo, Ia. (West)
30	Marty Ball	FB	6-2	205	Fr.	Dubuque, Ia. (Hempstead)
31	**Joe Hufford	DT	6-2	243	Sr.	Mt. Vernon, Ia. (Mt. Vernon)
32	*Bobby Hill	LB	6-1	222	Sr.	Mt. Clemens, Mich. (Mt. Clemens)
33	Jeff Jansen	TB	5-11	185	Fr.	Davenport, Ia. (Assumption)
34	Dwayne Williams	TB	5-11	180	Fr.	Bayonne, N.J. (Bayonne)
35	Dean McKillip	FB	6-1	227	So.	Galesburg, Ill. (Senior)
36	Pat Dean	DE	6-1	229	So.	W. Islip, N.Y. (W. Islip)
37	Joe Aulisi	DB	5-11	189	Fr.	South Orange, N.J. (Seton Hall)
38	Jeff Brown	WB	5-11	161	Fr.	Fremont, O. (Fremont)
39	*Kent Ellis	DB	6-2	182	So.	DeWitt, Ia. (DeWitt-Clinton)
40	Tom Riley	FB	6-0	192	So.	Iowa City, Ia. (City)
41	Tegre Taylor	DB	5-11	182	So.	Detroit, Mich. (Inkster)
42	**Leven Weiss	LB	6-2	215	Jr.	Detroit, Mich. (Cass Tech)
43	Lou King	DB	6-2	174	Fr.	Jersey City, N.J. (Snyder)
44	***Jon Lazar	FB	6-1	215	Sr.	Tama, Ia. (South Tama)
45	***Steve Vazquez	DE	6-1	227	Sr.	Lodi, N.J. (Lodi)
46	***Charles Danzy	DB	5-11	192	Sr.	Massillon, O. (Washington)
47	***Tom Rusk	LB	6-2	224	Sr.	Dubuque, Ia. (Hempstead)
48	Milton Turner	TB	5-9	190	So.	Cedar Rapids, Ia. (Washington)
49	Vince Campbell	DB	6-2	188	Fr.	Alachua, Fla. (Santa Fe)
50	Tim Schlatter	DT	6-1	256	Jr.	Wayland, Ia. (Waco)
51	**Sam Palladino	OT	6-2	245	Jr.	Lindenhurst, N.Y. (Lindenhurst)
52	Dave Oakes	C	6-3	236	Fr.	Mason City, Ia. (Mason City)
53	Todd Schumacher	OG	6-0	223	So.	Massillon, O. (Washington)
54	*Jay Hilgenberg	C	6-2	242	So.	Iowa City, Ia. (City)
55	John Hogarty	C	6-1	251	Jr.	Staten Island, N.Y. (Tottenville)
56	Jim Webb	LB	6-0	201	Fr.	Glen Ellyn, Ill. (Beret)
57	Herman Krieher	DE	6-2	225	Sr.	Chicago, Ill. (St. Rita)
58	Keith Frisk	OT	6-5	271	So.	Ackley, Ia. (Ackley-Geneva)
59	*Tim Holmstrom	C	6-4	239	Sr.	Clinton, Ia. (Clinton)
60	***Mike Mayer	OG	6-2	250	Sr.	Taylorville, Ill. (Taylorville)
61	*Bryan Skradis	LB	6-1	213	So.	Omaha, Neb. (South)
63	John Rushton	OG	6-2	241	Sr.	Boulder, Colo. (Boulder)
64	*Lemuel Grayson	OG	6-3	234	Jr.	Detroit, Mich. (Cass Tech)
65	Dave Mayhan	OG	6-4	205	Fr.	Omaha, Neb. (Gross)
66	Jim Cody	OT	6-3	263	Sr.	Racine, Wis. (Case)
68	*Don Willey	OG	6-2	244	Jr.	St. Louis, Mo. (Bishop-Dubourg)
69	Tom Woodland	DE	6-1	236	So.	St. Louis, Mo. (Central)
70	Jeff DeVilder	OG	6-2	271	So.	Brooklyn, Ia. (B-G-M)
71	Paul Postler	OT	6-3	236	So.	Madison, Wis. (West)
72	*Matt Petrzelka	OT	6-6	258	So.	Cedar Rapids, Ia. (Regis)
73	Steve Flood	C	5-10	213	Fr.	Des Moines, Ia. (Valley)
74	*Greg Gilbaugh	OG	6-3	241	So.	Rockford, Ill. (Harlem)
75	*John Harty	DT	6-5	263	So.	Sioux City, Ia. (Heelan)
76	Brian Ward	OT	6-4	257	So.	Lindenhurst, N.J. (Lindenhurst)
77	*Mark Mahmens	DT	6-2	250	Jr.	Clinton, Ia. (N.E. Gooselake)
78	John Hager	OT	6-5	267	Jr.	Sioux City, Ia. (Heelan)
79	Bruce Kittle	DE	6-4	227	So.	Cedar Falls, Ia. (Cedar Falls)
80	*Doug Dunham	SE	6-1	192	So.	Iowa City, Ia. (City)
81	Bill Bradley	LB	6-2	221	Fr.	Cedar Falls, Ia. (Cedar Falls)
82	Mel Cole	LB	6-2	221	Fr.	Elgin, Ill. (Elgin)
83	**Jim Molini	LB	6-4	228	Jr.	Norfolk, Neb. (Norfolk)
84	Ben Wozniak	TE	6-6	220	Jr.	Lombard, Ill. (Glenbard East)
85	Todd Simonsen	LB	6-2	217	Fr.	Racine, Wis. (Case)
86	Mike Dalton	TE	6-2	212	Fr.	Dubuque, Ia. (Wahlert)
87	*Brad Reid	SE	5-11	170	Jr.	Marion, Ia. (Linn-Mar)

No.	Name	Pos.	Hgt.	Wgt.	Class	Hometown
88	**Mike Brady	SE	5-10	175	Sr.	Canoga Park, Cal. (Carmelite)
89	Bill Ross	TE	6-2	230	Sr.	LeMars, Ia. (LeMars)
90	Phil Michel	DE	6-3	225	Jr.	Iowa City, Ia. (Regina)
91	***Jim Swift	TE	6-5	238	Jr.	Des Moines, Ia. (Dowling)
92	*Darrell Hobbs	DE	6-5	242	Sr.	Cedar Rapids, Ia. (Washington)
93	Frank Harty	DE	6-1	236	Fr.	Des Moines, Ia. (Dowling)
94	**Steve Wagner	DE	6-3	234	Sr.	Chicago, Ill. (St. Rita)
95	Tom Schroeder	DE	6-5	214	Fr.	Bloomington, Ill. (Bloomington)
96	Jeff Davis	TE	6-4	222	Fr.	Riverside, Ia. (Highland)
97	***Doug Benschoter	DT	6-3	250	Sr.	Waverly, Ia. (Shell Rock)
98	Clay Uhlenhake	DT	6-2	255	Fr.	Moravia, Ia. (Moravia)
99	**Dan Schultz	DT	6-3	262	Sr.	Detroit, Mich. (St. Ladislaus)

1978 MICHIGAN ALPHABETICAL TEAM ROSTER

(* Denotes letters won)

No.	Name	Pos.	Hgt.	Wgt.	Class	Hometown
35	Agnew, Doug	OLB	6-2¼	190	Fr.	Plymouth
21	Allen, Jay	FB	6-0	212	Jr.	McDonald, PA
58	Angood, David	C	6-4½	232	Jr.	Battle Creek
64	*Arbeznik, John	OG	6-3½	243	Sr.	University Heights, OH
36	Azar, George	PK	6-0	161	Fr.	Fort Wayne, IN
61	**Bartnick, Greg	OG	6-2	241	Sr.	Detroit
12	Bates, Brad	DB	6-1	181	So.	Port Huron
65	Becker, Kurt	OG	6-6	240	So.	Aurora, IL
42	*Bell, Gene	Wolf	6-1½	199	Jr.	East Liverpool, OH
85	Betts, Norm	OLB	6-5	206	Fr.	Midland
3	Body, Marion	DB	5-10½	175	Fr.	Detroit
28	*Braman, Mark	DHB	6-1¼	197	Sr.	Midland
8	Breaugh, Jim	QB	6-2	189	So.	West Bloomfield
48	Brewster, David	FB	6-1	203	Fr.	Grafton, WI
57	Butts, Mike	C	6-4½	214	Fr.	Fenton
19	Calindrino, Gaspare	DB	6-1	188	Sr.	Grand Rapids
41	Cannavino, Andy	ILB	6-1	217	So.	Cleveland, OH
9	Carpenter, Brian	DB-SE	5-11	163	Fr.	Flint
85	Christian, Chuck	TE	6-3	217	So.	Detroit
22	*Clayton, Ralph	WB	6-3½	210	Jr.	Detroit
79	Coles, Cedric	DT	6-2	247	Fr.	Detroit
37	Czarnata, Mike	LB	6-2	230	Fr.	Detroit
33	***Davis, Russell	FB	6-2	223	Sr.	Woodbridge, VA
92	**DeSantis, Mark	OLB	6-4	215	Sr.	Harper Woods
10	Dickey, B.J.	QB	5-11½	188	So.	Ottawa, OH
29	Diggs, Gerald	DB	6-0	185	Jr.	Chicago, IL
73	***Dufek, Bill	OT	6-4½	262	Sr.	Kent, OH
18	Feaster, Rodney	WR	6-1	188	So.	Flint
51	Felten, Jeff	C	6-2	216	Fr.	Centerville, OH
20	Fischer, Brad	QB	6-0	190	Fr.	Ortonville
54	Garrity, Tom	C	6-4	229	Fr.	Grafton, WI
14	Gaudette, Roger	DHB	6-0	191	Jr.	Riverview
68	**Giesler, Jon	OT	6-5	254	Sr.	Woodville, OH
29	Gilligan, Kevin	QB	5-11½	155	Fr.	Ann Arbor
90	*Godfrey, Chris	DT	6-4	240	Jr.	Miami Lakes, FL
95	**Greer, Curtis	DT	6-5	236	Sr.	Detroit

4	*Harden, Michael	DHB	6-½	183	Jr.	Detroit
31	Harris, Stuart	DB	6-3	196	So.	Chagrin Falls, OH
75	Hetts, Chuck	OG	6-4½	231	Jr.	Taylor
94	Hollway, Bob	OLB	6-2½	206	Sr.	West Bloomfield
25	***Huckleby, Harlan	TB	6-1	198	Sr.	Detroit
58	Humphries, Jim	MG	5-10½	216	Jr.	Detroit
97	Jackson, Jeff	OLB	6-7¼	224	So.	Toledo, OH
21	Jackson, Tony	WB	5-10½	170	Fr.	Cleveland, OH
93	*Jackson, William	DT	6-3	241	Sr.	Richmond, VA
13	Jelinek, Jerome	QB	6-0	175	Fr.	Ann Arbor
88	***Johnson, Gene	TE	6-4	234	Sr.	Flint
15	Johnson, Irvin	OLB	6-2¼	206	Jr.	Warren, OH
81	Johnson, Oliver	OLB	6-3¼	202	So.	Detroit
16	**Jolly, Michael	DHB	6-3½	181	Jr.	Melvindale
44	Jones, Rick	ILB	6-3	199	So.	Detroit
81	Kasparek, Ed	WR	6-½	182	Sr.	Dearborn
55	*Keitz, Dale	DT	6-1¼	233	Sr.	Columbus, OH
99	Keller, Tom	OLB	6-2½	208	Jr.	Grand Rapids
13	Kelsie, Tony	DB	5-11¼	197	Fr.	Dover, DE
57	Keough, Kelly	DT	6-3	237	So.	Merrillville, IN
39	Kligis, Mike	DHB	6-2	188	So.	Lombard, IL
69	Kwiatkowski, Dan	OT	6-5	246	So.	Detroit
7	***Leach, Rick	QB	6-½	194	Sr.	Flint
17	Lee, Gary	QB	6-3	193	Fr.	Flint
93	Lemirande, Mike	OLB	6-4½	207	Fr.	Grafton, WI
76	Leoni, Mike	OT	6-2½	246	Jr.	Flint
34	Leoni, Tony	TB	5-11	192	Jr.	Flint
59	*Lilja, George	C	6-4½	247	Jr.	Palos Park, IL
63	Lindsay, Rock	OG	6-2	241	Sr.	Lapeer
45	Malinak, Tim	ILB	6-1½	225	Sr.	Flemington, PA
80	*Marsh, Doug	TE	6-3	230	Jr.	Akron, OH
38	*Melita, Tom	MG	6-1	220	Sr.	Penns Grove, NJ
46	**Meter, Jerry	ILB	6-2½	210	Sr.	Bloomfield Hills
30	Mitchell, Alan	WR	6-1½	185	So.	Detroit
54	Moss, Tom	MG	5-8¼	204	Jr.	Detroit
52	Motley, Fred	MG	6-2	216	So.	Dayton, OH
72	Muransky, Edward	OT	6-7	257	Fr.	Youngstown, OH
27	Murray, Dan	Wolf	6-½	195	Jr.	Ann Arbor
50	**Nauta, Steve	C	6-2	229	Sr.	Norristown, PA
78	Neal, Tom	OG	6-5¼	254	Fr.	Edgewater, FL
83	Needham, Ben	OLB	6-4	214	So.	Groveport, OH
96	Nicolau, Dave	DT	6-5	232	So.	Arlington Heights, IL
78	Osbun, Tony	DT	6-5	243	So.	Kenton, OH
53	*Owens, Mel	ILB	6-2	226	Jr.	DeKalb, IL
12	Paciorek, James	QB	6-3	208	Fr.	Orchard Lake
31	Page, Craig	TB	6-2	195	Sr.	Saginaw
75	Paris, Bubba	OT	6-6¼	284	Fr.	Louisville, KY
89	Payne, David	DE	6-1¼	199	Jr.	Detroit
86	Petsch, Michael	TE	6-4½	208	Fr.	Detroit
67	*Powers, John	OG	6-3	256	Jr.	Oak Park, IL
71	Prepolec, John	OG	6-4	249	So.	Bloomfield Hills
70	Quinn, Gary	OG	6-3	246	Jr.	Quincy, MA
43	Reeves, Jeff	DB	6-1	189	Fr.	Columbus, OH
23	Reid, Lawrence	FB	6-1½	213	Jr.	Philadelphia, PA
65	Reilly, Steve	OT	6-5	242	Fr.	Boston, MA
74	Rowland, Charles	OT	6-4½	260	Fr.	Barberton, OH
39	Sandberg, John	FB	5-11¼	197	So.	Wheaton, IL

82	***Schmerge, Mark	TE	6-3¼	230	Sr.	Cincinnati, OH
91	***Seabron, Tom	OLB	6-4½	214	Sr.	Detroit
40	**Simpkins, Ron	ILB	6-1½	225	Jr.	Detroit
6	Smith, Kevin	FS	6-2½	182	Fr.	Dallas, TX
26	*Smith, Roosevelt	TB	5-10¼	200	Jr.	Detroit
45	Snell, Gary	ILB	6-3	210	Fr.	Mundelein, IL
84	Strenger, Richard	TE	6-7	221	Fr.	Grafton, WI
99	Thompson, Robert	DE	6-3½	211	Fr.	Blue Island, IL
77	*Trgovac, Mike	MG	6-2	227	So.	Austintown, OH
2	Virgil, Bryan	PK	5-9½	185	Jr.	Buchanan
37	Wallace, Zeke	WR	6-4	185	Fr.	Pompano Beach, FL
66	Wandersleben, Tom	OG	6-2½	245	So.	Euclid, OH
60	Warth, Mark	OG	6-5½	235	Fr.	Zanesville, OH
49	Washington, Sanford	ILB	6-2¼	206	Fr.	Youngstown, OH
62	Weber, Gary	DT	6-2	236	Jr.	Matawan, NJ
49	Webster, Mike	TB	6-½	192	So.	Dearborn
1	*Willner, Gregg	PK	5-10	158	Sr.	Miami Beach, FL
24	Woolfolk, Butch	TB	6-2	202	Fr.	Westfield, NJ
56	Wunderli, Greg	C	6-6	227	So.	St. Louis, MO

1978 MICHIGAN STATE ALPHABETICAL TEAM ROSTER

(* Denotes letters won)

	(High School and Coach in Parentheses)	Pos.	HT.	WT.	AGE	CL.§
8	ANDERSEN, MORTEN Struer, Denmark (Indianapolis, Ind. Davis—Bob Wilbur)	PK	6-1	180	18	Fr.
16	**ANDERSON, MARK Akron, Ohio (Springfield—Les Cheney)	DB	6-2	189	20	Jr.
59	*AUDAS, SEDRIC Saginaw (Arthur Hill—George Ihler)	C	6-3	231	20	So.
94	BACA, BEN Montebello, Calif. (Los Angeles Loyola—Steve Grady)	DT	6-3	239	18	Fr.
49	**BASS, DAN Bath (Bath—Ron Skorich)	ILB	6-1	221	20	Jr.
31	BLANK, STEVEN Grand Rapids (Northview—Mike Siwek)	ILB	6-2	214	18	Fr.
62	BOAK, BRYAN New Castle, Pa. (New Castle—Lindy Lauro)	OG	6-3	234	18	Fr.
91	**BRAMMER, MARK Traverse City (Traverse City—James Ooley)	TE	6-4	233	20	Jr.
38	BROWN, DARRYL Jacksonville, Fla. (Wolfson—Tom Grant)	OLB	6-4	215	17	Fr.
28	*BURROUGHS, JAMES Pahokee, Fla. (Pahokee—Antoine Russell)	DB	6-1	183	20	So.

117

#	Name	Pos	Ht	Wt	Age	Yr
84	**BYRD, EUGENE E. St. Louis, Ill. (E. St. Louis —Cornelius Perry)	SE	6-0	178	21	Jr.
14	CLARK, BRYAN Bloomfield Hills (Los Altos, Calif.—Bob Baird)	QB	6-2	178	18	Fr.
97	*CONVERSE, CRAIG Utica (Eisenhower—Robert Lantzy)	MG	5-11	207	21	So.
39	COOPER, GEORGE Detroit (Northern—John Dean)	OLB	6-2	207	17	Fr.
27	*DAVIS, ALAN Huntington Woods (Berkley— Jerry Catalina)	DB	6-1	179	20	Jr.
50	*DECKER, MICHAEL Roseville (Detroit DeLaSalle —John Maronto)	ILB	6-2	224	21	Jr.
66	**DENSMORE, MICHAEL Lapeer (West—Ken Nelson)	OG	6-3	257	20	Jr.
70	FEHLAN, JEFFREY Wellington, Ohio (Wellington —Jim Berarducci)	OT	6-5	239	18	Fr.
53	**FIELDS, ANGELO Washington, D.C. (Wilson— Bernard Hogans)	DT	6-6	284	20	Jr.
67	**FOSTER, MATTHEW Livonia (Churchill—Ken Kaestner)	C	6-3	228	20	Jr.
23	***GIBSON, KIRK Waterford (Kettering, Mel Patterson)	FL	6-2	217	21	Sr.
75	*GRABENHORST, TED Mt. Morris (Johnson—Frank Garofalo)	OT	6-6	270	21	Jr.
10	***GRAVES, THOMAS Norfolk, Va. (Lake Taylor— Bert Harrell)	DB	6-3	221	22	Sr.
29	GREENE, RICKEY Miami, Fla. (Carol City—Jerry Anderson)	DB	6-0	181	17	Fr.
24	*GRIFFIN, CURTIS Southfield (Birmingham Brother Rice—Al Fracassa)	OLB	6-3	217	21	Jr.
89	GRIFFIN, ISAAC Gary, Ind. (Lew Wallace— Mike Jennings)	DT	6-5	230	18	Fr.
5	*HANS, MICHAEL Pittsburgh, Pa. (Central Catholic—Joe Scully)	FB	5-11	200	22	Sr.
68	HAREWICZ, JOE Pittsburgh, Pa. (Upper St. Clair—Fred Wickstrom)	OG	6-3	230	18	Fr.
83	*HARRIS, BARRY San Diego, Calif. (Crawford— Bill Hall)	FL	5-11	176	22	Sr.

No.	Name	Pos	Ht	Wt	Age	Class
17	HARRIS, TONY Niles (Brandywine—Peter McCauley)	DB	6-2	197	18	Fr.
93	*HAY, BERNARD Riviera Beach, Fla. (Palm Beach Gardens—Larry Hood)	MG	6-3	235	19	So.
86	HAYNES, JOHNNY LEE Delray Beach, Fla. (Boca Raton—Roger Coffey)	OLB	6-2	225	19	So.
73	***HINESLY, JAMES Detroit (Country Day—Eugene Reilly)	OT	6-2	254	21	Sr.
4	HOWARD, SAMSON Miami, Fla. (Northwestern—Walt Frazier)	SE	5-8	165	19	Fr.
42	HUGHES, DEREK Charleston, S.C. (Bishop England—Jack Cantey)	TB	6-2	194	18	Fr.
51	JACQUEMAIN, JOE Mt. Clemens (L'Anse Creuse—Wes Carlos)	C	6-5	228	19	Fr.
64	**JONES, ERIC Grosse Pointe (South—Russ Hepner)	DT	5-11	238	22	Jr.
6	*JONES, MARK Ypsilanti (Ypsilanti—Ralph Pierriello)	SE	5-8	167	20	So.
25	JONES, MIKE South Haven (South Haven—Gary Steudle)	FL	6-3	180	18	Fr.
74	KAISER, JAMES Alpena (Alpena—Dutch Schrotenboer)	OT	6-3	232	20	Fr.
95	KIMICHIK, ALAN Norway (Norway—Robert Giannunzio)	TE	6-2	195	19	Fr.
60	KIRKLING, JACK Greensburg, Pa. (Hempfield Area—Bill Abraham)	MG	6-1	240	19	Fr.
33	KOLODZIEJ, JOSEPH Nashville, Tenn. (Overton—Nick Coutras)	ILB	6-2	202	20	Fr.
47	***LAND, MELVIN Campbell, Ohio (Memorial—Tony Cougros)	DT	6-3	240	22	Sr.
76	**LONCE, CRAIG Canton, Ohio (Central Catholic—Lowell Klinefelter)	OT	6-3	246	21	Jr.
43	MAIDLOW, STEVEN East Lansing (East Lansing—Jeff Smith)	ILB	6-2	223	18	Fr.
71	MANTOS, MARVIN Bloomingdale, Ohio Saccoccia) Wintersville—Rich	OG	6-4	222	18	Fr.

#	Name	Pos	Ht	Wt	Age	Yr
2	*MARSHALL, MICHAEL Detroit (Southwestern—Joe Hoskins)	DB	6-3	190	21	So.
79	MAZUR, SCOT Bowling Green, Ohio (Bowling Green—Hubert Reed)	OT	6-4	248	18	Fr.
41	McCLELLAND, DARRIN Detroit (Central—Dave Snead)	FB	6-0	216	18	Fr.
40	*McCORMICK, JOHN Marquette (Marquette—John Srholec)	OLB	6-2	211	19	So.
55	*McCULLOH, JAMES Youngstown, Ohio (Cardinal Mooney—Don Bucci)	OG	6-2	232	20	Jr.
34	McDOWELL, TERRY Flint (Ainsworth—Gary Cole)	ILB	6-2	180	19	So.
22	*McGEE, LEROY El Cajon, Calif. (El Cajon—Jim Mann)	TB	6-0	197	22	Sr.
77	*McQUAIDE, REGIS Pittsburgh, Pa. (Brentwood—George Radosevich)	OT	6-6	251	21	Jr.
44	**MIDDLETON, ALONZO Orangeburg, S.C. (Orangeburg-Wilkinson—Les Evans)	FB	6-1	217	19	Jr.
88	MITCHEM, RONALD South Bend, Ind. (Adams—Ed Faulkens)	DT	6-4	247	18	Fr.
92	MITTEN, PATRICK Naperville, Ill. (Central—John Perry)	DT	6-5	221	18	Fr.
48	MUSTER, MICHAEL Utica (Eisenhower—Robert Lantzy)	ILB	6-2	214	17	Fr.
52	**OTIS, STEVEN Chicago, Ill. (Gordon Tech.—Tom Winiecki)	ILB	6-3	210	20	Jr.
96	PERKINS, CALVIN Atlanta, Ga. (Harper—Henry Earls)	MG	6-4	275	17	Fr.
56	PIETTE, THOMAS Redford Township (Detroit Redford Union—Harvey Heitman)	C	6-4	221	18	Fr.
21	RAYE, GRAIG Fayetteville N.C. (Smith—D.T. Carter)	FL	5-8	176	22	Sr.
30	*REEVES, BRUCE Irmo, S.C. (Irmo—Reed Charpia)	TB	5-11	177	19	So.
9	*ROBINSON, KENNETH Ypsilanti (Ypsilanti—Ralph Pierriello)	DB	6-1	191	21	Jr.
82	SAUNDERS, CRAIG Huron, Ohio (Huron—Tony Munafo)	TE	6-4	220	18	Fr.

No.	Name	Pos.	Ht.	Wt.	Age	Class
57	**SAVAGE, LARRY Warren, Ohio (Howland—Jack Pierson)	OLB	6-3	213	21	Jr.
26	SCARLETT, TODD Okemos (Okemos—Pete Schmidt)	DB	5-11	175	18	Fr.
3	SCHARIO, RICHARD Lyndhurst, Ohio (Brush—Frank Gibson)	PK	6-0	181	18	Fr.
45	*SCHRAMM, ANDREW Findlay, Ohio (Findlay—Bill Jones)	FB	6-2	226	19	So.
65	SCIARINI, MICHAEL Fort Wayne, Ind. (Bishop Dwenger—Larry Bartolameolli)	OG	6-2	225	19	Fr.
80	*SHAFER, CHARLES Stevensville (Lakeshore—Dave Topping)	TE	6-6	229	22	Sr.
81	SHEERAN, BRETT West Bloomfield (Birmingham Groves—Bill Rankin)	DT	6-3	240	19	Fr.
7	**SMITH, EDWARD Hallandale, Fla. (Pittsburgh Central Catholic—Jim Scully)	QB	6-1	174	22	Sr.
20	*SMITH, STEVE Louisville, Ky. (DuPont Manual—Buddy Pfaadt)	TB	5-8	175	18	So.
19	*STACHOWICZ, RAYMOND Broadview Hts., Ohio (Cleveland Brecksville—Joe Vadini)	K	6-1	190	19	So.
61	*STANTON, EDMUND Battle Creek (Lakeview—Ron Lynch)	OT	6-3	239	21	Jr.
1	**STANTON, JEROME Detroit (Central—Dave Snead)	DB	6-1	181	21	Jr.
69	*STRATA, RODNEY Canton, Ohio (Massillon Perry—Tom Winkhart)	OG	6-2	240	21	So.
54	*TAPLING, MARK Chicago, Ill. (Gordon Tech—Tom Winiecki)	C	6-0	207	21	Jr.
15	*VAUGHN, BERT Mogadore, Ohio (Mogadore—Norm Lingle)	QB	6-4	215	19	So.
11	VIELHABER, JOHN Findlay, Ohio (Findlay—Bill Jones)	FL	5-11	178	21	Jr.
98	WEBB, TANYA Augusta, Ark. (Augusta—Larry Greene)	DT	6-7	254	21	Jr.
63	WHITTLE, DAVID Seattle, Wash. (Shoreline—Tom Wiley)	OT	6-5	244	20	Jr.

No.	Name		Pos.	Hgt.	Wgt.	Age	Class
99	WILLIAMS, BRUCE		MG	6-3	220	19	Fr.
	Wheaton, Ill. (North—Jim Rexilius)						
85	WILLIAMS, JAMES		SE	6-0	160	19	So.
	San Diego, Calif. (Madison—Bob Bishop)						
18	WILLIAMS, TERRY		DB	6-1	186	22	Sr.
	Cincinnati, Ohio (Princeton—Pat Mancuso)						
32	WILLIAMS, VAN		DB	5-9	175	19	So.
	Delray Beach, Fla. (Boca Raton—Roger Coffey)						
72	WISKA, JEFFREY		OG	6-3	238	18	Fr.
	Farmington Hills (Detroit Catholic Central—Tom Mach)						

Physical Data Certified as of Aug. 30, 1978

1978 MINNESOTA ALPHABETICAL TEAM ROSTER

(* Denotes letters won)

No.	Name	Pos.	Hgt.	Wgt.	Age	Class
90	ALLISON, MARK	DE	6-1	192	21	Sr.
	Edina, MN (West)					
62	ANDERSON, JIM	OG	6-1½	233	19	Fr.
	Fairbault, MN					
40	*ARTIS, ROY	TB	6-1½	179	19	So.
	Lawnside, NJ (Hadden Heights)					
1	*AVERY, WENDELL	QB	6-0	182	22	Jr.
	Corpus Christi, TX (Moody)					
32	BACH, CURT	LB	6-3	211	19	Fr.
	Wheaton, MN					
20	*BAILEY, ELMER	SE	6-0½	193	20	Jr.
	St. Paul, MN (Mechanic Arts)					
71	BANKSON, KURT	NG	5-10	241	18	Fr.
	Franklin Park, IL (E. Leyden)					
41	*BARBER, MARION	TB	6-2½	204	18	So.
	Detroit, MI (Chadsey)					
58	BEBEL, CHRIS	OG	6-3½	226	19	Fr.
	St. Paul, MN (ST. Thomas)					
30	BIFULK, ED	SB	6-1	196	18	Fr.
	St. Paul, MN (St. Thomas)					
93	BISCH, STEVE	DT	6-4½	234	18	Fr.
	LeSeuer, MN					
95	*BLANSHAN, ALAN	DT	6-5½	251	20	Jr.
	Mankato, MN (East)					
83	**BOURQUIN, GLENN	TE	6-3½	231	21	Jr.
	Cottage Grove, MN (St. Paul Park)					
22	BREAULT, GARY	CB	5-11	185	19	Fr.
	Hudson, WI					
31	**BREAULT, STEVE	SB	6-0	194	21	Sr.
	Hudson, WI					

34	***BROWN, KEITH St. Louis, MO (Soldan)	SS	5-11	192	20	Sr.
2	BURDITTE, ELWIN Minnetonka, MN	CB	5-10	191	20	Jr.
36	**BURNS, ED RAcine, WI (Horlick)	LB	6-1	212	23	Sr.
14	CARDELLI, GLENN Elmwood Park, IL (Holy Cross)	CB	5-10	171	18	Fr.
12	*CARLSON, MARK Deerfield, IL	QB	5-11	186	20	Jr.
39	*CARR, JEFF Palmyra, WI	NG	6-1	223	22	Sr.
43	COOPER, CHESTER Paulsboro, N.J.	SE	6-2	183	19	Fr.
70	**CUNNINGHAM, STEVE Waseca, MN	DE	6-6	241	20	Jr.
87	CURTIS, MIKE Eau Claire, WI	TE	6-3	202	18	Fr.
67	DAHLSON, RICK St. Cloud, MN (Tech)	OG	6-2½	227	19	Fr.
72	DALLAFOIR, KEN Madison Heights, MI	OT	6-4	251	19	Fr.
86	DAVIS, ANTHONY Detroit, MI (Chadsey)	DE	6-0	201	18	Fr.
42	DILULO, RAY Boise, ID	SB	6-0	203	20	So.
11	*EDWARDS, KEITH Grand Rapids, MI (Creston)	FS	5-11	201	20	Jr.
89	FAHNHORST, JIM St. Cloud, MN (Tech)	LB	6-3½	218	19	So.
64	FARNES, SCOTT Albert Lea, MN	OT	6-2½	238	21	Jr.
97	FEINE, DEAN Rushford, MN	DT	6-3	236	19	Fr.
57	FITZPATRICK, TOM Rochester, MN (Mayo)	OG	6-4½	231	20	Jr.
17	*FOXWORTH, KEN St. Louis, MO (University)	CB	5-11	176	20	Jr.
65	**FRIBERG, DOUG St. Paul, MN (Hill-Murray)	NG	6-3	228	21	Sr.
50	GARDNER, DAVE Rochester, MN (Mayo)	DT	6-4	236	21	Jr.
46	GREGORY, DUANE Chicago, IL (Priviso East)	TB	5-10	194	19	Fr.
27	HAIRSTON, BRIAN Columbus, OH (DeSales)	CB	5-9	177	21	Sr.
94	HALLSTROM, TODD Brook Park, MN (Mora)	LB	6-4½	221	18	Fr.
38	HARMS, BRENT Rice Lake, WI	LB	6-2	212	19	Fr.
16	HESSE, SCOTT Stillwater, MN	SS	5-10	173	19	Fr.
8	HOFFMAN, JOHN Duluth, MN (Morgan Park)	SS	5-11	199	20	Jr.
16	HOVERMAN, RANDY Osceola, WI	QB	6-2½	186	18	Fr.

#	Name	Pos	Ht	Wt	Age	Yr
3	**HOWARD, GLENN** Paulsboro, N.J.	DE	6-1½	211	19	So.
76	**HUMPHRIES, BILL** Detroit, MI (Chadsey)	OT	6-2	234	17	Fr.
49	**IZBAN, PAUL** Mount Prospect, IL (Prospect)	LB	6-2	206	19	Fr.
29	**JOHANSON, TOM** Cloquet, MN	LB	6-3	224	19	Fr.
56	**JOHNSON, JACK** Minnetonka, MN	LB	6-1½	218	20	Jr.
19	**JONES, WALTER** St. Louis, MO (Soldan)	SE	6-3	178	20	So.
24	**JURGENS, DUANE** Mundelein, IL	P	6-2	182	17	Fr.
91	**KELLIN, KEVIN** Grand Rapids, MN	DT	6-5½	229	19	Fr.
44	****KITZMANN, KENT** Rochester, MN (John Marshall)	FB	6-2½	204	21	Jr.
37	**LEWIS, GLENN** Edina, MN (West)	TB	6-1	205	20	So.
47	**LOWELL, CHUCK** White Bear Lake, MN	TB	6-0	181	18	Fr.
33	**MANGUM, KURT** Evanston, IL	DE	6-1½	208	19	Fr.
85	**MARCELLA, JIM** Virginia, MN	SE	6-2½	181	20	Jr.
25	**MARCUSON, LANCE** Bayport, MN	SB	5-11	180	19	So.
24	**MARKO, LARRY** Northfield, MN	P	5-10½	182	20	So.
59	***MEYER, DON** Arlington Hgts., IL (Prospect)	LB	6-2	219	20	Jr.
92	**MIA, DARRYL** Detroit, MI (Highland Park)	DE	6-1	209	18	Fr.
80	**MILLER, VAN** Columbia Hgts., MN	TE	6-2	214	18	Fr.
88	**MURPHY, TOM** Watertown, S.D.	DE	6-2½	218	21	Jr.
63	**MURTHA, GREG** Minneapolis, MN (Southwest)	OT	6-6½	251	21	Sr.
77	**NASH, McKINLEY** Evanston, Il	OT	6-3	244	18	Fr.
23	**NOEL, DANA** Wheaton, IL (Central)	CB	5-10	178	20	So.
51	**ODEGARD, BRAD** Agoura, CA	C	6-5	227	19	Fr.
66	**OLSON, ED** Crystal, MN (Armstrong)	C	6-3	219	19	Fr.
75	**ORGAS, FRED** Brooklyn Center, MN (Park Center)	DE	6-4	213	18	Fr.
61	**ORGAS, MIKE** Brooklyn Center, MN (Park Center)	OG	6-4	232	19	Fr.
73	**OWENS, MARK** Rochester, MN (Mayo)	DT	6-4	244	20	So.

No.	Name	Pos.	Ht.	Wt.	Age	Yr.
60	*PAQUETTE, PAT Superior, WI	OG	6-5	259	20	So.
69	PENOVICH, KENT Muskego, WI	OT	6-6½	267	20	So.
45	PEPPE, MIKE Brooklyn Park, MN (Cooper)	SS	5-11	182	19	Fr.
35	PETERS, KEVIN Cloquet, MN	FB	5-11	199	20	Fr.
84	PETERSON, TODD Richfield, MN	LB	6-1½	207	18	Fr.
6	PRAIRIE, BILL Rosemount, MN	FS	6-0	172	19	Fr.
10	PYLATIUK, GREG Columbia Heights, MN	QB	6-1	184	19	Fr.
49	QUAM, DAN Minneapolis, MN (Cooper)	TB	5-8½	166	20	Jr.
26	ROBB, MIKE Cottage Grove, MN (Woodbury)	SS	6-2	192	18	Fr.
13	**ROGIND, PAUL Farmington, MI (Harrison)	CB-K	5-10½	176	20	Jr.
98	**RONAN, JIM West Chester, PA (Carroll)	DT	6-5½	249	21	Sr.
99	SAPP, TOM Bloomington, MN (Jefferson)	DT	6-3	214	21	Jr.
96	SCHUH, JEFF Crystal, MN (Armstrong)	DE	6-2½	219	19	Jr.
52	*SCHWEN, DARELL Great Falls, MT	OG	6-4	232	20	Jr.
18	SHAREEF, AHMAD Pittsburgh, PA (Westinghouse)	QB	5-10	169	19	Fr.
15	*SIMMONS, TERRY Birmingham, MI (Brother Rice)	TE-P	6-1	191	20	Jr.
28	SMITH, TOM Edina, MN (East)	P	6-0½	186	20	So.
79	SNODGRASS, JEFF Valparaiso, IN	NG	6-2	228	19	Fr.
21	**SNYDER, BRIAN Washington, D.C. (Anacostia)	CB	5-10	172	21	Sr.
81	SONNENFELD, RANDY Robbinsdale, MN	TE	6-5	226	20	So.
68	*STEIN, MARTY Eau Claire, WI (Memorial)	OT	6-4	247	21	Jr.
5	**SYTSMA, STAN (Capt.) Hutchinson, MN	DE	6-2½	228	22	Sr.
48	*THOMPSON, JEFF Bloomington, MN (Jefferson)	FB	6-2	216	20	Jr.
53	**TOBIN, STEVE Moorhead, MN	C	6-4½	247	21	Jr.
7	TONN, MARK Green Bay, WI (Preble)	QB	6-6	216	20	Jr.
82	VELDMAN, GREG South St. Paul, MN	TE	6-3½	211	18	Fr.
78	WEINZIERL, MIKE Shakopee, MN	DT	6-5½	238	20	Jr.
9	*WHITE, GARY Rockdale, TX	FB-TB	5-11	197	19	So.

4	WITTUS, RICK Glencoe, MN	FS	6-3	186	19	Fr.
74	WOZNIAK, ANTHONY Lombard, IL (Glenbard)	OT	6-4½	209	18	Fr.
55	**WYPYSZYNSKI, KEN	C-OG	6-5½	243	21	Jr.

1978 NORTHWESTERN ALPHABETICAL ROSTER

(* Denotes letters won)

No.	Name	Pos.	Hgt.	Wgt.	Class
20	*Adams, Mark Detroit, MI (MacKenzie)	DB	6-0	188	So.
63	*Ahern, Tom Warren, OH (Howland)	OG	6-3	225	Jr.
84	Bahoric, Dave Johnstown, PA (Bishop McCourt)	WR	5-10	175	Fr.
94	Bambauer, Don North Royalton, OH (North Royalton)	DT	6-4	240	Fr.
98	*Berg, Kevin St. Paul, MN (St. Thomas Academy)	OLB	6-2	211	Jr.
95	Biancamano, Bob Dover, OH (Central Catholic)	OLB	6-3	185	So.
18	**Bobowski, Steve Arlington Heights, IL (St. Viator)	DB	5-10	175	Sr.
83	Bogan, Steve Weston, CT (Weston)	WR	6-1	175	Fr.
15	*Breitbeil, Steve Rolling Meadows, IL (Rolling Meadows)	QB	5-11	185	Sr.
66	Brown Kelby Mt. Pelier, OH (Mt. Pelier)	OG	6-4	220	Fr.
24	Burns, John Warren, OH (Howland)	DB	6-3	195	So.
37	Butler, Ben Chicago, IL (Mt. Carmel)	DB	6-4	191	Fr.
33	*Cammon, Mike Detroit, MI (University)	RB	5-11	185	So.
11	Capstran, Chris Menominee, WI (Menominee Falls)	QB	6-4	212	Fr.
50	*Carnicom, Todd Trenton MI (Trenton)	C	6-0	225	Jr.
1	Carver, Brett Northbrook, IL (Glenbrook North)	DB	5-7	135	So.
7	Christensen, Jeff Gibson City, IL (Gibson City)	K/QB	6-4	190	Fr.
14	Coleman, Ron Evanston, IL (Evanston Township)	RB	6-1	185	So.
78	***Corona, Joe Saline, MI (Saline)	DT	6-5	245	Sr.
67	Crowder, Jim Hinsdale, IL (Fenwick)	OT	6-4	220	Fr.
17	*Dierberger, Bill West St. Paul, MN (Bradley)	QB	6-0	185	Jr.
49	Dorsey, Doug Freeport, IL (Freeport)	LB	6-3	200	Fr.

#	Name	Pos	Ht	Wt	Yr
65	*Draznik, Bill Joliet IL (Joliet Catholic)	OG	6-4	225	So.
38	*Duncan, Scott Findlay, OH (Findlay)	LB	6-2	215	Sr.
53	Dunlea, Jim Youngstown, OH (Ursuline)	DT	6-2	225	Sr.
57	*Fiedler, Mike Toledo, OH (Whitmer)	C	6-3	235	Jr.
68	Finn, John Wadsworth, OH (Wadsworth)	LB	6-6	210	Fr.
76	*Ford, Jim Burbank, IL (St. Laurence)	OT	6-4	225	Jr.
45	**Geegan, Pat Rolling Meadows, IL (Rolling Meadows)	DB	6-0	190	Sr.
88	Gildner, Bill Springfield, OH (Griffin)	TE	6-4	219	Fr.
70	**Greer, Bill Athens, OH (Athens)	OT	6-4	240	Jr.
99	*Grelle, Curt Indianapolis, IN (Warren Central)	DE	6-2	215	Jr.
86	*Hemphill, Dana Gaithersburg, MD (Gaithersburg)	QB	6-0	170	So.
31	Hickey, Dave Burbank, IL (St. Laurence)	TE	6-3	215	So.
23	Hill, Tim Cincinnati, OH (St. Xavier)	RB	6-1	175	So.
41	Hoffman, David Cincinnati, OH (LaSalle)	DB	6-1	183	So.
9	Humphreys, Charlie Mt. Herman, MA (Mt. Herman)	QB	6-2	185	Fr.
69	Hunter, Hal Belle Vernon, PA (Belle Vernon)	LB	6-1	220	Fr.
93	Jenkins, Darryl Detroit, MI (University)	WR	6-0	173	Fr.
36	*Johnson, Donald Evanston, IL (Evanston Township)	RB	6-3	210	So.
77	Karstan, Adrian Horicorn, WI (Horicorn)	DE	6-7	220	Fr.
85	*Kasprycski, Wally Hammond, IN (Bishop Noll)	TE	6-4	225	Sr.
92	**Kendzicky, Mike Detroit, MI (Redford St. Mary)	DE	6-3	215	Sr.
10	Kenny, Gene Burbank IL (St. Laurence)	QB	5-9	185	Jr.
59	*Kenyon, Kevin Buffalo, NY (Nicholas)	C	6-4	225	Jr.
21	*Kern, Chuck New Castle, IN (Chrysler)	MLB	6-2	210	So.
12	Kerrigan, Mike Chicago, IL (Mt. Carmel)	QB	6-3	190	Fr.
6	***Knafelc, Guy Green Bay, WI (Premontre)	CAT	6-0	185	Sr.
61	*Kranz, Mike Glen Ellyn, IL (Glenbard South)	OT	6-4	240	Sr.
54	Krelder, Jack Pittsburgh, PA (Jefferson)	C	6-4	227	Fr.

#	Name		Pos	Ht	Wt	Yr
35	*Lawrence, Tim	Oak Lawn, IL (Brother Rice)	OLB	5-11	211	Jr.
72	Ley, Michael	Hialeah, FL (Hialeah)	OG	6-3	221	Fr.
48	Lizak, Matt	Oak Forest, IL (Oak Forest)	LB	6-1	218	Fr.
8	Lyons, Darryl	Chicago, IL (Corliss)	QB	6-2	185	Fr.
39	Maul, Tom	Belleville, IL (Althoff)	FB	6-1	209	Fr.
80	Maycan, Jim	Palatine, IL (Fremd)	TE	6-2	210	Sr.
81	McGee, Mike	Plant City, FL (Plant City)	WR	6-2	185	So.
43	*McGlade, Tom	Park Ridge, IL (Maine South)	DB	6-1	182	So.
52	Miklaszewski, John	Chicago, IL (Lane Tech)	OT	6-2	260	Fr.
62	***Miller, Jim	Kohler, WI (Kohler)	MLB	6-2	225	Sr.
4	***Mirkopulos, Nick	Cincinnati, OH (Withrop)	K	6-1	195	Sr.
32	*Mishler, Dave	Metamora, IL (Spaulding Institute)	FB	6-0	215	So.
82	North, Tom	Arlington Heights, IL (Arlington)	WR	6-3	180	So.
47	***Ogilvie, Blaine	Lancaster, OH (Lancaster)	MLB	5-11	210	Sr.
91	Pals, Steve	Glen Ellyn, IL (Glenbard West)	OLB	6-3	215	So.
97	*Payne, Dean	Chester, PA (Chester)	OLB	6-4	210	So.
27	Pearsall, Al	Akron, OH (Phillips Academy)	DB	5-10	190	Fr.
89	**Poulos, Sam	Northbrook, IL (Glenbrook North)	K/TE	6-2	201	Sr.
87	Prichard, Clarke	Lima, OH (Bath)	TE	6-6	220	Fr.
55	**Reitz, Phil	Brown Deer, WI (Brown Deer)	OG	6-2	235	Jr.
73	*Robinett, Bruce	Xenia, OH (Xenia)	DE	6-5	225	Jr.
90	**Rogers, Chuck	Toledo, OH (Bowshen)	DE	6-4	225	Sr.
34	Rooney, Tim	Riverside, IL (Fenwick)	SE	6-1	190	Sr.
16	Schanzer, Dave	Williamsville, NY (East)	DB	6-3	200	Fr.
60	*Schmidt, Bill	Clintonville, WI (Clintonville)	OG	6-2	230	Jr.
28	*Schmitt, Bob	Sun Prairie, WI (Prairie)	FB	6-2	200	So.
71	*Schober, John	Findlay, OH (Findlay)	OT	6-5	245	Jr.
26	**Sheets, Todd	Nappanee, IN (Northwood)	WR	6-0	175	Jr.

No.	Name	Pos	Hgt	Wgt	Cl.
58	Slater, Bob	LB	6-2	220	So.
	St. Paul, MN (St. Thomas Academy)				
46	Sobeck, Fred	DB	6-2	185	Fr.
	Miami, FL (Columbus)				
40	Stasiewicz, Brian	DT	5-11	220	So.
	Columbus, OH (Watterson)				
13	Strasser, Kevin	QB	6-3	190	Jr.
	Elmhurst, IL (Immaculate Conception)				
5	Taylor, Matt	P/QB	6-2	190	Fr.
	Pleasant Hill, CA (DeLaSalle)				
75	Taylor, Rob	DT	6-6	250	Fr.
	Kettering, OH (Fairmont East)				
42	Tiberi, Lou	FB	6-0	185	Fr.
	Blue Island, IL (Eisenhower)				
3	Vucovich, Dan	QB	6-0	185	Fr.
	Mt. Prospect, IL (Hersey)				
22	Washington, Greg	RB	6-0	185	Fr.
	Miami, FL (Gulliver Academy)				
29	Webb, Jo Jo	TB	5-7	160	Fr.
	Clairton, PA (Clairton)				
25	Weir, Bill	WR	6-1	180	So.
	Coshocton, OH (Coshocton)				
56	***Weitzman, Mike	DT	6-3	245	Sr.
	Eastlake, OH (North)				
74	**Wells, Norman	DT	6-4	236	Sr.
	Warren, MI (Mott)				
19	Westerhausen, Don	DB	6-0	200	So.
	Apple Valley, MN (Rosemont)				
51	Wilson, Paul	DE	6-0	205	Fr.
	Chicago, IL (Kenwood)				

1978
OHIO STATE NUMERICAL TEAM ROSTER

(* Denotes letters won)

No.	Name	Pos.	Wgt.	Hgt.	Age	Cl.	Hometown
1	*McKee, Dave	P	182	6-2	21	Sr.	Columbus
1	Atha, Bob	PK	185	6-1	19	Fr.	Worthington
2	McEldowney, Doug	PK	186	5-11	19	So.	Centerville
2	Budd, Dave	P	176	6-1	20	Jr.	Chester, N.J.
3	Hall, Ted	DB	212	6-2	18	Fr.	Gahanna
4	Burrows, Norman	QB	176	5-11	19	So.	Portsmouth
4	Mercer, Kyle	TB	185	5-9	20	Jr.	Columbus
5	*Laughlin, Jim	LB	214	6-2	20	Jr.	Lyndhurst
6	*Strahine, Mike	QB	194	6-0	20	Jr.	Lakewood
7	*Castignola, Greg	QB	180	6-2	20	Jr.	Tenton, Mich.
8	***Gerald, Rod	QB	177	6-1	21	Sr.	Dallas, Texas
9	Taylor, Alvin	FL	182	6-0	20	Jr.	Newport News Va.
9	Jusek, Jerry	DB	200	6-3	19	So.	Eastlake
10	Schlichter, Arthur	QB	190	6-3	18	Fr.	Bloomingburg
11	Watson, Otha	DB	200	6-0	19	Fr.	Dayton
12	**Guess, Mike	DB	176	5-11	20	Jr.	Columbus
13	*Janakievski, Vlade	PK	157	5-8	21	Jr.	Columbus

No.	Name	Pos	Wt	Ht	Age	Yr	Hometown
14	**Schwartz, Brian	DB	190	6-1	20	Jr.	Simi Valley, Calif.
15	Washington, Al	LB	222	6-3	19	So.	Cleveland
16	**Ross, Paul	LB	232	6-1	21	Sr.	Fort Valley, Georgia
17	Belmer, Cliff	FB	203	6-1	20	So.	Mansfield
17	James, Greg	LB	210	6-2	20	So.	Bloomfield, Conn.
18	O'Cain, Tim	TB	170	5-10	19	Fr.	Gahanna
19	*Orosz, Tom	P-PK	207	6-1	19	So.	Fairport Harbor
20	***Mills, Lenny	DB	184	6-3	21	Sr.	Miami, Fla.
21	*Johnson, Ricky	TB	192	6-0	19	Jr.	Santa Maria, Calif.
22	*Volley, Ric	FB	208	6-0	20	Jr.	Lynchburg, Va.
23	**Springs, Ron	TB	198	6-2	21	Sr.	Williamsburg, Va.
24	Lamb, Steve	DB	190	6-0	18	Fr.	Findlay
25	*Bell, Todd	DB	202	6-1	19	So.	Middletown
26	Gayle, Jim	TB	190	5-10	18	Fr.	Hampton, Va.
27	*Ellis, Ray	DB	194	6-2	19	So.	Canton
28	Murphy, Bob	DB	193	6-1	20	So.	Santa, Ynez, Calif.
29	**Blinco, Tom	LB	221	6-2	20	Jr.	Lewiston, N.Y.
30	*Payton, Joel	FB	221	6-2	19	So.	Mentor
32	***Dansler, Kelton	LB	208	6-1	22	Sr.	Warren
33	Epitropoulos, John	LB	225	6-2	19	So.	Warren
34	Greene, Tony	FB	240	6-0	19	Fr.	Detroit, Mich.
35	Lee, Felix	FB	229	6-1	19	So.	Highland Park, N.J.
35	Harris, Dennis	FL	165	5-11	21	Jr.	Cleveland
36	***Cousineau, Tom	LB	227	6-3	21	Sr.	Fairview Park
37	Hicks, Ty	FL	180	5-11	21	So.	Warren
38	**Campbell, Paul	FB	217	6-1	21	Jr.	Ravenna
39	Ellison, Leon	LB	211	6-2	20	So.	Washington, D.C.
41	Eberts, Mark	SE	187	5-11	19	Fr.	Canton
42	Willis, Ken	DB	181	6-0	19	So.	Columbus
42	Manning, Rob	LB	210	6-1	19	So.	Columbus
43	*Murray, Calvin	TB	185	5-11	19	So.	Woodbine, N.J.
44	Brown, Harold	TB	197	6-2	18	Fr.	Kent
44	Jacobs, Ron	FL	183	6-2	20	Sr.	Youngstown
46	***Griffin, Duncan	DB	188	5-11	20	Sr.	Columbus
47	*Donley, Doug	FL	180	6-1	19	So.	Cambridge
48	*Skillings, Vince	DB	172	6-0	19	So.	Brenzier, Pa.
49	Williams, Gary	DB	197	6-2	18	Fr.	Wilmington
50	DeLeone, Jim	C	217	5-11	20	So.	Kent
50	Rolf, Rex	TE	213	6-2	21	Jr.	Gibsonburg
51	Gatewood, Russell	LB	225	6-3	18	Fr.	Orlando, Fla.
52	**Vogler, Tim	C	223	6-3	21	Sr.	Covington
53	Pack, Craig	LB	218	6-2	18	Fr.	Orrville
54	*Henson, Luther	DT	241	6-2	19	So.	Sandusky
55	Foster, Jerome	DT	240	6-4	18	Fr.	Detroit, Mich.
56	**Fritz, Ken	OG	238	6-3	20	Jr.	Ironton
57	***Savoca, Jim	OG	228	6-2	22	Sr.	Solon
58	**Waugh, Tom	OG	242	6-1	21	Sr.	Norwalk
59	Epitropoulos, Ernie	OG	225	6-2	19	So.	Warren
59	Moberger, Steve	OG	220	6-2	21	Jr.	Lima
60	**Dulin, Gary	DT	258	6-4	21	Jr.	Madisonville, Ky.
61	Medich, Dave	OG	237	6-2	19	So.	Steubenville
20	Mills, Ed	OT	263	6-7	20	Jr.	Columbus
62	Balen, Alan	DT	217	6-1	19	So.	Lackawanna, N.Y.
63	Burris, Scott	OG	236	6-3	20	Jr.	Point Pleasant, W. Va.
64	Miller, Nick	DT	226	6-3	18	So.	Upland, Pa.
65	Ferguson, Keith	OT	232	6-5	19	So.	Miami, Fla.
66	Palahnuk, Mike	OG	235	6-2	18	Fr.	Hicksville, N.Y.

No	Name	Pos	Wt	Ht	Age	Yr	Hometown
66	Sullivan, Mark	MG	205	5-9	19	Fr.	Cleveland
67	Smith, Joe	DT	242	6-3	18	Fr.	Cincinnati
68	*Sawicki, Tim	MG	217	6-0	20	Jr.	Mayfield
69	**Andria, Ernie	OG	238	6-3	21	Sr.	Wintersville
70	**Robinson, Joe	OT	254	6-5	21	Sr.	Paulding
71	***Cato, Byron	DT	241	6-2	21	Sr.	Lorain
72	***Sullivan, Mark	MG	238	6-4	21	Sr.	New Bedford, Mass.
73	**Mackey, Doug	OT	250	6-4	21	Jr.	Saugus, Mass.
74	Brown, Tim	OT	272	6-6	21	Jr.	Warren
75	Hutchings, John	C	215	6-0	20	So.	Fremont
76	Burke, Tim	OT	252	6-5	21	Sr.	Wapakoneta
77	Phillips, Dave	C	221	6-5	20	So.	Vienna, W. Va.
78	Levenick, Tom	OT	234	6-4	18	Fr.	Washington, Ill.
79	Akins, Kevin	OT	254	6-5	18	Fr.	Webster, N.Y.
80	Houston, Jim	TE	218	6-3	18	Fr.	Akron
81	Light, Jim	DT	220	6-3	18	Fr.	Toledo
82	*Barwig, Ron	TE	250	6-8	20	Jr.	Willoughby Hills
83	***Hornik, Joe	DT	234	6-3	21	Sr.	North Olmsted
84	Pauley, Doug	FL	180	6-1	19	So.	Carpinteria, Calif.
84	Hafner, Ed	LB	215	6-0	19	Fr.	Sandusky
85	Meade, John	TE	237	6-5	18	Fr.	Mokena, Ill.
86	Lee, Ben	LB	196	6-0	19	Fr.	Canton
87	**Jaco, Bill	TE	248	6-5	21	Sr.	Toledo
88	Allen, Dave	LB	216	6-2	19	So.	Warren
89	*Hunter, Chuck	TE	203	6-2	21	Jr.	Newark, Delaware
90	*Megaro, Tony	LB	227	6-2	19	So.	Chicago, Ill.
91	Miller, Ron	LB	216	6-3	19	So.	Auburn, N.Y.
92	Laser, Joel	OT	234	6-2	21	Sr.	Akron
92	Echols, Reggie	DT	230	6-1	20	Jr.	Chardon
93	*Bach, Terry	LB	210	5-10	20	So.	Centerville
94	Berner, Joe	LB	215	6-3	18	Fr.	Avon Lake
95	Phillips, Larry	DT	230	6-3	19	Fr.	Vienna, W. Va.
96	D'Andrea, Mike	LB	218	6-4	18	Fr.	Akron
97	*Vogler, Terry	LB	221	6-2	21	Sr.	Covington
98	Kellum, Wendell	MG	227	5-8	27	Sr.	Columbus
98	Faler, Mike	LB	200	6-1	21	Jr.	Piqua
99	***Moore, Jimmy	TE	242	6-5	21	Sr.	Tempe, Arizona

1978
PURDUE ALPHABETICAL TEAM ROSTER

(* Denotes letters won)

No	Name	Pos	Ht/Wt	Yr.	Hometown (High School)
10	*Adamle, Mark	DB	6-0/197	Jr.	Kent, OH (Roosevelt)
5	Albaugh, Dick	DB	6-0/194	Jr.	Toledo, OH (Anthony Wayne)
75	Allison, Jay	OT	6-7/285	Fr.	Gahanna, OH (Westerville)
23	Augustyniak, Mike	FB	6-1/217	Jr.	Leo, IN (Leo)
2	Barioli, Giuseppe	PK	5-9/190	Fr.	Ft. Lauderdale, FL (St. Thomas Aquinas)
90	Barr, Jim	MG	5-10/230	Jr.	Greensburg, IN (New Castle Chrysler)
7	*Barr, Steve	QB	6-0/189	Sr.	Canton, OH (St. Thomas Aquinas)
84	Barr, Tom	TE	6-3/223	Fr.	Greensburg, IN (Greensburg)

16	Betulius, Joe	QB	6-2/200	So.	Evansville, IN (Reitz)
98	Bunchek, Matt	OL	6-0/202	Fr.	Chesterton, IN (Chesterton)
87	*Burrell, Bart	WR	6-2/180	So.	Carmel, IN (Carmel)
98	Bury, Jeff	DE	6-0/210	Jr.	Findlay, OH (Findlay)
94	*Clark, Calvin	DT	6-5/234	So.	Atlanta, GA (Brown)
51	Dodge, Dennis	OL	6-5/238	So.	Port Clinton, OH (Port Clinton)
33	Doria, Frank	FB	5-11/210	So.	Flushing, NY (St. Francis)
61	Dunn, Troy	LB	6-3/222	Fr.	Frankfort, IN (Clinton Central)
1	**Eagin, Dave	P	6-2/196	Sr.	Alexandria, VA (Fort Hunt)
57	East, Guy	OL	6-5/222	Fr.	Indianapolis, IN (NC)
68	Ernst, John	DE	6-4/218	So.	Cincinnati, OH (St. Xavier)
88	**Eubank, Tim	TE	6-6/241	Sr.	Paoli, IN (Paoli)
96	Farris, Mike	LB	6-3/233	Jr.	Cleveland, OH (Benedictine)
76	*Feil, Henry	OT	6-4/255	So.	Long Island, NY (Berner)
92	***Floyd, Ruben	DE	6-2/217	Sr.	Canton, OH (McKinley)
79	Fritzche, Jim	OL	6-8/245	Fr.	Parma, OH (Valley Forge)
27	Fuetterer, Mike	WR	6-3/191	Fr.	Columbus, IN (East)
49	*Gallivan, Tony	WR	5-11/174	Sr.	Wauconda, IL (Wauconda)
97	Gooden, Ike	DE	6-3/202	Fr.	Detroit, MI (Cass Tech)
54	*Grimmett, Keevan	DE	6-4/226	Jr.	Harvey, IL (Thornton)
52	Gunner, Ray	OL	6-2/225	Fr.	Toledo, OH (Woodward)
31	Guyton, Don	RB	5-11/178	Fr.	Memphis, TN (Northside)
55	*Hall, Don	OL	6-4/224	Jr.	Glen Ellyn, IL (Glenbard West)
96	Hanna, Paul	DL	6-4/230	Fr.	Westlake, OH (Westlake)
19	Harris, Labraunt	WR	5-10/187	Fr.	Miami, FL (Carol City)
41	Harris, Mike	WR	6-0/182	Jr.	Los Angeles, CA (Cerritos)
45	*Harris, Willie	DB	6-0/186	Sr.	Chicago, IL (Vocational)
9	*Herrmann, Mark	QB	6-5/194	So.	Carmel, IN (Carmel)
57	Hull, Tim		6-3/227	So.	Indianapolis, IN (N. Central)
77	**Jackson, Marcus	DT	6-4/260	Jr.	Lima, OH (Lima)
42	*Johanson, Mark	LB	6-2/211	Jr.	Indianapolis, IN (Lawrence Central)
99	Jones, Robert	DL	6-3/211	So.	McKenney, VA (Dinwiddie)
32	Jones, Wallace	RB	6-1/192	Fr.	Detroit, MI (Central)
51	*Josten, Mark	DE	6-3/214	Jr.	Indianapolis, IN (Warren Central)
38	Kay, Bill	DB	6-2/183	So.	Chicago, IL (Proviso East)
39	Keith, Ron	RB	6-1/185	Fr.	St. Marys, OH (Memorial)
56	Kerchner, Mike	OL	6-2/238	Jr.	LaPorte, IN (LaPorte)
15	*Kingsbury, Tom	OL	5-11/198	So.	Chicago, IL (St. Rita)
3	Kingseed, Terry	P	5-11/196	Sr.	Greentown, IN (Eastern)
73	Krol, Steve	OT	6-5/238	So.	Chicago, IL (De La Salle)
71	**LeFeber, John	OG	235	Sr.	Geneva, IL (Geneva)
14	Linville, Joe	P-WR	6-1/161	Fr.	Carmel, IN (Carmel)
72	*Loushin, Ken	MG	6-2/248	Jr.	Richmond Hts., OH (Richmond)
95	Luckianow, Neil	TE	6-2/213	Sr.	Brooklyn, OH (Brooklyn)
37	*Macon, John	FB	6-1/205	So.	Marion, IN (Marion)
16	Maher, Bryan	WR	6-1/195	Fr.	Highland, Falls, NY (Choate)
62	Marks, Mike	LB	6-3/229	So.	Chicago, IL (Leo)
30	McAfee, Don	RB	5-9/175	Jr.	Eau Claire, MI (Eau Claire)
13	McCall, Ben	RB	6-0/193	So.	Chicago, IL (Mendel)
74	**McKenzie, Steve	OT	6-5/260	Jr.	Chicago, IL (De La Salle)
34	McKinnie, Marcus	DB	6-2/178	Fr.	Barberton, OH (Barberton)
46	Meyer, Jim	FB	5-11/202	Fr.	Elk Grove, IL (Elk Grove)
21	Mihal, Tom	WR	6-0.184	Jr.	Muncie, IN (Northside)
58	**Motts, Kevin	LB	6-2/230	Jr.	South Bend, IN (Mishawaka Marian)
27	**Moss, Rick	DB	6-0/192	Sr.	Mattoon, IL (Mattoon)

No.	Name	Pos.	Ht.	Wt.		Hometown (School)
53	Munro, Tom	LB	6-6/212	Fr.	Elk Grove, IL (Elk Grove)
78	Myers, Don	OL	6-4/240	Fr.	Greenfield, IN (Central)
4	Oliver, Chuck	QB	6-1/189	Fr.	Valparaiso, IN (Valparaiso)
69	Palumbo, Greg	OL	6-3/226	Jr.	Cleveland, OH (Cathedral Latin)
17	Peete, Cleo	WR	6-3/182	Fr.	Memphis, TN (Northside)
11	Perry, Cedric	DB	6-0/169	Jr.	Gary, IN (Emerson)
40	***Pope, Russell	RB	5-11/186	Sr.	Rockford, IL (East)
40	Pruitt, Robert	RB	6-0/193	So.	Chicago, IL (Phillips)
63	*Quinn, Pete	C	6-2/243	Jr.	Indianapolis, IN (Scecina)
86	Rastovski, Dave	TE	6-5/212	Jr.	Merrillville, IN (Merrillville)
66	Rastovski, Tim	DE	6-3/213	Sr.	Merrillville, IN (Merrillville)
28	*Robinson, Dwight	RB	5-11/184	Jr.	Ft. Wayne, IN (Snider)
61	*Schlundt, Steve	OL	6-5/230	Jr.	Mishawaka, IN (Mishawaka)
66	*Schwan, Dale	OL	6-4/228	Sr.	Westlake, OH (Westlake)
15	Seibel, John	PK	5-11/176	Jr.	Cincinnati, OH (Princeton)
43	Seneff, Tim	DB	6-1/195	Fr.	Merrillville, IN (Merrillville)
81	**Smith, Raymond	WR	6-2/197	Jr.	Paris, KY (Paris)
44	Smith, Wayne	DB	6-0/180	Jr.	Chicago, IL (Harper)
8	**Sovereen, Scott	PK	6-3/213	Sr.	Midland, MI (Midland)
18	Speedy, Jeff	WR	6-3/186	Fr.	Louisville, KY (Fairdale)
20	**Supan, Rock	DB	6-1/192	Sr.	Parma, OH (Padua Franciscan)
60	Thorson, Jeff	OL	6-5/214	Jr.	Pittsburgh, PA (Upper St. Clair)
67	Townsend, Steve	DL	6-2/228	Fr.	Hartford City, IN (Blackford County)
85	**Turner, Keena	DE	6-3/212	Jr.	Chicago, IL (Vocational)
35	Vargyas, Gary	DB	5-9/187	Jr.	South Bend, IN (Mishawaka Marian)
59	Virkus, Scott	DE	6-5/242	Fr.	Rochester, NY (Greece Olympia)
70	Webber, Ed	DE	6-4/210	Fr.	Hazelwood, MO (Hazelwood)
65	Weissert, Mike	OL	5-11/236	So.	Ft. Wayne, IN (Bishop Dwenger)
71	Wilkinson, Jim	OL	6-3/227	Fr.	Munster, IN (Munster)
92	Wynn, Ammon	LB	6-2/196	Fr.	Chicago, IL (Vocational)
80	*Young, Dave	TE	6-6/222	So.	Akron, OH (East)
82	Zordani, John	DE	6-3/209	So.	Chicago, IL (Brother Rice)

1978 WISCONSIN ALPHABETICAL TEAM ROSTER

(* Denotes letters won)

No.	Name	Pos.	Ht.	Wt.	Age	Class
41	*Ahrens, Dave	OLB	6-3	216	19	So
	Oregon—Calvin Callaway					
69	Aldrich, Mark	OT	6-5½	251	18	Fr
	Angola, IN—Joe Sirk					
3	Aldrich, Tom	B	5-10	187	18	Fr
	Burlington (St. Mary's)—Donald Dalton					
29	Anderson, Ross	CSC	5-9	175	19	So
	Madison (LaFollette)—Dave Maas					
86	**Barber, Greg	Y	6-4	208	21	Sr
	Menomonee Falls (Sussex Hamilton)—Stan Grove					

No.	Name	Pos	Ht	Wt	Age	Yr
85	**Blaskowski, Curt** Schofield (D.C Everest)— Richard Ambrosino	DT	6-3	220	19	So
95	**Boliaux, Guy** Des Plaines, Il(Maine East)— Al Eck	OLB	6-½	203	18	Fr
19	**Braker, Tom** Beaver Dam—Charles McDonald	X-Z	6-5	205	20	Jr
15	**Brennan, Chris** Kenilworth,Il (Loyola Academy)— Tom Powers	TB	5-7	152	20	So
2	**Brhely, Mike** West Allis (Thomas Moore)— Jim Haluska	KS	5-10	192	21	Sr
65	**Burney, Richard** Norfolk, VA (Lake Taylor)— Wilbert Harrell	ILB	6-1	201	20	Jr
82	****Burt, Mike** Chicago, IL (Mendel)— Lou Guida	DT	6-5	221	21	Sr
3	**Buss, Jeff** Wisconsin Dells—Fred Kuhl	QB	6-1½	211	19	Jr
67	***Cabral, Kasey** New Bedford, MA—Bruce McPherson	DT	6-3½	244	20	Jr
30	**Casey, Mickey** Eau Claire (Regis)—Peter Koupal	WSC	5-11	180	21	Jr
72	**Chakos, Tom** Country Club Hills, IL (Hillcrest)—Carl Zambo	OT	6-4	235	19	So
10	****Charles, David (CC)** Houston, TX (Jefferson Davis)—Paul Garrison	X	6-2	192	22	Sr
48	**Christenson, Dennis** Oregon—Calvin Callaway	ILB	6-1	222	21	Jr
39	***Cohee, Kevin** Kansas City, MO (Paseo)— Bill Elliott	TB	5-11	185	20	Sr
74	**Coleman, Tim** Balt., MD (Douglass)—John Nash, IA Lakes JC Estherville, IA—Don Birmingham	OT	6-5	269	21	Jr
60	**Collins, Willie** Detroit, MI (McKenzie)— Robert Dozier	N	6-3	218	18	Fr
14	*****Crossen, Dave (CC)** Rhinelander—Juan Mentink	ILB	6-3	218	21	Sr
16	**Delaney, Patrick** Stratford—Bob Delaney	CSC	5-9½	178	20	So
61	**Dixon, John** Wisconsin Dells—Fred Kuhl	OG	5-10	233	19	So

No.	Name	Pos	Ht	Wt	Age	Yr
70	**Doerger, Jerry**	OT	6-5	230	18	Fr
	Cincinnati, OH (LaSalle)—Joe Clark					
21	***Erdmann, Scott**	S	6-1	195	21	Sr
	Footville (Parkview-Orfordville)—Rod Olsen					
44	**Fixmer, Mike**	Y	6-2	196	19	So
	Rhinelander—Juan Mentink					
32	**Goff, Mark**	FB	6-1	194	18	Fr
	Monona (Monona Grove)—Dick Rundle					
8	***Gordon, Greg**	CSC	6-2	206	21	Sr
	Mobile, Ala. (Blount)—Albert Terry					
93	**Gorsuch, Terry**	Z	6-0	189	20	So
	Pardeeville—Robert Bostad					
11	****Green, Charles**	QB	6-1	207	21	SR
	Mobile, Ala. (Blount)—Albert Terry					
35	**Griffith, Gene**	FB	6-0	205	19	So
	Stow, OH—John Bucey and Joe Denton					
22	**Hable, Ben**	OLB	6-4	200	20	Jr
	Madison (Memorial)—Wally Schoessow					
15	***Holm, Kurt**	ILB	6-3	228	23	Sr
	Waukesha (South)—Ken Hollub					
90	***Houston, Thomas**	N	6-3	238	20	Jr
	Washington, D.C. (Woodson)—Bob Headen					
56	****Jackomino, Brad**	OG	5-10	212	22	Sr
	Rhinelander—Juan Mentink					
37	****Johnson, Lawrence**	WSC	5-11	201	21	Sr
	Gary, IN (Roosevelt)—Claude Taliaferro					
13	**Josten, John**	QB	6-1	187	17	Fr
	Palatine, IL (St. Viator, Arlington Hgts., IL)—Jim Lyne					
71	**Joyce, Leo**	OG	5-11	243	19	So
	Wisconsin Dells—Fred Kuhl					
18	**Kalasmiki, Mike**	QB	6-4	210	20	Jr
	Addison, IL (Trail)—Don Layne					
66	***Kelly, Patrick**	OG	6-1	228	22	Sr
	Northbrook IL (Glenbrook North)—Harold Samorian; Woodruff, WI					
31	**Kiltz, John**	KS	6-4	215	19	So
	Hartland (Arrowhead)—Larry Reinhold					
68	****Krall, Dave**	OT	6-4½	253	21	Sr
	Milwaukee (Brown Deer)—George Blanchard					
91	**Krein, Joel**	DT	6-2	231	19	Jr
	Racine (Park)—Phil Dobbs					

No.	Name	Pos.	Ht.	Wt.	Age	Yr.
88	**Krepfle, Mike** Potosi—Craig Moldenhauer	Y	6-2	218	19	So
47	***Levenick, Dave** Grafton—Clifford Cramer	ILB	6-2	208	19	So
57	**Lewis, Richard** Akron, OH (Springfield)— Les Cheney	ILB	6-2½	220	19	So
43	**Lorenz, Don** Marshfield—Jack Jansen	OLB	6-4	215	20	Sr
62	**Luko, Jeff** Oconomowoc—Edward Rux	OG	6-3	212	19	Fr
63	**Martine, Jim** Neenah—Gary Parker	OG	6-1	231	20	Jr
92	**Matthews, Ed** Verona—Ralph Frank	OLB	6-1	180	19	Fr
23	**Matthews, Kyle** Monona (Monona Grove)— Dick Rundle	S	5-10	166	18	Fr
25	*****Matthews, Ira** Rockford, IL (East)— Bob Pellant	TB	5-9	182	20	Sr
50	***McCoy, Jim** Monona (Monona Grove)— Dick Rundle	C	6-1½	233	21	Sr
40	**McKinnon, Kyle** Verona—Ralph Frank	X	5-10½	173	18	Fr
1	**Messenger, Dan** Marinette, WI—John Harris	WSC	6-1	177	18	Fr
78	**Miskinis, Greg** Racine (Horlick)—Dick Wojick	OT	6-5½	262	19	So
17	**Moeschl, Scott** Cincinnati, OH (Elder)—Ray Bachus	QB	6-3	204	18	Fr
28	**Mohapp, Dave** Woodstock, IL—Robert Bradshaw	FB	5-11	202	18	Fr
52	****Moore, Jim** Rhinelander—Juan Mentink	C	6-4	250	21	Sr
16	**Motl, Kevin** Sun Prairie—Mike Hahn	QB	6-2	185	18	So
73	**Namnick, Steve** Morton Grove, IL (Gordon Tech., Chicago IL)—Tom Winiecki	OT	6-5	230	17	Fr
34	**Nelson, Patrick** Merrill—Ira Rebella	FB	6-2	210	20	Jr
20	****Relich, Dan (CC)** Wauwatosa (West)—Tom Janssen	N	6-0	214	21	Sr
33	**Richardson, Curtis** Youngstown, OH (North)— Jerry Fields	TB	6-1	182	19	Fr
9	**Rogness, Mark** Osseo (Osseo-Fairchild)— Duane Matye	TB	6-0	214	18	Fr

No.	Name	Pos	Ht	Wt	Age	Yr
99	**Rozkuska, Richard** Chicago, IL (Lane Tech)—Al Manasin	ILB	5-11	215	19	So
59	**Rothbauer, Joe** Oshkosh (Lourdes)—Bob Collins	C	6-0	226	21	Jr
53	**Ruetz, Joe** Racine (St. Catherine)—Bob Letsch	OG	6-1½	215	19	So
64	**Rutenberg, Bill** Waunakee—Gayle Quinn	OG	5-10½	207	19	So
24	**Savage, Nick** Baltimore, MD (Northwestern)—Jim Welsch	S	6-0	170	18	Fr
45	**Sawicki, Mark** Chicago, IL (Mendel)—Lou Guida	OLB	6-0	209	20	So
9	****Schieble, Dan** Mequon (Homestead)—John Brodie	B	5-11	194	21	Sr
76	***Schremp, Tom** Antigo—Gordon Schofield	DT	6-3½	251	20	Jr
97	**Seamonson, Al** Stoughton—Charles Schulte	X	6-0	178	19	Fr
4	**Seiler, Jay** Schofield, (D.C. Everest)—Richard Ambrosino	S	6-1	190	18	Fr
81	**Seis, Dean** Antigo—Gordon Schofield	DT	6-4	221	20	So
46	**Schumate, Mark** Poynette—Larry Thurston	DT	6-3	205	18	Fr
36	**Schumway, Andy** Wisconsin Dells—Fred Kuhl, Condordia JC, Mil. Andy Luptak	FB	6-2	215	19	So
55	**Skoglund, Dan** LaGrange Park, IL (Fenwick, Oak Park, IL)—George Badke	N	6-1	212	17	Fr
38	**Sletten, Dave** Madison (East)—Wayne Kelliher	X	6-1	175	19	So
75	***Snell, Ray** Baltimore, MD (Northwestern)—James Welsch	OT	6-3	251	20	Jr
6	***Souza, Wayne** New Bedford, Mass.—Bruce MacPherson	Z	6-2	187	20	Jr
49	**Spurlin, Larry** Albany, GA (Dougherty)—Luther Welsh	ILB	6-0	217	18	Fr
26	***Stauss, Tom** Jefferson—James Knoblauch	FB	5-11	194	20	Jr
42	**Stracka, Tim** Madison (West)—Burt Hable	X	6-4	195	18	Fr

5	**Stroede, Terry**	B	6-0	188	19	Jr
	Baraboo—Benny Pederson					
21	**Sutton, Dan**	WSC	5-11	182	18	Fr
	Wauwatosa (West)—Donald Brenner					
87	**Sydnor, Ray**	Y	6-8	225	20	Jr
	Baltimore, MD (Northwestern)—James Welsch					
27	**Thomas, Vaughn**	Z	6-0	175	17	Fr
	Columbus, OH (Eastmoor)—Robert Stuart					
94	**Timmer, Jeff**	CSC	6-2	177	18	Fr
	Oconomowoc—Edward Rux					
79	**Turturro, Ralph**	OT	6-3	227	21	Sr
	Howard Beach, NY (St. Francis)—Vincent O-Connor					
7	*****Veith, Steve**	KS	6-1	196	21	Jr
	Sun Prairie—Mike Hahn					
58	**Versnik, Ron**	C	6-4	226	17	Fr
	West Allis, (Hale)—George Cwiklowski					
89	******Vine, Jeff**	OLB	6-3	202	20	Jr
	Granton (Neillsville)—Harlen Sunsdahl					
84	**Wagner, Bob**	LB-FB	6-2	222	21	Sr
	Chicago, IL (St. laurence)—Tom Kavanaugh					
51	**Walter, Ted**	OG	-6-2	220	19	So
	Akron, OH (St. Mary)—John Cistone					
98	**Wasikowski, Paul**	DT	6-3	219	21	Sr
	Cudahy—Gerald Bowe					
12	*****Welch, George**	S	6-1	195	20	Jr
	Benton Harbor, MI (St. Joseph)—Terry Rose					
18	**Westphal, John**	B	5-11	191	18	Fr
	Janesville (Craig)—Robert Suter					
54	**Wicks, Doug**	ILB	6-2	219	19	So
	Blue Island, IL (Eisenhower)—Dick Weiner					
77	**Wojtowicz, George**	DT	6-3	215	21	Sr
	Rockford, IL (East)—Robert Pellant					
96	**Wray, Richard**	CSC	6-1	176	18	Fr
	Toledo, OH (Witmer)—Pat Gucciardo					
61	**Yourg, Dan**	N	6-1	209	19	Jr
	Arlington Hgts., IL (St. Viator)—Jim Lyne					

Key: X—Split End; Y—Tight End; Z—Wide Receiver; OLB—Outside Linebacker; ILB—Inside Linebacker; N—Nose Guard; B—Buck (Strong Safety); S—Free Safety; WSC—Wide Side Cornerback; CSC—Close Side Cornerback.

COMPOSITE 1978 BIG TEN FOOTBALL SCHEDULE

SEPTEMBER 9
NORTHWESTERN AT ILLINOIS

SEPTEMBER 16
ILLINOIS AT MICHIGAN
INDIANA AT LSU
MICHIGAN ST AT PURDUE
NORTHWESTERN AT IOWA
TOLEDO AT MINNESOTA
PENN STATE AT OHIO STATE
RICHMOND AT WISCONSIN

SEPTEMBER 23
STANFORD AT ILLINOIS
WASHINGTON AT INDIANA
IOWA STATE AT IOWA
MICHIGAN AT NOTRE DAME
SYRACUSE AT MICHIGAN STATE
OHIO STATE AT MINNESOTA
WISCONSIN AT NORTHWESTERN
OHIO U. AT PURDUE

SEPTEMBER 30
ILLINOIS AT SYRACUSE
NEBRASKA AT INDIANA
IOWA AT ARIZONA
DUKE AT MICHIGAN
MICHIGAN STATE AT SOUTHERN CAL.
MINNESOTA AT UCLA
NORTHWESTERN AT COLORADO
BAYLOR AT OHIO STATE
PURDUE AT NOTRE DAME
OREGON AT WISCONSIN

OCTOBER 7
ILLINOIS AT MISSOURI
INDIANA AT WISCONSIN
UTAH AT IOWA
ARIZONA AT MICHIGAN
NOTRE DAME AT MICHIGAN STATE
OREGON STATE AT MINNESOTA
ARIZONA STATE AT NORTHWESTERN
SO. METHODIST AT OHIO STATE
WAKE FOREST AT PURDUE

OCTOBER 14
WISCONSIN AT ILLINOIS
NORTHWESTERN AT INDIANA
IOWA AT MINNESOTA
MICHIGAN STATE AT MICHIGAN
OHIO STATE AT PURDUE

OCTOBER 21
PURDUE AT ILLINOIS
INDIANA AT MICHIGAN STATE
IOWA AT OHIO STATE
MICHIGAN AT WISCONSIN
MINNESOTA AT NORTHWESTERN

OCTOBER 28
ILLINOIS AT INDIANA
PURDUE AT IOWA
MINNESOTA AT MICHIGAN
WISCONSIN AT MICHIGAN STATE
NORTHWESTERN AT OHIO STATE

NOVEMBER 4
MICHIGAN STATE AT ILLINOIS
INDIANA AT MINNESOTA
MICHIGAN AT IOWA
NORTHWESTERN AT PURDUE
OHIO STATE AT WISCONSIN

NOVEMBER 11
ILLINOIS AT OHIO STATE
IOWA AT INDIANA
MICHIGAN AT NORTHWESTERN
MINNESOTA AT MICHIGAN STATE
PURDUE AT WISCONSIN

NOVEMBER 18
ILLINOIS AT MINNESOTA
OHIO STATE AT INDIANA
WISCONSIN AT IOWA
PURDUE AT MICHIGAN
MICHIGAN STATE AT NORTHWESTERN

NOVEMBER 25
INDIANA AT PURDUE
IOWA AT MICHIGAN STATE
MICHIGAN AT OHIO STATE
MINNESOTA AT WISCONSIN

1978 SEASON: PLAY-BY-PLAY

Publisher's Note:

We have arranged the complete game descriptions in alphabetical order of the home teams each week. When the home team has possession of the ball, the type is in bold face.

We regret certain inconsistencies of format in the play-by-plays. Our material was gathered from a number of sources and as a result there are differences in the handling of abbreviations, descriptions, etc. We have attempted to standardize the play-by-plays as much as possible, but because of time limitations we could not do so completely. It is hoped, however, that they are clear and that they capture the individual flavor of each game.

In most instances the name of player(s) making the tackle is in parentheses.

Game statistics have been included whenever available.

SEPTEMBER 9, 1978

NORTHWESTERN VS. ILLINOIS
Memorial Stadium,
Champaign, Illinois
Temp.: 93°
Wind: ESE 5 mph
Skies: Sunny, clear
FIRST QUARTER

Northwestern wins toss elects to receive and defend north goal. Jones kicks off to Hill in end zone returns to 18.

14:56 NORTHWESTERN
1/10 -N18 - Hill takes pitch around re for 7 (Venegoni)
2/3 -N25 - Mishler over rg for 1 (Scott)
3/2 -N26 - Mishler takes pitch over rt for 5 (Levitt)
1/10 -N31 - Cammen takes pitch over lt for 3 (Sullivan, Gillen)
2/7 -N34 - Strasser sideline pass complete to Cammen for 10 (Scott)
1/10 -N44 - Mishler over center for loss of 2 (Sullivan)
2/12 -N42 - Strasser swing pass dropped by Cammen
3/12 -N42 - Mishler on draw for 3 (Gillen, Scott)
4/9 -N45 - Poulos punt to Hardy at I23, fair catch (32 yard punt)

11:29 ILLINOIS
1/10 -I23 - Carter dances over lg for 4 (Rogers, Payne)
2/6 -I27 - Carter takes pitch around re for 10 (Geegan)
1/10 -I37 - Strader dive for 3 (Berg, Miller)
2/7 -I40 - Weiss keeps around re for 6
3/1 -I46 - PENALTY: Illinois clipping downfield
3/8 -I39 - Weiss keeps over rg for 6 (Knafelc, Payne)
4/2 -I45 - Finzer punt downed at NU 35 (19 yard punt)

8:13 NORTHWESTERN
1/10 -N35 - Strasser pass to McGee is caught out of bounds
2/10 -N35 - Mishler bounces outside on draw for 5 (Adams)
3/5 -N40 - Strasser pass for Webb broken up by Tucker
4/5 -N40 - Poulos punts out of bounds at I30 (30 yd punt)

7:17 ILLINOIS
1/10 -I30 - Weiss slips turning right side for 2
2/8 -I32 - Carter takes pitch around le for 1 (Hoffman)
3/7 -I33 - Weiss dropped for loss attempting to pass by Wells; loss of 2
4/9 -I31 - Finzer punt downed at N1 (68 yard punt)

5:09 NORTHWESTERN
1/10 -N1 - Strasser sneaks for 4 (Sullivan)
2/6 -N5 - Mishler up middle for loss of 2 (Sullivan, Flynn)
3/8 -N3 - Mishler slants off lt for 3 (Sullivan, Levitt)
4/5 -N6 - Poulos punts to Hardy at NU40, returns 9 (37 yard punt)

ILLINOIS
1/10 -N31 - Foster over rg for 4 (Payne, Corona)
2/6 -N27 - Foster takes pitch, dropped for loss of 8 (Rogers)
3/14 -N35 - Weiss pass over middle for Sherrod overthrown, Knafelc breaks up pass
4/14 -N35 - Finzer punt downed at N1 (34 yard punt)

1:35 NORTHWESTERN
1/10 -N1 - Strasser sneaks for 2 (Sullivan, Meyer)
2/8 -N3 - Mishler over rg for 4 (Flynn)
3/4 -N7 - Mishler takes pitch around re for 8 (Sullivan)

**END OF FIRST QUARTER:
ILLINOIS 0, NORTHWESTERN 0**

SECOND QUARTER

NORTHWESTERN
1/10 -N15 - Mishler takes pitch around re for 3 (Scott)
2/7 -N18 - Strasser pass complete to McGee for 12 (Levitt)
1/10 -N30 - Hill takes pitch around le for 2 (Meyer, Flynn)
2/8 -N32 - Strasser screen pass to Hill for 4 (Levitt)
3/4 -N36 - Strasser pass intended for Poulos, broken up by Adams
4/4 -N36 - Poulos PENALTY Northwestern: Poulos fumbles snap intentional grounding

13:18 ILLINOIS
1/10 -N17 - Carter over rg for 5 (Robinett, Knafelc)
2/5 -N12 - Weiss keeps around le for 2 (McGlade, Weitzman)
3/3 -N10 - Carter slants over rt for 1 (Miller)
4/2 -N9 - 26 yard field goal attempt is wide right (Jones)

11:05 NORTHWESTERN
1/10 -N20 - Strasser sideline pass for McGee overthrown
2/10 -N20 - Johnson up middle for loss of 1 (Thornton)
3/11 -N19 - Strasser screen pass for North incomplete; Adams breaks up pass
4/11 -N19 - Poulos punt to Hardy at I26, returns 11 (55 yard punt)
PENALTY: Illinois clipping on return

142

SEPTEMBER 9, 1978

10:00 ILLINOIS
1/10-I14 - Strader up middle for 3 (Weitzman)
2/7 -I17 - Carter over lg for 3 (Miller)
3/4 -I20 - Carter takes pitch around le for 22 (Geegan)
1/10-I42 - Weiss pass to Sherrod for 22 (Hoffman)
1/10-N36 - Carter takes pitch around re for 6 (Miller)
2/4 -N30 - Weiss on qb draw for 2 (Weitzman)
3/2 -N28 - Weiss keeps around le for 4 (Payne)
1/10-N24 - PENALTY ILLINOIS: illegal procedure
1/15-N29 - Carter takes pitch around re for 9 (Hoffman)
2/6 -N20 - Dismuke over rg for 2 (Kern, Stasiewicz)
3/4 -N18 - Weiss pass for Sherrod overthrown
TIME OUT ILLINOIS (4:25)
TIME OUT NORTHWESTERN (4:25)
4/4 -N18 - Weiss scrambles up middle for 3 (Berg)

4:17 NORTHWESTERN
1/10-N15 - Cammen around le for 5 (Levitt)
2/5 -N20 - Mishler over lg for 4 (Doney)
3/1 -N24 - Cammen slants over re for 6 (Adams, Gillen)
1/10-N30 - Strasser sideline pass to McGee complete for 9 (Scott)
2/1 -N39 - Strasser sideline pass complete to Miller for 12 (Tucker)
1/10-I49 - Cammen around re for 7 (Levitt)
2/3 -I42 - Strasser pass to Cammen for 7 (Sullivan)
1/10-I35 - Strasser dropped for loss of 8 by J. Gillen
2/18-I43 - Strasser sacked by Adams; loss of 13
3/31-N44 - Mishler's quick kick rolls dead at 16 (50 yard punt)

0:21 ILLINOIS
1/10-I6 - Weiss sneak for 6 (Miller)

**END OF FIRST HALF:
ILLINOIS 0, NORTHWESTERN 0**

Note: Illinois won toss at start of game and elected to defend south goal.

THIRD QUARTER

Jones kicks off north to Hill; downed in end zone)
NORTHWESTERN
1/10-N20 - Mishler takes pitch around le for 2 (Sullivan, Gillen)
2/8 -N22 - Strasser sideline pass complete to McGee for 7 (Levitt)
3/1 -N29 - Cammen over rg for no gain (Thiede)
4/1 -N29 - Poulos punts to Hardy at I30, fair catch (41 yard punt)

13:27 ILLINOIS
1/10-I30 - Carter fumbles pitch out of bounds for 4
2/6 -I34 - Weiss over rg for 4 (Corona, Rogers)
3/2 -I38 - Carter takes pitch around re for 9 (Geegan)
1/10-I47 - Weiss pass over middle to Sherrod complete for 17
1/10-N36 - Foster takes pitch around re for 2 (Kendzicky)
2/8 -N34 - Foster up middle for 1 (Weitzman)
3/7 -N33 - Weiss pass complete to Foster for 7 (Berg, Pals)
1/10-N26 - Weiss keeps around le for 2 (Miller)
2/8 -N24 - Strader over rg for 2 (Miller)
3/6 -N22 - Rouse takes pitch on reverse around re for 14 (Geegan)
1/8 -N8 - Carter on delay for 6 (Berg, Geegan)
2/2 -N2 - Weiss pitch goes behind Carter, recovered by Payne (N) for loss of 7

8:17 NORTHWESTERN
1/10-N9 - Mishler for 1 yd (Adams)
2/9 -N10 - Mishler over lg for 3 (Ralph, Thiede)
3/6 -N13 - Mishler on draw for 5 (Meyer, Adams)
4/1 -N18 - Poulos punt to Hardy at N48, fair catch (30 yard punt)

6:19 ILLINOIS
1/10-N48 - Strader over rg for no gain (Payne)
2/10-N48 - Weiss pass for Carter broken up by Robinett
3/10-N48 - Weiss sacked for loss of 12 by Miller
4/22-I40 - Finzer punt to Geegan at N20, returns 6 (40 yard punt)

143

4:55 NORTHWESTERN
- 1/10-N26 - Strasser pass complete to McGee for 10 (Scott)
- 1/10-N36 - PENALTY NORTHWESTERN: illegal procedure
- 1/15-N31 - Strasser swing pass for Mishler complete for 4 (Sullivan)
- 2/11-N35 - Strasser pass complete to North for 11 (Tucker)
- 1/10-N46 - Mishler over rg for 8 (Sullivan, Adams)
- 2/2 -I46 - Strasser deep sideline pass for Webb incomplete
- 3/2 -I46 - Mishler over rg for no gain (Flynn)
- 4/2 -I46 - Poulos punt to Hardy at I13 (33 yard punt)

2:16 ILLINOIS
- 1/10-I13 - Weiss keeps up middle for 8 (Lawrence)
- 2/2 -I21 - Weiss quick pass over middle to Sherrod for 13 (Geegan)
- 1/10-I34 - Weber over rt for 1 (Miller, Weitzman)
- 2/9 -I35 - Weiss fumbles for loss of 15 (recovered by Rogers (N) Robinett caused fumble

0:17 NORTHWESTERN
- 1/10-I20 - PENALTY NORTHWESTERN: illegal procedure
- 1/15-I25 - Cammen around le for loss of 1 (Flynn)

END OF THIRD QUARTER:
ILLINOIS 0, NORTHWESTERN 0

FOURTH QUARTER

NORTHWESTERN
- 2/15-I26 - Strasser screen complete to Cammen for loss of 3 (Scott, Flynn)
- 3/18-I29 - Mishler around le for loss of 1 (Gillen)
- 4/19-I30 - Mirkopulos 47 yard field goal attempt is no good

13:36 ILLINOIS
- 1/10-I30 - Foster over le for 2 (Rogers)
- 2/8 -I32 - Weiss keeps around re for 1 (Miller)
- 3/7 -I33 - Weiss pass to Strader for 3 (Knafelc)
- 4/4 -I36 - Finzer punt to North at N26, returns 10 (38 yard punt)

11:34 NORTHWESTERN
- 1/10-N36 - Strasser sideline pass complete to McGee for 7 (Levitt)
- 2/3 -N43 - Strasser quick out pass for McGee incomplete
- 3/3 -N43 - Strasser sideline pass for North broken up by Tucker
- 4/3 -N43 - Poulos punt fair caught by Hardy at I28 (29 yard punt)

10:47 ILLINOIS
- 1/10-I28 - Carter takes pitch around re for 6 (Geegan)
- 2/4 -I34 - Carter takes pitch around re for 1 (Kendzicky)
- 3/3 -I35 - Weiss keeps over rt, cuts back for 27 (Geegan)
TIME OUT ILLINOIS 9:52
- 1/10-N38 - Dismuke over rg for 1 (Stasiewicz)
- 2/9 -N37 - Dismuke trips over rg for loss of 1
- 3/10-N38 - Weiss sideline pass complete to Schooley for 19
- 1/10-N19 - Carter takes pitch around le for 1 (Rogers, Stasiewicz)
- 2/9 -N18 - Weiss keeps around re for 1 (Kern)
TIME OUT ILLINOIS 7:18
- 3/8 -N17 - Carter takes pitch around re for loss of 1 (Geegan, McGlade)
- 4/9 -N18 - Offsetting penalties on pass attempt from field goal
- 4/9 -N18 - Finzer 35 yard field goal attempt is wide right

6:28 NORTHWESTERN
- 1/10-N20 - Strasser pass complete to McGee for 9
- 2/1 -N29 - Strasser pass broken up by Thiede
- 3/1 -N29 - Strasser keeps for 3 (Sullivan)
- 1/10-N32 - Strasser pass down sidelines for McGee overthrown
- 2/10-N32 - Strasser sideline pass for McGee incomplete
TIME OUT NORTHWESTERN 5:14
- 3/10-N32 - Strasser sideline pass to McGee complete for 12 (Levitt)
- 1/10-N44 - Strasser sideline pass to Bogan complete for 7
- 2/3 -I49 - Mishler slants off lt for 2 (Ralph)
- 3/1 -I47 - PENALTY ILLINOIS: offsides
- 1/10-I41 - Strasser sideline pass complete to McGee for 11
- 1/10-I30 - PENALTY NORTHWESTERN: illegal procedure
- 1/15-I35 - Strasser pass for North, tipped by Sullivan, intercepted by Adams at I19 return 1

4:07 ILLINOIS
- 1/10-I20 - Carter takes pitch around re for 7 (Kern)
- 2/3 -I27 - Weiss pass complete to Sherrod for 17 (Geegan)
- 1/10-I44 - Weber over lt for 9 (Kern)
- 2/1 -N47 - PENALTY ILLINOIS: Clipping
- 2/29-I25 - Weiss pass to Rouse broken up by Hoffman
- 3/29-I25 - Carter on draw for 7 (Lawrence)
- 4/22-I32 - Finzer punt fair catch by North at N30 (38 yard punt)

SEPTEMBER 9, 1978

1:27 NORTHWESTERN
1/10-N30 - Strasser screen complete to Cammen for 8 (Levitt)
2/2 -N38 - PENALTY: Northwestern holding
2/17-N23 - PENALTY NORTHWESTERN: illegal procedure
2/22-N18 - Webb on double reverse for loss of six (Flynn)
TIME OUT ILLINOIS
3/28-N12 - Strasser pass for McGee intercepted by Levitt at N49, 20 ret.

1:05 ILLINOIS
1/10-N31 - Weiss pass for Schooley incomplete
2/10-N31 - Offsetting penalties
2/10-N31 - Carter takes pitch around re for 6 (Geegan)
3/4 -N25 - Weiss sideline pass complete to Rouse for 11, fumbles, recovered by Geegan NU

0:23 NORTHWESTERN
1/10-N14 - Hill over rg for 5 (Gillen)
TIME OUT NORTHWESTERN
2/5 -N20 - Strasser sideline pass for Webb incomplete
3/5 -N20 - Mishler takes pitch around re for 15 (Adams, Levitt)
TIME OUT NORTHWESTERN
1/10-N35 - Strasser long pass for Webb broken up by Levitt as game ends

FINAL SCORE:
ILLINOIS 0, NORTHWESTERN 0

145

NORTHWESTERN
VS.
IOWA
Kinnick Stadium
Temp.: 75
Wind: 20 mph SSW
Sky: cloudy and chance of rain
FIRST QUARTER

Northwestern wins toss and elects to receive. Iowa will kick off and defend south goal. Schilling kicks off into endzone to Webb for touchback.

NORTHWESTERN
1/10-N20 - Mishler over LG for gain of 2. (Vasquez)
2/8 -N22 - Cammon around RE for gain of 2. (Hobbs)
3/6 -N24 - Mishler over LT for gain of 2. (Harty)
4/4 -N26 - Poulos punts to Becker for return of 2. (27 yard punt) (Kern)

13:15 IOWA
1/10-I49 - Lazar over RG for gain of 2. (Corona)
2/8 -N49 - Mosley over LG for gain of 2. (Corona)
3/6 -N47 - Commings thrown for loss of 9. (Rogers)
4/15-I44 - Northwestern penalized for 5 yards illegal procedure.
4/10-I49 - Holsclaw punts to Northwestern 1 yard line. (downed by Lazar)
(50 yard punt)

11:42 NORTHWESTERN
1/10-N1 - Johnson over RT for gain of 5. (Shaw)
2/5 -N6 - Johnson over RG for gain of 1. (Shaw)
3/4 -N7 - Johnson around RE for gain of 2.
4/2 -N9 - Poulos punts to Reid, fumbles, return of 2. Recovered by Rogers.
1/10-N32 - Johnson around RE for gain of 5. (Danzy)
2/5 -N37 - Cammon around LE for gain of 6. (Molini)
1/10-N43 - Northwestern penalized 5 yds for delay of game.
1/15-N38 - Johnson over RG for gain of 2. (Vasquez)
2/13-N40 - Strasser pass to Johnson for gain of 7
Northwestern penalized for pass interference
3/28-N25 - Johnson over LG for gain of 3. (Rusk)
4/25-N28 - Poulos punts to Reid for no return. (28 yard punt)

7:23 IOWA
1/10-I44 - Mosley around LE for gain of 1. (Kern)
2/9 -I45 - Morton passes to Reid for TD. Green holds, Schilling kicks, PAT is good.
SCORE: IOWA 7 NORTHWESTERN 0

Schilling kicks off to Bahoric, downed in endzone for touchback.

6:19 NORTHWESTERN
1/10-N20 - Johnson around LE for no gain. (Danzy)
2/10-N20 - Cammon around RE for loss of 4 (Becker)
3/14-N16 - Mishler over RG for loss of 2 (Harty)
4/16-N14 - Poulos fumbles, recovered by Simonsen, for TD (return of 4)
Green holds, Schilling kicks, PAT is good
SCORE: IOWA 14 NORTHWESTERN 0

Schilling kicks off to Bahoric, downs in endzone for touchback.

4:26 NORTHWESTERN
1/10-N20 - Strasser passes to North for gain of 15.
1/10-N35 - Strasser pass intended for Cammon is incomplete.
2/10-N35 - Strasser passes to Mishler for gain of 8 (Hardy)
3/2-N43 - Schmitt over RT for gain of 2 (Becker)
1/10-N45 - Strasser passes to Schmitt for no gain (Pace)
2/10-N45 - Strasser pass intended for North is incomplete.
3/10-N45 - Strasser passes to Schmitt for gain of 6 (Rusk)
4/4 -I49 - Christensen punts to Reid for return of 1 (31 yard) (Kern)

SEPTEMBER 16, 1978

146

SEPTEMBER 16, 1978

1:37 IOWA
1/10-I19 - Mosley over RG for gain of 4 (Kern)
2/6 -I23 - Mosley over RT for gain of 3 (Corona)
3/3 -I26 - Commings thrown for loss of 12 (Rogers)

**FIRST QUARTER SCORE:
IOWA 14 NORTHWESTERN 0**

SECOND QUARTER

IOWA
4/15-I14 - Holsclaw punts to Knafelc, fumbles recovered by Simonsen
1/10-I43 - Commings pass intended for Reid is incomplete.
2/10-I43 - Lazar over RG for gain of 12 (Kern)
1/10-N45 - Lazar over LG for gain of 3 (Kern)
2/7 -N42 - Iowa penalized 5 yds for delay of game.
2/12-N47 - Commings thrown for loss of 3 (Weitzman)
3/15- 50 - Commings pass intended for Morton, intercepted by Knafelc, return of 13 (Swift)

12:39 NORTHWESTERN
1/10-N42 - Hill around RE for gain of 5. NW penalized 5 yds for illegal motion.
1/15-N37 - Mishler over RG for gain of 2 (Mahmens)
2/13-N39 - Strasser passes to North for gain of 11 (Becker)
3/2 - 50 - Hill around LE for gain of 1 (Page)
4/1 -I49 - Christensen punts to Reid for return of 6 (40 yard punt)

11:10 IOWA
1/10-I15 - Mosley over RT for gain of 4 (Weitzman)
2/6 -I19 - Lazar over LT for gain of 5, fumbles, recovered by Kendzicky.

10:26 NORTHWESTERN
1/10-I24 - Hill around RE for gain of 2 (Hobbs)
2/8 -I22 - Strasser pass intended for Hill is incomplete.
3/8 -I22 - Strasser thrown for loss of 5.
4/13-I27 - Breitbeil holds, Mirkopulos kicks, field goal attempt is good.
SCORE: IOWA 14 NORTHWESTERN 3

Mirkopulos kicks off to Mosley in endzone for touchback.
9:02 IOWA
1/10-I20 - Commings around RE for gain of 7 (Kern)
2/3 -I27 - Mosley around LE for loss of 3 (Knafelc)

3/6 -I24 - Commings pass intended for Morton is incomplete.
4/6 -I24 - Holsclaw punts dead on Iowa 34.

7:27 NORTHWESTERN
1/10-I34 - Strasser pass intended for Mishler is incomplete.
2/10-I34 - Strasser passes to Hill for gain of 20 (Danzy)
1/10-I14 - Mishler around RE for loss of 1 (Gutshall)
2/11-I15 - Mishler pass intended for McGee is incomplete.
3/11-I15 - Strasser passes to Mishler for gain of 10 (Rusk)
4/1 -I5 - Mishler over LT for loss of 3 (Molini)

5:42 IOWA
1/10-I8 - Mosley over LT for gain of 10 (Geegan)
2/10-I18 - Commings around RE for gain of 2 (Payne)
2/8 -I20 - Mosley around LE for loss of 3 (Adams)
3/11-I17 - Commings passes to Mosley for gain of 8 (McGlade)
4/3 -I25 - Holsclaw punts to Geegan for fair catch (35 yard kick)

3:05 NORTHWESTERN
1/10-N40 - Mishler over RT for gain of 5 (Hufford)
2/5 -N45 - Strasser passes to McGee for gain of 13 (Shaw)
1/10-I42 - Mishler over RG for no gain (Rusk)
2/10-I42 - Strasser thrown for loss of 8 (Vasquez)
3/18- 50 - Strasser pass intended for North is incomplete.
4/18- 50 - Christensen punts into endzone for touchback.

1:12 IOWA
1/10-I20 - Lazar over RG for gain of 5 (Knafelc)
2/5 -I25 - Commings pass intended for Dunham is incomplete.
3/5 -I25 - Mosley around RE for gain of 3 (McGlade)
4/2 -I28 - Holsclaw punts to Geegan for fair catch.

0:25 NORTHWESTERN
1/10-N41 - Strasser passes to Webb for gain of 21.
1/10-I38 - Breitbeil holds, Mirkopulos kicks, field goal attempt is no good.

0:02 IOWA
1/10-I38 - Commings pass intercepted by Butler, return of 25.

**HALF TIME SCORE:
IOWA 14 NORTHWESTERN 3**

THIRD QUARTER

Iowa will receive. Northwestern will kick off and defend south goal.
Mirkopulos kicks off to Mosley for return of 29 (Berg)

IOWA
1/10-I29 - Mosley over LT for gain of 4 (Berg)
2/6 -I33 - Morton over RT for gain of 19 (Berg)
1/10-N48 - Iowa penalized 5 yds for offsides.
1/15-I47 - Morton around RE for gain of 1 (Berg)
2/14-I48 - Gales around RE for gain of 8, fumbles, recovered by Rogers (Weitzman)

13:28 NORTHWESTERN
1/10-N44 - Mishler over RT for gain of 2 (Rusk)
2/8 -N46 - Strasser pass intended for Poulos is incomplete.
3/8 -N46 - Mishler over LG for no gain (Hufford)
4/8 -N46 - Christensen punts fo Becker for return of 3 (36 yard punt) (Tiberi)

12:16 IOWA
1/10-I21 - Mosley around LE for no gain (Payne)
2/10-I21 - Morton over LT for gain of 3 (Berg)
3/7 -I24 - Gales passes to Dunham for gain of 15 (Adams)
1/10-I40 - Mosley over RG for gain of 2 (Weitzman)
2/8 -I42 - Gales around LE for loss of 1 (Knafelc)
3/9 -I41 - Mosley fumbles out of bounds for gain of 2.
4/7 -I43 - Holsclaw punts to Geegan for fair catch (32 yard kick)

9:15 NORTHWESTERN
1/10-N25 - Johnson over LG for gain of 1 (Hufford)
2/9 -N26 - Strasser passes to Hill for gain of 3 (Hufford)
3/6 -N29 - Strasser thrown for loss of 10 (Hufford)
4/16-N19 - Christensen punts to Becker for return of 2 (36 yard punt) (Robinett)

7:21 IOWA
1/10-I47 - Mosley over RG for gain of 2 (Weitzman)
2/8 -I49 - Gales around RE for gain of 8 (Payne)
1/10-N43 - Lazar over RT for gain of 6.
2/4 -N37 - Mosley over RG for gain of 2 (Grelle)
3/2 -N35 - Mosley around LE for gain of 1.
4/1 -N34 - Gales sneaks for gain of 2.
1/10-N32 - Mosley over LT for gain of 2 (Rogers)
2/8 -N30 - Lazar over RG for gain of 5 (Weitzman)
3/3 -N25 - Mosley around RE, fumbles, recovered by NW (gain of 1)
NW penalized half distance to goal for facemask grabbing.
1/10-N11 - Lazar over LG for gain of 1 (Weitzman)
2/9 -N10 - Gales pass intended for Lazar is incomplete.
3/9 -N10 - Reid around LE for TD. Green holds, Schilling kicks, PAT is no good.
SCORE: IOWA 20 NORTHWESTERN 3

Schilling kicks off to Schmitt for return of 13 (Hollaway)

2:07 NORTHWESTERN
1/10-N26 - Strasser passes to North for gain of 17 (Becker)
1/10-N43 - Mishler over LG for gain of 2 (Benshoter)
2/8 -N45 - Strasser pass intended for North is incomplete.
3/8 -N45 - Strasser passes to Mishler for gain of 7 (Pace)
4/1 -I48 - Strasser sneaks for gain of 1 (Mahmens)

**THIRD QUARTER SCORE:
IOWA 20 NORTHWESTERN 3**

FOURTH QUARTER

NORTHWESTERN
1/10-I47 - Strasser pass intended for North is incomplete.
2/10-I47 - Strasser pass intended for Hill is incomplete.
3/10-I47 - Strasser pass intended for Poulos is incomplete.
4/10-I47 - Christensen passes to Tiberi for gain of 26 (Reid)
1/10-I21 - Strasser pass intended for North is incomplete.
2/10-I21 - Hill around RE for gain of 2, fumbles, recovers own fumble (Hufford)
3/8 -I19 - Strasser pass intended for Poulos is incomplete.
4/8 -I19 - Strasser pass intended for McGee incomplete.

SEPTEMBER 16, 1978

13:33 IOWA
1/10-I19 - Morton over RT for gain of 5 (Kern)
2/5 -I24 - Iowa penalized 5 yds for delay of game.
2/10-I24 - Gales around LE for gain of 6 (Berg) NW penalized for personal foul.
1/10-I40 - Dunham thrown for loss of 9 (Rogers)
2/19-I31 - Iowa penalized 5 yds for delay of game.
2/24-I26 - Turner over LG for gain of 6.
3/18-I32 - Gales pass intended for McKillip is incomplete.
4/18-I32 - Holsclaw punts to Geegan for fair catch (29 yard kick)

11:00 NORTHWESTERN
1/10-N39 - Breitbeil pass intended for Hill is incomplete.
2/10-N39 - Breitbeil pass intended for Schmitt is incomplete.
3/10-N39 - Breitbeil pass intended for Poulos is incomplete.
4/10-N39 - Christensen punts to Reid for return of 7 (36 yard punt) NW penalized 15 yds for personal foul (Robinett)

10:37 IOWA
1/10-I47 - Mosley over LG for gain of 3 (Berg)
2/7 - 50 - Lazar over RG, gain of 9, fumbles, recovered by Adams (Payne)

10:04 NORTHWESTERN
1/10-N41 - Hill around RE for gain of 4 (Skradis)
2/6 -N45 - Breitbeil pass intended for Poulos is incomplete.
3/6 -N45 - Breitbeill pass intended for Bogan, intercepted by Skradis, fumbles and recovered by Schober.
1/10-N23 - Schmitt over LG for gain of 2 (Hill)
2/8 -N25 - Hill around RE for gain of 4 (Hill) NW penalized 15 yds for clipping.
2/18-N15 - Schmitt over RT for gain of 3 (Mahmens)
3/15-N18 - Breitbeil pass intended for Kaspryscki is incomplete.
4/15-N18 - Christensen punts to Becker for fair catch (30 yard punt)

7:14 IOWA
1/10-N48 - Mosley around RE for gain of 13 (Butler)
1/10-N35 - Crocker over LG for gain of 7 (Berg)
2/3 -N28 - Green around LE for gain of 1 (Oglivie)
3/2 -N27 - Mosley over LG for gain of 2 (Dunlea)
1/10-N25 - McKillip over RG for gain of 3 (Dunlea)

2/7 -N22 - Turner around RE for gain of 13 (Geegan)
1/G -N9 - Green around RE for loss of 2 (Stasiewicz)
2/G -N11 - Turner around LE for gain of 3 (Payne)
3/G -N8 - Green thrown for loss of 6 (Oglivie)
4/G -N14 - Green holds, Schilling kicks, field goal attempt is no good.

2:11 NORTHWESTERN
1/10-N20 - Hill around RE for gain of 2 (Persons)
2/8 -N22 - Schmitt over RG for gain of 1 (Simonson)
3/7 -N23 - Breitbeil pass intended for Hill is incomplete.
4/7 -N23 - Christensen punts dead on the Iowa 47 yard line. Iowa penalized for substitution infraction
1/10-N37 - Breitbeil pass intended for Bogan is incomplete.
2/10-N37 - Schmitt over RG for gain of 8 (Webb)
3/2 -N45 - Breitbeil pass intended for Webb is incomplete.

**FINAL SCORE:
IOWA 20 NORTHWESTERN 3**

National Collegiate Athletic Association
FINAL TEAM STATISTICS

STATISTICS	IOWA	NORTH-WESTERN
FIRST DOWN	13	10
RUSHES - YARDS	54-167	38-31
PASSING YARDS	79	158
RETURN YARDS	58	38
PASSES	3-9-2	13-37-1
PUNTS	7-217 (31.0)	10-339 (33.9)
FUMBLES - LOST	5-5	3-2
PENALTIES - YARDS	5-35	8-81

Scoring	1	2	3	4	Final
Iowa	14	0	6	0	20
Northwestern	0	3	0	0	3

IA-55 yd Pass, Morton to Reid, Schilling (kick) .... 6:19 1st Qtr.
IA-4yd Fumble Return Simonson, Schilling (kick) .... 4:26 1st Qtr.
NW-44 yd FG, Mirkopulos .... 9:01 2nd Qtr.
IA-10 yd Run, Reid, (kick failed) .. 2:07 3rd Qtr.

ATTENDANCE: 56,840.

ILLINOIS VS. MICHIGAN

Ann Arbor Stadium
Temp: 70's
Wind WSW 15 mph
Skies Sunny and warm

FIRST QUARTER

Illinois won the toss and elected to receive. Michigan defends the n. goal.

Virgil kicked off out of the Illinois endzone.
15:00 ILLINOIS
1/10-I20 - Strader at rg for 3; Greer tackle.
2/7 -I23 - Carter at center for 5 (Simpkins)
3/2 -I28 - Weiss kept at le for 5 (Meter)
1/10-I33 - Carter at rt for 1 (Green)
2/9 -I34 - Weiss elected to run for 8 (Owens)
3/1 -I42 - Weiss kept at re for 8 (Meter)
1/10- 50 - Carter at rt for 4 (Simpkins)
2/6 -M46 - Weiss passed low for Carter incomplete.
3/6 -M46 - Weiss tried rg for no gain (Greer)
4/6 -M46 - Finzer punted to the M 22 (24 yd punt where downed)

10:01 MICHIGAN
1/10-M22 - Huckleby at lt for 2 (Flynn)
2/8 -M24 - Huckleby at rg for 4 (Flynn)
3/4 -M28 - Davis at rt for 2 (Gillen)
4/2 -M30 - Willner punted to Hardy on the I29, ret'd 4 (41 yd punt)

8:08 ILLINOIS
1/10-I33 - Carter took pitchback at le for -2 (Seabron)
2/12-I31 - Weiss passed to Strader for 9 (Simpkins)
3/3 -I40 - Weiss passed to Strader for 10 (Simpkins)
1/10- 50 - Weber at rg for 2 (Greer)
2/8 -M48 - Weiss spun off lt for 9 (Harden)
1/10-M39 - Weiss caught by Trgovac for -8.
2/18-M47 - Weiss passed for Sherrod incomplete.
3/18-M47 - Weiss was forced to run and lost 3 (Godfrey)
4/21- 50 - Finzer punted to Jolly on the M 6 and he ret'd 6 (44 yd punt)

3:44 MICHIGAN
1/10-M12 - Huckleby at lt for 3 (Flynn)
2/7 -M15 - Leach passed for Feaster incomplete.
3/7 -M15 - Leach passed for G. Johnson incomplete.
4/7 -M15 - Willner punted to Hardy on the I43 and ret'd 6 (43 yd punt)

2:50 ILLINOIS
1/10-I34 - Strader at lg for 1 (Greer)
2/9 -I35 - Weiss passed for Schooley incomplete.
3/9 -I35 - Weiss passed to Sherrod for 11.
1/10-I46 - Weiss passed for Sherrod and Owens intercepted for M at the M41 and ret'd 2.

1:30 MICHIGAN
1/10-M43 - Davis at rt for 2
2/8 -M45 - Leach elected to run at re for 15 (Flynn)
1/10-I40 - Huckleby at le for no gain (Adams)

END OF THE QUARTER:
MICHIGAN 0 ILLINOIS 0

M had 9 plays for 28 yds. I hand 21 plays for 63 yds.

SECOND QUARTER

MICHIGAN
2/10-I40 - Leach passed to G. Johnson for 15.
1/10-I25 - Huckleby at le for 5 (Scott)
2/5 -I20 - Davis at rg for 2 (Sullivan)
3/3 -I18 - Leach kept at re for 5 (Adams)
1/10-I13 - Huckleby took pitchback and cut inside le for 3 (Sullivan)
2/7 -I10 - Leach passed over Clayton incomplete
3/ 7-I10 - Leach faded and was chased by 4 Illini and he slipped down for -19 (Gillen and others were the pursuers)
4/26-I29 - Dickey held while Willner kicked a 46 yd field goal from the I36.
MICHIGAN 3 ILLINOIS 0 Time: 11:23

Virgil kicked off to Careron the I3 and he ret'd to the I18 where he fumbled and G. Boeke recovered for I and advanced it to the I25.

SEPTEMBER 16, 1978

11:18 ILLINOIS
1/10-I25 - Carter at lt for 3.
2/7 -I28 - Carter at rg for 2.
3/5 -I30 - Carter at le for 4.
4/1 -I34 - Finzer punted to Jolly on the M26 and he ret'd 5 (40 yd punt)

MICHIGAN
1/10-M31 - Huckleby at le for 7.
2/3 -M38 - Huckleby at le for 11.
1/10-M49 - Huckleby at lt for 5.
2/5 -I46 - Leach fumbled and Flynn recovered for I at the I49 (-3 on play)

7:25 ILLINOIS
1/10-I49 - Weiss at le for 2 (Seabron)
2/8 -M49 - Weiss passed for Strader broken up by Braman.
3/8 -M49 - Weiss passed for Strader incomplete.
4/8 -M49 - Finzer punted to Harden, fair catch on M15 (34 yd punt)

6:34 MICHIGAN
1/10-M15 - Davis at rg for 4.
2/6 -M19 - Leach passed to Clayton for 13 (Kelly)
1/10-M32 - Huckleby at rt for 6, BUT M penalized 5 for ill. substitution.
1/15-M27 - Leach was forced to run and went out of bounds for -3.
2/18-M24 - Leach passed to Huckleby for 2.
3/16-M26 - Leach threw a screen to Davis for 14 (Scott)
4/2 -M40 - Willner punted to Hardy on the I26 and he ret'd 2 (34 yd punt) (Needham)

4:26 ILLINOIS
1/10-I28 - Powell at re lost 1 (Meter)
2/22-I27 - Strader at center for 1 (Keitz)
3/10-I28 - Weiss passed for Sherrod incomplete.
4/10-I28 - Finzer punted to Harden on the M28 and he ret'd 21 (44 yd punt) (Rouse)

2:51 MICHIGAN
1/10-M49 - Huckleby at re for 8 (Sullivan)
2/2 -I43 - Leach passed to Mitchell for 13.
1/10-I30 - Huckleby at le for 4 (Ralph)
2/6 -I26 - Leach passed to Huckleby for 18 (Adams)
1/0 -I8 - Leach passed for G. Johnson incomplete out of the endzone.
2/0 -I8 - Leach faded to pass and then rolled around le for 8 and the M TD. Dickey held while Willner converted. 51 yds in 6 plays
MICHIGAN 10 ILLINOIS 0 Time: 0:32

Virgil kicked off to Carter on the I4 and he ret'd 17.

0:27 ILLINOIS
1.10-I21 - Weber at rg for 4

**END OF THE HALF:
MICHIGAN 10 ILLINOIS 0**

M had 22 plays for 112 yds. I had 10 plays for 15 yds.

THIRD QUARTER

M elects to receive. I defends the north goal. Jones kicked off to Huckleby on the M goal and he ret'd 25.
14:54 MICHIGAN
1/10-M25 - Davis at lg for 3 (Gillen)
2/7 -M28 - Leach rolled inside re for 9 (Kelly)
1/10-M37 - Leach dropped by Gillen for -3.
2/13-M34 - Leach rolled around re for 11 (Sullivan)
3/2 -M45 - Smith at rt for 1.
4/1 -M46 - Willner punted into the I endzone (54 yd punt.)

11:28 ILLINOIS
1.10-I20 - Powell at rg for 3 (Seabron)
2/7 -I23 - Weiss at lt for 3 (Owens)
3/4 -I26 - Weiss passed to Sherrod for 6 (Meter)
1/10-I32 - Strader at center for 1 (Simpkins)
2/9 -I33 - Powell caught behind re by Bell for -4.
3/13-I29 - Weiss passed to Strader for 9 (Meter and Simpkins)
4/4 -I38 - Finzer's punt went out of bounds on the M26, 36 yd punt.

8:00 MICHIGAN
1/10-M26 - Smith at rt for 4 (Durrell)
2/6 -M30 - Davis at lg for 5 (Adams)
3/1 -M35 - Smith took pitchout at re for 5 (Tucker)
1/10-M40 - Leach at lt for no gain (Durrell)
2/10-M40 - Smith took pitchout at re for 4 (Venegoni)
3/6 -M44 - Leach passed for Fester incomplete.
4/6 -M44 - Willner punted to Hardy on the I18, fair catch, 38 yd punt.

5:04 ILLINOIS
1/10-I18 - Weiss rolled at le for 15.
1/10-I33 - Powell at lt for 2.
2/8 -I35 - Weiss lost 3 behind le (Godrey)
3/11-I32 - McCullough at lt for no gain (Keitz)
4/11-I32 - Finzer punted out of bounds on the M21, 47 yd punt.

151

2:42 MICHIGAN
1/10-M21 - Leach rolled around le, broke 2 tackles and went for 45 yds before he was caught by Levitt.
1/10-I34 - Smith at rt for 7.
2/3 -I27 - Davis at lg for 5 (Durrell)
1/10-I22 - Smith at lt for no gain (Thiede)
2/10-I22 - Leach rolled inside le for 13 (Adams)
1/G -I9 - Leach picked his way inside le for 6 (Adams)

**END OF THE QUARTER:
MICHIGAN 10 ILLINOIS 0**

M had 17 plays for 115 yds. I had 10 plays for 32 yds.

FOURTH QUARTER

2/G -I3 - Davis at center for no gain (Durrell)
3/G -I3 - Smith took pitchback around re for 3 and the M TD. Time 14:11
Dickey held while Willner converted.
MICHIGAN 17 ILLINOIS 0 79 yds in 8 plays

Virgil kicked off out of the side of the endzone.
14:11 ILLINOIS
1/10-I20 - Powell took pitchout at re for 5 (DeSantis)
2/5 /I25 - Powell took pitchout at le for 8 (Simpkins)
1/10-I33 - McCullough kept off rt for 4 (Seabron)
2/6 -I37 - Powell took pitchback at re for 8 (Meter)
1/10-I45 - Weber at rg for 2 (Keitz)
2/8 -I47 - McCullough passed to Schooley for 16 (Harden)
1/10-M37 - Weber at center for 2 (Keitz)
2/8 -M35 - Weber at lt for 5 (Seabron)
3/3 -M30 - McCullough stopped by Keitz for -1.
4/4 -M31 - Rouse on an end around reverse was hit by Meter and many others for -4.

10:12 MICHIGAN
1/10-M35 - Smith at lt for 4 (Flynn)
2/6 -M39 - Leach passed for Clayton incomplete.
3/6 -M39 - Leach passed for Mitchell incomplete.
4/6 -M39 - M penalized 5 for delay.
4/11-M34 - Willner punted to Hardy on the I31, 35 yd punt, fair catch.

9:23 ILLINOIS
1/10-I31 - McCullough pitched out badly and Humphries rec'd for M at I30.

9:12 MICHIGAN
1/10-I30 - Leach kept at re for 10 (Gillen)
1/10-I20 - Clayton at lt for 4
2/6 -I16 - Leach pitched out to Smith at re for 12.
1/G -I4 - Smith at rg for 3 (Gillen)
2/G -I1 - Smith at rt for -1 (Tucker)
3/G -I2 - Leach rolled left around le for the M TD. Time: 6:35
Dickey held while Willner converted.
MICHIGAN 24 ILLINOIS 0 30 yds in 6 plays

Virgil kicked off out of the endzone.
6:35 ILLINOIS
1/10-I20 - Dismuke at rt for 3 (Humphries)
2/7 -I23 - Dismuke took pitchout at re for 2 (Owens)
3/4 -I26 - Dismuke caught behind le for -5 (Seabron)
4/9 -I21 - Finzer punted to Jolly, fair catch at M46, 33 yd punt.

4:39 MICHIGAN
1/10-M46 - Reid at rg for 3 (Gillen)
2/7 -M49 - Smith at rt for no gain (Gillen)
3/7 -M49 - Dickey rolled inside re and cut to the sideline for 35 (Venegoni)
1/10-I16 - Smith over center for 7 (Durrell)
2/3 -I9 - Dickey at rt for 2.
3/1 -I7 - Reid at lg for 2 (Flynn)
1/G -I5 - Dickey off rt for 4.
2/G -I1 - Clayton at lt for no gain.
3/G -1 - Dickey rolled around le for the M TD. Time: 0:39 rem.
Dickey held while Willner converted.
MICHIGAN 31 ILLINOIS 0
54 yds in 9 plays

Virgil kicked off to Powell in the I endzone and he ret'd 18 (Bell)

0:34 ILLINOIS
1/10-I38 - Strader at rg for 2.
2/8 -I20 - McCullough's pass to Schooley dropped incomplete.

**END OF THE GAME:
MICHIGAN 31 ILLINOIS 0**

M had 20 plays for 91 yds. I had 16 plays for 47 yds.

SEPTEMBER 16, 1978

**MICHIGAN STATE
VS.
PURDUE**
Ross-Ade Stadium
Temp.: 87
Wind: NNW 4-6
Skies: Partly Cloudly
FIRST QUARTER

Michigan State wins toss and will receive.
Purdue will kick and defend south Goal.
Sovereen kickoff out of end zone, 60 yd kick,
no return
MICHIGAN STATE
1/10-M20 - McGee RG, 2 yds (Loushin & Motts)
2/8 -M22 - S. Smith at LE, 2 yds (Marks)
3/6 -M24 - Reeves RT, 4 yds (Motts & Marks)
4/2 -M28 - Stachowicz punt to Purdue end
zone 72 yd kick, no return

13:05 PURDUE
1/10-P20 - Macon LG, 2 yds (Land & Bass)
2/8 -P22 - Williams at LE, loses 3 yds
(Marshall & Land)
Michigan personal foul 15 yd penalty,
Purdue first down on penalty
1/10-P34 - Macon LG on draw, 3 yds (Savage &
Hay)
2/7 -P37 - Herrmann to Young intercepted
Savage on P38 returned to P17, 21 yd
return (Herrmann)

11:39 MICHIGAN STATE
1/10-P17 - S. Smith LG, 2 yds (Clark & Marks)
2/8 -P15 - Reeves RG, 1 yd (Marks)
3/7 -P14 - Williams on draw up middle, 10 yds
(Kay)
1/G -P4 - S. Smith LG, no gain (Loushin)
2/G -P4 - Smith to Gibson, 4 yds, touchdown,
5 plays, 17 yds.
Andersen PAT kick good
SCORE: MICHIGAN STATE 7 PURDUE 0

Schario kickoff to Speedy on P12 yd line return
to P25, 48 yd kick, 13 yd return (Griffin)
9:00 PURDUE
1/10-P25 - Williams LG, cut right, 1 yd.
(Graves & Otis)
2/9 P26 - Herrmann to Williams over line, 11
yds (Graves)
1/10-P37 - Macon RG, 4 yds (Hughes)
2/6 -P41 - Williams RG, 3 yds (Otis)
3/3 -P44 - Herrmann to Harris, incomplete
4/3 -P44 - Eagin punt to M15, dead, 41 yd kick
no return

6:31 MICHIGAN STATE
1/10-M15 - Smith roll left, no gain (Motts)
2/10-M15 - S. Smith at LE, fumbles out of
bounds, lost 1 recovered by Clark
3/11-M14 - Reeves RE, 10 yds (W. Smith)
4/1 -M24 - Stachowicz punt to Pope on P30,
46 yd kick no return

5:09 PURDUE
1/10-P30 - Hermann to Smith, 45 yds
1/10-M25 - Macon RG, 3 yds (Fields & Bass)
2/7 -M22 - Herrmann to Smith, incomplete
3/7 -M22 - Herrmann to pass, loses 9 yds
(Savage)
4/16-M31 - Purdue time out 3:51
4/16-M31 - Sovereen attempt 48 yd field goal
Burrell hold, short

3:46 MICHIGAN STATE
1/10-M31 - Middleton RE on reverse 9 yds
(W. Smith)
2/1 -M40 - Reeves RT, 3 yds (Motts)
1/10-M43 - Smith to S. Smith, incomplete
(Harris)
2/10-M43 - Reeves RT, no gain (Loushin &
Johanson)
3/10-M43 - McGee on pitchout left, 2 yds
(W. Smith &-Turner)
4/8 -M46 - Stachowicz punt to P1 yd line, dead
no return

1:11 PURDUE
1/10-P1 - McCall LG, 3 yds, fumbles recovered
by Marshall (Michigan)

1:05 MICHIGAN STATE
1/G -P4 - McGee pitch right, 1 yd (Clark)
2/G -P3 - Smith roll right, 3 yds, touchdown,
2 plays, 4 yds.
Andersen PAT good
SCORE: MICHIGAN STATE 14 PURDUE 0

Schario kickoff to R. Moss on goal line return to
P23, 60 yd kick 23 yd return (Robinson)
0:27 PURDUE
1/10-P23 - Williams pitch left, loses 2 yds
(Graves)
**END OF FIRST QUARTER
MICHIGAN STATE 14 PURDUE 0**

153

SECOND QUARTER

PURDUE
2/12-P21 - Herrmann to pass, loses 11 yds (Land)
3/23-P10 - Macon on draw, 8 yds (Otis)
4/15-P18 - Eagin punt to M16 to Anderson, return to M23, 66 yd kick 7 yd return. Michigan clipping while ball in air 15 yd penalty (Josten-Kay)
1/10-P33 - Macon inside RE, 9 yds (Graves)
2/1 -P42 - Macon LG, 5 yds (Land & Otis)
1/10-P47 - Herrmann to Smith, incomplete
2/10-P47 - Herrmann to Pope, hit as released intercepted by Savage on M33

12:22 MICHIGAN STATE
1/10-M33 - Vaughn to Davis, incomplete
2/10-M33 - S. Smith RT, 3 yds (Motts)
3/7 -M36 - Michigan delay of game, 5 yd penalty
3/12-M31 - Vaughn to McGee, 5 yds (Clark)
4/7 -M36 - Stachowicz punt to Gallivan on P18 return to P29, 46 yd kick 11 yd return (Schramm)

10:48 PURDUE
1/10-P29 - Macon LE, 5 yds (Griffin)
2/5 -P34 - Pope RG, 3 yds (Bass & Otis)
3/2 -P37 - Macon RT, no gain
4/2 -P37 - Eagin punt to Anderson fair catch on M17, 46 yd kick, no return

9:25 MICHIGAN STATE
1/10-M17 - Michigan illegal procedure 5 yd penalty
1/15-M12 - McGee LT, 7 yds (W. Smith & Supan)
2/8 -M19 - Reeves pitch right, 7 yds (Clark & Johanson)
3/1 -M26 - Vaughn keeper at RG, 3 yds (Motts & Clark)
1/10-M29 - McGee RG, 2 yds (Loushin & Jackson)
2/8 -M31 - Vaughn to Brammer, incomplete
3/8 -M31 - Vaughn to Schramm, on screen, 4 yds (Clark)
3/4 -M35 - Stachowicz punt to Purdue end zone, 65 yd kick no return

6:23 PURDUE
1/10-P20 - Pope pitch right, 16 yds (Haynes)
1/10-P36 - Herrmann to Young, 8 yds (Graves & Otis)
2/2 -P44 - Herrmann to Pope, over the line, 8 yds (Fields & Savage)
1/10-M48 - Herrmann to Young, incomplete
2/10-M48 - Herrmann to Eubank, incomplete
3/10-M48 - Hermann to pass loses 9 yds (Savage)
4/19-P43 - Eagin punt to Anderson on M15, return to M18, 42 yd kick, 3 yd return (Adamle & Josten)

4:14 MICHIGAN STATE
1/10-M18 - Michigan illegal procedure, 5 yd penalty
1/15-M13 - Michigan illegal procedure, 5 yd penalty
1/20-M 8 - Vaughn keep right, 2 yds (Loushin)
2/18-M10 - McGee RE, no gain (Supan)
3/18-M10 - S. Smith up middle, 19 yds (Moss)
1/10-M29 - Michigan illegal procedure 5 yd penalty
1/15-M24 - McGee RG, 2 yds (Loushin)
2/13-M26 - S. Smith RT, 23 yds (Supan)
1/10-M49 - Reeves RT, 1 yd (Supan)
2/9 - 50 - Vaughn to McGee, incomplete
3/9 - 50 - S. Smith at RE, 1 yd (Marks)
Purdue time out 0:17
4/8 -P49 - Stachowicz punt to Purdue end zone 49 yd kick, no return

0:10 PURDUE
1/10-P20 - Macon LT, 11 yds (Land)
1/10-P31 - Purdue time out 0:02
1/10-P31 - Herrmann to Pope, incomplete
HALF TIME SCORE
MICHIGAN STATE 14 PURDUE 0

SEPTEMBER 16, 1978

THIRD QUARTER

Purdue will receive, Michigan will kickoff and defend south goal
Schario kickoff out of bounds on P22. 5 yd penalty and will kickoff from M35 yd line
Schario kickoff to Rick Moss on P2 yd line return to M22, 63 yd kick 76 yd return. Michigan face mask penalty assessed from M35

PURDUE
1/10-M20 - Williams pitch right, 3 yds (Land & Bass)
2/7 -M17 - Herrmann to Pope, dropped
3/7 -M17 - Williams pitch left, 6 yds (Haynes & Bass)
4/1 -M11 - Williams pitch left, 1 yd. (Bass)
1/G -M10 - Herrmann to Williams, Michigan defensive holding, 5 yd penalty
2/G -M5 - Macon up middle, 3 yds (Bass & Fields)
3/G M1 - Herrmann to Young, 1 yd touchdown
6 plays, 20 yds
PAT Sovereen kick, Burrell hold good
SCORE: MICHIGAN STATE 14 PURDUE 7

Sovereen kickoff to Reeves in end zone, 60 yd kick no return

12:02 MICHIGAN STATE
1/10-M20 - McGee at RE, loses 2 yds (Jackson)
2/12-M18 - Vaughn to Byrd, 20 yds (W. Harris)
1/10-M38 - S. Smith RT, 5 yds (Clark & Seneca)
2/5 -M43 - McGee LT, 4 yds (Jackson & Supan)
3/1 -M47 - Reeves RG, loses 1 yd (Jackson)
4/2 -M46 - Michigan State time out 9:15
4/2 -M46 - Stachowicz punt to Gallivan on P8, return to P13, 46 yd kick 5 yd return (Decker & Schramm)

9:05 PURDUE
1/10-P13 - Williams RT, 4 yds (Bass-Fields)
2/6-P17 - Pope RT, 5 yds (Bass & Graves)
3/1 -P22 - Pope pitch right, 2 yds
1/10-P24 - Herrmann to Smith, 14 yds
1/10-P38 - Williams LT, no gain (Land)
2/10-P38 - Herrmann to Smith, incomplete
3/10-P38 - Pope pitch left reverse field right cut cut left, 62 yds for touchdown, 7 plays, 87 yds
PAT Sovereen kick Burrell hold good
SCORE: MICHIGAN STATE 14 PURDUE 14

Sovereen kickoff to Reeves in end zone return to M15, 60 yd kick 15 yd return. Michigan clip, penalty 7 yds. (Kingsbury)

6:28 MICHIGAN STATE
1/10-M8 - Vaughn to Brammer incomplete
2/10-M8 - S. Smith RE, loses 1 yd
3/11-M7 - Vaughn to Middleton on draw, no gain (Motts)
4/11-M7 - Stachowicz punt to P48 out of bounds, 45 yd kick no return

4:59 PURDUE
1/10-P48 - Oliver at QB, Macon LT 2 yds (Savage)
2/8 - 50 - Oliver option right, 4 yds (Otis)
3/4 -M46 - McCall RT, no gain (Land & Haynes)
4/4 -M46 - Michigan time out 3:23
4/4 -M46 - Eagin punt to S. Smith M18 return to M19, 28 yd kick 1 yd return

3:15 MICHIGAN STATE
1/10-M19 - Vaughn to Gibson, 14 yds
1/10-M33 - Vaughn to Gibson, incomplete
2/10-M33 - Vaughn to Byrd, 22 yds (Supan & Motts)
1/10-M45 - McGee RT loses 5 yds, fumbles K. Turner recovers, FC Clark

2:27 PURDUE
1/10- 50 - Williams pitch right, no gain (Land)
2/10- 50 - Herrmann to Williams, incomplete
3/10- 50 - Herrmann to Pope, loses 2 yds. (Anderson)
4/12-P48 - Eagin punt to M9 yd line, dead, 43 yd kick, no return

1:01 MICHIGAN STATE
1/10-M9 - Vaughn to Brammer, 15 yds (W. Smith)
1/10-M24 - Middleton RG, 1 yd (Jackson)
2/9 -M25 - Vaughn to Byrd, incomplete (Harris
3/9 -M25 - Vaughn to Brammer, 13 yds

END OF THIRD QUARTER
PURDUE 14 MICHIGAN STATE 14

FOURTH QUARTER

MICHIGAN STATE
1/10-M38 - Middleton RT, 2 yds (Floyd)
2/8 -M40 - Vaughn to Byrd, 16 yds
1/10-P44 - Vaughn to Byrd, 16 yds
1/10-P28 - Vaughn to Gibson, incomplete
2/10-P28 - Vaughn to pass, loses 4 yds (Motts & Turner)
3/14-P32 - Vaughn to pass, Michigan offensive pass interference, 15 yd penalty, loss of down
4/29-P47 - Stachowicz punt to Purdue end zone, 47 yd kick no return

13:06 PURDUE
1/10-P20 - Macon inside RE, 6 yds (Hay & Land)
2/4 -P26 - Pope LT, 10 yds (Graves & Anderson)
1/10-P36 - Macon RG, 2 yds (Hay & Bass)
2/8 -P38 - Pope pitch out right, 4 yds (Fields & Bass)
3/4 -P42 - R. Smith on reverse, loses 11 yds (Haynes)
4/15-P31 - Eagin punt to Anderson on M26 return to M37, 43 yd kick, 11 yd return

155

10:18 MICHIGAN STATE
1/10-M37 - Vaughn to Brammer, 8 yds (Marks)
2/2 -M45 - Reeves RT, 1 yd (Marks & Clark)
3/1 -M46 - Vaughn keeper middle, 2 yds (Marks)
1/10-M48 - Vaughn to McGee, 13 yds (Josten)
1/10-P39 - Vaughn to Brammer, 15 yds. (Harris)
1/10-P24 - Reeves at LE, fumbles, recovers, no gain
2/10-P24 - Vaughn to Shafer, incomplete
3/10-P24 - Vaughn to Gibson, incomplete
4/10-P24 - Andersen attempt 41 yd field goal Anderson hold wide right

7:14 PURDUE
1/10-P24 - Herrmann to Harris, incomplete
2/10-P24 - Herrmann to Burrell, incomplete
3/10-P24 - Herrmann to Harris, incomplete
4/10-P24 - Eagin punt to S. Smith on M25, return to M28, 51 yd kick, 3 yd return (Kingsbury & Josten)

6:47 MICHIGAN STATE
1/10-M28 - Vaughn to pass, loses 8 yds (Loushin & Turner)
2/18-M20 - Vaughn to pass, loses 11 yds (Turner)
3/29-M 9 - McGee on draw 6 yds (Clark & Johanson)
4/23-M15 - Stachowicz punt out of bound on P44 yd line, 41 yd kick no return

4:43 PURDUE
1/10-P44 - Macon RT, 5 yds (Bass & Land)
2/5 -P49 - Macon on RT, 1 yd (Land & Fields)
3/4 - 50 - Herrmann to Smith, incomplete (Stanton)
4/4 - 50 - Michigan illegal procedure 5 yd penalty
1/10-M45 - Herrmann to Harris, incomplete (Marshall)
1/10-M33 - Macon LG, 33 yds, touchdown, 6 plays, 56 yds
PAT Sovereen kick, Burrell hold good
SCORE: PURDUE 21 MICHIGAN STATE 14

Sovereen kickoff to Reeves on M5 yd line return to M28 yd line 55 yd kick, 23 yd return fumbled (W. Smith recovers)

3:07 PURDUE
1/10-M28 - Williams pitch right, 1 yd. (Otis & Bass)
2/9 -M27 - Macon LG, 7 yds (Hay & Land)
3/2 -M20 - Williams pitch left, 5 yds (Marshall & Anderson)
1/10-M15 - Macon LG, 2 yds (Hay & Hughes)
2/8 -M13 - Williams pitch right, cut left, 3 yds (Fields)
3/5 -M10 - Michigan time out 0:37
3/5 -M10 - Williams LT, loses 1 yd (Bass & Otis)

FINAL SCORE
PURDUE 21 MICHIGAN STATE 14

National Collegiate Athletic Association
FINAL TEAM STATISTICS

	MSU	PURDUE
First Downs	15	19
Rushing	6	10
Passing	9	4
Penalty	0	5
Rushing Attempts	44	49
Yards Rushing	142	253
Yards Lost Rushing	36	39
Net Yards Rushing	106	214
Net Yards Passing	166	85
Passes Attempted	23	23
Passes Completed	13	7
Had Intercepted	0	2
Total Offensive Plays	67	72
Total Net Yards	272	299
Average Gain Per Play	4.1	4.2
Fumbles: Number—Lost	4/2	1/1
Penalties: Number—Lost	13/107	0/0
Interceptions: Number—Yards	2/18	0/0
Number of Punts—Yards	10/511	7/294
Average Per Punt	51.1	42.0
Punt Returns: Number—Yards	4/18	3/16
Kickoff Returns: Number—Yards	2/38	3/99

SEPTEMBER 16, 1978

TOLEDO
VS.
MINNESOTA
Memorial Stadium, Minneapolis
Temp: 65
Wind: SE 11 mph

FIRST QUARTER

Minnesota wins toss—to receive west goal
Ridgway kickoff to Noel on MN5 18 yd return (Ridgway)
14:53 MINNESOTA
1/10-MN23 - Kitzmann at left tackle 10 yards (Sutter)
1/10-MN33 - Kitzmann straight ahead 4 yd gain (Williams, Kennedy)
2/6 -MN37 Barber quick pitch left 17 yd gain (Long)
1/10-UT46 - Barber quick delay right no gain (Penza, Williams)
2/10-UT46 - Barber quick pitch left 8 yd gain (Kenerly)
3/2 -UT38 - Kitzmann at left tackle 5 yd gain (Williams)
1/10-UT33 - Barber quick pitch right, breaks into secondary 12 yard gain (Kenerly)
1/10-UT21 - Barber quick pitch cuts back left tackle 7 yd (Williams)
2/3 -UT14 - Kitzmann straight ahead 9 yards (Laraway)
1/G -UT5 - Kitzmann straight ahead no gain (Penza)
2/G -UT5 - Barber sweeps right, Kennedy tackle for 1 yd loss
3/G -UT4 - Avery Keeper left, Kennedy hit for 5 yd loss
4/G -UT9 - Rogind field goal good from 27 yards 5:47 elapsed 9:13 to go 57 yards in 12 plays goal on 13th play
MINNESOTA 3, TOLEDO 0

Rogind kickoff to Bell on goal line returns 18 yards (Hairston)
TOLEDO
1/10-UT18 - McCulley at left tackle 3 yd gain (Murphy)
2/7 -UT21 - Alston at right tackle 2 yard gain (Sytsma, Ronan)
3/5 -UT23 - Hall rolls left to pass, runs 4 yd gain (J. Johnson)
4/1 -UT27 - Wurst punts to Edwards on MN 35 25 yd return (Lanari) 38 yard punt MN clipping 15 yard penalty

7:11 MINNESOTA
1/10-MN41 - Barber quick pitch left, breaks into open 25 yard gain (Conroy)
1/10-UT34 - Kitzmann at left tackle 3 yd gain (Williams, Penza)
2/7 -UT31 - Barber slips down at right side 1 yd gain (Sherman)
3/6 -UT30 - Avery pass complete to Barber 4 yd gain (Sherman)
4/2 -UT26 - Kitzmann dives right tackle 1 yd gain (Williams)

4:56 TOLEDO
1/10-UT25 - Hall keeps option right, Brown tackle for no gain
2/10-UT25 - Toledo in motion 5 yd penalty
2/15-UT20 - McCully up middle, breaks open for 13 yards but fumbles and Murphy recovers for Gophers on UT33

4:04 MINNESOTA
1/10-UT33 - Barber breaks open over left tackle 8 yards (James)
2/2 -UT25 - Kitzmann runs 10 yards (Conroy)
1/10-UT15 - Barber left end no gain (Conroy)
2/10-UT15 - Dilulo left side for 5 yards (James)
3/5 -UT10 - Barber at left tackle 3 yd gain (Jefferson, Long)
4/2 -UT7 - Artis straight ahead 3 yd gain (Cross)
1/G -UT4 - Kitzmann left side no gain (Williams, Penza)
2/G -UT4 - Avery option keeper left 1 yd loss (Conroy, Long)
3/G -UT5 - Artis sweep right 2 yd gain (Cross, Kenerly)

**END OF FIRST QUARTER:
MINNESOTA 3, TOLEDO 0**

SECOND QUARTER

15:00 MINNESOTA
4/G -UT3 - Barber quick pitch right, dives into end one 33 yard drive in 10 plays elapsed time is :04, 14:56 to go 3 yd Rogind kick good
MINNESOTA 10, TOLEDO 0
Rogind's 32nd straight PAT kick is **MINNESOTA RECORD**

157

Rogind kickoff to Alston on UT1 returns 16 yds (Carr)
14:51 TOLEDO
1/10-UT17 - Alston hit behind line by Murphy and fumbles Blanshan recovers for Gophers 5 yd rushing loss

14:45 MINNESOTA
1/10-UT12 - Artis quick left 3 yd gain (Gotwals)
2/7 -UT9 - Artis straight ahead fumbles when hit by Sherman, Tobin recovers for Gophers 2 yd gain
3/5 -UT7 - Breault sweep left no gain (Gotwald)
4/5 -UT7 - Avery slant in to Bailey, Kenerly interference 6 yd penalty Minnesota first down on UT1
1/G -UT1 - Artis dives straight ahead 1 yd TD run 12 yards in 4 plays 2:00 elapsed 13:56 to go Rogind kick good
MINNESOTA 17, TOLEDO 0

Rogind kickoff to Alston on UT7 return 12 yards (Peppe)
12:50 TOLEDO
1/10-UT19 - Alexander at left tackle no gain (Johnson)
2/10-UT19 - Kasper straight ahead 3 yd gain (Ronan)
3/7 -UT22 - Hall pass at left sidelines, incomplete batted down
4/7 -UT22 - Wurst punt blocked by Jack Johnson who also recovers ball on UT6

11:31 MINNESOTA
1/G -UT6 - Artis straight ahead 1 yd gain (Williams, Kennedy)
2/G -UT5 - Artis quick pitch right, cuts back for 5 yard TD 4:13 elapsed, 10:57 left 6 yard drive in 2 plays Rogind kick good
MINNESOTA 24, TOLEDO 0

Rogind kickoff to Alston in end zone who downs it
10:57 TOLEDO
1/10-UT20 - Alexander at right tackle no gain (Johnson, Burns)
2/10-UT20 - Hall back to pass, Carr hits arm, causes fumble, Carr recovers for 5 yd loss
3/15-UT15 - Alexander sweeps left no gain (Burns)
4/15-UT15 - Wurst punt off side of foot, short, blown dead on UT44 29 yard punt

8:53 MINNESOTA
1/10-UT44 - Avery pass at right sides, intercepted by Long on UT 33, tackle by Artis after 11 yd return

8:45 TOLEDO
1/10-UT44 - Alexander at left tackle 5 yd gain (Blanshan)
2/5 -UT49 - Hall pass complete to Mitchell at left sidelines 8 yd gain (Foxworth)
1/10-MN43 - Kasper straight ahead 2 yd gain (Johnson)
2/8 -MN41 - Toledo illegal procedures 5 yd penalty
2/13-MN46 - Hall pass knocked down in line by Blanshan incomplete
3/13-MN46 - Hall back to pass, forced 20 yards deep and passes incomplete
4/13-MN46 - Wurst punt to Baily to MN8, returns right and steps out of bounds at MN18 38 yard punt

7:02 MINNESOTA
1/10-MN18 - Artis slant outside left tackle 4 yd gain (Cross, Penza)
2/6 -MN22 - Avery back to pass, runs right, passes incomplete intended for Bourquin MN ineligible receiver downfield 11 yd penalty
3/17-MN11 - Artis quick pitch right 12 yard gain (Sutter)
4/5 -MN23 - Smith punt bounces out of bounds at midfield 27 yard punt

5:36 TOLEDO
1/10- 50 - Alexander option pitch right 7 yd gain (Murphy)
2/3 -MN43 - Alexander at right tackle 3 yard gain (Johnson)
1/10-MN39 - Kasper at left tackle 2 yd gain (Johnson, Ronan)
2/8 -MN37 - Hall back to pass, forced out of pocket to right, steps out of bounds for 12 yard loss
3/20-MN49 - Alexander breaks open at left tackle 5 yd gain (Burns)
4/15-MN44 - Wurst punt bounces into end zone for touchback 44 yard punt

3:40 MINNESOTA
1/10-MN20 - White up middle, fumbles when hit and Conroy recovers for UT on MN19

3:36 TOLEDO
1/10-MN19 - Alexander at right end 1 yd gain (Friberg, Johnson)
2/9 -MN18 - Kasper at left tackle 3 yd gain (Burns)
3/6 MN15 - Kasper straight ahead 2 yd gain (Ronan, Friberg)
4/4 -MN13 - Hall pass knocked down at goalline by Foxworth

SEPTEMBER 16, 1978

1:40 MINNESOTA
1/10-MN13 - White up middle 4 yd gain (Cecutti)
2/6 -MN17 - Avery pass to Bourquin up middle 22 yd gain
1/10-MN39 - Avery pass complete to Bailey at UT49 12 yd gain :53 seconds left
1/10-UT49 - Avery back to pass, MN Thompson holding 25 yd penalty
1/35-MN27 - Avery pass over middle short and incomplete
2/35-MN27 - Artis at right tackle 3 yd gain (Jefferson)
3/32-MN30 - Avery back to pass, forced out of pocket and throws short and incomplete
4/32-MN30 - Smith punt to Alexander on UT 25, tackled by Peppe no return 45 yard punt

:17 TOLEDO
1/10-UT25 - Kasper straight ahead 5 yard gain (Johnson)

**END OF FIRST HALF:
MINNESOTA 24, TOLEDO 0**

THIRD QUARTER

Rogind kickoff to Bell who downs ball in end zone
15:00 TOLEDO
1/10-UT20 - Kasper at left tackle 1 yd gain (Ronan, Burns)
2/9 -UT21 - Hall option keeper right 3 yd loss (Murphy, Blanshan)
3/12-UT18 - Hall pass up right sidelines complete to Hunyadi 33 yd pass (Edwards)
1/10-MN49 - Kasper at right tackle 1 yd gain (Johnson, Friberg)
2/9 -MN48 - Hall option keeper right 2 yd gain (Sytsma)
3/7 -MN46 - Wurst punt/fake short snap to Fericks runs 8 yds
1/10-MN38 - Hall option keeper right 7 yd gain (Edwards)
3/3 -MN31 - Kasper at left tackle 1 yd gain
3/2 -MN30 - Alexander quick delay right, Brown hit for 1 yd loss
4/3 -MN31 - Hall pass option left, breaks two tackles 5 yd gain (Johnson)
1/10-MN26 - Hall rolls right to pass, rushed and passes incomplete
2/10-MN26 - Alexander quick delay right, hit by Eriberg for no gain
3/10-MN26 - Hall scrambles to right, stops and throws back across the field complete to Hunyadi for 26 yard TD Ridgway kick off to left no good 80 yards in 13 plays 4:59 elapsed 10:01 left
MINNESOTA 24, TOLEDO 6

Ridgway kickoff to Edwards on 9, runs right and cuts back to middle returns 36 yards (Laraway)
9:52 MINNESOTA
1/10-MN45 - Barber at right tackle no gain (Conroy)
2/10-MN45 - Avery back to pass, runs up middle 1 yd loss (Kennedy)
3/11-MN44 - Avery pass over middle intended for Bourquin, Long defending
4/11-MN44 - Smith punt to Alexander hit in tracks by Pepper no return 34 yd punt

8:34 TOLEDO
1/10-UT22 - Alexander option pitch right 7 yd gain (Systsma, Edwards)
2/3 -UT29 - Kasper up middle, Friberg hit for no gain
3/3 -UT29 - Bell scissors left 4 yd gain (Snyder)
1/10-UT33 - Hall pass long intended for Mitchell knocked down by Edwards
2/10-UT33 - Toledo illegal procedure 5 yd penalty
2/15-UT28 - Bell deep reverse right 7 yd gain (Brown)
3/8 -UT35 - Alexander at right tackle, bounces to outside 5 yd gain (Ronan, Snyder)
4/3 -UT40 - Wurst punt to Edwards returns 5 yds (Mitchell) 47 yd punt

5:11 MINNESOTA
1/10-MN18 - Barber quick pitch right 6 yd gain (Sherman)
2/4 -MN24 - Thompson at left tackle 2 yd gain (Williams)
3/2 -MN26 - Barber at left end 3 yd gain (Conroy)
1/10-MN29 - Thompson up middle 1 yd gain (team tackle)
2/9 -MN30 - Avery pass intended for Thompson flutters incomplete
3/9 -MN30 - Avery pass complete to Bourquin but holding on Gophers 17 yd penalty
3/26-MN13 - Avery pass complete to Bourquin 28 yd gain (Conroy)
1/10-MN41 - Barber quick delay up middle 1 yd gain (Williams)
2/9 -MN42 - Avery to Thompson over middle 13 yd pass (Williams)
1/10-UT45 - Brault at right end 4 yd loss by Long
2/14-UT49 - Avery pass complete to Bourquin 9 yd gain (Williams, Kennedy)
3/5 -UT40 - Barber quick pitch right/sweep outlegs defenders down right sidelines for 40 yd TD run :33 remaining, 14:27 elasped 82 yards in 11 plays
Rogind kick good
MINNESOTA 31, TOLEDO 6

Rogind kickoff floats out of bounds 5 yd illegal procedure penalty. 2nd kickoff to Alston on 11 returns 24 yards (Cooper)

159

:27 **TOLEDO**
1/10-UT35 - Hall option keeper left 1 yd loss (Pepper)

**END OF THIRD QUARTER:
MINNESOTA 31, TOLEDO 3**

FOURTH QUARTER

15:00 **TOLEDO**
2/11-UT34 - Hall complete to Hunyadi up right sidelines 14 yd gain steps OOB
1/10-UT48 - Alexander slides outside left end 8 yd run (Faunhorst)
2/2 -MN49 - McCulley up middle 11 yards (Wein zerl)
1/10-MN33 - Hall pass to Hunyadi dropped/incomplete
2/10-MN33 - Hall flare/swing pass left complete to Alexander 8 yd gain (Johnson)
3/2 -MN25 - Alexander at right tackle no gain (Snyder)
4/2 -MN25 - Hall flare left to Alexander, breaks open down sidelines for 21 yards (Burns)
1/10-MN4 - Alexander at right tackle no gain (team tackle)
2/G -MN4 - Hall sprints right, passes for 4 yd TD to McCulley 65 yard drive in 10 plays 3:40 elasped, 11:20 left Hall pack to pass for 2 point play, Sytsma tackle **MINNESOTA 31, TOLEDO 12**

Ridgway kickoff to Dilulo on 8, returns 20 yards (Delwiche)
11:12 **MINNESOTA**
1/10-MN29 - Artis quick pitch left 3 yd loss (Laraway)
2/13-MN26 - Artis at left tackle 3 yd gain (Conroy)
3/10-MN29 - Carlson delay pass complete over middle to White 10 yd gain (Long)
1/10-MN40 - White quickopener up middle MN illegal procedure 5 yd penalty
1/15-MN35 - Artis sweeps right end 6 yd gain (Sutter)
2/9 -MN41 - Artis sweeps left end 7 yd gain (Penza)
3/2 -MN48 - White quick opener over left tackle 8 yd gain (Sutter)
1/10-UT44 - Carlson pass complete to Breault right sidelines 12 yds (Kenerly)
1/10-UT32 - Artis at left tackle 4 yd gain (Cecutti)
2/6 -UT28 - Carlson pass complete over middle to Sonnenfeld 17 yds (Kennedy)
1/10-UT11 - Carlson option keeper right no gain (Laraway)
2/10-UT11 - Carlson complete over middle to Artis 6 yds (Cecutti)
3/4 -UT5 - White up middle but MN illegal procedure 5 yd penalty
3/9 -UT10 - Carlson pass intended for Bailey, Long knocks it away
4/9 -UT10 - Carlson back to pass, rushed and tackled by Grayson & Laraway 7 yd loss

5:09 TOLEDO
1/10-UT17 - McCulley breaks open over left tackle 20 yd gain (Prairie)
1/10-UT37 - Hall flare pass left to Alston off hands and incomplete
2/10-UT37 - Hall pass intercepted by MN Meyer on UT47 returns 4 yds to UT43

4:32 MINNESOTA
1/10-UT43 - Lewis quick pitch left no gain (Laraway)
2/10-UT43 - MN illegal procedure 5 yd penalty
2/15-UT48 - Tonn pass intercepted by UT Laraway on UT40, returns 3 yds

3:51 TOLEDO
1/10-UT43 - Fericks dive left 6 yd gain (Fahnhorst)
2/4 -UT49 - Hall sprints left to pass, rush up middle 5 yd gain (Meyer)
1/10-MN46 - Fericks at right tackle 4 yds (Meyer)
2/6 -MN42 - Gandee pass complete to Alston 4 yd gain (Noel)
3/2 -MN38 - Gandee pass complete to Michell at left sidelines 11 yd pass
1/10-MN27 - Gandee pass off hands of UT Walsh, intercepted MN14 by Hairston

2:04 MINNESOTA
1/10-MN14 - White up middle 6 yd gain (Brownlee)
3/4 -MN20 - Tonn pass complete to Cooper at left sidelines 18 yd gain
1/10-MN38 - Tonn pass complete to White, breaks two tackles, runs out of bounds after 26 yd gain
1/10-UT36 - Tonn pass/fly to Cooper for 36 yd TD pass up left sidelines 14:17 elapsed, :43 left 86 yd drive in 4 plays Rogind kick good
MINNESOTA 38, TOLEDO 12

Rogind kickoff to Alston on 2, returns 20 yds (Burdette)

:36 TOLEDO
1/10-UT22 - Gandee fumbles handoff but recovers for 1 yd gain
2/9 -UT23 - Gandee keeps left and runs for 14 yds before tackle by Burdette

**END OF GAME:
MINNESOTA 38, TOLEDO 12**

National Collegiate Athletic Association
FINAL TEAM STATISTICS
September 16, 1978

	TOLEDO	MINNE-SOTA
First Downs	12	22
Rushing	7	11
Passing	5	10
Penalty	0	1
Rushing Attempts	49	56
Yards Rushing	178	245
Yards Lost Rushing	27	18
Net Yards Rushing	151	227
Net Yards Passing	129	216
Passes Attempted	18	22
Passes Completed	9	14
Total Offensive Plays	67	78
Total Net Yards	280	443
Average Gain Per Play	4.2	5.7
Fumbles: Number—Lost	5/3	2/1
Penalties: Number—Lost	5/3	2/1
Interceptions: Number—Yards	2/4	2/14
Number of Punts—Yards	6/200	3/106
Average Per Punt	33.3	35.3
Punt Returns: Number—Yards	1/0	4/52
Kickoff Returns: Number—Yards	5/90	3/84

**PENN STATE
VS.
OHIO STATE**
Ohio Stadium
Columbus, Ohio
Temp: 80°
Wind: SW 10 mph
Skies: Overcast
FIRST QUARTER

Ohio State won the toss and elected to receive; Penn State to defend the south goal
Bahr kicked off at 1:58 P.M. thru the end zone for the touchback
15:00 OHIO
1/10-020 - Schlichter passed on short out right to Donley for 6
2/4 -026 - Springs option pitch at le, fumble recovered by Gerald for -1
3/5 -025 - Schlichter passed to Gerald on slant over middle for 13
1/10-038 - Campbell into lg for 4
2/6 -042 - Springs pitch thru rt for (measurement) 6
1/10-048 - Springs pitch at le for (measurement) 11
1/10-P41 - Campbell into rg for 2
2/8 -P39 - Schlichter passed on swing right to Springs; deflected Ragucci incomplete
3/8 -P39 - Schlichter passed deep right for Donley; P. Harris intercepted, return 33

11:45 PENN
1/10-046 - Guman lt 7
2/3 -039 - Penn Illegal procedure -5
2/8 -044 - Fusina passed short right in for Fitzkee incomplete
3/8 -044 - Fusina passed over middle on delay to Guman, cut right for 27
1/10-017 - Guman at rt for 4
2/6 -013 - Fusina passed too long for Guman in deep left flat incomplete
3/6 -013 - Fusina rolled left, passed too high for Donovan at the flag incomplete
4/6 -013 - Bahr's FG was from 30 yards at 9:52 - 33 yards, 7 plays,
SCORE: PENN STATE 3, OHIO STATE 0

Bahr kicked off 55; Hicks returned 19
9:47 OHIO
1/10-024 - Springs rt 1
2/9 -025 - Campbell draw lg 8
3/1 -033 - Volley at rt for (measurement) 1
1/10-034 - Ohio illegal procedure -5
1/15-029 - Schlichter rolled left passed to Campbell for 7
2/8 -036 - Schlichter kept inside re for 1
3/7 -037 - Schlichter faked, passed to Springs on safety right, cut in for 6
4/1 -043 - Orosz punted out of bounds right 35

6:30 PENN
1/10-P22 - Suhey cut outside re for 4
2/6 -P26 - Guman into lt for 4
3/2 -P30 - Suhey over rt for 3
1/10-P33 - Fusina faked, passed to Scovill cutting over middle for 9
2/1 -P42 - Fusina passed on screen left to Guman; stopped by Dansler for -2
3/3 -P40 - Fusina passed behind Donovan deep right incomplete
4/3 -P40 - Fitzkee punted 45; Guess returned 2

3:48 OHIO
1/10-017 - Springs option pitch at re for 2
2/8 -019 - Springs pitch at le for 13
1/10-032 - Campbell at center for 2
2/8 -034 - Schlichter faked passed to Gerald deep right; fumble recovered by Donaldson

2:20 PENN
1/10-P22 - Guman lt for 3
2/7 -P25 - Suhey turned le for 9
1/10-P34 - Suhey at middle 3
2/7 -P37 - Suhey counter lt for 4
3/3 -P41 - Fusina passed too high for Scovill right incomplete
4/3 -P41 - Fitzkee punted 44; Guess returned 2

0:21 OHIO
1/10-017 - Schlichter passed to Gerald left; Nehl deflected incomplete
2/10-017 - Springs draw middle for 1

**END OF FIRST QUARTER:
PENN STATE 3, OHIO STATE 0**

SECOND QUARTER

OHIO
3/9 -018 - Springs into rt for 4
4/5 -022 - Orosz punted 72 downed by Ohio

14:15 PENN
1/10-P6 - Moore counter le for no gain
2/10-P6 - Fusina rolled right passed behind Bassett incomplete
3/10-P6 - Torrey thru rg 5
4/5 -P11 - Fitzkee punted 44; faircatch Guess

12:56 OHIO
1/10-045 - Springs pitch left; downed by Kubin for -3
2/13-042 - Schlichter faked, passed to Springs on delay over middle for 14
1/10-P44 - Springs pitch at re for 3
2/7 -P41 - Springs pitch into le for 10
1/10-P31 - Volley rt no gain
2/10-P31 - Schlichter faked, faded; tackle and fumble recovery by Kubin -10

162

SEPTEMBER 16, 1978

10:51 PENN
1/10-P41 - Fusina passed to Torrey on delay over middle for 13
1/10-O46 - Fusina passed too low for Fitzkee right incomplete
2/10-O46 - Torrey draw rg for 4
3/6 -O42 - Fusina rolled left, chased, tackled by Cousineau -5
4/11-O47 - Fitzkee punted 39 out of bounds left

9:15 OHIO
1/10-O8 - Campbell center 5 (Gerald at QB)
2/5 -O13 - Campbell lt 2
3/3 -O15 - Springs option pitch le for 9
1/10-O24 - Springs pitch into re for 1
2/9 -O25 - Gerald faked, kept into lt for 4
3/5 -O29 - Gerald faked, stopped by Clark for -5
4/10-O24 - Orosz punted out of bounds left 39

6:15 PENN
1/10-P37 - Moore off rt for 5
2/5 -P42 - Torrey into rg for 3
3/2 -P45 - Fusina rolled left, chased, sacked by Sullivan, Ross -14
4/16-P31 - Fitzkee punted 39; Guess returned right for 6

4:23 OHIO
1/10-O36 - Schlichter passed to Donley over middle after deflection by Gilsenan 14
1/10- 50 - Schlichter passed deep right for Hunter, too long incomplete
2/10- 50 - Schlichter passed on delay to Campbell; deflected by Nehl incomplete
3/10- 50 - Schlichter passed deep left to Gerald for 21
1/10-P29 - Schlichter passed on delay over middle; intercepted Petruccio return 4

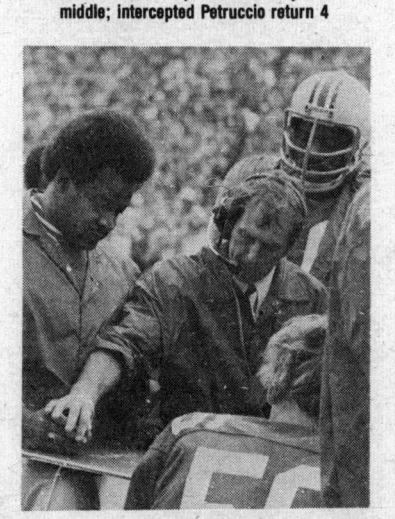

3:49 PENN
1/10-P36 - Fusina passed in right flat to Guman for 9
2/1 -P45 - Guman at rt for 6
1/10-O49 - Fusina passed over middle to Fitzkee 9
2/1 -O40 - Torrey middle 5
1/10-O35 - Fusina passed deep right for Donovan out of bounds incomplete
2/10-O35 - Fusina rolled right, chased out of bounds by Dulin -10
3/20-O45 - Guman lt for 2
4/18-O43 - Fitzkee punted out of bounds right 32

1:08 OHIO
1/10-O11 - Campbell at lg for 3 Time out Penn State at 1:02
2/7 -O14 - Campbell rg 1 Time out Penn State at 0:56 (injury Robinson - wheeled off)
3/6 -O15 - Springs pitch at le for 2 Penn State time out at 0:51
4/4 -O17 - Orosz punted 52; Guman FC; Penn offside 5
1/10-O22 - Gerald kept right for -2
2/12-O20 - Springs pitch at le for 2

END OF SECOND QUARTER:
PENN STATE 3, OHIO STATE 0

THIRD QUARTER

Penn State elected to receive; Ohio State to defend the south goal
Orosz kicked off at 3:33 P.M. six yards deep for the touchback

15:00 PENN
1/10-P20 - Suhey middle for 2
2/8 -P22 - Fusina faked, passed to Fitzkee right for 16
1/10-P38 - Guman rt 2
2/8 -P40 - Guman pitch at re for no gain - Dansler
3/8 -P40 - Fusina faded, chased left, sacked by Dulin -10 (Fusina hurt - ran off)
4/18-P30 - Fitzkee punted left; Guess' fumble recovered by Drazenovich
1/10-O34 - Suhey rt 3
2/7 -O31 - Fusina faded, sacked by Bell Cato -11
3/18-O42 - Fusina faded, looked, passed left; intercepted by Washington; return 27

11:50 OHIO
1/10-P42 - Campbell middle 2
2/8 -P40 - Springs into lt for 1
3/7 -P39 - Schlichter passed deep right for Gerald; deflected Gilsenan incomplete
4/7 -P39 - Orosz punted for the touchback Ohio illegal procedure - declined

163

10:40 PENN
1/10-P20 - Suhey at rt 4
2/6 -P24 - Suhey thru lt for 4 more
3/2 -P28 - Suhey cut outside le 4
1/10-P32 - Guman counter at lt for 8
2/2 -P40 - Suhey middle for 4
1/10-P44 - Guman into lt 4
2/6 -P48 - Suhey at center for 7
1/10-045 - Suhey lg for 6
2/4 -039 - Guman counter at le for no gain
3/4 -039 - Fusina passed to Bassett cutting over middle 17
1/10-022 - Suhey pushed thru lg, broke tackle for 11
1/10-011 - Guman cut over middle for 8
2/2 -03 - Suhey cut outside re for the TD Bahr PAT 80 yards in 13 plays
SCORE: PENN STATE 10, OHIO STATE 0

Bahr kicked off 60; Hicks returned 12
4:50 OHIO
1/10-012 - Campbell at rt for 3 (Gerald at QB)
2/7 -015 - Springs middle 5
3/2 -020 - Volley thru lg for 7
1/10-027 - Campbell spun at lg for 5
2/5 -032 - Springs option pitch right for -6 - Donaldson
3/11-026 - Schlichter faded, chased right, sacked -6 - Lally
4/17-020 - Orosz punted 44; Guman returned left 15

2:05 PENN
1/10-049 - Torrey over le for 5
2/5 -044 - Torrey rg 2
3/3 -042 - Fusina spun, passed down left sideline to Guman for 23
1/10-019 - Moore over rt for 2
2/8 -017 - Suhey cut into le for 1

**END OF THIRD QUARTER:
PENN STATE 10, OHIO STATE 0**

FOURTH QUARTER

PENN
3/7 -016 - Fusina pass to Fitzkee over middle was wide incomplete
4/7 -016 - Bahr's FG try was wide right at 14:53 for the touchback

14:53 OHIO
1/10-020 - Schlichter faded, ducked out, rolled left, passed to Springs for 15
1/10-035 - Schlichter faked, passed deep right for Donley; too long incomplete
2/10-035 - Schlichter was hit as he passed short right for Gerald; intercepted by Nehl returned center for 14; Ohio personal foul 15

14:31 PENN
1/10-020 - Penn illegal procedure -5
1/15-025 - Moore into rt on delay for 2
2/13-023 - Penn illegal procedure -5
2/18-028 - Fusina passed deep right for Fitzkee/too long incomplete
3/18-028 - Suhey draw right for 4
4/14-024 - Bahr's FG was from 41 yards - minus 4 yards, 4 plays,
SCORE: PENN STATE 13, OHIO STATE 0

Bahr kicked off 62 yards; Hicks returned 12
13:07 OHIO
1/10-012 - Springs draw lg for 1
2/9 -013 - Schlichter was hit as he passed short right for Campbell incomplete
3/9 -013 - Schlichter passed to Donley over middle for 22
1/10-035 - Schlichter rolled left, passed to Gerald for 11
1/10-046 - Springs option pitch right for -4 - Kubin
2/14-042 - Schlichter passed right for Gerald; intercepted by Lally; returned 14

11:14 PENN
1/10-044 - Guman at rt for 2
2/8 -042 - Suhey at rg for 2
3/6 -040 - Fusina faked, passed in right flat to Seevill for 13
1/10-027 - Guman delay into re for 2 (Ellis hurt - ran off)
2/8 -025 - Suhey fell at middle for no gain
3/8 -025 - Fusina passed to Bassett on right sideline for 14
1/10-011 - Suhey into rt for 3
2/7 -08 - Suhey turned le, caught by Bell for -2
3/9 -010 - Suhey centered the ball at rg for 1
4/8 -09 - Bahr's FG was from 25 yards - 10 plays, 35 yards
SCORE: PENN STATE 16, OHIO STATE 0

Bahr kicked off 54 yards; Hicks returned 14
6:40 OHIO
1/10-020 - Schlichter passed short over middle for Hicks incomplete
2/10-020 - Ohio illegal procedure -5
2/15-015 - Schlichter passed deep over middle for Gerald wide incomplete; Penn interference 28
1/10-043 - Schlichter passed deep left for Hicks; broken up by Gilsenan incomplete Ohio State holding -15
1/25-028 - Schlichter passed deep right for Hicks; too long incomplete
2/25-028 - Schlichter passed to Hunter short right for 7
3/18-035 - Schlichter passed over middle for Donley; intercepted P. Harris returned 33

164

SEPTEMBER 16, 1978

5:33 PENN
1/10-035 - Moore at re for 5
2/5 -030 - Torrey middle 4
3/1 -026 - Suhey cut outside re for 6
1/10-020 - Suhey at lg for 2
2/8 -018 - Moore countered at re for 5
3/3 -013 - Moore was stopped at re by Dansler for no gain
4/3 -013 - Bahr's FG was from 30 yards - 22 yards in 7 plays
SCORE: PENN STATE 19, OHIO STATE 0

Bahr kicked off six yards deep for the touchback

2:53 OHIO
1/10-020 - Castignola passed to Payton over middle for 6
2/4 -026 - Castignola passed to Murray over middle for 11
1/10-037 - Murray thru rt, broke tackle for 5
2/5 -042 - Castignola faked, passed to Barwig short right for (measurement) 5
1/10-047 - Castignola passed deep right for Gerald, too long incomplete
2/10-047 - Castignola passed low and behind Payton over middle incomplete
3/10-047 - Castignola passed over middle for Donley, broke tackle, for 49, stopped by Wise for the TD save
1/4 -P4 - Castignola kept left for -1
2/5 -P5 - Johnson fumbled out of bounds right after taking option pitch right from Gerald for no gain
3/5 -P5 - Castignola rolled left, passed too long for Murray incomplete
4/5 -P5 - Castignola passed too high for Moore right incomplete

0:21 PENN
1/10-P5 - Coles at re for -2 - Bell

**FINAL SCORE:
PENN STATE 19, OHIO STATE 0**

165

RICHMOND
VS.
WISCONSIN
Camp Randall Stadium
Temp: 68
Wind: SE 5-10 mph
Skies: Cloudy
FIRST QUARTER

RICHMOND wins the toss and will DEFEND the South Goal. WISCONSIN will receive.
Roach kicks off for Richmond to open the game, to the 15, Souza returns to 22 yards to the 37.

14:51 WISCONSIN
1/10-W37 - Matthews runs right, gets 4 to W41 (Cheshire)
2/6 -W41 - Josten runs right, gets 3 to 44 (Cheshire)
3/3 -W44 - Josten passes to Charles, incomplete
4/3 -W44 - Kiltz, punts 44 yards to R 12
Wisconsin is penalized 5 yards for illegal procedure
4/8 -W39 - Kiltz punts 44 yards to R 17, Nixon runs 4 yards to R 21 (Snell)

13:24 RICHMOND
1/10-R21 - Kornegay runs right tackle, gets 2 to 23 (Christenson)
2/8 -R23 - Kornegay runs right guard, gets 4 to 27 (Christenson)
3/4 -R27 - Williams runs right, gets 5 to 32 (Ahrens) (Christenson)
1/10-R32 - Kornegay runs up middle, gets 2 to 34 (Ahrens)
2/8 -R34 - Short passes to Beckstead, gets 11 to 45 (Christenson)
1/10-R45 - McCoig runs right tackle, gets 6 to W49 (Sawicki)
2/4 -W49 - Kornegay runs right guard, gets 4 to 45 (Ahrens)
1/10-W45 - Short runs wide right, gets 4 to 41 (Relich)
2/6 -W41 - Williams runs up middle, gets 8 to 33 (Schremp)
1/10-W33 - McCoig runs left guard gets 3 to 30 (Schremp)
2/7 -W30 - Short passes to Frick, incomplete
3/7 -W30 - Short passes to Beckstead, intercepted by Holm at 15, return 13 to W28 (Frick)

8:28 WISCONSIN
1/10-W28 - Stauss runs up middle, gets 4 to 32 (Nixon)
2/6 -W32 - Josten runs wide right, gets 2 to 34 (Kelly)
3/4 -W34 - Matthews runs reverse right, gets 3 to 37 (Braun)
4/1 -W37 - Kiltz punts 45 yards to R18, Nixon returns 73 yards to W9 (Stauss)

6:41 RICHMOND
1/G -W9 - Richmond is penalized 5 yards for illegal procedure
1/G -W14 - Evans runs wide right, gets 5 to 9 (Crossen)
2/G -W9 - Short runs right guard, gets 2 to 7 (Christenson)
3/G -W7 - Short sacked for 2 to 9 (Ahrens)
4/G -W9 - Adams kicks field goal for 25 yards. 3 plays, no yards
RICHMOND 3, WISCONSIN 0

Roach kicks off for Richmond after field goal to W14, Johnson returns 9 yards to W23 (Starr)
Wisconsin is penalized 11 yards for clipping to W12

4:43 WISCONSIN
1/10-W12 - Matthews runs wide right, gets 3 to 15 (Gallihugh)
2/7 -W15 - Matthews runs up middle, gets 6 to 21 (Starr)
3/1 -W21 - Matthews runs left tackle, gets 2 to 23 (Klaren)
1/10-W23 - Josten runs wide left, gets -1 to 22 (Gillian)
2/11-W22 - Souza runs reverse, loses 5 to 17 (Nixon)
3/16-W17 - Stauss runs left tackle, gets 4 to 21 (Coppola)
4/12-W21 - Kiltz punts 46 yards to R33, Nixon returns 9 to R42 (Johnson)

:46 RICHMOND
1/10-R42 - Williams runs right tackle, gets 1 to 43 (Schremp)
2/9 -R43 - Short runs up middle, gets 3 to 46 (Relich)

END OF THE FIRST QUARTER:
RICHMOND 3, WISCONSIN 0

SECOND QUARTER

15:00 RICHMOND
3/6 -R46 - Evans runs left end, gets 3 to 49 (Schieble)
4/3 -R49 - Philp punts 34 yards to W17, Stauss fair catch

14:17 WISCONSIN
1/10-W17 - Josten passes wide left to Charles, incomplete
2/10-W17 - Josten runs right tackle, gets no gain (Gilliam)
3/10-W17 - Josten backed to pass, sacked for loss of 5 to 12 (Coppola)
4/15-W12 - Kiltz punts 36 yards to W48, Nixon fair catch

SEPTEMBER 16, 1978

12:42 RICHMOND
1/10-W48 - Kornegay runs up middle, gets 1 to 47 (Schremp)
2/9 -W47 - Redden runs wide left, gets 6 to 41 (Erdmann)
3/3 -W41 - McGoig runs up middle, gets 6 to 35 (Christenson)
1/10-W35 - Short passes up middle to Beckstead gets 25 to 10 (Holm)
1/G -W10 - Short back to pass, sacked loses 3 to 13 (Holm)
2/G -W13 - Short passes to William in end zone, incomplete
3/G -W13 - Short passes up middle to Frick in end zone, broken up (by Johnson)
4/G -W13 - Adams kicks a field goal of 29 yards
RICHMOND 6, WISCONSIN 0

Roach kicks off for Richmond out of bounds and is penalized 5 yards for illegal procedure.

Roach kicks off from R35 into W end zone for touchback.

10:22 WISCONSIN
1/10-W20 - Josten passes over middle to Charles, gets 80 yards for touchdown. Veith kicks the extra point.
WISCONSIN 7 RICHMOND 6

Brhely kicks off for Wisconsin to goal line, Williams fumbles returns to 20. Wisconsin is penalized 5 yards, off sides

Brhely kicks off for Wisconsin from W35 to R2, Williams returns 26 to R28 (Burt)

10:13 RICHMOND
1/10-R28 - Evans runs up middle, no gain to 28 (Cabral) Wisconsin is penalized 15 yards for face mask
1/10-R43 - Evans runs wide right, gets 3 to 46 (Relich)
2/7 -R46 - McGoig runs up middle gets 3 to 49 (Cadral)
3/4 -R49 - Short passes up the middle to Spriggs, gets 5 to W46 (Erdhann)
1/10-W46 - Redeen runs left tackle, gets 3 to 43 (Crossen)
2/7 -W43 - Short runs wide left, gets no gain to 43 (Crossen)
3/7 -W43 - Gregory passes to Arval, overthrown
4/7 -W43 - Philp punts 29 yards to 14, ball goes out of bounds

6:59 WISCONSIN
1/10-W14 - Souza runs right tackle, gets 2 to 16 (Turner)
2/8 -W16 - Stauss runs right tackle, gets 8 to 24 (Gallihugh)
1/10-W24 - Stauss runs up middle, gets 2 to 26 (Loughran)

2/8 -W26 - Josten hit in backfield, losses 3 to 23 (Coppola)
3/11-W23 - Josten passes left to Krepple, underthrown
4/11-W23 - Kiltz punts 42 yards to R35, Nixon returns 16 yards to W49 (Casey)

4:20 RICHMOND
1/10-W49 - Korngay runs up middle, gets 1 to 48 (Ahrens)
2/9 -W48 - Gregory passes up middle to Spriggs incomplete
3/9 -W48 - McGoig draw up middle, gets no gain to 48 (Cabral)
4/9 -W48 - Philip punts 37 yards to W11, downed by Greaser

2:59 WISCONSIN
1/10-W11 - Matthews runs wide right, gets 5 to 16 (Gilliam)
2/5 -W16 - Matthews runs up middle, gets 6 to 22 (Cheshire)
1/10-W22 - Wisconsin calls timeout 2:19 Josten runs left, gets no gain to 22 (Chase)
2/10-W22 - Matthews runs right end, gets 2 to 24 (Coppola)
3/6 -W24 - Stauss runs up the middle, gets 2 to 26 (Chase)
4/6 W26 - Kiltz punts 17 yards to W43, downed by Rothbauer

:12 RICHMOND
1/10-W43 - Gregory passes right to Frick, incomplete
2/10-W43 - Gregory passes deep to W10, incomplete
3/10-W43 - Gregory passes screen right to Williams, gets 10 to 33 (Johnson), Richmond is penalized 15 yards for clipping, Wisconsin declines.

**END OF HALF:
WISCONSIN 7 RICHMOND 6**

THIRD QUARTER

Roach kicks off to open the start of the second half to W5, Souza returns 15 yards to W20 (Shelton)
14:25 WISCONSIN
1/10-W20 - Matthews runs left tackle to get 5 to 25 (Braun)
2/5 -W25 - Wisconsin is penalized 5 yards for illegal procedure
2/10-W20 - Josten runs right end, gets 1 to 21 (Braun)
3/9 -W21 - Josten runs left end to pass, gets 1 yard to 22 (Gilliam)
4/8 -W22 - Kiltz punts 53 yards to R25, Nixon returns 18 yards to 43 (Casey)

12:37 RICHMOND
1/10-R43 - Kornegay runs up midde, gets no gain (Crossen)
2/10-R43 - Kornegay runs up middle, gets 11 to W46 (Erdmann)
1/10-W46 - Kornegay runs right tackle, gets 2 to 44 (Schremp)
2/8 -W44 - Redden runs right tackle, gets 2 to 42 (Blaskowski)
3/6 -W42 - McCoig runs up middle, gets 3 to 39 (Crossen)
4/3 -W39 - Philp punts 39 yards to W end zone, touchback

10:18 WISCONSIN
1/10-W20 - Matthews runs right end gets, no gain to 20 (Chase)
2/10-W20 - Josten passes to Souza, intercepted by Turner, returns 25 yards to W39 (Moore)

9:20 RICHMOND
1/10-W39 - Kornegay runs up middle, gets 2 to 37 (Cabral)
2/8 -W37 - Redden runs left end, gets 7 to 30 (Johnson)
3/1 -W30 - Kornegay runs right tackle, gets 1 to 29 (Relich)
1/10-W29 - Kornegay runs up middle, gets 3 to 26 (Relich)
2/7 -W26 - Short keeps runs left end, gets 1 to 25 (Crossen)
3/6 -W25 - Short passes to Frick, incomplete (Schieble)
4/6 -W25 - Adams field goal attempt hits goal post, no good; bounces back into end zone.

6:58 WISCONSIN
1/10-W25 - Green passes to Charles, gets 9 to 34, runs out of bounds
2/1 -W34 - Matthews runs left tackle, retreats, losses 7 to 27 (Cheshire)
3/8 -W27 - Green rolls left, runs up middle, gets 7 to 34 (Starr)
4/1 -W34 - Kiltz punts 35 yards to R31, Nixon returns 27 to W42 (Ahrens)

5:12 RICHMOND
1/10-W42 - Evans runs right tackle, gets 2 to 40 (Relich)
2/8 -W40 - Short passes to Beckstead, overthrown
3/8 -W40 - Short passes to Evans, wide left incomplete
4/8 -W40 - Philp punts 30 yards to W10, Stauss fair catch

4:19 WISCONSIN
1/10-W11 - Stauss runs up middle, gets 3 to 14 (Cheshire)
2/7 -W14 - Stauss runs right tackle, gets 8 to 22 (Starr)

1/10-W22 - Green runs right tackle, gets 3 to 25 (Turner)
2/7 -W25 - Wisconsin calls timeout 2:35 Green passes left to Charles, gets 11 to 36, runs out of bounds
1/10-W36 - Green runs right end, gets 10 to 46
1/10-W46 - Matthews runs right tackle, gets no gain to 46 (Cheshire)
2/10-W46 - Green rolls left, losses 7 to 39 (Chase)
3/17-W39 - Green passes right to Krepfle, gets 5 to 44
4/12-W44 - Kiltz punts 41 yards to R15, Nixon returns 13 to R28 (Martine)

:53 RICHMOND
1/10-R28 - Williams runs right end, gets 5 to 33 (Erdmann)
2/5 -R33 - Short passes up middle to Sprigg, gets 4 to 37 (Sawicki)
3/1 -R37 - McCole runs up middle, gets 4 to 41 (Holm)

**END OF THIRD QUARTER:
WISCONSIN 7 RICHMOND 6**

FOURTH QUARTER

15:00 RICHMOND
1/10-R41 - Short runs up middle, gets -1 to 40 (Sawicki)
2/11-R40 - Short runsleft end, gets 7 to 47 (Christenson)
3/4 -R47 - Short runs left end, gets 1 to 48 (Anderson)
4/3 -R48 - Philp punts 34 yards to W18, Stauss fair catch

13:07 WISCONSIN
1/10-W18 - Matthews runs right end, gets 8 to 26 (Turner)
2/2 -W26 - Matthews runs up middle gets 1 to 27, fumbles, recovered by Starr

168

SEPTEMBER 16, 1978

12:21 RICHMOND
1/10-W27 - Williams runs left tackle, gets 3 to 24 (Christenson)
2/7 -W24 - Short runs left tackle gets 4 to 20 (Sawicki)
3/3 -W20 - Short runs up middle, gets 6 to 14 (Aherns)
1/10-W14 - Kornegay runs up middle gets 1 to 13 (Ahrens)
2/9 -W13 - Evans runs left guard, gets 3 to 10 (Schremp)
3/6 -W10 - Short pitches to Redden, fumbles loses 7 to 17, recovered by Relich

9:56 WISCONSIN
1/10-W17 - Green passes left to Charles, incomplete
2/10-W17 - Matthews runs left guard, loses 2 to 15 (Klaren)
3/12-W15 - Matthews runs right end gets 3 to 18 (Klaren)
4/9 -W18 - Kiltz punts 41 yards to R41, downed by McCoy

8:20 RICHMOND
1/10-R41 - Short passes to Arval, incomplete
2/10-R41 - Redden runs right guard, gets 3 to 44 (Crossen)
3/7 -R44 - Short pitches to Williams right, gets 10 to W46, fumbles out of bounds
1/10-W46 - McCoig runs left tackle; gets 5 to 41 (Christenson)
2/5 -W41 - McCoig runs left tackle; gets 3 to 38 (Crossen)
3/2 -W38 - Kornegay runs up middle, gets 4 to 34 (Crossen)
1/10-W34 - Short pitches right to Williams fumbles and recovers, loses 4 to 38 (Johnson)
2/14-W38 - Short rolls right, gets 13 to 25 (Erdmann)
3/1 -W25 - Richmond calls timeout 5:17 Short runs up middle gets 6 to 19 [Erdmann)
1/10-W19 - McCoig runs left end, gets 3 to 16 (Crossen)
2/7 -W16 - Evans runs up middle, gets no gain to 16 (Relich)
3/7 -W16 - Short sneaks up middle, gets 2 to 14 (Christenson)
  Richmond is penalized 15 yards for holding
3/22-W29 - Richmond calls timeout 3:59 Short passes screen right to Redden gets 9 to 20 (Christenson)
4/13-W20 - Adams field goal attempt is blocked (by Relich) downed on W9

3:33 WISCONSIN
1/10-W9 - Stauss runs up middle, gets 2 to 11 (Braun)
2/8 -W11 - Matthews runs right end, gets 57 to R32 (D. Havnie)
1/10-R32 - Matthews runs right tackle, gets no gain to 32 (Braham)
2/10-R32 - Matthews runs pitch left, loses 9 to 41 (Turner)
3/19-R41 - Wisconsin is penalized 5 yards for delay of game
3/24-R46 - Stauss runs up middle, gets 3 to 43 (Gilliam)
4/21-R43 - Kiltz punts 32 yards to R11, downed by Collins

:41 RICHMOND
1/10-R11 - Short roll left, passes to Arval, incomplete
2/10-R11 - Short passes left to Williams, incomplete
3/10-R11 - Kornegay runs draw up middle, gets 9 to 20 (Sawicki)
4/1 -R20 - Richmond calls timeout :18 Short runs up middle gets 3 to 23 (Levenick)
1/10-R23 - Short passes to Arval, gets to 29, Runs out of bounds
2/4 -R29 - Short passes deep to Williams, intercepted on W35, returns 3 yards to W38 (Williams)

END OF GAME:
WISCONSIN 7 RICHMOND 6

169

INDIANA
VS.
LSU
Tiger Stadium
Temp.: 80°
Wind: SE 3 mph
Skies: Partly Cloudy
FIRST QUARTER

Coin Toss: Indiana wins toss, will receive.
LSU will kick off and defend north goal
Conway kicks off for LSU to Indiana 1.
Hopkins (Kimball, Hensley) returns 19 to I20
14:53 INDIANA
1/10-I20 - Johnson (Minaldi) gets 6 at rt
2/4 -I26 - Johnson at middle (Atiyeh) gets 1
3/3 -I27 - Johnson right side (Frizzell) gets 4
1/10-I31 - Burnett left side (Broha) gets 1
2/9 -I31 - Burnett right side (L. White) gets 2, fumbles—Burrell covered

12:45 LSU
1/10-I34 - Woodley runs left, fumbles after gain of 17 (Adams recovers)

12:35 INDIANA
1/10-I17 - Johnson gets 15 (Frizzell)
1/10-I32 - Johnson at right side for 6 (Atiyeh)
2/4 -I38 - Burnett at middle (Atiyeh, Frizzell) gets 2
3/2 -I40 - Burnett right side (Teal) gets 14
1/10-L46 - Johnson left side (Teal) gets 21
1/10-L25 - Burnett right side (Radecker, Atiyeh) no gain
2/10-L25 - Burnett at middle (Adams, Teal) gets 11
1/10-L14 - Johnson at middle (Fizzell) gets 5
2/5 -L9 - Burnett right side (Quinn, Radecker) gets 3
3/2 -L6 - Burnett swings right side for 6 and TOUCHDOWN 8:25
Drive was 83 yards in 10 plays
Freud PAT
SCORE: INDIANA 7, LSU 0

Straub kicks off for Indiana at LSU 6—Gajan returns (Norman) 21 to LSU 27
8:20 LSU
1/10-L27 - Alexander right side (Hodge) gets 2
2/8 -L29 - Alexander (Norman, McIntosh) left side for 1
3/7 -L30 - Alexander left side (McIntosh, Arbuckle) for 5
4/2 -L35 - Adams punts to Indiana 9, ball rolls dead for 56-yard-punt

6:37 INDIANA
1/10-I9 - Arnett pass deep for Lundy is overthrown (Indiana calls time)

2/10-I9 - Johnson right side for 10, fumbles (Minaldi tackles) Quinn recovers for LSU

6:24 LSU
1/10-I19 - LB Jones left side (Tisdale) gets 6
2/4 -I13 - Alexander left side (Willhite, McIntosh) gains 5
1/G -I8 - Alexander right side (Norman, Arbuckle) gets 6
2/G -I2 - Alexander on dive for 2 and TOUCHDOWN—Time (4:58) Drive was for 19 yards in four plays—Conway PAT
SCORE: LSU, 7 INDIANA 7

Conway kicks off to Indiana 6—Hopkins (DeRutte) returns 26 to Indiana 32
4:53 INDIANA
1/10-I32 - Burnett right side (Atiyeh) loses 1
2/11-I31 - Burnett right side (Radecker, White) gets 1
3/10-I32 - Burnett left side (Minaldi) gets 3
4/7 -I35 - Lovett punts—ball rolls dead at LSU-27—38-yard kick

2:52 LSU
1/10-L27 - Alexander runs right (McIntosh, Arbuckle) for 8
2/2 -L35 - Alexander left side (Hodge, Norman) gets 3
1/10-L38 - Alexander left side (Arbuckle) gets 5
2/5 -L43 - Woodley (Arbuckle) keeps left for 1
3/4 -L44 - Woodley swings left (Hodge) goes down side line for 42 yards
1/10-I14 - LB Jones at left side (Stewart tackles), gets 2, fumbles—DeBord recovers for Indiana

0:32 INDIANA
1/10-I12 - Arnett pass for Friede broken up by C. Williams
2/10-I12 - Hopkins at middle (Radecker, Adams) gets 2

**END OF FIRST QUARTER:
LSU 7, INDIANA 7**

SEPTEMBER 16, 1978

SECOND QUARTER

15:00 INDIANA
3/8 -I14 - Burnett (Broha) left side loses 1
4/9 -I13 - Lovett punts to L48 39-yard kick C. Williams fair caught

14:11 LSU
1/10-L48 - Gajan at right side for 5 (DeBord)
2/5 -I47 - Ensminger pass left side to Murhpree, no play, LSU illegal procedure 5 yds
2/10-L48 - Ensminger pass left for Murphree incomplete
3/10-L48 - Ensminger pass for Quintela almost intercepted by Keneipp
4/10-L48 - Adams punts into Indiana end zone for 52-yard punt

13:15 INDIANA
1/10-I20 - Harkrader left side (Atiyeh, Broha) no gain
2/10-I20 - Harkrader (Atiyeh, Broha) at left side gains 2
3/8 -I22 - Arnett pass deep for Johnson is incomplete
4/8 -I22 - Lovett punts dead to L29-49-yard punt

11:52 LSU
1/10-L29 - LB Jones at right side (Abrams, Swinehart) gets 20
1/10-L49 - Alexander left side on pitch (Smith) loses 3-L15-yd clip (17 officially)
1/30-L29 - Alexander on right on pass from Woodley loses 1 (Smith)
2/31-L28 - LB Jones right side (Norman, McIntosh) gets 12
3/19-L40 - Woodley pass down middle to Quintela (Keneipp) for 19
1/10-I41 - Alexander right side (Hodge) for 8
2/2 -I33 - Alexander right side (Stewart) gets 3
1/10-I30 - Alexander right side (DeBord) gets 5
2/5 -I25 - LSU penalized 5 yards illegal procedure
2/10-L30 - Woodley on keeper at middle (Keneipp) for 13
1/10-I17 - Alexander right side (Keneipp) for 14 Indiana Time (6:58)
1/G -I3 - Alexander left side for 3 and TOUCHDOWN (Time: 6:55)
Drive—71 yards in 11 plays—Conway PAT SCORE: LSU 14, INDIANA 7

Conway kicks off to Indiana 4—Burnett returns (Hill, DeRutte) 24 to Indiana 28
6:48 INDIANA
1/10-I28 - Arnett pass incomplete intended for Fishel
2/10-I28 - Burnett at middle (Adams, Broha) gets 3
3/7 -I31 - Burnett right side (Teal, Burrell) gets 6
4/1 -I37 - Arnett keeps at middle for no gain (Atiyeh)

5:54 LSU
1/10-I37 - Alexander left side minus 3 (Smith)
2/13-I40 - Alexander right side (Iatorola, McIntosh) gets 1
3/12-I39 - Ensminger pass left side to Alexander (Oakley) gets 6
4/6 -I33 - Ensminger pass right to Soileau incomplete, LSU 15-yard offensive interference and loss of down to Indiana 48

4:26 INDIANA
1/10-I48 - Arnett keeps left side (Atiyeh) gets 3
2/7 -L49 - Harkrader left side (Williams, Adams) gets 2
3/5 -L47 - Arnett pass broken up by Minaldi
4/5 -L47 - Lovett punted to LSU-32-yard punt Williams fumbled and Gajan recovered

3:00 LSU
1/10-L15 - Alexander left side for 2 (Willhite)
2/8 -L17 - Woodley (Leeks, Willhite) loses 4
3/12-L13 - LSU penalized 5 yards illegal procedure
3/17-L8 - Alexander (Tisdale) at middle loses 3   Indiana Time Out (1:24)
4/20-L5 - Adams punts from deep in end zone to L36 punt for 31 yards

1:16 INDIANA
1/10-L36 - Burnett gets 6 (DeBord)
2/4 -L30 - Arnett pass intercepted at L27, by Adams, returns all the way—73 yards—for touchdown (Time: 0:43) Conway PAT
SCORE: LSU 21, INDIANA 7

Conway kicks off to Indiana 33 - Wilbur returns 7 and LSU 15 yards personal foul
0:38 INDIANA
1/10-L45 - Arnett pass right side to Friede for 25 (Williams, Quinn)
1/10-L20 - Arnett passes out of bounds to stop clock
2/10-L20 - Arnett passes right side to Burnett for 5 (Cupit, Burrell)
3/5 -L15 - Arnett pass in end zone intended for Fisher, broken up by Williams
4/5 -L15 - Freud field goal from 32 yards-good   drive-45 yards in 5 plays
SCORE: LSU 21, INDIANA 10

Straub kicks off to LSU 15—Hernandez returns 19 to LSU 34 (Norman)
0:05 LSU
1/10-L36 - Alexander runs right for 14, (Wilbur)

**END OF HALF:
LSU 21, INDIANA 10**

THIRD QUARTER

Straub kicks off for Indiana to LSU 5—Gajan (Patton) returns 20 to LSU 25

14:56 LSU
1/10-L25 - Alexander right side (Stewart) no gain
2/10-L25 - Woodley pass to Quintela for 2 (Swinehart) at right side
3/8 -L27 - Woodley pass for Jones intercepted by Abrams for no return at L33

13:45 INDIANA
1/10-L33 - Arnett right side (Quinn) gets 8
2/2 -L25 - Burnett carries for 2, but play called back, Indiana offside 5 yards
2/7 -I30 - Friede on reverse at right side for 9, play called back, Indiana 5 procedure
2/12-L35 - Huck pass for Corso intercepted by Williams at L13 (Powers) and returns 7

12:41 LSU
1/10-L20 - Alexander right side for 3 (Abrams)
2/7 -L23 - Quintela swings left (Abrams) for 6
3/1 -L29 - Alexander at middle (Tisdale) gains 2
1/10-L31 - Alexander left side (Todd) gets 4
2/6 -L35 - Woodley right side (Hodge) gets 11
1/10-L46 - LB Jones at middle (Norman) gets 4
2/6- 50 - Jones at left side (Arbuckle) gets 5
3/1 -I45 - Alexander right side (Arbuckle) gets 4
1/10-I41 - Woodley pass deep for Carson broken up by Swinehart
2/10-I41 - Soileau runs left for (Hodge) 16
1/10-I25 - LSU penalized 5 yards illegal procedure
1/15-I30 - Woodley keeps right side (Iatarola, Norman) gets 4
2/11-I26 - Woodley passes right side to Carson (Swinehart, Abrams) for 14
1/10-I12 - Woodley keeps middle (Norman, Arbuckle) gets 3
2/7 -I9 - Woodley keeps (Leake) loses 3
3/10-I12 - Woodley keeps right side for 1 (Leake)
4/9 -I11 - Convey attempts 27-yard field goal. GOOD
Drive—80 yards in 16 plays
SCORE: LSU 24, INDIANA 10

Convey kicks off for LSU to Indiana in end zone—Burnett returns (DeRutts, Bill) 30 to Indiana 30

5:03 INDIANA
1/10-I30 - Arnett pass to Fishel for 16 (Teal)
1/10-I46 - Burnett (Teal) left side for 8
2/2 -L46 - Burnett at right side (Thibodeaux) gets 3
1/10-L43 - Burnett right side for 4 (Minaldi, Quinn)
2/6 -L39 - Johnson right side (Minaldi) gets 5
3/1 -L34 - Burnett (Atiyeh) at right side held for no gain
4/1 -L34 - Burnett right side for 4 (Burrell)
1/10-L30 - Arnett pass is incomplete right side
2/10-L30 - Arnett pass to Harkrader for 6 (Teal)
3/4 -L24 - Arnett pass left to Stephenson for 10 (Williams)
1/10-L14 - Johnson (Atiyeh) at middle gets 2

**END OF THIRD QUARTER:
LSU 24, INDIANA 10**

FOURTH QUARTER

15:00 INDIANA
2/8 -L12 - Harkrader swings left (Williams) for 5
3/3 -L7 - Arnett keeps at left side (Cupit, Teal) gets 5
1/G -L2 - Burnett at left side no gain (stopped by Quinn, Atiyeh)
2/G -L2 - Burnett right side, fumbles ball into end zone, recovered by Indiana's Powers for TOUCHDOWN Time: 13:47
Burnett gets 2-yard gain on play
C. Williams forced the fumble
Drive—70 yards in 15 plays—
Freud PAT good
SCORE: LSU 24, INDIANA 17

Straub kicks off for Indiana to LSU 12. Gajan returns (Abrams, Straub) 25

13:39 LSU
1/10-L37 - Gajan at middle (Willhite) held for no gain
2/10-L37 - Gajan at left side (Tisdale, Tillery) gets 1
3/9 -L38 - Woodley pass down middle good to Quintela for 17
1/10-I45 - Soileau at middle (Leake) gets 4
2/6 -I41 - Gajan runs right (Ahrens) gets 9, LSU 15 yards clipping
2/12-I47 - Woodley keeps (Stewart, Willhite) gets 2
3/10-I45 - Woodley pass down middle for Quintela broken up by Norman
4/10-I45 - Adams punts into Indiana end zone kick 45 yards

172

SEPTEMBER 16, 1978

10:49 INDIANA
1/10-I20 - Burnett left side (Adams, Cupit) gets 5
2/5 -I25 - Johnson at right side (Atiyeh) gets 2
3/3 -I27 - Burnett at middle (Minaldi) held for no gain
4/3 -I27 - Lovett punts L30—kick for 43 yards—C. Williams fair catch

8:52 LSU
1/10-L30 - Murphree right side (Iatarola) gets 6
2/4 -L36 - Alexander right side (Stewart, Tallen) gets 7
1/10-L43 - Jones left side (Patton) gets 5 LSU Time Out 7:55
2/5 -L48 - Alexander (Hodge) at right side for 15 yards
1/10-I37 - Alexander at middle (Norman) gets 2
2/8 -I35 - Carson on reverse (McIntosh) loses 10
3/18-I45 - Woodley pass down middle to Quintela (Keipe) 29 no play LSU 5 illegal procedure
3/23- 50 - Gajan at middle (Oakley) gets 2
4/21-I48 - Adams punts to Indiana 17 - punt for 31 yards

5:33 INDIANA
1/10-I17 - Burnett runs middle (Teal) for 14
1/10-I31 - Johnson (Broha) at middle gets 2
2/8 -I33 - Burnett left side for 4 (Quinn, Adams)
3/4 -I37 - Arnett pass incomplete to Powers over middle
4/4 -I37 - Lovett punts 40 yards to L23, C. Williams lost 10 yards on return

3:42 LSU
1/10-L13 - Alexander at right tackle for 3 (Swinehart) Indiana time out 3:29
2/7 -L16 - Gajan at left side (Tisdale) gets 2
3/5 -L18 - Woodley left side (Tisdale) gets 3 Indiana time 2:49
4/2 -L21 - Willis punts to Indiana 46 33-yard kick—Fair catch by Wilbur

2:43 INDIANA
1/10-I46 - Arnett passes long 42 yard penalty pass interference by LSU
1/10-L12 - Arnett pitch was blocked by White, minus 22 yards for Arnett
2/32-L34 - Arnett pass intercepted by Frizzell, returns 12 (Burnett)

1:40 LSU
1/10-L34 - Alexander left side (McIntosh) gets 1
2/9 -L35 - Alexander left side (Keneipp, Leake) gets 12
1/10-L47 - LSU call time out
1/10-L47 - Gajan runs middle for 8, fumbles, DeLee gets 9
1/10-I36 - Alexander left side for 6 (31) (Stewart)

END OF GAME:
LSU 24, INDIANA 17

National Collegiate Athletic Association
FINAL TEAM STATISTICS

	INDIANA	LSU
First Downs	12	19
Rushing	9	16
Passing	3	3
Penalty	0	0
Rushing Attempts	48	63
Yards Rushing	208	369
Yards Lost Rushing	24	23
Net Yards Rushing	184	346
Net Yards Passing	62	57
Passes Attempted	17	12
Passes Completed	5	6
Had Intercepted	3	0
Total Offensive Plays	65	75
Total Net Yards	246	403
Average Gain Per Play	3.8	5.4
Fumbles: Number—Lost	3/2	3/2
Penalties: Number—Yards	2/10	10/129
Interceptions: Number—Yards	0/0	3/92
Number of Punts—Yards	6/241	6/248
Average Per Punt	40.2	41.3
Punt Returns: Number—Yards	0/0	2/(-10)
Kickoff Returns: Number—Yards	5/106	4/85

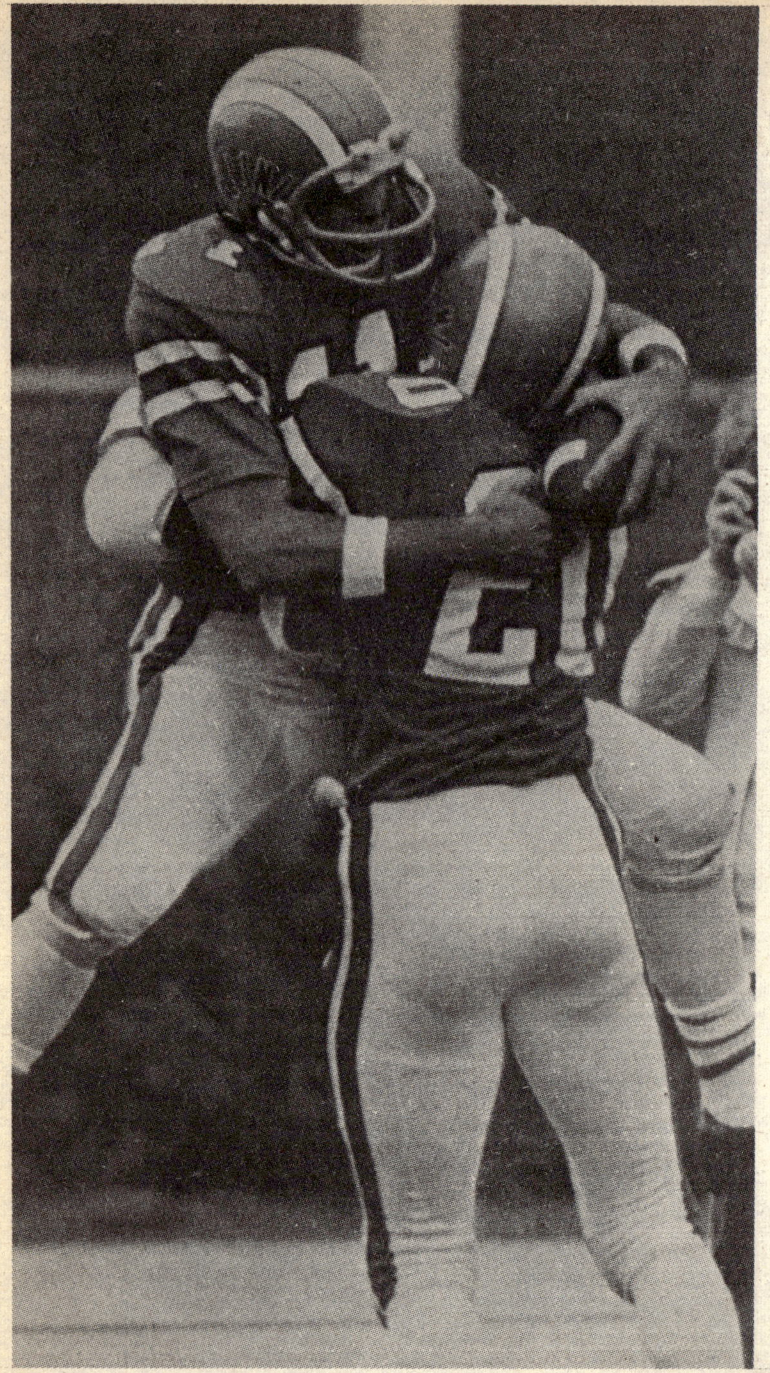

SEPTEMBER 23, 1978

STANFORD
VS.
ILLINOIS
Memorial Stadium
Champaign, IL
Temp.: 68
Wind: NE 7 mph
Skies: Sunny, clear
FIRST QUARTER

Stanford wins toss will receive, Illinois defends north goal
Finzer kicks off south Chapman at goal, returns 2 yards
14:54 STANFORD
1/10-S 2 - Nelson takes pitch around RE for 18
1/10-S20 - Dils flare for Margerum, intercepted by Tucker at S27 no return

14:43 ILLINOIS
1/10-S27 - Strader over LG for 3 (Ceresino, Hall)
2/7 -S24 - McCullough keeps around LE for 1 (Ceresino)
3/6 -S23 - McCullough sacked for loss of 7 (Evans)
4/13-S30 - Finzer 47 yard field goal attempt is good
SCORE: ILLINOIS 3 STANFORD 0

Finzer kicks off south through end zone for touchback
12:46 STANFORD
1/10-S20 - Dils pass over middle complete to Margerum for 6 (J. Gillen, Tucker)
Penalty: Illinois unnecessary roughness
1/10-S41 - Nelson around LT for 16 (Tucker)
1/10-I43 - Nelson takes pitch around LE, dropped for loss of 6 (Ramshaw)
2/16-Penalty: Stanford holding
2/34-S33 - Dils swing pass for Nelson incomplete
3/34-S33 - Dils pass over middle complete to Nelson for 9 (J. Gillen)
4/25-S42 - Kicker punts to Hardy, fair catch at I25 33 yd punt

10:55 ILLINOIS
1/10-I25 - Powell on delay over LG for 2 (Ceresino)
2/8 -I27 - McCullough keeps around LE for 3 (Wilson)
3/5 -I30 - McCullough keeps around LE for 3 (Hall)
4/2 -I33 - Finzer punt to Nelson at S23, return 18, 44 yd punt

9:17 STANFORD
1/10-S41 - Francis cuts over LG for 2 (Ralph)
2/8 -S43 - Dils swing pass for Pleis complete for 8 (Ramshaw)
1/10-I49 - Francis over LG for 9 (Tucker)
2/1 -I40 - Francis over LG for 2 (Ralph)

1/10-I38 - Dils swing pass to Nelson for loss of 1 (Tucker)
2/11-I39 - Penalty: Stanford illegal use of hands
2/30-S42 - Dils swing pass to Nelson complete for 8 (Tucker)
3/22- 50 - Dils flat pass for Pleis complete for 7 (Adams)
4/15-I43 - Fox punts downed at I25, 18 yd punt

5:20 ILLINOIS
1/10-I25 - Strader up middle for 1 (Budinger & Evans)
Penalty: Stanford facemask
1/10-I41 - McCullough pass complete to Rouse for 9 (Pigott)
2/1 - 50 - Strader off LG for 1 (McColl)
1/10-S49 - Powell takes pitch around RE for 6 (Chapman & Evans)
2/4 -S43 - Strader over RG for 2 (Ceresino & Hall)
3/2 -S41 - McCullough dropped for loss of 4 (Pigott)
4/6 -S45 - Time Out Illinois 2:04
Snap goes over Finzer's head, recovered by Rennaker at I26, loss of 29

1:57 STANFORD
1/10-I26 - Francis over LG for 3 (Flynn)
2/7 -I23 - Nelson around LE for 5 (Hardy)
3/2 -I18 - Dils swing pass to Francis for 6 (Hardy)
1/10-I12 - Nelson around LE for 4
2/6 -I8 - Dils swing pass to Francis for 4 (Gillen)
3/2 -I4 - Nelson takes pitch around LE for touchdown, 4 yds
Naber extra point is good
SCORE: STANFORD 7 ILLINOIS 3

Naber kicks off north, downed in end zone
0:15 ILLINOIS
1/10-I20 - Strader over RT for 3 (Norris)

END OF FIRST QUARTER
STANFORD 7 ILLINOIS 3

SECOND QUARTER

15:00 ILLINOIS
2/7-I23 - Strader up middle for 1 (Ceresino & Budinger)
3/6 -I24 - McCullough dropped for loss of 8 (Rennaker)
4/14-I16 - Finzer punt to Nelson at S40, fair catch, 44 yd punt

175

13:49 STANFORD
1/10-S40 - Francis slants over RT for 1 (Adams)
2/9 -S41 - Nelson takes pitch around RE for 13 (Tucker)
1/10-I46 - Dils pass to Banks complete for 24 (Levitt & Kelly)
1/10-I22 - Dils pass over middle to Pleis complete for 7 (Venegoni & Sullivan)
2/3 -I15 - Francis over LG for 1 (Ralph)
3/2 -I14 - Dils pass to Bowe complete for touchdown, 14 yds
Naber extra point good
SCORE: STANFORD 14 ILLINOIS 3

Naber kicks off south to Foster who downs in end zone
10:55 ILLINOIS
1/10-I20 - Powell over LG for loss of 1 (Norris)
2/11-I19 - McCullough sideline pass to Rouse overthrown
3/11-I19 - McCullough pass for Powell incomplete
4/11-I19 - Penalty: Stanford offsides (nullifies punt)
4/6 -I24 - Strader carries out of punt formation for 20 (St. Geme)
1/10-I44 - McCullough sideline pass to Sherrod complete for 9 (Chapman)
2/1 -S47 - Weber over RG for 5 (Hall & Piggott)
1/10-S42 - Powell delays over LG for 1 (Wilson)
2/9 -S41 - Penalty: Illinois illegal procedure
2/14-S46 - McCullough scrambles for 11 (Ceresino)
3/3 -S35 - Penalty: Illinois illegal procedure
3/8 -S40 - Weber picks up fumbled snap, carries for 3 (Budinger & Wilson)
4/5 -S37 - Finzer punt downed by Illinois at S10, 27 yd punt

6:55 STANFORD
1/10-S10 - Dils swing to Nelson complete for 7 (Ralph)
2/3 -S17 - Nelson carries around RE for 1 (Tucker)
3/2 -S18 - Nelson carries around LE for loss of 1 (Tucker)
4/3 -S17 - Fox punt to Hardy, fair catch at I49 34 yd punt

4:56 ILLINOIS
Penalty: Stanford unnecessary roughness
1/10-S36 - Dismuke takes pitch around RE for 1 (Hall)
2/9 -S35 - McCullough fumbles for loss of 5; recovered by Dismuke
3/14-S40 - McCullough pass for Rouse incomplete
4/14-S40 - Finzer punt to Nelson, fair catch at S12, 28 yd punt

3:57 STANFORD
1/10-S12 - Dils flat pass complete to Francis for 13 (Tucker)
1/10-S25 - Nelson takes pitch around RE for 7 (Ramshaw & Kelly)

2/3 -S32 - Nelson carries around LE for 4 (J. Gillen)
1/10-S36 - Dils swing pass for Francis is dropped
2/10-S36 - Dils slant in pass to Tyler complete for 17 (Hardy)
1/10-I47 - Nelson takes pitch around RE for no gain (Adams)
2/10-I47 - Dils sideline pass to Smith complete for 6 (Tucker)
3/4 -I41 - Dils scrambles out of bounds for 3
4/1 -I38 - Time Out Stanford 1:06
Dils bootlegs around LE for 5 (Sullivan)
1/10-I33 - Dils swing pass to Francis complete for 12 (Venegoni)
1/10-I21 - Dils sideline pass complete to Nelson for 13 (Levitt & Sullivan)
1/G -I8 - Francis over LG for touchdown
Naber kick is good
SCORE: STANFORD 21 ILLINOIS 3

Naber kicks off to Foster, downed in end zone
0:47 ILLINOIS
1/10-I20 - McCullough keeps around LE for 14 (Parker)
1/10-I34 - McCullough keeps around RE for 1 (Evans)
2/9 -I35 - McCullough keeps around LE for loss of 2 (Evans) TO Stanford 0:06
3/11-I33 - Weber up middle for 3 (Ceresino)

**HALFTIME
STANFORD 21 ILLINOIS 3**

SEPTEMBER 23, 1978

THIRD QUARTER

Naber kicks off to Dismuke at I8, returns to I25
14:55 ILLINOIS
1/10-I25 - Powell on delay over LG for 1 (Hall)
2/9 -I26 - Strader up middle for 2 (Wilson)
3/7 -I28 - McCullough fumbles for loss of 5 recovered by McColl

13:36 STANFORD
1/10-I23 - Dils sideline pass for Mulroy incomplete
2/10-I23 - Nelson takes pitch around RE for 18 (Tucker)
1/G -I5 - Dils sideline pass complete to Bowe for 3 (Tucker)
2/G -I2 - Francis dives over middle for 1 (Flynn)
3/G -I1 - Francis blasts over RG for touchdown
Naber kick is good
SCORE: STANFORD 28 ILLINOIS 3

Naber kicks off south through end zone
12:39 ILLINOIS
1/10-I20 - Powell takes pitch around RE for 8 (Chapman)
2/2 -I28 - Powell takes pitch for Sherrod incomplete
3/2 -I28 - Weber up middle for no gain (Norris)
4/2 -I28 - Finzer punt to Nelson at S27, returns 7, 45 yd punt

11:19 STANFORD
1/10-S34 - PENALTY: Stanford illegal use of hands
1/27-S17 - Dils scrambles for 1 (J. Gillen)
2/26-S18 - Nelson up middle, fumbles and recovers own for loss of 5
3/31-S13 - Dils on qb draw for no gain (Thiede, Flynn)
4/31-S13 - Fox punt to Hardy at I48, returns 0 (39 yard punt)

9:14 ILLINOIS
1/10-I48 - McCullough sideline pass for Sherrod, broken up by Hall
2/10-I48 - McCullough keeps around re for 7, fumbles recovers own (Hall caused)
3/3 -S45 - Strader up middle for 5 (Norris)
1/10-S40 - McCullough around le for loss of 3 (Hall, McColl)
2/13-S43 - McCullough sideline pass dropped by Schooley
3/13-S43 - McCullough pass down sidelines for Schooley, incomplete
4/13-S43 - Finzer punt to Tyler, fair catch at S18 (25 yard punt)

7:01 STANFORD
1/10-S18 - Francis around re for 7 (Sullivan)
2/3 -S25 - Brown up middle for 4 (Sullivan)
1/10-S29 - Dils swing pass to Nelson complete for 6 (Ralph)

2/4 -S35 - Nelson takes pitch around le for 5 (Tucker)
1/10-S40 - Nelson around re for 16 (Ramshaw)
1/10-I44 - Dils scrambles up middle for 8 (Levitt)
2/2 -I36 - Brown up middle for 9 (Adams)
1/10-I27 - Dils sideline pass complete to Margerum for 8 (Holm)
2/2 -I19 - Brown slants over lt for loss of 1 (Venegoni, J. Gillen)
3/3 -I20 - Dils swing pass complete to Brown for 4 (Adams)
1/10-I16 - Dils completes slant in to Tyler for 14 (Kelly)
1/10-I2 - Dils pass in end zone for Smith incomplete
2/G -I2 - Brown over rt for 1 (Kelly)
TO Stanford 2:32
3/G -I1 - Banks takes pitch around re for no gain (Gillen)
4/G -I1 - Brown over middle, fumbles, recovered in end zone by Levitt (I)

2:22 ILLINOIS
1/10-I20 - McCullough keeps over rg for 2 (Zellmer)
2/8 -I22 - McCullough sideline pass for Rouse incomplete
3/8 -I22 - Dismuke on draw play for 10 (Chapman)
1/10-I32 - Dismuke takes pitch around re for 14 (Parker)
1/10-I46 - McCullough keeps over rt for 2 (Dapper, Williams)
2/8 -I48 - Dismuke takes pitch around re for loss of 2 (Piggott)

END OF THIRD QUARTER
STANFORD 28 ILLINOIS 3

FOURTH QUARTER

15:00 ILLINOIS
3/10-I46 - McCullough pass incomplete for Schooley
4/10-I46 - Finzer punt to Tyler, fair catch at S8 (46 yard punt)

177

14:47 STANFORD
1/10-S8 - Nelson over lg for 1 (J. Gillen, Sullivan)
2/9 -S9 - Nelson takes handoff around re for 1 (Bonner)
3/8 -S10 - Dils sideline pass to Mulroy complete for 16 (Levitt)
1/10-S26 - Nelson takes pitch around re for 4 (Flynn)
2/6 -S30 - Dils sideline pass for Mulroy incomplete, broken up by Levitt
3/6 -S30 - Dils sacked by Thornton for loss of 9
4/15-S21 - PENALTY: Illinois roughing the kicker
4/1 -S35 - PENALTY: Illinois roughing the kicker TO Stanford: 11:18
1/10- 50 - Dils slant incomplete to Margerum for 29 (Tucker, Hardy) Dils out
1/10-I21 - Nelson carries around le for 18 (Adams, Tucker)
1/G -I3 - Brown slants over rg for 2 (J. Gillen, Sullivan)
2/G -I1 - Brown huddles rg for no gain (J. Gillen)
3/G -I1 - Brown over lg for no gain (Sullivan)
4/G -I1 - Schonert roll out pass to Bowe complete for Touchdown
Naber kick is good PENALTY: Illinois offsides assessed on kickoff
SCORE: STANFORD 35, ILLINOIS 3

Naber kicks off north from 45, Foster downs in end zone

8:41 ILLINOIS
1/10-I20 - Powell takes pitch around re for 9 (Zellmer)
2/1 -I29 - Dismuke over rg for 5 (Norris)
1/10-I34 - McCullough pass for Rouse incomplete
2/10-I34 - Dismuke on draw play for 10 (Boxold)
1/10-I44 - McCullough pass to Weber complete for 7 (Boxold)
2/3 -S49 - Dismuke on delay up middle for loss of 3 (Rennaker, Zellmer)
3/6 -I48 - McCullough pass for Schooley on turn incomplete
4/6 -I48 - Finzer punt goes through end zone (52 yard punt)

5:28 STANFORD
1/10-S20 - Schonert bootlegs around re for no gain (Squirek)
2/10-S20 - Mordell over lt, fumbles recovered by Smith (I), gain of 3

4:45 ILLINOIS
1/10-S23 - McCullough dropped for loss of 6 (Werstler)
2/16-S29 - PENALTY: Stanford roughing passer (nullifies Stanford interception)
2/1 -S14 - TO Illinois 3:57 Dismuke up middle for 2 (Bates)

1/10-S12 - McCullough keeps around le for loss of 1 (Norris, Mitre)
2/11-S13 - Dismuke takes pitch around le for touchdown
Finzer kick is good
SCORE: STANFORD 35 ILLINOIS 10

Finzer onside kick recovered by Chapman (S) at S40

2:37 STANFORD
1/10-S40 - Mordell over lg for 4 (Ramshaw)
2/6 -S44 - Mordell over lg for 4 (Ramshaw, Squirek)
3/2 -S48 - Mordell slants over lt for 4 (Ramshaw)
1/10-I48 - Schonert fumbles snap, falls on ball for no gain
2/10-I48 - Shonert sideline pass for Schimpf incomplete
3/10-S48 - Mordell over lg for 2 (Pavesic, Smith)
4/8 -I46 - Fox punt partially blocked by Durrell, fielded by Hardy at I30, no return

0:06 ILLINOIS
1/10-I30 - McCullough scrambles for 11 (Foley)

END OF GAME
STANFORD 35 ILLINOIS 10

National Collegiate Athletic Association
FINAL TEAM STATISTICS

	ILLINOIS	STANFORD
First Downs	12	28
Rushing	11	13
Passing	0	13
Penalty	1	2
Rushing Attempts	49	50
Yards Rushing	192	220
Yards Lost Rushing	76	22
Net Yards Rushing	116	198
Net Yards Passing	25	241
Passes Attempted	14	32
Passes Completed	3	25
Passes Intercepted	0	1
Total Offensive Plays	63	84
Total Net Yards	141	439
Fumbles: Number—Lost	5/2	5/2
Penalties: Number-Yards	6/60	7/104
Interceptions: Number— Return		
Punts: Number—Yards	7/266	4/101
Average Per Punt	38.0	25.3
Blocked Punts	0	1
Punt Returns: Number— Yards	0/0	2/25
Kickoff Returns	1/17	2/2
Time of Possession	27:06	32:54

SEPTEMBER 23, 1978

WASHINGTON
VS.
INDIANA
Memorial Stadium
Bloomington, Indiana
Temp.: 73°
Wind: NE 10 mph
FIRST QUARTER

Washington wins toss and will receive, Indiana will defend north goal.
Straub kicks off to Steele at W2, returned to W44, 42 return
14:53 WASHINGTON
1/10-W44 - Steele rt to 50, 6 yards
2/4 - 50 - Washington offsides
2/9 -W45 - Gipson rg to W47, 2 yards
3/7 -W47 - Porras pass incomplete at I25
4/7 -W47 - Wilson punts to Swinehart at I15, fair catch 38 punt

13:20 INDIANA
1/10 -I15 - Burnett rg to I17, 2 yards
2/8 -I17 - Burnett rt to I19, 2 yards
3/6 -I19 - Harkrader re to I18, loss of 1
4/7 -I18 - Lovett punts to Glasgow at W44, fair catch 38 punt

11:30 WASHINGTON
1/10-W44 - Steele re to W44, no gain
2/10-W44 - Steele re to W45, 1 yard
3/9 -W45 - Porras pass complete to Steele to W38, loss of 7
4/16-W38 - Casarino punts to Swinehart at I21, fair catch 41 punt

9:59 INDIANA
1/10-I21 - Johnson rg to I30, 9 yards
2/1 -I30 - Johnson lg to I29, loss of 1
3/2 -I29 - Burnett lg to I32, 3 yards
1/10-I32 - Burnett rt to I34, 2 yards
2/8 -I34 - Harkrader rt to I36, 2 yards
3/6 -I36 - Arnett pass incomplete to Corso at W30
4/6 -I36 - Lovett punts to Glasgow at W24, returned to W39, 15 return 40 punt

7:10 WASHINGTON
1/10-W39 - Steele rt to W38, loss of 1
2/11-W38 - Porras re to W40, 2 yards
3/9 -W40 - Porras pass incomplete to Richardson at 50
4/9 -W40 - Wilson punts dead to I1, 59 yards, but Washington personal foul
4/24-W25 - Wilson punts dead to I47, 28 punt

5:24 INDIANA
1/10-I47 - Arnett re to W49, 4 yards
2/6 -W49 - Bowers lg to W41, 8 yards
1/10-W41 - Harkrader le to W39, 2 yards
2/8 -W39 - Bowers rt to W31, 8 yards
1/10-W31 - Harkrader lg to W22, 9 yards

2/1 -W22 - Harkrader lg to W20, 2 yards
1/10-W20 - Harkrader re to W12, 8 yards
2/2 -W12 - Harkrader rg to W11, 1 yard
3/1 -W11 - Arnett lg to W9, 2 yards
1/G -W9 - Harkrader re to W1, 8 yards
2/G -W1 - Harkrader lg to W1, no gain

END OF FIRST QUARTER:
INDIANA 0 WASHINGTON 0

SECOND QUARTER

INDIANA
3/G -W1 - Harkrader lg for touchdown, 1 yard
PAT Freud kick good
SCORE: INDIANA 7 WASHINGTON 0

Straub kicks off to Coby to W7, no return
14:52 WASHINGTON
1/10-W7 - Steele le to W13, 6 yards
2/4 -W13 - Steele rt to W21, 8 yards
1/10-W21 - Porras pass complete to Briggs at W31, 10 yards
1/10-W31 - Steele rt to W37, 6 yards
2/4 -W37 - Steele le to W40, 3 yards
3/1 -W40 - Steele rg to W46, 6 yards
1/10-W46 - Porras pass complete to Briggs to I48, 6 yards
2/4 -I48 - Steele le to I47, 1 yard
3/3 -I47 - Washington offsides
3/8 -W48 - Porras pass complete to Briggs to I32, 20 yards
1/10-I32 - Porras le to I36, loss of 4
2/14-I36 - Smith lg to I32, 4 yards
3/10-I32 - Porras pass incomplete to Gaines at I18
4/10-I32 - Lansford 49 field goal attempt wide right

9:20 INDIANA
1/10-I32 - Arnett pass intercepted by Lee at W29

9:12 WASHINGTON
1/10-W29 - Steele fumbles, recovered by Keneipp at W36, 7 yards

9:07 INDIANA
1/10-W36 - Indiana penalized for holding 18-yard penalty
1/28-I46 - Friede re to W48, 6 yards
2/22-W48 - Burnett rg to W37, 11 yards
3/11-W37 - Bowers rg to W34, 3 yards
4/8 -W34 - Lovett punts into end zone, 34 punt

6:58 WASHINGTON
1/10-W20 - Steele le to W23, 3 yards
2/7 -W23 - Porras pass complete to Richards to W37, 14 yards
1/10-W37 - Porras pass intercepted by Abrams at I43, returned to I45, 2 return

179

6:10 INDIANA
1/10-I45 - Bowers rg to I49, 4 yards
2/6 -I49 - Harkrader lg to W49, 2 yards
3/4 -W49 - Harkrader lg to W42, 7 yards
1/10-W42 - Harkrader le to W41, 1 yard
2/9 -W41 - Indiana penalized for holding
2/24-I44 - Burnett rg to W44, 12 yards
3/12-W44 - Arnett pass incomplete
4/12-W44 - Lovett punts dead to W9, 35 punt

2:53 WASHINGTON
1/10-W9 - Steele le to W14, 5 yards
2/5 -W14 - Tyler lg to W21, 7 yards
1/10-W21 - Steele le to W20, loss of 1
2/11-W20 - Porras pass complete to Gaines to W41, 21 yards
1/10-W41 - Porras pass incomplete
2/10-W41 - Porras pass incomplete
3/10-W41 - Porras pass intercepted by Wilbur at 50, returned to W27, 23 return

0:55 INDIANA
1/10-W27 - Harkrader re to W27, no gain
2/10-W27 - Fishel re to W35, loss of 8
3/18-W35 - Arnett re to W25, 10 yards
4/8 -W25 - Arnett re to W28, loss of 3

0:08 WASHINGTON
1/10-W28 - Steele to 50, 22 yards
1/10- 50 - Porras pass incomplete

**END OF HALF:
INDIANA 7 WASHINGTON 0**

THIRD QUARTER

Lansford kicks off into end zone
14:55 INDIANA
1/10-I20 - Burnett lg to I21, 1 yard
2/9 -I21 - Burnett lg to I23, 2 yards
3/7 -I23 - Burnett rg to I26, 3 yards
4/4 -I26 - Lovett punts out of bounds at W42, 32 punt

13:03 WASHINGTON
1/10-W42 - Gipson rg to W44, 2 yards
2/8 -W44 - Steele re to I47, 9 yards
1/10-I47 - Porras le to W49, loss of 4
2/14-W49 - Porras pass complete to Greenwood to I45, 6 yards
3/8 -I45 - Porras trapped at I48, loss of 3
4/11-I48 - Casarino punts out of bounds at I29, 19 punt

10:25 INDIANA
1/10-I29 - Hopkins rg to I34, 5 yards
2/5 -I34 - Burnett rt to I37, 3 yards
3/2 -I37 - Bowers rg to I39, 2 yards
1/10-I39 - Burnett re to I43, 4 yards
2/6 -I43 - Burnett rg to I47, 4 yards
3/2 -I47 - Burnett le to I48, 1 yard

4/1 -I48 - Lovett punts to Glasgow at W7, returned to W9, 2 return 45 punt

6:59 WASHINGTON
1/10-W9 - Steele re to W11, 2 yards
2/8 -W11 - Porras pass complete to Richards to W23, 12 yards
1/10-W23 - Smith lg to W28, 5 yards
2/5 -W28 - Washington offsides
2/10-W23 - Porras pass complete to Greenwood to I39, 38 yards
1/10-I39 - Steele rg to I28, 11 yards
1/10-I28 - Smith rg to I24, 4 yards
2/6 -I24 - Steele le to I17, 7 yards
1/10-I17 - Steele le to I15, 2 yards
2/8 -I15 - Porras re trapped at I21, loss of 6
3/14-I21 - Steele lt to I16, 5 yards
4/9 -I16 - Lansford 33 field goal attempt wide left

1:44 INDIANA
1/10-I20 - Burnett rg to I37, 17 yards
1/10-I37 - Burnett rg to I40, 3 yards
2/7 -I40 - Bowers rg to W44, 16 yards
1/10-W44 - Burnett lt to W40, 4 yards

**END OF THIRD QUARTER,
INDIANA 7 WASHINGTON 0**

FOURTH QUARTER

INDIANA
2/6 -W40 - Washington offsides
2/1 -W35 - Burnett lg to W33, 2 yards
1/10-W33 - Bowers rt to W26, 7 yards
2/3 -W26 - Burnett lt to W25, 1 yard
3/2 -W25 - Burnett le to W25, no gain
4/2 -W25 - Burnett re to W2, 23 yards
1/G -W2 - Burnett lg for touchdown, 2 yards
PAT—Freud kick good
SCORE: INDIANA 14, WASHINGTON 0

SEPTEMBER 23, 1978

Straub kicks off to Steele, reverse to Blacken to W10, 10 return (KO into end zone)
12:40 WASHINGTON
1/10-W10 - Steele rg to W31, 21 yards
1/10-W31 - Steele rg to W37, 6 yards, and Indiana personal foul
1/10-I48 - Steele rg to I45, 3 yards
2/7 -I45 - Steele re to I39, 6 yards
3/1 -I39 - Steele re to I38, 1 yard
1/10-I38 - Flick pass complete to Briggs at I28, 10 yards
1/10-I28 - Steele le to I23, 5 yards
2/5 -I23 - Flick pass intercepted by Abrams at I13, returned to I17

9:54 INDIANA
1/10-I17 - Burnett rg to I23, 6 yards
2/4 -I23 - Bowers lg to I32, 9 yards
1/10-I32 - Indiana offsides
1/15-I27 - Burnett rg to I30, 3 yards
2/12-I30 - Burnett lg to I30, no gain
3/12-I30 - Burnett re to I30, no gain
4/12-I30 - Lovett punts to Glasgow at W30, returned to W36, 6 return 41 punt

6:33 WASHINGTON
1/10-W36 - Flick pass incomplete
2/10-W36 - Porras pass complete to Greenwood to I46, 18 yards
1/10-I46 - Porras pass complete to Gaines at I25, 21 yards
1/10-I25 - Steele le to I20, 5 yards
2/5 -I20 - Porras re to I14, 6 yards
1/10-I14 - Gipson rg to I9, 5 yards
2/5 -I9 - Porras pass complete to Gaines for touchdown, 9 yards
PAT—Lansford kick good
SCORE: INDIANA 14, WASHINGTON 7

Lansford kicks off at I9, returned to I24, 15 return
4:41 INDIANA
1/10-I24 - Burnett rg to I27, 3 yards
2/7 -I27 - Burnett lg to I27, no gain
3/7 -I27 - Burnett lg to I30, 3 yards
4/4 -I30 - Lovett punts to Glasgow at W29, returned to W36, 6 return 41 punt

3:12 WASHINGTON
1/10-W36 - Porras pass complete to Greenwood to I49, 15 yards, but Washington personal foul
1/25-W36 - Porras pass complete to Gaines to W48, 12 yards
2/13-W48 - Porras pass complete to Briggs to I42, 10 yards
3/3 -I42 - Porras pass complete to Steele to I32, 10 yards
1/10-I32 - Porras re to I30, 2 yards
2/8 -I30 - Porras pass incomplete to Blacken at I20
3/8 -I30 - Porras pass incomplete in end zone to Greenwood

4/8 -I30 - Porras pass incomplete to Gaines at I5

1:20 INDIANA
1/10-I30 - Arnett rg to I30, no gain
2/10-I30 - Arnett rg to I28, loss of 2
3/12-I28 - Indiana offsides
3/17-I23 - Arnett rg to I23, no gain
4/17-I23 - Indiana delay of game
4/22-I18 - Arnett rg to I18, no gain

FINAL SCORE:
INDIANA 14, WASHINGTON 7

National Collegiate Athletic Association
FINAL TEAM STATISTICS

	WASH-INGTON	INDIANA
First Downs	23	12
Rushing	10	12
Passing	12	0
Penalty	1	0
Rushing Attempts	43	63
Yards Rushing	196	253
Yards Lost Rushing	19	15
Net Yards Rushing	177	238
Net Yards Passing	225	0
Passes Attempted	29	3
Passes Completed	17	0
Had Intercepted	3	1
Total Offensive Plays	72	66
Total Net Yards	402	238
Average Gain Per Play	5.5	3.6
Fumbles: Number—Lost	4/1	0/0
Penalties: Number—Yards	6/50	6/63
Interceptions: Number—Yards	1/0	3/29
Number of Punts—Yards	4/126	8/306
Average Per Punt	31.5	38
Punt Returns: Number—Yards	4/29	0/0
Kickoff Returns: Number—Yards	3/52	1/15

**IOWA STATE
VS.
IOWA**
Kinnick Stadium
Temp.: mid 70's
Wind: 10-12 mph South
Skies: clear and sunny
FIRST QUARTER

Iowa State wins toss and elects to receive. Iowa will kick off and defend south goal.
Schilling kicks off to Hardee for return of 20. (Skradis)
IOWA STATE
1/10-S23 - Green around RE for loss of 1. (Gutshall)
2/11-S22 - Rubley passes to Hixon for gain of 14 (Shaw)
1/10-S36 - Green over RG for gain of 5. (Molini)
2/5-S41 - Rubley passes to Hardee, fumbles out of bounds for gain of 13.
1/10-I46 - Rubley pass intended for Hixon is incomplete. (Danzy)
Iowa penalized for pass interference (9yds)
1/10-I37 - Seabrooke over RG for gain of 2 (Hobbs)
2/8 -I35 - Green over RG for gain of 9 (Danzy)
1/10-I26 - Rubley around RE for loss of 1. (Rusk)
2/11-I27 - Green over LT for gain of 1. (Danzy)
3/10-I26 - Rubley pass intended for Hardee is incomplete.
4/10-I26 - Hixon holds, Johnson kicks, field goal attempt is no good.

10:36 IOWA
1/10-I26 - Mosley over RG for gain of 4. (C. Boskey)
2/6 -I30 - Gales passes to Morton for gain of 9.
1/10-I39 - Mosley over RT for gain of 7. (Cole)
2/3 -I46 - Lazar over RG for gain of 4. (C. Boskey)
1/10- 50 - Mosley over RG for gain of 5. (T. Boskey)
2/5 -S45 - Lazar over RG for gain of 2. (Weidemann)
3/3 -S43 - Gales around RE for gain of 6. (Cole)
1/10-S37 - Mosley over RT for gain of 3. (C. Boskey)
2/7 -S34 - Mosley around LE for loss of 2. (White)
3/9 -S36 - Iowa penalized 5 yds for delay of game.
3/14-S41 - Gales pass intended for Mosley is incomplete.
4/14-S41 - Holsclaw punts into end zone for touchback.

5:01 IOWA STATE
1/10-S20 - Green around RE for gain of 7.
2/3 -S27 - Green over RG for loss of 1. (Gutshall)

3/4 -S26 - Rubley passes to Hardee for gain of 12.
1/10-S38 - Green over RG for loss of 1. (Harty)
2/11-S37 - Hardee passes to Hixon for gain of 24. Iowa State penalized 5 yds. for illegal motion.
2/16-S32 - Green around RE for gain of 6. (Pace)
3/10-S38 - Rubley carries for no gain. (Hufford)
4/10-S38 - Miller punts to Iowa 19 yard line. (43 yard punt)

0:53 IOWA
1/10-I19 - Lazar over RG for gain of 1. (C. Boskey)
2/9 -I20 - Morton around RE for gain of 2. (Washington)
**FIRST QUARTER SCORE:
IOWA 0, IOWA STATE 0**

SECOND QUARTER

IOWA
3/7 -I22 - Gales scrambles for gain of 4.
4/3 -I26 - Holsclaw punts out of bounds on Iowa 47 yard line. (21 yard punt)

14:20 IOWA STATE
1/10-I47 - Grant passes to Hixon for TD. Hixon holds, Johnson kicks, PAT is good. SCORE: IOWA STATE 7, IOWA 0

Ligons kicks off into end zone for touchback.
14:13 IOWA
1/10-I20 - Mosley over RT for no gain. (T. Boskey)
2/10-I20 - Gales over RT for gain of 9. (Cole)
3/1 -I29 - Gales fumbles, C. Boskey recovers for State, gain of 1.

12:53 IOWA STATE
1/10-I30 - Grant passes to Kennedy, fumbles, for gain of 22.
1/G -I8 - Green around LE for 2. (Molini)
2/G I6 - Grant passes to Hardee for TD. Hixon holds, Johnson kicks, PAT is good.
SCORE IOWA STATE 14, IOWA 0

Ligons kicks off to Reid for return of 17. (B. Johnson)
11:55 IOWA
1/10-I26 - Lazar over RG for gain of 2. (Stensrud)
2/8 -I28 - Iowa penalized 5 yds for delay of game.
2/13-I23 - Gales passes to Lazar for loss of 2. (T. Boskey)
3/15-I21 - Gales around RE for gain of 9. (Cole)
4/6 -I30 - Holsclaw punts to Iowa State 36 yard line. (34 yard kick)

SEPTEMBER 23, 1978

9:47 IOWA STATE
1/10-S36 - Grant passes to Smith for gain of 20.
1/10-I44 - Green over LT for gain of 1. (Skradis)
2/9 -I43 - Grant passes to Hixon for gain of 20. (Becker)
1/10-I23 - Green around RE for loss of 2. (Gutshall)
2/12-I25 - Grant around RE for gain of 9. (Mahmens)
3/3 -I16 - Green pass intended for Cerrato is incomplete.
4/3 -I16 - Hixon holds, Johnson kicks, field goal attempt is good.
SCORE IOWA STATE 17, IOWA 0

Ligons kicks off to Reid for return of 15. (Earnest)
6:47 IOWA
1/10-I30 - Gales pass intended for Mosley is incomplete.
2/10-I30 - Reid around RE for gain of 2. (Cole)
3/8 -I32 - Gales pass intended for Frazier is incomplete.
4/8 -I32 - Holsclaw punts to Buck for fair catch. (32 yard punt)

5:57 IOWA STATE
1/10-S36 - Cerrato around LE for gain of 3. (Pace)
2/7 -S39 - Iowa State penalized 5 yds for delay of game.
2/12-S34 - Grant scrambles for gain of 8. (Shaw)
3/4 -S43 - Grant, fumbles, recovers, for no gain
4/4 -S43 - Miller punts to Reid for fair catch. (44 yard kick)

3:43 IOWA
1/10-I14 - Mosley over LG for gain of 6.
2/4 -I20 - Mosley over LT for gain of 3. (C. Boskey)
3/1 -I23 - Mosley over LT for gain of 2. (White)
1/10-I25 - Gales passes to Lazar for gain of 6. (Perticone)
2/4 -I31 - Iowa penalized for holding.
2/22-I12 - Mosley over LT for gain of 5. (Perticone)
3/17-I17 - Mosley over LT for gain of 13. (Schwartz)
4/4 -I30 - Holsclaw punts to Buck for fair catch. (24 yard kick)

0:34 IOWA STATE
1/10-S46 - Iowa State penalized 5 yds for illegal procedure.
1/15-S41 - Grant around LE for no gain. (Benschoter)

**FIRST HALF SCORE:
IOWA STATE 17 IOWA 0**

THIRD QUARTER

Iowa will receive. Iowa State will kick off and defend south goal.
Ligons kicks off to Kevin Ellis for return of 17. (Kennedy)
IOWA
1/10-I33 - Frazier over LG for gain of 2. (Cole)
2/8 -I35 - Gales around RE for gain of 5. (Perticone)
3/3 -I40 - Gales thrown for loss of 13. (White)
4/16-I27 - Holsclaw punts to Buck for return of 3. (33 yard kick) (Gutshall)

13:09 IOWA STATE
1/10-S42 - Grant around LE for gain of 16. (Danzy)
1/10-I42 - Green over RT for gain of 13. (Danzy)
1/10-I29 - Kennedy over LG for gain of 4. (Harty)
2/6 -I25 - Grant thrown for loss of 7. (Vasquez)
3/13-I32 - Rubley pass intended for Preston is incomplete.
4/13-I32 - Miller punts into endzone for touchback.

10:42 IOWA
1/10-I20 - Green around RE for gain of 5. (Weidemann)
2/5 -I25 - Mosley over LG for gain of 3. (C. Boskey)
3/2 -I28 - Frazier around LE for loss of 3. (White)
4/5 -I25 - Holsclaw punts to Buck for fair catch. (31 yard kick)

8:56 IOWA STATE
1/10-S44 - Kennedy over LG for gain of 2. (Mahmens)
2/8 -S46 - Grant over LT for gain of 3. (Rusk)
3/5 -S49 - Green over RT for gain of 3. (Gutshall)
4/2 -I48 - Miller punts to into endzone for touchback. (48 yard kick)

183

6:55 IOWA
1/10-I20 - Iowa penalized 5 yds for illegal motion
1/15-I15-Green around LE for no gain. (Stensrud)
2/15-I15 - Green pass intended for Reid is incomplete. Iowa State penalized for pass interference. (13 yds)
1/10-I28 - Green around LE, fumbles, recovered by Palladino, gain of 6. (White)
2/4 -I34 - Mosley over LT for gain of 3. (Neil)
3/1 -I37 - Lazar over LG for gain of 2. (Cole)
1/10-I39 - Green thrown for loss of 3. (Weidemann)
2/13-I36 - Green passes to Dunham for gain of 14. (Clemons)
1/10- 50 - Green fumbles, recovered by Mosley for loss of 11. (White)
2/21-I39 - Green pass intended for Mosley is incomplete.
3/21-I39 - Green around RE for gain of 18. (Vieceli)
4/3 -S43 - Green thrown for loss of 12. (Weidemann)

2:36 IOWA STATE
1/10-I45 - Grant pass intended for Smith is incomplete.
2/10-I45 - Grant around RE for gain of 3. (Gutshall)
3/7 -I42 - Grant pass intended for Hixon is incomplete. Iowa penalized for pass interference.
1/10-I24 - Green over RG for gain of 3. (Rusk)
2/7 -I21 - Green around LE for gain of 1. (Shaw)
3/6 -I20 - Grant pass intended for Green is incomplete.
4/6 -I20 - Green around RE for gain of 8. (Danzy)

THIRD QUARTER SCORE:
IOWA STATE 17 IOWA 0

FOURTH QUARTER

IOWA STATE
1/10-I12 - Mack over LT for gain of 1.
2/9 -I11 - Green over LT for gain of 2. (Rusk)
3/7-I9 - Grant passes to Preston for gain of 4. (Pace)
4/3 -I5 - Grant around RE for gain of 1. (Moloni)

12:47 IOWA
1/10-I4 - Turner over LG for gain of 2. (Stensrud)
2/8 -I6 - Green pass intended for Frazier is incomplete.
3/8 -I6 - Green pass intended for Frazier is incomplete
4/8 -I6 - Holsclaw punts to Buck for return of 20. (37 yard kick)

11:47 IOWA STATE
1/10-I23 - Curry over LG for gain of 2. (Harty)
2/8 -I21 - Grant around RE for gain of 1 (Rusk)
3/7 -I20 - Grant pass intended for Cerrato is incomplete.
4/7 -I20 - Grant passes to Hixon for TD. Hixon holds, Johnson kicks, PAT is good.
SCORE IOWA STATE 24 IOWA 0

Ligons kicks off to Reid for return of 19 (Earnest)

10:26 IOWA
1/10-I31 - Iowa penalized for illegal procedure (5 yds)
1/15-I26 - Green pass intended for Reid is incomplete.
2/15-I26 - Lazar around LE for gain of 5. (White)
3/10-I31 - Green around LE for gain of 2. (Meis)
4/8 -I33 - Holsclaw punts to Buck for return of 1. (50 yard punt) (Kent Ellis)

8:38 IOWA STATE
1/10-S19 - Curry over LG for gain of 2. (Benschoter)
2/8 -S21 - Mack over RT for gain of 3. (Mahmens)
3/5 -S24 - Mack over LG for gain of 2. (Benschoter)
4/3 -S26 - Miller punts to Reid for return of 4. (28 yard punt) (Henricksen)

6:45 IOWA
1/10- 50 - Green thrown for loss of 6. (Neil)
2/16-I44 - McKillip over RG for gain of 5. (Perticone)
3/11-I49 - Green scrambles for gain of 6. (Less)
4/5 -S45 - Turner around LE, fumbles, recovered by B. Johnson, gain of 3. (Vieceli)

184

SEPTEMBER 23, 1978

4:48 IOWA STATE
1/10-S42 - Mack over RG for gain of 7. (Wagner)
2/3 -S49 - Mack over LT for gain of 5. (Benschoter)
1/10-I46 - Mack around LE for gain of 7. (Benschoter)
2/3 -I39 - Curry over LG for gain of 4. (Shaw)
1/10-I35 - Gillis around RE for gain of 2. (Dean)
2/8 -I33 - Gillis over LT for gain of 9. (Skradis)
1/10-I24 - Gillis around LE for gain of 3. (Pace)
2/7 -I21 - Gillis around LE for gain of 1. (Simonsen)
3/6 -I20 - Smith around RE, fumbles, recovered by Iowa State, gain of 7. (Skradis) Iowa penalized for face mask grabbing.
1/G -I7 - Mack around LE for TD. Hixon holds, Johnson kicks, PAT is good.
SCORE IOWA STATE 31 IOWA 0

Ligons kicks off to Reid for return of 13. (Solus)
0:39 IOWA
1/10-I24 - Green around LE for gain of 4. (Stensrud)
2/6 -I28 - Green around RE for gain of 2.

FINAL SCORE:
IOWA STATE 31 IOWA 0

National Collegiate Athletic Association
FINAL TEAM STATISTICS

	IOWA	IA. STATE
First Downs	7	18
Rushes—Yards	45/113	48/162
Passing Yards	27	178
Return Yards	4	23
Passes	4/11/0	10/16/0
Punts	9/33.6	5/39.0
Fumbles—Lost	4/2	3/0
Penalties—Yards	8/72	4/28

SYRACUSE
VS.
MICHIGAN STATE

Temp: high 60s to low 70s Current: 67
Winds: N-NE up to 10 mph
Skies: Sunny, no chance of rain

FIRST QUARTER

S wins the toss elects to receive. MS defending the south goal.
Schario kicks to Monk at S7, fumbles, recovered by Kolodziej, return of 3.

14:54 MICHIGAN STATE
1/G -MS10 - McGee around right end, run out by Arkeilpane & Hartman, gain of 8
2/G -MS2 - S. Smith off right tackle, touchdown
Time: :15 10 yards in 2 plays
Anderson PAT good, Elapsed Time: :15
MICHIGAN STATE 7, SYRACUSE 0

14:45 SYRACUSE
Schario kicks to Harvey at S5, tackle by Cooper return of 13
1/10-S18 - Monk off right tackle, tackle by Bass, gain of 2
2/8 -S20 - Wilson carries on broken play, tackle by Land, loss of 2
3/18 -S18 - Wilson around left end on keeps, tackle by Bass, gain of 5
4/5 -S23 - Goodwill kicks to S. Smith, tackle by Goodwill, 32 yd punt, 30 yd return

12:48 MICHIGAN STATE
1/10-S25 - Middleton through the middle, tackle by O'Leary, gain of 11
1/10-SU14 - Middleton off left guard, tackle by Tate & Collins, gain of 3
2/7 -S11 - Vaughn pass, S holding, 7 yd penalty
2/1 -S4 - McGee off right guard, touchdown, Time: 3:23, 25 yds in 3 plays, 4 yd rush
Andersen PAT good, Elapsed Time: 1:11
SCORE: MICHIGAN STATE 14, SYRACUSE 0

11:37 SYRACUSE
Schario kicks to Harvey in end zone, tackle by Davis & T. Williams, return of 32
1/10-S32 - Wilson fumbles, recovered by Wilson, loss of 1
2/11-S31 - Wilson pass to Semall overthrown
3/11-S31 - Wilson back to pass, keeps through the middle, tackle, by Hay, gain of 4
4/7 -S35 - Goodwill punts to S. Smith, fair catch, 41 yd punt, no return

10:22 MICHIGAN STATE
1/10-M24 - Vaughn pass to Gibson on left sideline overthrown
2/10-M24 - Reeves on pitchout to left side, tackle by Collins, gain of 2 To/MS. 10:06

3/8 -M26 - Vaughn pass to Byrd long on left side, caught out of bounds
4/8 -M26 - Stachowicz punt downed by MS at 15 yd line, punt of 59, no return

9:27 SYRACUSE
1/10-S15 - Morris around left side on pitchout, tackle by Anderson, gain of 1
2/9 -S16 - Wilson pass to Monk, 27 yd pass completion, falls
1/10-S43 - Hartman off right guard, tackle by Hay & Land, gain of 1 To/SU. 9:04
2/9 -S44 - Wilson fumbles on snap, recovers, loss of 3
3/12-S41 - Wilson pass to Monk along left sideline, dropped
4/12-S41 - Goodwill punts to S. Smith, fair catch, 35 yd punt, no return

7:51 MICHIGAN STATE
1/10-M24 - Vaughn pass to Byrd on left sideline, steps out, gain of 16
1/10-M40 - Vaughn pass to Gibson on right sideline incomplete
2/10-M40 - Vaughn pass to Byrd on left sideline, steps out, gain of 14
1/10-S46 - Schramm off right guard, tackle by Collins, gain of 7
2/3 -S39 - Vaughn pass to Byrd over the middle, tackle by O'Leary, gain of 23
1/10-S16 - Reeves around left end on pitch, tackle by Tate, Lang & Arkeilpane, no gain
2/10-S16 - Gibson on reverse, touchdown, 16 yd run, Time: 9:17 76 yds in 7 plays
Andersen PAT attempt good. Elapsed time: 2:08
SCORE: MICHIGAN STATE 21 SYRACUSE 0

5:43 SYRACUSE
Schario kicks to Harvey in endzone, downs for touchback
1/10-S20 - Morris off left tackle, tackle by Hay, gain of 1
2/9 -S21 - Morris around left end on pitchout, tackle by Stanton, gain of 3
3/6 -S24 - Wilson pass to Trapasso on left sideline, overthrown
4/6 -S24 - Goodwill punts to Anderson, fair catch, 32 yd punt, no return

4:41 MICHIGAN STATE
1/10-M44 - Vaughn pass long to Byrd, interference by S, 45 yd penalty
1/10-S11 - Schramm through the middle, tackle by Richardson & Collins, gain of 3
2/7 -S8 - Vaughn sacked by Gyetvay, loss of 9
3/16-S17 - Vaughn pass over the middle McGee incomplete
4/16-S17 - Andersen 34 yd field goal attempt wide right

SEPTEMBER 23, 1978

3:12 SYRACUSE
1/10-S20 - Hartman through the middle, tackle by Land, gain of 3
2/7 -S23 - Hartman through the middle, tackle by Webb & Hay, gain of 6
3/1 -S29 - Hartman off left tackle, tackle by Land & Savage, gain of 8
1/10-S37 - Monk off left guard on counter, tackle by Hay, gain of 3
2/7 -S40 - Farneski fumbles, recovered, gain of 2
3/5 -S42 - Farneski back to pass, sacked by Bass & Savage, loss of 5

**FIRST QUARTER SCORE:
MICHIGAN STATE 21, SYRACUSE 0**

SECOND QUARTER

15:00 SYRACUSE
4/10-S37 - Goodwill punts to S. Smith, 45 yd punt, 4 yd return, tackle by Spinney

14:49 MICHIGAN STATE
1/10-M21 - Vaughn pass to Brammer overthrown
2/10-M21 - Vaughn pass to Schramm in left flat, tackle by Hinton, gain of 9
3/1 -M30 - McGee outside right end, tackle by Arkeilpane & Collins, no gain
4/1 -M30 - Stachowicz punts to O'Leary, 32 yd punt, no return, fair catch

13:24 SYRACUSE
1/10-S38 - Hartman through the middle, tackle by Hay, gain of 3
2/7 -S41 - Farneski pass on right side, to Zambuto, tackle by Marshall, gain 13
1/10-M46 - Farneski pass to Monk, tackle by Otis, gain of 12
1/10-M34 - Hartman off right tackle, tackle by Hay & Otis, gain of 6
2/4 -M28 - Hartman inside right guard, tackle by Land & Hay, gain of 3
3/1 -M25 - Hartman outside right guard, tackle by Webb, gain of 4
1/10-M21 - Monk outside right end on pitch, tackle by Anderson, gain of 7
2/3 -M14 - SU illegal procedure, 5 yd penalty
2/8 -M19 - Farneski pass to Semall, touchdown, Time: 4:37 62 yards in 8 plays Jacobs PAT attempt good. Elapsed time: 3:01
SCORE: MICHIGAN STATE 21, SYRACUSE 7

10:23 MICHIGAN STATE
Jacobs kicks to S. Smith in endzone, tackle by Sickles 25 yd return
1/10-M25 - McGee off right guard, tackle by Rotunda, gain of 3
2/7 -M28 - Vaughn pass to Brammer on left side, tackle by O'Leary, gain of 18

1/10-M46 - Middleton through the middle, tackle by Collins, gain of 4
2/6 -M50 - Vaughn pass to Gibson incomplete tripped by official
3/6 -M50 - Vaughn pass to Gibson, tackle by Patterson, gain of 14
1/10-S36 - Vaughn pass to Gibson long on right side, touchdown 36 yd pass
Andersen PAT good, 75 yds in 6 plays, Time: 7:07 elapsed Time: 2:30
SCORE: MICHIGAN STATE 28, SYRACUSE 7

7:53 SYRACUSE
Schario kicks to Harvey at S7, tackle by McCormick, 22 yd. return
1/10-S29 - Farneski off left tackle on keeper, tackle by Savage, gain of 3
2/7 -S32 - Farneski pass to Jones, fumble recovered, tackle by Marshall, gain of 16
1/10-S48 - Farneski through the middle, tackle by Bass, gain of 3
2/7 -M49 - Monk through the middle, tackle by Hay, gain of 5
3/2 -M44 - Monk on pitchout to the right, tackle by Bass, gain of 3
1/10-M41 - Farneski pass to Small on left sideline thrown out of bounds
2/10-M41 - Farneski back to pass, sacked by Hay, loss of 14
3/24-S45 - Farneski pass to Monk intercepted by Anderson, 26 yd return, tackle Hartman

4:16 MICHIGAN STATE
1/10-S49 - Reeves outside right tackle by Hinton, gain of 9
2/1 -S40 - Vaughn pass to Gibson on left sideline incomplete
3/1 -S40 - Vaughn on keeper through the middle, tackle by Gyetvay & Collins, gain of 2
1/10-S38 - Vaughn pass long on left sideline to Byrd, touchdown, Time: 12:06
Andersen PAT is good. 49 yds in 4 plays Elapsed Time: 1:22 38 yd TD play
MICHIGAN STATE 35, SYRACUSE 7

187

2:54 SYRACUSE
Schario kicks to Monk in end zone, touchback
1/10-S20 - Farneski pass thrown out of bounds on right sideline
2/10-S20 - Farneski on keeper outside right end, tackle by Stanton, gain of 2
3/8 -S22 - Farneski around left end on keeper, tackle by Savage, gain of 4
4/4 -S26 - Goodwill punts to S. Smith, tackle by Jones, 36 yd punt, 3 yd return

1:40 MICHIGAN STATE
1/10-M43 - Vaughn pass to Brammer on left side, tackle by O'Leary, gain of 15
1/10-S42 - Gibson on reverse, tackle by Shaffer, loss of 8
2/18-S50 - Vaughn back to pass runs, MS holding, 25 yd penalty
2/43-M25 - Schramm through the middle, tackle by Gyetvay, gain of 11

**END OF HALF SCORE:
MICHIGAN STATE 35, SYRACUSE 7**

THIRD QUARTER

MS elects to receive. S defending the south goal Jacobs kicks to Reeves in the endzone, tackle by McCullough & Sickles, return of 46 yds
MICHIGAN STATE
1/10-M46 - Vaughn back to pass, sacked by Rotunda, loss of 10
2/20-M36 - Reeves outside right tackle, tackle by Collins, gain of 5
3/15-M41 - S. Smith off left guard, tackle by McCullough, gain of 4
4/11-M45 - Stachowicz kicks ball out of bounds at S22, 33 yd punt, no return

SYRACUSE
1/10-S22 - Hartman outside right guard, team tackle, gain of 3
2/7 -S25 - Monk outside right end on pitch, tackle by Bass, gain of 7
1/10-S32 - Monk around left end on pitchout, tackle by Stanton & Anderson, gain of 5
2/5 -S37 - Hartman off right tackle, fumbles, recovered by Bass, gain of 2

11:07 MICHIGAN STATE
1/10-S39 - Vaughn pass to Byrd on right sideline incomplete To/MS. 10:54
2/10-S39 - Schramm through the middle, tackle by Richardson & Rotunda, gain of 5
3/5 -S34 - McGee through the middle, tackle by Kinley, gain of 2
4/3 -S32 - Reeves through the middle, tackle by Rotunda, loss of 1

SYRACUSE
1/10-S33 - Morris off left guard on counter tackle by Hay & Anderson, gain of 10
1/10-S43 - Morris off left guard, tackle by Land, gain of 1
2/9 -S44 - Farneski pass to Semall on right sideline incomplete, out of bounds
3/9 -S44 - Farneski keeps on option, tackle by Haynes, loss of 1
4/10-S43 - Goodwill fumbles, recovered by Hay, loss of 16

7:39 MICHIGAN STATE
1/10-S27 - Vaughn pass intercepted by Arkeilpane, tackle by Byrd

SYRACUSE
1/10-S26 - Farneski fumbles, tackle by Otis gain of 3
2/7 -S29 - Farneski pass to Zambuto incomplete
3/7 -S29 - Farneski pass to Monk on right side underthrown
4/7 -S29 - Goodwill punt downed by S at M44, 27 yd punt, no return

6:33 MICHIGAN STATE
1/10-M44 - Schramm outside right tackle, tackle by Arkeilpane, gain of 4
2/6 -M48 - Reeves inside left guard on counter, tackle by Gyetvay, gain of 5
3/1 -S47 - Schramm through the middle, team tackle, gain of 3
1/10-S44 - Vaughn pass to Byrd long on left side broken up by Harvey
2/10-S44 - Vaughn back to pass, sacked by Neugebauer, loss of 9
3/19-M47 - Hans off left guard on draw play, tackle by Tate, gain of 14
4/6 -S40 - Stachowicz punts through the endzone, touchback, 40 yd punt

SYRACUSE
1/10-S20 - Morris around right end on pitchout, tackle by Otis, gain of 2
2/8 -S22 - Farneski fumbles, recovered by Savage, loss of 3

3:05 MICHIGAN STATE
1/10-S19 - McGee outside right end on pitchout, tackle by Arkeilpane, gain of 9
2/1 -S10 - Hans inside left guard, tackle by Collins, gain of 7
1/G -S3 - Schramm inside left guard, tackle by Tate & McCullough, gain of 2
2/G -S1 - Reeves dives over left guard, touchdown, 1 yd play Time:13:46 Andersen PAT good. 19 yards in 4 plays Elapsed Time: 1:51
SCORE: MICHIGAN STATE 42, SYRACUSE 7

SEPTEMBER 23, 1978

SYRACUSE
Schario kicks to Monk at S5, tackle by Davis, 17 yd return
1/10-S22 - Wilson outside left end on keeper, tackle by Anderson, gain of 12
1/10-S34 - Morris outside right tackle by Hay, gain of 3
2/7 -S37 - Wilson back to pass, runs right side keeper, tackle by Otis, gain of 5

**THIRD QUARTER SCORE:
MICHIGAN STATE 42, SYRACUSE 7**

SYRACUSE
1/10-S20 - Matichak off right tackle, tackle by McCormick, no gain
2/10-S20 - Matichak around right end on pitchout, run out of bounds by Burroughs gain 2
3/8 -S22 - Wilson back to pass, sacked by Land & Decker, loss of 6
4/14-S16 - Goodwill punts to S. Smith, tackle Neugebauer, 5 yd return, 44 yd punt

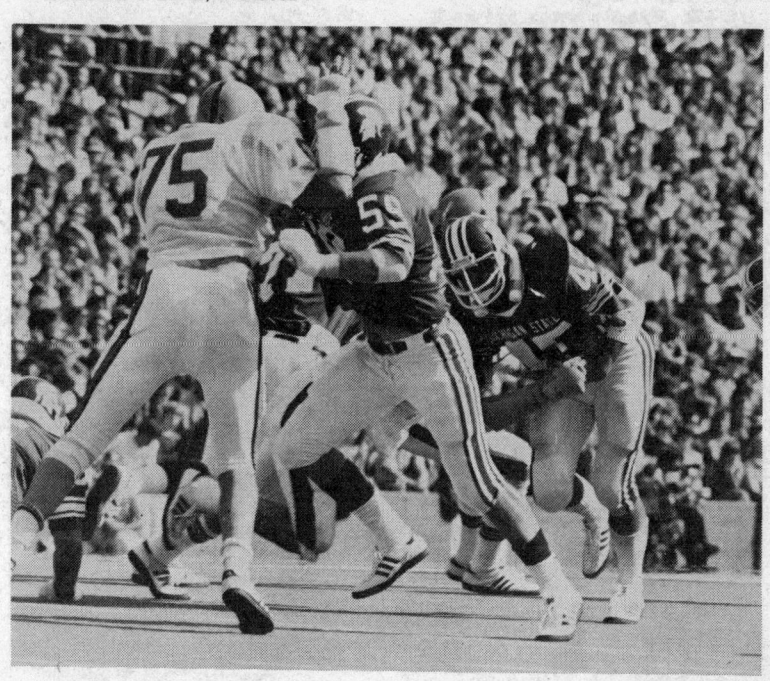

FOURTH QUARTER

SYRACUSE
3/2 -S42 - Wilson off right guard, tackle by Bass, gain of 3
1/10-S45 - Wilson back to pass, sacked by Hay, loss of 5
2/15-S40 - Morris fumbles, recovered by Bass, gain of 2

13:56 MICHIGAN STATE
1/10-S42 - Hughes off left tackle, tackle Cameron & Kinley, gain of 4
2/6 -S38 - Hans through the middle, tackle by Shaffer, no gain
3/6 -S38 - Schramm through the middle, tackle by Kinley, gain of 2
4/4 -S36 - Stachowicz punts through the end zone, touchback, 36 yd punt, no return

10:52 MICHIGAN STATE
1/10-M45 - Hughes outside left tackle, tackle by Kollar, gain of 4
2/6 -M49 - Schramm outside tackle, tackle by Collins, gain of 4
3/2 -S47 - Hughes outside left end on pitchout, tackle by O'Leary & Collins, gain of 6
1/10-S41 - Schramm inside right tackle, fumbles, recovered by Harvey, tackle by Collins, gain of 7

SYRACUSE
1/10-S34 - Morris on pitchout around right end, knocked out of bounds by Davis, gain 27
1/10-M39 - Matichak around left end on pitchout, fumbles, recovered by Decker, tackle by Maidlow & Decker, gain of 3

189

8:46 MICHIGAN STATE
1/10-M36 - Schramm through the middle, tackle by Zunic & Lang, gain of 6
2/4 -M42 - Clark pass to B. Harris, overthrown
3/4 -M42 - Clark screen pass to S. Smith, tackle by Hinton, gain of 18
1/10-S40 - Clark pass to B. Harris incomplete
2/10-S40 - Hughes around right end, tackle by Patterson, gain of 13
1/10-S27 - S. Smith off left tackle, tackle by O'Leary, gain of 4
2/6 -S23 - M illegal procedure, 5 yd penalty
2/11-S28 - Hughes outside left end on pitchout, touchdown 64 yds in 7 plays 28 yd run
Andersen PAT good Time: 9:01 Elapsed Time: 2:47
SCORE: MICHIGAN STATE 49, SYRACUSE 7

SYRACUSE
Schario kicks out of bounds 5 yd penalty kicking from 35 yard line
Schario kicks to Morris at SU5, tackle by Schario, 19 yd return
1/10-S24 - Morris outside right end, tackle by Marshall, gain of 8
2/2 -S32 - Farneski pass to G. Williams, falls down, gain of 13
1/10-S45 - Farneski off left guard, tackle by Burroughs, gain of 19
1/10-M36 - Morris through the middle, tackle by Sheeran, gain of 7
2/3 -M29 - Farneski through the middle, tackle by B. Jones, gain of 1
3/2 -M28 - Farneski through the line, tackle by Maidlow, no gain
4/2 -M28 - Monk around right end, tackle by D. Williams, gain of 4
1/10-M24 - Farneski pass to Hairston broken up by Davis
2/10-M24 - Farneski pass to Monk in left corner of field, touchdown, 76 yds in 9 plays
Jacobs PAT good, Time 12:42 Elapsed Time: 3:41
SCORE: MICHIGAN STATE 49, SYRACUSE 14

2:18 MICHIGAN STATE
Jacobs kicks to Schramm at M14 tackle by Arkeilpane, return of 14 TO/MS 2:13
1/10-M28 - Petross off left tackle by Richardson, gain of 2
2/8 -M30 - Hughes outside right end, fumbles, recovered by Richardson, gain of 2 TO/MS 1:34

SYRACUSE
1/10-M32 - Farneski pass to Monk, tackle by Davis, gain of 19 TO/SU 1:16
1/10-M13 - Morris around right end steps out of bounds, gain of 7

2/3 -M6 - Farneski pass to Monk tipped by Otis
3/3 -M6 - Farneski outside right end, touchdown, 6 yd run, 32 yards in 4 plays
Jacobs PAT is good, Time: 13:59 Elapsed Time: :44
SCORE: MICHIGAN STATE 49, SYRACUSE 21

1:01 MICHIGAN STATE
Jacobs kicks onside to Land at M49, no return
1/10-M49 - Hans through the middle, tackle by Lang, gain of 3
2/7 -S48 - Reeves outside left end, tackle by Cameron & Neugebauer, loss of 1

**END OF GAME SCORE:
MICHIGAN STATE 49, SYRACUSE 21**

National Collegiate Athletic Association
FINAL TEAM STATISTICS
September 23, 1978

	SYRACUSE	MICHIGAN STATE
FIRST DOWNS	19	19
Rushing	11	9
Passing	8	9
Penalty	0	1
RUSHING ATTEMPTS	58	48
YARDS RUSHING	224	230
YARDS LOST RUSHING	56	38
NET YARDS RUSHING	168	192
NET YARDS PASSING	143	201
Passes Attempted	19	22
Passes Completed	8	10
Had Intercepted	1	1
TOTAL OFFENSIVE PLAYS	77	70
TOTAL NET YARDS	311	393
Average Gain Per Play	4.0	5.6
FUMBLES: NUMBER—LOST	10/6	2/2
PENALTIES: NUMBER—YARDS	3/57	3/35
INTERCEPTIONS: NUMBER—YARDS	1/6	1/26
NUMBER OF PUNTS—YARDS	8/292	5/200
Average Per Punt	36.5	40.0
PUNT RETURNS: NUMBER—YARDS	0/0	4/43
KICKOFF RETURNS: NUMBER—YARDS	6/106	4/85

SEPTEMBER 23, 1978

OHIO STATE VS. MINNESOTA

Memorial Stadium, Minneapolis
Temp: 71
Wind: SW 20 mph
Skies: Clear

FIRST QUARTER

Ohio State wins toss and elects to defend west goal. Minnesota to receive. Orosz kicks off to Edwards on the 3, returns 18 yards to UM21 (Laughlin).

14:54 MINNESOTA
1/10-MN21 - Barber quick pitch left, Minnesota clipping 37 yard penalty (Washington, Cousineau)
1/17-MN15 - Barber quick pitch left 1 yard (Cato, Ellis)
2/16-MN16 - Barber up the middle no gain (Cato)
3/16-MN16 - Barber at LT, Avery fumble on handoff, Danzler recovers

13:27 OHIO STATE
1/10-MN17 - Schlichter keeper left 6 yards (Murphy)
2/4 -MN11 - Campbell dive LT 3 yards (Tam)
3/1 -MN8 - Schichter keeper right side 4 yards (Friberg)
1/G -MN4 - Payton at LT no gain (Johnson, Burns)
2/G -MN4 - Payton slant right side 1 yard (Blanshan)
3/G -MN3 - Schlichter keeper right TD from 3 yards out. 17 yards in 6 plays 3:58 elapsed 11:02 left. Janakievski kick good
OHIO STATE 7, MINN 0

Orosz kicks off to Edwards on 2, returns 26 yards (Griffin)

10:57 MINNESOTA
1/10-MN28 - Barber at LT 3 yard gain (Cato)
2/7 -MN31 - Avery pass complete Barber 13 yard gain (Skillings, Griffin)
1/10-MN44 - Barber at RT 2 yards (Laughlin, Washington)
2/8 -MN46 - Avery fullback delay pass complete to Kitzmann 7 yard gain. Bailey made key block (Ellis)
3/1 -OS47 - Kitzmann dive at RT 2 yard gain (Cato)
1/10-OS45 - Avery pass intercepted by Ohio State's Danzler on OS28

8:32 OHIO STATE
1/10-OS28 - Springs at RT 2 yards (Blanshan)
2/8 -OS30 - Springs quick pitch left 1 yard gain (Friberg, Ronan)
3/7 -OS31 - Schlitchter pass complete to Donley diving 24 yard gain

1/10-MN45 - Springs option pitch left 9 yards (Edwards, Brown)
2/1 -MN36 - Springs at LT 2 yd gain (team)
1/10-MN34 - Campbell dive RT 5 yd gain (Ronan)
2/5 -MN29 - Schlichter option keeper right 4 yard gain (Murphy, Brown)
3/1 -MN25 - Payton at LT 2 yd gain (Burns)
1/10-MN23 - Schlichter pass flare to Springs no gain (Burns, Brown)
2/10-MN23 - Schlichter pass knocked into air by Ronan, intercepted by Friber on MN26

4:29 MINNESOTA
1/10-MN26 - Barber at RT 2 yd. gain (Cousineau)
2/8 -MN28 - Barber quick pitch right 2 yd gain (Cousineau)
3/6 -MN30 - Avery complete to Kitzmann fullback delay middle (Springs) but Gophers called for offensive interference on Dilulo 15 yd penalty
4/21 - MN15 - Smith punts to Guess on OS49 (Sytsma) no return (36 yd punt)

3:02 OHIO STATE
1/10-OS49 - Springs at RT 5 yd gain (Friberg)
2/5 -MN46 - Campbell power dive RT 7 yd gain (Burns)
1/10-MN39 - Campbell at RT 2 yd gain (Johnson)
2/8 -MN37 - Spring option pitch right 7 yard (Sytsma)
3/1 -MN30 - MN Friberg illegal procedure 5 yd penalty
1/10-MN25 - Campbell option dive LT 12 yd gain (Brown)
1/10-MN13 - Campbell same play 9 yd gain (Sytsma)
2/1 -MN4 - Payton at LT no gain (Burns)
3/1 -MN4 - Payton at LT 2 yd gain (Burns)
1/G -MN2 - MN illegal procedure 1 yd penalty as quarter comes to end

**END OF FIRST QUARTER:
OHIO STATE 7 MINNESOTA 0**

SECOND QUARTER

OHIO STATE
1/G -MN1 - Payton dive RT no gain (Burns, Brown)
2/G -MN1 - Payton at LT scores from 1 standing up 51 yards in 10 plays :32 secs elapsed 14:28 left Janakievski kick good
OHIO STATE 14, MINN 0

Orosz kicks off lands beyond endzone touchback

191

14:28 MINNESOTA
1/10-MN20 - Barber breaks open at RT 9 yd gain (Bell) (Ellis)
2/1 -MN29 - Kitzmann springs at LT 2 yd gain (Cato) (Cousineau)
1/10-MN31 - Barber up the middle 2 yd gain (Washington)
2/8 -MN33 - Avery back to pass, runs up middle 13 yd gain (Cousineau)
1/10-MN46 - Avery pass over middle to Bourquin off his hands incomplete
2/10-MN46 - Avery back to pass, runs and fumbles but recovers own fumble 1 yd loss (team)
3/11-MN45 - Barber quick delay at LT 3 yd gain (Cousineau)
4/8 -MN48 - Smith punts short, downed by MN Carr on OS38 14 yd punt

10:57 OHIO STATE
1/10-OS38 - Campbell up middle 6 yd gain (Blanshan)
2/4 -OS44 - Schlichter keeper, runs 8 yards, pitches to Springs for 6 yards
1/10-MN42 - Schlichter pass long down right sidelines for Gerald incomplete (Foxworth)
2/10-MN42 - Springs option pitch left 5 yd gain (Snyder)
3/5 -MN37 - Schlichter option keeper right 4 yd gain (Burns)
4/1 -MN33 - Schlichter option keeper left 3 yd gain (Burns)
1/10-MN30 - Campbell dive at RT 5 yd gain (Brown)
2/5 -MN25 - Schlichter option keeper right 3 yd gain (Brown, Murphy)
3/2 -MN22 - Schlichter option keeper left, breaks tackle 5 yds (Blanshan)
1/10-MN17 - Springs quick pitch right 1 yd (Murphy)
2/9 -MN16 - Schlichter knocked down in back field by Sytsma 2 yd loss
3/11-MN18 - Schlichter pass intended for Gerald beyond end zone incomplete
4/11-MN18 - Janakievski field goal try wide left no good from 35 yards out

6:51 MINNESOTA
1/10-MN20 - Artis quick pitch right no gain (Washington, Danzler)
2/10-MN20 - Artis at RT 4 yd gain (Cousineau, Ellis)
3/6 -MN24 - Avery back to pass tackled by Henson for no gain
4/6 -MN24 - Smith punts to Guess on OS38, returns 8 yards 38 yd punt (Faunhorst)

4:43 OHIO STATE
1/10-OS46 - Springs quick pitch right, breaks open 20 yards (Foxworth)
1/10-MN34 - Ohio State illegal procedure 5 yd penalty
1/15-MN39 - Schlichter pass intended for Donely knocked away by Foxworth

2/15-MN39 - Schlichter option right, falls down for 1 yd loss
3/16-MN40 - Schlichter pass down left sidelines, Edwards defending, ball knocked into air, Donley catches it while on ball 33 yard gain
1/G -MN7 - Springs option pitch right, Foxworth/Edwards tackle for 5 yd loss
2/G -MN12 - Schlichter options pass/run left runs 10 yds (Carr, Brown)
3/G -MN2 - Payton at LT 1 yd gain (Burns)
4/G -MN1 - Schlicther keeper left for 1 yd TD 54 yds in 8 plays 13:29 elapsed 1:31 left Janakievski kick good (47 PATs straight)
OHIO STATE 21, MINN 0

Orosz kick off to Edwards in end zone where he downs it for touchback
1:31 MINNESOTA
1/10-MN20 - Barber quick pitch right 5 yd gain (Skillings)
2/5 -MN25 - Barber at LT 5 yd gain (team)
1/10-MN30 - Avery back to pass, runs left 4 yd gain (Megaro, Danzler)
2/6 -MN34 - Avery pass complete to Bailey down right sidelines 45 yard gain :04 remaining
1/10-OS21 - Rogind field goal from 39 yards out GOOD 58 yards in 4 plays, field goal on 5th play

END OF FIRST HALF:
OHIO STATE 21 MINNESOTA 3

THIRD QUARTER

Orosz kicks off lands beyond endzone touchback
15:00 MINNESOTA
1/10-MN20 - Barber quick pitch right no gain (Cousineau)
2/10-MN20 - Avery pass over middle complete to Bailey 12 yds (Bell)
1/10-MN32 - Barber at RT, slips through for 8 yards (Guess)
2/2 -MN40 - Avery quick pass right flat complete to Bailey 5 yds (Bell)
1/10-MN45 - Barber at RT, breaks two tackles 10 yards (Ross, Guess)
1/10-OS45 - Artis quick pitch left Ross tackle for 2 yd loss
2/12-OS47 - Bailey end around right to left, Ellis trips him down from ground 10 yards
3/2 -OS37 - Artis up middle 1 yd gain (Sullivan)
4/1 -OS36 - Ohio State jumps offside 5 yd penalty
1/10-OS31 - Avery pass intended to Artis goes through hands incomplete
2/10-OS31 - Breault flanker reverse left 2 yd loss (Cato)
3/12-OS33 - Avery pass intended pass for Bailey low and incomplete
4/12-OS33 - Smith punt downed in endzone touchback

192

SEPTEMBER 23, 1978

8:51 OHIO STATE
1/10-OS20 - Campbell up middle 3 yd gain (Burns)
2/7 -OS23 - Springs quick pitch left 4 yd gain (Johnson)
3/3 -OS27 - Donley flanker reverse left (Sytsma)
OSU clipping 11 yard penalty to OS11
3/19-OS11 - Campbell up middle 9 yd gain (Johnson)
4/10-OS20 - Orosz punt rolls dead on MN29 51 yd punt

6:59 MINNESOTA
1/10-MN29 - Avery pass off hands of Bailey to Bourquin (Guess) 13 yd gain
1/10-MN42 - Barber quick pitch left 2 yards (Griffin)
2/8 -MN44 - Avery rolls right to pass, chased and throws out of bounds incomplete
3/8 -MN44 - Artis quick draw at LT 1 yd gain (Sullivan)
4/7 -MN45 - Smith punt to Guess on OS12 3yd runback (Peppe) (43 yd punt)

5:34 OHIO STATE
1/10-OS15 - Spring at LT 3 yd gain (Ronan, Burns)
2/7 -OS18 - Schlichter option keeper left 5 yd gain (Burns)
3/2 -OS23 - Springs quick pitch left 1 yd gain (Burns, Ronan)
4/1 -OS24 - Orosz punt to Edwards to MN27 12 yd runback (Volley) 49 yd punt

3:43 MINNESOTA
1/10-MN39 - Avery pass over middle to Bourquin low and incomplete
2/10-MN39 - Bailey flanker reverse left 11 yd gain (Guess)
1/10- 50 - Artis up middle 1 yd gain (Washington)
2/9 -OS49 - Avery pass incomplete to Bailey on flea flicker play
3/9 -OS49 - Avery back to pass, Cousineau crashing from linebacker 11 yd loss

4/20-MN40 - Smith punt to Guess to OS18 41 yd runback (Smith) 42 yd punt

1:59 OHIO STATE
1/10-MN41 - Springs quick pitch left 7 yd gain (Burns)
2/3 -MN34 - Campbell at LT 4 yd gain (Johnson)
1/10-MN30 - Springs over at RT 4 yd gain (Faunhorst)
2/6 -MN26 - Schlichter option keeper left 3 yd gain (Johnson, Sytsma)
3/3 -MN23 - Campbell dive at Rt 2 yd gain (Friberg, Blanshan)

END OF THIRD QUARTER:
OHIO STATE 21 MINNESOTA 3

FOURTH QUARTER

OHIO STATE
4/1 -MN21 - Payton at LT 4 yd gain (Ronan)
1/10-MN17 - Springs over LT 7 yd gain (Ronan)
2/3 -MN10 - Payton dive RT 2 yd gain (Cunningham, Burns)
3/1 -MN8 - Payton at LT 3 yd gain (Snyder Brown)
1/G -MN5 - Campbell dive LT 2 yd gain (Johnson, Burns)
2/G -MN3 - Springs option pitch left 3 yd TD 41 yard drive in 11 plays 2:12 elapsed, 12:48 left Janakievski kick no good fails on 48th consecutive PAT kick
OHIO STATE 27, MINNESOTA 3

Orosz kicks off to Edwards who downs ball in endzone

12:48 MINNESOTA
1/10-MN20 - Avery pass down left sidelines intercepted by Ellis on OS39

12:41 OHIO STATE
1/10-OS39 - Castignola (new QB) option keeper left 3 yds (Burns)
2/7 -OS42 - Castignola option keeper right 3 yd gain (Ronan)
3/4 -OS45 - Castignola pass knocked down in line by Blanshan incomplete
4/4 -OS45 - Orosz punt to Edwards on MN10 10 yd runback (Hutchings) 45 yd punt

11:24 MINNESOTA
1/10-MN20 - Thompson up middle 5 yd gain (Cousineau)
2/5 -MN25 - Carlson delay pass over middle complete to Dilulo 6 yds (Ellis)
1/10-MN31 - Carlson back to pass, Dulin tackle for 9 yd loss
2/19-MN22 - Carlson pass complete to Dilulo over middle 5 yds (Megaro)
3/14-MN27 - Carlson pass complete to Bourquin 10 yd gain (Megaro)
4/4 -MN37 - Smith punt to Guess on OS17 4 yd return (Burns) 46 yd punt

193

8:34 OHIO STATE
- 1/10-OS21 - Volley dive at RT 3 yd gain (Johnson)
- 2/7 -OS24 - Castignola option keeper left 8 yd run (Fahnhorst)
- 1/10-OS32 - Castignola dropped in back field by Sytsma (3 yd loss)
- 2/13-OS29 - Castignola back to pass, runs & fumbles but recovers himself for 2 yd gain (Johnson)
- 3/11-OS31 - Volley quick opener 18 yd run (Foxworth)
- 1/10-OS49 - Castignola option keeper right 16 yds (Snyder)
- 1/10-MN35 - Volley dive at LT 2 yd gain (Faunhorst)
- 2/8 -MN33 - Castignola option keeper right, Johnson tackle for no gain
- 3/8 -MN33 - Castignola option keeper left 4 yd gain (Gardner)
- 4/4 -MN29 - Johnson option pitch left 3 yd gain (Snyder) OSU fails on downs

4:07 MINNESOTA
- 1/10-MN25 - Carlson back to pass complete to Sonnefeld crossing right to left (Griffin) 22 yd gain
- 1/10-MN47 - Bailey flanker reverse left 11 yd gain (Schwartz)
- 1/10-OS42 - Carlson delay to Thompson complete over middle 8 yds (Megaro)
- 2/2 -OS34 - Carlson pass complete to Barber right flat OSU offside 5 yd penalty
- 1/10-OS29 - Carlson screen right to Thompson 13 yd gain (Griffin)
- 1/10-OS16 - Barber at LT 1 yd gain (Griffin)
- 2/9 -OS15 - Carlson crossing pattern right to left complete to Dilulo 15 yd TD pass (Dilulo's first career TD) 75 yds in 6 plays 13:38 elapsed, 1:42 left Rogind kick good **OHIO STATE 27 , MINNESOTA 10** (Also, Carlson's 1st TD pass)

Rogind kicks off onside recovered by Castignola on OS46

1:42 OHIO STATE
- 1/10-OS46 - Castignola option keeper left 1 yd gain (Carr)
- 2/9 -OS47 - Payton dive RT 8 yd gain (Fahnhorst)

- 3/1 -MN45 - Castignola option keeper right 3 yd gain (Fahnhorst)
- 1/10-MN42 - Belmer dive LT 3 yds (Allison)
- 2/7 -MN39 - Murray quick pitch right 3 yd gain (Fahnhorst)

END OF GAME:
OHIO STATE 27 MINNESOTA 10

National Collegiate Athletic Association
FINAL TEAM STATISTICS
September 23, 1978

	OHIO STATE	MINNE-SOTA
First Downs	20	17
Rushing	17	7
Passing	2	9
Penalty	1	2
Rushing Attempts	73	36
Yards Rushing	311	122
Yards Lost Rushing	11	23
Net Yards Rushing	300	99
Net Yards Passing	57	174
Passes Attempted	8	21
Passes Completed	3	13
Had Intercepted	1	2
Total Offensive Plays	81	57
Total Net Yards	357	273
Average Gain Per Play	4.4	4.8
Fumbles: Number—Lost	1/0	2/1
Penalties: Number—Yards	4/26	5/33
Interceptions: Number—Yards	2/0	1/0
Numbers of Punts—Yards	3/145	7/252
Average Per Punt	48.3	36.0
Punt Returns: Number—Yards	5/62	2/22
Kickoff Returns: Number—Yards	0/0	2/44

SEPTEMBER 23, 1978

WISCONSIN VS. NORTHWESTERN
Dyche Stadium, Evanston
FIRST QUARTER

Northwestern co-captains Pat Geegan and Mike Kranz meet at midfield with Wisconsin tri-captains David Charles, Dave Crossen, and Dan Relich for the toss of the coin. Wisconsin wins the toss and elects to receive. Northwestern will kickoff and defend the south goal.
Mirkopulos kickoff for NU taken by Souza at the UW11 and returned 34 yds PENALTY: clipping UW accepted

14:51: WISCONSIN
1/10-UW27 - Matthews rt for 6 yds (Corona)
2/4 -UW33 - Stauss lt for 12 yds (Geegan)
1/10-UW45 - Matthews rg for 4 yds (Weitzman)
2/6 -UW49 - Matthews lt for 1 yd (Berg)
3/5 -50 - Stauss draw play middle for 22 yds (Geegan)
1/10-NU28 - Josten keeper re for 13 yds (Berg, Adams)
1/10-NU15 - Josten fumbles, recovered by NU Payne at NU17 (loss of 2 yds)

11:53 NORTHWESTERN
1/10-NU17 - Strasser pass to Mishler complete for six yds (Levenick)
2/4 -NU23 - Strasser pass for McGee incomplete PENALTY: motion NU accepted
2/9 -NU18 - Strasser pass for North incomplete
3/9 -NU18 - Hill sweep for 3 yds (Crossen)
4/6 -NU21 - Christensen punt for NU taken by Matthews at the UW 40 for -1 yds
PENALTY: clipping UW accepted

10:22 WISCONSIN
1/10-UW24 - Matthews re for no gain (Kendzicky)
2/10-UW24 - Josten pass to Souza complete for 9 yds (Adams, Knafelc)
3/1 -UW33 - Stauss middle for 2 yds (Stasiewicz)
1/10-UW35 - Josten keeper over rg fo 2 yds (Kern)
2/8 -UW37 - Matthews pitchout re for 7 yds (Kern) PENALTY: personal foul NU accepted
1/10-NU41 - Josten pass to Krepfle for 25 yds
1/10-NU16 - Josten pass to Souza incomplete PENALTY: pass interference NU accepted
1/G -NU7 - Stauss middle for 3 yds (Berg)
2/G -NU4 - Stauss re for 2 yds (Robinett, Kern)
3/G -NU2 - Stauss for 2 yds and a touchdown (6:19) PAT: Veith kick good 76 yards in 10 plays
SCORE: WISCONSIN 7 NORTHWESTERN 0

Brhely kickoff for UW taken by Webb at the NU10 and returned 3 yds

6:14 NORTHWESTERN
1/10-NU13 - Strasser pass to McGee complete for 5 yds (Gordon)
2/5 -NU18 - Hill sweep re for 3 yds (Cabral)
3/2 -NU21 - Strasser pass to McGee complete for 79 yds and a touchdown (4:46) PAT: Mirkopulos kick good 87 yards in 3 plays
SCORE: NORTHWESTERN 7 WISCONSIN 7

Mirkopulos kickoff for NU goes out of bounds. Penalty: ill. procedure NU Mirkopulos kickoff for NU taken by Souza at UW13 and returned 24 yds

4:38 WISCONSIN
1/10-UW37 - Stauss lt for 8 yds (Kern)
2/2 -UW45 - Matthews re for 2 yds (Geegan)
1/10-UW47 - Stauss lt for 8 yds (Hoffman)
2/2 -NU45 - Stauss middle for 1 yd (Kern)
3/1 -NU44 - Josten keeper middle for 2 yds (Corona)
1/10-NU42 - Josten pass to Krepfle complete for 9 yds (Hoffman)
2/1 -NU33 - Stauss lt for 4 yds
1/10-NU29 - Josten pass for Sydnor complete for 6 yds (Schanzer)
2/4 -NU23 - Stauss rg for 23 yds and a touchdown (0:39) PAT: Veith kick good 63 yards in 9 plays
SCORE: WISCONSIN 14 NORTHWESTERN 7

Bhrely kickoff for UW taken by Webb at the NU 2 and returned 2 yards

0:34 NORTHWESTERN
1/10-NU4 - Strasser sneak for 2 yards

END OF FIRST QUARTER:
WISCONSIN 14, NORTHWESTERN 7

SECOND QUARTER

NORTHWESTERN
2/8 -NU6 - Strasser pass to Poulos incomplete
3/8 -NU6 - Strasser pass to Poulos complete for 15 yds (Anderson)
1/10-NU21 - Strasser sacked by Relich for -4 yds
2/14-NU17 - Mishler draw play for 4 yds (Sawicki)
3/10-NU21 - Strasser pass to North complete for 9 yds
4/1 -NU30 - Strasser sneak for 1 yd (Schremp)
1/10-NU31 - Strasser pass to Hill complete for 11 yds (Ahrens)
1/10-NU42 - Strasser pass to Hill complete for 8 yds
2/2 -50 - Strasser pass to North incomplete
3/2 -50 - Strasser pass to Poulos incomplete
4/2 -50 - Christensen punt taken by Stauss at UW19 and returned 5 yds 31 yd kick

195

WISCONSIN
1/10-NW24 - Josten pass to complete to Stauss for 3 yds
2/7 -UW27 - Mathews middle for 6 yds
3/1 -UW33 - Josten sacked by Kendzicky for -3 yds
4/4 -UW30 - Kiltz punt for UW taken by Geegan at the NU31 and returned 3 yds 39 yds kick

9:04 NORTHWESTERN
1/10-NU34 - Strasser pass intercepted by Anderson and returned to NU34

9:01 WISCONSIN
1/10-NU34 - Matthews lt for 9 yds (Hoffman)
2/1 -NU25 - Josten sneak for 2 yds (team)
1/10-NU23 - Matthews middle for 17 yds (Geegan)
1/G -NU6 - Matthews re for 3 yds (Lawrence, McGlade)
2/G -NU3 - Stauss middle for 2 yds (Dunlea)
3/G -NU1 - Matthews middle for no gain
4/G -NU1 - Richardson middle for 1 yd and a touchdown (5:37) PAT: Veich kick good 34 yards in 7 plays SCORE:
SCORE: WISCONSIN 21 NORTHWESTERN 7

Brhely kickoff taken by Hill at NU4 and returned 68 yards
5:27 NORTHWESTERN
1/10-UW28 - Mishler lt for 3 yds (Crossen)
2/7 -UW25 - Strasser pass to Hill complete for 4 yds (Sawicki)
3/3 -UW21 - Strasser pass to Hill complete for 6 yds (Ahrens)
1/10-UW15 - Mishler re for 4 yds (Crossen)
2/6 -UW11 - Strasser thrown for -5 yds loss by Crossen
3/11 -UW16 - Strasser sacked by Cabrak -7 yds
4/18-UW23 - Mirkopulos field goal attempt from 39 yards no good

2:28 WISCONSIN
1/10-UW23 - Matthews middle for 2 yds (Kendzicky)
2/8 -UW25 - Matthews rt for 4 yds (Kern)
3/4 -UW29 - Josten keeper re for 2 yds (McGlade)
4/2 -UW31 - Kiltz punt taken by Geegan at NU18 and returned 9 yds 51 yard kick
PENALTY: holding NU accepted
0:14 NORTHWESTERN
1/10-NU14 - Mishler middle for 8 yds (Ahrens)

END OF HALF:
WISCONSIN 21, NORTHWESTERN 7

THIRD QUARTER

Brhely kickoff taken by Hill at NU1 and returned 19 yds (Levenick)

14:55 NORTHWESTERN
1/10-NU20 - PENALTY: ill. procedure NU accepted
1/15-NU15 - Strasser pass to Poulos complete for 14 yds (Gordon)
2/1 -NU29 - Mishler middle for 2 yds (Crossen)
1/10-NU31 - Mishler lg for 4 yds (Cabral)
2/6 -NU35 - Strasser pass to Mishler complete for -2 yds (Cabral)
3/8 -NU33 - Strasser pass to North broken up by Johnson
4/8 -NU33 - Christenson punt fair caught by Stauss at UW42 25 yd punt

12:16 WISCONSIN
1/10-UW42 - Josten keeper for 1 yd (Berg)
2/9 -UW43 - Josten pass to Charles complete for 19 yds (Kern)
1/10-NU38 - Josten pass to Souza incomplete
PENALTY: ineligible receiver downfield UW accepted
1/25-UW47 - Matthews re for 12 yds (Berg, Payne)
2/13 -NU41 - Josten keeper le for 3 yds (Schanzer)
3/10-NU38 - Josten pass to Mathews complete for 8 yds (Hoffman)
4/2 -NU30 - PENALTY: delay of game UW accepted
4/7 -NU35 - Stauss carried 4 yds off fake punt (Schanzer)

8:40 NORTHWESTERN
1/10-NU31 - Strasser pass to Poulos incomplete
2/10-NU31 - Strasser pass to McGee incomplete
3/10-NU31 - Strasser pass to Schmidt complete for 4 yds (Gordon)
4/6 -NU35 - Christenson punt taken by Matthews at the UW22 and returned 78 yds for a touchdown (8:07) 43 yard punt
PAT: Veith kick good
SCORE: WISCONSIN 28 NORTHWESTERN 7

SEPTEMBER 23, 1978

Brhely kickoff rolls into end zone for a touchback
8:07 NORTHWESTERN
1/10-NU20 - Mishler middle for 14 yds (Johnson)
1/10-NU34 - Mishler rt for 3 yds (Cabral)
2/7 -NU37 - Strasser pass to McGee incomplete
3/7 -NU37 - Strasser pass to Mishler complete for 6 yds (Holm)
4/1 -NU43 - Hill pitch le for 2 yds (Schremp)
1/10-NU45 - Strasser sacked by Athems fo -9 yds
2/19-NU36 - Strasser pass complete to Hill for 3 yds (Levenick)
3/16-NU39 - Strasser pass to McGee complete for 14 yds (Gordon)
4/2 -UW47 - Strasser pass to North complete for 20 yds (Gordon)
1/10-UW27 - Mishler pass to McGee incomplete
2/10-UW27 - Strasser pass to Poulos incomplete
3/10-UW27 - Strasser pass to Hill complete for -5 yds (Cabral)
4/15-UW32 - Strasser pass to McGee incomplete PENALTY: pass interference UW
1/10-UW11 - Strasser pass to McGee incomplete
2/10-UW11 - Strasser pass to Hill incomplete
3/10-UW11 - Strasser pass to Hill incomplete
PENALTY: roughing the passer UW
3/5 -UW6 - Hill re for 5 yds (Crossen)
1/G -UW1 - Mishler fumble recovered by Erdmann at the UW1

2:47 WISCONSIN
1/10-UW1 - Josten keeper for 3 yds (Dunlea)
2/7 -UW4 - Stauss rt for 22 yds (McGlade)
1/10-UW26 - Stauss rt for 7 yds
2/3 -UW33 - Matthews re for 5 yds (Kendzicky)
1/10-UW38 - Josten recovers his own fumble for no gain

**END OF THIRD QUARTER:
WISCONSIN 28, NORTHWESTERN 7**

FOURTH QUARTER

WISCONSIN
2/10-UW38 - Stauss draw for 3 yds (Kern)
3/7 -UW41 - Stauss lt for 3 yds (Dunlea)
4/4 -UW44 - Klitz punt rolls out of bounds at NU19 37 yard punt

13:33 NORTHWESTERN
1/10-NU19 - Strasser pass to North complete for 14 yds (Johnson)
1/10-NU33 - Strasser pass to Schmitt complete for 16 yds (Erdmann)
1/10-NU49 - Strasser sacked by Aherns for -7 yds
2/17-NU42 - Strasser sacked by Vine for -7 yds
3/24-NU35 - Strasser pass to Schmitt complete for 11 yds (Anderson)
4/13-NU46 - Christenson punt rolls dead at UW 10 44 yard punt

197

10:46 WISCONSIN
1/10-UW10 - Matthews re for 7 yds (Geegan)
2/3 -UW17 - Josten keeper for 2 yds (Geegan)
3/1 -UW19 - Josten sneak for 3 yds (Taylor)
1/10-UW22 - Matthews middle for 11 yds (McGlade)
1/10-UW33 - Josten keeper re for 9 yds (Rogers, Geegan)
2/1 -UW42 - Matthews middle for 15 yds (Berg)
1/10-NU43 - Matthews fumble recovered by NU Knafelc at NU35 8 yd gain

7:30 NORTHWESTERN
1/10-NU35 - Schmitt middle for 1 yd (Krepfle)
2/9 -NU36 - Strasser pass broken up by Vine at line of scrimmage (Strasser pass)
3/9 -NU36 - Strasser pass to Schmitt incomplete
4/9 -NU36 - PENALTY: illegal touch by lineman
4/14-NU31 - Christenson fair caught by Matthews 36 yd punt

6:42 WISCONSIN
1/10-UW33 - Greene keeper for -1 yd
2/11-UW32 - Greene keeper for 1 yd (Berg)
3/10-UW33 - Greene keeper le for 10 yds (McGlade)
1/10-UW43 - Mohapp lg for 5 yds (Geegan)
2/5 -UW48 - Richardson middle for 7 yds (Minn)
1/10-NU45 - Shumway middle for 4 yds, recovers own fumble (Berg)
2/6 -NU41 - Greene keeper lt for 2 yds (Dunlea)
3/4 -NU39 - Greene keeper le for 4 yds (Finn)
1/10-NU35 - Greene pass to Braker batted down by Berg
2/10-NU35 - Shumway lt for 4 yds
3/6 -NU31 - Cohee middle 3 yds (Taylor)
4/3 -NU28 - Greene pass to Stracka incomplete

0:55 NORTHWESTERN
1/10-NU28 - Washington re for 5 yds (team)
2/5 -NU33 - Mishler middle for 1 yd (Spurlin)

END OF GAME:
WISCONSIN 28, NORTHWESTERN 7

National Collegiate Athletic Association
FINAL TEAM STATISTICS

	WISCONSIN	NORTHWESTERN
First Downs	23	13
Rushing	19	5
Passing	2	7
Penalty	2	1
Rushing Attempts	61	24
Yards Rushing	332	54
Yards Lost Rushing	-6	-39
Net Yards Rushing	326	15
Net Yards Passing	79	238
Passes Attempted	9	35
Passes Completed	7	20
Had Intercepted	0	1
Total Offensive Plays	70	59
Total Net Yards	405	253
Average Gain Per Play	5.8	4.3
Fumbles: Number—Lost	4/2	1/1
Penalties: Number—Yards	6/77	7/58
Interceptions: Number—Yards	1/6	0/0
Number of Punts—Yards	3/127	6/218
Average Per Punt	42.3	36.3
Punt Returns: Number—Yards	3/82	2/12
Kickoff Returns: Number—Yards	2/58	4/92

SEPTEMBER 23, 1978

OHIO UNIVERSITY
VS.
PURDUE
Ross-Ade Stadium
Temp: 72°
Wind: ESE 10 mph
Skies: Partly Cloudy
FIRST QUARTER

Coin Flip: Purdue wins toss will receive, Ohio will kickoff and defend south goal Green kickoff to Moss on P1 yd line return to P27, 59 yd kick, 26 yd return.

PURDUE
1/10-P27 - Pope pitch left, 8 yds. (Green)
2/2 -P35 - Macon rg, 3 yds. (Lucas-Groves)
1/10-P38 - Pope re, 7 yds. (Green)
2/3 -P45 - Pope rt, 1 yd. (Ryan-Johnson)
3/2 -P46 - Pope rt, 1 yd. fumble Groves recovered for Ohio

13:42 OHIO
1/10-P47 - Yoho lg, 3 yds. (Marks-Jackson)
2/7 -P44 - Turpin roll left, 2 yds. (Marks-Clark)
3/5 -P42 - Turpin roll right, lost 4 yds. (Loushin)
4/9 -P46 - Green punt to Pope, fair catch on P10 yd line, 36 yd kick no return

12:05 PURDUE
1/10-P10 - Macon rt, 16 yds. (Hulburt)
1/10-P26 - Macon lt, 4 yds. (Lucas)
2/6 -P30 - Herrmann to pass, lost 7 yds. (Seymour)
3/13-P23 - Macon on draw, 2 yds. (Ryan-Johnson)
4/11-P25 - Eagin punt to Ohio 41, dead, 34 yd kick, no return

10:01 OHIO
1/10-O41 - Babcock rt, 17 yds. (Harris)
1/10-P42 - Babcock rt, 2 yds. (Floyd)
2/8 -P40 - Turpin to Summers, incomplete
3/8 -P40 - Babcock on draw, 4 yds. (Loushin-Marks)
4/4 -P36 - Green punt to P2, 34 yd kick, no return

8:18 PURDUE
1/10-P2 - Pope rg, 12 yds. (Lemon)
1/10-P14 - Pope pitch left, 30 yds.
1/10-P44 - Williams cut in at rt, 4 yds. (team)
2/6 -P48 - Herrmann to Burrell, incomplete
3/6 -P48 - Herrmann to Burrell, incomplete
4/6 -P48 - Eagin punt to Givens on 023, return to O33, 29 yd kick 10 yd return

7:13 OHIO
1/10-O33 - Babcock lg, 1 yd. (Loushin)
2/9 -O34 - Turpin keep right, 2 yds. (Motts)
3/7 -O36 - Turpin to Geisler, incomplete Ohio clipping declined
4/7 -O36 - Green punt to Pope on P18, return to P17, 46 yd kick -1 return

5:58 PURDUE
1/10-P17 - Williams up middle, 5 yds. (Ryan)
2/5 -P22 - Augustyniak at le, 4 yds. (Ryan)
3/1 -P26 - Augustyniak lg, 5 yds. (Ryan)
1/10-P31 - Herrmann to Young, 7 yds. (Carifa)
2/3 -P38 - Williams pitch left, lost 1 yd. (Carifa-Lucas)
3/4 -P37 - Macon pitch right, 1 yd. (Ryan-Seymour)
4/3 -P38 - Eagin punt to Givens on O16 return to O15, 46 yd punt -1 return Ohio clip on return, 7 yd. penalty

2:52 OHIO
1/10-O8 - Turpin keep, rg, 3 yds. (Johanson-Motts)
2/7 -O11 - Turpin keep, rg, 2 yds. (Johanson-Motts)
3/5 -O13 - Turpin QB draw, 2 yds. (Johanson-Clark)
4/3 -O15 - Green punt to W Smith on O48 fumbled, recovered Puthoff O47

1:04 OHIO
1/10-O47 - Turpin to Geisler, 8 yds. (Motts)
2/2 -P45 - Babcock lg, 1 yd. (Jackson-Floyd)
3/1 -P44 - time out Ohio
3/1 -P44 - Turpin keep lg, 2 yds. (Turner-Motts)

END OF FIRST QUARTER:
PURDUE 0, OHIO UNIVERSITY 0

199

SECOND QUARTER

OHIO
1/10-P42 - Turpin roll right, lost 3 yds. fumbled but recovered
2/13-P45 - Babcock lg, 1 yd. (Loushin)
3/12-P44 - Turpin to pass, run, 6 yds. (Marks)
4/6 -P38 - Green punt to Purdue end zone, 38 yd punt no return

12:55 PURDUE
1/10-P20 - Macon on draw, 2 yds. (Hulbert-Groves)
2/8 -P22 - Macon le, 3 yds. (Lucas)
3/5 -P25 - Herrmann to Macon, 4 yds. (Lucas)
4/1 -P29 - Macon rg, 2 yds. (Lucas-Ryan)
1/10-P31 - Herrmann to Harris, incomplete
2/10-P31 - Pope le, 24 yds.
1/10-045 - Herrmann to Harris, 11 yds. (Carifa)
1/10-034 - Pope inside re, no gain
2/10-034 - Pope lt, 5 yds. (Groves)
3/5 -029 - Herrmann keep right, 3 yds. (Lucas-Ryan)
4/2 -026 - Pope le, 6 yds. (Givens)
1/10-020 - Harris reverse right, 13 yds. (Lucas-Lemon)
1/G -07 - Pope pitch left, lost 3 yds. (Lemon)
2/G -010 - Herrmann to Young, incomplete
3/G -010 - Herrmann to Harris, 10 yds. TOUCHDOWN, 15 plays, 80 yds. PAT Sovereen, kick, Burrell hold good
SCORE: PURDUE 7, OHIO 0

Sovereen kickoff to Yoho on O10, return to O21, 50 yd kick, 11 yd return.

7:57 OHIO
1/10-021 - Yoho rg, 17 yds. (Moss-Supan)
1/10-038 - Turpin to Geisler, 15 yds. (Moss)
1/10-P47 - Yoho rt, 5 yds. (Clark-Jackson)
2/5 -P42 - James lt, lost 1 yd. (Loushin)
3/6 -P43 - Turpin to Geisler, 10 yds. (Marks)
1/10-P33 - Yoho rt, 2 yds. Cooper injured (Clark-Jackson)
2/8 -P31 - Grogan pitch left, Ohio illegal motion, 5 yd penalty
2/13-P36 - James rg, 5 yds. fumbled, W Harris recovered

5:15 PURDUE
1/10-P31 - Augustyniak rg. 9 yds. (Oliver at QB) (Johnson-Seymour)
2/1 -P40 - Augustyniak rt, 1 yd.
1/10-P41 - Oliver keep left, 4 yds. (Jontony)
2/6 -P45 - Oliver roll right, Purdue holding, (1st penalty for Purdue in 6 quarters) 17 yd penalty
2/23-P28 - Oliver lost 4 yds.
3/27-P24 - McCall le on draw, 11 yds. (Seymour-Lucas)
4/16-P35 - Eagin punt to Ohio 21 yd line, dead, 44 yd punt no return

3:10 OHIO
1/10-021 - Turpin to Geisler, 14 yds. (Marks)
1/10-035 - Grogan rt, no gain (Jackson-Clark)
2/10-035 - Babcock rg, 6 yds. (Marks)
3/4 -041 - Babcock rg, 2 yds. (Motts-Clark)
4/2 -043 - Green punt to Babcock on short snap le, 5 yds. (Thompson)
1/10-048 - Turpin to Volkmer, incomplete
2/10-048 - Turpin roll left, 8 yds. (Marks-Loushin)
3/2 -P44 - time out Ohio
3/2 -P44 - Babcock rg, 1 yd. (Motts-Loushin)
4/1 -P43 - Turpin roll left, lost 1 yd. (Turner) Purdue time out

0:28 PURDUE
1/10-P44 - Herrmann to Pope, 34 yds. (Kelch)
1/10-022 - Herrmann to Young on screen left, 13 yds. (Seymour-Carifa) Purdue time out
1/G -09 - Herrmann to Harris, incomplete
2/G -09 - Herrmann to R Smith, incomplete
3/G -09 - Sovereen attempt 27 yd field goal, Burrell hold pass from center bobbled no good

**END OF SECOND QUARTER:
PURDUE 7, OHIO UNIVERSITY 0**

THIRD QUARTER

Miami will receive, Purdue will kickoff and defend south goal. Sovereen kickoff to Summers in Ohio end zone, 60 yd kick no return

OHIO
1/10-020 - Turpin right keeper, 2 yds. (Turner-Marks)
2/8 -022 - Turpin roll left, 4 yds. (Loushin-Motts)
3/4 -026 - Turpin to Geisler, incomplete
4/4 -026 - Green punt to Pope on P24, fumbled recovered, 50 yd kick, 1 yd return

13:38 PURDUE
1/10-P25 - Macon up middle, 2 yds. (Lucas-Johnson)
2/8 -P27 - Herrmann to Young, 14 yds. (Kelch-Hulburt)
1/10-P41 - Pope swing left, no gain (Hulburt-Johnson)
2/10-P41 - Herrmann to Young, 21 yds. (Short)
1/10-038 - Pope left, 2 yds.
2/8 -036 - Herrmann to Harris, incomplete
3/8 -036 - Shotgun: Herrmann to Burrell, incomplete
4/8 -036 - Eagin punt out of bounds on Ohio 12 yd line, 24 yd kick no return

SEPTEMBER 23, 1978

11:12 OHIO
1/10-O12 - Turpin roll right, 1 yd loss (Motts)
1/11-O11 - Turpin roll left, 1 yd. (Marks-Loushin)
3/10-O12 - Grogan lt, 3 yds. (Jackson-Loushin)
4/7 -O15 - Green punt to Gallivan fair catch at midfield, 35 yd kick no return

9:18 PURDUE
1/10- 50 - Herrmann to Harris, 46 yds. (Kelch)
1/G -04 - Macon up middle, 3 yds. (Lucas)
2/G -01 - Pope lt, no gain (Lemon-Lucas)
3/G -01 - Pope pitch right, lost 4 yds. (Carifa)
4/G -05 - Sovereen attempt 22 yd field goal Burrell hold, good 5 plays, 50 yds.
SCORE: PURDUE 10, OHIO 0

Sovereen kickoff to Perkins on O16 return to O21, 44 yd kick 5 yd return.

7:18 OHIO
1/10-O21 - Grogan rg, 2 yds. (Marks-Motts)
2/8 -O23 - Grogan rt, lost 1 yd. (Floyd-Clark)
3/9 -O22 - Yoho rt, 4 yds. (Clark)
4/5 -O26 - Green punt to Sullivan on P40 return to P45, 34 yd kick, 5 yd return

5:15 PURDUE
1/10-P45 - Pope up middle, 1 yd. (Moore)
2/9 -P46 - Pope pitch right, 1 yd. (Johnson-Carifa)
3/8 -P47 - Shotgun: Screen over middle to Pope, 5 yds. (Johnson-Ryan)
4/3 -O48 - Eagin punt to Givens on O2 return to O2, 46 yd kick no return

3:32 OHIO
1/10-O2 - Turpin keep middle, 2 yds. (Loushin)
2/8 -O4 - Yoho rt, lost 1 yd. (Floyd)
3/9 -O3 - Yoho rg, no gain (Motts)
4/9 -O3 - Green punt to O44 dead, 41 yd kick no return

1:43 PURDUE
1/10-O44 - Herrmann to Burrell, 22 yds. (Short)
1/10-O22 - Macon rt, 3 yds. (Ryan-Johnson)
2/7 -O19 - Herrmann to Burrell, 19 yds. touchdown 3 plays 44 yds PAT Sovereen kick Burrell hold, good
SCORE: PURDUE 17, OHIO 0

Sovereen kickoff to Carifa on O6 return to O20, 54 yd kick 14 yd return. Summers injured on play

0:55 OHIO
1/10-O20 - Turpin to Geisler, 9 yds. (Supan-Johanson)
2/1 -O29 - Turpin fumble hand off, recovered, no gain

END OF THIRD QUARTER:
PURDUE 17, OHIO UNIVERSITY 0

FOURTH QUARTER

OHIO
3/1 -O29 - Yoho inside re, 1 yd (Floyd, Loushin)
1/10-O30 - Grogan pitch right, 3 yds (Supan)
2/7 -O33 - Turpin to Geisler, incomplete
3/7 -O33 - Turpin to pass, lost 6 yds (Floyd)
4/13-O27 - Green punt to Gallivan on P27 47 yd kick, no return

13:22 PURDUE
1/10-P27 - Oliver at QB: L Harris on reverse, 2 yds (Lemon, Carifa)
2/8 -P29 - Oliver to Speedy, incomplete
3/8 -P29 - Augustyniak rt, 7 yds (Groves, Johnson)
4/1 -P36 - Eagin punt to O18 dead, 46 yd kick no return

11:48 OHIO
1/10-O18 - Turpin fumbles snap, lost 3 yds
2/13-O15 - James on draw, no gain (Loushin, Turner)
3/13-O15 - Turpin rolled left, lost 12 yds (Jackson)
4/25-O3 - Green punt to O48 dead, 45 yd kick no return

9:48 PURDUE
1/10-O48 - McCall le, 1 yd (Groves)
2/9 -O47 - Herrmann to Burrell, 17 yds
1/10-O30 - Jones pitch left, 1 yd (Givens, Johnson)
2/9 -O29 - Herrmann to Eubank, incomplete offensive pass interference Purdue penalty 15 yds
3/24-O44 - Herrmann to Burrell, incomplete
4/24-O44 - Eagin punt to Ohio end zone, 44 yd kick no return

8:02 OHIO
1/10-O20 - Turpin keep right, 4 yds. (Floyd, Supan)
2/6 -O24 - James pitch right, 9 yds (Harris, Moss)
1/10-O33 - Turpin to pass, lost 8 yds (Loushin, Floyd)
2/18-O25 - Turpin to Yoho, 11 yds (Floyd, Moss)
3/7 -O36 - Turpin to James, intercepted by Johanson on O43 return to O35, 8 yd return

5:31 PURDUE
1/10-O35 - Oliver at QB: Robinson rg, 4 yds (Ryan, Lemon)
2/6 -O31 - L Harris swing right, lost 4 yds
3/10-O35 - Oliver to McCall, 35 yd. touchdown, 3 plays 35 yds
PAT Sovereen kick Barr hold, good
SCORE: PURDUE 24, OHIO 0

201

Penalty on touchdown play assessed against Ohio 15 yds
Purdue will kick off on Ohio 45 yd line
Sovereen kickoff to Carifa on O8 return to O25, 37 yd kick 17 yd return

OHIO
1/10-O25 - Turpin to Volkmer, 10 yds, Purdue personal foul 15 yds (Seneff)
1/10- 50 - Turpin to Yoho, 14 yds (Key)
1/10-P36 - James pitch right, 3 yds (Pope)
2/7 -P33 - Turpin to Yoho, incomplete, Yoho injured time 3:13
3/7 -P33 - Turpin keep left, 9 yds. (Adamle)
1/10-P24 - Grammison pitch left, fumbles lost 9 yds Purdue recovered

PURDUE
1/10-P33 - Purdue 3rd offensive team in
1/10-P33 - Myer rg, lost 1 yd (Lucas, Lemon)
2/11-P32 - Keith pitch left, no gain
3/11-P32 - Doria lt, 12 yds (Givens)
1/10-P44 - Robinson rg, 3 yds (Groves, Lucas)
2/7 -P47 - Pruitt rg, 12 yds
1/10-O41 - Pruitt lg, 1 yd
2/9 -O40 - Guyton pitch left, Ohio 15 yd penalty (Lemon, Moore) face mask
1/10-O25 - McAfee lt, 3 yds (Seymour)

FINAL SCORE
PURDUE 24 OHIO UNIVERSITY 0

National Collegiate Athletic Association
FINAL TEAM STATISTICS

	OHIO	PURDUE
First Downs	13	23
Rushing	7	12
Passing	5	10
Penalty	1	1
Rushing Attempts	52	55
Yards Rushing	147	245
Yards Lost Rushing	49	32
Net Yards Rushing	98	213
Net Yards Passing	91	258
Passes Attempted	15	25
Passes Completed	8	14
Had Intercepted	1	0
Total Offensive Plays	67	80
Total Net Yards	189	471
Average Gain Per Play	2.8	5.9
Fumbles: Number—Lost	5/2	4/3
Penalties: Number—		
Yards	4/42	3/47
Interceptions: Number—		
Yards	0/0	1/8
Number of Punts—Yards	11/437	8/313
Average Per Punt	39.7	39.1
Punt Returns: Number—		
Yards	3/9	5/5
Kickoff Returns:		
Number—Yards	4/46	1/26

SEPTEMBER 23, 1978

MICHIGAN VS. NOTRE DAME
Notre Dame Stadium
Temp.: 66
Wind: E/5mph
FIRST QUARTER

Michigan won the toss and elected to receive.
Notre Dame to defend south goal
Huckleby returned Male's kick 18 to M18 (Hartwig)
MICHIGAN
1/10-M18 - Davis fumbled and Zettek recovered on M17

14:45 NOTRE DAME
1/10-M17 - Heavens pulled for 8 (Owens)
2/2 -M9 - Heavens smashed for 3 (Owens)
1/G -M7 - Ferguson slanted for no gain
2/G -M7 - Montana passed to Grindinger for a TD Unis extra point good.
SCORE: NOTRE DAME 7 MICHIGAN 0

Male kicked into the end zone, but Notre Dame was penalized for a personal foul, placing the ball on the M35.
13:07 MICHIGAN
1/10-M35 - Huckleby gained 3 (Leopold)
2/7 -M38 - Huckleby hit center for 5 (Golic)
3/2 -M43 - Notre Dame drew an illegal procedure penalty
1/10-M48 - Huckleby lost 1 (Calhoun)
2/11-M47 - Leach passed to Davis for 2, but Notre Dame was penalized 15 for personal foul
1/10-N34 - Leach overthrew Feaster in the end zone
2/10-N34 - Leach pass to Huckleby was incomplete
3/10-N34 - Leach's pass intended for Marsh was incomplete
4/10-N34 - Willner then punted into the end zone (34 yd punt)

10:26 NOTRE DAME
1/10-N20 - Heavens broke over right end for 23 yds. (Simpkins)
1/10-N43 - Ferguson hit for 4 (Owens)
2/6 -N47 - Ferguson hit for 3 (Godfrey)
3/3 - 50 - Montana passed to Grindinger for 17 (Harden)
1/10-M33 - Heavens gained 3 (Godfrey)
2/7 -M30 - Notre Dame penalized for illegal procedure
2/12-M35 - Montana kept for 4 (Keitz)
3/8 -M31 - Montana's pass intended for Masztak was incomplete
4/8 -M31 - Restic then punted out of bounds on the Michigan 4 (27 yd punt)

7:49 MICHIGAN
1/10-M4 - Huckleby hit for 1, but Notre Dame charged with illegal procedure
1/5 -M9 - Leach was nailed for no gain by Weston
2/5 -M9 - Leach picked up 5 (Golic)
1/10-M14 - Huckleby was hit by Leopold, fumbled and Leach recovered on the M5 for a loss of 9
2/19-M5 - Davis picked up 3 (Golic)
3/16-M8 - Davis picked up 5 on draw (Heimkreiter)
4/11-M13 - Willner punted to Waymer who returned for 9 to M46 (42 yd punt)

4:17 NOTRE DAME
1/10-M46 - Heavens got 1 at le (Simpkins)
2/9 -M45 - Courey gained 8 (Bell)
3/1 -M38 - Ferguson hit center for 1 (Braman)
1/10-M36 - Heavens gained 3 at center (Braman)
2/7 -M33 - Montana passed to Masztak for 15 (Harden)
1/10-M18 - Ferguson picked up 2 (Keitz)
2/8 -M16 - Heavens gained 1 (DeSantis)
3/7 -M15 - Montana's pass was dropped by Haines at the M4
4/7 -M15 - Unis, with Restic holding, had the attempted field goal blocked by Michael Jolley, the ball rolling into the end zone for a touchback

1:00 MICHIGAN
1/10-M20 - Huckleby took a pitchout for 5 (Calhoun)
2/5 -M25 - Leach overthrew Feaster at N44
3/5 -M25 - Leach was smothered by Zettek and Case for an 8 yd loss

**END OF FIRST QUARTER
NOTRE DAME 7, MICHIGAN 0**

SECOND QUARTER

MICHIGAN
4/13-M17 - Willner, from his 3, punted to Waymer who was downed immediately on the N33. (50 yd punt)

14:50 NOTRE DAME
1/10-N33 - Ferguson hit for 3 (Meter)
2/7 -N36 - Heavens failed to gain (Owens)
3/7 -M36 - Montana's pitchout to Courey who fumbled and Stone recovered for a 15 yd loss
4/22-N21 - Restic punted to the 49 where Notre Dame downed the ball

13:08 MICHIGAN
1/10-N49 - Davis cracked for 8 (Leopold)
2/2 -N41 - Leach's pass to Feaster was incomplete
3/2 -N41 - Leach kept for 5 (Harrison)

203

1/10-N36 - Huckleby swept re for 11 (Restic)
1/10-N25 - Huckleby hit center for 3 (Weston)
2/7 -N22 - Davis added 3 (Golic)
3/4 -N19 - Huckleby drove for 13 (Browner)
1/G -N6 - Huckleby hit for 2 (Calhoun)
2/G -N4 - Leach faked a handoff and scored the T.D. Willner, with Dickey holding, converted from placement
SCORE: NOTRE DAME 7, MICHIGAN 7

J. Stone returned Virgil's kick from the goal line to the N25 where Virgil downed him
9:39 NOTRE DAME
1/10-N25 - Heavens hit for 1 (Godfrey)
2/9 -N26 - Montana passed to Vehr for 23 yds (Braman)
1/10-N49 - Ferguson slanted for 11 (Godfrey)
1/10-M41 - Heavens cracked for 7 (Simpkins)
2/3 -M34 - Notre Dame penalized for illegal procedure
2/8 -M39 - Ferguson smashed center for 7 (Meter)
3/1 -M32 - Ferguson bulled for 1 (Meter)
1/10-M31 - Montana passed to Heavens for 12 (DeSantis)
1/10-M19 - Ferguson circled le for 8 (DeSantis)
2/2 -M11 - Ferguson plunged for 3 (Owens)
1/G -M8 - Montana kept on a broken play, failed to gain but Michigan was called for a personal foul, the ball being placed on the Michigan 4
1/G -M4 - Ferguson then plunged through the middle for the T.D. Unis, with Restic holding, converted from placement
SCORE: NOTRE DAME 14, MICHIGAN 7

Smith took Male's kick on the M5 and returned 8 to M13
5:21 MICHIGAN
1/10-M13 - Huckleby circled le for 9 (Heimkreiter)
2/1 -M22 - Davis hit for 2 (Golic)
1/10-M24 - Leach overthrew Mitchell
2/10-M24 - Leach's pass was incomplete as Weston poured in on him
3/10-M24 - Leach's screen pass to Davis lost 3 (Browner)
4/13-M21 - Willner punted to Waymer who returned 4 to N40 (43 yd punt)

3:15 NOTRE DAME
1/10-N40 - Ferguson gained 2 (Greer)
2/8 -N42 - Montana's pass to Condeni was broken up by Simpkin's
3/8 -N42 - Montana passed to Ferguson for 7 (Simpkins)
4/1 -N49 - Restic punted to Jolly who returned 15 to the M28 (38 yd punt)

1:45 MICHIGAN
1/10-M28 - Davis hit center for 4 (Case)
2/6 -M32 - Leach's pass intended for Marsh was incomplete

3/6 -M32 - Leach passed to Clayton for 20 (Harrison)
1/10-N48 - Huckleby dropped Leach's swing pass
2/10-N48 - Leach's pass to Huckleby was incomplete as Browner again poured in on Leach
3/10-N48 - Leach's swing pass to Huckleby was incomplete
4/10-N48 - Willner then punted into the end zone for a touchback (47 yd punt)

:45 NOTRE DAME
1/10-N20 - Montana just fell on the ball for a 1 yd loss
2/11-N19 - Montana passed to Ferguson for 0 yds

END OF FIRST HALF
NOTRE DAME 14, MICHIGAN 7

THIRD QUARTER

Stone returned Virgil's kick 21 to N24 (Seabron)
NOTRE DAME
1/10-N24 - Ferguson picked up 7 (Simpkins)
2/3 -N31 - Heavens bulled for 12 (Bell)
1/10-N43 - Ferguson failed to gain (Greer)
2/10-N43 - Heavens gained 2 (Seabron)
3/8 -N45 - Montana passed to Condeni for 8 (Harden)
1/10-M47 - Heavens failed to gain (Greer)
2/10-M47 - Montana's pass to Condeni was ruled complete because of interference It was a gain of 9
1/10-M38 - Ferguson slashed for 3 (Greer)
2/7 -M35 - Ferguson broke two tackles for 4 (Diggs)
3/3 -M31 - Montana faked a pass and picked up 5 then stepped out
1/10-M26 - Ferguson fumbled and Greer recovered on M28

10:35 MICHIGAN
1/10-M28 - Huckleby gained 5 (Heimkreiter)
2/5 -M33 - Davis gained 2
3/3 -M35 - Huckleby took a pitchout for 5 (Golic)
2/10-M40 - Leach scrambled for 8 (Leopold)
3/2 -M48 - Leach scrambled for 9 (Browner)
1/10-N43 - Huckleby smashed for 11 (Leopold)
1/10-N32 - Huckleby got 3 (Golic)
2/7 -N29 - Huckleby lost 1 (Whittington)
3/8 -N30 - Michigan was called for illegal procedure
3/13-N35 - Leach passed to Marsh for 14 (Restic)
1/10-N21 - Huckleby took a pitchout for 7 (Golic)
2/3 -N14 - Huckleby smashed for 11 (Heimkreiter)

SEPTEMBER 23, 1978

1/G -N3 - Leach was spilled for 2 yd loss (Zettek)
2/G -N5 - Huckleby spilled by Leopold for no gain
3/G -N5 - Leach passed to Marsh in the end zone for a T.D. Willner, with Dickey holding, converted from placement
SCORE: NOTRE DAME 14, MICHIGAN 14

Stone returned Virgil's kick 22 to the N24 (Greer)
3:29 NOTRE DAME
1/10-N24 - Ferguson plunged for 5 (Simpkins)
2/5 -N29 - Heavens gained 3 (Meter)
3/2 -N32 - Ferguson slashed for 3 (DeSantis)
1/10-N35 - Ferguson failed to gain (Simpkins)
2/10-N35 - Montana's pass was dropped by Ferguson
3/10-N35 - Montana's pass was intercepted by Meter who returned to the N34, 14 ret

1:06 MICHIGAN
1/10-N34 - Huckleby failed to gain (Leopold)
2/10-N34 - Smith was dropped by Weston for no gain
1/10-N21 - Smith gained 3 (Leopold)

**END OF THIRD QUARTER
NOTRE DAME 14, MICHIGAN 14**

FOURTH QUARTER

MICHIGAN
2/7 -N18 - Leach passed to Marsh alone in the end zone for a T.D. Willner, with Dickey holding, failed to convert
SCORE: MICHIGAN 20, NOTRE DAME 14

Waymer returned Virgil's kick 5 yds to the N10 (Greer)
14:48 NOTRE DAME
1/10-N10 - Heavens slashed for 5 (Meter)
2/5 -N15 - Heavens hit for 3 (Simpkins)
3/2 -N18 - Montana's screen pass to Ferguson failed to gain (Meter)
4/2 -N18 - Restic punted dead to the M31, (50 yd punt from scrimmage)

13:07 MICHIGAN
1/10-M31 - Davis hit for 9 (Harrison)
2/1 -M40 - Davis cracked for 3 (Calhoun)
1/10-M43 - Leach was stopped by Case and Leopold for no gain
2/10-M43 - Smith circled le for 7 (Restic)
3/3 - 50 - Clayton lost 3 (Zettek)
4/6 -M47 - Willner punted 31 yds to Gibbons who signalled for a fair catch at the N22

11:20 NOTRE DAME
1/10-N22 - Montana's pass intended for Heavens was incomplete
2/10-N22 - Heavens took a screen pass for 4 (Meter)

3/6 -N26 - Montana passed to Haines for 18, but Notre Dame was penalized for a personal foul, placing the ball on the N27
1/25-N27 - Montana overthrew Holchan for an incomplete pass
2/25-N27 - Montana's pass was intercepted by Harden at the N41 where he stepped out of bounds

10:03 MICHIGAN
1/10-N41 - Davis hit center for 1 (Golic)
2/9 -N40 - Leach passed to Clayton who caught the ball on the N2 and went in for the T.D. Leach was smothered by Browner on an attempted two-point conversion
SCORE: MICHIGAN 26, NOTRE DAME 14

Stone returned Virgil's kick 16 to the N21 (Needham)
9:14 NOTRE DAME
1/10-N21 - Ferguson gained 2 (Meter)
2/8 -N23 - Montana's pass intended for Heavens was incomplete
3/8 -N23 - Montana's pass intended for Vehr was incomplete
4/8 -N23 - Restic punted to Harden who returned 1 to the M42 (Heimkreiter) 36 yd punt

8:16 MICHIGAN
1/10-M42 - Huckleby gained 1 (Weston)
2/9 -M43 - Huckleby picked up 4 (Browner)
3/5 -M47 - Leach's pass barely missed being intercepted by Leopold
4/5 -M47 - Willner punted to Waymer who was downed without a return (34 yd punt)

6:39 NOTRE DAME
1/10-N19 - Ferguson gained 2 (Greer)
2/8 -N21 - Montana passed to Haines, who fumbled after being hit by Jolly and Diggs recovered for Michigan at the N45

MICHIGAN
1/10-N45 - Reid gained 1 (Golic)
2/9 -N44 - Clayton picked up 2 (Case)
3/7 -N42 - Reid gained 4 (Golic)
4/3 -N38 - Willner then punted into the end zone for a touchback

3:48 NOTRE DAME
1/10-N20 - Montana passed to Mitchell for 11
1/10-N31 - Montana's pass to Haines was incomplete at the M44
2/10-N31 - Montana passed to Condini for 17 (Meter)
Notre Dame was called for personal foul after the previous play
1/25-N33 - Montana passed to Stone for 15
2/10-N48 - Montana passed to Masztak, who fumbled and Michigan recovered on the M43

205

2:27 MICHIGAN
1/10-M43 - Huckleby gained 2 (Calhoun)
2/8 -M45 - Huckleby slashed for 5 (Heimkreiter)
3/3 - 50 - Smith gained 2 (Whittington)
4/1 -N48 - Willner punted dead to the N5 (43 yd punt from scrimmage)

1:24 NOTRE DAME
1/10-N5 - Montana's pass intended for Masztek was incomplete
2/10-N5 - Montana's pass was dropped by Masztak
3/10-N5 - Montana was spilled by Greer for a safety, it being a 5 yd loss
SCORE: MICHIGAN 28, NOTRE DAME 14

Restic, with a free kick, punted to Clayton on the Michigan 15 and he returned 25 to the Michigan 40

1:01 MICHIGAN
1/10-M40 - Dickey at QB for Michigan. Reid slashed for 4 (Johnson)
2/6 -M44 - Reid added 3 more (Golic)
3/3 -M47 - Reid hit for 5

FINAL SCORE
MICHIGAN 28, NOTRE DAME 14

SEPTEMBER 30, 1978

**IOWA
VS.
ARIZONA**
Arizona Stadium
Temp.: 85
Wind: SSE 8 mph
Skies: Sunny
FIRST QUARTER

Iowa wins toss and elects to receive. Arizona will defend south goal.
Zivic kickoff taken on 1 yd. line by Blatcher, returned to A30
14:49 IOWA
1/10-A30 - Lazar middle for 3 yds. (Ingraham, Smith & Giangardella)
2/7 -A27 - Mosley middle for 1 yd. (Wunderli)
3/6 -A26 - Commings pass to Swift for 14 yds. (Liggins)
1/10-A12 - Mosley middle for no gain (Wunderli)
2/10-A12 - Lazar right for no gain. Lazar fumble recovered by Lazar for Iowa on A12
3/10-A12 - Commings pass to Lazar for 8 yds. (Smith)
4/2 -A4 - Schilling 21 yd. field goal good
SCORE: IOWA 3, ARIZONA 0

Schilling kickoff taken by Butler on A15, returned to A24
11:55 ARIZONA
1/10-A24 - Krohn right for 12 yds. (Hufford)
1/10-A36 - Krohn right for 1 yd. (Hobbs)
2/9 -A37 - Oliver left for 1 yd. (Gutshall)
3/8 -A38 - Krohn pass incomplete
4/8 -A38 - Garcia punt of 36 yds. received by Becker on I25 returned to I26

10:35 IOWA
1/10-I26 - Mosley middle for no gain (Crosby)
2/10-I26 - Mosley middle for 9 yds. (Smith, Ware)
3/1 -I35 - Mosley left for 1 yd. loss (Crawford)
4/2 -I34 - Holsclaw 52 yd. punt received by Streeter on A14, returned to A14

8:53 ARIZONA
1/10-A14 - Oliver middle for 2 yds. (Hufford)
2/8 -A16 - Krohn pass to Beyer for 18 yds. (Skradis)
1/10-A34 - Krohn pass to Beyer for 23 yds. (Becker)
1/10-I43 - Krohn pass to Ziegler incomplete
2/10-I43 - Krohn pass to Beyer incomplete
3/10-I43 - Krohn pass to Beyer for 13 yds.
1/10-I30 - Krohn pass to Beyer incomplete
2/10-I30 - Krohn left for 4 yd. loss (Rusk, Vasquez)
3/14-I34 - Ziegler middle for no gain (Skradis)
4/14-I34 - Zivic 51 yd. field goal good
SCORE: ARIZONA 3, IOWA 3

Zivic kickoff taken by Blatcher on I1, returned to I23
5:39 IOWA
1/10-I23 - Gales right for 13 yds. (Streeter)
1/10-I36 - Gales middle for 7 yd. loss. (Crawford)
2/17-I29 - Lazar middle for 10 yds. (Crawford, Crosby)
3/7 -I39 - Turner right for 1 yd. loss (Crosby, Smith)
4/8 -I38 - Holsclaw 32 yd. punt received by Horton on A30, returned A30

3:27 ARIZONA
1/10-A30 - Double penalty, no play
1/10-A30 - Krohn pass to Harvey incomplete
2/10-A30 - Krohn pass to Oliver incomplete
3/10-A30 - Oliver middle for 5 yds. (Skradis)
4/5 -A35 - Garcia 65 yd. punt into endzone

2:39 IOWA
1/10-I20 - Lazar middle for 1 yd. (Whitton, Crawford)
2/9 -I21 - Turner right for 6 yds. (Whitton)
3/3 -I27 - Turner right for 6 yds. (Ware, Giangardella)
1/10-I33 - Lazar middle for 1 yd. (Ingraham, Giangardella)
2/9 -I34 - Lazar left for 5 yds. (Streeter, Crawford)
3/4 -I39 - Lazar middle for no gain (Smith)
4/4 -I39 - Holsclaw 42 yd. punt received by Horton on A19, returned to A21

:05 ARIZONA
1/10-A21 - Heater middle for 2 yds.

END OF FIRST QUARTER
ARIZONA 3, IOWA 3

SECOND QUARTER

15:00 ARIZONA
2/8 -A23 - Heater right for 2 yds. (Gutshall, Hufford)
3/6 -A25 - Krohn left for 4 yds. (Danzy)
4/2 -A29 - Garcia 41 yd punt received by Reid on I30, returned to I30
15 yd. penalty against Iowa for clipping
1/10-A44 - Oliver middle for 3 yds. (Rusk)
2/7 -A47 - Heater left for 4 yd. loss (Molini)
3/11-A43 - Oliver middle for 3 yds. (Rusk, Hobbs)
4/8 -A46 - Garcia 54 yd. punt into endzone

12:17 IOWA
1/10-I20 - Holloway middle for 6 yds. (Ware)
2/4 -I26 - Turner middle for no gain (Wunderli, Whitton)
3/4 -I26 - Gales pass to Swift incomplete
4/4 -I26 - Holsclaw 54 yd. punt received by Horton on A20, returned to A19

207

10:58 ARIZONA
1/10-A19 - Heater right for 9 yds (Rusk, Vasquez)
2/1 -A28 - 5 yd. penalty against Iowa offsides
1/10-A33 - Oliver right for 5 yds. (Hobbs, Rusk)
2/5 -A38 - Heater middle for 3 yds. (Rusk)
3/2 -A41 - Krohn middle for 4 yds. (Rusk)
1/10-A45 - Heater right for 9 yds. (Rusk)
2/1 -I46 - Krohn pass to Oliver for 6 yds. (Steverson)
1/10-I40 - Heater middle for 9 yds. Heater fumble recovered by Danzy for Iowa on I31

7:38 IOWA
1/10-I31 - Gales pass to Reid broken up by Harris
2/10-I31 - Turner middle for 2 yds. (Crosby)
3/8 -I33 - Gales pass to Swift incomplete
4/8 -I33 - Holsclaw 33 yd punt received by Horton on A34 returned to A34

6:40 ARIZONA
1/10-A34 - Krohn pass to Beyer for 14 yds. (Becker, Steverson)
1/10-A48 - Heater middle for 2 yds. (Molini)
2/8 - 50 - Oliver left for 21 yds. (Becker)
1/10-I29 - Oliver for 3 yds. (Hufford, Hobbs)
2/7 -I26 - Oliver middle for 1 yd. (Hufford)
3/6 -I25 - Krohn pass to Harvey for 25 yds. Touchdown, Zivic kick good
SCORE: ARIZONA 10, IOWA 3

Zivic kickoff out of bounds. 5 yd. penalty. Zivic kickoff taken on I6 by Blatcher, returned to I21, (Bledsoe)
4:19 IOWA
1/10-I21 - Turner left for 3 yd. loss (Smith, Solomon)
2/13-I18 - Turner right for 1 yd. loss (Smith)
3/14-I17 - Turner middle for 3 yds. (Ingraham)
4/11-I20 - No Play, 15 yd. penalty against Arizona for roughing kicker
1/10-I35 - Gales pass incomplete (Giangardella)
2/10-I35 - Gales pass to Morton for 8 yds. (Harris)
3/2 -I43 - Holloway middle for 2 yds. (Giangardella)
1/10-I45 - Gales pass incomplete
2/10-I45 - Gales pass to Turner for 1 yd. (Wunderli)
3/9 -I46 - Time Out Iowa, Gales pass to Reid incomplete
4/9 -I46 - Holsclaw 39 yd. punt received by Streeter on A15, returned to A15

1:02 ARIZONA
1/10-A15 - Oliver middle for 2 yd. loss (Wagner)
2/12-A13 - Time Out Iowa. Oliver for 4 yds. (Hobbs, Rusk)
3/8 -A17 - Time Out Iowa. Heater right for 1 yd (Gutshall, Rusk)
4/7 -A18 - Garcia 45 yd. punt received on I37

:30 IOWA
1/10-I37 - Gales pass to Frazier for 9 yds.

HALF TIME SCORE
ARIZONA 10, IOWA 3

THIRD QUARTER

Schilling kickoff for Iowa taken by Butler on goal line, returned to A20 (Holloway)
15:00 ARIZONA
1/10-A20 - Heater middle for 2 yds. (Vasquez, Rusk)
2/8 -A22 - Oliver left for no gain (Vasquez, Gutshall)
3/8 -A22 - Krohn pass incomplete
4/8 -A22 - Garcia 40 yd. punt received by Becker on I38, returned to I38

13:30 IOWA
1/10-I38 - Commings right for no gain (Crosby)
2/10-I38 - 18 yd. penalty against Iowa for clipping
2/28-I20 - Green for 11 yd. loss (Smith)
3/39-I9 - Lazar middle for 4 yds.
4/35-I13 - Holsclaw 35 yd. punt received by Horton on I48, returned to I48

11:29 ARIZONA
1/10-I48 - Krohn pass to Haynes incomplete
2/10-I48 - Heater middle for 3 yds. (Harty)
3/7 -I45 - Krohn pass to Haynes for 12 yds.
1/10-I33 - Heater middle for 15 yds. (Pace)
1/10-I18 - Krohn left for 3 yds. (Rusk, Hobbs)
2/7 -I15 - Krohn pass incomplete. (Gutshall)
3/7 -I15 - No Play. Heater right for 6 yds.
15 yds. penalty against Arizona for personal foul
4/15-I23 - Zivic 40 yd. field goal failed

9:01 IOWA
1/10-I23 - Blatcher left for 5 yds. (Liggins)
2/5 -I28 - Holloway middle for 3 yds. (Whitton, Giangardella)
3/2 -I31 - Blatcher right for 12 yds. (Converse, Liggins)
1/10-I43 - Lazar middle for no gain (Whitton)
2/10-I43 - Mosley middle for 3 yds. (Whitton, Ingraham)
3/7 -I46 - Commings fumble after 3 yd. loss, recovered by Whitton for Arizona on I43

6:14 ARIZONA
1/10-I43 - Heater left for 6 yds. (Rusk)
2/4 -I37 - Oliver left for 2 yds. 15 yd penalty against Iowa for Personal Foul (Hufford, Rusk)
1/10-I20 - Krohn pass to Holmes for 17 yds. (Pace)
1/G -I3 - Oliver left for no gain (Molini)
2/G -I3 - Krohn right for 3 yds. Touchdown Zivic kick good
SCORE: ARIZONA 17, IOWA 3

208

SEPTEMBER 30, 1978

Zivic kickoff taken by Blatcher on I5, returned to I20

5:14 IOWA
1/10-I20 - Lazar middle for 5 yds. (Ingraham, Giangardella)
2/5 -I25 - Lazar middle for 6 yds. (Wunderli, Giangardella)
1/10-I31 - Turner left for 7 yd. loss (Wunderli)
2/17-I24 - Green pass to Frazier for 4 yds. (Ingraham)
3/13-I28 - Green pass to Reid incomplete. (Glass)
4/13-I28 - Holsclaw punt with off-setting penalties. Holsclaw 41 yd. punt received by Streeter on A31 returned to A38

2:08 ARIZONA
1/10-A38 - Oliver left for no gain (Rusk, Molini)
2/10-A38 - Krohn pass to Beyer for 16 yds. (Becker)
1/10-A46 - Krohn pass to Beyer for 18 yds. (Rusk, Becker)
1/10-I28 - Time Out Arizona. Oliver middle for no gain (Hobbs)
2/10-I28 - Krohn pass to Holmes for 28 yds. Touchdown Zivic kick failed
SCORE: ARIZONA 23, IOWA 3

Zivic kickoff taken by Blatcher on I1, returned to I40. Run out of bounds by Zivic

**END OF THIRD QUARTER
ARIZONA 23, IOWA 3**

FOURTH QUARTER

15:00 IOWA
1/10-I40 - Dunham pass incomplete
2/10-I40 - Green pass incomplete
3/10-I40 - Green sacked for 11 yd. loss (Ingraham)
4/21-I29 - Holsclaw 42 yd. punt received by Horton on A29, returned to A25 Fumble by Horton recovered by Iowa on A25

14:09 IOWA
1/10-A25 - Lazar right for 3 yds. (Giangardella)
2/7 -A22 - Green pass to Swift incomplete (Horton)
3/7 -A22 - Turner right for 2 yds. (Crosby, Wunderli)
4/5 -A20 - Time Out Iowa. Green pass to Swift incomplete (Liggins)

12:44 ARIZONA
1/10-A20 - Heater left for 5 yds. 15 yd. penalty against Iowa for personal foul (Rusk)
1/10-A40 - Oliver left for 3 yds. (Rusk, Woodland)
2/7 -A43 - Heater right for 1 yd. (Skradis, Wagner)
3/6 -A44 - Krohn pass incomplete

4/6 -A44 - Garcia 40 yd. punt taken by Reid on I16, returned to I18

11:05 IOWA
1/10-I18 - Green pass incomplete (Liggins)
2/10-I18 - Burke for 4 yds.
3/6 -I22 - Burke for no gain
4/6 -I22 - Holsclaw 52 yd. punt received by Horton on A25, returned to A27
13 yd. penalty against Arizona for clipping

9:37 ARIZONA
1/10-A14 - Carter left for 10 yds
1/10-A24 - Nelson right for 1 yd. (Hobbs, Gutshall)
2/9 -A25 - Carter pass to Jackson for 19 yds. (Steverson)
1/10-A44 - Dickerson middle for 2 yds. (Harty)
2/8 -A46 - Nelson left for 6 yds. (Hill)
3/2 -I48 - Robertson right for 8 yds (Danzy, Steverson)
1/10-I40 - Time Out Iowa. Carter left for 6 yds. (Kent, Ellis)
2/4 -I34 - Nelson for 1 yd. (Harty)
3/3 -I33 - Nelson right—no play 16 yd penalty against Arizona for clipping
3/19-I49 - Carter pass to Harvey for 13 yds. 15 yd. penalty against Arizona for face mask (Pace, Steverson)
4/21-A49 - Garcia 45 yd. punt received by Becker on I6, returned to I8

209

5:40 IOWA
- 1/10-I8 - Burke middle for 20 yds. (Ware)
- 1/10-I28 - Commings pass incomplete
- 2/10-I28 - Burke left for 4 yds. (Streeter)
- 3/6 -I32 - Commings pass to Holloway incomplete. 15 yd. penalty against Arizona for Personal Foul
- 1/10-I47 - Burke middle—no play 5 yd. penalty against Iowa for illegal motion
- 2/15-I42 - Commings left for 12 yds. (Liggins)
- 2/3 -A46 - Commings fumble, recovered by Flournoy for Arizona on A46

3:52 ARIZONA
- 1/10-A46 - Nelson middle for 9 yds. (Skradis)
- 2/1 -I45 - Nelson for 4 yd. loss (Mahmens)
- 3/5 -I49 - Dickerson for 8 yds. (Danzy)
- 1/10-I41 - Dickerson middle for 5 yds. (Simonsen)
- 2/5 -I36 - Nelson middle for 6 yds. (Simonsen, Gutshall)
- 1/10-I30 - Nelson left for no gain (Gutshall, Simonsen)
- 2/10-I30 - Carter pass to Linzy dropped
- 3/10-I30 - Stevenson right for 6 yds. (Stevenson)

FINAL SCORE
ARIZONA 23, IOWA 3

National Collegiate Athletic Association
FINAL TEAM STATISTICS

	ARIZONA	IOWA
First Downs	24	9
Rushing	8	6
Passing	12	1
Penalty	4	2
Rushing Attempts	55	46
Yards Rushing	223	152
Yards Lost Rushing	14	45
Net Yards Rushing	209	107
Net Yards Passing	222	44
Passes Attempted	24	20
Passes Completed	13	6
Had Intercepted	0	0
Total Offensive Plays	79	66
Total Net Yards	431	151
Average Gain Per Play	5.5	2.3
Fumbles: Number—Lost	3/2	3/2
Penalties: Number—Lost	7/94	6/73
Interceptions: Number—Yards	0	0
Number of Punts—Yards	7/225	10/422
Average Per Punt	46.4	42.2
Punt Returns: Number—Yards	6/6	2/4
Kickoff Returns: Number—Yards	2/29	5/161

SEPTEMBER 29, 1978

MICHIGAN STATE UNIVERSITY
VS.
UNIVERSITY OF SOUTHERN CALIFORNIA
Los Angeles Coliseum
FIRST QUARTER

Michigan State wins toss, elects to receive; USC defends West goal Kerr kicks off to Reeves on 9, returned 21

MICHIGAN STATE UNIVERSITY
1/10-MS30 - pitch to McGee around re for 9
2/1 -MS39 - 14:17 S. Smith at lg makes 5
1/10-MS44 - Reeves at rt stopped for no gain
2/10-MS44 - pitch to McGee over lt makes 4
3/6 -MS48 - Smith pass intercepted by Smith, 6 yd return

UNIVERSITY OF SOUTHERN CALIFORNIA
1/10-SC45 - 12:16 White at le makes no gain
2/10-SC45 - McDonald pass intended for Sweeney on MS45 too wide
3/10-SC45 - McDonald pass tipped up by Sweeney, intercepted by Mark Andersen, no return

MICHIGAN STATE UNIVERSITY
1/10-MS36 - 11:31 Smith pass intended for Brammer on 50 incomplete, but holding penalty, 16 yds
1/26-MS20 - Schramm at rt makes 3
2/23-MS23 - Smith pass complete to Byrd on 45, and run for 35
1/10-SC42 - Schramm plunges through rg for 5
2/5 -SC37 - Smith pass to Gibson on 15 incomplete
3/5 -SC37 - Middleton up middle makes 13
1/10-SC24 - Middleton at rg gains 3
2/7 -SC21 - S. Smith at rt makes no gain
3/7 -SC21 - Smith pass intended for Schramm on 15 dropped
4/7 -SC21 - Anderson holding, Morton Andersen makes FIELD GOAL, 38 yds 7:24 played
SCORE: MICHIGAN STATE 3, SOUTHERN CALIFORNIA 0

Schario kicks off to Butler on 6, returned 13
UNIVERSITY OF SOUTHERN CALIFORNIA
1/10-SC19 - 7:32 White around le makes 6
2/4 -SC25 - Cain through lt for 9
1/10-SC34 - White at lg gains 6
2/4 -SC40 - McDonald pass complete to Garcia for 6
1/10-SC46 - Cain at rt makes 3
2/7 -SC49 - Cain at lt gains 5
3/2 -MS46 - White at lt makes 6
1/10-MS40 - Ford at re loses 2
2/12-MS42 - McDonald pass in flat complete to White, 14 yd

1/10-MS28 - Cain at lt makes 6
2/4 -MS22 - White through lg for 9
1/10-MS13 - McDonald pass complete to Hunter on 6, run over for 13 and TOUCHDOWN King holding, Jordan makes
CONVERSION 14:52 played
SCORE: SOUTHERN CALIFORNIA 7, MICHIGAN STATE 3

Kerr kicks to Reeves, on 9, returned 5
MICHIGAN STATE UNIVERSITY
1/10-MS14 - :08 Smith on broken play at rt for no gain

FIRST QUARTER SCORE:
SOUTHERN CALIFORNIA 7 MICHIGAN STATE 3

SECOND QUARTER

MICHIGAN STATE UNIVERSITY
2/10-MS14 - Middleton at lg makes 5
3/5 -MS19 - Middleton at lt gains 4
4/1 -MS23 - Stachowicz punts to Butler on 32, returned 15; 45 yd punt

UNIVERSITY OF SOUTHERN CALIFORNIA
1/10-SC47 - 13:56 White at rg makes 4
2/6 -MS49 - Ford at le stopped for no gain
3/6 MS49 - McDonald pass intended for Butler on 45 incomplete
4/6 MS49 - King punts into end zone, no return; 49 yd kick

MICHIGAN STATE UNIVERSITY
1/10-MS20 - 12:33 Smith pass complete to Gibson on 23, run for 20
1/10-MS40 - Smith pass intended for Byrd on 20 tipped away by Crawford
2/10-MS40 - Smith pass complete to Gibson for 11
1/10-SC49 - Middleton at rg makes 3
2/7 -SC46 - McGee at lt makes 6
3/1 -SC40 - Smith pass intended for Gibson on 35 incomplete
4/1 -SC40 - Schramm at lt makes 4
1/10-SC36 - Smith pass intended for Byrd on 10 tipped away by Smith
2/10-SC36 - Smith, back to pass, runs re for 5
3/5 -SC31 - Schramm at lg makes 3
4/2 -SC28 - from 35, Anderson holding, Andersen field goal attempt wide south

UNIVERSITY OF SOUTHERN CALIFORNIA
1/10-SC29 - 9: White at rt makes 3
2/7 -SC32 - Cain up middle for 2, but SC holding, 15 yd penalty, 1 yd gain
2/21-SC18 - White at re makes 1
3/21-SC18 - McDonald pass intended for Williams, intercepted by Stanton on MS40, no return

211

MICHIGAN STATE UNIVERSITY
1/10-MS40 - E. Smith pass complete to Byrd, who fumbles, recovered by (8:04) Dennis Smith, gain of 10

UNIVERSITY OF SOUTHERN CALIFORNIA
1/10- 45 - 7:56 Cain at rt makes 5
2/5 -MS45 - White inside re makes 6
1/10-MS39 - White at rt for 2, but SC holding, 15 yds (2 gain)
1/23-SC48 - McDonald pass intended for Sweeney incomplete
2/23-SC48 - Butler on reverse around re makes 11
3/12-MS41 - McDonald pass complete to Sweeny on 25, run for 20
1/10-MS21 - Cain at rg makes 2
2/8 -MS19 - end around to Williams makes 6
3/2 -MS13 - White inside re gains 6
1/G -MS7 - Cain at lg makes 3
2/G -MS4 - White hits lt for 3
3/G -MS1 - White dives over rt for 1 and TOUCHDOWN (12 min. played) King holding, Jordon makes CONVERSION SCORE: SOUTHERN CALIFORNIA 14, MICHIGAN STATE 3

Kerr kicks off to S. Smith on goal, returned 17
MICHIGAN STATE UNIVERSITY
1/10-MS17 - 2:56 pitch to McGee at lt makes 5
2/5 -MS22 - Middleton at middle hit by Dimmler for no gain
3/5 -MS22 - E. Smith pass complete to Schramm for 8
1/10-MS30 - Schramm slips through rt for 7
2/3 -MS37 - Schramm at rt makes 6
1/10-MS43 - E. Smith pass complete for 18
1/10-SC39 - E. Smith pass intended for Gibson, out of bounds
2/10-SC39 - Anderson holding, Andersen attempted field goal short

END OF HALF:
SOUTHERN CALIFORNIA 14 MICHIGAN STATE 3

THIRD QUARTER

Schario kicks off to White on 4, Bobbles, goes for 43 yds

UNIVERSITY OF SOUTHERN CALIFORNIA
1/10-SC47 - White at rg makes 3
2/7 - 50 - Cain at middle gains 4
3/3 -MS46 - McDonald pass complete to Hunter on 40, gain of 8
1/10-MS38 - White at le makes 4
2/6 -MS34 - Cain plows through rt for 10
1/10-MS24 - White at lg gains 4
2/6 -MS20 - White inside re makes 2
3/4 -MS18 - McDonald pass for Williams just out of reach on 2
4/4 -MS18 - King holding on 25, Jordan makes 35-yd FIELD GOAL (3:29 played) SCORE: SOUTHERN CALIFORNIA 17, MICHIGAN STATE 3

Kerr kicks off to Reeves on 5, returned 14
MICHIGAN STATE UNIVERSITY
1/10-MS20 - (11:36) McGee at lt makes 2
2/8 -MS22 - Reeves hit by Lott for loss of 1
3/9 -MS21 - too much time, delay of game penalty, 5 yds
3/14-MS16 - S. Smith at lg caught for loss of 2
4/16-MS14 - Stachowicz punts out of bounds on 50; 36 yd punt

UNIVERSITY OF SOUTHERN CALIFORNIA
1/10- 50 - 9:29 McDonald pass complete to Sweeney on 4, over for TOUCHDOWN, 50 yds (x 5:38 played) King holding, Jordan makes Conversion SCORE: SOUTHERN CALIFORNIA 24, MICHIGAN STATE 3

Kerr kicks off to Reeves in end zone, no return, but SC offside, 5 yd penalty From 35, Kerr kicks off to Reeves on 11, returned 15
MICHIGAN STATE UNIVERSITY
1/10-MS26 - E. Smith pass intended for Byrd on 45 incomplete
2/10-MS26 - E. Smith pass intended for Gibson tipped up intercepted on MS47, returned 7

UNIVERSITY SOUTHERN CALIFORNIA
1/10-MS40 - 9:01 Cain makes 3
2/7 -MS37 - White all over le makes 11
1/10-MS26 - Cain at lg gains 4
2/6 -MS22 - end around to Williams, le, makes 7, but SC holding, 16 yd penalty
2/22-MS38 - McDonald pass to William complete in end zone, but offensive pass interference on Williams, 15 yds, loss of down
3/37-SC47 - McDonald pass intended for Cain on 50 incomplete
4/37-SC47 - King punts through end zone, 53 yd punt

SEPTEMBER 29, 1978

MICHIGAN STATE UNIVERSITY
1/10-MS20 - 7:22 Schramm at rg makes 2
2/8 -MS22 - E. Smith pass intended for Byrd incomplete, but interference called on SC, 16 yd penalty
1/10-MS38 - E. Smith pass complete to Schramm for 4, but interference called for 12 yd penalty
1/10- 50 - McGee at rg makes 3
2/7 -SC47 - E. Smith pass intended for Byrd on 30 incomplete
3/7 -SC47 - E. Smith pass intended for Schramm on 50 incomplete
4/7 -SC47 - Schario punts into end zone, 47 yd kick

UNIVERSITY OF SOUTHERN CALIFORNIA
1/10-SC20 - 5:00 Cain at rt makes 5
2/5 -SC25 - White around le for 4
3/1 -SC29 - Ford goes through rt for 12
1/10-SC41 - Cain inside lt, goes for 36
1/10-MS23 - Ford at rt makes 4; late hit, half distance, 10 yd penalty
1/G -MS9 - Ford at rt makes 7
2/G -MS2 - White inside le makes 2 and TOUCHDOWN (12:10 played) King holding, Jordan misses attempted conversion SCORE: SOUTHERN CALIFORNIA 30, MICHIGAN STATE 3

Kerr kicks off to Reeves on 4, returned 9
MICHIGAN STATE UNIVERSITY
1/10-MS13 - 2:45 E. Smith pass complete to McGee for 7
2/3 -MS20 - McGee at rt makes 7
1/10-MS27 - Schramm at rt makes 6
2/4 -MS33 - E. Smith pass to Byrd ruled incomplete
3/4 -MS33 - E. Smith pass complete to Howard on 45, run for 21 yds
1/10-SC46 - Schramm at lt makes 8
2/2 -SC38 - S. Smith at rt no gain

**END OF THIRD QUARTER:
SOUTHERN CALIFORNIA 30, MICHIGAN STATE 3**

FOURTH QUARTER

MICHIGAN STATE UNIVERSITY
3/2 -SC38 - Schramm at lg for 1
4/1 -SC37 - Middleton at rg makes 1
1/10-SC36 - E. Smith caught by Dimmler for loss of 9
2/19 -SC45 - Reeves at lg no gain
3/19-SC45 - E. Smith keeps at le for 5 yd gain, 15 yd penalty SC
1/10-SC25 - Middleton at rt makes 2
2/8 -SC23 - E. Smith pass to Byrd, Lott tips it up, Hartwig recovers

UNIVERSITY SOUTHERN CALIFORNIA
1/10-SC9 - 12:40 DiLulo makes 5 (Preston at qb)
2/5 -SC14 - Allen at lt makes 10
1/10-SC24 - DiLulo at lt makes 5
2/5 -SC29 - Allen around le gains 6
1/10-SC35 - Allen at re rolls for 17
1/10-MS48 - Allen at rt makes 6
2/4 -MS42 - Allen fumbles on handoff for loss of 8, recovered by Land

MICHIGAN STATE UNIVERSITY
1/10- 50 - 9:34 Middleton at rg gains 3
2/7 -SC47 - E. Smith pass to Howard on 10 incomplete
3/7 -SC47 - E. Smith pass complete to McGee for 5
4/2 -SC42 - S. Smith at re makes 1

UNIVERSITY OF SOUTHERN CALIFORNIA
1/10-SC41 - 8:14 DiLulo at rg makes 4
2/6 -SC45 - Preston pass intended for DiLulo incomplete
3/6 -SC45 - Allen at le makes 4
4/2 -SC49 - King punts to Anderson on 22, fair catch, 29 yd kick

MICHIGAN STATE UNIVERSITY
1/10-MS22 - 6:50 pitch to Hughes around le good for 10
1/10-MS32 - Middleton up middle for 5
2/5 -MS37 - E. Smith pass complete to Harris for loss of 1
3/6 -MS36 - Reeves at le makes 1
4/5 -MS37 - Stachowicz punts to Hayes at SC21, 9 yd return

UNIVERSITY OF SOUTHERN CALIFORNIA
1/10-SC30 - 4:21 Allen at le for 3, but 5 yd penalty for illegal motion
1/15-SC25 - DiLulo at rg gains 1
2/14-SC26 - Preston back to pass, runs middle for loss of 3
3/17-SC23 - Preston fumbles, recovered by Land (gain of 3)

213

MICHIGAN STATE UNIVERSITY
1/10-SC26 - 2:53 Middleton at rg makes 3
2/7 -SC23 - E. Smith complete to Reeves for 5
3/2 -SC18 - S. Smith at rt makes 4
1/10-SC14 - E. Smith tripped by Ussery for loss of 2
2/12-SC16 - Hughes at le makes 11
3/1 -SC5 - S. Smith hits rg for 2
1/G -SC3 - E. Smith pas intended for Harris in and zone broken up
2/G -SC3 - E. Smith pass complete to Hans on goal, over for TOUCHDOWN (14:40 played) Anderson holding, Andersen kick wide to south
SCORE: SOUTHERN CALIFORNIA 30
       MICHIGAN STATE 9,

Andersen kicks out of bounds on onside attempt,
UNIVERSITY OF SOUTHERN CALIFORNIA
1/10-SC39 - Preston downs ball for no gain (20 s remaining)
2/10-SC39 - Preston again falls on ball for no gain

END OF GAME
SOUTHERN CALIFORNIA 30
MICHIGAN STATE 9

National Collegiate Athletic Association
FINAL TEAM STATISTICS
September 29, 1978

	MICHIGAN STATE	USC
First Downs	18	19
Rushing	9	12
Passing	6	6
Penalty	3	11
Rushing Attempts	46	55
Yards Rushing	166	279
Yards Lost Rushing	14	15
Net Yards Rushing	152	264
Net Yards Passing	141	111
Passes Attempted	27	15
Passes Completed	12	6
Had Intercepted	3	2
Total Offensive Plays	73	70
Total Net Yards	293	375
Average Gain Per Play	4.01	5.36
Fumbles: Number—Lost	1/1	2/2
Penalties: Number—		
Yards	3/31	9/114
Interceptions: Number—		
Yards	2/0	3/17
Number of Punts—Yards	4/170	3/131
Average Per Punt	42.5	43.7
Punt Returns: Number—		
Yards	0/0	2/24
Kickoff Returns:		
Number—Yards	6/81	2/56
Third Down Efficiency	7-19-36.8	6-13-46.2
Time of Possession	32:34	27:26

SEPTEMBER 30, 1978

NORTHWESTERN VS. COLORADO
Boulder Stadium
Temp.: 67°
Wind: N 5 mph
Skies: Clear
FIRST QUARTER

Northwestern wins the toss of the coin. Northwestern elects to receive and defend the north goal. Colorado will defend the south goal.
Dadiotis kicks off for Colorado from the C40 Deep for Northwestern are Hill, Geegan; the kick by Dadiotis is taken by Geegan at the N2 and returned to the N24 for a return of twenty-two yards

13:51 COLORADO
1/10-C22 - Kozlowski over the right side to the C23 and a gain of one yard
2/9 -C23 - Solomon overthrows Ballage in the left flat incomplete pass
3/9 -C23 - Solomon throws to Kozlowski in the right flat It is complete to the C32 for a gain of nine yards
1/10-C32 - Solomon rolls left along the line and is hit down for a loss of one yard at the C31
2/11-C31 - Solomon throws over the middle to Kozlowski who gains to the C36 and a gain of five yards
3/6 -C36 - Solomon pitches to Kozlowski who is hit at the C37 and a gain of one yard
4/5 -C37 - Olander punts to North on a fair catch, punt is good for thirty-seven yards North takes the ball on the N26

14:50 NORTHWESTERN
1/10-N24 - Mishler over the left side to the N31 for a gain of seven yards
2/3 -N31 - Pitch to Hill who fumbles it out of bounds at the N30 for a loss of one yard
3/4 -N30 - Pitch right to Mishler who gains to the N33 for a gain of three yards
4/1 -N33 - Christensen punts for Northwestern Roberts and Davis are deep for Colorado Davis takes the punt at the C13 and returns it to the C22 for a return of nine yards Punt for fifty-four yards

11:21 NORTHWESTERN
1/10-N26 - Mishler over the right side to the N29 for a gain of three yards
2/7 -N29 - Strasser keeps, tries the right side, and is hit for a loss of three yards to the N26
3/10-N26 - Strasser passes incomplete to North along the east sidelines
4/10-N26 - Christensen punts for Northwestern, Davis and Roberts are deep Davis takes the punt at the C30 and is run out of bounds along the east sidelines at the N36, punt is for forty-four yards, return is for thirty-four yards

215

9:40 COLORADO
1/10-N36 - Kozlowski over the middle to the N30 for a gain of six yards
2/4 -N30 - Mayberry gains three yards over the middle to the N27
3/1 -N27 - Kozlowski sweeps left but gains nothing, ball is at the N27
4/1 -N27 - Mayberry over the middle and hits to the N25 for a gain of two yards
1/10-N25 - Mayberry over left tackle to the N11 and a gain of fourteen yards
1/10-N11 - Kozlowski over left guard to the N8 and a gain of three yards
2/7 -N8 - Kozlowski over right guard to the N2 and a gain of six yards
3/1 -N2 - Mayberry over the left guard for no gain, ball is on the N2
4/1 -N2 - Mayberry tries right tackle and is stopped at the N3 for a loss of one yard, Northwestern takes the ball

5:35 NORTHWESTERN
1/10-N3 - Mishler over left tackle to the N5 and a gain of two yards
2/8 -N5 - Misler turns the left corner and gains to the N20 for a first down and a gain of fifteen yards
1/10-N20 - Strasser throws complete to kill in the right flat, Hill gains to the N28 for a gain of eight yards
2/2 -N28 - Pitch right to Mishler who goes over right tackle to the N33 and a gain of five yards
1/10-N33 - Mishler over the middle to the N35 for a gain of two yards
2/8 -N35 - Strasser throws over the side to North, Haynes breaks up the pass, incomplete
3/8 -N35 - Strasser throws over the middle to Poulos, it is incomplete
4/8 -N35 - Christensen punts for Northwestern, Roberts, Davis, and Cullins are deep for Colorado, Davis takes the punt at the C29 and returns it two yards to the C31, punt is good for thirty-six yards

2:37 COLORADO
1/10-C31 - Mayberry over the right side to the C39 and a gain of eight yards
2/2 -C39 - Kozlowski over the middle to the C47 for a gain of eight yards
1/10-C47 - Mayberry gains to the mid-field stripe for three yards
2/7 - 50 - Solomon throws incomplete to Ballage along the west sidelines
3/7 - 50 - Solomon drops to throw, keeps, and streaks up the middle to the N32 for a gain of eighteen yards, penalty against Northwestern for face mask violation moves the ball to the N18
1/10-N18 - Mayberry over left guard, he fumbles at the N18 for no gain, Northwestern recovers the ball at the N28

1:00 NORTHWESTERN
1/10-N28 - Strasser passes but the ball is tipped and falls incomplete
2/10-N28 - Mishler over right tackle to the N33 for a gain of five yards
3/5 -N33 - Pitch to Hill who tries right end and gains to the N39 with a gain of six yards, Northwestern is guilty of holding ball is moved to the N23
3/15-N23 - Draw to Mishler who gains two yards to the N25
4/13-N25 - Christensen punts for Northwestern, deep for Colorado are Roberts, Davis, and Cullins, the punt is taken by Davis at the C28 and returned to the C32 for a return of four yards, punt is good for forty-seven yards

**END OF FIRST QUARTER:
COLORADO 0, NORTHWESTERN 0**

SECOND QUARTER

14:53 COLORADO
1/10-C32 - Solomon keeps and goes over the middle for ten yards to the C42
1/10-C42 - Mayberry over the left side to the N44 and a gain of fourteen yards
1/10-N44 - Mayberry around the left side and along the east sidelines to the N16 for a gain of twenty-eight yards
1/10-N16 - Kozlowski for a one yard gain over right tackle to the N15
2/9 -N15 - Kozlowski over the right tackle to the N9 for a gain of six yards
3/3 -N9 - Kozlowski sweeps left and gains to the N5 for a gain of four yards and a first down
1/G -N5 - Kozlowski tries the right end and fumbles at the N1, the gain is for four yards, Kendzicky recovers at the N1 for Northwestern, Kozlowski is hurt on the play, Northwestern takes possession at the N1

SEPTEMBER 30, 1978

12:36 NORTHWESTERN
1/10-N1 - Strasser keeps, tries the middle, and gains the the N4 for a gain of three yards
2/7 -N4 - Mishler tries left guard, Northwestern is guilty of illegal procedure, Colorado declines the penalty there is no gain for Mishler
3/7 -N4 - Strasser pitches to Mishler who goes over left tackle to the N13 for a gain of nine yards
1/10-N13 - Hill tries left end and gains two yards to the N15
2/8 -N15 - Hill on a counter play to the N19 for a gain of four yards
3/4 -N19 - Strasser passes incomplete to North over the right side
4/4 -N19 - Christensen punts for Northwestern, deep for Colorado are Davis, Cullins, and Roberts, Davis takes the punt at the C34, he fumbles but recovers his fumble at the C49 for a return of fifteen yards, punt is good for forty-seven yards

10:06 COLORADO
1/10-C49 - Solomon passes complete to Ballage on the right side to the N42 for a gain of nine yards
2/1 -N42 - Mayberry gains to the N38 for a gain of four yards
1/10-N38 - Solomon keeps, streaks up the middle, cuts back to the west side, and scores by cutting into the corner of the end zone
Time: 9:33
PAT by Dadiotis is good
SCORE: COLORADO 7, NORTHWESTERN 0

Dadiotis kicks off for Colorado from the C40. Deep for Northwestern are Hill and Breitbeil. The kick is taken by Hill and he comes out of the end zone to the N19. Return is for nineteen yards.

9:30 NORTHWESTERN
1/10-N19 - Hill takes a handoff who in turn hands it off to Bogan who gains thirteen yards to the N32
1/10-N32 - Hill sweeps right and gains to the N37 for a gain of five yards
2/5 -N37 - Strasser passes complete over the right side to Poulos at the C47 and a gain of sixteen yards
1/10-C47 - Strasser passes complete to Hill on the left side, Hill loses three yards to the mid-field stripe
2/13- 50 - Strasser passes complete to Mishler in the right flat, he gains to the C43 for a gain of seven yards
3/6 -C43 - Strasser passes complete to McGee in the left flat who gains to the C34 for a nine yard gain

1/10-C34 - Strasser passes off to Mishler who goes over left tackle for five yards to the C29
2/5 -C29 - Strasser passes complete to Hill in the right flat to the C25 for a gain of four yards
3/1 -C25 - Strasser keeps, goes over right guard, and gains to the C22 for a gain of three yards
1/10-C22 - Strasser overthrows Hill along the west sidelines, it falls incomplete
2/10-C22 - Strasser throws over the middle and hits Poulos who gains to the C13 and a gain of nine yards
3/1 -C13 - Johnson over right guard to the C11 for a gain of two yards
1/10-C11 - Pitch to Johnson who goes over left tackle to the C1 for ten yards
1/G -C1 - Strasser keeps, goes over the middle for a touchdown
Time: 3:29
PAT by Mirkopulos is good
SCORE: COLORADO 7, NORTHWESTERN 7

Mirkopulos kicks off for Northwestern from the N40. Deep for Colorado are Ballage, Hornberger, and Green. The kick is taken by Ballage at the C2. He cuts to the west sidelines and streaks to the N36. Return is for sixty-two yards. Colorado is guilty of clipping, the ball is placed on the C20.

3:20 COLORADO
1/10-C20 - Solomon keeps, goes over right guard, and gains to the C24 for a gain of four yards
2/6 -C24 - Pitch to Hornberger who tries the right side to the C29 and a gain of five yards
3/1 -C29 - Hornberger over the middle and breaks into the open to the C42 for a gain of thirteen yards
1/10-C42 - Solomon rolls right and throws complete to Howard on the left side to the N35 and a gain of twenty-three yards
1/10-N35 - Solomon keeps, turns the right corner, and gains fourteen yards to the N21
1/10-N21 - Mayberry over the middle to the N19 and a gain of two yards
2/8 -N19 - Solomon throws complete to Ballage on the left side, he steps out of bounds at the N5 for a gain of fourteen yards
1/G -N5 - There are fifty-two seconds on the clock, Mayberry over the middle to the N1 for a gain of four yards
2/G -N1 - Solomon keeps, tries the middle, and gains nothing
3/G -N1 - Solomon keeps, goes the one yard, and scores
PAT by Dadiotis is good
SCORE: COLORADO 14 NORTHWESTERN 7

217

Dadiotis kicks off for Colorado from the C40 to Hill and Geegan. The kick goes over the end zone. There is no return.

:10 NORTHWESTERN
1/10-N20 - Strasser hands off to Washington who gains to the N22 for a gain of two yards.

**END OF FIRST HALF:
COLORADO 14, NORTHWESTERN 7**

THIRD QUARTER

Mirkopulos kick off for Northwestern from the N40. Northwestern will defend the south goal. Colorado will defend the north goal. Deep for Colorado are Hornberger, Ballage, and Mayberry. The kick by Mirkopulos is taken by Ballage at the goal line. He goes up the west side to the C32 for a return of thirty-two yards.

14:54 COLORADO
1/10-C32 - Mayberry over the middle to the C38 for a gain of six yards. Mayberry is injured on the play, leaves the field on his own
2/4 -C38 - Solomon keeps, goes over the middle, and gains to the C46 for a gain of eight yards, Mayberry returns to the field
1/10-C46 - Solomon sweeps left and gains to mid-field for a gain of four yards
2/6 - 50 - Solomon throws complete to Ballage in the right flat, the gain is to the N45 for five yards
3/1 -N45 - Hornberger goes left on a sweep and gets to the N40 for a gain of five yards
1/10-N40 - Solomon throws complete to Howard on the right side, the pass is complete to the N14 for a gain of twenty-six yards
1/10-N14 - Mayberry over left guard to the N11 for a gain of three yards
2/7 -N11 - Solomon rolls left and goes over left tackle to the N9 for a gain of two yards
3/5 -N9 - Mayberry over left guard to the N6 for a gain of three yards
4/2 -N6 - Mayberry cracks over right tackle to the N2 for a gain of two yards
1/G -N2 - Mayberry bulls his way into the end zone by going over right tackle
Time: 10:29
PAT by Dadiotis is not good
SCORE: COLORADO 20 NORTHWESTERN 7

Dadiotis kicks off for Colorado from the C40. Geegan and Hill are deep for Northwestern. The kick is taken by Geegan in the end zone and downed. There is no return.
10:29 NORTHWESTERN
1/10-N20 - Mishler over left guard to the N24 for a gain of four yards

2/6 -N24 - Strasser passes incomplete to Schmitt in the right flat
3/6 -N24 - Strasser passes into the right flat, it is intercepted by McCabe at the N25 and returned one yard to the N24, intended receiver was Poulos

9:38 COLORADO
1/10-N24 - Solomon keeps and goes to the N20 for a gain of four yards
2/6 -N20 - Mayberry over left guard to the N12 for a gain of eight yards
1/10-N12 - Mayberry over left guard to the N7 for a gain of five yards
2/5 -N7 - Mayberry over the left end, he loses one yard to the N8
3/6 -N8 - Solomon keeps, rolls right, goes over right tackle, and gets to the N1 for a gain of seven yards
1/G -N1 - Mayberry over right guard for no gain
2/G -N1 - Solomon keeps, goes over the middle, but does not make the one yard
3/G -N1 - Solomon keeps, goes over the middle, no gain
4/G -N1 - Mayberry over the right side for a touchdown
Time: 5:23
PAT by Dadiotis is good
SCORE: COLORADO 27 NORTHWESTERN 7

Dadiotis kicks off for Colorado from the C40. Deep for Northwestern are Bahoric and Geegan. The kick is taken in the end zone and fumbled. Bahoric picks it up and tries to come out of the end zone. He fumbles. It is recovered by Cullins for Colorado at the N1. Colorado has possession.
5:23 COLORADO
1/G -N1 - Mayberry over right tackle for a touchdown
Time: 5:20
PAT by Dadiotis is good
SCORE: COLORADO 34 NORTHWESTERN 7

Dadiotis kicks off for Colorado from the C40. Breitbeil and Hill are deep for Northwestern. The kick is taken in the end zone by Hill who returns the ball to the N16 for a return of sixteen yards

5:17 NORTHWESTERN
1/10-N16 - Washington gains to the N21 for a gain of five yards
2/5 -N21 - Washington is hit for a loss at the N17
3/9 -N17 - Washington gains three yards to the N20
4/6 -N20 - Christensen punts for Northwestern, Davis and Roberts are deep Davis takes the punt at the C40 no return

SEPTEMBER 30, 1978

3:19 COLORADO
1/10-C40 - Mayberry over the middle to the C44 for a gain of four yards
2/6 -C44 - Hornberger over the right side to the N44 for a gain of twelve yards
1/10-N44 - Mayberry over the left tackle to the N41 for a gain of three yards
2/7 -N41 - Hornberger over the right end to the N35 for a gain of six yards
3/1 -N35 - Hornberger over the middle to the N29 for a gain of six yards
1/10-N29 - Mayberry over left tackle to the N27 for a gain of two yards
2/8 -N27 - Solomon over the right side and goes to the N2 and a gain of twenty-five yards
1/G -N2 - Mayberry over the right side into the end zone for a touchdown
Time: 00:03
PAT by Dadiotis is good
SCORE: COLORADO 41 NORTHWESTERN 7

Dadiotis kicks off for Colorado from the C40. Deep for Northwestern are Hill and Geegan. Hill takes the kick in the end zone and returns it to the N23 for a return of twenty-three yards.

END OF THIRD QUARTER:
COLORADO 41, NORTHWESTERN 7

FOURTH QUARTER

15:00 NORTHWESTERN
1/10-N23 - Strasser throws a quick pass to Hill on the left side, it is complete and Hill gains to the N37 for a gain of fourteen yards
1/10-N37 - Pitch to Hill who goes left to the N42 for a gain of five yards
2/5 -N42 - Mishler tries right guard and loses one yard to the N41
3/6 -N41 - Strasser throws Bogan complete for nine yards to the mid-field stripe
1/10- 50 - Mishler tries the right side and gains nothing
2/10- 50 - Strasser throws incomplete to Poulos, it is broken up by Cullins in the right flat
3/10- 50 - Strasser passes complete to Schmitt in the right flat Schmitt gains to the C45 for a gain of five yards
4/5 -C45 - Christensen punts to Davis, the punt is allowed to roll and is downed at the C3, punt is good for forty-two yards

12:34 COLORADO
1/10-C3 - Davis is quarterback for Colorado, he keeps, breaks over the middle, and goes to the C11 for a gain of eight yards
2/2 -C11 - Davis keeps, goes over the left side, and gains ten yards to the C21

1/10-C21 - Davis rolls right and overthrows Boyd who was clear along the east sidelines, incomplete pass
2/10-C21 - Davis keeps, rolls right, and tries right end, he gains one yard to the C22
3/9 -C22 - Davis drops to pass and throws to Pugh, Pugh drops the pass along the east sidelines
4/9 -C22 - Olander punts for Colorado, Geegan and North are deep for Northwestern, North calls for a fair catch at the N37, punt is good for forty-one yards

10:37 NORTHWESTERN
1/10-N37 - Johnson over the left side to the N39 for a gain of two yards
2/8 -N39 - Washington around the left end to the N44 for a gain of five yards
3/3 -N44 - Pitch to Johnson who goes left, scrambles, and loses six yards to the N38
4/9 -N38 - Christensen punts to Davis at the C17, he returns the ball to the C23 for a return of five yards, punt is good for forty-five yards

8:37 COLORADO
1/10-C23 - Davis is quarterback, Humble over the middle to the C26 for a gain of three yards
2/7 -C26 - Pitch to Beebe who turns the right corner, along the sidelines and gains nine yards to the C35
1/10-C35 - Davis keeps, rolls left, goes over the left end, and gains nine yards to the C44
2/1 -C44 - Humble over the middle to the N49 for a gain of seven yards
1/10-N49 - Davis keeps, goes left, and loses two yards to the C49
2/12-C49 - Davis rolls right and throws complete to Harden who gains to the N43 for a gain of eight yards
3/4 -N43 - Beebe over the middle to the N30 for a gain of thirteen yards
1/10-N30 - Davis fakes, goes over right guard to the N9 for a gain of twenty-one yards
1/G -N9 - Humble over right guard to the N7 for a gain of two yards
2/G -N7 - Davis draws the opposition offsides by moving too soon, ball is moved to the N12
2/G -N12 - Humble over left guard to the N6 for a gain of six yards
3/G -N6 - Davis keeps and goes over the right side to the N1 for a gain of five yards
4/G -N1 - Davis keeps, rolls left, goes over the left guard, and scores
Time: 3:17
PAT by Dadiotis is good
SCORE: COLORADO 48 NORTHWESTERN 7

219

Dadiotis kicks off for Colorado from the C40. Geegan and Hill are deep for Northwestern. The kick by Dadiotis is taken by Hill at the N5. It is fumbled and recovered by Hill at the N12. The return is for seven yards

3:14 NORTHWESTERN
- 1/10-N12 - Breitbeil is quarterback, Washington goes over the left side to the N21 for a gain of nine yards
- 2/1 -N21 - Schmitt over right guard to the N24 for a gain of three yards
- 1/10-N24 - Washington rolls right and is hit down at the N17 for a loss of seven yards
- 2/17-N17 - Schmitt over right guard to the N20 for a gain of three yards
- 3/14-N20 - Pitch to Washington is dropped, he picks it up, tries to go left, and loses nine yards to the N11
- 4/23-N11 - Christensen punts for Northwestern, deep for Colorado is Olander. Olander takes the punt at the C49 and goes to the N42, return is for nine yards, punt is for forty yards

1:04 COLORADO
- 1/10-N42 - Beebe gains four yards to the N38
- 2/6 -N38 - Davis sweeps left to the N30 for a gain of eight yards
- 1/10-N30 - Beebe sweeps right and streaks to the N3 for a first down and a gain of twenty-seven yards
- 1/G -N3 - Beebe over the left side for a touchdown
  Time: :03
  PAT by Dadiotis is good
  SCORE: COLORADO 55 NORTHWESTERN 7

Dadiotis kicks off for Colorado from the C40. Hill and Breitbeil are deep for Northwestern. The kick is short. It is recovered by Northwestern on the N30.

END OF GAME:
COLORADO 55, NORTHWESTERN 7

National Collegiate Athletic Association
FINAL TEAM STATISTICS

	NORTH-WESTERN	COLO-RADO
First Downs	12	39
Rushing	9	35
Passing	3	4
Penalty	0	0
Rushing Attempts	37	79
Yards Rushing	134	488
Yards Lost Rushing	31	5
Net Yards Rushing	103	483
Net Yards Passing	86	98
Passes Attempted	20	12
Passes Completed	12	8
Had Intercepted	1	0
Total Offensive Plays	57	91
Total Net Yards	189	581
Average Gain Per Play	3.3	6.4
Fumbles: Number—Lost	2/1	2/2
Penalties: Number—Yards	2/30	2/20
Interceptions: Number—Yards	0/0	1/1
Number of Punts—Yards	9/395	2/78
Average Per Punt	43.9	39.0
Punt Returns: Number—Yards	8/79	0/0
Kickoff Returns: Number—Yards	2/94	6/88

220

SEPTEMBER 30, 1978

**PURDUE
VS.
NOTRE DAME**
Notre Dame Stadium
Temp: 65°
Wind: WSW 10-12 mph
FIRST QUARTER

ND won the toss and elected to receive, Purdue to defend southern goal.
Stone returned Sovereen's kick 22 to ND 29. (Biorkus)
NOTRE DAME
1/10-N29 - Ferguson hit for 3. (Motts)
2/7 -N32 - Ferguson gained 2. (Turner)
3/5 -N34 - Montana kept for 4. (Motts)
4/1 -N38 - Restic punted to Pope who signalled for a fair catch at Purdue 13, a kick of 49 yds.

13:27 PURDUE
1/10-P13 - Macon broke for 13 (Harrison)
1/10-P26 - Pope slanted for 3. (Case)
2/7 -P29 - Pope fumbled and recovered for 3. (Weston)
3/4 -P32 - Macon picked up 2. (Heimkreiter)
4/2 -P34 - Eagin kicked to Waymer who returned 31 yds. to P46, 43 yd punt.

11:15 NOTRE DAME
1/10-P46 - Ferguson failed to gain, but ND was penalized for holding to the Irish 39.
1/25-N39 - Montana passed to Ferguson for 5. (Jackson)
2/20-N44 - Ferguson hit for 2. (Clark)
3/18-N46 - Montana overthrew Haines at the P25.
4/18-N46 - Restic punted to Pope who signalled for a fair catch, but Gallivan caught the ball, a kick of 41 yds. to the P13.

9:42 PURDUE
1/10-P13 - Pope circled right end for 9 yds. (Gibbons)
2/1 -P22 - Macon hit center for 3 (Golic)
1/10-P25 - Herrmann's first pass intended for Harris was incomplete.
2/10-P25 - Herrmann passed to Harris for 24 (Gibbons)
1/10-P49 - Macon was stopped for no gain by Heimkreiter.
2/10-P49 - Herrmann passed to Young for 13 (Golic)
1/10-N38 - Pope slanted around right end for 7.
2/3 -N31 - Macon cracked for 6 (Golic)
1/10-N25 - Pope was stopped by Heimkreiter and Leopold after 2.
2/8 -N23 - Herrmann passed to Young for 12 (Leopold)
1/10-N11 - Herrmann's pass intended for Harris was incomplete in the end zone.
2/10-N11 - Herrmann, from the shotgun overthrew Smith in the end zone.
3/10-N11 - Herrmann hit Smith in the end zone but Waymer stripped the ball from his hands for an incomplete pass.
4/10-N11 - Sovereen, with Burrell holding, then booted a field goal of 28 yds. with 5:15 to go.
SCORE: PURDUE 3, NOTRE DAME 0

Stone returned Sovereen's kick 15 yds. to N22.
5:15 NOTRE DAME
1/10-N22 - Ferguson was slammed after 1 by Clark.
2/9 -N23 - Montana's pass intended for Holohan was intercepted by W. Smith on the Irish 44.

4:31 PURDUE
1/10-N44 - Herrmann's long pass intended for Young was incomplete at the N11.
2/10-N44 - Herrmann's swing pass to Augustyniak was good for 5 yds. (Johnson)
3/5 -N39 - Herrmann passed to Young for 8 (Whittington)
1/10-N31 - Macon gained 3. (Whittington)
2/7 -N28 - Pope slanted for 2. (Weston)
3/5 -N26 - Herrmann passed to Smith for 13 (Waymer)
1/10-N13 - Pope gained 1. (Weston)
2/9 -N12 - Herrmann's pass intended for Harris in the end zone was incomplete.
3/9 -Herrmann was nailed by Browner at the N28 and he recovered the fumble at the N37, a loss of 25 yds. for Herrmann.

:55 NOTRE DAME
1/10-N37 - Ferguson gained 6. (Moss)
2/4 -N43 - Ferguson added 2 more(Jackson)

END OF FIRST QUARTER:
PURDUE 3, NOTRE DAME 0

SECOND QUARTER

NOTRE DAME
3/2 -N45 - Ferguson popped for 6 (Moss)
1/10-P49 - Ferguson picked up 1. (Motts)
2/9 -P48 - Montana's pass intended for Ferguson was incomplete.
3/9 -P48 - Montana passed to Grindinger for 5.
4/4 -P43 - Restic then punted out of bounds on the Purdue 20, a 23 yd punt.

13:21 PURDUE
1/10-P19 - Pope lost 2. (Whittington)
2/12-P17 - Macon hit for 4 on a delay. (Heimkreiter)
3/8 -P21 - Macon broke over right end for 24 yds. (Gibbons)
1/10-P45 - Pope cracked for 5. (Whittington)
2/5 - 50 - Augustyniak gained 2. (Case)
3/3 -N48 - Herrmann failed to find a receiver and raced for 10: (Whittington)
1/10-N38 - Herrmann's pass intended for Smith was broken up by Harrison.
2/10-N38 - Pope picked up 4. (Heimkreiter)
3/6 -N34 - Herrmann's swing pass to Augustyniak gained 5. (Browner)
4/1 -N29 - Herrmann passed to Pope in the flat for 5 (Leopold)
1/10-N24 - Macon slashed for 4. (Heimkreiter)
2/6 -N20 - Pope took a pitchout for 4. (Gibbons)
3/2 -N16 - Pope took another pitchout for 1, missing a 1st down by inches.
4/1 -N15 - Macon then jumped over center for 4 (Golic)
1/10-N11 - Herrmann overthrew Young in the end zone.
2/10-N11 - Hankerd nailed Herrmann for a 13 yd loss.
3/23-N24 - Herrmann pitched to Pope who was spilled by Browner for a 6 yd loss.
4/29-N30 - Sovereen then booted a 47 yd field goal with 5:27 to go, with Burrell holding.
SCORE: PURDUE 6, NOTRE DAME 0

Stone returned Sovereen's kick 21 yds. but N was penalized for clipping to the Irish 11.

5:22 NOTRE DAME
1/10-N11 - Heavens was nailed by Motts for a 2 yd loss.
2/12-N9 - Montana passed to Masztak for 17 (Motts)
1/10-N26 - Ferguson picked up 12 (Harris)
1/10-N38 - Ferguson fumbled, but Huffman recovered for the Irish for a 4 yd loss.
2/14-N34 - Montana passed to Ferguson for 8. (Moss)
3/6 -N42 - Montana passed to Heavens for 16 (Moss)
1/10-P42 - Heavens then slanted over right tackle for 17 (Harris)
1/10-P25 - Ferguson was upended by Harris after 5.

2/5 -P20 - Montana kept for 1, being forced out of bounds by Motts.
3/4 -P19 - 1:40 to go with N taking time out. Courey was stopped by Loushin for a loss of 5.
4/9 -P24 - Unis, with Knafel holding, missed a field goal which dropped in front of the goal posts. It was a 41 yd attempt.

:54 PURDUE
1/10-P24 - Macon slashed for 11 (Whittington)
1/10-P35 - Augustyniak fumbled and recovered for Purdue for a 1 yd loss

**END OF SECOND QUARTER:
PURDUE 6, NOTRE DAME 0**

THIRD QUARTER

Male kicked out of the end zone for a touchback.
PURDUE
1/10-P20 - Macon hit for 8. (Heimkreiter)
2/2 -P28 - Pope added 3 (Calhoun)
1/10-P31 - Pope lost 1. (Heimkreiter)
2/11-P30 - Pope took a pitchout for 2. (Case)
3/9 -P32 - Herrmann's pass to Gallivan was incomplete as Waymer was on the play.
4/9 -P32 - Eagin punted to Waymer who returned to the N36, a 35 yd punt.

13:11 NOTRE DAME
1/10-N37 - Ferguson hit center for 3. (Turner)
2/7 -N40 - Montana passed to Holohan for 28 yds. (Moss)
1/10-P33 - Heavens slanted for 11 (Harris)
1/10-P22 - Heavens slipped and fell for no gain.
2/10-P22 - Courey picked up 3. (Moss)
3/7 -P19 - Montana was spilled by Turner for a 17 yd loss
4/24-P36 - Restic then kicked out of bounds on the Purdue 9, a 28 yd punt.

10:42 PURDUE
1/10-P9 -Pope was nailed by J. Case after 1.
2/9 -P10 - Macon failed to gain. (Calhoun)
3/9 -P10 - Macon stopped by Calhoun after 1.
4/8 -P11 - Eagin then kicked dead to the Purdue 47, a 36 yd punt.

8:55 NOTRE DAME
1/10-P47 - Ferguson broke up the middle for 6. (Johanson)
2/4 -P41 - Ferguson crashed for 7 (Motts)
1/10-P34 - Ferguson went around right end for 7 more. (Harris)
2/3 -P27 - Heavens failed to gain. (Motts)
3/3 -P27 - Heavens then broke over left tackle and raced into the end zone for a T.D. He broke a tackle from Wayne Smith. Unis, with Knafel holding, booted the conversion.
SCORE: NOTRE DAME 7, PURDUE 6

SEPTEMBER 30, 1978

Male kicked into the end zone for a touchback.
7:51 PURDUE
1/10-P20 - On an attempted flea flicker play, Herrmann's pass was intercepted by Randy Harrison on the Purdue 48 and he returned to the Purdue 14, a 34 yard return.

NOTRE DAME
1/10-N24 - Ferguson gained 3. (Moss)
2/7 -N27 - Ferguson gained 1 more.
3/6 -N28 - Heavens was stopped by Jackson after 3.
4/3 -N31 - Restic punted to Pope who returned 3 to the Purdue 33. (Heimkreiter)

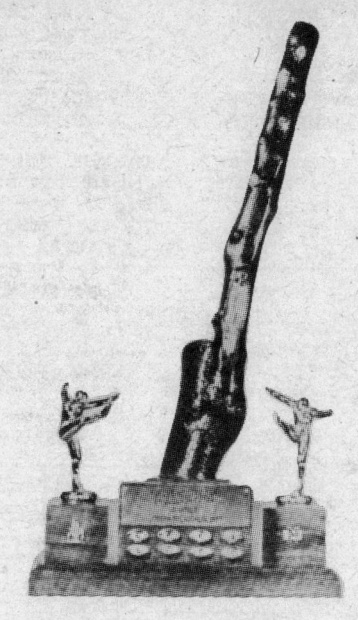

NOTRE DAME
1/10-P14 - Ferguson hit for 6. (Motts)
2/4 -P8 - Ferguson was stopped by Turner and Moss for a yard loss.
3/5 -P9 - Ferguson was nailed by Loushin for no gain.
4/5 -P9 - Unis, with Knafel holding, then booted a 27 yard field goal with 6:03 to go.
SCORE: NOTRE DAME 10, PURDUE 6

Male kicked to Moss who returned 17 to the Purdue 22, but the Irish were offside and had to kick over from the N35. This time Male kicked to Moss who returned 26 to the Purdue 28.
6:03 PURDUE
1/10-P28 - Pope circled right end for 9. (Calhoun)
2/1 -P37 - Macon plunged for 3 (Golic)
1/10-P40 - Herrmann's pass to Pope was incomplete.
2/10-P40 - Oliver at QB for N. Oliver fumbled and recovered for a 3 yd. loss.
3/13-P37 - Oliver passed to Pope for 6. (Whittington)
4/7 -P43 - Eagin punted to Waymer who was nailed immediately on the Irish 24 by Kingsbury, a punt of 33 yds.

2:02 PURDUE
1/10-P33 - Macon gained 3. (Heimkreiter)
2/7 -P36 - Macon hit for 2. (Calhoun)
3/5 -P38 - Oliver was nailed by Gibbons attempting to pass, and picked up 3.
4/2 -P41 - Eagin punted to Gibbons on the N18 and he returned 10 to the Irish 28, the punt being good for 41 yards.

:18 NOTRE DAME
1/10-N29 - Montana passed to Hart for 15.

END OF THIRD QUARTER:
NOTRE DAME 10, PURDUE 6

FOURTH QUARTER

NOTRE DAME
1/10-N44 - Ferguson slanted for 2. (Johanson)
2/8 -N46 - Montana was dumped by Jackson and Turner for a 10 yd loss.
3/18-N36 - Montana's pass was intercepted by Moss on the P44 where Haines, for whom the pass was intended, dropped him after a 3 yd gain.

13:33 PURDUE
1/10-P47 - Herrmann back in for Purdue. Macon picked up 3. (Heimkreiter)
2/7 - 50 - Herrmann's safety valve pass to Macon gained 5. (Gibbons)
3/2 -N45 - Pope took a pitchout but was stopped for no gain by Heimkreiter.
4/2 -N45 - Eagin then punted into the end zone for a touchback, a 45 yd punt.

11:41 NOTRE DAME
1/10-N20 - Heavens slashed for 1. (Turner)
2/9 -N21 - Ferguson picked up 3. (Motts)
3/6 -N24 - Heavens took a pitchout for 4. (Clark)
4/2 -N28 - Restic punted to Pope who signalled for a fair catch at the P21, a kick of 51 yds.

9:50 PURDUE
1/10-P21 - Herrmann's long pass to Young was broken up by Waymer. But Purdue was called for holding and the ball put on the P10.
1/21-P10 - Pope gained 6.
2/15-O16 - Herrmann's long pass to Harris was overthrown on the N35.
3/15-P16 - Herrmann passed to Burrell for 23 yds.
1/10-P39 - Macon hit center for 5. (Golic)
2/5 -P44 - Pope was spilled by Waymer for no gain.
3/5 -P44 - Herrmann passed to Pope, but Browner nailed him after a gain of 1.
4/4 -P45 - Eagin shanked a punt to the Irish 16 where Waymer downed it. The kick was good for 39 yds.

7:11 NOTRE DAME
1/10-N16 - Ferguson circled right end for 11 (Floyd)
1/10-N27 - Heavens broke over the middle for 10 more (Moss)
1/10-N37 - Ferguson slashed for 3. (Moss)
2/7 -N40 - Heaven hit center for 3 more. (Loushin)
3/4 -N43 - Ferguson was pinned by Loushin on an attempted sweep for a 3 yd loss.
4/7 -N40 - Restic punted to Gallivan who signalled for a fair catch on the Purdue 19, a 41 yd punt from scrimmage

4:35 PURDUE
1/10-P19 - Herrmann passed to Macon for 7. (Browner)
2/3 -P26 - Herrmann's swing pass was dropped by Macon.
3/3 -P26 - Herrmann passed to Young for 11 (Browner)
1/10-P37 - Weston dropped Herrmann for a 7 yd loss
2/17-P30 - Herrmann's pass intended for Raymond Smith was called for offensive pass interference by Smith and the ball placed on the P15.
2/32-P15 - Herrmann's pass to Young was good for 29 yds. before Harrison dropped him.
4/3 -P44 - Herrmann tossed a swing pass to Macon for 9.
1/10-N47 - Herrmann's pass to Pope was incomplete at the N26.
2/10-N47 - Herrmann was sacked by Weston, but N was called for holding and the ball placed on the N37.
1/10-N37 - Herrmann's pass was then intercepted by Heimkreiter on the Irish 21 where Harris then tackled him for a 2 yd loss on the return

1:47 NOTRE DAME
1/10-N19 - Heavens gained 2. (Johanson)
2/8 -N21 - Heavens slanted for 3. (Clark)
3/5 -N24 - Montana on a keeper circled right end for 5.
1/10-N29 - Montana fell on the ball, but Purdue was called for a personal foul.
1/10-N43 - Montana lost 1 at center. (Moss)
2/11-N42 - Montana kept the ball for a 1 yd loss (Clark)
3/11-N41 - Montana again kept the ball

FINAL SCORE:
NOTRE DAME 10, PURDUE 6

National Collegiate Athletic Association
FINAL TEAM STATISTICS

	PURDUE	NOTRE DAME
First Downs	18	14
Rushing	9	9
Passing	9	4
Penalty	0	1
Rushing Attempts	47	48
Yards Rushing	174	184
Yards Lost Rushing	56	45
Net Yards Rushing	118	139
Net Yards Passing	167	95
Passes Attempted	31	11
Passes Completed	16	7
Had Intercepted	2	2
Total Offensive Plays	78	59
Total Net Yards	285	234
Average Gain Per Play	3.7	4.0
Fumbles: Number—Lost	3/1	1/0
Penalties: Number—Yards	3/41	4/51
Interceptions: Number—Yards	2/3	2/32
Number of Punts—Yards	7/264	7/271
Average Per Punt	37.7	38.7
Punt Returns: Number—Yards	1/3	4/38
Kickoff Returns: Number—Yards	1/26	3/57

SEPTEMBER 30, 1978

**ILLINOIS
VS.
SYRACUSE**
Archbold Stadium
Temp: 65°
Wind: S 10-20 mph
Skies: Partly Cloudy
FIRST QUARTER

Syracuse lost the toss. Syracuse will kick off from the west goal. Jacobs kicks to Foster and he returned it for 82 yards by Sickles
ILLINOIS
1/10-S15 - Weber for 10 by O'Leary and Newman
1/G -S5 - Paul for 3 by Collins
2/G -S2 - Paul carries for TD Finzer kicks good PENALTY: Syracuse offsides

Finzer kicks to Monk, returns for 23 yards by Bonner
SYRACUSE
1/10-S27 - Farneski to Monk for 3 by Adams and Venegoni
2/7 -S30 - Hartman carries for 3 by Flynn and Ralph
3/4 -S33 - Farneski incomplete to Ishman PENALTY: illegal procedure on Syracuse penalty refused
4/4 -S33 - Goodwill punts to the I31

ILLINOIS
1/10-I31 - Powell for two by Richardson
2/8 -I33 - Weber for 3 by Collins
3/5 -I36 - McCullough incomplete to Barnes by Patterson
4/5 -I36 - Finzer kicks to Patterson who downs it on the S39 by Brzyszkiewicz

SYRACUSE
1/10-S39 - Monk for 9 by Kelley
2/1 -S48 - Monk carries for 3 by Sullivan
1/10-I49 - Hartman for no gain Flynn and Ralph
2/10-I49 - Farneski to Ishman incomplete
3/10-I49 - Farneski incomplete to Jones by Venegoni and Gillen
4/10-I49 - Goodwill punts into the end zone

ILLINOIS
1/10-I20 - McCullough keeps for no gain by Collins
2/10-I20 - McCullough to Barnes complete for 11 by Patterson
1/10-I31 - Weber carries for 5 by Collins and Cameron
2/5 -I36 - Powell for 5 by Collins and McCullough

3/1 -I41 - McCullough keeps for 1 by center of line
1/10-I42 - Strader for 3 by Richardson
2/7 -I45 - Strader for 15 by Newman and O'Leary
1/10-S40 - Strader for 8 by O'Leary and Collins
2/2 -S32 - McCullough complete to Rouse for 29 by Harvey
1/G -S3 - Powell carries for TD Finzer kicks good

Finzer kicks to Monk carries for 15 by Venegoni
SYRACUSE
1/10-S27 - Farneski to Zambuto for 6 by Levitt and Ramshaw
2/4 -S33 - Morris for 4 by Sullivan
1/10-S37 - Farneski to Monk for 5 by Thiede
2/5 -S42 - Monk carries for 2 by Gillen
3/3 -S44 - Farneski to Monk for 3 by Levitt
4/1 -S47 - Monk carries for 2 by Thiede
1/10-S49 - Farneski keeps for 9 by Sullivan
2/1 -I42 - Monk carries for 2 by Levitt and Ramshaw
1/10-I40 - Farneski to Morris for 7 by Flynn
2/3 -I33 - Farneski incomplete to Jones covered by Levitt
3/3 -I33 - Farneski keeps for 3 by Flynn and Sullivan
4/1 -I30 - Hartman carries for 3 by Sullivan
1/10-I27 - Monk carries for 11 by Venegoni
1/10-I16 - Farneski to Monk for 1 by Venegoni and Tucker
2/9 -I15 - Farneski complete to Semall for 15 by Levitt
1/G -IG - Hartman carries for TD, Jacobs kicks good

225

Jacobs kicks to Foster returns for 36 by Sickles

ILLINOIS
1/10-I38 - Weber carries for 12 by O'Leary
1/10- 50 - Powell for 3 by Conners

**END OF FIRST QUARTER:
ILLINOIS 14, SYRACUSE 7**

SECOND QUARTER

ILLINOIS
2/7 -S47 - Weber carries for 2 (team)
3/5 -S45 - McCullough back to pass loses 3 by Cameron and Gyetvay facemask against Syracuse
1/10-S30 - Weber for 4 by Collins and Connors
2/6 -S26 - Weber to Powell for 4 by Tate and Collins
3/2 -S22 - Weber carries for 3 by Cameron and Connors
1/10-S19 - Powell for 6 by Harvey
2/4 -S13 - Powell for 3 by O'Leary
3/1 -S10 - Weber for 8 by McCullough
1/G -S2 - Powell carries for 1 by Kollar and Gyetvay
2/G -S1 - Powell carries hit by center of line and fumbles
Fumble recovered by McCullough of Syracuse at the 1 yard line

SYRACUSE
1/10-S1 - Monk carries for no gain by Gillen
2/10-S1 - PENALTY: offsides on Illinois
2/5 -S6 - Hartman for 3 (Levitt)
3/2 -S9 - Hartman carries for 4 by Gillen
1/10-S13 - Monk for 3 by Ramshaw and Thiede
2/7 -S16 - Farneski to Morris for 9 by Venegoni
1/10-S25 - Farneski to Morris for 48 by Venegoni
1/10-I27 - Hartman carries for 13 by Levitt and Venegoni
1/10-I14 - Farneski for -3 by Venegoni
2/13-I17 - Farneski intercepted by Levitt

ILLINOIS
1/10-I18 - Weber for 3 by Collins and Gyetvay
2/7 -I21 - McCullough keeps for 4 by Collins and Newman
3/3 -I25 - Powell for 1 by Collins and Gyetvay
4/2 -I26 - Finzer kicks to Monk returns for 11 by Boeke

SYRACUSE
1/10-S36 - Monk carries for 1 by Thornton and Ralph
2/9 -S37 - Monk inc. to Zambuto by Tucker
3/9 -S37 - Farneski keeps for -3 by Pazesic
4/12-S34 - Goodwill punts ball downed by Syracuse on the I30

ILLINOIS
1/10-I30 - Powell for 1 (team)
2/9 -I31 - McCullough to Barnes complete for 14 by Patterson
1/10-I45 - McCullough keeps for 6 by Gyetvay
2/4 -S49 - McCullough inc. to Barnes by Patterson
3/4 -S49 - McCullough complete to Boeke for 6 by Newman
1/10-S43 - Rouse carries for 1 by Patterson
2/9 -S42 - Dismuke for 3, fumbles recovered by Gyetvay but ball blown dead before fumble
3/6 -S39 - McCullough complete to Strader for 23 by Tate
1/10-S16 - McCullough keeps for 14 by O'Leary and Harvey
1/G -S2 - McCullough keeps for -1 by Collins
2/G -S3 - Dismuke carries for 2 by Newman and Collins
3/G -S 1 - McCullough keeps for TD 14:40 of the 2nd quarter Finzer kicks good
PENALTY illegal procedure on Syracuse. Finzer kicks good.

Finzer kicks to Monk returns for 27 by Durrell

SYRACUSE
1/10-S27 - Farneski keeps for no gain by Adams

**END OF FIRST HALF:
ILLINOIS 21, SYRACUSE 7**

226

SEPTEMBER 30, 1978

THIRD QUARTER

Syracuse wins toss, elects to receive at the east goal.
Finzer kicks to Morris returns for 39 by Finzer

SYRACUSE
1/10-S42 - Monk carries for no gain by Ralph and Gillen
2/10-S42 - Farneski keeps for 2 by Sullivan and Ramshaw
3/8 -S44 - Farneski complete to Jones for 9 by Gillen
1/10-I47 - Morris for 2 (team)
2/8 -I45 - Morris for no gain by Ralph
3/8 -I45 - Farneski inc. to Morris
4/8 -I45 - Goodwill punts into the end zone for a touchback

ILLINOIS
1/10-I20 - Weber carries for 2 by Gyetvay
2/8 -I22 - McCullough keeps for 8 by O'Leary
1/10-I30 - Strader carries for 19 by O'Leary
1/10-I49 - Powell carries for 5 (team)
2/5 -S46 - Strader carries for 2 by Rotunda McCullough
3/3 -S44 - McCullough complete to Barnes for 10 by Harvey
1/10-S34 - McCullough sweeps on right end for 9 by Patterson
2/1 -S25 - Weber carries for 2 by Richardson
1/10-S23 - Powell for 2 by Richardson
2/8 -S21 - McCullough keeps for 6 by Collins and McCullough
PENALTY: illegal procedure Illinois
2/13-S26 - McCullough keeps for 9 by Collins
3/4 -S17 - McCullough keeps for 11 by Harvey
1/G -S6 - Lateral to Powell fumbles and recovered by Illinois for 5
2/G -S1 - McCullough keeps for TD
Finzer kicks good

Finzer kicks to Harvey returns for 30 by Finzer PENALTY: clipping

SYRACUSE
1/10-S11 - Farneski keeps for -2 by Ramshaw and Ralph
2/12-S9 - Farneski to Monk for 6 by Levitt
3/5 -S16 - Farneski back to pass by Thornton tackled for -8
4/13-S8 - Goodwill punts to Hardy for fair catch
PENALTY: personal foul Illinois
1/10-S23 - Monk for 2 by Ramshaw and Ralph
2/8 -S25 - Hartman carries for 3 by Sullivan
PENALTY: piling on Illinois
1/10-S43 - Farneski to Morris for 18 by Hardy
1/10-I39 - Monk carries for 3 by Ralph and Thornton
2/7 -I36 - Morris for 8 by Levitt
1/10-I28 - Monk carries for 7 by Gillen
2/3 -I21 - Morris carries for 4 by Ralph and Gillen
1/10-I17 - Morris carries for no gain by Levitt
2/10-I17 - Farneski complete to Monk for 9 by Venegoni and Tucker
3/1 -I8 - Monk carries for 3 by Durrell
PENALTY: illegal procedure Illinois
1/G -I4 - Monk carries for TD
Jacobs kicks good

227

Jacobs kicks to Foster returns for 22 by Sickles
ILLINOIS
1/10-I24 - Weber carries for 4 by Kinley

END OF THIRD QUARTER:
ILLINOIS 28, SYRACUSE 14

FOURTH QUARTER

ILLINOIS
2/6 -I28 - McCullough to Powell for 1 by Kinley and Arkeilpane
3/5 -I29 - McCullough to Barnes complete for 10 by Patterson
1/10-I39 - PENALTY delay of game Illinois
1/15-I34 - McCullough to Powell for 11 by Kinley
2/4 -I45 - McCullough to Weber for 6 by Collins and Kinley
1/10-S49 - Powell carries for 3 by Arkeilpane and Collins
2/7 -S46 - Strader carries for 10 by Patterson
1/10-S36 - Strader for 2 by Kinley
2/8 -S34 - McCullough keeps for 1 by Kinley, Collins and Richardson
3/7 -S33 - McCullough keeps for 3 up the middle by Rotunda
4/4 -S30 - McCullough intended for Rouse intercepted by Tate

SYRACUSE
1/10-S16 - Farneski intended to Semall inc. by Sullivan
2/10-S16 - Farneski keeps for 9 by Gillen
3/1 -S25 - Morris for 2 by Ralph
1/10-S27 - Farneski to Morris complete for 7 by Ramshaw
2/3 -S34 - Morris carries for 6 by Durrell
1/10-S40 - Morris carries for 3 by Durrell and Ramshaw
2/7 -S43 - Farneski complete to Williams for 16 by Sullivan
1/10-I40 - Farneski keeps for 4 by Hardy
2/6 -I36 - Farneski to Morris for no gain by Levitt
3/6 -I36 - Farneski intended to Monk intercepted by Venegoni (Hodges)

ILLINOIS
1/10-I30 - Weber carries for 2 by O'Leary and Connors
2/8 -I32 - McCullough to Powell for 17 by O'Leary
1/10-I49 - Weber carried for 6 by Kinley
2/4 -S45 - Strader for 3 by Connors
3/1 -S42 - Powell carries for 1 by Collins
1/10-S41 - Powell carries for 4 by Kinley
2/6 -S37 - Strader for 12 by Connors and Arkeilpane
1/10-S25 - Powell for 3 by Cameron and Collins
2/7 -S22 - Strader for 2 by Neugebauer and Arkeilpane
3/5 -S20 - Strader for 7 by Neugebauer

1/10-S13 - Strader carries for 4 by Kollar
2/6 -S9 - Powell carries for no gain by Collins
3/6 -S9 - McCullough keeps for -4 by Kollar and Gyetvay
4/10-S13 - Finzer kicks FG no good

SYRACUSE
1/10-S20 - Farneski inc. to Jones by Sullivan
2/10-S20 - Farneski complete to Morris for 6 by Ramshaw
3/4 -S26 - Farneski inc. to Monk by Gillen
4/4 -S26 - Farneski intended for Jones intercepted by Levitt

ILLINOIS
1/10-S46 - Stieger carries for 2 by Gyetvay and Connors
2/8 -S44 - Dismuke carries for 5 (team)

END OF GAME:
ILLINOIS 28, SYRACUSE 14

National Collegiate Athletic Association
FINAL TEAM STATISTICS

	ILLINOIS	SYR-ACUSE
First Downs	25	21
Rushing	17	15
Passing	7	3
Penalty	1	3
Rushing Attempts	71	52
Yards Rushing	329	244
Yards Lost Rushing	5	17
Net Yards Rushing	324	227
Net Yards Passing	101	62
Passes Attempted	10	18
Passes Completed	7	6
Had Intercepted	1	3
Total Offensive Plays	81	70
Total Net Yards	429	289
Average Gain Per Play	5.2	4.1
Fumbles: Number—Lost	3/1	0
Penalties: Number—Yards	6/49	4/32
Interceptions: Number—Yards	3/13	1/3
Number of Punts—Yards	2/80	4/166
Average Per Punt	40	41.5
Punt Returns: Number—Yards	0	1/12
Kickoff Returns: Number—Yards	3/139	5/123

SEPTEMBER 30, 1978

MINNESOTA
VS.
UCLA
Los Angeles Memorial Stadium
Temp.: 70°
Skies: Slightly hazy
FIRST QUARTER

UCLA won toss, chose to receive. Minnesota kicks off, defending west goal. Rogind (M) kicks off, received by Brown on goal line, returned 34 from L1.
UCLA
1/10-L35 - Brown off lt for 1
2/9 -L36 - Brant reverses to right, laterals to Owens for 6 around re
3/3 -L42 - Owens around re for 9
1/10-M49 - Owens over lg for 5
2/5 -M44 - Brant reverses to right, loses 2
3/7 -M46 - Bashore passes incomplete, intended for Reece on M33
4/7 -M46 - UCLA penalized illegal procedure
4/12-L49 - McFarland punts to Edwards on M6, no return, fumbles, recovered by Baggott

12:45 UCLA
1/G -M6 - Owens on pitch into le for 1
2/G -M5 - Brown over rt for 3
3/G -M2 - Owens around le for 1
4/G -M1 - Bashore stopped for no gain on QB sneak

10:56 MINNESOTA
1/10-U1 - Kitzmann over rg for no gain
2/10-U1 - Kitzmann gains nothing at lg
3/10-U1 - Kitzmann at rt for 3
4/7 -U4 - Smith punt from deep in endzone, partially deflected by Morris, goes out on M14

9:21 UCLA
1/10-M14 - Owens at rg for 4
2/6 -M10 - Owens on counter over rg for 4
3/2 -M6 - Brown at rt for 2
1/G -M4 - Brown at lt for no gain
2/G -M4 - Bashore keeps into rt for 3
3/G -M1 - Bashore keeps inside le for TD. Boormeester kicks conversion good (Brant holder), UCLA went 14 yds in 6 plays to score.
SCORE: UCLA 7, MINNESOTA 0

Johnson (UCLA) kicks off, downed by Edwards in end zone for touchback
MINNESOTA
1/10-M20 - Barber into lg for 5
2/5 -M25 - Barber on pitch inside le for 3
3/2 -M28 - Kitzmann tries rg for 2; but play nullified—Minn penalized offside
3/6 -M24 - Avery passes middle to Bourquin on M40, down on M41 for 17

1/10-M41 - Kitzmann into lg for 5
2/5 -M46 - Kitzmann over lg for 4
3/1 - 50 - Kitzmann over rt for 4
1/10-L46 - Kitzmann over lt for 5
2/5 -L41 - Kitzmann over rt for 1
3/4 -L40 - Barber sweeps le for 5
1/10-L35 - Kitzmann over lt for 7
2/3 -L28 - Barber over rg, breaks tackle for 11 down middle
1/10-L17 - Barber at lt for 4
2/6 -L13 - Kitzmann over lg for 4

**END OF FIRST QUARTER:
UCLA 7, MINNESOTA 0**

SECOND QUARTER

MINNESOTA
3/2 -L9 - Kitzmann over lg for 4 but play nullified -Minnesota penalized for holding
3/17-L24 - Avery back to pass, sacked by Hopwood for 8 yd loss
4/25-L32 - Carlson holder, Rogind's 50 yd field goal try from L40 wide left—no good

14:09 UCLA
1/10-L32 - Brown at rg for 3
2/7 -L35 - Bashore passes incomplete, intended for Coffman on L41
3/7-L35 - Bashore passes to Reece on L49 middle, down at M37 for 28
1/10-M37 - Brown at lg for 4
2/6 -M33 - Bashore passes incomplete, intended for Brant on M29, but UCLA pen. illegal motion
2/11-M38 - Brown at lg for 6
3/5 -M32 - Bashore on scramble to right, passes to McNeil at M11, and he prances down south sideline for 32 yd TD Boormeester kicks conversion good (Brant holder). L went 68 yds in 6 plays
SCORE: UCLA 14, MINNESOTA 0

Johnson (UCLA) kicks off into end zone, downed by Edwards for touchback
MINNESOTA
1/10-M20 - Kitzmann into lg for 3
2/7 -M23 - Barber into rt gains nothing
3/7 -M23 - Avery passes incomplete intended for Barber on M32
4/7 -M23 - Smith's punt taken on fair catch by Brant at L41, 36 yd kick

(10:20) UCLA
1/10-L41 - Brown at lt for 4 (Bukich now at QB)
2/6 -L45 - Bukich on scramble loses 3 in middle
3/9 -L42 - McNeil at le trapped by Sytsma for 2 yd loss
4/11-L40 - McFarland's punt taken on fair catch by Bailey at M22, 38 yd kick

8:28 MINNESOTA
1/10-M22 - Avery passes left to Bailey on M30, down at M37 for 15
1/10-M37 - Kitzmann breaks over rg for 9
2/1 -M46 - MINN penalized delay of game
2/6 -M41 - Barber at le for 1
3/5 -M42 - Avery passes right to Barber on M44, down there for 2 (Barber injured)
4/3 -M44 - Smith's punt taken on fair catch by Reece at L19, 37 yd kick

6:41 UCLA
1/10-L19 - Brown at lg for 4
2/6 -L23 - Coffman reverse rt for 8
1/10-L31 - Brown over rg for 3
2/7 -L34 - Bukich passes left to McNeil at L31, stopped at L32 for 2 yd loss
3/9 -L32 - Bukich back to pass, sacked by Edward on safety blitz for 11 yd loss
4/20-L21 - McFarland's punt taken on fair catch by Bailey on L48, 27 yd punt

3:53 MINNESOTA
1/10-L48 - Avery passes left to Bailey on L40, goes out at L39 for 9
2/1 -L39 - Avery recovers own fumble on snapback, loses 1
3/2 -L40 - Kitzmann tries lt, fumble apparently recovered by Tuinei (UCLA), but play nullified, UCLA penalized off side
1/10-L35 - Artis outside rt for 1
2/9 -L34 - Avery back to pass, sacked by Windom for 8 yd loss
3/17-L42 - Avery passes, incomplete, intended for Cooper at L23
4/17-L42 - Smith's punt taken on fair catch by Reece at L11, 31 yd punt

1:52 UCLA
1/10-L11 - McNeil around le for 6
2/4 -L17 - Brown over lt for 4
1/10-L21 - McNeil at le for 5
2/5 -L26 - Morris at rg for 6
1/10-L32 - Bukich keeps around le for 9

**END OF FIRST HALF:
UCLA 14, MINNESOTA 0**

THIRD QUARTER

UCLA kicks off, defending east goal. Johnson kicks off to Edwards on goal line, returned right up south sideline for 54 yds.
MINNESOTA
1/10-L46 - Barber hurdles rg for 3
2/7 -L43 - Barber around le for 5 but UCLA penalized offside
2/2 -L33 - Kitzmann at rg for 4
1/10-L34 - Barber inside re stopped for no gain by Robinson
2/10-L34 - Avery screen passes left to Kitzmann on L40, down on L37 for 3 yd loss
3/13-L37 - MINN penalized illegal procedure
3/18-L42 - Dilulo reverses right, slips for 2 yd loss
4/20-L44 - Smith's punt taken on fair catch by Reece at L8, 36 yd punt

11:59 UCLA
1/10-L8 - Owens at rt for 4 (Bashore at QB)
2/6 -L12 - Owens outside rt for 3
3/3 -L15 - Bashore keeps at re gains nothing
4/3 -L15 - McFarland's punt taken on fair catch by Bailey at L46, 31 yd kick

SEPTEMBER 30, 1978

FOURTH QUARTER

10:18 MINNESOTA
1/10-L46 - Avery keeps over center for 4
2/6 -L42 - Barber reverses lg for 1 yd loss
3/7 -L43 - Avery back to pass, hit by Robinson, fumble recovered by Plemmons (UCLA) on 50

9:00 UCLA
1/10- 50 - Coffman reverses rt for 2
2/8 - M48 - Brown at rg for 3
3/5 -M45 - Bashore on scramble keeps up middle for 4
4/1 - M41 - Bashore sneaks middle for 1, but UCLA penalized illegal motion
4/6 -M46 - McFarland punts to M10, 36 yd punt out of bounds.

6:58 MINNESOTA
1/10-M10 - Kitzmann outside lt for 5
2/5 -M15 - Kitzmann at rg for 4
3/1 -M19 - Avery sneaks middle for 3 but play nullified—Minn penalized illegal motion
3/6 -M14 - Barber over rg for 9
1/10-M23 - Kitzmann over lt for 2
2/2 -M25 - Avery passes middle to Bourquin on M40, down on M44 for 19
1/10-M44 - Barber sweeps le for 11
1/10-L45 - Kitzmann over for 3 into lt
2/7 -L42 - White into rt for 8
1/10-L34 - Avery on roll out to right loses 6
2/16-L40 - Avery back to pass, sacked by Robinson and Tuiasosopo for 5 yd loss
3/21-L45 - Avery passes middle to Bourquin on L29, down there for 16
4/5 -L29 - Carlson holding on L36, Rogind kicks 36 yd field goal good
SCORE: UCLA 14, MINNESOTA 3

Rogind kicks off into endzone for touchback, downed by Brown
2:15 UCLA
1/10-L20 - Owens on pitch at re for 1
2/9 -L21 - Bashore passes right to Brisbin on L23, goes out there for 2
3/7 -L23 - Bashore passed incomplete, intended for Reece on L39
4/7 -L23 - McFarland's punt taken on fair catch by Bailey at M47, 30 yd kick

1:17 MINNESOTA
1/10-M47 - Barber over rg for 1
2/9 -M48 - Barber at rg for 1
3/8 -M49 - Avery passes middle to Bourquin at L37, down at L26 for 25
1/10-L26 - Kitzmann over lt for 10

**END OF THIRD QUARTER:
UCLA 14, MINNESOTA 3**

MINNESOTA
1/10-L16 - Kitzmann at lt for 4
2/6 -L12 - Avery keeps into middle for 2
3/4 -L10 - Barber on pitch at le for 3
4/1 -L7 - Avery keeps at middle for 2
1/G -L5 - Avery keeps into middle for 1
2/G -L4 - Barber hurdles rt for 2
3/G -L2 - Barber bucks lt for 1
4/G -L1 - Avery stopped short of goal-line on QB sneak

11:40 UCLA
1/10-L1 - Bashore keeps into lg for 1
2/9 -L2 - Brown at lt for 1
3/8 -L3 - Brown at rg for 2
4/6 -L5 - McFarland's punt taken on fair catch by Bailey at L28, 23 yd kick

9:46 MINNESOTA
1/10-L28 - Barber on late pitch around le for 1
2/9 -L27 - Kitzmann breaks over lt for 8
3/1 -L19 - Kitzmann at lg for 1
1/10-L18 - Barber at rg for 2
2/8 -L16 - Avery passes incomplete, intended for Bailey in end zone (Bailey injured)
3/8 -L16 - Avery back to pass under pressure, sacked by Robinson for 14 yd loss
4/22-L30 - Carlson holding at L37, Rogind's 47 yd field goal try wide right, no good

231

7:07 UCLA
1/10-L30 - Owens on pitch around re for 14
1/10-L44 - Owens inside le for 9
2/1 -L47 - Brown into lg for 4
1/10-M43 - Brown at rg for 3 (Brown goes over 2000 career yds)
2/7 -M40 - Owens at lt for 1
3/6 -M39 - Bashore back to pass, dropped by Murphy and Ronan for 9 yd loss
4/15-M48 - McFarland's punt taken on fair catch by Edwards on M10 but Minn is penalized for roughing kicker
1/10-M33 - Owens around re for 5
2/5 -M28 - Brown over lt for 4 (Brown shaken up)
3/1 -M24 - Morris outside lt for 5
1/10-M19 - Owens at right side slips for 2 yd loss
2/12-M21 - Bashore passes incomplete, dropped by Morris at M18
3/12-M21 - Bashore passes incomplete, intended for Coffman on M3
4/12-M21 - Boormeester kicks 38 yd field goal good (Brant holder at M28)
SCORE: UCLA 17, MINNESOTA 3

Johnson kicks off to Edwards just inside end zone, returned 16
MINNESOTA
1/10-M16 - Carlson (at QB) passes middle to Bourquin on M30, down there for 14
1/10-M30 - Carlson passes incomplete, intended for Artis on M37
2/10-M30 - Carlson back to pass, sacked by Raymond Robinson for 10 yd loss
3/20-M20 - Carlson passes incomplete, intended for White on M16
4/20-M20 - Smith's punt downed on L42, 38 yd punt

1:11 UCLA
1/10-L42 - (Bukich at QB) Morris over lg for 5
2/5 -L47 - McNeil at le loses 2
3/7 -L45 - Saipale at lg for 10

**FINAL SCORE:
UCLA 17, MINNESOTA 3**

National Collegiate Athletic Association
FINAL TEAM STATISTICS
September 30, 1978

	MINNE-SOTA	UCLA
First Downs	16	12
Rushing	10	9
Passing	5	2
Penalty	1	1
Rushing Attempts	56	53
Yards Rushing	167	183
Yards Lost Rushing	62	31
Net Yards Rushing	105	152
Net Yards Passing	114	60
Passes Attempted	14	9
Passes Completed	9	4
Had Intercepted	0	0
Total Offensive Plays	70	62
Total Net Yards	219	212
Average Gain Per Play	3.13	3.42
Fumbles: Number—Lost	3/2	0/0
Penalties: Number—Yards	6/49	5/25
Interceptions: Number—Yards	0/0	0/0
Number of Punts—Yards	6/188	7/230
Average Per Punt	31.3	32.9
Punt Returns: Number—Yards	1/0	0/0
Kickoff Returns: Number—Yards	2/70	1/34
Third Down Efficiency	7/20/35.0	7/18/38.9
Time of Possession	31:45	28:15

SEPTEMBER 30, 1978

NEBRASKA VS. INDIANA
Memorial Stadium
Bloomington, Indiana
Temp: 66°
Wind: SS 8-12 mph
FIRST QUARTER

Indiana wins toss and will receive, Nebraska will defend south goal Todd kicks off to Hopkins at I4, returned to I31, 27 return
14:54 INDIANA
1/10-I31 - Darring re to I33 (2 yards)
2/8 -I33 - Darring lt to I33, no gain
3/8 -I33 - Darring le to I37 (4 yards)
4/4 -I37 - Lovett punts dead to N45, 18 punt

13:35 NEBRASKA
1/10-N45 - Hipp rt to I46 (9 yards)
2/1 -I46 - Hipp lg to I43 (3 yards)
1/10-I43 - Sorley le to I42 (1 yard)
2/9 -I42 - Sorley pass complete to
  Miller to I20 (22 yards)
1/10-I20 - Hipp lt to I11 (9 yards)
2/1 -I11 - Berns rg to I9 (2 yards)
1/G -I9 - Hipp le for touchdown (9 yards)
  PAT—Todd kick good
  SCORE: NEBRASKA 7, INDIANA 0

Todd kicks off to Burnett at I1, returned to I21, 20 return
11:08 INDIANA
1/10-I21 - Johnson lg to I23 (2 yards)
2/8 -I23 - Burnett rt to I27 (4 yards)
3/4 -I27 - Burnett re to I28 (1 yard)
4/3 -I28 - Lovett punts out of bounds at
  I49 (21 yards)

9:00 NEBRASKA
1/10-I49 - Sorley pass complete to Brown at
  I13 (36 yards)
1/10-I13 - Hipp rg to I10 (3 yards)
2/7 -I10 - Hipp re to I6 (4 yards)
3/3 -I6 - Hipp le for touchdown (6 yards)
  PAT—Todd kick good
  SCORE: NEBRASKA 14, INDIANA 0

Todd kicks off to Burnett at goal, returned to I25, 25 return
7:41 INDIANA
1/10-I25 - Arnett pass complete to Fishel
  at I28 (3 yards)
2/7 -I28 - Harkrader lg to I37 (9 yards)
1/10-I37 - Arnett pass incomplete to Fishel
  at N40
2/10-I37 - Harkrader lg to I34, loss of 3
3/13-I34 - Harkrader re to I38 (4 yards)
4/9 -I38 - Lovett punts to Brown at N16
  46 punt, returned to I47, 37 return

5:43 NEBRASKA
1/10-I47 - Sorley le to I41 (6 yards)
2/4 -I41 - Hipp re to I31 (10 yards)
  and Indiana personal foul
1/10-I16 - Berns lg to I13 (3 yards)
2/7 -I13 - Wurth re to I2 (11 yards)
1/G -I2 - Wurth lt for touchdown (2 yards)
  PAT—Todd kick good.
  SCORE: NEBRASKA 21, INDIANA 0

Todd kicks off into end zone
4:23 INDIANA
1/10-I20 - Johnson lg to I22 (2 yards)
2/8 -I22 - Harkrader lg to I27 (5 yards)
3/3 -I27 - Arnett fumble recovered by Nelson
  at I24, loss of 3

3:12 NEBRASKA
1/10-I24 - Hipp re to I11 (13 yards)
1/10-I11 - Franklin rg to I8 (3 yards)
2/7 -I8 - Hipp le for touchdown (8 yards)
  PAT—Todd kick good.
  SCORE: NEBRASKA 28, INDIANA 0

Todd kicks off to Hopkins at I6, returned to I28, 22 return
2:23 INDIANA
1/10-I28 - Harkrader lt to I32 (4 yards)
2/6 -I32 - Harkrader le to I37 (5 yards)
3/1 -I37 - Harkrader lt to I40 (3 yards)
1/10-I40 - Johnson lg to I43 (3 yards)
2/7 -I43 - Harkrader lg to I44 (1 yard)

**END OF FIRST QUARTER:
NEBRASKA 28, INDIANA 0**

SECOND QUARTER

INDIANA
3/6 -I44 - Arnett trapped at I31, loss of 13
4/19-I31 - Lovett punts to Brown at N20,
  returned to N31, 11 return 49 punt

14:12 NEBRASKA
1/10-N31 - Berns le to N35 (4 yards)
2/6 -N35 - Brown rt to N43 (8 yards)
1/10-N43 - Berns fumble recovered by
  Tisdale at N44 (1 yard)

13:45 INDIANA
1/10-N44 - Arnett le to N42 (2 yards)
2/8 -N42 - Arnett re to N29 (13 yards)
1/10-N29 - Johnson lg to N26 (3 yards)
2/7 -N26 - Burnett rg to N24 (2 yards)
3/5 -N24 - Arnett pass complete to Freide
  for touchdown (24 yards) PAT—Freud
  kick good.
  SCORE: NEBRASKA 28, INDIANA 7

Straub kicks off to Berns at N3, returned to N23, 20 return

11:27 NEBRASKA
1/10-N23 - Hipp le fumble recovered by Keneipp at N21, loss of 2

11:19 INDIANA
1/10-N21 - Harkrader rg to N18 (3 yards)
2/7 -N18 - Burnett rg to N17 (1 yard)
3/6 -N17 - Arnett pass incomplete in end zone
4/6 -N17 - Freud 35 field goal good.
SCORE: NEBRASKA 28, INDIANA 10

Straub kicks off to Berns in end zone
10:00 NEBRASKA
1/10-N20 - Hipp lg to N29 (9 yards)
2/1 -N29 - Hipp lg to N32 (3 yards)
1/10-N32 - Nebraska offsides
1/15-N27 - Hipp re to N31 (4 yards)
2/11-N31 - Sorley pass incomplete to Hipp
3/11-N31 - Nebraska illegal procedure
3/16-N26 - Sorley pass complete to Brown at N39 (13 yards)
4/3 -N39 - Smith punts to Swinehart at I29 returned to I32, 32 punt, 3 return

7:33 INDIANA
1/10-I32 - Arnett pass complete to Lundy at N29 (39 yards)
1/10-N29 - Arnett re to N26 (3 yards) but Indiana penalized clipping
1/22-N41 - Burnett rt to N39 (2 yards)
2/20-N39 - Bowers rg to N35 (4 yards)
3/16-N35 - Clifford pass intercepted by Cole at N33, returned to N41, 8 return

5:51 NEBRASKA
1/10-N41 - Franklin lg to I42 (17 yards)
1/10-I42 - Sorley pass complete to Brown to I16 (26 yards)
1/10-I16 - Franklin lg to I14 (2 yards)
2/8 -I14 - Berns le to I4 (10 yards)
1/G -I4 - Berns re to I3 (1 yard)
2/G -I3 - Franklin lg to I1 (2 yards)
3/G -I1 - Berns rg for touchdown (1 yard)
PAT—Todd kick good.
SCORE: NEBRASKA 35, INDIANA 10

Todd kicks off to Burnett, dead at I13
3:18 INDIANA
1/10-I13 - Harkrader rg to I14 (1 yard)
2/9 -I14 - Harkrader lg to I20 (6 yards)
3/3 -I20 - Harkrader lg to I22 (2 yards)
4/1 -I22 - Lovett punts to Brown at N43, fair catch, 35 punt

1:58 NEBRASKA
1/10-N43 - Sorley pass complete to Hipp at 50 (7 yards)
2/3 - 50 - Hipp lt to I44 (6 yards)
1/10-I44 - Sorley pass incomplete
2/10-I44 - Sorley pass incomplete
3/10-I44 - Nebraska illegal procedure
3/15-I49 - Sorley pass incomplete
4/15-N49 - Smith punts into end zone, 49 punt

0:34 INDIANA
1/10-I20 - Arnett pass incomplete
2/10-I20 - Arnett re to I26 (6 yards)

END OF HALF:
NEBRASKA 35, INDIANA 10

THIRD QUARTER

Straub kicks off to Brown at N3, returned to N26, 23 return
14:55 NEBRASKA
1/10-N26 - Franklin lg to N35 (9 yards)
2/1 -N35 - Franklin rg to N42 (7 yards)
1/10-N42 - Hipp re to N49 (7 yards)
2/3 -N49 - Hipp le to 50 (1 yard)
3/2 - 50 - Franklin lg to I29 (21 yards)
1/10-I29 - Sorley pass incomplete
2/10-I29 - Hipp le to I23 (6 yards)
3/4 -I23 - Sorley pass complete to Miller at I9 (14 yards)
1/G -I9 - Hipp le for touchdown (9 yards)
PAT—Todd kick good
SCORE: NEBRASKA 42, INDIANA 10

Todd kicks off to Burnett at I2, returned to I30, 28 return
11:47 INDIANA
1/10-I30 - Burnett re to I32 (2 yards)
2/8 -I32 - Bowers lg to I35 (3 yards)
3/5 -I35 - Arnett pass complete to Bowers to I45 (10 yards)
1/10-I45 - Burnett le to I46 (1 yard)
2/9 -I46 - Burnett lg to I46, no gain
3/9 -I46 - Burnett re to N44 (10 yards)
1/10-N44 - Burnett lg to N43 (1 yard)
2/9 -N43 - Arnett pass incomplete
3/9 -N43 - Fishel le to N35 (8 yards)
4/1 -N35 - Arnett lg to N35, no gain

8:23 NEBRASKA
1/10-N35 - Wurth lt to N47 (12 yards)
1/10-N47 - Wurth lg to I49 (4 yards)
2/6 -I49 - Sorley re to 50, loss of 1
3/7 - 50 - Sorley pass complete to Miller to I27 (23 yards)
1/10-I27 - Sorley pass complete to Lockett for touchdown (27 yards) PAT—Todd kick good.
SCORE: NEBRASKA 49, INDIANA 10

Todd kicks off to Burnett at I9, returned to I44, 35 return
6:34 INDIANA
1/10-I44 - Harkrader re to I45 (1 yard)
2/9 -I45 - Arnett pass complete to Johnson to N47 (8 yards)
3/1 -N47 - Arnett pass incomplete
4/1 -N47 - Lovett punts to Pillen at N6, fair catch (41 yards)

234

SEPTEMBER 30, 1978

5:33 NEBRASKA
1/10-N6 - Hipp lg to N7 (1 yard)
2/9 -N7 - Hipp le to N12 (5 yards)
3/4 -N12 - Hager pass complete to Brown to N24 (12 yards)
1/10-N24 - Wurth re to N28 (4 yards)
2/6 -N28 - Wurth rt to N35 (7 yards)
1/10-N35 - Hager pass complete to Miller to I47 (18 yards)
1/10-I47 - Hager le to I44 (3 yards)
2/7 -I44 - Wurth rt to I26 (18 yards)
1/10-I26 - Nebraska penalized personal foul
1/25-I41 - Kotera rg to L38 (3 yards)
2/22-I38 - Hager pass incomplete
3/22-I38 - Hager pass incomplete
4/22-I38 - Smith punts dead at I7, 31 punt

1:11 INDIANA
1/10-I7 - Darring lg fumble recovered by Johnson at I18 (11 yards)
1/10-I18 - Arnett le to I5, loss of 13
2/23-I5 - Arnett pass incomplete

**END OF THIRD QUARTER:
NEBRASKA 49, INDIANA 10**

FOURTH QUARTER

INDIANA
3/23-I5 - Harkrader le to I1, loss of 4
4/27-I1 - Nebraska penalized for roughing the kicker
4/12-I16 - Lovett punt blocked by Nelson, recovered by Dunning in end zone for touchdown PAT—Sukup run failed.
SCORE: NEBRASKA 55, INDIANA 10

Sukup kicks off to Pennick at I5, returned to I24, 19 return
14:01 INDIANA
1/10-I24 - Clifford pass incomplete
2/10-I24 - Darring rt to I29 (5 yards)
3/5 -I29 - Clifford pass incomplete
4/5 -I29 - Lovett punts to Brown at N34, returned to I37, 29 return 35 punt

13:03 NEBRASKA
1/10-I37 - Wurth rt for touchdown (37 yards) PAT—Sukup kick good
SCORE: NEBRASKA 62, INDIANA 10

Sukup kicks off to Pennick at I5, returned to I23, 18 return
12:48 INDIANA
1/10-I23 - Darring lg to I23, no gain
2/10-I23 - Clifford pass incomplete
3/10-I23 - Darring lg to I29 (6 yards) and Nebraska penalized personal foul
1/10-I44 - Darring rt to I45 (1 yard)
2/9 -I45 - Clifford pass complete to Bowers at N49 (6 yards)
3/3 -N49 - Clifford pass incomplete
4/3 -N49 - Lovett punts to Liegl at N17, fair catch 32 punt

10:36 NEBRASKA
1/10-N17 - Johnson rg to N20 (3 yards)
2/7 -N20 - Quinn le to N40 (20 yards)
1/10-N40 - McCloney lt to N44 (4 yards)
2/6 -N44 - Quinn le to N46 (2 yards)
3/4 -N46 - Kotera rg to N49 (3 yards)
4/1 -N49 - Todd punts out of bounds at I16 35 punt

8:09 INDIANA
1/10-I16 - Bowers rg to I24 (8 yards)
2/2 -I24 - Bowers lg to I25 (1 yard)
3/1 -I25 - Darring lt to I27 (2 yards)
1/10-I27 - Darring lg to I30 (3 yards)
2/7 -I30 - Darring lg to I32 (2 yards)
3/5 -I32 - Darring re to I35 (3 yards)
4/2 -I35 - Lovett punts to Liegl, fair catch fumbled at N33 and recovered by Wilbur 32 punt

5:28 INDIANA
1/10-N33 - Clifford pass incomplete
2/10-N33 - Clifford pass incomplete
3/10-N33 - Clifford pass intercepted at N25, 24 return and Indiana personal foul

5:06 NEBRASKA
1/10-I36 - Quinn re to I32 (4 yards)
2/6 -I32 - Quinn le to I25 (7 yards)
1/10-I25 - Johnson rg to I19 (6 yards)
2/4 -I19 - Quinn le to I17 (2 yards)
3/2 -I17 - Nebraska clipping
3/17-I32 - McCloney le to I25 (7 yards) but Nebraska penalized for clipping
3/25-I40 - Quinn le to I30 (10 yards) fumbled recovered by Dart Ramsey

235

3:00 INDIANA
1/10-I30 - Clifford le to I29, loss of 1
2/11-I29 - Darring fumble recovered by Bryant at I21, loss of 8

2:46 NEBRASKA
1/10-I21 - Kotera rg to I16 (5 yards)
2/5 -I16 - Johnson lt to I11 (5 yards)
1/10-I11 - Quinn re to I4 (7 yards)
2/3 -I4 - Johnson re to I2 (2 yards)
3/1 -I2 - Kotera rg for touchdown (2 yards) PAT—Sukup kick good.
SCORE: NEBRASKA 69, INDIANA 10

Sukup kicks off to Pennick at I12, returned to I34, 22 return

0:28 INDIANA
1/10-I34 - Clifford pass complete to Lundy N19 (47 yards)
1/10-N19 - Clifford pass incomplete
2/10-N19 - Clifford pass complete to Fishel for touchdown (19 yards) PAT—Freud kick good.
SCORE: NEBRASKA 69, INDIANA 17

Straub kicks off to Lockett at N20, returned to I40 40 return

**FINAL SCORE:
NEBRASKA 69, INDIANA 17**

**National Collegiate Athletic Association
FINAL TEAM STATISTICS**

	NEBRASKA	INDIANA
First Downs	32	12
Rushing	22	6
Passing	8	5
Penalty	2	1
Rushing Attempts	65	55
Yards Rushing	418	165
Yards Lost Rushing	3	45
Net Yards Rushing	415	120
Net Yards Passing	198	156
Passes Attempted	17	23
Passes Completed	10	8
Had Intercepted	0	2
Total Offensive Plays	82	78
Total Ney Yards	613	276
Average Gain Per Play	7.5	3.6
Fumbles: Number—Lost	4/4	4/2
Penalties: Number—Yards	9/95	3/45
Interceptions: Number—Yards	2/32	0/0
Number Of Punts—Yards	4/147	10/304
Average Per Punt	37	30.7
Punt Returns: Number—Yards	4/93	1/3
Kickoff Returns: Number—Yards	3/83	8/198

SEPTEMBER 30, 1978

DUKE VS. MICHIGAN
Michigan Stadium
Temp: 64°
Wind: S 10-20 mph
Skies: Cloudy and mild

FIRST QUARTER

TOSS: Duke won the toss and elected to receive. Michigan elects to defend the south goal.
Virgil kicked off to Rhett in the D endzone where he downed it.
15:00 DUKE
1/10-D20 - Rhett took a pitchback at re for no gain (Seabron)
2/10-D20 - Rhett at lg for 3 (Godfrey)
3/7 -D20 - Dunn back to pass was hit by Greer and others for -10
4/17-D13 - Brummitt punted to Jolly on the M44 and he ret'd 6 (Kelly, 43 yd punt)

13:02 MICHIGAN
1/10- 50 - Huckleby at lg for 5 (Mashore)
2/5 -D45 - Davis at rg for 3 (Schoenhoft)
3/2 -D42 - Huckleby at rt for 5 (King)
1/10-D37 - Davis at rg for 13 (Hoskins)
1/10-D24 - Leach kept at lt for 2; Pritchard
2/8 -D22 - Huckleby took pitchback at re for 5 (Sommers)
3/3 -D17 - Huckleby took a pitchout from Leach at le for 9 (McGee)
1/G -D 8 - Huckleby at center for 5 (Mashore)
2/G -D 3 - Leach kept at lt for 2 (Gawdun)
3/G -D 3 - Huckleby at rg for no gain (Shoenhoft)
4/G -D 1 - Davis at center for the Michigan TD 50 yds in 11 plays. Dickey held while Wilner converted. MICHIGAN 7 DUKE 0 Time: 7:51

Virgil kicked off to Hoskins on the Duke goal line and he ret'd 20 (Needham)
7:46 DUKE
1/10-D20 - Rhett at lg for no gain (Greer)
2/10-D20 - Stopper around le lateralled to Rhett who made 26 (Harden)
1/10-D46 - Gonet at lt for 2 (Greer)
2/8 -D48 - Rhett at le for 1 (Greer)
3/7 -D49 - Dunn passed for Comer, broken up by Meter
4/7 -D49 - Brummitt punted out of bounds on the M19, 32 yd punt

8:30 MICHIGAN
1/10-M19 - Huckleby at center for 13 (King)
1/10-M19 - Davis at lg for 4 (Algor)
2/6 -M36 - Huckleby at rg for 2 (Shoenhoft)
3/4 -M38 - Leach passed to Smith in left for 8 (Brooks)
1/10-M46 - Huckleby at lg for 5 (McGee)

2/5 -D49 - Huckleby took pitchback at re for 1 (Sommers)
3/4 -D48 - Leach elected to run right and made 8 (Penn)
1/10-D40 - Davis cut back over lt for 7 (Mashore)
2/3 -D33 - Huckleby took and cut inside le for 3 (McGee)
1/10-D30 - Huckleby outside for 5 (Gawdun)
2/5 -D25 - Davis at rg for 4 (King)

END OF FIRST QUARTER: MICHIGAN 7 DUKE 0

Michigan had 23 plays for 114 yds.
Duke had 8 plays for 22 yds.

SECOND QUARTER

MICHIGAN
1/10-D17 - Huckleby at rg for 5 (Pelosky)
2/5 -D12 - Leach pitched out to Huckleby at re for no gain (Brooks)
3/5 -D12 - Leach rolled left and elected to run and went for the Michigan TD, aided by a block from Davis. Time: 13:36. Dickey held while Willner converted.
MICHIGAN 14 DUKE 0 81 yds in 15 plays.

Virgil kicked off the Rhett on the goal line and he ret'd 11 (Bell)
13:31 DUKE
1/10-D11 - Gonet at rt for 2 (Greer)
2/8 -D13 - Dunn at lt for 2 (Seabron)
3/6 -D15 - Dunn went back to pass, dropped the ball, tried to recover it, chased it back to the D1, where Keitz recovered for Michigan

12:09 MICHIGAN
1/G D 1 - Huckleby at rt for the Michigan TD. Time: 12:06 Dickey held while Wilner converted MICHIGAN 21 DUKE 0 1 yd in 1 play.

237

Virgil kicked off to Rhett who downed it in the endzone, BUT Michigan offside. Virgil's second from M35 to Rhett on the D2 and he ret'd 17 (Trgovac)

11:58 DUKE
1/10-D19 - Brower took pitchout at le for 12
1/10-D31 - Dunn elected to run left for 3 (DeSantis)
2/7 -D34 - Dunn passed for Brown incomplete, broken up by Braman
3/7 -D34 - Brower took pitchback at re for 14 (Harden)
1/10-D48 - Brower took pitchback at re for no gain (Simpkins)
2/10-D48 - Dunn kept at rt for 2 (Simpkins)
3/8 - 50 - Dunn passed for Brower incomplete, But Michigan penalized for interference to the M39, 11 yd penalty
1/10-M39 - Dunn pitched out to Rhett who fumbled and recovered at the 50
2/21- 50 - Dunn passed over the middle to Rhett for 11 (Meter)
3/10-M39 - Dunn was chased down by Greer for -18
4/28-D43 - Brummitt punted to Jolly on the M12 and he ret'd 7 (Drescher)

4:05 DUKE
1/10-D29 - Dunn at re no gain (Keitz)
2/10-D29 - Dunn's pass for Patten intercepted by Jolly at the D38 where he downed it also

3:20 MICHIGAN
1/10-D33 - Huckleby at rt for 5 (Algor)
2/5 -D33 - Leach's pass for Mitchell inc. off his fingers
3/5 -D33 - Leach passed to Feaster for 19 (Sommers)
1/10-D14 - Huckleby at re for 4 (King)
2/6 -D10 - Huckleby took pitchout at le and lost 2 (Brooks)
3/8 -D12 - Leach passed to Huckleby in the endzone for an apparent TD, BUT offsetting penalties nullify play—Duke personal foul, Michigan inelig.
3/8 -D12 - Leach passed to Schmerge caught out of bounds, BUT Michigan penalized illegal forward pass
4/13-D18 - Dickey held while Willner kicked a 35 yd field goal from the D25. Time: 0:26. 38 yds in 7 plays
MICHIGAN 24 DUKE 0

7:07 MICHIGAN
1/10-M19 - Huckleby at rg for 5 (Shoenhoft)
2/5 -M24 - Davis at center for 4 (Shoenhoft)
3/1 -M28 - Leach rolled right for 10 (Sommers)
1/10-M38 - Davis at rg for 3 (Pritchard)
2/7 -M41 - Leach made no gain at re (McGee)
3/7 -M41 - Leach passed for Feaster inc.
4/7 M41 - Willner punted to Gawdun on the D26 and he ret'd 3 (Weber)

Virgil kicked off to Rhett on the D3 and he ret'd 24
0:19 DUKE
1/10-D27 - Brower at lt for 3

END OF FIRST HALF
MICHIGAN 24 DUKE 0

SEPTEMBER 30, 1978

THIRD QUARTER

Michigan elects to defend the north goal. Duke elects to receive. Virgil kicked off out of the endzone.
15:00 DUKE
1/10-D20 - Gonet at rg for 7 (Meter)
2/3 -D27 - Gonet off rt for 5 (Simpkins)
1/10-D32 - Dunn's pass for Brower incomplete.
2/10-D32 - Dunn was dropped by Keitz for '7.
3/17-D25 - Dunn passed to Gonet for 8 (DeSantis)
4/9 -D33 - Brummitt punted to Jolly on the M25 and he ret'd 6 (Hoskins)

13:05 MICHIGAN
1/10-M31 - Davis at lg for 14 (Mashore)
1/10-M45 - Huckleby at center for 5 (Algor)
2/5 -M50 - Davis at rg for 7 (King)
1/10-D41 - Leach's pass for Marsh broken up by Sommers.
2/10-D41 - Leach went back to pass and then elected to run left and made 19, aided by block from Arbeznik (Gawdun)
1/10-D22 - Leach rolled inside re for 19 (Hoskins)
1/G -D3 - Huckleby at rt for 2 (Schoenhoft.)
2/G -D1 - Huckleby at rt for 1 and the M TD. Time: 9:42. Dickey held while Willner converted.
MICHIGAN 31 DUKE 0 69 yds in 9 plays.

Virgil kicked off to Hoskins on the goal line and he ret'd 26 (Meter)
9:36 DUKE
1/10-D26 - Driskell at rt for 2 (Seabron)
2/3 -D28 - Driskell passed for Castor intercepted by Harden at the M32.

MICHIGAN
1/10-M32 - Reid at rg for 5 (Pritchard)
2/5 -M37 - Dickey at center for no gain (Penn)
3/5 -M37 - Dickey passed to Marsh for 16 (Gawdun)
1/10-D47 - Smith at rg for 4 (Pelosky)
2/6 -D43 - Dickey rolled at re for 5 (Penn)
3/1 -D38 - Smith at rg for 1 (Pelosky)
1/10-D37 - Dickey passed to Marsh for 25 (Sommers)
1/10-D12 - Smith took pitchback at re for 4 (King)
2/6 -D8 - Dickey kept inside re for 6 (Pritchard)
1/G -D2 - Reid at lt for 2 and the M TD. Time: 3:29 Dickey held while Willner converted.
MICHIGAN 38 DUKE 0 68 yds in 10 plays.

Virgil kicked off to Hoskins on the D goal line and he ret'd 23, AND 11 penalized 15 for personal foul.

3:21 DUKE
1/10-D38 - Rhett at rt lost 1 (Greer)
2/11-D37 - Brower took pitchback at le for 1 (Jolly)
3/10-D38 - Dunn passed to Brower for 5 (Hollway)
4/5 -D43 - Brummitt punted to Harden on the M13 and he ret'd 7 (44 yard punt) (Garstkiewicz)

1:14 MICHIGAN
1/10-M20 - Reid at lt for 4 (Mashore)
2/6 -M24 - Dickey kept inside re for 8 (King)
1/10-M32 - Smith at rt for 4 (Penn)

**END OF THE QUARTER:
MICHIGAN 38 DUKE 0**

FOURTH QUARTER

MICHIGAN
2/6 -M36 - Dickey at le for 2 (McGee)
3/4 -M36 - Reid at rt for 7 (Penn)
1/10-M45 - Reid at center for 21 (Brooks)
1/10-D34 - Smith at lt for 3, fumbled when hit by Algor, and King recovered for D at the D31.

13:13 DUKE
1/10-D31 - Brower at le for 9 (Harris)
2/1 -D40 - Stopper passed for Brown and Jolly intercepted at the M21, no return (Brown)

12:56 MICHIGAN
1/10-M21 - Reid at lg for 3 (King)
2/7 -M24 - Dickey passed for Schmerge incomplete.
3/7 -M24 - Dickey's pass for Smith incomplete, broken up by King.
4/7 -M24 - Willner punted to Gawdun on the D40 and he ret'd 4 (36 yd. punt) (Smith)

239

11:55 DUKE
1/10-D44 - Driskell's pass for Brown incomplete, broken up by Jolly.
2/10-D44 - Driskell lost 4 behind lt (Trgovac)
3/14-D40 - Driskell's pass for Brown incomplete.
4/14-D40 - Brummitt punted to Harden on the M19 and he ret'd 2 (41 yd. punt) (Hoskins)

10:44 MICHIGAN
1/10-M21 - Smith at lt for 2
2/8 -M23 - Dickey rolled right and passed for Kasparek incomplete, caught out of bounds.
3/8 -M23 - Dickey passed to Kasparek for 14 (Tabron)
1/10-M37 - Dickey rolled at re for 2 (King)
2/8 -M39 - Smith at lt for 12 (Stroud)
1/10-D49 - Smith took pitchback at le for 10 (Pelosky)
1/10-D39 - Reid at rg for 8 (McGee)
2/2 -D31 - Smith took a pitchout at le for 17 (Stroud)
1/10-D14 - Dickey kept inside le for 5 (Stroud)
2/5 -D9 - Smith at lg for 3 (Algor)
3/2 -D6 - Smith at rg for 6 and the M TD. Time: 6:21 Dickey held while Willner converted. MICHIGAN 45 DUKE 0 79 yds. in 11 plays.

Virgil kicked off to Hoskins on the D5 and he ret'd 32 (Virgil)

6:13 DUKE
1/10-D37 - Martin at lt for 3 (Hollway)
2/7 -D40 - Driskell's pass intercepted by Bell at the comp M40 and he ret'd 20 to the D40

5:27 MICHIGAN
1/10-D40 - Leoni at lt for 3 (Mashore)
2/7 -D37 - Reid at rt for 6 (Doby)
3/1 -D31 - Reid at center lost 1 (Algor)
4/2 -D32 - Leoni took pitchback at le for 5, AND D penalized for personal foul to the D13.
1/10-D13 - Reid at rt for 3 (King)
2/7 -D10 - Leoni took pitchout at le for 2 (Mashore)
3/5 -D8 - Dickey passed to Clayton for the M TD. Time: 2:08.
Dickey held while Willner converted. MICHIGAN 52 DUKE 0 40 yds. in 7 plays.

Virgil kicked off to Brower on the D15 and he ret'd 12 (Trgovac)

2:02 DUKE
1/10-D27 - Driskell passed through Jones hands incomplete.
2/10-D27 - Driskell's pass for Castor broken up by Jones.
3/10-D27 - Driskell passed to Small for 11 (Cannavino)
1/10-D38 - Driskell passed to Small for 9 (Harris)
2/1 -D47 - Driskell's pass for Castor broken up by Jones.
3/1 -D47 - Driskell hit by Weber for '5.
4/6 -D42 - Driskell passed to Small for 5.

0:18 MICHIGAN
1/10-D47 - Page at rt for 4 (Penn)

END OF THE GAME:
MICHIGAN 52 DUKE 0

M had 26 plays for 145 yds. D had 14 plays for 28 yds.

National Collegiate Athletic Association
FINAL TEAM STATISTICS
September 30, 1978

	MICHIGAN	DUKE
Total First Downs	29	6
Rushing/Passing/Penalty	23/6/0	4/1/1
Rushing Attempts	74	29
Yards Gained/Lost/Net	391/3/398	97/70/27
Net Yards Passing	90	49
Passes Att/Comp/Int	12/6/0	18/6/4
Total Offensive Plays/Yards	86/4/78	47/76
Average Gain Per Play	5.5	1.6
Interceptions/Yards Returned	4/20	0/0
Punts/Average/Blocked	2/34.5/10	6/41.3/0
Field Goals Att/Made	1/1	0/0
Extra Points Att/Made	7/7	0/0
Punt Returns No/Net Yards	5/28	2/7
Kickoff Returns No/Net Yards	0/0	8/165
Penalties No/Yards	4/36	1/13
Fumbles No/Lost	1/1	2/1

SEPTEMBER 30, 1978

BAYLOR
VS.
OHIO STATE
Ohio Stadium,
Columbus, Ohio
Temp: 75
Wind: S 10-20 mph
Skies: Overcast
FIRST QUARTER

Ohio State won the toss and elected to defend the south goal; Baylor to receive.
Orosz kicked off at 1:32 P.M. five yards deep for the TB

15:00 BAYLOR
1/10-B20 - Howell middle for 6
2/4 -B26 - Hawthorne cut into lg for 2
3/2 -B28 - Hawthorne pitch into re for 1
4/1 -B29 - Prestridge punted 45; Guess returned left 9

12:50 OHIO
1/10-035 - Springs spun into center for 2
2/8 -037 - Schlichter kept inside re for 7
3/1 -044 - Campbell dove thru lg for 5; Baylor Personal Foul 15
1/10-B36 - Schlichter passed too low for Springs in short right flat incomplete
2/10-B36 - Schlichter kept inside le for 3
3/7 -B33 - Campbell thru rg for 4; Baylor offside 5
3/2 -B28 - Campbell pushed thru lt for 4
1/10-B24 - Schlichter kept on counter option right for the TD at the flag at 10:52
Janakievski PAT - 65 yards in 7 plays
OHIO STATE 7, BAYLOR 0
Orosz kicked off nine yards deep for the TB

10:52 BAYLOR
1/10-B20 - Smith rolled right, passed sideline for Marshall; deflected Skillings incomplete
2/10-B20 - Hawthorne cut into middle for 3
3/7 -B23 - Smith passed on hook over middle to Marshall for 20
1/10-B43 - Hawthorne countered at re for no gain - Skillings
2/10-B43 - Smith passed to Hawthorne on swing left, broke tackle for 5; Baylor dead ball Pers. foul -15
3/20-B33 - Smith passed deep right flat to Marshall for 16
4/4 -B49 - Prestridge punted short left 22; downed by Baylor

8:08 OHIO
1/10-029 - Springs cut into lg for 5
2/5 -034 - Springs option pitch at le for 3
3/2 -037 - Campbell hit into lg for 5
1/10-042 - Springs pitch at re for 5
2/5 -047 - Campbell lg 4

3/1 -B49 - Campbell lg 2
1/10-B47 - Springs option pitch re for 1
2/9 -B46 - Schlichter passed to Moore in left flat; deflected by Fields incomplete
3/9 -B46 - Schlichter, faked passed over middle for Gerald; intercepted by Goodwin, returned right 57; Vogler TD save

5:11 BAYLOR
1/10-O11 - Hawthorne at lt for 2
2/8 -09 - Smith faked, passed to Marshall cutting into left end zone for the TD, Bledsoe PAT - 11 yards, 2 plays,
OHIO STATE 7, BAYLOR 7
Black kicked off left 46; Hicks returned left 10

4:23 OHIO
1/10-024 - Springs pitch le for 6
2/4 -030 - Campbell bumped thru lg for 6
1/10-036 - Campbell into rt for 2
2/8 -038 - Springs option pitch right for -3 - Brothers
3/11-035 - Schlichter faked, passed over middle for Gerald; Singletary intercepted, returned middle for 12

2:48 BAYLOR
1/10-034 - Hawthorne lg for 6
2/4 -028 - Hawthorne cut over rg for 3
3/1 -025 - Hawthorne option pitch le, clear for 21; Guess TD save
1/4 -04 - Hawthorne dove over lg for 1
2/3 -03 - Smith faked, pitch to Laws on option left for the TD at 0:50 at flag Bledsoe PAT - 34 yards in five plays,
BAYLOR 14, OHIO STATE 7
Black kicked off short middle; bounce recovered by Hicks for zero

241

0:47 OHIO
1/10 -O27 - Springs pitch at le for 8
2/2 -O35 - Campbell lg for 5
1/10 -O40 - Springs at rg for 3 as the quarter came to an end

BAYLOR 14, OHIO STATE 7

SECOND QUARTER

OHIO
2/7 -O43 - Springs pitch at le for 4
3/3 -O47 - Schlichter faked, kept inside re for 7
1/10-B46 - Campbell was clear at lt for 18
1/10-B28 - Springs pitch at re for 5
2/5 -B23 - Springs into rg for 3 (Singletary hurt - limped off)
3/2 -B20 - Schlichter faked, kept inside le for 3
1/10-B17 - Campbell cut thru center for 5
2/5 -B12 - Springs pitch at le for 4
3/1 -B8 - Campbell bumped thru lt for 1; Baylor Sub infraction 4 (stepped off short)
1/4 -B4 - Campbell hit into rg for the TD at 11:10 - Janakievski PAT 73 yards in 12 plays - OHIO STATE 14, BAYLOR 14
Orosz kicked off 42 yards; Elam returned right 13

11:03 BAYLOR
1/10-B31 - Smith faked, passed to Lee cutting across middle, broke tackle for 23
1/10-O46 - Hawthrone cut over middle for 6
2/4 -O40 - Howell at lg for 3 Time out Baylor
3/1 -O37 - Hawthorne cut outside lt for 4
1/10-O33 - Howell option pitch on the short left side for 11
1/10-O22 - Smith faked, passed to Fisher on short out left; wide incomplete
2/10-O22 - Taylor took reverse pitch le for 1
3/9 -O21 - Smith passed for Lee deep over middle; too high incomplete
4/9 -O21 - Bledsoe's FG try from 38 yards was short and wide right - TB

8:15 OHIO
1/10 -O21 - Volley lg 4
2/6 -O25 - Murray pitch at re for 5
3/1 -O30 - Volley fought at rg for 3
1/10 -O33 - Schlichter kept inside le for 12
1/10 -O45 - Murray at rg for 5
2/5 - 50 - Murray pitch around le for 6
1/10-B44 - Schlichter faked, passed deep over middle for Moore; Young deflect incomplete
2/10-B44 - Murray took counter option pitch at re for 15
1/10-B29 - Schlichter kept right on broken play - 1 - Jiral
2/11-B30 - Murray pitch on counter right for 23
1/7 -B7 - Springs option pitch le for 2
2/5 -B5 - Volley hit by Singletary at rg for -1
3/6 -B6 - Campbell middle for 4 Time out Ohio State at 4:05 - then Baylor

4/2 -B2 - Janakievski's FG was from nineteen yards at 4:02 77 yards on 14 plays
OHIO STATE 17, BAYLOR 14
Orosz kicked off 48 yards right; Elam returned 14

3:57 BAYLOR
1/10-B26 - Hawthorne took option pitch right on counter - 2 Cousineau
2/12-B24 - Smith faked, passed too deep for Fisher down left sideline incomplete
3/12-B24 - Smith rolled left, pass on side line to Holt for 13
1/10-B37 - Hawthorne cut thru middle 7
2/3 -B44 - Smith faked, passed deep over middle to Holt between 3 defenders for 34
1/10-O22 - Howell into rg 4
2/6 -O18 - Hawthorne thru rt for 3
3/3 -O15 - Smith moved left, passed into left end zone corner to Fisher for the TD Bledsoe PAT - 74 yards, 8 plays, BAYLOR 21, OHIO STATE 17
Black kicked off 57 yards; Hicks returned 21

0:31 OHIO
1/10-O24 - Springs pitch cut over rt for 4
2/6 -O28 - Springs option pitch at le for 4 as the first half ended at 2:41 P.M.

BAYLOR 21, OHIO STATE 17

THIRD QUARTER

Baylor elected to receive as rain comes down hard; Ohio to defend the south goal
Orosz kicked off 19 yards deep for the TB
15:00 BAYLOR
1/10-B20 - Hawthorne option pitch on counter left for 11
1/10-B31 - Smith faked, faded, chased, passed way too short for Lee right incomplete
2/10-B31 - Howell lg 1
3/9 -B32 - Smith pass too low to Hawthorne on screen left incomplete
4/9 -B32 - Prestridge punted 40; Guess returned 4

13:37 OHIO
1/10-O32 - Campbell middle for 4
2/6 -O36 - Springs pitch, cut into lt for 2
3/4 -O38 - Springs on counter le for 1
4/3 -O39 - Orosz' punt, partially blocked, rolled for 42 dead (McGeary)

11:53 BAYLOR
1/10-B19 - Smith rolled right, passed for lee on sideline, too long incomplete
2/10-B19 - Smith kept on counter option left for -1 - Ross
3/11-B18 - Smith passed to Howell on safety swing right for 3
4/8 -B21 - Prestridge punted 33; Schwartz FC

SEPTEMBER 30, 1978

10:57 OHIO
1/10-O46 - Campbell middle for 4
2/6 - 50 - Murray cut left on deep handoff for - 1 - Singletary
3/7 -O49 - Schlichter rolled right, passed to Donley on the sideline (23 yard line) for the TD - Janakievski PAT 54 yards in 3 plays (all alone)
OHIO STATE 24, BAYLOR 21
Orosz kicked off 14 yards deep for the TB

9:49 BAYLOR
1/10-B20 - Hawthorne lt 2
2/8 -B22 - Howell center 5
3/3 -B27 - Smith rolled right, passed to Holt on sideline for 11
1/10-B38 - Pollard cut thru rt for 13
1/10-O49 - Smith faked, passed quick to Lee over middle for 14
1/10-O35 - Smith kept on counter option right for 5
2/5 -O30 - Smith faked, passed quick right for Marshall; deflected by Cato incomplete
3/5 -O30 - Smith rolled left, passed to Lee; broken up by Ross incomplete
4/5 -O30 - Smith passed left to Holt as hit by Sullivan; way short incomplete

6:57 OHIO
1/10-O30 - Springs pitch le for 3
2/7 -O33 - Ohio State illegal procedure -5
2/12-O38 - Schlichter passed to Donley on slant over middle for 13
1/10-O41 - Schlichter kept inside le for 1
2/9 -O42 - Murray hit into re for 6
3/3 -O48 - Campbell on robust into le for 7
1/10-B45 - Murray fought thru middle for 7
2/3 -B38 - Campbell at lg for 1
3/2 -B37 - Campbell center for just 1
4/1 -B36 - Campbell, on second effort, into lg for 2
1/10-B34 - Volley was clear at rt for 14
1/10-B20 - Murray option pitch at le for no gain
2/10-B20 - Schlichter rolled right, ran for 5 out of bounds on clothesline
3/5 -B15 - Campbell off lt for 4 as he broke a tackle Time out Ohio State at 1:27
4/1 -B11 - Campbell jumped over lt for 2
1/9 -B9 - Ohio State illegal procedure -5
1/14-B14 - Campbell lt 3
2/11-B11 - Schlichter kept inside re for 7
3/4 -Campbell thru rg for 3 as the quarter ended

OHIO STATE 24, BAYLOR 21

FOURTH QUARTER

OHIO
4/1 -B1 - Time out Baylor at 15:00
4/1 -B1 - Campbell stretched thru rt for the TD Janakievski PAT 70 yards in 18 plays
OHIO 31, BAYLOR 21
Orosz kicked off 49 yards; Taylor returned right for 15

14:50 BAYLOR
1/10-B26 - Hawthorne turned right end for 4 on deep hand off
6 -B30 - Smith passed behind Taylor on right sideline incomplete; Baylor III. Proc. -5
2/11-B25 - Pollard cut outside rt for 2
3/9 -B27 - Smith passed on safety swing right to Howell, broke tackle for 11
1/10-B38 - Smith rolled left, passed in deep flat to Holt; broken up Skillings incomplete
2/10-B38 - Smith faded, passed on screen right to Howell; hit by cousineau -5
3/15-B33 - Smith passed way too high to Holt right incomplete
4/15-B33 - Prestridge punted 42; Guess fumble recovered by Skillings for -7

11:45 OHIO
1/10-O18 - Volley thru lt for 9
2/1 -O27 - Murray pitch at re for 12
1/10-O39 - Volley thru lt for 3
2/7 -O42 - Murray rt 5
3/2 -O47 - Campbell clear at center for 12
1/10-B41 - Murray rt for 2
2/8 -B39 - Schlichter kept inside lt for 2
3/6 -B37 - Schlichter passed to Gerald down left side line for 33; dead ball personal foul Ohio State -15
1/10-B19 - Schlichter kept right for - 1 - Brown
2/11-B18 - Schlichter passed quick to Donley on slant over middle; broken up in complete.
3/20-B20 - Volley pushed thru rg for 3
4/17-B17 - ATHA's FG was from 34 yards
OHIO STATE 34, BAYLOR 21
65 yards in 12 plays
Orosz kicked off 54 yards; Taylor returned left 22

6:59 BAYLOR
1/10-B28 - Smith faked, passed to Holt deep right, just too high incomplete
2/10-B28 - Pollard over le for
3/5 -B33 - Smith passed left for Fisher for 21
1/10-O46 - Smith kept inside le for 17
1/10-O29 - Smith passed down left side line to Hawthorne for 17
1/10-O12 - Pollard option pitch re for 4
2/6 -O8 - Smith rolled left, passed way too high for Fisher at the flag incomplete
3/6 -O8 - Smith passed to Taylor over middle; intercepted Dansler, return 3

4:17 OHIO
1/10-O7 - Volley rt 2
2/8 -O9 - Schlichter kept inside le for 2
3/6 -O11 - Volley at lg for 2 more
4/4 -O13 - Orosz punted 32, Fields returned right 11; Baylor Clip -16 (stepped off long)

243

2:33 BAYLOR
- 1/10- 50 - Smith passed deep left on flea flicker to Hawthorne who tripped incomplete
- 2/10- 50 - Smith passed deep right to Taylor for 18 /(Hawthorne hurt, wheeled off)
- 1/10-O32 - Smith Passed on screen right to Lee; illegal pass receiver down field -7
- 2/17-O39 - Smith passed into deep left flat; intercepted by Cousineau down sideline for the TD; Ohio State penalty Pers foul 15
- 2/2 -O34 - Smith passed deep left into the end zone to Mitchell for the TD Bledsoe PAT - 50 yards in four plays
  OHIO STATE 34, BAYLOR 28
  Bledsoe kicked off squibb left; Volley recovered deflection for no yards

1:47 OHIO
- 1/10-O43 - Campbell middle for 1
- 2/9 -O44 - Murray pitch (in the rain) at le for 5 Time out Baylor at 1:04
- 3/4 -O49 - Murray pitch at re for (measurement) 3 time out Baylor at 0:57
- 4/1 -B48 - Orosz punted 37; Fields returned 4

0:48 BAY
- 1/10-B15 - Smith rolled right passed over middle for Taylor; broken up Cousineau incomplete
- 2/10-B15 - Smith faded, sacked by Ross; fumbled recovered by Sullivan for -5

0:48 BAYLOR
- 1/10-B15 - Smith rolled right passed over middle for Taylor; broken up Cousineau incomplete
- 2/10-B15 - Smith faded, sacked by Ross; fumbled recovered by Sullivan for -5

0:36 OHIO
- 1/10-B10 - Castignola fell on ball for -1
- 2/11-B11 - The game ended at 4:18 P.M. (The rain was limited to a few minutes at the beginning and end of the second half)

OHIO STATE 34, BAYLOR 28

244

SEPTEMBER 30, 1978

OREGON
VS.
WISCONSIN
Camp Randall Stadium
Temp: 59
Wind: WNW 10-12 mph
Skies: Cloudy and warm
FIRST QUARTER

WISCONSIN WON THE TOSS AND ELECTED TO RECEIVE. Oregon will kickoff and defend the NORTH goal.

Pat English will kickoff for Oregon to open the game, to the W11, Green returns the kick 20 yards to W 31.
14:55 WISCONSIN
1/10-W31 - Stauss runs up the middle, gets 1 to 32. (Vobora)
2/9 -W32 - Josten passes to right to Souza, gets 10 yards to 42. Wisconsin is penalized 5 yards for illegal procedure
2/14-W27 - Stauss runs left end, gets 13 to W 40. (Nolan)
3/1 -W40 - Josten sneaks over the middle, gets 4 to 44. (Beekley)
1/10-W44 - Josten passes left to Charles, incomplete
2/10-W44 - Mohapp runs right tackle, gets 1 to 45. (Bryant)
3/9 -W45 - Wisconsin is penalized for delay of game 5 yards
3/14-W40 - Josten is back to pass, loses 9 to 31 (Dion)
4/23-W31 - Kiltz punt 42 yards to O 27, Richmond returns 16 to 43 (Cohee)

11:46 OREGON
1/10-O43 - Radcliff runs wide left, loses 1 to 42 (Gordon)
2/11-O42 - Kennedy passes to Williams, incomplete
3/11-O42 - Kennedy passes to Beyer, incomplete
4/11-O42 - Babb punts 36 yards to W 22, Matthews returns -1 to 21.

10:56 WISCONSIN
1/10-W21 - Matthews runs right tackle, gets no gain (Setterlund)
2/10-W21 - Josten passes right to Charles, gets 16 to 37. (Nolan)
1/10-W37 - Wisconsin calls timeout (9:52) Josten keeps on option right; gets 2 to 39 (Setterlund)
2/8 -W39 - Josten passes left Braker, gets 4 to 43.
3/4 -W43 - Josten runs right end, gets 7 to 50. (Hinkle)
1/10- 50 - Souza runs right on reverse, gets 7 to O 43. (Bryant)

2/3 -O43 - Josten pitched to Matthews on left end, gets 11 to 32.(Covington)
1/10-O32 - Matthews runs up the middle, loses 3 to 35. (Kesler) Wisconsin illegal procedure penalty refused.
2/13-O35 - Josten runs left end, gets 4 to 31, (Blasher)
3/9 -O31 - Green runs out of bounds on pass, loses 16 to 47
4/25-O47 - Kiltz punts 38 yards to O 9, Richmond fair catch

6:44 OREGON
1/10-O9 - Williams runs left tackle, gets 2 to 11 (Schremp)
2/8 -O11 - Kennedy passes to Radcliff, gets 3 to 14 (Crossen)
3/5 -O14 - Kennedy back to pass is sacked; loses 4 to 10 (Relich)
4/9 -O10 - Babb punts to 36 yards to O 46, Matthews fair catch

4:41 WISCONSIN
1/10-O46 - Wisconsin is penalized 5 yards for illegal procedure
1/15-W49 - Green runs reverse, loses 14 to 35, fumbles recovered by O Blasher.

4:31 OREGON
1/10-W35 - Kennedy passes to Jackson, incomplete
2/10-W35 - Williams runs right tackle, gets 2 to 33 (Ahrens)
3/8 -W33 - Kennedy passes left to Jackson, gets 2 to 31. (Crossen)
4/6 -W31 - English field goal attempt is short.

3:03 WISCONSIN
1/10-W31 - Mohapp runs up the middle, gets 7 to 38 (Goldsmith)
2/3 -W38 - Mohapp runs up middle gets, gets 3 to 41 (Kesler)
1/10-W41 - Green keeps left, gets 6 to 47 (Dion)
2/4 -W47 - Green keeps up the middle, gets 8 to O 45 (Beekley)
1/10-O45 - Green passes incomplete; knocked down at line
2/10-O45 - Mohapp runs left tackle, gets 8 to 37 (Blasher)
3/2 -O37 - Green pitch left to Matthews, gets 1 to 36. (Schwartz)

END OF FIRST QUARTER SCORE:
WISCONSIN 0, OREGON 0

SECOND QUARTER

15:00 WISCONSIN
4/1 O36 - Richardson runs up the middle, gets no gain (Dion)

245

14:56 OREGON
1/10-0:36 - Young runs up the middle, gets 5 to 41 (Christenson)
2/5 -041 - Young runs right tackle, gets 2 to 43 (Schremp)
3/3 -043 - Young runs left tackle, gets no gain (Cabral)
4/3 -043 - Babb punts 46 yards to W 11, Matthews returns 7 to W18 (Wood)

13:09 WISCONSIN
1/10 W18 - Mohapp runs up the middle, gets 13 to 31 (Nolan)
1/10-W31 - Mohapp runs up middle, gets 4 to 35 (Cosgrove)
2/6 -W35 - Souza runs reverse, loses 6 to 29, fumbles, recovered by Dion

12:10 OREGON
1/10-W29 - Young runs left end, gets 12 to W 17
1/10-W17 - Kennedy rolls right passes to Heyer, gets 16 to 1
1/G -W1 - Kennedy sneaks over middle, gets no gain (Crossen)
2/G -W1 - Young runs right tackle, gets 1 for TD 10:29 English kick is good.
(4 plays, 29 yards)
SCORE: OREGON 7, WISCONSIN 0

English kicks off for Oregon following the score to W11, Anderson returns 18 yards to 29 (Anderson)

10:25 WISCONSIN
1/10-W29 - Kalasmiki is sacked, loses 6 to 23 (Goldsmith)
2/16-W23 - Kalasmiki passes right to Souza, gets 10 to 33 (Richmond)
3/6 -W33 - Kalasmiki passes left to Souza, gets 8 to 41 (Bryant)
1/10-W41 - Mohapp runs up the middle, gets 3 to 44 (Kesler)
2/7 -W44 - Kalasmiki passes to Sydnor, incomplete
Oregon is penalized 35 yards for pass interference
1/10-021 - Wisconsin is penalized 5 yards for illegal procedure
1/15-026 - Kalasmiki passes right to Souza, incomplete
2/15-026 - Kalasmiki passes incomplete, deflected (by Hinkle)
3/15-026 - Wisconsin is penalized 5 yards for delay of game
3/20-031 - Kalasmiki passes left to Souza, intercepted by Covington

8:02 OREGON
1/10-05 - Wood runs tackle, gets 6 to 11 (Relich)
2/4 -011 - Williams runs left end, gets 1 to 12 (Crossen)
3/3 -012 - Young runs up the middle, gets 2 to 14 (Ahrens)

4/1 -014 - Bass punts 33 yards, to 047, Gordon returns 3 yards, fumbles, recovered by Clough.

6:22 OREGON
1/10-044 - Kennedy passes to Jackson, incomplete
2/10-044 - Williams runs left end, gets 7 to W49 (Crossen)
3/3 -W49 - Kennedy rolls right, loses 2 to 049 (Crossen)
4/5 -049 - Babb punts 51 yards to W endzone for touchback

4:46 WISCONSIN
1/10-W20 - Mohapp runs left guard, gets 6 to 26 (Dion)
2/4 -W26 - Kalasmiki passes right to Sydnor, incomplete
Wisconsin is penalized 16 yards for intentional grounding and loss of down
3/20-W10 - Mohapp runs up the middle, gets 4 to 14 (Kesler)
4/16-W14 - Kiltz punts 45 yards to 042. Richmond returns 0 to 42 (Johnson)

3:25 OREGON
1/10-042 - Kennedy passes right to Coleman, incomplete
2/10-042 - Kennedy passes over middle to Clark, incomplete
3/10-042 - Williams runs right tackle, gets 4 to 46 (Christenson)
4/6 -046 - Babb punts 28 to W26, Erdmann fair catch

2:34 WISCONSIN
1/10-W26 - Kalasmiki passes left to Charles, gets 7 to 33
2/3 -W33 - Kalasmiki passes right to Charles, 22 to 045 (Richmond)
1/10-045 - Kalasmiki passes right to Sydnor, overthrown
2/10-045 - Wisconsin calls timeout (1:55)
Kalasmiki passes right to Charles, gets 9 to 36 (Richmond)
3/1 -036 - Kalasmiki passes left to Souza, broken up (by Covington)
4/1 -036 - Kalasmiki pitches right to Cohee, gets 4 to 32 (Bryant)
1/10-032 - Kalasmiki passes right to Charles, overthrown
2/10-032 - Kalasmiki passes over middle to Charles, broken up (by Dale)
3/10-032 - Wisconsin calls timeout (1:13)
Cohee runs right tackle, gets 9 to 23 (Richmond)
4/1 -023 - Wisconsin is penalized 5 yards for illegal procedure
4/6 -028 - Veith field goal attempt is wide left

SEPTEMBER 30, 1978

:41 OREGON
1/10-O28 - Williams runs right guard, gets 4 to 32 (Relich)
2/6 -O32 - Williams runs right tackle, gets 1 to 33 (Relich)

**END OF THE FIRST HALF
SCORE: OREGON 7, WISCONSIN 0**

THIRD QUARTER

OREGON WILL RECEIVE and WISCONSIN WILL defend the north goals.
Mike Brhley will kickoff for Wisconsin to open the second half, to the 0 endzone for the touchback.

15:00 OREGON
1/10-O20 - Radcliff runs right tackle, gets to 22 (Sawicki)
2/8 -O22 - Kennedy passes screen right to Williams, gets 21 to 43 (Relich)
1/10-O43 - Williams runs right end, gets 9 to W48 (Erdmann)
2/1 -W48 - Radcliff runs right end, gets no gain (Sawicki)
Wisconsin is penalized 15 yards for personal foul
1/10-W33 - Kennedy falls going back to pass, loses 3 o 36
2/13-W36 - Kennedy passes left to Williams, gets 9 to 27, fumbles, recovered by Christenson

12:49 WISCONSIN
1/10-W27 - Cohee runs right tackle, loses 3 to 24 (Goldsmith)
2/13-W24 - Green pitches right, gets 7 to 31 (Bryant)
3/6 -W31 - Green runs off pass, gets 8 to 39 (Berkich)
1/10-W39 - Green pitches right to Gohee, gets 10 to 49 (Beekley)
1/10-W49 - Mohapp runs right tackle, gets 4 to O47 (Dale)
2/6 -O47 - Green pitches right to Cohee, gets 5 to 42 (Beekley)
3/1 -O42 - Green keeps left guard, gets 4 to 38 (Blasher)
1/10-O38 - Mohapp runs right tackle, gets 3 to 35 (Beekley)
2/7 -O35 - Mohapp runs left guard, gets 3 to 32 (Bryant)
3/4 -O32 - Mohapp runs right tackle, gets 2 to 30 (Dale)
4/2 -O30 - Green keeps on option, gets no gain (Setterlund)

7:38 OREGON
1/10-O30 - Wood runs left guard, gets 4 to 34 (Crossen)

2/6 -O34 - Radcliff runs right end, no gain
Wisconsin is penalized 5 yards for off sides
2/1 -O39 - Wood runs up the middle, gets 2 to 41 (Christenson)
1/10-O41 - Kennedy passes to Clark, broken up (by Crossen)
2/10-O41 - Kennedy passes over middle to Bachtold, gets 17 to W42
1/10-W42 - Wood runs up the middle, gets 3 to 39 (Christenson)
2/7 -W39 - Radcliff runs right end, gets 33 to W6 (Gordon)
1/G -W6 - Kennedy passes left to Wood, incomplete
2/G -W6 - Radcliff runs left tackle, gets 6 for TD (5:15)
English extra point kick is wide right (8 plays 70 yards)
SCORE: OREGON 13, WISCONSIN 0

English will kickoff for Oregon following the score to W10, Souza returns 9 to W19
5:09 WISCONSIN
1/10-W19 - Mohapp left tackle, gets 3 to 22 (Beekley)
2/7 -W22 - Green keeps on option, loses 3 to 19 (Setterlund)
3/10-W19 - Mohapp runs draw, gets 1 to 20 (Goldsmith)
4/9 -W20 - Kiltz punts 43 yards to O37, Robertson fair catch

3:07 OREGON
1/10-O37 - Wood runs up the middle, gets 6 to 43 (Crossen)
2/4 -O43 - Oregon calls timeout (2:42)
Young runs right end, gets 3 to O46 (Christenson)
3/1 -O46 - Wood runs up the middle, gets 5 to W49 (Erdmann)
1/10-W49 - Wisconsin is penalized 5 yards for substitution penalty
1/5 -W44 - Kennedy passes over middle to Bachtold, gets 17 to 27 (Anderson)
1/10-W27 - Wood runs right guard, gets 3 to 24 (Relich)
2/7 -W24 - Young runs left tackle, gets 4 to 20, fumbles, recovered by Lorenz

:51 WISCONSIN
1/10-W20 - Cohee runs right tackle, 19 to 39 (Bryant)
1/10-W39 - Kalasmiki passes right to Sydnor, gets 48 to O13 (Richmond)

**END OF THIRD QUARTER:
SCORE: OREGON 13, WISCONSIN 0**

247

FOURTH QUARTER

15:00 WISCONSIN
1/10-013 - Kalasmiki passes over middle to Souza, incomplete
2/10-013 - Kalasmiki passes left to Charles, incomplete
3/10-013 - Kalasmiki keeps and runs left end, gets 3 to 10 (Beekley)
4/7 -010 - Oregon calls timeout (14:15)
Kalasmiki passes left to Sydnor on fake field goal, gets 3 to 7 (Blasher)

14:09 OREGON
1/10-07 - Wood runs up the middle gets 4 to 11 (Schremp)
2/6 011 - Kennedy pitches right to Wood, gets 5 to 16 (Erdmann)
3/1 -016 - Wood runs right tackle, gets 2 to 18 (Christenson)
1/10-018 - Radcliff runs right end, gets 3 to 21 (Christenson)
2/7 -021 - Radcliff runs up the middle, gets 1 to 22 (Cabral)
3/6 -022 - Kennedy sacked, loses 4 to 18 (Lorenz)
4/10-018 - Babb punts 42 yards to W40, Erdmann returns 5 to W45 (Covington)

11:23 WISCONSIN
1/10-045 - Kalasmiki passes to Charles, gets 11 to O44 (Covington)
1/10-044 - Kalasmiki passes over middle to Sydnor, gets 18 to 26 (Nolan)
1/10-026 - Kalasmiki passes right to Charles, gets 26 for TD (10:29)
Veith kicks the extra point (3 plays, 55 yards) SCORE: OREGON 13, WISCONSIN 7

Oregon is penalized 20 yards for personal foul and offsides on extra point.
Brhley kicks off for Wisconsin O40 to O30, Delegato recovers the onside kick

10:29 OREGON
1/10-030 - Wood runs left guard, gets 9 to 39 (Holm)
2/1 -039 - Wood runs left tackle, gets 5 to 44 (Lorenz)
1/10-044 - Kennedy passes over middle to Clark, gets 9 to W47
2/1 -W47 - Kennedy passes over middle to Bachtold, incomplete
3/1 -W47 - Wood runs left guard, gets 2 to W45 (Burt)
1/10-W45 - Wood runs right tackle, gets 1 to 44 (Christenson)
2/9 -W44 - Kennedy pitches left to Radcliff, gets 42 to W2 (Holm)
1/G -W2 - Kennedy pitches right to Radcliff, gets 1 to W1 (Gordon)
2/G -W1 - WISCONSIN is penalized for illegal procedure
2/G W1 - Wood runs up the middle, gets no gain (Holm)
3/G -W1 - Radcliff runs left tackle, gets 1 for TD (7:07)
Oregon calls timeout (7:07) (10 plays, 70 yards)
Kennedy passes for extra point, incomplete
SCORE: OREGON 19, WISCONSIN 7

English will kickoff for Oregon following the score to W endzone for touchback.

7:07 WISCONSIN
1/10-W20 - Kalasmiki passes long to Souza, incomplete
2/10-W20 - Kalasmiki passes over the middle, to Charles get 7 to 27 (Bryant)
3/3 -W27 - Kalasmiki passes over the middle to Souza, gets 29 yds to O44 (Covington)
1/10-O44 - Wisconsin is penalized 5 yards for illegal procedure
1/15-O49 - Kalasmiki passes long right to Sydnor, gets 49 for TD
Wisconsin is penalized 15 yards for offensive pass interference and loss of down
2/30-W36 - Kalasmiki passes long left to Stracka, incomplete
3/30-W36 - Kalasmiki passes left to Souza, incomplete
4/30-W36 - Kiltz, punts 50 yards to O14 and out of bounds

5:23 OREGON
1/10-014 - Kennedy pitches left to Radcliff, gets 6 to 20 (Levenick)
2/4 -020 - Wood runs left guard, gets 5 to 25, (Crossen)
1/10-025 - Kennedy ptiches left to Radcliff, gets 7 to 32 (Crossen)
2/3 -030 - Kennedy passes to Clark, intercepted by Levenick, at O42 returned 18 to O24 (Matthews)

SEPTEMBER 30, 1978

4:04 WISCONSIN
1- -O24 - Kalasmiki passes up the middle to Cohee, gets 4 to 20 (Nolan)
2/6 -O20 - Kalasmiki passes left to Braker, gets 8 to 12
1/10-O12 - Kalasmiki passes to Stracka, incomplete
2/10-O12 - Kalasmiki passes to Sydnor, incomplete
3/10-O12 - Kalasmiki passes long right to Stracka, gets 12 for TD
Veith kicks the extra point (5 plays, 24 yards)
SCORE: OREGON 19, WISCONSIN 14

Veith kicks off for Wisconsin following the score, to O25 Covington fumbles recovered by Casey.
2:12 WISCONSIN
1/10-O25 - Kalasmiki passes left to Souza, gets 10 to 15 (Covington)
1/10-O15 - Kalasmiki passes to Souza, incomplete
2/10-O15 - Kalasmiki passes over the middle to Sydnor, incomplete
3/10-O15 - Kalasmiki passes left to Souza, incomplete
Oregon is penalized 8 yards for roughing the passer
3/2 -O7 - Wisconsin calls timeout (1:56)
Kalasmiki pitches left to Cohee, gets 3 to 4 (Beekley)
1/G -O4 - Cohee runs left tackle, get 4 for TD
Wisconsin calls timeout (1:32) (6 plays, 25 yards)
Kalasmiki passes to Charles for 2 point conversion
SCORE: WISCONSIN 22, OREGON 19

Brhley kicks off for Wisconsin following the score to O14, Young returns 18 to O32. (Anderson)
1:26 OREGON
1/10-O32 - Kennedy passes left to Jackson, incomplete
2/10-O32 - Kennedy passes over the middle to Jackson, incomplete
3/10-O32 - Kennedy passes right to Jackson, get 13 to 45 (Crossen)
1/10-O45 - Kennedy passes to Jackson, incomplete
2/10-O45 - Kennedy passes right incomplete
3/10-O45 - Kennedy passes to Wood, incomplete (hit by Ahrens)

4/10-O45 - Kennedy passes right to Bachtold, gets 22 to W33 (Levenick)
1/10-W33 - Kennedy is sacked, loses 10 to 43 (by Ahrens)
2/20-W43 - Kennedy passes right to Bachtold, gets 2 to 41
3/18-W41 - Kennedy passes to Bachtold, incomplete
4/18-W41 - Kennedy passes right to Jackson 14 to 27

:05 WISCONSIN
1/10-W27 - Kalasmiki 1 to 26

**FINAL SCORE:
WISCONSIN 22, OREGON 19**

National Collegiate Athletic Association **FINAL TEAM STATISTICS**		
	OREGON	WISCONSIN
First Downs	16	24
Rushing	9	12
Passing	6	11
Penalty	1	1
Rushing	52	49
Yards Rushing	225	205
Yards Lost Rushing	26	61
Net Yards Rushing	199	144
Net Yards Passing	143	252
Passes Attempted	28	39
Passes Completed	12	18
Had Intercepted	1	1
Total Offensive Plays	80	88
Total Net Yards	342	396
Average Gain Per Play	4.27	4.5
Fumbles: Number—Lost	3/3	3/3
Penalties: Number—Yards	4/63	13/91
Interceptions: Number—Yards	1/0	1/18
Number of Punts—Yards	7/272	5/217
Average Per Punt	39	43.4
Punt Returns: Number—Yards	2/16	4/14
Kickoff Returns: Number—Yards	1/18	3/47

OCTOBER 7, 1978

ILLINOIS VS. MISSOURI
Temp: 56°
Winds: NW 10-15 mph
Skies: Partly Cloudy
FIRST QUARTER

Missouri wins toss, elects to receive. Illinois defends south goal. Finzer kicks to Meyer at 3. 22 yd return (Venegoni)

14:55 MISSOURI
- 1/10-M25 - Bradley pass to Lewis incomplete (Venegoni)
- 2/10-M25 - Bradley option lt, gain of 7 (Sullivan)
- 3/3 -M32 - Newman lt tackle, gain of 6 (Hardy)
- 1/10-M38 - Bradley lt pass to Lewis, gain of 16 (Venegoni)
- 1/10-I46 - Wilder lt guard, gain of 3 (Ralph)
- 2/7 -I43 - Wilder pitch right, gain of 13 (Levitt) Personal foul, Illinois 15 yds.
- 1/10-I15 - Bradley pass lt flat to Wilder, gain of 14 (Venegoni)
- 1/G -I1 - Wilder lt, touchdown. 1 yd run Brockhaus PAT good 8 plays 75 yds.
MISSOURI 7, ILLINOIS 0

Brockhaus kicks to Foster, downed in endzone. Touchback.

12:49 ILLINOIS
- 1/10-I20 - Powell up middle, gain of 2 (Petersen)
- 2/8 -I22 - Powell lg, gain of 5 (Petersen)
- 3/3 -I27 - McCullough pass for Rouse broken up by Lauderdale.
- 4/3 -I27 - Finzer punts 20 yds, out of bounds. No return.

11:25 MISSOURI
- 1/10-I47 - Bradley left keeper, gain of 6 (J. Gillen)
- 2/4 -I41 - Wilder lg, gain of 3 (Sullivan, Atkins)
- 3/1 -I38 - Wilder rt, loss of 2 (Gillen)
- 4/3 -I40 - Brockhaus punt is out of bounds at 18. 22 yd. kick.

9:43 ILLINOIS
- 1/10-I18 - Powell le, gain of 1 (Garlich)
- 2/9 -I19 - Weber lg, gain of 2 (Miltenberger)
- 3/7 -I21 - Weber rg, gain of 2 (Petersen, Bess)
- 4/5 -I23 - Finzer punts 37 yards. Whitaker minus one return. (Weber)

7:52 MISSOURI
- 1/10-M39 - Bradley scrambles rt, gain of 9 (Sullivan, Adams) Personal foul, Illinois 15 yds.
- 1/10-I37 - Newman lt, gain of 8 (Adams)
- 2/2 -I29 - Penalty offsides, Illinois 5 yds.
- 1/10-I24 - Wilder le, gain of 12 (Thornton)
- 1/10-I12 - Bradley pass left to Winslow incomplete, (Adams)
- 2/10-I12 - Ellis le, gain of 9 (Sullivan)
- 3/1 -I3 - Ellis lg, loss of 1 (Venegoni)
- 4/2 -I4 - Brockhaus 21 yd field goal good. 7 plays, 61 yards
MISSOURI 10, ILLINOIS 0

Brockhaus kicks to Rouse at 6, 12 yd. return (Goodman)

5:42 ILLINOIS
- 1/10-I18 - Illegal procedure, Illinois. 5 yd. penalty.
- 1/15-I13 - McCullough left keeper, gain of 1 (Bess, Goodman)
- 2/14-I14 - McCullough pass to Barnes, gain of 21 (Calabrese)
- 1/10-I35 - McCullough pass to Barnes, incomplete (Wright)
- 2/10-I35 - Weber rt, gain of 5 (Bess)
- 3/5 -I40 - McCullough pass to Barnes incomplete (Wright)
- 4/5 -I40 - Finzer kicks 25 yards to Lauderdale at 35.
(Delay of Game, Missouri, 5 yds.)

4:01 MISSOURI
- 1/10-M30 - Bradley pass to Sly. Sly carries 70 yards for touchdown. Brockhaus PAT good. 1 play, 70 yards, 9 seconds.
MISSOURI 17, ILLINOIS 0

Brockhaus kicks to Foster at 1, return 20 yds (Green) Personal foul, Missouri. 15 yd penalty.

3:47 ILLINOIS
- 1/10-I36 - Powell re gain of 2 (Garlich) Penalty, holding Illinois, 15 yards.
- 1/23-I23 - McCullough pass to Powell, gain of 10
- 2/13-I33 - McCullough pass to Barnes incomplete (Wright)
- 3/13-I33 - McCullough pass to Barnes incomplete
- 4/13-I33 - Finzer punts 26 yards, downed at 41.

2:40 MISSOURI
- 1/10-M41 - Wilder up middle, no gain.
- 2/10-M41 - Bradley sacked, loss of 5 (J. Gillen, Adams)
- 3/15-M36 - Bradley pass rt to Wilder, gain of 10 (J. Gillen)
- 4/5 -M46 - Brockhaus punts 42 yards to Hardy, return of 10. Clipping, Illinois, 11 yd. penalty.

ILLINOIS
- 1/10-I11 - Strader rt, no gain, (Stephens)
- 2/10-I11 - Strader rg, gain of 5 (Bungarda)

**END OF FIRST QUARTER:
MISSOURI 17, ILLINOIS 0**

250

SECOND QUARTER

15:00 ILLINOIS
3/15-I16 - McCullough pass complete to L. Boeke, gain of 20 (Lauderdale)
1/10-I36 - McCullough pass to Barnes, gain of 17 (Wright)
1/10-M47 - McCullough pass to Powell, gain of 12 (Lauderdale, Poe)
1/10-M35 - Strader up middle, gain of 2 (Garlich)
2/8 -M33 - McCullough rt end, gain of 6 (Hamilton, Wright)
3/2 -M27 - Weber lg gain of 3 (Garlich)
1/10-M24 - Powell up middle, gain of 4 (Bess)
2/6 -M20 - McCullough pass for Schluter broken up by Whitaker.
3/6 -M20 - Finzer 37 yard field goal good. 11 plays, 89 yards,
MISSOURI 17, ILLINOIS 3

Finzer kicks to Lewis, return of 20 yds, (Durrell)

11:48 MISSOURI
1/10-M20 - Bradley rt option, gain of 7 (Sullivan)
2/3 -M27 - Bradley pass to Downer, gain of 7 (Sullivan)
1/10-M34 - Bradley scrambles left, for a gain (Tucker) penalty, Missouri, personal foul, 15 yards.
1/28-M16 - Bradley scrambles right, gain of 8
2/20-M24 - Wilder re, gain of 8. Fumble, Thornton recovers.

ILLINOIS
1/10-M32 - McCullough pass to Powell, gain of 7 (Wright)
2/3 -M25 - Powell lg, gain of 1 (Bungarda)
3/2 -M24 - McCullough pass to Barnes incomplete, (Calabrese)
4/2 -M24 - Powell fumbles pitch, recovers, loss of 4.

9:21 MISSOURI
1/10-M28 - Newman rg, gain of 8 (Ralph)
2/2 -M36 - Newman rt, gain of 3.
1/10-M39 - Bradley pass to Wilder incomplete
2/10-M39 - Bradley pass to Newman, gain of 7 (Ramshaw)
3/3 -M46 - Bradley scrambles lt, gain of 4 (Sullivan)
1/10- 50 - Bradley keeps, no gain (Sullivan)
2/10- 50 - Bradley pass to Downer rt, gain of 4 (Levitt)
3/6 -I46 - Bradley pass to Downer, gain of 16 (Hardy)
1/10-I30 - Bradley pass to Lewis out of bounds, gain of 8. (George)
2/2 -I22 - Bradley pass for Winslow, incomplete (George)

OCTOBER 7, 1978

3/2 -I22 - Bradley keeps, lt option, gain of 3. (Flynn)
1/10-I19 - Bradley pass to Wilder, loss of 1 (Hardy)
2/11-I20 - Bradley scrambles up middle, gain of 8 (Sullivan)
3/3 -I12 - Bradley rt option, gain of 2 (Flynn)
4/1 -I11 - Brockhaus 28 yd. field goal attempt wide to the right

4:36 ILLINOIS
1/10-I20 - Powell rg, gain of 2 (Ray)
2/8 -I22 - McCullough lt option, no gain (Ray, Garlich)
3/8 -I22 - McCullough pass intercepted by Garlich at 28.

3:17 MISSOURI
1/10-I28 - Bradley rt option, gain of 8 (Hardy)
2/2 -I20 - Wilder lg gain of 6 (Sullivan)
1/10-I14 - Newman rt, gain of 4 (Thornton)
2/6 -I10 - Bradley lt option, gain of 3 (J. Gillen)
3/3 -I7 - Wilder pitchout rt, loss of 4 (Ramshaw) Missouri timeout.
4/7 -I11 - Brockhaus 28 yd. field goal wide to the right.

1:05 ILLINOIS
1/10-I20 - Powell re, no gain (Petersen), timeout, Missouri.
2/10-I20 - McCullough keeps right, gain of 2 (Petersen), timeout, Missouri.
3/8 -I22 - McCullough, bad pitch to Dismuke, loss of 6. Calabrese recovers.

:34 MISSOURI
1/10-I16 - Bradley pass to Lewis out of bounds at 1, gain of 15.
1/G -I1 - Bradley pass to Lewis, rt, touchdown 1 yd. 2 plays, 16 yards, 9 seconds. Brockhaus PAT good.
MISSOURI 24, ILLINOIS 3

Brockhaus kicks to Rouse at 11, 7 yd. return. (Whitaker, Green)

:20 ILLINOIS
1/10-I18 - Delay of game, Illinois, 5 yd. penalty.
1/15-I13 - Dismuke rt gain of 7 (Lauderdale, Hamilton)

END OF HALF:
MISSOURI 24, ILLINOIS 3

251

THIRD QUARTER

Brockhaus kicks to Foster at 4, 16 yd. return (Gaylord)

14:55 ILLINOIS
1/10-I20 - Powell rg gain of 4 (Bess)
2/6 -I24 - Weiss lt option, gain of 4 (Bess)
3/2 -I28 - Weiss rt option, gain of 1 (Bess, Goodman)
4/1 -I29 - Finzer punts 34 yards to Whitaker, 12 yd return (Cozen)

12:53 MISSOURI
1/10-M49 - Newman up middle, gain of 5 (Sullivan)
2/5 -I46 - Wilder lt gain of 4 (J. Gillen)
3/1 -I42 - Wilder lt, gain of 16 (Hardy)
1/10-I26 - Newman up middle, gain of 3 (Sullivan, Ramshaw)
2/1 -I23 - Bradley pass complete to Downer, gain of 15 (Hardy)
1/G -I8 - Bradley rt option, fumbles, Illinois recovers, Hardy, Bradley, gain of 2.

10:37 ILLINOIS
1/10-I6 - Dismuke rg gain of 3 (Garlich)
2/7 -I9 - Dismuke rt pitch, gain of 2 (Whitaker), Timeout, Illinois.
3/5 -I11 - Dismuke rt pitch, gain of 2 (Petersen)
4/3 -I13 - Finzer punts 28 yards to Whitaker, no return

9:24 MISSOURI
1/10-I41 - Wilder fumbles pitch. Bradley recovers, gain of 2.
2/8 -I39 - Bradley pass to Lewis intercepted by George. 28 yd. return (Lewis)

8:34 ILLINOIS
1/10-I41 - Powell le, gain of 8 (Wright)
2/2 -I49 - Weiss fumbles snap, Taylor recovers, gain of 1 (Goodman)
3/1 - 50 - Dismuke lg gain of 2 (Berg)
1/10-M48 - Weiss le, gain of 1 (Ray)
2/9 -M47 - Weiss sacked by Lauderdale, Hamilton. Loss of 3.
3/12- 50 - Weiss pass to Dismuke, gain of 5 (Wright)
4/7 -M45 - Finzer punts 17 yards to Lauderdale. Fair catch.

5:55 MISSOURI
1/10-M28 - Newman lt gain of 5 (J. Gillen)
2/5 -M33 - Newman lt no gain (Thiede)
3/5 -M33 - Bradley pass to Dansdill incomplete (Hardy)
4/5 -M33 - Brockhaus punts 36 yards to Hardy, fumbles fair catch, but recovers. No yards no return.

4:40 ILLINOIS
1/10-I31 - Weiss scrambles left, gain of 2 (Bungarda)
2/8 -I33 - Weber lg, gain of 4 (Garlich)
3/4 -I37 - Weber rg, gain of 2 (Hamilton)
4/2 -I39 - Finzer punts 38 yards to Whitaker at 23. 2 yd. return (L. Boeke)

2:33 MISSOURI
1/10-M25 - Bradley pass lt to Downer, gain of 7
2/3 -M32 - Newman up middle, gain of 17 (Durrell)
1/10-M49 - Bradley pass to Lewis broken up by Ramshaw
2/10-M49 - Bradley rt option, no gain (Thornton)
3/10-M49 - Bradley sacked by Sullivan, loss of 13. Timeout, Missouri
4/23-M36 - Brockhaus punts 38 yards to Hardy. Fair catch.

:26 ILLINOIS
1/10-I26 - Weiss pass for Strader intercepted by Garlich for 29 yard touchdown Brockhaus PAT good.
MISSOURI 31, ILLINOIS 3

Brockhaus kicks to Foster, 22 yd. return (Goodman)
ILLINOIS
1/10-I26 - Powell draw lt, gain of 18 (Lauderdale)

**END OF THIRD QUARTER:
MISSOURI 31, ILLINOIS 3**

FOURTH QUARTER

McClintock returns as referee.
15:00 ILLINOIS
1/10-I44 - Weiss pass for L. Boeke incomplete (Calabrese)
2/10-I44 - Weiss pass for L. Boeke, gain of 9 (Litzelfelner)
3/1 -M47 - Weiss sneak, gain of 2. (Goodman)
1/10-M45 - Weiss pass for Rouse incomplete (Whitaker)
2/10-M45 - Weiss re gain of 1 (Garlich, Green)
3/9 -M44 - Weiss pass to Barnes, gain of 10. (Whitaker)
1/10-M34 - Powell draw play, loss of 3 (Whitaker)
2/13-M37 - Weiss sacked by Whitaker for loss of 12.
3/25-M49 - Weiss pass to L. Boeke out of bounds and incomplete (Wright)
4/25-M49 - Finzer punts 32 yards to Whitaker, 2 yd. return (Taylor)

OCTOBER 7, 1978

11:21 MISSOURI
1/10-M19 - Ellis rt, gain of 8 (J. Gillen)
2/2 -M27 - Jeffrey keeps lt, gain of 1 (Thiede)
3/1 -M28 - Ellis lg, gain of 6. (Hardy, J. Gillen)
1/10-M34 - Jeffrey pass for Wilder incomplete (Adams)
2/10-M34 - Jeffrey pass for Blair incomplete (George)
3/10-M34 - Jeffrey pass for Anderson incomplete (Levitt)
4/10-M34 - Brockhaus punts 37 yards. Hardy fumbles. Gadt recovers. Minus 8 return.

MISSOURI
1/10-I21 - Ellis rg gain of 6 (J. Gillen)
2/4 -I15 - Jeffrey keeps lt, gain of 6 (Hardy)
1/G -I9 - Meyer lt gain of 6 (J. Gillen)
2/G -I3 - Ellis up mdl, gain of 2 (Ramshaw)
3/G -I1 - Ellis dives lt, TD 5 plays, 21 yards
MISSOURI 38, ILLINOIS 3
Gie kicks to Foster at 1, 18-yard return (Whitaker, Goodman)

ILLINOIS
1/10-I19 - Weiss scrambles, loss of 5 (Berg)
2/15-I14 - Perez draw lt, gain of 1 (Garlich) illegal procedure Illinois declined
3/14 -I15 - Weiss pass for Rouse incomplete (Litzelfelner)
4/14-I15 - Finzer kicks to Whitaker at 50 Whitaker runs 50 yds touchdown
Finzer 35 yard kick Timeout MISSOURI PAT good
MISSOURI 45, ILLINOIS 3

Gie kicks to Foster at 5. 25-yd. return (Gie, Powell)
6:09 ILLINOIS
1/10-I30 - Perez rg gain of 6 (Judd)
2/4 -I36 - Weiss pass to Barnes, gain of 28 (T. Newman) holding against Illinois, 22-yd. penalty
2/26-I14 - Weiss keeps rt, loss of 1 (Green, Matthews)
3/27-I13 - Thomas lt gain of 4 (Boone) Timeout, Illinois
4/23-I17 - Finzer punts 49 yards to Lewis at 34 (Taylor) 5-yd. return

4:08 MISSOURI
1/10-M39 - Meyer lg, gain of 15 (Hardy)
1/10-I46 - McBride le, gain of 12 (Hardy)

1/10-I34 - McBride lg gain of 4
2/6 -I30 - Jeffrey keeps rt, loss of 2 (Thornton)
3/8 -I32 - Meyer draw lt, gain of 2 (Carmien) holding, Missouri, nullified gain with 15-yard penalty
3/23-I47 - Jeffrey fumbles snap, Salder recovers. No gain
4/23-I47 - Brockhaus punts 36 yards to Hardy at 11

1:40 ILLINOIS
1/10-I11 - Thomas carries, no gain (Miltenberger)
2/10-I11 - Perez rg, loss of 2 (Boone)
3/12-I9 - Thomas lg, gain of 5 (Berg)

FINAL SCORE:
MISSOURI 45, ILLINOIS 3

National Collegiate Athletic Association
FINAL TEAM STATISTICS

	ILLINOIS	MISSOURI
First Downs	9	26
Rushing	4	15
Passing	5	8
Penalty	0	3
Rushing Attempts	49	55
Yards Rushing	125	270
Yards Lost Rushing	35	30
Net Yards Rushing	90	240
Net Yards Passing	111	189
Passes Attempted	23	24
Passes Completed	9	14
Had Intercepted	2	1
Total Offensive Plays	72	79
Total Net Yards	201	429
Average Gain Per Play	2.8	5.4
Fumbles: Number— Lost	5/2	4/2
Penalties: Number— Yards	9/98	4/50
Interceptions: Number— Yards	1/28	2/29
Number of Punts— Yards	11/341	6/211
Average Per Punt	31.0	35.2
Punt Returns: Number— Yards	3/1	7/70
Kickoff Returns: Number—Yards	7/120	2/42

INDIANA VS. WISCONSIN
Camp Randall Stadium
Temp.: 46
Wind: NNW 12-13 mph
Skies: Cloudy
FIRST QUARTER

INDIANA won the toss and elected to defend the North goal. WISCONSIN will receive. Steve Straud will kick off for Indiana to open the game, to the W7, Green returns 13 yards to W20. (Abrams).

14:55 WISCONSIN
1/10-W20 - Wisconsin is penalized 5 yards for illegal procedure
1/15-W15 - Matthews runs right tackle, gets 4 to 19 (Norman)
2/11-W19 - Kalasmiki passes left to Charles, gets 12 to 31
1/10-W31 - Mohapp runs left guard, loses 1 to 30 (Tisdale)
2/11-W30 - Kalasmiki passes right to Charles, incomplete
3/11-W30 - Kalasmiki passes over the middle to Charles, incomplete
4/11-W30 - Kiltz punts 32 yards to I 38, Wilbur fair catch

13:27 INDIANA
1/10-I38 - Arnett passes left to Fisher, gets 11 to 49 (Johnson)
1/10-I49 - Burnett runs right tackle, gets 2 to W49 (Ahrens)
2/8 -W49 - Arnett passes right to Johnson, gets 6 to 43 (Christenson)
3/2 -W43 - Burnett runs left tackle, gets 4 to 39 (Gordon)
1/10-W39 - Arnett passes to Johnson, broken up (by Ahrens)
2/10-W39 - Arnett passes screen left to Johnson, incomplete
3/10-W39 - Arnett pitches left to Burnett, gets no gain
4/10-W39 - Lovett punts 39 yards to W endzone for touchback

11:16 WISCONSIN
1/10-W20 - Schapp runs left guard, gets 2 to 22 (Wilhite)
2/8-W22 - Kalasmiki passes over the middle to Charles, gets 14 to 36
1/10-W36 - Kalasmiki passes left to Souza, incomplete
2/10-W36 - Mohapp runs draw up middle, gets 5 to 41 (Tisdale)
3/5 -W41 - Mohapp runs right guard, gets 4 to 45 (Doehia)
4-1 -W45 - Kiltz punts 28 yards to I 27.

8:48 INDIANA
1/10-I27 - Burnett runs left tackle, gets 3 to 30 (Crossen)
2/7 -I30 - Arnett pitches left to Burnett, gets no gain (Anderson)
3/7 -I30 - Burnett runs left tackle, gets 3 to 33 (Schremp)
4/4 -I33 - Lovett punts 38 yards to W 29, Matthews returns 71 yards for TD (6:50) Veith extra point kick is good
SCORE: WISCONSIN 7, INDIANA 0

Brhley kicks off for Wisconsin following the score, to I 6, Hopkins fumbles the return gets 10 to 16

6:47 INDIANA
1/10-I16 - Burnett runs right tackle, gets 2 to 18 (Cabral)
2/8 -I18 - Burnett runs right tackle, gets no gain (Cabral)
3/8 -I18 - Burnett runs right tackle, gets 2 to 20 (Christenson)
4/6 -I20 - Lovett punts 39 yards to W 41, Matthews fair catch

4:51 WISCONSIN
1/10-W41 - Matthews runs right tackle, gets 8 to 49 (Norman)
2/2 -W49 - Kalasmiki passes right to Sydnor, gets 38 to I 13
1/10-I13 - Kalasmiki keeps on option right, gets 5 to 8 (Sybert)
2/5 -I8 - Kalasmiki pitches left to Matthews gets 2 to 6 (Norman)
3/3-I6 - Kalasmiki pitches right to Matthews, gets 6 for TD (2:40) Veith kicks extra point (5 plays, 59 yards)
SCORE: WISCONSIN 14, INDIANA 0

OCTOBER 7, 1978

Brhley kicks off for Wisconsin following the score, to the I 7, Burnett returns 12 yards to 19. (Stroede)

2:34 INDIANA
1/10-I19 - Burnett runs up the middle, gets 4 to 23 (Cabral)
2/6 -I23 - Arnett passes right to Powers, incomplete
3/6 -I23 - Arnett passes left to Friede, incomplete
4/6 -I23 - Lovett punts 41 yards to W 36, Matthews returns 21 to I 43 (Hopkins)

1:38 WISCONSIN
1/10-I43 - Matthews runs right end, gets 1 to 42 (Doehia)
2/9 -I42 - Mohapp runs up the middle, gets 2 to 40 (Leake)
3/7 -I40 - Kalasmiki passes over middle to Sydnor, incomplete
4/7 -I40 - Kiltz punts 40 yards to I endzone

:15 INDIANA
1/10-I20 - Harkrader runs left end, gets 6 to 26 (Erdmann)
2/4 -I26 - Johnson runs up the middle, gets 2 to 28 (Crossen)

**END OF FIRST QUARTER:
WISCONSIN 14, INDIANA 0**

SECOND QUARTER

15:00 INDIANA
3/2 -I28 - Arnett pitches right to Harkrader, loses 8 to 20
4/10-I20 - Lovett punts 39 yards W 41, Matthews fumbles return loses 1 to 40. (Swinehart)

14:15 WISCONSIN
1/10-W40 - Kalasmiki passes right to Charles, incomplete
2/10-W40 - Mohapp runs up the middle, gets 12 to I 47 (Alexander)
1/10-I47 - Kalasmiki passes right to Charles, incomplete
2/10-I47 - Matthews runs right guard, gets 2 to 45 (Norman)
3/8 -I45 - Kalasmiki passes over the middle to Sydnor, gets 12 to 33 (Hodge)
1/10-I33 - Kalasmiki passes left to Charles, gets 8 to 25 (Swinehart)
2/2 -I25 - Mohapp runs right guard, gets 3 to 22 (Leake)
1/10-I22 - Kalasmiki pitches to Matthews, passes to Braker, intercepted by Keneipp in endzone

11:37 INDIANA
1/10-I20 - Harkrader runs up the middle, gets 4 to 24 (Relich)

2/6 -I24 - Arnett keeps on option left, gets 3 to 27 (Christenson)
3/3 -I27 - Burnett runs up the middle, loses 1 to 26 (Relich)
4/4 -I26 - Lovett punts 35 yards to W 39

9:34 WISCONSIN
1/10-W39 - Kalasmiki passes left to Charles, incomplete
2/10-W39 - Mohapp runs right guard, gets 4 to 43 (Tisdale)
3/6 -W43 - Kalasmiki passes over the middle to Sydnor, incomplete
4/6 -W43 - Kiltz punts 48 yards to I 9, Swinehart returns no gain (Snell)

8:38 INDIANA
1/10-I9 - Harkrader runs left tackle, gets 5 to 14 (Erdmann)
2/5 -I14 - Harkrader runs left end, gets 3 to 17 (Anderson)
3/2 -I17 - Harkrader runs up middle, loses 1 to 16 (Boliaux)
4/3 -I16 - Lovett punts 24 yards to I 40 downed by Smith

7:12 WISCONSIN
1/10-I40 - Matthews runs left guard, loses 1 to 41 (Doehia)
2/11-I41 - Kalasmiki passes right to Sydnor, incomplete
3/11-I41 - Kalasmiki passes right to Sydnor, incomplete Indiana is penalized 15 yards for holding
1/10-I26 - Kalasmiki pitches right to Matthews, gets 26 yards for TD (6:24) (3 plays, 40 yards) Veith kicks the extra point SCORE: WISCONSIN 21, INDIANA 0

Brhley kicks off for Wisconsin following the score, to I endzone, Burnett returns 5 to I5 (Schieble)

6:22 INDIANA
1/10-I5 - Arnett runs left end, gets no gain (Schremp)
2/10-I5 - Johnson runs left tackle, gets 2 to 7 (Crossen)
3/8 -I7 - Clifford passes left to Friede, incomplete
4/6 -I7 - Lovett punts 28 yards to I35, Erdmann fair catch

4:48 WISCONSIN
1/10-I35 - Kalasmiki passes long right to Sydnor, incomplete
2/10-I35 - Matthews runs left guard, gets no gain (Sybert)
3/10-I35 - Kalasmiki keeps right on option, gets 1 to 34 (Doehia)
4/9 -I34 - Veith field goal attempt is wide left

255

3:22 INDIANA
- 1/10-I35 - Clifford passes right to Lundy, incomplete
- 2/10-I35 - Clifford pitches to Harkrader passes to Clifford, gets 17 to W48
- 1/10-W48 - Clifford passes right to Friede, gets 5 to 43 (Johnson)
- 2/5 -W43 - Harkrader runs right tackle, gets 5 to 38 (Holm)
- 1/10-W38 - Clifford pitches over the middle to Friede, broken up (by Johnson)
- 2/10-W38 - Clifford passes left to Friede, passes to Fishel, incomplete
- 3/10-W38 - Clifford passes right to Powers, intercepted by Gordon on I24 returned 7 to I31 (Harkrader)

1:58 WISCONSIN
- 1/10-W31 - Mohapp runs left guard, gets 3 to 34 (Norman)
- 2/7 -W34 - Matthews runs right tackle, gets 4 to 38 (Doehia)
- 3/3 -W38 - Wisconsin calls time out (:42) Matthews runs reverse right end, gets 4 to 42 (Leake)
- 1/10-W42 - Wisconsin calls timeout (:36) Kalasmiki passes long right to Charles, incomplete
- 2/10-W42 - Mohapp runs right guard, gets 3 to 45 (Leake)
- 3/7 -W45 - Matthews runs right tackle gets to I49 (Norman)

END OF FIRST HALF: WISCONSIN 21, INDIANA 0

THIRD QUARTER

Steve Straub will kick off for Indiana to open the second half, to the W2, Anderson return for no gain.

14:57 WISCONSIN
- 1/10-W2 - Kalasmiki keeps left guard, gets 2 to 4 (Hunter)
- 2/8 -W4 - Matthews runs right tackle, gets 6 to 10 (Norman)
- 3/2 -W10 - Kalasmiki keps right guards, gets 1 to 11 (Leake)
- 4/1 -W11 - Kiltz punts 51 yards to I38 downed by Sawicki

13:17 INDIANA
- 1/10-I38 - Arnett left to Burnett, loses 2 to 36 (Gordon)
- 2/12-I36 - Arnett passes over the middle to Powers, incomplete
- 3/12-I36 - Arnett passes right to Powers, broken up (by Erdmann)
- 4/12-I36 - Lovett recovers long snap, loses 21 to I15 (Ahrens)

12:22 WISCONSIN
- 1/10-I15 - Kalasmiki keeps on the option left, gets 9 to 6 (Keneipp)
- 2/1 -I6 - Mohapp runs right guard, gets 2 to 4 (Patton)
- 1/G -I4 - Mohapp runs up middle, gets no gain (Arbuckle)
- 2/G -I4 - Kalasmiki passes left to Charles, incomplete
  Indiana is penalized 3 yards for pass interference
- 1/G -I1 - Kalasmiki keeps for 1 for TD (10:08) Veith extra point kick is wide right (5 plays, 15 yards)
  SCORE: WISCONSIN 27, INDIANA 0

Brhley kicks off for Wisconsin following the score, to I8, Hopkins returns 13 fumbled recovered by I Willhite.

10:04 INDIANA
- 1/10-I21 - Arnett passes to Friede, incomplete
- 2/10-I21 - Arnett passes left to Bowers, gets 14 to 35, fumbled out of bounds (Gordon)
- 1/10-I35 - Arnett keeps on option right, gets 2 to 37 (Relich)
- 2/8 -I37 - Arnett passes to Bowers, incomplete
- 3/8 -I37 - Burnett runs draw up middle, gets 2 to 39 (Schremp)
- 4/6 -I39 - Lovett punts 39 yards to W22, Matthews fumbles loses 3 to 19

8:33 WISCONSIN
- 1/10-W19 - Kalasmiki keeps runs right end, gets 8 to 27 (Wilbur)
- 2/2 -W27 - Matthews runs right tackle, gets 5 to 32 (Norman)
- 1/10-W32 - Matthews runs left tackle, gets 2 to 34 (Patton)
- 2/8 -W34 - Wisconsin is penalized 5 yards for illegal procedure
- 2/13-W29 - Kalasmiki is sacked on pass, loses 6 to 23 (Tallen)
- 3/19-W23 - Mohapp runs draw off right guard, gets 5 to 28 (Norman)
- 4/14-W28 - Kiltz punts 35 yards to I37, Swinehart fair catch

5:28 INDIANA
- 1/10-I37 - Arnett passes left to Friede, gets 12 to I49
- 1/10-I49 - Arnett pitches left to Burnett, gets 3 to W48 (Boliaux)
- 2/7 -W48 - Arnett passes right to Fishel, gets 10 to 38 (Schieble)
- 1/10-W39 - Burnett runs right tackle, gets 7 to 31 (Boliaux)
- 2/3 -W31 - Burnett runs right tackle, gets 8 to 23 (Crossen)
- 1/10-W23 - Harkrader runs left tackle, gets 1 to 22 (Schremp)
- 2/9 -W22 - Arnett keeps and runs right end, gets 3 to 19 (Boliaux)
- 3/6 -W19 - Arnett back to pass fumbles, loses 12 to 31 (Ahrens recovered)

OCTOBER 7, 1978

1:50 WISCONSIN
- 1/10-W31 - Mohapp runs up the middle, gets 3 to 34 (Iatarola)
- 2/7 -W34 - Kalasmiki passes over middle to Sydnor, gets 13 to 47 (Abrams)
- 1/10-W47 - Matthews rush right tackle, gets no gain (Patton)
- 2/10-W47 - Kalasmiki passes long left to Stracka, broken up (by Abrams)
- 3/10-W47 - Kalasmiki passes right to Sydnor, incomplete
- 4/10-W47 - Kiltz punts 23 yards to I30; kick goes out of bounds

END OF THIRD QUARTER: WISCONSIN 27, INDIANA 0

FOURTH QUARTER

15:00 INDIANA
- 1/10-I30 - Arnett back to pass loses 3 to 27 (Ahrens)
- 2/13-I27 - Arnett passes right to Lundy, broken up (by Gordon)
- 3/13-I27 - Arnett passes over the middle, to Friede, broken up (by Levenick)
- 4/13-I27 - Lovett punts 31 yards to W42, Matthews returns 5 to 47

14:01 WISCONSIN
- 1/10-W47 - Green keeps on option right, gets 7 to I46 (Tisdale)
- 2/3 -I46 - Green pitches right to Matthews, gets no gain (Norman)
  Wisconsin is penalized 15 yards for personal foul
- 3/18-W39 - Green keeps on option right, gets 9 to 48 (Tisdale)
- 4/9 -W48 - Kiltz punts 29 yards, to I23, downed by Snell

12:35 INDIANA
- 1/10-I23 - Clifford passes right to Fishel, broken up (by Johnson)
- 2/10-I23 - Clifford passes long left to Friede, incomplete
- 3/10-I23 - Clifford passes left to Bowers, gets 11 to 34 (Levenick)
- 1/10-I34 - Clifford passes right to Lundy, incomplete
  Wisconsin is penalized 15 yards for personal foul
- 1/10-I49 - Clifford passes right to Bowers, gets 19 to W32 (Welch)
- 1/10-W32 - Clifford passes screen right to Bowers, incomplete
- 2/10-W32 - Clifford passes right to Bowers, gets 3 to 29 (Anderson)
- 3/7 -W29 - Clifford passes right to Bowers, overthrown
- 4/7 -W29 - Clifford passes left to Stephenson, overthrown

11:20 WISCONSIN
- 1/10-W30 - Green keeps on option left, gets 8 to 38 (McIntosh)
- 2/2 -W38 - Shumway runs right guard, gets 1 to 39 (Willhite)
- 3/1 -W39 - Richardson runs right guard, gets 4 to 43 (Norman)
- 1/10-W43 - Green fumbles the snap, gets no gain (recovered by Arbuckle)

9:41 INDIANA
- 1/10-W43 - Clifford passes right to Friede, incomplete
- 2/10-W43 - Clifford passes over the middle to Stephenson, gets 7 to 36
- 3/3 -W36 - Burnett runs draw left, gets no gain (Relich)
- 4/3 -W36 - Clifford passes left to Johnson, gets 15 yards to 21 (Welch)
- 1/10-W21 - Clifford passes right to Burnett, gets 12 to 9 (Johnson)
- 1/G -W9 - Burnett runs right tackle, gets 3 to W6 (Boliaux)
- 2/G -W6 - Clifford keeps on option left, gets 1 to 5 (Crossen)
- 3/G -W5 - Friede runs reverse right, gets 5 for TD (6:24)
  Freud kicks the extra point (8 plays, 43 yards)
  SCORE: WISCONSIN 27, INDIANA 7
  Straub kicks off, for Indiana following the score, to W5 returns 5 to W10 runs out of bounds

6:19 WISCONSIN
- 1/10-W10 - Matthews runs right tackle, gets 15 to 25 (Keneipp)
- 1/10-W25 - Matthews runs right end, loses 3 to 22 (Iatarola)
- 2/13-W22 - Kalasmiki passes long right, intercepted by Keneipp on I34

5:12 INDIANA
1/10-I34 - Clifford passes screen left, to Bowers, gest 6 to 40 (Boliaux)
2/4 -I40 - Clifford passes left to Bowers, gets 6 to 46 (Christenson)
1/10-I46 -Clifford passes right to Lundy, gets 3 to 49 (Schieble)
2/7 -I49 - Clifford passes right to Pennick, gets 16 to W35
1/10-I35 - Clifford passes over the middle to Stephenson, gets 5 to 30 (Schieble)
2/5 -W30 - Clifford passes long to Lundy, incomplete
3/5 -W30 - Clifford passes left to Bowers, incomplete
4/5 -W30 - Indiana calls time out (2:41) Clifford passed right to Johnson, incomplete

2:34 WISCONSIN
1/10-W30 - Richardson runs right tackle, gets 11 to 41 (Arbuckle)
1/10-W41 - Richardson runs right tackle, gets 5 to 46 (Arbuckle)
2/5 -W46 - Green keeps on option, gets 10 to I44 (Iatarola)
1/10-I44 - Richardson runs left tackle, gets 1 to 43 (Patton)
2/9 -I43 - Richardson runs pitch right, gets 5 to 38, fumbled out of bounds
3/4 -I38 - Shumway runs left tackle, gets 5 to 33 (Arbuckle)
1/10-I33 - Green keeps up the middle, gets 17 to 16 (Swinehart)
1/10-I16 - Green passes over the middle to Stracka, gets 16 for TD (:13)
Veith kicks the extra point (8 plays, 70 yards)
SCORE: WISCONSIN 34, INDIANA 7

Brhley kicks off for Wisconsin following the score, to I2, Hopkins returns 16 to I18 (Brhley)
:08 INDIANA
1/10-I18 - Clifford passes long right to Lundy, broken up (by Casey)
2/10-I18 - Clifford passes long left to Lundy intercepted by Schieble at W44 returned 30 to I26 (Johnson)

FINAL SCORE:
WISCONSIN 34, INDIANA 7

National Collegiate Athletic Association
FINAL TEAM STATISTICS

	INDIANA	WISCONSIN
First Downs	15	21
Rushing	3	13
Passing	11	6
Penalty	1	2
Rushing Attempts	37	55
Yards Rushing	85	249
Yards Lost Rushing	48	11
Net Yards Rushing	37	238
Net Yards Passing	178	113
Passes Attempting	45	22
Passes Completed	18	7
Had Intercepted	2	2
Total Offensive Plays	82	77
Total Net Yards	215	351
Average Gain Per Play		
Fumbles: Number—Lost	5/0	4/1
Penalties: Number—Yards	2/18	4/40
Interceptions: Number—Yards	2/0	2/37
Number of Punts—Yards	10/352	8/286
Average Per Unit	35.2	35.8
Punt Returns: Number—Yards	1/0	5/93
Kickoff Returns: Number—Yards	5/56	3/18

OCTOBER 7, 1978

UTAH
VS.
IOWA
Kinnick Stadium
Temp.: 50's
Wind: NNE at 25 mph
Skies: Cloudy
FIRST QUARTER

Utah wins toss and elects to receive. Iowa will kick off and defend north goal. Schilling kicks off to Solomon for return of 11. (Cole)
UTAH
1/10-U17 - Moseley over LG for gain of 3 (Rusk)
2/7 -U20 - Gomez passes to Hansen for gain of 18 (Danzy)
1/10-U38 - Lindsay around LE for no gain (Harty)
2/10-U38 - Gomez pass intended for Henry is incomplete
3/10-U38 - Lindsay over LG for gain of 6 (Harty)
4/4 -U44 - Partridge punts to Reid for return of 7. (42 yard punt) (Solomon)

12:46 IOWA
1/10-I21 - Burke for RG for gain of 4 (Kinsella)
2/6 -I25 - Lazar over LG for gain of 4 (Negrete)
3/2 -I29 - Commings around LE for gain of 4 (Reed)
1/10-I33 - Lazar over LT for gain of 5 (Sobolewski)
2/5 -I38 - Burke over RG for gain of 1
3/4 -I39 - Burke around RE for loss of 3 (Kinsella)
4/7 -I36 - Holsclaw punts to Wilson for return of 4 (40 yard punt) (McKillip)

9:29 UTAH
1/10-U28 - Lindsay around LE for no gain (Gutshall)
2/10-U28 - Gomez pass intended for Henry is incomplete
3/10-U28 - Gomez thrown for loss of 9 (Harty)
4/19-U19 - Utah penalized 5 yards for offsides
4/24-U14 - Partridge punts to Becker for fair catch. (32 yard punt)

8:12 IOWA
1/10-U46 - Burke over RG for gain of 4
2/6 -U42 - Burke over RG for gain of 37 (Reed)
1/G -U5 - Lazar over LG for gain of 1 (La Rocque)
2/G -U4 - Burke over LG for gain of 1 (Washington)
3/G -U3 - Commings around RE for loss of 6 (Padjen)
4/G -U9 - Green holds, field goal attempt good. (Schilling kicks)
SCORE IOWA 3 UTAH 0

Schilling kicks off into endzone for touchback.
5:27 UTAH
1/10-U20 - Lindsay over LG for gain of 3 (Rusk)
2/7 -U23 - Gomez pass intended for Henry is incomplete
3/7 -U23 - Gomez passes to Lindsay for gain of 13 (Danzy)
1/10-U36 - Moseley over RT for gain of 2 (Hufford)
2/8 -U38 - Gomez passes to Lindsay for gain of 5 (Weiss)
3/3 -U43 - Lindsay around LE for loss of 1 (Rusk)
4/4 -U42 - Partridge punts to Reid for return of 4 (39 yard punt) (Bailey)

2:30 IOWA
1/10-I23 - Burke over LG for no gain. Utah penalized 15 yards for face mask grabbing (Bailey)
1/10-I38 - Frazier over RT for no gain (Lyall)
2/10-I38 - Commings passes to Lazar for gain of 12
1/10- 50 - Lazar over RG for gain of 3 (Sobolewski)
2/7 -U47 - Burke over LG for gain of 2 (Lyall)
3/5 -U45 - Iowa penalized 5 yards for illegal motion
3/10- 50 - Commings pass intended for Lazar incomplete.
4/10- 50 - Holsclaw punts to Solomon for return of 7 (37 yard punt Webb)

**FIRST QUARTER SCORE:
IOWA 3 UTAH 0**

259

SECOND QUARTER

UTAH
1/10-U20 - Walker around LE for gain of 12
1/10-U32 - Gomez passes to Henry for gain of 17
1/10-U49 - Gomez fumbles, recovers, for no gain
2/10-U49 - Gomez pass intended for Hansen is incomplete
3/10-U49 - Gomez pass intended for Lindsay is incomplete
4/10-U49 - Partridge punt is blocked by Hill, Person returns for 19

13:21 IOWA
1/10-U19 - Commings fumbles, recovered by Reed, for loss of 4
Utah penalized 5 yards for offsides
1/5 -U14 - Burke around RE for no gain
2/5 -U14 - Burke over RG for gain of 4 (Lyall)
3/1 -U10 - Lazar over RG for gain of 2 (Bailey)
1/G -U8 - Frazier around RE for no gain (Griffin)
2/G -U8 - Commings pass intended for Swift is incomplete
3/G -U8 - Burke around LE for gain of 6 (Washington)
4/G -U2 - Burke over RG for gain of 1 (Bailey)

UTAH
1/10-U1 - Gomez pass intended for Teahan is incomplete
2/10-U1 - Richeson over LG for gain of 4 (Rusk)
3/6 -U5 - Richeson over LT for gain of 3 (Hufford)
4/3 -U8 - Partridge punts to Becker for return of 11 (49 yard punt) (Henry)

9:24 IOWA
1/10-U46 - Commings pass intended for Swift, intercepted by Reed

9:17 UTAH
1/10-U10 - Richeson over LT for gain of 3 (Gutshall)
2/7 -U13 - Moseley over LG for gain of 1 (Benschoter)
3/6 -U14 - Gomez passes to Richeson for gain of 1
4/5 -U15 - Partridge punts to Reid for return of 11 (52 yard punt) (Brock)

7:24 IOWA
1/10-I44 - Frazier over RT for gain of 3 (Padjen)
2/7 -I47 - Burke over RT for gain of 2 (Alvey)
3/5 -I49 - Burke around LE for gain of 10 (Reed)

1/10-U41 - Morton over RG for loss of 3 (Lyall)
2/13-U44 - Lazar over RG for gain of 6 (Morell)
3/7 -U38 - Commings passes to Burke for gain of 15 (Reed)
1/10-U23 - Commings around LE for gain of 2 (Lyall)
2/8 -U21 - Commings pass intended for Reid is incomplete
3/8 -U21 - Mosley over RG for gain of 2 (LaRocque)
4/6 -U19 - Green holds, Schilling kicks, field goal attempt is good
SCORE: IOWA 6 UTAH 0

Schilling kicks off to Solomon for return of 21. (Schilling) (King)

3:53 UTAH
1/10-U24 - Lindsay around LE for gain of 5 (Danzy)
2/5 -U29 - Lindsay over RT for gain of 24 (Pace)
1/10-I47 - Gomez passes to Lindsay for gain of 9 (Gutshall)
2/1 -I38 - Gomez pass intended for Henry is incomplete
3/1 -I38 - Lindsay around LE for gain of 11 (Danzy)
1/10-I27 - Gomez passes to Teahan for gain of 26
1/G -I1 - Gomez fumbles, recovered by Hobbs (Loss of 1)

2:28 IOWA
1/10-I2 - Commings sneaks for gain of 3 (Clark)
2/7 -I5 - Lazar over RT for gain of 2 (Clark)
3/5 -I7 - Lazar over RG for gain of 1 (Negrete)
4/4 -I8 - Holsclaw around RE for gain of 8
Iowa penalized half distance to goal for clipping.
4/4 -I8 - Hosclaw punts to Solomon for no return

1:20 UTAH
1/10-I35 - Gomez passes to Henry for gain of 13 (Weiss)
1/10-I22 - Gomez pass intended for Lindsay is incomplete
2/10-I22 - Gomez passes to Folsom for gain of 14 (Rusk)
1/G -I8 - Gomez pass intended for Teahan is incomplete
2/G -I8 - Gomez pass intended for Folsom is incomplete
4/G -I8 - Partridge holds, Hucko kicks, field goal attempt is good
SCORE: IOWA 6 UTAH 3

Hucko kicks off to Holloway for return of 13 (Solomon)

260

OCTOBER 7, 1978

0:46 IOWA
1/10-I18 - Burke over LG for gain of 2 (Lyall)

**FIRST HALF SCORE:
IOWA 6 UTAH 3**

THIRD QUARTER

Iowa will receive. Utah will kick off and defend south goal. Hucko kicks off to Holloway, fumbles, recovered by Holloway, return of 8.
IOWA
1/10-I19 - Burke over LT for gain of 3 (Lyall)
2/7 -I22 - Lazar over RT for gain of 5 (Bailey)
3/2 -I27 - Commings fumbles, recovered by Lyall for Utah. (loss of 8) (Bailey)

13:46 UTAH
1/10-I23 - Lindsay around RE for gain of 8
Utah penalized 15 yds for holding
1/25-I38 - Lindsay over LG for no gain (Benschoter)
2/25-I38 - Gomez passes to Moseley for gain of 6. Iowa penalized 15 yards for personal foul. (Weiss)
3/4 -I17 - Lindsay over LG for gain of 4 (Gutshall)
1/10-I13 - Walker around RE for no gain (Weiss)
2/10-I13 - Gomez pass intended for Teahan is incomplete
3/10-I13 - Gomez passes to Teahan for gain of 8 (Steverson)
4/2 -I5 - Partridge holds, Hucko kicks, field goal attempt is no good

11:13 IOWA
1/10-I20 - Commings around RE for gain of 3 (Bailey)
2/7 -I23 - Mosley over RG for no gain (Sobolewski)
3/7 -I23 - Dolan passes to Mosley for gain of 6
4/1 -I29 - Holsclaw thrown for loss of 14 (Griffin)

9:30 UTAH
1/10-I15 - Richeson fumbles, recovered by Rusk, gain of 1

9:23 IOWA
1/10-I14 - Mosley over RT for gain of 3 (Padjen)
2/7 -I17 - Dolan pass intended for Swift is incomplete
3/7 -I17 - Dolan passes to Blatcher for gain of 10 (Griffin)
1/10-I27 - Dolan around RE for gain of 1
2/9 -I28 - Dolan passes to Lazar for loss of 2 (Sobolewski)

3/11-I26 - Dolan pass intended for Lazar is incomplete
4/11-I26 - Holsclaw punts to Solomon for fair catch. (39 yard kick)

6:40 UTAH
1/10-U35 - Barrett over RT for gain of 1
2/9 -U36 - Walker fumbles, recovered by Rusk loss of 5

6:03 IOWA
1/10-U31 - Blatcher around RE for gain of 7 (Reed)
2/3 -U24 - Lazar over RT for gain of 6 (Bailey)
1/10-U18 - Lazar over RG for gain of 6 (Sobolewski)
2/4 -U12 - Lazar over LT for no gain (Reed)
3/4 -U12 - Dolan around RE for loss of 2 (Sobolewski)
4/6 -U14 - Green holds, Schilling kicks, field goal attempt is good
SCORE: IOWA 9 UTAH 3

Schilling kicks off to Solomon, fumbles, recovered by Solomon, gain of 17. (Cole)

3:46 UTAH
1/10-U19 - Lindsay around LE for gain of 10 (Rusk)
2/10-U29 - Moseley over LG for gain of 3 (Benschoter)
2/7 -U32 - Lindsay over RT for gain of 31 (Pace)
1/10-I37 - Moseley over RG for gain of 5 (Gutshall)
2/5 -I32 - Lindsay over RT for gain of 1 (Benschoter)
3/4 -I31 - Lindsay around RE for gain of 1 (Harty)
4/3 -I30 - Gomez passes to Moseley for gain of 11 (Becker)
1/10-I19 - Lindsay around RE for gain of 8 (Becker)

**THIRD QUARTER SCORE:
IOWA 9 UTAH 3**

FOURTH QUARTER

UTAH
2/2 -I11 - Gomez pass intended for Hansen is incomplete
Iowa penalized for defensive pass interference
1/G -I4 - Lindsay around LE for loss of 1
2/G -I5 - Gomez pass intended for Teahan is incomplete
3/G -I5- Gomez passes to Lindsay for TD. Partridge holds, Hucko kicks, PAT is good.
SCORE: UTAH 10 IOWA 9

261

Hucko kicks off to Blatcher for return 32 (Barrett)
14:07 IOWA
1/10-I33 - Blatcher around RE for gain of 18
1/10 50 - Lazar over RG for gain of 5
2/6 -U45 - Lazar over RG for gain of 2 (Bailey)
3/4 -U43 - Dolan around LE for gain of 1 (Lyall)
4/3 -U42 - Blatcher over RT for no gain

11:42 UTAH
1/10-U42 - Lindsay over LT for gain of 8 (Hill)
2/2 - 50 - Lindsay over RG for no gain (Hobbs)
3/2 - 50 - Lindsay around LE for gain 1 (Skradis)
4/1 -I49 - Partridge punts downed on one yard line

9:42 IOWA
1/10-I1 - Dolan pass intended for Swift intercepted by Griffin for return of 10 (Reed)

9:34 UTAH
1/G -I5 - Moseley over RG for gain of 2 (Rusk)
2/G -I3 - Lindsay over LT for no gain (Hill)
3/G -I3 - Gomez pass intended for Teahan, intercepted by Becker, gain of 22 Iowa penalized for clipping

8:24 IOWA
1/10-I6 - Dolan around RE for gain of 1 (Bailey)
2/9 -I7 - Dolan pass intended for Blatcher is incomplete
3/9 -I7 - Iowa penalized for illegal motion.
3/13-I3 - Dolan passes to Blatcher for gain of 4 (Griffin)
4/9 -I7 - Holsclaw punts to Iowa 49 yard line (42 yard punt)

6:52 UTAH
1/10-I49 - Lindsay around LE for gain of 2 (Rusk)
2/8 -I47 - Lindsay around LE for gain of 8 (Pace)
1/10-I39 - Gomez pass intended for Henry is incomplete
2/10-I39 - Lindsay around RE for gain of 9 (Danzy)
3/1 -I30 - Lindsay over LT for no gain. (Benschoter)
4/1 -I30 - Lindsay over LT for no gain. (Benschoter)

4:19 IOWA
1/10-I30 - Dolan pass intended for Frazier is incomplete

2/10-I30 - Dolan fumbles, recovered by Sobolewski, loss of 2

4:08 UTAH
1/10-I28 - Lindsay over LT for gain of 2 (Harty)
2/8 -I26 - Lindsay around LE for gain of 10 (Danzy)
1/10-I16 - Richeson around LE for no gain (Harty)
2/10-I16 - Richeson over LT for gain of 6 (Danzy)
3/4 -I10 - Lindsay around RE for gain of 4 Utah penalized for holding
3/16-I22 - Lindsay around LE for loss of 6 (Molini)
4/22-I28 - Partridge holds, Hucko kicks, field goal attempt is good
SCORE: UTAH 13 IOWA 9

Hucko kicks off to Blatcher for return of 31
1:38 IOWA
1/10-I31 - Dolan pass intended for Reid is incomplete
2/10-I31 - Dolan pass intended for Blatcher, intercepted by Morrell, return of 4

1:19 UTAH
1/10-I30 - Gómez falls on ball for loss of 3
2/13-I33 - Utah penalized 5 yards for delay of game
2/18-I38 - Gomez falls on ball for loss of 4
3/22-I42 - Gomez around LE for gain of 1

**FINAL SCORE:
UTAH 13 IOWA 9**

**National Collegiate Athletic Association
FINAL TEAM STATISTICS**

	IOWA	UTAH
First Downs	10	16
Rushes - Yards	52-138	50-161
Passing Yards	45	148
Return Yards	75	25
Passes	6-17-3	13-28-1
Punts	5-37.0	7-37.4
Fumbles - Lost	3-2	5-3
Penalties - Yards	4-22	6-57

Scoring	1	2	3	4	Final
IOWA	3	3	3	0	9
UTAH	0	3	0	10	13

OCTOBER 7, 1978

ARIZONA
VS.
MICHIGAN
Michigan Stadium
Temp: 49
Wind: NW 15-30 mph
Skies: Partly cloudy and cool
FIRST QUARTER

M won the toss and elected to receive. A defends the north goal.

Zivic kicked off to Clayton on the M8 and he ret'd 48 to the A44 (Hardville)
14:52 MICHIGAN
1/10-A44 - Huckleby at lg for 3 (Crosby)
2/7 -A41 - Davis at rg for 4 (Ingraham)
3/3 -A37 - Huckleby at rt for 1 (Ingraham)
4/2 -A36 - Leach rolled off rt for 1 (Ware)

13:13 ARIZONA
1/10-A35 - Oliver at center for 5 (Godfrey)
2/5 -A40 - Heater at le for 2 (Simpkins)
3/3 -A42 - Oliver at rt for 1 (Ketiz)
4/2 -A43 - Garcia punted to Jolly at the M14 (Streeter) (43 yd punt.)

11:30 MICHIGAN
1/10-M14 - Huckleby lost 1 behind rt (Whitton)
2/11-M13 - Leach hit are re for no gain (Liggins)
3/11-M13 - Leach passed to Marsh for 4 (Ingraham)
4/7 -M17 - Willner's punt was downed at the A42, 41 yd punt.

9:33 ARIZONA
1/10-A42 - Krohn, back to pass, hit by Keitz for -4.
2/14-A38 - Oliver at center for 7 (Meter)
3/7 -A45 - Krohn elected to run and made 7 (Bell)
1/10-M48 - Oliver at center for 8 (Bell)
2/2 -M40 - Krohn passed for Holmes incomplete.
3/2 -M40 - Oliver at rg for 10 (Bell)
1/10-M30 - Heater took pitchback at re for 6 (Jolly)
2/4 -M24 - Oliver at center for 3 (Godfrey)
3/1 -M21 - Heater took a pitchback at le for no gain (Godfrey)
4/4 -M21 - McKee held while Zivic's 37 yd field goal attempt from the M27 was wide to the left. Time: 5:04.

5:04 MICHIGAN
1/10-M21 - Huckleby took pitchback at le for 26 (Crosby)
1/10-M47 - Davis at lg for 4 (Crosby)
2/6 -A49 - Leach kept off lt for 5 (Ingraham)

3/1 -A44 - Leach kept at rt for no gain (G. Harris)
4/1 -A44 - Willner's punt downed by Weber at the A4, 40 yd punt.

2:42 ARIZONA
1/10-A4 - Oliver, at lg, fumbled when hit by Greer and Seabron recovered for M at the A2.

2:38 MICHIGAN
1/G -A2 - Huckleby took a pitchout at le and went in for 2 and the M TD.
Dickey held while Willner converted.
Time: 2:32
MICHIGAN 7 ARIZONA 0 2yds in 1 play.

Virgil kicked off to Butler on the A6 and he ret'd 22 (Trgovac)
2:28 ARIZONA
1/10-A28 - Oliver hit by Keitz at center for no gain.
2/10-A28 - Heater at rg for 5 (Simpkins
3/5 -A33 - Krohn passed for Beyer incomplete.
4/5 -A33 - Garcia punted to Harden, who fumbled the ball, and Housley recovered it for A at the M19.
1/10-M19 - Heater at lg for 5 (Meter)
2/5 -M14 - Krohn passed to Oliver for 9 (Jolly td save)
1/G -M5 - Oliver at lg for 4 (Simpkins)
2/G -M1 - McKee held white Zivic converted.
MICHIGAN 7 ARIZONA 7 19 yds in 4 plays

M had 12 plays for 49 yds. A had 20 plays for 62 yds.

END OF FIRST QUARTER

SECOND QUARTER

Zivic kicked off to Clayton on the M 11 and he ret'd 11 (Hardville)
14:53 MICHIGAN
1/10-M22 - Davis at rg for 1 (Ingraham).
2/9 -M23 - Leach passed to Feaster incomplete.
3/9 -M23 - Leach's pass to Davis dropped incomplete.
4/9 -M23 - Willner punted to Streeter who slipped as he caught it at the A33 (44 yd punt.)

14:01 ARIZONA
1/10-A33 - Heater took a pitchback at re for 9 (Harden)
2/1 -A42 - Oliver at rt for 9 (Meter)
1/10-M49 - Oliver at lg for 3 (Greer)
2/7 -M46 - Krohn passed to Holmes for 11 (Seabron)
1/10-M35 - Oliver at rt for 4 (Meter)
2/6 -M31 - Krohn passed to Oliver for 11 (Jolly)
1/10-M20 - Krohn rolled off rt for 9 (Simpkins)
2/1 -M11 - Heater at lt for 3 (Simpkins)
1/G -M8 - Krohn's pass for Beyer broken up by Bell.
2/G -M8 - Krohn's pass for Holmes broken up by Bell.
3/G -M8 - Oliver at lt for 1 (Simpkins)
4/G -M7 - McKee held while Zivic kicked a 24 yd field goal from the M14.
Time: 10:11 67 yds in 12 plays.
ARIZONA 10 MICHIGAN 7

Zivic kicked off to Calayton on the M11 and he ret'd 14 (Housley)
10:07 MICHIGAN
1/10-M25 - Leach pitched out badly for Huckleby and Bledsoe recovered for A at the M21.

10:02 ARIZONA
1/10-M21 - Krohn's pass was deflected by Seabron and Katnik caught it and made 3 (Simpkins)
2/7 -M18 - Krohn passed to Oliver for 6 (Jolly)
3/1 -M12 - Oliver at center for 2;
1/G -M10 - Oliver took pitchback at le, and aided by block from Holmes, went for 10 and the A TD. Time: 7:52.
McKee held while Zivic converted.
21 yds in 5 plays.
ARIZONA 17 MICHIGAN 7

Zivic kicked off to Smith on the M10 and he ret'd 17;
7:47 MICHIGAN
1/10-M27 - Huckleby took pitchback at re for 2 (Converse)

2/8 -29 - Leach's pass went through Clayton's hands incomplete.
3/8 -M29 - Leach passed to Clayton for 16 (Liggins)
1/10-M45 - Davis off rt for 8 (Liggins)
2/2 -A47 - Huckleby at lt for 2 (Wunderli)
1/10-A45 - Leach cut back at rg for 9 (Giangardella)
2/1 -A36 - Davis at lt for 4 (Giangardella)
1/10-A32 - Davis at rg for 2 (Wunderli)
2/8 -A30 - Leach passed to Marsh who caught it at the 9 and went in untouched for the M TD.
Time 3:58.
Dickey held while Willner converted.
ARIZONA 17 MICHIGAN 14 73 yds in 9 plays

Virgil kicked off to Butler in the A endzone where he downed it.
3:58 ARIZONA
1/10-A20 - Oliver at lg for 2 (Keitz)
2/8 -A22 - Oliver at rt for 5 (Keitz)
3/3 -A27 - Krohn's pass for Haynes broken up by Harden.
4/3 -A27 - Garcia punted to Jolly, fair catch at the M39 (34 yd punt.)

2:30 MICHIGAN
1/10-M39 - Leach passed through Huckleby's hands incomplete.
2/10-M39 - Davis on draw at lt for 4 (Ingrahama)
3/6 -M43 - Leach under pressure thre for Huckleby just incomplete.
4/6 -M43 - Willner punted to Streeter on the A21 and he ret'd 6 (Huckleby) 36 yd punt.

OCTOBER 7, 1978

1:30 ARIZONA
1/10-A27 - Oliver at center for 4;
2/6 -A31 - Heater at center for 8 (Simpkins)
1/10-A39 - Oliver at rg for 4 (Humphries)
2/6 -A43 - Krohn passed to Harvey for 35 (Jolly)

**END OF THE HALF:
ARIZONA 17 MICHIGAN 14**

M had 15 plays for 74 yds. A had 23 plays for 139 yds.

THIRD QUARTER

A elects to Receive. M defends the north goal.

Virgil kicked off to Butler in the A endzone where he downed it.
15:00 ARIZONA
1/10-A20 - Krohn at rg for 2 (Keitz)
2/8 -A22 - Krohn kept inside re for 7 (Seabron)
3/1 -A29 - Krohn at lg for 2 (Meter)
1/10-A31 - Krohn pitched out to Heater at re for 12 (Harden)
1/10-A43 - Krohn kept at le for 3 (Meter)
2/7 -A46 - Krohn passed to Oliver for 10 (Jolly)
1/10-M44 - Heater at lg for 4 (Meter)
2/6 -M40 - Heater at lt for 2 (Simpkins)
3/4 -M38 - Krohn hit by Meter for -5.
4/9 -M43 - Garcia punted to the M 6 where Streeter downed it, 37 yd punt.

10:29 MICHIGAN
1/10-M6 - Davis at rg for 4 (Giangardella)
2/6 M-10 - Huckleby took at pitchout at re for 23;
1/10-M33 - Leach kept at rt for 1 (Ingraham)
2/9 -M34 - Leach elected to keep and run right for 6.
3/3 -M30 - Davis at lg for 3 (Whitton)
1/10-M43 - Davis at lg for 10 (Giangardella)
1/10-A47 - Huckleby took pitchout at re for 3 (Ware)
2/7 -A44 - Huckleby cut back over lg for 5 (Witton)
3/2 -A39 - Leach kept off rt for 4 (Liggins)
1/10-A35 - Huckleby at rt for 2 (C. Smith)
2/8 -A33 - Davis at lt for 5 (Giangardella)
3/3 -A28 - Leach kept off rt for 8 (Liggons)
1/10-A20 - Leach hit by Crosby for -1 behind center.
2/11-A21 - Leach hit by Ware for -8.
3/19-A29 - Leach hit by Wunderli for -6.
4/25-A35 - Willner's punt went out of bounds on the A 15, 20 yd. punt.

2:45 ARIZONA
1/10-A15 - Oliver at rt for 1 (Keitz)
2/9 -A16 - Heater took pitchback at re for no gain (Seabron)
3/9 -A16 - Nelson took pitchout at re and lost (Braman)
4/10-A15 - Garcia's punt blocked by Keitz and it went out of bounds on the A 1.

0:53 MICHIGAN
1/G -A1 - Leach hit by Crawford for -4.
2/G -A5 - Leach kept at lt for 3 (Crawford)

**END OF THIRD QUARTER:
ARIZONA 17 MICHIGAN 14**

M had 17 plays for 58 yds. A had 12 plays for 27 yds.

FOURTH QUARTER

15:00 MICHIGAN
3/G A2 - Leach's pass for Schmerge intercepted by Ingraham in the A endzone.

14:52 ARIZONA
1/10-A20 - Oliver at r for 5 (Greer)
2/5 -A25 - Oliver at rg for 3 (Keitz)
3/2 -A28 - Nelsone took a pitchback at re for 3 (Harden)
1/10-A31 - Oliver at rg for 4 (deSantis)
2/6 -A35 - Nelson took a pitchback at re for 5 (Simpkins)
3/1 -A40 - Oliver at rt for no gain (Meter)
4/1 -A40 - Garcia punted to Jolly on the M 21 and he ret'd 11, 39 yd punt'

11:31 MICHIGAN
1/10-M32 - Huckleby took pitchout at re for 8 (Liggins)
2/2 -M40 - Davis at lg for 2 (Witton)
1/10-M42 - Leach rolled and kept off lt for 7 (Witton)
2/3 -M49 - Huckleby took pitchout at re for 7 (Ware)
1/10-A44 - Leach passed for Huckleby incomplete, A blitzing.
2/10-A44 - Leach back to pass rolled left and went for 21 (Crosby)
1/10-A23 - Davis at rg for 4 (Crosby)
2/6 -A19 - Huckleby at re for 4 (Ware)
3/2 -A15 - Davis at lg for 5 (Liggons)
1/10-A10 - Davis at rt for 5 (Crosby)
2/5 -A5 - Huckleby took pitchout at le for 3 (Giangardella)
3/2 -A2 - Huckleby at rg for 1 (Ingraham)
4/1 -A1 - Davis at lg for the M TD. Time:
5:25 Dickey held while Willner converted.
MICHIGAN 21 ARIZONA 17 68 yds in 13 plays

Virgil kicked off to Butler on the A 3 and he ret'd 16 (Bell)

265

5:21 ARIZONA
1/10-A19 - Krohn hit by Godfrey for -9.
2/19-A10 - Oliver on draw at lg for 6 (Simpkins)
3/13-A16 - Krohn passed for Dickerson incomplete, pressure by Godfrey.
4/13-A16 - Garcia punted to Jolly on the M 31 and he ret'd it 1 (Streeter)

3:54 MICHIGAN
1/10-M32 - Huckleby took pitchback at re for 4 (C. Smith)
2/6 -M36 - Davis at lt for 4 (Crawford)
3/2 -M40 - Leach kept at lt for 1 (Crosby)
4/1 -M41 - Willner punted to Streeter on the A 12 and he ret'd 2, 47 yd punt (Clayton)

2:27 ARIZONA
1/10-A14 - Krohn passed to Deyer for 7 (Simpkins)
2/3 -A21 - Krohn passed for Haynes broken up by Braman.
3/3 -A21 - Krohn hit by Simpkins and then Godfrey for -11.
4/14-A10 - Garcia punted to Jolly, fair catch at A 45, 35 yd punt.

1:12 MICHIGAN
1/10-A45 - Davis at lg for 3 (Crosby)
2/7 -A42 - Huckleby off lt for 9 (Liggins)
1/10-A33 - Davis at lg for 4, BUT M penalized 5 for offside.
1/15-A38 - Davis at lt for 3 (Crawford)
2/12-A35 -

END OF THE GAME:
MICHIGAN 21 ARIZONA 17

M had 19 plays for 92 yds. A had 12 plays for 13 yds.

OCTOBER 7, 1978

NOTRE DAME
VS.
MICHIGAN STATE
Spartan Stadium
East Lansing, Mich.
FIRST QUARTER

Michigan won the toss and elects to receive.
Notre Dame defending the north goal
Male kicks through end zone touchback
MICHIGAN STATE
1/10-M20 - McGee around RE on pitchout (Golic) no gain
2/10-M20 - Pass by Smith to Byrd along right sideline, steps out, gain of 8
3/2 -M28 - Reeves around LE on pitchout (Leopold) gain of 10
1/10-M38 - Smith around LE on pitchout (Leopold & Hankerd) gain of 5
2/5 -M43 - Smith pass to Schramm in right flat (Browner) loss of 2
3/7 -M41 - Smith pass to Brammer on left side (Waymer) gain of 14
1/10-N45 - S. Smith outside LE (Gibbons & Leopold) gain of 4
2/6 -N41 - E. Smith around LE, ran out of bounds, gain of 3
3/3 -N38 - Gibson around LE on reverse (Waymer & Golic) gain of 6
1/10-N32 - Middleton outside RG (Harrison) gain of 12
1/10-N20 - Smith pass to Byrd caught out of end zone
2/10-N20 - E. Smith around LE (Leopold) gain of 3
3/7 -N17 - Middleton off RT (Browner & Harrison) gain of 8
1/G -N9 - E. Smith pass to Byrd at goal line, incomplete, Michigan illegal procedure, declined
2/G -N9 - E. Smith pass to Byrd, tipped by Gibbons
3/G -N9 - Middleton off LG (Calhoun) gain of 1
4/G -N8 - Andersen 25 yd field goal attempt good
SCORE: MICHIGAN STATE 3, NOTRE DAME 0

8:20 NOTRE DAME
Schario kicks to Beldon at the N20 (Cooper) return of 12
1/10-N32 - Ferguson off RT (Fields) gain of 6
2/4 -N38 - Mitchell through the middle (Land) gain of 2
3/2 -N40 - Ferguson around RE (Hay & Marshall) gain of 3
1/10-N43 - Montana pass to Grindinger incomplete
2/10-N43 - Montana back to pass runs around LE, runs out of bounds, gain of 6
3/4 -N49 - Heavens off LT (Land) gain of 3

4/1 -M48 - Montana on QB sneak, team tackle gain of 3
1/10-M45 - Montana pass to Haines, steps out of bounds at M10, gain of 35
1/10-M10 - Ferguson outside LE (Land) gain of 3
2/7 -M7 - Montana pass to Grindinger in end zone, Notre Dame ineligible receiver, 15 yd penalty
2/22-M22 - Montana pass to Grindinger, forced out (McCormick & Anderson) gain of 21
3/1 -M1 - Heavens off RT on dive, touchdown 68 yards in 11 plays, 1 yd run
Unis PAT attempt good
SCORE: NOTRE DAME 7, MICHIGAN STATE 3

4:49 MICHIGAN STATE
Male kicks to Reeves in end zone, touchback.
1/10-M20 - Smith pass to Byrd on left side (Gibbons) gain of 9
2/1 -M29 - Middleton off RT, team tackle, no gain
3/1 -M29 - McGee off LT (Gibbons) gain of 2
1/10-M31 - Reeves outside RE on pitchout (Case) gain of 2
2/8 -M33 - S. Smith off LT (Calhoun) gain of 1
3/7 -M34 - Smith screen pass attempt incomplete
4/7 -M34 - Stachowicz punts to Waymer (Savage) punt 34 yds, no return

1:24 NOTRE DAME
1/10-N32 - Heavens off RT (Land) gain of 7
2/3 -N39 - Ferguson through the middle (Hay) gain of 1
3/2 -N40 - Ferguson off RT (Bass) gain of 5

**FIRST QUARTER SCORE
NOTRE DAME 7, MICHIGAN STATE 3**

267

SECOND QUARTER

NOTRE DAME
1/10-N45 - Heavens off right tackle, tackle by Stanton, gain of 27
1/10-M28 - Ferguson outside left end, tackle by Otis & Haines, gain of 4
2/6 -M24 - Stone on reverse, tackle by Land, loss of 10
3/16-M34 - Montana pass along left side line, incomplete
4/16-M34 - Restic punt into end zone, 34 yd punt, touchback

13:30 MICHIGAN STATE
1/10-M20 - Smith pass over the middle to Brammer, tackle by Browner, gain of 15
1/10-M35 - Smith around left end on pitchout, MS holding, 15 yd penalty
1/25-M20 - Smith back to pass, sacked by Hankerd, loss of 3
2/28-M17 - Reeves outside left end on pitchout, team tackle, gain of 4
3/24-M21 - S. Smith outside right end, tackle by Case, gain of 8
4/16-M29 - Stachowicz punts to Harrison at N31, fair catch, 40 yd punt, no return

10:48 NOTRE DAME
1/10-N31 - Ferguson outside end, tackle Anderson & Hay, gain of 12
1/10-N43 - Heavens through the middle, tackle by Bass, gain of 1
2/9 -N44 - Montana pass over the middle to Haines, knocked out by Bass & Anderson, gain of 44
1/10-M12 - Heavens outside right tackle, tackle by Anderson, gain of 2
2/8 -M10 - Montana pass to Courey overthrown
3/8 -M10 - Heavens through the middle, tackle by Anderson, gain of 7
4/1 -M3 - Unis 20 yard field goal attempt wide left

8:37 MICHIGAN STATE
1/10-M20 - Smith pass over the middle to Gibson incomplete
2/10-M20 - MS illegal procedure 5 yd penalty
2/15-M15 - Smith pass over the middle, tackle by Waymer, gain of 58
1/10-N26 - Schramm through the middle, tackle by Case & Restic, gain of 7
2/3 -N19 - Smith pass to Byrd along right sideline overthrown
3/3-N19 - Schramm through the middle, tackle by Golic & Calhoun, no gain
4/3 -N19 - Andersen 36 yard field goal attempt good. Time: 8:13 Elapsed Time: 1:50
SCORE: NOTRE DAME 7, MICHIGAN STATE 6

6:47 NOTRE DAME
Schario kicks to Pallas at ND17, fumbles, recovered by Mitchell
1/10-N22 - Ferguson off right tackle, tackle by Otis & Bass, gain of 8
2/2 -N30 - Ferguson off left tackle, tackle by Bass, gain of 7
1/10-N37 - Heavens off right tackle, tackle by Bass, gain of 2
2/8 -N39 - Montana pass to Masztak, falls down, gain of 23
1/10-M38 - Ferguson off left tackle, tackle by Hay & Savage, gain of 7
2/3 -M31 - Ferguson outside right end, tackle by Savage, gain of 4
1/10-M27 - Pallas off left tackle, tackle by Anderson, gain of 13
1/10-M14 - Heavens through the middle, tackle by Hay & Land, gain of 1
2/9 -M13 - Montana pass to Haines on right sideline, tackle by Stanton, gain of 11
1/G -M2 - Heavens off right guard, team tackle, gain of 1
2/G -M1 - Montana on quarterback sneak, touchdown, 1 yd run, 78 yards in 11 plays
Knafelc pass to Vehr good for PAT attempt
Time: 12:47 Elapsed Time: 4:34
SCORE: NOTRE DAME 15, MICHIGAN STATE 6

2:13 MICHIGAN STATE
Unis kicks to S. Smith at MS4, tackle by Harwick, gain of 24
1/10-M28 - McGee outside right tackle, tackle by Golic, gain of 3
2/7 -M31 - Smith pass to Middleton incomplete, ND pass interference, 10 yd penalty
1/10-M41 - Smith pass to Schramm, ball stolen by Browner, 45 yard pass interception return touchdown
Unis PAT is good
SCORE: NOTRE DAME 22, MICHIGAN STATE 6
Male kicks to Reeves at MS17, returns 7 yards
MICHIGAN STATE
1/10-M24 - Smith back to pass, runs down middle, falls down, gain of 2 TO/MS 1:01
2/8 -M26 - Smith pass over the middle to Byrd incomplete
3/8 -M26 - Smith pass over the middle to Gibson, bobbled, broken up by Restic
4/8 -M26 - Stachowicz punts to Belden, tackle by Davis, 38 yd punt, ND clipping 15 yd penalty

:40 NOTRE DAME
1/10-N21 - Montana keeps it, falls down, no gain
2/10-N21 - Montana keeps it, falls down, loss of 2
3/12-N19 - Montana falls down, loss of 1

**HALF TIME SCORE:
NOTRE DAME 22, MICHIGAN STATE 6**

OCTOBER 7, 1978

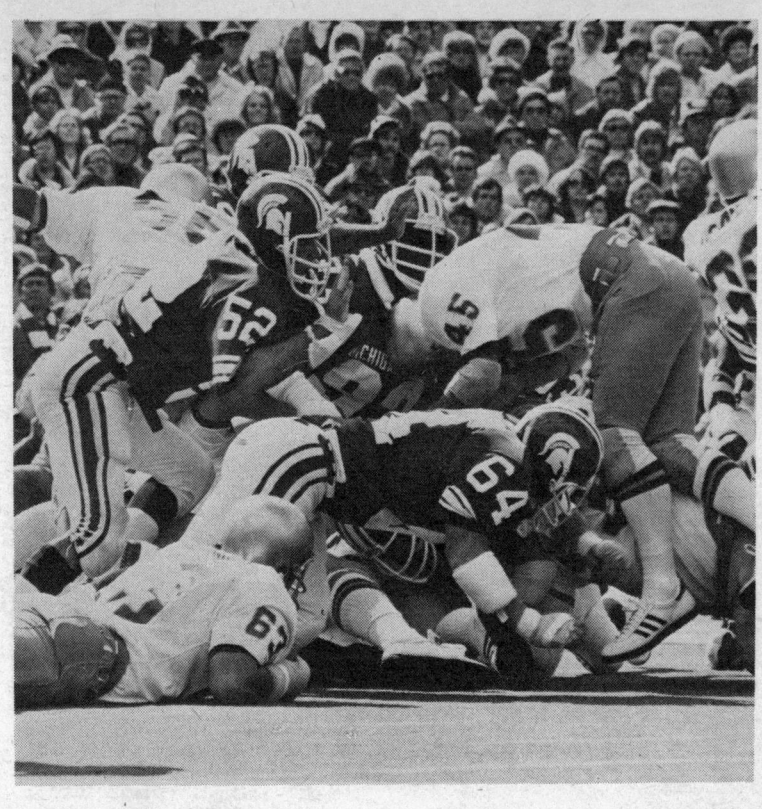

THIRD QUARTER

ND elects to receive. MS defending the north goal.
Schario to Stone at the ND 8, returns to ND 23, return 15 yards

NOTRE DAME
1/10-N23 - Ferguson around right end on pitchout, tackle by Marshall, gain of 6
2/4 -N29 - Pallas through the middle, tackle by Fields, gain of 1
3/3 -N30 - Montana pass to Stone, tackle by Marshall, gain of 15
1/10-N45 - Ferguson, tackle by Otis, Haines, gain of 1
2/9 -N46 - Heavens outside right guard, tackle by Land, Bass & Graves, gain of 9
1/10-N45 - Heavens through the middle, tackle by Haynes, gain of 2
2/8 -M43 - Montana pass on right side line to Courey, MS pass interference 29 yd penalty
1/10-M14 - Heavens through the middle, tackle by Savage & Fields, gain of 6
2/4 -M8 - Ferguson around right end, ND holding 15 yd penalty
2/19-M23 - Montana pass to Stone in end zone overthrown
3/19-M23 - Montana pass to Stone overthrown
4/19-M23 - Male 40 yd field goal attempt short

10:34 MICHIGAN STATE
1/10-M23 - Smith pass long to Gibson broken up by Waymer
2/10-M23 - S. Smith outside right tackle, tackle by Case, gain of 7
3/3 -M30 - MS delay of game, 5 yd penalty
3/8 -M25 - Smith pass to Reeves in left side flats, tackle by Leopold, no gain
4/8 -M25 - Stachowicz punts through end zone, touchback, 75 yd punt

9:01 NOTRE DAME
1/10-N20 - Ferguson outside right end, tackle by Graves, gain of 4
2/6 -N24 - Heavens through the middle, tackle by Land & Haynes, gain of 3
3/3 -N27 - Ferguson outside left end on pitchout, tackle by Hay & Bass, no gain
4/3 -N27 - Restic punts to Anderson at MS40, 28 yd punt

7:08 MICHIGAN STATE
1/10-M45 - Hughes outside left end, tackle by Browner, loss of 1
2/11-M44 - Smith back to pass, sacked by Weston, loss of 6
3/17-M38 - Smith pass to Gibson over the middle, tackle by Waymer, gain of 16
4/1 -N46 - Smith pass on left sideline to Byrd, tackle by Restic, gain of 16
1/10-N30 - S. Smith through the middle, tackle by Weston, gain of 3
2/7 -N27 - Smith pass to Middleton, tackle by Heimkreiter, gain of 1
3/6 -N26 - Smith pass over the middle to Gibson, tackle by Gibbons, gain of 20
1/G -N6 - Schramm through the middle, tackle by Calhoun & Case, gain of 2
2/G -N4 - Smith back to pass, tackle by Calhoun, loss of 6
3/G -N10 - Smith pass to Samson Howard, touchdown, Time: 13:45 Elapsed Time: 5:53
Andersen PAT attempt good 55 yards in 10 plays
SCORE: NOTRE DAME 22, MICHIGAN STATE 13

1:15 NOTRE DAME
Schario kicks to Stone in end zone, returns 19, tackle by by T. Williams.
1/10-N19 - Ferguson outside right end, tackle by Graves, gain of 4
2/6 -N23 - Ferguson outside left end, tackle by Bass, gain of 5
THIRD QUARTER SCORE
NOTRE DAME 22, MICHIGAN STATE 13

FOURTH QUARTER

NOTRE DAME
3/1 N28 - Heavens around right end, tackle by Bass & Marshall, gain of 5
1/10-N33 - Heavens outside right tackle, tackle by Bass, loss of 1
2/11-N32 - Ferguson outside left guard along right sideline, tackle by Stanton, gain of 38
1/10-M30 - Heavens through the middle, tackle by Hay, gain of 3
2/7 -M27 - Montana pass to Haines in end zone overthrown
3/7 -M27 - Montana along left sideline, steps out of bounds, gain of 13
1/10-M14 - Pallas through the middle, tackle by Bass, gain of 3
2/7 -M11 - Ferguson outside left end, touchdown, Time: 2:51 Elapsed Time: 4:06
Unis PAT attempt good, 81 yards in 10 plays
SCORE: NOTRE DAME 29, MICHIGAN STATE 13

12:09 MICHIGAN STATE
Male kicks to S. Smith in end zone, return to MS17, tackle by Belden.
1/10-M17 - Smith pass to Brammer, tackle by Leopold, gain of 9
2/1 -M26 - Smith pass to Byrd, tackle by Leopold, gain of 10
1/10-M36 - Smith pass over the middle, tackle by Gibbons & Golic, gain of 18
1/10-N46 - Smith pass incomplete
2/10-N46 - S. Smith outside right end on pitchout, tackle by Case, gain of 11
1/10-N35 - Schramm through the middle, tackle by Heimkreiter, Calhoun, gain of 2
2/8 -N33 - Smith pass to Gibson, falls, gain of 12
1/10-N21 - McGee outside right tackle on pitchout, tackle by Browner, gain of 4
2/6 -N17 - Schramm off left tackle, tackle by Golic, gain of 1
3/5 -N16 - Smith pass to Howard on left sideline, knocked but by Gibbons, gain 10
1/G -N6 - McGee inside left guard on counter, tackle by Calhoun & Leopold, no gain
2/G -N6 - Smith pass to Gibson, touchdown, 6 yd play Time: 7:51 Elapsed Time: 5:00
Anderson pass intercepted 83 yards 12 plays
SCORE: NOTRE DAME 29, MICHIGAN STATE 19

OCTOBER 7, 1978

7:09 NOTRE DAME
Schario kicks to Pallas returns 18 yards to ND35
1/10-N35 - Heavens outside right tackle, tackle by Haynes, gain of 3
2/7 -N38 - Ferguson outside end, run out of bounds by Bass, gain of 9
1/10-N47 - Heavens off right tackle, tackle by Fields & Hay, gain of 5
2/5 -M48 - Mitchell outside left tackle, tackle by Bass, gain of 6
1/10-M42 - Mitchell off right tackle, tackle by Haynes, no gain
2/10-M42 - Heavens off left tackle, tackle by Land & Hay, gain of 7
3/3 -M35 - Heavens outside left end, tackle by Bass & Graves, loss of 1
4/4 -M36 - Restic punts out of bounds at the MS2, 34 yard punt, no return

3:12 MICHIGAN STATE
1/10-M2 - Smith pass to Gibson, incomplete
2/10-M2 - Smith pass to Gibson on left sideline overthrown
3/10-M2 - Smith pass to Middleton, tackle by Browner, gain of 6
4/4 -M8 - Smith pass to Brammer on right side, tackle by Waymer, gain of 8
1/10-M16 - Smith pass to S. Smith on right sideline, knocked out K. Johnson, gain of 4
2/6 -M20 - Middleton on draw, tackle by Johnson & Harrison, gain of 22
1/10-M42 - Smith to Gibson over the middle, tackle by Harrison, gain of 20
1/10-N38 - Smith pass to Gibson over the middle, tackle by Harrison, gain of 22
1/10-N16 - Smith pass to Brammer, tackle by Harrison, gain of 6
ND roughing the passer, 5 yd penalty
1/G -N5 - Smith pass to Gibson incomplete
2G -N5 - Smith pass to Byrd in end zone incomplete
3/G -N5 - Smith pass to Brammer, tackle by Harrison, gain of 1 TO/MS :49
4/G -N4 - Smith pass to Byrd, touchdown, 98 yards in 13 plays Time: 14:14
Elapsed 1:28
Smith pass intercepted
SCORE: NOTRE DAME 29, MICHIGAN STATE 25

:44 NOTRE DAME
Schario kicks to Masztak at the ND49 no return
1/10-N49 - Montana falls down, loss of 2
2/12-N47 - Montana falls down, loss of 1

**FINAL SCORE:
NOTRE DAME 29, MICHIGAN STATE 25**

**National Collegiate Athletic Association
FINAL TEAM STATISTICS**
October 7, 1978

	NOTRE DAME	MICHIGAN STATE
FIRST DOWNS	22	20
Rushing	16	7
Passing	5	11
Penalty	1	2
RUSHING ATTEMPTS	56	33
YARDS RUSHING	279	133
YARDS LOST RUSHING	18	16
NETS YARDS RUSHING	26	117
NETS YARDS PASSING	149	306
Passes Attempted	12	41
Passes Completed	6	27
Had Intercepted	0	0
TOTAL OFFENSIVE PLAYS	68	74
TOTAL NET YARDS	410	413
Average Gain Per Play	6.0	5.6
FUMBLES: NUMBER - LOST	1/0	1/1
PENALTIES: NUMBER - YARDS	5/60	4/54
INTERCEPTIONS: NUMBER - YARDS	1/45	0/0
NUMBER OF PUNTS - YARDS	3/96	4/187
Average Per Punt	32.0	46.8
PUNT RETURNS: NUMBER - YARDS	1/0	0/0
KICKOFF RETURNS: NUMBER - YARDS	6/69	3/48

OREGON STATE VS. MINNESOTA

Memorial Stadium, Minneapolis
Temp: 50
Wind NW 9 mph
Skies: Overcast

FIRST QUARTER

Minnesota wins toss, elects to receive at east goal. Walford kicks off to Edwards on own 2, returns 22 yds (Rae)

14:53 MINNESOTA
1/10-MN24 - Kitzmann straight ahead 1 yard gain (Payton, Schillinger)
2/9 -MN25 - Carlson on broken play 1 yard (team)
3/8 -MN26 - Carlson pass delay complete over middle to Kitzman for first down at MN34 but Gophers clipping 15 yard penalty
3/18-MN16 - Barber at RT 2 yard gain (Schillinger)
4/16-MN18 - Smith punt to Tim Smith returns 11 yards (Hoffman) 40 yard punt

12:10 OREGON STATE
1/10-MN47 - Johnson at RT 2 yards (Blanshan)
2/8 -MN45 - Bardosi at RT 6 yards (Burns)
3/2 -MN39 - Tim Sim option pitchout left, 12 yards, steps out of bounds
1/10-MN27 - Steve Smith pass at left sidelines complete to Sims 12 yard (Snyder)
1/10-MN15 - Sim option pitch right 3 yard loss (Sytsma, Johnson)
2/13-MN18 - Steve Smith pass intended for Hall, short and incomplete
3/13-MN18 - Steve Smith complete to Mike Smith 8 yards, steps out of bounds
4/5 -MN10 - Walford field goal from 27 yards GOOD. 37 yards in 7 plays, kick on 8th play 4:26 elapsed, 10:34 to play
OREGON STATE 3, MINN 0

Walford kick off bounds away from Noel, picks up on 3 and Wells makes tackle for no return.

10:31 MINNESOTA
1/10-MN3 - Kitzmann up middle 2 yards (Sommes, Priest)
2/8 -MN5 - Kitzmann at LT, cuts back to middle 2 yards (Priest)
3/6 -MN7 - Barber quick pitch left, slips down after 2 yard gain
4/4 -MN9 - Smith punt to Coury who signals fair catch on MN44 35 yard punt

8:51 OREGON STATE
1/10-MN44 - Mike Smith sweep left 1 yard gain (Sytsma)

2/9 -MN43 - Sim delay left no gain (Ronan, Blanshan)
3/9 -MN43 - Steve Smith rolls left to pass, run down by Burns for 2 yard loss
4/11-MN45 - Misko punt downed by Stateplayer at MN17 28 yard punt

7:57 MINNESOTA
1/10-MN17 - Barber quick pitch right, breaks one tackle 19 yards (Franklin)
1/10-MN36 - Kitzmann at middle 2 yards (Childress)
2/8 -MN38 - Kitzmann slips tackle at left side, breaks open for 11 yards (Franklin)
1/10-MN49 - Barber breaks open up middle for 14 yards (Holmes)
1/10-OS37 - Barber quick pitch right 1 yard gain (Franklin)
2/9 -OS36 - Carlson pass over middle complete to Bourquin 13 yards (Franklin)
1/10-OS23 - Thompson flanker reverse left 4 yard gain
2/6 -OS19 - Kitzmann quick opener up middle 7 yards (Howe)
1/10-OS12 - Barbar at RT, slides outside 2 yards (Childress, Williams)
2/8 -OS10 - Kitzman at RT, 1 yd gain (Priest)
3/7 -OS9 - Carlson pass complete to Bourquin 9 yard TD pass into right corner of endzone 83 yards in 11 plays 11:20 elapsed, 3:40 to go. Rogind kick good.
MINNESOTA 7, OREGON STATE 3

Rogind kickoff to Tim Smith on run, breaks open from right to left, 90 yard TD run. Snyder and Prairie last two to get shot along left sideline at 10-15 yard line. Walford kick good.
OREGON STATE 10, MINNESOTA 7

Walford kicks off for OSU to Edwards 1 yard deep in end zone, ret. 20 yards (Rae)

3:22 MINNESOTA
1/10-MN20 - Barbar quick pitch RE, hit, fumbles when hit by Franklin, Williams recovers for OSU at UM28 (8 yd. gain for Barber)

3:20 OREGON STATE
1/10-MN28 - Mike Smith up middle breaks loose at RT, gains 13 (Brown)
1/10-MN15 - Sim on option pitch at RE, dropped loss of 3 by Forxworth
2/13-MN18 - Steve Smith rolls L, pass int. by Foxworth at UM11, ret. 13 yds to UM24

2:17 MINNESOTA
1/10-MN24 - Barber stacked up gain of 1 at RG (Childress, Priest)
2/9 -MN25 - Carlson pass intended for Barber thrown behind at R sideline, no good
3/9 -MN25 - Carlson pass on delay over middle for Kitzman no good, overthrown
4/9 -MN25 - Tom Smith punts 40 yards to Coury, fair catch at OSU35

272

OCTOBER 7, 1978

1:28 OREGON STATE
1/10-OS35 - Mike Smith up middle, gains 4 (Blanshan, Johnson)
2/6 -OS39 - Sim gains 3 yards at LT (Burns, Johnson)
3/3 -OS42 - Steve Smith to pass, sacked for loss of 8 by Sytsma

**END OF FIRST QUARTER:
OREGON STATE 10, MINNESOTA 7**

SECOND QUARTER

4/11-OS34 - Misko punt fair catch by Edwards, who fumbles and recovers on MN18 Oregon State illegal motion to kick over
4/16-OS29 - Misko punt to Bailey fair catch on MN38 32 yard punt

14:47 MINNESOTA
1/10-MN38 - Kitzmann at RT 1 yard (Priest)
2/9 -MN39 - Barber quick pitch left 5 yards (Stevens, Williams)
3/4 -MN44 - Carlson pass intended for Thompson, interference on Stevens of OSU First down on OS48 8 yard penalty
1/10-OS48 - Kitzmann up middle 4 yards (Schillinger)
2/6 -OS44 - Carlson fumbles snap, picks up and goes straight ahead for 2 yards (team)
3/4 -OS42 - Kitzmann at LT 3 yards (Childress)
4/1 -OS39 - Kitzmann at RT 2 yard gain (Wilkinson)
1/10-OS37 - Carlson pass fly down right sidelines incomplete intended for Bailey, Franklin covering
2/10-OS37 - Carlson pass complete to Bailey over middle 18 yards (Franklin)
1/10-OS19 - Barmer at LT 3 yards (Westeberg)
2/7 -OS16 - Kitzman at LT 3 yard gain (Childress)
3/4 -OS13 - Barber sweep right 2 yard gain (Franklin)
4/1 -OS11 - Kitzman at RT 4 yard gain (Payton)
1/G -OS7 - Kitzman at LT no gain (Priest)
2/G OS7 - Dilulo flanker sweep left no gain (Tim Smith)
3/G OS7 - Carlson pass complete to Barber for TD but Minnesota holding 19 yd penalty
3/G OS26 - Carlson pass intercepted on OS6 by Franklin but Carlson beyond line of scrimmage, interception stands return 8 yards (Bouquin)

6:57 OREGON STATE
1/10-OS14 - Smith complete to Coury at left sidelines 6 yard gain
2/4 -OS20 - Smith pass complete to Halberg 11 yards (Foxwoth)
1/10-OS31 - Sim fumbles at LT, recovers own after no gain (Burns)
2/10-OS31 - Smith pass complete to Halberg 13 yards (Brown)
1/10-OS34 - Smith pass quick stop/100 k-in right high and incomplete
2/10-OS34 - Smith back to pass, prime receiver covered, Blanshan sack for 5 yard loss
3/15-OS29 - Smith back to pass, Sytsma sack for 8 yard loss
4/23-OS21 - Misko punt fair catch by Bailey on MN40 39 yard punt

4:19 MINNESOTA
1/10-MN40 - Thompson flanker reverse left 2 yard loss (Westerberg)
2/12-MN38 - Carlson pass complete to Barbar over middle, OS Williams personal foul roughing passer, penalty from point of foul, 15 yards (Priest)
1/10-OS42 - Carlson back to pass, sacked by Schillinger 6 yard loss
2/16-OS48 - Carlson pass complete to Thompson (right to left) 17 yards (Stevens)
1/10-OS31 - Kitzmann at RT 1 yd (Peyton) (2:35)
2/9 -OS30 - Carlson pass intended for Bourquin thrown behind him and incomplete
3/9 -OS30 - Carlson pass intended for Thompson wide open high and incomplete
4/9 -OS30 - Rogind field goal try for 47 yards out short ball goes over

2:04 OREGON STATE
1/10-OS20 - Mike Smith up middle 3 yards (Friberg)
2/7 -OS23 - Mike Smith breaks open at LT, Brown makes tackle after 38 yard gain
1/10-MN39 - Smith pass complete flair out to Sim 2 yds (Ronan) (1:00 left)
2/8 -MN37 - Smith tries to roll right, Burns tackle for no gain (:29 left)
3/8 -MN37 - Smith pass intended for Coury incomplete out of bounds (:25 left)
4/8 -MN37 - Misko punt goes into end zone 37 yard punt

:17 MINNESOTA
1/10-MN20 - Carlson pass intercepted by Tim Smith on OS41

:10 OREGON STATE
1/10-OS41 - Oregon illegal procedure 5 yd penalty
2/15-OS36 - Mike Smith at LT no gain (Blanshan)

**END OF FIRST HALF:
OREGON STATE 10 MINNESOTA 7**

THIRD QUARTER

Rogind kickoff to Jim Smith on OS5, returns 18 yards (Hairston)

14:55 OREGON STATE
1/10 -OS23 - Mike Smith at LT 2 yards (Brown, Ronan)
2/8 -OS25 - Smith pass knocked down in line by Blanshan
3/8 -OS25 - Sim delay off RT 5 yd gain (Blanshan, Sytsma)
4/3 -OS30 - Misko punt short and allowed to roll dead at MN33 37 yard punt

13:38 MINNESOTA
1/10 -MN33 - Barber at LT 1 yd gain (Westerberg)
2/9 -MN34 - Carlson pass short and incomplete as Priest is hitting him
3/9 -MN34 - Carlson back to pass, intended for Bailey who slips down as pass incomplete
4/9 -MN34 - Smith punt to Tim Smith, returns 2 yards (Burns) 31 yard punt Oregon State clipping (Coury) 15 yard penalty

12:48 OREGON STATE
1/10 -OS22 - Johnson option pitch right 6 yards
2/4 -OS28 - Mike Smith at RT 2 yards (Blanshan, Ronan)
3/2 -OS30 - Smith tries to option right, Sytsma meets him in backfield for 3 yard loss
4/5 -OS27 - Misko punt to Bailey, returns 2 yards, slips down 38 yard punt

11:27 MINNESOTA
1/10 -MN37 - Barber at LT, breaks open 8 yards (Williams)
2/2 -MN45 - Kitzmann at LT, 2 yd loss (Williams)
3/4 -MN43 - Barber sweep right (Minnesota holding) (Murtha) 16 yard penalty
3/20 -MN27 - Barber at LT, fumbles recovered by OS Holmes, hit by Williams

10:28 OREGON STATE
1/10 -MN30 - Mike Smith up middle 1 yard (Burns)
2/9 -MN29 - Johnson option pitch right, break open for 21 yards (Brown)
1/G -MN8 - Smith option right, slips down for no gain
2/G MN8 - Smith keeper right 1 yd gain (Johnson, Burns)
3/G -MN7 - Smith pass complete to Halxberg 7 yd TD play 6:27 elapsed 8:33 to go 30 yard drive in 5 plays Walford kick good OREGON STATE 17, MINN 7

Walford kick off to Edwards who downs ball in end zone

8:32 MINNESOTA
1/10-MN20 - Carlson pass intended for Thompson off target and incomplete
2/10-MN20 - Artis delay up middle no gain (Schillinger)
3/10-MN20 - Carlson back to pass, rushed and sacked by Schillinger for 8 yd loss
4/18-MN12 - Smith punt to Coury and tackled by Burns 1 yd return 46 yd punt

7:06 OREGON STATE
1/10 -OS43 - Smith pass complete to Hall 21 yards
1/10-MN36 - Mike Smith at RT 3 yd gain (Blanshan, Sytsma)
2/7 -MN33 - Smith rolls left, Burns makes tackle for 1 yd loss
3/8 -MN34 - Smith quick fly down left sidelines intended for Hall long and incomplete
4/8 -MN34 - Misko punt goes into end one touchback 34 yard punt

5:17 MINNESOTA
1/10-MN20 - Carlson keeper rollout left 9 yd gain (Holmes)
2/1 -MN29 - Kitzmann at LT 4 yd gain (Westerberg)
1/10-MN33 - Carlson pass complete to Bailey 9 yards (Tim Smith)
2/1 -MN42 - Kitzmann at LT 5 yd gain (Tim Smith, Westerberg)
1/10-MN47 - Carlson pass incomplete tipped in line by Westerberg
2/10-MN47 - Carlson option right 3 yards (Peyton)
3/7 -50 - Carlson back to pass, rushed out of pocket, tackled by Messenger for 3 yd loss
4/10-MN47 - Smith punt fair catch by Tim Smith 36 yard punt

2:08 OREGON STATE
1/10 -OS17 - Smith pass complete to Hall 8 yards (Foxwoth, Burns)
2/2 -OS25 - Mike Smith straight ahead 3 yards (Johnson, Burns)
1/10 -OS28 - Hall flanker reverse left 2 yards (Snyder)
2/8 -OS30 - Smith rolls right Cunningham tackle for 6 yard loss

**END OF THIRD QUARTER:
OREGON STATE 17, MINNESOTA 7**

FOURTH QUARTER

3/14 -OS24 - Smith keeps on off-count snap Carr and Sytsma for 3 yard loss
4/17 -OS21 - Misko punt to Bailey returns 16 yards 42 yard punt

OCTOBER 7, 1978

14:30 MINNESOTA
1/10-OS47 - Bailey flanker reverse, Wilkinson Franklin tackle for 3 yd loss
2/13-50 - Carlson 50 yd TD pass to Bailey who takes ball away from Franklin about 20 yd line and goes in 1:16 elapsed 13:14 to play 47 yd drive in two plays Rogind kick good **MINNESOTA 14, ORE STATE 17**

Rogind kick off to Tim Smith on 7 returns 27 yards (Harms)
13:37 OREGON STATE
1/10-OS34 - Steve Smith keeps, State offside refused no gain (Blanshan)
2/10-OS34 - Smith flare left to Johnson. slips down for 2 yd loss
3/12-OS32 - Smith back to pass. Burns crashes through tackle for 8 yard loss
4/20-OS24 - Misko punt fair catch by Bailey on MN41 35 yard punt

12:21 MINNESOTA
1/10-MN41 - Carlson rolls right to pass, slips down after 5 yard gain
2/5 -MN46 - Barber at RT 3 yards (Franklin)
3/2 -MN49 - Barbar at RT no gain (team)
4/2 -MN49 - Smith punt fair catch by Tim Smith 36 yard punt

10:36 OREGON STATE
1/10-OS15 - Johnson quick pitch left 1 yd gain (team)
2/9 -OS16 - Johnson draw up middle 9 yards (Brown)
1/10-OS25 - Smith rolls right, runs and Friberg makes tackle for 5 yd loss
2/15-OS20 - Smith pass complete to Sim 4 yds (Sytsma)
3/11-OS24 - Smith pass rollout left thrown short and incomplete
4/11-OS24 - Misko punt to Bailey no return 39 yard punt

8:07 MINNESOTA
1/10-MN37 - Carlson pass to Barber open down right sidelines overthrown and incomplete
2/10-MN37 - Carlson pass off target but Holmes called for pass interference on Bourquin 11 yard penalty
1/10-MN48 - Carlson complete to Thompson at right sidelines 5 yards (Stevens)
2/5 -OS47 - Carlson complete to Bailey 8 yards (Franklin)
1/10-OS39 - Artis quick pitch right 4 yards (Peyton)
2/6 -OS35 - Carlson pass to Barber down right sidelines overthrown and incomplete
3/6 -OS35 - Carlson pass intercepted by Franklin on 22 no return (Barber)

275

6:55 OREGON STATE
- 1/10-OS22 - Mike Smith up middle 3 yards (Cunningham)
- 2/7 -OS25 - Smith pass complete to Hall 3 yards (Foxworth)
- 3/4 -OS28 - Smith option right, Johnson penetrates and Cunningham makes tackle no gain
- 4/4 -OS28 - Misko punt bounds past Bailey who picks up on own 12, returns 11 yards 60 yard punt

5:14 MINNESOTA
- 1/10-MN23 - Carlson complete over middle to Kitzmann 2 yards (Peyton)
- 2/8 -MN25 - Carlson back to pass, Howe sack 8 yard loss from left side
- 3/16-MN17 - Carlson complete to White (screen) Stevens tackle for 6 yd loss
- 4/22-MN11 - Smith punt to Coury on OS47, returns 6 yards (Burns) 42 yard punt

3:18 OREGON STATE
- 1/10-MN47 - Mike Smith up middle 2 yards (Friberg, Ronan)
- 2/8 -MN45 - Mike Smith at LT 4 yards (Cunningham, Ronan)
- 3/4 -MN41 - Smith pass complete to Sims at right sidelines, breaks tackle and runs 32 yards to MN9 before tackle by Burns
- 1/G -MN9 - Mike Smith up middle 4 yards (Burns)
- 2/G -MN5 - Mike Smith at RT 2 yards (team)
- 3/G -MN3 - Mike Smith at LT 2 yards (Burns)
- 4/G -MN1 - Mike Smith at RT 1 yd loss (Burns, Snyder) (1:03)

1:03 MINNESOTA
- 1/10-MN2 - Carlson pass incomplete over thrown at left sidelines
- 2/10-MN2 - Carlson pass complete to Barber 8 yards (Franklin)
- 3/2 -MN10 - Carlson pass complete to White 4 yards (Franklin)
- 1/10-MN14 - Carlson pass intended for Barber Stevens knocks ball down
- 2/10-MN14 - Minnesota Schwen illegal motion 5 yard penalty
- 2/15-MN9 - Carlson pass complete to Barber over middle 7 yards

END OF GAME:
OREGON STATE 17 MINNESOTA 14

National Collegiate Athletic Association
FINAL TEAM STATISTICS
October 7, 1978

	OREGON STATE	MINNESOTA
First Downs	17	14
Rushing	6	8
Passing	6	7
Penalty	0	3
Rushing Attempts	47	49
Yards Rushing	145	154
Yards Lost Rushing	54	32
Net Yards Rushing	91	122
Net Yards Passing	125	151
Passes Attempted	20	31
Passes Completed	13	15
Had Intercepted	1	3
Total Offensive Plays	67	80
Total Net Yards	216	273
Average Gain Per Play	3.2	3.4
Fumbles: Number—Lost	1/0	3/2
Penalties: Number— Yards	6/59	4/54
Interceptions: Number— Yards	3/10	1/13
Number of Punts—Yards	11/410	8/308
Average Per Punt	37.3	38.5
Punt Returns: Number— Yards	4/20	3/42
Kickoff Returns: Number—Yards	3/135	3/42

OCTOBER 7, 1978

ARIZONA STATE VS. NORTHWESTERN
Dyche Stadium Evanston

FIRST QUARTER

Northwestern co-captains Geegan and Kranz meet at midfield with Arizona State co-captains Williams, Felix, and Harris for the toss of the coin. Northwestern wins the toss and elects to receive; ASU will kick and defend the north goal.

Lewis kickoff taken by Mill one yard deep and returned 37 yards
14:45 NORTHWESTERN
1/10-NU36 - Strasser pass to Bogan complete for 39 yds (Williams)
1/10-AS25 - Johnson draw play middle for 13 yds
1/10-AS12 - Hill LE for -1 yds (Kohrs)
2/11-AS13 - Strasser pass to North incomplete
3/11-AS13 - Hill RT for -1yds, fumbles, recovered by ASU Gill

13:17 ARIZONA STATE
1/10 -AS14 - Williams RT for 4 yds (Kern)
2/6 -AS18 - Malone keeper for 4 yds (Kern)
3/2 -AS22 - Moore pitch RE for 3 yds (Berg)
1/10-AS25 - Williams LT for 1 yd (Berg, Kendzicky)
2/9 -AS26 - Malone pass to DeFrance incomplete
3/9 -AS26 - Malone pass to Edwards complete for 17 yds (Hoffman)
1/10-AS43 - Moore middle for 3 yds (Kern)
2/7 -AS46 - Malone keeper LE for 28 yds (Hoffman)
1/10-NU26 - Williams middle for 8 yds (Knafelc)
2/2 -NU18 - Moore pitch RE for 3 yds (Berg)
1/10-NU15 - Malone keeper RE for 3 yds (Kern)
2/7 -NU12 - Moore middle for 1 yd, fumbles, recovered by NU Kendzicky

8:11 NORTHWESTERN
1/10-NU11 - Johnson RT for 3 yds (Apuna)
2/7 -NU14 - Johnson LT for 1 yd (Peters)
3/6 -NU15 - Johnson middle for 1 yd (Allison)
4/5 -NU16 - Christensen punt rolls dead at the AS49 35 yrd kick

6:21 ARIZONA STATE
1/10-AS49 - Malone pass to Edwards complete for 15 yds (McGlade)
1/10-NU36 - Moore middle for 1 yd (Robinett)
2/9 -NU35 - Moore LE for 19 yds
1/10-NU16 - Williams middle for 2 yds (Kern)
2/8 -NU14 - Williams middle for 5 yds (Kern)
3/3 -NU9 - DeFrance pitch LE for 9 yds and a touchdown (4:07)
PAT: Hicks kick good 51 yards in 6 plays
SCORE: ARIZONA STATE 7
NORTHWESTERN 0

Lewis kickoff taken by Hill at the NU1 and returned 51 yds (Wilson, Lee)
3:57 NORTHWESTERN
1/10-AS48 - Strasser pass for Washington incomplete
2/10-AS48 - Strasser screen pass for Cannon incomplete
3/10-AS48 - Strasser pass to Poulos incomplete. PENALTY: holding NU declined
4/10-AS48 - Christensen punt rolls out of bounds on the AS18 30 yrd kick

3:38 ARIZONA STATE
1/10-AS18 - Malone keeper RE for 4 yds (Kendzicky)
2/6 -AS22 - Moore LT for 5 yds (Payne)
3/1 -AS27 - Malone pass to DeFrance complete for 43 yds (Kenfelc)
1/10-NU30 - Malone keeper LE for 19 yds (Geegan)
1/10-NU11 - Williams middle for 3 yds (Corona)
2/7 -NU8 - Moore pitch LE for 4 yds (Corona)
4/3 -NU4 - Malone pass to DeFrance incomplete
4/3 -NU4 - PENALTY: offside NU accepted
4/1 -NU2 - Malone keeper LE for 2 yds and a touchdown (1:03)
PAT: Hicks kick good 82 yards in 8 plays
SCORE: ARIZONA STATE 14
NORTHWESTERN 0

Lewis kickoff downed by Geegan in the endzone
1:03 NORTHWESTERN
1/10-NU20 - Strasser pass to North incomplete
2/10-NU20 - Strasser fumbles the snap, recovered by AS Peters (2 yd loss)

0:57 ARIZONA STATE
1/10-NU18 - Malone pass to Hoover complete for 18 yds and a touchdown
PAT: penalty ASU holding accepted 18 yds in 1 play (0:53)
PAT: Hicks kick good
SCORE: ARIZONA STATE 21
NORTHWESTERN 0

Lewis kickoff rolls out of the endzone for a touchback
0:53 NORTHWESTERN
1/10-NU20 - Johnson pitch RE for 1 yd (Puna)
2/9 -NU21 - Hill middle for 2 yds (Carl)

**END OF FIRST QUARTER:
ARIZONA STATE 21 NORTHWESTERN 0**

277

SECOND QUARTER

NORTHWESTERN
3/7 -NU23 - Strasser screen pass to Cammon complete for 44 yds (Anderson)
1/10-AS33 - Strasser sacked by Kohrs for a 10 yd loss
2/20-AS43 - Johnson draw middle for -1 yd (Peters)
3/21-AS44 - Strasser sacked by Kohrs for -14 yds—play nullified by penalty
PENALTY: face masking ASU accepted
3/7 -AS30 - Strasser pass to Bogan complete for 30 yds and a touchdown (13:20)
PAT: Mirkopolous kick good
ARIZONA STATE 21 NORTHWESTERN 7

Mirkopolous kickoff taken by Moore at the NU4 and returned 13 yds (McGlade)
13:17 ARIZONA STATE
1/10-AS17 - Moore pitch LE for 6 yds (Kendzicky)
2/4 -AS23 - Malone keeper RE for 3 yds — PENALTY: holding ASU accepted
2/14-AS13 - Malone pass to Williams incomplete
3/14-AS13 - Moore draw play middle for 6 yds (Berg)
4/8 -AS19 - Butledge punt fair caught by North 23 yds

11:49 NORTHWESTERN
1/10-AS42 - Hill LE for -1 yds (Kohrs)
2/11-AS43 - Bogan reverse LE for 3 yds (McIntyre)
3/7 -AS40 - Strasser pass to Bogan complete for 23 yds (Anderson)
1/10-AS17 - Johnson LT for 2 yds (Allison)
2/8 -AS15 - Strasser pass to Bogan incomplete
3/8 -AS15 - Strasser pass to North incomplete
4/8 -AS15 - Mirkopolous 32 yd field goal attempt wide to right

9:52 ARIZONA STATE
1/10-AS20 - Moore middle for -2 yds (Robinett)
2/12-AS18 - Malone pass to Hoover complete for 22 yds (Hoffman)
1/10-AS40 - Moore pitch RE for 15 yds (Payne)
1/10-NU45 - Malone keeper RE for 4 yds (Kern)
2/6 -NU41 - Moore LT for 7 yds (Stasiewicz)
1/10-NU34 - Williams middle for 5 yds (Berg)
2/5 -NU29 - Moore middle for 3 yds (Robinett)
3/2 -NU26 - Malone keeper middle for 4 yds (Berg)
1/10-NU22 - Moore LE for 5 yds (Robinett)
2/5 -NU17 - Moore RE for 8 yds (Kern, Geegan)

1/G -NU9 - Moore pitch RE for -1yd (Bobowski)
2/G -NU10 - Malone keeper RE for 5 yds (Geegan)
3/G -NU5 - Malone pass to Williams complete for 5 yds and a touchdown (4:51)
PAT: Hicks kick good 80 yds in 13 plays
ARIZONA STATE 28 NORTHWESTERN 7

Lewis kickoff taken by Schmitt at the NU 16 and returned 10 yds
4:48 NORTHWESTERN
1/10-NU26 - Johnson RE for 3 yds (Allison)
2/7 -NU29 - Strasser keeper RE for -1 yds (Harris)
3/8 -NU28 - Hill pitch RE for 7 yds (Peters)
4/1 -NU35 - PENALTY: delay of game NU accepted
4/6 -NU30 - Christensen punt take by Hoover at the AS29 and returned -2 yds 41 yd punt

2:26 ARIZONA STATE
1/10-AS27 - Moore pitch LE for 7 yds (McGlade)
2/3 -AS34 - Williams LT for 4 yds (Corone)
1/10-AS38 - Malone pass to Hoover incomplete
2/10-AS38 - Gittens pitch RE for 5 yds (Shanzer) PENALTY: personal foul NU
1/10-NU42 - Malone pass to Edwards incomplete
2/10-NU42 - Malone pass to DeFrance complete for 23 yds
1/10-NU19 - Malone keeper LE for 5 yds (Corona)
2/5 -NU14 - Malone pass to DeFrance incomplete
3/5 -NU14 - Malone pass to Edwards for 9 yds (Hoffman)
1/G -NU5 - Malone pass to DeFrance complete for 5 yds and a touchdown (0:21)
PAT: Hicks kick good 73 yards in 10 plays
ARIZONA STATE 35 NORTHWESTERN 7

Lewis kickoff taken by Geegan at the NU9 and returned 14 yds
0:17 NORTHWESTERN
1/10-NU23 - Hill sweep RE for 7 yds (Allison)
2/3 -NU30 - Johnson RT for 5 yds (McIntyre)

**END OF HALF:
ARIZONA STATE 35 NORTHWESTERN 7**

THIRD QUARTER

Mirkopolous kickoff taken by DeFrance at the AS 5 and returned 14 yds

OCTOBER 7, 1978

14:56 ARIZONA STATE
1/10-AS19 - Moore middle for 5 yds (McGlade)
2/5 -AS24 - Malone pass to Hoover complete for 16 yds (Geegan)
1/10-AS40 - Moore pitch RE for 5 yds (Corona)
2/5 -AS45 - Gitten pitch RE for 8 yds (Hoffman)
1/10-NU47 - Gitten pitch RE for 3 yds
2/7 -NU44 - Giten RE for 5 yds (Kendzicky)
3/2 -NU39 - Malone keeper middle for 5 yds (Kern)
1/10-NU34 - Williams middle for 3 yds (Robinett)
2/7 -NU31 - Malone keeper RE for 7 yds (McGlade)
1/10-NU24 - Gitten RT for -2 yds (Berg)
2/12-NU26 - Malone pass to Hoover incomplete PENALTY: Pass interference NU
1/10-NU15 - Malone keeper RE for 15 yds and a touchdown (10:38)
PAT: Hicks kick good 81 yards in 11 plays
ARIZONA STATE 42 NORTHWESTERN 7

Lewis kickoff taken by Geegan at NU 6 and returned 18 yds (Wilson)

10:33 NORTHWESTERN
1/10-NU24 - Strasser sacked by Harris for loss of 14 yds
2/24-NU10 - Hill pitch RE for 1 yd (Williams)
3/23-NU11 - Johnson LT for 5 yds (Padjen)
4/18-NU16 - PENALTY: ill/procedure NU accepted
4/23-NU11 - Christensen punt downed at the 50 39 yard punt

9:07 ARIZONA STATE
1/10- 50 - Scott middle for 8 yds (Payne)
2/2 -NU42 - Scott middle for 1 yd (Stasiewicz)
3/1 -NU41 - Pagel keeper RE for 2 yds (Stasiewicz)
1/10-NU39 - Gitten pitch RE for 2 yds (McGlade)
2/8 -NU37 - Pagel pass to Pollard incomplete
3/8 -NU37 - Pagel keeper LE for 7 yds (Hoffman)
4/1 -NU30 - Scott RT for 8 yds (Hoffman)
1/10-NU22 - Gitten pitch RE for 3 yds (McGlade)
2/7 -NU19 - Pagel pass to Pollard complete for 19 yds and a touchdown (5:41)
PAT: Hicks kick good 50 yards in 9 plays
ARIZONA STATE 49 NORTHWESTERN 7

Lewis kickoff taken by Geegan at the NU 8 and returned 20 yds

5:36 NORTHWESTERN
1/10-NU28 - Strasser pass to Cannon complete for 6 yds (Gill)
2/4 -NU34 - Strasser pass to McGee complete for 5 yds
1/10-NU39 - Strasser pass to North complete for 9 yds (Barge)
2/1 -NU48 - Cannon RT for 24 yds (Gill)
1/10-AS28 - Strasser keeper LE for -3 yds (Apuna)
2/13-AS31 - Strasser pass to McGee incomplete
3/12-AS31 - Strasser pass to Johnson incomplete
4/13-AS31 - PENALTY: delay of game NU accepted
4/18-AS36 - Strasser pass to Bogan complete for 36 yds and a touchdown (2:49)
PAT: Mirkopolous kick good 72 yards in 8 plays
ARIZONA STATE 49 NORTHWESTERN 14

Mirkopolous kickoff taken by Hoover at the AS3 and returned 16 yds

2:44 ARIZONA STATE
1/10-AS19 - Scott middle for 4 yds (Berg)
2/6 -AS23 - Gitten pitch RE for 5 yds (Geegan)
3/1 -AS28 - Scott RT for 3 yds (McGlade)
1/10-AS31 - Felix middle for 1 yd (Ahern)
2/9 -AS32 - Pagel pass to Mistler complete for 12 yds
1/10-AS44 - Gitten pitch LE for 2 yds (Schanzer)
2/8 -AS46 - Scott LT for 4 yds (Payne)

END OF THIRD QUARTER:
ARIZONA STATE 49 NORTHWESTERN 14

FOURTH QUARTER

ARIZONA STATE
3/4 - 50 - Pagel pass to Scott incomplete
4/4 - 50 - Rutledge punt downed at the NU28 22 yard punt

14:43 NORTHWESTERN
1/10-NU28 - Strasser hit attempting to pass, fumble recovered by ASU Padjen (9 yd loss)

14:37 ARIZONA STATE
1/10-NU19 - Gitten RE for 2 yds (Kern)
2/8 -NU17 - Scott middle for 3 yds (Taylor)
3/5 -NU14 - Pagel pass to Mistler complete for 11 yds (Hoffman)
1/G -NU3 - Gitten RT for 1 yd (Kern)
2/G -NU2 - Scott middle for 2 yds and a touchdown (12:42)
PAT: Hicks kick good 19 yards in 5 plays
ARIZONA STATE 56 NORTHWESTERN 14

Lewis kickoff taken by Geegan at the goalline and returned 23 yds

12:38 NORTHWESTERN
1/10 -NU23 - Cammon RE for -4 yds (Lumpkin)
2/14 -NU19 - Cammon LE for 6 yds (Lumpkin)
3/9 -NU25 - Strasser pass to McGee incomplete
4/9 NU25 - Christensen punt downed at the NU48 23 yd punt

11:11 ARIZONA STATE
1/10 -NU48 - Scott LT for 5 yds (Schanzer)
2/5 -NU43 - Gitten middle for 2 yds (Taylor)
3/3 -NU41 - Gitten LE for -2 yds (McGlade)
4/5 NU43 - Pagel punt rolls out of bounds at NU1 42 yd punt

9:13 NORTHWESTERN
1/10 -NU1 - Breitbeil sneak for 1 yd (team)
2/9 -NU2 - Breitbeil sneak for 1 yd (team)
3/8 -NU3 - Johnson pitch RE for -1 yd (Barge)
4/9 -NU2 - Christensen punt taken by Hoover at NU33 and returned -6 yds 31 yd kick

7:06 ARIZONA STATE
1/10 -NU39 - Scott middle for 1 yd (Bambauer)
2/9 -NU38 - Gitten middle for 2 yds (Taylor)
3/7 -NU36 - Scott RT PENALTY: holding ASU accepted, play nullified
3/22 -AS49 - Gitten middle for 3 yds
4/19 -NU48 - Pagel punt down at NU 30 18 yard punt

5:04 NORTHWESTERN
1/10 -NU30 - PENALTY: ill. procedure NU accepted
1/15 -NU25 - Breitbeil pass to North incomplete
2/15 -NU25 - Washington RE for no gain (Sanders)
3/15 -NU25 - Breitbeil pass to Schmitt complete for -4 yds, play nullified by penalty PENALTY: roughing the passer ASU accepted
1/10 -NU40 - Washington RE for 3 yds (Lumpkin)
2/7 -NU43 - Breitbeil pass to Bogan incomplete
3/7 -NU43 - Breitbeil pass to Hemphill incomplete
4/7 -NU43 - Christensen punt fair catch by Hoover at AS28 29 yd punt

3:21 ARIZONA STATE
1/10 -AS28 - Scott middle for 4 yds (Olgivie)
2/6 -AS32 - Scott RT for 2 yds (Gildner)

3/4 -AS34 - Gitten Re for -1 yds (Taylor)
4/5 -AS33 - Pagel punt downed at NU24 43 yd punt

1:24 NORTHWESTERN
1/10 -NU24 - Washington LE for 4 yds (Felix)
2/6 -NU28 - Washington RT for -1 yds (Bowles)
3/7 -NU27 - Washington RE for -2 yds
4/9 -NU25 - Christensen punt fair caught by Hoover at AS42 33 yd punt

0:07 ARIZONA STATE
1/10 -AS42 - Scott middle for 3 yds (Harris)

END OF GAME:
ARIZONA STATE 56 NORTHWESTERN 14

National Collegiate Athletic Association
FINAL TEAM STATISTICS

	ARIZONA STATE	NORTH-WESTERN
First Downs	32	10
Rushing	19	3
Passing	11	6
Penalty	2	1
Rushing Attempts	76	35
Yards Rushing	358	92
Yards Lost Rushing	-8	-51
Net Yards Rushing	350	41
Net Yards Passing	216	192
Passes Attempted	21	21
Passes Completed	13	8
Had Intercepted	0	0
Total Offensive Plays	97	56
Total Net Yards	566	233
Average Gain Per Play	5.8	4.2
Fumbles: Number—Lost	1/1	3/3
Penalties: Number—Yards	6/88	6/33
Interceptions: Number—Yards	0/0	0/0
Number of Punts—Yards	5/148	8/262
Average Per Punt	29.6	32.8
Punt Returns: Number—Yards	2/-8	0
Kickoff Returns: Number—Yards	3/43	7/172

281

SOUTHERN METHODIST
VS.
OHIO STATE
Ohio Stadium
Columbus, Ohio
Temp.: 53°
Wind: WNW 10-20 mph
Skies: Partly Cloudy
FIRST QUARTER

SMU won the toss and elected to receive; Ohio State to defend the south goal
Orosz kicked off at 1:32 P.M. eleven yards deep for the touchback
15:00 SMU
1/10-S20 - Turner into rg for 2
2/8 -S22 - Shelton le for -4 - Ross
3/12-S18 - Johnson middle for 5
4/7 -S23 - Rosenthal punted 31; Guess returned middle for 15

13:29 OHIO
1/10-S39 - Murray pitch at le, broke tackle for (measurement) 10
1/10-S29 - Campbell at lg for 6
2/4 -S23 - Schlichter faked, kept inside le, down sideline for the TD at 12:26
Janakievski PAT - 39 yards in three plays
SCORE: OHIO STATE 7, SMU 0

Orosz kicked off 60 yards; Perry returned middle 19
12:21 SMU
1/10-S19 - Ford passed to Fisher in right flat for 10
1/10-S29 - Ford faked, passed on screen to Turner cutting over middle for 9
2/1 -S38 - turner pitch at re for no gain - Ellis
3/1 -S38 - Ford faked, passed quick on swing to Turner 5; Personal foul Ohio 15
1/10-042 - Turner pitch into rt, clear for 8
2/2 -034 - Ford passed too high for Smith right sideline incomplete
3/2 -034 - Shelton into rt for (measurement) 1
4/1 -033 - Ford sneak rg 1
1/10-032 - Ford passed to Garrett on out cut left for 6
2/4 -026 - Shelton over le for 2
3/2 -024 - Ford passed quick to Tolbert in deep right flat for 6
1/10-018 - Ford passed deep left for Tolbert, out of bounds for 17
1/G -01 - Shelton pushed into rt for the TD 8:09; Ohio offside declined
Garcia PAT - 81 yards in 13 plays
SCORE: OHIO STATE 7, SMU 7

Garcia kicked off out of bounds right -5
Garcia kicked off out of bounds right -5
Garcia kicked off out of bounds left -5
Garcia kicked off 47 yards; Hicks returned right 25

8:01 OHIO
1/10-S47 - Schlichter kept inside le for 1
2/9 -S46 - Campbell into lt for 4
3/5 -S42 - Schlichter passed for Donley on right sideline; intercepted by Hill returned 14

6:52 SMU
1/10- 50 - Ford passed deep over middle for Tolbert for 28
1/10-022 - Turner rt 2
2/8 -020 - Ford passed over middle to Tolbert for 7
3/1 013 - Shelton turned le for 2
1/10-011 - Ford passed over middle into end zone for Garrett after deflection by Tolbert for the TD 5:00 - 50 yards in 5 plays
Garcia's PAT try was wide left
SCORE: SMU 13, OHIO STATE 7

Garcia kicked off 46 yards; Murray returned middle for 19
4:55 OHIO
1/10-033 - Schlichter kept inside re for 4
2/6 -037 - Schlichter kept inside le for 3
3/3 -040 - Campbell at lt for 2; fumble recovered by Ferguson

3:44 SMU
1/10-042 - Ford faded, sacked by Ross for -9
2/19-S49 - Ford passed to Tolbert in left flat - dropped incomplete
3/19-S49 - Turner at lt for 2
4/17-049 - Rosenthal punted 37; Guess no return

2:36 OHIO
1/10-012 - Murray cut into middle, broke tackle for 8
2/2 -020 - Murray pushed thru rg for 7
1/10-027 - Campbell at lg for 6
2/4 -033 - Murray pitch at rt for 8
1/10-041 - Murray off lt, broke tackle, cut left for 20
1/10-S39 - Murray pitch at le, broke tackle for 7
2/3 -S32 - Johnson at lt for 2
3/1 -S30 - Campbell at rt for (measurement) 1
1/10-S29 - Schlichter kept inside le, clear down sideline out of bounds by Perry for 28

END OF FIRST QUARTER:
SMU 13, OHIO STATE 7

SECOND QUARTER

OHIO
1/G -S1 - Cambell dove over left guard for the TD 14:56 - Janakievski PAT
88 yards in ten plays
SCORE: OHIO STATE 14, SMU 13

282

OCTOBER 7, 1978

Orosz kicked off 60 yards; Perry returned left for 45
14:47 SMU
1/10-S45 - Ford passed in short left flat to Turner for 7
2/3 -048 - Johnson was clear at center, cut right for 10
1/10-038 - Ford passed too low left for Smith incomplete
2/10-038 - Ford passed quick in left flat to Smith for 5
3/5 -033 - Ford passed to Shelton short over middle for 7
1/10-026 - Shelton into lg for 4
2/6 -022 - Ford passed deep right for Tolbert, just out of bounds in end zone incomplete
3/6 -022 - Ford faked, passed on delay short left to Shelton for (measurement) 5
4/1 -017 - Ford sneak lg 2
1/10-015 - Ford passed way to high over middle for Garrett incomplete
2/10-015 - Ford passed over middle for Smith; knocked down by Ellis incomplete
3/10-015 - Ford passed at right goal line for Tolbert, knocked down Bell inc., Ohio pass interference 14
1/G -01 - Shelton at lt for no gain
2/G -01 - Ford sneak at left guard for the TD
10:55 - Ford, on conversion attempt, faked, passed quick on lob in left flat to Shelton for the score
55 yards in 13 plays
SCORE: SMU 21, OHIO STATE 14

Garcia kicked off 52 yards; Gerald returned 16
10:50 OHIO
1/10-024 - Murray into le for 2
2/8 -026 - Murray option pitch at le for -1 - Simmons
3/9 -025 - Campbell middle 2
4/7 -027 - Orosz punted right 45; Perry returned 4

9:03 SMU
1/10-S32 - Johnson cut thru rg, broke tackles for 13
1/10-S45 - Turner was stood up lg for 1
2/9 -S46 - Ford passed deep down sideline, too high, deflected Ellis incomplete
3/9 -S46 - Ford passed on screen right to Johnson for no gain - Cousineau
4/9 -S46 - Rosenthal punted 34; Guess returned right for 7

7:28 OHIO
1/10-027 - Ohio illegal procedure -5
1/15-022 - Schlichter kept left on broken play for 1
2/14-023 - Schlichter kept inside re for 5
3/9 -028 - Schlichter passed deep down right side line for Murray; broken up Hill inc.
4/9 -028 - Orosz punted right 53; Perry returned right for no gain

6:00 SMU
1/10-S19 - Ford passed on Johnson on delay left, dropped incomplete
2/10-S19 - Ford passed on swing right to Turner for 4
3/6 -S23 - Ford faded, looked, ran middle for 4
4/2 -S27 - Rosenthal punted 44; Guess returned 2

5:10 OHIO
1/10-031 - Johnson pitch into rt for 3
2/7 -034 - Schlichter kept inside re for 3
3/4 -037 - Schlichter passed over middle for Barwig: Choate deflected incomplete
4/4 -037 - Orosz punted right 48; Perry returned sideline 27

3:55 SMU
1/10-S42 - Ford passed deep right to Fisher for 12
1/10-046 - Shelton at lg, broke tackle for (measurement) 11
1/10-035 - Turner pitch at re for 3 Time out SMU 2:46
2/7 -032 - Ford passed to Garrett on out cut left for 5
3/2 -027 - Ford passed over middle deep for Smith; Ellis intercept after juggle

2:01 OHIO
1/10-01 - Murray lt 3
2/7 -04 - Schlichter kept inside le for 4 Time out SMU at 1:18
3/3 -08 - Schlichter kept inside re for 1 Time Out SMU at 1:10
4/2 -09 - Orosz punted 46; Perry returned right then left for 4

0:57 SMU
1/10-S49 - Ford passed into deep right flat to Garrett 6
2/4 -045 - Ford passed quick right flat to Tolbert 3
3/1 -042 - Ford passed too low for Garrett right flat incomplete
4/1 -042 - Johnson at rg for 4
1/10-038 - Garcia's FG try was short and wide left

END OF FIRST HALF:
SMU 21, OHIO STATE 14

THIRD QUARTER

Ohio State elected to receive; SMU to defend the north goal
Garcia kicked off at 3:12 50 yards; Murray returned left 38

283

14:53 OHIO
1/10-O48 - Schlichter passed deep down right sideline to Donley out of bounds inc.
2/10-O48 - Schlichter kept inside re for 3
3/7 -S49 - Schlichter faked, passed too low for Moore short right incomplete
4/7 -S49 - Orosz punted right 32; Perry's muff recovered by Volley
1/10-S24 - Murray cut into center for 4
2/6 -S20 - Campbell thru lg for 4 more
3/2 -S16 - Campbell hit into lt for 2; fumble recovered by Perry

12:48 SMU
1/10-S14 - Ford passed into right flat for Garrett for 9
2/1 -S23 - Shelton cut over le for 3
1/10-S26 - Ford passed on hook right to Smith for 23; SMU holding -13
1/23-S13 - Johnson at lg for 5
2/18-S18 - Ford faked to Shelton then passed to him cutting over middle for 9
3/9 -S27 - Ford passed to Smith in right flat, fell down inc., SMU pass interfer. -13
4/22-S14 - Rosenthal's punt was blocked by J. Epitropoulos, caught on play by Washington who carried in left for the TD 11:34 - Janakeivski's PAT was wide right
SCORE: SMU 21, OHIO STATE 20

Orosz kicked off 10 yards deep for the touchback

11:34 SMU
1/10-S20 - Ford faked, passed to Smith on hook left for 15
1/10-S35 - Shelton turned le for 3
2/7 -S38 - Ford passed for Tolbert deep cutting over middle; broken up Guess incomplete
3/7 -S38 - Ford passed for Smith deep left sideline; broken up by Ellis incomplete
4/7 -S38 - Rosenthal punted 38; Guess returned right 15

10:15 OHIO
1/10-O39 - Schlichter passed in deep left flat for Donley for 8
2/2 -O47 - Schlichter kept inside le for 3
1/10- 50 - Murray pitch at re for 3
2/7 -S47 - Schlichter faked, passed to Donley left for 13
1/10-S34 - Schlichter kept on counter option inside le for 8
2/2 -S26 - Johnson pitch at re, clear for 11
1/10-S15 - Johnson into lg for 4
2/6 -S11 - Johnson took option pitch at right end for the TD 7:54 - Time Out Ohio Schlichter, on conversion try, rolled right, passed to Donley for the score - 61 yards in eight plays
SCORE: OHIO STATE 28, SMU 21

Orosz kicked off 60 yards; Perry returned left for 28

7:48 SMU
1/10-S28 - Ford passed for Shelton on safety left, thru hands, dropped incomplete
2/10-S28 - Ohio illegal procedure 5
2/5. -S33 - Ford faded, sacked by Henson, Ross -8
3/13-S25 - Ford passed on delay over middle to Shelton 10
4/3 -S35 - Rosenthal punted 40; Guess returned 4; SMU holding -15
4/18-S20 - Rosenthal punted 31; Guess returned middle 7

6:22 OHIO
1/10-S44 - Schlichter passed to Campbell short, too low incomplete
2/10-S44 - Schlichter faked, passed too low for Donley over middle incomplete
3/10-S44 - Schlichter passed deep down left sideline to Murray for 29
1/10-S15 - Johnson pitch at re for 3
2/7 -S12 - Johnson option pitch at re for 6
3/1 -S6 - Campbell into le for 1
1/G -S5 - Schlichter kept inside left end for the TD 5:03 - Janakievski PAT - 44 yards in 7 plays
SCORE: OHIO STATE 35, SMU 21

Orosz kicked off 51 yards; Perry returned left 15

4:59 SMU
1/10-S24 - Ford passed to Tolbert cutting over middle between four defenders 17
1/10-S41 - Ford passed to Johnson on delay over middle for 9
2/1 - 50 - Shelton pitch at le for no gain - Dansler
3/1 - 50 - Shelton was clear at rg for 10
1/10-O40 - Ford passed deep right for Tolbert; Skillings intercepted returned 14

3:09 OHIO
1/10-O35 - Volley lg 2
2/8 -O37 - Schlichter faked, faded, looked, ran center for 5, lateralled to Volley for 22
1/10-S36 - Johnson re 2
2/8 -S34 - Schlichter on counter option pitched behind Hicks for -12
3/20-S46 - Volley was clear at lg for 12
4/8 -S34 - Schlichter's pass on delay over middle for Johnson was deflected C. Hunt incomplete

0:30 SMU
1/10-S34 - Ford passed over middle on delay to Shelton for 13

**END OF THIRD QUARTER:
OHIO STATE 35, SMU 21**

284

OCTOBER 7, 1978

FOURTH QUARTER

SMU
1/10-S47 - Ohio State offside 5
1/5 -048 - Johnson thru rg for 6
1/10-042 - Shelton cut thru rt for 9
2/1 -033 - SMU illegal procedure -5
2/6 -038 - Shelton at rt for 4
3/2 -034 - Ford faked, passed quick to Shelton on left swing lob for 4
1/10-030 - Shelton turned le for 6
2/4 -024 - Turner cut outside rt for no gain
3/4 -024 - Ford passed into short right flat to Turner for 2
4/2 -022 - Ford passed on hook over middle to Smith for 16
1/G -06 - Shelton clear at rt for 5
2/G -01 - Shelton was stopped at rt for no gain
3/G-01 - Ford sneak at right guard for the TD 10:03 - Garcia's PAT try was blocked by Ross - 66 yards in 13 plays
SCORE: OHIO STATE 35, SMU 27

Garcia kicked off 48 yards; Hicks returned 10
9:57 OHIO
1/10-022 - Schlichter kept left, slipped down for no gain
2/10-022 - Murray was clear at lg, cut right for 19
1/10-041 - Murray pitch at le, clear for 12
1/10-S47 - Murray leaped at rg for 3
2/7 -S44 - Schlichter kept right for no gain
3/7 -S44 - Schlichter passed deep down right sideline for Johnson, just out of bounds
4/7 -S44 - Orosz punted 38 right; B. Smith returned 3

7:28 SMU
1/10-S9 - Ford passed just too long for Tolbert deep over middle incomplete
2/10-S9 - Ford passed behind Smith cutting over middle incomplete (Washington hurt - helped off)
3/9-S9 - Ford passed to Tolbert cutting across middle for 21
1/10-S30 - Shelton turned le for 8
2/2 -S38 - Shelton cut into middle for (measurement) 2
1/10-S40 - Ford passed to Smith on left sideline for 12
1/10-048 - Johnson draw thru center for 9
2/1 -039 - Shelton leaped thru rg for 3
1/10-036 - Ford passed quick to Garrett right flat, broke tackle, fumbled out of bounds for 11
1/10-025 - Johnson pushed thru rg, cut left for 13
1/10-012 - Turner, on deep handoff left, was stopped for -1 by Dulin
2/11-013 - Ford faked, passed for Tolbert cutting across across middle; broken up Guess, dropped incomplete
3/11-013 - Ford passed over middle to Garrett, drove for 12
1/G -01 - Ford sneak at lg for the TD 3:41 - T.O. Ohio 3:43
Ford, on conversion try, rolled right and slid in for the score 91 yards in 14 plays
SCORE: SMU 35, OHIO STATE 35

Garcia kicked off 47 yards; Guess returned 19
3:35 OHIO
1/10-032 - Johnson at le for 2
2/8 -034 - Schlichter faded, chased left, ran for 3
3/5 -037 - Schlichter passed deep left for Johnson; Simmons intercepted, returned 23

2:48 SMU
1/10-039 - Shelton into rt for 3
2/7 -036 - Johnson center for 4
3/3 -032 - Shelton at lg for 2 Time out SMU 1:32
4/1 -030 - Shelton was stopped for no gain by Cousineau

OHIO STATE
1/10-031 - Schlichter faded, sacked by Nelson for -11 Time out SMU at 1:15
2/21-020 - Schlichter passed deep over middle for Gerald, short incomplete
3/21-020 - Schlichter passed deep right sideline for Murphy; interception Hill, no return

1:03 SMU
1/10-S37 - Ford passed in right flat to Johnson for 3
2/7 -S40 - Ford passed in right flat to Smith for 4
3/3 -S44 - Ford passed to Garrett over middle, ran for 21
1/10-035 - Ford passed over Tolbert's head in right flat to stop clock incomplete
2/10-035 - Ford faded, ran left for 6, Skillings kept him in bounds
3/4 -029 - Garcia's FG try was just wide left from 47 yards at 0:02 - touchback

0:02 OHIO
1/10-020 - Schlichter's pass deep over middle for Gerald was intercepted by Hill for no return; Ohio illegal procedure declined (Schlichter hurt - helped off)

END OF GAME:
SMU 35, OHIO STATE 35

WAKE FOREST VS. PURDUE
Ross-Ade Stadium
Temp.: 61°
Wind: NW 10-15 mph
Skies: Cloudy

FIRST QUARTER

Coin Flip: Purdue wins toss will receive, Wake Forest will kickoff and defend north goal. Schonert kickoff to Purdue end zone, 60 yd kick no return.

PURDUE
1/10-P20 - Macon rg, 1 yd. (Hopkins, Hester)
2/9 -P21 - Pope at re, 2 yds. (Bradley, Hester)
3/7 -P23 - Herrmann to Pope, 9 yds.
1/10-P32 - Macon pitch left, 3 yds. (Bradley, Hester)
2/7 -P35 - Pope re, 8 yds. (Ingram)
1/10-P43 - Macon rt, 6 yds. (Hopkins)
2/4 -P49 - Macon inside le, 3 yds. (Lancaster, Wisher)
3/1 -W48 - Macon rt, no gain, fumble recovered by WF Lancaster

11:57 WAKE FOREST
1/10-W48 - Kirby le, no gain (Turner)
2/10-W48 - Kirby lg, 2 yds. (Jackson, Moss)
3/8 - 50 - McDougald lg, 2 yds. (Clark, Jackson)
4/6 -P48 - Mullen punt to Purdue off sides, 5 yd penalty
4/1 -P43 - Webber roll right, no gain (Floyd)

PURDUE
1/10-P43 - Macon pitch left, 6 yds. (Ervin, Bradley)
2/4 -P49 - Pope pitch right, 1 yd. (Lancaster, Wisher)
3/3 - 50 - Macon rt. 1 yd. (Parker)
4/2 -W49 - Macon pitch right, lost 1 yd. (Bradley, Hester)

WAKE FOREST
1/10- 50 - Webber to Wright, incomp.
2/10- 50 - Webber to McDougald, 4 yds. (Johanson)
3/6 -P46 - Webber to McDougald, incomp. (PBU, Jackson)
4/6 -P46 - Mullen punt to P7 yd line, dead 39 yd kick no return

7:14 PURDUE
1/10-P7 - Macon up middle 4 yds. (Parker)
2/6 -P11 - Herrmann to Burrell, 25 yds.
1/10-P36 - Herrmann to pass, lost 12 yds. (Crayton)
2/22-P24 - Macon on draw, 1 yd. (Parker)
3/21-P25 - Herrmann to Young, incomp.
4/21-P25 - Eagin punt to Duckett on W41, return to W42, 34 yd kick

4:55 WAKE FOREST
1/10-W42 - McDougald rg, no gain (Clark-Floyd)
2/10-W42 - WF illegal procedure 5 yd. penalty
2/15 - W37 - Webber to Baumgardner, incomp. (PBU, Moss)
3/15-W37 - Webber to pass, run, 11 yds. (Moss)
4/4 -W48 - Mullen punt to Gallivan fair catch on P17, 35 yd kick no return

PURDUE
1/10-P17 - Pope pitch left, no gain (Lancaster)
2/10-P17 - Herrmann to pass, lost 10 yds. (Hopkins, Parker)
3/20-P7 - Macon lg, 5 yds. (Barley, Hester)
4/14-P12 - Eagin punt to P39, dead, 27 yd. kick no return

1:40 WAKE FOREST
1/10-P39 - Kirby rg, 2 yds. (Floyd)
2/8 -P37 - Webber to Rolark, 6 yds.
3/2 -P31 - McDougald pitch right, 4 yds. (Seneff, Kay)
1/10-P27 - Webber roll left, 2 yds. (Motts, Smith)

**END OF FIRST QUARTER
PURDUE 0, WAKE FOREST 0**

SECOND QUARTER

WAKE FOREST
2/8 -P25 - McDougald reverse right, 7 yds. (Seneff, Motts)
3/1-P18 - Webber roll right, 4 yds. (Seneff)
1/10-P14 - McDougald pitch right, 1 yd. (Floyd, Motts)
2/9 -P13 - Webber keep left, lost 2 yds. (Loushin)
3/11-P15 - Webber to Baumgardner, incomp.
4/11-P15 - Schonert att. 32 yd. field goal, Mullen hold, partially blocked no good

12:59 PURDUE
1/10-P20 - Macon rg, 2 yds. (Hopkins)
2/8 -P22 - Herrmann to Pope, 7 yds. (Yarnell)
3/1 -P29 - Macon up middle, no gain
4/1 -P29 - Eagin punt to time out Purdue time 11:16
4/1 -P29 - Eagin punt to Duckett, fair catch on W23, 48 yd. kick no return

OCTOBER 7, 1978

11:09 WAKE FOREST
1/10-W23 - Kirby inside re, 3 yds. (Clark, Loushin)
2/7 -W26 - Kirby inside le, 7 yds. (Smith)
1/10-W33 - Kirby on draw, 4 yds. (Loushin)
2/6 -W37 - Webber fumble, recov. Kirby, lost 6 yds. (Loushin, Johanson)
3/12-W31 - Webber to Wright, incomp. (PBU, Turner)
4/12-W31 - Mullen punt to Gallivan, fair catch on P34, 35 yd kick no return

8:47 PURDUE
1/10-P34 - Pope rt, 16 yds.
1/10- 50 - WF illeg. proc. 5 yd. penalty
1/5- W45 - Pope slide left, 2 yds. (Lancaster)
2/3 -W43 - Pope on draw, lost 2 yds. (Hopkins, Crayton)
3/5 -W45 - Herrmann to Macon, incomp.
4/5 -W45 - Eagin punt to W12 out of bounds, 33 yd kick no return

7:23 WAKE FOREST
1/10-W12 - Webber roll right, lost 4 yds. (Floyd)
2/14-W8 - Kirby rt, 3 yds. (Loushin)
3/11-W11 - Webber roll left, lost 3 yds. (Jackson)
4/14-W8 - Mullen punt to Pope on W44 return to W41, 36 yd. kick 3 yd return

5:38 PURDUE
1/10-W41 - Herrmann to Harris, 14 yds. (Royster)
1/10-W27 - Herrmann to Macon, 10 yds. (Lancaster)
1/10-W17 - Pope rt, 10 yds. (Lancaster, Ervin)
1/G -W7 - Pope rt, 2 yds. (Bradley)
2/G -W5 - Macon lg, 2 yds. (Crayton)
3/G -W3 - Pope rg, 2 yds. (Hester, Bradley)
4/G -W1 - Sovereen att. 18 yd. field goal Burrell hold, good, 7 plays, 40 yds.
SCORE: PURDUE 3, WAKE FOREST 0

Sovereen kickoff to Buckett on WF end zone 60 yd. kick no return.

2:58 WAKE FOREST
1/10-W20 - Kirby right, lost 4 yds. (Clark)
2/14-W16 - Daly to Baumgardner, incomp. (PBU, Moss)
3/14-W16 - Daly to pass, lost 7 yds. (Loushin)
4/21-W9 - Mullen punt to Gallivan on W49 return to W46, 40 yd. kick, 3 yd. return

1:36 PURDUE
1/10-W46 - Herrmann to Macon, 8 yds. (Bradley, Royster)

2/2 -W38 - Shotgun, Herrmann to Pope, 6 yds.
1/10-W32 - Macon on draw, 17 yds. fumbled WF recov. time 1:01 recov. Jackson

WAKE FOREST
1/10-W15 - McDougald lt, 3 yds.
2/7 -W18 - McDougald lt, 4 yds. (Clark)

**END OF FIRST HALF:
PURDUE 3, WAKE FOREST 0**

THIRD QUARTER

WF will receive, Purdue will kickoff and defend north goal. Sovereen kickoff to Duckett on WF goal line return W22, 60 yd. kick 22 yd. return.

WAKE FOREST
1/10-W22 - Kirby lg, 2 yds. (Loushin)
2/8 -W24 - Webber to Baumgardner, 13 yds.
1/10-W37 - McDougald le, 3 yds. (Johanson)
2/7 -W40 - Webber to pass, lost 9 yds.
3/16-W31 - Webber to Rolark, 5 yds. (Smith)
4/11 -W36 - Mullen punts to P26 dead, 38 yd. kick no return

12:17 PURDUE
1/10-P26 - Pope pitch left, 3 yds.
2/8 -P29 - Herrmann to Young, 8 yds. (Royster)
1/10-P37 - Pope pitch right, 6 yds. (Bradley, Hester)
2/4 -P43 - Pope lt, 1 yd. (Crayton)
3/3 -P44 - Pope pitch left, lost 7 yds. (Lancaster)
4/10-P37 - Eagin punt to W15 dead, 48 yd. kick no return

9:50 WAKE FOREST
- 1/10-W15 - McDougald re, 1 yd. (Motts, Loushin)
- 2/9 -W16 - Webber to Baumbardner, 16 yds.
- 1/10-W32 - Purdue pass interf. 10 yd. penalty (Robinson injured)
- 1/10-W42 - McDougald inside re, 7 yds. (Kay, Johanson)
- 2/3 -W49 - Kirby re, 2 yds. (Clark, Motts)
- 3/1-P49 - Kirby rg, 2 yds. (Clark, Loushin)
- 1/10-P47 - Webber to McDougald, 13 yds.
- 1/10-P34 - Webber to pass, lost 11 yds. (Turner)
- 2/21-P45 - McDougald rg, 5 yds. (Motts, Clark)
- 3/16-P40 - Webber to pass, lost 10 yds (Jackson)
- 4/26- 50 - Mullen punt to Purdue off sides, 5 yd penalty
- 4/21-P45 - Mulen punt to Pope fair catch P18, 27 yd. kick no return

5:23 PURDUE
- 1/10-P18 - Pope inside re, 15 yds. (Ervin)
- 1/10-P33 - Macon re, 20 yds. (Ervin, Wisher)
- 1/10-W47 - Pope left end, 3 yds. (Lancaster)
- 2/7 -W44 - Herrmann to Harris, 15 yds. (Hester)
- 1/10-W29 - Pope re, 14 yds. (Hopkins, Ervin)
- 1/10-W15 - Macon rt, 9 yds. (Hester)
- 2/1 -W6 - Pope lt, no gain (Maxwell, Parker)
- 3/1 -W6 - Pope pitch right, fumbled out of bounds, 2 yds. (Hopkins inj.)
- 1/G -W4 - Macon up middle, 1 yd. (Parker, Bradley)
- 2/G -W3 - Herrmann roll left, lost 3 yds. (Osborne)
- 3/G -W6 - Shotgun, Herrmann to Harris, incomp. (Herrmann injured)
- 4/G -W6 - Sovereen att. 23 yd. field goal, Burrell hold, good, 12 plays 76 yds.
- SCORE: PURDUE 6, WAKE FOREST 0

Sovereen kickoff to McMillan on W9 ret to W29, 51 yd kick 20 yd return.

1:13 WAKE FOREST
- 1/10-W29 - Kirby slide re, 4 yds. (Turner, Johanson)
- 2/6 -W33 - Kirby lt, 2 yds. (Jackson)

END OF THIRD QUARTER: PURDUE 6, WAKE FOREST 0

FOURTH QUARTER

WAKE FOREST
- 3/4 -W35 - Kirby rg, 2 yds.
- 4/2 -W37 - Mullen punt to Gallivan on P22, return to P30, fumbled Jackson recov. for W, 41 yd. kick, 8 yd. return
- 1/10-P30 - Webber roll right, 17 yds.
- 1/10-P13 - Kirby lt, 4 yds. (Jackson)
- 2/6 -P9 - McDougald re, 9 yds. touchdown, 3 plays 30 yds.
- PAT WF off sides 5 yd. penalty
- PAT from 8, time out WF 13:18
- PAT from 8, Schonert kick Webber hold good
- SCORE: WAKE FOREST 7, PURDUE 6

Roughing kicker against Purdue on PAT, 15 yd. penalty assessed on kickoff, WF kick on P45. Schonert kickoff to Moss out of end zone, 45 yd. kick no return.

PURDUE
- 1/10-P20 - Pope pitch right, 7 yds. (Lancaster)
- 2/3 -P27 - Pope re, 4 yds. (Bradley)
- 1/10-P31 - Herrmann to Young, 3 yds. (Ervin)
- 2/7 -P34 - Herrmann to Macon, 13 yds. (Ingram)
- 1/10-P47 - Herrmann to Harris, 11 yds. (Hester, Bradley)
- 1/10-W42 - Macon le, 6 yds. (Hester, Yarnell)
- 2/4 -W36 - Macon inside le, 6 yds. (Yarnell)
- 1/10-W30 - Herrmann to Pope, 11 yds. (Ingram)
- 1/10-W19 - Macon rt, 9 yds. (Irvin)
- 2/1 -W10 - Macon rg, 2 yds. LeFeber inj. (Parker)
- 1/G -W8 - Pope le, lost 1 yd. (Lancaster)
- 2/G -W9 - Herrmann to Young, lost 1 yd. (Royster, Lancaster)
- 3/G -W10 - Herrmann to Harris, interc. Ervin in end zone

8:40 WAKE FOREST
- 1/10-W20 - Weber roll right, 1 yd. (Maus)
- 2/9 -W21 - Kirby lt, 3 yds. (Turner)
- 3/6 -W24 - McDougald rt, 3 yds. (Turner, Jackson)
- 4/3 -W27 - Mullen punt to Gallivan fair catch on P38, 35 yd. kick no return

6:53 PURDUE
- 1/10-P38 - Herrmann to Young, incomp. (PBU, Lancaster)
- 2/10-P38 - Macon on draw, 3 yds. (Hopkins)
- 3/7 -P41 - Herrmann to Harris, 15 yds. (Royster, Jackson)

OCTOBER 7, 1978

1/10-W44 - Macon at re, 1 yd. (Hopkins)
2/9-W43 - Shotgun Herrmann to Burrell, 34 yds. (Royster, Lancaster)
1/G -W9 - Pope rg, 4 yds. (Lancaster, Crayton)
2/G -W5 - Pope rg, 3 yds. (Hopkins, Wisher)
3/G -W2 - Pope inside re, 2 yds. touchdown, 8 plays 62 yds.
PAT Sovereen kick, Purdue time out 3:50
PAT Herrmann to Burrell two-point conversion
SCORE: PURDUE 14, WAKE FOREST 7

Sovereen kickoff to Rolark on W21 return to W27, 39 yd. kick 6 yd. return.

WAKE FOREST
1/10-W27 - Webber to pass, incomp. (PBU, Johanson)
2/10-W27 - Webber to McDougald, 32 yds. (Smith, Kay)
1/10-P41 - Webber to McDougald, incomp.
2/10-P41 - Kirby lt, 1 yd. (Turner)
3/9 -P40 - Webber to pass, lost 15 yds. (Loushin)
4/24-W45 - Mullen punt to P22 yd. line, dead, 33 yd. kick no return

1:56 PURDUE
1/10-P22 - Pope re, 6 yds. (Royster, Lancaster)
Wake Forest time out time 1:47
2/4 -P28 - Pope lg, 3 yds. (Hester, Lancaster)
3/1 -P31 - Pope on broken play, lost 4 yds. (Wisher)
WF time out 1:05
4/5 -P27 - Eagin punt to Duckett on W37 return to W43, 36 yd. kick 6 yd. return

0:55 WAKE FOREST
1/10-W43 - Daly to Mullen, incomp.
2/10-W43 - Daly to pass, run hit by Turner, fumbled recov. WF, lost 14 yds.
3/24-W29 - Daly to Wright, incomp.
4/24-W29 - Daly to Baumgardner, incomp.

0:14 PURDUE
1/10-W29 - Oliver at qb, fell on ball, lost 4 yds.

FINAL SCORE:
PURDUE 14, WAKE FOREST 7

National Collegiate Athletic Association
FINAL TEAM STATISTICS

	PURDUE	WAKE FOREST
First Downs	21	11
Rushing	10	6
Passing	11	4
Penalty	0	1
Rushing Attempts	56	46
Yards Rushing	225	127
Yards Lost Rushing	44	85
Net Yards Rushing	181	42
Net Yards Passing	188	89
Passes Attempted	21	18
Passes Completed	16	7
Had Intercepted	1	0
Total Offensive Plays	77	64
Total Net Yards	369	131
Average Gain Per Play	4.8	2.0
Fumbles: Number—Lost	4/3	2/0
Penalties: Number—Yards	4/35	3/15
Interception: Number—Yards	0/0	1/0
Number of Punts—Yards	6/226	10/359
Average Per Punt	37.7	35.9
Punt Returns: Number—Yards	3/14	2/7
Kickoff Returns: Number—Yards	0/0	3/48

OCTOBER 14, 1978

OHIO STATE
VS.
PURDUE
Ross-Ade Stadium
Temp: 54°
Wind: NNW 12-14 mph
Skies: Party cloudy and cool

FIRST QUARTER

Coin Flip: Ohio State wins toss, and elects to kickoff and defend north goal Purdue will receive Orosz kickoff to Moss on P goal line return to P26, 60 yd kick
PURDUE
1/10-P26 - Macon rt, 4 yds. (Henson)
2/6 -P30 - Pope lt, no gain (Henson-Dansler)
3/6 -P30 - Herrmann to Burrell, 20 yds. (Ellis)
1/10- 50 - Purdue illegal motion, 5 yd penalty
1/15-P45 - Pope inside re on draw, 4 yds. (Cousineau)
2/11-P49 - Macon up middle, 3 yds. (Washington-Cousineau)
3/8 -O48 - Herrmann to Burrell, 9 yds.
1/10-O39 - Macon inside re, 4 yds. (Cousineau-Dulin)
2/6 -O35 - Macon inside re, 5 yds. (Cousineau)
3/1 -O30 - Macon rt, 1 yd (Dansler)
1/10-O29 - Herrmann to Harris, 11 yds.
1/10-O18 - Macon up middle, 2 yds. (Washington)
2/8 -O16 - Herrmann to Burrell, incomplete
3/8 -O16 - Herrmann roll right, 5 yds. (Mills)
4/3 -O11 - Sovereen 28 yd field goal attempt Burrell hold good 14 plays 63 yds.
SCORE: PURDUE 3, OHIO STATE 0

Sovereen kickoff to Murray on O32, 50 yd kick 22 yd return.
10:04 OHIO STATE
1/10-O32 - Volley lg, 3 yds. (Clark-Motts)
2/7 -O35 - Schlichter to Johnson, 14 yds. (Johanson)
1/10-O49 - Volley rg, 1 yd. (Loushin-Turner)
2/9 - 50 - Volley rg, 17 yds. (Jackson)
1/10-P33 - Schlichter pitch right Johnson, 9 yds. (Moss)
2/1 -P24 - Johnson rt, 4 yds. (Loushin)
1/10-P20 - Johnson pitch left, fumbled Clark recovered for Purdue, 2 yds.

8:14 PURDUE
1/10-P18 - Pope rt, 8 yds. (Cousineau)
2/2 -P26 - Pope lt, 3 yds. (Cousineau)
1/10-P29 - Macon lg, 7 yds. (Ross)
2/3 -P36 - Pope re, 6 yds. (Ellis)
1/10-P42 - Macon rg, 3 yds. (Cato)
2/7 -P45 - Herrmann to Burrell, incomplete
3/7 -P45 - Pope on draw, 4 yds. (Cousineau-Mills)

4/3 -P49 - Eagin punt to O10, 41 yd kick no return 4:58 personal foul Purdue 15 yd penalty
4/18-P34 - Eagin punt to Guess on O28, return to O26, 38 yd kick -2 return.

4:42 OHIO STATE
1/10-O26 - Johnson pitch right, 2 yds. (Motts-Clark) Purdue time out 4:42.
2/8 -O28 - Schlichter roll right, 39 yds. (Smith)
1/10-P33 - Volley lg, 6 yds. (Moss-Marks)
2/4 -P27 - Schlichter to Johnson, 3 yds. (Johanson)
3/1 -P24 - Johnson lt, 2 yds. (Loushin-Marks)
1/10-P22 - Schlichter slide right, 1 yd.
2/9 -P21 - Schlichter to Donley, Purdue unsportsmanlike conduct, 11 yd penalty
1/10-P11 - Schlichter roll right, 1 yd. (Motts-Loushin)
2/9 -P10 - Volley lg, lost 1 yd. fumbled recovered Clark

2:03 PURDUE
1/10-P11 - Pope lg, 1 yd. (Dansler)
2/9 -P12 - Herrmann to Macon, dropped
3/9 -P12 - Macon lt, 4 yds. (Washington-Sullivan)
4/5 -P16 - Eagin punt to Guess on 50 yd line, fumbled recovered returned to P48 34 yd kick 2 yd return

0:29 OHIO STATE
1/10-P48 - Johnson pitch left, 1yd (Moss)
2/9 -P47 - Johnson pitch left, 1 yd. (Moss-Harris)

**END OF FIRST QUARTER:
PURDUE 3, OHIO STATE 0**

SECOND QUARTER

OHIO STATE
3/8 -P46 - Schlichter to Gerald, 15 yds.
1/10-P31 - Johnson pitch right, 6 yds. (Johnson-Jackson)
2/4 -P25 - Campbell up middle, 2 yds.
3/2 -P23 - Ohio illegal motion, 5 yd penalty
3/7 -P28 - Schlichter to Gerald, 9 yds.
1/10-P19 - Johnson pitch right, fumble, recovered lost 2 yds.
2/12-P21 - Schlichter to Campbell on draw, 8 yds. (Turner-Johanson)
3/4 -P13 - Johnson pitch right, 2 yds. (Jackson)
4/2 -P11 - Atha 28 yd field goal attempt, Castignola hold, wide right

11:49 PURDUE
1/10-P20 - Macon rt, 3 yds. (Cato-Sullivan)
2/7 -P23 - Herrmann to Macon, 9 yds. (Mills-Cousineau)
1/10-P32 - Herrmann to Pope, 3 yds. (Mills)
2/7 -P35 - Macon lt, 4 yds. (Cato-Sullivan)

OCTOBER 14, 1978
THIRD QUARTER

3/3 -P39 - Pope inside le, 1 yd. (Washington)
4/2 -P40 - Eagin punt to Guess on O12 return to O17 48 yd kick 5 yd return.

9:36 OHIO STATE
1/10-O17 - Schlichter roll left, 3 yds. (Floyd)
2/7 -O20 - Schlichter to Donley, incomplete
3/7 -O20 - Schlichter to Hicks, 15 yds. (Johanson)
1/10-O35 - Hicks pitch right, lost 1 yd. (Smith)
2/11-O34 - Schlichter to Volley, 5 yds. (Turner-Marks)
3/6 -O39 - Schlichter to Donley, Purdue pass interference 11 yd penalty
1/10- 50 - Hicks lt, 1 yd. (Turner-Marks)
2/9 -P49 - Schlichter to Volley forward handoff 49 yds. touchdown 7 plays 83 yds. PAT Janakievski kick, Castignola hold good
SCORE: OHIO STATE 7, PURDUE 3

Orosz kickoff to Augustyniak on P20 return to P30, 40 yd kick 10 yd return.
6:50 PURDUE
1/10-P30 - Pope re, lost 2 yds. (Ross)
2/12-P28 - Herrmann to Pope, 6 yds. (Dansler)
3/6 -P34 - Herrmann to Harris, 22 yds. (Ellis)
1/10-O44 - Herrmann to Young, intercepted Murphy on O21

5:40 OHIO STATE
1/10-O21 - Ohio State illegal procedure 5 yd penalty
1/15-O16 - Hicks pitch right 1 yd. (Loushin)
2/14-O17 - Schlichter keep left, 7 yds. (Floyd)
3/7 -O24 - Schlichter to Donley, Purdue pass interference 13 yds penalty
1/10-O37 - Schlichter left to Hicks 3 yds. (Kay)
2/7 -O40 - Schlichter to Donley, 11 yds. (Kay)
1/10-P49 - Volley on draw, lost 3 yds. (Clark)
2/13-O48 - Hicks lt, 4 yds. (Floyd-Motts)
3/9 -P48 - Schlichter to pass, lost 5 yds. (Turner-Jackson) Schlichter injured
4/14-O47 - Orosz punt to P17, Purdue roughing kicker, 15 yd penalty
1/10-P37 - Schlichter to Hicks, 8 yds.
2/2 -P29 - Hicks pitch right, Ohio State holding 14 yd penalty
2/16-P43 - Volley on draw, 4 yds. (Johanson-Motts)
3/12-P39 - Schlichter to Donley, incomplete
4/12-P39 - Orosz punt to end zone, 39 yd kick no return

0:42 PURDUE
1/10-P20 - Macon up middle, 5 yds. (Cato-Cousineau)
2/5 -P25 - Macon inside le, 2 yds. (Sullivan-Cousineau)

HALF TIME SCORE:
OHIO STATE 7, PURDUE 3

Purdue has option and will receive Ohio State will kickoff and defend north goal

Orosz kickoff to Moss on P1 ret. to P23 59 yd kick 22 yd ret.
PURDUE
1/10-P23 - Herrmann to Pope, 2 yds. (Dansler)
2/8 -P25 - Herrmann to Pope, incomplete
3/8 -P25 - Herrmann to Harris, 10 yds (Guess)
1/10-P35 - Macon inside RE, 3 yds (Sullivan)
2/7 -P38 - Herrmann to Macon, 4 yds (Ross-Guess)
3/3 -P42 - Herrmann to Augustyniak, 11 yds (Washington)
1/10-O47 - Herrmann to Burrell, Ohio State pass interf. 16 yd. penalty
1/10-O31 - Herrmann to Harris, 3 yds (Guess)
2/7 -O28 - Herrmann to Burrell, incomplete
3/7 -O28 - Herrmann to Burrell, 10 yds
1/10-O18 - Herrmann to Burrell, incomplete
2/10-O18 - Shotgun, Herrmann to Young 17 yds. (Ross)
1/G -O1 - Macon RT, 1 yd. touchdown, time 10:47, 12 plays 77 yds.
PAT Sovereen kick, Burrell hold good
SCORE: PURDUE 10, OHIO STATE 7

Sovereen kickoff to Hicks on O12 ret. to O18 48 yd kick 6 yd ret.
OHIO STATE
1/10-O18 - Hicks LT, 12 yds (Clark-Johanson)
1/10-O30 - Schlichter roll left, 6 yds (Jackson)
2/4 -O36 - Schlichter to Donley incomplete
3/4 -O36 - Schlichter roll right, 5 yds (Motts-Johanson)
1/10-O41 - Schlichter to Gerald incomplete
2/10-O41 - Schlichter to Donley, 22 yds (Motts)
1/10-P37 - Hicks LE, lost 1 yd (Turner-Harris)
2/11-P38 - Schlichter to Barwig, 13 yds (Harris)
1/10-P25 - Hicks pitch left, 1 yd. (Marks-Jackson)
2/9 -P24 - Schlichter roll left, 3 yds (Jackson)
3/6 -P21 - Schlichter to pass, lost 4 yds (Loushin)
4/10-P25 - Atha 42 yd field goal attempt Castignola hold good, 12 plays 57 yds. time 6:20
SCORE: PURDUE 10, OHIO STATE 10

Orosz kickoff to Moss on goal line ret. to P25, 60 yd kick 25 yd ret

PURDUE
1/10-P25 - Pope RE, 3 yds (Ross-Cousineau)
2/7 -P28 - Herrmann to Harris, incomplete
3/7 -P28 - Purdue time out 5:40
3/7 -P28 - Herrmann to Macon, 10 yds (Mills)
1/10-P38 - Herrmann to Pope, 3 yds (Ellis)
2/7 -P41 - Macon draw RG, 4 yds (Washington-Skillings)
3/3 -P45 - Pope RT, 2 yds (Dansler)
4/1 -P47 - Eagin punt to O26, downed, 27 yd kick no ret. time: 4:26

OHIO STATE
1/10-026 - Hicks RG, 4 yds
2/6 -O30 - Hicks pitch left, 10 yds (Harris)
1/10-040 - Volley RG, 3 yds (Jackson-Johanson)
2/7 -043 - Hicks pitch right, no gain (Floyd)
3/7 -043 - Schlichter to Hicks, incomplete
4/7 -043 - Orosz punt to Pope on P16, ret. to P39, 41 yd kick, 23 yd ret. Ohio State personal foul, 15 yd penalty time 3:03

PURDUE
1/10-046 - Herrmann to Eubank (Guess-Mills) Purdue illeg. rec. downfield 15 yd penalty
1/25-P39 - Macon on draw, 3 yds (Henson)
2/22-P42 - Shotgun, Herrmann to Pope, 11 yds. Ohio State personal foul 15 yd. pen.
1/10-032 - Shotgun, Herrmann to Macon, 21 yds. (Guess-Mills)
1/10-011 - Herrmann to Burrell, incomplete
2/10-011 - Shotgun, Herrmann to Macon, incomplete
3/10-011 - Pope pitch left, 11 yds, touchdown time 1:13, 6 plays 46 yds.
PAT Sovereen kick Burrell hold good
SCORE: PURDUE 17 OHIO STATE 10

Sovereen kickoff to Hicks on O11 ret. to O22 49 yd kick 11 yd ret.
OHIO STATE
1/10-022 - Schlichter roll right, 2 yds
2/8 -024 - Schlichter to pass, run left, 3 yds (Jackson)

END OF THIRD QUARTER: PURDUE 17 OHIO STATE 10

FOURTH QUARTER

OHIO STATE
3/5 -027 - Schlichter roll left, 8 yds. (Marks)
1/10-035 - Volley rg, 4 yds. (Jackson)
2/6 -039 - Schlichter to Barwig, incomplete
3/6 -039 - Schlichter to pass, lost 14 yds. fumbled recovered Floyd for Purdue

14:05 PURDUE
1/10-025 - Macon inside re, 3 yds. (Washington-Sullivan)
2/7 -022 - Shotgun, Herrmann to Burrell, incomplete

3/7 -022 - Herrmann to Macon, lost 2 yds. (Cousineau)
4/9 -024 - Sovereen 41 yd field goal attempt Burrell hold, good 4 plays, 1 yd.
SCORE: PURDUE 20, OHIO STATE 10

Sovereen kickoff to Johnson in end zone, 60 yd kick no return
12:46 OHIO STATE
1/10-020 - Hicks rt, 1 yd. (Marks-Loushin)
2/9 -021 - Schlichter to Moore, 19 yds. (Moss) Moore injured
1/10-040 - Schlichter to Gerald, incomplete
2/10-040 - Schlichter to Donley, incomplete
3/10-040 - Schlichter to Gerald, 60 yds. touchdown, 5 plays, 80 yds. Ohio State time out PAT Schlichter to Donley, incomplete no good
SCORE: PURDUE 20, OHIO STATE 16

Orosz kickoff to Moss on P5 return to P22, 55 yd kick 17 yd return
11:37 PURDUE
1/10-P22 - Macon up middle, 5 yds. (Skillings-Cousineau)
2/5 -P27 - Herrmann to pass, run, 11 yds.
1/10-P38 - Macon rt on draw, 9 yds. (Washington-Skillings)
2/1 -P47 - Herrmann to Pope, no gain (Washington)
3/1 -P47 - Herrmann to Macon, 12 yds. (Washington)
1/10-041 - Macon inside re, 3 yds. (Washington)
2/7 -038 - Herrmann to Harris, Ohio State roughing passer 15 yd penalty
1/10-023 - Macon lg, 2 yds. (Sullivan-Washington)
2/8 -021 - Shotgun, Herrmann to pass, lost 14 yds. (Cato)
3/22-035 - Herrmann to Pope, incomplete
4/22-035 - Eagin punt to Ohio State time out time: 8:00
4/22-035 - Eagin punt out of bounds on Ohio State 6, 29 yd kick no return

7:51 OHIO STATE
1/10-06 - Schlichter to Gerald, 3 yds. fumbled, W Smith recovered for Purdue

7:40 PURDUE
1/G -09 - Macon rt, 1 yd.
2/G -08 - Harris on end around, lost 11 yds. (Bell)
3/G -019 - Herrmann to Harris, 19 yds. Touchdown, 3 plays 9 yds. PAT Sovereen kick Burrell hold, good
SCORE: PURDUE 27, OHIO STATE 16

Sovereen kickoff to Hicks on O10 return to O35, 50 yd kick 25 yd return.

OCTOBER 14, 1978

6:16 OHIO STATE
1/10-O35 - Schlichter roll left, 17 yds. (Floyd)
1/10-P48 - Schlichter to Johnson, incomplete
2/10-P48 - Schlichter to Johnson, 10 yds.
 (Johanson-Motts)
1/10-P38 - Schlichter to Hunter, incomplete
2/10-P38 - Schlichter to Barwig, 29 yds.
 (Harris-Kay)
1/G -P9 - Schlichter to Donley, incomplete
2/G -P9 - Schlichter to Donley, incomplete
3/G -P9 - Schlichter to Volley, on forward draw, lost 2 yds.
4/G -P11 - Schlichter to Donley, 4 yds.

4:05 PURDUE
1/10-P7 - Pope rt, 7 yds.
2/3 -P14 - Pope rg, 2 yds.
3/1 -P16 - Macon rt, no gain (Washington)
4/1 -P16 - Eagin punt to Guess on O42, return to O41, 42 yd kick -1 return. Ohio State clip on return 15 yd penalty

2:12 OHIO STATE
1/10-O26 - Schlichter to Donley, Ohio State holding, 14 yd penalty
1/24-O12 - Schlichter to Volley, 3 yds.
2/21-O15 - Schlichter to Donley, 24 yds. (Harris)
1/10-O39 - Schlichter to pass, fell, lost 8 yds.
2/18-O31 - Schlichter to Volley, 11 yds. (Motts)
3/7 -O42 - Schlichter to Donley, 10 yds. (Grimmett)
1/10-P48 - Ohio State time out 0:18
1/10-P48 - Schlichter to Donley, intercepted Supan in end zone

0:08 PURDUE
1/10-P20 - Oliver at QB, Oliver downs ball, lost 5 yds.

FINAL SCORE:
PURDUE 27, OHIO STATE 16

National Collegiate Athletic Association
FINAL TEAM STATISTICS

	PURDUE	OHIO STATE
First Downs	20	27
Rushing	5	10
Passing	12	13
Penalty	3	4
Rushing Attempts	43	52
Yards Rushing	150	259
Yards Lost Rushing	32	41
Net Yards Rushing	118	518
Net Yards Passing	210	289
Passes Attempted	34	34
Passes Completed	22	20
Had Intercepted	1	1
Total Offensive Plays	77	86
Total Net Yards	328	507
Average Gain Per Play	4.3	5.9
Fumbles: Number—Lost	0/0	6/4
Penalties: Number—Yards	7/85	9/116
Interceptions: Number—Yards	1/0	1/0
Number of Punts—Yards	6/218	2/80
Average Per Punt	36.3	40.0
Punt Returns: Number—Yards	1/23	4/4
Kickoff Returns: Number—Yards	5/100	4/64

WISCONSIN VS. ILLINOIS
Memorial Stadium
Champaign, Illinois
Temp.: 48°
Wind: WNW 20-25 mph
Skies: Partly cloudy
FIRST QUARTER

Wisconsin wins toss, elects to defend North goal; Illinois will receive Brhely kicks off south over end zone

ILLINOIS
1/10-I20 - Weber slants over rt for 3 (Boliaux)
2/7 -I23 - Powell dances over re for 3 (Boliaux)
3/4 -I26 - Weiss keeps around re for 3 (Christenson, Welch)
4/1 -I29 - Weiss sneaks over rg for 2 (Relich, Crossen)
1/10-I31 - Strader over rg for no gain (Crossen)
2/10-I31 - Weiss rolls right completes pass to Barnes for 13 (Boliaux)
1/10-I44 - Strader up middle for 4 (Boliaux, Christenson)
2/6 -I48 - Powell wiggles over rg for 5 (Ahrens, Welch)
3/1 -W47 - Powell on delay over lg for 2 (Christenson)
1/10-W45 - PENALTY: Illinois illegal procedure
1/15-50 - Weiss pass complete to Barnes for 7 (Anderson, Christenson)
2/8 -W43 - Weiss keeps around re for 7 (Welch)
3/1-W36 - Weiss sneaks over middle for 3 (Relich, Holm)
1/10-W33 - Weber up middle for 3 (Holm, Crossen)
2/7 -W30 - Powell slants over lt for 4 (Holm, Welch)
2/3 -W27 - Weiss keeps around re for no gain (Crossen, Relich)
4/3 -W26 - Finzer 43 yard field goal is GOOD
SCORE: ILLINOIS 3, WISCONSIN 0

5:26 WISCONSIN
Finzer kicks off north to Mohapp who falls on ball at 20.
1/10-W20 - Matthews around le for 6 (Sullivan, George)
2/4 -W26 - Pitch to Matthews around le for 2 (Ralph)
3/2 -W28 - Josten keeps around re for 6 and stumbles
1/10-W34 - Stauss over rg for no gain (Ramshaw, Ralph)
2/10-W34 - Josten keeps around re for 4 (Sullivan)
3/6 -W38 - Josten sideline pass for Charles, broken up by George
4/6 -W38 - Kiltz punts to Foster falls on at I23) 39 yard punt

2:18 ILLINOIS
1/10-I23 - Weber over middle for 3 (Crossen, Schremp)
2/7 -I26 - Strader over rg for 4 (Crossen, Holm)
3/3 -I30 - Powell takes pitch around re for 11 (Ahrens)
1/10-I41 - Powell over rg for 2 (Relich, Holm)
PENALTY: Wisconsin personal foul on dead ball
1/10-W42 - Powell takes pitch around re for 6 (Welch)
2/4 -W36 - Strader up middle for 2 (Holm, Schremp)

END OF FIRST QUARTER:
ILLINOIS 3, WSCONSIN 0

SECOND QUARTER
ILLINOIS
3/2 -W34 - Powell over rg for 3 (Cabral, Crossen)
1/10-W31 - Powell up middle for no gain (Relich)
2/10-W31 - Weiss scrambles up middle for 1 (Relich)
3/9 -W30 - Weiss pass complete to Weber for 5, fumbles, recovered by Johnson (W) (Gordon)

13:07 WISCONSIN
1/10-W25 - Stauss up middle for 1 (Thiede)
2/9 -W26 - Josten pass for Charles incomplete
3/9 -W26 - Josten scrambles for 6 (George)
4/3 -W32 - Kiltz punt to Hardy at I33, returns for no gain (35 yard punt)

11:30 ILLINOIS
1/10-I33 - Strader up middle for 5 (Crossen, Cabral)
2/5 -I38 - Weiss keeps around le for 8 (Welch, Johnson)
1/10-I46 - PENALTY: Illinois illegal receiver downfield (nullifies pass to W19)
2/14-I42 - Dismuke on draw for loss of 4, fumbles, Westerlind recovers (Ahrens)
3/18-I38 - Weiss pass to Strader complete for 6 (Holm, Boliaux)
4/12-I44 - Finzer punt to Matthews at W10, returns 9 (46 yard punt)

8:30 WISCONSIN
1/10-W19 - Matthews over rt for 6 (Gillen, Thiede)
2/4 -W25 - Matthews slants over rt for 2 (Sullivan, Ralph)

294

OCTOBER 14, 1978

3/2 -W27 - Josten keeps around re for 4 (Sullivan)
1/10-W31 - Stauss over lg for no gain (Thiede)
2/10-W31 - Stauss up middle for 4 (Thiede)
3/6 -W35 - Josten sacked for loss of 2 (J. Gillen)
4/8 -W33 - Kiltz punt to Hardy, fair catch at I31 (36 yard punt)

5:03 ILLINOIS
1/10-I31 - Weber over rg for 2 (Cabral, Cabral, Crossen)
2/8 -I33 - Powell takes pitch around le for 4 (Anderson)
3/4 -I37 - Weiss scrambles up middle for 8 (Schremp)
1/10-I45 - Powell over rg for 3 (Ahrens, Holm)
2/7 -I48 - Weiss pass for Powell tipped, intercepted by Welch at I33, no return

2:27 WISCONSIN
1/10-W33 - Josten pass to Sydnor complete for 17 (Hardy, Venegoni)
1/10- 50 - Matthews on draw for loss of 2 (Thornton)
2/12-W48 - Matthews on draw for 5 (Thiede)
PENALTY: Illinois personal foul on dead ball
1/10-I32 - Josten pass for Charles, broken up by Venegoni
2/10-I32 - Josten roll out pass for Souza, broken up by Ramshaw
3/10-I32 - Charles takes pitch on reverse, passes to Souza for TOUCHDOWN (Veith extra point is good)
SCORE: WISCONSIN 7, ILLINOIS 3

1:20 ILLINOIS
Brhely kicks off south to Foster at I11 returns 67 yards (Johnson)
1/10-W22 - Scrambles up middle, maintains balance for 13 (Anderson, Johnson)
1/G -W9 - Powell over rt for 1 (Crossen) TO I11 0:36
2/G -W8 - Weiss keeps around re for 4 (Welch) TO Illinois 0:28
3/G -W4 - Weiss slips down attempting to pass for loss of 8
4/G -W12 - Finzer 29 yard field goal is GOOD
SCORE: WISCONSIN 7, ILLINOIS 6

0:14 WISCONSIN
Finzer kicks off south through end zone for touchback
1/10-W20 - Matthews slants over rt for 9 (J. Gillen)

**END OF FIRST HALF:
WISCONSIN 7, ILLINOIS 6**

THIRD QUARTER

ILLINOIS
Brhely kicks off south over end zone for touchback
1/10-I20 - Weiss keeps around rt for 5 (Boliaux)
2/5 -I25 - PENALTY: Wisconsin offsides
1/10-I30 - Weiss keeps around re for 18 (Welch, Gordon)
1/10-I48 - Powell over rg for 6 (Schieble)
2/4 -W46 - Powell over lg for 3 (Ahrens, Schremp)
3/1 -W43 - Weber over rg for 2 (Crossen, Gordon)
1/10-W41 - Powell takes pitch down sidelines for 15 (Johnson)
1/10-W26 - Strader slants over rt for 2 (Holm, Blaskowski)
2/8 -W24 - Powell delay over lg for 8 (Welch)
1/10-W16 - Strader up middle for 2 (Schremp, Relich)
2/8 -W14 - Weiss keeps around re for 7 (Crossen)
3/1 -W7 - Weiss dives for 2 (Ahrens, Blaskowski)
1/G -W5 - Weiss pass to Boeke in end zone for TOUCHDOWN - 5 yards (Foster on reverse for loss of 2 on conversion attempt) TO Illinois (Gordon, Blaskowski)
SCORE: ILLINOIS 12, WISCONSIN 7

10:28 WISCONSIN
Finzer kick to Anderson at W10, returns 26 yards (Doney)
1/10-W36 - Matthews up middle for 16 (Adams) Kalasmiki in at qb
1/10-I48 - Matthews on delay over rg for 1 (Sullivan)
2/9 -I47 - Kalasmiki pass for Charles is dropped
3/9 -I47 - Kalasmiki long pass for Charles broken up by Hardy
4/9 -I47 - Kiltz punts through end zone for touchback (47 yard punt)

9:07 ILLINOIS
1/10-I20 - Weiss keeps around le for 11 (Crossen)
1/10-I31 - Weber over lg for 1 (Holm, Boliaux)
2/9 -I32 - Powell over lg for 3, fumbles recovered by Boliaux (Welch, Anderson)

7:47 WISCONSIN
1/10-I35 - Kalasmiki pass for Souza is overthrown
2/10-I35 - Matthews over rg for 2 (Ramshaw, Flynn)
3/8 -I33 - Kalasmiki pass to Sydnor complete for 11 (Levitt, Ramshaw)
PENALTY: Illinois personal foul after dead ball
1/10-I11 - Matthews takes pitch around re for 1 (Thiede, Ramshaw)
2/9 -I10 - Kalasmiki sacked by Adams for loss of 4
3/13-I14 - Kalasmiki pass for Sydnor incomplete
4/13-I14 - Veith 32 yard field goal attempt is no good

5:30 ILLINOIS
1/10-I20 - Weiss keeps around re for 6 (Holm, Relich)
2/4 -I26 - Powell takes pitch around le for 3 (Anderson)
3/1 -I29 - Weiss sneaks over rg for 3 (Gordon, Boliaux)
1/10-I32 - Powell on delay over lg for no gain (Relich)
2/10-I32 - Weiss keeps around re for 9, fumbles recovered by Anderson (W)

3:54 WISCONSIN
1/10-I41 - Matthews over lg for 1 (Sullivan, Flynn)
2/9-I40 - Kalasmiki turn in pass for Souza complete for 8 (Levitt)
3/1 -I32 - Kalasmiki sneaks over rg for 3 (Sullivan, Thiede)
1/10-I29 - Stauss up middle for 3 (Sullivan)
2/7 -I26 - Souza on reverse around le for 5 (Hardy)
3/2 -I21 - Matthews takes pitch around le for 2 (Ramshaw, Levitt)
1/10-I19 - Kalasmiki pass for Souza incomplete
2/10-I19 - Kalasmiki rollout pass complete to Charles for TOUCHDOWN
(Kalasmiki pass for Charles incomplete TO Wisconsin
SCORE: WISCONSIN 13, ILLINOIS 12

1:39 ILLINOIS
Brhely kicks off south to Dismuke, downed in endzone
1/10-I20 - Weiss keeps around le for 1 (Holm, Boliaux)
2/1 -I21 - Powell takes pitch around re for loss of 5 (Holm)
3/14-I16 - Weiss scrambles up middle for 12 (Holm, Gordon)

**END OF THIRD QUARTER:
WISCONSIN 13, ILLINOIS 12**

FOURTH QUARTER

ILLINOIS
4/2 -I28 - Finzer punt downed at W24 (48 yard punt)

14:51 WISCONSIN
1/10-W24 - Matthews takes pitch around re for 1 (Hardy)
2/9-W25 - Kalasmiki pass for Sydnor, broken up by Ramshaw
3/9 -W25 - Kalasmiki sideline pass complete to Charles for 13 (Venegoni, Tucker)
1/10-W38 - Kalasmiki pass for Charles, intercepted by Hardy at I31, returns 21
PENALTY: Wisconsin personal foul after play dead

13:44 ILLINOIS
1/10-W33 - Weiss dropped loss of 2 (Holm)
2/12-W35 - Weiss pass for Rouse incomplete
3/12-W35 - Weiss sacked for loss of 10 by Boliaux
4/22-W45 - Snap goes over Finzer's head recovered by Holm, loss of 34

12:14 WISCONSIN
1/10-I21 - Kalasmiki carries for 2 (Sullivan)
2/8 -I19 - Kalasmiki scrambles for 1 before stumbling
3/7 -I18 - PENALTY: Illinois pass interference
1/10-I5 -Stauss over rg for 1 (J. Gillen)
2/G -I4 - Matthews around le for 1 (Ramshaw, Venegoni)
3/G -I3 - Kalasmiki alley oop pass to Sydnor for TOUCHDOWN (Veith kick is good)
SCORE: WISCONSIN 20, ILLINOIS 12

9:29 ILLINOIS
Brhely kick to Cozen at I25, returns 6
1/10-I31 - Powell takes pitch around le for loss of 1 (Anderson)
2/11-I30 - Weber over rg for 6 (Crossen, Gordon)
3/5 -I36 - Weiss complete to Rouse for 16 (Gordon, Schieble)
1/10-W48 - Weiss around le for loss of 1 (Relich)
1/10-W49 - Weiss pass for Barnes incomplete

OCTOBER 14, 1978

3/11-W49 - Weiss pass over middle for Barnes complete for 11 (Anderson)
1/10-W38 - Weiss pass to Rouse complete for 9
2/1 -W29 - Powell on draw play for 3 (Crossen, Gordon)
1/10-W26 - Weiss keeps over rg for 6 (Crossen)
2/4 -W20 - Weiss keeps around le for 3 (Crossen)
3/1 -W17 - Weiss over lg for 2 (Ahrens, Crossen)
1/10-W15 - Powell takes pitch around le for 1 (Crossen, Schieble)
2/9 -W14 - Weiss sacked for loss of 7 (Cabral)
3/16-W21 - PENALTY: Wisconsin pass interference
1/10-W11 - Weber over lg for 3 (Holm)
2/7 -W8 - Weiss keeps over rt for TOUCHDOWN (8 yards) Boeke diving catch of Weiss pass for conversion
SCORE: ILLINOIS 20, WISCONSIN 20

2:50 WISCONSIN
(Finzer kicks to Matthews at W3, returns 13)
1/10-W16 - Matthews over lg for 7 (Hardy)
2/3 -W23 - Kalasmiki pass complete to Krepfle for 11
1/10-W34 - Kalasmiki pass for Charles incomplete
2/10-W34 - Kalasmiki pass for Sydnor down sidelines incomplete
3/10-W34 - Kalasmiki turn in pass for Sydnor complete for 17 (Sullivan)
1/10-I49 - Kalasmiki sideline pass for Charles incomplete
2/10-I49 - Kalasmiki pass for Souza is overthrown
3/10-I49 - Kalasmiki pass for Sydnor off his hands
4/10-I49 - Kiltz kick rolls dead at Illinois 22 (27 yard punt)

0:46 ILLINOIS
1/10-I22 - Weiss pass for Burt broken up
2/10-I22 - Weiss long pass down sidelines for Foster incomplete (0:34)
3/10-I22 - Weiss sacked for loss of 7 (Relich) TO Wisconsin
4/17-I15 - Finzer punt to Matthews at W45, returns 7 (40 yard punt)

0:13 WISCONSIN
1/10-I47 - Kalasmiki pass to Matthews complete for 4 (Ramshaw) TO Wisconsin
2/6 -I43 - Kalasmiki pass for Souza broken up by Hardy in end zone

**END OF GAME:
ILLINOIS 20, WISCONSIN 20**

**National Collegiate Athletics Association
FINAL TEAM STATISTICS**
October 14, 1978

	ILLINOIS	WISCON-SIN
First Downs	25	14
By Rushing	18	5
By Passing	3	6
By Penalty	4	3
Rushing Attempts	70	32
Yards Rushing, Gross	257	102
Yards Lost Rushing	69	8
Net Yards Rushing	188	94
Net Yards Passing	71	135
Passes Attempted	13	27
Passes Completed	8	10
Passes Intercepted	1	1
Total Offensive Plays	83	59
Total Net Yards	259	229
Fumbles (No-Lost)	5/4	0/0
Penalties (No-Yards)	5/49	4/45
Interceptions (No-Ret)	1/21	1/0
Punts (No-Yds)	3/134	5/183
Avg. per punt	44.7	36.6
Blocked punts	0	0
Punt Returns (No-Yards)	2/0	3/29
Kickoff Returns	2/73	2/26
Time Of Possession	38:19	21:41

NORTHWESTERN VS. INDIANA
Bloomington, Indiana
Memorial Stadium
Temp: 51°
Wind: NNW 9-10 mph
FIRST QUARTER

Indiana wins toss and will receive,
Northwestern will defend north goal
Mirkopulos kicks off to Johnson at goal,
returned to I25, 25 return

14:55 INDIANA
1/10-I25 - Harkrader le to I37 (12 yards)
1/10-I37 - Johnson rg to I40 (3 yards)
2/7 -I40 - Harkrader re to I43 (3 yards) and Indiana clipping
2/19-I28 - Harkrader le to I30 (2 yards)
3/17-I30 - Harkrader rg to I49 (19 yards)
1/10-I49 - Johnson rg to N48 (3 yards)
2/7 -N48 - Harkrader re to N46 (2 yards)
3/5 -N46 - Arnett pass incomplete to Johnson
4/5 -N46 - Lovett punts to North, fumbled and recovered by Doehla at N7 39 punt

11:44 INDIANA
1/G -N7 - Arnett le for touchdown (7 yards)
PAT—Freud kick good.
SCORE: INDIANA 7, NORTHWESTERN 0

Straub kicks off to Hill at N5, returned to N23, 18 return

11:32 NORTHWESTERN
1/10-N23 - Johnson rg to N25 (2 yards)
2/8 -N25 - Strasser pass intercepted by Wilbur at N40, returned to N24, 16 return

10:54 INDIANA
1/10-N24 - Harkrader lt to N18 (6 yards)
2/4 -N18 - Johnson rg to N16 (2 yards)
3/2 -N16 - Harkrader re to N9 (7 yards)
1/G -N9 - Harkrader lt to N6 (3 yards)
2/G -N6 - Arnett pass complete to Hopkins at N3 (3 yards)
3/G -N3 - Harkrader le to N1 (2 yards)
4/G -N1 - Arnett re for touchdown (1 yard)
PAT—Freud kick good.
SCORE: INDIANA 14, NORTHWESTERN 0

Straub kicks off to Geegan at N8, returned N26, 13 return, fumble recovered by Hunter

8:20 INDIANA
1/10-N26 - Harkrader le to N17 (9 yards)
2/1 -N17 - Johnson rg for touchdown (17 yards)
PAT—Freud kick good.
SCORE: INDIANA 21, NORTHWESTERN 0

Straub kicks off to Hill at N7, returned to I42, 51 return

7:33 NORTHWESTERN
1/10-I43 - Johnson rg to I39 (4 yards)
2/6 -I39 - Strasser pass complete to Poulos to I15 (24 yards)
1/10-I15 - Johnson rg to I10 (5 yards)
2/5 -I10 - Strasser pass complete to Bogan for touchdown (10 yards) PAT—Mirkopulos kick good.
SCORE: INDIANA 21, NORTHWESTERN 7

Mirkopulos kicks off to Johnson at I3, returned to I28, 25 return

6:00 INDIANA
1/10-I28 - Arnett pass complete to Fishel at I33 (5 yards)
2/5 -I33 - Harkrader rg to I32, loss of 1
3/6 -I32 - Harkrader rg to I31, loss of 1
4/7 -I31 - Lovett punts dead at N36, 33 punt

4:14 NORTHWESTERN
1/10-N36 - Hill le to N39 (3 yards)
2/7 -N39 - Strasser trapped to N31, loss of 8
3/15-N31 - Strasser pass complete to Schmitt to N37 (6 yards)
4/9 -N37 - Christenson punts out of bounds at N47 (10 yards)

2:25 INDIANA
1/10-N47 - Harkrader le to N42 (5 yards) but Indiana holding
1/20-I43 - Harkrader lt to 50 (7 yards)
2/13- 50 - Johnson rg to N49 (1 yard)
3/12-N49 - Friede pass incomplete
4/12-N49 - Lovett 1 punt to Geegan at N22, returned to N32 10 return 27 punt

0:57 NORTHWESTERN
1/10-N32 - Cammon rg to N34 (2 yards)
2/8 -N34 - Strasser pass complete to Cammon at N39 (5 yards)

END OF FIRST QUARTER: INDIANA 21, NORTHWESTERN 7
SECOND QUARTER

NORTHWESTERN
3/3 -N39 - Hill re to N38, loss of 1
4/4 -N38 - Christenson punts to Wilbur at I32, no return 30 punt

14:00 INDIANA
1/10-I32 - Harkrader le to I32, no gain
2/10-I32 - Arnett pass intercepted by Kern at I39, no return

13:26 NORTHWESTERN
1/10-I39 - Strasser pass incomplete
2/10-I39 - Strasser lg to I37 (2 yards)
3/8 -I37 - Strasser pass incomplete
4/8 -I37 - Christenson punts dead at I11, 26 punt

OCTOBER 14, 1978

4:05 NORTHWESTERN
1/10-N31 - Hill rg to N35 (4 yards)
2/6 -N35 - Strasser pass complete to Schmitt to N38 (3 yards)
3/3 -N38 - Strasser pass complete to Hill to N42 (4 yards)
1/10-N42 - Schmitt lg to N43 (1 yard)
2/9 -N43 - Strasser pass complete to Poulos at I49 (8 yards)
3/1 -I49 - Johnson re to I44 (5 yards)
1/10-I44 - Strasser pass incomplete
2/10-I44 - Strasser pass complete to Schmitt to I44, no gain
3/10-I44 - Strasser pass complete to Poulos to I28 (16 yards)
1/10-I28 - Strasser pass complete to Poulos to I20 (8 yards)
2/2 -I20 - Strasser pass incomplete in end zone
3/2 -I20 - Strasser pass complete to North at I8 (12 yards)
1/G -I8 - Strasser pass incomplete
2/G -I8 - Strasser pass complete to Hill to I8, no gain
3/G -I8 - Mirkopulos 25 field goal attempt good.
SCORE: INDIANA 24, NORTHWESTERN 10

Mirkopulos kicks off to Pennick at I12, returned to I37, 25 return

**END OF HALF:
INDIANA 24, NORTHWESTERN 10**

THIRD QUARTER

Mirkopulos kicks off to Johnson at goal, returned to I26, 26 return
14:55 INDIANA
1/10-I26 - Arnett pass complete to Fishel to I36 (10 yards)
1/10-I36 - Harkrader lg to I41 (5 yards)
2/5 -I41 - Harkrader rg to I43 (2 yards)
3/3 -I43 - Arnett pass complete to Johnson to N42 (15 yards)
1/10-N42 - Harkrader lt to N33 (9 yards)
2/1 -N33 - Harkrader re to N26 (7 yards)
1/10-N26 - Johnson lg to N23 (3 yards)
2/7 -N23 - Harkrader re to N17 (6 yards)
3/1 -N17 - Arnett pass complete to Hopkins to N11 (6 yards)
1/10-N11 - Harkrader rg to N5 (6 yards)
2/4 -N5 - Harkrader rg for touchdown (5 yards) PAT—(Northwestern offsides) Freud kick good.
SCORE: INDIANA 31, NORTHWESTERN 10

Straub kicks off to Geegan at N5, returned to N19, 14 return
11:04 NORTHWESTERN
1/10-N19 - Johnson rg to N21 (2 yards)
2/8 -N21 - Strasser fumble recovered by Tisdale at N12, loss of 4

12:33 INDIANA
1/10-I11 - Arnett pass incomplete
2/10-I11 - Arnett pass intercepted by Geegan at I44, returned to I20, 24 return

12:16 NORTHWESTERN
1/10-I20 - Johnson lg to I18 (2 yards)
2/8 -I18 - Strasser pass complete to Cammon at I12 (6 yards) and Indiana face mask
1/G -I6 - Johnson rg to 5 (1 yard) fumble recovered by Leake

11:28 INDIANA
1/10-I5 - Harkrader lg to I18 (13 yards)
1/10-I18 - Harkrader lg to I22 (4 yards)
2/6 -I22 - Harkrader lg to I21, loss of 1
3/7 -I21 - Harkrader rg to I34 (13 yards)
1/10-I34 - Johnson lg to I38 (4 yards)
2/6 -I38 - Johnson lg to I46 (8 yards)
1/10-I46 - Johnson lg to N43 (11 yards)
1/10-N43 - Harkrader re to N36 (7 yards)
2/3 -N36 - Johnson rg to N34 (2 yards)
3/1 -N34 - Arnett rg to N31 (3 yards)
1/10-N31 - Harkrader lt to N24 (7 yards)
2/3 -N24 - Johnson lg to N9 (15 yards)
1/G -N9 - Harkrader lg to N9, no gain
2/G -N9 - Arnett lt to N8 (1 yard)
3/G -N8 - Harkrader lg to N5 (3 yards)
4/G -N5 - Freud 22 field goal attempt good.
SCORE: INDIANA 24, NORTHWESTERN 7

Straub kicks off to Hill at N13, returned to N31, 18 return

299

10:02 INDIANA
1/10-N17 - Johnson rg to N12 (5 yards)
2/5 -N12 - Arnett le to N6 (6 yards)
1/G -N6 - Harkrader lt to N5 (1 yard)
2/G -N5 - Johnson rg to N2 (3 yards)
3/G -N2 - Arnett rt for touchdown (2 yards)
PAT—Freud kick good.
SCORE: INDIANA 38, NORTHWESTERN 10

Straub kicks off to Geegan at N10, returned to N28, 18 return
7:51 NORTHWESTERN
1/10-N28 - Washington lg to N34 (6 yards)
2/4 -N34 - Washington le to N32, loss of 2
3/6 -N32 - Strasser pass incomplete
4/6 -N32 - Christenson punts to Wilbur at I28, no return 40 punt

6:26 INDIANA
1/10-I28 - Darring le to I31 (3 yards)
2/7 -I31 - Bowers rt to I37 (6 yards)
3/1 -I37 - Clifford rg to I40 (3 yards)

1/10-I40 - Bowers rg to I39, loss of 1
2/11-I39 - Darring le to I42 (3 yards)
3/8 -I42 - Darring rt to I47 (5 yards)
3/3 -I47 - Lovett punts to Geegan at N17, returned to N20, 3 return 36 punt

3:01 NORTHWESTERN
1/10-N20 - Cammon lg to N19, loss of 1
2/11-N19 - Strasser pass complete to Poulos at N44 (25 yards)
1/10-N44 - Strasser pass incomplete
2/10-N44 - Strasser pass incomplete
3/10-N44 - Strasser trapped at N32, loss of 12
4/22-N32 - Christenson punts to Wilbur at I35, returned to I38, 3 return 33 punt

1:14 INDIANA
1/10-I38 - Darring re to I41 (3 yards)
2/7 -I41 - Darring rt to I47 (6 yards)

**END OF THIRD QUARTER:
INDIANA 38, NORTHWESTERN 10**

OCTOBER 14, 1978

FOURTH QUARTER

INDIANA
3/1 -I47 - Bowers lg to N46 (7 yards)
1/10-N46 - Darring rg to N44 (2 yards)
2/8 -N44 - Bowers lg to N29 (15 yards)
1/10-N29 - Bowers rg to N20 (9 yards)
2/1 -N20 - Bowers rg to N16 (4 yards)
1/10-N16 - Darring re to N12 (4 yards)
2/6 -N12 - Darring re to N14, loss of 2
3/8 -N14 - Bowers rg to N9 (5 yards)
4/3 -N9 - Clifford fumble recovered by Taylor at N12, loss of 3

11:16 NORTHWESTERN
1/10-N12 - Northwestern illegal procedure
1/15-N7 - Johnson lt to N13 (6 yards)
2/9 -N13 - Johnson rg to N20 (7 yards)
3/2 -N20 - Johnson lt to N21 (1 yard)
4/1 -N21 - Christenson punts to Swinehart at N45, fair catch, 24 punt

9:31 INDIANA
1/10-N45 - Brooks fumble recovered by Hemphill at N49, loss of 4

9:24 NORTHWESTERN
1/10-N49 - Strasser pass incomplete
2/10-N49 - Strasser pass complete to Pritchard at I35 (16 yards)
1/10-I35 - Johnson re to I27 (8 yards)
2/2 -I27 - Johnson re to I25 (2 yards) fumbled recovered by Keneipp

8:16 INDIANA
1/10-I25 - Hopkins lg to I38 (13 yards)
1/10-I38 - Hopkins lg to I40 (2 yards)
2/8 -I40 - Hopkins rg to N49 (11 yards)
1/10-N49 - Hopkins rg to N45 (4 yards)
2/6 -N45 - Brooks re to N45, no gain
3/6 -N45 - Hopkins lg to N40 (5 yards)
4/1 -N40 - Hopkins lg to N32 (8 yards)
1/10-N32 - Brooks lg to N32, no gain
2/10-N32 - Hopkins lg to N31 (1 yard)
3/9 -N31 - Brooks re to N28 (3 yards)
4/6 -N28 - Hopkins rg to N24 (4 yards)

2:31 NORTHWESTERN
1/10-N24 - Cammon lg to N29 (5 yards)
2/5 -N29 - Washington rt to N31 (2 yards)
3/3 -N31 - Cammon lt to N34 (3 yards)
1/10-N34 - Breitbeil pass incomplete
2/10-N34 - Breitbeil pass complete to Washington at N39 (5 yards)
3/5 -N39 - Breitbeil pass incomplete
4/5 -N39 - Cammon lg to N42 (3 yards)

0:11 INDIANA
1/10-N42 - Clifford lg to N44, loss of 2

FINAL SCORE:
INDIANA 38, NORTHWESTERN 10

National Collegiate Athletic Association
FINAL TEAM STATISTICS

	NORTH WESTERN	INDIANA
First Downs	10	23
Rushing	2	20
Passing	7	3
Penalty	1	0
Rushing Attempts	28	80
Yards Rushing	75	388
Yards Lost Rushing	28	15
Net Yards Rushing	47	373
Net Yards Passing	148	39
Passes Attempted	28	10
Passes Completed	16	5
Had Intercepted	1	2
Total Offensive Plays	56	90
Total Net Yards	195	412
Average Gain Per Play	3.5	4.6
Fumbles: Number—Lost	6/5	2/2
Penalties: Number—Yards	2/11	3/36
Interceptions: Number—Yards	2/24	1/16
Number Of Punts—Yards	6/163	4/135
Average Per Punt	27	34
Punt Returns: Number—Yards	2/13	3/3
Kickoff Returns: Number—Yards	6/137	4/101

MICHIGAN STATE
VS.
MICHIGAN
Michigan Stadium
Temp: 50°
Wind: NE 11 mph
Skies: Partly cloudy and cool
FIRST QUARTER

TOSS: S won the toss and elected to receive. M defends the north goal.
Virgil kicked off to S. Smith in the S endzone and he ret'd 20 (Needham)
14:54 STATE
1/10-S20 - Smith passed for Gibson incomplete.
2/10-S20 - Smith passed to Middleton for 13 (Simpkins)
1/10-S33 - S.Smith at lt for no gain (Seabron)
2/10-S33 - Smith passed to Brammer for 18 (DeSantis)
1/10-M49 - S.Smith on delay over rt for 14 (Seabron)
1/10-M35 - McGee cut back at rg for 3 (Keitz)
2/7 -M32 - Smith passed for Gibson incomplete.
3/7 -M32 - Smith passed for Byrd incomplete.
4/7 -M32 - Anderson held while Andersen's 49 yd. field goal attempt from the M39 was short. Time: 11:51.

11:51 MICHIGAN
1/10-M32 - Leach passed to Kasparek for 35 (Marshall)
1/10-S33 - Huckleby at rg for 2 (Land)
2/8 -S31 - Davis at rg for 3 (Decker)
3/5 -S28 - Huckleby hit behind le for Land for -3.
4/8 -S31 - Dickey held while Willner's 48 yd. field goal attempt hit the left upright and bounced back no good. Time: 9:31.

STATE
1/10-S31 - S. Smith at lg for 8 (Meter)
2/2 -S39 - Smith passed for Gibson incomplete
3/2 -S39 - Smith passed to Brammer for 13 (Meter)
1/10-M48 - Smith passed to Gibson for 13 (Harden)
1/10-M35 - S. Smith at lt for 7 (Meter)
2/3 -M28 - Middleton at rg for 2 (Simpkins)
3/1 -M26 - Middleton at rg for 1 (Simpkins)
1/10-M25 - McGee took a pitchout at re for 5 (Simpkins)
2/5 -M20 - Smith passed for S. Smith incomplete.
3/5 -M20 - Smith's pass for Byrd broken up by Braman.
4/5 -M20 - Anderson held while Andersen kicked a 38 yd. field goal from the M28. Time: 5:34 69 yds. in 11 plays.
STATE 3 MICHIGAN 0

Schario kicked off to R.Smith on the M5 and he ret'd 2 (McCormick)
5:27 MICHIGAN
1/10-M7 - Leach rolled inside le and sprinted for 37 (Graves)
1/10-M44 - Leach passed for Clayton incomplete at about the S10.
2/10-M44 - Huckleby took a pitchout at re for 5 (Graves)
3/5 -M49 - Leach's pass for Clayton intercepted by Masrshall at the S23 where Clayton tackled him.

4:18 STATE
1/10-S23 - Smith elected to run at center for 6 (Godfrey)
2/4 -S29 - Smith passed to Gibson for 25 (Meter)
1/10-M46 - S. Smith at rt for 5 (Needham)
2/5 -M41 - Smith passed to McGee over center for 10 (Simpkins)
1/10-M31 - Middleton at lg for 1 (Greer)
2/9 -M30 - Smith passed to Brammer for 7 (Bell)
3/2 -M23 -Middleton at center for 1 (Simpkins)

END OF THE QUARTER:
STATE 3 MICHIGAN 0

M had 8 plays for 79 yds. S had 25 plays for 152 yds.

SECOND QUARTER

STATE
4/1 -M22 - McGee took a pitchout at le for 9 (Bell)
1/10-M13 - Middleton at lg for 8 (DeSantis)
2/2 -M5 - Middleton at lg for no gain, BUT S penalized 5 for delay.
2/7 -M10 - Smith passed to Middleton all alone to the right and he went in for the TD. Time: 13:34. Anderson held while Andersen converted.
STATE 10 MICHIGAN 0 77 yds in 10 plays.

Schario kicked off to Clayton in the M endzone and he ret'd 18 (Williams)
MICHIGAN
1/10-M18 - Huckleby took a pitchout at re for 1 Stanton.
2/9 -Leach's pass for Kasparek intercepted by Anderson at the M41 and he ret'd 21 to the M20 (Leach)

12:38 STATE
1/10-M20 - Smith passed to Brammer for 9 (Simpkins)
2/1 -M11 - McGee at rt for 8 (Bell)
1/G -M3 - Middleton at lg for 2 (Keitz)
2/G -M1 - Middleton dove over lg for 1 and the S TD. Time: 10:59
Anderson held while Andersen converted.
20 yds in 4 plays. STATE 17 MICHIGAN 0

OCTOBER 14, 1978

Schario kicked off to R. Smith on the M5 and he ret'd 16 to the M21 (Hans)
10:54 MICHIGAN
1/10-M21 - Davis at rt for 4 (Hay)
2/6 -M25 - Huckleby took a pitchback at re for 6 (Fields)
1/10-M31 - Leach rolled left and kept and Hay hit him for −4.
2/14-M27 - Huckleby on delay at lg for 8 (Savage)
3/6 -M35 - Leach passed over Kasparek incomplete.
4/6 -M35 - Willner punted to S. Smith on the S 30 and he ret'd 5 (35 yd. punt) (DeSantis)

8:18 STATE
1/10-S35 - Middleton at lg for 4 (Simpkins)
2/6 -S39 - Smith passed to Brammer for 11 (DeSantis)
1/10- 50 - Schramm at lt for 2 (Trgovac)
2/8 -M48 - Smith passed to McGee for 3 (Simpkins)
3/5 -M45 - Smith elected to run and went down the left sideline for 30, where Harden pushed him out at the M15.
1/10-M15 - McGee at rt for 4 (Trgovac)
2/6 -M11 - S. Smith at lt for 1 (Greer)
3/5 -M10 - Smith passed incomplete in the endzone over Brammer.

4/5 -M10 - Smith passed for Schramm incomplete with coverage by Seabron.

4:23 MICHIGAN
1/10-M10 - Davis at lg for 15 (McCormick)
1/10-M25 - Davis at center for 3 (Hay)
2/7 -M28 - Davis at rt for 7 (Hay)
1/10-M35 - Davis at lg for 5 (Decker)
2/5 -M40 - Leach rolled right and made 8
1/10-M48 - Leach passed for Schmerge and Marshall intercepted on the S30 and he ret'd 22 BUT S penalized for clipping to the S15.

2:17 STATE
1/10-S15 - Middleton at center for no gain (Trgovac)
2/10-S15 - S. Smith on draw at lt for 18 (Bell)
1/10-S33 - McGee hit by Keitz for '2.
2/12-S31 - S. Smith on draw at center for 11 (Simpkins)
3/1 -S42 - Schramm at lg for 2 (Keitz)
1/10-S44 - Smith's pass for Gibson caught out of bounds by Jolly.
2/10-S44 - McGee on draw at rg for 23 (Bell)
END OF THE HALF:
STATE 17 MICHIGAN 0

M had 13 plays for 53 yds. S had 23 plays for 155 yds.

303

THIRD QUARTER

M elects to receive. S defends the north goal. Schario kicked off to Leoni on the M19 and he ret'd 11 (Cooper).
14:53 MICHIGAN
1/10-M30 - Huckleby took pitchout at re for 3 (Graves)
2/7 -M33 - Huckleby took pitchback at le for 15 (Anderson)
1/10-M48 - Leach slipped at le for 1 (Decker)
2/9 -M49 - Leach passed to Huckleby in right flat for 5 (Fields)
3/4 -S46 - Huckleby on delay at lg for 6 (Decker)
1/10-S40 - Davis at lg for 3 (Land)
2/7 -S37 - Leach cut up at lt for 3 (Fields)
3/4 -S34 - Huckleby at rg for 4 (Land)
1/10-S30 - Davis at center for 7 (Bass)
2/3 -S23 - Davis at lt for 2 (Hay)
3/1 -S21 - Davis at rg for 4 (Fields)
1/10-S17 - Huckleby off rt for 3 (Anderson)
2/7 -S14 - Huckleby at re for 4 (Stanton)
3/3 -S10 - Huckleby cut off rt for 4 (Bass)
1/G -S6 - Huckleby at rt for 2 (Bass)
2/G -S4 - Leach kept off lt for 1 (Land)
3/G -S3 - Leach rolled right and dove over Davis for the M TD.
Dickey held while Willner converted.
Time: 6:42 STATE 17 MICHIGAN 7 70 yds in 17 plays

Virgil kicked off to Schramm on the S19 and he ret'd 11; Trgovac.

6:38 STATE
1/10-S30 - Smith passed to Gibson for 15
1/10-S45 - McGee cut back at rt for 3 (Simpkins)
2/7 -S48 - Smith passed to S. Smith for 7 (Seabron)
1/10-M45 - Smith's pass for Brammer almost intercepted by Bell.
2/10-M45 - S. Smith hit by Simpkins for 15 on delay.
3/15- 50 - Smith passed to Byrd for 20 (DeSantis)
1/10-M30 - Smith passed to Schramm for 7, AND M penalized for personal foul to the M11.
1/10-M11 - Smith passed to Brammer in the right flat and he went in for the S TD, shaking off Jolly for the last 3 yds. Anderson held while Andersen converted.
Time: 3:45 STATE 24 MICHIGAN 7 70 yds. in 8 plays.

Schario kicked off to Huckleby on the M5 and he ret'd 21, BUT M penalized for clipping to the M10.
3:37 MICHIGAN
1/10-M10 - Leach spun and went over lt for 3 (Savage)
2/7 -M13 - Leach passed to Clayton for 9 (Graves)
1/10-M22 - Davis at rg for 5 (Bass)
2/5 -M27 - Huckleby took a pitchback and cut up for 10 (Bass)
1/10-M37 - Leach passed to Marsh for 45 (Stanton)
1/10-S18 - Huckleby at re for 3 (Decker)
2/7 -S15 - Leach rolled left for 1 (Decker)
3/6 -S14 - Huckleby at rg for 5 (Land)
4/1 -S9 -

END OF THE QUARTER:
STATE 24 MICHIGAN 7

M had 25 plays for 151 yds. S had 8 plays for 58 yds.

FOURTH QUARTER

MICHIGAN
4/1 -S9 - Huckleby took a pitchback at re for 6 (Graves)
1/G -S3 - Davis at lt for 3 and the M TD.
Time: 14:37 Leach passed to Huckleby for the 2 extra points.
STATE 24 MICHIGAN 15 90 yds in 10 plays

OCTOBER 14, 1978

Virgil kicked off to S. Smith in the S endzone where he downed it.

14:37 STATE
1/10-S20 - S. Smith caught behind rt by Godfrey for '3.
2/13-S17 - Gibson on a double reverse at re for 10 (Jolly)
3/3 -S27 - Smith passed for Brammer incomplete.
4/3 -S27 - Stachowicz punted to Jolly who ret'd from the M27 to the M34, BUT M penalized 15 for illegal substitution.
1/10-S42 - Smith passed to Gibson for 15 (DeSantis)
1/10-M43 - Smith passed to Brammer for 10, BUT S penalized for clipping to the M49.
1/16-M49 - Smith's pass for Gibson incomplete
2/16-M49 - Smith's pass for Gibson incomplete
3/16-M49 - Smith passed to Gibson for 14 (Braman)
4/2 -M35 - Smith passed for Gibson incomplete

12:09 MICHIGAN
1/10-M35 - Davis at lt for 10 (Land)
1/10-M45 - Davis at rg for 4 (Fields)
2/6 -M49 - Leach passed for Kasparek incomplete.
3/6 -M49 - Leach's pass for Marsh incomplete.
4/6 -M49 - Willner punted to S. Smith, fair catch at the S 8 (43 yd. punt)

10:52 STATE
1/10-S8 - Schramm at lt for 6 (Simpkins)
2/4 -S14 - Reeves hit by Greer behind lt for '3.
3/7 -S11 - Smith passed to S. Smith for 17 (Bell)
1/10-S28 - Smith passed for Howard incomplete.
2/10-S28 - S. Smith got 1 at rt (Bell)
3/9 -S29 - Smith's pass for Brammer broken up by Bell.
4/9 -S29 - Stachowicz' punt downed on the M25 (46 yd. punt)

8:05 MICHIGAN
1/10-M25 - Huckleby at center for 5 (Decker)
2/5 -M30 - Leach passed to Huckleby for 4 (McCormick)
3/1 -M34 - Leach at rt for 2 (Decker)
1/10-M36 - Huckleby at center for 4, BUT M penalized 5 for ill. motion.
1/15-M31 - Davis at rt for 4 (Fields)
2/11-M35 - Leach's pass broken up by Hay.
3/11-M35 - Huckleby on delay at lt for 9 (McCormick)
4/2 -M44 - Davis rolled off rt for 6 (Graves)
1/10- 50 - Leach's pass for Kasparek incomplete.
2/10- 50 - Leach's pass for Davis incomplete BUT M penalized for ineligible receiver downfield.
2/25-M35 - Leach's pass for Davis incomplete, broken up by Anderson.
3/25-M35 - Leach hit by Fields for —5.
4/30-M30 - Willner punted to S. Smith on the S31, where he fumbled it out of bounds. (39 yd. punt)

3:29 STATE
1/10-S31 - Hans at center for no gain (Meter)
2/10-S31 - Reeves took a pitchback at re for 5 (Meter)
3/5 -S36 - Hans at center for 5 (Simpkins)
1/10-S41 - Reeves hit behind le by Simpkins for '2.
2/12-S39 - S. Smith at lt for 16 (Harden)
1/10-M45 - Hughes took a pitchback at re for 26 (Harden).
1/10-M19 - S. Smith on delay at rt for 14 (Harden)
1/G -M5 - Smith kept at center, BUT S penalized 5 for ill. proc.
1/G -M10 - Smith fell down at center for no gain.

END OF THE GAME:
STATE 24   MICHIGAN 15

M had 16 plays for 48 yds. S had 22 plays for 131 yds.

305

IOWA VS. MINNESOTA
Memorial Stadium
Minnesota
Temp.: 44°
Wind: SW at 7
Skies: Cloudy

FIRST QUARTER

Minnesota wins toss, to receive and defend east goal.
Schilling kick off to Edwards downs ball in end zone.

15:00 MINNESOTA
1/10-M20 - Carlson pass down middle to Bourquin off hands and incomplete
2/10-M20 - Barber quick pitch left 8 yards (Molini)
3/2-M28 - Barber quick pitch right 3 yd loss (Becker, Hobbs)
4/5 -M25 - Smith punt fair catch by Becker (38 yd punt)

13:39 IOWA
1/10-I37 - Gales pass into right flat intercepted by Johnson, stumbles down after 4 yd runback

13:33 MINNESOTA
1/10-I34 - Kitzmann up middle 3 yards (Benschoter)
2/7 -I31 - Barber quick pitch left, cuts back 3 yards (Hobbs)
3/4 -I28 - Carlson pass complete to Barber 8 yards (Gutschall)
1/10-I20 - Kitzmann at lt 2 yards (Harty)
2/8 -I18 - Carlson rollout keeper right 4 yards (Hill, Danzy)
3/4 -I14 - Kitzmann at rt 2 yards (Hill, Harty)
4/2 -I12 - Kitzmann at lt no gain (team)

IOWA
1/10-I12 - Burke sweep right 1 yard (Ronan, Brown)
2/9 -I13 - Gales pass beyond line of scrimmage/penalty/ 4 yds
3/13-I9 - Burke sweep left/runs out of bounds 3 yard gain (Johnson)
4/10-I12 - Holsclaw punt to Bailey fair catch on M45 43 yard punt

8:00 MINNESOTA
1/10-M45 - Carlson pass off Kitzmann's hands, almost intercepted by Hill
2/10-M45 - Carlson back to pass, rushed and tackled by Beschoter & Hobbs 5 yd loss
3/15-M40 - Carlson pass complete to Bailey crossing right to left (Pace) 20 yd gain
1/10-I40 - Barber pitch left, cuts back for 7 yards (Pace)

2/3 -I33 - Barber up middle 5 yards (Harty)
1/10-I28 - Kitzmann straight ahead 2 yards (Benschoter, Molini)
2/8 -I26 - Carlson pass to Kitzmann left flat/delayed release 8 yds (Pace)
1/10-I18 - Kitzmann up middle no gain (Molini)
2/10-I18 - Carlson pass to Bailey in end zone high and incomplete
3/10-I18 - Carlson pass complete to Dilulo delay into left flat 11 yards (Becker, Danzy)
1/G -I7 - Kitzmann at lt 3 yards (Danzy, Hobbs)
2/G -I4 - Kitzmann at rt 3 yards (Becker, Rusk)
3/G -I1 - Kitzmann scored TD from 1 yard out (rt) 55 yard drive in 13 plays
Rogind to kick, bad pass from center, Carlson picks up ball and passes incomplete to Sonnenfeld
SCORE: MINNESOTA 6, IOWA 0

Rogind kick off to Reed on I1, returns 24 yards (Fahnhorst)

IOWA
1/10-I25 - Gales pass intended for Burke high and incomplete
2/10-I25 - Burke pitch/sweep left no gain (Friberg, Foxworth)
3/10-I25 - Lazar pass from Gales 1 yard gain (Johnson)
4/9 -I26 - Hollslaw punt to Edwards returns 16 yards (Hilgenberg) Minnesota clipping (Blanshan) 15 Yard penalty 47 yard punt

MINNESOTA
1/10-M28 - Barber quick pitch right 5 yards (Hobbs)
2/5 -M33 - Kitzmann at rt 3 yards (Harty)
3/2 -M36 - Kitzmann at rt 4 yards (Dean)
1/10-M40 - Carlson pass complete to Thompson right flat 11 yds (Pace)
1/10-I49 - Barber quick pitch right, runs out of bounds 9 yards
2/1 -I40 - Kitzmann breaks open at rt 5 yards (Rusk)

END OF FIRST QUARTER: MINNESOTA 6, IOWA 0

SECOND QUARTER

MINNESOTA
1/10-I35 - Carlson pass complete to Barber right to left 17 yds (Becker)
1/10-I18 - Barber quick pitch left 1 yd gain (Mahmens)
2/9 -I17 - Carlson pass complete to Bailey in end zone 17 yd TD :51 elapsed 72 yd drive in 9 plays Carlson pass intended for Barber NO GOOD
SCORE: MINNESOTA 12, IOWA 0

OCTOBER 14, 1978

Rogind kick off to Reid on goal line returns 25 yards (Fahnhorst)
IOWA
1/10-I25 - Lazar at rt 3 yds (Friberg)
2/7 -I28 - Green fumbles handoff, picks up and passes complete to Lazar 5 yds
3/2 -I33 - Green pass complete to Dunham, comes back for catch 25 yds (Foxworth)
1/10-M42 - Lazar at lt 2 yds (Johnson)
2/8 -M40 - Morton flanker reverse 5 yds (Sytsma, Burns)
3/3 -M35 - Mosley quick pitch right 3 yds (Johnson)
1/10-M32 - Lazar at lt 2 yds (Friberg)
2/8 -M30 - Green pass diving interception by Sytsma on I25

10:40 MINNESOTA
1/10-M25 - Artis quick pitch left 3 yds (Molini, Hill)
2/7 -M28 - Artis quick pitch right, breaks open 8 yds (Danzy)
1/10-M36 - White at rt 2 yds (Molini, Skradis)
2/8 -M38 - Carlson back to pass, Vazquez tackle for 6 yd loss
3/14-M32 - Minnesota in motion 5 yd penalty
3/19-M27 - Carlson to White pass complete 9 yd gain (Rusk)
4/10-M38 - Smith punt fair catch but Iowa penalized for running into kicker 15 yds
1/10-I49 - Barber quick pitch left 9 yards (Danzy)
2/1 -I40 - Carlson quick look-in left to Bourquin 11 yds (Pace, Danzy)
1/10-I29 - Barber runs left, runs out of bounds after 6 yd gain
2/4 -I23 - White at rt 1 yd (Harty)
3/3 -I22 - Kitzmann at rt 5 yds (Gutschall, Danzy)
1/10-I17 - Carlson pass complete to Bailey 17 yd TD complete on 75 yds in 12 plays Rogind kick good (40th straight)
SCORE: MINNESOTA 19, IOWA 0

Rogind kickoff to Blatcher on I3, returns 17 yards (Brown)
IOWA
1/10-I20 - Green keeper rollout left 3 yds (Cunningham)
2/7 -I23 - Green pass complete to Dunham, runs to M47 30 yds (Sytsma)
1/10-M47 - Green pass complete to Mosley 12 yds (Brown)
1/10-M35 - Mosley pitch right 1 yd gain (Foxworth)
2/9 -M34 - Green back to pass, rushed, escapes up middle 20 yds (Foxworth)
1/10-M14 - Green passes complete to Mosley 3 yds (Johnson)
2/7 -M11 - Green pass incomplete, Iowa illegal procedure, declined

3/7 -M11 - Mosley quick pitch left 3 yd gain (Brown)
4/4 -M8 - Green pass knocked down by Brown in end zone, Minnesota takes over

MINNESOTA
1/10-M8 - White up middle 2 yds (team)
2/8 -M10 - Artis quick pitch left 1 yd (Mahmens)
3/7 -M11 - Kitzmann at lt 4 yds (Mahmens)
4/3 -M15 - Smith punt to Becker, runs OOB (49 yd punt) 5 yd runback

IOWA
1/10-I41 - Green pass knocked down in line by Blanshan incomplete
2/10-I41 - Green pass complete to Lazar 3 yds (Foxworth)
3/6 -I45 - Green pass intended for Swift, Burns called for interference 7 yd penalty
1/10-M48 - Green complete to Morton right flat 9 yards (Brown)
2/1 -M39 - Green pass to Morton down right sidelines long and incomplete
3/1 -M39 - Green back to pass, Brown blitz from rightside, tackle for 9 yd loss
4/10-M48 - Holsclaw punt allowed to roll dead on M1 47 yard kick

MINNESOTA
1/10-M1 - Carson QB sneak 2 yds (team)

END OF FIRST HALF:
MINNESOTA 19, IOWA 0

307

THIRD QUARTER

Rogind kickoff to Blatcher, runs up right sidelines for 32 yards (Brown)
14:53 IOWA
1/10-I35 - Green back to pass, short and incomplete
2/10-I35 - Lazar draw up middle 2 yds (Blanshan, Friberg)
3/8 -I37 - Green back to pass, runs up middle for 3 yds (Sytsma)
4/5 -I40 - Holsclaw punt/Iowa illegal procdure 5 yd penalty
4/10-I35 - Holsclaw punt fair catch by Failey, fumbles and recovers 30 yd punt

13:24 MINNESOTA
1/10-M36 - Barber quick pitch left 19 yards (Skradis)
1/10-I45 - Kitzmann at lt 3 yds (Mahmens)
2/7 I42 - Carlson pass complete to Kitzmann over middle 15 yds (Pace)
1/10-I27 - Barber quick pitch, slides off lt 9 yds (Rusk)
2/1 -I18 - Kitzmann at lt 3 yards (Mahmens)
1/10-I15 - Kitzmann at lt 2 yards (Mahmens)
2/8 -I13 - Barber up middle 3 yards (Mahmens, Becker)
3/5 -I10 - Artis quick pitch left no gain (Pace)
4/5 -I10 - Rogind field goal attempt from 27 yards GOOD, 54 yards in 8 plays, field goal on 9th play
SCORE: MINNESOTA 22, IOWA 6

Rogind kickoff to Blatcher on goal line, returns 16 yards (Cunningham)
9:38 IOWA
1/10-I16 - Mosley at rt 3 yards (Burns)
2/7 -I19 - Green moves right, Murphy makes tackle for 3 yd loss
3/9 -I17 - Green pass long and OOB incomplete intended for Reid
4/9 -I17 - Holsclaw punt to Edwards on M44, gets 13 yds (Gutshall) 39 yd punt

8:07 MINNESOTA
1/10-I43 - Carlson pass intended for Dilulo over middle long and incomplete
2/10-I43 - Carlson pass complete to Barber over middle 9 yds (Weiss, Vazquez)
3/1 -I34 - Kitzmann running/Bourquin off side 5 yd penalty
3/6 -I39 - Carlson back to pass, rushed, escapes two tackles 2 yds (Harty, Schlickman)
4/4 -I37 - Smith punt downed by Gophers on I7 30 yd punt

6:15 IOWA
1/10-I7 - Mosley quick pitch/right no gain (Sytsma)
2/10-I7 - Green pass complete to Swift 24 yds (Edwards) face mask call adds 15 yd penalty

1/10-I46 - Reid flanker reverse right 9 yards
2/1 -M45 - Lazar draw, breaks away up middle, 33 yards (Edwards)
1/10-M12 - Green keeper right 1 yard (Cunningham)
2/9 -M11 - Mosley quick pitch left 9 yards (Johnson)
1/G -M2 - Lazar at rt 1 yard (Johnson)
2/G -M1 - Green QB sneak no gain (team)
3/G -M1 - Green QB sneak for 1 yd TD 93 yard drive in 9 plays, Green pass for 2 points, knocked down by Johnson
SCORE: IOWA 6, MINNESOTA 22

Schilling kickoff to Edwards returns 26 yards (Woodland) M clipping 15 yd penalty
2:30 MINNESOTA
1/10-M12 - Barber at rt 1 yard (Pace, Weiss)
2/9 -M13 - Barber at lt 2 yards (Harty, Hill)
3/7 -M15 - Barber quick pitch left, breaks tackle and into open 29 yards (Pace)
1/10-M44 - Kitzmann at rt 3 yards (Benschoter)
2/7 -M47 - Carlson pass complete over middle to Kitzmann 6 yds (Molini)
3/1-I47 - Kitzmann at rt 2 yards (Rusk)

END OF THIRD QUARTER:
MINNESOTA 22, IOWA 6

FOURTH QUARTER

MINNESOTA
1/10-I45 - Carlson pass intended for Bailey intercepted by Becker

14:54 IOWA
1/10-I11 - Green pass (fly up right sidelines) complete to Reid 60 yds (Edwards)
1/10-M29 - Green pass down middle for Mosley long and incomplete
2/10-M29 - Mosley at lt, Friberg crashing/tackle for 3 yd loss
3/13-M32 - Green screen pass right complete to Mosley 21 yards (Murphy)
1/10-M11 - Reid flanker reverse left (Swift makes key block) 11 yd TD 89 yard drive in 5 plays, Morton runs right (2 pts)
SCORE: MINNESOTA 22, IOWA 14

OCTOBER 14, 1978

Schilling kickoff goes over end line touchback
13:15 MINNESOTA
1/10-M20 - Kitzmann at lt 2 yards (Simonsen)
2/8 -M22 - Barber quick pitch right, fumbles after 8 yards, Danzy recovers for Iowa

12:29 IOWA
1/10-M30 - Morton halfback pass intended for Reid, Burns knocks ball away incomplete
2/10-M30 - Mosley option pitch right 2 yards (Foxworth, Brown) IA Palladino holding 15 yd penalty
2/23-M43 - Lazar draw up middle 5 yards (Burns)
3/18-M38 - Green pass over middle short and incomplete
4/18-M38 - Holsclaw punt high and allowed to roll dead on M8 30 yd punt

11:53 MINNESOTA
1/10-M8 - Barber pitch left 5 yards (Simonsen, Danzy)
2/5 -M13 - Kitzmann at lt 2 yards (Simonsen)
3/3 -M15 - Kitzmann up middle, fumbles when hit, ball rolls for first down and Thompson covers for Gophers Kitzmann gets 7 yd gain
1/10-M22 - Barber fumbles pitch, I's Harty recovers on M19 3 yd rushing loss

10:13 IOWA
1/10-M19 - Mosley sweep right 5 yards (Murphy)
2/5 -M14 - Lazar up middle 1 yard (Ronan, Friberg)
3/4 -M13 - Green screen pass left to Mosley 9 yds (Edwards)
1/G -M4 - Lazar up middle 3 yards (team)
2/G -M1 - Lazar up middle no gain (team)
3/G -M1 - Lazar at lt no gain (team)
4/G -M1 - Green rolls right/keeper 1 yd TD 19 yard drive in 7 plays, Green rolls left, trapped, rolls back and chased/tackle
• Friberg conversion fails
SCORE: MINNESOTA 22, IOWA 20

Schilling kickoff sails over end line touchback
7:07 MINNESOTA
1/10-M20 - Kitzmann at lt 3 yards (Harty, Simonsen)
2/7 -M23 - Artis pitch left 2 yd loss (Molini, Pace)
3/9 -M21 - Carlson pass complete to Thompson, breaks two tackles 16 yds (Becker)
1/10-M37 - Kitzmann up middle 2 yards (Harty, Simonsen)
2/8 -M39 - Artis pitch right 1 yd loss (Schlickman)
3/9 -M38 - Carlson back to pass, rushed and tackled for 13 yd loss Harty and Dean

4/22-M25 - Smith punt hits short and rolls dead on I37 38 yd punt

3:10 IOWA
1/10-I37 - Green back to pass, rushed, runs, finally throws incomplete
2/10-I37 - Green option keeper right 3 yards (Johnson)
3/7 -I40 - Green pass complete to Mosley 3 yards (Foxworth)
4/4 -I43 - Green pass for Swift long and incomplete

1:59 MINNESOTA
1/10-I43 - Barber at rt Kitzmann 3 yds (Pace)
2/7 -I40 - Minnesota delay of game 5 yd penalty
2/12-I45 - Kitzmann at rt 2 yards (Dean)
3/10-I43 - Kitzmann at rt no gain (Weiss)
4/10-I43 - Minnesota delay of game 5 yd penalty
4/15-I48 - Carlson rolls out left loses 3 yds as time runs out

END OF GAME:
MINNESOTA 22, IOWA 20

National Collegiate Athletic Association
FINAL TEAM STATISTICS
October 14, 1978

	IOWA	MIN-NESOTA
First Downs	14	21
Rushing	5	10
Passing	7	11
Penalty	2	0
Rushing Attempts	37	62
Yards Rushing	141	234
Yards Lost Rushing	14	35
Net Yards Rushing	127	199
Net Yards Passing	206	175
Passes Attempted	27	19
Passes Completed	13	14
Had Intercepted	2	1
Total Offensive Plays	64	81
Total Net Yards	333	374
Average Gain Per Play	5.2	4.6
Fumbles: Number—Lost	1/0	4/2
Penalties: Number—Yards	4/40	8/72
Interceptions: Number—Yards	1/0	2/6
Number of Punts—Yards	6/236	4/155
Average Per Punt	39.3	38.8
Punt Returns: Number—Yards	1/5	3/29
Kickoff Returns: Number—Yards	5/114	1/27

OCTOBER 21, 1978

PURDUE VS. ILLINOIS
Memorial Stadium
Temp: 67°
Wind S 19 mph
Skies: Sunny, clear

FIRST QUARTER

Illinois wins toss and elects to receive, Purdue will defend south goal
Sovereign kicks off north to Foster at goal line, return to I20
ILLINOIS
1/10-I20 - Weber over rg for no gain (Loushin)
2/10-I20 - Weber over rg for 4 (Johanson)
3/6 -I24 - Weiss scrambles up middle for 4 (Mott, Johanson)
4/2 -I28 - Finzer punts to Gallivan at P36, returns 5 (36 yard punt)

12:51 PURDUE
1/10-P41 - Herrmann sideline pass to Burrell for 6 (Levitt, Ramshaw)
2/4 -P47 - PENALTY: Purdue illegal procedure
2/9 -P42 - Macon around re for 5 (Sullivan)
3/4 -P47 - Macon spins around re for 6 (Sullivan, Gillen)
1/10-I47 - Pope on delay up middle for 2 (Ralph)
2/8 -I45 - Pope slants over rg for 3 (Adams)
3/5 -I42 - Herrmann sideline pass to Burrell complete for 5 (Levitt)
1/10-I37 - Herrmann sacked for loss of 5 (Flynn, Adams)
2/15-I42 - Ball slips from Herrmann's hands for incomplete pass
3/15-I42 - Herrmann pass over middle to Pope complete for 5 (Sullivan, Venegoni)
4/10-I37 - Linville punts through end zone (37 yard punt)

9:20 ILLINOIS
1/10-I20 - Weber over rg for 3 (Johanson)
2/7 -I23 - Strader up middle fumbles, recovered by Floyd (P)

8:40 PURDUE
1/10-I25 - Macon around le for 9
2/1 -I16 - Macon fumbles into line for 1, fumbles, recovered by Hardy

8:27 ILLINOIS
1/10-I15 - Strader over lg for 2 (Motts)
2/8 -I17 - Weiss around re for 4 (Moss)
3/4 -I21 - Powell on delay over lg for 1 (Jackson, Motts)
4/3 -I22 - Finzer punt downed at I49 (27 yard punt)

6:30 PURDUE
1/10-I49 - Herrmann sacked by Thornton for loss of 10
2/20-P41 - Macon over lt for 3 (Sullivan)
3/17-P44 - Macon on draw over lt for 8 (Ramshaw, J. Gillen)
4/9 -I48 - Linville punts through end zone (48 yard punt)

4:50 ILLINOIS
1/10-I20 - Weber over rg for 2 (Motts)
2/8 -I22 - Weiss roll out pass to Strader complete for 17 (Johanson)
1/10-I39 - Weiss over lg for 3 (Moss)
2/7 -I42 - Weiss hit attempting to throw by Clark, incomplete pass
3/7 -I42 - Weiss sacked for loss of 11 (Turner)
4/18-I31 - Finzer punt to Pope at P34, returned 4 (35 yard punt)

2:32 PURDUE
1/10-P38 - Pope around le for loss of 1 (J. Gillen)
2/11-P37 - Herrmann pass to Macon is dropped
3/11-P37 - Herrmann pass over middle to Pope complete for 6 (Adams)
4/5 -P43 - PENALTY: Illinois illegal substitution (12 men)
1/10-I41 - Macon up middle for 1 (Flynn)
2/9 -I40 - Herrmann sideline pass thrown behind Burrell
3/9 -I40 - Herrmann pass over middle to Macon complete for 10 (J. Gillen)
1/10-I30 - Macon around le for 6 (Sullivan, J. Gillen)

END OF FIRST QUARTER
ILLINOIS 0 PURDUE 0

SECOND QUARTER

PURDUE
2/4 -I24 - Pope slants over re for 1 (Sullivan, Flynn)
3/3 -I23 - PENALTY: Purdue illegal procedure
3/8 -I28 - Pope on delay over le for 3 (Durrell, Flynn)
4/5 -I25 - Herrmann pass intercepted by Adams at I20, intended for Young

13:43 ILLINOIS
1/10-I20 - Weber over lg for 3 (Jackson)
2/7 -I23 - Weiss sideline pass complete to Rouse for 9 and out of bounds
1/10-I32 - Weiss keeps around re for 1 (Marks)
2/9 -I33 - Weiss on quarterback draw up middle for 12 (Floyd, Motts)
1/10-I45 - Strader over lg for 18 (W. Smith)
1/10-P37 - Strader up middle for 3 (Loushin)
2/7 -P34 - Weiss pass complete to Strader for 20 (W. Smith)
1/10-P14 - Weiss keeps over lg for 1 (Turner)
2/9 -P13 - Perez fumbles going up middle for loss of 3, recovered by Jackson (P)

310

OCTOBER 21, 1978

9:33 PURDUE
1/10-P16 - Macon up middle for 3 (Flynn)
2/7 -P19 - Herrmann swing pass to Pope complete for loss of 3 (Ramshaw)
3/10-P16 - Macon on draw play for 9 (Hardy)
4/1 -P25 - Linville punt to Hardy, fair catch at I48 (27 yard punt)

8:14 ILLINOIS
1/10-I48 - Weiss keeps around le for 3 (Jackson, Johanson)
2/7 -P49 - Weiss around le for loss of 4 (Turner)
3/11-I47 - Powell on draw play for 4 (Motts)
4/7 -P49 - Finzer punt rolls through end zone (49 yard punt)

6:20 PURDUE
1/10-P20 - Macon up middle for 6 (Adams, Sullivan)
2/4 -P26 - Macon on delay over rt for 3 (Ramshaw)
3/1 -P29 - Macon on delay over rg for 1 (Ramshaw)
1/10-P30 - Macon around re for 5 (Sullivan)
2/5 -P35 - PENALTY: Purdue illegal procedure
2/10-P30 - Herrmann pass over middle complete to Burrell for 20 (Sullivan)
1/10- 50 - Macon around re for 7 (Sullivan)
2/3 -I43 - Pope on delay over lg for 2 (J. Gillen)
3/1 -I41 - Macon up middle for 4 (Ramshaw)
1/10-I37 - Herrmann sideline pass to Harris complete for 2 (Tucker)
2/8 -I35 - Pope on inside reverse for 11 (Venegoni)
1/10-I24 - Herrmann pass for Burrell near goal line incomplete
2/10-I24 - Herrmann pass in end zone for Young, broken up by Levitt
3/10-I24 - Herrmann pass over middle to Young for 11 (Sullivan)
1/10-I13 - Macon on draw for loss of 1 (Ralph)
2/11-I14 - Herrmann pass over middle to Harris complete for touchdown
Sovereen extra point is good
SCORE: PURDUE 7 ILLINOIS 0

Sovereen kicks off to Rouse at I14, returns 14 fumbles but recovers
0:35 ILLINOIS
1/10-I28 - Powell takes option pitch around re for no gain (W. Smith)

END OF FIRST HALF
PURDUE 7 ILLINOIS 0

THIRD QUARTER

Finzer kicks off to Moss in end zone, downed for touchback
PURDUE
1/10-P20 - Pope over rt for 2 (Sullivan)
2/8 -P22 - Macon up middle for 1 (Ralph, J. Gillen)
3/7 -P23 - Herrmann pass to Pope for 17 (Tucker)
1/10-P40 - Pope around re for 5 (Hardy)
2/5 -P45 - Macon over rt for no gain (Flynn)
3/5 -P45 - Herrmann delay pass to Pope complete for 6 (Venegoni)
1/10-I49 - Macon over lt for 9 (Adams, Hardy)
2/1 -I40 - Macon over lg for 4 (Sullivan)
1/10-I36 - Pope around le for 9 (Sullivan)
2/1 -I27 - Macon up middle for 4 (Thornton, Sullivan)
1/10-I23 - Macon over lt for 4 (J. Gillen)
2/6 -I19 - Macon around le for 8 (Sullivan)
1/10-I11 - Macon up middle for 2 (Flynn, Durrell)
2/8 -I9 - Pope around re for 4 (Adams)
3/4 -I5 - Herrmann sideline pass for Harris is incomplete in end zone
4/4 -I5 - Sovereen 22 yard field goal attempt is no good

8:36 ILLINOIS
1/10-I20 - Powell slants over lt for 1 (Clark)
2/9 -I21 - Powell takes pitch around le for 4 (Motts)
3/5 -I25 - Weiss on quarterback draw for 8 (Clark)
1/10-I33 - Weiss around re for no gain (Floyd)
2/10-I33 - Weiss scrambles up middle for 5 (Clark)
3/5 -I38 - Weiss pass down sidelines to Rouse is incomplete, broken up by Moss
4/5 -I38 - Finzer punt goes through end zone (62 yard punt)

5:25 PURDUE
1/10-P20 - Macon around re for 6 (Flynn)
2/4 -P26 - Pope around le for 5 (Thornton)
1/10-P31 - Macon slants over re for 2 (Ramshaw)
2/8 -P33 - Pope over lt for 5 (Venegoni)
3/3 -P38 - Macon around re for 4 (Ramshaw)
1/10-P42 - Macon up middle for 4 (Sullivan)
2/6 -P46 - Herrmann sideline pass complete to Harris for 9 (Tucker)
1/10-I45 - Macon over rg for 3 (Adams)
2/7 -I42 - Macon around le for 1 (J. Gillen)
3/6 -I41 - Herrmann pass to Pope complete for 6 (Levitt)
1/10-I35 - Pope takes pitch around re for 1 (Sullivan)
2/9 -I34 - Herrmann pass to Burrell incomplete on sidelines
3/9 -I34 - Pope on draw for 12 (Hardy, Tucker)

END OF THIRD QUARTER
PURDUE 7 ILLINOIS 0

FOURTH QUARTER

PURDUE
1/10-I22 - Pope slants over lt stumbles for 1
2/9 -I21 - Macon around le for loss of 2 (Flynn)

3/11-I23 - Herrmann pass for Pope is incomplete
4/11-I23 - Sovereen 41 yard field goal attempt is good
SCORE: PURDUE 10 ILLINOIS 0

Sovereen kicks off north, rolls through end zone for touchback

13:39 ILLINOIS
1/10-I20 - Weiss pass complete to Barnes on sideline for 6 and out of bounds
2/4 -I26 - Weber over lg for 4 (Johanson)
1/10-I30 - Weiss scrambles up middle for 7 (Motts, Loushin)
2/3 -I37 - Powell takes pitch, reverses field for 1 (Moss)
3/2 -I38 - Weber over lg for 1 (Turner)
4/1 -I39 - Strader over rg for 2 (Motts)
1/10-I41 - PENALTY: Purdue personal foul, roughing the passer
1/10-P44 - Weiss keeps for loss of 1 (Loushin)
2/11-P45 - Weiss sacked for loss of 9 (Turner)
3/20-I46 - Weiss scrambles up middle for 2 (Jackson)
4/18-I48 - Finzer punt rolls dead at P17 (35 yard punt)

8:42 PURDUE
1/10-P17 - Macon over rg for 19 (Hardy)
1/10-P35 - Pope up middle for 7 (Venegoni)
2/3 -P42 - Pope slants over rt for 6 (Tucker)
1/10-P49 - Pope around le for 7 (Kelly)
2/3 -I44 - Augustyniak up middle for 7 (J. Gillen)
1/10-I37 - Pope slants over lt for 3 (Levitt)
2/7 -I34 - Pope up middle for 5 (J. Gillen)
3/2 -I29 - Pope over lt for 2 (Sullivan, J. Gillen)
1/10-I27 - Pope around le for 5 (Levitt, Sullivan)
2/5 -I22 - Pope takes pitch around le for loss of 1 (Ramshaw)
3/6 -I23 - Herrmann pass complete to Pope for 2 (Sullivan)
4/4 -I21 - Sovereen 38 yard field goal attempt is good
SCORE: PURDUE 13 ILLINOIS 0

Sovereen kicks off north to Dismuke, downs in end zone

3:23 ILLINOIS
1/10-I20 - Weiss sacked for loss of 12 by Turner
2/22-I8 - Powell on draw play for 10 (Turner)
3/12-I18 - Weiss sacked for loss of 5 (Jackson)
4/17-I13 - Finzer punt downed at I46, (33 yard punt)

1:25 PURDUE
1/10-I46 - McCall up middle for 4 (Durrell) Time Out Illinois 1:18
2/6 -I42 - Augustyniak up middle for 8 (Hardy)
1/10-I34 - Robinson up middle for 1 (Durrell)
2/9 -I33 - Keith over lg for 4 (Adams, Squirek)
3/5 -I29 - Robinson around re for 6 (Sullivan, Ramshaw)

FINAL SCORE
PURDUE 13 ILLINOIS 0

National Collegiate Athletic Association
FINAL TEAM STATISTICS
October 21, 1978

	ILLINOIS	PURDUE
First Downs	9	26
Rushing	5	16
Passing	3	9
Penalty	1	1
Rushing Attempts	38	64
Yards Rushing	115	277
Yards Lost Rushing	45	20
Net Yards Rushing	70	257
Net Yards Passing	52	116
Passes Attempted	6	24
Passes Completed	4	15
Passes Intercepted	0	1
Total Offensive Plays	44	88
Total Net Yards	122	373
Fumbles: Number—Lost	3/2	1/1
Penalties: Number—Yards	1/15	4/30
Interceptions: Number—Return	1/0	0/0
Punts: Number—Yards	7/277	3/112
Average Per Punt	39.6	37.3
Blocked Punts	0	0
Punt Returns: Number—Yards	0/0	2/9
Kickoff Returns	2/34	0/0
Time of Possession	23:49	36:11

OCTOBER 21, 1978

INDIANA
VS.
MICHIGAN STATE
FIRST QUARTER

Indiana won the toss and elects to receive. Michigan State defending the south goal Schario kicks to Hopkins at the goal, returns 25 yards, tackle by V. Williams

INDIANA
- 1/10-IU25 - Arnett pass to Fishel, tackle by Bass, gain of 11
- 1/10-IU36 - Fishel off right tackle, tackle by Savage, gain of 4
- 2/6 -IU40 - Harkrader around left end, tackle by Bass, gain of 2
- 3/4 -IU42 - Harkrader inside right guard, tackle by Bass & Savage, gain of 5
- 1/10-IU47 - L. Johnson through the middle, tackle by Webb & Bass, gain of 3
- 2/7 -IU50 - Arnett back to pass keeps through the middle, tackle by Hay, gain of 0
- 3/7 -IU50 - Arnett pass to Powers over the middle, tackle by Bass & Savage, gain of 6
- 4/1 -MS44 - Arnett on quarterback sneak, team tackle, gain of 4
- 1/10-MS40 - Harkrader on draw off left tackle, tackle by Hay & Webb, gain of 4
- 2/6 -MS36 - Harkrader off right guard on counter, tackle by Anderson, gain of 15
- 1/10-MS21 - Harkrader off left tackle on draw, tackle by team, gain of 2
- 2/8 -MS19 - Arnett pass to Stephenson dropped
- 3/8 -MS19 - Harkrader off left guard on draw, tackle by Hay & Decker, gain of 4
- 4/4 -MS15 - Freud 32 yard field goal attempt blocked by Hay, picked up by Bass, 8 yd return tackle by Johnson

9:40 MICHIGAN STATE
- 1/10-MS13 - Smith off right tackle, tackle by Patton, gain of 1
- 2/9 -MS14 - Smith pass to Gibson over the middle, touchdown, 86 yard pass play 87 yards in two plays, Time: 6:10 Elapsed Time: :50 Andersen PAT attempt good
  MICHIGAN STATE 7, INDIANA 0

Schario kicks to Hopkins in end zone, downed for touchback

8:50 INDIANA
- 1/10-IU20 - Harkrader through the middle on draw, tackle by Savage & Graves, gain of 2
- 2/8 -IU22 - Harkrader through the middle, IU holding, 12 yard penalty
- 2/20-IU10 - Harkrader through the middle on draw, tackle by Bass, gain of 7
- 3/13-IU17 - L. Johnson through the middle, tackle by Decker, gain of 4
- 4/9 -IU21 - Lovett punt to S. Smith at MS45, fair catch, no return

6:54 MICHIGAN STATE
- 1/10-MS45 - Smith pass over the middle to Howard, touchdown. 55 yards in 1 play Time: 8:17 Elapsed Time: :11 Andersen PAT attempt good
  MICHIGAN STATE 14, INDIANA 0

Schario kicks to Hopkins in endzone, downed for touchback

6:43 INDIANA
- 1/10-IU20 - Arnett pass to Friede incomplete
- 2/10-IU20 - Harkrader off right tackle, tackle by Webb & Savage, gain of 4
- 3/6 -IU24 - Arnett back to pass sweeps left end, knocked out by Decker, no gain
- 4/6 -IU24 - Lovett punts to S. Smith, 43 yard punt, MS clipping, 15 yard penalty, 7 yd return

5:42 MICHIGAN STATE
- 1/10-MS25 - MS illegal motion, 5 yd penalty,
- 1/15-MS20 - Smith pass to S. Smith over the middle, tackle by Norman, gain of 10
- 2/5 -MS30 - McGee off left guard, tackle by team, loss of 1
- 3/6 -MS29 - Smith pass to S. Smith, tackle by McIntosh, gain of 6
- 1/10-MS35 - Smith back to pass runs through middle, tackle by McIntosh, loss of 1
- 2/11-MS34 - Smith pass to Middleton in the right flat, tackle by Abrams, Doehla, gain 2
- 3/9 -MS36 - McGee off right tackle on draw, tackle by Keneipp, gain of 17
- 1/10-IU47 - S. Smith off left tackle, tackle by Patton, no gain
- 2/10-IU47 - Smith pass to McGee in left flat, tackle by McIntosh, gain of 1
- 3/9 -IU46 - Smith pass long to Howard, falls down, gain of 42
- 1/G -IU4 - Reeves off right guard, tackle by Doehla, gain of 2

**END OF FIRST QUARTER:
MICHIGAN STATE 14, INDIANA 0**

SECOND QUARTER

MICHIGAN STATE
- 2/G -IU2 - McGee off left tackle, touchdown, 2 yd. run. 80 yards in 11 plays Time: :03 Elapsed Time: 5:45 Andersen PAT attempt good
  MICHIGAN STATE 21, INDIANA 0

Schario kicks to L. Johnson at IU2, tackle by Davis & Kolodziej

14:57 INDIANA
- 1/10-IU10 - Arnett pass to Fishel underthrown
- 2/10-IU10 - Harkrader off right guard, tackle by McCormick, gain of 4
- 3/6 -IU14 - Arnett back to pass runs outside left end, tackle by Hay & Savage, gains 2
- 4/4 -IU16 - Lovett punts out of bounds at MS 45, 39 yd punt, no return

13:28 MICHIGAN STATE
1/10-MS45 - Smith pass to Howard on right sideline, incomplete
2/10-MS45 - Smith pass to McGee over the middle, steps out of bounds, gain of 9
3/1 -IU46 - S. Smith through the middle on draw, tackle by Norman, gain of 3
1/10-IU43 - Middleton off left guard, tackle by Norman, gain of 5
2/5 -IU38 - Middleton off left guard, tackle by Tisdale, gain of 2
3/3 -IU36 - Smith pass to Brammer incomplete
4/3 -IU36 - S. Smith sweeps right, touchdown, 36 yd run. 55 yards in 7 plays
Time: 3:34 Elapsed Time: 2:12
Andersen PAT attempt good
MICHIGAN STATE 28, INDIANA 0

Schario kicks to Hopkins at IU2, tackle by Hay, 18 yd return
INDIANA
1/10-IU20 - Harkrader outside right end, forced out by Decker, gain of 1
2/9 -IU21 - Clifford pass to Friede, caught on the ground, gain of 9
1/10-IU30 - Clifford pass to Powers, tackle by Decker, gain of 22
1/10-MS48 - Harkrader off left guard, tackle by Decker, gain of 3
2/7 -MS45 - Harkrader off right guard on draw, tackle by Fields, gain of 7
1/10-MS38 - Clifford pass Powers over the middle, 19 yard gain, MS personal foul on dead ball 10 yard penalty
1/G -MS9 - Harkrader off right tackle, tackle by Bass, gain of 4
2/G -MS5 - Clifford pass to Stephenson in end zone, touchdown, 80 yards in 8 plays
Time: 6:15 Elapsed time: 2:41
Freud PAT attempt good
MICHIGAN STATE 28, INDIANA 7

Straub kicks to S. Smith at the MS 1, returns to MS 32, 31 yd return, tackle by D. Ramsey
8:45 MICHIGAN STATE
1/10-MS32 - Smith pass to Howard on left sideline, tackle by Wilbur, gain of 16
1/10-MS48 - Smith pass to Brammer incomplete, broken up by Wilbur
2/10-MS48 - Reeves around right end on sweep, tackle by Leake, gain of 17
1/10-IU35 - Smith back to pass keeps, goes left, gain of 1
2/9 -IU34 - Smith passes, incomplete, MS holding, 16 yard penalty
2/25- 50 - Reeves through the middle, tackle by Tisdale, gain of 3
3/22-IU47 - Smith back to pass, keeps runs down left side, tackle by Tayler, gain of 8
4/14-IU39 - Stachowicz punts into corner end zone, touchback 39 yard punt

5:13 INDIANA
1/10-IU20 - Clifford pass to Fishel along left sideline, overthrown
2/10-IU20 - Clifford screen pass to L. Johnson, tackle by McCormick, no gain
3/10-IU20 - Clifford back to pass, keeps sweeps right, tackle by Bass & Hay, gain of 1
4/9 -IU21 - Lovett punts to S. Smith fumbles, recovers, 37 yd punt, 1 yd return

4:04 MICHIGAN STATE
1/10-MS43 - Howard on end around to the right, tackle by Norman, Keneipp, gain of 5
2/5 -MS48 - Smith pass to Reeves over the middle, tackle by McIntosh, gain of 5
1/10-IU47 - Middleton off left guard, tackle by Willhite & Tallen, gain of 3
2/7 -IU44 - Smith pass long to Gibson along right sideline, steps out, gain of 40
1/G -IU4 - McGee outside left end, tackle by Doehla & Abrams, gain of 2
2/G -IU2 - Reeves over the middle, tackle by Norman, no gain
3/G -IU2 - S. Smith through the middle, touchdown 57 yards in 7 plays
Time: 14:14 Elapsed Time: 3:18
MS illegal motion 5 yd penalty
Andersen PAT attempt good
MICHIGAN STATE 35, INDIANA 7

Schario kicks out of end zone, touchback
:46 INDIANA
1/10-IU20 - Harkrader off left tackle, tackle by Savage, gain of 1
2/9 -IU21 - L. Johnson off right tackle, tackle by Hay, gain of 4

**END OF HALF:
MICHIGAN STATE 35, INDIANA 7**

THIRD QUARTER

Michigan State will receive. Indiana University defending the south goal. Straub kicks to Reeves in endzone, touchback.
MICHIGAN STATE
1/10-MS20 - S. Smith outside left tackle, tackle by Norman, gain of 6
2/4 -MS26 - McGee off right tackle, tackle by Patton, loss of 1
3/5 -MS25 - Smith pass to Gibson over the middle, broken up by Norman
4/5 -MS25 - Stachowicz punts to Swinehart, tackle by Hans, 33 yd punt

13:36 INDIANA
1/10-IU44 - Harkrader off left guard on draw, tackle by Bass, gain of 3
2/7 -IU47 - Clifford pass to Friede broken up by Bass
3/7 -IU47 - Clifford pass to Friede overthrown
4/7 -IU47 - Lovett punts to S. Smith at MS18, 35 yd punt, 7 yd return

314

OCTOBER 21, 1978

12:42 MICHIGAN STATE
1/10-MS25 - Reeves outside left tackle, tackle by Tisdale, Arbuckle, gain of 5
2/5 -MS30 - McGee outside right end on pitchout, tackle by Norman, gain of 6
1/10-MS36 - S. Smith outside right tackle on draw, tackle by Norman, gain of 7
2/3 -MS43 - Schramm off left tackle, tackle by Arbuckle, gain of 4
1/10-MS47 - Smith pass to Howard in right flat, falls down, gain of 6
2/4 -IU47 - McGee outside right tackle, tackle by Arbuckle & McIntosh, gain of 5
1/10-IU42 - Smith pass to Howard on right sideline, overthrown
2/10-IU42 - McGee outside right tackle, run out of bounds by Wilbur, gain of 10
1/10-IU32 - Smith pass to Gibson in endzone overthrown
2/10-IU32 - S. Smith over the middle, tackle by Abrams, gain of 14
1/10-IU18 - Smith pass to Howard on left sideline overthrown
2/10-IU18 - Smith pass to Brammer in left corner, touchdown 75 yards in 12 plays
Time: 6:31 Elapsed Time: 4:14
Andersen PAT attempt good
MICHIGAN STATE 42 INDIANA U. 7

Schario kicks to L. Johnson in endzone touchback
8:29 INDIANA
1/10-IU20 - Harkrader around right end, tackle by Webb, McCormick gain of 1
2/9 -IU21 - L. Johnson off right tackle, tackle by Decker, gain of 11
1/10-IU32 - Clifford to Fishel, tackle by Burroughs, Bass, gain of 15
1/10-IU47 - Clifford around right end on keeper, tackle by Webb, gain of 4
2/6 -MS49 - Harkrader around left end, tackle by Bass, gain of 6
1/10-MS43 - L. Johnson through the middle, tackle by Hay, gain of 4
2/6 -MS39 - Clifford pass over the middle to Powers overthrown
3/6 -MS39 - Darring off right tackle, tackle by Hay & Savage, loss of 3
4/9 -MS42 - Lovett punts to MS1, downed, 41 yd punt

4:45 MICHIGAN STATE
1/10-MS1 - Smith pass to Gibson over the middle, tackle by Wilbur, gain of 20
1/10-MS21 - Hughes off right tackle, tackle by Tallen, gain of 4
2/6 -MS25 - Smith pass to Reeves, tackle by Doehla, gain of 7
1/10-MS32 - Hughes off right tackle, tackle by Norman, gain of 7
2/3- MS39 - Reeves outside left tackle, tackle by Willhite, gain of 3
1/10-MS42 - Smith pass to Howard intercepted by Wilbur, no return

2:04 INDIANA
1/10-IU35 - Clifford screen pass to L. Johnson, tackle by Bass, no gain
2/10-IU35 - Clifford pass thrown out of bounds, MS penalty, holding 15 yd penalty
1/10- 50 - Friede on end around to the left, fumbles, recovers, tackle by Graves, loss of 7
2/17-IU43 - Hopkins through the middle, tackle by Decker, gain of 6

END OF THIRD QUARTER:
MICHIGAN STATE 42 INDIANA 7

FOURTH QUARTER

INDIANA
3/11-IU49 - Clifford pass to Fishell on right sideline incomplete
4/11-IU49 - Lovett punts to S. Smith at MS 18, 33 yd punt, 5 yd return

14:46 MICHIGAN STATE
1/10-MS23 - Smith pass on right sideline to Byrd, tackle by Wilbur, gain of 11
1/10-MS34 - Hughes off left guard, tackle by Tallen, gain of 1
2/9 -MS35 - Reeves around left end, tackle by Norman, gain of 21
1/10-IU44 - Smith pass over the middle to Byrd incomplete
2/10-IU44 - Smith pass to Reeves on left sideline, tackle by C. Smith, gain of 4
3/6 -IU40 - Smith pass over the middle to Hughes, tackle by Alexander, gain of 10
1/10-IU30 - Smith pass to Byrd on right sideline, steps out of bounds, gain of 8
2/2 -IU22 - Hans over the middle, tackle by Alexander & Keneipp, gain of 15
1/G -IU7 - Smith pass intercepted by Wilbur at IU2, returns 98 yards, touchdown
Freud PAT attempt good Time: 4:32
MICHIGAN STATE 42 INDIANA 14

Straub kicks to S. Smith at MS2, 17 yd return, tackle by Ramsey
11:23 MICHIGAN STATE
1/10-MS19 - Reeves off right guard, tackle by Tallen, no gain
2/10-MS19 - Smith back to pass, fumbles, caused by Norman, recovered by Norman, loss of 8

10:38 INDIANA
1/10-MS11 - Clifford screen pass to Darring, tackle by Graves, loss of 4
2/14-MS15 - Clifford pass intercepted by Graves at goal line, tackle by Wallace, 13 yd return

315

9:54 MICHIGAN STATE
1/10-MS13 - Hans off right guard on counter, tackle by Arbuckle, gain of 4
2/6 -MS17 - Hughes off left tackle, tackle by Norman, gain of 1
3/5 -MS18 - Reeves around right end on pitchout, tackle by Stewart & Norman, gain of 4
4/1 -MS22 - Stachowicz punts to Swinehart, fair catch, 36 yd punt no return

7:53 INDIANA
1/10-IU42 - Clifford back to pass keeps runs around right end, tackle by Cooper, no gain
2/10-IU42 - Clifford pass to Hopkins, tackle by Anderson, gain of 3
3/7 -IU45 - Clifford pass to Fishel broken up by Graves
4/7 -IU45 - Lovett punts to MS21 out of bounds, 34 yd punt

6:19 MICHIGAN STATE
1/10-MS21 - Hughes off left tackle, tackle by Norman & Alexander, gain of 4
2/6 -MS25 - Reeves off left tackle, tackle by C. Smith, gain of 2
3/4 -MS27 - Smith dump pass over the middle to Hughes, tackle by Arbuckle, Stewart, gain of 13
1/10-MS40 - Schramm through the middle tackle by Norman, gain of 3
2/7 -MS43 - Hughes off right tackle, tackle by Keneipp, gain of 46
1/10-IU11 - Hans through the middle, tackle by Patton, gain of 1
2/9 -IU10 - Hughes off right tackle on draw, touchdown 79 yards in 7 plays
Time: 12:16 Elapsed Time: 3:35
Andersen PAT attempt good
MICHIGAN STATE 49 INDIANA 14

2:44 INDIANA
Schario kicks to Huck in endzone, downed for touchback
1/10-IU20 - Darring through the middle on draw, tackle by Muster, gain of 4
2/6 -IU24 - Darring through the middle, tackle by McDowell, gain of 3
3/3 -IU27 - Clifford pass over the middle to Powers dropped
4/3 -IU27 - Lovett punts to Anderson, 23 yd punt, no return

1:24 MICHIGAN STATE
1/10- 50 - McClelland through the middle, tackle by Willhite, gain of 1
2/9 -IU49 - Hughes off left tackle, tackle by Arbuckle, gain of 4
3/5 -IU45 - McClelland off right guard, tackle by Ramsey, M., gain of 3

**END OF GAME:
MICHIGAN STATE 49 INDIANA 14**

FINAL TEAM STATISTICS

	Indiana	Michigan State
FIRST DOWNS	12	27
Rushing	6	14
Passing	5	13
Penalty	1	0
RUSHING ATTEMPTS	36	49
YARDS RUSHING	129	286
YARDS LOST RUSHING	10	11
NET YARDS RUSHING	119	275
NET YARDS PASSING	86	369
Passes Attempted	22	30
Passes Completed	11	20
Had Intercepted	1	2
TOTAL OFFENSIVE PLAYS	58	79
TOTAL NET YARDS	205	644
Average Gain Per Play	3.5	8.2
FUMBLES: NUMBER-LOST	1-0	2-1
PENALTIES: NUMBER-YARDS	1-12	5-61
INTERCEPTIONS: NUMBER-YARDS	2-98	1-13
NUMBER OF PUNTS - YARDS	9-319	3-108
Average Per Punt	35.4	36.0
PUNT RETURNS: NUMBER-YARDS	1-2	4-20
KICKOFF RETURNS: NUMBER-YARDS	3-51	2-48

OCTOBER 21, 1978

MINNESOTA VS. NORTHWESTERN
Dyche Stadium, Evanston
FIRST QUARTER

Minnesota wins the toss and elects to kick off
Northwestern will receive and defend the north goal
Rogind kickoff for Minnesota downed by Geegan in end zone for touchback

15:00 NORTHWESTERN
1/10 -N20 - Cammon lt for 6 yds (Ronan)
2/4 -N26 - Hill pitch le for 6 yds (Edwards)
1/10 -N32 - Cammon middle for 7 yds (Meyer)
2/3 -N39 - Hill rt for 4 yds (Murphy)
1/10 -N43 - Strasser pass to Bogan incomplete
2/10 -N43 - Strasser pass to Hill complete for 1 yd (Sytsma)
3/9 -N44 - Strasser pass to Hill incomplete
4/9 -N44 - Christensen punt taken by Edwards and downed at M24

12:31 MINNESOTA
1/10 -M25 - Barber pitch le for no gain (Robinett)
2/10 -M25 - Barber rt for 3 yds (McGlade)
3/7 -M28 - Carlson pass complete to Dilulo for 3 yds (Berg)
4/4 -M31 - Smith punt taken by Geegan N26 and returned 4 yds 43 yd punt

10:35 NORTHWESTERN
1/10 -N30 - Strasser pass to Bogan complete for 9 yds
2/1 -N39 - Cammon middle for 3 yds (Ronan)
1/10 -N42 - Hill pitch le for 3 yds (Snyder)
2/7 -N45 - Strasser pass to Kasprycski complete
PENALTY: holding Northwestern accepted
PENALTY: illegal procedure Minnesota accepted
2/22 -N30 - Cammon middle for 5 yds
PENALTY: face mask Minnesota accepted
3/2 - 50 - Strasser pass to McGee complete for 5 yds
1/10 -N45 - Hill re for 5 yds (Meyer)
2/5 -M40 - Strasser pass to McGee incomplete
3/5 -M40 - Strasser pass to Poulos complete for 11 yds (Snyder)
1/10 -M29 - Webb re for no gain
2/10 -M29 - Strasser fumbles attempting to pass, recovered by Minnesota Blanshan (14 yd loss)

7:50 MINNESOTA
1/10 -M43 - Barber re for 6 yds (Lawrence)
2/4 -M49 - Kitzman middle for 4 yds
PENALTY: personal foul Northwestern
1/10 -N32 - Kitzman middle for 3 yds (Robinett)
2/7 -N29 - Barber re for 1 yd (Bobowski)
3/6 -N28 - Carlson pass to Bailey complete for 12 yds
1/10 -N16 - Barber le for 7 yds (Taylor)
2/3 -N9 - Barber middle for 8 yds (McGlade)
1/G -N1 - Kitzman rt for 1 yd and a TD
PAT: Rogind kick good 57 yds in 8 plays
SCORE: MINNESOTA 7 NW 0

Rogind kickoff downed by Hill in end zone
4:45 NORTHWESTERN
1/10 -N20 - Cammon middle for 4 yds (Ronan)
2/6 -N24 - Strasser pass to Bogan incomplete
PENALTY: holding Northwestern accepted
2/18 -N12 - Hill middle for 3 yds (Murphy)
3/15 -N15 - Cammon re for 6 yds, fumbles, recovered by Northwestern Ford
4/9 -N21 - Christensen punt downed by Northwestern at N44 23 yard punt

2:49 MINNESOTA
1/10 -N44 - Kitzman rt for 9 yds (Berg)
2/1 -N35 - Barber middle for 9 yds (McGlade)
1/10 -N26 - Kitzman middle for 9 yds (Bobowski)
2/1 -M17 - Barber lt for 7 yds (Berg)
1/10 -N10 - Barber pitch le for 2 yds (Kern)
2/8 -N8 - Carlson pass to Barber complete for 8 yds and a touchdown
PAT: Rogind kick good
SCORE: MINNESOTA 14 NW 0

Rogind kickoff goes out of the end zone for a touchback
0:51 NORTHWESTERN
1/10 -N20 - Hill middle for 5 yds (Meyer)
2/5 -N25 - Strasser pass to Tiberi complete for 6 yds (Brown)

END OF FIRST QUARTER
MINNESOTA 14
NORTHWESTERN 0

SECOND QUARTER

15:00 NORTHWESTERN
1/10 -N31 - Strasser pass to Bogan incomplete
2/10 -N31 - Tiberi middle for 16 yds (Snyder)
1/10 -N47 - Tiberi re for 4 yds (Friberg)
2/6 -N49 - Strasser pass to Poulos complete for 16 yds (Edwards)
1/10 -M33 - Tiberi middle for 4 yds (Murphy)
2/6 -M29 - Hill middle for no gain (Murphy)
3/6 -M29 - Bogan reverse le for -13 yds (Brown)
4/19 -M42 - Christensen pass from punt formation complete to Tiberi for 24 yds
1/10 -M18 - Strasser pass to Bogan incomplete
2/10 -M18 - Strasser scrambles le for 18 yds and a TD PAT: Mirkopulos kick good
SCORE: MINNESOTA 14 NW 7

317

Mirkopulos kickoff downed in end zone
11:00 MINNESOTA
1/10-M20 - White middle for 4 yds (Taylor)
2/6 -M24 - Barber pitch re for 8 yds (Berg)
1/10-M32 - White middle for 2 yds (Kendzicky)
2/8 -M34 - Barber pitch le for 6 yds (Berg)
3/2 -M40 - Barber middle for 6 yds (Kern)
1/10-M46 - White rt for 6 yds (Kern)
2/4 -N48 - Barber pitch le for 3 yds (Geegan)
3/1 -N45 - Kitzman lt for 4 yds (Bobowski)
1/10-N41 - White middle for 4 yds (Corona)
2/6 -N37 - Artis pitch le for 3 yds (Kern)
3/3 -N34 - Carlson pass to Artis complete for 3 yds (Payne)
1/10-N31 - Artis middle for 6 yds (Kern)
2/4 -N25 - White rt for 9 yds (Geegan)
1/10-N16 - Artis lt for 7 yds (Bobowski)
2/3 -N9 - White lt for 7 yds (Berg)
1/G -N2 - Kitzman rt for 2 yds and a TD PAT: Rogind kick good
80 yards in 16 plays
SCORE: MINNESOTA 21 NW 7

Rogind kickoff taken by Hill at N10 and returned 22 yds
3:26 NORTHWESTERN
1/10-N32 - Cammon draw middle for 4 yds (Weinzierl)
2/6 -N36 - Strasser pass to McGee incomplete
3/6 -N36 - Strasser pass to Hill batted down by Blanshan
4/6 -N36 - Christensen punt taken by Edwards at M22 and return 2 yds 42 yd punt

2:44 MINNESOTA
1/10-M24 - White middle for 4 yds (Kern)
2/6 -M28 - Artis pitch le for 72 yards and a TD PAT: Rogind kick good
76 yds in 2 plays
SCORE: MINNESOTA 28 NW 7

Rogind kickoff taken by Cammon at N15 and returned 11 yds
1:49 NORTHWESTERN
1/10-N26 - Strasser pass to Hill complete for 4 yds (Cunningham)
PENALTY: personal foul Northwestern accepted (after the play)
2/21-N15 - Cammon lt for 29 yds (Cunningham)
1/10-N44 - Strasser pass to Bogan incomplete
2/10-N44 - Strasser pass to Bogan incomplete
3/10-N44 - Strasser pass to Poulos incomplete
4/10-N44 - Christensen punt taken by Edwards at M12 and returned 2 yds 44 yd punt
PENALTY: clipping Minnesota accepted

0:55 MINNESOTA
1/10-M7 - Carlson sneak middle for 2 yds (Taylor)
2/8 -M9 - Barber middle for 3 yds (Hoffman)

3/5 -M12 - Barber pitch le for 1 yd (Robinett)
4/4 -M13 - Smith punt fair caught by Geegan at M38 25 yard punt

0:30 NORTHWESTERN
1/10-M38 - Strasser pass to McGee complete for 21 yds
1/10-M17 - Strasser pass to McGee incomplete
2/10-M17 - Strasser fumbles attempting to pass, recovered by Minnesota (Sytsma) (22 yd loss)

0:05 MINNESOTA
1/10-M39 - Carlson pass complete to Thompson for 16 yds (Geegan)

END OF FIRST HALF
MINNESOTA 28
NORTHWESTERN 7

THIRD QUARTER

Rogind kickoff downed by Hill in end zone
15:00 NORTHWESTERN
1/10-N20 - Tiberi middle for 2 yds (Weinzierl)
2/8 -N22 - Strasser pass to Poulos incomplete
3/8 -N22 - Strasser pass to Poulos complete for 20 yds (Edwards)
PENALTY: pass interference Minnesota declined
1/10-N42 - Washington rt for 3 yds (Meyer)
2/7 -N45 - Webb reverse le for no gain (Snyder)
3/7 -N45 - Strasser pass to Kaspryscki complete for 15 yds (Snyder)
1/10-M40 - Washington middle
PENALTY: illegal procedure Northwestern accepted
1/15-M45 - Strasser pass to Bogan incomplete (broken up by Burns)
2/15-M45 - Strasser pass to Webb incomplete
3/15-M45 - Strasser pass to Bogan intercepted by Edwards at M20 and returned 50 yds

OCTOBER 21, 1978

12:30 MINNESOTA
1/10-N30 - Kitzman middle for 7 yds (Knafelc)
2/3 -N23 - Barber rt for 3 yds (Bobowski)
1/10-N20 - Barber pitch le for 3 yds (Kern)
2/7 -N17 - Dilulo reverse le for 6 yds (team)
3/1 -N11 - Kitzman middle for 2 yds (Geegan)
1/G -N9 - Carlson keeper le for 1 yd (Taylor)
2/G -N8 - Barber pitch re
PENALTY: illegal motion Minnesota accepted
2/G -N13 - Carlson pass to Bailey knocked down by Taylor
3/G -N13 - Carlson pass to Kitzman incomplete
4/G -N13 - Rogind field goal attempt of 30 yards is good 17 yards in 9 plays
SCORE: MINNESOTA 31 NW 7

Rogind kickoff goes out of end zone for a touchback
8:57 NORTHWESTERN
1/10-N20 - Cammon le for 3 yds (Sytsma)
PENALTY: personal foul Minnesota accepted
1/10-N38 - Hill pitch le for 8 yds (Snyder)
2/2 -N46 - Washington rt for 3 yds (Blanshan)
1/10-N49 - Cammon pitch re for 12 yds (Weinzierl)
1/10-M39 - Cammon lt for 4 yds (Weinzierl)
2/6 -M35 - Hill lt for 4 yds (Meyer)
3/2 -M31 - Hill pitch LE for 3 yds (Friberg)
1/10-M28 - Tiberi re for 2 yds (Burns)
2/8 -M26 - Hill pitch rt for 2 yds (Sytsma)
3/6 -M24 - Strasser sacked by Hoffman for -15
4/21-M39 - Geegan middle off punt formation for 2 yds (Burns)

4:27 MINNESOTA
1/10-M37 - Barber pitch le for 4 yds (Kern)
2/6 -M41 - Barber middle for 4 yds (Payne)
3/2 -M45 - Kitzman rt for 4 yds (Payne)
1/10-M49 - Barber re for 16 yds (Hoffman)
1/10-N35 - Barber pitch re for -1 yd (Bobowski)
2/11-N36 - Carlson pass to Bailey complete for 14 yds (Bobowski)
1/10-N22 - Barber rt for 7 yds (Berg)
2/3 -N15 - Kitzman rt for 3 yds (Kern)

END OF THIRD QUARTER
MINNESOTA 31
NORTHWESTERN 7

FOURTH QUARTER

15:00 MINNESOTA
1/10-N12 - Barber lt for no gain (Hemphill)
2/10-N12 - Carlson sacked by Bambauer for -1 yd
PENALTY: face-masking Northwestern (6 yds)
2/5 -N7 - Barber rt for 7 yds and a TD
PAT Rogind kick good 63 yds in 11 plays
SCORE: MINNESOTA 38 NW 7

Rogind kickoff goes out of bounds
PENALTY: illegal procedure Minnesota accepted
Rogind kickoff taken by North at N26 and returned 10 yds

14:10 NORTHWESTERN
1/10-N36 - Tiberi lt for 3 yds
2/7 -N39 - Washington lt for 3 yds (Carr)
3/4 -N42 - Strasser pass to Prichard for 12 yds (Hoffmann)
1/10-M46 - Tiberi rt for 7 yds (Murphy)
2/3 -M39 - Washington fumbles pitchout out of bounds for -1 yd
3/4 -M40 - Strasser pass to Bogan complete for 15 yds (Noel)
1/10-M25 - Washington lt, fumbles, recovered by Minnesota Prairie (gain of 1 yd)

11:37 MINNESOTA
1/10-M24 - Lewis pitch le for 7 yds (Lawrence)
2/3 -M31 - Lewis middle for 4 yds (Pals)
1/10-M35 - Avery sacked by Lawrence for -4 yds
2/14-M31 - White draw play middle for -2 yds (Bambauer)
3/16-M29 - Lewis pitch le for 3 yds (Lawrence)
4/13-M32 - Smith punt rolls dead at M48 16 yd punt

8:33 NORTHWESTERN
1/10-M48 - Hill rt for -3 yds (Gardner)
2/13-N49 - Webb pitch re, fumbles, recovers his own for 1 yd (Gardner)
3/12- 50 - Strasser pass to Tiberi incomplete
4/12- 50 - Christensen punt rolls out of endzone for touchback 50 yd punt

7:24 MINNESOTA
1/10-M20 - Artis pitch re for no gain (Lizak)
2/10-M20 - Avery pass to Cooper complete for 11 yds
1/10-M31 - Artis pitch re for 3 yds (Lizak)
2/7 -M34 - Avery pass to Cooper incomplete
3/7 -M34 - Artis lt for 2 yds (Dunlea)
4/5 -M36 - Smith punt taken by Carver at N39 and returned 5 yds 25 yd punt

4:53 NORTHWESTERN
1/10-N44 - Cammon le for 1 yd (Cunningham)
2/9 -N45 - Strasser pass to Bogan complete for 18 yds (Prairie)
1/10-M37 - Washington lt for -1 yd (Cunningham)
2/11-M38 - Strasser pass to Prichard incomplete
3/11-M38 - Strasser pass to Prichard incomplete
4/11-M38 - Strasser pass to Bahoric incomplete
PENALTY: pass interference Minnesota (3 yd penalty)
1/10-M35 - Webb LE for 2 yds (Sapp)
2/8 -M33 - Tiberi rt for 1 yd (Carr)
3/7 -M32 - Strasser pass to Bogan incomplete
4/7 -M32 - Strasser pass to Bahoric incomplete

2:24 MINNESOTA
1/10-M32 - Lewis middle for 3 yds, fumbles, recovered by Northwestern Burns

2:18 NORTHWESTERN
1/10-M34 - Webb pitch re for 5 yd (Fahnhorst)
2/5 -M29 - Webb lt for 6 yds (Hoffman)
1/10-M23 - Strasser pass to North incomplete
2/10-M23 - Strasser pass to Poulos
PENALTY: pass interference Minnesota (4 yd penalty)
1/10-M19 - Tiberi pass to Bogan complete for 19 yds and a TD
PAT Mirkopulos kick good 34 yds in 4 plays
SCORE: MINNESOTA 38 NW 14

Mirkopulos kickoff recovered by Northwestern Bobowski at M39
1:09 NORTHWESTERN
1/10-M39 - Breitbeil fumbles attempting to pass, recovered by Minnesota Murphy (Loss of 7 yds)

1:04 MINNESOTA
1/10-M46 - Artis pitch le for 10 yds
1/10-N44 - Avery keeper for 2 yds

2/8 -N42 - Avery pass for Cooper intercepted by Northwestern Butler at N21, no return

END OF GAME
MINNESOTA 38
NORTHWESTERN 14

National Collegiate Athletic Association
FINAL TEAM STATISTICS

	MINNE-SOTA	NORTH-WESTERN
First Downs	25	25
Rushing	18	10
Passing	6	12
Penalty	1	3
Rushing Attempts	61	51
Yards Rushing	328	210
Yards Lost Rushing	8	76
Net Yards Rushing	320	134
Net Yards Passing	67	196
Passes Attempted	11	37
Passes Completed	7	15
Had Intercepted	1	1
Total Offensive Plays	72	88
Total Net Yards	387	330
Average Gain Per Play	5.4	3.8
Fumbles: Number—Lost	1/1	7/4
Penalties: Number—Yards	8/59	6/68
Interceptions: Number—Yards	1/50	1/0
Number of Punts—Yards	4/109	5/190
Average Per Punt	27.25	38
Punt Returns: Number—Yards	1/2	2/9
Kickoff Returns: Number—Yards	0/0	3/43

OCTOBER 21, 1978

**IOWA
VS.
OHIO STATE**
Ohio Stadium
Columbus, Ohio
Temp.: 70°-75°
Wind: SW 10-20 mph
Skies: Sunny
FIRST QUARTER

OHIO STATE won the toss and elected to receive; IOWA to defend the South goal
Schilling kicked off at 1:32 P.M. eight yards deep for the TB
15:00 OHIO
1/10-O20 - Schlichter faked, rolled right, passed too wide for Hunter inc.
2/10-O20 - Springs at left end for just one
3/9 -O21 - Schlichter faked, chased right, ran, broke tackle for 14
1/10-O35 - Campbell into lg for 5
2/5 -O40 - Springs was hit at rt but made 3
3/2 -O43 - Schlichter kept inside re for 1
4/1 -O44 - Orosz punted 41; rolled dead

12:21 IOWA
1/10-I15 - Mosley pitch at re for 9
2/1 -I24 - Lazar cut into middle for 5
1/10-I29 - Green faked, passed over middle for Swift, wide, broken up Ellis inc.
2/10-I29 - Green faded, chased left, passed over middle for Dunham; intercepted by Skillings, returned 6

11:46 OHIO
1/10-I44 - Springs on option pitch re for 3
2/7 -I41 - Campbell lg 2
3/5 -I39 - Springs took option pitch at right end, down sideline for the TD at 10:40
Janakievski PAT - forty-four yards in three plays
SCORE: OHIO STATE 7, IOWA 0

Orosz kicked off 50 yards; Reid returned middle 32
10:33 IOWA
1/10-I42 - Lazar cut into rg for 2
2/8 -I44 - Mosley pitch at re for 3
3/5 -I47 - Mosley pitch into rt for 2
4/3 -I49 - Holsclaw punted 36 left; downed by Iowa

8:38 OHIO
1/10-O15 - Springs leaped into center for no gain
2/10-O15 - Campbell clear at rt, spun for 10
1/10-O25 - Campbell clear at lg for 10
1/10-O35 - Springs turned into rt for 3
2/7 -O38 - Schlichter faked, turned, passed too low for Donley over middle inc.

3/7 -O38 - Schlichter faded, looked, ran middle for 1
4/6 -O39 - Orosz punted 43; Booker returned 1

6:39 IOWA
1/10-I19 - Mosley pitch at re for 2
2/8 -I21 - Green passed to Swift short over middle for 7
3/1 -I28 - Green sneak at rg for 2
1/10-I30 - Morton counter at lg for 2
2/8 -I32 - Green kept at re for 2 (Green hurt - helped off)
3/6 -I34 - Gales passed deep over middle, too long for Dunham inc.
4/6 -I34 - Holsclaw punted 39; Guess no return

3:48 OHIO
1/10-O27 - Campbell hit rg for 3
2/7 -O30 - Campbell thru rt for 4
3/3 -O34 - Schlichter passed over middle to Moore for 9; Iowa roughing passer 15
1/10-I42 - Campbell burst thru lg for 6
2/4 -I36 - Springs option pitch at le for 2
3/2 -I34 - Campbell spun into lg for 2
1/10-I32 - Campbell, from robust, off lt for 4
2/6 -I28 - Springs pitch at le for 2
3/4 -I26 - Campbell slanted thru rt for 2
4/2 -I24 - Campbell thru lt for 3 as the quarter came to an end

**END OF FIRST QUARTER:
OHIO STATE 7, IOWA 0**

SECOND QUARTER
OHIO
1/10-I21 - Campbell clear at lg, bumped for 11
1/10-I10 - Campbell again at lg for 3
2/7 -I 7 - Schlichter rolled right, passed too long for Doniey inc.
3/7 -I 7 - Schlichter tripped left for -3
4/10-I10 - Atha's FG was from 27 yards at 13:37; Iowa offside was declined
63 yards in 15 plays
SCORE: OHIO STATE 10, IOWA 0

Orosz kicked off 11 yards deep for the TB
13:37 IOWA
1/10-I20 - Mosley pitch at le for 2
2/8 -I22 - Gales faked, faded, looked, ran middle for 4
3/4 -I26 - Gales passed to Dunham in left flat for 6
1/10-I32 - Lazar on delayed draw at rg for no gain
2/10-I32 - Mosley cut outside re for 3
3/7 -I35 - Gales passed to Morton left for 7; Ohio pass interference 7
1/10-I42 - McKillip, on option pass play right, stopped by team for -6
2/16-I36 - Mosley turned le for 4
3/12-I40 - Gales passed deep right for Morton; Ross intercepted, returned 23

321

8:52 OHIO
1/10-I28 - Ohio illegal procedure -5
1/15-I33 - Schlichter passed to Campbell on delay over middle; wide - dropped inc.
2/15-I33 - Campbell on delayed draw over right side, broke clear for 19
1/10-I14 - Springs option pitch at le for 9
2/1 -I 5 - Campbell over rg for the TD at 7:51 - Janakievski PAT
28 yards in 4 plays
SCORE: OHIO STATE 17, IOWA 0

Orosz kicked off eleven yards deep for the TB
7:51 IOWA
1/10-I20 - Mosley at rg for 3
2/7 -I23 - Gales faked, passed on screen left, Ross deflected, Sullivan intercepted and ran in for the TD 6:57 - Janakievski PAT - SCORE: OHIO STATE 24, IOWA 0

Orosz kicked off eleven yards deep again for the TB
6:57 IOWA
1/10-I20 - Lazar option pitch at le for 8
2/2 -I28 - Dolan faded, sacked by Dulin for-8 Time out Iowa at 6:12
3/10-I20 - Dolan faded, chased left, passed too short for Morton on sideline inc.
4/10-I20 - Holsclaw punted 44; Guess returned 2; Ohio Clipping -16

5:53 OHIO
1/10-022 - Schlichter passed deep over middle for Donley at the Iowa 30, cut left and was clear for the TD 5:41 - Janakievski PAT 78 yards in one play
SCORE: OHIO STATE 31, IOWA 0

Orosz kicked off 55 yards; Crocker returned 23
5:33 IOWA
1/10-I28 - Turner pitch left for -5 - Ross
2/15-I23 - Dolan faded, ran middle, cut left for 3
3/12-I26 - Dolan faded, ran middle, sack for -6 - Dulin (Gilbaugh hurt - helped off)
4/18-I20 - Holsclaw punted 33; Guess FC; Ohio State Pers. foul 16
4/2 -I36 - Holsclaw punted 36 left; downed by Iowa

3:33 OHIO
1/10-028 - Murray pitch at le for 5; Ohio clipping -15
1/20-018 - Volley clear at rg for 11 Time out Iowa at 3:03
2/9 -029 - Castignola kept inside re for 6
3/3 -035 - Castignola kept inside le for 9
1/10-044 - Volley middle 4
2/6 -048 - Volley jumped over lt for 8
1/10-I44 - Murray option pitch at re for 8
2/2 -I36 - Castignola, on broken play kept around re for 9
1/10-I27 - Volley lg 6
2/4 -I21 - Castignola kept left for no gain Time out Ohio State at 0:24
3/4 -I21 - Castignola passed too wide for Meade left inc.
4/4 -I21 - Castignola passed way wide for Murray in short left flat inc.

0:16 IOWA
1/10-I21 - Morton option pitch at le for 4
2/6 -I25 - Dolan faded, chased out of bounds right for -8 by Dulin as the first half ended at 2:46 P.M.

**END OF FIRST HALF:
OHIO STATE 31, IOWA 0**

THIRD QUARTER

Iowa elected to recieve; Ohio State to defend the South goal
Orosz kicked off at 3:13 P.M. six yards deep for the TB
15:00 IOWA
1/10-I20 - Lazar at rg for 2
2/8 -I22 - Mosley was stopped at le for no gain
3/8 -I22 - Dolan passed quick into short left flat, broke tackle for 14 (Dunham)
1/10-I36 - Mosley lt 4
2/6 -I40 - Lazar at rg for 5
3/1 -I45 - Lazar was stopped at center by Sullivan for no gain
4/1 -I45 - Holsclaw punted 36; Guess FC

OCTOBER 21, 1978

11:48 OHIO
1/10-019 - Volley cut outside rt for 7
2/3 -026 - Schlicher kept inside le, broke tackle for 7
1/10-033 - Volley was clear up middle for 17
1/10- 50 - Schlicter rolled right, out of bounds for -1
2/11-049 - Schlichter passed short on delay to Volley left for 6
3/5 -I45 - Springs option pitch at le for 6
1/10-I39 - Schlichter faded, broke tackle, rolled right, passed too high for Volley
2/10-I39 - Schlichter shovel pass middle to Springs no gain on safety right
3/10-I39 - Schlichter faded, chased, passed too wide to Volley on safety right inc.
4/10-I39 - Orosz punted into left end zone for the TB

8:57 IOWA
1/10-I20 - Lazar option pitch re for no gain
2/10-I20 - Mosley pitch at le for 2 (Willey, Cousineau hurt - both walked off)
3/8 -I22 - Dolan faded, chased left, passed deep to Morton for 28
1/10- 50 - Lazar, on pitch left, passed way too long for Reid inc.
2/10- 50 - Mosley stopped at lt by Henson for no gain
3/10- 50 - Dolan faded, ran right for 15; Ohio Pers. foul, late hit out of bounds 15
1/10-020 - Lazar cut into middle for 5
2/5 -015 - Dolan passed short left to Crocker for 4
3/1 -011 - Dolan sneak 2
1/9 -0 9 - Mosley turned re for 3
2/6 -0 6 - Lazar thru lg for the TD 5:10 - Schilling PAT; Iowa illegal Procedure -5 Schilling PAT - 80 yards in 11 plays
SCORE: OHIO STATE 31, IOWA 7

Schilling kicked off 55 yards; Springs returned 18
5:05 OHIO
1/10-023 - Volley rt 3
2/7 -026 - Volley lt 4
3/3-030 - Schlichter kept inside le for 9
1/10-039 - Volley at lt for 1
2/9-040 - Volley into rg for 3
3/6 -043 - Schlichter passed into short left flat for Meade, broken up Kevin Ellis; Iowa pass interference 5
1/10-048 - Volley middle 2
2/8 - 50 - Ohio illegal procedure -6 (stepped off long) Ohio Time Out 2:23
2/14-044 - Schlichter faked, faded, chased, passed to volley on safety right for 2
3/12-046 - Schlichter faked, passed to Hunter in short right flat for 7
4/5 -I47 - Orosz punt into right end zone for the TB

1:03 IOWA
1/10-I20 - Lazar off left tackle for 3
2/7 -I23 - Dolan faked, faded, chased left, passed out of bounds inc.
3/7 -I23 - Dolan passed to Dunham in left flat for 11
1/10-I34 - Dolan passed just out of bounds to Mosley in left flat inc.
2/10-I34 - Mosley pitch around re for 5; Ohio face mask 15 - Cato, Ross both hurt - walked off)
1/10-046 - Dolan passed very deep right for Reid; broken up by Ellis inc. as the quarter came to an end

**END OF THIRD QUARTER:
OHIO STATE 31, IOWA 7**

FOURTH QUARTER

IOWA
2/10-046 - Mosley pitch around le for 4
3/6 -042 - Lazar pushed into center for 5
4/1 -037 - Lazar at lg for 5
1/10-032 - Dolan faded, chased, sacked by Dulin, Lee -12
2/22-044 - Mosley pitch and turned re for 3; Iowa clipping -15
2/37-I41 - Dunham took pitch backward on reverse, passed deep left to Swift for 45 Ohio pass interference declined
1/10-014 - Mosley pitch off rt for 1
2/9 -013 - Dolan faked, faded, chased left, passed to no one at the flag inc.
3/9-013 - Dolan faked, rolled left, blind sided by Bell for -8
4/17-021 - Schillings FG was wide right from 38 yards - TB

323

10:51 OHIO
1/10-021 - Castignola kept inside le for 3
2/7 -024 - Castignola kept inside lt for 3 more
3/4 -027 - Springs option pitch re for another 3
4/1 -030 - Orosz punted out of bounds right 27

9:12 IOWA
1/10-143 - Lazar on delayed draw for 6
2/4 -149 - Dolan passed high in short right flat, Reid leaped high for 7
1/10-044 - Dolan faded, chased right, sacked by Henson, Ellison -14
2/24-142 - Reid took pitch on reverse, fumble recovered by Reid -13
3/37-129 - Ohio State offside 5
3/32-134 - Mosley cut over rg for 3
4/29-137 - Lazar took direct snap on punt formation, ran center for 19 (Lazar hurt - walked off)

5:53 OHIO
1/10-044 - Payton into rt for 3
2/7 -047 - Murray pitch at re for just 1
3/6 -048 - Murray cut into middle for 4

4/2 -148 - Castignola kept inside le for (measurement) 1

4:15 IOWA
1/10-146 - Dolan passed to Reid on right sideline for 16
1/10-038 - Dolan faded, sacked by Hornik for -10
2/20-048 - Mosley pitch around le for 3 (Ross hurt - limped off)
3/17-045 - Mosley pitch around re for 3 more
4/14-042 - Reid took pitch on reverse left for 7; Iowa clip declined

1:47 OHIO
1/10-035 - **Payton thru lt for 5**
2/5 -040 - **Johnson pitch at re for 7**
1/10-047 - **Johnson pitch at le for 3**
2/7 - 50 - **Payton hit rg for 6**
3/1 -144 - **Johnson pitch at le for 4 as the game ended at 4:16 P.M.**

END OF GAME:
OHIO STATE 31, IOWA 7

324

OCTOBER 21, 1978

MICHIGAN VS. WISCONSIN
Camp Randall Stadium
Temp: 70
Wind: SSW 15-20 mph
Skies: Partly cloudy and warm
FIRST QUARTER

Wisconsin won the toss and elected to receive, Michigan will defend the south goal.
Brian Virgil will kickoff for Michigan to open the game, to the W endzone, for a touchback
15:00 WISCONSIN
1/10-W20 - Stauss runs right guard, gets 3 to W23. (Cannavino)
2/7 -W23 - Kalasmiki pitches right to Matthews, gets 4 to 27 (Cannavino)
3/3 -W27 - Matthews runs right tackle, gets 4 to 31 (Simpkins)
1/10-W31 - Kalasmiki passes over the middle to Sydnor, gets 15 to 46, fumbles recovered by Bell

13:20 MICHIGAN
1/10-W46 - Davis runs right tackle, gets 2 to 44 (Cabral)
2/8 -W44 - Leach pitches right to Huckleby, gets 24 to 20 (Gordon)
1/10-W20 - Huckleby runs right guard, gets 7 to 13 (Crossen)
2/3 -W13 - Leach pitches right to Huckleby, gets 2 to 11 (Holm)
3/1 -W11 - Wisconsin is penalized 5 yards for false start
1/G -W6 - Leach keeps on option left, gets 5 to 1 (Welch)
2/G -W1 - Davis dives over middle, gets no gain (Crossen)
3/G -W1 - Leach keeps on option right, gets 1 for TD (9:57)
Willner kicks the extra point (7 plays, 46 yards)
SCORE: MICHIGAN 7, WISCONSIN 0

Virgil will kickoff for Michigan following the score, to W endzone, Matthews returns 14 yards to W14. (Bell)
9:52 WISCONSIN
1/10-W14 - Matthews runs left tackle, gets 4 to 18 (Cannavino)
2/6 -W18 - Kalasmiki pitches right to Matthews, gets 5 to 23 (Harden)
3/1 -W23 - Matthews runs right tackle, gets 13 to 36 (Scabron)
1/10-W36 - Stauss runs right guard, gets 9 to 45 (Braman)
2/1 -W45 - Kalasmiki passes to Charles, gets 5 to 50, fumbles, recovered Trgovac

8:11 MICHIGAN
1/10-50 - Leach keeps on option right, gets 3 to 47 (Boliaux)
2/7 -W47 - Leach pitches left to Huckleby, loses 2 to 49 (Gordon)
3/9 -W49 - Leach passes over the middle to Marsh, gets 9 to 40 (Gordon)
Michigan is penalized 15 yards for clipping
3/14-M45 - Huckleby runs right tackle, gets 2 to M47 (Boliaux)
4/12-M47 - Willner punts 52 yards to Wisconsin endzone for touchback

6:35 WISCONSIN
1/10-W20 - Matthews runs right tackle, gets 1 to 21 (Meeter)
2/9 -W21 - Kalasmiki passes right to, Souza, broken up (by Harden)
3/9 -W21 - Kalasmiki passes screen right to Stauss, gets 1 to 22 (Trgovac)
4/8 -W22 - Kiltz punts 31 yards to M47, out of bounds

5:05 MICHIGAN
1/10-M47 - Huckleby runs left tackle, gets 3 to 50 (Cabral)
2/7 -M50 - Leach pitches right to Huckleby, gets 5 to 45 (Ahrens)
Wisconsin is penalized 15 yards for face mask
1/10-W30 - Leach pitches right to Huckleby, gets 3 to 27 (Holm)
2/7 -W27 - Leach pitches on right reverse to Clayton gets 27 for TD (4:07)
Willner kicks the extra point (4 plays, 53 yards)
SCORE: MICHIGAN 14, WISCONSIN 0

Virgil kicks off for Michigan following the score, to Wisconsin endzone for touchback.

4:07 WISCONSIN
1/10-W20 - Kalasmiki passes right to Charles, gets 10 to 30
1/10-W30 - Matthews runs right tackle, gets 2 to 32 (Keitz)
2/8 -W32 - Matthews runs left guard, gets 2 to 34 (Keitz)
3/6 -W34 - Kalasmiki passes left to Stracka, incomplete
4/6 -W34 - Kiltz punts 33 yards to M33, Jolly returns 14 to M47 (Snell)

2:39 MICHIGAN
1/10-M47 - Davis runs left guard, gets 7 to W46 (Crossen)
2/3 -W46 - Huckleby runs left end, gets no gain (Schremp)
3/3 -W46 - Wisconsin is penalized 5 yards for false start
1/10-W41 - Leach passes left to Smith, incomplete
2/10-W41 - Reed runs left guard, gets 2 to 39 (Boliaux)
3/8 -W39 - Leach pitches right to Smith, gets 7 to 32 (Ahrens)

END OF FIRST QUARTER:
MICHIGAN 14, WISCONSIN 0

SECOND QUARTER

15:00 MICHIGAN
4-1 -W32 - Leach keeps left on option, gets 3 to 29 (Relich)
1/10-W29 - Huckleby runs right tackle, gets 4 to 25 (Crossen)
2/6 -W25 - Reid runs left guard, gets 5 to 20 (Crossen)
Wisconsin calls timeout (13:36)
3/1 -W20 - Reid runs left tackle, gets 1 to 19 (Schremp)
1/10-W19 - Leach keeps on the option right, gets 2 to 17 (Schremp)
2/8 -W17 - Leach pitches right to Huckleby gets 17 yards for TD (12:28)
Willner kicks the extra point (11 plays, 53 yards)
SCORE: MICHIGAN 21, WISCONSIN 0

Virgil kicks off for Michigan following the score, to W endzone for the touchback.

12:28 WISCONSIN
1/10-W20 - Kalasmiki passes right to Charles, broken up (by Bell)
2/10-W20 - Matthews runs left tackle, gets 3 to 23 (Cannavino)
3/7 -W23 - Kalasmiki keeps up the middle, gets 2 to 25 (Keitz)
4/5 -W25 - Kiltz punts 36 yards to M39, Jolly returns 1 to 40 (Levenick)

10:56 MICHIGAN
1/10-M40 - Smith runs left guard, gets 11 to W49 (Gordon)
1/10-W49 - Leach pitches left to Smith, gets 2 to 47 (Boliaux)
2/8 -W47 - Leach keeps on option right, gets 5 to 42 (Relich)
3/3 -W42 - Smith runs right tackle, gets no gain (Johnson)
4/3 -W42 - Willner punts, 38 yards to W4, (downed by Clayton)

9:01 WISCONSIN
1/10-W4 - Kalasmiki runs right tackle, gets 2 to 6 (Trgovac)
2/8 -W6 - Kalasmiki pitches left to Mathews, gets 7 to 13 (Diggs)
3/1 -W13 - Kalasmiki sneaks right guard, gets 1 to 14 (Simpkins)
1/10-W14 - Kalasmiki pitches left to Matthews, gets 3 to 17 (Cannavino)
2/7 -W17 - Stauss runs left tackle, gets 17 to 34 (Harden)
1/10-W34 - Kalasmiki keeps on option right, gets 8 to 42 (Diggs)
2/2 -W42 - Stauss runs right guard, gets 1 to 43 (Simpkins)
3/1 -W43 - Kalasmiki pitches right to Mathews, gets 4 to 47 (Cannavino)
1/10-W47 - Mathews runs left tackle, gets 1 to 48 (Greer)
2/9 -W48 - Kalasmiki passes long left to Stracka, incomplete
3/9 -W48 - Kalasmiki back to pass is sacked, loses 1 (Keitz)
4/10-W47 - Kiltz punts 24 yards to M29, out of bounds

3:37 MICHIGAN
1/10-M29 - Reid runs right guard, gets 4 to 33 (Ahrens)
2/6 -M33 - Leach pitches right to Smith, gets 3 to 36 (Christenson)
3/3 -M36 - Leach pitches left to Smith, gets 5 to 41 (Ahrens)
1/10-M42 - Leach passes long left to Clayton, incomplete
2/10-M41 - Leach pitches left to Smith, loses 2 to 39 (Relich)
3/12-M39 - Leach passes over the middle to Huckleby, gets 9 to 48 (Holm)
4/3 -M48 - Willner punts 46 yards to W6, Matthews returns 4 to 10 (Weber)

:37 WISCONSIN
1/10-W10 - Matthews runs right tackle, gets 3 to 13 (Cannavino)
Wisconsin calls timeout (:24)
2/7 -W13 - Mathews runs left tackle, loses 2 to 11 (Greer)

END OF FIRST HALF:
SCORE: MICHIGAN 21, WISCONSIN 0

OCTOBER 21, 1978

THIRD QUARTER

Mike Brhley will kick off for Wisconsin to open the second half, to M3, Clayton returns 22 to M25. (Stracka)

14:54 MICHIGAN
1/10-M25 - Reid runs right tackle, gets 2 to 27 (Schremp)
2/8 -M27 - Leach keeps on the option left, gets 44 to W29 (Anderson)
1/10-W29 - Reid runs left guard, gets 1 to 28 (Schremp)
2/9 -W28 - Leach keeps on option right, gets 2 to 26 (Cabral)
3/7 -W26 - Leach passes over the middle to Clayton, gets 17 to W9
1/G -W9 - Leach pitches left to Huckleby, gets 3 to 6 (Welch)
2/G -W6 - Leach keeps on the option right gets 6 for TD (11:30)
Willner kicks the extra point (7 plays, 75 yards)
SCORE: MICHIGAN 28, WISCONSIN 0

Virgil will kick off for Michigan following the score, to W goal line, Matthews returns 12 to W12 (DeSantis)

11:23 WISCONSIN
1/10-W12 - Kalasmiki keeps on the option left, gets 7 to 19 (Bell)
2/3 -W19 - Kalasmiki keeps on the option left, gets 2 to 21 (Trgovac)
3/1 -W21 - Matthews runs right guard, gets 2 to 23 (Bell)
1/10-W23 - Kalasmiki runs out of pass, gets 13 to 36 (Seabron)
1/10-W36 - Kalasmiki passes over the middle to Charles, gets 14 to 50 (Harden)
1/10-W50 - Stauss runs right guard, gets 2 to M48 (Greer)
2/8 -M48 - Matthews runs right tackle, gets 4 to 44 (Simpkins)
3/4 -M44 - Kalasmiki pitches right to Matthews gets no gain (Braman)
4/4 -M44 - Wisconsin calls timeout (7:07)
Crossen punts 33 yards to M11, Jolly fair catch

7:02 MICHIGAN
1/10-M11 - Huckleby runs right guard, gets 5 to 16 (Sawicki)
2/5 -M16 - Reid runs left guards, gets 5 to 21 (Relich)
1/10-M21 - Leach keeps on the option left, gets 5 to 26 (Holm)
2/5 -M26 - Huckleby runs left tackle, gets 3 to 29 (Sawicki)
3/2 -M29 - Leach keeps on the option left, gets 5 to 34 (Sawicki)
1/10-M34 - Leach keeps on the option left, gets 1 to 35 (Schremp)

2/9 -M35 - Leach passes long over the middle to Clayton, gets 65 yards for TD (3:34)
Willner kicks the extra point (7 plays, 89 yards)
SCORE: MICHIGAN 35, WISCONSIN 0

Virgil will kickoff for Michigan following the score, to Wisconsin goal line, Matthews returns 12 to Wisconsin 12 (DeSantis)

3:34 WISCONSIN
1/10-W20 - Kalasmiki pitches to Green, who passes long to Charles, incomplete
2/10-W20 - Kalasmiki passes right to Sydnor, gets 7 to 27 (Bell)
3/3-W27 - Kalasmiki passes left to Braker, incomplete
4/3 W27 - Crossen punts 40 yards to M33, Jolly fair catch

3:12 MICHIGAN
1/10-M33 - Dickey pitches right to Huckleby, gets 16 To 49 (Anderson)
1/10-M49 - Huckleby runs left tackle, gets 4 to W47 (Holm)
2/6 -W47 - Reid runs right guard, gets 4 to 43 (Holm)
3/2 -W43 - Dickey keeps on the option left, gets 4 to 39 (Christenson)
1/10-W39 - Dickey runs right end, gets 12 to 27 (Relich)
1/10-W27 - Leach pitches left to Huckleby, loses 7 to 34 (Stroede)
2/17-W34 - Leach passes right to Huckleby, incomplete
3/17-W34 - Leach pitches right to Huckleby, gets 9, fumbles, recovered by Schieble

:06 WISCONSIN
1/10-W25 - Kalasmiki passes over the middle to Syndor, gets 16 to 41 (Bell)

**END OF THIRD QUARTER:
MICHIGAN 35, WISCONSIN 0**

FOURTH QUARTER

15:00 WISCONSIN
1/10-W41 - Kalasmiki passes right to Charles, incomplete
2/10-W41 - Kalasmiki passes over the middle to Braker, gets 9 to 50
3/1 - 50 - Souza runs reverse right, gets 5 to M45 (Simpkins)
1/10-M45 - Kalasmiki back to pass is sacked, loses 13 to W42 (Weber)
2/23-W42 - Kalasmiki passes left to Souza gets 10 to M48 (Jolly)
3/13-M48 - Kalashmiki passes over the middle to Charles, broken up (by Jolly)
4/13-M48 - Crossen punts 21 yards to M27, downed by Burt

327

12:45 MICHIGAN
- 1/10-M27 - Reid runs right guard, gets 5 to 32 (Relich)
- 2/5 -M32 - Woolfolk runs right tackle, gets 5 to 37 (Ahrens)
- 1/10-M37 - Woolfolk runs right tackle, gets 11 to M48 (Johnson)
- 1/10-M48 - Reid runs left guard, gets 13 to W39 (Schieble)
- 1/10-W39 - Dickey keeps on the option, loses 2 to 41 (Ahrens)
- 2/12-W41 - Dickey runs left end, gets 16 to W25 (Christenson)
- 1/10-W25 - Woolfolk runs left tackle, gets 1 to 24 (Crossen)
- 2/9 -W24 - Woolfolk runs right tackle, gets 2 to 22 (Relich)
- 3/7 -W22 - Dickey passes over the middle to Johnson, gets 16 to W6 (Anderson)
- 1/G -W 6 - Reid runs right guard, gets 3 to W3 (Crossen)
- 2/G -W 3 - Dickey keeps on the option right, gets 3 for TD (7:09) Willner kicks the extra point (11 plays, 73 yards)
  SCORE: MICHIGAN 42, WISCONSIN 0

Virgil kicks off for Michigan following the score to Wisconsin endzone for a touchback.

7:09 WISCONSIN
- 1/10-W20 - Stauss runs right guard, gets 3 to 23 (Jones)
- 2/7 -W23 - Kalasmiki passes right to Charles, gets 7 to 30
- 1/10-W30 - Josten pitches right to Matthews, gets 1 to 31 (Diggs)
- 2/9 -W31 - Josten passes over the middle to Souza, overthrown
- 3/9 -W31 - Josten runs up the middle, gets 2 to 33 (Meeter)
- 4/7 W33 - Kiltz punts 31 yards to M35, Jolly returns 4 yards to 39. Michigan is penalized 15 yards for clipping

5:04 MICHIGAN
- 1/10-M25 - Reid runs right tackle, gets 7 to 32 (Christenson)
- 2/3 -M32 - Leoni runs up the middle, gets 1 to 33 (Burt)
- 3/2 -M33 - Reid runs up the middle, gets 1 to 34 (Blaskowski)
- 4/1 M34 - Willner punts 66 yards to Wisconsin for touchback

2:58 WISCONSIN
- 1/10-W20 - Josten rolls right and throws to Krepfle, incomplete
- 2/10-W20 - Mohapp runs right tackle, gets 7 to 27 (Jones)
- 3/3 -W27 - Richardson runs right end, gets 3 to 30 (Jones)
- 1/10-W30 - Josten passes over the middle to Souza, incomplete
- 2/10-W30 - Josten passes left to Stracka, incomplete
  Wisconsin is penalized 15 yards for ineligible man down field
- 2/25-W15 - Cohee runs right tackle, gets 2 to 17 (Hollway)
- 3/23-W17 - Josten back to pass is sacked, loses 3 to 14 (Melita)
- 4/26-W14 - Crossen punts 31 yards to W45, Harden fair catch

:26 MICHIGAN
- 1/10-W45 - Woolfolk runs right tackle, gets 12 to 33 (Johnson)

**END OF GAME:
MICHIGAN 42, WISCONSIN 0**

National Collegiate Athletic Association
FINAL TEAM STATISTICS

	MICHIGAN	WISCONSIN
First Downs	24	15
Rushing	18	9
Passing	3	6
Penalty	3	0
Rushing Attempts	65	39
Yards Rushing	373	152
Yards Lost Rushing	13	19
Net Yards Rushing	360	133
Net Yards Passing	117	94
Passes Attempted	8	21
Passes Completed	5	10
Had Intercepted	0	0
Total Offensive Plays	73	60
Total Net Yards	477	227
Average Gain Per Play	6.5	3.8
Fumbles: Number—Lost	1/1	2/2
Penalties: Number—Yards	2/30	4/40
Interceptions: Number—Yards	—	—
Number of Punts—Yards	4/202	9/280
Average Per Punt	50.5	31.1
Punt Returns: Number—Yards	3/19	1/4
Kickoff Returns: Number—Yards	1/22	2/26

OCTOBER 28, 1978

**ILLINOIS
VS.
INDIANA**
Memorial Stadium
Bloomington, Ind.
Temp: 61
Wind: NW 10-12
FIRST QUARTER

Illinois wins toss, will receive and defend south goal. Freud kicks off into end zone to Foster, returned to IL26, 26 return.
14:54 ILLINOIS
1/10-IL26 - Weiss pass complete to Barnes to IL39 (13 yards)
1/10-IL39 - Dismuke le to IN46 (15 yards)
1/10-IN46 - Dismuke lg to IN44 (2 yards)
2/8 -IN44 - Dismuke lg to IN42 (2 yards)
3/6 -IN42 - Weiss trapped to IN48 (loss of 6)
4/12-IN48 - Indiana illegal procedure
4/7 -IN43 - Strader re to IN26 (17 yards)
1/10-IN26 - Weiss re to IN22 (4 yards)
2/6 -IN22 - Weiss rg to IN15 (7 yards)
1/10-IN22 - Dismuke re for touchdown (15 yards)
PAT—Finzer kick good Score: Illinois 7 Indiana 0

Finzer kicks off to Wilbur at IN22, 12 return to IN34
10:32 INDIANA
1/10-IN34 - Harkrader re to IN38 (4 yards)
2/6 -IN38 - Johnson lg to IN41 (3 yards)
3/4 -IN41 - Arnett pass incomplete
4/4 -IN41 - Lovett punts into end zone (59 punt)

9:17 ILLINOIS
1/10-IL20 - Weiss re to IN18, loss of 2
2/12-IL18 - Weiss pass complete to Barnes to IL21 (3 yards)
3/9 -IL21 - Dismuke rt to IL20, loss of 1
4/10-IL20 - Finzer punts to Wilbur to IN47, returned to IL45 (8 return 33 punt)

7:17 INDIANA
1/10-IL45 - Arnett re to IL42 (3 yards)
2/7 -IL42 - Harkrader lg to IL31 (11 yards)
1/10-IL31 - Indiana illegal procedure
1/15-IL36 - Harkrader le to IL25 (11 yards)
2/4 -IL25 - Harkrader lg to IL18 (7 yards)
1/10-IL18 - Johnson rg to IL10 (8 yards)
2/2 -IL10 - Johnson lg to IL1, 9 yards
1/G -IL1 - Arnett rg for touchdown (1 yard)
PAT—Freud kick good Score: Indiana 7 Illinois 7

Straub kicks off out of end zone
5:02 ILLINOIS
1/10-IL20 - Powell rg to IL21 (1 yard)
2/9 -IL21 - Weiss pass complete to Strader to IL29 (8 yards)
3/1 -IL29 - Weiss fumble recovered by Doehla, loss of 1 to IL28

3:38 INDIANA
1/10-IL28 - Harkrader lg to IL25 (3 yards)
2/7 -IL25 - Johnson lg to IL25 (2 yards)
3/5 -IL23 - Harkrader re to IL27 (loss of 4)
4/9 -IL27 - Freud 44 field goal attempt good
Score: Indiana 10, Illinois 7

Straub kicks off to Foster at goal line, returned to IL21, 21 return
1:40 ILLINOIS
1/10-IL21 - Strader lg to IL25 (4 yards)
2/6 -IL25 - Dismuke re to IL26 (1 yard)
3/5 -IL26 - Illinois holding
3/18-IL13 - Weiss rt to IL25 (12 yards)
4/6 -IL25 - Finzer punts to Wilbur at IN42, returned to IN39 (loss of 3 return 33 punt)

**END OF QUARTER:
INDIANA 10, ILLINOIS 7**

SECOND QUARTER

15:00 INDIANA
1/10-IN39 - Arnett pass incomplete
2/10-IN39 - Harkrader re to IL47 (14 yards)
1/10-IL47 - Harkrader lt to IL48 (loss of 1)
2/11-IL48 - Arnett pass complete to Stephenson to IL42, 6 yards and Illinois personal foul
1/10 IL27 - Harkrader lt to IL29 (loss of 2)
2/12-IL29 - Harkrader rg to IL30 (loss of 1)
3/13-IL30 - Arnett lt to IL28 (2 yards)
4/11-IL28 - Freud 45 field goal attempt wide left

12:15 ILLINOIS
1/10-IL28 - Strader lg to IL43 (15 yards)
1/10-IL43 - Strader rg to IL45 (2 yard)
2/8 -IL45 - Weiss re to IL46 (1 yard)
3/7 -IL46 - Weiss pass incomplete
4/7 -IL46 - Finzer punts to Wilbur at IN8, returned to IN48, 40 return (46 punt)

10:15 INDIANA
1/10-IN48 - Arnett re to IL46 (6 yards)
2/4 -IL46 - Bowers lg to IL41 (5 yards)
1/10-IL41 - Harkrader le to IL34 (7 yards)
2/3 -IL34 - Harkrader lg to IL34 (no gain)
3/3 -IL34 - Harkrader le to IL34 (no gain)
4/3 -IL34 - Arnett re to IL32 (2 yards)

7:59 ILLINOIS
1/10-IL32 - Weiss pass complete to Barnes to IN49 (19 yards)
1/10-IN49 - Dismuke le to IN44 (5 yards)
2/5 -IN44 - Weiss pass incomplete
3/5 -IN44 - Weiss trapped to IN49 (loss of 5)
4/10-IN49 - Finzer punts dead to IN10 (39 punt)

6:15 INDIANA
1/10-IN10 - Arnett pass incomplete
2/10-IN10 - Harkrader rg to IN24 (14 yards)
1/10-IN24 - Indiana holding
1/22-IN12 - Harkrader re to IN28 (16 yards)
2/6 -IN28 - Harkrader rt to IN27 (loss of 1)
3/7 -IN27 - Arnett pass complete to Bowers to IN23 (loss of 4)
4/11-IN23 - Lovett punts to Tucker at IL43 (fair catch 34 punt)

3:43 ILLINOIS
1/10-IL43 - Powell lt to IL46 (3 yards)
2/7 -IL46 - Weiss pass complete to Boeke to IN36 (18 yards)
1/10-IN36 - Dismuke rg to IN34 (2 yards)
2/8 -IN34 - Strader lg to IN21 (13 yards)
1/10-IN21 - Dismuke recovers own fumble back at IL47 (loss of 32)
2/42-IL47 - Strader rg to IN41 (12 yards)
3/30-IN41 - Weiss rg to IN23 (18 yards)
4/12-IN23 - Finzer 40 field goal attempt good
Score: Indiana 10, Illinois 10

Finzer kicks off to M. Ramsey at IN25, returned to IN32, 7 return
0:13 INDIANA
1/10-IN32 - Johnson rg to IN38 (6 yards)
2/4 -IN38 - Arnett pass incomplete

**END OF HALF:
INDIANA 10, ILLINOIS 10**

THIRD QUARTER

Finzer kicks off into end zone
15:00 INDIANA
1/10-IN26 - Johnson rg to IN26 (6 yards)
2/4 -IN26 - Harkrader lt to IN27 (1 yard)
3/3 -IN27 - Harkrader re to IN45 (18 yards)
1/10-IN45 - Harkrader rt to IL41 (14 yards)
1/10-IL41 - Johnson lg to IL38 (3 yards)
2/7 -IL38 - Harkrader re to IL36 (2 yards)
3/5 -IL36 - Arnett pass complete to Johnson to IL16 (20 yards)
1/10-IL16 - Arnett re to IL13 (3 yards)
2/7 -IL13 - Harkrader rg to IL8 (5 yards)
3/2 -IL8 - Harkrader re to IL7 (1 yard)
4/1 -IL7 - Illinois offsides
1/G -IL3 - Harkrader rg to IL1 (2 yards)
2/G -IL1 - Arnett lg to IL1 (no gain)
3/G -IL1 - Harkrader rt for touchdown (1 yard)
PAT—Freud kick good
Score: Indiana 17, Illinois 10

Straub kicks off to Dismuke at IL8, returned to IL25, 17 return
9:12 ILLINOIS
1/10-IL25 - Dismuke re to IL28 (3 yards)

2/7 -IL28 - Strader lg to IL34 (6 yards)
3/1 -IL34 - Strader rg to IL41 (7 yards)
1/10-IL41 - Weiss pass incomplete
2/10-IL41 - Strader lg to IL44 (3 yards)
3/7 -IL44 - Weiss pass complete to Barnes to IN49 (7 yards)
1/10-IN49 - Strader rg to IN46 (3 yards)
2/7 -IN46 - Weiss re to IN43 (3 yards)
3/4 -IN43 - Weiss lg to IN40 (3 yards)
4/1 -IN40 - Strader lg to IN38 (2 yards)
1/10-IN38 - Strader rg to IN32 (6 yards)
2/4 -IN32 - Weiss pass incomplete
3/4 -IN32 - Strader rg to IN31 (1 yard)
4/1 -IN31 - Finzer 49 field goal attempt wide right

2:20 INDIANA
1/10-IN31 - Harkrader rt to IL42 (27 yards)
1/10-IL42 - Johnson rg to IL26 (16 yards)
1/10-IL26 - Johnson rg to IL22 (4 yards)
2/6 -IL22 - Darring lg to IL19 (3 yards)
3/3 -IL19 - Harkrader re to IL17 (2 yards)
4/1 -IL17 - Arnett pass complete to Powers for touchdown (17 yards)
PAT—Freud kick good
Score: Indiana 24, Illinois 10

**END OF QUARTER:
INDIANA 24, ILLINOIS 10**

FOURTH QUARTER

Straub kicks off to Foster in end zone, returned to IL19 (19 return)
14:55 ILLINOIS
1/10-IL19 - Dismuke re to IL26 (7 yards)
2/3 -IL26 - Weiss pass complete to Dismuke at IL32 (6 yards)
1/10-IL32 - Weber rg to IL41 (9 yards)
2/1 -IL41 - Weiss pass incomplete
3/1 -IL41 - Weber rg to IN43 (16 yards)
1/10-IN43 - Weiss pass incomplete
2/10-IN43 - Weber lg to IN40 (3 yards)
3/7 -IN40 - Illinois illegal receiver
4/12-IN45 - Finzer punts to Wilbur at IN10 returned to IN9 (loss of 1 return 35 punt)

12:35 INDIANA
1/10-IN9 - Harkrader lg to IN14 (5 yards)
2/5 -IN14 - Johnson rg to IN17 (3 yards)
3/2 -IN17 - Harkrader rt to IN21 (4 yards)
1/10-IN21 - Johnson lg to IN25 (4 yards)
2/6 -IN25 - Johnson rg to IN28 (3 yards)
3/3 -IN28 - Arnett pass incomplete
4/3 -IN28 - Illinois roughing kicker
1/10-IN43 - Johnson rg to IN44 (1 yard) but Indiana holding
1/24-IN29 - Johnson lg to IN33 (4 yards)
2/20-IN33 - Johnson lt to IN48 (15 yards)
3/5 -IN48 - Burnett rg to 50 (2 yards)
4/3 - 50 - Lovett punts to Hardy at IL9, returned to ILl5, 6 return 41 punt

330

ILLINOIS
1/10-ILI5 - Strader lg to IL8 (3 yards)
2/7 -IL8 - Weiss pass complete to Cozen to IL40 (22 yards) first down and Indiana personal foul roughing passer
1/10-IN45 - Illinois holding
1/37-IL28 - Strader rg to IL32 (4 yards)
2/33-IL32 - Weiss trapped to IL23, loss of 9
3/42-IL23 - Weiss pass complete to Dismuke to IL29 (6 yards)
4/36-IL29 - Finzer punts out of bounds on IN48,
23 punt, and Illinois penalized for interference

4:50 INDIANA
1/10-IL37 - Burnett lt to IL33 (4 yards)
2/6 -IL33 - Bowers rg to IL31 (3 yards)
3/3 -IL31 - Bowers rg to IL26 (5 yards)
1/10-IL26 - Bowers rg to IL23 (3 yards)
2/7 -IL23 - Burnett rg to IL20 (3 yards)
3/4 -IL20 - Burnett rg to ILl3 (7 yards)
1/10-IL13 - Burnett rg to IL10 (3 yards)
2/7 -IL10 - Bowers rg to IL8 (2 yards)
3/5 -IL8 - Burnett rt to IL4 (4 yards)
4/1 -IL4 - Burnett lg to IL2 (2 yards)
1/G -IL2 - Burnett rg for touchdown (2 yards)
PAT—Freud kick good. Score: Indiana 31, Illinois 10

**FINAL SCORE:
INDIANA 31 ILLINOIS 10**

**National Collegiate Athletic Association
FINAL TEAM STATISTICS**

	ILLINOIS	INDIANA
First Downs	16	19
Rushing	9	14
Passing	6	2
Penalty	1	3
Rushing Attempts	43	65
Yards Rushing	230	320
Yards Lost Rushing	56	9
Net Yards Rushing	174	311
Net Yards Passing	102	39
Passes Attempted	15	9
Passes Completed	9	4
Had Intercepted	0	0
Total Offensive Plays	58	74
Total Net Yards	276	350
Average Gain Per Play	4.7	4.7
Fumbles: Number—Lost	3/1	1/0
Penalties: Number—Yards	8/106	4/40
Interceptions: Number—Yards	0/0	0/0
Number of Punts—Yards	6/209	3/134
Average Per Punt	35	48
Punt Returns: Number—Yards	1/6	4/44
Kickoff Return: Number—Yards	4/83	2/19

PURDUE VS. IOWA
Temp: mid 50's
Wind: 10-12 mph East
Skies: sunny
FIRST QUARTER

Purdue wins toss and elects to receive. Iowa will kick off and defend north goal.
Schilling kicks off to Moss in endzone for touchback
PURDUE
1/10-P20 - Herrmann passes to Harris for gain of 40
1/10-I40 - Herrmann pass intended for Harris is incomplete
2/10-I40 - Herrmann passes to Burrell for gain of 21 (King)
1/10-I19 - Macon around re for gain of 4 (Kevin Ellis)
2/6 -I15 - Herrmann thrown for loss of 7 (Vazquez)
3/13-I22 - Herrmann passes to Pope for no gain (Gutshall)
4/13-I22 - Burrell holds, Sovereen kicks, field goal attempt is good
SCORE: PURDUE 3, IOWA 0

Sovereen kicks off to Blatcher for return of 19 (Seneff)
12:45 IOWA
1/10-I19 - Lazar over lg for gain of 17 (Clark)
1/10-I36 - Mosley around le for gain of 2 (Motts)
2/8 -I38 - Mosley over rg for gain of 3 (Motts)
3/5 -I41 - Mosley around re for gain of 8 (Floyd)
1/10-I49 - Morton over rt for gain of 2 (Johanson)
2/8 -P49 - McKillip over lg for gain of 7 (Jackson)
3/1 -P42 - McKillip over rg for no gain (Johanson)
4/1 -P42 - Lazar over lt for gain of 2 (Johanson)
1/10-P40 - Mosley around re for loss of 1
Iowa penalized 15 yds for holding
1/26-I44 - Dolan thrown for loss of 10 (Turner)
2/36-I34 - Mosley around re for gain of 3 (Motts)
3/33-I37 - Mosley over lg for gain of 6 (Clark)
4/27-I43 - Holsclaw punts to Gallivan for fair catch (35 yard punt)

6:44 PURDUE
1/10-P22 - Macon over rg for gain of 3 (Hobbs)

2/7 -P25 - Herrmann pass intended for Harris incomplete
3/7 -P25 - Macon over lg for gain of 2 (Vazquez)
4/5 -P27 - Linville punts to Reid for fair catch (33-yard punt)

5:34 IOWA
1/10-I40 - Dolan pass intended for Morton is incomplete
2/10-I40 - Dolan thrown for loss of 1 (Jackson)
3/11-I39 - Dolan pass intended for Dunham, intercepted by Moss, return of 4

4:36 PURDUE
1/10-P47 - Pope over lt for gain of 2 (Rusk)
2/8 -P49 - Herrmann passes to Macon, fumbles, recovered by Burrell (13 yard gain)
1/10-I38 - Pope around le for gain of 3
2/7 -I35 - Herrmann pass intended for Burrell is incomplete
3/7 -I35 - Herrmann passes to Harris for gain of 9
1/10-I26 - Macon over rg for gain of 3 (Weiss)
2/7 -I23 - Mason around re for gain of 2 (Weiss)
3/5 -I21 - Herrmann scrambles for gain of 10 (Pace)
1/10-I11 - Herrmann pass intended for Young is incomplete
2/10-I11 - Pope around NC for TD
Burrell holds, Sovereen kicks, PAT is good
SCORE: PURDUE 10, IOWA 0

332

OCTOBER 28, 1978

Sovereen kicks off to Blatcher for return of 18 (Josten)
1:34 IOWA
1/10 -I23 - Lazar over rt for gain of 1 (Loushin)
2/9 -I24 - Mosley around re for gain of 2 (Motts)
3/7 -I26 - Dolan thrown for loss of 8 (Clark)

FIRST QUARTER SCORE: PURDUE 10, IOWA 0
SECOND QUARTER

IOWA
4/15-I18 - Holsclaw punts to Pope for fair catch. (39 yard kick)

14:53 PURDUE
1/10-P43 - Pope around RE for no gain (Hobbs)
2/10-P43 - Herrmann passes to Burrell for gain of 19. (King)
1/10-I38 - Herrmann pass intended for Eubank is incomplete
2/10-I38 - Herrmann passes to Macon for gain of 5
3/5 -I33 - Pope around RE for gain of 8 (Rusk)
1/10-I25 - Herrmann passes to Young for gain of 25 for TD. Burrell holds, Sovereen kicks, PAT is good.
SCORE: PURDUE 17, IOWA 0

Sovereen kicks off to Reid for return of 4. (Kingsbury)
13:47 IOWA
1/10-I20 - Burke around LE for gain of 4. (Supan)
2/6 -I24 - Dolan over LT for gain of 1. (Loushin)
3/5 - I25 - Dolan passes to Lazar for gain of 4. (Floyd)
4/1 -I29 - Dolan sneaks for gain of 2. (Motts)
1/10-I31 - Burke over LT for gain of 2. (Clark)
2/8 -I33 - Burke over LT for gain of 1. (Jackson)
3/7 -I34 - Dolan pass intended for Reid is incomplete. Iowa penalized for offensive pass interference (15 yds)
4/22-I19 - Holsclaw punts out-of-bounds on Purdue 24 yard line (57 yard punt)

10:42 PURDUE
1/10-P24 - Herrmann passes to Burrell for gain of 8 (Shaw)
2/2 -P32 - Pope over RT for gain of 5 (Shaw)
1/10-P37 - Pope around LE for gain of 7 (Becker)
2/3 -P44 - Herrmann pass intended for Harris is incomplete
3/3 -P44 - Pope around RE, fumbles, recovered by Hall, gain of 7 (Shaw)
1/10-I49 - Herrmann pass intended for Burrell is incomplete
2/10-I49 - Macon over LG for loss of 1 (Hobbs)
3/11- 50 - Herrmann passes to Macon for gain of 9 (Vazquez)
4/2 -P41 - Linville punts dead on Iowa 14 yard line. Offsetting penalties.
4/2 -P41 - Linville punts out of bounds on I17 yard line (42 yard)

6:50 IOWA
1/10-I17 - Burke around LE for gain of 5 (Johanson)
2/5 -I22 - Burke over RT for gain of 9 (Motts)
1/10-I31 - Burke over LT for gain of 5 (Seneff)
2/5 -I36 - Dolan over LT for gain of 2 (Jackson)
3/3 -I38 - Burke over RT for gain of 5 (Johanson)
1/10-I43 - Lazar over LT for gain of 2 (Jackson)
2/8 -I45 - Burke over RT for gain of 5 (Loushin)
3/3 - 50 - Dolan over RT for no gain. (Motts)
4/3 - 50 - Holsclaw punts to Pope for fair catch (26 yard kick)

1:48 PURDUE
1/10-P24 - Herrmann pass intended for Harris is incomplete
2/10-P24 - Pope over RT for gain of 9 (Vazquez)
3/1 -P33 - Pope around LE for no gain (Vazquez)
4/1 -P33 - Linville punts to Reid for return of 7 (29 yard kick) (Adamie)

333

0:50 IOWA
1/10-I45 - Dolan passes to Reid for gain of 20 (Seneff)
1/10-P35 - Dolan thrown for loss of 15 (Floyd)
2/25- 50 - Dolan pass intended for Crocker is incomplete
3/25- 50 - Dolan around LE for no gain (Turner)
4/25- 50 - Burke around RE for gain of 3 (Turner)

0:02 PURDUE
1/10-P47 - Herrmann pass intended for Harris is incomplete

**FIRST HALF SCORE:
PURDUE 17 IOWA 0**

11:12 PURDUE
1/10-P12 - Pope over RT for loss of 3 (Weiss)
2/13-P9 - Herrmann pass intended for Harris is incomplete
3/13-P9 - Pope around LE for loss of 5 (Becker) Iowa penalized for piling on
4/3 -P19 - Eagin punts to Reid for return of 4 (42 yard kick)

10:11 IOWA
1/10-I43 - Reid around LE for TD
Morton holds, Schilling kicks, PAT is good
SCORE: PURDUE 17 IOWA 7

THIRD QUARTER

Iowa will recieve. Purdue will kick off and defend north goal. Sovereen kicks off to Reid for return of 12. (Kingsbury)
IOWA
1/10-I18 - Mosley over LG for gain of 1 (Jackson)
2/9 -I19 - Dolan pass intended for Mosley is incomplete
3/9 -I19 - Dolan passes to Morton for gain of 11
1/10-I30 - Mosley over LG for gain of 4 (Loushin)
2/6 -I34 - Burke over RG for gain of 1 (Loushin)
3/5 -I35 - Lazar over RG for gain of 20 (Moss)
1/10-P45 - Dolan passes to Swift for gain of 27 (Harris)
1/10-P18 - McKillip over RT for gain of 1 (Jackson)
2/9 -P17 - Burke over RT for gain of 5, fumbles, recovered by Turner.

Schilling kicks off into endzone for touchback
9:57 PURDUE
1/10-P20 - Augustyniak over LG for gain of 3 (Rusk)
2/7 -P23 - Herrmann pass intended for Young is incomplete
3/7 -P23 - Herrmann pass intended for Augustyniak is incomplete
4/7 -P23 - Eagin punts to Reid for return of 1 (39 yard punt) (Seneff)

9:08 IOWA
1/10-I39 - Burke over RT for no gain (Ernst)
2/10-I39 - Dolan around RE for gain of 2 (Floyd)
3/8 -I41 - Dolan around RE for gain of 2 (Motts)
4/6 -I43 - Holsclaw punts to Pope, fumbles, recovered, no gain (29 yard kick)

7:07 PURDUE
1/10-P30 - Pope over LT for no gain. (Vazquez)
2/10-P30 - Herrmann pass intended for Burrell, intercepted by King, return of 3

OCTOBER 28, 1978

6:33 IOWA
1/10 -P40 - Burke around LE for gain of 1 (Jackson)
2/9 -P39 - Dolan pass intended for Burke is incomplete
3/9 -P39 - Dolan passes to Reid for gain of 8 (Supan)
4/1 -P31 - Mosley over RG for gain of 4 (Clark)
1/10 -P27 - Mosley over RG for gain of 2 (Motts)
2/8 -P25 - Dolan pass intended for Reid is incomplete
3/8 -P25 - Dolan over LG for no gain (Turner)
4/8 -P25 - Morton holds, Schilling kicks, field goal attempt is no good.

3:26 PURDUE
1/10 -P25 - Macon around LE for gain of 6 (Weiss)
2/4 -P31 - Pope over LG for gain of 1 (Gutshall)
3/3 -P32 - Pope around RE for gain of 3 (Rusk)
1/10 -P35 - Macon over RT for gain of 3 (Vazquez)
2/7 -P38 - Herrmann passes to Young for gain of 14 (Pace)
1/10 -I48 - Pope around LE for gain of 3 (King)
2/7 -I45 - Herrmann passes to Harris for gain of 7
1/10 -I38 - Herrmann pass intended for Young is incomplete
2/10 -I38 - Herrmann passes to Augustyniak for gain of 5 (Gutshall)

**THIRD QUARTER SCORE:
PURDUE 17 IOWA 7**

FOURTH QUARTER

PURDUE
3/5 -I33 - Herrmann around RE for gain of 6 (Becker)
1/10 -I27 - Macon over LG for gain of 2 (Mahmens) Iowa penalized half distance to goal for personal foul.
1/10 -I12 - Pope over RT for gain of 1 (Mahmens)
2/9 -I11 - Herrmann passes to Burrell for TD Burrell holds, Sovereen kicks, PAT is good.
SCORE: PURDUE 24 IOWA 7

Sovereen kicks off to Crocker, fumbles, recovered by Seneff. Return of 17 (Kingsbury)
14:08 PURDUE
1/10 -I23 - McCall over RT for gain of 1. Purdue penalized 15 yds for holding (Gutshall)
1/25 -I38 - Oliver passes to Gallivan for gain of 14 (Pace)
2/11 -I24 - Oliver passes to Eubank for gain of 9 (Becker)
3/2 -I15 - McCall over LG for gain of 2 (Vazquez)
1/10 -I13 - Oliver around LE for gain of 9
2/1 -I4 - McCall around RE for loss of 6 (Becker)
3/7 -I10 - Oliver pass intended for Smith is incomplete.
4/7 -I10 - Burrell holds, Sovereen kicks, field goal attempt is good
SCORE: PURDUE 27 IOWA 7

Sovereen kicks off to Blatcher for return of 15 (Smith)
11:47 IOWA
1/10 -I20 - Dolan pass intended for Reid is incomplete
2/10 -I20 - Dolan pass intended for Morton, intercepted by Supan, return of 2

11:24 PURDUE
1/10 -I32 - Augustyniak around RE for loss of 5 (Dean)
2/15 -I37 - Oliver around LE for gain of 5 (Woodland)
3/10 -I32 - Oliver passes to Turner, fumbles, recovered by Pace, gain of 12 (King)

10:33 IOWA
1/10 -I20 - Burke around RE for gain of 6 (Marks)
2/4 -I26 - Lazar over LG for gain of 9 (Motts)
1/10 -I35 - Lazar over LG for gain of 1 (Marks)
2/9 -I36 - Dolan pass intended for Swift is incomplete
3/9 -I36 - Dolan scrambles for gain of 4 (Marks)
4/5 -I40 - Holsclaw punts to Purdue (36 yard kick)
Iowa penalized 15 yards for interference

7:57 PURDUE
1/10 -P39 - McCall around RE for no gain (Pace)
2/10 -P39 - Augustyniak over RT for gain of 2 (Dean)
3/8 -P41 - Oliver around LE for gain of 7 (Woodland)
4/1 -P48 - Eagin punts to Reid for gain of 14 (42 yard punt) (Adamie)

6:43 IOWA
1/10 -P24 - Dolan passes to Wozniak for gain of 9
2/1 -P33 - Dolan pass intended for Reid, intercepted by Smith, return of 40.

5:53 PURDUE
1/10 -I7 - Augustyniak over LG for gain of 2 (Hill)
Iowa penalized for too many men on field.
2/6 -I3 - Oliver passes to Eubank for TD. Burrell holds, Sovereen kicks, field goal attempt is good
SCORE: PURDUE 34 IOWA 7

335

Sovereen kicks off to Blatcher for return of 29 (Moss)

5:26 IOWA
1/10-I33 - Blatcher over RT for gain of 11 (Kingsbury)
1/10-I44 - Dolan passes to Reid for gain of 13 (Moss)
1/10-P43 - Frazier over RG for gain of 2 (Munro)
2/8 -P41 - Dolan pass intended for Dunham is incomplete
3/8 -P41 - Dolan pass intended for Blatcher, intercepted by Marks, return of 5

3:43 PURDUE
1/10-P48 - Robinson over RT for gain of 4 (Skradis)
2/6 -I48 - Augustyniak over LT for gain of 3 (Woodland)
3/3 -I45 - Robinson around RE for no gain (King)
4/3 -I45 - Eagin punts to Iowa 15 yard line (30 yard punt)

2:17 IOWA
1/10-I15 - Blatcher around RE for gain of 2 (Marks)
2/8 -I17 - Ball over LT for gain of 1 (Loushin)

3/7 -I18 - Dolan around LE for gain of 4 (Barr)
4/3 -I22 - Holsclaw punts to Purdue 28 yard line. (50 yard kick)

0:11 PURDUE
1/10-P28 - Robinson around LE, fumbles out of bounds, gain of 5 (Simonsen)
2/5 -P33 - McCall over LG for gain of 2 (Dean)

**FINAL SCORE:
PURDUE 34 IOWA 7**

FINAL TEAM STATISTICS

Statistics	Iowa	Purdue
First Downs	15	18
Rushes - Yards	54-205	43-116
Passing Yards	92	224
Return Yards	29	53
Passes	7-20-4	18-33-1
Punts	7-39.7	7-34.1
Fumbles - Lost	2-2	5-1
Penalties - Yards	6-78	1-15

OCTOBER 28, 1978

MINNESOTA VS. MICHIGAN
Michigan Stadium
Temp: 53º
Wind: N 14 mph
Skies: Sunny and Mild
FIRST QUARTER

TOSS: Minnesota won the toss and elected to receive. Michigan defends the north goal. Minnesota will be referred to as m—Michigan will be referred to as M. Virgil kicked off out of the m endzone.

15:00 MINNESOTA
1/10-m20 - Barber at lg for 1; Simpkins.
2/9 -m21 - Carlson rolled right, elected to run and cut back for 7; Greer.
3/2 -m28 - Kitzmann hit behind rt by Simpkins for -1.
4/3 -m27 - Smith's punt downed by m at the M41; 32 yd punt.

13:09 MICHIGAN
1/10-M41 - Davis at rg for 2; Friberg.
2/8 -M43 -Woolfolk took a pitchback at re for 11, BUT M penalized for clipping to the M39.
2/12-M39 - Leach elected to run right for 1; Sytsma.
3/11-M40 - Woolfolk on draw at center for 1; Friberg.
4/10-M41 - Willner punted into the m endzone, 59 yd punt.

11:05 MINNESOTA
1/10-m20 - Barber took a pitchback at lt for 1; Keitz.
2/9 -m21 - Carlson passed to Kitzmann for 3; Cannavino.
3/6 -m24 - Carlson was forced to run for -1 hit by Trgovac.
4/7 -m23 - Smith punted to Harden, fair catch at the 50, 27 yd punt.

9:10 MICHIGAN
1/10- 50 - Woolfolk took pitchout at re for 4; Johnson.
2/6 -m46 - Leach rolled left for 1; Burns.
3/5 -m45 - Leach passed to G. Johnson for 14; Brown.
1/10-m31 - Woolfolk on delay at center, cut out to his left for 6; Sytsma.
2/4 -m25 - Woolfolk took pitchback at re for 3; Brown.
3/1 -m22 - Davis off lt for 11; Foxworth.
1/10-m11 - Woolfolk took pitchout at le for 4, BUT M penalized for holding to the m26.

1/25-m26 - Leach passed to Clayton cutting across the middle at about the m20 and Clayton outraced 2 defenders for the M TD. Dickey held while Willnerr converted. 50 yds in 7 plays
MICHIGAN 7, MINNESOTA 0.

Virgil kicked off to Edwards who muffed the catch and downed it for touchback.

6:01 MINNESOTA
1/10-m20 - Kitzmann at center for 5; Keitz.
2/5 -m25 - Barber at rg for 3; Simpkins.
3/2 -m28 - Barber took pitchback at re for 1; Jolly.
4/1 -m29 - Smith punted to Jolly, fair catch at M47, 24 yd punt.

4:09 MICHIGAN
1/10-M47 - Davis at rt for 2; Murphy.
2/8 -M49 - Leach passed to Marsh for 16; Foxworth.
1/10-m35 - Woolfolk took the ball at rt for 11; Edwards.
1/10-m24 - Davis at lg for 4; Friberg.
2/6 -m20 - Woolfolk at re for 3; Snyder.
3/3 -m17 - Davis at lg for 2, BUT M penalized 5 for illegal procedure.
3/8 -m22 - Leach, back to pass, caught by Sytsma for -11.
4/19-m33 - Dickey held while Willner's 50 yd field goal attempt was far short.

0:43 MINNESOTA
1/10-M33 - Kitzmann at center for 2; Greer.
2/8 -m35 - Barber on delay at lg for 3; Simpkins.

**END OF THE FIRST QUARTER:
MICHIGAN 7, MINNESOTA 0**

SECOND QUARTER

MINNESOTA
3/5 -m38 - Carlson, back to pass, hit by Cannavino for -11.
4/16-m27 - Smith punted to Jolly on the M23 and he returned 9; Snyder.

14:19 MICHIGAN
1/10-M32 - Davis at lt for 5; Burns.
2/5 -M37 - Woolfolk took pitchout at le for 3; Johnson.
3/2 -M40 - Davis at lg for 4; Friberg.
1/10-M44 - Leach kept at re for 4; Blanshan.
2/6 -M48 - Woolfolk took pitchback off re for 10; Brown.
1/10-m42 - Woolfolk at rt cut wide for 3; Blanshan.
2/7 -m39 - Leach's pass for Clayton incomplete.
3/7 -m39 - Leach passed to Clayton complete at the m20 and he went to the m8 where Snyder stopped him—TD save credited to Snyder.
1/G -m8 - Leach kept at re for the M TD. Dickey held while Willner converted. 68 yds in 9 plays.
MICHIGAN 14, MINNESOTA 0

Virgil kicked off to Edwards on the m1 and he returned 15 to the m16; T. Leoni.
10:07 MINNESOTA
1/10-m16 - Carlson passed to Barber who dropped it incomplete.
2/10-m16 - Barber on delay at lt for 3; Cannavino.
3/7 -m19 - Carlson passed for Bourquin, broken up by Braman.
4/7 -m19 - Smith punted to Jolly on the M44 and he returned to the m46, 10 yd return, 37 yd punt; Odegard.

9:11 MICHIGAN
1/10-m46 - Davis at rt was hit by Burns, fumbled and Brown recovered for m at the m46.

9:07 MINNESOTA
1/10-m46 - Barber took a pitchback inside re for 45; Braman credited with TD save.
1/G -M9 - Barber at re for 3; Harden.
2/G -M6 - Barber at lt for 3; Trgovac.
3/G -M3 - Carlson kept at lt for no gain; Simpkins.
4/G -M3 - Carlson held while Rogind kicked a 20 yd field goal from the M10 54 yds in 5 plays
MICHIGAN 14, MINNESOTA 3

Rogind kicked off to Clayton in the M endzone where he downed it.

6:53 MICHIGAN
1/10-M20 - Leach cut inside le for 8; Burns.
2/2 -M28 - Davis at rg for 7; Johnson.
1/10-M35 - Woolfolk at lt for 3; Blanshan.
2/7 -M38 - Woolfolk cut off lt for 6; Edwards.
3/1 -M44 - Davis dove over lg for 2; Johnson.
1/10-M46 - Smith took pitchout at re for 5; Brown.
2/5 -m49 - Davis at lg for 2; Ronan.
3/3 -m47 - Leach rolled left for 4; Burns.
1/10-m43 - Woolfolk at lt for 5; Sytsma.
2/5 -m38 - Clayton on pitchback to the right lost 1, Brown.
3/6 -m39 - Leach passed to Mitchell for 15; Foxworth.
1/10-m24 - Leach back to pass, elected to run and lost 1; Murphy.
2/11-m25 - Leach passed for Mitchell incomplete.
3/11-m25 - Woolfolk took pitchout at le for 14; Brown.
1/10-m11 - Woolfolk took pitchout at le for 7; Snyder.
2/3 -m4 - Woolfolk took a pitchout at re, fumbled, and the ball was eventually knocked out of bounds at the m31, -27 on play.
3/30-m31 - Leach passed to Clayton for 18; Edwards.
4/12-m13 - Dickey held while Willner's 30 yd field goal attempt was wide to the right.

0:30 MINNESOTA
1/10-m20 - White at lt for 5; Simpkins.
2/5 -m25 - Barber at le on pitchback for 7; Simpkins.

**END OF THE HALF:
MICHIGAN 14, MINNESOTA 3**

THIRD QUARTER

M elects to receive. m kicks off and defends the north goal. Rogind kicked off out of the M endzone.

15:00 MICHIGAN
1/10-M20 - Davis at lg for 3; Ronan.
2/7 -M23 - Smith at center for 3; Murphy.
3/4 -M26 - Smith took pitchout at le for no gain; Murphy.
4/4 -M26 - Willner punted to Brown, fair catch at m44, 30 yd punt.

13:06 MINNESOTA
1/10-m44 - Carlson's pass intended for Bailey, intercepted by Harden on the m49, and returned to the m27; Barber.

OCTOBER 28, 1978

12:58 MICHIGAN
1/10-m27 - Smith outside le for 5; Sytsma.
2/5 -m22 - Davis at lg for 5; Blanshan.
1/10-m17 - Leach pitched the ball off Smith's hands and out of bounds for 1.
2/9 -m16 - Leach elected to run at center and fought his way for 10; Sytsma.
1/G -m6 - Leach rolled left and fumbled out of bounds for 3.
2/G -m3 - Leach's pass knocked down by Murphy incomplete.
3/G -m3 - Leach passed to Marsh in the endzone for the M TD. Dickey held while Willner converted.
27 yds in 7 plays
MICHIGAN 21, MINNESOTA 3

Virgil kicked off to Edwards on the m15 where he fumbled and Diggs recovered for M.
11:04 MICHIGAN
1/10-m15 - Leach pitched to Smith who fumbled the ball out of bounds at the m9, 6 yd gain.
2/4 -m9 - Davis at center for 7; Burns.
1/G -m2 - Leach rolled at re for 2 and the M TD. Dickey held while Willner converted. 15 yds in 3 plays.
MICHIGAN 28, MINNESOTA 3

Virgil kicked off to Edwards who fumbled and fell on it at the m13; Needham.
10:23 MINNESOTA
1/10-m13 - m penalized 5 for illegal procedure.
1/15-m8 - Barber took pitchback at le for 2; Trgovac.
2/13-m10 - Barber at center for no gain; Keitz, secured by Meter.
3/13-m10 - Avery faded to pass and then ran up the center for 22; Jolly.
1/10-m32 - Kitzmann at lg for 3; Simpkins.
2/7 -m35 - Avery passed for Bourquin incomplete.
3/7 -m35 - Avery faded and rolled left for 6; Simpkins.
4/1 -m41 - Barber at lt for 2; Cannavino.
1/10-m43 - Avery passed for Kitzmann incomplete.
2/10-m43 - Barber hit by Trgovac for -1.
3/11-m42 - White at center for 4; Trgovac.
4/7 -m46 - Smith punted to Jolly, fair catch at M19, 35 yd punt.

6:05 MICHIGAN
1/10-M19 - Woolfolk took pitchout at le for 8; Sytsma.
2/2 -M27 - Reid at lg for 3; Burns.
1/10-M30 - Woolfolk off lg for 6; Ronan.
2/4 -M36 - Leach passed to Mitchell for 19; Edwards.
1/10-M45 - Woolfolk off rt for 2; Johnson.
2/8 -m43 - Leach's pass for Marsh broken up by Foxworth.

3/8 -m43 - Leach faded and ran left across the field for 13; Burns.
1/10-m30 - Reid over lt for 5; Sytsma.
2/5 -m25 - Leach rolled left, faked a pitch, and cut up for 17; Foxworth.
1/G -m8 - Reid at rg for 4; Murphy.
2/G -m4 - Leach at le for 3; Burns.
3/G -m1 - Clayton took a pitchback at le for no gain; Burns.
4/G -m1 - Leach passed to Clayton in the endzone for the M TD. Dickey held while Willner converted.
81 yds in 13 plays
MICHIGAN 35, MINNESOTA 3

Virgil kicked off to Edwards on the m12 and he returned 15; Hollway.
1:33 MINNESOTA
1/10-m27 - Artis at lt for 1; Seabron.
2/9 -m28 - Artis at lg for 13; Meter.
1/10-m41 - White at lg for 4; Greer.

END OF THE THIRD QUARTER:
MICHIGAN 35, MINNESOTA 3

FOURTH QUARTER

MINNESOTA
2/6 -m45 - Artis at lg for 1; Trgovac.
3/5 -m46 - Avery's pass for White incomplete.
4/5 -m46 - Smith punted to Jolly, fair catch at M16, 38 yd punt.

14:11 MICHIGAN
1/10-M16 - Dickey at le for 3; Friberg.
2/7 -M19 - Woolfolk cut back at rt for 3; Fahnhorst.
3/4 -M22 - Dickey rolled left for 6; Johnson.
1/10-M28 - Woolfolk at rt for 1; Cunningham.
2/9 -M29 - Woolfolk took pitchout at re for 2; Edwards.
3/7 -M31 - Dickey hit by Brown for -8.
4/15-M23 - Willner punted to Edwards, fair catch at m32, 45 yd punt.

339

10:42 MINNESOTA
1/10-m32 - Avery passed to White for 15, but m penalized for holding to the m26.
1/16-m26 - Avery's pass for Bourquin incomplete—dropped by Harden.
2/16-m26 - Artis at center for no gain.
3/16-m26 - Avery's pass for Bourquin incomplete, almost intercepted by Harden.
4/16-m26 - Smith's punt downed at the M48, but M penalized 15 for roughing the kicker.
4/1 -m41 - Kitzmann at lt for 2; Cannavino.
1/10-m43 - Bailey on double reverse at le for 4; Jolly.
2/6 -m47 - Avery passed to Bourquin for 14; Diggs.
1/10-M39 - White at lg for 5; Jones.
2/5 -M34 - Avery passed to Thompson for 16; Jolly.
1/10-M18 - Barber at rg for 2; Needham.
2/8 -M16 - Avery passed to Kitzmann for 8; Page.
1/G -M8 - Artis cut up at re for 6; Harden.
2/G -M2 - Kitzmann at rg for 2 and the m TD. Carlson held while Rogind converted. 68 yds in 12 plays.
MICHIGAN 35, MINNESOTA 10

Rogind kicked off to Clayton at the M6 and he returned 14; Hoffman.
6:41 MICHIGAN
1/10-M20 - Reid at lg for 7; Johnson.
2/3 -M27 - Woolfolk on pitchback at re for no gain; Gardner.
3/3 -M27 - Dickey hit by Ronan for -3.
4/6 -M24 - Willner punted to Bailey on the m31 and he returned 7; Mitchell 45 yd punt.

4:35 MINNESOTA
1/10-m38 - Avery passed to White for 3; Cannavino.
2/7 -m41 - Avery's pass for Thompson incomplete.
3/7 -m41 - Avery kept and Jones hit him for -5.
4/12-m36 - Smith punted to Harden, fair catch at M25, 39 yd punt.

3:05 MICHIGAN
1/10-M25 - Reid at lg for 3; Carr.
2/7 -M28 - Dickey's fumble recovered by Schmerge for 3 yd gain;
3/4 -M31 - Leoni on draw at lt for 20; Foxworth.

1/10-m49 - Woolfolk took a pitchback at re, cut to the west sideline and outran the defenders for the M TD. Dickey held while Willner converted. 75 yds in 4 plays.
MICHIGAN 42, MINNESOTA 10

Virgil kicked off to Noel on the m12 and he fumbled it ahead to the m18.
1:13 MINNESOTA
1/10-m18 - Avery passed to Thompson for 12; Jones.
1/10-m30 - White at rg for 1; Jones.
2/9 -m31 - Avery passed for Lewis incomplete, broken up by Jones.
3/9 -m31 - Avery passed to White for 5; Page.

END OF THE GAME:
MICHIGAN 42, MINNESOTA 10

National Collegiate Athletic Association
FINAL TEAM STATISTICS
October 28, 1978

	MICHIGAN	MINNE-SOTA
First Downs	23	10
Rushing	17	6
Passing	6	4
Penalty	0	0
Rushing Attempts	69	39
Net Yards Gained	352	169
Net Yards Lost	51	19
Net Yards	301	150
Net Yards Passing	143	61
Passes Attempted	13	17
Passes Completed	9	7
Had Intercepted	0	1
Total Offensive Plays	82	56
Total Net Yards	444	211
Average Gain Per Play	5.4	3.7
Fumbles: Number—Lost	6/1	3/1
Penalties: Number—Yards	3/45	3/26
Interceptions: Number—Yards	1/22	0/0
Number of Punts—Yards	4	8
Average Per Punt	44.7	35.2
Punts Blocked	0	0
Punt Returns: Number—Yards	2/19	1/7
Kickoff Returns: Number—Yards	1/14	4/37
Field Goals	2/0	1/1
Extra Points	6/6	1/1

OCTOBER 28, 1978

WISCONSIN VS. MICHIGAN STATE

FIRST QUARTER

Wisconsin won the toss and elects to receive. Michigan State defending the north goal.
Wisconsin Co-Captains: Dave Crossen, David Charles, Dan Relich
Michigan State Co-Captains: Craig Lonce, Melvin Land, Charles Shafer
Schario kicks to Matthews returns to UW34, 22 yard return

WISCONSIN
1/10-UW34 - Kalasmiki back to pass, around right end on keeper, tackle by Decker, 6 yd gain
2/4 -UW40- Kalasmiki pass to Stracka, tackle by Bass & Decker, gain of 14
1/10-MS46 - Matthews fumbles, recovers, loss of 5, team tackle
2/15-UW49 - Kalasmiki pass to Sydnor incomplete
3/15 - UW49 - Kalasmiki pass to Matthews, tackle by McCormick & Decker, gain of 12
4/3 -MS39 - Kiltz punts to the MS5, downed by UW, 34 yd punt, no return

12:08 MICHIGAN STATE
1/10-MS5 - S. Smith off right tackle, tackle by team, gain of 3
2/7 -MS8 - Smith back to pass, tackle by Erdmann, loss of 8, safety, Time: 3:38
SCORE: WISCONSIN 2, MICHIGAN STATE 0

Stachowicz punting from 20 (free kick) to Stauss, 8 yd return

11:22 WISCONSIN
1/10-UW43 - Kalasmiki back to pass around right end, tackle by McCormick, no gain
2/10-UW43 - Kalasmiki pass to Seis overthrown
3/10-UW43 - Stauss around left end, tackle by Burroughs, gain of 6
4/4 -UW49 - Kiltz punts to MS12, downed by UW, 39 yd punt, no return

9:42 MICHIGAN STATE
1/10-MS12 - Smith pass to Middleton in left flat, tackle by Johnson, gain of 5
2/5 -MS17 - Smith pass over the middle to Brammer, tackle by Anderson, gain of 12
1/10-MS29 - Smith pass long to Byrd on left sideline incomplete
2/10-MS29 - McGee outside right end on pitchout, tackle by Anderson, gain of 53
1/10-UW18 - Middleton into the middle, tackle Ahrens, no gain

2/10-UW18 - Smith back to pass, around left end, tackle by Schremp, gain of 2
3/8 -UW16 - Smith pass to Hans, clipping MS, 15 yd penalty, 3 yd pass play
3/20-UW28 - Smith pass to Byrd overthrown
4/20-UW28 - Andersen 45 yard field goal attempt wide left

6:12 WISCONSIN
1/10-UW28 - Matthews around right end, tackle by Hay, gain of 27
1/10-MS45 - Stauss off left guard, tackle by Savage, gain of 1
2/9 -MS44 - Matthews inside right guard on counter, tackle by Savage, gain of 1
3/8 -MS43 - Kalasmiki shovel pass to Matthews, tackle by Burroughs, gain of 24
1/10-MS19 - Matthews outside right tackle, tackle by Bass, gain of 17
1/G -MS2 - Stauss through the middle, team tackle, gain of 1
2/G -MS1 - Green through the middle, team team tackle, no gain
3/G -MS1 - Kalasmiki on keeper into right side of line, team tackle, no gain
4/G -MS1 - Matthews on pitchout into right side of line, tackle by Bass & Hay, no gain

1:45 MICHIGAN STATE
1/10-MS1 - S. Smith off right tackle, tackle by Crossen & Relich, gain of 1
2/9 -MS2 - Smith pass to Gibson, knocked out by Johnson, gain of 13
1/10-MS15 - S. Smith around left end on pitchout, tackle by Sawicki, gain of 10
1/10-MS25 - Reeves outside right end, tackle by Blaskowsi, gain of 3
2/7 -MS28 - S. Smith off right tackle on draw, tackle by Christenson, gain of 3

**END OF FIRST QUARTER
WISCONSIN 2, MICHIGAN STATE 0**

SECOND QUARTER

MICHIGAN STATE
3/4 -MS31 - Smith screen pass to Middleton, tackle by Johnson, gain of 8
1/10-MS39 - S. Smith off right tackle on draw, tackle by Schremp, gain of 4
2/6 -MS43 - Smith pass over the middle to Byrd, incomplete
3/6 -MS43 - Smith pass over the middle to McGee goes down right side, tackle by Welch, gain of 40
1/10-UW17 - Smith screen pass to Hans, incomplete
2/10-UW17 - Smith pass to Byrd on right sideline, touchdown. 99 yards in 11 plays
Time: 1:34 Elapsed Time: 3:19
Andersen PAT attempt wide left
SCORE: MICHIGAN STATE 6 WISCONSIN 2

Schario kicks to Stracka at the UW 25, no return
13:26 WISCONSIN
1/10-UW25 - Kalasmiki pass to Charles, tackle by Decker, gain of 16
1/10-UW41 - Kalasmiki pass to Stracka, tackle by Bass, gain of 26
TO/UW 12:26
1/10-MS33 - Stauss off right tackle, tackle by Bass & Decker, gain of 6
2/4 -MS27 - Matthews through the middle, tackle by Bass & Fields, gain of 3
3/1 -MS24 - Green through the middle, tackle by Bass, gain of 2
1/10-MS22 - Kalasmiki off right tackle, tackle by Fields, Savage, gain of 5
2/5 -MS17 - Matthews outside left end on pitchout, tackle by Marshall, gain of 9
1/G -MS8 - Stauss off right tackle, tackle by Decker & Savage, gain of 4
2/G -MS4 - UW delay of game, 5 yd penalty
2/G -MS9 - Kalasmiki pass to Krepfle over the middle incomplete
3/G -MS9 - Kalasmiki pass to Sydnor incomplete (underthrown)
4/G -MS9 - Attempted field goal attempt faked, Kalasmiki pass to Vieth in end zone broken up by Savage

9:06 MICHIGAN STATE
1/10-MS10 - S. Smith outside left end, tackle by Anderson & Gordon, gain of 21
1/10-MS31 - Schramm inside right guard, tackle by Sawicki, gain of 9
2/1 -MS40 - S. Smith off right tackle on draw, Schieble & Sawicki, gain of 12
1/10-UW48 - Smith pass over the middle to Gibson, broken up by Holm
2/10-UW48 - Smith pass in flat to S. Smith, tackle by Holm, no gain, MS penalty declined

3/10-UW48 - Smith pass to Byrd incomplete
4/10-UW48 - Stachowicz punts to Stauss, fair catch, 27 yard punt, no return

7:18 WISCONSIN
1/10-UW21 - Kalasmiki pass to Seis, broken up by Anderson
2/10-UW21 - Kalasmiki pass to Souza, tackle by Graves, gain of 9
3/1 -UW30 - UW illegal procedure, 5 yard penalty
3/6 -UW25 - Kalasmiki back to pass, keeps through middle, tackle by McCormick, gain of 5
4/1 -UW30 - Kiltz punts to S. Smith, fair catch, 41 yd punt, no return

5:47 MICHIGAN STATE
1/10-MS29 - Schramm off left tackle, tackle by Relich & Welch, gain of 6
2/4 -MS35 - McGee around left end on pitchout, steps out of bounds, gain of 7
1/10-MS42 - Smith pass in right flat to Gibson, tackle by Johnson, gain of 7
2/3 -MS49 - Smith pass to Byrd on right side line, tackle by Sawicki, gain of 11
1/10-UW40 - Smith pass to Gibson over the middle, tackle by Johnson, gain of 28
1/10-UW12 - S. Smith outside right tackle, tackle by Sawicki & Welch, gain of 8
2/2 -UW4 - S. Smith off left tackle, tackle by Ahrens, gain of 1 TO/MS 2:13
3/1 -UW3 - Reeves dives over right tackle, tackle by Welch & Crossen, gain of 2
1/G -UW1 - Reeves off left tackle on dive, tackle by Welch & Crossen, no gain
2/G -UW1 - S. Smith outside left end on pitchout, touchdown 71 yards in 10 plays
Time: 13:50 Elapsed Time: 4:37
Andersen PAT attempt good
SCORE: MICHIGAN STATE 13 WISCONSIN 2

Schario kicks to Sydnor, no return, tackle by Savage
1:10 WISCONSIN
1/10-UW18 - Kalasmiki pass to Matthews, runs out of bounds, gain of 7
2/3 -UW25 - Kalasmiki pass to Matthews, tackle by Bass, gain of 6
1/10-UW31 - Kalasmiki pass to Sydnor, broken up by Burroughs
2/10-UW31 - Kalasmiki pass to Matthews, tackle by Bass, gain of 11
1/10-UW42 - Kalasmiki pass to Charles incomplete
2/10-UW42 - Kalasmiki pass to Souza, tackle by McCormick & Burroughs, gain of 21

END OF HALF:
MICHIGAN STATE 13 WISCONSIN 2

OCTOBER 28, 1978

THIRD QUARTER

Michigan State elects to receive. Wisconsin defending the north goal Vieth kicks to Reeves at the goal, returns to the MS 23, tackle by Casey
MICHIGAN STATE
1/10-MS23 - Middleton inside LE (Relich) gain of 3
2/7 -MS26 - Smith pass to Brammer in right side line (Sawicki) gain of 6
3/1 -MS32 - S. Smith off RT (Gordon) gain of 4
1/10-MS36 - McGee outside LE, touchdown, 77 yards in 4 plays
Andersen PAT attempt good
SCORE: MICHIGAN STATE 20 WISCONSIN 2

Schario kicks out of end zone, touchback
12:56 WISCONSIN
1/10-UW20 - Kalasmiki around right end on the keeper (Burroughs) gain of 8
2/2 -UW28 - Stauss through the middle (Bass & Hay) gain of 2
1/10-UW30 - Kalasmiki on keeper (Land) gain of 1
2/9 -UW31 - Kalasmiki pass to Stracka incomplete
3/9 -UW31 - Kalasmiki pass to Stauss (Marshall) gain of 21
1/10-MS48 - Kalasmiki pass to Reutz incomplete (McCormick)
2/10-MS48 - Kalasmiki pass to Matthews (Hay) gain of 7
3/3 -MS41 - Kalasmiki pass incomplete
4/3 MS41 - Faked punt carried by Stauss (Bass & Hay) no gain

10:15 MICHIGAN STATE
1/10-MS42 - Smith pass to Byrd on right side line (Schieble) gain of 19

1/10-UW39 - Smith pass long to Gibson, touchdown, 2 plays 58 yards 39 yd pass play
Andersen PAT attempt good. Wisconsin offside, 5 yd penalty assessed on kickoff
SCORE: MICHIGAN STATE 27 WISCONSIN 2

Schario kicks from MS45 out of end zone, touchback
10:05 WISCONSIN
1/10-UW20 - Kalasmiki pass to Charles overthrown
2/10-UW20 - Souza through the middle (Burroughs) gain of 1
3/9 UW21 - Kalasmiki pass intercepted by Graves, steps out of bounds

9:17 MICHIGAN STATE
1/10-UW46 - Smith pass to Byrd long down right side line, incomplete
2/10-UW46 - Michigan holding, 22 yd penalty
2/32-MS32 - Smith pass to Byrd on right side line, incomplete
3/32-MS32 - S. Smith around left end pitchout (Schieble) gain of 12
4/20-MS44 - Stachowicz punts to UW8, 48 yd punt, downed by Michigan

8:14 WISCONSIN
1/10-UW 8 - Matthews around RE (Burroughs & Savage) loss of 3
2/13-UW 5 - Kalasmiki fumbles, recovered in end zone by McCormick, loss of 5
Andersen PAT attempt good
SCORE: MICHIGAN STATE 34 WISCONSIN 2

Schario kicks to Souza on the UW8 (Hans) 13 yd return

343

7:29 WISCONSIN
1/10-UW21 - Matthews off RE (Decker) gain of 3
2/7 UW24 - Kalasmiki back to pass, keeps around RE (Land) gain of 8
1/10-UW32 - Kalasmiki pass to Souza on right side line, steps out of bounds, gain of 9
2/1 -UW41 - Matthews around RE on pitchout (Webb) gain of 9
1/10- 50 - Kalasmiki pass to Matthews incomplete (Anderson)
2/10- 50 - Stauss off RG (Graves) gain of 23
1/10-MS27 - Matthews around RE on pitchout (Hay) gain of 3
2/7 -MS24 - Kalasmiki pass to Souza in left corner incomplete (Marshall)
3/7 -MS24 - Kalasmiki pass to Souza (Anderson & Graves) gain of 13
1/10-MS11 - Kalasmiki pass to Matthews (Decker) gain of 2
2/8 MS 9 - Kalasmiki pass to Matthews (Decker) gain of 4
Michigan personal foul, late hit, 3 yd penalty
3/1 -MS 2 - Matthews around LE on pitchout (Land & Decker) no gain
4/1 -MS 2 - Kalasmiki pass to Sydnor intercepted by Bass returns 98 yards, touchdown
Andersen PAT attempt good
SCORE: MICHIGAN STATE 41 WISCONSIN 2

Schario kicks out of end zone, touchback
3:04 WISCONSIN
1/10-UW20 - Kalasmiki pass to Souza, steps out of bounds, gain of 10
1/10-UW30 - Kalasmiki pass to Sydnor, Michigan interference, 50 yd penalty
1/10-MS20 - Kalasmiki pass to Charles bobbled & dropped
2/10-MS20 - Kalasmiki back to pass, keeps runs out of bounds (Bass & Land) gain of 6
3/4 -MS14 - Matthews around RE on pitchout (Webb) gain of 2
4/2 -MS12 - Kalasmiki back to pass, sacked by McCormick, loss of 13

1:51 MICHIGAN STATE
1/10-MS25 - Smith pass to Howard on left side line incomplete (Anderson)
2/10-MS25 - Hughes around RE on pitchout, fumbles, recovered by Schieble, gains 8

1:38 WISCONSIN
1/10-MS32 - Kalasmiki pass to Souza (Graves) gain of 8
2/2 -MS24 - Kalasmiki pass to Sydnor incomplete (Webb)
3/2 -MS24 - Kalasmiki pass to Matthews, incomplete
4/2 -MS24 - Kalasmiki pass broken up by Burroughs

:50 MICHIGAN STATE
1/10-MS25 - Reeves carries through middle, tackle, gain of 6
2/4 -MS31 - Hans through the middle (Levenick) gain of 4
END OF THIRD QUARTER
MICHIGAN STATE 41 WISCONSIN 2

FOURTH QUARTER

MICHIGAN STATE
1/10-MS35 - Smith pass to Brammer, gain of 14
1/10-MS49 - Smith pass to Williams, gain of 14
1/10-MS37 - Reeves through the middle (Relich) gain of 10
1/10-MS27 - Smith pass incomplete
2/10-MS27 - Schramm through the middle, gain of 6
3/4 -MS21 - Hughes off RE (Relich) loss of 1
4/5 -MS22 - Reeves around LE on pitchout (Gordon & Ahrens) gain of 1

12:14 WISCONSIN
1/10-UW22 - Kalasmiki pass to Charles bobbled
2/10-UW22 - Kalasmiki back to pass, sacked by Land, loss of 8
3/18-UW14 - Kalasmiki pass intercepted by T. Williams (Mohapp) 25 yd return

11:15 MICHIGAN STATE
1/10-UW15 - Smith pass to Howard in right corner of end zone, touchdown, 15 yds in 1 play
Andersen PAT attempt good
SCORE: MICHIGAN STATE 48 WISCONSIN 2

Schario kicks to Green at UW9 (Griffin)
11:10 WISCONSIN
1/10-UW21 - Matthews around right end (I. Griffin) loss of 3
2/13-UW18 - Kalasmiki pass to Mathews (Decker) gain of 4
3/9 UW22 - Kalasmiki pass to Sydnor on right side (Decker) gain of 14
1/10-UW36 - Kalasmiki pass to Cohee on left side (T. Williams) gain of 2
2/8 -UW38 - Kalasmiki pass to Souza incomplete
4/8 -UW38 - Kiltz punts to MS33, downed by Wisconsin, 29 yd punt, no return

8:49 MICHIGAN STATE
1/10-MS33 - Smith screen pass to Schramm on left side (Schieble) gain of 14
1/10-MS47 - Smith pass to Hans on right side touchdown, 53 yd pass play, 67 yds in 2 plays. Andersen PAT attempt good, Wisconsin offside, 5 yd penalty
SCORE: MICHIGAN STATE 55 WISCONSIN 2

OCTOBER 28, 1978

Schario kicks from MS45 out of end zone, touchback

8:22 WISCONSIN
- 1/10-UW20 - Josten around RE on keeper (Townsend) gain of 3
- 2/7 -UW23 - Richardson through the middle (Converse & Tapling) no gain
- 3/7 -UW23 - Josten pass to Reutz (Cooper) gain of 13
- 1/10-UW36 - Mchapp outside RT (C. Griffin) gain of 3
- 2/7 -UW39 - Josten pass to Souza overthrown
- 3/7 -UW39 - Josten pass to Richards incomplete TO/UW 5:56
- 4/7 -UW39 - Kiltz punts to MS33, 28 yd punt, no return

5:46 MICHIGAN STATE
- 1/10-MS33 - Reeves outside LE (Levenick & Welch) gain of 13
- 1/10-MS46 - Clark pass to Shafer (Welch) gain of 17
- 1/10-UW37 - Michigan illegal procedure 5 yd penalty
- 1/15-UW42 - Reeves outside LT (Burt) gain of 1
- 3/6 -UW33 - Clark pass to Shafer (Levenick & Spurlin & Stroede) gain of 13
- 1/10-UW20 - Hughes outside RE on pitchout (Blaskowski) gain of 4
- 2/6 -UW16 - Schramm through middle (Yourg) gain of 4
- 3/2 -UW12 - Hans off RT (Vine & Welch) gain of 7
- 1/G -UW5 - Schramm through the middle, team tackle, gain of 2
- 2/G -UW3 - Hughes outside LE on pitchout (Ahrens) gain of 1

**FINAL SCORE
MICHIGAN STATE 55 WISCONSIN 2**

**National Collegiate Athletic Association
FINAL TEAM STATISTICS**
October 28, 1978

	WISCON-SIN	MICHIGAN STATE
First Downs	21	28
Rushing	8	12
Passing	12	16
Penalty	1	0
Rushing Attempts	40	39
Yards Rushing	162	304
Yards Lost Rushing	37	9
Net Yards Rushing	125	295
Net Yards Passing	253	350
Passes Attempted	48	31
Passes Completed	22	21
Had Intercepted	3	0
Total Offensive Plays	88	70
Total Net Yards	378	645
Average Gain Per Play	4.3	9.2
Fumbles: Number—Lost	2/1	1/1
Penalties: Number—Yards	3/15	5/95
Interceptions: Number—Yards	0/0	3/123
Number of Punts—Yards	5/171	2/65
Average Per Punt	34.2	32.5
Punt Returns: Number—Yards	0/0	0/0
Kickoff Returns: Number—Yards	6/53	1/23

NORTHWESTERN
VS.
OHIO STATE
Ohio Stadium, Columbus Ohio
Temp.: 58°
Wind: SW 8-15 mph
Skies: Sunny
FIRST QUARTER

Northwestern won the toss and elected to receive;
Ohio State to defend the south goal
Orosz kicked off at 1:34 P.M. 7 yards deep for the touchback
15:00 NORTHWESTERN
1/10-N20 - Cammon into lg for 3
2/7 -N23 - Strasser faked, passed deep left for Bogan, too long incomplete
3/7 -N23 - Strasser passed on screen right to Cammon for 10
1/10-N33 - Strasser passed left to Hill for 11
1/10-N44 - Hill pitch at le for 5
2/5 -N49 - Strasser faded, chased right, reversed left for 3
3/2 -O48 - Strasser passed on hook left to Prichard for 9
1/10-O39 - Cammon thru rg for 5
2/5 -O34 - Strasser passed high and wide for Bogan cutting deep over middle incomplete
3/5 -O34 - Strasser kept right on broken play for -7 Ross, Sullivan; NW motion declined
4/12-O41 - Christensen punted left for the touchback

11:15 OHIO
1/10-O20 - Springs pitch at le, leaped over for 13
1/10-O33 - Springs cut over lg for 8
2/2 -O41 - Campbell middle for 4 (Robinett helped off)
1/10-O45 - Murray pitch at re, outran defenders and went over at the flag Janakievski PAT 80 yards in four plays
SCORE: OHIO 7 NORTHWESTERN 0

Orosz kicked off out of bounds right -5
Orosz kicked off out of bounds right -5
Orosz kicked off out of bounds right -5
Atha kicked off 69 yards left, Geegan returned 24
10:07 NORTHWESTERN
1/10-N30 - Cammon up middle for 7
2/3 -N37 - Hill cut back thru lg for 7
1/10-N44 - Cammon at lg for 4
2/6 -N48 - Strasser faded, sacked by Ross for -10
3/16-N38 - Cammon draw at rg, clear for 15 Northwestern time out at 7:34
4/1 -O47 - Hill pitch at re, clear for 7
1/10-O40 - Hill pitch at re, clear for 10
1/10-O30 - Cammon powered into lg for 3

2/7 -O27 - Bogan took reverse hand off left for 5; Ohio face mask 11
1/10-O11 - Tiberi took handoff right, passed left Strasser for the TD at the flag Mirkopulos PAT 70 yards in 10 plays
SCORE: OHIO 7 NORTHWESTERN 7

Mirkopulos kicked off 54 yards; Murray returned middle 39
5:45 OHIO
1/10-O45 - Campbell stopped at center for 2
2/8 -O47 - Schlichter faked, rolled left, chased, sacked for -1 (Gildner)
3/9 -O46 - Schlichter passed on hook to Springs over middle for 7; Northwestern pass interference 18
1/10-N36 - Springs thru center for 9
2/1 -N27 - Schlichter kept inside le, for 2
1/10-N25 - Schlichter kept inside re, was clear for 12
1/10-N13 - Springs pitch at le for 8
2/2 -N5 - Campbell pushed thru lt for the TD Janakievski PAT 55 yards in 7 plays
SCORE: OHIO 14 NORTHWESTERN 7

Atha kicked off thru the end zone for the touchback
2:53 NORTHWESTERN
1/10-N20 - Cammon lg 2
2/8 -N22 - Strasser faked, passed deep left for Bogan was broken up by Ellis incomplete
3/8 -N22 - Strasser faded, sacked by Ross for -5
4/13-N17 - Christensen punted short right for 26; downed by Northwestern

1:34 OHIO
1/10-N43 - Springs cut into rg for 6
2/4 -N37 - Springs slanted thru rg for 6
1/10-N31 - Schlichter kept inside le for 12
1/10-N19 - Schlichter rolled right, passed off Springs hands in flat incomplete
2/10-N19 - Springs at rt for 4
3/6 -N15 - Schlichter passed too low for Donley over middle left incomplete
4/6 -N15 - Atha's FG try from 32 yards was wide right for the touchback

END OF FIRST QUARTER
OHIO 14 NORTHWESTERN 7

SECOND QUARTER

15:00 NORTHWESTERN
1/10-N20 - Northwestern illegal procedure -5
1/15-N15 - Cammon draw left side for no gain (Sullivan)
2/15-N15 - Cammon at lg for 3
3/12-N18 - Strasser passed on safety swing left to Cammon - dropped incomplete
4/12-N18 - Christensen punted 37; Guess returned 1
Time out Northwestern at 13:31

346

OCTOBER 28, 1978

13:31 OHIO
1/10-O46 - Campbell into middle for 2
2/8 -O48 - Murray option pitch at le for -2 (Bobowski)
3/10-O46 - Schlichter faded, chased, sacked by Stasiewicz -5
4/15-O41 - Orosz punted right 36; Carver fair catch

12:22 NORTHWESTERN
1/10-N23 - Cammon at rt for 2
2/8 -N25 - Strasser passed to Hill on swing right for 5
3/3 -N30 - Strasser passed to Bogan cutting over middle for 16
1/10-N46 - Cammon hesitated at rt for 2
2/8 -N48 - Strasser faded, moved right, passed to Hill on sideline for 4
3/4 -O48 - Strasser passed on safety left to Cammon for -7 (Cousineau)
4/11-N45 - Christensen punted 37; Guess broke tackles, cut right for 33

9:47 OHIO
1/10-N49 - Murray pitch at le for 5
2/5 -N44 - Murray option pitch at re for (measurement) 6
1/10-N38 - Murray option pitch around le for 6
2/4 -N32 - Schlichter kept inside re, cut back left and went over for the TD Janakievski PAT 49 yards, 4 plays
SCORE: OHIO 21 NORTHWESTERN 7
Atha kicked off one yard deep for the touchback

8:42 NORTHWESTERN
1/10-N20 - Hill cut into middle for 2
2/8 -N22 - Strasser passed deep over middle for Poulos, too high; intercepted by Skillings, returned left 28

7:56 OHIO
1/10-N19 - Campbell middle 6
2/4 -N13 - Murray over lt for 1
Time out Northwestern at 7:09
3/3 -N12 - Campbell into rg for 2
4/1 -N10 - Campbell lt for 4
1/G -N6 - Campbell into rg for 5
2/G -N1 - Campbell fell at lt for no gain
3/G -N1 - Campbell again into lt for the TD - Janakievski PAT Northwestern sub infraction, 15 on kickoff 19 yards, 7 plays
SCORE: OHIO 28 NORTHWESTERN 7

Orosz kicked off 19 yards deep for the touchback

5:43 NORTHWESTERN
1/10-N20 - Hill turned re for 5
2/5 -N25 - Hill pitch at re, cut in for 8
1/10-N33 - Cammon into middle for 4
2/6 -N37 - Strasser faked, passed deep right for Bogan, just wide incomplete

3/6 -N37 - Strasser passed to Cammon on swing for 4
4/2 -N41 - Northwestern delay of game -5
4/7 -N36 - Christensen punted 37; Guess returned right, cut left to the N35 Ohio clipping -5 (Guess return was 38 yards)

3:04 OHIO
1/10-N40 - Schlichter passed to Donley right cut left for 20
1/10-N20 - Schlichter faded, chased, ran left for 1
2/9 -N19 - Schlichter passed too low for Donley open over middle incomplete
3/9 -N19 - Volley delayed draw middle for 4
4/5 -N15 - Schlichter faded, chased right passed to Donley in middle of end zone for the TD Janakievski PAT 40 yards, 5 plays
SCORE: OHIO 35 NORTHWESTERN 7

Atha kicked off 58 yards; Hill returned 22
1:44 NORTHWESTERN
1/10-N24 - Hill at le for 3
2/7 -N27 - Cammon at rg for 4
3/3 -N31 - Cammon at rg for 2

END OF HALF:
OHIO 35 NORTHWESTERN 7

THIRD QUARTER

Ohio State elected to receive; Northwestern to defend the south goal Mirkopulos kicked off at 3:16 P.M. 45 yards; Hicks returned 4 Northwestern face mask 15
14:45 OHIO
1/10-O34 - Springs lg 3
2/7 -O37 - Springs option pitch re for 10
1/10-O47 - Springs clear at rg for 15
1/10-N38 - Springs pitch at le 3
2/7 -N35 - Springs option at re, fell for 1
3/6 -N34 - Schlichter's pass over middle was deflected, then intercepted by Kendzicky for no return

13:01 NORTHWESTERN
1/10-N37 - Strasser passed to Bogan left for 14
1/10-O49 - Hill at rg for 2
2/8 -O47 - Strasser passed in deep right flat to Bogan, incomplete
3/8 -O47 - Strasser passed deep right to Bogan for 36
1/10-O11 - Strasser faked, rolled right, sacked by Laughlin for -7
2/17-O18 - Strasser passed quick to Hill in right flat for 5
3/12-O13 - Strasser passed to Bogan who was wide open in left end zone for the TD Mirkopulos PAT 63 yards in 7 plays
SCORE: OHIO 35 NORTHWESTERN 14

Mirkopulos kicked off 57 yards;
Hicks returned 10
10:17 OHIO
1/10-O13 - Springs pitch inside re 12
1/10-O25 - Springs option pitch le for 1
2/9 -O26 - Murray option pitch at re for 5;
fumble recovered by Geegan

9:21 NORTHWESTERN
1/10-O31 - Strasser's pass deep right for
Bogan was intercepted by Skillings,
no return

9:15 OHIO
1/10-O9 - Murray pitch at re for 4
2/6 -O13 - Campbell into lt for 5
3/1 -O18 - Schlichter kept inside le for 10
1/10-O28 - Murray pitch re 3
2/7 -O31 - Murray option pitch le, clear
for 19
1/10- 50 - Schlichter faked, passed deep
down left sideline, wide incomplete
2/10- 50 - Johnson option pitch re, clear
for 13
1/10-N37 - Campbell thru lg for 5
2/5 -N32 - Johnson option pitch at le for -1
3/6 -N33 - Schlichter kept inside re for 5
4/1 -N28 - Campbell at lt, dove for 3
1/10-N25 - Johnson option pitch re for 4
2/6 -N21 - Johnson cut back over rg for
(measurement) 6
1/10-N15 - Johnson pitch at re for 5
2/5 -N10 - Johnson at rg, broke tackle for 8
1/G -N2 - Campbell pushed at rt for 1
(inches short)
2/G -N1 - Campbell thru lt for the TD
Kern hurt, walked off Janakievski PAT
91 yards in 17 plays
SCORE: OHIO 42 NORTHWESTERN 14

Atha kicked off two yards deep; Hill
returned 23
3:02 NORTHWESTERN
1/10-N23 - Tiberi at lt for 2
2/8 -N25 - Webb pitch at re for -1
Skillings, Ross
3/9 -N24 - Strasser passed over middle for
McGee; deflected Sullivan incomplete
4/9 -N24 - Christensen punted 29, downed
by Northwestern

1:36 OHIO
1/10-O47 - Johnson pitch at re for 12
1/10-N41 - Castignola kept inside le for 5
2/5 -N36 - Volley at rt for 2
3/3 -N34 - Castignola kept inside re for 12
1/10-N22 - Johnson pitch at re 3

END OF THIRD QUARTER
OHIO 42 NORTHWESTERN 14

FOURTH QUARTER

15:00 OHIO
2/7 -N19 - Johnson thru lg for 8
1/10-N11 - Volley cut into middle for 4
2/6 -N7 - Volley clear thru lg, just over
for the TD
Janakievski PAT 53 yards in 8 plays
SCORE: OHIO 49 NORTHWESTERN 14

Atha kicked off seven yards deep for the
touchback
14:06 NORTHWESTERN
1/10-N20 - Webb at rt, cut right for 5
2/5 -N25 - Webb at rt, fumble recovered
by Hornik 5

13:21 OHIO
1/10-N30 - Castignola kept inside le for 9
2/1 -N21 - Hicks pitch at le for 4
1/10-N17 - Hicks at lg, fumble recovered
by Butler 1

12:49 NORTHWESTERN
1/10-N16 - Tiberi at lt for 2
2/8 -N18 - Strasser faded, sacked by Lee
for -7
3/15-N11 - Strasser passed deep left for
Bogan wide incomplete
4/15-N11 - Christensen punted 30; Volley
fair catch

11:21 OHIO
1/10-N41 - Johnson pitch at re, cut in for 4;
sub. infraction - declined (on NW)
2/6 -N37 - Castignola kept inside le for 7
after breaking tackle
1/10-N30 - Johnson pitch at re for 7
2/3 -N23 - Johnson into rg for 8
1/10-N15 - Payton lg 3
2/7 -N12 - Johnson thru rg for 6
3/1 -N6 - Payton hit at lt for 2
1/G -N4 - Castignola around le for 3
(McGlade hurt - ran off)
2/G -N1 - Castignola into rt for the TD
Janakievski PAT Northwestern offside
41 yards in 9 plays
SCORE: OHIO 56 NORTHWESTERN 14

Atha kicked off from the O45 six yards
deep for the touchback
8:04 NORTHWESTERN
1/10-N20 - Hill rt no gain
2/10-N20 - Tiberi lg 3
3/7 -N23 - Strasser passed left to Prichard
dropped incomplete
4/7 -N23 - Christensen punted right 26;
downed by Northwestern

6:42 OHIO
1/10-N49 - Strahine kept inside re for 5
2/5 -N44 - Strahine kept inside le for 3
3/2 -N41 - Hicks cut over middle for 11
1/10-N30 - Strahine kept inside le for 1

OCTOBER 28, 1978

2/9 -N29 - Hicks slanted into middle, clear broke tackle for the TD
Janakievski PAT 49 yards in 5 plays
SCORE: OHIO 63 NORTHWESTERN 14

Atha kicked off 4 yards deep for the touchback
4:45 NORTHWESTERN
1/10-N20 - Tiberi into center for no gain
2/10-N20 - Hill cut outside re for 4
3/6 -N24 - Strasser passed on swing right for 10
1/10-N34 - Tiberi middle 5
2/5 -N39 - Webb cut outside le for 2
3/3 -N41 - Strasser passed quick on screen left to Webb for 5
1/10-N46 - Tiberi middle 3
2/7 -N49 - Strasser passed into short left flat to Webb, dropped incomplete
3/7 -N49 - Strasser passed to Tiberi on screen right for 7
1/10-044 - Webb pitch at re, clear for 7
2/3 -037 - Strasser passed to Tiberi on delay over middle for 7
1/10-030 - Strasser passed into short right flat to Tiberi for 10
1/10-020 - Strasser passed deep right for McGee, too long incomplete
2/10-020 - Strasser passed to Tiberi short left for 2
Time out Northwestern 0:05
3/8 -018 - Strasser passed over middle into end zone, deflected, intercepted by J. Epitropoulos; Ohio pass interference 17
1/1 -01 - Webb pitch at rt, dove for TD with no time on clock
Mirkopulos' PAT try was wide left
80 yards, 15 plays

**END OF GAME
OHIO 63 NORTHWESTERN 20**

349

MICHIGAN VS. IOWA
Kinnick Stadium
Temp: 68
Wind: light and variable
Skies: clear and sunny
FIRST QUARTER

MICHIGAN
Michigan wins toss and elects to receive. Iowa will kick off and defend north goal.
Schilling kicks off to Jackson for return of 26. (Skradis)
- 1/10-M30 - Leach pass intended for Smith is incomplete
- 2/10-M30 - Smith around re for loss of 1 (Weiss)
- 3/11-M29 - Leach passes to Clayton for gain of 27 (Pace)
- 1/10-I44 - Smith around re for gain of 8 (Becker)
- 2/2 -I36 - Davis over rt for gain of 5 (Mahmens)
- 1/10-I31 - Leach pass intended for Clayton is incomplete
- 2/10-I31 - Smith around le for loss of 4 (Becker)
- 3/14-I35 - Leach pass intended for Clayton incomplete. Iowa penalized for offsides—Michigan for illegal procedure—offsetting
- 3/14-I35 - Leach passes to Smith for gain of 15 (Danzy)
- 1/10-I20 - Leach over lt for gain of 2 (Rusk)
- 2/8 -I18 - Smith over rg for gain of 4 (Benschoter)
- 3/4 -I14 - Leach around re for gain of 8 (Becker)
- 1/G -I6 - Smith around re for TD. Dickey holds, Willner kicks, PAT is good
SCORE: MICHIGAN 7, IOWA 0

10:06 IOWA
Virgil kicks off out of bounds. Michigan penalized 5 yds for delay of game. Virgil kicks off to Blatcher for return of 18 (Needham)
- 1/10-I18 - Mosley over rg for gain of 3 (Cannavino)
- 2/7 -I21 - Dolan passes to Mosley for gain of 3 (Cannavino)
- 3/4 -I24 - Dolan over rg for gain of 2
- 4/2 -I26 - Holsclaw punts to Jolly for return of 18 (44-yard punt) (McKillip)

7:55 MICHIGAN
- 1/10-M49 - Smith over lg for gain of 3 (Benschoter)
- 2/7 -I49 - Leach around re for gain of 11
- 1/10-I38 - Smith around re for loss of 3 (Weiss)
- 2/13-I41 - Leach passes to Clayton for gain of 14 (Pace)
- 1/10-I27 - Smith over rg for gain of 3 (Benschoter)
- 2/7 -I24 - Leach around le for gain of 6 (Benschoter)
- 3/1 -I18 - Iowa penalized 5 yds for offsides
- 1/10-I13 - Leach around re for loss of 3 (Dean)
- 2/13-I16 - Leach pass intended for Marsh is incomplete
- 3/13-I16 - Smith over rg for gain of 4 (Weiss)
- 4/9 -I12 - Dickey holds, Willner kicks, field goal attempt is good
SCORE: MICHIGAN 10, IOWA 0

3:42 IOWA
Virgil kicks off into endzone for touchback
- 1/10-I20 - Mosley over lt for gain of 7 (Meter)
- 2/3 -I27 - Morton over lt for gain of 7 (Simpkins)
- 1/10-I34 - Dolan thrown for loss of 8 (Meter)
- 2/18-I26 - Dolan passes to Mosley for gain of 2. Iowa penalized for holding
- 2/31-I13 - Mosley over rg for gain of 5 (Meter)
- 3/26 - I18 - Dolan thrown for loss of 5 (Greer)
- 4/31-I13 - Holsclaw punts to Harden for fair catch. Iowa penalized for faircatch interference

0:24 MICHIGAN
- 1/10-I23 - Smith over rt for gain of 5 (Dean)

FIRST QUARTER SCORE:
MICHIGAN 10, IOWA 0

SECOND QUARTER

MICHIGAN
- 2/5 -I18 - Leach fumbles, recovered by Smith, for loss of 18 (Dean)
- 3/23-I36 - Leach passes to Mitchell for TD Dickey holds, Willner kicks, PAT is good
SCORE: MICHIGAN 17, IOWA 0

14:09 IOWA
Virgil kicks off to Blatcher for return of 15. (Jones)
- 1/10-I15 - Mosley around le for loss of 2 (Bell)

NOVEMBER 4, 1978

2/12-I13 - Dolan passes to Lazar for loss of 1. Michigan penalized 15 yds for roughing the passer.
1/10-I27 - Mosley over lg for 7 (Simpkins)
2/3 -I34 - Lazar over rt for gain of 5 (Weber)
1/10-I39 - Mosley over rg for gain of 2 (Keitz)
2/8 -I41 - Mosley around re for no gain (Bell)
3/8 -I41 - Dolan passes to Lazar for loss of 4 (Seabron)
4/12-I37 - Holsclaw punts to Jolly for no return (40-yard punt)

10:03 MICHIGAN
1/10-M23 - Davis over lg for no gain (Vazquez)
2/10-M23 - Leach thrown for loss of 3 (Molini)
3/13-M20 - Leach passes to Mitchell for gain of 18 (Becker)
1/10-M38 - Davis over lt for gain of 4 (Rusk)
2/6 -M42 - Leach pass intended for Clayton is incomplete
3/6 -M42 - Davis over rg for no gain (Vazquez)
4/6 -M42 - Willner punts to Becker for fair catch (40 yard punt)

6:54 IOWA
1/10-I18 - Mosley pass intended for Morton is incomplete
2/10-I18 - Dolan thrown for loss of 3 (Greer)
3/13-I15 - Dolan passes to Mosley for gain of 9 (Simpkins)
4/4 -I24 - Holsclaw punts to Jolly for return of 3 (38-yard punt) (Kent Ellis)

5:10 MICHIGAN
1/10-M41 - Leach pass intended for Clayton is incomplete
2/10-M41 - Smith over lt for gain of 11 (Woodland)
1/10-I48 - Smith over rt for gain of 9 (King)
2/1 -I39 - Leach passes to Schmerge for gain of 20 (Rusk)
1/10-I19 - Smith over lt for gain of 3 (Harty)
2/7 -I16 - Smith around re for gain of 3 (Becker)
3/4 -I13 - Leach pitch, fumbles, recovered by Molini. Iowa penalized 5 yds for offsides
1/G -I8 - Smith around re for loss of 6 (Danzy)
2/G -I14 - Leach pass intended for Clayton is incomplete
3/G -I14 - Leach passes to Smith for TD Dickey holds, Willner kicks, PAT is good
SCORE: MICHIGAN 24, IOWA 0

1:46 IOWA
Virgil kicks off to Reid for return of 16
1/10-I18 - Dolan pass intended for Reid is incomplete

2/10-I18 - Mosley around le for gain of 2 (Greer)
3/8 -I20 - Mosley over lg for gain of 2 (Simpkins)
4/6 -I22 - Holsclaw punts to Harden for fair catch (34 yard punt)

0:01 MICHIGAN
1/10-M44 - Woolfolk over lt for loss of 1 (Skradis)
**FIRST HALF SCORE:
IOWA 0, MICHIGAN 24**

THIRD QUARTER

IOWA
Michigan will kick off. Iowa will receive and defend north goal. Virgil kicks off to endzone for touchback
1/10-I20 - Mosley over rt for gain of 2 (Greer)
2/8 -I22 - Lazar over rt for gain of 3 (Meter)
3/5 -I25 - Iowa penalized 5 yds delay of game
3/10-I20 - Dolan thrown for loss of 9 (Keitz)
4/19-I11 - Holsclaw punts to Harden for fair catch (35 yard punt)

13:01 MICHIGAN
1/10-I46 - Smith over rt for gain of 1, fumbles, recovered by King (Danzy)

12:55 IOWA
1/10-I45 - Lazar over rg, fumbles, recovered by Simpkins, loss of 2

12:47 MICHIGAN
1/10-I43 - Davis over rg for gain of 5 (Weiss)
2/5 -I38 - Woolfolk around re for gain of 4 (Danzy)
3/1-I34 - Davis over rg for gain of 4 Michigan penalized for illegal motion (5yds)
3/6 -I39 - Leach around re for gain of 5
4/1 -I34 - Davis over rg for gain of 2 (Rusk)
1/10-I32 - Smith around re for gain of 14 (Pace)
1/10-I18 - Davis over lg, fumbles, recovered by Dean, loss of 1

10:20 IOWA
1/10-I19 - Dolan pass intended for Reid is incomplete
2/10-I19 - Burke over rt for gain of 8
3/2 -I27 - Lazar over lg for no gain (Cannavino)
4/2 -I27 - Holsclaw punts to Jolly for fair catch (40-yard punt)

8:42 MICHIGAN
1/10-M33 - Smith over rg for gain of 1 (Dean)
2/9 -M34 - Smith around re for gain of 5 (King)

351

3/4 -M39 - Leach around re for gain of 5 (Weiss)
1/10-M44 - Leach thrown for loss of 4 (Dean)
2/14-M40 - Clayton around re for gain of 6. Michigan penalized 15 yds for clipping
2/32-M22 - Woolfolk over rg for gain of 2 (Dean)
3/30-M24 - Leach passes to Clayton for gain of 40
1/10-I36 - Woolfolk around re for no gain (Dean)
2/10-I36 - Davis over lg for gain of 1 (Rusk)
3/9 -I35 - Leach pass intended for Johnson is incomplete
4/9 -I35 - Davis around re for gain of 24 (Kevin Ellis)
1/10-I11 - Leach thrown for loss of 2 (Vazquez)
2/12-I13 - Leach passes to Marsh for gain of 7 (Pace)
3/5 -I6 - Leach pass intended for Clayton is incomplete
4/5 -I6 - Dickey holds, Willner kicks, field goal attempt is good
SCORE: MICHIGAN 27, IOWA 0

2:36 IOWA
Virgil kicks off to Blatcher in endzone for touchback.
1/10-I20 - Gales pass intended for Reid is incomplete
2/10-I20 - Gales passes to Morton for gain of 19
1/10-I39 - Gales thrown for loss, fumbles, recovers for loss of 11
2/21-I28 - Iowa penalized 5 yds for illegal procedure
2/26-I23 - Burke around le for gain of 1 (Simpkins)
3/25-I24 - Gales pass intended for Morton, intercepted by Harden, return of 31 (Swift)

1:02 MICHIGAN
1/10-I15 - Smith over rt for gain of 4
2/6 -I11 - Smith around re for no gain (Skradis)

THIRD QUARTER SCORE:
MICHIGAN 27, IOWA 0

352

NOVEMBER 4, 1978

FOURTH QUARTER

MICHIGAN
3/6-I11 - Dickey passes to Marsh for TD
Dickey holds, Willner kicks, PAT is good
SCORE: MICHIGAN 34, IOWA 0

14:54 IOWA
Virgil kicks off to Blatcher for return of 11 (Leoni)
1/10-I19 - Gales pass intended for Morton is incomplete
2/10-I19 - Burke over rg, fumbles, recovered by Mayham, gain of 9
2/1-I28 - Burke over rg for gain of 3
1/10-I31 - Gales pass intended for Morton is incomplete
2/10-I31 - Gales pass intended for Burke is incomplete
3/10-I31 - Gales passes to Dunham for gain of 23 (Jolly)
1/10-M46 - Lazar over rg for gain of 5 (Needham)
2/5 -M41 - Gales passes to Swift for gain of 5 (Bell)
1/10-M36 - Gales thrown for loss of 14 (Simpkins)
2/24-50 - Gales pass intended for Frazier is incomplete
3/24-50 - Gales passes to Lazar for loss of 2 (Needham)
4/26-I48 - Holsclaw punts into endzone for touchback (52 yard punt)

10:51 MICHIGAN
1/10-M20 - Woolfolk around re for gain of 5 (Danzy)
2/5 -M25 - Woolfolk over lt for gain of 4 (Hufford)
3/1 -M29 - Dickey around le for gain of 11 (Dean)
1/10-M40 - Dickey pass intended for Jackson is incomplete
2/10-M40 - Reid over lg for gain of 6 (Benschoter)
3/4 -M46 - Dickey thrown for loss of 4 (Benschoter)
4/8 -M42 - Willner punts to Reid for fair catch (25 yard punt)
(Offsetting penalties)

8:05 IOWA
1/10-I33 - Burke around le for loss of 5 (Harris)
2/15-I28 - Gales passes to Burke for gain of 4 (De Santis)
3/11-I32 - Gales passes to Lazar for gain of 9 (Digs)
4/2 -I41 - Blatcher over rg for gain of 3 (Godfrey)
1/10-I44 - Blatcher over rt for gain of 5 (Jones)
2/5 -I49 - Gales pass intended for McKillip is incomplete
3/5 -I49 - Blatcher over rg, fumbles, recovered by Jolly, gain of 1

5:00 MICHIGAN
1/10-50 - Dickey around re for no gain (Hufford)
2/10-50 - Dickey pass intended for Jackson is incomplete
3/10-50 - Dickey pass intended for Johnson is incomplete
4/10-50 - Willner punts to Becker for fair catch (32 yard punt)

4:00 IOWA
1/10-I18 - Gales pass intended for Wozniak is incomplete
2/10-I18 - Gales pass intended for McKillip is incomplete
3/10-I18 - Gales thrown for loss of 15 (Weber)
4/25-I3 - Holsclaw punts to Harden for return of 4.(51 yard punt) (Kevin Ellis) Michigan penalized 15 yard for clipping

2:54 MICHIGAN
1/10-M35 - Woolfolk around re for gain of 4 (Bradley)
2/6 -M39 - Dickey around le for gain of 2
Iowa penalized 15 yards for facemask grabbing (Simonsen)
1/10-I45 - Woolfolk around le for gain of 13 (Kevin Ellis)
1/10-I32 - Reid over lg for gain of 1 (Simonsen)
2/9 -I31 - Dickey pass intended for Johnson incomplete
3/9 -I31 - Woolfolk over rg for gain of 7 (Skradis)
4/2 -I24 - Woolfolk over lt for gain of 3 (Schultz)
1/10-I21 - Jackson around le for loss of 4
2/14-I25 - Leoni over lt for no gain (Simonsen)

FINAL SCORE:
MICHIGAN 34, IOWA 0

MSU VS. ILLINOIS
Memorial Stadium
Temp: 75
Wind: 15 mph SSW
Skies: Partly cloudy and warm

FIRST QUARTER

(Illinois wins toss, elects to receive; Michigan State will defend south goal) (Schario kicks off north to Foster at I6, returns 16)
ILLINOIS
1/10-I22 - Weiss long pass down sidelines to Foster is incomplete, broken up by Anderson
2/10-I22 - Weiss sideline pass to Barnes complete for 22 (Land)
1/10-I44 - Weiss pass over middle to Strader complete for 4 (Bass)
2/6 -I48 - Weiss on quarterback draw for 2 (Hay, Bass)
3/4 - 50 - Weiss sideline pass to Boeke complete for 6 (Graves)
1/10-M44 - Strader over rg for 7 (Webb)
2/3 -M37 - Strader up middle for 20 (Burroughs)
1/10-M17 - Strader slants over lt for TOUCHDOWN (Finzer kick is wide left)
ILLINOIS 6, MICHIGAN STATE 0

(Finzer kick goes out of bounds; PENALTY: illegal procedure 5 yards) (Finzer kicks off to S.Smith at M10, returns 20 fumbles recovered Atkins)
ILLINOIS
1/10-M30 - McCullough takes pitch from Weiss, pass for Rouse is overthrown
2/10-M30 - Weiss sideline pass to Barnes complete for 19
1/10-M11 - Dismuke over lt for 1 (Hay)
2/9 -M10 - Weiss pass in end zone for Cozen is complete for TOUCHDOWN Weiss conversion run is no good (McCormick)
ILLINOIS 12, MICHIGAN STATE 0

(Finzer kicks off south to Reeves at M7, returns 36)
MICHIGAN STATE
1/10-M43 - S. Smith slants over rt for 1 (Ralph)
2/9 -M44 - McGee slants over lt for 15 (J. Gillen)
1/10-I41 - E. Smith sideline pass to Gibson complete for 11 and out of bounds
1/10-I30 - PENALTY: Michigan St. clipping
1/26-I46 - Middleton over rg for 13 (Hardy)
2/13-I33 - Middleton over rt for 4 (Thiede)
3/9 -I29 - E. Smith pass over middle complete to Reeves for 4 (Carmien)
4/5 -I25 - S. Smith around re for TOUCHDOWN (Andersen kick is good)
ILLINOIS 12, MICHIGAN STATE 7

(Schario kicks off north to Dismuke at I11, returns 8)
ILLINOIS
1/10-I19 - Weiss pass complete to Cozen for 15 (Graves)
1/10-I34 - Weiss sideline pass complete to L. Boeke for 6 (McCormick)
2/4 -I40 - Weber fights over rg for 4 (Hay, Decker)
1/10-I44 - Strader over rg for 2 (Fields)
2/8 -I46 - Weiss keeps around re for 6 (Hay)
3/2 -M48 - Weiss pass for L. Boeke is incomplete
4/2 -M48 - Finzer punt downed at M31 (17 yard punt)

MICHIGAN STATE
1/10-M31 - Middleton up middle for 3 (Sullivan)
2/7 -M34 - E. Smith sideline pass for Byrd is overthrown
3/7 -M34 - S. Smith on draw for 11 (Sullivan, J. Gillen)
1/10-M45 - McGee around re for 3 (Levitt)
2/7 -M48 - E. Smith pass to Middleton complete for 3 (Adams)
3/4 -I49 - S. Smith on draw for 13 (Sullivan, J. Gillen)
1/10-I36 - McGee takes pitch around re for 4 (Adams)
2/6 -I32 - S. Smith on draw for 1 (J. Gillen, Sullivan)
3/5 -I31 - Reeves over lg for 12 (Hardy)
1/10-I19 - E. Smith pass over middle Byrd complete for 18 (George)
1/G -I1 - Middleton over rg for TOUCHDOWN (Andersen kick is good)
MICHIGAN STATE 14, ILLINOIS 12

(Schario kicks off north to Foster, downs in end zone for touchback)
ILLINOIS
1/10-I20 - Strader over lg for 11 (Bass)

**END OF FIRST QUARTER:
MICHIGAN STATE 14, ILLINOIS 12**

SECOND QUARTER

ILLINOIS
1/10-I31 - Weiss pass over middle complete to Rouse for 14 (Anderson)
1/10-I45 - Strader up middle for 9 fumbles, recovered by McCormick (Land)

14:23 MICHIGAN STATE
1/10-M46 - S. Smith slants over rt for 2 (J. Gillen)
2/8 -M48 - E. Smith out pass for Byrd is incomplete
3/8 -M48 - E. Smith pass over middle for McGee complete for 5 (Sullivan)
4/3 -I47 - Stachowicz punt goes out of bounds at I23 (24 yard punt)

NOVEMBER 4, 1978

13:05 ILLINOIS
1/10-I23 - Dismuke over rt for 5 (Hay)
2/5 -I28 - Weiss pass over middle complete to Dismuke for 6 (Decker)
1/10-I34 - Strader up middle for 4 (Land, Hay)
2/6 -I38 - Weiss keeps around le for loss of 3 (Land)
3/9 -I35 - Weiss sacked for loss of 9 (Decker)
4/18-I26 - Finzer punt to S. Smith at M39, fumbles, recovers own for 1 (35 yards)

9:05 MICHIGAN STATE
1/10-M40 - E. Smith long sideline pass for Byrd incomplete
2/10-M40 - E. Smith sideline pass for Middleton complete for 8 (Adams)
3/2 -M48 - McGee up middle for 4 (J. Gillen, Carmien)
1/10-I48 - Smith slants over rt for 11 (Levitt)
1/10-I37 - E. Smith pass for Gibson intercepted by Hardy at I8, returns 36

7:57 ILLINOIS
1/10-I44 - Weiss pass for Rouse broken up by Decker
2/10-i44 - Weiss keeps around le for loss of 1 (Land)
3/11-I43 - Weiss sacked for loss of 10 (McCormick)
4/21-I33 - Finzer punt to S. Smith, fair catch at M37 (30 yard punt)

6:25 MICHIGAN STATE
1/10-M37 - S. Smith on draw for no gain (Flynn)
2/10-M37 - PENALTY: Michigan State illegal use of hands
2/30-M17 - E. Smith screen pass complete to McGee for loss of 2 (Sullivan)
3/32-M15 - S. Smith on draw up middle for 3 (J. Gillen)
4/29-M18 - Stachowicz punt to Hardy, fair catch at I43 (39 yard punt)

4:17 ILLINOIS
1/10-I43 - Strader over rg for 2 (Savage)
2/8 -I45 - Weiss pass for Strader is incomplete
3/8 -I45 - Dismuke on draw for 7 (Burroughs)
4/1 -M48 - Finzer punt rolls through end zone (48 yard punt)

2:42 MICHIGAN STATE
1/10-M20 - Middleton over rg for 5 (Sullivan)
2/5 -M25 - E. Smith pass for Brammer is incomplete
3/5 -M25 - E. Smith sideline pass complete to Byrd for 23 (Sullivan, Bonner)
1/10-M48 - Middleton over rg for 3 (J. Gillen)
2/7 -I49 - E. Smith pass for Howard deflected by Sullivan intercepted by Levitt at I27, returns 33.

1:10 ILLINOIS
1/10-M40 - Weiss pass over middle complete to Rouse for 21 (Anderson)
1/10-M19 - Strader over rg for 3 (Bass)
2/7 -M16 - Weiss on qb draw middle for 5 (Bass)
3/2 -M11 - Dismuke over rg for 1 (Webb)
4/1-M10 - Weiss scrambles for no gain

0:10 MICHIGAN STATE
1/10-M10 - S. Smith around le for 17

END OF FIRST HALF:
MICHIGAN STATE 14, ILLINOIS 12

THIRD QUARTER

(Finzer kicks off north to Reeves in endzone, returns 15)
MICHIGAN STATE
1/10-M15 - Smith on counter play for loss of 1(Ralph)
2/11-M14 - E. Smith sideline pass complete to Brammer for 9 (Venegoni)
3/2 -M23 - S. Smith up middle for 2 (J. Gillen)
1/10-M25 - McGee on delay for 1 (J. Gillen)
2/9 -M26 - E. Smith sideline pass complete to Byrd for 13 (Levitt)
1/10-M39 - E. Smith sideline pass complete to Gibson for 16 and out of bounds
1/10-I45 - S. Smith slants over rt for 2 (Flynn, Carmien)
2/8 -I43 - E. Smith sideline pass complete to Byrd for 19 (Levitt)
1/10-I24 - E. Smith pass in endzone for Byrd, broken up by Hardy
2/10-I24 - S. Smith takes pitch around le for 13 (George, Bonner)
1/10-I11 - McGee around le for 3 (Levitt)
2/7 -I8 - E. Smith sideline pass to Brammer complete for 7 (Bonner)
1/G -I1 - Middleton leaps over lg for TOUCHDOWN (Andersen kick is good)
MICHIGAN STATE 21, ILLINOIS 12

(Schario kicks to Foster at goal, returns 16)
ILLINOIS
1/10-I16 - Weiss pass over middle to Rouse complete for 19 (Anderson)
1/10-I35 - PENALTY: Illinois illegal motion
1/15-I30 - Weiss pass for Cozen incomplete, broken up by Graves
2/15-I30 - Weiss pass over middle complete to Rouse for 18 (Graves)
1/10-I48 - Dismuke takes pitch around re for 30 (Land, Burroughs)
1/10-M22 - Dismuke takes pitch around re for 12 (Anderson)
1/10-M10 - PENALTY: Michigan State interference
1/G -M1 - Weiss sneaks over rg for TOUCHDOWN (Finzer kick is good)
MICHIGAN STATE 21, ILLINOIS 19

(Finzer kicks off north to Reeves, downed in end zone for touchback)
MICHIGAN STATE
1/10-M20 - E. Smith fumbles, recovers own for loss of 1
2/11-M19 - E. Smith pass complete to Brammer for 22 (Carmien)
1/10-M41 - E. Smith sideline pass complete to Gibson for 16 (George)
1/10-I43 - E. Smith sideline pass complete to Byrd for 8 (Levitt)
2/2 -I35 - McGee slants over lt for 7 (J. Gillen) PENALTY: Illinois personal foul on dead ball
1/10-I13 - E. Smith pass for Gibson is incomplete in end zone
2/10-I13 - E. Smith pass for McGee broken up by Levitt
3/10-I13 - E. Smith pass complete to Schramm for 5 (Bonner)
4/5 -I8 - Andersen 25 yard field goal is good
MICHIGAN STATE 24, ILLINOIS 19

(Schario kicks off south to Rouse at I11, returns 12)
ILLINOIS
1/10-I23 - Strader slants over rt for 4 (Savage)
2/6 -I27 - Dismuke over rg on delay for 1 fumbles, recovered by Savage (M)

MICHIGAN STATE
1/10-I28 - Middleton up middle for 3 (Flynn, Ralph)
2/7 -I25 - McGee over lt fumbles for loss of 9 recovered by E. Smith
3/16-I34 - E. Smith pass over middle to S. Smith for 8 (J. Gillen)
4/8 -I26 - McGee slants over lt for 12 (Hardy)
1/10-I14 - S. Smith takes pitch around re for 10 (Hardy, Sullivan)
1/G -I4 - Schramm over rg for 3 (Carmien, Thiede)
2/G I1 - Schramm over rg for no gain (Thiede)
3/G I1 - Middleton twists in for TOUCHDOWN (Anderson kick is good)

MICHIGAN STATE 31, ILLINOIS 19

(Schario kicks off south to Foster at 15, returns 13)
ILLINOIS
1/10-I18 - Weiss sideline pass for Barnes is incomplete
2/10-I18 - Weiss sideline pass for Barnes is incomplete
2/10-I18 - Dismuke takes pitch around re for 15 (Land, Anderson)
1/10-I33 - Weiss scrambles for loss of 1 (Land)

END OF THIRD QUARTER:
MICHIGAN STATE 31, ILLINOIS 19

FOURTH QUARTER

ILLINOIS
2/11-I32 - Weiss pass for Dismuke is incomplete
3/11-I32 - Weiss keeps around le for 6 (Anderson)
4/5 -I38 - Finzer punt to S. Smith at M34, returns 6 (38 yard punt)

14:18 MICHIGAN STATE
1/10-M40 - S. Smith on delay over lt for loss of 3 (Flynn, Ralph)
2/13-M37 - Gibson on reverse for 21 (Hardy)
1/10-I42 - S. Smith up middle for 2 (Ralph, Carmien)
2/8 -I40 - E. Smith pass complete to McGee for 3 (Carmien)
3/5 -I37 - Hughes on delay over lt for 10
1/10-I27 - S. Smith over lt for 7 (Sullivan)
2/3 -I20 - E. Smith pass for Byrd on sideline incomplete
3/3 -I20 - Hans up middle for no gain (Thornton)
4/3 -I20 - PENALTY: Illinois illegal procedure
1/10-I15 - S. Smith takes pitch around re for 9 (Squirek)
2/1 -I6 - Reeves takes pitch around le for TOUCHDOWN (Anderson kick is good)
MICHIGAN STATE 38, ILLINOIS 19

(Schario kicks off north to Foster in end zone, returns 11)
ILLINOIS
1/10-I11 - Weiss pass for Dismuke, intercepted by Graves at I17, fumbles recovered by McCormick, return for loss of 7

9:12 MICHIGAN STATE
1/10-I24 - E. Smith pass over middle to Gibson complete for 23
1/G -I1 - Hans up middle for TOUCHDOWN (Anderson kick is good)
MICHIGAN STATE 45, ILLINOIS 19

(Schario kicks off deep to Foster in end zone, touchback)
ILLINOIS
1/10-I20 - PENALTY: Illinois illegal procedure
2/15-I15 - Powell takes pitch around re fumbles for loss of 2, recovered by Savage

8:30 MICHIGAN STATE
1/10-I13 - E. Smith pass over middle for Shafer, broken up by Levitt
2/10-I13 - Reeves takes pitch around re for TOUCHDOWN (Anderson kick is good)
MICHIGAN STATE 52, ILLINOIS 19

(Schario kicks off north to Foster in endzone, returns 16)

NOVEMBER 4, 1978

ILLINOIS
1/10-I16 - McCullough pass to Powell complete for 14 (Graves, Marshall)
1/10-I30 - McCullough sideline pass to Lopez complete for 12 (Burroughs)
1/10-I42 - Weber over lg for 5 (Land)
2/5-I47 - McCullough pass complete to Powell for loss of 1, fumbles recovered by Norman
3/6 -I46 - McCullough scrambles for 3 (Bass, Burroughs)
4/3 -I49 - Finzer punt to S. Smith at M16, returns 4 (35 yard punt)

5:54 MICHIGAN STATE
1/10-M20 - Reeves over lt for 7 (Blalock)
2/3 -M27 - PENALTY: Michigan State blocking below waist
2/12-M18 - Reeves around le for 17 (Kelly)
1/10-M35 - Hans up middle for 3 (Squirek)
2/7 -M38 - Reeves over rg for 5 (Burlingame)
3/2 -M43 - Hans over lg for 9 (Burlingame)
1/10-I48 - Schramm over lg for loss of 1 (Burlingame)
2/11-I49 - Hughes takes pitch around re for TOUCHDOWN (Andersen kick is good)
MICHIGAN STATE 59, ILLINOIS 19

(Schario kick to Foster in end zone, downed for touchback)
ILLINOIS
1/10-I20 - Thomas over rg for 4 (Otis, Converse)
2/6 -I24 - Strader over lt for 4 (C. Griffin, Otis)
3/2 -I28 - PENALTY: Illinois illegal procedure
3/7 -I23 - McCullough keeps around le for 4 (Muster)
4/3 -I27 - PENALTY: Illinois illegal procedure
4/8 -I22 - Finzer punt to Reeves at M39, returns 8 (39 yard punt)

0:18 MICHIGAN STATE
1/10-M47 - Clark sneaks up middle for 7 (Burlingame)

**FINAL SCORE:
MICHIGAN STATE 59, ILLINOIS 19**

FINAL TEAM STATISTICS

	ILLINOIS	MSU
First Downs	20	28
By Rushing	7	16
By Passing	12	10
By Penalty	1	2
Rushing Attempts	35	55
Yards Rushing, Gross	194	375
Yards Lost Rushing	26	15
Net Yards Rushing	168	360
Net Yards Passing	185	219
Passes Attempted	24	31
Passes Completed	15	20
Passes Intercepted	1	2
Total Offensive Plays	59	86
Total Net Yards	253	579
Fumbles (No-Lost)	4/3	6/1
Penalties (No-Yards)	7/45	3/44
Interceptions (No-Ret)	2/69	1/7
Punts (No-Yds)	7/242	2/63
Avg. per punt	34.6	31.5
Blocked punts	0	0
Punt Returns (No-Yards)	0/0	4/19
Kickoff Returns	7/92	3/71
Time Of Possession	23.38	36.22

INDIANA
VS.
MINNESOTA
Memorial Stadium, Minneapolis
Temp.: 56°
Wind: Southeast at 8 mph
FIRST QUARTER

Indiana wins toss, elects to receive at west end Rogind kick off sails out of bounds inside I10. 5 yd penalty. Second kick off to Johnson at I6, returns 27 yards (Fahnhorst)

14:54 INDIANA
1/10-I33 - Harkrader up middle on delay 4 yd gain (Ronan)
2/6 -I37 - Harkrader up middle 1 yd gain (Blanshan)
3/5 -I38 - Clifford pass fly up left sidelines complete to Friede complete 62 yard TD pass Freud PAT kick good
SCORE: INDIANA 7, MINNESOTA 0

Straub kick off to Noel on M5, returns 17 yards (Alexander)

13:39 MINNESOTA
1/10-M22 - Barber cuts left up middle, 3 yds (Tallen, Norman)
2/7 -M25 - Carlson pass off Bourquin's hands, intercepted by Keneipp, 12 yd run back (Thompson)

12:37 INDIANA
1/10-M33 - Harkrader up middle 2 yds (Ronan)
2/8 -M31 - Johnson at le 4 yds (Johnson, Blanshan)
3/4 -M27 - Johnson at le 2 yds (Brown)
4/2 -M25 - Clifford back to pass, rushed by Friberg, throw is incomplete

11:08 MINNESOTA
1/10-M25 - Barber quick pitch right, breaks open at right sidelines 12 yds (Norman)
1/10-M37 - Kitzmann slants off lg 4 yds (Norman)
2/6 -M41 - Kitzmann straight ahead Minnesota illegal procedure 5 yd penalty
2/11-M36 - Carlson back to pass, no one open rush for 10 yds (Keneipp)
3/1 -M46 - Kitzmann straight ahead 3 yds (Arbuckle)
1/10-M49 - Carlson pass complete to Thompson 18 yds (Wilbur)
1/10-I33 - Barber quick pitch left, cuts back and runs for TD, but Bailey clipping for Gophers, 15 yd penalty Barber 11 yd gain
1/14-I37 - Carlson keeps on busted play no gain (Walls)
2/14-I37 - Carlson back to pass, rushed and Smith makes tackle for 9 yd loss
3/23-I46 - Carlson pass intended for Bourquin knocked down by Abrams
4/23-I46 - Smith punt to Wilbur fair catch on I12 34 yard punt

7:08 INDIANA
1/10-I12 - Clifford fly pass down left sidelines complete Friede 82 yds (Edwards)
1/G -M6 - Harkrader up middle 2 yds (Blanshan)
2/G -M4 - Harkrader at lg 2 yds (Burns)
3/G -M2 - Clifford keeps left no gain (Johnson Burns)
4/G -M2 - Freud field goal good 19 yds out 86 yd drive in 5 plays
SCORE: INDIANA 10, MINNESOTA 0

Straub kick off to Noel on M10, returns 19 yds

4:45 MINNESOTA
1/10-M29 - Barber quick pitch left, cuts back for 5 yds (Doehla)
2/5 -M34 - Barber up middle 1 yard (Willhite, Arbuckle)
3/4 -M35 - Carlson pass complete to Bailey 21 yds, fumbles when hit, Norman recovers for Indiana at I44

3:23 INDIANA
1/10-I44 - Harkrader at rt 3 yds (Friberg)
2/7 -I47 - Harkrader at lt 5 yds (Ronan)
3/2 -M48 - Harkrader option pitch left 3 yds (Burns)
1/10-M45 - Johnson up middle 5 yds (Blanshan)
2/5 -M40 - Johnson at lt 1 yd (Brown, Friberg)
3/4 -M39 - Harkrader option pitch left 2 yds (Snyder, Sytsma)
4/2 -M37 - Lovett punt covered by Keneipp on M5 32 yd punt

1:04 MINNESOTA
1/10-M5 - Barber quick pitch right, breaks open 16 yds (Abrams, Tallen)
1/10-M21 - Kitzmann at lt 3 yds (Norman)
2/7 -M24 - Barber quick pitch left, cuts back for 12 yds (Tallen)

END OF FIRST QUARTER:
INDIANA 10 MINNESOTA 0

SECOND QUARTER

MINNESOTA
1/10-M36 - Kitzmann at lt 1 yd (Arbuckle)
2/9 -M37 - Carlson pass complete to Bailey, stumbles down 17 yds
1/10-I46 - Barber quick pitch left no gain (Norman)
2/10-I46 - Carlson pass intended for Dilulo incomplete behind him
3/10-I46 - Carlson complete to Bourquin at left sidelines 20 yds (Keneipp)
1/10-I26 - Barber quick up middle 4 yds (Norman)
2/6 -I22 - Barber slides inside rt 11 yards (Keneipp)

358

NOVEMBER 4, 1978

1/10-I11 - Barber quick pitch left, fumbles and Keneipp recovers in air, runs 96 yds for TD
Freud PAT kick good
SCORE: INDIANA 17, MINNESOTA 0

Straub kick off to Noel on M7, returns 32 yds up left sidelines (Friede)
11:10 MINNESOTA
1/10-M39 - Barber up middle, breaks one tackle, runs 15 yds (Hunter)
1/10-I46 - Kitzmann at left tackle 3 yards (Norman)
2/7 -I43 - Dilulo flanker reverse left 5 yds (Norman)
3/2 -I38 - Barber at rt 4 yds (Arbuckle)
1/10-I34 - Carlson look-in to Bailey, dropped incomplete
2/10-I34 - Bourquin look-in left Bourquin complete 13 yds (Keneipp, Wilbur)
1/10-I21 - Barber quick pitch right 1 yd (Norman)
2/9 -I20 - Carlson pass complete to Bailey 11 yds (Wilbur)
1/G -I9 - Barber quick hit up middle 6 yds (Doehla)
2/G -I3 - Minnesota Stein illegal procedure, 5 yard penalty
2/G -I8 - Carlson pass intercepted by Keneipp on M3, returns 25 yds (Kitzmann)

7:24 INDIANA
1/10-I28 - Clifford complete to Lundy up left sidelines 30 yds (Snyder)
1/10-M42 - Harkrader breaks into clear outside lt, rushs 41 yds to M1 (Foxworth)
1/G -M1 - Harkrader at rt no gain (team)
2/G -M1 - Harkrader at lt 1 yd TD run
Freud PAT kick good
72 yd drive in 4 plays
SCORE: INDIANA 24, MINNESOTA 0

Straub kick off to Bailey on M4, returns 33 yds (Wilbur)
6:12 MINNESOTA
1/10-M38 - Artis quick pitch left 7 yds (Keneipp)
2/3 -M45 - White straight ahead 2 yds, stumbles down
3/1 -M47 - Artis up middle no gain (Zilkowski)
4/1 -M47 - White at rt no gain (Norman)

5:09 INDIANA
1/10-M47 - Harkrader quick pitch left 5 yds (Murphy, Foxworth)
2/5 -M42 - Johnson at rt 1 yd (Friberg)
3/4 -M41 - Harkrader halfback pass right, Edwards intercepts on M12, returns 22 yds

4:21 MINNESOTA
1/10-M34 - Carlson release pass left to White 8 yds (Wilbur)
2/2 -M42 - Artis quick pitch left 1 yd (Wilbur, Smith)
3/1 -M43 - Barber up middle 5 yds (Doehla)

1/10-M48 - Carlson pass complete to Bailey 25 yds, rush out of bounds
1/10-I27 - Carlson pass intended for Bailey short and incomplete
2/10-I27 - Carlson hit by Smith as he's passing falls incomplete
3/10-I27 - Carlson pass complete to Cooper 18 yds (Swinehart)
1/G -I9 - Barber up middle 4 yds (Willhite)
2/G -I5 - Barber up middle 4 yds (Iatarola, Ramsey)
3/G -I1 - Barber over top at left side TD 1 yd
Rogind PAT kick good
66 yd drive in 11 plays
SCORE: INDIANA 24, MINNESOTA 7

Rogind kick off on side covered by Tillery on I47
1:15 INDIANA
1/10-I47 - Harkrader at rt 3 yds (Burns)
2/7 - 50 - Harkrader delay up middle, Indiana Peacock holding 15 yd penalty 1 yd rush
2/21-I36 - Harkrader runs right, 3 yds and runs out of bounds
3/18-I39 - Harkrader at lt 9 yds (Johnson)
4/9 -I48 - Lovett punt fair catch by Edwards on M26 26 yd punt

0:21 MINNESOTA
1/10-M26 - Carlson pass over middle intended for Bailey short and incomplete
2/10-M26 - Tonn release left to White 19 yds decline interference penalty
1/10-M45 - Tonn pass sails out of bounds around I15

**END OF HALF:
INDIANA 24 MINNESOTA 7**

359

THIRD QUARTER

Straub kick off to Noel, returns 21 yards, fumbles and recovered by IND Arbuckle

14:55 INDIANA
1/10-MN25 - Harkrader at right tackle 4 yards (Burns)
2/6 -MN21 - Johnson slants left 5 yards (Friberg)
3/1 -MN16 - Burnett hit behind line by Johnson and Burns for 1 yard loss
4/2 -MN17 - Freud field goal sails wide left no good 34-yard attempt

13:03 MINNESOTA
1/10-MN20 - White at right tackle 5 yards (Norman)
2/5 -MN25 - White breaks open at left tackle 11 yards (Abrams)
1/10-MN36 - Carlson pass dropped by Bailey cutting over middle
2/10-MN36 - Barber quick pitch left, fumbles and recovered by White 1 yd (Doehla)
3/9 -MN37 - Carlson rushed by Smith, hits Carlson while passing incomplete
4/9 -MN37 - Smith punt (Minnesota illegal procedure/5 yard penalty)
4/14-MN32 - Smith punt to Wilburs (Harms) 1 yd return 44 yd punt

10:59 INDIANA
1/10-IN25 - Johnson up middle 9 yards (Brown)
2/1 -IN34 - Harkrader quick delay right 1 yd loss (Friberg)
3/2 -IN33 - Harkrader tackled behind line for 1 yd loss, submarined by Friberg
4/3 -IN32 - Lovett punt to Bailey fair catch on MN42 26 yd punt

9:17 MINNESOTA
1/10-MN42 - Barber breaks open on quick delay up middle 14 yards (Norman, Abrams)
1/10-IN44 - White quick opener up middle 8 yards (Norman)
2/2 -IN36 - Barber quick pitch right 5 yards (Leake)
1/10-IN31 - White at left guard 3 yards (Leake)
2/7 -IN28 - Barber quick pitch left, cuts back for 5 yards (Smith, Arbuckle)
3/2 -IN23 - Barber at right tackle 3 yards (Norman, Wilbur)
1/10-IN20 - Carlson complete to Barber over middle 5 yards (Swinehart)
2/5 -IN15 - Artis up middle 4 yards (Willhite)
3/1 -IN11 - White at right guard 6 yards (Keneipp)
1/G -IN5 - Barber up middle 1 yard (Iatarala)
2/G -IN4 - Barber pitch right, Leake crashes and makes tackle for 3 yard loss
3/G -IN7 - Carlson pass intended for Bailey, intercepted in end zone by Wilbur

3:55 INDIANA
1/10-IN20 - Harkrader pitch left, fumbles, recovered by Sytsma 2-yd rush

3:47 MINNESOTA
1/10-IN22 - Barber quick delay slant right 4 yards (Willhite)
2/6 -IN18 - Carlson pass complete to Bailey (IND pass int., declined) 15 yards (Wilbur)
1/G -IN3 - White at right tckle 1 yard (team)
2/G -IN2 - Barber dives for 2-yd TD over right side 12:32 ET, 2:28 TL 22 yard drive in 4 plays Rogind PAT good
SCORE: INDIANA 24, MINNESOTA 14

Rogind kick off to Johnson in end zone, returns 18 yards (Fahnhorst)

2:24 INDIANA
1/10-IN18 - Clifford pass complete to Stephenson 15 yards (Brown)
1/10-IN33 - Harkrader up middle 3 yards (Sytsma)
2/7 -IN36 - Clifford pass complete to Fishel 7 yards (Foxworth)
1/10-IN43 - Johnson at left tackle 5 yards (Ronan, Burns)
2/5 -IN48 - Harkrader hit behind line by Brown for 1 yd loss
3/6 -IN47 - Johnson up middle 4 yards (Blanshan)

**END OF THIRD QUARTER:
INDIANA 24, MINNESOTA 14**

FOURTH QUARTER

INDIANA
4/2 -MN49 - Lovett punt to Bailey, returns 7 yards (Doehla) 34 yard kick

14:50 MINNESOTA
1.10-MN22 - Carlson pass complete to Thompson 4 yards (Abrams)
2/6 -MN26 - Artis quick delay off left tackle 4 yards (Tillery, Norman)
3/2 -MN30 - Artis pitch left 3 yards (Iatarola)
1/10-MN33 - Carlson pass incomplete up middle
2/10-MN33 - Carlson back to pass, hit by Doehla, fumbles and Leake recovers for IND

13:33 INDIANA
1/10-MN19 - Harkrader breaks outside left 12 yards (Snyder)
1/G -MN7 - Harkrader slants left 5 yards (Friberg)
2/G -MN2 - Harkrader up middle scores from 2 yards out (TD) 2:09 ET, 12:51 TL 19 yard drive in 3 plays Freud PAT good
SCORE: INDIANA 31, MINNESOTA 14

360

NOVEMBER 4, 1978

Straub kick off to Noel on MN6, returns 22 yards (Smith)
12:45 MINNESOTA
1/10-MN29 - Bailey flanker reverse left 6 yards (Norman)
2/4 -MN35 - Avery pass for Bailey at left sideline incomplete
3/4 -MN35 - Barber quick pitch right, breaks open for 25 yards (Keneipp)
1/10-IN40 - Avery back to pass, runs for 6 yards (Doehla)
2/4 -IN34 - Barber slants left 1 yard (Willhite, Doehla)
3/3 -IN33 - Artis pitch right, cuts back for 4 yards (Smith)
1/10-IN29 - Avery release pass left to White complete 11 yards (Wilbur)
1/10-IN18 - Avery pass dropped by Bailey incomplete
2/10-IN18 - Artis at right tackle 4 yards (Willhite)
3/6 -IN14 - Avery pass hits ground in front of Bailey incomplete
4/6 -IN14 - Avery screen pass to Bailey 14 yd TD 5:15 ET, 9:32 EL (Wypyszynski throws key block) Rogind PAT good
SCORE: INDIANA 31, MINNESOTA 21

Rogind kick off to Burnet, returns 11 yards (Fahnhorst, Cunningham)
9:28 INDIANA
1/10-IN26 - Harkrader delay left 1 yard (Cunningham, Ronan)
2/9 -IN27 - Harkrader at right tackle 1 yard (Meyer)
3/8 -IN28 - Harkrader draw 3 yd loss Brown (Meyer, Burns)
4/11-IN25 - Lovett punt to Bailey, runs into punter/15 yard penalty
1/10-IN40 - Johnson up middle 2 yards (team)
2/8 -IN42 - Harkrader slants left 2 yards (Burns, Cunningham)
3/6 -IN44 - Clifford pass to Powers high off hands and incomplete
4/6 -IN44 - Lovett punt to Bailey, returns 23 yards (Lovett) 35 yard punt

6:01 MINNESOTA
1/10-MN44 - Avery pass intended for Bourquin behind him/incomplete
2/10-MN44 - Avery complete pass to Dilulo 7 yards (Keneipp)
3/3 -IN49 - Barber quick delay left tackle 1 yard (Norman)

361

4/2 -IN48 - Avery keeps right, 3 yards (Arbuckle)
1/10-IN45 - Avery back to pass, runs for 4 yards (Swinehart)
2/6 -IN41 - Avery complete to Barber 5 yards (Wilbur)
3/1 -IN36 - White slants left 5 yards (Norman)
1/10-IN31 - Avery complete to Bourquin 12 yards (Keneipp) (3:19)
1/10-IN19 - Avery pass batted down in line by Smith incomplete
2/10-IN19 - Avery screen left to Barber complete (19 yd) 3:04 TL, 11:56 ET 56 yard drive in 10 plays
Avery pass to Bailey for 2 points
SCORE: INDIANA 31, MINNESOTA 29

Rogind kick off to Johnson on IND 6 returns 19 yds (Peppe)
3:00 INDIANA
1/10-IN19 - Harkrader at right tackle no gain (Ronan)
2/10-IN19 - Harkrader at left tackle 4 yards (Burns) (2:46)
3/6 -IN23 - Harkrader slants left/IND holding (team) (2:42) 12 yard penalty
3/18-IN11 - Clifford pass intercepted by Edwards (no return) on MN41 (2:34)

MINNESOTA
1/10-MN41 - Avery pass to Barber dropped/incomplete (2:30)
2/10-MN41 - Avery pass complete to Barber 7 yards (Keneipp)
3/3 -MN48 - Avery to pass, runs for 5 yards (Norman)
1/10-IN47 - White up middle 7 yards (Tallen)
2/3 -N40 - Avery pass complete to Bailey 10 yards (Wilbur)
1/10-IN30 - (1:20) White slants left 3 yards (Norman)
2/7 -IN27 - Avery to pass, runs for 9 yards (Norman)
1/10-IN18 - White slants left 3 yards (Arbuckle)
2/7 -IN15 - White slants right 1 yard (Burtis) MN Time out (:05 secs)
3/6 -IN14 - Rogind field goal from 21 yards GOOD 45 yard drive in 10 plays, 14:59 ET, :02 TL
SCORE: MINNESOTA 32, INDIANA 31

Rogind kickoff to Burnet who downs ball with 1 sec left
:01 INDIANA
1/10-IN25 - Clifford pass intercepted by Edwards

END OF GAME:
MINNESOTA 32, INDIANA 31

National Collegiate Athletic Association
FINAL TEAM STATISTICS
November 4, 1978

	INDIANA	MIN-NESOTA
First Downs	9	34
Rushing	3	20
Passing	5	14
Penalty	1	0
Rushing Attempts	44	68
Yards Rushing	161	324
Yards Lost Rushing	7	26
Net Yards Rushing	154	298
Net Yards Passing	196	279
Passes Attempted	10	41
Passes Completed	5	21
Had Intercepted	3	3
Total Offensive Plays	54	109
Total Net Yards	350	577
Average Gain Per Play	6.48	5.29
Fumbles: Number-Lost	1/1	6/4
Penalties: Number-Yards	2/27	7/65
Interceptions: Number-Yards	3/129	3/22
Number of Punts-Yards	5/149	2/78
Average Per Punt	29.8	39.0
Punt Returns: Number-Yards	1/1	2/30
Kickoff Returns: Number-Yards	4/69	6/146

NOVEMBER 4, 1978

NORTHWESTERN VS. PURDUE
Ross-Ade Stadium
Temp: 79°
Wind: SW 5-7 mph
Skies: clear
FIRST QUARTER

Coin Flip: Purdue wins toss will receive Northwestern will kickoff and defend south goal. Poulos kickoff out of end zone.
PURDUE
1/10-P20 - Macon re, 3 yds. (Lizak-Geegan)
2/7 -P23 - Herrmann to Harris, incomplete
3/7 -P23 - Herrmann to Burrell, incomplete
4/7 -P23 - Eagin punt to Carver on N44 return to N47 (33 yard kick)

14:10 NORTHWESTERN
1/10-N47 - Hill lt, 2 yds. (Johnson)
2/8 -N49 - Strasser to Tiberi, incomplete
3/8 -N49 - Strasser to Bogan, Purdue offsides, 5 yd penalty
3/3 -P46 - Tiberi pitch left, 5 yds. (Johanson-Supan)
1/10-P41 - Tiberi lt, 5 yds. (Jackson-Loushin)
2/5 -P36 - Strasser to McGee, 19 yds. (Supan)
1/10-P17 - Tiberi pitch left, lost 1 yd. (Turner)
2/11-P18 - Tiberi pitch left, pass to North, incomplete
3/11-P18 - Strasser to Bogan, incomplete
4/11-P18 - Poulos attempt 36 yd field goal hit right upright no good

12:11 PURDUE
1/10-P20 - Pope inside le, 6 yds. (Gildner)
2/4 -P26 - Macon rg, 3 yds.
3/1 -P29 - Macon up middle, 2 yds.
1/10-P31 - Pope rt, 1 yd. (Berg-McGlade)
2/9 -P32 - Herrmann to Young, 19 yds. (Geegan)
1/10-N49 - Herrmann to Harris, intercept Geegan on N9

9:41 NORTHWESTERN
1/10-N9 - Cammon lt, 4 yds.
2/6 -N13 - Strasser to Hill, 4 yds.
3/2 -N17 - Hill pitch left, lost 4 yds. (Turner)
4/6 -N13 - Christenson punt to Pope on P24 return to P32 (63 yd punt 9 yd return)

8:19 PURDUE
1/10-P33 - Macon lt, 12 yds. (Geegan-Berg)
1/10-P45 - Pope inside le, 4 yds. (Lizak-Kern)
2/6 -P49 - Pope lt, 3 yds. (Taylor)
3/3 -N48 - Pope pitch right, 5 yds. (McGlade)
1/10-N43 - Herrmann to Burrell, incomplete
2/10-N43 - Macon on draw, 4 yds. (Gildner)
3/6 -N39 - Herrmann to Burrell, incomplete

4/6 -N39 - Eagin punt to end zone, 39 yd kick no return

5:43 NORTHWESTERN
1/10-N20 - Strasser to pass, lost 11 yds. (Jackson)
2/21-N9 - Cammon on draw, 1 yd (Loushin-Clark)
3/20-N10 - Strasser to Tiberi, 7 yds. (Marks)
4/13-N17 - Christenson punt to P38 dead, 45 yd kick no return

3:47 PURDUE
1/10-P38 - Macon at re, 3 yds. (Lizak)
2/7 -P41 - Herrmann to Burrell, 22 yds. (Geegan-Kern)
1/10-N37 - Macon lg, 5 yds. (Kendzicky)
2/5 -N32 - Pope at re, 10 yds. (Butler)
1/10-N22 - Pope rg, 2 yds. (Taylor-Dunlea)
2/8 -N20 - Herrmann to Macon, 8 yds. (Lizak)
1/10-N12 - Macon lg, 4 yds. (Dunlea-Corona)
2/6 -N8 - Pope pitch right, 8 yds. touchdown, 8 plays, 62 yds. PAT Sovereen kick Burrell hold good
SCORE: PURDUE 7, NORTHWESTERN 0

Sovereen kickoff to Hill on N4 return to N29, 56 yd kick 24 yd return
0:55 NORTHWESTERN
1/10-N28 - Strasser to McGee, intercept W Harris on N34 return to N26 fumbled out of bounds, 18 yd return.

0:41 PURDUE
1/10-N26 - Pope le, 7 yds. (McGlade-Lizak)
2/3 -N19 - Herrmann to Smith, 19 yds. touchdown, 2 plays 26 yds. PAT Sovereen kick Burrell hold good
SCORE: PURDUE 14, NORTHWESTERN 0

**END OF FIRST QUARTER:
PURDUE 14, NORTHWESTERN 0**

363

SECOND QUARTER

Sovereen kickoff to N end zone, 60 yd kick no return
NORTHWESTERN
1/10-N20 - Cammon up middle, 3 yds. (Loushin-Marks)
2/7 -N23 - Hill rg, 3 yds. (Jackson)
3/4 -N26 - Strasser to Hill, incomplete
4/4 -N26 - Christenson punt to Gallivan on P44 return to P48, 30 yd kick 4 yd return

13:41 PURDUE
1/10-P48 - Macon lt, 9 yds. (McGlade-Kern)
2/1 -N43 - Pope re, 3 yds. (Hoffman)
1/10-N40 - Herrmann to Harris, 11 yds. (McGlade)
1/10-N29 - Macon on draw, 6 yds. (Kern-Berg)
2/4 -N23 - Herrmann to Harris, 23 yds. touchdown, 5 plays 52 yds. PAT Sovereen kick Burrell hold good
SCORE: PURDUE 21, NORTHWESTERN 0

Sovereen kickoff to Hill on goal line return to N21, 60 yd kick 21 yd return
12:27 NORTHWESTERN
1/10-N21 - Cammon lg, 4 yds. (Johanson)
2/6 -N25 - Northwestern time out 11:47
2/6 -N25 - Strasser to Kaspryski, 3 yds.
3/3 -N28 - Strasser to McGee, 9 yds. (Turner-Johanson)
1/10-N37 - Strasser to McGee, 9 yds.
2/1-N46 - Cammon rg, 2 yds (Johanson)
1/10-N48 - Strasser to Bogan, incomplete
2/10-N48 - Strasser to pass, fumbled, Loushin recovered for P, lost 1 yd.

10:03 PURDUE
1/10-N47 - 2nd team offense McCall re, 4 yds. (Hoffman)
2/6 -N43 - Augustyniak inside re, 3 yds. (Dunlea)
3/3 -N40 - McCall pitch right, 5 yds. (Rogers)
1/10-N35 - Oliver to Gallivan, Purdue ineligible receiver down field 15 yd penalty
1/25- 50 - Shotgun: McCall le, 11 yds. (Hoffman)
2/14-N39 - Oliver to Eubank, incomplete
3/14-N39 - Oliver to Luckianow, 13 yds. (Butler)
4/1 -N26 - McCall inside re, lost 1 yd. (Butler)

7:00 NORTHWESTERN
1/10-N27 - Hill pitch left, 1 yd. (Loushin-Smith)
2/9 -N28 - Strasser to Hill, 4 yds. (Johanson)
3/5 -N32 - Strasser to McGee, incomplete
4/5 -N32 - Christenson punt to Pope on P34 return to P31 34 yd kick -3 return Northwestern personal foul 15 yd penalty

5:30 PURDUE
1/10-P46 - 1st team offense: Pope lt, 5 yds. (McGlade)
2/5 -N49 - Macon re, cut back, 2 yds. (Kern-Dunlea)
3/3 -N47 - Herrmann to Burrell, 9 yds. (Geegan)
1/10-N38 - Herrmann to Burrell, 18 yds. (Berg-Geegan)
1/10-N20 - Pope pitch right, 3 yds. (Dorsey)
2/7 -N17 - Macon lg, 8 yds. (Berg-McGlade)
1/G -N9 - Macon lg, 4 yds. (Dorsey)
2/G -N5 - Pope lt, 2 yds. (Kern-Dunlea)
3/G -N3 - Purdue time out 2:07
3/G -N3 - Pope lg, 1 yd. (Dorsey-Kern)
4/G -N2 - Sovereen attempt 19 yd field goal good, 10 plays, 51 yds.
SCORE: PURDUE 24, NORTHWESTERN 0

Sovereen kickoff to Carver in end zone, 60 yd kick no return
1:31 NORTHWESTERN
1/10-N20 - Strasser to Hill, 3 yds. (Barr)
2/7 -N23 - Strasser to pass, lost 19 yds. (Turner)
3/26-N4 - Strasser keep, 2 yds.

**HALF TIME SCORE:
PURDUE 24, NORTHWESTERN 0**

THIRD QUARTER

Northwestern elected to receive Purdue will kick off and defend south goal
Sovereen kickoff to Carver on N2 return to N21, 58 yd kick 19 yd return
NORTHWESTERN
1/10-N21 - Cammon rt, 2 yds. Kaspryscki injured 14:42
2/8 -N23 - Strasser to Tiberi, 7 yds. (Moss-Motts)
3/1 -N30 - Hill slide re, 4 yds. Hill injured (Moss)
1/10-N34 - Tiberi lt, 4 yds. (Loushin)
2/6 -N38 - Strasser to Bogan intercept Harris on P34 return to N22, 44 yd return

13:05 PURDUE
1/10-N22 - Pope le, lost 2 yds. (McGlade)
2/12-N24 - shotgun Herrmann to Pope, 24 yds. touchdown, 2 plays 22 yds PAT Sovereen kick Burrell hold good
SCORE: PURDUE 31, NORTHWESTERN 0

Sovereen kickoff to Carver on goal line return to N14 60 yd kick 14 yd return
12:18 NORTHWESTERN
1/10-N14 - Webb lt, 6 yds. (Jackson-Smith)
2/4 -N20 - Tiberi lt, no gain (Barr-Marks)
3/4 -N20 - Webb rg, 3 yds. (Marks-Motts)
3/1 -N23 - Christenson punt to Gallivan on P32 return to P33, 45 yd kick 1 yd return

364

NOVEMBER 4, 1978

10:28 PURDUE
1/10-P33 - second offense: Augustyniak lg, 4 yds. (Rogers-Berg)
2/6 -P37 - Oliver roll left, 5 yds. (Hoffman)
3/1 -P42 - Augustyniak lg, 5 yds. (Kern)
1/10-P47 - Oliver to Smith, incomplete
2/10-P47 - Augustyniak on draw, 5 yds. (Berg-Kern)
3/5 -N48 - Oliver to pass, run, 9 yds. (Kern)
1/10-N39 - McCall pitch right, 7 yds. (Kendzicky)
2/3 -N32 - McCall lg, 2 yds. (Taylor-Berg)
3/1 -N30 - Oliver to Smith, 7 yds. Smith injured (Geegan)
1/10-N23 - McCall pitch right, lost 1 yd. (Gildner)
2/11-N24 - Oliver to Gallivan, incomplete
3/11-N24 - Oliver to Speedy, incomplete
4/11-N24 - Sovereen atttempt 42 yd field goal Burrell hold, no good wide right

7:05 NORTHWESTERN
1/10-N24 - Webb rg, 1 yd. (Marks-Barr)
2/9 -N25 - Strasser to Washington, 6 yds. (Moss)
3/3 -N31 - Strasser to Poulos, 10 yds. (Kay)
1/10-N41 - Webb pitch left, 4 yds. (Barr)
2/6 -N45 - Webb rt, 1 yd. (Seneff)
3/5 -N46 - Strasser to Tiberi, 11 yds. (Smith)
1/10-P43 - Tiberi lt, 3 yds. (Barr-Marks)
2/7 -P40 - Webb inside le, 6 yds. (Johanson-Seneff)
3/1 -P34 - Tiberi lt, no gain (Johanson-Jostin)
4/1-P34 - Strasser keep, 1 yd. (Motts-Johanson)
1/10-P33 - Strasser to Poulos, 9 yds. (Supan-Jostin)
2/1 -P24 - Webb rt, lost 3 yds. (Motts-Kingsbury)
3/4 -P27 - Strasser to Bogan, 6 yds. (Smith)
1/10-P21 - Tiberi rt, lost 1 yd. (Motts)
2/11-P22 - Strasser to pass, lost 11 yds. (Barr)
3/22-P33 Strasser to Bahoric, incomplete
4/22-P33 - Tiberi swing left, pass back to Strasser, incomplete

0:51 PURDUE
1/10-P33 - Augustyniak inside re, 47 yds. (Geegan)
1/10-N20 - Jones pitch left, 5 yds. fumble, Taylor recovered N

0:31 NORTHWESTERN
1/10-N15 - Washington pitch right, 2 yds. (Kingsbury)

END OF THIRD QUARTER: PURDUE 31, NORTHWESTERN 0

FOURTH QUARTER

NORTHWESTERN
2/8 -N17 - Tiberi up middle, 7 yds. (Barr)
3/1 -N24 - Webb pitch right, 2 yds. (Moss)
1/10-N26 - Tiberi lg, 4 yds. (Ernst)
2/6 -N30 - Strasser to Webb, incomplete
3/6 -N30 - Tiberi on delay, lost 1 yd. (Barr)
4/7 -N29 - Christenson punt to P23 dead, 48 yd kick no return

12:47 PURDUE
1/10-P23 - Robinson rg, 5 yds. (Taylor)
2/5 -P28 - Robinson le, 7 yds. (Geegan)
1/10-P35 - Oliver to pass, run, 12 yds. (McGlade)
1/10-P47 - Augustyniak rg, 2 yds. (Gildner)
2/8 -P49 - Oliver to Linville, incomplete
3/8 -P49 - Oliver to pass, lost 5 yds.
4/13-P44 - Eagin punt to Carver on N11 return to N29, 45 yd kick 18 yd return

9:11 NORTHWESTERN
1/10-N29 - Breitbeil at QB: Webb at rt, 5 yds. (Moss)
2/5 -N34 - Breitbeil to Tiberi, 6 yds.
1/10-N40 - Tiberi lg, 1 yd. (Harris, M)
2/9 -N41 - Breitbeil to pass Bahoric, intercept Kingsbury on N47, Northwestern face mask on return 15 yd. penalty

7:37 PURDUE
1/10-N32 - Steve Barr at QB: Barr roll right, 9 yds. (Hoffman-Dorsey)
2/1 -N23 - Robinson lt, 7 yds. (Berg)
1/10-N16 - Jones pitch back right, 5 yds. fumbled Jim Meyer recovered
2/5 -N11 - Meyer rt, tripped, 4 yds.
3/1 -N7 - Meyer rt, no gain, fumbled, recovered
4/1 -N7 - Robinson lg, 2 yds. (Kern)
1/G -N5 - Robinson rt, 2 yds. (Berg)
2/G -N3 - Robinson pitch left, lost 1 yd. (Berg-Hoffman)
3/G -N4 - Barr roll right, 2 yds. (McGlade-Rogers)
4/G -N2 - Barr to pass, lost 11 yds. (Rogers)

2:44 NORTHWESTERN
1/10-N13 - Webb rg, 1 yd. (Bury-Virkus)
2/9 -N14 - Tiberi rg, 1 yd. (R Jones-Kingsbury)
3/8 -N15 - Breitbeil to Webb, 7 yds. (R. Jones-Kingsbury)
4/1 -N22 - time out Northwestern 0:57
4/1 -N22 - Christenson punt to P24 dead 54 yd kick no return

0:46 PURDUE
1/10-P24 - Beteulis at QB: Beteulis fumbled recovered 1 yd.
2/9 -P25 - Pruitt rt, lost 2 yds. (Dorsey)

**FINAL SCORE:
PURDUE 31, NORTHWESTERN 0**

National Collegiate Athletic Association
FINAL TEAM STATISTICS

	NORTH-WESTERN	PURDUE
First Downs	11	25
Rushing	5	15
Passing	6	10
Penalty	0	0
Rushing Attempts	41	60
Yards Rushing	90	293
Yards Lost Rushing	52	22
Net Yards Rushing	38	271
Net Yards Passing	120	173
Passes Attempted	28	21
Passes Completed	16	11
Had Intercepted	3	1
Total Offensive Plays	69	81
Total Net Yards	158	444
Average Gain Per Play	2.29	5.48
Fumbles: Number—Lost	2/1	5/1
Penalties: Number—Yards	2/30	2/20
Interceptions: Number—Yards	1/0	3/62
Number of Punts—Yards	7/318	3/116
Average Per Punt	45.4	38.7
Punt Returns: Number—Yards	2/20	4/12
Kickoff Returns: Number—Yards	4/78	0/0

NOVEMBER 4, 1978

OHIO STATE
VS
WISCONSIN
Camp Randall Stadium
Temp: 63
Wind:ENE 6 mph
Skies: Sunny and cool
FIRST QUARTER

OHIO STATE won the toss and will receive. WISCONSIN will defend the north goal.
Mike Brhley will kickoff for Wisconsin to open the game, to the 02, Murray returns 21 yards to the 0 23. (Spurlin)

1:55 OHIO STATE
1/10-023 - Campbell runs up the middle, gets 7 to 30 (Burt)
2/3 -030 - Campbell runs right tackle, gets 6 to 36 (Burt)
1/10-036 - Campbell runs up the middle, gets 2 to 38 (Crossen)
2/8 -038 - Schlichter pitches left to Springs, gets 6 to 44 (Anderson)
3/2 -044 - Schlichter keeps on the option right, gets 46 to W10 (Casey)
1/10-010 - Campbell runs right tackle, gets 3 to7 (Cabral)
2/G -07 - Schlichter keeps on the option left, gets 7 for TD (12:44)
Janakievski kicks the extra point (7 plays, 77 yards)
SCORE: OHIO STATE 7, WISCONSIN 0

Orosz kicks off for Ohio State following the score, to W5, Green returns 17 yards to the W22. (Laughlin)

12:39 WISCONSIN
1/10-W22 - Kalasmiki pitches right to Matthews, gets 9 to 31 (Skillings)
2/1 -W31 - Stauss runs right tackle, gets 3 to 34 (Cato)
1/10-W34 - Matthews runs up the middle, gets 4 to 38 (Cousineau)
2/6 -W38 - Kalasmiki pitches left to Matthews, gets 7 to 45 (Washington)
1/10-W45 - Stauss runs up the middle, gets 7 to O48 (Cousineau)
2/3 -O48 - Kalasmiki pitches right to Green, gets 6 to 42 (Dulin)
1/10-042 - Green runs left tackle, gets 3 to 39 (Washington)
2/7 -039 - Kalasmiki passes left to Stauss, gets 8 to 31 (Washington)
1/10-031 - Kalasmiki passes right to Souza, incomplete
2/10-031 - Kalasmiki passes over the middle to Green, intercepted by Washington on 02. (Sydnor)

8:15 OHIO STATE
1/10-02 - Campbell runs right tackle, gets 5 to 7 (Ahrens)
2/5 -07 - Campbell runs right tackle, gets 4 to 11 (Casey)
3/1 -011 - Campbell runs right tackle, gets 3 to 14 (Lorenz)
1/10-014 - Schlichter pitches right to Springs, gets 4 to 18 (Lorenz)
2/6 -018 - Campbell runs up the middle, gets 6 to 24 (Christenson)
1/10-024 - Schlichter back to pass is sacked, loses 12 to 12 (Lorenz and Christenson)
2/22-012 - Campbell runs up the middle, gets 7 to 19, fumbles recovered by Lorenz

5:30 WISCONSIN
1/10-019 - Green runs right tackle, gets 3 to 16 (Washington)
2/7 -016 - Kalasmiki pitches left to Green, gets no gain (Skillings)
3/7 -016 - Stauss runs right tackle, gets 1 to 15 (Cousineau)
4/6 -015 - Veith 32 yard field goal attempt wide left

3:35 OHIO STATE
1/10-020 - Murray runs right tackle, gets 3 to 23 (Ahrens)
2/7 -023 - Schlichter keeps on the option left, gets no gain (Lorenz)
3/7 -023 - Volley runs draw up the middle, gets 9 to 32 (Casey)
1/10-032 - Volley runs up the middle, gets 6 to 38 (Holm)
2/4 -038 - Volley runs up the middle, gets 8 to 46 (Welch)
1/10-046 - Schlichter pitches right to Murray, gets 10 to W44 (Welch)
1/10-W44 - Murray runs right end, gets 1 to 43 (Relich)
2/9 -W43 - Schlichter is sacked, loses 5 to 48 (Schieble)
3/14-W48 - Schlichter passes up the middle, incomplete
4/14-W14 - Orosz punts 41 yards to W7

:02 WISCONSIN
1/10-W7 - Cohee runs up the middle, gets no gain (Sullivan)

**END OF THE FIRST QUARTER:
OHIO STATE 7, WISCONSIN 0**

SECOND QUARTER

15:00 WISCONSIN
2/10-W7 - Stauss runs right tackle, gets 5 to 12 (Dansler)
3/5 -W12 - Kalasmiki patches right to Green, gets 11 to 23 (Skillings)

367

1/10-W23 - Stauss runs up the middle, gets 4 to 27 (Cato)
2/6 -W27 - Stauss runs up the middle, gets 1 to 28 (Cato)
3/5 -W27 - Kalasmiki passes over the middle to Ruetz, incomplete
4/5 -W27 - Kiltz punt is blocked by Skillings, recovered by Watson in the W endzone for TD Janakievski kicks the extra point
SCORE: OHIO STATE 14, WISCONSIN 0

Orosz kicks off for Ohio State following the score to the W3, Anderson returns 23 yards to W26 (Laughlin)

12:42 WISCONSIN
1/10-W26 - Kalasmiki keeps right on the option, gets 4 to 30 (Bell)
2/6 -W30 - Kalasmiki passes right to Souza, incomplete
3/6 -W30 - Kalasmiki pitches right to Cohee, gets 3 to 33 (Ellis)
4/3 -W33 - Kiltz punts 45 yards to O22, Guess returns 5 to 27 (Kelly)

11:36 OHIO STATE
1/10-O27 - Schlichter pitches right to Springs, loses 3 to 24 (Schieble)
2/13-O24 - Schlichter passes left to Donley, gets 11 to 35 (Anderson)
3/2 -O35 - Campbell runs up the middle, get 2 to 37 (Christenson)
1/10-O37 - Campbell runs left tackle, gets 4 to 41 (Christenson)
2/6 -O41 - Schlichter passes to Donley, broken up (by Schieble)
3/6 -O41 - Campbell runs up the middle, loses 1 to 40 (Christenson)
4/7 -O40 - Orosz punts 40 yards to W20, Stauss returns 1 yard to 21

9:04 WISCONSIN
1/10-W21 - Stauss runs right tackle, gets 10 to 31 (Mills)
1/10-W31 - Green runs left tackle, gets 11 to 42 (Bell)
1/10-W42 - Green runs right tackle, gets 5 to 47 (Washington)
2/5 -W47 - Kalasmiki pitches to Charles, passes to Souza, intercepted by Skillings on O18

7:19 OHIO STATE
1/10-O18 - Schlichter pitches right to Springs, gets 8 to 26 (Anderson)
2/2 -O26 - Campbell runs up the middle, gets 6 to 32 (Holm)
1/10-O32 - Schlichter passes over the middle, to Taylor, intercepted by Welch at O46 returned 13 yards to O33

6:22 WISCONSIN
1/10-O33 - Stauss runs right tackle, gets 7 to 26 (Skillings)
2/3 -O26 - Green runs left tackle, gets 7 to 19 (Bell)
1/10-O19 - Kalasmiki keeps on the option left, gets 3 to 16 (Cato)
2/7 -O16 - Kalasmiki pitches right to Green, loses 1 to 17 (Dulin)
3/8 -O17 - Kalasmiki passes left to Stauss, incomplete
4/8 -O17 - Veith field goal attempt is wide left

3:41 OHIO STATE
1/10-O20 - Schlichter pitches left to Springs, gets 4 to 24 (Welch)
2/6 -O24 - Campbell runs up the middle, gets 5 to 29 (Holm)
3/1 -O29 - Campbell runs left tackle, gets 9 to 38 (Welch)
1/10-O38 - Schlichter passes over the middle, intercepted by Schieble at W42, returns 21 yards to O37

2:22 WISCONSIN
1/10-O37 - Kalasmiki passes left to Charles, incomplete
2/10-O37 - Kalasmiki is sacked, loses 7 (Henson) Ohio State is penalized 15 yards for holding
1/10-O22 - Kalasmiki pitches right to Green, gets 10 to 12 (Bell)
1/10-O12 - Green runs left guard, gets 2 to 10 (Washington)
Wisconsin calls timeout (1:25)
2/8 -O10 - Kalasmiki pitches right to Green, gets 3 to 7 (Cato)
Wisconsin calls timeout (1:17)
3/5 -O7 - Kalasmiki passes left to Charles, gets 7 to TD (1:10) Veith kicks the extra point (5 plays, 37 yards)
SCORE: OHIO STATE 14, WISCONSIN 7

Brhley kicks off for Wisconsin following the score to O4, Hicks returns 96 yards for the TD Janakievski kicks the extra point
SCORE: OHIO STATE 21, WISCONSIN 7

Artha kicks off for Ohio State following the score, to the W 27, Sydnor returns 8 yards to W35. (Laughlin)

:53 WISCONSIN
1/10-W35 - Kalasmiki back to pass is sacked, loses 9 to 26 (Cato)
2/19-W26 - Kalasmiki passed left to Charles, gets 13 to 39
3/6 -W39 - Kalasmiki passes over the middle to Souza, intercepted by Cousineau at W45, returned 3 to W42. (Krall)

**END OF THE FIRST HALF:
OHIO STATE 21, WISCONSIN 7**

NOVEMBER 4, 1978

THIRD QUARTER

Orosz will kickoff for Ohio State to open the second half, to W10, Anderson returns 19 yards to W29 (Murphy)
14:46 WISCONSIN
1/10-W29 - Stauss runs right tackle, gets 2 to 31 (Cousineau)
2/8 -W31 - Kalasmiki passes left to Souza, gets 11 to 42
1/10-W42 - Green runs left guard, gets no gain (Sullivan)
2/10-W42 - Kalasmiki passes over the middle to Charles, intercepted by Skillings at O39, returns 61 yards for TD (13:21) Janakievski kicks the extra point
SCORE: OHIO STATE 28, WISCONSIN 7

Orosz will kickoff for Ohio State following the score, to W14, Anderson returns 19 yards to W33 (Laughlin)
13:16 WISCONSIN
1/10-W33 - Stauss runs right guard, gets 3 to 36 (Washington)
2/7 -W36 - Kalasmiki keeps and runs right, gets 11 to 47 (Ross)
1/10-W47 - Kalasmiki pitches left to Green, gets 1 to 48 (Mornik)
2/9 -W48 - Kalasmiki passes right to Charles, incomplete
3/9 -W48 - Green runs up the middle on draw, gets 3 to O49 (Mornik)
4/6 -O49 - Kiltz punts 49 yards to O endzone for touchback

10:51 OHIO STATE
1/10-O20 - Springs runs right tackle, gets 3 to 23 (Lorenz)
2/7 -O23 - Schlichter pitches left to Springs, gets 3 to 26 (Holm)
3/4 -O26 - Schlichter keeps on the option left, gets no gain (Schremp)
4/4 -O26 - Orosz punts 63 yards to W11, Stauss returned 0 yards (Ferguson)

9:17 WISCONSIN
1/10-W11 - Green runs left tackle, gets 4 to 15 (Cousineau)
2/6 -W15 - Souza runs reverse right, gets 7 to 22 (Cousineau)
1/10-W22 - Kalasmiki keeps on option right, gets 9 to 31 (Cousineau)
2/1 -W31 - Green runs right tackle, gets 3 to 34 (Washington)
1/10-W34 - Kalasmiki keeps on faked reverse left, gets 5 to 39 (Bell)
2/5 -W39 - Kalasmiki runs up middle, gets no gain (Mornik)
3/5 -W39 - Kalasmiki passes right to Charles, incomplete
4/5 -W39 - Kiltz punts 42 yards to O19, Guess returns 11 yards to O30 (Kelly)

5:44 OHIO STATE
1/10-O30 - Campbell runs left tackle, gets 1 to 31 (Schremp)
2/9 -O31 - Schlichter passes over the middle to Gerald, gets 15 to 46 (Holm)
1/10-O46 - Schlichter pitches left to Murray gets 5 to W49
2/5 -W49 - Murray runs right tackle, gets 5 to 44 (Blaskowski)
1/10-W44 - Ohio State is penalized 5 yards for illegal procedure
1/15-W49 - Schlichter passes left to Campbell, gets 3 to 46 (Lopenz)
2/12-W46 - Campbell runs draw up the middle, gets 5 to 41 (Holm)
3/7 -W41 - Schlichter passes right to Gerald, gets 10 to 31 (Ahrens)
1/10-W31 - Murray runs left tackle, gets 6 to 25 (Stroede)
2/4 -W25 - Volley runs up the middle, gets 11 to 14 (Schiebke)
1/10-W14 - Murray runs left, reverses to right, gets 14 for TD (1:58)
Janakievski kicks the extra point (10 plays, 70 yards)
SCORE: OHIO STATE 35, WISCONSIN 7

Artha kicks off for Ohio State following the score to W2 Anderson returns 17 yards to 19 (Epotopoulos)
1:54 WISCONSIN
1/10-W19 - Green runs left end, gets 10 to 29, fumbles, recovered by Bell

1:43 OHIO STATE
1/10-W29 - Murray runs left tackle, gets 3 to 26 (Stroede)
2/7 -W26 - Castignola leeps left on option, gets 1 to 25 (Ahrens)
3/6 -W25 - Castignola passes right to Taylor, incomplete
4/6 -W25 - Castignola passes to Hunter Wisconsin is penalized 11 yards for pass interference
1/10-W14 - Castignola keeps on the option right, gets 3 to 11 (Holm)
2/7 -W11 - Castignola passes right to Hicks, gets 1 to 10 (Christenson)

END OF THE THIRD QUARTER
OHIO STATE 35, WISCONSIN 7

FOURTH QUARTER

15:00 OHIO STATE
3/6 -W10 - Ohio State is penalized 5 yards for illegal procedure
3/11-W15 - Wisconsin calls timeout 14:55
Castignola keeps on the option right, gets 15 to TD (14:47)
Janakievski kicks the extra point (6 plays, 29 yards)
SCORE: OHIO STATE 42, WISCONSIN 7

Artha kicks off for Ohio State following the score to W4, Anderson returns 18 yards to 22 (Burrows)

14:41-WISCONSIN
1/10-W22 - Josten keeps on the option right, loses 9 to 13, fumbles, recovered by Bell

14:32-OHIO STATE
1/10-W13 - Castignola pitches right to Hicks, gets 5 to 8 (Houston)
2/5 -W8 - Ohio State is penalized 5 yards for illegal procedure
2/10-W13 - Hicks runs right tackle, gets 4 to 9 (Yourg)
3/6 -W9 - Castignola keeps up the middle, gets 3 to 6 (Casey)
4/3 -W6 - Castignola keeps on the option left, gets 6 for TD (13:03) Janakievski kicks the extra point (4 plays, 13 yards)
SCORE: OHIO STATE 49, WISCONSIN 7

Artha kicks off for Ohio State following the score to W endzone for touchback.
13:03 WISCONSIN
1/10-W20 - Cohee runs right tackle, gets 6 to 26 (Epitropoulos, J)
2/4 -W26 - Josten pitches right to Cohee, gets 1 to 27 (Henson)
3/3 -W27 - Braker runs reverse right, gets 6 to 33 (Megaro)
1/10-W33 - Josten keeps on option right, gets 9 to 42 (Epitropoulos, J)
2/1 -W42 - Cohee runs left tackle, gets 3 to 45 (Lee)

1/10-W45 - Josten keeps on the option right, gets 2 to 47 (Megaro)
2/8 -W47 - Green runs left end, gets 13 to O40 (Epitropoulos, J)
1/10-O40 - Mohapp runs up the middle, gets 28 to 12 (Sullivan)
1/10-O12 - Josten keeps on the option right gets 7 to 5 (Griffin)
2/3 -O5 - Cohee runs up the middle, gets 1 to 4 (Sullivan)
3/2 -O4 - Josten pitches to Souza, loses 1 to 5 (Guess)
4/3 -O5 - Josten keeps on the option right, gets 4 to 1 (Cousineau)
1/G -O1 - Green runs right tackle, gets 1 for TD (6:18)
Veith kicks the extra point (13 plays, 80 yards)

SCORE: OHIO STATE 49, WISCONSIN 14

Brhely kicks off for Wisconsin following the score to O endzone for touchback.

6:18 OHIO STATE
1/10-O20 - Volley runs up the middle, gets 1 to 21 (Yourg)
2/9 -O21 - Volley runs left tackle, gets 2 to 23 (Cabral)
3/7 -O23 - Castignola keeps on the option left gets 2 to 25 (Scheible)

NOVEMBER 4, 1978

4/5 -O25 - Orosz punts 56 yards to W19, Stauss returns 3 to 22 (Laughlin)

4:35 WISCONSIN
1/10-W22 - Josten passes left to Stracka, incomplete
2/10-W22 - Josten passes left to Stracka, incomplete
3/10-W22 - Josten passes right to Mohapp, gets 23 to 45 (Murphy)
1/10-W45 - Ohio State calls timeout (4:13) Josten pitches right to Cohee, gets 5 to 50 (Griffin)
2/5 - 50 - Mohapp runs up the middle, gets 3 to O47 (J. Epitropoulos) Ohio State is penalized 15 yards for personal foul
1/10-O32 - Josten keeps on the option right, gets 3 to 29 (Lee)
2/7 -O29 - Green runs left tackle, gets 5 to 24 (Watson)
3/2 -O24 - Green runs end, gets no gain (Hornik)
4/2 -O24 - Wisconsin calls timeout (2:12) Green runs right tackle, gets 1 to 23 (Megaro)

2:07 OHIO STATE
1/10-O23 - Johnson runs left tackle, gets 6 to 29 (Levenick)
2/4 -O29 - Castignola keeps on the option left, gets 3 to 32 (Spurlin)
3/1 -O32 - Castignola fumbles the handoff to Hicks, no gain (Spurlin)
4/1 -O32 - Hicks runs left tackle, gets 5 to 37 (Lorenz)
1/10-O37 - Hicks runs right tackle, gets 4 to 41 (Yourg)

**END OF THE GAME:
OHIO STATE 49, WISCONSIN 14**

National Collegiate Athletic Association
FINAL TEAM STATISTICS

	OHIO STATE	WISCONSIN
First Downs	19	22
Rushing	16	16
Passing	2	4
Penalty	1	2
Rushing Attempts	57	61
Yards Rushing	297	285
Yards Lost Rushing	21	20
Net Yards Rushing	276	265
Net Yards Passing	40	62
Passes Attempted	10	18
Passes Completed	5	5
Had Intercepted	2	4
Total Offensive Plays	67	79
Total Net Yards	316	327
Average Gain Per Play	4/7	4.1
Fumbles: Number—Lost	2/1	2/2
Penalties: Number—Yards	5/45	2/16
Interceptions: Number—Yards	4/64	2/34
Number of Punts—Yards	4/200	4/136
Average Per Punt	50.0	34.0
Punt Returns: Number—Yards	3/44	3/4
Kickoff Returns: Number—Yards	2/117	7/121

NOVEMBER 11, 1978

IOWA
VS.
INDIANA
Memorial Stadium
Bloomington, Indiana
Temp.: 66°
Wind: SSW 12mph
FIRST QUARTER

Indiana wins toss and will receive, Iowa will defend south goal
Schilling kicks off out of end zone
15:00 INDIANA
1/10-IN20 - Arnett pass complete to Harkrader to IN25, 5 yards
2/5 -IN25 - Burnett rt to IN27, 2 yds
3/3 -IN27 - Harkrader re to IN35, 8 yds
1/10-IN35 - Burnett le to IN35, no gain
2/10-IN35 - Harkrader lt to IN35, no gain
3/10-IN35 - Indiana penalized for holding
3/25-IN20 - Burnett re to IN24, 4 yds
4/21-IN24 - Lovett punts to Reid, fair catch at IN33, 43 punt

11:51 IOWA
1/10-Io33 - Mosley le to Io37, 4 yds
2/6 -Io37 - Mosley rg to Io44, 12 yds
1/10-Io44 - Turner re to 50, loss of 6
2/16- 50 - Green trapped to I32, loss of 18
3/34-I32 - Green pass incomplete
4/34-I32 - Holsclaw punts to Swinehart at I27 returned to I30, 3 return 41 punt

8:34 INDIANA
1/10-IN30 - Harkrader re to IN37, 7 yards
2/3 -IN37 - Harkrader lg to IN45, 8 yards
1/10-IN45 - Arnett pass incomplete
2/10-IN45 - Burnett rg to Io48, 7 yards
3/3 -Io48 - Burnett rt to Io41, 7 yards
1/10-Io41 - Indiana penalized holding
1/25-IN44 - Burnett lt to IN45, 1 yard
2/24-IN45 - Arnett pass incomplete
3/24-IN45 - Arnett pass incomplete
4/24-IN45 - Iowa penalized for roughing the kicker
4/9 -I40 - Lovett punts into end zone, 40 punt

5:24 IOWA
1/10-I20 - Mosley rg to I22, 2 yards
2/8 -I22 - Green le to I22, no gain
3/8 -I22 - Green pass intercepted by Wilbur at I34, returned to I33 1 return

3:59 INDIANA
1/10-I33 - Harkrader re to I20, 13 yards
1/10-I20 - Burnett rg for touchdown, 20 yards
PAT Freud kick good
SCORE: INDIANA 7 IOWA 0

Straub kicks off to Blatcher at I9, returned to I28, 19 return

3:44 IOWA
1/10-I28 - Turner rg to I35, 7 yards
2/3 -I35 - Turner lg to I38, 3 yards
1/10-I38 - Iowa illegal motion
1/15-I33 - Turner re to I35, 2 yards
2/13-I35 - Iowa penalized for holding
2/33-I15 - Reid le to I10 loss of 5
3/38-I10 - Turner le to I7, loss of 3
4/41-I 7 - Holsclaw punts to Wilbur at IN48 returned to I45, 7 return 45 punt

0:36 INDIANA
1/10-I45 - Harkrader le to I39, 6 yards
2/4 -I39 - Johnson rg to I35, 4 yards
END OF FIRST QUARTER:
INDIANA 7 IOWA 0

SECOND QUARTER

INDIANA
1/10-Io35 - Johnson rg to Io22 (13 yards)
1/10-Io22 - Harkrader re to Io 14 (8 yards)
2/2 -Io14 - Harkrader rt to Io10 (4 yards)
1/10-Io10 - Arnett pass complete to Hopkins for touchdown (10 yards)
PAT—Freud kick good.
SCORE: INDIANA 14, IOWA 0

STRAUB kicks off to Blatcher in end zone, returned to Io23, 23 return.
13:57 IOWA
1/10-Io23 - Lazar rg to Io24 (1 yard)
2/9 -Io24 - Green pass incomplete
3/9 -Io24 - Turner le to Io29 (5 yards)
4/4 -Io29 - Holsclaw punts to Wilbur at In34, returned to In37, 3 return. 37 punt

12:29 INDIANA
1/10-In37 - Arnett trapped to In34, loss of 3.
2/13-In34 - Harkrader rg to In39 (5 yards)
3/8 -In39 - Harkrader le to Io49 (12 yards)
1/10-Io49 - Indiana penalized for holding
1/25-In36 - Burnett re to In35, loss of 1
2/26-In35 - Harkrader rt to Io48 (17 yards)
3/9 -Io48 - Arnett le to Io45 (3 yards)
4/6 -Io45 - Lovett punts into end zone 45 punt

9:34 IOWA
1/10-Io20 - Turner rg to Io25 (5 yards)
2/5 -Io25 - Blatcher le to Io27 (2 yards)
3/3 -Io27 - Blatcher re to Io27, no gain
4/3 -Io27 - Holsclaw punts to Wilbur at In43, returned to In46, 3 return

7:34 INDIANA
1/10-In46 - Arnett pass complete to Johnson to Io36 (18 yards)
1/10-Io36 - Harkrader lt to Io27 (9 yards)
2/1 -Io27 - Bowers rg to Io24 (3 yards)
1/10-Io24 - Burnett rg to Io12 (12 yards)

NOVEMBER 11, 1978

1/10-Io12 - Burnett rg to Io8 (4 yards)
2/6 -Io8 - Burnett rt to Io6 (2 yards)
3/4 -Io6 - Burnett rt to Io3 (3 yards)
4/1 -Io3 - Arnett pass completed to Powers for touchdown (3 yards) PAT—Freud kick good.
SCORE: INDIANA 21, IOWA 0

Straub kicks off to Blatcher in end zone, returned to Io43, 43 return.

3:53 IOWA
1/10-Io43 - Green pass incomplete
2/10-Io43 - Turner rg to Io48 (5 yards)
3/5 -Io48 - Turner le to Io47, loss of 1
4/6 -Io47 - Holsclaw punts to Wilbur, fair catch at In26, 27 punt

2:34 INDIANA
1/10-In26 - Harkrader re to In23, loss of 3
2/13-In23 - Harkrader to In36 (13 yards)
1/10-In36 - Johnson lg to In42 (6 yards)
2/4 -In42 - Harkrader rg to In45 (3 yards)
3/1 -In45 - Burnett lt to In45, no gain
4/1 -In45 - Lovett punts to Becker at Io12, returned to Io37, 25 return 42 punt

0:36 IOWA
1/10-Io37 - Green pass incomplete
2/10-Io37 - Green pass complete to Dunham Io46 (9 yards)
3/1 -Io46 - Iowa penalized for holding
3/25-Io22 - Mortoan pass complete to Green to Io39, 17 yards, but fumble recovered by Abrams

0:08 INDIANA
1/10-Io39 - Clifford pass complete to Friede to Io19, 20 yards
1/10-Io19 - Freud 37 field goal attempt good

**END OF HALF:
INDIANA 24, IOWA 0**

THIRD QUARTER

Straub kicks off to Reid in end zone, returns to In46, 54 return

14:48 IOWA
1/10-In46 - Turner rg to In41 (5 yards)
2/5 -In41 - Turner le to In39 (2 yards)
3/3 -In39 - Morton lt to In38 (1 yard)
4/2 -In38 - Turner rg to In36 (2 yards)
1/10-In36 - Green pass incomplete
2/10-In36 - Turner rg to In25 (11 yards)
1/10-In25 - Lazar rg to In18 (7 yards)
2/3 -In18 - Turner rg to In16 (2 yards)
3/1 -In16 - Turner re to In16, no gain
4/1 -In16 - Green re to In10 (6 yards)
1/10-In10 - Turner lg to In4 (6 yards)
2/4 -In4 - Turner lg to In2 (2 yards)
3/2 -In2 - Turner re to In4, loss of 2
4/4 -In4 - Green pass complete to Morton for touchdown (4 yards) PAT—Schilling kick good.
SCORE: INDIANA 24, IOWA 7

Schilling kicks off to Johnson at goal line, returned to Io42, 58 return

8:49 INDIANA
1/10-Io42 - Burnett rg to Io40 (2 yards)
2/8 -Io40 - Arnett pass complete to Friede to Io25 (15 yards)
1/10-Io25 - Harkrader re to Io18 (7 yards)
2/3 -Io18 - Harkrader rt to Io13 (5 yards)
1/10-Io13 - Burnett rg to Io8 (5 yards)
2/5 -Io8 - Johnson lt to Io6 (2 yards)
3/3 -Io6 - Harkrader le for touchdown, (6 yards) PAT—Freud kick good.
SCORE: INDIANA 31, IOWA 7

(Iowa penalized for offsides on PAT)
Straub kicks off to Kevin Ellis at Io2, returned to Io25, 23 return

5:37 IOWA
1/10-Io25 - Indiana penalized for roughing passer
1/10-Io40 - Turner rt to Io47 (7 yards)
2/3 -Io47 - Lazar lg to Io49 (2 yards)
3/1 -Io49 - Green lg to In49 (2 yards)
1/10-In49 - Green pass incomplete
2/10-In49 - Turner re to Io49, loss of 2
3/12-Io49 - Green pass incomplete
4/12-Io49 - Holsclaw punts to Wilbur, fair catch at In14, 37 punt

3:09 INDIANA
1/10-In14 - Arnett pass complete to Friede at Io47 (39 yards)
1/10-Io47 - Johnson rg to Io44 (3 yards)
2/7 -Io44 - Arnett le to Io38 (6 yards)
3/1 -Io38 - Arnett rg to Io36 (2 yards)
1/10-Io36 - Burnett rt to Io33 (3 yards)
2/7 -Io33 - Burnett rg to Io21 (12 yards)
1/10-Io21 - Burnett rg to Io15 (6 yards)
2/4 -Io15 - Arnett re to Io14 (1 yard)
3/3 -Io14 - Burnett rg to Io13 (1 yard)

**END OF THIRD QUARTER:
INDIANA 31, IOWA 7**

373

FOURTH QUARTER

INDIANA
4/2 -Io13 - Freud 30 field goal attempt good. SCORE: INDIANA 34, IOWA 7

Straub kicks off to Kevin Ellis at Io8, returned to Io28, 20 return
14:49 IOWA
1/10-Io28 - Green pass complete to Lazar to Io33 (5 yards)
2/5 -Io33 - Iowa illegal motion
2/10-Io28 - Green pass complete to McKillip to 50 (22 yards)
1/10- 50 - Turner rg to In49 (1 yard)
2/9 -In49 - Green pass incomplete
3/9 -In49 - Green pass complete to Morton to In37 (12 yards)
1/10-In37 - Green pass incomplete
2/10-In37 - Lazar rg to In38, loss of 1
3/11-In38 - Commings trapped to In45, loss of 7
4/18-In45 - Lazar rg to In48, loss of 3

11:17 INDIANA
1/10-In48 - Harkrader le to In48, no gain
2/10-In48 - Burnett recovers own fumble at In39, loss of 9
3/19-In39 - Burnett lt to In38, loss of 1
4/20-In38 - Lovett punts out of bounds at Io37, 25 punt

9:58 IOWA
1/10-Io37 - Green pass complete to Reid at Io49 (12 yards)
1/10-Io49 - Green pass incomplete
2/10-Io49 - Turner re to Io47, loss of 2
3/12-Io47 - Green pass incomplete
4/12-Io47 - Indiana personal foul
1/10-In38 - Green pass complete to Reid at In19 (19 yards)
1/10-In19 - Green trapped to In32, loss of 13
2/23-IN32 - Green pass complete to Swift at In25 (7 yards)
3/16-In25 - Green pass intercepted by Abrams at In12, returned to In25, 13 return

7:24 INDIANA
1/10-In25 - Harkrader rt to In26 (1 yard)
2/9 -In26 - Clifford pass incomplete
3/9 -In26 - Clifford pass complete to Stephenson to In42 (16 yards)
1/10-In42 - Harkrader lt to In42, no gain
2/10-In42 - Darring lt to In45 (3 yards)
3/7 -In45 - Bowers rg to In47 (2 yards)
4/5 -In47 - Lovett punts to Reid at Io16, returned to Io40, 24 return 37 punt

4:24 IOWA
1/10-Io40 - Commings pass incomlete to Swift at In39 (21 yards)
1/10-In39 - Commings pass complete to Reid at In23 (16 yards)

1/10-In23 - McKillip rt to In7 (16 yards)
1/G -In7 - Turner le to In2 (5 yards)
2/G -In2 - Turner rg to In1 (1 yard)
3/G -In1 - Commings rg for touchdown (1 yard) PAT—Schilling kick good. SCORE: INDIANA 34, IOWA 14

Schilling kicks off short, recovered by Friede, no return at In44
2:20 INDIANA
1/10-In44 - Darring lt to In49 (5 yards)
2/5 -In49 - Darring lt to Io45 (6 yards)
1/10-Io45 - Darring lt to Io46, loss of 1
2/11-Io46 - Darring lg to Io42 (4 yards)
3/7 -Io42 - Darring le to Io43, loss of 1

**FINAL SCORE:
INDIANA 34, IOWA 14**

National Collegiate Athletic Association
FINAL TEAM STATISTICS

	IOWA	INDIANA
First Downs	17	24
Rushing	8	17
Passing	7	7
Penalty	2	0
Rushing Attempts	45	60
Yards Rushing	134	286
Yards Lost Rushing	63	19
Net Yards Rushing	71	267
Net Yards Passing	144	126
Passes Attempt	25	12
Passes Completed	11	8
Had Intercepted	2	0
Total Offensive Plays	70	72
Total Net Yards	215	393
Average Gain Per Play	3.0	5.4
Fumbles: Number—Lost	2/1	1/0
Penalties: Number—Yards	6/74	5/65
Interceptions: Number—Yards	0/0	2/14
Number Of Punts—Yards	6/217	6/232
Average Per Punt	36	39
Punt Returns: Number—Yards	2/49	4/16
Kickoff Returns: Number—Yards	6/182	1/58

NOVEMBER 11, 1978

MINNESOTA VS. MICHIGAN STATE
at Spartan Stadium
East Lansing
FIRST QUARTER

Michigan State won the toss, elects to receive, Minnesota defending the north goal Rogind kicks to Reeves, tackle by Fahnhorst, 30 yd return from out of end zone

MICHIGAN STATE
1/10-S30 - Smith pass to Gibson on left side, (Foxworth) gain of 19
1/10-S49 - McGee outside right end on pitchout, MS holding, 13 yd penalty
1/23-S36 - Smith pass to Byrd on left sideline thrown out of bounds
2/23-S36 - Middleton through the middle (Burns) gain of 2
3/21-S38 - Smith screen pass to S. Smith (Myer) loss of 1
4/22-S37 - Stachowicz punts to Edwards at UM26 pushed out by Stachowicz 39 yd punt
45 yd return

12:47 MINNESOTA
1/10-S31 - Barber off RT (Decker) gain of 2
2/8 -S29 - Barber through the middle (Anderson) gain of 9
1/10-S20 - White through the middle (Land & Fields) gain of 4
2/6 -S16 - Barber off RT (Hay) gain of 2
3/4 -S14 - Barber through the middle gain of 4
1/10-S10 - Barber outside LE, (Anderson) gain of 2
2/8 -S 8 - Avery pass broken up by Savage
3/8 -S 8 - Avery pass to Barber in right flat incomplete
4/8 -S 8 - Rogind 25 yard field goal attempt wide left

9:38 MICHIGAN STATE
1/10-S20 - Smith pass to Brammer on left side (Snyder) gain of 4
2/6 -S24 - Smith pass to Byrd on left side line steps out of bounds, gain of 14
1/10-S38 - Smith pass to Gibson on right side, (Foxworth) gain of 16
1/10-M46 - Smith pass to Middleton in left flat (Foxworth) gain of 6
2/4 -M40 - McGee through the middle (Ronan) gain of 3
3/1 -M37 - Smith pass to Gibson on right side (Foxworth) gain of 17
1/10-M20 - Smith pass to Byrd on right side (Snyder) gain of 13
1/G -M 7 - Smith pass to Gibson overthrown
2/G M 7 - Smith back to pass keeps around RE (Systma) gain of 6

3/G -M 1 - Middleton over the middle, touchdown 80 yards in 10 plays Andersen PAT attempt good
SCORE MICHIGAN STATE 7, MINNESOTA 0

Schario kicksoff to Bailey at UM9, returns to 19
6:38 MINNESOTA
1/10-M19 - Barber around LE (Hay & Decker) gain of 7
2/3 -M26 - Barber through the middle, Minnesota holding 11 yd penalty
2/14-M15 - Avery pass to Baily incomplete
3/14-M15 - Barber through the middle on draw (Fields) loss of 2
4/16-M13 - Smith punts to S. Smith at S40 47 yd punt, 13 yd return

5:35 MICHIGAN STATE
1/10-M47 - Smith pass to Brammer on left side (Edwards) gain of 1
2/9 -M46 - Reeves outside RE on sweep (Murphy) gain of 9
1/10-M37 - S. Smith off RT (Blanshan) gain of 4
2/6 -M33 - Smith pass to Gibson on left sideline steps out of bounds gain of 13
1/10-M20 - Smith pass to Gibson on right side incomplete
2/10-M20 - Smith pass to Schramm overthrown
3/10-M20 - Smith pass to Schramm incomplete tipped by (Carr)
4/10-M20 - Andersen 37 yd field goal attempt good
SCORE MICHIGAN STATE 10, MINNESOTA 0

Schario kicks to Bailey at M19, returns to M30
3:20 MINNESOTA
1/10-M30 - White off LE (McCormick) gain of 5
2/5 -M35 - White off LG (Bass & Decker) gain of 3
3/2 -M38 - Barber through the middle (Decker) gain of 3
1/10-M41 - Avery pass to Barber on left side (McCormick & Burroughs) gain of 4
2/6 -M45 - White off RT (Decker & Fields) gain of 1
3/5 -M46 - Avery pass to Barber (Decker) gain of 18

**END OF FIRST QUARTER
MICHIGAN STATE 10, MINNESOTA 0**

SECOND QUARTER
MINNESOTA
1/10-S36 - Barber through the middle (Bass & Decker) gain of 5
2/5 -S31 - Barber into the middle (Bass) gain of 1
3/4 -S30 - Avery back to pass sacked by Decker loss of 5
4/9 -S35 - Rogind 52 yard field goal attempt short

375

12:55 MICHIGAN STATE
1/10-S35 - S. Smith outside RE on pitchout (Brown) gain of 3
2/7 -S38 - Smith pass to Brammer long down the middle, overthrown
3/7 -M38 - Smith flat pass to Brammer (Brown) gain of 1
4/6 -S39 - Stachowicz punts to the M28 34 yd punt, downed

11:25 MINNESOTA
1/10-M28 - White off RT (Hay) gain of 3
2/7 -M31 - Avery pass to Bailey (Fields & Anderson) gain of 19
1/10- 50 - Barber off RT (Fields & Hay) gain of 3
2/7 -S47 - Avery pass to Bailey on right side line underthrown
3/7 -S47 - Barber of RT (Anderson) gain of 4
4/3 -M43 - Smith punts to S. Smith, fair catch 29 yd punt

8:59 MICHIGAN STATE
1/10-S14 - Middleton off RG (Brown) gain of 9
2/1 -S23 - Smith pass to Brammer (Brown) gain of 5
1/10-S28 - Smith pass to Gibson on left sideline (Foxworth) gain of 12
1/10-S40 - Smith pass to Byrd on left side line overthrown
2/10-S40 - Smith pass to Gibson on right side line (Foxworth) gain of 22
1/10-M38 - Middleton through the middle (Meyer) gain of 2
2/8 -M36 - Smith pass to Schramm incomplete
3/8 -M36 - Smith pass long over the middle to Byrd incomplete, Minnesota personal foul 15 yds.
1/10-M21 - McGee outside LT (Burns & Murphy) gain of 3
2/7 -M18 - Smith pass to Byrd on the left side line, touchdown, 86 yds on 10 plays Minnesota illegal motion, half the distance to goal, Anderson PAT attempt good
SCORE MICHIGAN STATE 17, MINNESOTA 0

Schario kicks out of end zone, touchback, Minnesota personal foul, 10 yd penalty, 1/2 the distance to goal line

5:16 MINNESOTA
1/20-M10 - Artis outside LE (Land) gain of 6
2/14-M16 - White off RT (Land) loss of 5 MSU personal foul, 15 yds
3/5 -M25 - Artis through the middle (McCormick) gain of 6
1/10-M31 - Avery pass to Dilulo incomplete
2/10-M31 - Avery pass to White (Savage & Fields) gain of 5
3/5 -M36 - Avery back to pass sacked by Decker, loss of 7
4/12-M29 - Smith punts to S. Smith at S29 34 yd punt, 8 yd return

2:32 MICHIGAN STATE
1/10-S37 - S. Smith outside RE (Systma) gain of 33
1/10-M30 - Smith pass to Gibson on left side (Foxworth & Brown) gain of 12
1/10-M18 - S. Smith off left guard on draw (Meyer) gain of 11
1/G -M 7 - Smith pass to Byrd in left end zone corner, overthrown
2/G -M 7 - Smith pass to Gibson in right end zone corner overthrown
3/G -M 7 - Reeves off left guard on draw (Snydner & Murphy) gain of 6
4/G -M 1 - Smith (S.) outside right end, fumbles, picked up by Carr, returns 71 yds (Gibson)

:51 MINNESOTA
1/10-M29 - Avery pass to Bailey (Bass) gain of 16
1/10-M13 - Avery pass to Bourkinquin (Graves) gain of 9
2/1 -M 4 - Barber outside left end on pitchout (Bass & Graves) loss of 3
3/4 -M 7 - Avery pass to Bourquin incomplete
4/4 -M 7 - Rogind 25 yard field goal attempt good
SCORE: MICHIGAN STATE 17, MINNESOTA 3

Rogind kicks to McGee (Fahnhorst) return of 6
:17 MICHIGAN STATE
1/10-S17 - Smith pass to Byrd on right side line overthrown
2/10-S17 - Smith pass to Byrd over the middle (Burns) gain of 20
1/10-S37 - Smith screen pass to McGee (Edwards) gain of 18
END OF HALF
MICHIGAN STATE 17, MINNESOTA 3

THIRD QUARTER

Minnesota elects to receive. Michigan State defending the north goal
Schario kicks to Bailey at M2 (Schario) 24 yd return
MINNESOTA
1/10-M26 - Avery fumbles, recovered, loss of 1
2/11-M25 - Avery pass to Barber on right side (Bass) gain of 4
3/7 -M29 - Avery pass to White on left side (Graves) fumble recovered by Savage loss of 1

13:41 MICHIGAN STATE
1/10-M28 - S. Smith off RT (Friberg) no gain
2/10-M28 - Smith pass to Brammer over the middle (Brown & Edwards) gain of 13
1/10-M15 - Schramm off LT (Meyer) gain of 7
2/3 -M 8 - Schramm outside RT (Ronan & Burns) gain of 4
1/G -M 4 - S. Smith over the middle (Meyer) gain of 1

NOVEMBER 11, 1978

2/G -M 4 - Smith pass to Byrd in left end zone corner, touchdown, 28 yards in 6 plays Andersen PAT attempt good Minnesota offside, 5 yd penalty assessed at kickoff
SCORE MICHIGAN STATE 24, MINNESOTA 3

Schario kicks from S45 to Bailey in end zone, downed for touchback
10:41 MINNESOTA
1/10-M20 - Barber outside right end on pitchout (Hay) gain of 3
2/7 -M23 - Avery pass broken up by Land
3/7 -M23 - Avery pass (screen) to Barber (McCormick) gain of 3
4/4 -M26 - Smith punts to S. Smith, fumbles, recovered by Systma, 34 yd punt

9:44 MINNESOTA
1/10-S43 - Barber off RT gain of 5
2/5 -S38 - Barber through the middle (Land & Burroughs) gain of 7
1/10-S31 - Barber outside RE on pitchout (Decker) no gain
2/10-S31 - Artis around LE on pitchout (Bass & Graves) Minnesota clipping 15 yd penalty
2/25-S46 - Avery pass to Bailey long on right side overthrown
3/25-S46 - Avery pass to Artis on left side (McCormick) gain of 2
4/23-S44 - Smith punts into end zone, touchback, 44 yd punt, no return

7:14 MICHIGAN STATE
1/10-S20 - Hans off RG (Meyer) gain of 3
2/7 -S23 - Michigan delay of game 5 yd penalty
2/12-S18 - Smith pass to Reeves in left flat incomplete (Snyder)
3/12-S18 - McGee off LT on draw (Burns & Murphy) gain of 8
4/4 -S26 - Stachowicz punts to Bailey at M22 (Hans) 52 yd punt, 5 yd return

5:43 MINNESOTA
1/10-M27 - Bailey around RE on end around runs out of bounds, gain of 27
1/10-S46 - Barber through the middle, team tackle, gain of 2
2/8 -S44 - Barber off LT on counter (Land) loss of 1
3/9 -S45 - Avery back to pass (Decker & Savage) loss of 11
4/20-M44 - Smith punts to Reeves at S22, 33 yd punt (T. Smith) 29 yd return

3:19 MICHIGAN STATE
1/10-M49 - Hans off LT (Murphy) gain of 3
2/7 -M46 - Smith screen pass to Hans incomplete
3/7 -M46 - Smith pass across middle to Byrd falls down, gain of 13
1/10-M33 - Reeves off RT (Meyer & Systma) gain of 2

2/8 -M31 - Smith pass to McGee (Edwards & Murphy) gain of 12
1/10-M19 - Smith pass to Gibson overthrown
2/10-M19 - McGee outside LE on pitchout (Burns) gain of 7
3/3 -M12 - Hans over the middle, fumbles, recovered by Snyder, gain of 11

:08 MINNESOTA
1/10-M 1 - Avery pass to Bailey on right side line overthrown
2/10-M 1 - Barber outside RE on pitchout (Bass) gain of 5

**END OF THIRD QUARTER
MICHIGAN STATE 24, MINNESOTA 3**

FOURTH QUARTER

MINNESOTA
3/5 -M 6 - Barber outside RE on pitchout (Burroughs) gain of 2
4/3 -M 8 - Smith punt blocked by Land, hit out of end zone by Savage for safety
SCORE MICHIGAN STATE 26, MINNESOTA 3

Smith punts (free kick) from M20 to Reeves at S22, (Brown) 16 yd return Minnesota offside, 5 yd penalty
Smith punts (free kick) from M15 to S. Smith at S34, (Artis) 22 yd return
14:06 MICHIGAN STATE
1/10-M44 - Reeves outside RE (Burns & Brown) gain of 5
2/5 -M39 - Hans off LT (Foxworth & Brown) gain of 17
1/10-M22 - Smith pass to Gibson on right side (Foxworth) gain of 11
1/10-M11 - Hughes outside LE on pitchout (Burns & Brown) gain of 6
2/4 -M 5 - Reeves off RT touchdown, 44 yds in 5 plays
Andersen PAT attempt good
SCORE MICHIGAN STATE 33, MINNESOTA 3

Schario kicks to Bailey on M2, runs left sideline, knocked out by Andersen, 29 yd return
11:57 MINNESOTA
1/10-M31 - White through the middle (Land) gain of 4
2/6 -M35 - White inside LG (Decker) gain of 5
3/1 -M40 - Artis off LT (Bass) gain of 2
1/10-M42 - Avery back to pass, sacked by Savage, loss of 11
2/15-M37 - Barber through the middle on draw (Savage, Burroughs & Anderson) 7 gain
3/8 -M44 - Avery pass to Bailey on left sideline incomplete
4/8 -M44 - Smith punts Reeves at S13, Fahnhorst, 4 yd return, 43 yd punt

377

8:37 MICHIGAN STATE
1/10-S17 - Michigan delay of game, 5 yd penalty
1/15-S12 - Hans outside LT (Cunningham & Burns) gain of 3
2/12-S15 - Gibson around LE on reverse (Burns) gain of 1
3/11-S16 - Smith screen pass to Hans incomplete
4/11-S16 - Stachowicz punts to Bailey at M40 returns to S20 (Schramm) 44 yd punt, 40 yd return

6:49 MINNESOTA
1/10-S20 - Barber off LE (Bass) gain of 1
2/9 -S19 - Avery pass to Barber in flat, (Bass & Cooper) gain of 5
3/4 -S14 - Barber outside LE on pitchout (Anderson & Land) gain of 7
1/G -S 7 - Barber through the middle (Otis) no gain
2/G -S 7 - Avery pass to Dilulo in end zone incomplete
3/G -S 7 - Avery back to pass, sacked by Anderson on safety blitz, loss of 8
4/G -S15 - Avery pass to Bailey in end zone right corner, touchdown 20 yards in 7 plays

Carlson pass conversion attempt broken up by Cooper
SCORE: MICHIGAN STATE 33, MINNESOTA 9

Rogind kicks to S. Smith at S5 (Artis) 34 yd return

3:28 MICHIGAN STATE
1/10-S39 - Smith back to pass, sacked by Cunningham, loss of 11
2/21-S28 - Smith pass to Howard on left side line, steps out, gain of 7
3/14-S35 - Hughes through the middle on draw (Gardner) gain of 14
1/10-S49 - Hughes off RT on draw (Gardner & Ronan) no gain
2/10-S49 - Smith pass to Williamson right side line, steps out, gain of 14
1/10-M37 - Smith pass to J. Williams on left side line, gain of 13
1/10-M24 - Hans off LT (Edwards) gain of 10
1/10-M14 - Stachowicz outside RT (Gardner) loss of 1

FINAL SCORE:
MICHIGAN STATE 33, MINNESOTA 9

FINAL TEAM STATISTICS
November 11, 1978

	MINNE-SOTA	MICHIGAN STATE
First Downs	11	28
Rushing	8	8
Passing	3	19
Penalty	0	1
Rushing Attempts	43	35
Yards Rushing	147	199
Yards Lost Rushing	48	12
Net Yards Rushing	99	187
Net Yards Passing	99	296
Passes Attempted	23	42
Passes Completed	12	26
Had Intercepted	0	0
Total Offensive Plays	66	77
Total Net Yards	198	483
Average Gain Per Play	3.0	6.3
Fumbles: Number—Lost	2/1	3/3
Penalties: Number—Yards	4/51	5/43
Interceptions: Number—Yards	0/0	0/0
Number of Punts—Yards	8/264	4/169
Average Per Punt	33.0	42.3
Punt Returns: Number—Yards	3/86	4/58
Kickoff Returns: Number—Yards	4/74	5/98

NOVEMBER 11, 1978

MICHIGAN VS. NORTHWESTERN
Dyche Stadium
Evanston, Illinois
FIRST QUARTER

Northwestern co-captains Pat Geegan, Steve Bobowski, and Mike Kranz meet at midfield with Michigan co-captains Russell Davis and Jerry Mater for the toss of the coin. Michigan wins the toss and elects to defend the north goal; Northwestern will receive and defend the south goal.

Virgil kickoff rolls out of the endzone for a touchback
15:00 NORTHWESTERN
1/10-NU20 - Strasser pass to Bahoric complete for 16 yds (Jolly)
1/10-NU36 - Tiberi RT for 3 yds (Keitz)
2/7 -NU39 - Strasser pass to Bogan incomplete
3/7 -NU39 - Strasser pass to Tiberi incomplete
4/7 -NU39 - Christensen punt fair caught at UM29 32 yd punt

13:55 MICHIGAN
1/10-UM29 - Davis middle for 4 yds (Kern)
2/6 -UM33 - Huckleby pitch LE for 1 yd (Kendzicky)
3/5 -UM34 - Leach pass to Clayton complete for 14 yds (Butler)
1/10-UM48 - Huckleby RG for 8 yds (Lizak)
2/2 -NU44 - Huckleby LT for 9 yds (Butler)
1/10-NU35 - Davis middle for 15 yds (Butler)
1/10-NU20 - Huckleby LE for 12 yds (Geegan)
1/G -NU8 - Davis middle for 7 yds (Kern)
2/G -NU1 - Davis middle for no gain (Dorsey)
3/G -NU1 - Leach keeper LE for 1 yard and a touchdown
PAT: Willner kick good 71 yards in 10 plays
SCORE: MICHIGAN 7 NORTHWESTERN 0

Virgil kickoff downed in endzone for a touchback
9:36 NORTHWESTERN
1/10-NU20 - Strasser pass to Schmitt incomplete
2/10-NU20 - Cammon pitch LE for 8 yds (Cannavino)
3/2 -NU28 - Cammon RE for 4 yds (Simpkins)
1/10-NU32 - Cammon middle for 1 yd (Simpkins)
2/9 -NU33 - Strasser pass to Cammon incomplete
3/9 -NU33 - Strasser pass to Bahoric complete for 21 yds (Bell)
1/10-UM46 - Cammon middle for no gain (Simpkins)
2/10-UM46 - Strasser pass to Bogan incomplete

3/10-UM46 - Strasser pass to Bahoric incomplete
4/10-UM46 - Christensen punt rolls dead on the UM25 21 yd punt

7:15 MICHIGAN
1/10-UM25 - Huckleby LT for 6 yds (Kern)
2/4 -UM31 - Leach keeper RE for 7 yds (Corona)
1/10-UM38 - Huckleby RG for 4 yds (Gildner)
2/6 -UM42 - Leach pass to Clayton complete for 31 yds (Hamphill)
1/10-NU27 - Davis LG for 4 yds (Dunlea)
2/6 -NU23 - Huckleby pitch LE for 9 yds (Hemphill)
1/10-NU14 - Davis LT for 5 yds (Kern)
2/5 -NU9 - Huckleby pitch RE for no gain (McGlade)
3/5 -NU9 - Leach pass to Clayton complete for 9 yds and a touchdown (3:01)
PAT: Willner kick good 75 yds in 9 plays
SCORE: MICHIGAN 14 NORTHWESTERN 0

Virgil kickoff goes out of the endzone for a touchback
3:01 NORTHWESTERN
1/10-NU20 - Cammon RT for 1 yd (Lilja)
2/9 -NU21 - Cammon sweep RE for 20 yds (Harden)
1/10-NU41 - Strasser pass to Cammon complete for 3 yds (Jolly)
2/7 -NU44 - Strasser pass to Schmitt complete for 2 yds (Seabron)
3/5 -NU46 - Strasser pass to Poulos incomplete
4/5 -NU46 - Christensen pass in punt formation to Hemphill complete for 20 yds
1/10-UM34 - Strasser keeper RE for no gain (Trgovac)
2/10-UM34 - Tiberi pass to Bogan incomplete
PENALTY: pass interference UM (30 yds)
1/G -UM4 - Cammon RT for 2 yds (Simpkins)

**END OF FIRST QUARTER:
MICHIGAN 14 NORTHWESTERN 0**

379

SECOND QUARTER

NORTHWESTERN
1/G -UM2 - Strasser pass to Bogan complete for 2 yds and a touchdown (14:57)
PAT: Poulos kick good 80 yds in 9 plays
SCORE: MICHIGAN 14 NORTHWESTERN 7

Poulos kickoff rolls out of the endzone for a touchback
14:57 MICHIGAN
1/10-UM20 - Leach keeper RE for 11 yds (Berg) PENALTY: personal foul NU
1/10-UM46 - Huckleby RT for 9 yds (Kern)
2/1 -NU45 - Davis middle for 5 yds (Kern)
1/10-NU40 - Huckleby pitch RE for 4 yds (Kendzicky)
2/6 -NU36 - PENALTY: ill. procedure UM
2/11-NU41 - Leach pass to Clayton complete for 41 yds and a touchdown (13:22)
PAT: Willner kick good 80 yds in 5 plays
SCORE: MICHIGAN 21 NORTHWESTERN 7

PENALTY: personal foul NU (on touchdown play)
Virgil kickoff downed in endzone for a touchback
13:22 NORTHWESTERN
1/10-NU20 - Cammon LG for 2 yds (Trgovac)
2/8 -NU22 - Strasser pass to Tiberi complete for -3 yds (Simpkins)
3/11-NU19 - Cammon LT for 1 yd (Simpkins)
4/10-NU20 - Christensen punt taken by Jolly at UM38 and returned 5 yds 42 yd punt

11:32 MICHIGAN
1/10-UM43 - Huckleby pitch RE for 14 yds (Butler)
1/10-NU43 - David middle for 4 yds (Bambauer)
2/6 -NU39 - Huckleby middle for 5 yds (Kern)
3/1 -NU34 - Davis middle for 6 yds (Kern)
1/10-NU28 - Huckleby RT for 8 yds (Lizak)
2/2 -NU20 - Davis LT for 5 yds (Payne)
1/10-NU15 - Huckleby pitch RE for 3 yds (Butler)
2/7 -NU12 - Leach keeper LE for 12 yds and a touchdown (8:37)
PAT: Willner kick good 57 yds in 8 plays
SCORE: MICHIGAN 28 NORTHWESTERN 7

Virgil kickoff taken by North at NU22 and returned 8 yds
8:33 NORTHWESTERN
1/10-NU30 - Strasser pass to Bogan complete for 9 yds (Jolly)
2/ 1-NU39 - Tiberi pitch LE for 2 yds (Meter)
1/10-NU41 - Strasser pass to Bogan complete PENALTY: ill. motion NU
1/15-NU36 - Strasser pass to Bahoric incomplete
2/15-NU36 - Strasser pass to Poulos complete for 7 yds (Cannavino)
3/8 -NU43 - Strasser pass to Poulos complete for 24 yds (Warden)

1/10-UM33 - Strasser pass to Poulos incomplete
2/10-UM33 - Strasser pass to Bahoric for 13 yds (Simpkins)
1/10-UM20 - Strasser keeper RE for 8 yds
PENALTY: personal foul UM (6 yds)
1/G -UM6 - Cammon sweep RE for 2 yds
2/G -UM4 - Strasser pass to Kasprywcki incomplete
3/G -UM4 - Strasser pass to Poulos complete for 3 yds (Bell)
4/G -UM1 - Cammon RT for 1 yd and a touchdown (5:21)
PAT: Poulos kick good 70 yds in 12 plays
SCORE: MICHIGAN 28 NORTHWESTERN 14

Poulos kickoff taken by Smith at the UM1 and returned 20 yds
5:16 MICHIGAN
1/10-UM21 - Huckleby RE for 9 yds (Geegan)
2/1 -UM30 - Leach pass to Clayton complete for 27 yds (Hoffman)
1/10-NU43 - Huckleby middle for 4 yds (Kern)
2/6 -NU39 - Huckleby pitch RE for 10 yds (Butler)
1/10-NU29 - Huckleby RT for 2 yds (Berg)
2/8 -NU27 - Leach pass to Marsh complete for 9 yds
1/10-NU18 - Huckleby RT for 4 yds (Bambauer)
2/6 -NU14 - Huckleby pitch LE for 4 yds (Kern)
3/2 -NU10 - Leach keeper RE for 8 yds (Kern)
1/G -NU2 - Huckleby RG for 2 yds and a touchdown (1:32)
PAT: Willner kick good 79 yds in 10 plays
SCORE: MICHIGAN 35 NORTHWESTERN 14

Virgil kickoff taken by Geegan at NU19 and returned 17 yds
1:26 NORTHWESTERN
1/10-NU36 - Strasser pass to Cammon incomplete (Trgovac)
2/10-NU36 - Cammon draw middle for 5 yds (Trgovac)
3/5 -NU41 - Strasser pass to Poulos incomplete (Needham)
4/5 -NU41 - Christensen punt taken by Jolly at UM18 and returned 3 yds 42 yd kick

380

NOVEMBER 11, 1978

0:40 MICHIGAN
1/10-UM20 - Huckleby RT for 3 yds (Rogers)
2/7 -UM23 - Jackson fumbles pitch, recovers for -6 yds

END OF HALF:
MICHIGAN 35 NORTHWESTERN 14

THIRD QUARTER

Virgil kickoff downed in endzone for a touchback
15:00 NORTHWESTERN
1/10-NU20 - Strasser pass to Cammon incomplete
2/10-NU20 - Strasser pass to Poulos incomplete
3/10-NU20 - Strasser pass to Cammon complete for 4 yds (Seabron)
4/6 -NU24 - Christensen punt fair caught at NU46 22 yd punt

14:15 MICHIGAN
1/10-NU46 - Huckleby fumbles handoff, recovers for 2 yd gain
2/8 -NU44 - Davis middle for 11 yds (Kendzicky)
1/10-NU33 - Huckleby pitch RE for 9 yds (Bambauer)
2/1 -NU24 - Davis middle for 12 yds (Butler)
1/10-NU12 - Clayton LT for 7 yds (Lizak)
2/3 -NU5 - Leach keeper RE, fumbles, recovered by NU Rogers (loss of 1 yd)

11:34 NORTHWESTERN
1/10-NU6 - Strasser pass to Cammon intercepted by Cannavino at the NU16 and returned 5 yds

11:28 MICHIGAN
1/10-NU11 - Davis middle for 6 yds (Bambauer)
2/4 -NU5 - Leach keeper RE for 5 yds and a touchdown (10:46)
PAT: Willner kick good 11 yards in 2 plays
SCORE: MICHIGAN 42 NORTHWESTERN 14

Virgil kickoff downed in endzone for a touchback
10:46 NORTHWESTERN
1/10-NU20 - Cammon middle for 1 yd (Simpkins)
2/9 -NU21 - Strasser pass to Bogan complete for 10 yds (Cannavino)
1/10-NU31 - Cammon pitch RE for -4 yds (Meter)
2/14-NU27 - Strasser sacked by Trgovac for -7 yds
3/21-NU20 - Schmitt quick kick taken by Harden at UM49 and returned 2 yds

8:28 MICHIGAN
1/10-NU49 - Reid LT for 5 yds (Kern)
2/5 -NU44 - Dickey keeper LE for 2 yds (Gildner)
3/3 -NU42 - Smith LT for 8 yds (Berg)
1/10-NU34 - Smith pitch RE for 12 yds (Hemphill)
1/10-NU22 - Reid LG for 3 yds (Taylor)
2/7 -NU19 - Smith middle for -1 yd (Kendzicky)
3/8 -NU20 - Smith pitch LE for 8 yds (Knafelc)
1/10-NU12 - Smith LG for 6 yds (Kern)
2/4 -NU6 - Jackson LG for 1 yd (Kern)
3/3 -NU5 - Smith pitch RE, fumbles, rolls out of bounds for -2 yds
4/5 -NU7 - Willner, 24 yard field goal (3:55) 42 yds in 11 plays
SCORE: MICHIGAN 45 NORTHWESTERN 14

Virgil kickoff taken by Carver at NU7 and returned 18 yds
3:49 NORTHWESTERN
1/10-NU25 - Strasser pass to Tiberi complete for 2 yds (Simpkins)
2/8 -NU27 - Webb middle for 1 yd (Cannavino)
3/7 -NU28 - Strasser keeper RE for 4 yds (Keitz)
4/3 -NU32 - Christensen punt fair caught at UM38 30 yd punt

2:05 MICHIGAN
1/10-UM38 - Smith RT for 5 yds (Rogers)
2/5 -UM43 - Dickey keeper RG for no gain (Gildner)
3/5 -UM43 - Smith pitch LE for 8 yds (Berg)
1/10-NU49 - Smith middle for 6 yds (Kendzicky)
2/4 -NU43 - Dickey pass to Johnson incomplete
3/4 -NU43 - Smith middle for 3 yds (Taylor)

END OF THIRD QUARTER:
MICHIGAN 45 NORTHWESTERN 14

381

FOURTH QUARTER

15:00 MICHIGAN
4/ 1-NU40 - Dickey keeper RE for 40 yds and a touchdown (14:51)
  PAT: Willner kick good 62 yds in 7 plays
  SCORE: MICHIGAN 52 NORTHWESTERN 14

Virgil kickoff taken by Geegan at NU15 and returned 19 yds

14:44 NORTHWESTERN
1/10-NU34 - Strasser pass to Bogan incomplete
2/10-NU34 - Strasser pass to Bahoric blocked by Greer
3/10-NU34 - Bogan sweep LE, fumbles, recovers for -9 yds
4/19-NU25 - Christensen punt taken by Harden at UM35 and returned 19 yds

13:56 MICHIGAN
1/10-NU46 - Smith RT for 6 yds (Kern)
2/4 -NU40 - Woolfolk pitch Le for 3 yds (Geegan)
3/1 -NU37 - Reid middle for 1 yd (Rogers)
1/10-NU36 - Woolfolk middle 9 yds (Butler)
2/1 -NU27 - Smith LG for 11 yds (Geegan)
1/10-NU16 - Woolfolk pitch RE for 15 yds (McGlade)
1/G NU1 - Woolfolk RT for 1 yd and a touchdown (10:51)
  PAT: Willner kick good 46 yds in 7 plays
  SCORE: MICHIGAN 59 NORTHWESTERN 14

Virgil kickoff taken by Geegan at NU19 and returned 12 yds

10:48 NORTHWESTERN
1/10-NU31 - Strasser pass to Schmitt complete for -2 yds (Jones)
2/12-NU29 - Strasser pass to Bogan complete for 9 yds (Jolly)
3/3 -NU38 - Strasser pass to Tiberi incomplete
4/3 -NU38 - Christensen punt fair caught at UM20 42 yd punt

9:21 MICHIGAN
1/10-UM20 - Reid RT for 6 yds (Payne)
2/4 -UM26 - Woolfolk RE for no gain (Bobowski)
3/4 -UM26 - Smith pitch LE for 8 yds (Lawrence)
1/10-UM34 - Woolfolk middle for 11 yds (Lawrence)
1/10-UM45 - Woolfolk pitch RE for 9 yds (Dorsey)
2/1 -NU46 - Reid middle for 5 yds (Bambauer)
1/10-NU41 - Dickey keeper RE for 5 yds (Lawrence)
2/5 -NU36 - Woolfolk RT for 5 yds (McGlade)
1/10-NU31 - Smith pitch RE for -2 yds (Burns)
2/12-NU33 - Dickey pass to Feaster incomplete
3/12-NU33 - Dickey pass to Feaster complete for 13 yds (McGlade)
1/10-NU20 - Woolfolk pitch RE
  PENALTY: ill. motion UM
1/15-NU25 - Woolfolk RT for 4 yds
2/11-NU21 - Dickey pass to Jackson complete for 12 yds
1/G -NU9 - Woolfolk RT for 5 yds (Rogers)
2/G -NU4 - Reid middle for 3 yds (Taylor)
3/G -NU1 - Leoni pitch RE for -4 yds
4/G -NU5 - Dickey pass to Johnson incomplete

1:40 NORTHWESTERN
1/10-NU5 - Schmitt RT for 1 yd (Humphries)
2/9 -NU5 - Cammon RE for 12 yds (Harris)
1/10-NU18 - Schmitt RE for 2 yds (Cannavino)
2/8 -NU20 - Christensen fumbles, recovered for -4 yds

**END OF GAME:
MICHIGAN 59 NORTHWESTERN 14**

National Collegiate Athletics Association
FINAL TEAM STATISTICS

	Michigan	Northwestern
First Downs	37	12
Rushing	28	4
Passing	8	6
Penalty	1	2
Rushing Attempts	82	26
Yards Rushing	486	81
Yards Lost Rushing	-16	-24
Net Yards Rushing	470	57
Net Yards Passing	156	140
Passes Attempted	11	35
Passes Completed	8	17
Had Intercepted	0	1
Total Offensive Plays	93	61
Total Net Yards	626	197
Average Gain Per Play	6.7	3.2
Fumbles: Number-Lost	4-1	2-0
Penalties: Number-Yards	4-46	3-35
Interceptions: Number-Yards	1-5	0-0
Number of Punts-Yards	0-0	9-301
Average Per Punt	0	33.4
Punt Returns: Number-Yards	4-29	0-0
Kickoff Returns: Number-Yards	1-20	5-74

NOVEMBER 11, 1978

ILLINOIS
VS.
OHIO STATE
Temp.: 65°
Wind: S 5-15 mph
Skies: Sunny
FIRST QUARTER

Ohio State won the toss and elected to receive; Illinois to defend the South goal
Finzer kicked off at 1:33 P.M. Murray returned 21 middle, cut right
14:54 OHIO STATE
1/10-O25 - Springs pitch at le for 5
(J. Gillen hurt - walked off)
2/5 -O30 - Campbell optioned at rt for 2
3/3 -O32 - Schlicter kept into rt for 1
4/2 -O33 - Orosz punted 67 yards for the touchback

13:34 ILLINOIS
1/10-I20 - Illinois illegal procedure -5
1/15-I15 - Weiss faded, fumbled, ran re for 5
2/10-I20 - Thomas lg 2
3/8 -I22 - Weiss faked, faded, sacked by Henson, Dansler, Cato for -12
4/20-I10 - Finzer punted 40; Guess return was zero

11:59 OHIO STATE
1/10- 50 - Springs option pitch le for 10
1/10-I40 - Campbell into lt for 5
2/5 -I35 - Campbell center for 4
3/1 -I31 - Schlicter, kept inside re for 2
1/10-I29 - Schlichter kept left for -2 (Adams)
2/12-I31 - Schlichter passed to Springs short right on delay for 8
3/4 -I23 - Campbell cut into middle for 1
4/3 -I22 - Schlicter passed to Springs on swing right for 7
1/10-I15 - Springs slanted thru middle for 8
2/2 -I7 - Schlicter kept inside re, dove in for touchdown at 8:24
Janakievski PAT - Fifty yards in ten plays
SCORE: OHIO STATE 7 ILLINOIS 0

Orosz kicked off 42 yards; Foster fair catch
8:23 ILLINOIS
1/10-I18 - Thomas rg 2
2/8 -I20 - Powell was clear at lt for 7 on delayed hand off
3/1 -I27 - Weiss kept inside le on counter option for 2
1/10-I29 - Weiss faked, faded ran middle for 6
2/4 -I35 - Powell cut into middle for 4
1/10-I39 - Weiss, faded chased right, ran for 1
2/9 -I40 - Powell was clear over right side on hand off for 12
1/10-O48 - Weiss faked, faded passed on deep hook over middle to Rouse for 17
1/10-O31 - Powell into middle for 4
2/6 -O27 - Powell draw, cut over left side for 4

3/2 -O23 - Weiss kept over lt on counter option fumble recovered by Cousineau for 6

2:56 OHIO STATE
1/10-O17 - Volley into lt for 4 (Gerald at quarterback)
2/6 -O21 - Volley thru rt, dodged for 7
1/10 -O28 - Murray pitch at le for 3
2/7 -O31 - Gerald, on option right; fumble recovered by Hardy for -6

1:29 ILLINOIS
1/10-O25 - Weiss faked, passed to Powell short over middle for 5
2/5 -O20 - Weiss faded, sacked by Bell for -9
3/14-O29 - Powell draw for -4 (Henson)

END OF FIRST QUARTER
OHIO STATE 7 ILLINOIS 0

SECOND QUARTER

15:00 ILLINOIS
4/18-O33 - Illinois delay of game -5
4/23-O38 - Finzer punted high and short; Illini bounce for 26; downed by Illinois

14:51 OHIO STATE
1/10-O12 - Schlichter kept inside re for 3
2/7 -O15 - Murray pitch at le for 3
3/4 -O18 - Murray option pitch at re for 5 (Ralph hurt, limped off)
1/10-O23 - Murray pitch at le for 2
2/8 -O25 - Schlichter faked, passed too wide for Donley cutting over middle incomplete
3/8 -O25 - Volley draw middle for 5
4/3 -O30 - Orosz punted 48; Hardy returned 14

12:26 ILLINOIS
1/10-I36 - Weiss, on option pitch right, fumble went out of bounds for 2
2/8 -I38 - Powell at rg for 2
3/6 -I40 - Weiss faked, faded, ran over right side for 8
1/10-I48 - Weiss kept inside le for 3
2/7 -O49 - Illinois illegal procedure -5
2/12-I46 - Powell was clear on draw thru middle, cut left for 10
3/2 -O44 - Weiss faked, faded, sacked by Dansler, Hornik for -9
4/11-I47 - Finzer punted 36; Guess for no return

9:05 OHIO STATE
1/10-O17 - Springs at rg for 4
2/6 -O21 - Springs pitch at re for 2
3/4 -O23 - Schlichter passed to Gerald on right sideline hook for 15
1/10-O38 - Schlichter passed to Gerald right intercepted by Carmien for no return

7:55 ILLINOIS
1/10-I48 - Weiss faked, passed too long to Barnes incomplete
2/10-I48 - Powell draw for -4 (Hornik, Sullivan)
3/14-I44 - Weiss counter option right, reversed thru middle for 2; Ohio face mask 15
1/10-039 - Thomas rg 1
2/9 -038 - Weiss passed too wide for Rouse in right flat incomplete
3/9 -038 - Weiss on delayed draw, cut right 11
1/10-027 - Thomas rg 2
2/8 -025 - Weiss kept on counter option inside re for 4
3/4 -021 - Thomas thru lt for 6 (Washington hurt - helped off)
1/10-015 - Powell draw thru lt for 2
2/8 -013 - Powell option pitch at re for 5
3/3 -08 - Powell on counter pitch at re for 6 (Megaro TD save)
1/G -02 - Weiss was stopped on sneak at re for no gain
2/G 02 - Powell dove thru lt for the TD Finzer PAT - Ohio offside to be marked off on kickoff - 52 yards in 14 plays
SCORE: OHIO STATE 7 ILLINOIS 7

Finzer kicked off 54 yards; Hicks returned middle for 28
2:06 OHIO STATE
1/10-029 - Campbell pushed thru center for 6
2/4 -035 - Schlichter, faded, chased, ducked out, passed short left to Campbell deflected incomplete
3/4 -035 - Schlichter passed into deep left flat to Moore for 9
1/10-044 - Schlichter passed to Donley slanting over middle for 23
1/10-I33 - Schlichter passed into deep left flat to Moore for 6
Time out Ohio 0:43
2/4 -I27 - Schlichter passed deep over middle to Gerald for 20
1/G -I7 - Schlichter kept inside le, went in untouched for the TD
Janakievski PAT - Illinois offside to be marked off on kickoff - 71 yards in 7 plays
SCORE: OHIO STATE 14 ILLINOIS 7

Atha kicked off 50 yards; Dismuke returned middle 25
0:17 ILLINOIS
1/10-I30 - Thomas slanted off lt for 5

**HALFTIME SCORE
OHIO STATE 14 ILLINOIS 7**

THIRD QUARTER

Illinois elected to receive; Ohio State to defend the South Goal
Orosz kicked off at 2:59 P.M. 57 yards; Foster returned 20
14:55 ILLINOIS
1/10-I23 - Thomas into rg for 6
2/4 -I29 - Weiss faked, passed quick on lob right; Murphy intercepted returned 3

14:09 OHIO STATE
1/10-I39 - Campbell rg for 7
2/3 -I32 - Volley slanted into middle for 2
3/1 -I30 - Payton into lt for no gain
4/1 -I30 - Campbell into lt, broke tackle for 8
1/10-I22 - Springs at rg for 2
2/8 -I20 - Campbell was clear at lg for 13
1/G -I7 - Payton hit into rg for 4
2/G -I3 - Payton over rt for 1; Ohio holding -15
2/G -I17 - Schlichter passed on delay over middle to Murray for 4
3/G -I13 - Schlichter passed into left end zone to Gerald, broken up by George incomplete
4/G -I13 - Atha's FG was from 31 yards at 11:15 - 26 yards in 11 plays
SCORE: OHIO STATE 17 ILLINOIS 7

Atha kicked off thirteen yards deep for the touchback
11:15 ILLINOIS
1/10-I20 - Thomas off lt for 2
2/8 -I22 - Weiss kept inside re for 3
3/5 -I25 - Powell was hit by Cousineau on draw for -4
4/9 -I21 - Finzer punted right 30; downed by Illinois

9:18 OHIO STATE
1/10-049 - Schlichter moved right faked pass, pitched to Murray for 20
1/10-I31 - Campbell middle 4
2/6 -I27 - Murray on deep handoff, broke clear over rt for 9
1/10-I18 - Schlichter kept inside re for 7
2/3 -I11 - Murray option pitch re for 3
1/G -I 8 - Campbell hit into rg for 4
2/G -I4 - Campbell lg for 3
3/G -I1 - Campbell rt standing for the TD
Janakievski PAT - 51 yards in 8 plays
SCORE: OHIO STATE 24 ILLINOIS 7

Atha kicked off 4 yards deep for the touchback
6:46 ILLINOIS
1/10-I20 - Weiss faked, passed on deep hook left to Barnes for 16
1/10-I36 - Thomas thru lg for 6
2/4 -I42 - Thomas at lg again for 2

NOVEMBER 11, 1978

3/2 -I44 - Weiss, on counter option left was stopped by Sullivan for -1
4/3 -I43 - Finzer punted out of bounds right for 26

4:17 OHIO STATE
1/10-O31 - Schlichter passed to Springs on delay over middle for 17
1/10-O48 - Volley was clear at rt for 11
1/10-I41 - Schlichter passed deep left to Donley (George) incomplete Ohio illegal motion - declined
2/10-I41 - Volley middle for 3
3/7 -I38 - Orosz punted right, just in for the touchback

2:58 ILLINOIS
1/10-I20 - Weiss faded, chased, knocked down by Dansler, Sullivan, Cato for -4
2/14-I16 - Powell on delay at It for 6
3/8 -I22 - Weiss faked, faded, ran middle for 6; fumble recovered by Dansler

1:31 OHIO STATE
1/10-I28 - Campbell into It for 6
2/4 -I22 - Campbell at center for another 6
1/10-I16 - Volley was stopped at rt for no gain
2/10-I16 - Schlichter kept left for 1

END OF THIRD QUARTER
OHIO STATE 24 ILLINOIS 7

FOURTH QUARTER

15:00 OHIO STATE
3/9 -I15 - Schlichter faked, passed right for Moore; intercepted by Carmien returned sideline for 23

14:52 ILLINOIS
1/10-I27 - Powell at rt for no gain
2/10-I27 - Weiss faked, ran middle for 3
3/7 -I30 - Weiss faked, faded, chased right passed to Barnes for 15
1/10-I45 - Thomas at rg for 3
2/7 -I48 - Weiss faked, moved right, sacked by Laughlin for -2
3/9 -I46 - Weiss faked, faded, sacked by Hornik, Dansler for -11
4/20-I35 - Finzer punted 47; Guess returned left, broke tackle for 62

11:00 OHIO STATE
1/10-I20 - Murray pitch at le for 5; Illinois Personal Foul 8 (Murray hurt, limped off)
1/G -I7 - Volley lg for 2
2/G -I5 - Schlichter kept left, hesitated, scored at the flag for the TD Janakievski's partially blocked PAT was good - Illinois offside to be marked off on kickoff - 20 yards in 3 plays
SCORE: OHIO STATE 31 ILLINOIS 7

Atha kicked off 3 yards deep for the touchback
10:24 ILLINOIS
1/10-I20 - Dismuke option pitch at re for 4 (Lawrence McCullough at QB)
2/6 -I24 - Dismuke pitch at le for 1
3/5 -I25 - Dismuke draw stopped by Dansler for -6
4/11-I19 - Finzer punted 39; Guess returned 15

8:54 OHIO STATE
1/10-I43 - Johnson lg 3 (Gerald at QB)
2/7 -I40 - Johnson pitch at le for 5
3/2 -I35 - Payton was clear at rg for 8
1/10-I27 - Johnson pitch at re for 4
2/6 -I23 - Gerald kept inside re, spun for 2
3/4 -I21 - Gerald faked, passed to Johnson left for 7; Illinois personal foul 7
1/G -I7 - Gerald kept inside re, cut right for the TD Janakievski PAT - 43 yards, 7 plays
SCORE: OHIO STATE 38 ILLINOIS 7

Atha kicked off right one yard deep; Foster returned 14
6:18 ILLINOIS
1/10-I14 - McCullough's fumble recovered by Cato for no gain

6:14 OHIO STATE
1/10-I14 - Johnson slanted thru center for 6
2/4 -I8 - Johnson on same play for the TD Janakievski PAT 14 yards in two plays
SCORE: OHIO STATE 45 ILLINOIS 7

385

Atha kicked off 5 yards deep for the touchback
5:44 ILLINOIS
1/10-I20 - Dismuke at rg for 5
2/5 -I25 - Dismuke draw middle, clear for 10
1/10-I35 - Thomas rg 4
2/6 -I39 - Dismuke on deep handoff was stopped by Lee, Miller for -1
3/7 -I38 - McCullough passed on delay to Thomas cutting short over middle for 8
1/10-I46 - Dismuke pitch at re for 6
2/4 -O48 - Thomas middle 4
1/10-O44 - McCullough faked, passed to Foster in right flat; Ellison intercepted no return

2:29 OHIO STATE
1/10-O35 - Hicks pitch at re for 14
1/10-O49 - Belmer lg 3
2/7 -I48 - Hicks pitch at re 9
1/10-I39 - Hicks into rg, cut right for 12
1/10-I27 - Hicks recovered his own fumble for -3
2/13-I30 - Castignola kept at re on broken play for 8
3/5 -I22 - Belmar thru lg for 3 (Fritz hurt - limped off)
4/2 -I19 - Hicks pitch at re 3

END OF GAME
OHIO STATE 45 ILLINOIS 7

National Collegiate Athletic Association
FINAL TEAM STATISTICS
November 11, 1978

	ILLINOIS	OHIO STATE
First Downs	14	26
Rushing	9	18
Passing	4	7
Penalty	1	1
Third Down Efficiency	5/17	8/18
Rushing Attempts	59	66
Yards Rushing	197	321
Yards Lost Rushing	67	8
Net Yards Rushing	130	313
Net Yards Passing	61	116
Attempted	9	16
Completed	5	10
Had Intercepted	2	2
Total Offensive Plays	68	82
Total Net Yards	191	429
Interceptions: Number—Yards	2/23	2/3
Punts—Yards—Had Blocked	7/244/0	3/153/0
Average Per Punt	34.8	51.0
Punt Returns—Yards	1/14	4/77
Kickoff Returns: Yards	3/59	2/49
Penalties—Yards	7/40	3/35
Fumbles—Lost	4/3	2/1
Touchdowns	1	6
Rushing—Passing—Other	1/0/0	6/0/0
Kicking Extra Points Attempted—Made	1/1	6/6
Other Extra Points Attempted—Made	0/0	0/0
Fields Goals Attempted—Made	0/0	1/1

NOVEMBER 11, 1978

PURDUE
VS
WISCONSIN
Camp Randall Stadium
Temp:38
Wind: 15-25 mph
Skies: Cloudy
FIRST QUARTER

PURDUE won the toss and will receive.
WISCONSIN will kickoff and defend the north goal
Mike Brhley will kickoff for Wisconsin to open the game, to the P2, Moss returns 24 yards to P26 (Stroede)

14:55 PURDUE
1/10-P26 - Pope runs right end, gets 2 to 28 (Crossen)
2/8 -P28 - Herrmann passes left to Burrell, broken up (By Johnson)
3/8 -P28 - Herrmann passes over the middle to Harris, incomplete
4/8 -P28 - Lagin punts 25 yards to W47. Out of bounds

14:05 WISCONSIN
1/10-W47 - Green runs up the middle, gets no gain (Loushin)
2/10-W47 - Kalasmiki passes right to Souza, incomplete
3/10-W47 - Kalasmiki keeps runs end, gets 6 to P47 (Johnson)
4/4 -P47 - Kiltz punts 38 yards to P9, Pope returns 2 to 11

13:09 PURDUE
1/10-P11 - Macon runs right end, gets 5 to 16 (Relich)
2/5 -P16 - Herrmann runs up middle, gets no gain (Relich)
3/5 -P16 - Herrmann passes right to Harris, gets 4 to 20 (Holm)
4/1 -P20 - Lagin punts 27 yards to P47, Stracka returns 0 to 47 (Seneff)

11:24 WISCONSIN
1/10-P47 - Stauss runs up the middle, gets 18 to 29 fumbles, recovered by Supan

11:15 PURDUE
1/10-P29 - Pope runs right tackle, gets 3 to 32 (Ahrens)
2/7 -P32 - Herrmann passes left to Macon, gets 4 to 36 (Ahrens)
3/3 -P36 - Pope runs draw up middle, gets 2 to 38 (Anderson)
4/1 -P38 - Lasin punts 35 yards to W27, Stauss returns 5 yards to 32 (Moss)

9:38 WISCONSIN
1/10 W32 - Stauss runs right guard, gets 2 to 34 (Clark)
2/8 -W34 - Kalasmiki passes long left to Charles, incomplete
3/8 -W34 - Stauss runs left tackle, gets 3 to 37 (Turner)
4/5 -W37 - Kiltz punts 35 yards to P28, Gallivan returns 1 to 29 (Ahrens)
Wisconsin is penalized 15 yards for personal foul

8:05 PURDUE
1/10-P44 - Macon runs right end, gets 2 to 46 (Ahrens)
2/8 -P46 - Macon runs right tackle, gets 2 to 48 (Ahrens)
3/6 -P48 - Herrmann passes over the middle to Harris, gets 14 to W38 (Johnson)
1/10-W38 - Pope runs right end, gets no gain (Ahrens)
2/10-W32 - Herrmann passes over middle to Harris, broken up (by Gordon)
3/10-W38 - Herrmann passes right to Burrell, incomplete
4/10-W38 - Lasin punts 29 yards to W29, Stracka fair catch

5:45 WISCONSIN
1/10-W9 - Stauss runs up middle, gets 3 to 12 (Motts)
2/7 -W12 - Green runs right tackle, gets 1 to 13 (Turner)
3/6 -W13 - Kalasmiki pitches left to Cohee, gets 7 to 20 (Harris)
1/10-W20 - Kalasmiki keeps on option left, gets 9 to 29 (Clark)
2/1 -W29 - Green runs right tackle, gets 10 to 39 (Clark)
1/10-W39 - Kalasmiki passes over the middle to Ruetz, broken up (by Johanson)
2/10-W39 - Kalasmiki keeps on the option left, gets 2 to 41 (Jackson)
3/8 -W41 - Kalasmiki passes over the middle to Green, gets 5 to 46 (Hotts)
4/3 -W46 - Kiltz punts 40 yards to P14, Pope loses 1 on return to 13 (Levenick)

1:52 PURDUE
1/10-P13 - Pope runs left end, loses 1 to 12 (Vine)
2/11-P12 - Pope runs left end, gets 1 to 13 (Ahrens)
3/10-P13 - Herrmann passes right to Harris, gets 12 to 25
1/10-P25 - Pope runs left tackle, gets 3 to 28 (Holm)
2/7 -P28 - Macon runs right end, gets 7 to 35 (Schieble)

END OF THE FIRST QUARTER
WISCONSIN 0, PURDUE 0

SECOND QUARTER

15:00 PURDUE
1/10-P35 - Macon runs right guard, gets 4 to 39 (Ahrens)
2/6 -P39 - Herrmann passes right to Burrell, incomplete
3/6 -P39 - Herrmann passes over the middle to Burrell, broken up (by Schieble)
4/6 -P39 - Eagin punts 38 yards to W23, Stauss returns 5 yards to 28 (Josten)

14:10 WISCONSIN
1/10-W28 - Stauss runs up the middle, gets 2 to 30 (Jackson)
2/8 -W30 - Kalasmiki passes right to Charles, incomplete
3/8 -W30 - Green runs right tackle, gets 7 to 37 (Motts)
4/1 -W37 - Kiltz punts 27 yards to P36 downed by Rothbauer

12:49 PURDUE
1/10-P36 - Herrmann passes left to Pope, incomplete
2/10-P36 - Herrmann passes over the middle to Pope, incomplete
3/10-P36 - Herrmann passes over the middle to Burrell, incomplete Wisconsin is penalized 16 yards for pass interference
1/10-W48 - Macon runs up the middle, gets no gain (Ahrens)
2/10-W48 - Herrmann back to pass, runs up middle, gets 2 to 46 (Relich)
3/8 -W46 - Herrmann passes left to Burrell, gets 20 to 26 (Schieble)
1/10-W26 - Macon runs right guard, gets 9 to 17 (Schieble)
2/1 -W17 - Macon runs right guard, gets 5 to 12 (Holm)
1/10-W12 - Macon runs draw right tackle, gets 3 to W9 (Schremp)
2/7 -W9 - Herrmann passes left to Burrell, broken up (by Schieble)
3/7 -W9 - Herrmann passes over the middle to Harris, incomplete
4/7 -W9 - Sovereen's 26 yard field goal attempt is good (9:30) (11 plays, 64 yards)
SCORE: PURDUE 3, WISCONSIN 0

Sovereen kicks off for Purdue following the score to W goal line, Green returns 22 yards to 22 (Josten)

9:25 WISCONSIN
1/10-W22 - Green runs right tackle, gets 4 to 26 (Turner)
2/6 -W26 - Wisconsin is penalized 5 yards for illegal procedure
2/11-W21 - Stauss runs right tackle, gets 7 to 28 (Motts)
3/4 -W28 - Kalasmiki keeps on the option right, gets no gain (Johanson)
4/4 -W28 - Kiltz punts 28 yards to P44, Gallivan fair catch

7:25 PURDUE
1/10-P44 - Macon runs up middle, gets 3 to 47 (Holm)
2/7 -P47 - Herrmann passes over the middle to Burrell, gets 17 to W36 (Schieble)
1/10-W36 - Herrmann passes left to Burrell, gets 9 to 27 (out of bounds)
2/1 -W27 - Macon runs left guard, gets 1 to 26 (Schremp)
1/10-W26 - Herrmann passes over the middle to Young, gets 9 to 17 (Gordon)
2/1 -W17 - Macon runs right tackle, gets 3 to 14 (Holm)
1/10-W14 - Macon runs right guard, gets 1 to 13 (Holm) Purdue is penalized 15 yards for holding
1/24-W28 - Pope runs left end, loses 4 to 32 (Vine)
2/28-W32 - Herrmann passes over the middle to Harris, gets 11 to 21
3/17-W21 - Herrmann passes over the middle to Burrell, broken up (by Schieble)
4/17-W21 - Sovereen's 38 yard field goal attempt-wide left

3:16 WISCONSIN
1/10-W21 - Wisconsin calls timeout (3:16) Green runs left end, gets 6 to 27 (Moss)
2/4 -W27 - Kalasmiki pitches to Green, gets 1 to 28 (Clark)
3/3 -W28 - Kalasmiki pitches left to Green, gets 9 to 37 (Motts)
1/10-W37 - Kalasmiki passes right to Souza, gets 8 to 45 (Motts)
2/2 -W45 - Wisconsin calls timeout (1:26) Stauss runs up the middle, gets no gain (Loushin)
3/2 -W45 - Kalasmiki passes left to Green gets 17 to P38
1/10- P38 - Kalasmiki passes long right to Souza broken up (by Supan)
2/10-P38 - Kalasmiki passes left to Sydnor, gets 38 for TD (:43)
Veith extra point kick is wide left (8 plays, 79 yards)
SCORE: WISCONSIN 6, PURDUE 3

Brhely will kick off for Wisconsin following the score to P17, McCall returns 14 yards to 31 (Spurlin)

:38 PURDUE
1/10-P31 - Macon runs up the middle, gets 3 to 34 (Relich)
2/7 -P34 - Herrmann pitches right to Pope, gets 3 to 37 (Ahrens)

**END OF THE FIRST HALF:
WISCONSIN 6, PURDUE 3**

NOVEMBER 11, 1978

THIRD QUARTER

Scott Sovereen will kickoff for Purdue to open the third quarter to W goal line Green returns 17 yards to W17 (Kay)
14:56 WISCONSIN
1/10-W17 - Kalasmiki keeps on the option right gets 17 to 34 (Clark)
1/10-W34 - Green runs right tackle, gets 2 to 36 (Floyd)
2/8 -W36 - Kalasmiki passes over the middle to Charles, incomplete
3/8 -W36 - Kalasmiki runs right end, gets 2 to 38 (Moss)
4/6 -W38 - Kiltz punts 41 yards to P20, downed by Ahrens

13:07 PURDUE
1/10-P21 - Herrmann passes right to Harris, gets 3 to 24
2/7 -P24 - Macon runs up middle, gets no gain (Crossen)
3/7 -P24 - Herrmann runs right tackle, gets 1 to 25 (Blaskowski)
4/6 -P25 - Eagin punt is blocked by Blaskowski Wisconsin is penalized 15 yards for personal foul
1/10-P40 - Herrmann passes over the middle to Young, gets 6 to 46 (Gordon)
2/4 -P46 - Macon runs right guard, gets 6 to W48 (Schremp)
1/10-W48 - Macon runs up the middle, gets 2 to 46 (Crossen)
2/8 -W46 - Herrmann passes right to Young, gets 26 to 20 (Johnson)
1/10-W20 - Macon runs left guard, gets 3 to 17 (Relich)
2/7 -W17 - Herrmann passes left to Harris, gets 9 to 8 (Johnson)
1/G -W8 - Macon runs left tackle, gets no gain (Ahrens)
2/G -W8 - Herrmann back to pass, runs left, gets 4 to 4 (Ahrens)
3/G -W4 - Herrmann passes over middle to Burrell, gets 4 for TD (7:02) Sovereen kicks the extra point (12 plays, 79 yards)
SCORE: PURDUE 10, WISCONSIN 6

Sovereen will kickoff for Purdue following the score, to W endzone for touchback
7:02 WISCONSIN
1/10-W20 - Kalasmiki pitches right to Green, gets no gain (Moss)
2/10-W20 - Kalasmiki runs left end, gets 5 to 25 (Clark)
3/5-W25 - Kalasmiki pitches left to Cohee, gets 6 to 31 (Turner)
1/10-W31 - Kalasmiki pitches to Green, runs right tackle, gets 3 to 34 (Clark)
2/7 -W34 - Stauss runs right tackle, gets 2 to 36 (Jackson)
3/5 -W36 - Kalasmiki passes over the middle to Souza, incomplete

4/5 -W36 - Kiltz punts 42 yards to P22, Pope returns 1 to P23 (Snell)

4:07 PURDUE
1/10-P23 - Pope runs left tackle, gets 2 to 25 (Relich)
2/8 -P25 - Herrmann passes over the middle to Young, gets 75 yards for TD (3:24) Sovereen kicks the extra point (2 plays, 77 yards)
SCORE: PURDUE 17, WISCONSIN 6

Purdue is penalized 5 yards for delay of game Sovereen will kickoff for Purdue following the score, to W goal line, Green returns 21 yards to W21 (Josten)
3:18 WISCONSIN
1/10-W21 - Kalasmiki runs left end, gets 6 to 27 (Turner)
2/4 -W27 - Kalasmiki runs right end, gets 3 to 30 (Turner)
3/1 -W30 - Kalasmiki pitches left to Green, loses 2 to 28 (Turner)
4/3 -W28 - Kiltz punts 31 yards to P41, Gallivan fair catch

1:03 PURDUE
1/10-P41 - Pope runs left end, gets 1 to 42 (Vine)
2/9 -P42 - Macon runs right tackle, gets 8 to gets 50 (Holm)

**END OF THE THIRD QUARTER:
PURDUE 17, WISCONSIN 6**

FOURTH QUARTER

15:00 PURDUE
1/10- 50 - Herrmann pitches left to Pope, gets 15 to W35 (Schieble)
1/10-W35 - Macon runs right guard, gets 3 to 32 (Crossen)
2/7 -W32 - Macon runs right end, gets 7 to 25 (Schieble)
1/10-W25 - Macon runs left guard, gets 4 to 21 (Crossen)
2/6 -W21 - Herrmann passes right to Burrell, gets 14 to W7
1/G -W7 - Macon runs left guard, gets 3 to 4 (Relich)
2/G -W4 - Macon runs right tackle, gets 4 for TD (11:42) Sovereen kicks the extra (9 plays, 59 yards)
SCORE: PURDUE 24, WISCONSIN 6

Sovereen will kickoff for Purdue following the score to W7, Green returns 5 yards to 12 (Speedy)

11:36 WISCONSIN
1/10-W12 - Kalasmiki passes long right to Sydnor, gets 45 to P43

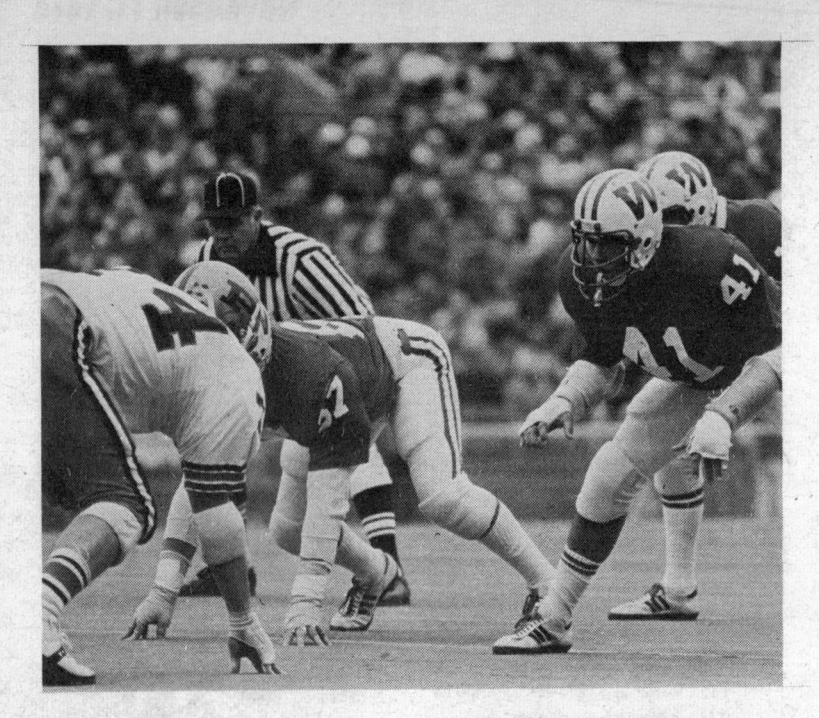

1/10-P43 - Kalasmiki runs left end, gets 4 to 39 (Clark)
2/6 -P39 - Green runs right tackle, gets 3 to 36 (Motts)
3/3 -P36 - Kalasmiki pitches right to Green, gets 5 to 31 (Motts)
1/10-P31 - Kalasmiki runs left end, gets no gain (Jackson)
2/10-P31 - Kalasmiki passes left to Sydnor, broken up (by Kay)
3/10-P31 - Kalasmiki passes over middle to Souza, gets 31 yards for TD (8:11) Veith kicks the extra point (7 plays, 88 yards)
SCORE: PURDUE 24, WISCONSIN 13

Brhley will kickoff for Wisconsin following the score to P4, Moss returns 14 yards to P18 (Welch)

8:05 PURDUE
1/10-P18 - Macon runs up middle, gets 2 to 20 (Crossen)
2/8 -P20 - Macon runs right tackle, gets 6 to 26 (Relich)
3/2 -P26 - Macon runs right tackle, gets 1 to 27 (Schremp)
4/1 -P27 - Lagin punts 10 yards to P37, downed by Macon

6:04 WISCONSIN
1/10-P37 - Kalasmiki passes right to Sydnor, gets 8 to 29 (Seneff)

2/2 -P29 - Stauss runs left guard, gets 3 to 26 (Johanson)
1/10-P26 - Kalasmiki passes right to Sydnor, incomplete
2/10-P26 - Kalasmiki passes right to Sydnor, incomplete Purdue is penalized 20 yards for pass interference
1/G -P6 - Kalasmiki keeps on the option right, gets no gain (Motts)
2/G -P6 - Kalasmiki rolls left, loses 9 to 15 (Turner)
3/G -P15 - Wisconsin calls timeout (4:24) Kalasmiki passes left to Sydnor, incomplete
4/G -P15 - Veith's 32 yard field goal attempts is good (4:13) (7 plays, 37 yards)
SCORE: PURDUE 24, WISCONSIN 16

Brhley will kickoff for Wisconsin following the score to goal line, Pope returns 6 to P6 (out of bounds)

4:09 PURDUE
1/10-P6 - Macon rush up the middle, gets 7 to 13 (Crossen)
2/3 -P13 - Macon runs left tackle, gets 4 to 17 (Vine)
1/10-P17 - Macon runs left guard, gets 8 to 25 (Crossen)
2/2 -P25 - Macon runs right guard, gets 1 to 26 (Schremp)
3/1 -P26 - Herrmann pitches right to Macon, gets no gain (Schieble)

NOVEMBER 11, 1978

4/1 -P26 - Lagin punts blocked by Cabral recovered by Christenson. Wisconsin calls timeout (1:39) Cabral 14 yard punt return

1:33 WISCONSIN
1/10-P12 - Kalasmiki passes over the middle to Sydnor, incomplete
2/10-P12 - Kalasmiki passes left to Sydnor, gets 11 to P1 (Moss)
1/G -P1 - Green runs left tackle, gets no gain
2/G -P1 - Green runs left tackle, loses 2 to 3 (Jackson)
3/G -P3 - Wisconsin calls timeout (:29) Kalasmiki passes right to Charles, gets 3 for TD (:25) Purdue calls timeout (:25) (5 plays, 12 yards) Kalasmiki passes over middle to Souza for 2 point conversion
SCORE: WISCONSIN 24, PURDUE 24

Veith will kickoff for Wisconsin following the score to P40, Luckianow returns 1 yard to P41 (Levenick)

:23 PURDUE
1/10-P41 - Herrmann passes right to Macon, gets 3 to 44
2/7 -P44 - Herrmann passes left to Pope, gets 22 to W34 (Vine)
1/10-W34 - Purdue calls timeout (:05) Sovereen's 51 yard field goal attempt is short Wisconsin was off side. Purdue personal fouls Sovereen's 50 yard field goal attempt is short, Green return 15 to W18.

**END OF THE GAME:
WISCONSIN 24, PURDUE 24**

National Collegiate Athletic Association
FINAL TEAM STATISTICS

	PURDUE	WISCONSIN
First Downs	20	13
Rushing	8	7
Passing	9	5
Penalty	3	1
Rushing Attempts	49	40
Yards Rushing	156	158
Yards Lost Rushing	5	13
Net Yards Rushing	151	145
Net Yards Passing	262	166
Passes Attempted	29	20
Passes Completed	18	9
Had Intercepted	0	0
Total Offensive Plays	78	60
Total Net Yards	413	311
Average Gain Per Play	5.3	5.2
Fumbles: Number—Lost	0/0	1/1
Penalties: Number—Yards	3/40	4/51
Interceptions: Number—Yards	—	—
Number of Punts—Yards	8/195	7/251
Average Per Punt	24.4	35.9
Punt Returns: Number—Yards	4/3	4/24
Kickoff Returns: Number—Yards	5/59	4/65

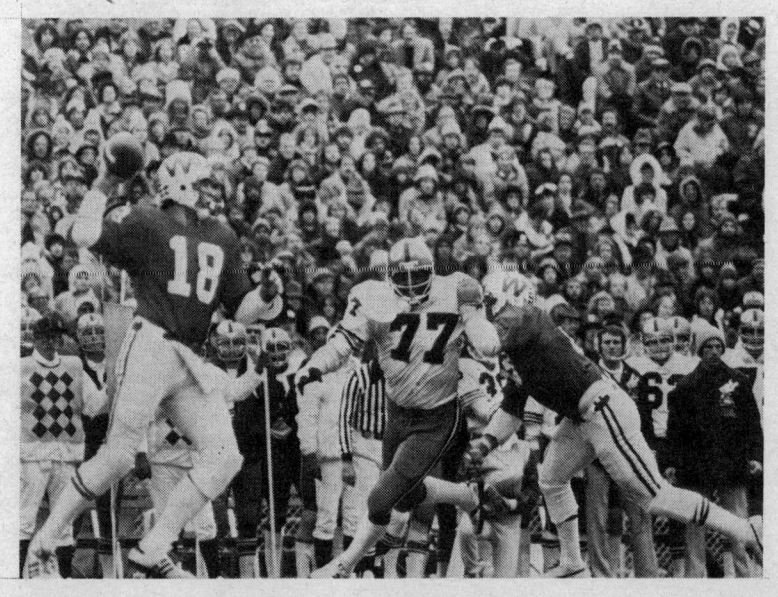

NOVEMBER 18, 1978

OHIO STATE
VS.
INDIANA
Memorial Stadium
Bloomington, Ind.
Temp.: 41°
Wind: W 8-10 mph
FIRST QUARTER

Indiana wins toss and will receive, Ohio State will defend south goal Atha kicks off out of end zone

15:00 INDIANA
1/10-I20 - Harkrader rt to I27, 7 yards
2/3 -I27 - Harkrader le to I31, 4 yards
1/10-I31 - Harkrader le to I31, no gain
2/10-I31 - Harkrader le to I31, no gain
3/10-I31 - Friede punts dead to O17, no return

13:49 OHIO STATE
1/10-O17 - Schlichter le to O30, 13 yards
1/10-O30 - Campbell rt to O36, 6 yards
2/4 -O36 - Schlichter rt to O40, 4 yards
1/10-O40 - Springs le to I44, 16 yards
1/10-I44 - Indiana penalized too many men on field
1/10-I29 - Murray le to I23, 6 yards
2/4 I23 - Campbell rg to I20, 3 yards
3/1 -I20 - Campbell lg to I17, 3 yards
1/10-I17 - Murray le to I16, 1 yard
2/9 -I16 - Springs le to I13, 3 yards
3/6 -I13 - Schlichter pass incomplete
4/6 -I13 - Indiana offside
4/1 -I8 - Campbell rt to I4, 4 yards
1/G -I4 - Campbell rt for touchdown, 4 yards
PAT—Janakievski kick good
SCORE: OHIO STATE 7, INDIANA 0

Atha kicks off into end zone
10:19 INDIANA
1/10-I20 - Arnett pass complete to Powers I27, 7 yards
2/3 -I27 - Johnson lg to I39, 12 yards
1/10-I39 - Arnett pass incomplete
2/10-I39 - Clifford pass complete to Stephenson to I46, 7 yards
3/3 -I46 - Harkrader re to I48, 2 yards
4/1 -I48 - Harkrader re to O49, 3 yards
1/10-O49 - Darrick lt to O46, 3 yards
2/7 -O46 - Arnett pass complete to Hopkins to O44, 2 yards
3/5 -O44 - Clifford pass complete to Powers to O36, 8 yards
1/10-O36 - Arnett pass complete to Hopkins to O30, 6 yds
2/4 -O30 - Darrick le to O25, 5 yards
1/10-O25 - Harkrader lt to O23, 2 yards
2/8 -O23 - Johnson rt to O23, no gain
3/8 -O23 - Clifford pass incomplete
4/8-O23 - Freud 40 field goal attempt short

5:54 OHIO STATE
1/10-O23 - Springs rt to O28, 5 yds
2/5 -O28 - Springs lt to O31, 3 yards
3/2 -O31 - Schlichter le to O32, 1 yard
4/1 -O32 - Campbell lt to O32, no gain

4:29 INDIANA
1/10-O32 - Harkrader le to O34, loss of 2
2/12-O34 - Clifford trapped to O41, loss of 7
3/19-O41 - Ohio State penalized pass interference
1/10-O28 - Darrick rg to O23, 5 yards
2/5 -O23 - Darrick lg to O4, 19 yards
1/G -O4 - Arnett re to O1, 3 yards
2/G -O1 - Harkrader rg for touchdown, 1 yard
PAT—Freud kick good
SCORE: INDIANA 7, OHIO STATE 7

Straub kicks off to Belmer at O31, no return
2:01 OHIO STATE
1/10-O31 - Campbell lt to O36, 5 yards
2/5 -O36 - Schlichter le to O35, loss of 1
3/6 -O35 - Schlichter pass incomplete
4/6 -O35 - Orosz punts to Wilbur at I15, returned to I11, minus 4 return 50 punt

0:52 INDIANA
1/10-I11 - Harkrader lt to I10, loss of 1
2/11-I10 - Johnson lg to I13, 3 yards
END OF FIRST QUARTER:
INDIANA 7, OHIO STATE 7

SECOND QUARTER

INDIANA
3/8 -I13 - Friede punt dead to O11, 76 punt

14:47 OHIO STATE
1/10-O11 - Campbell lg to O15, 4 yards
2/6 -O15 - Schlichter le to O15, no gain
3/6 -O15 - Springs re to O18, 3 yards
4/3 -O18 - Orosz punts to Swinehart at I48, fair catch

13:31 INDIANA
1/10-I48 - Burnett rg to O45, 7 yards
2/3 -O45 - Burnett rg to O43, 2 yards
3/1 -O43 - Harkrader rt to O37, 6 yards
1/10-O37 - Harkrader lt to O30, 7 yards
2/3 -O30 - Burnett rg to O28, 2 yards
3/1 -O28 - Burnett rt to O28, no gain
4/1 -O28 - Arnett le to O25, 3 yards
1/10-O25 - Arnett pass incomplete
2/10-O25 - Harkrader re to O17, 8 yards
3/2 -O17 - Arnett re to O16, 1 yard
4/1 -O16 - Arnett rg to O14, 2 yards
1/10-O14 - Burnett rt to O11, 3 yards
2/7 -O11 - Burnett re to O9, 2 yards
3/5 -O9 - Arnett pass complete to Johnson to O12, loss of 3
4/8-O12 - Freud 30 field goal attempt good
SCORE: INDIANA 10, OHIO STATE 7

NOVEMBER 18, 1978

Straub kicks off to Hicks at O2, returned to to O26, 24 return
6:52 OHIO STATE
1/10-O26 - Murray rt to O29, 3 yards
2/7 -O29 - Schlichter pass complete to Springs to O35, 6 yards
3/1 -O35 - Payton rt to O41, 6 yards
1/10-O41 - Springs re to I48, 11 yards
1/10-I48 - Springs lt to I42, 6 yards
2/4 -I42 - Schlichter re to I41, 1 yard
3/3 -I41 - Payton rt to I37, 4 yards
1/10-I37 - Springs rt to I33, 4 yards
2/6 -I33 - Springs lt to I31, 2 yards
3/4 -I31 - Johnson re to I30, 1 yard
4/3 -I30 - Schlichter pass incomplete

3:12 INDIANA
1/10-I30 - Arnett pass incomplete
2/10-I30 - Burnett trapped to I28, loss of 2
3/12-I28 - Friede punts dead O6, 66 punt

2:25 OHIO STATE
1/10-O6 - Schlichter pass intercepted by Swinehart at O48, returned to O43, 5 return

2:16 INDIANA
1/10-O43 - Burnett re to O42, 1 yard
2/9 -O42 - Johnson le to O43, loss of 1
3/10-O43 - Clifford pass incomplete
4/10-O43 - Lovett punts into end zone, 43 punt

0:59 OHIO STATE
1/10-O20 - Johnson lg to O33, 13 yards
1/10-O33 - Johnson rg to O39, 6 yards
2/4 -O39 - Schlichter pass complete to Johnson to O42, 3 yards
3/1 -O42 - Schlichter pass complete to Johnson to O47, 5 yards
1/10-O47 - Schlichter pass complete to Campbell to I46, 7 yards
2/3 -I46 - Schlichter pass incomplete

END OF FIRST HALF:
INDIANA 10, OHIO STATE 7

THIRD QUARTER

Straub kicks off to Hicks at O7, returned to O29, 22 return but OS illegal advance ball
14:46 OHIO STATE
1/10-O25 - Johnson rt to O24, loss of 1
2/11-O24 - Schlichter pass incomplete
3/11-O24 - Schlichter pass incomplete
4/11-O24 - Orosz punts to Wilbur at I23, returned to I19, minus 4 return 53 punt

13:49 INDIANA
1/10-I19 - Harkrader lt to O27, 8 yards
2/2 -I27 - Johnson rg to I28, 1 yard
3/1 -I28 - Harkrader re to I31, 3 yards
1/10-I31 - Burnett rg to I31, no gain
2/10-I31 - Johnson lg to I34, 3 yards
3/7 -I34 - Johnson rg to I38, 4 yards
4/3 -I38 - Lovett punts dead at O2, 60 punt

10:28 OHIO STATE
1/10-O2 - Volley rg to O8, 6 yards
2/4 -O8 - Johnson rg to O10, 2 yards
3/2 -O10 - Johnson le to O16, 6 yards
1/10-O16 - Volley rg to O19, 3 yards
2/7-O19 - Johnson re to O19, no gain, but Indiana penalized face mask
1/10-O34 - Schlichter re to O39, 5 yards
2/5 -O39 - Johnson rg to O41, 2 yards
3/3 -O41 - Volley rg to I47, 12 yards
1/10-I47 - Johnson le to I41, 6 yards
2/4 -I41 - Schlichter re to I40, 1 yard
3/3 -I40 - Volley lg to I30, 10 yards
1/10-I30 - Johnson re to I25, 5 yards
2/5 -I25 - Johnson lt to I21, 4 yards
3/1 -I21 - Schlichter rg to I15, 6 yards
1/10-I15 - Volley lg to I13, 2 yards
2/8 -I13 - Schlichter le to I8, 5 yards
3/3 -I8 - Payton rg to I7, 1 yard
4/2 -I7 - Payton rg to I3, 4 yards
1/G -I3 - Payton rg to I3, no gain
2/G -I3 - Schlichter re for touchdown, 3 yards
PAT—Janakievski kick good
SCORE: OHIO STATE 14, INDIANA 10

Atha kicks off to Burnett at I6, returned to I32, 26 return
2:52 INDIANA
1/10-I32 - Clifford pass complete to Powers I49, 17 yards
1/10-I49 - Clifford pass incomplete
2/10-I49 - Harkrader lt to I47, loss of 2
3/12-I47 - Harkrader rt to I46, loss of 1
4/13-I46 - Lovett punts to Guess at O12, returned to O21, 9 return 42 punt

1:15 OHIO STATE
1/10-O21 - Schlichter le to O28, 7 yards
2/3 -O28 - Volley rg to O30, 2 yards
3/1 -O30 - Schlichter rg to O33, 3 yards

END OF THIRD QUARTER
OHIO STATE 14, INDIANA 10

FOURTH QUARTER

OHIO STATE
1/10-O33 - Johnson le to O36, 3 yards
2/7 -O36 - Volley lg to O46, 10 yards
1/10-O46 - Johnson re to I48, 6 yards
2/4 -I48 - Volley rg to I46, 2 yards
3/2 -I46 - Johnson re for touchdown, 46 yards
PAT—Janakievski kick good
SCORE: OHIO STATE 21, INDIANA 10

393

Atha kicks off to Burnett in end zone, return to I20, 20 return

13:08 INDIANA
1/10-I20 - Burnett lt to I22, 2 yards
2/8 -I22 - Clifford pass complete to Powers to I31, 9 yards
1/10-I31 - Clifford re to I40, 9 yards
2/1 -I40 - Harkrader lt to I44, 4 yards
1/10-I44 - Clifford pass incomplete
2/10-I44 - Clifford pass complete to Harkrader to I46, 2 yards
3/8 -I46 - Clifford pass incomplete
4/8 -I46 - Lovett punts dead at O25, 29 punt

10:42 OHIO STATE
1/10-O25 - Johnson re to O29, 4 yards
2/6 -O29 - Johnson lt to O29, no gain
3/6 -O29 - Schlichter le to O31, 2 yards
4/4 -O31 - Orosz punts to Wilbur at I29, returned to I28, minus 1 return 40 punt

9:02 INDIANA
1/10-I28 - Clifford pass complete to Powers to I37, 9 yards
2/1 -I37 - Burnett lt to I37, no gain
3/1 -I37 - Clifford rg to I38, 1 yard
1/10-I38 - Clifford pass incomplete
2/10-I38 - Harkrader rg to I45, 7 yards
3/3 -I45 - Clifford pass complete to Lundy to O42, 13 yards
1/10-O42 - Clifford pass incomplete
2/10-O42 - Harkrader to O35, 7 yards
3/3 -O35 - Friede le to O33, 2 yards
4/1 -O33 - Burnett lg to O29, 4 yards
1/10-O29 - Clifford pass incomplete
2/10-O29 - Clifford pass incomplete
3/10-O29 - Ohio State penalized for pass interference in end zone
1/G -O1 - Burnett rg for touchdown, 1 yard
PAT—Indiana penalized delay of game
PAT—Friede pass from Clifford
SCORE: OHIO STATE 21, INDIANA 18

Straub kicks off to Hicks at O7, returned to O26, 19 return

4:55 OHIO STATE
1/10-O26 - Schlichter lt to O32, 6 yards
2/4 -O32 - Schlichter lt to O35, 3 yards
3/1 -O35 - Schlichter re to O38, 3 yards
1/10-O38 - Johnson le to O42, 4 yards
2/6 -O42 - Johnson le to O44, 2 yards
3/4 -O44 - Schlichter le to O47, 3 yards
4/1 -O47 - Orosz punts to Wilbur at I11, returned to I17, 6 return

2:15 INDIANA
1/10-I17 - Clifford pass complete to Johnson to I19, 2 yards
2/8 -I19 - Burnett re to I30, 11 yards
1/10-I30 - Clifford pass complete to Powers to I42, 12 yards
1/10-I42 - Friede pass intercepted by Guess at O25, returns to O27 and Indiana penalized for personal foul

1:37 OHIO STATE
1/10-O42 - Volley rg to O45, 3 yards
2/7 -O45 - Ohio State penalized delay of game
2/12-O40 - Schlichter rg to O41, 1 yard
3/11-O41 - Schlichter lg to O41, no gain

**END OF GAME:
OHIO STATE 21, INDIANA 18**

National Collegiate Athletic Association
FINAL TEAM STATISTICS

	OHIO STATE	INDIANA
First Downs	21	20
Rushing	18	14
Passing	1	4
Penalty	2	2
Rushing Attempts	72	53
Yards Rushing	334	180
Net Yards Rushing	332	164
Net Yards Passing	22	93
Passes Attempted	11	27
Passes Completed	4	14
Had Intercepted	1	1
Total Offensive Plays	83	80
Total Net Yards	354	257
Average Gain Per Play	4.3	3.2
Fumbles: Number—Lost	1/0	1/0
Penalties: Number—Yards	4/51	5/55
Interceptions: Number—Yards	1/2	1/5
Number of Punts—Yards	5/219	7/368
Average Per Punt	44	52.6
Punt Returns: Number—Yards	1/9	4/3
Kickoff Returns: Number—Yards	3/65	2/46

NOVEMBER 18, 1978

WISCONSIN
VS.
IOWA
Kinnick Stadium
Temp: mid 40's
Wind: 5-10 mph South
Skies: clear
FIRST QUARTER

Wisconsin wins toss and elects to receive. Iowa will kick off and defend south goal. Schilling kicks off to out of bounds. Iowa penalized 5 yds for illegal procedure. Schilling kicks off to Sousa for return of 20 yds. (Webb)
WISCONSIN
1/10-W30 - Kalasmiki around re for gain of 5 (Hufford)
2/5 -W35 - Matthews around le for loss of 1 (Vazquez)
3/6 -W34 - Kalasmiki pass intended for Sydnor is incomplete
4/6 -W34 - Kiltz punts to Iowa 34 yard line (32 yard punt)

13:18 IOWA
1/10-I34 - Lazar over lg for gain of 6 (Holm)
2/4 -I40 - Burke around le for gain of 7 (Schieble)
1/10-I47 - Green around le for gain of 1 (Holm)
2/9 -I48 - Green passes to Reid for gain of 10 (Anderson)
1/10-W42 - Burke over rg for gain of 4 (Relich)
2/6 -W38 - Lazar over rt for gain of 3 (Schremp)
3/3 -W35 - Burke around re for gain of 2 (Blaskowski)
4/1 -W33 - Burke over rg for gain of 1 (Crossen)
1/10-W32 - Lazar over rg for gain of 9 (Schieble)
2/1 -W23 - Iowa penalized 5 yds for illegal procedure
2/6 -W28 - Burke over rg for gain of 4 (Holm)
3/2 -W24 - Burke over lg for gain of 3 (Holm)
1/10-W21 - Burke around le for gain of 3 (Holm)
2/7 -W18 - Lazar over lg for gain of 9 (Ahrens)
1/G -W9 - Burke over rt for gain of 1 (Ahrens)
2/G -W8 - Burke over rg for gain of 3 (Vine)
3/G -W5 - Burke around re for no gain (Gordon)
4/G -W5 - Morton holds, Schilling kicks, field goal attempt is good.
SCORE: IOWA 3, WISCONSIN 0

4:43 IOWA
Schilling kicks off onside kick, Steverson recovers for Iowa.
1/10-W49 - Green passes to Green for gain of 39
1/10-W10 - Reid around re for TD
Morton holds, Schilling kicks, PAT is good.
SCORE: IOWA 10, WISCONSIN 0

4:27 WISCONSIN
Schilling kicks off into endzone for touchback
1/10-W20 - Kalasmiki passes to Sydnor for gain of 13 (Rusk)
1/10-W33 - Stauss over rg, fumbles, recovered by Becker, gain of 18 (Weiss)

3:58 IOWA
1/10-I49 - Burke over rg for gain of 3. Iowa penalized for holding. (12 yd penalty)
1/22-I37 - Lazar over rg for gain of 2 (Gordon)
2/20-I39 - Lazar over rg for no gain (Ahrens)
3/20-I39 - Burke around le for gain of 8 (Johnson)
4/12-I47 - Holsclaw punts out of bounds on 17 yard line. (36 yard punt)

1:58 WISCONSIN
1/10-W17 - Kalasmiki pass intended for Charles is incomplete
2/10-W17 - Stauss over lg for gain of 2 (Simonsen)
3/8 -W19 - Kalasmiki around re for gain of 4 (Becker)
4/4 -W23 - Kiltz punts to Reid, fumbles, recovered by McCoy (37 yard punt) Return of 1

0:55 WISCONSIN
1/10-I41 - Josten passes to Charles for gain of 17 (Rusk)
1/10-I24 - Stauss over rg for gain of 9 (Steverson)

**FIRST QUARTER SCORE:
IOWA 10, WISCONSIN 0**

SECOND QUARTER

WISCONSIN
2/1 -I15 - Stauss fumbles, recovered by Moore, loss of 1 (Benschoter)
3/2 -I16 - Souza around re for gain of 3
1/10-I13 - Josten pass intended for Charles is incomplete
2/10-I13 - Souza around re for TD
Kalasmiki holds, Veith kicks, PAT is good
SCORE: IOWA 10, WISCONSIN 7

13:45 IOWA
Brhely kicks off into endzone for touchback
1/10-I20 - Burke around re for gain of 12 (Crossen)
1/10-I32 - Green fumbles, recovers, for loss of 2
2/12-I30 - Green pass intended for Swift is incomplete
3/12-I30 - Green pass intended for Morton is incomplete
4/12-I30 - Holsclaw punts to Stauss for fair catch (36 yard punt)

12:29 WISCONSIN
1/10-W34 - Matthews over lg for gain of 1 (Molini)
2/9-W35 - Kalasmiki pass intended for Souza is incomplete
Wisconsin penalized for illegal receiver downfield.
3/24-W20 - Stauss over lg for gain of 5 (Rusk)
4/19-W25 - Kiltz punts to Becker for return of 1 (40 yard punt) (Levenick)

11:01 IOWA
1/10-I36 - Burke over lt for gain of 2 (Lorenz)
2/8 -I38 - Green passes to Reid for gain of 16
1/10-W46 - Burke passes to Morton for gain of 13 (Johnson)
1/10-W33 - Morton over rt gain of 6 (Anderson)
2/4 -W27 - Burke around re for gain of 5 (Relich)
1/10-W22 - Lazar over rt for gain of 4 (Crossen)
2/6 -W18 - Burke over lg for gain of 4 (Crossen)
3/2 -W14 - Lazar over lg for gain of 1 (Christenson)
4/1 -W13 - Green sneaks for gain of 1
1/10-W12 - Burke over lt for no gain (Schremp)
2/10-W12 - Green passes to Swift for TD
Morton holds, Schilling kicks, PAT is good
SCORE: IOWA 17, WISCONSIN 7

6:42 WISCONSIN
Schilling kicks off to Reutz, fumbles, recovered by Rothbauer, return of 2
1/10-W29 - Matthews around re for gain of 9 (Steverson)
2/1 -W38 - Matthews over rt for no gain (Dean)
3/1 -W38 - Green over rt for gain of 2 (Weiss)
1/10-W40 - Kalasmiki passes to Souza for gain of 25 (Danzy)
1/10-I35 - Kalasmiki passes to Sydnor for gain of 12 (Rusk)
1/10-I23 - Kalasmiki around re for gain of 6 (Vasquez)

2/4 -I17 - Stauss over rt for gain of 2 (Hufford)
3/2 -I15 - Green over lg for gain of 6 (Hufford)
1G -I9 - Matthews around le for loss of 4 (Danzy)
2/G -I13 - Kalasmiki passes to Charles for gain of 12
3/G -I1 - Green over re for TD
Kalasmiki holds, Veith kicks, PAT is good
SCORE: IOWA 17, WISCONSIN 14

1:40 IOWA
Brhely kicks off to Blatcher for return of 19 (Brhely)
1/10-I36 - Green pass intended for Morton is incomplete
2/10-I36 - Green passes to Lazar for no gain (Johnson)
3/10-I36 - Green pass intended for Lazar is incomplete
4/10-I36 - Holsclaw punts to Stauss for fair catch (34 yard punt)

0:29 WISCONSIN
1/10-W30 - Kalasmiki passes to Souza for gain of 3 (Becker)
2/7 -W33 - Kalasmiki pass intended for Souza is incomplete
3/7 -W33 - Kalasmiki pass intended for Matthews is incomplete
4/7 -W33 - Matthews around re for gain of 4
FIRST HALF SCORE:
IOWA 17, WISCONSIN 14

THIRD QUARTER

Iowa will receive. Wisconsin will kick off and defend south goal. Brhely kicks into endzone for touchback.
IOWA
1/10-I20 - Burke over lt for gain of 2 (Relich)
2/8 -I22 - Burke over lg for gain of 5 (Schremp)
3/3 -I27 - Burke over rg for gain of 2 (Relich)
4/1 -I29 - Holsclaw punts on the Wisconsin 42 yard line. (29 yard punt)

13:14 WISCONSIN
1/10-W42 - Matthews around re for loss of 1 (Weiss)
2/11-W41 - Kalasmiki passes to Souza for gain of 10
3/1 -I49 - Souza around le for no gain (Rusk)
4/1 -I49 - Kiltz punts into endzone for touchback (49 yard punt)

11:40 IOWA
1/10-I20 - Reid around re for TD
Morton holds, Schilling kicks, PAT is good
SCORE: IOWA 24, WISCONSIN 14

NOVEMBER 18, 1978

11:25 WISCONSIN
Schilling kicks off into endzone for touchback
1/10-W20 - Kalasmiki pass intended for Charles is incomplete
2/10-W20 - Kalasmiki passes to Souza for gain of 12 (Simonsen)
1/10-W32 - Kalasmiki passes to Charles for gain of 20 (Rusk)
1/10-I48 - Kalasmiki pass intended for Charles is intercepted by Pace, return of 7. Iowa penalized 15 yards for clipping.

10:27 IOWA
1/10-I19 - Burke around le for no gain (Lorenz)
2/10-I19 - Green pass intended for Swift is incomplete
3/10-I19 - Morton passes to Green for gain of 1 (Houston)
4/9 -I20 - Holsclaw punts out of bounds on 37 yard line
Wisconsin penalized 5 yds for too many men on field
4/4 -I25 - Holsclaw punts to Mathews for fair catch (36 yard punt)

9:00 WISCONSIN
1/10-W39 - Kalasmiki around le for gain of 9 (Weiss)
2/1 -W48 - Kalasmiki passes to Charles for gain of 16 (Pace)
Iowa penalized 15 yards for facemask grabbing
1/10-I21 - Kalasmiki passes to Sydnor for gain of 18 (Becker)
1/G -I3 - Green over rg for gain of 2 (Vazquez)
2/G I1 - Green over rg for loss of 2
3/G -I3 - Kalasmiki around le for loss of 2
4/G -I5 - Kalasmiki holds, Veith kicks, field goal attempt is good
SCORE: IOWA 24, WISCONSIN 17

6:35 IOWA
Brhley kicks off to endzone for touchback
1/10-I20 - Lazar over lg for gain of 4 (Vine)
2/6 -I24 - Green passes to Lazar for gain of 14 (Schieble)
1/10-I38 - Burke over lt for gain of 6 (Holm)
2/4 -I44 - Lazar over rg for gain of 1 (Schremp)
3/3 I45 - Burke around re for gain of 5 (Schieble)
1/10- 50 - Green scrambles for loss of 1 (Schremp)
2/11-I49 - Burke over lg for gain of 1
3/10- 50 - Green passes to Morton for gain of 6 (Anderson)
4/4 -W44 - Holsclaw punts to Matthews for fair catch (34 yard punt)

2:12 WISCONSIN
1/10-W10 - Green over rg for loss of 2 (Hobbs)
2/12-W8 - Wisconsin penalized for illegal motion, Iowa penalized for personal foul
2/12-W8 - Green over rg for gain of 2 (Benschoter)
3/10-W10 - Kalasmiki passes to Charles for gain of 12 (Pace)
1/10-W22 - Kalasmiki around le for gain of 6 (Benschoter)

THIRD QUARTER SCORE:
IOWA 24, WISCONSIN 17

FOURTH QUARTER

WISCONSIN
2/4 -W28 - Kalasmiki pass intended for Charles is intercepted by Pace.

14:54 IOWA
1/10-W44 - Burke over rg for gain of 1 (Crossen)
2/9 -W43 - Green around le for loss of 1 (Vine)
3/10-W44 - Green pass intended for Swift is incomplete
4/10-W44 - Holsclaw punts out of bounds on Wisconsin 2 yard line (42 yard line)

13:29 WISCONSIN
1/10-W2 - Green over rg for gain of 3 (Hobbs)
2/7 -W5 - Stauss over rt for gain of 3 (Weiss)
3/4 -W8 - Kalasmiki passes to Charles for gain of 6
Wisconsin penalized for illegal receiver downfield
3/8 -W4 - Stauss over rt for gain of 2 (Hobbs)
4/6 -W6 - Kiltz punts for Reid for no return (36 yard punt)

11:19 IOWA
1/10-W42 - Green passes to Reid for gain of 31 (Johnson)
1/10-W11 - Lazar over rg for gain of 1 (Holm)
2/9 -W10 - Blatcher around re for gain of 4 (Johnson)
3/5 -W6 - Blatcher around for TD
Morton holds, Schilling kicks, PAT is good
SCORE: IOWA 31, WISCONSIN 17

10:07 WISCONSIN
Schilling kicks off to Green for return of 7 (Webb)
1/10-W16 - Kalasmiki pass intended for Charles is intercepted by Becker

397

9:55 IOWA
1/10-W42 - Lazar over rg for gain of 3 (Relich)
2/7 -W39 - Green pass intended for Burke is incomplete
3/7 -W39 - Blatcher around re for gain of 2 (Gordon)
4/5 -W37 - Wisconsin penalized 5 yds for illegal procedure
4/1 -W33 - Lazar over rg for gain of 3
1/10-W30 - Blatcher around le for gain of 9 (Gordon)
2/1 -W21 - Lazar over rg for gain of 11 (Gordon)
Wisconsin penalized half distance to goal for personal foul
1/G -W5 - Blatcher over rg for TD
Morton holds, Schilling kicks, PAT is good
SCORE: IOWA 38, WISCONSIN 17

8:03 WISCONSIN
Schilling kicks off to out of bounds. Iowa penalized 5 yds for illegal procedure. Schilling kicks off to Matthews for return of 16. (Webb)
1/10-W26 - Kalasmiki passes to Sydnor for gain of 3 (Skradis)
2/7 -W29 - Souza around re for gain of 5. Wisconsin penalized for holding
2/17-W19 - Kalasmiki passes to Stauss for gain of 10
3/7 -W29 - Kalasmiki pass intended for Sydnor is incomplete
4/7 -W29 - Kiltz punts to Reid for return of 9 (40 yard punt) (McCoy)

6:17 IOWA
1/10-I40 - Blatcher over rt for gain of 5 (Houston)
2/5 -I45 - McKillip over lg for gain of 2 (Vine)
3/3 -I47 - Commings pass intended for McKillip is incomplete
4/3 -I47 - Holsclaw punts to Schieble for return of 1 (37 yard punt)

4:50 WISCONSIN
1/10-W17 - Kalasmiki pass intended for Charles is incomplete
2/10-W17 - Kalasmiki passes to Charles for gain of 15
1/10-W32 - Charles around re for gain of 5 (Krieher)
2/5 -W37 - Kalasmiki passes to Charles for gain of 13 (Kevin Ellis)
1/10-50 - Kalasmiki passes to Sydnor for gain of 3 (Kent Ellis)
2/7 -I47 - Kalasmiki passes to Charles for gain of 17
1/10-I30 - Kalasmiki passes to Charles for gain of 11 (Webb)

1/10-I19 - Kalasmiki pass intended for Charles, intercepted by Kent Ellis, fumbles, recovered by Souza, return of 1
1/10-I14 - Kalasmiki passes to Souza for TD
Kalasmiki holds, Veith kicks, PAT is good
SCORE: IOWA 38, WISCONSIN 24

1:43 IOWA
Brhely kicks off to Brady for no return
1/10-I49 - O'Hanlon around re for gain of 5
Iowa penalized for holding
1/26-I33 - Blatcher over rg for gain of 1 (Cabral)
2/25-I34 - Blatcher around le for gain of
Iowa penalized for clipping
3/39-I20 - Commings passes to O'Hanlon for loss of 7 (Souza)
4/46-I13 - Holsclaw punts to Mathews for fair catch (39 yard kick)

0:25 WISCONSIN
1/10-W48 - Kalasmiki passes to Sydnor for gain of 11 (Kent Ellis)
1/10-I37 - Kalasmiki pass intended for Charles is incomplete

FINAL SCORE:
IOWA 38, WISCONSIN 24

National Collegiate Athletic Association
FINAL TEAM STATISTICS

	IOWA	WISCONSIN
First Downs	20	20
Rushes—Yards	54/266	33/108
Passing Yards	135	266
Return Yards	19	1
Passes	11/19/0	21/35/4
Punts	9/35/9	6/39.0
Fumbles—Lost	3/2	3/1
Penalties—Yards	8/97	6/43

NOVEMBER 18, 1978

PURDUE
VS.
MICHIGAN
Michigan Stadium
Temp: 41°
Wind: SW 17mph
Skies: Overcast and cold
FIRST QUARTER

Purdue won the toss and elected to receive. Michigan defends the s goal.
Virgil kicked off to Moss in the P endzone where he downed it.
15:00 PURDUE
1/10-P20 - Herrmann passed for Young incomplete.
2/10-P20 - Herrmann rolled right for 2 (Meter)
3/8 -P22 - Herrmann passed to Harris for 7 (Jolly)
4/1 -P29 - Linville punted dead on the M32 (39 yd. punt)

14:04 MICHIGAN
1/10-M32 - Huckleby at rg for 4 (Loushin)
2/6 -M36 - Leach rolled off lt for 24 (Harris)
1/10-P40 - Leach rolled at lt for 4 (Clark)
2/6 -P36 - Davis at center for 5 (Loushin)
3/1 -P31 - Davis at rt for 4 (Clark)
1/10-P27 - Clayton at lt for 4 (Jackson)
2/6 -P23 - Leach rolled inside re for 5 (Johanson)
3/1 -P18 - M penalized 5 for ill. proc.
3/6 -P23 - Leach passed to Huckleby for 8 (Motts)
1/10-P15 - Davis at center for 3 (Motts)
2/7 -P12 - Huckleby was unable to control the pitch at re and fumbled it out for 1.
3/6 -P11 - Leach passed to Clayton in the P endzone for the M TD. Dickey held while Willner converted. 68 yds. in 11 plays.
MICHIGAN 7 PURDUE 7 Time: 8:57 rem.

Virgil kicked off to Moss in the P endzone where it was downed.
8:57 PURDUE
1/10-P20 - Macon at rg for 1 (Greer)
2/9 -P21 - Herrmann passed for Macon incomplete.
3/9 -P21 - Herrmann passed for Macon and Braman intercepted it on the P35 and he ret'd 3 (Macon, Eubank)

8:11 MICHIGAN
1/10-P32 - Davis at rt for 10 (Johanson)
1/10-P22 - Huckleby took a pitchout at le for 2 (Moss)
2/8 -P20 - Huckleby at lg for 5 (Johanson)
3/3 -P15 - Leach passed to Clayton complete out of bounds—incomplete.
4/3 -P15 - Dickey held while Willner kicked a 32 yd. field goal from the P22.
MICHIGAN 10 PURDUE 0 Time: 6:53.

Virgil kicked off to Moss who downed it in the P endzone.
6:53 PURDUE
1/10-P20 - Herrmann caught by Trgovac for 4.
2/14-P16 - Macon on draw at rg for 4 AND M penalized 15 for face-mask.
1/10-P35 - Macon at le for 3 (Trgovac)
2/7 -P38 - Herrmann passed to Young for 12.
1/10- 50 - Macon at center for 2 (Simpkins)
2/8 -M48 - Oliver was hit by Simpkins, fumbled and Seabron recovered for M at the P39 (13 on the play)

4:40 MICHIGAN
1/10-P39 - Davis at lg for 6 (Motts)
2/4 -P33 - Leach rolled inside le for 27 (Moss)
1/G -P6 - Leach caught behind rt for −1 (Motts)
2/G -P7 - Davis at center for 1 (Floyd)
3/G -P6 - Leach's pass for Feaster incomplete, broken up by Moss.
4/G -P6 - Dickey held while Willner's field goal attempt from the P13 was blocked, and downed at the P 10. Time: 2:18.

PURDUE
1/10-P10 - Macon at lg for 4 (Greer)
2/6 -P14 - Macon at re for 7 (Braman)
1/10-P21 - Macon at lt for 2 (Simpkins)
2/8 -P23 - Pope at lg for no gain (Greer)
3/8 -P23 - Oliver passed to Pope for 11 (Bell)
1/10-P34 - Augustyniak off rt for 22 (Simpkins)

**END OF THE QUARTER:
MICHIGAN 10 PURDUE 0**

M had 20 plays for 123 yds. P had 18 plays for 60 yds.

SECOND QUARTER

PURDUE
1/10-M44 - Augustyniak at re for 2
2/8 -M42 - Oliver lost 12 when hit by Cannavino
3/20-P46 - Oliver rolled left for 5 (Simpkins)
4/15-M49 - Linville punted to Harden on the M14, faircatch (35 yd. punt)

13:29 MICHIGAN
1/10-M14 - Huckleby at rt for 2
2/8 -M16 - Leach rolled right for 15 (Moss)
1/10-M31 - Davis inside le for 27 (Harris)
1/10-P42 - Huckleby at lt for 5 (Jackson)
2/5 -P37 - Davis at rt for 8 (Johanson)
1/10-P29 - Huckleby at center for 2 (Clark)
2/8 -P27 - Davis at center for 2 (Turner)
3/6 -P25 - Leach's pass for Clayton broken up by Johanson.
4/6 -P25 - Dickey held while Willner's 42 yd. field goal attempt was short.

399

9:24 PURDUE
1/10-P25 - Pope at rg for no gain (Cannavino)
2/10-P25 - Macon took pitchback at re for 14 (Harden)
1/10-P39 - Macon at center for 1 (Trgovac)
2/9 -P40 - Oliver passed for Burrell incomplete.
3/9 -P40 - Macon hit behind re for '3 by Meter.
4/12-P37 - Linville punted to Jolly, fair catch at M24 (39 yd. punt)

7:06 MICHIGAN
1/10-M24 - Davis at rg for 6 (Motts)
2/4 -M30 - Huckleby at lg for 5 (Johanson)
1/10-M35 - Leach at lt for 4 (Clark)
2/6 -M39 - Leach passed to Feaster for 18 (Harris)
1/10-P43 - Davis at lt for 4 (Loushin)
2/4 -P39 - Leach rolled off re for 17 (Supan)
1/10-P22 - Davis at rt for 17 (Harris)
1/G -P5 - Davis at rt for 2, BUT M penalized 5 for offside.
1/G -P10 - Huckleby at center for 5 (Johanson)
2/G -P5 - Leach hit by Supan for −5 behind lt.
3/G -P10 - Leach passed to Marsh in the P endzone for the M TD.
Dickey held while Willner converted.
76 yds in 10 plays. MICHIGAN 17 PURDUE 0 Time: 2:27.

Virgil kicked off out of bounds. Virgil's second kick from the M35 was taken by Augustyniak at the P27 where he downed it.

2:23 PURDUE
1/10-P27 - Oliver passed for Harris incomplete.
2/10-P27 - Macon at rg on draw for 4 (Trgovac)
3/6 -P31 - Oliver's pass for Harris incomplete.
4/6 -P31 - Linville's punt downed on the M17, 52 yd punt.

1:21 MICHIGAN
1/10-M17 - Huckleby at lt for 3 (Loushin)
2/7 -M20 - Davis at lg for 2 (Motts)
3/5 -M22 - Davis at rt for 7, BUT M penalized 5 for delay.
3/10-M17 - Leach fell down behind center for −2.

**END OF THE HALF:
MICHIGAN 17 PURDUE 0**

M had 21 plays for 145 yds. P had 11 plays for 11 yds.

THIRD QUARTER

M receives. P elects to defend the s goal. Sovereen kicked off to Jackson on the goalline and he ret'd to the M23

14:54 MICHIGAN
1/10-M23 - Davis at rg for 2 (Motts)
2/8 -M25 - Huckleby at lg for 9 (Turner)
1/10-M34 - Davis at lg for 2 (Loushin)
2/8 -M36 - Leach passed to G. Johnson for 7 (Motts)
3/1 -M43 - Davis at lg for 2 (Jackson)
1/10-M45 - Smith took pitchback at le and lost 2 (Turner)
2/12-M43 - Davis on draw at lt for 14 (Marks)
1/10-P43 - Davis at rt for 1 (Floyd)
2/9 -P42 - Woolfolk took pitchback at le for 10 (Clark)
1/10-P32 - Woolfolk took pitchout at re for 6 (Harris)
2/4 -P26 - Woolfolk at center for 7 (Loushin)
1/10-P19 - Davis at lg for 1 (Loushin)
2/9 -P18 - Leach's pass for Clayton broken up by Smith in the endzone.
3/9 -P18 - Leach elected to run up the center and made 10 (Floyd)
1/G -P8 - Woolfolk off rt for 3 (Moss)
2/G -P5 - Reid at center for the TD for M. Dickey held while Willner converted.
77 yds. in 16 plays. MICHIGAN 24 PURDUE 0 Time: 7:21 rem.

Virgil kicked off to Moss on the P9 and he ret'd 12 to the P21 (DeSantis)
PURDUE
1/10-P21 - Oliver hit by Trgovac for '8
2/18-P13 - Oliver's pass for Young broken up by Meter.
3/18-P13 - Oliver's pass for Pope incompiete.
4/18-P13 - Linville's punt taken by Jolly, fair catch at P43 (30 yd. punt)

6:15 MICHIGAN
1/10-P43 - Woolfolk on pitchout at re, forced out by Floyd for −1.
2/11-P44 - Woolfolk at lt for 9 (Turner)
3/2 -P35 - Davis at lg for 5 (Loushin)
1/10-P30 - Woolfolk took pitchout at re for 12 (Marks)
1/10-P18 - Davis at lt for 1 (Marks)
2/9 -P17 - Leach hit by Loushin for −7, back to pass.
3/16-P24 - Woolfolk took pitchout at le and was hit by Moss for −4.
4/20-P28 - Dickey held while Willner's 46 yd. field goal attempt was wide to the left. Time: 3:17.

NOVEMBER 18, 1978

3:17 PURDUE
1/10-P28 - Macon slipped at center for 2.
2/8 -P30 - Oliver's pass for Pope broken up by Harden.
3/8 -P30 - Oliver passed to Pope for 2 (Trgovac)
4/6 -P32 - Linville punted to Jolly on the M21 ret'd 6 (47 yd. punt) (Moss)

1:52 MICHIGAN
1/10-M27 - Woolfolk at rg for 3 (Clark)
2/7 -M30 - Leach elected to run right and made 10, AND P penalized 15 for personal foul.
1/10-P45 - Clayton at lt for 5 (Jackson)
2/5 -P40 - Dickey kept at le for no gain (Jackson)

**END OF THE QUARTER:
MICHIGAN 24 PURDUE 0**

M had 27 plays for 110 yds. P had 6 plays for −4 yds.

FOURTH QUARTER

MICHIGAN
3/5 -P40 - Leach caught by Turner for −14.
4/19-P46 - Willner punted to Pope, fair catch at P10 (44 yd. punt)

14:00 PURDUE
1/10-P10 - Macon at g for 2 (Greer)
2/8 -P12 - Oliver passed to Young for 10 (Jolly)
1/10-P22 - Pope fumbled on draw and Oliver recovered for '6.
2/16-P16 - Oliver passed to Pope for 7 (Bell)
3/9 -P23 - Oliver passed to Burrell for 5 (Needham)
4/4 -P28 - Linville punted to Harden on the M36 (36 yd punt) (Marks)

11:03 MICHIGAN
1/10-M36 - Woolfolk at rg for 3, BUT M penalized 18 for holding.
1/28-M18 - Woolfolk at center lost 2 (Loushin)
2/30-M16 - Leach's pass for Clayton incomplete.
3/30-M16 - Davis on draw at lg for 1 (Loushin)
4/29-M17 - Willner's punt blocked by Kingsbury and Adam le picked it up at the M10 and ran it in for the P TD. Time: 9:32 Oliver rolled to pass and Meter tackled him.
MICHIGAN 24 PURDUE 6

Sovereen's kickoff (onside attempt) taken by by Murray on the M49;
9:32 MICHIGAN
1/10-M49 - Leach kept at le for 4 (Marks)
2/6 -P47 - Leach rolled right for 5 (Kay)
3/1 -P42 - Davis at lg for 3 (Jackson)

1/10-P39 - Leach passed incomplete for Clayton in the P endzone, just off Clayton's fingertips.
2/10-P39 - Leach kept at le for 6 (Turner)
3/4 -P33 - Leach hit by Floyd for −12.
4/16-P45 - Willner punted into the P endzone (45 yd. punt)

6:08 PURDUE
1/10-P20 - Augustyniak at le for 13 (Harden)
1/10-P33 - Augustyniak at le for no gain.
2/10-P33 - Oliver elected to run and went out after 16, and M penalized 15 for personal foul.
1/10-M36 - Oliver's pass for Burrell broken up by Meter.
2/10-M36 - Oliver's pass for Young incomplete.
3/10-M36 - Oliver passed to Pope for 19 (Harden)
1/10-M17 - Oliver passed for Young incomplete, BUT M penalized 7 for pass interference.
1/10-M10 - Oliver passed for Pope incomplete.
2/10-M10 - Macon at center for 2 (Bell)
3/8 -M8 - Oliver hit by Simpkins for '12.
4/20-M20 - Oliver's pass for Pope incomplete.

2:49 MICHIGAN
1/10-M20 - Davis at rg for 4 (Motts)
2/6 -M24 - Woolfolk at rt for 6 (Marks)
1/10-M30 - Davis at rg for 3 (Marks)
2/7 -M33 - Woolfolk took pitchback at le for 10 (Kay)
1/10-M43 - Woolfolk at rg for 5 (Loushin)

**END OF THE GAME:
MICHIGAN 24 PURDUE 6**

M had 15 plays for 19 yds. P had 15 plays for 56 yds.

ILLINOIS
VS.
MINNESOTA
Memorial Stadium, Minneapolis
Temp: 28
Wind: W 7 mph
Skies -
FIRST QUARTER

Minnesota wins toss, elect to defend west goal, Illinois to receive Rogind kickoff hits into end zone and rolls out for touchback

15:00 ILLINOIS
1/10-IL20 - Weber right tackle 2 yds (Ronan)
2/8 -Il22 - Weiss option keeper right 1 yard
3/7 -IL23 - Weiss pass intended for Barnes on R. sidelines (Snyder hit knocks ball away)
4/7 -IL23 - Finzer punt fumbled by Brown, recovered by Edwards on M49 (27 yd punt)

13:28 MINNESOTA
1/10-MN49 - Barber up middle 2 yds (Flynn)
2/8 -IL49 - Barber quick pitch left, cuts back 5 yds (Sullivan)
3/3 -IL44 - White starts early, in motion 5 yd penalty
3/8 -IL49 - Avery pass for White R sidelines overthrown and incomplete
4/8 -IL49 - Smith punt to Hardy fair catch at IL15 34 yd punt

12:20 ILLINOIS
1/10-IL15 - Weiss option keeper left, breaks open 9 yds (Brown)
2/1 -IL24 - Weiss sneak L 1 yd gain (team)
1/10-IL25 - Weiss quick out pass to Barnes L sidelines complete 9 yds (Snyder)
2/1 -IL34 - Weber up middle 4 yds (Meyer)
1/10-IL38 - Weiss option R, throws bad pitchout but Weiss recovers own fumble 8 yd loss
2/18-IL30 - Weiss back to pass, runs R 7 yds (Meyer)
3/11-IL37 - Weiss back to pass, rushed from L outside, Brown sack for 10 yd loss
4/21-IL27 - Finzer punt to Bailey on MN 28, returns 10 yds 45 yd kick (Thomas) 15 yd clipping penalty on Minnesota

8:02 MINNESOTA
1/10-MN23 - Barber quick pitch right 7 yds (Gillen, Hardy)
2/3 -MN30 - Barber up middle 7 yds (Levitt)
1/10-MN37 - White off L side 7 yds (Boner, Tuchery)
2/3 -MN44 - White breaks open up middle 22 yds, fumbles but recovered by Avery
1/10-IL34 - Barber quick pitch right 9 yds (Hardy)
2/1 -IL25 - White off L side on fake pitch 4 yds (Gillen)
1/10-IL21 - Barber quick pitch L no gain (Gillen)
2/10-IL21 - Barber up middle 6 yds (Sullivan)
3/4 -IL15 - Barber quick pitch right, cuts back breaks two tackles 15 yd TOUCHDOWN run 77 yd drive in 9 plays 10:12 ET, 4:48 TL Rogind hits 50th straight EP kick
MINNESOTA 7, ILLINOIS 0

MM penalized 15 yds on kickoff/Barber spiked ball in end zone after TD run Rogind kickoff to Foster on IL 18, 9 yd return (Pepper)

4:44 ILLINOIS
1/10-IL27 - Dismuke at L tackle 3 yds (Burns, Brown)
2/7 -IL30 - Weiss back to pass, receivers cover, Cunningham sack for 2 yd loss
3/9 -IL28 - Dismuke delay L 4 yd gain (Roman, Friberg)
4/5 -IL32 - Finzer punt low and short, rolls dead on MN34 33 yd punt

2:41 MINNESOTA
1/10-MN34 - Barber up middle 4 yds (Thiede)
2/6 -MN38 - White off L side, on delay pitch 5 yds (Sullivan)
3/1 -MN43 - Barber off L side/tackle 6 yds (Carmien)
1/10-MN49 - Barber quick pitch right, Gillen crashes/hit for 1 yd loss
2/11-MN48 - Avery pass intercepted by Hardy, returns 17 yds MN45

:50 ILLINOIS
1/10-MN45 - Weiss back to pass, rushed/tackle by Friberg Blanshan for 5 yd loss
2/15- 50 - Weiss pass complete to Boeke L sideline 5 yd (Snyder)

**END OF FIRST QUARTER:
MINNESOTA 7, ILLINOIS 0**

SECOND QUARTER

ILLINOIS
3/10-MN45 - Weiss completes look-in L 12 yards (Snyder)
1/10-MN33 - Weber at R tackle 4 yards (Meyer, Friberg)
2/6 -MN29 - Dismuke takes option pitch L 9 yards (Edwards)
1/10-MN20 - Weber slants right tackle 2 yards (Meyer, Friberg)
2/8 -MN18 - Weiss option pitch R, fumbled and recovered by Burns 3 yd rushing loss

NOVEMBER 18, 1978

13:01 MINNESOTA
1/10-MN21 - White at L tackle 6 yards (Gillen)
2/4 -MN27 - Barber at middle Bailey in motion, MN penalized 5 yards
2/9 -MN22 - illegal procedure (Murtha) 5 yd penalty
2/14-MN17 - Artis delay up middle, breaks open for 15 yards (Gillen)
1/10-MN32 - White up middle 5 yards (Carmien)
2/5 -MN37 - Barber quick pitch R 13 yards (Blalock)
1/10- 50 - Barber quick pitch R. breaks open for 30 yards (Thiede, Adams)
1/10-IL20 - White slant left 3 yards (Gillen)
2/7 -IL17 - Barber quick pitch right, cuts back for 8 yards (Adams)
1/G -IL9 - Barber quick pitch right, 5 yards (Sullivan, Durrell)
2/G -IL4 - Barber at L tackle 3 yards (Adams, Bonney)
3/G -IL1 - Barber at L tackle 1 yd TOUCHDOWN run 0:55 ET, 8:05 TP 79 yard drive in 10 plays. Rogind kick off to Foster on IL9, returns 11 yards (Hoffman)

8:01 ILLINOIS
1/10-IL20 - Dismuke at L tackle 5 yards (Brown, Meyer)
2/5 -IL25 - Dismuke at R tackle 4 yards (Cunningham, Brown)
3/1 -IL29 - Weber slants R 5 yards (Blanshan)
1/10-IL34 - Weiss pass complete to Dismuke delay up middle 17 yards (Brown)
1/10-MN49 - Dismuke sweeps left, no gain tackle by Burns
2/10-MN49 - Weiss pass R sidelines to Barnes, Snyder knocks ball away
3/10-MN49 - Weiss pass intended for Lopez, Snyder knocks away, Foxworth intercepts and returns 16 yards (MN personal foul on runback, 15 yd penalty after play was over — Blanshan late hit)

4:49 MINNESOTA
1/10-MN22 - Barber delay up middle, breaks open for 15 yards (Hardy)
1/10-MN37 - Avery back to pass, runs R cut of bounds for no gain
2/10-MN37 - Barber at L tackle (MN illegal procedure/5 yd penalty)
3/15-MN32 - Avery pass L to R over middle complete to Bailey 20 yards
1/10-IL48 - White slants L, stumbles down after breaking open 4 yd gain
2/6 -IL44 - Barber quick pitch R (MN Stein holding/15 yd penalty)
2/21-MN41 - Avery screen L to White complete 11 yds (Hardy)
3/10-IL48 - Barber delay up middle 8 yards (Hardy, Carmien)

4/2 -IL40 - Smith punt covered by MN player on IL6 (34 yard punt)

1:51 ILLINOIS
1/10-IL6 - Thomas slants L no gain (Friberg)
2/10-IL6 - Weiss option R 3 yards (Ronan)
3/7 -IL9 - Weiss fake pass/run up middle 17 yards (Cunningham)
1/10-IL26 - Weiss pass intended for Sherrod, Cunningham defending incomplete
2/10-IL26 - Dismuke draw up middle 1 yard (Meyers, Burns)
3/9 -IL27 - Weiss option keeper R 3 yd gain (Snyder)
4/6 -IL30 - Finzer punt to Bailey on MN31 no return (Taylor) 39 yd punt

:02 MINNESOTA
1/10-MN31 - White at L tackle breaks open for 23 yds

**END OF HALF:
MINNESOTA 14, ILLINOIS 0**

THIRD QUARTER

Rogind kickoff to Foster on IL6, returns 31 yards (Rogind)
14:52 ILLINOIS
1/10-IL37 - Weber slides outside L tackle 9 yds (Foxworth, Cunningham)
2/1 -IL46 - Weiss option keeper L 4 yds (Fauhnhorst)
1/10- 50 - Weiss pass intended for Weber incomplete/low off hands
2/10- 50 - Weiss option L, bad pitchout but Weiss recovers for 1 yd gain
3/9 -MN49 - Weiss back to pass, runs R but Sytsma runs him down for 8 yd loss
4/17-IL43 - Finzer punt covered by II on MN 32 (25 yd punt)

12:17 MINNESOTA
1/10-MN32 - White up middle 2 yd gain (Durrell)
2/8 -MN34 - Barber quick pitch left 6 yards (Sullivan)
3/2 -MN40 - White slants left (Gillen, Durrell) 1 yd gain
4/1 -MN41 Smith punt to Bonner, returns 12 yards (Thompson) 41 yd punt

10:29 ILLINOIS
1/10-IL30 - Thomas slants R 5 yds (Burns, Cunningham)
2/5 -IL35 - Thomas slants R 1 yd (Friberg)
3/4 -IL36 - Weiss back to pass, runs up middle 15 yds (Fahnhorst, Cunningham)
1/10-MN49 - Weiss pass deflected in line by Cunningham/incomplete

403

2/10-MN49 - Weiss pass intended for Rouse off hands/incomplete
3/10-MN49 - Weiss back to pass/QB draw 5 yards (Ronan, Fahnhorst)
4/5 -MN44 - Finzer punt bounces into end zone/touchback 44 yd punt

7:45 MINNESOTA
1/10-MN20 - Barber quick pitch L 21 yd run (Tucker)
1/10-MN41 - MN Murtha illegal procedure/5 yd penalty
1/15-MN36 - White slants R no gain (Gillen, Flynn)
2/15-MN36 - Barber quick pitch RL 2 yds (Ranshaw)
3/13-MN38 - Smith punt to Hardy on IL30, returns 6 yds (Cunningham) 42 yd punt

5:26 ILLINOIS
1/10-IL36 - Weber slants R 3 yds (Friberg)
2/7 -IL39 - Weiss complete to Barnes on RL sidelines 6 yds
3/1 -IL45 - Weiss QB sneak 1 yd (Team)
1/10-IL46 - Weiss option keeper L, breaks open/runs thru two tackles 43 yd run (Foxworth)
1/10-MN11 - Strader at L tackle 3 yds
2/7 -MN8 - Weber at R tackle powers to 8 yd TOUCHDOWN 12:30 ET, 2:30 TL 64 yard drive in 6 plays IL ran for 2, no good (Brown)
  MINNESOTA 14, ILLINOIS 6

Finzer kickoff to Bailey on MN8, returns 14 yards (MN penalty for clipping/10 yds)

2:17 MINNESOTA
1/10-MN13 - Barber quick pitch L but MN Paqueate holding 7 yd penalty
1/17-MN6 - Barber up middle no gain (Sullivan)

2/17-MN6 - White off L tackle 5 yds Sullivan
3/12-MN11 - Barber quick pitch R 4 yds (Gillen)
4/8 -MN15 - Smith punt to Hardy on IL41, returns 8 yds (Burns) 44 yd punt

:12 ILLINOIS
1/10-IL49 - Weiss QB draw 4 yd gain (Blanshan)

END OF THIRD QUARTER:
MINNESOTA 14, ILLINOIS 6
FOURTH QUARTER

ILLINOIS
2/6 -MN47 - Strader draw R 2 yds (Meyer)
3/4 -MN45 - Weiss tries QB draw, Blanshan tackle for 2 yd loss
4/6 -MN47 - Finzer punt rolls dead on MN12 35 yd punt

13:41 MINNESOTA
1/10-MN12 - Barber quick pitch right 9 yards (Hardy)
2/1 -MN21 - Barber breaks up middle 12 yds (Flynn)
1/10-MN33 - Barber slants R 5 yds (Levitt, Hardy)
2/5 -MN38 - Barber up middle 4 yds (Durrell)
3/1 -MN42 - White slants right 3 yds (Gillen)
1/10-MN45 - Barber off L tackle 4 yds (Gillen, Bonner)
2/6 -MN49 - Barber quick pitch left 1 yd (Gillen, Thornton)
3/5 - 50 - Barber quick pitch R, breaks open for 18 yds (Gillen)
1/10-IL32 - White slants left 3 yds (Durrell, Gillen)
2/7 -IL29 - Barber quick pitch left 3 yds (Gillen, Adams)

404

NOVEMBER 18, 1978

3/4 -IL26 - Artis pitch right 3 yds (Gillen, Hardy)
4/1 -IL23 - White at R tackle 3 yds (Gillen, Hardy)
1/10-IL20 - Artis quick pitch right no gain (Ramshaw)
2/10-IL20 - Avery pass for Bailey overthrown and incomplete
3/10-IL20 - Artis draw L 9 yds (Ramshaw, Fonner)
4/1 -IL11 - White vaults over middle 3 yds (team)
1/G -IL8 - Artis up middle 2 yds (Flynn, Gillen)
2/G -IL6 - Barber quick pitch right no gain (Adams, Sullivan)
3/G -IL6 - Barber draw L 4 yds (Gillen)
4/G -IL2 - Rogind field goal GOOD from 19 yds 11:53 ET, 3:07 TP 88 yard drive with FG on 20th play
MINN 17, ILLINOIS 6

Rogind kickoff to Norman on IL 25, returns 5 yds (Car, Fahnhorst)

3:02 ILLINOIS
1/10-IL30 - Weiss pass intended for Barnes middle/behind him and incomplete
2/10-IL30 - Weiss pass intercepted by Snyder on IL45, returns 21 yds (Weber)

2:44 MINNESOTA
1/10-IL24 - Thompson slot/back reverse R 4 yds, slips down when cutting
2/6 -IL28 - Barber quick pitch left, Gillen tackle for 5 yd loss
3/11-IL25 - Carlson pass complete to Cooper 12 yds (Hardy)
1/10-IL13 - White up middle 2 yds (Gillen, Burlingame)
2/8 -ILL11 - Barbar at R tackle 2 yds (Ramshaw)
3/6 -IL9 - Artis quick pitch L, cuts back 8 yds to IL 1 (Rmashaw)
1/G -IL1 - White hits middle no gain (team)
2/G -IL - White scores 1 yd TOUCHDOWN at R tackle 14:48 ET, :12 TG 24 yd drive in 8 plays Roginds EPK good
MINNESOTA 24, ILLINOIS 6

Rogind kickoff to Norman, returns 10 yds (Pepper)

:09 ILLINOIS
1/10-IL36 - Weiss pass knocked a way by Edwards as game ends

END OF GAME:
MINNESOTA 24, ILLINOIS 6

National Collegiate Athletic Association
FINAL TEAM STATISTICS
November 18, 1978

	ILLINOIS	MINNESOTA
First Downs	12	19
Rushing	10	17
Passing	2	2
Penalty	0	0
Rushing Attempts	41	65
Yards Rushing	188	382
Yards Lost Rushing	38	16
Net Yards Rushing	150	366
Net Yards Passing	49	43
Passes Attempted	15	6
Passes Completed	5	3
Had Intercepted	2	1
Total Offensive Plays	56	71
Total Net Yards	199	409
Average Gain Per Play	3.55	5.76
Fumbles: Number—Lost	3/1	2/0
Penalties: Number—Yards	0/0	11/102
Interceptions: Number—Yards	1/17	2/37
Number of Punts—Yards	7/249	5/195
Average Per Punt	35.6	39.0
Punt Returns: Number—Yards	3/26	3/9
Kickoff Returns: Number—Yards	5/66	1/14

MICHIGAN STATE VS. NORTHWESTERN
Evanston, Ill.

Northwestern co-captains, the seniors on the squad, meet at midfield with the Michigan State co-captains Melvin Land, Leroy McGee, and Terry Williams. Michigan State wins the toss and elects to receive; Northwestern will kick and defend the south goal

FIRST QUARTER

Poulos kickoff taken by S. Smith at the MSU6 and returned 21 yds
14:55 MICHIGAN STATE
1/10-MS27 - McGee RT for 7 yds (Kendzicky)
2/3 -MS34 - E. Smith pass to Gibson incomplete
3/3 -MS34 - S. Smith LE for 5 yds (McGlade)
1/10-MS39 - McGee LT for 10 yds (Geegan)
1/10-MS49 - Reeves RT for 3 yds (Dunlea)
2/7 -NU48 - E. Smith pass to Gibson complete for 20 yds (McGlade)
1/10-NU28 - E. Smith pass to Gibson complete for 11 yds (Hemphill)
1/10-NU17 - McGee RT for 5 yds (Kern)
2/5 -NU12 - Reeves LE for 10 yds (Butler)
1/G -NU2 - Schramm middle for 1 yd (Corona)
2/G -NU1 - E. Smith pass to Gibson complete for 1 yd and a touchdown 10:47
PAT: Andersen kick good 73 yds in 11 plays
SCORE: MICHIGAN STATE 7 NORTHWESTERN 0

Schario kickoff taken by Hill at NU3 and returned 17 yds
10:42 NORTHWESTERN
1/10-NU20 - Cammon middle for 5 yds (Bass)
2/5 -NU25 - Strasser pass to McGee complete for 13 yds
1/10-NU38 - Cammon RT for 4 yds (Decker)
2/6 -NU42 - Strasser pass to Poulos incomplete (Bass)
3/6 -NU42 - Strasser pass to Bogan incomplete
4/6 -NU42 - Christensen punt taken by S. Smith at the MS21 and returned 21 yds; 37 yd. punt

9:15 MICHIGAN STATE
1/10-MS42 - McGee RE for 6 yds (Hoffman)
2/4 -MS48 - Reeves pitch LE for -3 yds (McGlade)
3/7 -MS45 - E. Smith pass to Byrd incomplete
4/7 -MS45 - Stachowicz punt blocked by Berg, rolls out of bounds at MS23

7:38 NORTHWESTERN
1/10-MS23 - Cammon pitch RE for 5 yds (Anderson)
2/5 -MS18 - Strasser pass to McGee incomplete
3/5 -MS18 - Strasser pass to Tiberi incomplete
4/5 -MS18 - Poulos, 36-yard field goal 6:48 5 yds in 4 plays
SCORE: MICHIGAN STATE 7 NORTHWESTERN 3

Poulos kickoff taken by Reeves at MS1 and returned 22 yds
6:43 MICHIGAN STATE
1/10-MS23 - Middleton LT for 11 yds (Butler)
1/10-MS34 - S. Smith pitch LE for 7 yds (Lawrence)
2/3 -MS41 - Middleton RT for 2 yds (Dunlea)
3/1 -MS43 - S. Smith LT for no gain (Dunlea)
4/1 -MS43 - Middleton middle for 2 yds (Corona)
1/10-MS45 - E. Smith pass to Byrd complete for 15 yds (Kern)
1/10-NU40 - McGee LE for 3 yds (Lawrence)
2/7 -NU37 - Reeves LT for 1 yd (Taylor)
3/6 -NU36 - S. Smith middle for 15 yds (McGlade)
1/10-NU21 - McGee LT for no gain (Dunlea)
2/10-NU21 - Smith pass to Gibson incomplete
3/10-NU21 - McGee middle for 5 yds (Kendzicky)
4/5 -NU16 - E. Smith pass to Schramm incomplete

1:20 NORTHWESTERN
1/10-NU16 - Strasser pass to Bogan incomplete
2/10-NU16 - Hill middle for 2 yds (Land)
3/8 -NU18 - Strasser pass to Poulos complete for 2 yds (Savage)
4/6 -NU20 - Christensen punt rolls dead at MS8; 72 yd punt (Play nullified)
PENALTY: face-masking MSU accepted
1/10-NU35 - Strasser pass to Bogan incomplete

**END OF QUARTER:
MICHIGAN STATE 7 NORTHWESTERN 3**

SECOND QUARTER
NORTHWESTERN
2/10-NU35 - Cammon pitch RE for 14 yds (Graves)
1/10-NU49 - Strasser pass to McGee complete for 5 yds (Stanton)
2/5 -MS46 - Tibert RT for 3 yds (Bass) was Tiberi
3/2 -MS43 - Strasser pass to Bogan incomplete
4/2 -MS43 - Hemphill run from punt formation for 3 yds (Land)

406

NOVEMBER 18, 1978

1/10-MS40 - Strasser pass to McGee incomplete
2/10-MS40 - Strasser pass to North intercepted by Savage at MS29 and returned 5 yds

13:17 MICHIGAN STATE
1/10-MS34 - Hans middle for 4 yds (Kern)
2/6 -MS38 - Reeves RT for 2 yds (Payne)
3/4 -MS40 - E. Smith to Brammer incomplete
4/4 -MS40 - Stachowicz punt taken by Geegan at NU17 and returned 10 yds

11:48 NORTHWESTERN
1/10-NU27 - Cammon RT for 3 yds (Bass)
2/7 -NU30 - Strasser pass to Tiberi complete for -1 yds (Stanton)
PENALTY: clipping NU accepted..... play nullified
2/22-NU15 - Cammon middle for 1 yd (Bass)
3/21-NU16 - Hill RE for 11 yds (Anderson)
4/10-NU27 - Christensen punt taken by S. Smith at MS35 and returned 18 yds; 38 yd punt

10:10 MICHIGAN STATE
1/10-NU47 - E. Smith pass to Byrd complete for 12 yds
1/10-NU35 - Hans middle for 9 yds (Gildner)
2/1 -NU26 - E. Smith pass to Gibson incomplete
3/1 -NU26 - Hans middle for 4 yds (Kern)
1/10-NU22 - E. Smith scrambles RE for 10 yds (Kern)
1/10-NU12 - E. Smith pass to Byrd incomplete
2/10-NU12 - Hans LT for 6 yds (Lawrence)
3/4 -NU6 - Middleton RG for 3 yds (Corona)
4/1 -NU3 - Middleton middle for 1 yd (Lawrence)
1/G -NU2 - Reeves LT for 2 yds and a touchdown 7:06
PAT: Andersen kick good 47 yds in 10 plays
SCORE: MICHIGAN STATE 14 NORTHWESTERN 3

Schario kickoff downed in endzone for a touchback
7:06 NORTHWESTERN
1/10-NU20 - Hill pitch RE for -7 yds (Anderson)
2/17-NU13 - Strasser fumbles snap, recovered by MS Decker at NU8 (loss of 5 yds)

6:15 MICHIGAN STATE
1/G -NU8 - S. Smith pitch RE for 7 yds (Lawrence)
2/G -NU1 - Schramm middle for 1 yd and a touchdown 5:37
PAT: PENALTY: Ill. motion MS accepted
PAT: Andersen kick good 8 yds in 2 plays
SCORE: MICHIGAN STATE 21 NORTHWESTERN 3

Schario kickoff downed in endzone for a touchback
5:37 NORTHWESTERN
1/10-NU20 - Hill RT for 3 yds (Graves)
2/7 -NU23 - Strasser pass to Bogan complete for 11 yds (Burroughs)
1/10-NU34 - Cammon pitch RE for 8 yds (Bass)
2/2 -NU42 - Hill RT for 1 yd (Fields)
3/1 -NU43 - Strasser pass to Hill incomplete
4/1 -NU43 - Christensen punt downed at MS 27

3:27 MICHIGAN STATE
1/10-MS27 - S. Smith RT for 5 yds (Kern)
2/5 -MS32 - Reeves RT for 8 yds (Taylor)
1/10-MS40 - E. Smith pass to Gibson incomplete
2/10-MS40 - E. Smith pass to Brammer complete for 11 yds (Lawrence)
1/10-NU49 - E. Smith pass to Byrd complete for 20 yds (McGlade)
1/10-NU29 - S. Smith middle for 3 yds (Taylor)
2/7 -NU26 - S. Smith RE for 18 yds (Geegan)
1/G -NU8 - Reeves RE for 8 yds, fumbles, recovered in endzone by Gibson for touchdown 0:40
PAT: Andersen kick good 73 yds in 8 plays
SCORE: MICHIGAN STATE 28 NORTHWESTERN 3

Schario kickoff goes out of endzone for touchback
0:40 NORTHWESTERN
1/10-NU20 - Strasser pass to Cammon incomplete (Fields)
2/10-NU20 - Cammon LT for 3 yds (Bass)

**END OF HALF:
MICHIGAN STATE 28 NORTHWESTERN 3**

THIRD QUARTER

Shario kickoff downed in endzone for touchback
14:56 NORTHWESTERN
1/10-NU20 - Hill LT for no gain (Decker)
2/10-NU20 - Strasser pass to Bogan incomplete
3/10-NU20 - Strasser pass to McGee incomplete
4/10-NU20 - Christensen punt downed at NU45 (25 yd punt)

14:04 MICHIGAN STATE
1/10-NU45 - S. Smith pitch RE for 4 yds...
PENALTY: CLIPPING MSU accepted
1/21-MS44 - E. Smith pass to Gibson complete for 6 yds
PENALTY: personal foul NU accepted
1/10-NU35 - Schramm middle for 7 yds (Kern)

407

2/3 -NU28 - Gibson reverse LE for 7 yds
1/10-NU21 - S. Smith LE for 12 yds
   (Lawrence)
1/10-NU9 - McGee RT for 9 yds and a
   touchdown 12:40
   PAT: Andersen kick good 45 yds in 6
   plays
   **SCORE: MICHIGAN STATE 35
   NORTHWESTERN 3**

Schario kickoff rolls out of bounds PENALTY:
ill. procedure MSU accepted
Schario kickoff taken by Hill at NU2 and
returned 18 yds
12:37 NORTHWESTERN
1/10-NU20 - Strasser pass to McGee
   incomplete PENALTY: pass interference
   MSU
1/10-NU26 - Hill middle for 6 yds (Otis)
2/4 -NU32 - Strasser pass to McGee
   incomplete
3/4 -NU32 - Strasser pass to Hill incomplete
4/4 -NU32 - Christensen punt fair caught at
   MS40 (28 yd punt)

11:48 MICHIGAN STATE
1/10-MS40 - E. Smith pass to S. Smith
   complete for 33 yds (Payne)
1/10-NU27 - Hans middle for 8 yds
   (Lawrence)
2/2 -NU19 - Smith pass to Byrd incomplete
3/2 -NU19 - McGee pitch RE for 2 yds (Kern)
1/10-NU17 - E. Smith pass to Schramm
   incomplete
2/10-NU17 - E. Smith sacked by Kern for -13
   yds
2/23-NU30 - S. Smith RT for 6 yds
   (Lawrence)
4/17-NU24 - Andersen, 42 yd field goal
   8:50 36 yds in 8 plays
   **SCORE: MICHIGAN STATE 38
   NORTHWESTERN 3**

Schario kickoff taken by North at NU15 and
returned 12 yds
8:46 NORTHWESTERN
1/10-NU27 - Cammon RT for 5 yds (Bass)
2/5 -NU32 - Strasser pass to Bogan
   incomplete
3/5 -NU32 - Strasser pass to Bogan
   incomplete
4/5 -NU32 - Christensen punt taken by S.
   Smith at MS33 and returned 24 yds
   35 yd kick

7:56 MICHIGAN STATE
1/10-NU43 - PENALTY: ill. procedure NU
   accepted
1/5 -NU38 - E. Smith pass to S. Smith
   complete for 6 yds (Kern)
1/10-NU32 - McGee RT for 4 yds (Geegan)
2/6 -NU28 - E. Smith pass to Brammer
   intercepted by Knafelc at NU19 and
   returned 1 yd.

6:48 NORTHWESTERN
1/10-NU20 - Tiberi pitch LE for 1 yd (Savage)
2/9 -NU21 - Strasser pass to McGee complete
   for 15 yds (Anderson)
1/10-NU36 - Tiberi middle for 5 yds (Land)
2/5 -NU41 - Strasser pass to Bogan complete
   for 12 yds (Stanton)
1/10-MS47 - Strasser pass to North
   incomplete (Otis)
2/10-MS47 - Strasser pass to Tiberi
   incomplete
3/10-MS47 - PENALTY: ill. procedure NU
   accepted
3/15-NU48 - Strasser scrambles RE for 4 yds
   (Hay)
4/11-MS48 - Christensen punt fair caught at
   MS24 (24 yd punt)

4:28 MICHIGAN STATE
1/10-MS24 - E. Smith pass to Gibson
   incomplete
2/10-MS24 - E. Smith pass to Byrd complete
   for 34 yds (Geegan)
1/10-NU42 - S. Smith middle for -2 yds
   (Dunlea)
2/12-NU44 - McGee pitch LE for -4 yds
   (Kern)
3/16-NU48 - E. Smith pass to Schramm
   complete for 11 yds (Butler)
4/5 -NU37 - Andersen field goal attempt of
   54 yds is short

1:54 NORTHWESTERN
1/10-NU37 - Tiberi middle for 3 yds (Land)
2/7 -NU40 - Strasser pass to Poulos complete
   for 5 yds (Bass)
3/2 -NU45 - Strasser keeper RE for 7 yds
   (Stanton)
1/10-MS48 - Tiberi RE for 2 yds (Stanton)

**END OF QUARTER:
MICHIGAN STATE 38 NORTHWESTERN 3**

FOURTH QUARTER

NORTHWESTERN
2/8 -MS46 - Strasser pass to North
   intercepted by MS Bass at MS35 and
   returned 2 yds

14:54 MICHIGAN STATE
1/10-MS37 - S. Smith RT for 15 yds (Kern)
1/10-NU48 - Hughes RE for 8 yds (Geegan)
2/2 -NU40 - E. Smith middle for -2 yds
   (Dunlea)
3/4 -NU42 - Middleton LT for 21 yds
   (Geegan)
1/10-NU21 - McGee LE for 7 yds (Lawrence)
2/3 -NU14 - Hughes RT for 2 yds (Kern)
3/1 -NU12 - S. Smith pitch RE for 12 yds
   and a touchdown 11:31
   PAT: Andersen kick good 63 yds in 7
   plays

NOVEMBER 18, 1978

SCORE: MICHIGAN STATE 45
NORTHWESTERN 3

Schario kickoff taken by Hill at NU3 and returned 13 yds (Muster)
11:27 NORTHWESTERN
1/10-NU16 - Tiberi LG for 2 yds (Otis)
2/8 -NU18 - Hill middle for 2 yds (Cooper)
3/6 -NU20 - Strasser sacked by Jones for -4 yds
4/10-NU16 - Christensen punt taken by Smith at MS46 and returned 2 yds (38 yd punt)

9:39 MICHIGAN STATE
1/10-MS48 - Schramm LT for 5 yds (Taylor)
2/5 -NU47 - Hughes pitch RE for 46 yds (Lawrence)
1/G -NU1 - Schramm middle for 1 yd and a touchdown 8:35
PAT: Andersen kick good 52 yards in 3 plays
SCORE: MICHIGAN STATE 52
NORTHWESTERN 3

Schario kickoff taken by North at NU16 and returned 9 yds
8:32 NORTHWESTERN
1/10-NU25 - Hill LT for 1 yd (Williams)
2/9 -NU26 - Strasser pass to McGee incomplete
3/9 -NU26 - Strasser pass to McGee incomplete
4/9 -NU26 - Christensen punt taken by Hughes at MS35 and returned 2 yds; (39 yard punt)
PENALTY: clipping MSU accepted

7:38 MICHIGAN STATE
1/10-MS22 - Schramm middle for 3 yds (Lawrence)
2/7 -MS25 - Hughes RE, reverses field for 18 yds (Butler)
1/10-MS43 - Reeves LT for 3 yds (Taylor)
2/7 -MS46 - Hughes RT for 3 yds (Payne)
3/4 -MS49 - Clark pass to Reeves complete for 11 yds (Butler)
1/10-NU40 - Clark keeper RE for 3 yds
2/7 -NU37 - Middleton up middle
PENALTY: ill. motion MSU accepted
2/12-NU42 - Clark pass to Williams incomplete
3/12-NU42 - Clark pass to Williams intercepted by Geegan at NU25 and returned 9 yds

4:08 NORTHWESTERN
1/10-NU34 - Tiberi LT for no gain (Converse)
2/10-NU34 - Webb RE for 1 yd (Converse)
3/9 -NU35 - Strasser sacked by Webb for -6 yds
4/15-NU30 - Christensen punt taken by Reeves at MS38 and returned -1 yds (32 yd punt)

2:20 MICHIGAN STATE
1/10-MS37 - Schramm middle for 4 yds (Dunlea)
2/6 -MS41 - Hughes LE for 15 yds (Bobowski) PENALTY: personal foul NU
1/10-NU29 - Reeves LT for 1 yd (Bambauer)
2/9 -NU28 - Schramm RT for 6 yds (Knafelc)
3/3 -NU22 - Schramm LT for 4 yds (Knafelc)
1/10-NU18 - Hughes pitch RE for 14 yds (Bambauer)

END OF GAME:
MICHIGAN STATE 52 NORTHWESTERN 3

National Collegiate Athletic Association
FINAL TEAM STATISTICS

	MICHIGAN STATE	NORTH-WESTERN
First Downs	34	9
Rushing	22	3
Passing	10	4
Penalty	2	2
Rushing Attempts	68	32
Yards Rushing	434	105
Yards Lost Rushing	-24	-22
Net Yards Rushing	410	83
Net Yards Passing	191	63
Passes Attempted	27	29
Passes Completed	13	7
Had Intercepted	2	2
Total Offensive Plays	95	61
Total Net Yards	601	146
Average Gain Per Play	6.3	2.4
Fumbles: Number—Lost	1/0	1/1
Penalties: Number—Yards	6/61	5/55
Interceptions: Number—Yards	2/7	2/10
Number of Punts—Yards	2/43	10/327
Average Per Punt	21.5	32.7
Punt Returns: Number—Yards	6/65	1/10
Kickoff Return: Number—Yards	2/43	5/69

NOVEMBER 25, 1978

IOWA
VS.
MICHIGAN STATE
Spartan Stadium
East Lansing

FIRST QUARTER

Michigan State Co-Captains: Senior Squad
Iowa: Gutshall, Rusk, Becker, Lazar
Iowa won the toss, elects to receive; Michigan State defending the south goal
Schario kicks to Reid at UI 18, tackle by T. Williams, return of 3

IOWA
1/10-UI21 - Burke around left end on pitchout, tackle by Graves & Webb, gain of 2
2/8 -UI23 - Burke around left end on pitchout, tackle by Webb, gain of 5
3/3 -UI28 - Burke through the middle, tackle by Hay, loss of 2
4/5 -UI26 - Holsclaw punts to S. Smith, fair catch, 34 yd. punt, no return

13:09 MICHIGAN STATE
1/10-MS40 - Smith pass to Byrd across the middle, underthrown
2/10-MS40 - McGee around left end on pitchout, tackle by Rusk, gain of 6
3/4 -MS46 - Smith pass to Gibson across the middle, touchdown, 54 yd pass play
60 yards in 3 plays Time: 2:45 Elapsed Time: 54 Andersen PAT attempt good
MICHIGAN STATE 7 IOWA 0

Schario kicks to Blatcher at the UI5, tackle by Davis & Schario, return of 26
12:15 IOWA
1/10-UI31 - Green through the middle, tackle by Land, gain of 4
2/6 -UI35 - Lazar through middle, tackle by Land & Bass, gain of 5
3/1 -UI40 - Burke around right end on pitchout, tackle by Anderson, gain of 8
1/10-UI48 - Lazar outside left guard, team tackle, gain of 2
2/8 - 50 - Burke off left tackle, tackle by Anderson, gain of 9
1/10-MS41 - Lazar off right tackle, tackle by Bass & Savage & Jones, gain of 3
2/7 -MS38 - Green drops back & falls down, team tackle, loss of 6
3/13-MS44 - Green pass across the middle to Morton, tackle by Burroughs, gain of 11
4/2 -MS33 - Burke off left tackle, tackle by Bass, no gain

7:23 MICHIGAN STATE
1/10-MS33 - Smith pass to Byrd on left sideline, tackle by Weiss & Danzy, gain of 18

1/10-UI49 - Smith pass to McGee incomplete
2/10-UI49 - Smith pass to Middleton on right side, tackle by Rusk, gain of 11
1/10-UI38 - Smith pass to Gibson long on left side, UI pass interference, 18 yd penalty
1/10-UI20 - Middleton through the middle, tackle Steverson, Becker, gain of 17
1/G -UI3 - McGee outside right tackle, tackle by Becker, gain of 2
2/G -UI1 - Middleton over the middle, tackle by Rusk, no gain
3/G -UI1 - S. Smith around right end on pitchout, touchdown, 1 yd play
67 yards in 7 plays, Time: 9:47 Elapsed Time: 2:10 Andersen PAT attempt good

MICHIGAN STATE 14 IOWA 0

Schario kicks to Blatcher at UI3, tackle by Schario, 38 yd return
IOWA
1/10-UI41 - Burke around right end on pitchout, tackle by Savage & Webb, no gain
2/10-UI41 - Lazar off left tackle, team tackle, gain of 7
3/3 -UI48 - Green pass to Reid incomplete
4/3 -UI48 - Holsclaw punts ball out of bounds on right side, 2 yd punt, no return

3:36 MICHIGAN STATE
1/10- 50 - Middleton off left tackle, run out of bounds by Becker, gain of 23
1/10-UI27 - Smith pass to Byrd in left end zone corner broken up by Steverson
2/10-UI27 - S. Smith around right end on pitchout, tackle by Danzy, gain of 12
1/10-UI15 - McGee outside left tackle, tackle by Becker, gain of 3
2/7 -UI12 - Smith pass to Byrd across the middle incomplete, MS holding 15 yd penalty
2/22-UI27 - Smith screen pass to S. Smith incomplete
3/22-UI27 - Smith pass across the middle to McGee incomplete
4/22-UI27 - Andersen field goal attempt (44 yds) wide left

2:04 IOWA
1/10-UI27 - Lazar off right tackle, tackle by Webb, gain of 2
2/8 -UI29 - Mosley around right end, tackle by Savage, loss of 4
3/12-UI25 - Frazier on reverse, tackle by Burroughs, gain of 1
4/11-UI26 - Holsclaw punts to S. Smith, fair catch, no return, 34 yd punt

:37 MICHIGAN STATE
1/10-MS40 - Smith pass to Brammer across the middle to left side, tackle by Steverson, gain of 19

410

NOVEMBER 25, 1978

1/10-UI41 - McGee outside right end on pitchout, knocked out of bounds by Danzy, gain of 33

1/G -UI8 - S. Smith outside left end on pitchout, touchdown, 8 yd play 60 yds in 3 plays Time: 15:00, Elapsed Time: 37
Iowa offside, ½ distance to goal, Andersen PAT attempt good
MICHIGAN STATE 21 IOWA 0

**END OF FIRST QUARTER:
MICHIGAN STATE 21 IOWA 0**

SECOND QUARTER

Schario kicks to Blatcher at UI1, tackle by Cooper, 18 yd return
IOWA
1/10-UI19 - Burke around right end on pitchout, tackle by Land, gain of 4
2/6 -UI23 - Frazier off right tackle on counter, tackle by Bass, gain of 1
3/5 -UI24 - Green pass to Reid long over the middle incomplete
4/5 -UI24 - Holsclaw punt to S. Smith, fair catch, 29 yd punt

13:30 MICHIGAN STATE
1/10-MS47 - Smith pass to Byrd across the middle, drops to knees, gain of 17
1/10-UI36 - Smith pass to Brammer, broken up by Gutshall
2/10-UI36 - Smith pass to S. Smith on right side, slips, gain of 1
3/9 -UI35 - Smith pass to McGee on right side line, incomplete, broken up by Simonsen
4/9 -UI35 - Andersen 52 yd field goal attempt short

12:02 IOWA
1/10-UI35 - Lazar through the middle on draw, tackle by Decker & Hay, loss of 1
2/11-UI34 - Burke halfback pass broken up by Stanton
3/11-UI34 - Green pass to Lazar, UI holding, ½ distance from foul 22 yd penalty
3/33-UI12 - Green screen pass to Mosley dropped.
4/33-UI12 - Holsclaw punts, MS roughing the kicker, 15 yd penalty
4/18-UI27 - Holsclaw punts to S. Smith at MS 39, 34 yd punt, steps out, 55 yd return

10:49 MICHIGAN STATE
1/G -MS6 - McGee around right end on pitchout, fumbles, rolls out of bounds, loss of 6
2/G -MS12 - S. Smith around left end on pitchout, tackle by Becker Molini, gain of 2
3/G -MS10 - Smith pass to Byrd broken up by Steverson TO/MS 9:53

4/G -MS10 - Smith pass to Byrd in left end zone corner, touchdown, 10 yd play 6 yards in 4 plays. Time: 5:10 Elapsed Time: :59 Andersen PAT attempt good
MICHIGAN STATE 28 IOWA 0

Schario kicks to Blatcher in end zone, returns to UI15, fumbles recovered by Muster, fumble caused by I. Griffin
9:44 MICHIGAN STATE
1/10-UI14 - S. Smith outside right tackle, tackle by Rusk, gain of 4
2/6 -UI10 - Middleton off left guard, tackle by Hufford & Rusk, gain of 3
3/3 -UI7 - Smith pass to Gibson in left end zone corner overthrown
4/3 -UI7 - Smith pass to Byrd across the middle in end zone, incomplete

8:09 IOWA
1/10-UI7 - Burke off right tackle, tackle by Savage, gain of 5
2/5 -UI12 - Lazar through the middle, tackle by Webb, gain of 2
3/3 -UI14 - Burke off left guard, tackle by Bass & Decker, gain of 6
1/10-UI20 - Green off left guard on broken play, by McCormick, gain of 2
2/8 -UI22 - Green pass long on right side to Reid, broken up by Stanton
3/8 -UI22 - Mosley around right end on pitchout, tackle by Decker, gain of 7
4/1 -UI29 - Lazar over the middle, team tackle, gain of 2
1/10-UI31 - Green back to pass, keeps through the middle, tackle by Bass & Decker, gain of 9
2/1 -UI40 - Mosley off left guard on counter, no gain
3/1 -UI40 - Green around right end, run out of bounds by Savage, loss of 2
4/3 -UI38 - Holsclaw punts to Reeves at MS28, 34 yd punt, fair catch, no return

3:06 MICHIGAN STATE
1/10-MS28 - S. Smith off left tackle on counter, tackle by Steverson, gain of 33
1/10-UI39 - Smith pass to Byrd on left sideline, overthrown
2/10-UI39 - S. Smith outside right end on pitchout, tackle by Molini, gain of 38
1/G -UI1 - Smith pass to Byrd in right endzone corner, touchdown, 1 yd pass play 72 yards in 4 plays Time: 12:58 Elapsed Time: 1:04 Andersen PAT attempt good
MICHIGAN STATE 35 IOWA 0

Schario kicks to Reid at UI4, tackle by C. Griffin, Muster, 9 yd return

411

2:02 IOWA
- 1/10 -UI15 - Green pass broken up by Savage
- 2/10 -UI15 - Green pass to Blatcher, fumbles, recovered by Reid, tackle by Webb, gain of 3
- 3/7 -UI18 - Green back to pass, sacked by Webb, loss of 2
- 4/9 -UI16 - Holsclaw punts to Reeves, 34 yd punt, MS clipping, 15 yd penalty, 4 yd return

:16 MICHIGAN STATE
- 1/10-MS39 - Middleton off left tackle, tackle by Mahmens & Marty, gain of 2

**END OF HALF:
MICHIGAN STATE 35 IOWA 0**

THIRD QUARTER

Michigan State elects to receive, Iowa defending the north goal
Schilling kicks to Reeves in the end zone, returns to MS17, tackle by Gutshall
MICHIGAN STATE
- 1/10-MS17 - S. Smith around right end on pitchout, tackle Weiss & Hobbes, gain of 5
- 2/5 -MS22 - Smith pass to Byrd on right sideline, knocked out by Steverson, gain of 7
- 1/10-MS29 - Smith pass to Middleton in left flat, tackle by Becker, gain of 2
- 2/8 -MS31 - Smith pass to Middleton in right flat, falls down, loss of 3
- 3/11-MS28 - S. Smith through the middle on draw, fumbles, recovers, tackle by Weiss, gain of 3
- 4/8 -MS31 - Stachowicz punts to Becker at UI 37, tackle by Davis, 32 yd punt, 10 yd return

12:31 IOWA
- 1/10-UI47 - Turner around left end, tackle by team, loss of 3
- 2/13-UI44 - Green pass to Frazier, intercepted by Stanton, MS interference, 2 yd penalty
- 1/10-UI46 - Turner off left tackle, tackle by Hay, gain of 4
- 2/6 - 50 - Green pass to Reid on right side line, broken up by Anderson
- 3/6 - 50 - Green pass to Lazar on right sideline, incomplete
- 4/6 - 50 - Holsclaw punts to S. Smith at MS12, fair catch, 38 yd punt, no return

10:57 MICHIGAN STATE
- 1/10-MS12 - S. Smith off right tackle by Hufford, Rusk, gain of 3
- 2/7 -MS15 - S. Smith outside left end, tackle by Danzy, loss of 3 offsetting penalty
- 3/10-MS12 - S. Smith off right tackle, tackle by Danzy & Becker, gain of 10

- 1/10-MS22 - Reeves outside left tackle, tackle by Rusk, gain of 7
- 2/3 -MS29 - S. Smith outside right end on pitchout, tackle by Rusk, gain of 17
- 1/10-MS46 - Middleton off left tackle, tackle by Benschoter, gain of 2
- 2/8 -MS48 - Smith pass to Howard long on left side, incomplete
- 3/8 -MS48 - Smith pass to Howard overthrown
- 4/8 -MS48 - Stachowicz punts the ball out of bounds at UI9, 43 yd punt, no return

7:50 IOWA
- 1/10-UI9 - Green pass to Reid on left sideline, broken up by Burroughs
- 2/10-UI9 - Green back to pass, sacked by Savage, loss of 6
- 3/16-UI3 - Green pass incomplete
- 4/16-UI3 - Holsclaw punts to S. Smith, fair catch, called, touches the ball, recovered by Bradley, 47 yd punt, no return

6:41 IOWA
- 1/10- 50 - Mosley around left end, tackle by Graves, loss of 3
- 2/13-UI47 - Green pass to Reid, overthrown
- 3/13-UI47 - Green pass to Swift, tackle by Anderson, 23 yd gain
- 1/10-MS30 - Turner through the middle, tackle by Otis, gain of 2
- 2/8 -MS28 - Green pass to Frazier across the middle, tackle by T. Williams, gain of 10
- 1/10-MS18 - Turner around left end, tackle by Savage, gain of 6
- 2/4 -MS12 - Turner around left end, tackle by Burroughs, gain of 1
- 3/3 -MS11 - Turner around right end, run out by Stanton & Otis, gain of 3
- 1/G -MS8 - Turner around left end, tackle by Land & Savage, loss of 2
- 2/G -MS10 - Green pass to Lazar, touchdown, 10 plays, 50 yards, Time: 12:22 Elapsed Time: 4:02
Schilling PAT attempt good
MICHIGAN STATE 35 IOWA 7

Schilling kicks to S. Smith at MS1, returns to 25, tackle by Kent, 24 yd return
2:39 MICHIGAN STATE
- 1/10-MS25 - S. Smith off left guard on counter, tackle by Rusk, gain of 7
- 2/3 -MS32 - Smith pass to Howard on left sideline, fumbles, rolls out of bounds, knocked out by Steverson, gain of 7
- 1/10-MS39 - Smith pass to Howard across the middle, broken up by Steverson
- 2/10-MS39 - Smith hands to S. Smith, fumbles, recovered by S. Smith, loss of 6
- 3/16-MS33 - Smith back to pass keeps runs out on left side line gain of 7
- 4/9 -MS40 - Stachowicz punts to Becker, 34 yd punt, 6 yd return

NOVEMBER 25, 1978

:44 IOWA
1/10-UI32 - Green back to pass, keeps around right end, tackle by Hay, no gain
2/10-UI32 - Turner off left tackle, tackle by Decker, gain of 8

**END OF THIRD QUARTER:
MICHIGAN STATE 35 IOWA 7**

FOURTH QUARTER

IOWA
3/2 -UI40 - UI illegal motion, 5 yd penalty
3/7 -UI35 - Green pass to Frazier in right flat, tackle by Hay, gain of 9
1/10-UI44 - Green screen pass to Turner incomplete
2/10-UI44 - Green pass to Swift broken up by Stanton
3/10-UI44 - Green pass to Frazier across the middle incomplete
4/10-UI44 - Holsclaw punts to Reeves, UI personal foul, facemask, 15 yard penalty
4/25-UI29 - Holsclaw punts to Reeves, tackle by McKillip, loss of 1 on return, 33 yd punt

14:05 MICHIGAN STATE
1/10-MS37 - Smith pass to J. Williams, overthrown
2/10-MS37 - Hughes outside right end, tackle by Danzy, gain of 9
3/1 -MS46 - Reeves outside left end, tackle by Steverson, gain of 41
1/10-UI13 - Hughes through the middle, fumbles, recovered by Steverson, loss of 3

12:43 IOWA
1/10-UI16 - Turner around right end on pitchout, knocked out by Anderson, UI illegal motion
1/15-UI11 - Turner around left end on pitchout, tackle by Stanton, loss of 3
2/18-UI8 - UI delay of game, ½ distance to goal, 4 yd penalty
2/22-UI4 - Green pass to Swift underthrown
3/22-UI4 - Green pass to Lazar in right flat incomplete
4/22-UI4 - Holsclaw punts to Reeves at UI37, 33 yd punt, tackle by Holsclaw, 26 yd return

11:28 MICHIGAN STATE
1/10-UI11 - Smith pass to Byrd in end zone dropped
2/10-UI11 - Smith pass to Brammer overthrown
3/10-UI11 - Hughes outside right end, touchdown, 11 yards in 3 plays, 11 yd run time: 3:45 Elapsed Time: :13 Andersen PAt attempt good
MICHIGAN STATE 42 IOWA 7

Schario kicks to K. Ellis at goal line, tackle by T. Williams, 17 yd return
11:15 IOWA
1/10-UI17 - Turner outside left tackle, tackle by Bass, gain of 5
2/5 -UI22 - Turner off right tackle, team tackle, gain of 3
3/2 -UI25 - Turner off right end, tackle by Bass, gain of 4
1/10-UI29 - Turner off left guard on counter, team tackle, fumble recovered, gain of 3
2/7 -UI32 - Lazar over the middle, tackle by Bass, gain of 3
3/4 -UI35 - Green pass to Lazar on right sideline, gain of 5
1/10-UI40 - Green pass to Swift on right sideline, knocked out by Bass & Marshall, 10 yd. gain
1/10- 50 - Turner outside right end, tackle by Haynes, gain of 1
2/9 -MS49 - Green pass long to Dunham, broken up by Anderson
3/9 -MS49 - Green pass to Swift across the middle, tackle by Anderson, gain of 16
1/10-MS33 - Green back to pass keeps around left end, tackle by I Griffin, gain of 4
2/6 -MS29 - Green back to pass, sacked by Otis, loss of 6
3/12-MS35 - Dunham on end around reverse, sacked by Haynes, loss of 9
4/21-MS44 - Holsclaw punts to Reeves at MS19, 25 yd punt

4:06 MICHIGAN STATE
1/10-MS19 - Smith pass to Howard overthrown
2/10-MS19 - MS illegal motion, 5 yd penalty
2/15-MS14 - Hughes off right tackle, tackle by Steverson, gain of 23
1/10-MS37 - Reeves outside right tackle, knocked out by Steverson, gain of 5
2/5 -MS42 - Hughes outside left end, tackle by Schlickman, gain of 4
3/1 -MS46 - Reeves outside right end, tackle by K. Ellis, gain of 10
1/10-UI44 - Hughes outside right end fumbles, recovered by Bradley, loss of 9

2:10 IOWA
1/10-MS46 - Green back to pass, keeps, tackle by Cooper, gain of 18
1/10-MS28 - Green pass to Frazier, tackle by Marshall, gain of 11
1/10-MS17 - Green pass to Turner on right sideline, incomplete
2/10-MS17 - Green pass to Frazier incomplete
3/10-MS17 - Green pass to Turner incomplete, UI personal foul, declined
4/10-MS17 - Green back to pass, sacked by Haynes, loss of 12

:58 MICHIGAN STATE
1/10-MS29 - Hughes off left tackle, tackle by Harty & Bradley, gain of 2
2/8 -MS31 - Reeves outside right end, tackle by K. Ellis, loss of 2

FINAL SCORE:
MICHIGAN STATE 42 IOWA 7

National Collegiate Athletic Association
FINAL TEAM STATISTICS

	IOWA	MICHIGAN STATE
First Downs	15	20
Rushing	7	12
Passing	7	7
Penalty	1	1
Rushing Attempts	52	38
Yards Rushing	151	350
Yards Lost Rushing	61	29
Net Yards Rushing	90	321
Net Yards Passing	108	144
Passes Attempted	30	30
Passes Completed	10	12
Had Intercepted	0	0
Total Offensive Plays	82	68
Total Net Yards	198	465
Average Gain Per Play	2.4	6.8
Fumbles: Number—Lost	3/1	7/3
Penalties: Number—Yards	6/69	5/52
Interceptions: Number—Yards	0/0	0/0
Number Of Punts—Yards	12/377	3/109
Average Per Punt	31.4	36.3
Punt Returns: Number—Yards	2/16	4/84
Kickoff Returns: Number—Yards	7/128	2/41

NOVEMBER 25, 1978

OHIO STATE
VS.
MICHIGAN
Ohio Stadium,
Columbus, Ohio
Temp: 40
Wind: SW 5-10 mph
Skies: Overcast
FIRST QUARTER

Michigan won the toss and elected to receive; Ohio State to defend the South goal
Atha kicked off at 12:56 P.M. 59 yards; Jackson returned 20
14:56 MICHIGAN
1/10-M21 - Davis into lg for 4
2/6 -M25 - Woolfolk at lg for 3
3/3 -M28 - Leach kept at le on option for (measurement) 3
1/10-M31 - Woolfolk cut over center, clear for 13
1/10-M44 - Davis was stopped at center by Sullivan for 1
2/9 -M45 - Woolfolk pitch at le for 1
3/8 -M46 - Leach faded, chased, ran middle for -1 - Dansler
4/9 -M45 - Willner punted center, Ohio bounce for 28; downed by Michigan

11:26 OHIO
1/10-O27 - Schlichter kept inside le for 4
2/6 -O31 - Volley over rt for 3
3/3 -O34 - Volley thru lt for 6
1/10-O40 - Schlichter rolled right, passed short to Springs for 5
2/5 -O45 - Springs pitch over rt for 4
3/1 -O49 - Volley pushed thru lt for 3
1/10-M48 - Volley at rt for 2
2/8 -M46 - Springs option pitch at re for 8
1/10-M38 - Springs pitch at re for just 2
2/8 -M36 - Schlichter rolled left, chased, ran for 7
3/1 -M29 - Campbell, on robust, over rt for 3
1/10-M26 - Schlichter, on option, kept at lt for 3
2/7 -M23 - Schlichter rolled right, chased out of bounds by Trgovac -6
3/13-M29 - Volley on delayed draw middle for 8
4/5 -M21 - Atha's FG try from 38 yards was wide left - TB

4:58 MICHIGAN
1/10-M21 - Woolfolk option pitch at le for 6
2/4 -M27 - Woolfolk was stopped at rg by Sullivan, Henson for no gain
3/4 -M27 - Davis into lt on draw for 3
4/1 -M30 - Willner punted 31; Guess returned center for 11

3:25 OHIO
1/10- 50 - Volley was clear at left guard for 21

1/10-M29 - Springs option pitch at le for 11
1/10-M18 - Schlichter cut over rt for 6
2/4 -M12 - Schlichter kept right slipped down for -1
3/5 -M13 - Springs pitch at re, slipped down for 1
4/4 -M12 - Atha's FG was from 29 yards
38 yards in six plays
OHIO STATE 3, MICHIGAN 0
Atha kicked off out of bounds right -5
Atha kicked off 62 yards; Jackson returned 27

1:08 MICHIGAN
1/10-M30 - Woolfolk pitch at le, stopped for no gain by Cato
2/10-M30 - Leach faked, passed deep right to Marsh for 26
1/10-O44 - Leach faked, passed short over middle to Woolfolk, cut right for 14
1/10-O30 - Leach faked, passed to Feaster cutting over middle for the TD
Willner PAT - 70 yards in four plays
MICHIGAN 7, OHIO STATE 3
Virgil kicked off our of bounds left -5
Virgil kicked off middle 52 yards; Murray returned center, slipped for 13

0:06 OHIO
1/10-O31 - Schlichter faded, chased, ran middle, cut right for 12 as the quarter came to an end

MICHIGAN 7, OHIO STATE 3

SECOND QUARTER

OHIO
1/10-O43 - Volley at lg for 2
2/8 -O45 - Springs on counter option re for 3
3/5 -O48 - Schlichter faded, chased, sacked for -1 - Keitz
4/6 -O47 - Orosz punted short middle for 32; downed by Ohio State

13:19 MICHIGAN
1/10-M21 - Davis at rt for 2
2/8 -M23 - Leach kept inside tackle on counter option left for 4
3/4 -M27 - Leach passed on short out right to Davis for 10
1/10-M37 - Woolfolk pitch at re for 1
2/9 -M38 - Leach faked, faded, chased, spun out and passed deep right to nobody incomplete
3/9 -M38 - Woolfolk took option pitch to the wide left side for no gain
4/9 -M38 - Willner punted 33; Guess returned 2

10:01 OHIO
1/10-O31 - Volley pushed into lt for 3
2/7 -O34 - Springs was stopped at rt for 1

415

3/6 -035 - Schlichter rolled left, chased, passed short down side line for Gerald incomplete
4/6 -035 - Orosz punted right 51; Jolly returned -1

8:45 MICHIGAN
1/10-M13 - Woolfolk on counter at rt for 6 (Woolfolk hurt - helped off)
2/4 -M19 - Davis was clear at rt for 14
1/10-M33 - Davis was stopped this time at lg for just one
2/9 -M34 - Leach faked, passed deep down right sideline for Marsh; broken up Bell incomplete
3/9 -M34 - Leach faded, faded, chased, sacked by Cousineau, Sullivan for -11
4/20-M23 - Willner punted 46; Guess returned 8

6:56 OHIO
1/10-039 - Schlichter faded, ran middle, sacked by Trgovac for -3
2/13-036 - Springs option pitch at le for 12
3/1 -048 - Schlichter turned into lt for 4
1/10-M48 - Schlichter cut into re, cut right for 8
2/2 -M40 - Schlichter kept inside le for 4
1/10-M36 - Schlichter passed to Moore left; Simpkins deflected incomplete
2/10-M36 - Springs option pitch at re for 11
1/10-M25 - Schlichter kept inside le for 4
2/6 -M21 - Ohio State illegal procedure -5
2/11-M26 - Volley rt 2
3/9 -M24 - Schlichter faded, sacked; fumble caused by Meter, recovered by Cannavino -8

3:20 MICHIGAN
1/10-M32 - Smith cut thru a big hole over left side, clear for 16
1/10-M48 - Leach faked, passed deep right for Feaster; knocked down by Guess incomplete
2/10-M48 - Smith into rg for 4
3/6 -048 - Leach passed to Clayton cutting over middle for 15
1/10-033 - Davis thru rg for 5 Time out Michigan at 1:36
2/5 -028 - Leach faked, faded, chased, ran middle for 5
1/10-023 - Leach faked, passed way too high for Feaster in right flat incomplete
2/10-023 - Leach passed to Smith on deep swing right for 9 Time out Michigan at 0:52
3/1 -014 - Leach faked, passed to Johnson cutting over middle; Skillings caused fumble on the one and then recovered in end zone for the TB

0:43 OHIO
1/10-020 - Schlichter fell on ball for -2
2/12-018 - Schlichter fell on ball again for -2 as the first half came to an end at 2:05 P.M.

MICHIGAN 7, OHIO STATE 3

THIRD QUARTER

Ohio State elected to receive; Michigan to defend the South goal
Virgil kicked off at 2:30 P.M. 59 yards; Hicks returned middle for 30

14:54 OHIO
1/10-031 - Volley hit center for 3
2/7 -034 - Volley thru lg for 5
3/2 -039 - Schlichter kept inside re for (measurement) 1
4/1 -040 - Orosz punted right 43; Jolly FC

13:26 MICHIGAN
1/10-M17 - Davis into lt for 4
2/6 -M21 - Leach kept inside re for 7
1/10-M28 - Smith was clear outside rt for 13
1/10-M41 - Reid into middle for 2
2/8 -M43 - Leach faked, passed too short for Clayton deep down right sideline incomplete
3/8 -M43 - Leach passed to Clayton cutting over middle; low, dropped incomplete
4/8 -M43 - Willner punted 45; Guess returned 8

11:21 OHIO
1/10-020 - Schlichter was stopped on counter option left by Greer for -3
2/13-017 - Springs on draw over left side for 10
3/3 -027 - Ohio State illegal procedure -5
3/8 -022 - Springs on draw over left side for 4
4/4 -026 - Orosz punted 50; Jolly returned 7

9:31 MICHIGAN
1/10-M31 - Smith option pitch around right end for 5
2/5 -M36 - Smith on counter at rt for 3
3/2 -M39 - Reid into rt for 4
1/10-M43 - Leach kept inside le for 5
2/5 -M48 - Smith was clear at lt, broke tackle for 14
1/10-038 - Reid at lg for 4
2/6 -034 - Leach faked, passed to Marsh on out cut right for 13
1/10-021 - Woolfolk into rg for 2
2/8 -019 - Leach faded, looked, passed over middle for Clayton at the goal line; deflected by Skillings incomplete
3/8 -019 - Leach faked, moved left, passed to Reid on screen back right for 11
1/8 -08 - Leach kept inside right end for 4
2/4 -04 - Leach kept left, stopped by Mills for -1
3/5 -05 - Michigan delay of game -6* (*stopped off a little long)
3/11-011 - Leach faded, rolled left, looked, passed to Smith on switch left for the TD at the flag at 4:12 - Willner PAT - 69 yards, 13 plays, MICHIGAN 14, OHIO STATE 3
Virgil kicked off 15 yards; Murray returned 19

416

NOVEMBER 25, 1978

4:07 OHIO
1/10-022 - Schlichter faked, passed to Moore on out cut left for 8
2/2 -030 - Springs option pitch at re for -4 - Bell
3/6 -026 - Schlichter faded, chased left, ran for 4
4/2 -030 - Orosz picked ball off ground, punted 45; Jolly returned -3

2:06 MICHIGAN
1/10-M22 - Leach kept on option at re for 8
2/2 -M30 - Davis at rg 1
3/1 -M31 - Woolfolk over rt for 5
1/10-M36 - Woolfolk into lt for 2
2/8 -M38 - Davis at rt for 2 as the quarter came to an end

MICHIGAN 14, OHIO STATE 3

FOURTH QUARTER

MICHIGAN
3/6 -M40 - Leach faked, passed to Clayton in left falt for 13-
1/10-047 - Smith thru middle for 2
2/8 -045 - Davis pushed thru lt for 6
3/2 -039 - Davis at lg for (measurement) 2
1/10-037 - Davis cut into middle for 3
2/7 -034 - Leach faked, passed behind Clayton cutting over middle incomplete
3/7 -034 - Leach passed too low and short for Feaster right incomplete
4/7 -034 - Willner punted 33; downed by Michigan

11:52 OHIO
1/10-01 - Gerald cut over rt for 2
2/8 -03 - Johnson into rt for 3
3/5 -06 - Volley at lg for 2
4/3 -08 - Orosz punted 37 yards right; Jolly returned 2

10:09 MICHIGAN
1/10-043 - Smith cut into middle for 5
2/5 -038 - Reid cut at center for 2
3/3 -036 - Smith into rt for (measurement) 3
1/10-033 - Clayton over lt for 5
2/5 -028 - Smith cut over re for 2 (Smith hurt - helped off) Time out Michigan 7:25
3/3 -026 - Leach faked, passed way too long for Feaster in left end zone incomplete
4/3 -026 - Willner's FG try was Wide left and short for the TB at 7:16

7:16 OHIO
1/10-026 - Gerald kept right, cut in for no gain
2/10-026 - Ohio State illegal procedure -5
2/15-021 - Gerald faded, chased, ran right for 5
3/10-026 - Gerald passed to Springs on delay over middle for 5 more
4/5 -031 - Payton, on direct snap from punt formation, ran over right side for zero

5:51 MICHIGAN
1/10-031 - Reid at rg for 4 (Dickey at quarterback)
2/6 -027 - Woolfolk into rt for 3
3/3 -024 - Dickey kept left, stopped by Cato from behind for -2
4/5 -026 - Woolfolk was stopped by Hornik at rt for no gain

3:44 OHIO
1/10-026 - Schlichter passed to Gerald slanting deep over middle for 25
1/10-M49 - Schlichter passed wide for Volley short left incomplete
2/10-M49 - Schlichter's pass for Gerald over middle was intercepted by Jolly, returned 7

3:15 MICHIGAN
1/10-M48 - Dickey passed too high for Clayton deep over middle incomplete
Ohio State personal foul 15
1/10-037 - Dickey kept left for -1 - Dulin
2/11-038 - Reid off left tackle for 3
3/8 -035 - Woolfolk at lg for -1 - Henson
Time out Ohio State at 1:43
4/9 -036 - Willner punted 31; downed by Michigan

1:36 OHIO
1/1005 - Schlichter faded, ran over right side for 4
2/6 -09 - Schlichter passed to Hunter right for 5
3/1 -014 - Schlichter faded, moved up, slipped down for -3
4/4 -011 - Schlichter passed too wide for Volley short right incomplete

0:20 MICHIGAN
1/10-011 - Dickey fell on ball for -2 as the game ended at 3:40 P.M.

MICHIGAN 14, OHIO STATE 3

The skys cleared during the second quarter and was sunny for the rest of the game.

417

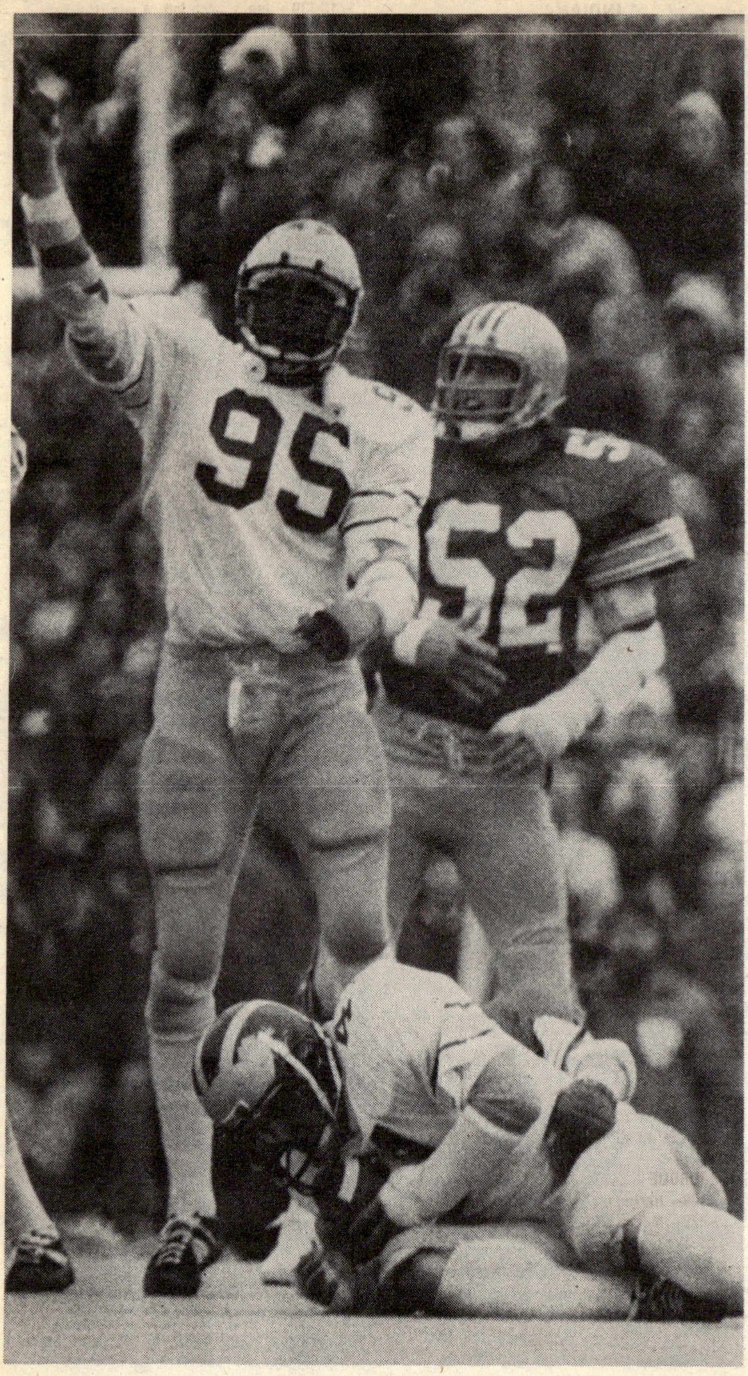
95
52

NOVEMBER 25, 1978

INDIANA VS. PURDUE

Ross-Ade Stadium
Temp.: 42°
Wind: SW 3-5 mph
Skies: Partly cloudy

FIRST QUARTER

Purdue wins toss and will receive Indiana will kickoff and defend south goal.
Straub kickoff to Speedy on P7 return to P25, 53 yd kick 18 yd return

PURDUE
1/10-P25 - Herrmann roll left, 4 yds (Wilbur)
2/6 -P29 - Macon inside re, 8 yds (Sybert, Ramsey)
1/10-P37 - Macon rt draw, 4 yds (Abrams, Norman)
2/6 -P41 - Herrmann to pass, lost 4 yds (Tallen)
3/10-P37 - Herrmann to Pope, 18 yds (Sybert, Keneipp)
1/10-I45 - Macon up middle, 2 yds (Tallen)
2/8 -I43 - Herrmann to Burrell, incomplete
3/8 -I43 - Draw, Macon, 7 yds. (McIntosh, Doehla)
4/1 -I36 - Macon pitch right, lost 4 yds (Norman)

11:11 INDIANA
1/10-I40 - Arnett to Friede, 14 yds
1/10-P46 - Burnett rt, 2 yds (Johanson)
2/8 -P44 - Johnson rt, 3 yds (Loushin)
3/5 -P41 - Arnett roll right, 1 yd. (Motts)
4/4 -P40 - Lovett punt to Purdue end zone, 40 yd kick no return

9:13 PURDUE
1/10-P20 - Macon lt, lost 2 yds (Norman)
2/12-P18 - Herrmann to Burrell, incomplete
3/12-P18 - Macon on draw, 2 yds (Walls)
4/10-P20 - Linville punt to I42 Wilbur, no return, 38 yd kick, clip on return 15 yd penalty

7:46 INDIANA
1/10-I28 - Burnett lt, no gain
2/10-I28 - Burnett rt, 1 yd (Loushin)
3/9 -I29 - Johnson rg, 7 yds (Floyd)
4/2 -I36 - Lovett punt to Pope on P21 return to P29, 43 yd kick 8 yd return

5:53 PURDUE
1/10-P29 - Herrmann to Young, incomplete
2/10-P29 - Macon rg, 2 yds Macon injured (Leake)
3/8 -P31 - Augustyniak on draw, 14 yds (Norman)
1/10-P45 - Jones up middle, 7 yds (Leake)
2/3 -I48 - Herrmann to Pope, 9 yds (Norman, Sybert)
1/10-I39 - Jones pitch left, 4 yds (Norman, Sybert)
2/6 -I35 - Jones rg, 2 yds (Walls)
3/4 -I33 - Herrmann to Young, 10 yds (Swinehart, Doehla)
1/10-I23 - Augustyniak inside re, 3 yds (Leake, Sybert)
2/7 -I20 - Augustyniak on draw, 4 yds (Sybert)
3/3 -I16 - Jones pitch right cut back, 3 yds (Tallen)
1/10-I13 - Augustyniak lg, 5 yds (Tisdale, Sybert)
2/5 -I8 - Jones rg, 4 yds (Keneipp)
3/1 -I4 - Augustyniak rg, 3 yds

**END OF FIRST QUARTER:
PURDUE 0 INDIANA 0**

SECOND QUARTER

PURDUE
1/G -I1 - Jones rg, no gain
2/G -I1 - Macon return to line, McCall lg, 1 yd touchdown, 16 plays 71 yards
PAT Sovereen kick Burrell hold good
SCORE: PURDUE 7 INDIANA 0

Sovereen kickoff out of bounds, 5 yd penalty illegal procedure, from P35 Sovereen kickoff to Burnett on I10 return to P34 55 yd kick 56 yd return

INDIANA
1/10-P34 - Harkrader inside le, 2 yds (Loushin)
2/8 -P32 - Arnett pass incomplete
3/8 P32 - Clifford at QB, Clifford to Johnson, 1 yd.
4/7 -P31 - Clifford to Stevenson interference by Harris on P14

13:17 PURDUE
1/10-P14 - Augustyniak lt, 3 yds (Ramsey)
2/7 -P17 - Jones pitch left, no gain (Oakley)
3/7 -P17 - Jones on draw, 6 yds (Doehla)
4/1 -P23 - Linville punt to Wilbur fair catch on P49, 26 yd kick no return

11:36 INDIANA
1/10-P49 - Burnett inside le, 3 yds (Supan, Motts)
2/7 -P46 - Clifford roll right, 5 yds. (Loushin)
3/2 -P41 - Harkrader lt, 1 yd (Motts, Johanson)
4/1 -P40 - Arnett sneak, 3 yds
1/10-P37 - Harkrader rg, lost 2 yds (Floyd)
2/12-P39 - Arnett roll left, 4 yds (Motts)
3/8 -P35 - Clifford to Powers, incomplete
4/8 -P35 - Indiana time out 8:40
4/8 -P35 - Clifford to Lundy, incomplete

419

8:34 PURDUE
1/10-P35 - Herrmann to Harris, 43 yds (Swinehart)
1/10-I22 - Jones pitch right, 11 yds (Sybert)
1/10-I11 - Jones pitch left, 5 yds (Keneipp)
2/5 -I6 - Jones pitch left, 3 yds (McIntosh, Tisdale)
3/2 -I3 - Pitch left Pope pass to Burrell, incomplete
4/2 -I3 - Sovereen attempt 20 yd field goal Burrell hold good 6 plays 62 yards
SCORE: PURDUE 10 INDIANA 0

Sovereen kickoff to Johnson on I9 return to I17 51 yd kick 8 yd return
6:40 INDIANA
1/10-I17 - Clifford to Johnson, 5 yd (Motts, Turner)
2/5 -I22 - Harkrader lt, 9 yds (Supan)
1/10-I31 - Clifford to Friede, 12 yds
1/10-I43 - Clifford to Friede, incomplete
2/10-I43 - Clifford to Powers, 7 yds. (Moss)
3/3 - 50 - Clifford to Johnson, 7 yds (Motts)
1/10-P43 - Clifford to Friede, Purdue defensive holding 15 yd penalty
1/10-P28 - Burnett inside left end, 2 yd (Jackson, Motts)
2/8 -P26 - Clifford to Harkrader, incomplete
3/8 -P26 - Clifford to Stevenson, incomplete
4/8 -P26 - Clifford to Friede, 22 yds
1/G -P4 - Arnett at QB, Arnett to Powers, incomplete
2/G -P4 - Arnett to Hopkins, incomplete
3/G -P4 - Clifford at QB, Clifford to Friede, 4 yds touchdown, 13 plays 83 yds
PAT kick Clifford hold good
SCORE: PURDUE 10 INDIANA 7

Straub kickoff to Speedy on P8 return to P23 52 yd kick 15 yd return
3:07 PURDUE
1/10-P23 - Augustyniak lt, 22 yds (Keneipp)
1/10-P45 - Herrmann to Burrell, 17 yds
1/10-I38 - Herrmann to pass, Indiana defensive holding 13 yd penalty
1/10-I25 - Herrmann to Burrell, incomplete
2/10-I25 - Augustyniak on draw, 9 yds (McIntosh, Doehla)
3/1 -I16 - Jones lg, 2 yds (Tallen)
1/10-I19 - Pope lt, no gain (Sybert, McIntosh) Purdue time out 1:41
2/10-I14 - Shotgun: Purdue illegal procedure 5 yd penalty
2/15-I14 - Shotgun: Herrmann to pass, run 5 yds
3/10-I14 - Time out Purdue 1:08
3/10-I14 - Herrmann to Burrell, incomplete
4/10-I14 - Sovereen attempt 31 yd field goal, Burrell hold, good, 9 plays 63 yds
SCORE: PURDUE 13 INDIANA 7

Sovereen kickoff to Burnett on I3 ret to I25, 57 yd kick 22 yd return
1:00 INDIANA
1/10-I25 - Clifford to Lundy, incomplete
2/10-I25 - Harkrader inside le, 27 yds (W. Smith)
1/10-P48 - Clifford Friede, incomplete
2/10-P48 - Clifford to Friede, 18 yds Indiana time out 0:27
1/10-P30 - Clifford to Friede, incomplete
2/10-P30 - Clifford lateral to Harkrader left, 3 yds (Turner) time out 0:14
3/7 -P27 - Clifford to Lundy, incomplete
4/7 -P27 - Freud attempted 44 yd field goal Indiana delay of game 5 yd penalty
4/12-P32 - Clifford to Lundy, incomplete

PURDUE
1/10-P32 - Augustyniak up middle, 9 yds (Sybert)

**HALFTIME SCORE:
PURDUE 13 INDIANA 7**

THIRD QUARTER

Sovereen kickoff to Johnson on I6 return to I18 54 yd kick 12 yd return
INDIANA
1/10-I18 - Burnett lt, 2 yds (Motts, Johnson)
2/8 -I20 - Clifford to Harkrader, 5 yds (Moss, Motts)
3/3 -I25 - Arnett at qb, Arnett roll right, 2 yds (Clark)
4/1 -I27 - Lovett punt to Gallivan fair catch on P45, 28 yd kick no return

13:03 PURDUE
1/10-P45 - Jones pitch left, 5 yds fumbled Indiana recovered

12:57 INDIANA
1/10- 50 - Clifford to Lundy, 5 yds (Supan)
2/5 -P45 - Indiana back in motion 5 yd penalty
2/10- 50 - Clifford to Bowers 5 yds Bowers injured (W. Smith)
3/5 -P45 - Harkrader inside le, 9 yds (Turner)
1/10-P36 - Clifford to Lundy, incomplete
2/10-P36 - Johnson rg, 5 yds (Motts)
3/5 -P31 - Clifford to Friede, incomplete
4/5 -P31 - Lovett punt to Purdue end zone 31 yd kick no return

11:00 PURDUE
1/10-P20 - Augustyniak rt, 6 yds (Sybert, Leake)
2/4-P26 - Augustyniak re, 5 yds (Mormon, Leake)
1/10-P31 - Herrmann to Harris, 12 yds (Swinehart)
1/10-P43 - Jones rt, 3 yds (Swinehart)
2/7 -P46 - Herrmann to Harris incomplete

NOVEMBER 25, 1978

3/7 -P46 - Purdue illegal procedure 5 yd penalty
3/12-P41 - Herrmann to Jones, incomplete
4/12-P41 - Linville punt to Wilbur on I24, no return 35 yd kick

8:44 INDIANA
1/10-I24 - Burnett up middle, 12 yds. fumbled recovered by Jackson

8:44 PURDUE
1/10-I36 - Jones rt, 4 yds
2/6 -I32 - Herrmann to Harris, 11 yds. (Swinehart)
1/10-I21 - Augustyniak up middle, 3 yds (Tisdale)
2/7 -I18 - Herrmann to Harris, 6 yds (Wilbur, Sybert)
3/1 -I12 - Augustyniak up middle, 3 yds (Sybert, Doehla)
1/G -I9 - Jones pitch right, cut back, 4 yds (Norman, Keneipp)
2/G -I5 - Augustyniak rt, 3 yds (Norman)
3/G -I2 - Jones rt, 2 yds touchdown, 8 plays 36 yds
PAT Sovereen kick Burrell hold good
SCORE: PURDUE 20 INDIANA 7

Sovereen kickoff to Burnett on I1 return to I23 59 yd kick 22 yd return

4:51 INDIANA
1/10-I23 - Clifford to Friede, 20 yds
1/10-I43 - Johnson lt, 15 yds (W. Smith)
1/10-P42 - Clifford to Johnson, 9 yds (Motts)
2/1 -P33 - Clifford to Lundy, incomplete
3/1 -P33 - Johnson slide off lg, 7 yds (Supan)
1/10-P26 - Clifford to pass, lost 11 yds (Turner)
2/21-P37 - Harkrader on draw rg, 2 yds (Johanson)
3/19-P35 - Clifford to Burnett, 10 yds (Supan)
4/9 -P25 - Freud attempted 42 yd field goal Clifford hold wide left and short

0:52 PURDUE
1/10-P25 - Augustyniak rg, 3 yds (Sybert)
2/7 -P28 - Augustyniak on draw, 2 yds (Norman, Sybert)

**END OF THIRD QUARTER:
PURDUE 20 INDIANA 7**

FOURTH QUARTER

PURDUE
3/5 -P30 - Herrmann to Young, incomplete
4/5 -P30 - Linville punt to Wilbur fair catch on I27 43 yd kick no return

14:47 INDIANA
1/10-I27 - Clifford to Harkrader on screen, incomplete
2/10-I27 - Harkrader on draw, 2 yds (Jackson)
3/8 -I29 - Clifford to Harkrader on screen, 2 yds (Motts, Moss)
4/6 -I31 - Lovett punt to Pope fair catch on P37 32 yd kick no return

13:21 PURDUE
1/10-P37 - Herrmann to Burrell, 9 yds (Sybert Keneipp)
2/1 -P46 - Augustyniak up middle, lost 1 yd (Wilhite)
3/2 -P45 - Jones lt, 1 yd (Tisdale)
4/1 -P46 - Linville punt to Wilbur on I21 return to I49, 33 yd kick 28 yd return

11:51 INDIANA
1/10-I49 - Clifford to Lundy, incomplete
2/10-I49 - Clifford screen left to Harkrader, 2 yds (Moss)
3/8 -P49 - Clifford to Friede, incomplete, out of bounds
4/8 -P49 - Lovett punt to Gallivan fair catch on P21, 28 yd punt no return

10:56 PURDUE
1/10-P21 - Augustyniak at re, 2 yds (Norman, Wilbur)
2/8 -P23 - Herrmann to Burrell, incomplete
3/8 -P23 - Augustyniak on draw 9 yds (Norman)
1/10-P32 - Jones up middle, 17 yds (Tisdale)
1/10-P49 - Jones rg, 1 yd (Sybert)
2/9 - 50 - Augustyniak inside re, 15 yds (Abrams)
1/10-I35 - Jones rg, 1 yd (Norman)
2/9 -I34 - Jones pitch right, 8 yds (Norman)
3/1 -I26 - Jones rg, no gain (Norman)
4/1 -I26 - Sovereen attempt 42 yd field goal Burrell hold, short

7:08 INDIANA
1/10-I26 - Clifford to Friede, 29 yds (Moss, Supan)
1/10-P45 - Clifford to Johnson, incomplete
2/10-P45 - Clifford to Lundy, incomplete
3/10-P45 - Clifford to Stevenson, incomplete
4/10-P45 - Lovett punt to Gallivan fair catch on P14, 31 yd kick no return

6:29 PURDUE
1/10-P14 - Augustyniak inside le, 9 yds (Tallen)
2/1 -P23 - Augustyniak rg, no gain (Doehla)
3/1 -P23 - Jones pitch right, 8 yds (Keneipp)
1/10-P31 - Augustyniak inside re, 4 yds (Wilbur)
2/6 -P35 - Jones pitch right, lost 1 yd
3/7 -P34 - Jones on draw, 4 yds
4/3 -P38 - Linville punt to I18 dead, 44 yd kick no return

3:03 INDIANA
1/10-I18 - Clifford to Lundy, incomplete
2/10-I18 - Clifford to Bowers, 7 yds (Turner)
3/3 -I25 - Clifford to Stevenson, incomplete
4/3 -I25 - Clifford to Bowers, 5 yds (Marks)
1/10-I30 - Clifford to Lundy intercepted,
   Supan on P35

1:51 PURDUE
1/10-P35 - Oliver at QB McCall pitch left,
   5 yds (Keneipp, Ramsey)
2/5 -P40 - McCall pitch right, no gain
   (Swinehart)
3/5 -P40 - McCall pitch, no gain (Doehla,
   Swinehart)
   Indiana time out 0:30
4/5 -P40 - Linville punt to Wilbur on I26
   return to I21 -5 return fumble Kingsbury
   recovered for Purdue 0:18
1/10-I21 - McCall rt, no gain (Doehla)

FINAL SCORE:
PURDUE 20 INDIANA 7

National Collegiate Athletic Association
FINAL TEAM STATISTICS

	PURDUE	INDIANA
First Downs	21	15
Rushing	13	6
Passing	7	8
Penalty	1	1
Rushing Attempts	67	27
Yards Rushing	285	128
Yards Lost Rushing	12	13
Net Yards Rushing	273	115
Net Yards Passing	135	189
Passes Attempted	19	46
Passes Completed	9	20
Had Intercepted	0	2
Total Offensive Plays	86	73
Total Net Yards	408	304
Average Gain Per Play	4.74	4.16
Fumbles: Number—Lost	1/1	2/2
Penalties: Number—Yards	4/30	4/35
Interceptions: Number—Yards	2/0	0/0
Number of Punts—Yards	7/253	7/234
Average Per Punt	36.1	33.4
Punt Returns: Number—Yards	1/8	4/24
Kickoff Returns: Number—Yards	2/33	5/120

NOVEMBER 25, 1978

MINNESOTA
VS.
WISCONSIN
Camp Randall Stadium
Temp: 30
Wind: 5-10 mph
Skies: Partly cloudy
FIRST QUARTER

WISCONSIN won the toss and will receive. Minnesota will kickoff and defend the north goal.
Paul Rogind will kickoff for Minnesota to open the game to W10, Matthews returns 16 yards to W26 (Edwards).
14:55 WISCONSIN
1/10-W26 - Kalasmiki pitches right to Matthews, gets no gain (Ronan)
2/10-W26 - Kalasmiki passes over the middle to Krepfle, incomplete
3/10-W26 - Kalasmiki runs right end, gets 5 to 31 (Blanshan)
4/5 -W31 - Kiltz punts 37 yards to M32, Edwards returns -1 (Johnson)

13:26 MINNESOTA
1/10-M31 - Dilulo runs right end, gets 3 to 34 (Crossen)
2/7 -M34 - White runs up middle, gets 5 to 39 (Crossen)
3/2 -M39 - Barber runs left end, gets 6 to 45 (Crossen)
1/10-M45 - White runs up the middle, gets 4 to 49 (Relich)
2/6 -M49 - Avery pitches left to Barber, gets 5 to W46 (Lorenz)
3/1 -W46 - White runs left tackle, gets no gain (Relich)
4/1 -W46 - Smith punts 40 yards to W6 downed by Peppe

9:59 WISCONSIN
1/10-W6 - **Matthews runs left end, gets 1 to 7 (Ronan)**
2/9 -W7 - Kalasmiki passes over the middle to Sydnor, incomplete
Minnesota is penalized 26 yards for pass interference
1/10-W33 - Kalasmiki passes long left to Sydnor, incomplete
2/10-W33 - Kalasmiki passes right to Sydnor, gets 3 to 36 (Edwards)
3/7 -W36 - Kalasmiki runs right end, gets 2 to 38 (Blanshan)
4/5 -W38 - **Kiltz punts 31 yards to M31, recovered by Brown**

8:06 MINNESOTA
1/10-M31 - Barber runs left end, gets 2 to 33 (Crossen)
2/8 -M33 - Avery pitches right to Barber, gets no gain (Crossen)
3/8 -M33 - Avery passes left to White, gets 2 to 35 (Stroede)
4/6 -M35 - Smith punts 44 yards to W21 Matthews returns 3 yards to 24 (Burns)

6:56 WISCONSIN
1/10-W24 - Stauss runs left tackle, gets 13 to 37 (Sytsma)
1/10-W37 - Kalasmiki passes right to Charles, gets 12 to 49
1/10-W49 - Matthews runs left guard, gets no gain (Blanshan)
2/10-W49 - Kalasmiki passes left to Souza, gets 20 to M31
1/10-M31 - **Kalasmiki options to Matthews left, gets 31 yards for TD (4:42)**
Veith kicks the extra point (5 plays, 76 yards)
SCORE: WISCONSIN 7, MINNESOTA 0

Mike Brhely will kickoff for Wisconsin following the score to M9, Bailey returns 16 yards to M25 (Schieble)
4:37 MINNESOTA
1/10-M25 - Avery passes left to Barber, gets 1 to 26 (Johnson)
2/9 -M26 - Avery passes right to Dilulo, gets 12 to 38 (Levenick)
1/10-M38 - White runs left guard, gets 5 to 43 (Crossen)
2/5 -M43 - Barber runs left tackle, gets 2 to 45 (Crossen)
3/3 -M45 - Barber runs left guard, gets 4 to 49 (Houston)
1/10-M49 - Avery back to pass runs up middle, gets 9 to W42 (Levenick)
2/1 -W42 - WISCONSIN calls timeout (1:57) Avery keeps on the option right, gets 2 to 40 (Crossen)
1/10-W40 - Avery pitches right to Barber, gets 5 to 35 (Lorenz)
2/5 -W35 - Avery pitches right to Barber, gets no gain (Lorenz)
3/5 -W35 - Avery passes left to Bailey, incomplete
4/5 -W35 - MINNESOTA calls timeout (:07) Smith punts 4 yards to W31, out of bounds

423

0:01 WISCONSIN
1/10-W31 - Stauss runs left tackle, gets 2 to 33 (Burns)

END OF THE FIRST QUARTER: WISCONSIN 7, MINNESOTA 0

SECOND QUARTER

15:00 WISCONSIN
2/8 -W33 - Kalasmiki keeps on the option left, gets no gain (Meyer)
3/8 -W33 - Kalasmiki passes over the middle to Souza, intercepted by Brown returned 14 yards to W32 (Krall)

14:10 MINNESOTA
1/10-W32 - Barber runs left end, gets 7 to 25 (Schieble)
2/3 -W25 - Thompson runs up the middle, gets 4 to 21 (Crossen)
1/10-W21 - Barber runs right guard, gets 2 to 19 (Relich)
2/8 -W19 - Avery passes right to Dilulo, gets 4 to 15 (Johnson)
3/4 -W15 - Barber runs left guard, gets 2 to 13 (Holm)
Minnesota is penalized 5 yards for delay of game.
4/7 -W18 - Rogind's 35 yard field goal attempt is good (11:19)
SCORE: WISCONSIN 7, MINNESOTA 3

Rogind will kickoff for Minnesota following the score to W15, Matthews returns 25 yards to W40 (Thompson)
11:11 WISCONSIN
1/10-W40 - Matthews runs up the middle, gets 3 to 43 (Blanshan)
2/7 -W43 - Kalasmiki passes right to Charles, gets 16 to M41
1/10-W41 - Kalasmiki passes left to Souza, incomplete
2/10-M41 - Kalasmiki passes long right to Sydnor, incomplete
3/10-M41 - Kalasmiki passes left to Charles, gets 4 to 37
4/6 -M37 - Minnesota is penalized 5 yards for false start
4/1 -M32 - Kalasmiki sneaks up the middle, gets 6 to 26 (Brown)
1/10-M26 - Kalasmiki pitches left to Matthews, gets 2 to 24 (Sytsma)
2/8 -M24 - Kalasmiki pitches right to Cohee, gets 16 to 8 (Snyder)
1/G -W8 - Kalasmiki keeps on the option right loses 1 to 9 (Sytsma)
2/G -W9 - Kalasmiki passes right to Stauss, gets 9 for TD (6:47)
Veith kicks the extra point (10 plays, 60 yards)
SCORE: WISCONSIN 14, MINNESOTA 3

Brhely will kickoff for Wisconsin following the score to M endzone for touchback.
6:47 MINNESOTA
1/10-M20 - Avery passes right to Thompson, gets 10 to 30 (Stroede)
1/10-M30 - Barber runs left tackle, gets 6 to 36 (Relich)
2/4 -M36 - Avery pitches right to Barber, gets 3 to 39 (Cabral)
Wisconsin is penalized 15 yards for holding
1/10-W45 - White runs up the middle, gets 1 to 44 (Christenson)
2/9 -W44 - Avery pitches left Barber, gets 9 to 35 (Levenick)
1/10-W35 - MINNESOTA calls timeout (5:04)
Avery passes over the middle to Bailey, gets 19 to 16 (Anderson)
1/10-W16 - Avery pitches right to Barber, gets 7 to 9 (Welch)
Wisconsin is penalized 5 yards for personal foul
1/G -W4 - Barber runs left tackle, gets 4 for TD (4:20)
Rogind kicks the extra point (8 plays, 80 yards)
SCORE: WISCONSIN 14, MINNESOTA 10

Rogind will kickoff for Minnesota following the score to W10, Matthews returns 22 yards to W32 (Snyder)
4:14 WISCONSIN
1/10-W32 - Stauss runs up the middle, gets 5 to 37 (Sytsma)
2/5 -W37 - Kalasmiki passes over the middle to Matthews, gets 6 to 43 (Burns)
1/10-W43 - Matthews runs left tackle, gets no gain (Cunningham)
2/10-W43 - Kalasmiki passes left to Charles, incomplete
3/10-W43 - Kalasmiki passes long right to Souza, broken up (by Edwards)
4/10-W43 - Kiltz punts 35 yards to M22, out of bounds

2:17 MINNESOTA
1/10-M22 - Avery runs left, gets 14 to 36 (Welch)
1/10-M36 - Avery passes over middle to Bailey, gets 16 to W48 (Cabral)
1/10-W48 - Avery passes over middle to Barber, gets 11 to W37 (Holm)
1/10-W37 - Thompson runs left guard, gets 4 to 33 (Holm)
2/6 -W33 - Avery back to pass, loses 7 to 40 (Schremp)
3/13-W40 - Avery passes to Dilulo, incomplete
4/13-W40 - Minnesota is penalized 5 yards for delay of game
4/18-W45 - Minnesota calls timeout (:34)
Smith punts 27 yards to W18, Stauss fair catch

424

NOVEMBER 25, 1978

:27 WISCONSIN
1/10-W18 - Kalasmiki passes right to Matthews, gets 14 to 32 (Sytsma)
1/10-W32 - WISCONSIN calls timeout (:17) Kalasmiki back to pass, loses 11 to 21 (Blanshan)

END OF HALF:
WISCONSIN 14, MINNESOTA 10

THIRD QUARTER

Brhely will kickoff for Wisconsin to open the second half to M endzone for the touchback.
15:00 MINNESOTA
1/10-M20 - Avery pitches left to Barber, gets 3 to 23 (Stroede)
2/7 -M23 - Avery passes right to Dilulo, gets 7 to 30
1/10-M30 - Thompson runs right guard, gets 5 to 35 (Relich)
2/5 -M35 - Barber runs left tackle, gets 7 to 42 (Welch)
1/10-M42 - Avery pitches left to Barber, gets 5 to 47 (Stroede)
2/5 -M47 - Thompson runs right tackle, gets 8 to 45 (Welch)
1/10-W45 - Avery pitches right to Barber, gets 5 to 40 (Christenson)
2/5 -W40 - Avery pitches left to Barber, gets 1 to 39 (Johnson)
3/4 -W39 - Avery runs right end, gets 8 to 31 (Relich)
1/10-W31 - Avery pitches right to Barber, loses 2 to 33 (Levenick)
2/12-W33 - Avery passes over the middle, to Bailey, broken up (by Holm)
3/12-W33 - Avery passes over the middle to Bailey, intercepted by Welch returned 6 yards to W31 (Schwen)
Wisconsin is penalized 15 yards for clipping

11:14 WISCONSIN
1/10-W15 - Stauss runs up the middle, gets 4 to 19 (Meyer)
2/6 -W19 - Kalasmiki keeps on the option right, gets 5 to 24 (Brown)
3/1 -W24 - Matthews runs right guard, gets 4 to 28 (Blanshan)
1/10-W28 - Kalasmiki options left to Cohee, gets 2 to 30 (Brown)
Wisconsin is penalized 15 yards for clipping
1/23-W15 - Stauss runs left tackle, gets 2 to 17 (Rowan)
2/21-W17 - Kalasmiki passes right to Charles, gets 27 to 44 fumbles out of bounds
1/10-W44 - Kalasmiki options left to Matthews, gets 9 to M47 (Foxworth)
2/1 -M47 - Kalasmiki passes over the middle to Charles, incomplete

3/1 -M47 - Kalasmiki runs right guard, gets 2 to 45 (Friberg)
1/10-M45 - Kalasmiki keeps on the option left, gets 7 to 38 (Burns)
2/3 -M38 - Stauss runs up the middle, gets no gain (Burns)
3/3 -M38 - Kalasmiki keeps on the option right, gets 5 to 33 (Friberg)
1/10-M33 - Kalasmiki passes left to Sydnor, loses 1 to 34 (Edwards)
2/11-M34 - Kalasmiki passes over the middle to Sydnor, incomplete
3/11-M34 - Kalasmiki passes over the middle to Matthews, gets 34 for TD (5:21)
Veith kicks the extra point (15 plays, 85 yards)
SCORE: WISCONSIN 21, MINNESOTA 10

Brhely will kickoff for Wisconsin following the score to M endzone, Bailey returns 18 yards to 18. Minnesota is penalized 9 yards for illegal block.
5:10 MINNESOTA
1/10-M9 - Dilulo reverses right gets 6 to 15 (Anderson)
2/4 -M15 - Barber runs up the middle, gets 7 to 22 (Welch)
Wisconsin is penalized 15 yards for personal foul
1/10-M37 - Avery passes left to Bourquinn, gets 5 to 42 (Stroede)
2/5 -M42 - Barber runs right guard, gets 3 to 45 (Relich)
3/2 -M45 - Barber runs right tackle, gets 1 to 46 (Lorenz)
4/1 -M46 - Barber runs right guard, gets no gain (Holm)

3:05 WISCONSIN
1/10-M46 - Kalasmiki passes right to Charles, gets 22 to 24 (Brown)
1/10-M24 - Matthews runs right tackle, gets 3 to 21 (Ronan)
2/7 -M21 - Kalasmiki passes over the middle to Charles, broken up (by Foxworth)
3/7 -M21 - Stauss runs right tackle, gets 14 to 7 (Brown)
1/G -M7 - Kalasmiki passes over the middle to Ruetz, gets 7 for TD (1:27)
Veith kick is wide left (5 plays, 46 yards)
SCORE: WISCONSIN 27, MINNESOTA 10

Brhely will kickoff for Wisconsin following the score to M23. Thompson returns 14 yards to 37 (Gordon)
1:20 MINNESOTA
1/10-M37 - Avery back to pass, is sacked loses 7 to 30 (Lorenz)
2/17-M30 - Avery passes right is blocked, (by Lorenz)
3/17-M30 - Barber runs right tackle, gets 1 to 31 (Lorenz)
END OF THE THIRD QUARTER:
WISCONSIN 27, MINNESOTA 10

425

FOURTH QUARTER

15:00 MINNESOTA
4/16-M31 - Smith punts 33 yards to W36, Matthews returns 64 yards for TD Veith kicks the extra point (14:43)
  SCORE: WISCONSIN 34, MINNESOTA 10

Brhley will kickoff for Wisconsin following the score to M15, Thompson returns 12 yards to M27 (Gordon)

14:38 MINNESOTA
1/10-M27 - Carlson passes left to Dilulo, broken up (by Gordon)
2/10-M27 - Barber runs left tackle, gets 3 to 30 (Holm)
3/7 -M30 - Carlson passes left to Dilulo, gets 15 to 45 (Gordon)
1/10-M45 - Carlson passes right to Bailey, broken up (by Holm)
2/10-M45 - Bailey runs the reverse left gets no gain (Anderson)
3/10-M45 - Carlson passes over middle to Bailey, incomplete
4/10-M45 - Smith punts 44 yards to W11, Matthews fair catch

12:39 WISCONSIN
1/10-W11 - Matthews runs right tackle, gets 82 to M7 (Edwards)
1/G -M7 - Wisconsin is penalized 5 yards for delay of game
1/G -M12 - Kalasmiki passes left to Souza incomplete
3/G -M12 - Souza runs reverse right, gets 1 to 11 fumbles recovered by Kelly.
4/G -M11 - Vieth's 28 yard field goal attempt is wide

11:22 MINNESOTA
1/10-M20 - Carlson passes over the middle to Barber, gets 8 to 28 (Welch)
2/2 -M28 - Carlson pitches right to Barber gets 5 to 33 (Welch)
1/10-M33 - Carlson passes over the middle to Thompson, gets 3 to 36 (Christenson)
2/7 -M36 - Carlson passes over the middle to Artis, incomplete
3/7 -M36 - Carlson passes over the middle to Bourquinn, broken up (by Welch)
4/7 -M36 - Smith punts 46 yards to W18, Matthews loses 6 on returns to W12

9:19 WISCONSIN
1/10-W12 - Souza runs reverse left, gets 3 to 15 (Sytsma)
2/7 -W15 - Green runs left end, gets 6 to 21 (Fahnhorst)
3/1 -W21 - Kalasmiki pitches right to Green, gets 4 to 25
1/10-W25 - Green runs up the middle, gets 2 to 27 (Cunningham)
2/8 -W27 - Stauss runs right tackle, gets 73 yards for TD (7:13)
Veith kicks the extra point (5 plays, 88 yards)
SCORE: WISCONSIN 41, MINNESOTA 10

NOVEMBER 25, 1978

Brhely will kickoff for Wisconsin following the score to M19, Thompson returns 8 yards to M27. (Gordon)
7:08 MINNESOTA
1/10-M27 - Minnesota is penalized 5 yards for illegal procedure
1/15-M22 - Carlson passes long right to Bailey, incomplete
2/15-M22 - Carlson pitches left to Barber, gets 7 to 29 (Johnson)
3/8 -M29 - Carlson passes right to Cooper, intercepted by Spurlin

6:11 WISCONSIN
1/10-M41 - Matthews runs left guard, loses 1 to 42 (Gardner)
2/11-M42 - Wisconsin calls timeout (6:02) Josten pitches to Cohee, gets 3 to 39 (Foxworth)
3/8 -M39 - Wagner runs right tackle, gets 4 to 35 (Fahnhorst)
Minnesota is penalized 15 yards for personal foul
1/10-M20 - Josten pitches left to Cohee, gets 6 to 14 (Foxworth)
2/4 -M14 - Josten pitches left to Richardson, gets no gain (Gardner)
3/4 -M14 - Josten pitches right to Richardson, gets 3 to 11 (Edwards)
4/1 -M11 - Richardson runs right tackle, gets 3 to 8 (Fahnhorst)
1/G -M8 - Josten keeps on the option right, gets 7 to 1 (Cunningham)
2/G -M1 - Wagner runs right tackle, gets no gain (Brown)
3/G -M1 - Josten pitches left to Braker, gets 1 for TD (1:42)
Brhely kicks the extra point (10 plays, 41 yards)
SCORE: WISCONSIN 48, MINNESOTA 10

Brhely will kickoff for Wisconsin following the score to M 15, Dilulo returns 17 yards to M32 fumbles recovered by Simmons.
1:36 MINNESOTA
1/10-M32 - Tonn passes left to Dilulo, intercepted by Johnson returned 14 yards to 36 (Thompson)

1:26 WISCONSIN
1/10-M36 - Wagner runs up the middle, gets 6 to 30 (Ronan)
Wisconsin is penalized 5 yards for illegal procedure
1/15-M41 - Wagner runs up the middle, gets 2 to 39 (Sapp)
2/13-M39 - Josten pitches left to Richardson loses 3 to 42 (Brown)
3/16-M42 - Josten keeps on the option left, gets 7 to 35 (Ronan)
Wisconsin is penalized 5 yards for illegal procedure

**END OF GAME:
WISCONSIN 48, MINNESOTA 10**

427

PEACH BOWL

November 18, 1978 proved to be one of those "good news-bad news" days for Purdue football fanatics. First the bad news. Star quarterback Mark Herrmann suffered a neck and shoulder injury early in the game against Michigan and didn't play the rest of the way as the Wolverines earned a relatively easy 24-6 victory, thus knocking the Boilermakers out of first place and into sole possession of fourth place. Whew! Can there be any such thing as good news after that?

Yes, there can definitely be good news if you happened to have been an avid follower of Purdue football the past dozen years or so. For despite the loss to Michigan, immediately after the game Purdue Athletic Director, George King, announced that the Boilermakers had received a bid to play in the Peach Bowl, the Christmas Day extravaganza in Atlanta, with Georgia Tech later picked as the opposition.

It meant for only the second time in the history of Purdue football, a Boilermaker team would be a participant in a post-season bowl game. The only other such occurrence came 11 years ago, when a Bob Griese-Leroy Keyes-led Boiler team represented the Big Ten in the 1967 Rose Bowl Game and emerged victorious by a 14-13 count over Southern California. But not only did the Peach Bowl invite help offset the long lapse between bowl games, it meant something more than just an immediate reward this year, according to King.

"Basically, the No. 1 thing it does for Purdue is give us good exposure," the popular Boilermaker AD stated. "It could serve to hike interest in the university and the athletic program and that should boost recruiting and perhaps allow us to get a few more 'blue chip' players."

"In addition, it should increase interest and help ticket sales next year and give us a chance to make a little money. It's just a great thing for the university."

There had been some concern about the game being played on Christmas Day, that date selected after a lucrative national TV contract had been signed with Peach Bowl officials and CBS-TV. But it didn't appear to have any negative affect on the Boilermaker players, as opinions seemed unanimous-the bowl game took precedence over the holiday.

"Oh sure it's worth it, even though it is Christmas Day," said starting fullback John Macon. "This is the first time I've been away from home, though. But my Mom and Dad are coming down and we're all really excited about the game. Just the fact that Purdue has been in only one other bowl—and that was 11 years ago—adds pressure for us to do a good job."

That being the case, Head Coach Jim Young may want his Boilermaker squad playing under the same kind of pressure every game in 1979. Purdue played probably its finest first half of the season and stormed to a 34-7 halftime lead, driving Boilermaker fans wild with glee but causing CBS officials to squirm uncomfortably in fear of losing a vast majority of their audience.

Actually the game may have been over before it got started. There wasn't much question that the Georgia Tech offense was at less than full strength without the elusive Eddie Lee Ivery, the Yellow Jackets' all-time leading rusher, who had to miss the game due to a tender ankle. And certainly by the end of the first quarter, there was little doubt which team had control of the game that particular day.

Purdue's defense, called the "junk defense", forced Tech into a pair of turnovers in the opening stanza and with Mark Herrmann engineering the way, the Boilers quickly jumped out to a 21-0 lead before most of the Christmas presents had been unwrapped on the West Coast. From there, the margin expanded to 34-7 at halftime, and the rest, as they say, was elementary.

"We were at our best in the first quarter," understated Young. "We've never been sharper than we were in that period. I'm sure Tech missed Ivery very much. I saw him in the films and he was the best back that I saw all year."

While the Boilermakers didn't dominate the second half as they did the first 30 minutes of the game, it didn't matter with the 27 point margin they held at the break. During the second half, Young was able to get all 95 players who dressed for the game into the action. It wasn't until this free-wheeling substitution on Young's part that the Tech offense was able to generate anything which resembled the type of attack that had carried the soon-to-become Atlantic Coast Conference member to seven straight wins during the regular season. The final score was Purdue 41 - Georgia Tech 21.

Purdue so controlled the first half that Georgia Tech actually ended it with a net of zero total yards on offense, based on 29 net passing yards and minus the same number of yards rushing. Sophomore tackle Calvin Clark, who along with 20 other Boilermaker players will return in 1979, was named the defensive player of the game. The 6-5, 234-pounder just may have been a bit more inspired than the rest, as, being an Atlanta native, he wanted to show Tech coaches the prize catch they failed to grab two years ago.

The romp was such an artistic success that both QB Herrmann and second year Coach Young immediately turned their attention and thoughts to a Big Ten title in 1979.

"I think we're on our way now," said Herrmann, who is well on his own way to establishing all-time Big Ten records in both passing and total offense. "We've got a lot of guys who are going to be back, and the winning attitude is going to be there. Purdue is going to be a national power the next few years. I think we've got a great shot at the Rose Bowl next season."

"This win puts us in an entirely new position," said Young, the former defensive whiz for Bo Schembechler's great teams in the early 70's. "Now we have established our winning program and I firmly believe we will continue to have winning seasons. Just how many we'll win remains to be seen. But this helps our recruiting program, and maybe next year it'll be the Rose Bowl."

Even Purdue President Arthur Hansen showed more than just a casual interest in the game. Hansen was so involved in the game's buildup that he took to the playing field before the game started and conducted the Boilermaker marching band. Hansen's added interest in this particular contest may have stemmed from his previous job prior to taking over at Purdue. And what, as if one hasn't guessed by now, was that job? Why, he was president at Georgia Tech, of course. But while serving as president of both schools, Hansen had no second thoughts about which side of the field he would sit on once the game began.

"As an alumnus of the university and as its president, my heart is completely with Purdue" he stated emphatically. There were no second thoughts about which school fielded the better football team that day either.

GEORGIA TECH VS. PURDUE
Temp.: 45
Wind: NW 1-5 mph
Skies: Clear
FIRST QUARTER

Tech win toss, will receive, Purdue defends south goal
Sovereen kickoff taken by Sumpter at 12, returns 10 yards to 22

14:55 GEORGIA
1/10-G22 - Kelley keeps wide left for 4 (Turner)
2/6 -G26 - Kelley pass intended for Hill incomplete
3/6 -G26 - Shamburger middle for 5 (Jackson)
4/1 -G32 - Peeples punt taken by Pope at P36 fair catch (32 yard punt)

13:52 PURDUE
1/10-P36 - Herrmann pass intended for Harris incomplete
2/10-P36 - Macon left side for 6
3/4 -P42 - Augustyniak left side for 5 to 47
1/10-P47 - Herrmann pass intended for Harris incomplete
2/10-P47 - Pope middle for 7 (Haley)
3/3 -G46 - Jones middle for no gain (Bradley)
4/3 -G46 - Linville punt out of bounds at 8 (38 yard punt)

11:19 GEORGIA
1/10-G8 - Shamburger fumble loss of 3 recovered by Clark

11:15 PURDUE
1/5 -G5 - Macon middle for 2 (Blanton)
2/G -G3 - Jones middle for 3 and TD Sovereen PAT good
SCORE: PURDUE 7, GEORGIA 0

Sovereen into end zone for touchback
10:40 GEORGIA
1/10-G20 - Kelley pass intended for Moore intercepted by Marks at 30, returns 10

10:31 PURDUE
1/10-G20 - Macon for 1 up middle (Bradley)
2/9 -G19 - Augustyniak right side for 11 (Bessillieu)
1/G -G8 - Jones right side for 8 and TD Sovereen PAT good
SCORE: PURDUE 14, GEORGIA 0

Sovereen kickoff taken by Hill at 4, returns 23 yards to 27
9:37 GEORGIA
1/10-G27 - Lee middle for 2 (Clark)
2/8 -G29 - Shamburger wide left no gain (Motts)
3/8 -G29 - Kelley pass complete to Shamburger for 5 (Turner)
4/3 -G34 - Peeples punt taken by Pope, returns for loss of 5 to P20 (41 yard punt)

7:49 PURDUE
1/10-P20 - Herrmann pass complete to Young for 28
1/10-P48 - Pope middle for loss of 1 (Richardson)
2/11-P47 - Herrmann pass intended for Young incomplete
3/11-P47 - Herrmann pass complete to Pope for 23 (Lowe)
1/10-G30 - Augustyniak right side for 3 (Harris)
2/7 -G27 - Herrmann pass intended for Burrell but Georgia penalized 17 yards (pass interference)
1/G -G10 - Herrmann pass complete to Smith for 10 and TD Sovereen PAT good
SCORE: PURDUE 21, GEORGIA 0

Sovereen kickoff out of end zone for touchback
6:04 GEORGIA
1/10-G20 - Shamburger middle for no gain (Floyd)
2/10-G20 - Kelley pass intended for Hill incomplete
3/10-G20 - Kelley pass complete to Rank for 19
1/10-G39 - Kelley back to pass, loses 5 (Jackson)
2/15-G34 - Shamburger middle for 2 (Marcus, Jackson)
3/13-G36 - Kelley pass intended for Rank incomplete
4/13-G36 - Peeples punt, bad snap, Peeples tackled at G13 for a team loss of 23 (Fuetterer)

3:42 PURDUE
1/10-G13 - Macon right side for loss of 2 (Blanton)
2/12-G15 - Oliver pass intended for Eubank incomplete
3/12-G15 - Oliver pass intended for Smith incomplete
4/12-G15 - Sovereen field goal attempt from 22 (32 yard attempt) no good wide right but Georgia penalized 8 yards (roughing kicker) ball on 7
4/14-G7 - Sovereen 25-yard field goal attempt no good wide left

2:51 GEORGIA
1/10-G20 - Shamburger right side for 2 (Clark)
2/8 -G22 - Kelley pass intended for Moore incomplete
3/8 -G22 - Kelley back to pass, slips down at 13, loss of 9
4/17-G13 - Peeples punt taken by Pope at P49 fair catch (38 yard punt)

431

1:34 PURDUE
- 1/10-P49 - Herrmann pass complete to Burrell for 11
- 1/10-G40 - Augustyniak middle for 6 (Helm)
- 2/4 -G34 - Macon right side for 1 (Helm, Volley)
- 3/3 -G33 - Herrmann back to pass, keeps left side for 2 (Harris)

END OF FIRST QUARTER
PURDUE 21, GEORGIA TECH 0

SECOND QUARTER
PURDUE
- 4/1 -G31 - Macon middle for 2 (Cooksey)
- 1/10-G29 - Pope right side for loss of 1 (Haley)
- 2/11-G30 - Herrmann pass complete to Harris for 27
- 1/G -G3 - Jones middle for 1 (Harris)
- 2/G -G2 - Herrmann keeps left side for 2 and TD Sovereen PAT good
  SCORE: PURDUE 28, GEORGIA 0

Sovereen kickoff taken by Hill at 3, returns 43 to 46 and Purdue penalized to P39 (personal foul)
12:55 GEORGIA
- 1/10-P39 - Lee middle for 10 (Soupan)
- 2/1 -P29 - Shamburger middle for no gain (Loushin)
- 3/1 -P29 - Mann left side for 6
- 1/10-P23 - Lanier keeps right side for 9 (Moss)
- 2/1 -P14 - Hill on reverse wide right for 10 (Clark)
- 1/G -P4 - Shamburger right side for 3 (Zordani)
- 2/G -P1 - Shamburger middle no gain (Johanson)
- 3/G -P1 - Lee middle for 1 and TD Smith PAT good
  SCORE: PURDUE 28, GEORGIA 7

Bessillieu kickoff out of end zone for touchback
9:35 PURDUE
- 1/10-P20 - Jones middle for 14 (Dyett)
- 1/10-P34 - Herrmann pass complete to Burrell for 18
- 1/10-G48 - Macon right side for 8, fumble recovered by Jones
- 2/2 -G40 - Augustyniak wide right for no gain (Fox)
- 3/2 -G40 - Herrmann keeps left side for 4 (Helm)
- 1/10-G36 - Macon left side for 7 (Shank)
- 2/3 -G29 - Herrmann keeps left side for 4 (Fox)
- 1/10-G25 - Macon middle for 5 (Haley)
- 2/5 -G20 - Herrmann pass intended for Harris incomplete
- 3/5 -G20 - Macon middle for 6 (Bessillieu)
- 1/10-G14 - Jones left side for 6 (Cooksey)
- 2/4 -G8 - Jones leftside for 7 (Perkins)
- 1/G -G1 - Macon middle for 1 and TD Sovereen PAT no good
  SCORE: PURDUE 34, GEORGIA 7

Sovereen kickoff taken by Marble at G24, returns 13 to 37 (McKinnie)
3:50 GEORGIA
- 1/10-G37 - Kelley pass complete to Hill for 5 (Smith)
- 2/5 -G42 - Shamburger right side for 1 (Clark)
- 3/4 -G43 - Kelley sacked by Turner at 30 for loss of 13
- 4/17-G30 - Peeples punt downed at P45 (25 yard punt), but Purdue penalized 15 yards to 45 (roughing kicker)
- 4/2 -G45 - Peeples back to punt, bad snap, Peeples downed ball at 13, team loss of 32 yards

1:49 PURDUE
- 1/10-G13 - McCall middle for 2 (Kelly)
- 2/8 -G11 - Oliver back to pass, loses 7 (Richardson)
- 3/15-G18 - Oliver back to pass, sacked by Blanton for loss of 12
- 4/27-G30 - Sovereen 47-yard field goal attempt no good short.

END OF FIRST HALF
PURDUE 34, GEORGIA TECH 7

THIRD QUARTER

Bessillieu kickoff out of bounds. Bessillieu kickoff from 35 (Georgia penalized 5 yards) taken by Moss at 2, returns 30 to 32 (Haley)
14:53 PURDUE
- 1/10-P32 - Macon left side for loss of 2
- 2/12-P30 - Herrmann pass intended Burrell incomplete
- 3/12-P30 - Herrmann pass intended for Augustyniak incomplete (Shank)
- 4/12-P30 - Eagan punt fair catch by Bessillieu (31 yard punt)

14:00 GEORGIA
- 1/10-G39 - Lee middle for 2 (Motts)
- 2/8 -G41 - Kelley pass intended for Moore incomplete
- 3/8 -G41 - Kelley pass intended for Moore incomplete
- 4/8 -G41 - Peeples punt taken by Pope at 16, returns 14 to 30 (43 yard punt)

13:04 PURDUE
- 1/10-P30 - Jones middle for 2 (Helm)
- 2/8 -P32 - Herrmann pass intended for Harris intercepted for Bessillieu at G38, no return

12:20 GEORGIA
- 1/10-G38 - Lee middle for 1 (Floyd)
- 2/9 -G39 - Lanier keeps right side for 4, fumbles, recovered by Moss

11:37 PURDUE
- 1/10-G43 - Macon middle for 2 (Harris)

2/8 -G41 - Pope right side for 5 (Lowe, Johnson)
3/3 -G36 - Herrmann pass intended for Macon incomplete
4/3 -G36 - Macon right side for 2 (Richardson)

10:19 GEORGIA
1/10-G34 - Kelley pass complete to Moore but Purdue penalized pass interference for 9
1/10-G43 - Shamburger middle for 2
2/8 -G45 - Kelley pass intended for Hill, intercepted by Wayne Smith at P47 returns 28 to G25

8:53 PURDUE
1/10-G25 - Purdue penalized 5 (illegal procedure)
1/15-G30 - Jones wide right for 1 (Haley)
2/14-G29 - Herrmann pass complete to Harris for 11 (Shank)
3/3 -G18 - Herrmann pass intended for Burrell incomplete
4/3 -G18 - Purdue penalized 5 to 23 (delay of game)
4/8 -G23 - Herrmann pass intended for Harris, intercepted by Shank at 5, returns 5 to 10

7:26 GEORGIA
1/10-G10 - Lanier right side, bad pitch to Shamburger, loses 2
2/12-G8 - Shamburger right side for 6
3/6 -G14 - Kelley pass intended for Rank incomplete
4/6 -G14 - Peeples punt fair catch by Pope at G49 (35 yard punt)

5:56 PURDUE
1/10-G49 - Macon middle for 4 (Harris)
2/6 -G45 - Jones right side for 5, fumble recovered by Schwann
3/1 -G40 - Jones middle for 2
1/10-G38 - Herrmann pass intended for Burrell incomplete, but Georgia penalized 13 yards (pass interference)
1/10-G25 - Macon middle for 3 (Johnson)
2/7 -G22 - Herrmann pass intended for Burrell incomplete
3/7 -G22 - Macon middle for 7 (Richardson)
1/10-G15 - Jones wide right for no gain (Harris)
2/10-G15 - Purdue penalized 5 yards (delay of game)
2/15-G20 - Herrmann pass to Pope complete for 2 (Bessillieu)
3/13-G18 - Herrmann back to pass, slips down for loss of 9
4/22-G27 - Linville in to punt, but Purdue penalized 15 (personal foul)
4/37-G42 - Linville punt fair catch by Bessillieu at 11 (31 yard punt)

1:38 GEORGIA
1/10-G11 - Kelley pass complete to Hill for 3 (Clark)

2/7 -G14 - Kelley pass intended to Newman incomplete
3/7 -G14 - Kelley pass complete to Davis for 6
4/1 -G20 - Peeples punt fair catch by Gallivan at P49 (31 yard punt)

:45 PURDUE
1/10-P49 - Augustyniak middle for 1 (Helm)
2/9 - 50 - Herrmann pass complete to Augustyniak for 10 (Shank)

END OF THIRD QUARTER
PURDUE 34, GEORGIA TECH 7

FOURTH QUARTER

PURDUE
1/10-G40 - Herrmann pass complete to Augustyniak for no gain (Helm)
2/10-G40 - Macon wide left for 16 (Richardson)
1/10-G24 - Herrmann pass intended for Harris incomplete
2/10-G24 - Macon middle for loss of 3 (Kelley, Harris)
3/13-G27 - Herrmann pass complete to Burrell for 14
1/10-G13 - Jones wide right for 1 (Kelley)
2/9 -G12 - Herrmann pass complete to Burrell for 12 and TD Sovereen PAT good
SCORE: PURDUE 41, GEORGIA 7

Tech penalized 5 to 45 (illegal procedure) Sovereen kickoff from 45 taken by Hill in end zone, returns 16 to 16

12:31 GEORGIA
1/10-G16 - Kelley pass intended for Hill incomplete
2/10-G16 - Kelley pass complete to Hill for 15
1/10-G31 - Kelley pass complete to Davis but Purdue penalized 5 yards to 36 (offsides)
1/5 -G36 - Kelley pass complete to Shamburger for 14 (Mark, Smith)
1/10- 50 - Kelly pass complete to Davis for no gain
2/10- 50 - Kelley pass intended for Moore incomplete
3/10- 50 - Kelley pass complete to Lee for no gain
4/10- 50 - Kelley pass intended for Hill incomplete

10:14 PURDUE
1/10- 50 - Oliver pass intended for Gallivan incomplete, but Purdue penalized declined
2/10- 50 - McCall middle for 4 (Richardson)
3/6 -G46 - Oliver back to pass, sacked by Blanton for loss of 9
4/15-P45 - Eagan punt taken by Bessillieu at 11 returns 10 to 21 (44 yard punt)

9:22 GEORGIA
1/10-G21 - Kelley pass intended for Moore incomplete

433

2/10-G21 - Hill end around, wide right for 11
1/10-G32 - Kelley keeps wide left for 11 (Grimmett)
1/10-G43 - Kelley back to pass, loses 3 (Kingsbury)
2/13-G40 - Kelley pass intended for Davis incomplete
3/13-G40 - Kelley pass intended for Moore incomplete
4/13-G40 - Peeples punt taken by Pope at 23, returns 0 to 23 (37 yard punt)

7:06 PURDUE
1/10-P23 - Doria left side for 2 (Dyett)
2/8 -P25 - Williams right side for 3
3/5 -P28 - Barr keeps right side for 2
4/3 -P30 - Linville punt taken by Bessillieu at 31, returns 4 (39 yard punt)

5:14 GEORGIA
1/10-G35 - Kelley pass complete to Hardie for 9
2/1 -G44 - Lee middle for 8
1/10-P48 - Kelley pass intended for Hill incomplete
2/10-P48 - Kelley pass complete to Moore for 4
3/6 -P44 - Kelley pass intended for Hardie incomplete
4/6 -P44 - Kelley pass complete to Hardie for 14 (Perry)
1/10-P30 - Kelley pass complete to Hill for 23
1/G -P7 - Kelley pass intended for Mann incomplete
2/G -P7 - Hardie pass intended for Kelley incomplete, but Purdue penalized 4 (holding)
2/G -P3 - Kelley pass complete to Moore for 3 yards and TD. Two-Point Conversion Attempt: Hill wide left run good.
SCORE: PURDUE 41, GEORGIA 15

Bessillieu onside kickoff covered by Marble at P48

2:37 GEORGIA
1/10-P48 - Kelley pass intended for Moore incomplete
2/10-P48 - Kelley pass complete to Hardie for 6
3/4 -P42 - Kelley pass intended for Hill incomplete
4/4 -P42 - Kelley pass complete to Hardie for 11
1/10-P31 - Kelley pass complete to Hill 31 yards and TD Two-Point Conversion Attempt: Kelley pass intended for Moore incomplete
SCORE: PURDUE 41, GEORGIA 21

Bessillieu kickoff taken by East at 50

1:15 PURDUE
1/10- 50 - Doria middle for 8 (Dyett, Fox)
2/2 -G42 - McAfee middle for no gain (Dyett)
3/2 -G42 - Harris left side for 9

**FINAL SCORE
PURDUE 41, GEORGIA TECH 21**

National Collegiate Athletic Association
FINAL TEAM STATISTICS

	PURDUE	GA TECH
First Downs Rushing	13	5
First Downs Passing	9	7
First Downs by Penalties	2	2
Total First Downs	24	14
Number Attempts Rushing	58	33
Yards Gained Rushing	203	102
Yards Lost Rushing	46	90
Net Yards Gained Rushing	157	12
Number Passes Attempted	27	38
Number of Passes Completed	12	17
Number of Passes Had Intercepted	2	2
Net Yards Gained Passing	166	168
Number Plays Rushing and Passing	85	71
Total Offense Yardage	323	180
Number Interceptions	2	2
Net Yard Interceptions Returned	38	5
Number Times Punted	5	7
Number Punts Had Blocked	0	0
Punting Average, Yards	36.6	36.7
Number Punts Returned	3	2
Net Yards Punts Returned	9	14
Number Kickoffs Returned	1	5
Net Yards Kickoffs Returned	30	105
Number Times Penalized	9	5
Total Yards Penalized	78	48
Number Times Fumbled	3	2
Number Own Fumbles Lost	1	2

GATOR BOWL

Ohio State freshman quarterback Art Schlichter established an all-time single season Buckeye record for total offense with 275 yards in the 34th annual Gator Bowl but your average sports fan isn't likely to remember that fact. He isn't even likely to recall the score of the game that December 29th night when Clemson edged the Buckeyes by a 17-15 count. Rather, the item which will be readily recalled by historians when referring to the '78 Gator Bowl, will be labeled "the Hayes incident".

The game itself had shaped up as one of contrasting styles, with Clemson's stingy defense having allowed its opposition only four touchdown passes and eight via rushing through an impressive 10-1 season and 7th place ranking in the national polls. Ohio State on the other hand, had been embarrassed on several occasions with a porous pass defense, to the extent that the Buckeyes' pass defense actually ranked 134th out of 134 teams in Division I play during the early part of the season. On the other hand, OSU had the rookie quarterback Art Schlichter, who after throwing five interceptions in his first collegiate start against Penn State, had only 16 more errant tosses in the next 10 games.

Ohio State coach Woody Hayes had labeled the '78 season a disappoinment, as the Buckeyes had finished fourth in the vastly improved Big Ten race. Now it was up to the OSU general of 28 years and 238 coaching victories to prepare his squad for another post-season confrontation. Possibly it was the remembrance of the year before when word got out that the Buckeye players were restless in New Orleans after arriving two weeks before the New Year's Day classic with Alabama which the Crimson Tide dominated by a 35-6 score. At any rate, Hayes decided this year to travel to the bowl site in Jacksonville just three days ahead of the game with the Atlantic Coast Conference champions.

"We're not practicing as often, but with more intensity," Hayes stated prior to the team's departure from Columbus. "We want to try to get ready without overdoing it this time."

It hadn't been a particularly good build-up to the game weatherwise anyway. Wind, rain and cold had washed away the dreams and hopes of both OSU and Clemson supporters to soak up some Florida sun. Game night found chilly conditions, but the crowds soon forgot about temperature readings as the ever-popular *Hang on Sloopy* got the OSU fans in high gear while Clemson partisans—in their overabundance of orange and preponderance of tiger paw prints, including ones painted on their faces—quickly got into the spirit of things as well.

Ohio State started off like it had the perfect game plan. After holding the vaunted Tiger attack to 5 yards in its first possession, the Buckeyes got the ball on their own 36 and promptly put together a 10-play drive that carried them down to the one yard line. But on a key fourth-down play, fullback Rick Volley was thrown for a one yard loss and the Tigers took over. The rest of the quarter was a battle between punters David Sims of Clemson and Tom Orosz of Ohio State as the period ended with a scoreless tie.

But the second stanza had just the opposite results as both teams gained possession twice and scored both times they had the ball. The Buckeyes used Schlichter's passing skills, with a 34 yard completion to Doug Donley setting up a Bob Atha field goal, while another 34-yarder to big Ron Barwig was followed two plays later by Schlichter's keeper around end for a 4-yard TD jaunt. Unfortunately for the Bucks, the PAT attempt by Vlade Janakievski was blocked to give Ohio State its only lead of the game, a 9-7 edge. Clemson had used a 15-play march to go 80 yards for its first score, and though there was just 1:20 showing on the clock following Ohio State's field goal, the Tigers used three quick pass completions by QB Steve Fuller to pick up 66 yards. That put the ball within field goal range for Obed Ariri who connected on a 47-yard effort with just five seconds left in the half, giving the Tigers a slim 10-9 advantage at the halfway mark.

The third quarter saw another time-consuming (over 7½ minutes) Clemson drive result in six points, though the Tigers did need three tries from the one yard line before reaching paydirt on the 19th play of the 84-yard march. Thus heading into the final 15 minutes of play, the ACC champs held a precarious 8-point lead.

But the gutsy Schlichter, who ended up with 16 completions in 20 attempts and over 200 yards, took the Bucks on an 87 yard march to the end zone, accounting for all but 13 yards himself. The all-important two-point conversion attempt by Schlichter was stopped just short of the goal line for Ohio's next and final march with less than 4½ minutes remaining in the game.

The Buckeyes had gotten the needed break when a bad pitch by Fuller was recovered back on the 44 yard line. The OSU offense took over at the point, and with Schlichter again performing like a seasoned veteran, the Buckeyes moved down to the 24 yard line, setting up a vital 3rd and 5 situation. What followed will rank among the most talked-about happenings in college football.

Schlichter, back to pass, hurried a throw over the middle that was picked off by middle guard Charlie Bauman and returned to the 40 yard line, where he was wrestled out of bounds. Accounts vary as to the happenings hereafter, but what was clear after viewing TV replays, was the altercation, that a very frustrated Hayes had with

Bauman. The resulting melee in front of the OSU bench not only gave the Tigers the ball, but an unsportsmanlike penalty added on another 15 yards to put the ball inside the 50. The very next play brought about another 15-yarder for the same infraction as Hayes vigorously complained to officials about the clock running too long after the Buckeyes had called time out. With the ball now well inside the 30 yard line, Clemson was able to run out the clock (thanks to a surprise 8-yard pass play on a 4th and 7 situation), the game ending 17-15.

For Hayes it proved to be his final game as head coach of the Buckeyes. The following morning Ohio State Director of Athletics Hugh Hindman informed Hayes he had been relieved of his coaching duties as of that day. It marked an unfortunate ending of a great coaching career for the man who owns the fourth highest victory total in the history of college football, and was the second winningest active coach at the time of his dismissal. The Woody Hayes era had come to a close.

CLEMSON VS. OHIO STATE
Jacksonville, Fla.
FIRST QUARTER

Clemson won toss and will receive, Ohio St. will defend the north goal Atha kicks off for State to the end zone, no return

15:00 CLEMSON
1/10-C20 - Fuller passes incomplete to Brown (Johnson)
2/10-C20 - Brown around left end gain 5 (Skillings)
3/5 -C25 - Fuller passes incomplete to Brown (Ross)
4/5 -C25 - Sims 39 yards no return

14:30 OHIO STATE
1/10-O36 - Schlichter passes incomplete to Donley (Varn)
2/10-O36 - Schlichter passes complete to Donley gain 12 (Brooks)
1/10-O48 - Springs up the middle gain 1 (Scott)
2/9 -O49 - Springs around left end gain 13 (Rollins)
1/10-C38 - Campbell off tackle gain 3 (Brown)
2/7 -C35 - Springs on the draw gain 8 (Stuckey)
1/10-C27 - Schlichter up the middle gain 3 (Varn)
2/7 -C24 - Springs around right end gain 14 (Adams)
1/10-C10 - Campbell off left tackle gain 4 (Brown)
2/6 -C6 - Schlichter off tackle gain 1 (Gibbs)
3/5 -C5 - Schlichter off left tackle gain 4 (Brown)
4/1 -C1 - Volley around left end loss 1 (Brown)

9:49 CLEMSON
1/10-C2 - Brown off right tackle gain 3 (Washington)
2/7 -C5 - Fuller around right end gain 2 (Ross)
3/5 -C7 - Fuller passes incomplete to Butler (Guess)
4/5 -C7 - Sims punts 40 yards to the 47, Guess returns 5

8:16 OHIO STATE
1/10-C42 - Schlichter almost intercepted by Scott intended for Gerald
2/10-C42 - Campbell off tackle gain 8 (Gibbs)
3/2 -C34 - Schlichter off tackle, motion Ohio State
3/7 -C39 - Murray off tackle on Draw, loss 1 (Scott)
4/8 -C40 - Orosz punts out of bounds to the 8

6:39 CLEMSON
1/10-C8 - Perry off tackle gain 5 (Cato)
2/5 -C13 - Perry off right tackle gain 1 (Ross)
3/4 -C14 - Perry around left end, loss 1 (Mills)
4/5 -C13 - Sims punts 32, no return

4:43 OHIO STATE
1/10-C45 - Schlichter keeps around right end gain 9 (Williams)
2/1 -C36 - Springs fumbles in the backfield, loss 4 (Scott)
3/5 -C40 - Schlichter keeps around left end, gain 9 (Ryan)
1/10-C31 - Johnson up the middle 2 (Brown)
2/8 -C29 - Campbell up the middle, gain 2 (Bauman)
3/6 -C27 - Motion Clemson
3/1 -C22 - Campbell up the middle, gain 0 (Williams)
4/1 -C22 - Campbell up the middle, gain 0 (Jordan)

1:26 CLEMSON
1/10-C21 - Fuller keeps up the middle after pass fails, gain 10 (Cousineau) personal foul Clemson
2/15-C16 - Fuller passes complete to Tuttle gain 5 personal foul Ohio State
1/10-C37 - Fuller passes incomplete to Clark (Guess)
2/10-C37 - Fuller around left end loss 5 (Bell)
3/15-C32 - Fuller passes incomplete to Clark (Guess)
4/15-C32 - Sims punts 40 no return

:39 OHIO STATE
1/10-O28 - Springs up the middle gain 2 (Scott)
2/8 -O30 - Schlichter passes complete to Barwig gain 17 (Hansford)

END OF FIRST QUARTER
CLEMSON 0, OHIO STATE 0

SECOND QUARTER

OHIO STATE
1/10-O47 - Springs off left tackle gain 3 (Brown)
2/7 - 50 - Schlichter passes complete to Donley gain 34 (Geathers)
1/10-C16 - Schlichter around right end gain 2 (Scott)
2/8 -C14 - Gerald around right end on reverse gain clipping Ohio State
2/16-C22 - Schlichter to Campbell gain 6 (Brown)
3/10-C16 - Springs off left tackle gain 7 (Gibbs
4/3 -C9 - Atha kicks a 27 yd FG 72 yards, 8 plays
SCORE: OHIO STATE 3, CLEMSON 0

Atha kicks off in the end zone

438

12:08 CLEMSON
1/10-C20 - Perry up the middle, gain 2 (Cato)
2/8-C22 - Fuller keeps around left end, gain 13 (Ellis)
1/10-C35 - Fuller runs out of the pocket gain 6 (Megaro)
2/4 -C41 - Perry up the middle gain 5 (Cousineau)
1/10-C46 - Fuller passes to Butler gain 6 (Guess)
2/4 -O48 - Brown around right and gain 2 (Henson)
3/2 -O46 - Fuller passes complete to Butler gain 13 (Skillings)
1/10-O33 - Perry up the middle gain 5 (Cato)
2/5 -O28 - Perry up the middle gain 4 (Cousineau)
3/1 -O24 - Goggins up the middle gain 0 (Henson)
4/1 -O24 - Brown off right tackle gain 4 (Cousineau)
1/10-O20 - Perry up the middle gain 3 (Sullivan)
2/7 -O17 - Fuller around left end gain 8 (Cato)
1/G -O9 - Fuller around left end gain 5 (Cousineau)
2/G -O4 - Fuller around left end for the touchdown gain 4
Ariri kicks the conversion
SCORE: CLEMSON 7, OHIO STATE 3

Ariri kicks off for Clemson to the 3, Donley returns 19 to the 22
4:58 OHIO STATE
1/10-O22 - Campbell off tackle gain 3 (Bryant)
2/7 -O25 - Schlichter around left end gain 6 (Brown)
3/1 -O31 - Campbell off tackle gain 3 (Brown)
1/10-O34 - Schlichter around right end gain 3 (Scott)
2/7 -O37 - Schlichter passes complete to Campbell gain 11 (Jordan)
1/10-O48 - Schlichter passes to Gerald gain 9 (Jordan)
2/1 -C43 - Schlichter passes to Barwig gain 34 (Rollins)
1/G -C9 - Schlichter off tackle gain 5 (Brown)
2/G -C4 - Schlichter around left end gain 4 touchdown Janakievski kick blocked by Gibbs motion Ohio State declined
SCORE: OHIO STATE 9, CLEMSON 7

Atha kicks off for Ohio State to the 2, Jordan returns 22 to the 24
1:15 CLEMSON
1/10-C24 - Fuller passes complete to Butler gain 17 (Guess)
1/10-C41 - Fuller passes to Clark gain 39 interference Clemson
2/24-C27 - Fuller passes to Clark gain 28 (Cousineau)
1/10-O45 - Fuller passes to Ratchford gain 10 (Ellis)

1/10-O35 - Fuller passes incomplete to Butler (Skillings)
2/10-O35 - Fuller passes incomplete to Tuttle (Megaro)
3/10-O35 - Sims off left tackle gain 5 (Cousineau)
4/5 -O30 - Ariri kicks 47 yd 76 yards, 8 plays
SCORE: CLEMSON 10, OHIO STATE 9

Ariri kicks off for Clemson to the 12, Murray returns 15 to the 27

END OF FIRST HALF
CLEMSON 10, OHIO STATE 9

THIRD QUARTER

Clemson will kickoff and defend the north goal......
Ariri kicks off for the Tigers to the goal, returned by Donley to the 21
14:50 OHIO STATE
1/10-O21 - Campbell off tackle gain 4 (Scott)
2/6 -O25 - Schlichter off tackle gain 2 (Scott)
3/4 -O27 - Schlichter passes to Donley loss 2 (Varn)
4/6 -O25 - Orosz punts 53 yards, Jordan returns to the 14, clipping Clemson Jordan minus 8 return, 7 yard penalty

13:03 CLEMSON
1/10-C7 - Ratchford around left end gain 5 (Cousineau)
2/5 -C12 - Ratchford around left end gain 4 (Megaro)
3/1 -C16 - Goggins up the middle gain 0
4/1 -C16 - Sims punts 38, Guess returns loss 1

11:47 OHIO STATE
1/10-O45 - Schlichter minus 3 (Scott)
2/13-O42 - Schlichter passes to Springs gain 0 (Brown)
3/13-O42 - Campbell up the middle loss 4 (Brown & Scott)
4/17-O38 - Orosz punts 46 no return

9:53 CLEMSON
1/10-C16 - Sims off left tackle gain 2 (Henson)
2/8 -C18 - Fuller around right end gain 4 (Cato)
3/4 -C22 - Fuller passes to Tuttle gain 15 (Guess)
1/10-C37 - Around left end Austin gain 9 (Dulin)
2/1 -C46 - Fuller passes incomplete to Tuttle (Ellis)
3/1 -C46 - Austin off left tackle gain 1 (Ellis)
1/10-C47 - Fuller passes incomplete to Butler (Mills)
2/10-C47 - Sims off left tackle gain 12 (Byron)
1/10-O41 - Fuller passes incomplete to Tuttle
2/10-O41 - Ratchford around left end gain 14 (Skillings)

439

1/10-027 - Sims off left tackle gain 6 (Cousineau)
2/4 -021 - Sims up the middle gain 2 (Henson)
3/2 -019 - Ratchford around right end gain 5 (Cousineau)
1/10-014 - Sims up the middle gain 4 (Dansler)
2/6 -010 - Fuller keeps around left end loss 1 (Guess)
3/7 -011 - Fuller runs from the pocket gain 10 (Mills)
1/G -01 - Ratchford up the middle no gain (Cato)
2/G -01 - Ratchford up the middle no gain (Cousineau)
3/G -01 - Austin up the middle gain 1 touchdown 2:16
Ariri kicks the conversion
SCORE: CLEMSON 17, OHIO STATE 9

Ariri kicks off for Clemson to the end zone, Donley returns 39 to the 39
2:06 OHIO STATE
1/10-039 - Schlichter passes to Springs, loss 5 (Scott)
2/15-034 - Schlichter passes incomplete to Hunter (Jordan)
3/15-034 - Schlichter to Murray gain 8 (Brooks)
4/7 -042 - Orosz punts out of bounds at the 23, 35 yard punt

:27 CLEMSON
1/10-C23 - Ratchford around left end gain 6 (Skillings)
2/4 -C29 - Perry up the middle gain 8 (Mills)

END OF THIRD QUARTER
CLEMSON 17, OHIO STATE 9

FOURTH QUARTER

CLEMSON
1/10-C37 - Perry up the middle gain 6 (Cousineau)
2/4 -C43 - Perry off right tackle gain 5 (Cousineau)
1/10-C48 - Perry up the middle gain 1 (Cousineau)
2/9 -C49 - Fuller off tackle gain 1 fumble recovered Kenney (Henson)
3/8 - 50 - Fuller fumbles again loss 1 (Cousineau)
4/9 -C49 - Sims punts to the 10, Guess returns 3 (Soowal)

11:57 OHIO STATE
1/10 -013 - Springs around right end gain 0 (B. Smith)
2/10-013 - Schlichter passes to Hunter gain 37 (Underwood)
1/10- 50 - Schlichter around left end no gain (Reed)
2/10- 50 - Schlichter passes to Murray gain 8 (Geathers)
3/2 -C42 - Campbell off right tackle gain 3 (B. Smith)
1/10-C39 - Schlichter passes to Gerald gain 10 (Geathers)
1/10-C29 - Schlichter off tackle gain 8 (Gibbs)
2/2 -C21 - Murray off tackle gain 9 (Rollins)
1/10-C12 - Schlichter around right end gain 6 (Brown)
2/4 -C6 - Schlichter around right end gain 3 (Brown)
3/1 -C3 - Volley off right tackle gain 2 (Latimer)
1/G -C1 - Schlichter off left tackle for gain 1 touchdown 8:11 4th Schlichter attempts around left end for 2 pts. no good (Stuckey)
SCORE: CLEMSON 17, OHIO STATE 15

Atha kicks off for Ohio State to the 4, Jordan returns kick to the 20, 16 yds
Personal Foul Ohio State, 15 yards
8:06 CLEMSON
1/10-C35 - Ratchford around left end gain 12 (Cousineau)
1/10-C47 - Sims up the middle gain 1 (Megaro)
2/9 -C48 - Holding Clemson 14 yards
2/23-C34 - Ratchford up the middle gain 4 (Sawiki)
3/19-C38 - Fuller passes to Tuttle gain 20 (Skillings)
1/10-042 - Ratchford around left end gain 4 (Skillings)
2/6 -038 - Sims off right tackle gain 2 (Megaro)
3/4 -036 - Fuller loss 20 bad pitch fumble, Sawiki recovers

440

4:22 OHIO STATE
1/10-C44 - Murray around right end gain clipping Ohio State
2/21-O45 - Schlichter passes to Gerald gain 14 (Jordan)
2/7 -C41 - Schlichter passes Hunter gain 12 (Varn)
1/10-C29 - Springs around left end loss 2 (Stuckey)
2/12-C31 - Schlichter around right end gain 7 (Brooks)
3/5 -C24 - Schlichter pass intercepted by Bauman intended for Springs, returned 15 yards Ohio State Unsportsmanlike penalty

1:59 CLEMSON
1/10-O45 - Perry off left tackle gain 3 Unsportsmanlike penalty Hayes
1/10-O28 - Perry off right tackle gain 3 (Megaro)
2/7 -O25 - Delay Clemson
2/12-O30 - Perry off left tackle gain 3 (Laughlin)
3/9 -O27 - Fuller on the keeper up the middle gain 2 (Cousineau)
4/7 -O25 - Fuller passes it Butler gain 8 (Ellis)
1/10-O17 - Fuller falls on ball no gain
2/10-O17 - Fuller falls on ball no gain

END OF GAME
CLEMSON 17, OHIO STATE 15

National Collegiate Association
FINAL TEAM STATISTICS
December 29, 1978

	OHIO STATE	CLEMSON			
First Downs	16	20	Had Intercepted	1	0
Rushing	8	12	Total Offensive Plays	64	80
Passing	8	6	Total Net Yards	355	330
Penalty	0	2	Average Gain Per Play	5.55	4.12
Rushing Attempts	44	60	Fumbles: Number—Lost	1/0	5/1
Yards Rushing	164	235	Penalties: Number—Yards	7/83	7/65
Yards Lost Rushing	14	28	Interceptions: Number—Yards	0/0	1/12
Net Yards Rushing	150	207	Number of Punts—Yards	4/166	6/230
Net Yards Passing	205	123	Average Per Punt	41.5	38.3
Passes Attempted	20	20	Punt Returns: Number Yards	3/7	1/8
Passes Completed	16	9	Kickoff Returns: Number—Yards	4/94	2/38

ROSE BOWL

As one veteran West Coast scribe pointed out the day before the 1979 Rose Bowl Game between Michigan and Southern California, "If there is such a thing as the law of averages, then Michigan should beat USC on New Year's Day in the 65th Rose Bowl Game." Apparently, there is no such thing as "the law of averages."

The team with the best won-lost record during the regular season, in the last ten years, Michigan is still looking for a way to transpose that success to a post-season bowl game. Since 1969, when Coach Bo Schembechler took over the coaching duties, the Wolverines have posted an incredible 96 wins against just 8 losses and 3 ties, a most impressive percentage of .911. However, during that same span, Schembechler's teams have yet to taste success in six tries at post-season play, including the '79 Rose Bowl loss to USC, 17-10. But, as Schembechler stated after the '78 game (in which a valiant Michigan rally fell seven points short in Washington's 27-20 win) and which he unfortunately had to restate after this year's classic, "we plan to keep coming out here until we get the job done right."

Certainly no one can argue this positive approach nor the fact that the Wolverines have become Pasadena residents for three consecutive years now during the Christmas and New Year's holidays, while nine other Big Ten teams can only read about and watch this collegiate classic with visions that maybe next year, they will be participants. It's not been a case of Michigan teams getting beat badly by so-so teams however. Three of the Wolverines' recent Rose Bowl losses have been to USC, and have come by just 7, 8 and 7 points. And following the final collegiate rankings after the bowl games, those three Trojan teams were rated 1st (last year), 2nd (1976 season) and 3rd (after the 1970 game). Even the other two New Year's Day losses were close—a one-pointer to Stanford in 1972 and the seven-point defeat to Washington two years ago. Both of those Pac Ten teams also finished among the nation's top 10 teams after the final national poll.

One can't fault Schembechler of failing to look for a new method of winning the '79 Rose Bowl. When the Michigan team arrived in Los Angeles 10 days prior to the January 2 game (due to the 1st falling on a Sunday), Schembechler took them directly to Newport Beach, a plush city by the Pacific Ocean and adjacent to such surroundings as Balboa Island, Newport Bay and Santa

Catalina Island. The hotel was a modern-day Marriott, featuring a huge swimming pool, a jucuzzi and an adjacent golf course. It also happened to be the residence of the previous year's Rose Bowl victors the Washington Huskies.

"The only thing we wanted to do was have a change of pace," Schembechler explained. "We wanted to get a little different look at Rose Bowl preparations, that's all."

"I've felt that our problem out here is that we haven't played with the same emotional pitch we're accustomed to playing big games with. You can accomplish anything you want if you're emotionally right. But if you're not, you won't accomplish much. We're going to work on that and we feel this may help."

Schembechler then proceeded to put his troops through several days of non-contact drills, and didn't actually start regular-game-week practice until after the team had moved into the Huntington-Sheraton Hotel (the Pasadena "home" for the Big Ten team and officials each year) on Christmas Eve. The week-long practice produced few surprises, though it did confirm Schembechler's earlier beliefs, that tailbacks Harlan Huckleby and Stanley Edwards would not be at full strength for the game.

The Big Ten Club Dinner was held in the Hollywood Paladium where over 2,000 U-M faithfuls repeatedly echoed chants of "Go Blue" and listened to the ever-popular Bob Hope toss digs at Schembechler and quarterback Rick Leach. Two days before the game, the annual Kiwanis Kickoff Luncheon was staged in the Civic Center in downtown Pasadena, and for the 65th straight year, the prediction of sunny skies and no rain on game day was by promised by the mayor of Pasadena.

Finally, Monday, January 2, arrived, much to the delight of the New Year's Eve party-goers who had an extra day to recover from the toasting and celebrating the welcoming of the final year of the 70s. And for about the 62nd time in 65 years, the local mayor was right as sunny skies and temperatures in the 60s greeted over 1.5 million people who awoke at dawn to find the choicest of seats remaining along the five-mile long Rose Parade route. Following the many snack lunches that were devoured along the adjacent Brookfield Golf Course and hillside, over 105,000 enthusiasts jammed the Rose Bowl to witness the Battle of Pac Ten and Big Ten representatives.

Schembechler had been heard to say during the week that he felt Michigan could pass on the Trojans, but that it couldn't be sloppy or else one of USC's numerous skilled players would pick it off. It turned out to be words of wisdom for on Michigan's second play from scrimmage, Leach's pass was overthrown and intercepted by Ron Lott at midfield and returned all the way to the 16 yard line. Three plays later USC held a 7-0 lead, just four minutes into the game. The rest of the quarter was scoreless, but the Wolverines got

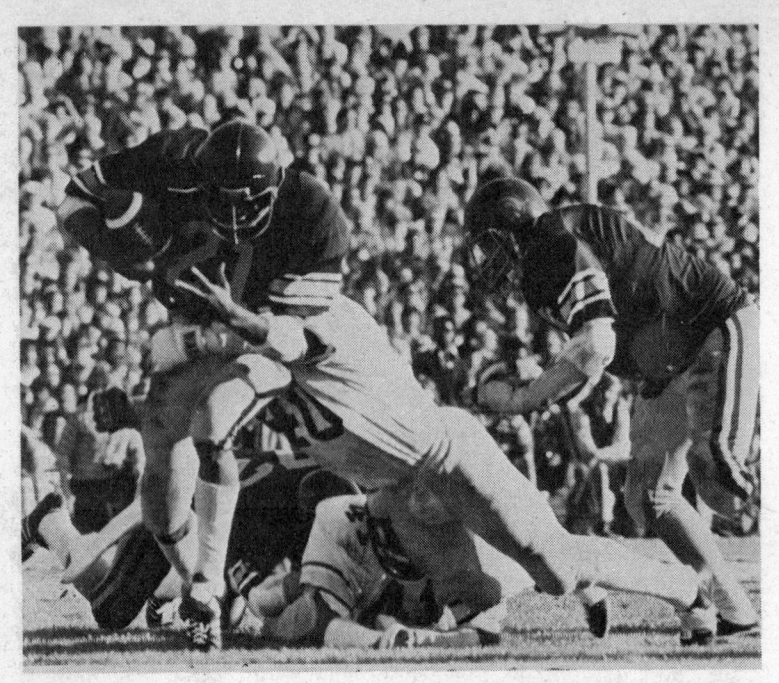

Michigan linebacker Ron Simpkins (40) hauls down Southern California's Lynn Cain (21).

a break early in the second period with a fumble recovery at the USC 23 yard line. Three plays netted only 4 yards however, and thus Gregg Willner was called on for a 36 yard field goal to narrow the margin to 7-3.

Midway in the same quarter USC took over at midfield and marched down to the 3 yard line. The play that followed will likely be grouped with those infamous Rose Bowl memories likely to be remembered for a long time, such as Roy Riegels wrong way run, the 1963 USC-Wisconsin game which produced 79 points, and USC's Pat Hayden to John McKay TD pass and two-point conversion afterwards which gave the Trojans a thrilling 18-17 win over Ohio State in 1975. The setting was a second and goal situation from the 3 yard line and USC's Charles White dove for the end zone. Somewhere around the goal line the ball popped free resulting in two different signals from the officials. The line judge had ruled that White had broken the goal line plane with the ball, thus producing a touchdown. the umpire, however, upon seeing the ball recovered by a Michigan lineman, signalled U-M possession on the one yard line. A quick conference with the referee followed, and the result was the line judge's call stood—a USC touchdown. TV replays later were to show that White did indeed appear to lose control of the ball prior to reaching the goal line.

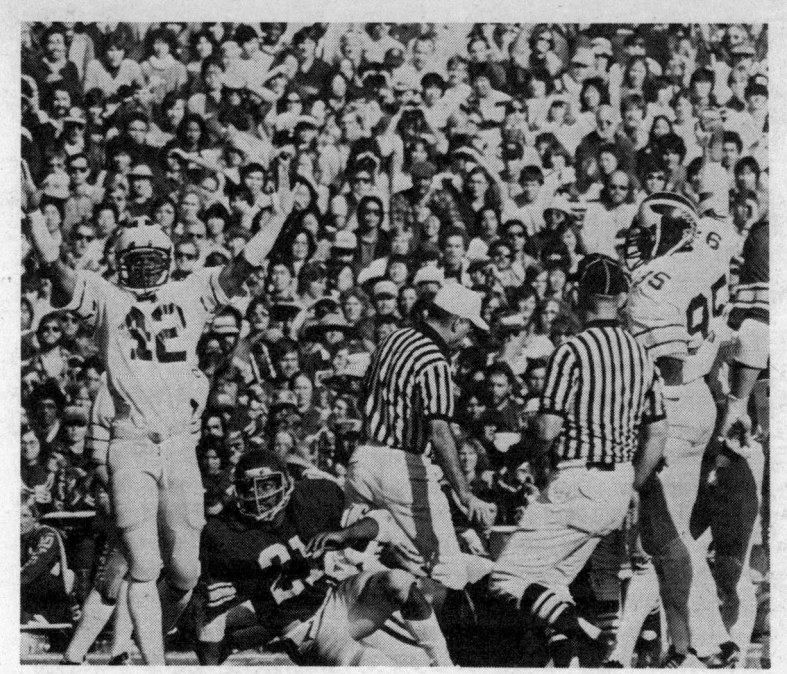

Gene Bell (42) and Curtis Greer (95) raise their arms after stopping USC's offense early in the Rose Bowl game.

Later in the quarter and now facing a 14-3 deficit, another Leach pass was picked off and returned to the Michigan 30 yard line with only 8 seconds remaining in the half. That was enough time however, for a USC pass completion to the 18 yard line followed by a quick timeout with just two seconds remaining to enable the Trojan field goal unit to get on the field and convert a 35 yard effort as the clock ran out, the Pac Ten thus holding a 17-3 margin at halftime.

To say that the first half had been a defensive standoff would be an understatement. The two teams combined for just 13 first downs, less than 100 yards rushing and only 51 through the air. The Wolverines had actually outgained the potent Trojan offense by a meager 84-63 margin and had held possession of the ball longer, but faced an uphill struggle with a 14-point deficit staring at them as the second half began.

Leach & Co. cut that margin in half midway in the third quarter as a short pass to 3rd string tailback Roosevelt Smith and a couple of good runs by Smith moved the ball down into USC territory. On the next play, Leach stepped back and threw a perfect strike to Smith cutting across the middle. The sophomore speedster never broke stride in hauling it in on the 5 yard line and going into the end zone for Michigan's first six-pointer of the day. Willner's extra point was good and with nearly 23 minutes still remaining in the game, Michigan fans increased their cries of "Go Blue" and pleas for the tying touchdown.

The latter went unanswered, as in the next 23 minutes of action, Michigan's chances for its first Rose Bowl win since 1965 faded away just as the sun was doing so behind the Wolverines bench. The U-M offensive attack, which entered the game averaging better than 400 total yards per game during the season, simply couldn't cope with the USC defensive charge. Only one time did Michigan manage to enter USC territory those final 23 minutes, and that was for one play, before Willner was called on to punt with less than three minutes left to play—the last time Leach and the offense would have the ball that day.

Biggest culprit in keeping the Wolverines out of scoring range was USC punter Marty King, who tied a Rose Bowl modern-day record for most punts in a game (9), and set an unofficial record of kicks stopping inside the 20. King punted a total of four times after Michigan's TD, and forced the Wolverines to start their offensive drives from the 11, 16, 20, and 11 yard lines.

Schembechler was later questioned about his decision to give up the ball with less than three minutes remaining and his team owning possession on the Southern Cal 46 yard line.

"There was plenty of time left and we had three time-outs left," he said. "We had a long-yardage situation and we didn't want to give them the ball at midfield."

The strategy looked like it might pay off for Michigan, as the defense stopped Troy runners twice and needed one more good effort on a third and 7 situation from the 15 yard line. But that's when USC fullback Lynn Cain broke through over left tackle and scampered 20 yards—the longest run of the game—enabling the Trojans to run out the clock the rest of the way.

The win was the fifth straight bowl game triumph in as many years for Southern California, while Michigan suffered its fourth consecutive post-season bowl defeat since 1976. It especially had to be tough for U-M quarterback Rick Leach who started all 48 of Michigan's games since joining the Wolverines in '75, yet couldn't find the success in four bowl games that had carried Michigan to 38 regular season victories in 44 games. But while so many Michigan followers were filled with frustration and bitterness as they filed out of the huge Bowl that night, such wasn't the case with Leach.

"Naturally I'm disappointed, but I've played in four bowl games and been to the Rose Bowl three straight years," Leach told members of the national media afterwards. "This isn't the end of the world for Rick Leach. I've worked with underprivileged kids in Ann Arbor and visited kids in the hospital who have cancer. There are things a lot more important than football."

Quarterback Rick Leach rolls out looking for a pass receiver while being chased by Riki Gray (35) and Garry Cobb (53).

The Gridiron Club of Greater Boston has an award it gives out at the conclusion of each collegiate football season in the name of the late Nils V. "Swede" Nelson. It is named for a former Harvard football player and coach and is given to the college player who exemplifies sportsmanship on and off the field. There was little surprise this year when the club selected Rick Leach as the 1979 recipient.

UNIVERSITY OF MICHIGAN VS. UNIVERSITY OF SOUTHERN CALIFORNIA
Pasadena, California
FIRST QUARTER

USC wins toss, elects to receive, defending north goal
Virgil kicks off out of bounds on 3, 5 yd penalty
From 35, Virgil kicks off to Dilulo on 17 no return from 17
SOUTHERN CALIFORNIA
1/10-S17 - Cain gains 4 at lt, but illegal procedure, 5 yd penalty
1/15-S12 - White at lt stopped for 3 loss (Greer)
2/18-S9 - White at le no gain
3/18-S9 - Cain at rg makes 4
4/14-S13 - King punt rolls dead on 28; 59 yd punt, no return

12:57 MICHIGAN
1/10-M28 - Huckleby at rt (D Johnson) 1 gain
2/9 -M29 - Leach pass intended for Clayton intercepted by Lott on M49, returned 33

12:07 SOUTHERN CALIFORNIA
1/10-M16 - White inside rt makes 5
2/5 -M11 - White at rg makes 2
3/3 -M9 - McDonald pass complete to Brenner in end zone for touchdown King holding, Jordan makes conversion
SCORE: SOUTHERN CALIFORNIA 7, MICHIGAN 0

Jordan kicks off to Jackson in end zone, no return
10:46 MICHIGAN
1/10-M20 - Davis (R) makes 6 at lg
2/4 -M26 - Huckleby on pitchout fumbles, recovers for loss of 3
3/7 -M23 - Leach pass intended for Clayton on S45 incomplete
4/7 -M23 - Willner punts to Butler on 33, returned 4, 44 yd punt

9:11 SOUTHERN CALIFORNIA
1/10-S37 - McDonald pass complete to White in backfield, run for 4
2/6 -S41 - White hits inside le for 11
1/10-M48 - Cain at lt makes 1
2/9 -M47 - McDonald back to pass, sacked by Godfrey for loss of 9
3/18-S44 - White at lt makes 5
4/13-S49 - King punts to Jolley 37 yds, 2 yd return from 14

6:18 MICHIGAN
1/10-M16 - Davis at rg makes 8
2/2 -M24 - Pitch to Huckleby around re for 4
1/10-M28 - Huckleby at lg makes 6

2/4 -M34 - Leach pass complete to Huckleby on 35, run for 7
1/10-M41 - Leach on broken play goes at le for 7
2/3 -M48 - Davis at rt makes 2
3/1 - 50 - Michigan offside, 5 yd penalty
3/6 -M45 - Leach back to pass, snowed under by Smith, Edwards for loss of 10
4/16-M35 - Willner punt rolls dead on S31, 34 yd kick, no return

2:49 SOUTHERN CALIFORNIA
1/10-S31 - White at le gains 2
2/8 -S33 - McDonald back to pass, sacked by Seabron for loss of 6
3/14-S27 - McDonald pass intended for Sweeney on S38 incomplete
4/14-S27 - King punts to Jolley on 35, returned 1, but roughing the kicker penalty 15 yd penalty
1/10-S42 - White at le stopped by Keitz for 3 yd loss
2/13-S39 - White at lt gains 2
3/11-S41 - Hit by Seabron, fumbles, recovered by Bell (18 yd loss for McDonald)

END OF FIRST QUARTER
SOUTHERN CALIFORNIA 7, MICHIGAN 0

SECOND QUARTER

MICHIGAN
1/10-S23 - Leach at re makes 2
2/8 -S21 - Leach pass on 17 dropped by Huckleby
3/8 -S21 - Davis at lg makes 2
4/6 -S19 - Dickey holding, Willner makes 36 yd field goal
SCORE: SOUTHERN CALIFORNIA 7, MICHIGAN 3

Virgil kicks off to Butler on 11, returned 40
13:28 SOUTHERN CALIFORNIA
1/10-M49 - White runs for 11 yd loss
2/21-M40 - Cain at middle makes 6
3/15-M46 - White at re no gain
4/15-M46 - King punts to Jolley on 12, returned 5, 42 yd punt

12:22 MICHIGAN
1/10-M17 - Leach keeps at le for 2
2/8 -M19 - Leach back to pass, caught by Lapka for loss of 12
3/20-M7 - Davis at le gains 2
4/18-M9 - Willner punts to Butler on S48, returned 3, 43 yd punt

10:03 SOUTHERN CALIFORNIA
1/10-M49 - Cain through lg for 8
2/2 -M41 - Cain at lt makes 7
1/10-M34 - White at rg makes 3
2/7 -M31 - Cain at rg gains 9
1/10-M22 - White at lt goes for 17
1/G -M5 - White dives at rg for 2

2/G -M3 - White dives at lg for 3 and touchdown King holding, Jordan makes conversion
SCORE: SOUTHERN CALIFORNIA 14, MICHIGAN 3

Jordan kicks off to Jackson on 7, returned 21
7:27 MICHIGAN
1/10-M28 - Huckleby at lt makes 7
2/3 -M35 - Davis at lt makes 4
1/10-M39 - Leach pass complete to Clayton for 21
1/10-S40 - R Smith loses 1 at lg
2/11-S41 - Huckleby at re on pitch gains 5
3/6 -S36 - Leach pass intended for Johnson on 10, almost intercepted by Smith
4/6 -S36 - Leach pass intended for R Davis on 30 dropped

4:47 SOUTHERN CALIFORNIA
1/10-S36 - McDonald pass complete to White for loss of 2
2/12-S34 - Cain at lg makes 3
3/9 -S37 - White at re slips, falls for no gain
4/9 -S37 - King punt rolls dead on M10, 53 yd punt

2:59 MICHIGAN
1/10-M10 - Huckleby falls at rg for 1 yd loss
2/11-M 9 - Huckleby at le makes 7
3/4 -M16 - Leach back to pass, runs rt for 7
1/10-M23 - Leach scrambles at re for 9
2/1 -M32 - Leach pass intended for Marsh midfield incomplete
3/1 -M32 - Huckleby at rg gains 2
1/10-M34 - Leach pass intended for Clayton on 15 incomplete
2/10-M34 - Leach pass intended for Johnson intercepted by Smith on S39, returned 31

:08 SOUTHERN CALIFORNIA
1/10-M30 - McDonald pass complete to Garcia for 12, out of bounds
1/10-M18 - King holding, King makes 35 yd field goal
SCORE: SOUTHERN CALIFORNIA 17, MICHIGAN 3

**HALFTIME SCORE
SOUTHERN CALIFORNIA 17, MICHIGAN 3**

THIRD QUARTER

Jordan kicks off to Jackson on 7, returned 14 yds
14:57 MICHIGAN
1/10-M21 - Smith at lt gains 5
2/5 -M26 - Davis at lg makes 2
2/3 -M28 - Leach pass complete to Smith to right for 4
1/10-M32 - Smith at lt makes 5
2/5 -M37 - Smith at rg gains 4
3/1 -M41 - Smith on pitch to left caught by Lott for loss of 4

4/5 -M37 - Willner punts to Crawford on fair catch on S35, 28 yd punt

11:38 SOUTHERN CALIFORNIA
1/10-S35 - Cain through rt makes 13
1/10-S48 - White at rt makes 4
2/6 -M48 - White at lt makes 2
3/4 -M46 - White at le gains 4, but SC illegal use of hands, 16 yd penalty
3/20-S38 - McDonald back to pass, hit by Meter, fumbles, recovered by Van Horne 9 yd loss
4/29-S29 - King punts to Jolley on M35, returned 5, 36 yd kick

9:09 MICHIGAN
1/10-M40 - Leach pass complete to Smith to left, run for 6
2/6 -M46 - Leach to Smith pitchout to right makes 7
1/10-S47 - Smith at rt makes 1
2/9 -S46 - Leach scrambles, fumbles out of bounds for 7 yds
3/2 -S39 - too much time, 5 yd penalty
3/7 -S44 - Leach pass complete to Smith on 5 run over for touchdown Dickey holding Willner makes conversion
SCORE: SOUTHERN CALIFORNIA 17 MICHIGAN 10

Virgil kicks off to Butler on 4, returned 20
6:57 SOUTHERN CALIFORNIA
1/10-S24 - White at lt makes 5
2/5 -S29 - Cain at lg gains 2
3/3 -S31 - White around le makes 5
1/10-S36 - White goes inside re for 14
1/10- 50 - White at re makes 2
2/8 -M48 - McDonald pass intended for Sweeney on 20 incomplete
3/8 -M48 - McDonald pass intended for Sweeney on 25 broken up by Braman
4/8 -M48 - King punts into end zone, 48 yd kick

4:21 MICHIGAN
1/10-M20 - pitch to Smith at re makes 2
2/8 -M22 - pass in flat to Smith good for 4 to left
3/4 -M26 - Leach, almost trapped, passes incomplete to nobody
4/4 -M26 - Willner punts to Butler on 36, returned 1, 38 yd kick

2:38 SOUTHERN CALIFORNIA
1/10-S37 - White through rt for 17
1/10-M46 - Cain at rt makes 1
2/9 -M45 - White at re makes 1
3/8 -M44 - McDonald pass intended for Williams on 30 incomplete
4/8 -M44 - King punts to Jolley on fair catch on 11, 33 yd kick

449

:43 MICHIGAN
1/10-M11 - Leach pass intended for Smith tipped away by Moses
2/10-M11 - Smith at lt makes 1

END OF THIRD QUARTER
SOUTHERN CALIFORNIA 17, MICHIGAN 10

FOURTH QUARTER

MICHIGAN
3/9 -M12 - Leach back to pass, runs lg for 5
4/4 -M17 - Willner punts to Butler on 42, returned 12, 41 yd kick

14:09 SOUTHERN CALIFORNIA
1/10-M46 - White at rg stopped for 2 loss
2/12-M48 - McDonald sacked by Greer for loss of 5
3/17-S47 - McDonald pass intended for Williams on 10 too long
4/17-S47 - King punts to Jolley on 13, returned 3, 40 yd punt

12:35 MICHIGAN
1/10-M16 - Davis at rt gains 2
2/8 -M18 - Leach, almost trapped, passes to Marsh for 9
1/10-M27 - Leach runs le for 4
2/6 -M31 - Woolfolk at rg loses 1
3/7 -M30 - Leach keeps and runs up middle for 4
4/3 -M34 - Willner punts to Butler on fair catch on 34, 32 yd punt

9:22 SOUTHERN CALIFORNIA
1/10-S34 - Cain at lg makes 4.

2/6 -S38 - White at le gains 5
3/1 -S43 - White at rg gains 3
1/10-S46 - Cain at rt makes 4
2/6 - 50 - White at rg makes 4
3/2 -M46 - White caught by Cannavino for 2 yd loss
4/4 -M48 - King punts to Jolley on 10, returned 1, 38 yd punt

5:42 MICHIGAN
1/10-M11 - pitchback to Jackson, passes incomplete out of bounds
2/10-M11 - Leach pass complete to Clayton for 19
1/10-M30 - Smith through rt for 2
2/8 -M32 - Leach pass complete to Johnson for 17
1/10-M49 - Leach running to right caught by Lapka for 3 yd loss
2/13-M46 - Leach pass complete to Johnson for 6
3/7 -S48 - Leach pass intended for Feaster knocked down on 3
4/7 -S48 - Willner punts to Butler on fair catch on 15, 33 yds

2:44 SOUTHERN CALIFORNIA
1/10-S15 - White at middle no gain
2/10-S15 - White inside le gains 3
3/7 -S18 - Cain through lt makes 20 (longest run of game)
1/10-S38 - Cain up middle for 8
2/2 -S46 - White at lg dives for 3
1/10-S49 - McDonald falls on ball for 3 yd loss
2/13-S46 - McDonald sits on ball for 2 yd loss
3/15-S44 - McDonald falls on ball for 3 yd loss

END OF GAME
SOUTHERN CALIFORNIA 17, MICHIGAN 10

1979 BIG TEN FOOTBALL PREVIEW

It's hard to imagine that anything could generate more enthusiasm, more excitement and more thrilling moments than the 1978 Big Ten football season. It was a year that featured record setting performances by three different quarterbacks and a Conference race that went down to the final weekend of play with four teams still in contention for a share of the league title. The latter contributed to a banner year at the gate that had an all-time record average in excess of 61,000 fans per game.

However, the final year of the 70s may produce an even better and tighter battle for the Big Ten championship than has been seen in the last dozen years. As always during fall drills, a strong feeling of excitement and optimism pervades Big Ten camps right up until the September 8 openers. But unlike in the past, a good case can be made for any one of the ten teams this year. Five schools (Purdue, Michigan State, Minnesota, Northwestern and Illinois) have at least 15 starters returning from a year ago, while no team has fewer than 10 regulars back. All but three schools (Michigan, Michigan State, and Indiana) have last year's starting quarterback back along with most of their backfield. Five schools (Michigan, Ohio State, Purdue, Wisconsin and Michigan State) were picked among the top 25 teams in the nation as having the best recruiting seasons this past winter.

In addition, a new style and flavor of football looks to be coming upon Big Ten play. With three new coaches starting their first year in the Big Ten this fall, two others with just one year of competition and yet another pair with only two years of Conference warfare behind them, there appears to be a growing trend towards the pass. League passing was near an all-time high in several categories in 1978, and even with the departure of such flingers as Ed Smith of Michigan State and Rick Leach of Michigan, fans can be assured of seeing plenty of air-action again this year. But lest one think that all this passing is because of a lack of quality runners, remember—four of the top five running backs in the Big Ten last year are back again this season.

There was little question who the premier running back in the Big Ten was in 1978 and who rates among the nation's best backs in 1979. Minnesota's Marion Barber had such an outstanding season a year ago that he led all other Conference rushers in four categories as the Detroit sophomore totaled 186 yards more than runnerup Mike Harkrader, and was the only running back to rush for over 165 yards in any game last year.

Barber was having just a mediocre year through the first half of the Conference season, having rushed for 372 yards in the first four Gopher games, a 93.0 average per contest. But starting with the Indiana game, in which he helped spark the Gophers to a thrilling 32-31 win after the Hoosiers had jumped to a 24-0 lead, Barber really put on a show the final four games. He gained 177 yards against Indiana, followed that with a 75 yard effort against a tough Michigan State defense, broke loose for 233 yards in the Gophers' win over Illinois and closed out the season with 111 yards in a losing cause to Wisconsin. That brought his four-game total to 596 yards over the last half of the season, good for a 149.0 per game effort.

Harkrader edged Michigan State's Steve Smith for runnerup honors to Barber, though it was a distant runnerup. Harkrader actually led the league in rushing with just two weeks remaining in the '78 season, but while Barber finished with a flurry, the Hoosier tailback managed only 116 in the final two weeks of play to leave him with a total of 782 yards and a 97.7 average. Smith needed one more strong showing and he might have surpassed Harkrader for No. 2 honors, as he rushed for 238 yards his final two Saturdays of action to run his season mark to 702 yards and an 87.7 per game average. Smith did capture one honor, his 7.3 per carry average being the best among the top 20 rushers in the league last year.

In addition to Barber, Harkrader and Smith, Purdue fullback John Macon, who finished fifth in the rushing derby a year ago, is also back this fall. But if those four runners figure it'll be a four-player battle to gain the top spot, they should be wary of Michigan tailback Butch Woolfolk, who started slow but came on strong at the end to finish in the No. 7 spot with a 61.8 average last year. That mark is somewhat misleading, as Woolfolk saw limited action behind standout Harlan Huckleby (the league's No. 4 rusher with an 85.8 average in '78) and had to share backup duties with two other top reserves, Stanley Edwards and Roosevelt Smith. With Huckleby graduated and Smith's status uncertain, Woolfolk could see a lot more action for the Wolverines this fall.

Among the league's other top running backs who will return this year are Wisconsin fullback Tom Stauss, Ohio State fullback Paul Campbell and quarterback Art Schlichter (the top returning "running" signal-caller), Iowa tailback Dennis Mosley, and Northwestern's Dave Mishler, who led the Wildcats in rushing as a freshman but suffered a knee injury in the fifth game of the '78 season. Newcomers who could break into the top 10 list this year include Mike Holmes of Illinois, who transferred from Colorado a year ago, and Jimmy Smith of Purdue, who was rated among the best high school running backs in the country a year ago.

Purdue's Mark Herrmann silently sat back and watched

Michigan's Rick Leach and Michigan State's Ed Smith set various Big Ten records for total offense and passing last year, but the Boilermaker quarterback may now be ready to surpass those recently established records in only his junior season at Purdue. At the completion of the 1978 season, Smith had rewritten the record book for career totals in three categories: most pass attempts (789), most completions (418), and most yards (5,706). Impressive figures indeed, but already on shakey ground when one looks at Herrmann's two-year figures in those departments: pass attempts (593), completions (327) and yards (4,357). What it means is that Herrmann need post the following totals in 1979: 91 completions, 196 passes, and 1,449 yards. Look for any one of those three figures by the Boilermaker ace around mid-season.

Herrmann is not the only standout quarterback returning this fall, however, as only one other usual starter (Scott Arnett of Indiana) has graduated from last year's regulars. After going through a freshman season of mistakes and learning, Ohio State's Art Schlichter and Illinois' Rich Weiss could be among the Big Ten's best in only their second full year of competition. Schlichter was a most pleasant surprise for the Buckeyes, totaling over 1,800 yards in offense to set an OSU single season in total offense. Weiss proved to be among the league's top running quarterbacks in 1978, gaining 568 yards on 154 carries, though the net total ended up slightly under 300 after he was dropped behind the line of scrimmage for a minus 271 yards, most of which came on pass attempts.

Indiana's Tim Clifford saw enough backup action behind Arnett last year to total over 800 yards in passing, nearly twice as many as Arnett finished with. Minnesota has both Mark Carlson and Wendell Avery returning for their senior seasons after having shared the quarterbacking duties the past two years. Carlson had slightly better passing credentials last year with 64 completions and 736 yards, but Avery is a more elusive runner. Wisconsin's Mike Kalasmiki took over signal-calling duties early in the season and was eventually named the Badgers' MVP, but has since had academic difficulties and missed the Badgers' spring drills as he attempted to make up scholastic deficiencies at Madison Area Technical College during the spring semester. If he doesn't return this fall, sophomore John Josten, who started the first three games in his rookie season until sidelined for a while with an injury, would probably get the starting call.

Quarterbacking is one position which seems solid at Northwestern, as record-setting Kevin Strasser is back after a strong junior year which saw him go from 3 pass attempts as a sophomore to 307 attempts in 1978. Strasser, who threw for 1,526 of NU's 1,650 yards by air, will be backed up by 6-4 Chris Capstran who was also No. 2 behind Strasser a year ago but did not get into a single game and thus "saved" his freshman year of eligibility. Iowa Coach

Hayden Fry had half a dozen quarterbacks out for spring practice, including last year's part-time starters Jeff Green and Pete Gales. The player who had the inside spot however, was Phil Suess, a 6-5 former defensive back who hasn't seen much action in three previous years with the Hawkeyes. Tony Ricciarduli, tabbed as one of the top JC quarterbacks in 1978, could also figure prominently in Fry's plans for his first Iowa team.

The two schools which face the biggest challenge to find a starter at the all-important QB spot are last year's co-champions Michigan and Michigan State. With Leach, a four-year Wolverine starter, and Smith, a three-year regular for the Spartans, both departed, several of last year's backups or a pair of highly-touted incoming frosh could get the nod this fall. B.J. Dickey saw the most backup action behind Leach a year ago, but either Gary Lee or Jim Paciorek, who didn't see much action during their freshman seasons a year ago, along with reserve John Wrangler could inherit Leach's position. Rich Hewlett and Steve O'Donnell both had outstanding prep careers, and would like nothing better than to match Leach's record of having started 47 of 48 games Michigan played during his career.

Lanky Burt Vaughn would appear to have the inside track to replace Smith at Michigan State. The 6-4 sophomore passed for 346 yards in State's first two games last year when Smith was out with an injury, but then Vaughn suffered a shoulder injury and he missed the remainder of the season, which should allow for an extra season of competition a couple of years from now. Should Vaughn's shoulder continue to hamper his play, then incoming frosh Jon English, rated the premier QB in Midwest high schools last year, may get an early call to display his highly-touted passing form.

Like the passing category, the total offense title will also be up for grabs as last year's top two finishers, Smith and Leach, have departed. Both players left their mark in the Conference Record Book, however, with Smith gaining a total of 1,808 yards in eight Big Ten games last year, while Leach increased his career mark to 6,460 yards in total offense. The old records were set by Mike Phipps during the 1969 season, enroute to a three-year total of 5,883 yards in total offense.

Three other Conference quarterbacks also finished with over 1,100 yards in this department, to rank as the three front-runners to succeed Smith as the most proficient yardage gainer. Wisconsin's Mike Kalasmiki finished in the No. 3 spot with a 164.9 average per game, Purdue's Mark Herrmann 4th at 143.2, and Ohio State's Art Schlichter 5th at 137.9. Illinois' Rich Weiss and Northwestern's Kevin Strasser were also among the top eight yardage producers last year, making this category one of the most competitive for the coming season.

The only other player among the top 14 offensive leaders who won't be returning (other than Leach and Smith) is Michigan tailback Harlan Huckleby.

Michigan State's Steve Smith and Minnesota's Barber both closed with a flurry in the all-purpose category last year, and should stage another close battle for the title this fall. Smith eventually won out in '78, gaining an incredible 570 yards via rush, receiving, punt and kickoff return in his last three league games (190.0 average), while Barber was pretty impressive also with 473 yards in the Gophers' last three games. Smith had a season ending total of 1,159 yards (46 more than Barber) to post a 144.9 per game average.

The battle to replace Michigan State's Kirk Gibson as the league's leading receiver could involve any of three pairs of outstanding pass catchers at Wisconsin, Michigan State and Purdue. The Spartans have the top two returning receivers in Eugene Byrd, who finished just one catch behind the talented Gibson last year, and big tight end Mark Brammer, who was 4th in the league with 25 receptions.

Wisconsin's 6-8 tight end Ray Sydnor and Purdue flanker Mike Harris were deadlocked in the No. 5 position with 24 grabs each, while Bart Burrell of the Boilermakers was eighth and the Badgers' Wayne Souza was tied for ninth. Tied with Souza last year were Minnesota's Elmer Bailey, and Northwestern's duo threat of Tim Hill and Mike McGee. All seven of the above will also return in 1979.

Three of the top four Big Ten kick-scorers have graduated, which will likely pave the way for Minnesota's Paul Rogind to dominate this category. Rogind doesn't have to prove his capabilities to anyone, however. He already holds the Gopher record for most field goals (35), most attempts (54), has converted on all but one of his 55 point-after-touchdown attempts, and is working on a string of 53 straight PATs.

A new and young breed of coaching has infiltrated the Big Ten ranks the past couple of years, to such an extent that only two of the league's ten coaches have been through more than three years of Conference competition. But while eight of the coaches have relatively short spans within the league, the experience they have gained at other schools makes them among the most knowledgeable in the profession.

The dean of the current group is Michigan's Bo Schembechler, who joined the Wolverines in 1969 and now ranks as one of the most successful head coaches ever in Big Ten play. His 10-year mark with Michigan stands at 96 wins, just 15 losses and 3 ties, for a .855 percentage. Coupled with a six year record of 40-17-3 at Miami O., Schembechler's collegiate coaching mark now shows 136 victories, 32 losses and 6 ties, for an even .800. Only one other man in Big Ten history that coached for at least ten years in the Conference has a better winning percentage than Schembechler, and that would be the immortal Fielding H. Yost who was 165-29-12 (.830) in his 25 years of collegiate coaching at Michigan.

Second in seniority in the league is Indiana's dynamic Lee Corso, who has been with the Hoosiers for six years now following his departure as head coach at Louisville in 1972. IU teams managed only five wins in the first three years under Corso, but the next three have found much more success with 14 victories, including back-to-back Old Oaken Bucket wins over rival Purdue in 1976 and 1977.

Michigan State's Darryl Rogers will begin his fourth year with the Spartans, and is the only coach to have his team improve its record each of the past three seasons. Rogers' first MSU team in 1976 compiled a 4-6-1 record, but the next two have come through with 7-3-1 and 8-3 marks, including a share of the 1978 championship. Rogers was selected Big Ten Coach-of-the-Year in 1977 when the Spartans finished just half a game out of first place.

Starting just their third season as head coaches in the Big Ten are a pair of former defensive coordinators at Michigan, Jim Young of Purdue and Gary Moeller of Illinois. Young served as Bo Schembechler's top defensive coach for the Wolverines for five seasons before moving to Arizona in 1973 in his first head coaching job. After four successful seasons with the Wildcats, Young came to Purdue in 1977, and wasted little time in turning the Boilermakers into a title contender, achieving this goal in just his second season. For his efforts last fall, Young was selected as Coach-of-the-Year in the Big Ten.

Moeller inherited the defensive coordinator spot at Michigan when Young departed the Wolverines' camp. He stayed in that capacity until 1977 when he accepted his first head coaching position with the Illini. Though Illinois has won just four games in two years, Moeller has been successful in attracting some of the state's top players to Champaign, an indication the Illini won't be down for long.

Wisconsin's Dave McClain and Northwestern's Rick Venturi became members of the Big Ten coaching fraternity last year, and happened on different results. Venturi inherited a veteran defensive club at Evanston but a fairly inexperienced team on offense, only to watch six defensive regulars sidelined for nearly the entire season due to injuries. McClain had the Badgers off to a fast start with four wins and a tie in the first five games, but three one-sided losses to Michigan, Michigan State and Ohio State dashed any hopes of a championship in his initial season. A late-season tie with Purdue prevented the Boilermakers from sharing the league title with the two Michigan schools.

Three new coaches will get their first taste of head coaching in the Big Ten when the season opens on September 8. Minnesota's Joe Salem, Ohio State's Earle Bruce and Hayden Fry at Iowa will be looking to bring new ideas and plays into the league this year in hopes of instant success. All three coaches were highly successful the past couple of seasons prior to taking over at their current jobs. Bruce led Iowa State to consecutive 8-3 records the past three years, twice taking the Cyclones to post-season bowl games and twice being selected as Big Eight Coach-of-the-Year.

As Bruce is at Ohio State, Salem is a graduate of the school he now serves as head coach. He's been a head coach since 1966, serving at South Dakota for nine seasons before assuming head coaching duties at Northern Arizona the past four years. From 1976-78, Salem's teams won 25 games and lost just 8. The third member of the trio of rookie head coaches in the Conference, Iowa's Fry is certainly no beginner to the coaching profession. He has restored two previous ailing football programs at Southern Methodist (where he served 11 years) and North Texas State (the past six seasons) back to sound condition. Iowa fans are hoping his work results in similar success for the Hawkeyes.

The three new coaches will find the schedule-maker possessed little sympathy ten years ago when preparing this year's list of opponents. Fry may get to know the Big Eight Conference better than the Big Ten the first month of the season, since, after opening at home with Indiana, he takes on three straight perennial Big Eight powers—Oklahoma, Nebraska and Iowa State. Fry may be putting in a quick call to Bruce at Ohio State come Sept. 29 when the Hawkeyes engage in their battle with state-rival Iowa State, but Bruce may not have much time to help his colleague as the Buckeyes will be encountering their own problems that week.

Ohio State is scheduled for an inter-sectional matchup with UCLA on the Bruins' home field that particular Saturday. It's the third and final non-conference foe for OSU in 1979. They will also play Syracuse (in the season opener) and Washington State in home contests. Minnesota has just two non-league games this year, opening with Ohio U. at home on Sept. 8, but then, after a Conference game with Ohio State, the Gophers must travel to Southern California to take on the powerful Trojans, likely to be rated No. 1 in the nation in the first pre-season poll.

Unfortunately, the three new coaches aren't likely to receive condolences from the other seven head mentors, who have their own tough non-conference schedules to tackle. UCLA and Notre Dame, two perennial national powers, will play Big Ten schools three times each next fall, with Michigan, Michigan State and Purdue taking on neighboring Notre Dame, and the Boilermakers and Wisconsin joining Ohio State in an attempt to saddle the Bruins with three quick early-season losses. Three other opponents—Syracuse, Oregon and the Air Force—will each oppose Big Ten schools twice.

Broken down by conference, the Pac Ten Conference continues

to provide the most opponents for Big Ten teams. A total of eight matchups between the two leagues which provide the Rose Bowl entries each year will take place in 1979. In addition there will be six Big Ten-Big Eight contests, along with a pair of meetings with teams from the Southeastern, Mid-American and Western Athletic Conferences. Eight games are scheduled with major independents, headed by three confrontations with Notre Dame.

Prior to that opening kickoff each season, all Big Ten teams feel this could be the year to finish up in the first division, and with a break here and there, a lucky bounce now and then, well... But how do the teams shape up, what are the team strengths, the weaknesses, and what do the ten coaches have to say about the coming year? Let's take a look....

ILLINOIS *Fighting Illini*

Generating optimism after a disappointing season and a ninth place Big Ten finish? It's not as difficult as you might think, especially for Fighting Illini coach Gary Moeller, now in his third year at the University of Illinois after serving as the number one assistant at Michigan. He knows what it takes to be a winner.

"We're starting to have upperclassmen who have grown up in our system of football," says the 38-year old mentor. "We'd like to get our program to the point where our seniors and juniors are the regulars with our freshmen and sophomores realizing that they will have to wait their turn to start. We're not quite at that point yet, but we're closer than we were two years ago."

Such was not the case last year with a team that began the season dubbed as the "Baby Brigade" because of its youth. As injuries and personnel shifts occurred during the season, the look got even younger. In 1978's final game at Minnesota, 32 of the 54 Illini players on the sidelines were freshmen or sophomores. Of the 22 UI starters, eight were sophomores and four were freshmen.

That is hardly the kind of experience necessary for success in the Big Ten grid wars. The result was below expectations—one win, two ties and eight losses, six of which came to teams ranked among the top 20 during the season. Five of those setbacks were also from squads which went on to post season bowl games. The campaign's lone victory came against Syracuse with ties against Northwestern and Wisconsin.

The positive thing is that while those youngsters were taking some lumps last year, they were building up game experience that will stand them in good stead in the 1979 season. Moeller can look to eight starters on both the offensive and defensive units to return this year.

The mistakes and inconsistencies caused by that evil culprit, inexperience, were particularly costly on offense a year ago. The Illini were only able to wrack up 103 points through the 11 game schedule, ranking 9th in the Big Ten in total offense and last in scoring. Fumbles and penalties continually blunted Illinois surges into enemy territory as U of I ball carriers coughed up the pigskin 41 times, losing it to the opposition on 23 occasions. Opponents only lost eight of 23 fumbles on the year.

"We obviously have to rid ourselves of the things that continued to hurt us when we had good sustained drives and momentum," emphasizes Moeller. "Once we've accomplished that, we must become a more balanced team offensively, one that is able to throw the football on any down, as well as having a good solid running attack."

So expect the Illini to pass more than the previous two seasons and run basically an option offense out of the I-formation. The key to how much the team is able to diversify its attack will depend on the development of the offensive line, a unit which began the 1978 season with four new faces surrounding senior center Randy Taylor and whose progress was hindered by injuries throughout the year.

The situation is completely reversed this season with four solid starters returning and a newcomer needed to replace the graduated Taylor, the MVP on offense last year. Junior Greg Boeke looks like the early bet to fill the critical role in the middle of the line although he will find competition from promising sophomore Mark Helle. Both have good size at 230 pounds but Helle was set back by missing spring ball with a fractured toe. The coaches are taking a look at converting linebacker John Scott here.

The Illini enjoy their greatest depth across the front line at the guard spot. The development of such depth was necessitated last season when injuries wiped out the top four guards on the team. Untested freshman Mike Carrington and sophomore Troy McMillin ended the season getting baptisms of fire in Big Ten competition but showing enough talent to challenge for starting positions this year. However, if Rich Antonacci returns healthy from last year's knee surgery, you can consider one guard spot nailed down. The Chicago native displayed outstanding potential two years ago as a freshman reserve and big things were expected of him as a sophomore starter in 1978. His injury in August drills ended those hopes, but early reports on his physical condition indicate the 6-3, 242 pounder is ready to go.

Bob McClure had finally earned himself a starting guard position opposite Antonacci as a senior last year and was a steady performer until sustaining a hand fracture in front of his home state fans at Missouri, requiring surgery. With a "human bowling ball" build at 6-0, and 230 pounds, the Ladue, Missouri product will return for an additional year of eligibility. In the battle for a starting spot, along with Carrington and McMillin, will be senior Bob Noelke who proved to be an able replacement for Antonacci. However, Illinois' incredibly bad luck streak at this position continued as Noelke went down with a season-ending knee injury in practice just two days after being named Offensive Player of the Game in the victory over Syracuse. Dan Westerlind, a junior who transferred to Illinois from Wisconsin, had his collegiate career ended a year ago with the re-occurrence of chronic neck injuries.

The offensive tackle slots show excellent front line talent but depth could be a question mark. The Illini coaches feel they have a player deserving of all-American consideration in giant Tim

Norman. At 6-6, and 265 pounds, Norman was agile enough to have won the Illinois high school heavyweight wrestling title as a prep senior. In his freshman year at the U of I, he displayed enough versatility to see action as a defensive tackle and tight end as well as offensive tackle. Although others garnered all-Big Ten honors in 1978, Norman's sophomore year, the UI staff did not feel they saw a better tackle in the Conference than the Winfield, Illinois native. At the other tackle spot, Mike Priebe returns for his red-shirt year. One of the strongest players on the squad, Priebe finally fulfilled the promise predicted of him when switched to the offensive line, after toiling as a reserve linebacker during his first two seasons.

Depth will come from senior Tom Kolloff, junior Tom Coady and sophomore Lou Belmont, all of whom saw limited action a year ago.

A front line of Norman, Antonacci, Boeke, McClure and Priebe would average a mobile 243 pounds and have the talent to develop into a unit that would give some promising backfield performers a chance to show their skills.

Junior quarterback Rich Weiss should make a solid bid to be recognized among the top quarterbacks in the Big Ten this year. A prep all-American from Wilmette, Illinois, Weiss lost a year of competition as a freshman due to back problems. However, he bounced back during his sophomore campaign to earn a starting role and showed he has the ability to direct a potent offensive attack. Weiss' 568 gross yards rushing a year ago would have led the team had they not been offset by a total of 271 yards lost behind the line of scrimmage. One of the squad's strongest backs, bench pressing 320 pounds, the 6-1, 205 pounder is a punishing runner when he turns the corner on the option. Don't think he can't throw the ball either. Weiss completed 53% of his passes in 1978, being intercepted just six times in 109 attempts.

"Rich has all the physical and leadership qualities to be an outstanding quarterback for us this year," asserts Moeller. "He's one of the classiest kids, not only on the team, but on the whole campus. I'm so glad we're going to have him around for three more years."

The Illini can feel confident in the depth they have behind Weiss at quarterback. Lawrence McCullough, a junior college transfer a year ago, stepped in for an injured Weiss and directed Illinois to its victory over Syracuse. With a whip arm and blazing speed, the UI coaches have no reservations about putting McCullough in the game. "We have a lot of confidence in Lawrence," says Moeller. "Last year he was slowed by having to pick up a new system but this season could be different." Tim McAvoy, who saw some action at QB as a freshman two years ago, will be returning to the signal calling spot this season after spending most of 1978 in the defensive secondary.

The team's leading rusher from a year ago returns in junior

fullback Wayne Strader. A prep all-American from Geneseo, Illinois, Strader has gained 737 yards in two years while splitting duties with Charlie Weber. In that time, the 6-3, 215 pounder has averaged 5.2 yards per carry and has never been caught behind the line of scrimmage. Weber has now graduated but Strader will again receive a strong challenge for the starting role, this time from sophomore Calvin Thomas. A muscular package at 5-10, 220 pounds, Thomas is very quick off the ball. The powerful running and blocking of the St. Louis native caught the coaches' eye last season, and should be the principal challenger to Strader.

"We want to see our running backs get more on their own, that is, make yardage after they reach the point where the play has been blocked. I believe we'll do better in that respect this year," says Moeller.

One of the keys will be finding a tailback who can be that kind of a game-breaking threat this season. Junior college transfer Larry Powell finished as the team's second leading rusher with 325 yards while dividing playing time with freshman Mark Dismuke. Both could improve with a year's experience along with freshmen Dave Perez and Joe Curtis. All are on the diminutive side, with Perez the only back over 180 lbs., and Curtis the only one at six feet. The answer could come in a new entry to this season's tailback derby. Mike Holmes, a transfer from the University of Colorado, at 6-3 and 210 pounds possesses the size and power of a fullback along with the speed and elusiveness of a tailback. The Chicago Leo High School product was impressive in drills a year ago, while sitting out last season, but he's raring to go this fall.

It's not unlikely that a freshman could assert himself at the tailback spot or at the two wide receiver positions where three of the top four players from a year ago are gone. Greg Foster, a kick return specialist, is the only returning letter winner, after being switched from tailback a year ago. Sophomore John Lopez figures to have good starting potential after seeing some playing time in 1978. They will be joined by Shawn Janus, a transfer from Yale a year ago who had an impressive spring game outing, and Kenny Shaw, a converted quarterback who Moeller feels has too much athletic ability to sit on the bench behind Weiss and McCullough.

Whereas inexperience will be a factor at the wide-out positions, the tight end spot will be manned by two talented veteran performers. Senior Mike Sherrod and junior Lee Boeke (twin brother of Greg) will give the Illini one of the best 1-2 punches in the Big Ten at this position. At 6-6 and 225 pounds with excellent speed and hands, Sherrod possesses all the potential to become an outstanding tight end but, each year, injuries have retarded his development and cut into his playing time. Fortunately, Boeke has been there to step into the breach the past two seasons, as a freshman and sophomore, to become the mainstay at this position and turn in solid performances. Both players are strong blockers and provide another offensive weapon for Moeller when called upon.

An improved offensive line and a better tailback situation will help the offense maintain better control of the football and allow the defense to get a bit more rest on the sidelines which it sorely lacked in 1978. The Illini defenders gave up 317 points on the year and the fatigue factor was readily apparent in the breakdown of scoring by quarters. Opponents scored 121 of those points in the final stanza, a total that nearly doubles every other quarter.

Illinois ranked seventh in overall defense and seventh in scoring defense in the Big Ten. In order to improve on those positions, Moeller aims to build depth in the defensive line and find capable replacements for a secondary weakened by graduation.

There has already been some position shifting done to attempt to strengthen the defensive front in Illinois' 5-2 alignment. The unexpected departure of starting tackle John Thiede due to a heavy academic schedule and the graduation of Bruce Thornton, has left the defensive tackle spot thin on experience. Moeller intends to take a strong look at last year's middle guard, Stanley Ralph, at defensive tackle with promising sophomore Ken Durrell moving up on the center's nose guard spot with Ralph stronger against the run and Durrell as an excellent pass rusher. Junior Dennis Flynn returns at the other tackle spot after an exceptional sophomore season when he registered 58 tackles and six sacks.

There are no returning letter winners to provide depth in the line behind the aforementioned three. Dave Dwyer, a 230 lb. linebacker will get a look at middle guard with sophomores Ken Gillen and Joe Moton making their challenge at tackles.

Some highly regarded freshmen could also have a shot in the defensive line or the secondary where depth is also a problem. Three-time letter winner Dale Hardy and four-time letter winner Derwin Tucker are gone with most of the unit's experience. Lloyd Levitt, a walk-on as a freshman, worked his way into a starting spot at defensive halfback last year as a senior and is back with an extra year of eligibility. He was the team's leading interceptor a year ago with four. Dave Kelly at safety and Rick George at the corner are also returning letter winners.

Kelly is one of the best all-around athletes on the team but the senior from LaGrange, Illinois has been hampered throughout his career by injuries. George, a sophomore, saw most of his action on specialty teams as a freshman in '78 but injuries pressed him into action against Missouri where he intercepted a pass and returned it 28 yards.

The critical "*warrior*" position in the Illini defense will likely be handled by two excellent athletes in John Venegoni or Bonji Bonner. Bonner was impressive in limited action as a freshman but could be moved to a safety or corner if needed. Venegoni, a junior, started most of last year at the warrior spot.

Tyrone Worthy, Eddie Mitchell, Jay Moton and Tim Holm were all newcomers a year ago and are eager to prove they can do the job in the secondary if called upon.

One of the proudest Fighting Illini traditions is the nearly unbroken lineage of excellence at linebacker, highlighted by Ray Nitschke in the '50s, Dick Butkus in the '60s and Scott Studwell and John Sullivan in recent years. With the graduation of Sullivan, the fine junior tandem of John Gillen and Earnest Adams appear well qualified to fill the gap. Gillen ranked number one in tackles ahead of Sullivan last year with 155 stops, including a team-leading 9 tackles-for-loss. Although weighing only 205 lbs., Adams used his outstanding 4.5 speed to get to ball carriers 68 times a year ago, including six stops behind the line of scrimmage, and picked off two enemy aerials. Both athletes could be in line for Conference honors this season.

Another excellent corps of young linebackers headed by sophomores Jack Squirek, Kelvin Atkins, Harold Blalock and Joe Barry will battle vets Bobby Smith, Tab Carmien and Jerry Ramshaw for the two additional vacant linebacker spots.

David Finzer returns as punter and place kicker in his junior year. The Chicago product made eight of nine extra points and five of eight field goals, including a 47-yarder, but his punting performance dropped off slightly. Cliff Jones will try to return from a leg muscle pull to battle Finzer for placekicking duties.

Illini followers were fearful of an "off" year in recruiting following last season's results, but Moeller and his staff appear to have proved them wrong. The group of signees is regarded by most observers as very comparable to the highly regarded class Mo has recruited the past two years. This season's crop is highlighted by a number of quick, game-breaking tailbacks as well as some big interior linemen. Five of the eight interior linemen signed weigh in at 235 lbs. or better including one giant at 6'10" and 280 lbs.

There are areas these newcomers could step in but more and more the upperclassmen are beginning to form the nucleus for Illinois, which is what Moeller is aiming for. The unit is beginning to take on the experienced look that had been lacking for the past two years and it all should spell an improved season for the Illini in 1979. It's a year that includes staunch Big Ten opponents on the schedule along with non-conference foes Navy, Air Force and Missouri. When you're going against competition like that, you like to bet on a vet!

INDIANA *Hoosiers*

There is no confusing where Indiana's priorities lie in preparing and playing its 1979 schedule.

It's defense and coach Lee Corso, whose bubbling, *extrovertish* approach to bigtime football sometimes misleads the casual observer into an erroneous impression opposed to the sound football practitioner he actually is, lays the baby and its future health on that doorstep.

Not that this represents any change in the Corso thinking and concept of what makes up championship football teams.

"That's as true now as it was when I arrived here seven years ago," he recounts. "I said then that every successful football program had to be built on: 1. Defense, 2. Kicking Game; 3. Offensive line. Nothing has changed. That is still my philosophy and it dictates the priorities we follow."

Unfortunately, that is the area of greatest Hoosier need, and the rebuilding demands there would appall anyone but a Corso, one of the world's few remaining great optimists.

Consider: Eight defensive starters are gone from a unit which gave up more than 403 yards and 26 points per game. Granted that the average is influenced unduly by a few games that just flat-out got away from the Hoosiers—the 69-17 debacle with Nebraska, the 49-14 loss to Michigan State—but the fact remains that few veteran hands remain from a defensive unit that had its problems in 1978.

At end, for example, George Doehla, Greg McIntosh and Carl Smith, who dominated the two positions, are gone; top defensive tackle Al Leake is an academic casualty; Indiana's greatest linebacker of all-time, Joe Norman, who was so good he could be selected the outstanding defensive player in a game his team was losing by 52 points, is gone, along with running mate Doug Sybert. And the secondary is shot to pieces with the departure of veteran safeties Dave Abrams and Dale Keneipp, three-year starters, both, and cornerback John Swinehart.

Obviously, the defense will require major attention and, if necessary, some offensive players will be shifted to shore it up.

"Offensively I think we'll be able to move the ball reasonably well," Corso concedes, "but this will be the greenest, least experienced defensive unit I've ever had."

Of course, the needs were well established long before recruiting began and it was aligned to the shortages. And it was a highly successful recruiting year, easily the best of Corso's seven classes at Indiana. And it's not unreasonable to expect some help from the newcomers.

"I had hoped our program was beyond that point," Corso admitted, "and that only the super-freshman would be able to make our lineup. But I think we'll see some freshmen here and there, particularly as we get into the season. I don't necessarily regard this as a weakness. I think we've got some quality players among the new people."

The offense lost just four starters and while they can't be minimized, there are some extenuating circumstances to lessen the loss.

For instance, tight-end Dan Powers graduated. But he was a fill-in for starter Dave Harangody, the 6-5, 240 pound junior who was lost before the start of last season with a broken leg incurred an auto accident. Coaches felt he was the equal of any tight end in the nation and his loss was felt even more keenly in that the offense in spring drills had been restructured around him.

Another plus is the return of fullback Tony D'Orazio, a two-year starter sidelined by a pre-season injury and subsequent surgery. Sophomore Lonnie Johnson did well as a replacement for him in '78 but D'Orazio is such a well-rounded player, a strong runner, a fine receiver and a superb blocker that he left an unfillable void. If his knee is sound, *and there's no reason to think otherwise,* his return could help greatly. And Johnson has so much talent there is some talk of moving him to the defense to fill one of those secondary gaps.

There's even less distress over the departure of three-year quarterback starter Scott Arnett than one would suspect. It's not that Arnett didn't do well. In fact, Corso dates Indiana's resurgence to the point where Arnett became the starter midway in the 1976 season. From that point the Hoosiers went 11-11-1 in Big Ten play, including a third and fourth-place finish, two out of three with arch-rival Purdue, and 13-14-1 overall against some of the nation's roughest opposition.

But Arnett played at 75 percent capacity all through 1978. An ankle injury in his summer conditioning work never mended and it cut down his mobility to a point where his running threat was nullified, with subsequent impairment of his passing potential. Arnett had his moments but figures reveal the problem. Sophomore Tim Clifford posted a 130-60, 726-yard passing record in relief to Arnett's 89-37, 421.

The year of experience should stand Clifford in good stead. He's rangy and has a good arm. He may not be as mobile as Arnett but he moves well enough to maintain the roll-out threat and retain an option phase to the offense.

The other missing starter is Mark Heidel, along with Norman an

All-Big Ten selection, and some jiggling may be required. Early plans call for Lucky Wallace, who moved from center to guard last year, to return to center, and a switch of guard John Taylor to center. Tackle Kevin Speer was a high school center and could get a shot there, although at the moment he's needed more at tackle.

Otherwise the offense is pretty much intact.

Arnett most likely will be succeeded by Clifford. Mike Harkrader proved his 1,003-yard freshman year was no fluke by netting 880 last fall after a year's lay-out with surgery, although he played very little through the early games. Fullback is well-manned with D'Orazio, Johnson and Jerry Bowers.

Corso likes the looks of his receivers. Mike Friede was coming with a rush at the last half of the season and he's a long-ball threat, as indicated by his two catches for 144 yards at Minnesota and the seven he caught at Purdue. Mark Fishel, at flanker last year, is coming up for his senior year with probably more experience than anyone else.

At tight end, Harangody provides a formidable target. He caught 11 passes as a sophomore. Bob Stephanson caught eight there as a freshman.

Frontline guards are veterans in Mark Johnson and Jeff Phipps and tackle Gerhard Ahting, about 15 pounds heavier, is back, leaving one replacement to be made at the other tackle. Doug Peacock departed there.

It's a team that should be able to both run and pass. Darrick Burnett is the lone running back loss, diminished to some extent by his chronic situation. His considerable talent was marred by injuries which never permitted him to play a complete season.

Defensive replacements may be harder to come by.

Out of the gate the defensive ends could revert to Dave Stewart, a two-game starter a year ago, and Eric DeBord, who lost most of the year after an injury in the second game. Brent Tisdale, matured and bigger, is back at tackle and Terry Tallen, who played some at middle-guard as well as tackle, could wind up the tackle pair. Randy Willhite started seven games at middle-guard and Mel Patton two, and one of them could be it. Corso's system makes defensive tackles and middle-guards interchangeable and various combinations are possible.

If the situation is "iffy" up front it gets downright puzzling in the next layers of defense.

Norman had been such a tower of strength, inspiration as well as physical, that replacing him at a linebacker post is impossible. As the IU all-time tackle leader, he had the capacity to pick up a defense and make it do things it never knew it could do. His 199 tackles were more than twice those of any other defender. And Sybert added another 76. Finding a comparable pair is really too much to expect.

"I've had some great linebackers," said Corso, "but no one like Joe Norman. That includes people like Tom Jackson, the All-Pro at Denver who I had at Louisville. Joe was that rare combination of the tremendously skilled athlete and intense competitor. He played hurt when others would have been on the sideline. He made plays that no mortal should make. Anyone who didn't enjoy watching Joe Norman play football doesn't enjoy football."

You can count on plenty of experimenting in searching out their replacements.

Aaron Arbuckle started four games last year when Sybert was on the shelf. Mark Ramsey played well in spots coming off freshman surgery. There will be a lot of looks taken at many of the candidates.

The same situation prevails among the deep backs. Loss of Abrams and Keneipp poses monumental problems. Lettermen Chuck Alexander and Dart Ramsey, a younger brother to Mark, stand first in line. It's anyone's guess at Swinehart's cornerback post, although there's little doubt that there will be a place for Tim Wilbur either at safety or cornerback.

Wilbur gathered in six interceptions as a freshman last fall, one of them at Michigan State for a 98 yard return and a Conference record that lasted just a short time. His 138 return yards, however, is an Indiana record.

Corso's kicking ingredient seems well on its way toward accomplishment.

True, little David Freud, the 5-6 Israeli army veteran, the 27-year-old father of one, is a hard act to follow. He hit a perfect 28 on PATS, knocked in eight of 13 field goal attempts, wound up as IU's leading scorer with 52 points, and finished his career with 65 consecutive conversions.

But Kevin Kellogg, a 1977 letterman redshirted last year, promises to be of the same caliber and, perhaps kicks with a bit more range. Last year Steve Straub handled most of the kickoffs in view of Freud's limitations in range, and he's better than a fair hand at FG-production also.

Larry Lovett is back at punting and with the year of experience, it is hoped, he will eliminate some of his inconsistencies. He would throw an occasional shank among his boomers, although once he foresook his barefoot style for a shoe his consistency took a turn for the better.

But it's a long way from Henderson Junior College in Texas to Indiana in the Big Ten, and Corso feels the year at the wars will show some benefit this time around.

Basically the Hoosiers will change little in style or system.

The offense will remain a basic Pro-I or split-back formation. It will not be oriented either to the pass or to the run.

"Normally I'd say our offense would be about two-to-one with the run," said Corso, "but it all depends upon what those people on the other side of the line are doing. I once coached a team that ran the ball 50 consecutive times. It all depends upon what the defense gives us."

It's possible that the Hoosiers might rely more on a dropback passing style to accomodate Clifford. But he can roll out on he option. In fact, against Iowa in his freshman year he did so for a 16-yard gain that set up a touchdown in a come-from-behind victory.

Corso is an extremely adaptable coach. He is not afraid to gamble or to change things, although if one analyzes it deeply enough, he usually finds the odds pretty good all along. But there's some of the "riverboat gambler" in Corso and opponents find it difficult to type-cast him.

Defensively the Hoosiers are a basic 5-2-4. But here also the variations are numerous and Corso will give you a lot of looks out of it. The Hoosiers have blitzed out of the safety, gambled on the ends, done a lot of unsettling things—which have worked much more often than not.

It presents a crowd pleasing aspect to Hoosier fans, who have been outmanned enough to appreciate unorthodox means to overcome it. The Corso flair for the unexpected reveals itself in many ways.

Such as last year when he brought split-end Mike Friede back to quick kick against Ohio State. Result? Friede kicked three times for 194 yards, a 64.7-yard average, and kept the Buckeyes back in their end of the field most of the afternoon. They recovered enough to win, 21-18, but the wrinkle kept the Hoosiers in contention nearly to the end in a game where man-for-man they were totally overmatched.

Another factor in Corso's favor toward attaining the championship he aspires at Indiana is his ability—and liking—to recruit. To most coaches the recruiting process is a distasteful and wearing chore. Not so for Corso. He truly loves the challenge of it and he relates so well to today's youth that he can sell his program on his personality alone.

And 1979 has been his premier recruiting class.

Understandably reluctant to rank players before even a workout, Corso feels they compare to any. Some carry special names. One is Jeff Gedman of Duquesne, Pa., whose uncle, Gene, was an All-Big Ten selection at Indiana went on to be an outstanding back on Detroit's NFL champions. Another, Rob Harkrader, younger brother of Indiana's fabulous Mike and son of Jerry, his coach at Middletown, O., and the anonymous "other back" in the Hopalong Cassady backfield at Ohio State in the mid 1950's.

John Mineo, from St. Louis, is another highly-sought running back. The Hoosiers appear well stocked with running backs but know from experience a team can't have too many. Fresh in mind is the 1976 season when the team lost No. 1 Courtney Snyder in the first game, No. 2 Tony Suggs in the second; No. 3 Darrick Burnett in the third. That was when Harkrader burst onto the scene as No. 4.

But the emphasis in recruiting was on interior linemen, which is where the current needs are greatest. As a result, some of the newcomers may be surfacing early in the season.

As far as the 1979 schedule goes, there's little gained or lost.

The Big Ten slate drops Michigan State and picks up Michigan.

The non-Conference season might be a shade more reasonable, particularly when one sees Washington, Louisiana State and Nebraska dropping off. Vanderbilt, Kentucky and Colorado replace them.

Whether it matters or not, five of Indiana's opponents will be showing up with new coaches. That's Iowa, Vanderbilt, Colorado, Ohio State and Minnesota. Probably it evens out—the advantage of meeting a team which has no established patterns as a guide.

But one thing is certain. The Hoosiers have turned things around, to a point where they are competitive with all. A taste of the upper reaches of the Big Ten, the third and fourth places, the pair of victories over Purdue, the heady feeling of going toe-to-toe with the likes of Ohio State and Michigan State and Purdue, does wonders for confidence and faith in what they're doing and being asked to do.

The Hoosiers are again a fullfledged member of the Big Ten football family. And Corso's eye is on the top of the heap.

Coach Leo Corso

Lee Corso's ultimate goal remains the same today as it was when he was appointed football coach at Indiana University on January 7, 1973—that of building a championship program at IU. Long-time Hoosiers followers are convinced the program is headed in that direction.

The Corso era at IU has been marked by considerable, consistent improvement. After struggling through the early years, the Hoosiers finished third and fourth in the Big Ten in 1976 and 1977, the first time in eight years IU posted consecutive first division finishes. And in both of those years that Hoosiers beat arch-rival Purdue, their first back-to-back victories in that long series in 30 years. And even in the injury-wrecked season of '78, when Corso was forced to continually juggle his starting lineup, the Hoosiers won four games, including a big 14-7 win over defending Rose Bowl champion Washington, and were just nipped in down-to-the-wire battles with Louisiana State, Minnesota and Ohio State.

It's no accident that the Hoosiers have progressed to a point where they pose a challenge to all comers. A self-imposed *workaholic*, Corso and his staff have labored long and hard to bring IU football to the top. When he's not working until midnight in the office, Corso is usually on the road. Speaking engagements take up a large portion of his time, and in an age where most coaches find recruiting a detestful part of their job, Corso looks upon it as challenging and rewarding.

Corso has a style and flair about him that creates excitement wherever he goes. He's that rarity among his kind, a football coach who has fun with the game. He can laugh at it, and himself, and feels the game was meant to be enjoyed by players and coaches, as well as fans.

His coaching philosophy is simple. Although he's widely recognized as a gambler and an innovator, he has never lost sight of what he believes to be the cornerstones to a winning program—a sound defense, a strong kicking game, and a good offensive line.

Those were the ingredients he used to mold together a fabulously successful program at the University of Louisville, which proved to be his springboard to the Indiana job. In four years there, he transformed a losing program into one of high national ranking.

His record there was 28-11-3 and twice the Cardinals were Missouri Valley Conference champions, their first-ever league titles. In 1970 he took the Cardinals to their first bowl game, where they tied favored Long Beach State in the Pasadena Bowl. In 1972 Louisville posted a 9-1 record and ranked 16th and 17th in the national polls. They also ranked first in the nation in both total and rushing defense and 12th in the country in scoring offense.

Lee Corso was born in Cicero, Ill., but his family moved to Miami, Fla., when he was ten. He was graduated from Miami's Jackson High School and went on to a fabled athletic career at Florida State University.

He enrolled at FSU in 1953 and four years later he graduated after having made a record for versatility rarely matched in the collegiate ranks. Playing both offense, where he was a quarterback and a halfback, and defense, Corso set school records in both rushing and interceptions. In 1956 he was the national back-of-the-week by one wire service after leading the Seminoles to a 14-0 victory over North Carolina State, their fourth consecutive victory over the Wolfpack. He played in the Blue-Gray all-star game that year and was an honorable mention All-America choice by AP.

In May of 1978, Corso was inducted into the Florida State Athletic Hall of Fame, a year behind a long-time friend who played in the same backfield with him, Buddy Reynolds, who now goes by the name of Burt, and can occasionally be seen in the motion picture theatres.

After receiving his B.S. in '57 in physical education, he stayed on to earn a Master's degree in educational administration in 1959. He assisted his head coach, Tom Nugent, and when Nugent took over at the University of Maryland, Corso went with him as an assistant. After seven years at Maryland, he joined Bill Elias' staff at Navy, where he served for three years before he secured the Louisville job.

Many look upon Corso as a jokester. It's simply not true. He's a serious man who says funny things. Or, as one writer proclaims: "a character with a lot of character."

He's made a personal vow to represent IU "with class and dignity." He's most proud of the fact that during his six years at IU, the bitter Purdue-Indiana rivalry has never spilled into a fight on the field.

Corso's stature both on and off the field is evident. He has served the football coaches' association in many capacities. He has been a member of various NCAA seminars and in 1978 was on the pre-season NCAA tour of players and coaches.

He has coached in the coaches' All-American Bowl and last year was head coach of the East team in the Japan Bowl, which won by a 33-14 margin and had as the game's most valuable player one of Corso's own Hoosiers, linebacker Joe Norman.

Off the field, Corso diverts his attention to other areas. He served as the Indiana March-of-Dimes chairman in '78 and this year served as the state's Easter Seal Chairman.

A devoted family man, Corso enjoys his private moments at home. The family jewels include wife Betsy, sons Steve, a senior on the Hoosier squad, Dave and Dan, and daughter Diane.

Indiana Tailback Mike Harkrader

Mike Harkrader doesn't fit the mold of your average collegiate running back. For one thing, the Indiana junior stands a mere 5-7, smallish by most standards. He's not exceptionally strong, nor blazingly fast, qualities which often earmark All-American runners.

And yet, Harkrader, barring injuries, will most likely be remembered as the most prolific yardage gainer in Indiana history.

He may also be the answer to one of the all-time great Big Ten trivia questions, as in name the only freshman in Big Ten history to gain 1,000 yards rushing.

Stop and reflect, if you will, back to the 1976 season. Mike Harkrader didn't exactly burst on the scene in a blaze of glory. In fact, he began the season as IU's No. 4 tailback, and moved into the starting lineup only by accident.

The scene was Seattle, Wash.; the Hoosiers were 0-2 on the season and battling a tough Washington team. The Hoosiers had already lost their top two tailbacks to injuries in the first two games and, yep, you guessed it, tailback No. 3 went out in the second quarter against the Huskies. Enter Harkrader, who in two games had carried four times for 15 yards. All the pintsized rookie did was gain 76 yards in 18 carries as the Hoosiers upset the Huskies, 20-13. A legend was born.

Harkrader became an overnight sensation for the Hoosiers. He had his first 100-yard day in a 7-0 Homecoming win over Northwestern, gaining 179 yards in only 22 carries, including a 72-yard sprint that bailed the Hoosiers out of a deep hole late in the game. He was selected as the AP Midwest Back-of-the-Week. The very next Saturday, against Iowa, he ran for 191 yards, including an 18-yard sprint in the final period that won the game for the Hoosiers, and for that effort was named to the UPI Backfield-of-the-Week.

On two other occasions he broke 100 yards and he went into the season finale against Purdue needing just 67 yards to reach 1,000 for the season.

Gutty is the appropriate word to describe how he did it. Late in the first half, after a run around right end, he ran into a fence and, it was discovered later, broke a bone in his leg. Undaunted, he started the second half, and after his second carry, which put him at 1,003 yards for the year, he broke his other leg. Two broken legs in the same game, on different plays.

But in gaining that 1,003 yards, he became the first Big Ten freshman ever to do that (*remember, trivia fans*) and the fourth leading rusher in one season in IU history. He was also only the fourth freshman in NCAA history to exceed 1,000 yards as a rookie.

Harkrader then missed the 1977 season, but not because of the broken legs. They healed fine. Trouble was, he hurt his knee before the opening game and underwent surgery, which left a few doubters wondering if he could ever come back. They soon found out.

Although he started slowly in 1978, by the Big Ten season it was the old Mike Harkrader, cutting, darting and slashing for every possible yard. Like '76, his first big game came against Northwestern, when he picked up 162 yards in 31 tries. Two weeks later, against Illinois, he was the AP Big Ten Offensive Player-of-the-Week after running for 164 yards and scoring a touchdown in that 31-10 win. He was good for 113 yards and two touchdowns at Minnesota and 129 yards and another score in the 34-14 win over Iowa.

Harkrader was challenging for the Big Ten rushing lead with two weeks to go, eventually finishing second. He gained 880 yards for the season and scored seven touchdowns, leading the Hoosiers in both categories. He was selected to a 2nd team berth on the All-Big Ten squad. And already, with two seasons to go, he ranks fifth on the all-time IU career rushing list with 1,883 yards, easily within the Hoosier record of 2,789.

IU Coach Lee Corso has often joked that Harkrader gains so much yardage because he's so small that the defense can't find him. It goes beyond that.

Harkrader comes from good stock. He was coached in high school by his father, Jerry, who was a starter with Howard

"Hopalong" Cassady at Ohio State when the Buckeyes won the national championship in 1953. Twice Mike was named Ohio's Class A "Player-of-the-Year" and in three seasons gained more than 4,000 yards and scored 50 TD's.

And now, the Harkrader's are trying to make it a family affair. Brother Rob, much bigger than Mike at 5-9, is a freshman at IU and all he did in two years at Middletown (O.) was net 2,654 yards, a 6.4 average and score 40 touchdowns.

"Mike is so good because he's such a great competitor," IU Coach Lee Corso says. "He'll battle for every yard he can get and it's that drive and determination that make him outstanding. And he's really tough in clutch situations. We're a tailback oriented offense and he's a big part of it."

As the season unfolds, it won't be at all surprising to see the Hoosiers' "Mighty Mike" among the Big Ten's leaders in rushing. Unless, of course, brother Rob pushes him aside.

Indiana Defensive Back Tim Wilbur

A budding star. That's the tag that Big Ten football observers have placed on Indiana's Tim Wilbur, who in just one season earned the recognition, and respect, of the league's brethren.

When the IU squad reported for practice last August, the general consensus among Hoosier coaches was that Wilbur stood the best chance of playing out of all the freshmen. For one thing, when Coach Lee Corso recruited him, he called him "one of the top two prospects in the state." That was after Wilbur led his Indianapolis Ben Davis High school team to an 11-1 record while playing both quarterback and safety. Secondly, the Hoosiers were lacking depth in the defensive secondary, so freshmen were getting immediate attention there.

Wilbur didn't disappoint the coaches, although it did take him awhile to settle into a position. He began drills with free safety in mind, but moved to strong safety behind 1977 star Dave Abrams, although he was utilized as the fifth back when the Hoosiers went into a prevent defense. Soon, however, he got a call at cornerback, and almost immediately moved into the starting lineup.

Once there, he didn't waste any time in establishing himself.

His first start came in the fifth game, against Northwestern, and early in the first quarter he intercepted a pass at the Wildcat 40, ran it back 16 yards to the 24, and set up a Hoosier touchdown. It was a day the Hoosiers came out winners, 38-10.

The next week he became an instant celebrity by making Indiana and Big Ten history. Michigan State quarterback Ed Smith had an exceptional day in leading the Spartans to a 49-19 win, but he went Wilbur's way twice too often. The rookie redhead picked off a pass in the third quarter, and in the fourth, after a defensive lineman hit Smith's arm when he was throwing, grabbed another errant toss and sped 98 yards down the sideline for a touchdown. That set a new Indiana record and tied the existing Big Ten standard.

"I just grabbed the ball and didn't look back," Wilbur said later. "I played quarterback in high school and I like to run."

With such an eye-startling beginning, three interceptions in his first two starts, it would have have been only natural for his interception rate to decrease, which it did. But not by much. By year's end, he had accumulated six, in just seven starts, which was the second best mark in IU history. And his five thefts in Big Ten play tied him for the league leadership.

Without question, 1978 was an exceptional freshman year for Tim Wilbur. In addition to his six interceptions, he knocked down four passes, recovered a fumble and was credited with 45 tackles.

He was also the Hoosier's No. 1 punt returner. Handling that job, from day one, proved just how much confidence the coaches had in the talented freshman. He almost broke one for a touchdown against Illinois, being run out of bounds after returning a punt 40 yards upfield.

What made Wilbur so good, so soon? Ability, for one thing. And secondary coach Trent Walters lists numerous other qualities.

"One of his biggest attributes is that he has so much poise," Walters says. "That's one of the reasons he returned punts. In our early drills, he always caught the ball, which is the No. 1 prerequisite for a punt returner.

"He's also a very intelligent player. He reads very well, which you have to be able to do when playing cornerback. Because reacting to the run is every bit as important as defending against the pass.

"And above everything else," Walters continued, "he's a great competitor. He's tough and tenacious and likes the pressure of the big games. He's already a good player who's going to get better."

What will Wilbur do for an encore? Well, out ahead of him is the IU career record of 11 interceptions...or the one-season mark of seven grabs. Although he'll only be a sophomore, Wilbur is one player who could be preceded by his reputation. He could be that good.

Indiana Quarterback Tim Clifford and Receiver Mike Friede

Tim Clifford did a lot of throwing for IU athletic teams back in April. Not only did Lee Corso's No. 1 quarterback spend three weeks in spring drills readying for the '79 season, he also spent his pre and post-spring practice session weeks hurling baseballs for Bob Lawrence's diamond squad as its No. 1 hurler.

Sound challenging? You can bet it was. But that's part of the makeup of Tim Clifford, who loves a challenge. He'll have one this fall, as he'll be leading the Hoosier offense after spending the last two years in relief roles, mainly as a "designated thrower."

When Clifford throws in '79, his main man on the receiving end could very well be split end Mike Friede, who is looking for a big season himself. The Clifford-Friede duo, which successfully clicked on a number of big plays towards the end of the 1978 season, could develop into one of the Big Ten's most feared combinations.

Clifford has to rank as the best pure thrower the Hoosiers have had in the Corso era at IU, and Friede is the big-play specialist the Hoosiers have lacked since the incomparable Jade Butcher put 30 touchdowns on the board from 1967-69. It will come as no surprise then if the Hoosiers shift their offensive emphasis from a tailback oriented ground attack to more of an aerial circus. Corso isn't about to waste the talents of Clifford and Friede.

It wasn't until the latter half of the '78 season, and maybe not even then, that Clifford and Friede drew much attention from Big Ten followers. Both had to overcome early season struggles.

Clifford's problems were all physical. He was suffering from a mysterious leg ailment that caused him to miss over two weeks of practice before the opening game, and later in the campaign was suffering from knee and hand injuries. Actually, he was never 100% healthy throughout the entire season.

Friede had to overcome other problems—like the transition from junior college to major college football. A standout at Garden City (Kan.) for two years, where he once caught 11 passes for 239 yards and five touchdowns in one game, Friede soon found out the Big Ten was the major leagues. And in the latter half of the campaign, he proved he belonged.

"I think Mike can become one of the outstanding receivers in the league, a very, very good player," says IU quarterback and receiver coach Morris Watts. "He has good speed, is smart, and has amazing concentration. Nothing distracts him when he's going for the ball. He never takes his eyes off of it."

Corso is impressed "by the way he plays on every down. He does a lot of little things that most people don't notice, like getting a piece of his man on downfield blocks, or making a good fake on a pass route that decoys the defense away from a play. That's the mark of a good football player."

Friede really started to assert himself when the Hoosiers played at Minnesota. Clifford was a surprise starter that day, and on the third play of the game he launched a deep pass down the sideline that Friede reached up and snared between two Gopher defenders and scampered 62 yards for a touchdown. It qualified as IU's longest play of the season, but not for long.

Just seven minutes later, Friede ran the same route, Clifford launched the same type of pass and the result was an 82-yard completion, the third longest pass play in IU history. Two throws, two completions, 144 yards of real estate.

Friede and Clifford hooked up on a big two-point conversion against Ohio State that put the Hoosiers within range of a tying field goal, and they worked their magic repeatedly against Purdue in the season finale. Friede freed himself long, short, over the middle and at the sidelines to catch seven passes for 119 yards and a touchdown. That performance should have served notice to the rest of the Big Ten of what to be aware of in '79.

Friede ended the season as IU's leading receiver with 17 catches for 412 yards and an amazing 24.2 yard average per catch, by far the best in the Big Ten. And, he uses his feet as well as his hands. Against Ohio State he quick-kicked three times for 52, 66 and 76 yards.

But no matter how good a receiver is, he has to have a quarterback who can deliver the goods. Clifford should fit the bill. Most of his playing time last year came in obvious passing situations, when the Hoosiers were in third-and-long or playing catchup from behind. An obvious advantage for a pass-playing defense.

Still, Clifford hit on 60-130 passes for 726 yards and four touchdowns and threw only nine interceptions, not bad considering he was throwing into five and six-man secondaries. Against Wisconsin, in a similar situation, he completed eight straight passes.

Affectionately known as "Sonny" because of his resemblance to former professional standout Sonny Jurgenson, Clifford is a person who believes in his own abilities.

"I'm always confident I can pass," he says. "And I feel like Mike Friede is one of the best split ends around. It will just be a matter of me getting the ball to him."

Corso agrees. "Clifford can throw the football," he says. "We could have a nicely balanced offense with our running and his throwing. He's gained some experience over the past two years, which should be of great benefit to him. There's no doubt in my mind that he will be a very good quarterback."

Remember the names—Clifford and Friede. They could become more than just a *passing fancy*.

IOWA *Hawkeyes*

Historians tell us Michelangelo could take a slab of marble and chisel it into a masterpiece in a matter of months. That's great if you're an artist, but what if you're a first-year football coach like Iowa's Hayden Fry? How long will it take you to mold your new team into a winner?

The 49-year-old Fry, a former North Texas State coach who is famous for wide-open football, has quite a chore on his hands this season. He inherits 13 starters from a team that was 2-9 overall and 2-6 in the Big Ten, and markedly inept offensively. Should Fry give Iowa his "master" touch, as he did in rebuilding sagging programs at Southern Methodist (1962-72) and North Texas State (1973-78), he would indeed have himself a work of art.

But how long will it take for the tall, determined Texan to get the job done?

"I didn't take this job and come all this way north to lose," says Fry. "We may not accomplish our goals in a year or in two years, but I can guarantee you that we are committed to win. I'm impressed with the attitude here and with the players returning from last year. I feel we have some excellent recruits who will help us immediately."

Consider the massive project facing Fry this year:

—The 1979 schedule is one of Iowa's toughest in years, with Big Eight powerhouses Oklahoma, Nebraska and cross-state rival Iowa State (all who played in bowl games last year) the foes prior to the heart of the Big Ten schedule. The Hawkeyes open Sept. 8 at home against Indiana. In the past, league cellar-dweller Northwestern was the first opponent.

—Fry must take an offense, with 10 starters returning, that was able to generate only 16 touchdowns (six by split end Brad Reid), was outscored 291-125 (and 133-10 in the second quarter), and was unable to mount serious offensive drives two Saturdays in a row.

—Iowa returns only three starters from a defensive unit that was porous in the defensive secondary. Biggest losses are all-Big Ten linebacker and safety Dave Becker.

—Iowa has not had a winning season since 1961.

Despite those obstacles, Fry brings a breath of fresh air to Iowa with his multiple, pro-type offense. He says he likes to pattern his teams after the Dallas Cowboys, and compares notes with another successful coach in the league, Michigan State's Darryl Rogers.

To get out of the gate, Fry recruited heavily in the junior college ranks, landing seven outstanding prospects. Iowa alternated four quarterbacks last season, and that is an area needing immediate attention if the Hawkeyes are to develop consistency.

Fry recruited junior college standouts Tony Ricciardulli (6-2, 195) from San Diego Mesa and Gordy Bohannan (6-2, 180) of South Pasadena, Calif., who started at Glendale, Calif. Ricciardulli was a JC all-American, setting school records for most yards in one game (452) and most pass completions (30 of 50). He completed 164 of 307 passes for 2,130 yards and 20 touchdowns in leading Mesa to the South Coast Conference title last year.

The fourth leading passer in the nation, Ricciardulli was topped by Bohannan, who was the nation's third-leading signal-caller, hitting on 181 of 303 passes for 2,396 yards and 22 touchdowns.

The standout pair will contend with veteran returnees Jeff Green (5-11, 185) and Pete Gales (6-3, 170) for the starter's role. Green, a junior from Newhall, Calif., helped the Hawkeyes to a 38-24 upset of Wisconsin and completed 41 of 103 passes for 556 yards and three touchdowns. Gales, a junior from Paterson, N.J., threw 40 passes, completing 15 for 112 yards. Fry says he's also taking a look at senior Phil Suess, a 6-5, 177-pounder from Des Moines, Ia., who was on the "scout team" last year.

Jeff Green   *Pete Gales*   *Mike Brady*

Brady is a curious case. He was almost a forgotten man last year under ex-coach Bob Commings. He saw action in only two games after leading Iowa in receptions with 26 for 357 yards and two touchdowns in 1977. He was sixth in the Big Ten in receiving that year.

Rounding out the JC talent in the Iowa camp are noseguard Glenn Manning (6-2, 275) of Waterloo, Ia., defensive end Andre Tippett (6-4, 225) of Newark, N.J., and defensive tackle Ron Hallstrom (6-6, 270) of Moline, Ill. Hallstrom was a second team all-America at Iowa Central of Fort Dodge, while Manning and Tippett played for Ellsworth of Iowa Falls.

Fry's colleagues consider him imaginative and daring in his offensive philosophy. That's pleasant news for both Iowa and the Big Ten, which has long waged a ground-oriented battle season after season. Fry took his 1968 Southern Methodist team to Ohio State and put the ball in the air an NCAA record 76 times.

In order for Iowa to enjoy such a passing game, it must have some protection for its signal-caller. Fry will look to junior center Jay Hilgenberg and tight end Jim Swift to anchor the offensive line. Swift (6-5, 238) is a gifted blocker and was seldom used as a receiver last year. When he is a target, Swift has shown outstanding ability to bother the opponents secondary. He caught 12 passes for 211 yards and one touchdown last season.

Jay Hilgenberg    *Jim Swift*

Sam Palladino    *Matt Petrzelka*

Rounding out the offensive line are tackles Sam Palladino and Matt Petrzelka, and guards Greg Gilbaugh and Dave Mayhan. Palladino (6-2, 245) showed the most consistency last season, helping Iowa to its only wins over Northwestern and Wisconsin.

The backfield will feature a variety of candidates for starting roles. Iowa used as many as 12 running backs last year in the wing-

T formation. Fry will run his multiple sets with a fullback, flanked by a halfback and wingback. The Hawkeyes will have ample speed at halfback with senior Dennis Mosley (5-10, 176), who gained 310 yards (second best on the team) and sophomores Kenny Burke (6-1, 194) and Phil Blatcher (5-8, 175). Burke carried 76 times for 303 yards, while Blatcher handled the ball only 19 times for 98 yards and turned in Iowa's longest kickoff return of 69 yards.

Dennis Mosley   *Dean McKillip*   *Brad Reid*

Dean McKillip, a rugged 6-1, 227-pounder from Galesburg, Ill., is the top candidate at fullback. Wingback should be a battle between talented Brad Reid and Doug Dunham, a duo which started at end last year.

Reid, a swift 5-11, 170-pounder from Marion, Ia., was perhaps the fastest player last year for the Hawkeyes. He was Mr. Everything during the disappointing year, averaging 20.4 yards every time he touched the ball. Named Most Valuable Player and twice Outstanding Midwest Back of the Week by United Press International, Reid scored five touchdowns via the end around play and caught one pass for another score. He rushed for 186 yards on 10 carries, caught 14 passes for 322 yards, returned 17 punts for 104 yards and ran back 13 kickoffs for 245 yards.

Dunham hurled in nine passes for 148 yards. He'll also be battling senior Rod Morton (5-11, 187) of Neptune, N.J., who is in his fifth year of eligibility after playing wingback last year. Morton showed his versatility by passing 55 yards to Reid for a touchdown against Northwestern, catching 11 passes for 130 yards and one TD and rushing 13 times for 57 yards.

Fry says he never enjoyed a strong kicking game at North Texas State. He may find the right prescription this season with veteran punter Dave Holsclaw and placekicker Scott Schilling handling the chores. The only problem the two seniors may have is the presence of freshman sensation Reggie Roby. The 6-3, 215-pound all-American from Waterloo is considered one of the top kickers in the country. He averaged 40 plus yards punting, had three field goals

Dave Holsclaw *Scott Schilling*

from beyond 45 yards, (one for 51) and booted 24 of 27 kickoffs out of the end zone. Holsclaw averaged 36.6 yards punting, while Schilling made 12 of 13 extra points and hit on five of eight field goal attempts to finish as Iowa's second leading scorer. It appears Holsclaw and Schilling will have to upgrade all phases of their game to beat out Roby.

Jim Molini *Bryan Skradis* *Mark Mahmens*

While Fry hopes to rebuild and inject life into the offense, it is the defense which will need perhaps the most concern. Only three starters are back, the most noticeable losses being standout linebacker Tom Rusk and safety Dave Becker. Fry says he will use the Oklahoma 5-2 defensive alignment as compared to the 4-3 formation Iowa fans have seen for the past five seasons.

With that move, Fry will probably switch standout senior linebacker Jim Molini (6-4, 228) and sophomore Brian Skradis (6-1, 213) to defensive end. Tackle Mark Mahmens (6-2, 250) returns at one spot, while the other slot may be a battle between junior college transfer Hallstrom, sophomore Clay Uhlenhake and senior Don Willey, who was an offensive guard last year.

Don Willey    Leven Weiss

The linebacker position where Iowa showed the most strength the past several years, will be manned by capable hands. Leven Weiss (6-2, 215) is a top candidate for one position, while sophomore Todd Simonsen (6-2, 217) of Racine Wis., and senior Bobby Hill (6-1, 222) of Mt Clemens, Mich., are battling for the other slot.

Noseguard should be a spirited clash in spring drills between JC transfer Manning, junior Pat Dean (6-1, 229) of West Islip, N.Y., and senior Phil Michel (6-3, 225) of Iowa City.

Bobby Hill    Mario Pace    Cedric Shaw

Iowa's defensive secondary, which allowed 138 passes by opponents for 1,947 yards, will need immediate upgrading. Fry will count on leadership from senior Mario Pace (5-11, 180) of Stow, Ohio, to trim their opponents' margin. Pace intercepted two passes last year, saved two touchdowns, recovered one fumble, had four passes defended and was the fifth leading tackler with 57.

Pace should have the lock on one cornerback position, while senior Cedric Shaw (6-0, 192) of Newark, N.J. is the top candidate at the other cornerback position. The safety slots are up for grabs between sophomore twins Kent and Kevin Ellis of DeWitt, Ia., freshmen red-shirts Joe Aulisi (6-0, 203) of South Orange, N.J., and Bobby Stoops (6-0, 175) of Youngstown, Ohio, and sophomore Lou King (6-2, 174) of Jersey City, N.J., who started in late season to finish with 23 tackles, two passes defended, one recovered fumble, one tackle forcing a fumble and one interception.

Fry also bolstered competition for the secondary positions by recruiting three freshmen defensive backs: Todd Suchomel (6-1, 185) of Sun Prairie, Wis., Jay Bachman (6-2, 180) of Whitewater, Wis., and Mike Hufford (6-3, 190) of Mt. Vernon, Ia. The newcomers should make their presence known in fall drills.

The Hawkeyes also welcome into their camp a rare "species"—a prep recruit from talent-rich Texas. He's Mark Barden, a 602, 217-pound fullback from Houston. The biggest prep on the roster is tackle Carl Peiffer of Keota. Peiffer, a 6-7, 255-pounder, follows in the footsteps of Hawk brothers Warren and Dan, now with the Chicago Bears.

The remainder of Iowa's prep recruits display versatility. Six played two different positions last year, five were quarterbacks.

Fry will change the practice format this year. Iowa scrimmaged eight times in the spring before the May 5 spring game. No scrimmages are slated for the fall. By that time, Iowa fans hope, Fry will have begun to mold his first Big Ten team into an exciting and competitive unit. "I can guarantee you that my staff and I will work day and night to get the job done," says Fry. "I hope that the good Iowa fans will continue to turn out and support us."

Some of the Top Hawkeye Players

Jeff Green emerged as Iowa's top quarterback during the 1978 campaign. A native of Newhall, Cal., Green's arm pulled the Hawkeye offense out of a slump at mid-season and he went on to complete 41 of 103 passes for the year. He compiled 556 yards via the air, with a long completion of 60 yards. The 6-0, 185-pound junior also ran for two TDs. His best game was the Hawkeyes' home finale against Wisconsin, as he passed for 128 yards, one touchdown, and scored another TD on a one-yard run in Iowa's 38-24 win.

Since moving to the defensive backfield from the quarterback position in his freshman year, **Mario Pace** has seen a lot of action for the Iowa Hawkeyes. Although only 5-11, and 173 pounds, Pace enters his senior season as a three-year letterman and the leader of the defensive secondary. Pace was the fifth-leading tackler on the Iowa squad in 1978, and topped the team in touchdown saves with two. He intercepted two passes from his cornerback position last year. Pace is from Stow, Ohio, and threw a 99-yard pass completion as a prep at Stow High School.

Split end **Brad Reid** was Iowa's big play man last season. The 5-11, 170 pound native of Marion, Ia., included an 80-yard touchdown run against Wisconsin and a 60-yard pass reception against Minnesota in his list of big gainers. Reid was named UPI Mid-West Offensive Player of the Week twice last season and was named Iowa's most valuable player. He scored six touchdowns to finish as the Hawkeyes' leading scorer with 36 points. Reid also led the team in punt returns with 17 for 104 yards, and averaged 18.9 yards on kickoff returns. The all-purpose wide receiver is equally as dangerous on the end around as he is receiving passes. Reid rushed for 168 yards and five touchdowns as a junior last year in addition to catching 14 passes for 322 yards. Each time he touched the ball his average gain was 20.4 yards.

Jay Hilgenberg, a 6-3, 240 pound center from Iowa City is part of a family tradition at Iowa. His father Jerry was an all-American center for the Hawkeyes, his uncle Wally Hilgenberg was a star at Iowa and is now a linebacker for the Minnesota Vikings, and older brother Jim was a co-captain at Iowa in 1977. Jay was a regular starter at center for the Hawkeyes as a sophomore last season, and is expected to be the anchor of the offensive line this year.

Iowa defensive tackle **John Harty** was one of the most sought after preps in the country after a brilliant career at Sioux City Heelen. As a sophomore in 1978 the 6-6, 260-pound giant was involved in 49 tackles, including four for losses. The former high school all-American is one of the few returning defensive linemen for the Hawkeyes. He is considered a top-notch pass rusher.

Senior **Jim Molini** returns at a linebacker slot for Iowa in 1979 after gaining semi-regular status last year. Molini spent two years in a reserve role as a defensive end before moving to linebacker. A 6-4, 225-pound native of Norfolk, Neb., Molini was one of the team leaders in tackles for losses in 1978 with five for minus-18 yards. His 19 solo and 43 total tackles were also among the team leaders. Molini made a name for himself as a freshman by blocking a kick.

Despite sitting out several games last season with an injury,

Cedric Shaw a 6-0, 190-pounder, Sr., defensive back from Newark, N.J. showed he was a valuable member of Iowa's defensive secondary. Shaw finished the season with 10 solo tackles and two passes defended. Iowa's secondary was hard hit by graduation and will need Shaw's experience and leadership this fall. Showing he has fully recovered from injury in spring drills, Shaw is counted on to return to his freshman season form when he had 41 solo tackles, eight assists and a fumble recovery.

Leven Weiss the 6-3, 215-pound, Sr. linebacker from Detroit, Mich. ranked third in solo tackles among Iowa's talented linebackers last season. He finished with 26 solos and 16 assists. His 42 total tackles placed him ninth among Iowa's defenders and fourth among those returning this season. Owns a career-high nine solo tackles against Michigan. A quick and powerful linebacker, Weiss is expected to have a big season for Iowa this year.

One of the key ingredients in new Coach Hayden Fry's passing game at Iowa in 1979 will be senior tight end **Jim Swift**. The 6-4, 238-pound former all-stater from Des Moines caught 12 passes for 211 yards in last year's ground oriented attack. Swift's size and speed make him an excellent blocker. He scored one touchdown for the Hawkeyes and included a 45-yard gainer in his 12 receptions. Swift was a three sport star at Dowling High School.

Tailback **Dennis Mosley** was Iowa's third leading rusher last season with 292 yards in 96 carries. The 5-9 speed-burner from Youngstown, Ohio also competes for the Iowa track team, sporting a 9.6 time in the 100-yard dash. Always a threat to break a big gainer, he is often used on sweeps and trap plays. Mosley scored Iowa's winning touchdown against Iowa State in 1977 as a sophomore with a 77-yard dash. He may also be used on kickoff returns. As a high school senior Mosley captured the Ohio State championships in the 100-, 220-, and 440-yard dashes. He also developed as a pass receiver last season, catching 9 tosses for 148 yards.

As a freshman **Kenny Burke** stepped into the Iowa backfield and became the team's second leading rusher. Burke's slashing style of running earned him 293 yards, including a long gainer of 37 yards. A native of Chicago, the 6-3, 197-pounder will enter his sophomore campaign as a top candidate for a starting position in the Hawkeyes' backfield.

Hayden Fry, Head Coach

A tall, square-jawed Texan has taken over as Iowa's head football coach. His name is Hayden Fry, and he has promised to make the Hawkeyes competitive, colorful, tough and exciting. Considering Fry's record at Southern Methodist and North Texas State, where he was head coach for a total of 17 years, those are not empty promises.

Both schools were in the doldrums when he arrived and it did not take him long to perk things up. At SMU, where he coached 11 seasons (1962-72), Hayden put the Mustangs in three bowl games with a free-wheeling, wide-open style of football. His 1966 team won the Southwest Conference championship with an 8-3 record, which is SMU's best season since 1948. That team earned a Cotton Bowl berth, and two years later the Mustangs went to the Bluebonnet Bowl and whipped Oklahoma.

At North Texas State, where he coached six seasons (1973-1978), Fry took an ailing program and was 19-3 in his last two years there. North Texas was 33-11 in Fry's final four years at the school, an outstanding mark considering the Mean Green had won only seven games in the four seasons prior to Hayden's arrival.

Fry is a man with a fertile football mind. He is certainly not reluctant to throw the football; his 1968 SMU team went to Ohio State and put the ball in the air 76 times! That's still an NCAA record. Hayden likes to open up his offense, but he believes that success starts with sound defense. His 1978 North Texas team proved that by leading the nation in three defensive categories.

Fry broke the color barrier in the Southwest Conference when he recruited Jerry Levias, the first black to play in that league. Men who have served under Hayden include Bum Phillips, the successful and respected coach of the Houston Oilers. A native of Odessa, Tex., who was a quarterback at Baylor, Fry was named Texas College Coach of the Year four times while at SMU and North Texas State. He has coached in the Hula Bowl, the East-West Shrine Game and the Blue-Gray Game. A former Marine Corps captain, Fry is the father of four sons and one daughter.

MICHIGAN Wolverines

Michigan's Wolverines move into their 100th season of intercollegiate football in 1979 with Coach Bo Schembechler trying to develop "strength down the middle.... just like in baseball."

The middle—from the center position right on through the tailback spot—is where the Wolverines lost four starters from their Big Ten championship and Rose Bowl squad of 1978.

Schembechler's main task is to retool an offensive unit that last season ranked among the finest in college football. The Wolverines were ninth in the nation in rushing and ranked fourth in scoring. Only three players return to the offense who started the Rose Bowl game.

The entire backfield, with the exception of wingback Ralph Clayton, is gone and only John Powers, an offensive guard, returns in the line. Wide receiver Rodney Feaster also was a Rose Bowl starter.

The offensive line picture could be a little deceiving, however. While the Wolverines did lose two exceptional tackles in Bill Dufek and Jon Giesler, as well as center Steve Nauta, there are several players who started games last year, including guard John Arbeznik, a 240-pound senior who was named to the All-Big Ten first team despite missing the last two games of the regular season and the Rose Bowl because of a damaged ankle.

Also returning is 6-foot-7, 280-pound Bubba Paris, who started two games as a freshman when injuries depleted the line. Line coach Jerry Hanlon says, "Bubba has the fastest feet of any lineman we've had here at Michigan in 10 years."

Mike Leoni, a 246-pound senior from Flint who filled in for Dufek much of the season, also returns. In fact, there are six lettermen back in the interior offensive line, including center George Lilja and guard Kurt Becker.

Paris is just one of a group of outstanding linemen who enrolled in Michigan last fall, a group that includes 6-7, 280-pound tackle Ed Muransky of Youngstown, Ohio, 6-5 245-pound Mark Warth of Zanesville, Ohio, and 6-6, 265-pound Chuck Rowland of Barberton, Ohio.

The center position should be solid with Lilja, a 6-4 247-pound senior returning after serving as a backup for Walt Downing and then Nauta. Behind Lilja, a two-year letterman from Palos Park, Ill., are a pair of promising sophomores, 6-4, 240-pound Tom Garrity (Grafton, Wis.) and 6-2, 225-pound Jeff Felten (Centerville, Ohio).

"I think we'll be all right at guard and tackle, but we've got a lot of work to do from our center position right on through to the tailback," offers Schembechler.

In addition to the loss of Nauta at center, gone are All-American quarterback Rick Leach, unanimous All-Big Ten fullback and team most valuable player in 1977 Russell Davis, and tailback Harlan Huckleby, who finished his career as the fourth leading rusher in Michigan history.

Michigan Quarterback B.J. Dickey (10) sprints out behind the blocking of guard John Arbeznik (64)

The quarterback position is the most vital and most uncertain. Battling for the right to succeed Leach are B.J. Dickey, who was the main backup last season as a sophomore; Gary Lee, who went to the Rose Bowl in his freshman season as the No. 3 quarterback; Jim Paciorek, a sophomore from Orchard Lake; John Wangler, injured as a junior with a pinched nerve in his neck, junior Jim Breaugh from West Bloomfield, and Jerome Jelinek from Ann Arbor.

Dickey has shown an ability to run the team. He completed eight of 19 passes for 115 yards and two touchdowns last year and added 154 yards in 33 rushing attempts for a fine 4.7 average. As a freshman two years ago he raced 74 yards on one play, the ninth longest run in Michigan history.

Wangler, from Royal Oak, emerged from spring drills a year ago as Leach's backup, but an injury sidelined him for the entire 1978 season.

Michigan fullback Lawrence Reid (23) gains six yards against Arizona.

Lee, who comes from the same high school that produced Leach (Flint Southwestern), has a strong, lively arm and good speed. Paciorek is one of the finest all-around athletes to attend Michigan in years.

"There was no quarterback in football who did all the things we asked of Rick Leach," says Schembechler. "He did it all and now we must go back to work and try to develop another quarterback who can run the Michigan team. We have some outstanding young men battling for that job and whoever comes out on top will be a take charge guy who will be able to handle the responsibilities. I'm sure of that."

Leach accounted for an NCAA record 79 touchdowns, broke virtually all Michigan's career passing records and was named the Wolverines' and the Big Ten's MVP last year. He started 47 of the 48 games Michigan played during his four years, but Schembechler points out:

"That was unusual. You really should not count on an 18-year old to come to Michigan and immediately take over at any position, let alone quarterback. I think it's only fair that they be given time to adjust to college life, college football and their new teammates. They don't need any added pressures."

Two promising quarterbacks are among the incoming 1979 freshmen—Rich Hewlett from Plymouth-Salem High in Michigan and Steve O'Donnell from Madison, N.J.

Schembechler also brought in seven running backs, including a pair of fullbacks, another extremely thin position going into the

1979 season. The only replacement for Davis with any game experience is Lawrence Reid, a sturdy, 213-pound senior from Philadelphia who carried the ball 50 times, gained 209 yards and scored twice. He has gained 373 yards and averaged 5 yards per carry over three seasons of limited action.

Tailback is another area where, "there's never enough players to completely satisfy me," says Schembechler. And he has a point.

Two years ago Michigan had to start a freshman tailback, Stanley Edwards, in the Rose Bowl game against Washington. It was a scramble again last year against Southern California to find a healthy tailback before Huckleby was pronounced fit.

Edwards, who missed the entire 1978 season because of injury, and Butch Woolfolk, who gained 378 yards in 78 carries as a freshman, are the prime candidates at tailback. Tony Leoni, a tough senior letterman from Flint, also is available.

There are several fine pass receivers returning, a group headed by the multi-talented Ralph Clayton and the vastly underrated Doug Marsh. "Ralph is an outstanding player," says Schembechler. "He can catch the ball, has very good speed and can block."

Clayton, a definite All-American candidate, caught 25 passes for 546 yards (21.8 average) and tied a Michigan record with eight touchdown receptions. In his three-year career, the speedy, 6-3, 210-pound wingback has caught 51 passes for 1036 yards, returned kickoffs 408 yards and rushed for 130 yards. The former Detroit prep 100 and 220 sprint champion (timed at 4.4 in the 40) was an All-Big Ten first team selection as a junior.

Marsh, 6-3, 233 senior from Akron, Ohio, caught six touchdown passes last year, including two against Notre Dame. He had 19 receptions for 283 yards and receiver coach Tirrel Burton said, "We never thought there was a dropoff in talent when Gene Johnson came out and Marsh went in. He's as good a tight end as we've had at Michigan in some time."

Feaster, a junior from Flint with blazing speed, Alan Mitchell, a junior from Detroit, and Tony Jackson, a sophomore from Cleveland who backed up Clayton and returned kickoffs, are all exceptional receivers.

Behind Marsh at tight end are Chuck Christian, a 219-pound junior, Rich Strenger, 6-7, 233-pound sophomore, and Vincent Shaw, 218-pound sophomore.

Michigan's football credentials for 1979 are mostly defensive. The Wolverines have the best record of any team in the nation over the last decade in defense against the score. Last year, according to final NCAA statistics, the Wolverine defenders were second in fewest points allowed (8.0 per game), eighth in rushing defense (112.7 yards per game) and fourth in total defense (215.6 yards).

Most of the players who contributed to that type of success are returning. Eight of the 11 starters are returning in addition to eight

Linebacker Andy Cannavino (41) chases down Ohio State's Art Schlichter (10) with Dale Keitz (55) and Mike Trgovac (77) in pursuit. Michigan won the game 14-3.

other defensive lettermen.

The Michigan defense again is led by Ron Simpkins, one of the finest inside linebackers to play for Schembechler in the last decade. Twice an All-Big Ten first-team selection, Simpkins set a Wolverine tackle record as a sophomore with 174 and in three seasons the 6-1, 220-pound senior has a staggering total of 362 tackles.

Last season he was honored by national wire services three times as the Midwest Defensive Player of the Week and four times he was judged the best player on Michigan's highly ranked defense by the coaches after a thorough study of game films.

Simpkins teamed with Mel Owens early last season to form a formidable linebacking set, but Owens was injured in the victory over Notre Dame and was lost for the season. Sophomore Andy Cannavino, a 220-pounder from Cleveland, took over and did a superb job.

Michigan's three down interior linemen—tackles Curtis Greer (Detroit) and Dale Keitz (Upper Arlington, Ohio) and middle guard Mike Trgovac (Austintown, O)—return intact.

Greer, who has great speed and was named to the All-American strength team (bench presses 425 pounds), has recorded 25 tackles for 127 yards in losses. Greer at 6-6, 236 pounds, and Keitz, at 6-1 and 233 pounds, are fifth year seniors.

Trgovac, voted Michigan's top freshman player two years ago, was named the Associated Press Defensive Player of the Game in Michigan's win over Purdue last year.

Versatile Michael Harden at free safety is the key to Michigan's

Michigan defensive tackle Curtis Greer (95) wards off a blocker.

experienced defensive secondary. The 6-0, 183-pound senior from Detroit came up with four interceptions and 57 tackles last season and doubled up as a punt returner. The former All-City track and basketball star has 4.5 speed in the 40.

Mike Jolly, who played baseball last spring and still made it to football practice, is a three-year starter at the wideside halfback spot. The slender senior from Melvindale had 41 tackles and three interceptions last season as well as 28 punt returns, a school record.

Returning to the shortside halfback position are Mark Braman, 197-pound fifth-year senior from Midland who was a starter there last year, and Gerald Diggs, a 185-pound senior letterman from Chicago.

Both starting outside linebackers from last year, Jerry Meter and Tom Seabron, have graduated, but Ben Needham, a 6-4, 214-pounder from Groveport, O., started the Ohio State game as a sophomore because of Seabron's injury.

In an attempt to shore up the perimeter defenses, defensive coordinator Bill McCartney moved Owens from inside to outside linebacker (Michigan operates with four linebackers). The 6-2, 230-pound senior is extremely quick (4.7 in the 40) for his size. Sophomore Bob Thompson and junior Oliver Johnson provide depth at outside linebacker.

There are very capable backups on defense for the middle and tackle spots. Behind Trgovac at middle guard are James Humphries, a 223-pound senior letterman, and Fred Motley, a 234-pound junior. Lettermen Chris Godfrey (240, senior) and Gary Weber (239, senior) and juniors Dave Nicolau (232) and Tony Osbun (253) and sophomore Cedric Coles (238) provide depth at tackle.

Brian Carpenter and Jeff Reeves are promising sophomores who figure in the defensive secondary somewhere. Reeves, a 192-pounder from Columbus, could start at free safety, while Carpenter, a 163-pounder from Flint, has the speed to play on the wide side and could return punts.

Stuart Harris, a letterman as a reserve defensive halfback last year, has been moved to strong safety where the 196-pound junior will battle Dan Murray and Mike Kligis for the starting job.

The Outlook for 1979

Michigan again will be one of the favorites in the Big Ten title race after winning three straight championships and making four straight bowl appearances—one in the Orange ('75) and three in the Rose Bowl ('76-77-78).

Ohio State, Purdue, Michigan State and possibly Wisconsin loom as challengers to Michigan's reign. The Buckeyes and Boilermakers went right down to the wire as title contenders last season, but the Wolverines and Spartans ended up sharing the crown.

Michigan opens its 1979 schedule at home against Northwestern, then meets three nonconference opponents. These include Notre Dame and Kansas in Michigan Stadium and the California Bears on the Coast. Michigan played the Irish in South Bend last season, the first game between these two schools in a quarter of a century. The Wolverines hold a 17-3-0 record against these three nonleague teams.

A key game for the Wolverines is October 6 in East Lansing against Michigan State. Then it's back home for Minnesota, on to Illinois, Indiana and Wisconsin in Michigan Stadium and finally two important games to wrap up the season—Nov. 10 at Purdue and Nov. 17 against Ohio State in Ann Arbor.

"Despite heavy losses on our offensive unit, we could open the season this Fall with six seniors and that means there is some experience there," reasoned Schembechler. There are five seniors who will start on the defense.

Schembechler, who has guided the Wolverines to a remarkable record of 96 victories, 14 losses and 3 ties and eight championships during a 10-year period, has never had a Michigan team finish out of Top Ten in either of the final wire service polls. "I do believe, however," cautions Schembechler, "that winning is becoming progressively more difficult. More and more balance is being established around the country and the lack of undefeated teams is evidence that the era of the superpower has gone."

"We recruited players of considerable size last season," said defensive coordinator Bill McCartney. "This year we needed some players to complement last season's recruiting effort, so we concentrated more on the skilled positions."

Eight of the 26 student-athletes are listed as linebackers while seven are considered running backs. Two quarterbacks, four receivers and four defensive backs along with one player listed as both an offensive and defensive back round out the list of 1979 freshmen.

Mike Cade (Eloy, Arizona), Winfred Carraway (Detroit) and Anthony Carter (Riviera Beach, Florida) were three scholastic All-Americans in high school.

The group includes ten high school players from Ohio, eight from Michigan, two from Florida, two from Pennsylvania, and one player each from New York, New Jersey, Arizona and Wisconsin.

Rich Hewlett (Plymouth, Mich.) and Steve O'Donnell (Madison, N.J.) were the only two quarterbacks recruited by the Wolverines. Hewlett ran for 2,261 yards and passed for 1,032 and accounted for 51 touchdowns at Plymouth-Salem. O'Donnell was an all-stater in New Jersey.

Cade, a 6-1, 205-pound running back, gained 2,253 yards last season, including 299 yards and six touchdowns in his team's state Class A title victory.

Carter, at 6 feet, 172, is a scatback-type runner and an exceptional kick returner.

Carraway, from Detroit MacKenzie, has 4.6 speed and is considered an excellent linebacking prospect as is Todd Triplett from St. Martin DePorres, where he earned all-state honors in track and football.

A couple of the largest players selecting Michigan were Robin Koschalk, whose brother Rick played at Michigan, and Dan Yarano, a 6-3, 230-pound tight end. Koschalk is a 6-1, 230-pound defensive lineman.

Wolverines To Watch In 1979 Candidates for All-American Teams

RON SIMPKINS........Linebacker, 6-1, 220, Sr., Detroit...Has 362 tackles in three seasons...Twice All-Big Ten linebacker selection...Set school record for tackles (174) as a sophomore...Last season was voted Defensive Player of the Week three times -UPI (Illinois game) and AP (Iowa and Purdue games) and was voted Michigan player of the game four times by a unit that was second in the nation against the score, eighth in rushing defense and fourth in total defense...Prep All-American (Cum Laude) at Western High in Detroit..one of the finest linebackers to play for 'M'.

CURTIS GREER........Defensive tackle, 6-4, 236, Sr., Detroit...One of the quickest tackles in college football...All-Big Ten first team...Led team with 11 tackles for 62 yards in losses. Coming back for a fifth year, has 209 tackles in his career, 25 of them for 127 yards in losses. Three-year starter for Michigan. Strongest defensive lineman (bench presses 425 pounds).

Ron Simpkins

Curtis Greer

Michael Harden

Ralph Clayton

MICHAEL HARDEN .... Defensive back (free safety), 6-1, 183, Sr., Detroit... runs 40 in 4.5, former all-city in basketball and track. All-Big Ten first team as a junior... had 57 tackles, four interceptions for 55 yards, seven pass deflections last season. Returns punts.

RALPH CLAYTON ...... Wingback, split receiver, 6-3, 210, Sr., Detroit... runs 40 in 4.4, former city track champion in 100 and 220... averaged nearly 22 yards per catch on 25 receptions last year... his 8 touchdown receptions in 1978 tied 'M' record... runs from scrimmage and returns kickoffs.

Doug Marsh

Mike Trgovac

Candidates for Conference and Regional Honors

DOUG MARSH .... Tight end, 6-3, 233, Sr., Akron, OH... as good as any tight end to play at Michigan in the last decade. Has size, 4.7 speed, excellent blocker, caught 19 passes for 283 yards, six touchdowns last year, including 2 against Notre Dame. Second team All-Big Ten.

MIKE TRGOVAC .... Middle guard, 6-2, 227, Jr., Austintown, OH... AP Co-Defensive Player of the Week against Purdue.. combines speed and strength at MG... already two-year letterman... voted top 'M' freshman award, was regular as soph.

Mike Jolly *Stanley Edwards*

JOHN ARBEZNIK ......Offensive guard, 6-3, 240, Sr., University Heights, OH...Has 4.8 speed. Great player, will be starter for third season...First team All-Big Ten last year despite missing last two games with ankle injury...Outstanding blocker, especially pulling and downfield. Strong, bench presses 435 pounds.

JOHN POWERS ....Offensive guard, 6-3, 265, Sr., Oak Park, IL...extremely quick, good blocker, strong enough to play tackle in '77, but moved back to guard in '78.

MIKE JOLLY ....6-3, 181, Sr., Melvindale...great all-around athlete..three-year starter for 'M'...All-Big Ten first team as junior...three interceptions, 41 tackles last season...returns punts. Defensive back.

Other Players of Note

TB - Stanley Edwards (injured in 1978); TB - Butch Woolfolk, gained 370 yards, 4.7 avg. as a freshman; DT - Dale Keitz; OT - Bubba Paris, started two games as a freshman.

Dale Keitz

Butch Woolfolk

Head Football Coach

MICHIGAN STATE *Spartans*

This will be a "new look" Michigan State football team, but hopefully it will perform as well as its immediate predecessor. That 1978 Spartan club tied Michigan for the Big Ten crown and rated 12th in the nation in the Associated Press rankings with its 8-3 record.

"Each team develops its own personality from the athletes," says Coach Darryl Rogers. "People like quarterback Eddie Smith, wide receiver Kirk Gibson, offensive tackle Jim Hinesly, defensive tackle Mel Land and strong safety Tom Graves created the look of the 1978 team and now they're gone. So I think our personality very definitely will change."

Return of the majority of key defensive players and loss of some vital offensive cogs lead to the belief this team will be stronger off the ball and perhaps down a little with it.

Much will depend on the performances of replacements for lost stars. Likely successor to consensus All-America Kirk Gibson at wide receiver is sophomore Samson (Light Bulb) Howard, a veritable midget at 5-8 and 166 pounds compared to Gibson's 6-2 and 220. But he is fast and has good hands. Moving in for Smith, the 1978 team's MVP and holder of the full set of Spartan passing records as well as several Big Ten standards, probably will be Bert Vaughn, a 6-4 sophomore who missed almost all of last season nursing a shoulder separation. He is a strong, accurate passer but will need time to develop the game management ability that was Smith's strong suit.

Leaders of the new club are certain to include All-America (Football Writers) tight end Mark Brammer, All-Big Ten split end Eugene Byrd, two time All-Big Ten punter Ray Stachowicz and All-Big Ten linebacker Dan Bass. Brammer is the consummate tight end, a big, fast, smart athlete who can block with authority and catch the ball with the best. Byrd was the team's top receiver last fall with 43 catches, one more than Gibson, good for 718 yards and seven TDs. Stachowicz led the nation for awhile in punting and wound up near the top with an average of 43.1 yards per boot. Bass led all defenders in tackles with 136, possibly an all-time Spartan record although complete statistics in this area have not been kept.

Other defensive veterans with pacemaker qualifications are weak safety Mark Anderson, whom Rogers thinks may be the best in his role in the college game, defensive backs Mike Marshall and

Jim Borroughs and middle guard Bernard Hay.

In the same category on offense are veteran guards Mike Densmore and Rod Strata, center Matt Foster and a set of running backs that includes tailbacks Steve Smith, Bruce Reeves and Derek Hughes and fullbacks Lonnie Middleton and Andy Schramm.

Smith, playing only about one third the time last fall, finished third in rushing, pass receiving and punt and kickoff returns. Coaches feel he can become a super performer.

Players who didn't see much action last season but could emerge strongly this fall include Howard, linebacker George Cooper, Hughes, defensive tackle Tanya Webb and linebacker Steve Maidlow.

The kicking game should be sound with punter Stachowicz, placekicker Morten Andersen (52 of 54 extra point tries, seven field goals) and kickoff specialist Rich Schario all back again.

Some 42 previous letterwinners are expected back. Among them will be 17 of the 22 starters in late season games last fall.

Several position shifts are likely. One already planned will send Angelo Fields, the biggest Spartan at 6-6 and 284, from defensive tackle to offensive tackle where both regulars of last season, Hinesly and Craig Lonce, have completed college play.

The schedule, while difficult, gives MSU a break in that the first three games against Illinois, Oregon and Miami (O.) are in Spartan Stadium. Then comes the bad news—Notre Dame away, Michigan at home, Wisconsin away, Purdue at home and Ohio State away. That quintet could wreck most any team. The final trio of Northwestern away, Minnesota at home and Iowa away also has dangerous portent.

Coach Rogers foresees a Big Ten race without a dominant power and hence with more teams in the title scramble. He thinks Purdue is the strongest in terms of numbers of proven players particularly with ace quarterback Mark Herrmann returning. Michigan and Ohio State will be contenders as usual and pressing them should be Minnesota and Wisconsin, he says.

Michigan State's spring football drills opened Tuesday, April 17, and concluded with the traditional Green and White intra-squad game on Saturday, May 19.

Spartan Best Bets For All-America And All-Big Ten Honors

Mark Brammer, All-America at tight end in 1978, lives in dangerous waters most of the year—sailing during the summer and playing football during the fall. He's proficient in both.

Michigan State's highly-talented tight end is a native of Traverse City, Mich. where he works at a nearby marina during the summer months, allowing him to pursue his hobbies of recreational sailing and sailboating racing.

But the 6-4, 233-pound senior returns to MSU when the leaves turn red and yellow to battle opposing defenders intent on banging the ball away from him.

Last fall, he was the third-leading receiver for the Spartans with 33 passes caught for 360 yards and two touchdowns. In Big Ten games he ranked fourth among loop pass catchers with 25 receptions for 274 yards and two scores. His standout, all-round play earned him first team selection on the All-America first unit picked by The Football Writers Association of America. He also was on first teams selected by AP, UPI and The Chicago Tribune, and was a second team selection All-America by UPI and honorable mention All-America by The Sporting News.

Mark started the first game of his collegiate career against Ohio State in place of Mike Cobb who was sidelined by NCAA suspension. He also was the starter in the next four games and then finished the campaign playing behind Cobb who later went to the Cincinnati Bengals as a first round draft choice. Mark has been the starter ever since and his splendid blocking and pass receiving has been a major factor in State's rise to national prominence.

Career stats show him with 84 receptions for 1,017 yards and four scores. He does it all on the field. He is highly-dedicated and consistent in his play. He's a dream player to Spartan offensive coaches.

For the past three years Michigan State football opponents have found a sturdy figure in the middle of the Spartan defense—inside linebacker **Dan Bass**—All-Big Ten in 1978.

Bass, a 6-1, 217-pound senior, has started every game at MSU, and that has meant trouble for opposing ball carriers.

The hard-hitting Bass has led the Spartan defense in tackles for three seasons, as well as in fumble recoveries two years ago, and that's what he thrives on—being in the thick of things.

Last fall, he was credited with 79 solo tackles and 57 assists for a total of 136, tops in MSU defensive statistical history. He also recovered two fumbles, broke up two pass plays and had two pass interceptions—one of them resulting in a return of 99 yards for a score, longest such return in Big Ten and Spartan history.

"I like being the middle of the action because we're always hitting someone and something is always going on," explains the Bath native.

Inside linebacking coach Walt Harris agrees. "Linebackers are supposed to make the most tackles," says the second-year coach, "but Dan is not satisfied with leading the team in tackles or starting every game. He wants to be great and believes he can be great."

And it is his self-confidence that has driven Bass from small Class C Bath High School to the limelight of the Big Ten.

"During my first two years at State I had to learn to read play actions," says the three-year letterwinner. "In my junior year I gained so much more confidence. I'm really looking forward to having a strong final season."

Mark Anderson is a two-way stopper for Michigan State's football team, excelling at putting the brakes on an opponent's running and passing attacks.

The senior safety out of Akron, Ohio is set to be a starter for the third year in the defensive backfield, and for the second consecutive season in 1978, he led the Spartan defensive backs in pass interceptions as well as in tackles.

"Mark plays well against the run and pass," says defensive backfield coach Sherm Lewis. "His strong suit is his general lateral range. Few backs play both the run and pass as well as Mark does."

Anderson, a 6-2, 189-pounder, had 56 tackles (35 solo) in 11 games and three times nabbed enemy passes.

Perhaps his finest showing was in State's 33-9 victory over Minnesota. Although he didn't intercept any errant tosses, Anderson was all over the field frustrating the Gopher running game time and again. For the day he made eight tackles, including one for an eight-yard loss, and broke up a pass.

Anderson, who made first team All-Big Ten in 1978, is a fisheries and wildlife major. As a prepster at Springfield High he was a National Honor Society member and an honor roll student.

Spartan head coach Darryl Rogers has great respect for his star defender, commenting, "Mark is an outstanding free safety. There aren't many better."

Eugene Byrd regained top-notch playing form at split end for Michigan State in 1978 after injuries kept him out of the 1977 campaign. A tremendous performance as the team's leading pass receiver led to his being named to the All-Big Ten first teams picked by AP and UPI at split end. He could be one of the nation's best in 1979.

Byrd snared 42 serials for 806 yards and seven TDs for State as the club went on to earn a Big Ten co-championship. The great year added to those of 1975 and 1976 show his career totals at 83 catches for 1,611 yards and 11 touchdowns.

In Big Ten stats, he was No. 2 for the season with 30 catches for 458 yards and five scores—ranking behind All-America teammate Kirk Gibson.

Eugene is a fleet 6-0, 178-pound senior athlete who had many fine games in 1978 including an effort against Notre Dame that saw him snare seven aerials—two short of MSU's single game reception mark.

"Our passing attack depends on an opponent's coverage, and my success in 1978 cannot be attributed to any one factor," said Byrd. "But I felt I was at the top of my game in 1978."

Before he graduates, Byrd has some ideas about what he'd like to see happen to MSU football in 1979.

"Most importantly, I want to be involved in a highly-successful winning program, a 10-1 or 11-0 and maybe a bowl game, and I would like to be a part of that."

The East St. Louis, Ill. native was an All-Southern Illinois and East St. Louis All-Metro pick as a prepster.

Michigan State junior punter **Ray Stachowicz** will again bid to be among the nation's top punters, following two seasons in which he's been All-Big Ten in his specialist role.

He boomed out punts for State last fall averaging 43.1 per kick to set an all-time MSU record. His longest was a 75-yarder against Notre Dame which also set an MSU mark. Earlier in the season at Purdue he came through with a 72-yard effort.

It was in the Purdue game that Ray had one of the finest punting days seen in the midwest. He kicked 10 times, averaging 51.1 yards per kick.

"It was one of the finest displays of punting I've ever seen," praised head coach Darryl Rogers. "Ray had an exceptionally fine day. He kept us in the game."

Stachowicz ended the Big Ten campaign as the second man in average, his 43.2 ranking behind Tom Orosz of Ohio State at 44.4. On national listings which he led for a number of weeks, Ray ended up in eighth place.

During summer months, the 6-1, 186-pound graduate of Brecksville, Ohio, works out every day honing his skills. "I run a lot and lift leg weights as well as kicking every night and stretching my legs," Ray says.

Ray started his punting as a youngster competing in the Punt, Pass and Kick competition sponsored by a national automotive firm. He's now one of the nation's gifted specialists who looks for a fine junior campaign.

Rogers Announces MSU Grid Recruiting List....

Coach Darryl Rogers announced the names of 21 student-athletes who've accepted scholarships and will enroll at MSU and play football in 1979.

"I feel we had a very good recruiting year," Rogers said. "First and foremost, we were looking for quarterbacks and we were fortunate to sign four promising prospects to join the several candidates for Eddie Smith's position already on campus.

"The great majority of the young men who will be joining us committed to us in the first days of the signing period. This is a high priority group of which we are quite proud."

Besides the four quarterbacks, there are four linebackers and four defensive backs listed among the new Spartans. Rounding out the list of newcomers are two tailbacks, two wide receivers, two tight ends, two offensive linemen and one defensive lineman.

In the group are seven preps from Michigan, five from Ohio, two from Indiana, two from California, and one each from Georgia, Arizona, Pennsylvania, Montana and Illinois.

The quarterbacks recruited are Jon English, All-America pick from Birmingham Brother Rice and all-staters Denis Lavelle (Rocky River, Ohio), John Leister (Great Falls, Mon.) and Otis Grant (Atlanta, Ga.).

One of the Californians is linebacker Terry Bailey, 6-4, 230, who has transferred to MSU from San Francisco City College where he was an All-California J.C. pick. The other is Howard McAdoo, a 6-2, 250 pound linebacker from Rolling Hills High School in Rancho Palos Verdes.

Among the offensive linemen is Walter Schramm, 6-4, 235-pound all state player from Findlay, Ohio, who's a younger brother of current Spartan fullback Andy Schramm.

Darryl Rogers

Big Ten "Coach of the Year" in 1977, Michigan State head football coach Darryl Rogers made his squad the Big Ten team of the year in 1978.

Rogers guided his Spartans to a 24-15 win over Michigan and a share of the Big Ten title, the first for Michigan State since 1966. The overall mark was 8-3 and the Big Ten record 7-1.

MSU's high-powered aerial game drew national attention, placing State in the top five in many NCAA offensive statistical categories and in the AP's national top 20 for much of the season's second half.

MSU and Big Ten records fell week by week with quarterback Ed Smith and wide receiver Kirk Gibson establishing new marks with each pass, reception and touchdown.

Two Spartans—Gibson and tight end Mark Brammer—attained first team All-America ratings. Numerous others achieved All-America mentions and nine made All-Big Ten status.

MSU now ends its three-year football probation and again becomes eligible for national television appearances and consideration for bowl bids.

Battling a shortage of quality performers and a rash of serious injuries in 1976, Rogers' first season at Michigan State resulted in a 4-6-1 record and runner-up position for Rogers in Big Ten "Coach of the Year" balloting.

Both the team and the coach moved up in 1977 when the Spartans finished the season with a 7-3-1 record and third place at 6-1-1 in the Big Ten behind Michigan and Ohio State. Media representatives voted Darryl the 1977 Big Ten "Coach of the Year."

The 43-year-old mentor came from San Jose State University where he put together a nifty 22-9-3 record in three years at the California school.

"In Darryl Rogers, we brought to Michigan State one of the nation's bright young coaches," noted MSU Athletic Director Dr. Joe Kearney. "He presents in Spartan Stadium a wide open offense that spectators love to watch."

Rogers has revolutionized the Big Ten's style of play with his passing philosophy: "The way I look at it, if you complete the pass on the first down, you don't have to worry about the next two downs.

"I enjoy football and I enjoy the relationship between a coach and a player. But I can't stand to lose, and if anybody can stand losing, he shouldn't be in coaching."

Rogers was born May 28, 1935, and received his B.A. degree in physical education in 1957 and his M.A. in physical education in 1964, both from Fresno State University.

He began his coaching career in 1961 as the defensive backfield coach for Fresno City College, a position he held until 1964. He then became the first head football coach for Hayward State University, holding that post one year, 1965, after which he returned to his alma mater to lead the Bulldogs to a 43-32-1 mark from 1966 through 1972. The Bulldogs competed in the Camellia

Bowl in 1968 and in the Mercy Bowl in 1971.

Rogers started as head coach of San Jose State in 1973 and promptly turned the struggling Spartan program around. That year, the Spartans posted a 5-4-2 record, their first winning season since 1961.

During the 1974 season, Rogers led the Spartans to an 8-3-1 record, their best in 25 years. In the 1975 season, San Jose posted a 9-2 mark and became the Pacific Coast Conference champions. That same year, Rogers was voted Conference Coach of the Year, Northern California Coach of the Year and American Football Coaches Association District 9 Coach of the Year.

Rogers' 1975 mark at San Jose was the best the Spartans had recorded since 1946. One of the highlights of the campaign came when San Jose played San Diego State for the PCAA title in front of a record paid crowd of 20,339, in San Jose's Spartan Stadium, defeating the Aztecs, 31-7. The win put San Jose into the national rankings (15th by UPI and 20th by AP) for the first time in the history of the school.

The total record compiled by teams coached by Rogers over 14 seasons is 87 wins, 60 losses and six ties, for a winning percentage of .588.

Rogers was a wide receiver and defensive back while playing at Fresno State from 1955-57. As a professional football player for the Los Angeles Rams and the Denver Broncos from 1958-60, he was a defensive back.

Rogers and his wife, Marsha, have three daughters.

MINNESOTA *Gophers*

Seldom, if ever, had new University of Minnesota head football coach "Smokey" Joe Salem been at a loss for words. Well, as this piece was put to print before the opening of the season Salem, plus his staff, were stymied when it came to describing or predicting anything about the 1979 football season in store for Golden Gopher fans.

As stated, seldom is Joe left hanging when it comes to a quick quip, or a lengthy answer to the smallest question. But for right now it's "take a good look at who is returning and base your predictions on what experience we have and how good do you think we coaches will do."

Salem returns to his alma mater after 13 years as a head coach. He piloted the University of South Dakota Coyotes for nine seasons, and then moved over to Northern Arizona University at Flagstaff for another four seasons.

At both stops he inherited programs immersed in losing and red ink. When he left, things were winning, black and rosy.

However, the question is asked immediately... can he win at a major school, a school running in the middle of the pack in the Big Ten? Joe's answer: "Why not? We'll never know until we've tried. I'm just personally happy that Athletic Director Paul Giel and the University administration gave me the opportunity to see if I could do the job. If my staff and I succeed, well, that's what we are in this business for. If I fail, well, at least I've had my chance. But I'm not coming here to fail. I believe we can get the job done. It will not be easy, but it can be done."

The Minnesota program is no where near the mess Salem found at South Dakota and Northern Arizona. Both the latter spots were at the bottom of their cycles. It only took Joe two years to provide a winning program at Vermillion. In 1966, his first season, he was 5-5-0. Two years later the Coyotes came in with a 9-1-0 season record.

His last three seasons at USD produced 6-1, 6-1 and 5-2 records as the Coyotes tied for the 1972-73-74 North Central Conference championships.

Then came the move to NAU at Flagstaff. Again a program left for dead is what Joe found. He was 1-9 the first year, and then came home with 8-3, 9-3, and 8-2 records. Last fall he won the Big Sky Conference title outright with a 6-0-0 league mark.

At South Dakota U. he ended 52-38-2 in nine seasons, and was 26-17-0 at Northern Arizona giving coach Salem a career record of

78-55-2 for 13 seasons on the job.

"When I left the coaching staff in 1966 at Minnesota under Murray Warmath, the man I played under at UM, I honestly hoped that some day I could return here as a coach," Salem offers. "Well, in some ways my dream has come true."

"Maybe it will turn into a nightmare, but as I said earlier, at least I've been given the chance. I cannot remember any man who went into coaching and would not have liked to return some day as boss of the football program at the school where he played. Like I said, it's some kind of dream."

Joe's playing days were spent mostly on the bench at Minnesota. It seems there was a young fellow named Sandy Stephens who led UM to a national championship in 1960 and two straight Rose Bowl appearances. Even at that, Joe was still a crowd favorite whenever he entered the game.

One thing coach Salem is positive about and can talk about is that Minnesota will play exciting football in 1979.

"When I went west I was primarily a wishbone, ground attack coach," Joe states. "But when out in Arizona it was like I suddenly found the true value of the forward pass. Passing, combined with multiple formations, is now the key to our game plan."

"But at the same time we'll grind it out if need be. We'll run sweeps, counters, end arounds, flanker reverses, and everybody who lines up on a spot other than the interior line will practice on throwing the football.

"My belief is that you must keep changing, you must keep your offensive game plans flexible. To my way of thinking there are five or six plays that win ball games. The big play is what has done it for us in the past. I'm always searching for that big play, the game breaker. If we have to use something different, something tricky, off beat, we'll use it if the situation presents itself.

"I no longer believe you can simply grind it out game after game and both win and keep the interest of your fans. We'll throw from any spot on the field, even the six inch line if need be. We'll do anything to both win and excite our fans. Hey, college football is in the entertainment business, too, you know. You can bet Minnesota will be entertaining if nothing else in 1979...and beyond."

As to Gopher personnel, well, coach Joe Salem has inherited some pretty fair country ball players who return from last year's team that posted a 5-6 season record and was 4-4 in the Big Ten.

Many of these same men are lads who still remember the thrill of defeating UCLA, Washington and Michigan, the latter two Rose Bowl opponents, during the 1977 season. Among them are several who helped set team records and then went out and broke all kinds of individual NCAA, Big Ten and school marks, too.

The letterman list shows 37 men who won their "M" either last fall or the year before. Oh sure, like always there are holes to fill.

But most of these spots are on defense. In fact, every man, with the possible exception of one guard, returns from last year's offensive starting lineup.

So experience will not be lacking. However, Joe does have to fill six starting positions on defense, a problem that could cause troubles. But again there are numerous good looking young men who either saw some playing duty, or maybe his replacements could come from the entire 1978 freshman class which was red shirted last fall.

By sections, here is a look at Minnesota's key personnel for 1979.

Offensive Backfield

The key here, as it is for just about every college football team, is who pulls the trigger. The quarterback situation appears confusing, at best, just as it has been the last two years. Two letterman return in Wendell Avery (6-0, 182, Sr., Corpus Christi, TX) and Mark Carlson (5-11, 186 Sr., Deerfield, IL).

Mark Carlson, QB

Wendell Avery

Avery and Carlson have split starting duty the last two years, but Avery saw more duty covering that span. Avery is the quicker, able to turn flanks better on the option play. But Carlson is rated the more accurate passer. Both are good field generals who make things happen. And they own the big item...experience. Carlson threw for 736 yards and six touchdowns last fall while Avery passed for three scores and 663 yards. Carlson led the Big Ten in accuracy connecting on 44 of 74 attempts in league games for a .595 percent efficiency rating.

However, a towering figure looms just behind Avery and

Carlson in Mark Tonn (6-6, 216, Sr., Green Bay, WI). Tonn, pronounced TON, saw limited action last fall, but may be the best pure thrower on the ball club.

He owns a powerful arm and has been known to throw the football 80 yards in the air. But he lacks game experience and this could affect his chances. Tonn tranferred to Minnesota two years ago from St. Norbert College in Wisconsin after leading the NCAA Division III in passing two straight years.

Two more candidates that can't be overlooked are Greg Pylatiuk (6-1, 184, So., Columbia Heights, MN) and incoming freshman Tom Pence (6-2, 190, Fr., Crystal Lake, IL). Pylatiuk has yet to take a snap at Minnesota, but came to the University with good credentials. The same can be said for Pence who was ranked as one of the outstanding prep quarterbacks in the Chicago area as a prep star last season.

Marion Barber, RB

Kent Kitzmann, FB

The running back situation is loaded with vets and stars. Minnesota's most prodigious ground gaining duo ever is back for another try in tailback Marion Barber (6-2, 204, Jr., Detroit, MI) and fullback Kent Kitzmann (6-2, 204, Sr., Rochester, MN). This pair has run in tandem most of the last two seasons and their All-America credentials are impressive.

Kitzmann, in three years, has 1,682 yards in 419 carries for a 4.1 average. He has been thrown for losses exactly twice in three seasons. And all remember his "day in the sun" when he set an all-time NCAA record of 57 carries when Minnesota defeated Illinois 21-0 in 1977. He broke by one the previous high of 56 carries set by former Oklahoma great Steve Owens.

Last season Kitzmann was second to Barber in rushing with 339 yards in 100 carries. His fall-off in production came as he missed much of the last half of the season due to injuries. But "Kitz" is expected back at full strength next fall.

The other half of the torrid duo is possibly Minnesota's All-American candidate, Barber. Last season he demolished Minnesota's single season rushing record by gaining 1,210 yards for a 4.8 per carry average.

He led the Big Ten in rushing by averaging 121 yards per game and was named to every post season conference first team. He was the only sophomore in the Big Ten thus honored.

Barber will easily break the all-time Minnesota rushing record set by the man who now holds down the Gopher athletic director's chair, Paul Giel, in 1951-52-53. Giel gained 2,188 career yards, and Barber already has 1,792 in just two seasons.

Roy Artis

Garry White, FB

Besides his rushing prowess, Barber also was second in pass receptions for the 1978 Gophers with 22 catches. He scored 10 touchdowns, eight rushing, and did just about everything but sell peanuts in the stands. His best day was 233 yards vs. Illinois, well short of the UM record 266 set by Kitzmann on his "day" in 1977.

But the rushing talents on Minnesota's roster do not stop with Kitzmann and Barber. Also returning at tailback is lettermen Roy Artis (6-1, 179, Jr., Lawnside, NJ). Last fall Artis peeled off the longest Gopher run from scrimmage in more than a decade when he traveled 72 yards to score at Northwestern. He gained 280 yards on 60 trips for a 4.7 average last fall and may be the fanciest high stepper on the squad.

Behind Barber and Artis at tailback are Glenn Lewis (6-1, 205, Jr., Edina, MN) and Duane Gregory (5-10, 194, So., Chicago, IL), plus one or two promising freshmen who could make their presence felt.

At fullback Kitzmann, despite his amazing career, will be pressed by three additional lettermen. The most experienced is possibly the fastest man on the Gopher varsity, Garry White (5-11, 197, Jr., Rockdale, TX). White was fourth in rushing last season with 272 yards and a 4.1 average. He comes off the blocks in a streak. He gained that ability as a prep track man in Texas where he ran a 9.6 100-yards in the state regional meet, but couldn't qualify for the state finals. (Yes, the DO run fast in Texas).

Two others who last fall played mostly at a slot back position are Jeff Thompson (6-2, 216, Sr., Bloomington MN), who came to UM originally as a fullback, and Ray Dilulo (6-0, 203, Jr., Boise, ID), originally a tailback.

Combined this group mentioned has already earned 12 letters (Kitzmann three, Barber, Artis, Thompson, White two each and

Elmer Bailey, FL

Glenn Bourquin, TE

Dilulo one). Experience will be far from lacking when Minnesota goes to the ground in 1979.

The flanker position is also well stocked as Minnesota's leading receiver last year returns in the likes of Elmer Bailey (6-0, 193, Sr., St. Paul, MN). Bailey may possibly be the best athlete on the varsity with matching speed and hands. Backing him up is Chester Cooper (6-2, 183, So., Paulsboro, NJ). But both could be pressed by a pair of newcomers, transfer Kelvin Jenkins (5-9, 175, Jr., Long Beach, CA) or freshman Lonnie Farrow (5-10, 165, Fr., Pompano, FL). Both the latter have been clocked in 4.5 for 40-yards.

Offensive Line

Here is where the Gophers and Salem are again blessed with tried and true performers. Every starter from last year, with the possible exception of guard Pat Paquette (6-4, 254, Sr., Superior,

Marty Stein OT

Ken Wypysynski, TE-P

WI). Paquette had been ordered to bypass spring drills because of a knee injury, and it is hoped that he can return by fall.

So the Gopher offensive front wall could line up again this way for the 1979 season opener: LT-Marty Stein (6-4, 247, Sr., Eau Claire, WI); LG-Darell Schwen (6-4, 232, Sr., Great Falls, MT); C-Steve Tobin (6-4, 247, Sr., Moorhead, MN); RG-Ken Wypyszynski (6-5, 243, Sr., DePere, WI); RT-Greg Murtha (6-6, 251, Sr., Minneapolis, MN); and TE-Glenn Bourquin (6-3, 231, Sr., Cottage Grove, MN). Combined, this unit averages out to 6-4 and 242 pounds per man. The only problem is what does Salem do for starters in 1980. All the men mentioned are seniors this fall!

However, in checking back, the best years Minnesota football has enjoyed in the last decade were 7-4 campaigns in 1973 and 1977. In both years the Gophers lined up with an all veteran front wall.

However, the six returning starters are not about the only ones who will man the trenches for Minnesota this season. Salem and Co. find several other young men who have either lettered or seen some action. Among additional returning lettermen in the offensive line are TE Randy Sonnenfeld (6-5, 226, Jr., Robbinsdale, MN), tackle Ken Dallafior (6-4, 251, So., Madison Heights, MI), and guard Jim Anderson (6-1, 233, So., Fairbault, MN).

Others expected to step in when called on include centers Brad Odegard (6-5, 227, So., Agoura, CA) and Ed Olsen (6-3, 219, Fr., Crystal, MN). Together this pair shared much of the long snapping duties last fall.

Also watch for a pair of last year's red shirted rookies to move up in guards McKinley Nash (6-3, 244, So., Evanston, IL) and Bill Humphries (6-2, 234, Fr., Detroit, MI). Both own unlimited potential and only need game experience to prove themselves.

Wypyszynski proved to be the most versatile player on the Gopher varsity last fall. He, at one time or another, started at every interior line position from tackle to tackle filling in for men sidelined by injuries. In addition, he graded out as high as any other regular in terms of efficiency. So you can bet to see "Kenny alphabet" somewhere in the Gopher lineup this fall. And he came to Minnesota lettering as a tight end his rookie year.

The final line spot on offense is split end where another crop of good looking candidates line up. A promising freshman red shirt from last season, Ed Bifulk (6-1, 196, Fr., St. Paul, MN), will be given a long look, but may have to fight off the talents of Jenkins, who could double at both flankerback and split end, plus speedster Elwin Burditte (5-11, 187, Sr., Minnetonka, MN), and Jeff Anhorn (6-2, 186, Sr., Blue Island, IL). Anhorn lettered at Minnesota in 1976 and 1977, but sat out last season. He has one year remaining. Two year's ago he was Minnesota's leading receiver with 16 catches for 217 yards and a pair of scores.

Whoever lines up at the wide receiver spots for Minnesota will have two things going...a lot of speed and plenty of aerials thrown their way. If Salem lives up to his promises about throwing the football, Minnesota may resemble a Southwest Conference team in 1979.

Defensive Line

The biggest vacancies from last fall are found in this area where three starters have completed their days of wearing the maroon and gold. All-Big Ten end Stan Sytsma, MVP and captain last season, is gone along with starting right tackle Jim Ronan, a 6-5, 260-pound giant, and outstanding nose guard Doug Friberg. Both the latter made second team All-Big Ten, so quality as much as quantity was lost.

However, again Salem is looking at several young men who know what it takes to win in the Big Ten. Returning starters in the defensive wall include end Tom Murphy (6-2, 218, Sr., Watertown, SD) and tackle Alan Blanshan (6-5, 251, Sr., Mankato, MN). Both excelled and showed as much improvement from start to finish as any other 1978 squad member. They are expected to be the anchors next fall.

Another who lettered and saw considerable action late in the season was end Steve Cunningham (6-6, 241, Sr., Waseca, MN). Cunningham played most of two years before severe injuries forced him to sit on the sidelines during the 1977 season. But he came back strong last fall and is expected to line up opposite Murphy in 1979 giving Salem's defense excellent strength at the defensive flanks.

Men expected to make a run at starting jobs in the defensive line include John Kuduk (6-2, 220, Sr., Minneapolis, MN) at nose guard, plus Dave Gardner (6-4, 236, Sr., Rochester, MN) and Mike Weinzierl (6-5, 238, Sr., Shakopee, MN) at tackle. Both the latter saw limited duty last year. Weinzierl transferred to UM a year ago. Kuduk sat out last fall with injuries but could be ready to take Friberg's nose spot in '79.

Expected to provide most of the backup material are several members of last year's red shirted freshman class, and possibly a newly recruited transfer, Jim Anderson (6-5, 235, Jr., Windom, MN), or maybe one or two newly recruited freshmen. Only time will tell how Salem and his defensive coaches shape up the interior line.

Steve Tobin, C-OG

Tom Murphy, DE

Linebackers

One is gone, team tackle leader Ed Burns (63 solo, 42 assists, 105 tackles), but everyone else who saw duty at linebacker last fall is back in harness. Three leading candidates who will battle it out for starting berths include Jack Johnson (6-1, 218, Sr., Minnetonka, MN), Don Meyer (6-2, 219, Sr., Arlington Heights, IL), and Jim Fahnhorst (6-3, 218, Jr., St. Cloud, MN).

However, Johnson underwent knee surgery in the winter and missed spring drills. But hopes are high for a complete recovery so he can be on the field in the fall. Johnson was one of the hardest hitters on last year's club. His presence would be missed.

Meyer came on strong when Johnson was felled last fall and could be the man to move in. He plays the game very smartly and will be ready.

Fahnhorst, the younger brother of former Gopher Keith, now a lineman with the S.F. '49'ers, could be the next great Minnesota bred linebacker.

Many are already comparing this rangy youngster with Steve Stewart, now at Atlanta in the NFL. Two years ago Stewart was one of the best linebackers in the Big Ten. The younger Fahnhorst plays the game with much the same style that Stewart used...all out. But he also plays heady. With continued growth and experience, he already wears the "can't miss" label.

Several others, including last year's rookies Paul Izban (6-2, 206, Fr., Mt. Prospect, IL) and Todd Peterson (6-1, 207, Fr., Richfield, MN) will be given strong consideration if they continue to show the same level of improvement. Both are considered solid "futures" for the Gopher program. And, as always, there will be others who come to the front, too.

Jim Fahnhorst, TE

Keith Edwards, FS

So if Johnson recovers and the others continue to come along, Minnesota's long tradition of outstanding linebackers should continue in 1979. Salem places huge responsibilities on the men at this position, but with defensive coordinator Bruce Vandersall coaching men at this spot, the Gophers should be OK at linebacker.

Defensive Secondary

Again Salem is blessed with a majority of returning starters and plenty of experience. Back for another campaign are two of last year's regulars in free safety and return specialist Keith Edwards (5-11, 201, Sr., Grand Rapids, MI) and scrappy cornerback Ken Foxworth (5-11, 176., Sr., St. Louis, MO). Both these gentlemen have been through the wars and come out with flying colors. Edwards will challenge any and all as to who is the fastest man on the Gopher roster. He averaged 20.7 and 12.3 yards on kickoff and punt returns, respectively, last fall. Many times he was just a step away from breaking for the distance.

Foxworth hits surprisingly hard for his size and is also adept at covering deep on the downfield passes.

Salem will have to replace one giant key in the Gopher defense as he looks at the strong safety slot vacated by Keith Brown. Brown was one of the hardest Gopher tacklers last year ending second only to Burns in total figures with 77 stops. He also made seven tackles behind enemy lines.

The heir apparent to Brown's strong safety slot appears to be the wild man of the kickoff return team, Mike Peppe (5-11, 182, So., Brooklyn Park, MN). Peppe is known as the "wedge buster" on the Gopher special teams. But he is expected to be pressed by vet John Hoffman (5-11, 199, Sr., Duluth, MN) and rookie Mike Robb (6-2, 192, Fr., Cottage Grove, MN). Robb is another of last year's fresh crop who sat out all season.

With cornerback Brian Snyder also gone via the graduation route, it now looks as if converted running back Dana Noel (5-10, 178, Jr., Wheaton, IL) could become heir. Noel moved to DB a year ago and progressed rapidly. He could team with Foxworth to give the Gophers a strong pair at the corners in 1979. Both support the run well and defend against the pass strongly.

But Minnesota's veteran placekicker, Paul Rogind (5-10, 176, Sr., Farmington, MI) would like nothing better than to get a shot at playing cornerback besides his regular booting chores. He will be given the chance, but will have to battle several other candidates for playing time, including a 1978 rookie in Glenn Cardelli (5-10, 171, Fr., Elmwood Park, IL).

Behind Edwards at free safety expect to see hard-nosed Bill Prarie (6-0, 172, So., Rosemount, MN) pushing for all he's worth, and possibly another of last year's rookie crop, Rick Witthus (6-3, 186, Fr., Lombard, IL).

Of course, as with all the positions already covered, there always looms the question, can any of the newly recruited freshmen and transfers cut the mustard and move up in their first year? It's not probable, but always possible. But more on these lads later.

Kicking Game

Half this vital part of any coaches' program is in excellent hands, or feet, in this case. Sidewinder Paul Rogind already owns all but one record for place kicks in the Gopher book. An All-Big Ten selection on every squad chosen last fall, Rogind has accounted for several key Gopher wins in the past two years with his amazing instep.

Salem says... "this is one young gentleman I can talk about. I mean, a kicker is a kicker, and he is something else."

Paul Rogind, K-CB

"According to records in the sports information office, he is on a current streak of 53 consecutive extra points. He has only missed one try in three years. He has converted a school record 35 of 54 field goal attempts, and his last second kicks have accounted for six of seven victories. I already knew about Paul Rogind before I came here. Anybody who follows college football knows this young man's name. He may be the premier kicker in the nation this fall."

"And I'm no different than any other coach. The kicking game is a vital part of any game plan. With Rogind back for one more season, I realize this part of our program is A-OK. Paul is a great kicker, and from what I hear he wants to play some cornerback, too. We'll just have to wait and see about the latter."

Tom Smith (6-0, 186, Jr., Edina, MN) transferred to Minnesota and handled the punting last season. Although a bit inconsistant at first, Smith ended with a 36.6 average and finished strong. He, himself, believes he had a sub-par year and expects to do much better in 1979.

Smith, along with quarterback Mark Carlson, played on the Minnesota baseball team last spring, Smith as a pitcher and Carlson as a power hitting catcher.

The New Coaching Staff

Salem retained three members of the Gophers coaching staff, all on defense, for the coming season in end coach Butch Nash, interior line coach Cal Jones, and defensive coordinator and linebacker coach Bruce Vandersall.

Nash is a legend in his own time at Minnesota. As an undergrad he played on the great national championship team under coach Bernie Bierman in the late 1930's, and has been on the Gopher staff since 1947. This fall marks his 33rd year with the program. He has turned out more All-American players than any other past or present assistant coach at Minnesota.

In 1977 he was credited with both the game plan and the emotional charge that led Minnesota 16-0 over then number one and undefeated Michigan.

Jones joined the Gopher staff in 1977 and has turned the Gopher defensive interior into something rough and ready. A member of the NAIA Hall of Fame as a player for Adams State in Colorado, Jones has enjoyed successful coaching stops at Southern University, Florida State and Western Illinois before he chose Minnesota. He also led Central Union High of El Centro, CA, to five consecutive league championships during his days as a prep coach.

Vandersall came to Minnesota in 1973 and has become widely known as one of the best linebacker coaches in collegiate circles. His tandem of Michael Hunt and Steve Stewart were called by many one of the best duos in the Big Ten during the 1975-76-77 season. Both are now fixtures in the pro ranks.

Vandersall once served on the staff of Massillon High in his native state of Ohio before moving on to the college ranks at Wichita State, his last stop before Minnesota. His assignment as defensive coordinator is new this season under Salem. But there is little question that Bruce will more than handle the job.

The remaining assistant coaches are all new to Minnesota, but none are new to Salem.

Mike Shanahan last fall coached the Eastern Illinois University offense to the 1978 NCAA Division II championship. He had previously coached with Salem at Northern Arizona where he also concentrated on the offense that reached the NCAA Division II quarterfinals in 1977. Shanahan will serve as offensive coordinator and handle the running backs at Minnesota.

One of two offensive line coaches is Jim Clements. Although a product of Detroit, MI, Clements played at Arizona State and later coached at Flagstaff High School from 1970 through 1974. He joined Salem at NAU in '75 and has been with the new Minnesota boss ever since.

The other young man helping with offensive line chores is Pat Morris. Morris played offensive guard for the Southern Cal powerhouses of 1973-74-75. The middle year saw USC win a national championship, and in all three years he played on Rose Bowl teams.

Morris stayed on at USC as a graduate assistant coach for two years before joining Salem last fall. His primary function in going to NAU, says Salem, was to teach the offensive linemen, and the backs, the famed USC power sweep.

"Let's face it," Joe now says, "with backs like Marion Barber, Roy Artis, Kent Kitzmann and others, we may pull the entire line to lead the end sweep. But however it's done, coaches Morris and

Clements will show our men how to do it the right way."

Morris is the youngest UM staff member at 25 years of age.

Pat Levin joined Salem at Northern Arizona last fall following one of the most successful high school coaching careers in the history of Arizona prep football. An undergraduate of Arizona State who later gained a masters degree at NAU, Lavin coached prep ball for seven years posting a 64-13-2 record for which he was twice named Arizona Coach of the Year. He will handle the receivers on Salem's staff, a heady assignment considering Joe's aerial plans.

The final staff member mentioned here is defensive secondary coach Dan Runkle. Another of Salem's crew at Northern Arizona, Runkle joined his present boss back in the days at South Dakota, and later moved with him to NAU. Prior to the S.D. stay, Runkle coached high school ball and also served on the staff of the University of Utah.

Each man mentioned as an assistant to coach Salem was an outstanding high school and collegiate athlete. So knowing what it takes to produce a winner is part of each man's football background.

In closing, let's just say that pre season excitement is running at a high pitch in Minnesota. A favorite son has returned to take the job of the king of sports, football.

There isn't a fan in Minnesota right now that doesn't believe Joe will get the job done. How long will it take? Well, that's another matter.

"No football power gained that distinction just by handing out press releases," Salem adds. "It's something that has to be earned."

"But the University of Minnesota owns a long and proud heritage of winning, championship football. The fans are there and they want to back a winner. Any winner."

"Just look at the way our fans support basketball, hockey and baseball. It's amazing. Coach Jim Dutcher had an off year in basketball last winter, so all Minnesota did was lead the Big Ten in attendance again and was ranked second or third nationally in average game attendance. Of course you can hardly get into a Gopher hockey game, and not just because Herb Brooks won his third NCAA championship in six years, either."

"Both those sports feature exciting winners at Minnesota. We want to feature the same thing, an exciting winner. And I think we can do it, too."

"I'm awfully proud of the way we were able to round out our staff. I believe we were lucky to convince Nash, Jones and Vandersall to stay on and become part of a new team. And I already know what the other staff members can do as they have all been with me before."

"If it sounds like I'm a bit excited, well, that's exactly the way I feel. I mean, how many men get to return as head coach at the institution which helped them gain an educational degree by providing scholarship aid? Not many. So I consider myself one of the luckier men around."

"As to football itself, well, on paper we have what appears to be a good looking crop of players coming back. They own that one ingredient you can't buy, Big Ten experience."

"I also believe we were able to come up with a very representative group of new freshmen and transfers. We didn't have much time to recruit, about five or six weeks, but my staff members did just one helluva job. Their hard work may not be evident for a year or two, but I believe their efforts started us out in the right direction."

"Now it's up to us, the coaches. We've got to convince our Minnesota varsity squad members they can be winners. We've got to teach them our system, our ideas, our program in one big hurry. But you know kids are sharp today. You can't con them. But I find if you're honest with them the players will return the trust tenfold."

"Excitement and winning football. That's exactly what we plan to place on the playing surface of Memorial Stadium starting this fall. If we don't, it's our fault. But I just hope our fans give us the time needed to fully install our ideas, our own program. I sincerely believe that in time we can return Minnesota to its winning days of the past."

"But brother, in the Big Ten, that's some kind of challenge."

Joe Salem, new as a coach at Minnesota, but far from anything new as a familiar name and face.

Yes, excitement is running high in Paul Bunyan land. Now the proof comes on Saturday afternoons in Memorial Stadium. Minnesota football fans may be on the verge of a new, winning era. At least that's what everyone in this part of the country is hoping.

Listed below are Minnesota's 1979 recruits (alphabetically):

Jim Anderson*- 6-5, 235, DL, Windom, MN
Chris Bennett - 6-3, 220, C, Stillwater, MN
Rene Cape - 6-1, 215, LB, Hialeah, FL
Paul Dagner - 6-1, 185, DB, Richfield, MN
Nick Davidson - 5-10, 170, QB, Miami, FL
Howard Davis - 6-0, 190, DB, Detroit, MI
Jeff Denney - 6-2, 220, DL, Washington, DC
Lonnie Farrow - 5-10, 165, WR, Pompano, FL
Keith Gehrke - 6-5, 225, OL, Prospect, IL
John Houle - 6-2, 210, LB, St. Paul, MN
Kelvin Jenkins*- 5-9, 175, WR, Long Beach, CA
Mike Laliberte - 6-3, 210, LB, Hibbing, MN

Tom Pence - 6-2, 190, QB, Crystal Lake, IL
Randy Rasmussen - 6-2, 212, LB, New Brighton, MN
Ronnie Renzi - 6-2, 210, LB, Arlington, VA
Marvell Ross - 5-9, 170, QB, Detroit, MI
Mike Stensrud - 6-4, 190, WR, Apple Valley, MN
Bob Stroup - 6-1, 190, DB, Fargo, ND
Tracy Thomas - 6-4, 220, TE, Detroit, MI
Virgil Thomas - 6-2, 200, OB, Detroit, MI
Terry Thompton - 6-3, 240, OL, Fridley, MN
Reed Wiecks - 6-3, 230, TE, Walnut Grove, MN
DeWayne Williams - 6-2, 215, OB, Waukegan, IL
* - J.C. transfer

NORTHWESTERN *Wildcats*

"That was a year of investment," says Rick Venturi, referring to the 1978 football season, his first campaign as head coach at Northwestern, his alma mater.

Venturi survived the 0-10-1 season, in which a 0-0 tie at Illinois was the highlight, and remarkably put together a superb recruiting year. He signed 27 players to National Letters of Intent, culminating what Venturi and his staff feel was a very, very successful effort.

"This completes our second successful recruiting year in a row," Venturi said after having all his tenders signed within the first day of the letter-signing period. "I feel this will be the nucleus of a successful football team in Big Ten competition in the near future. I said when I came here we needed two outstanding recruiting years back-to-back to get things headed in the right direction. I definitely feel we are now headed in the right direction. This gives us 51 new players in our first two years."

Of last year's 24 freshmen, 22 wound up playing in 1978, as many as 19 went on road trips and 16 won letters. By the end of the season, seven freshmen were in the starting lineup and 15 were listed in the two-deep lineup on offense and defense. Similar immediate help is expected from the 1979 freshman group.

"At this stage of our program," Venturi notes, "we view our freshmen more as rookies than as true freshmen. We expect them to make contributions and take significant roles in the 1979 season. We recruited with balance both offensively and defensively with the emphasis on running backs and the perimeter defense. In an attempt to improve our defense, we have recruited kids with mobility in both the defensive secondary and outside linebacker positions. Offensively, we feel we have shored up our running game with three fullbacks and three tailbacks along with five offensive linemen who average 6-feet, 5-inches and weigh an average of 257 pounds.

"In addition to recruiting almost a full team, offensively and defensively," Venturi adds, "we have also improved our specialty areas. Jay Anderson (Lusten, MN) is one of the best high school placekickers in the country, as well as being a fine tight end. Ricky Edwards (White Plains, NY) has speed and quickness and is an excellent kick return man."

Freshmen will be counted on heavily to shore up the defense, which last year after its opening-game shutout of Illinois, suffered a multitude of injuries and surrendered 440 points in the last 10 games. Best candidate to move into a starting berth is 6-4,

218-pound outside linebacker Chris Hinton, perhaps the finest all-around prep athlete in the City of Chicago last year as a senior at Phillips High School. Venturi also figures as many as three freshmen could earn starting spots in his defensive secondary, where the 1978 Wildcats were short on speed.

The center of the defense will be anchored by junior linebacker Chuck Kern (New Castle, IN), who was on the field enough to be credited with 218 tackles — 121 solo and 97 assisted — last year, and a pair of red-shirt seniors in tackle Norm Wells (Warren, MI) and middle linebacker Jim Miller (Kohler, WI), both of whom were knocked out of 1978 with severe knee injuries in the opener at Illinois.

Offensively, the Wildcats will also be bolstered by the return of a red-shirt player in junior Todd Sheets (Nappanee, IN), a superb wide receiver and kick return artist who missed all of last year with knee surgery. To get his starting job back, however, Sheets will have to beat out one of last year's finest freshmen, speedy Steve Bogan (Weston, CT), who, although starting only the second half of the season, was the team's second leading pass receiver with 22 catches for 353 yards. Bogan also had six touchdown receptions, most ever by a freshman in the Big Ten and second most by a freshman in NCAA history.

In addition to Bogan, several other offensive statistics leaders return for Venturi. Tailback Tim Hill (Cincinnati, OH) missed two games last year as a sophomore but still led the Big Ten in kickoff returns with an average of 25.1 yards on 14 returns, led the Cats in pass receptions with 24 and was second in rushing with 195 yards in 65 carries. Fullback Dave Mishler (Metamora, IL) missed the last seven games of 1978 with a knee injury, after being the team's leading ground-gainer as a freshman in 1977 and through the first four games of '78. Also, last year's top rusher Mike Cammon (Detroit, MI), who was used at fullback and tailback while picking up 322 yards in 73 attempts, returns for his junior year.

At quarterback, an interesting battle could develop between the veteran Kevin Strasser (Elmhurst, IL), who started every game last year as a junior and set numerous Northwestern and Big Ten records for offensive plays (363), passing attempts (307) and completed passes (151) while throwing for 1526 yards, and inexperienced Chris Capstran (Menominee, WI), who was Strasser's understudy all last year as a freshman without getting into a game. That part of it was intentional as Venturi decided to 'save' Capstran a year of eligibility, meaning he'll have him for the next four years. At 6-4 and 212 pounds, Capstran is an inch taller and 20 pounds heavier than Strasser. Capstran has a strong arm and is a good runner, making him very suitable for Venturi's pass-oriented offense.

In all, Venturi has 53 lettermen returning (28 on offense and 25 on defense), including nine each on offense and defense who were considered starters at the end of the season last year. Of the 15 senior letterwinners, only nine had the opportunity to start, if even occasionally during the 1978 campaign. And, two of those seniors may be back with an additional year of eligibility.

Northwestern Offense

Offensively, the Wildcats under Venturi's direction showed outstanding improvement from the start of last season until the end. Implementing an entirely new offense, with the pass as the main method of attack, the Wildcats began moving the ball consistently around mid-season, giving the coach and players confidence in their new philosophy.

That confidence should carry over to this year as nearly all of the principal figures are back for 1979. Venturi has 28 lettermen returning on offense (22 from last year and 6 from 1977). A total of 17 different players drew starting assignments last fall, only three of which were seniors.

"We want to become the Stanford of the Big Ten," says Venturi. "To do that, we knew we had to establish a passing attack. In that respect, I was very pleased with our offense last season. The passing attack is solid. But, to become like a Stanford, we need a running attack as well. Too many teams were able to key on our passing attack last year because they knew we were not a strong running team. With the offensive backs and linemen we recruited this year, I'm confident our running game will be much more efficient."

Venturi's passing attack generated 1650 yards last fall with 160 completions in 336 attempts. The running game, meanwhile, netted only 747 yards in 392 rushes (an average of 1.9 yards per carry). That means out of an offense that produced 2397 yards, nearly 70 per cent came by virtue of the aerial attack. According to Venturi, that is not a desirable percentage.

"Ideally, we'd like our offense to be 50 percent passing and 50 percent running," he says. "We definitely need to achieve better balance, but that doesn't mean our style of play will vary at all. We were efficient with the forward pass last year. We simply must be as efficient when we run as we are when we pass. We are still going to be a passing team, but total offense is our goal."

There is little doubt the passing game will be efficient, effective and explosive. Last year's deep threat Bogan (with his 22 catches for 353 yards and 6 touchdowns) will be joined on deep patterns by wingback Sheets, who two years ago as a sophomore — prior to last year's red-shirt season — averaged nearly 25 yards per catch with eight receptions for 199 yards and a TD.

The Wildcats figure to be extremely well-blessed with depth at the two key receiving positions. Behind Bogan at wide receiver could be last year's leading receiver Hill, who grabbed 24 passes for 122 yards as a tailback last season and who was tested as a wide receiver in spring practice. Hill's ability to play both positions gives Venturi added versatility. Also at wide receiver is sophomore Dave Bahoric (Johnstown, PA), who came into his own late last year when he caught three passes for 50 yards in the 10th game of the season against Michigan.

Behind Sheets at wingback is junior Tom North (Arlington Heights, IL), a starter in eight games last fall with 10 receptions for 130 yards, and freshman Jeff Maher (Highland Falls, NY), a prep All-American who in his senior year in high school caught 27 passes for 638 yards and 11 touchdowns, seven of which came from 50 yards and out.

Getting the ball to this bevy of receivers is the responsibility of quarterbacks Strasser and Capstran. Strasser, a senior, who two years ago threw only three passes during the entire season (all incomplete), made up for it last year with 307 tosses and was responsible for 1526 of NU's 1650 yards by air. Capstran had no passes and no yardage and didn't play in a single game, but that was by design. Even though he was Venturi's No. 2 quarterback, Capstran was held out of competition to 'save' his freshman year of eligibility. Now the big, strong lad from Wisconsin has a year of practice experience behind him and is ready to take charge of the situation when called into the game.

"The quarterback position is very important to us," says Venturi. "We can never be caught without an excellent quarterback, because that's the trigger of our offense. I feel very comfortable with Strasser and Capstran as our top two quarterbacks and there are three sophomores whom I'm expecting to see develop in the same line."

Also a major factor in the receiving patterns in Northwestern's pro-set offense is the tight end position, where the candidates for 1979 are numerous. Last year's two starters, Wally Kaspryscki (Hammond, IN) and Sam Poulos (Northbrook, IL), both have a possibility of being back for a fifth season. Poulos, also a pitcher on the Wildcat baseball team, possesses deft hands (19 catches for 242 yards) while Kaspryscki, better known for his blocking, caught two passes for 18 yards. If neither returns, sophomore Clark Prichard (Lima, OH) figures to handle the position well with his 6-6, 220-pound frame. He had three receptions for 37 yards as a frosh. Another sophomore of similar size, John Finn (Wadsworth, OH), will also get a shot at tight end after being a linebacker on defense last year. Two freshmen could also figure at tight end, the placekicker Jay Anderson and Dave Callaway (Appleton, WI).

Catching the ball in the NU offense is not restricted to the ends and receivers, however. Last year, 78 passes were completed to backs coming out of the Wildcat backfield and this year figures to provide more of the same. Plenty of experience returns to that backfield with the likes of juniors Mishler (out most of last year with a knee injury), Hill (when not working out at wide receiver), Cammon (last year's top ground gainer and a Big Ten All-Academic pick) and Bob Schmitt (Sun Prairie, WI) along with sophomores Jo Jo Webb (Clairton, PA) and Lou Tiberi (Blue Island, IL), who was *Mr. Versatility* in 1978 with 36 rushes for 103 yards, 14 receptions for 122 yards and two pass completions (both for touchdowns) out of four attempts for 30 yards.

However, as Venturi sees the situation, incoming freshmen may shake things up considerably in the backfield. Four all-state prepsters, Edwards and Jeff Cohn (Chicago, IL) at running back plus Bill Kornegay (Grand Blanc, MI) and Jerome Woods (St. Louis, MO) at fullback, will be given solid shots at their respective positions when they arrive in the fall.

"These freshmen will be very good," says Venturi. "I'll be very disappointed if they don't come in and really push for starting jobs. We need that kind of good competition in the backfield. That will help us become a better team."

But the work up front will be important as well.

The front wall returns almost completely intact. With the exception of graduated co-captain Mike Kranz, who started every game last year at right tackle, the other Wildcats will be back and improved. Seniors Mike Fiedler (Toledo, OH), who Venturi considers one of the finest centers in the Big Ten after starting all 11 games there last year, Jim Ford (Burbank, IL), who started every game at right guard last fall but will move to right tackle this season, and John Schober (Findlay, OH), a starter during all 1978 at left tackle, give the Wildcats plenty of leadership on the line. Another senior Kevin Kenyon (Buffalo, NY) started twice at left guard last year and figures to inherit that position with junior Bill Draznik (Joliet, IL) moving from left guard to right guard.

"This is a veteran front which improved a great deal from the start of last season to the end," Venturi says. "They became particularly good with the pass protection and in our offense that is highly important. The five outstanding freshmen we have coming in will give us instant depth and, by the end of the season, I wouldn't be surprised if some of those kids are starting. The offensive line is probably the toughest area for a kid to come into, but I expect our freshmen to contribute quickly."

The first-year players Venturi is counting on are 6-6, 260-pound Walt Currie (Washington, MI), 6-5, 265-pound James 'Bubba' Thornton (Atlanta, GA), 6-4, 250-pound Tom Crist (Kenosha, WI), 6-5, 255-pound Bob Pratt (Sharon, PA) and 6-4, 205-pound center Bob Szpak (Parma, OH).

"The freshman linemen will definitely add needed bulk to our line," says Venturi. "We didn't really expect to take that many good offensive linemen in one recruiting class, but when all the top kids we were looking at decided to come to Northwestern, we figured we'd take them all. In the long run, that should help us considerably because now we've got a young offensive line unit that will be with us for a long time."

Venturi figures it will take less time to get freshmen ready to play major college football now than it did in the past, thanks largely to a new NCAA rule, which Venturi introduced to the latest convention and lobbied for, allowing freshmen to be brought in four days early this fall for a 'rookie camp'.

"I think that will help us a great deal," he says. "It will give us a chance to concentrate on the freshmen for four days. I believe we can get a lot done in teaching fundamentals and just preparing the youngsters for what they're going to be up against in those first three or four weeks of practice. When a first-year player comes in with the entire squad, he is usually overwhelmed. He sometimes gets neglected because the coaches naturally want to spend as much time as possible getting the front-line players ready for the opener. That often leads the freshman into being discouraged and sometimes even causes him to quit the team. I think the new 'rookie camp' will serve to remedy that. It will help those of us who need the freshmen most in getting our programs turned around."

Getting the program turned around at Northwestern is the goal of Venturi. Having an offense with flair, passing the ball and using unusual formations, plus finding a home for his outstanding freshmen is all part of realizing that goal. Venturi is getting the job done and it will be obvious in 1979.

Northwestern Defense

Key injuries forced Venturi to shuffle his defensive starting lineup several times in 1978, but it could pay off with instant dividends in 1979. Numerous freshmen gained game experience last fall and this year 25 lettermen return (including red-shirts Miller, Wells and Scott Duncan).

Only two defensive players started every game last fall, sophomore Tom McGlade and senior Pat Geegan, as 23 Wildcats started on different occasions. Only six of those 23 defensive players graduated, so Venturi is confident that he has a solid base to build on in 1979.

"In essence, we had two different teams playing defense last year due to our injury situation," Venturi says. "We must play great defense week in and week out, in order to win consistently. Injuries just depleted our defense all of last year. We obviously need to improve in some areas and I think we will be better this fall."

On paper, the strength of the Northwestern defense will be its inside linebackers. The return of Miller will be a welcome addition to the young Wildcat defense. The senior recorded 14 tackles last year at Illinois, including one sack for a loss of 12 yards. Kern moved in and started the last ten games of the season after Miller suffered the knee injury.

In addition to leading the team in tackles, Kern broke up three passes, saved a touchdown and recorded an interception. Miller and Kern together will give Northwestern a rugged duo to confront the opponent's running game.

"Chuck Kern and Jim Miller are a fine pair of linebackers," Venturi says. "Having them back in the middle of our defense will give us a real boost. However, the sleeper could be Scott Duncan. He's a doggone good football player."

Duncan (Findlay, OH), a fifth-year player who missed the entire 1978 season with knee problems, led the Wildcats in tackles in 1977 with 103. His return to the Northwestern lineup would certainly be a bonus. Sophomore Doug Dorsey (Freeport, IL) and senior Tim Lawrence (Oak Lawn, IL) give the Wildcats experience and depth at that position.

"At the outside linebackers, a lot of rookies will get a chance," Venturi says. "We recruited a lot of perimeter players so we can have some depth and not be so thin."

Two of the Wildcats' leading tacklers from 1978 return this fall. All-Big Ten Academic selection Kevin Berg (St. Paul, MN) secured 120 tackles last year (58 solos) for the second-highest total on the squad. Also, junior Dean Payne (Chester, PA) has a good chance at a starting berth after recording 78 tackles last fall.

Steve Pals (Glen Ellyn, IL) played extensively in a reserve role last fall and will compete for a starting nod along with freshmen Hinton, Steve Kaiser (Bloomfield Hills, MI), Jim Karstens (Melrose Park, IL) and Tom Epich (Evergreen Park, IL).

Competition will be keenest at the tackle positions. Sophomores Bill Gildner (Springfield, IL), Rob Taylor (Kettering, OH) and Don Bambauer (North Royalton, OH) all earned letters as freshmen and junior Brian Stasiewicz (Columbus, OH) started six games despite knee trouble. In addition, two veterans Norm Wells (Warren, MI) and Bruce Robinett (Xenia, OH) are coming off knee surgery and will be hungry for game competition.

"There will be tremendous competition at tackle with the move of Bill Gildern from end to tackle and the return of a healthy Wells and Robinett," says Venturi. "We'll have plenty of depth there this fall. We came up a little short there with all the injuries last year so we are moving some perimeter players inside.

"We have a lot of talent at tackle and there will definitely be some drastic improvement at those positions," Venturi adds. "Those three sophomores got plenty of game experience last year. They were in there like colts. Unfortunately, we never got a lot of them in the game at the same time. This year we decided to move different players inside to try to quicken and strengthen the position."

Five freshmen, including Venturi's biggest recruit, Jack Mead (Whitewater, WI), a 6-foot-7, 225-pound prospect, provide other competition at tackle. Candidates at tackle include: Pat Erdman (Erie, PA), Tim Kadlec (Robbins, IA), Richard Moore (Harvey, IL) and Terry Harrell (Beloit, WI).

One of the main areas of concentration this fall will be the Wildcat secondary. McGlade (Park Ridge, IL), who started all 11 games last fall as Cat, should start again this year. Venturi wanted a little more speed in his secondary and he recruited some speedsters who could play a significant role in the fall.

"If we can shore up our secondary completely, we'll be a good defensive team," Venturi says. "Our strength in the secondary is inside with McGlade at Cat and Ben Butler at safety. However, at the corners our new kids will get a chance. I really look for the incoming ball players to compete with the heirs-apparent for the outside positions. On the inside, I feel McGlade and Butler are two capable Big Ten football players."

Butler (Chicago, IL) started the final two games of the 1978 season and impressed Venturi with his speed and desire. Junior John Burns (Warren, OH) will back up Butler.

At the cornerback position, several players are vying for the two starting berths. Juniors Mark Adams (Detroit, MI), Dana Hemphill (Gaithersburg, MD) and David Hoffman (Cincinnati, OH) all saw action in 1978 in the secondary. However, some speedy recruits will compete vigorously with those lettermen. Bobby Anderson (Rockford, IL), Rich Raffin (Valparaiso, IN) and Dave Shaw (Peoria, IL) are all freshmen who could provide immediate help. Venturi has also entertained the thought of moving speedy wide receiver Roosevelt Groves (St. Louis, MO) to the cornerback spot. Another possibility is switching Tiberi, a multi-talented sophomore who played three offensive backfield positions last year, to the secondary.

"Our strengths would seem to be our inside linebackers and safeties," says Venturi. "We just have to work hard at the other positions and improve ourselves. I expect a lot of freshmen to contribute, if not early in the season, certainly by late in the fall."

Specialty Teams

One of the areas where Northwestern figures to improve most this fall is in the performance of its specialty teams. Placekicker Nick Mirkopulos graduated but the Wildcats landed a super recruit in Jay Anderson. Punter Jeff Christensen (Gibson City, IL) returns after averaging 36 yards per kick last fall.

"Christensen did a pretty good job last year," Venturi says, "However, he won't be handed the job. Chris Capstran and Matt Taylor will battle him for the position. Our placekicker will probably be Jay Anderson. I'm really thrilled about him — he's one of the top kickers in the country. He can hit field goals consistently."

As far as kickoff and punt returns, the Wildcats will be very explosive. One of the nation's leading kick return artists, Tim Hill, returns for his junior season in 1979. The speedster averaged 25.2 yards on kickoff returns last fall on the season and led the Big Ten in that category. His best effort came against Wisconsin when he scampered 68 yards with a kickoff return.

This season, Hill will be complemented by junior Sheets, who was a devastating kick return specialist in 1977 before sitting out the 1978 campaign with a serious knee injury. In 1977, Sheets averaged 8.3 yards on punt returns and 18.7 on kickoff returns. However, Sheets had an even better year as a freshman. The speedy Sheets averaged 21.5 yards on kickoff returns in 1976, including a 93-yard jaunt for a touchdown against Iowa.

"We're putting a lot of emphasis on our kickoff and punt returns," says Venturi. "Having Todd Sheets back on kickoffs will really give us an explosive player to go along with Hill. Obviously, Hill had a great season last year returning kicks. With Sheets back there also, our opposition won't be able to kick away from Hill anymore."

"Another player who figures to give us a lift in that area is Ricky Edwards," Venturi adds. "He is electrifying and will be a big contribution to our punt return unit. Hill, Sheets and Edwards all have the potential to break away and score six points for us."

Last year, the Wildcats averaged 6.7 yards on punt returns and, with the exception of Hill, no Northwestern player returned a kickoff longer than 24 yards. For his career, Sheets averages 20.0 yards on kickoff returns and 6.5 yards on punt returns.

"We will really be improved in our return game," Venturi says. "In fact, it should be one of our strengths. Last year, we put ourselves in a hole a few times when we mishandled kicks and gave the opposition great field position. With two experienced, proven specialists and a freshman with speed to burn, we should really be improved in that area of the game."

In addition to Hill, Sheets and Edwards, Venturi plans on giving sophomore Bogan and freshman Cohn a shot at returning kickoffs in the fall.

Wildcats To Watch

Kevin Berg, St. Paul, MN, (St. Thomas Academy), OLB, 6-2, 211, Sr.

All-Academic Big Ten player in 1978...second leading tackler on the team last year with 120...played an outstanding game against Michigan State securing 11 tackles and a blocked punt...started eight games in 1978...bothered by neck injury most of last year...solid Big Ten player who will receive stern competition for the starting job this fall...all-state player as a senior in high school...earned five letters in high school as a football (3) and baseball (2) player...majoring in arts and sciences.

Steve Bogan, Weston, CT, (Weston), WR, 6-1, 185, So.
One of the finest freshmen in the Big Ten last year...caught six touchdown passes in 1978 — the most ever by a freshman in the Big Ten and second most by a freshman in NCAA history...exploded onto the scene against Arizona State with two touchdown receptions...Northwestern's second-leading receiver last year with 22 receptions...averaged 16 yards per catch...led team in scoring with 36 points...has tremendous speed...played just one year of high school football...just scratching the surface of his true potential, according to Venturi...excellent baseball player...plays centerfield for Northwestern baseball team...earned seven varsity letters in high school...majoring in business management.

Steve Bogan   Mike Cammon

Ben Butler, Chicago, IL, (Mount Carmel), S, 6-4, 191, So.
Started the final two games last year at free safety...hard hitter with extremely good range...intercepted two passes last year and recorded 47 tackles...should start at safety in the fall...very quick player...earned five letters in high school, including three in baseball and two in football...majoring in arts and sciences.

Mike Cammon, Detroit, MI, (University of Detroit), FB, 5-11, 190, Jr.
Started the last five games of the 1978 season and enjoyed his best day against Minnesota, rushing for 84 yards on 12 carries...His longest jaunt of the season was 29 yards against the

Tim Hill

Chuck Kern

Jim Miller

Kevin Strasser

Golden Gophers...led the Wildcats in rushing with 322 yards and averaged 4.4 yards per carry...also caught 13 passes for 97 yards...bothered by nagging injuries throughout the season...scored one touchdown against Michigan...good speed and agility...scored four touchdowns on the varsity reserve team as a freshman...voted the Most Valuable running back on that team...chosen as the top fullback in the Catholic League as a senior in high school...All-Big Ten Academic choice last year...enjoys music and reading...majoring in communication studies.

Mike Fiedler, Toledo, OH, (Whitmer), C, 6-3, 235, Sr.
One of the best centers in the Big Ten...has not received the

Receiver Steve Bogan (83) makes a juggling reception during action in Northwestern's non-conference battle with Arizona State last fall. Bogan, a Chicago native prep product from Weston, CT, came into his own in this game with four pass receptions good for 128 yards and two touchdowns. In the background is sophomore runningback Mike Cammon (33), who finished the season as NU's leading ball carrier with 322 yards. Coach Venturi expects a fine contribution from these two returning players.

acclaim he should have, according to Venturi...very good balance and leverage...will start again at center this fall...started every game last fall despite nagging injuries...also started six games as a sophomore...experienced lineman with All-Big Ten credentials ...lettered in football twice in high school...enjoys fishing...his cousin Dag Azam was an All-American guard at West Texas State...aspires to work in the public relations field...works for a construction company in the summer...played in Ohio All-Star football game as a prep...played soccer in high school...majoring in arts and sciences.

Tim Hill, Cincinnati, OH, (St. Xavier), RB/WR, 6-1, 175, Jr.

Started the first nine games last fall, before suffering knee injury at Purdue...led the team in receiving last year with 24... excellent receiver coming out of the backfield...could be moved to split end this fall to take advantage of his catching ability...one of the top kickoff return artists in the country...led the Big Ten with a 25.1 average...averaged 25.2 yards per return overall...Northwestern's second-leading rusher last year with 195 yards...Has earned two letters at Northwestern...exceptional quickness ...returned a kickoff 68 yards against Wisconsin for his season best...leading scorer and rusher in high school, averaging 4.9 yards per carry...enjoys electronics...played on varsity reserve team as a freshman and returned a kickoff 96 yards for a touchdown...majoring in psychology.

Chuck Kern, New Castle, IN, (Chrysler), LB, 6-2, 210, Jr.

Stepped in at middle linebacker and started the last ten games of the 1978 season after Jim Miller was injured in the opener at Illinois...led Northwestern in tackles with 218, including 121 solos... intercepted one pass and broke up three others last fall... recorded two sacks resulting in 14 yards in losses...will be counted on to plug the middle of the Wildcat defense along with Miller in 1979...class valedictorian in high school...earned eight letters in high school in football (3), basketball (2) and track (3)...reads plays very well...UPI and AP All-State player in high school, doubling as a linebacker and offensive halfback...limited playing time as a freshman — saw most of his action on the specialty teams...plans a career in medicine...enjoys camping and backgammon...Most Valuable Player of his high school team...majoring in biochemistry and economics.

Tom McGlade, Park Ridge, IL, (Maine South), Cat, 6-1, 182, Jr.

Only returning player on defense to start every game last

year...has found a home at the Cat position and his primary concern will be stopping the run...a walk-on as a freshman...very durable player...earned a scholarship after starting as a freshman...member of Alpha Tau Omega...his father, Thomas, also played football at Northwestern...awarded five letters in high school, including two in football and baseball and one in track...captained his baseball team as a prep...plans a career in business management...enjoys water and snow skiing...majoring in communication studies and economics.

Jim Miller, Kohler, WI, (Kohler), LB, 6-2, 225, Sr.

Fifth-year player who will bolster the Wilcat defense tremendously...sat out nearly the whole year in 1978, playing only in the season opener at Illinois before suffering a severe knee injury...had an outstanding game against the Fighting Illini, recording 14 tackles and sacked the quarterback once for a loss of 12 yards...Venturi hopes he can pick up where he left off last year and give the Wildcat defense "a shot in the arm"...good speed and strength...made 104 tackles in his sophomore and junior years at Northwestern...National Honor Society member in high school ...received 14 letters in high school, including four in wrestling and baseball and three in football and track...an outstanding prep wrestler, recording a 75-19-1 career record...heavyweight wrestler and letterwinner at Northwestern...received the Most Desire Award from his Wildcat wrestling teammates two years ago...plans to teach and coach in the future...majoring in physical education.

Dave Mishler, Metamora, IL, (Spaulding Institute), RB, 6-0, 215, Jr.

Started the first four games of the season before suffering a knee injury at Colorado, which sidelined him for the rest of the season...his best game of the 1978 season came at Colorado, where he gained 58 yards on 14 carries...totaled 168 yards rushing last fall, the third highest individual total on the team...also caught nine passes for 49 yards...rushed for 520 yards as a freshman to lead Northwestern in that department...good inside quickness and fine pass receiver...gained 128 yards against Wisconsin in 1977 for the best effort of his career...ran for 60-yard touchdown against Purdue as a freshman...his brothers, Bob ('69), Larry ('72) and Jim ('75) all played at Northwestern...member of Beta Theta Pi...plans to enter medical school in the future...earned six letters in high school...majoring in arts and sciences.

Todd Sheets, Nappanee, IN, (Northwood), WR, 6-0, 175, Jr.

Missed the entire 1978 season with a knee injury...his return will give Northwestern another deep threat in its passing game...very exciting player...grabbed eight passes in 1977, averaging 24.9 yards per catch...outstanding kick return specialist...averaged 8.3 yards on punt returns and 18.7 on kickoff returns in 1977...his freshman year, he returned a kickoff 93 yards for a touchdown against Iowa...averages 20 yards per kickoff return for his career...All-Big Ten potential...his return gives Venturi the option of using three receivers on certain occasions ...National Honor Society member in high school...MVP in basketball and track...majoring in physical education and health.

Kevin Strasser, Elmhurst, IL, (Immaculate Conception), QB, 6-3, 190, Sr.

Started every game last year and broke several school and conference records...owns Big Ten record for most pass attempts in a conference season (270), most completions (132) and most offensive plays (316)...he finished as the fourth-leading passer in the conference last year...he also ranked eighth in total offense...set Northwestern school record for offensive plays (363), passing attempts (307) and completed passes (151) while throwing for 1526 yards...his best game was against Wisconsin when he completed 20 of 34 attempts for 238 yards — including a 79-yard touchdown pass to Mike McGee, the fourth longest in Northwestern history...he ranks 11th on the all-time Northwestern passing list with 1526 yards...he is the trigger to the Wildcat offense...only threw three passes as a sophomore at Northwestern prior to last fall...very strong arm...durable player...good height for a quarterback...earned nine letters in high school...his father, Don, played basketball at Notre Dame...could set more records this fall...Venturi is counting on him to guide Northwestern's passing attack...captained the football and basketball teams in high school as a senior...majoring in communication studies.

Northwestern Head Football Coach
Rick Venturi

Northwestern head football coach Rick Venturi has a manner about him that makes people believe in what he says. Venturi promised an exciting offensive attack last year and he followed through. The 1979 season, Venturi's second as head coach, will also be full of excitement as the 32-year-old mentor and his youthful staff continue to turn the Wildcat program toward winning ways.

Despite an 0-10-1 record in his initial season, Venturi still believes Northwestern can have a good year in 1979.

"I haven't lost any enthusiasm nor the belief that we can get the job done at Northwestern," Venturi says. "We've put two successful recruiting years back-to-back. Our young kids gained a lot of playing experience last year and we've recruited some players that can step right in and give us a lift right away."

A 1968 graduate of Northwestern, Venturi is very confident in his players and their abilities on the gridiron.

"A Northwestern kid is a winner in the real sense of the word," Venturi says. "These kids play hard all the time. I don't know of a Northwestern player that quits. We had a tough year in 1978, but these players can bounce back. With a few breaks, we can be on our way.

"I love Northwestern and played here when we won and I know we can win again," Venturi added. "I honestly think we can have a winning football program here. That's what our staff works around the clock for. I won't sleep until we become a winner."

A native of Pekin, IL, Venturi is the 22nd head coach in Wildcat history. At Pekin High School, Venturi starred in football, basketball and baseball. He earned nine varsity letters during his prep career and was selected to the all-state team as a senior quarterback, coached by his father Joe Venturi.

As a freshman at Northwestern, Venturi was a quarterback but switched to the defensive secondary as a sophomore and remained there for the rest of his Wildcat career. However, in his first year at Northwestern Venturi etched his name in the Wildcat record book.

Against Illinois in 1965, Venturi connected with Ron Rector on an 80-yard touchdown pass, the third longest in Northwestern history.

Fresh out of college, Venturi began his coaching career as a graduate assistant at Northwestern. He moved up to become Wildcat freshman coach 12 months later and eventually progressed to become defensive coach at Purdue, when Alex Agase left Northwestern to take the job in West Lafayette.

In 1976, Gary Moeller left Michigan in hopes of rebuilding the Illinois program and tapped Venturi as a member of his staff. After his brief stint in Champaign, Venturi returned to his alma mater in December of 1977. At that time, he was the youngest Wildcat field general since 31-year-old Bob Voigts accepted the post in 1947.

The former Wildcat quarterback wanted to establish a sound passing game in his rookie season at Northwestern.

"I wanted to set up a style in my first year and build from there," Venturi said. "What I really wanted to do was teach them to throw and catch and I think we were successful. Now, I believe we are crisp in our passing game and Kevin Strasser is doing a fine job for us."

This fall, the tireless Venturi will start his 16th season (either as a coach or player) of association with Big Ten football. His positive attitude carries through to the players and his coaching experience has made him a well-respected man throughout the country.

"We never go into a ball game thinking we can't win," Venturi says. "My staff is tremendous. They are a group of aggressive, selfless, enthusiastic coaches who can relate to the players. We're working hard together and are totally absorbed in the program."

"We hope to reap the benefits of the 1978 investment season this fall," Venturi added. "The biggest key is how fast we can bring on our youngsters. In recruiting, we've been very competitive with some top-notch schools and this is beginning to show on the field."

Venturi's entire staff from his rookie season will return in the fall. Veteran **Nick Mourouzis** handles the quarterbacks and will start his 15th season as an assistant coach in the Big Ten in 1979. The offensive line is handled by coaches **Gene Mitz** and **Mike Westhoff**. The wide receiving corps is guided by **Venturi's** younger brother, **Tom**.

On the other side of the line, **Bruce Hoffman** serves as the defensive coordinator. Northwestern grad **Johnny Cooks** is in charge of the outside linebackers and **Greg Mattison** helps the defensive line. **Jim Muehling** is responsible for the linebackers and **Bill Rees** handles the running backs. **Ralph Dintino** serves as Venturi's chief scout.

The colorful Venturi has not only added an exciting flavor to the Northwestern football program. His personable and radiant style away from the gridiron is also contagious.

Venturi and his wife, Cheri, live in Evanston and have two children, Marin, 6, and Jason, 4.

OHIO STATE Buckeyes

A new era has dawned for Ohio State University football. For the first time in 29 years Woody Hayes will not be the head coach. The new mentor is Earle Bruce, a 1953 graduate of Ohio State, and for the past six years, head coach at Iowa State.

About The New Coach

Earle Bruce is unusually well qualified for the head coaching job at Ohio State University. Not only is he an Ohio State graduate but he spent six years on the Ohio State football staff under former Coach Hayes from 1966-1971. Earle is familiar with the talent-rich Ohio high schools, having spent 12 years coaching in the state, including ten as a head coach.

Bruce started as an assistant at Mansfield, Ohio in 1953 and became convinced he wanted to make a career of football coaching. His first opportunity as head coach came in 1956 at Salem, Ohio, where in four years, his teams compiled an impressive 28-9 record. His next stop was at Sandusky, Ohio, where he stayed four years and had a glittering 34-3-3 mark. In 1960 Bruce was named "Ohio High School Coach of the Year." In 1964 he went to Massillon, Ohio, long considered the top high school football job in Ohio and one of the most prestigious high school positions in the nation. Earle coached at Massillon for two years and both his teams went undefeated and each year Bruce was named "Ohio High School Coach of the Year." At this point Earle left the high school ranks to become an assistant at Ohio State in 1966. His ten-year high school record was a brilliant 82-12-3. He concluded his high school stint with a 42-game winning streak intact.

Earle joined the Buckeye football staff as a defensive backfield coach. Two years later a staff realignment took place and he moved to offense to coach the guards and centers. During the six years as an assistant at Ohio State, the Buckeyes won three Big Ten championships, one national championship, played in two Rose Bowls and compiled a 43-14 record.

He left Ohio State to become head coach at the University of Tampa in 1972. His record that year was 10-2, including a Tangerine Bowl victory over Mid-American Conference champion Kent State. The following year, 1973, Earle accepted the head coaching job at Iowa State University in the powerful Big Eight Conference. For years Oklahoma and Nebraska had dominated Big Eight football with occasional challenges from Missouri and Colorado. Winning had not been easy at Iowa State, where the school had enjoyed only two winning seasons in ten years.

Earle Bruce tackled the Iowa State job with rare dedication and hard work. It took time, more time than Earle believed would be needed, but he meticulously assembled a winning football program that developed pride in winning. His first two seasons at Iowa State were 4-7 each and there were high hopes in 1975, but a rash of injuries caused a third straight 4-7 season. Discouraged but not disheartened, Bruce saw his untiring efforts reap dividends the next season when the Cyclones finished 8-3, the best record any Iowa State team had enjoyed in 32 years. He followed with successive 8-3 regular season records in 1977 and '78, although Iowa State lost bowl games both years. Not since 1925, '26 and '27 had Iowa State's football team been able to enjoy three straight winning seasons, and those years produced modest 4-3-1 marks. For his outstanding coaching job at Iowa State, Earle Bruce was twice named "Big Eight Coach of the Year."

With these impressive credentials, Earle Bruce is uniquely qualified to tackle the demanding Ohio State University head football coaching duties. He knows the school, he knows the area and he has been a notable coaching success on each level, starting as an assistant in high school to head coach of a major football powerhouse in one of the top college conferences in the nation.

About The Staff

Just as head coach Earle Bruce is unfamiliar with the Buckeye playing personnel, so too is the entire staff, with two exceptions. Tight end and tackle coach Bill Myles and Glen Mason, who will coach the offensive guards and centers, are the only two holdovers from the previous Ohio State staff. Myles has been with Ohio State for two years and Mason one. The other six assistants are new to Ohio State and unfamiliar with the talent.

Four of the assistants accompanied Coach Bruce from Iowa State, so they have a working knowledge with the system and the coaching techniques to be used. These include; Steve Szabo, who will coach the defensive line; Bob Tucker, outside linebackers; Pete Carroll, the defensive secondary, and Wayne Stanley, the offensive running backs. Dennis Fryzel was hired from the Air Force academy to be defense coordinator and coach of linebackers, and Fred Zechman has been hired from the ranks of Ohio high schools to coach the Buckeye quarterbacks. The staff must make a quick transition to Big Ten football at a university where winning is taken for granted.

About The Returning Personnel

Coach Bruce and his staff inherit a squad that returns 11 starters, five on offense and six from defense. There are 39 lettermen returning from last year's team plus three kicking specialists. In addition, five players who lettered in earlier years but not in 1978 will be available. The total number of returning lettermen sounds impressive but football awards have been given generously at Ohio State, thus creating a picture that is not entirely true as far as experience is concerned.

About The System

Coach Earle Bruce has been discretely, perhaps deliberately vague, when asked about his system. One gets the feeling he prefers to let the opponents worry about what system he will use. If Ohio State uses the same style as Iowa State, you can expect an I-formation with two wide receivers. But again, a split back formation was used, not infrequently, with one wide-out and two tight ends. All of which proves one thing: Iowa State was not predictable as to offensive alignment. There is no reason to think this will change at Ohio State this year.

When asked about passing, Earle replied, "We will try to feature whatever we do best. If our strength is with our fullback, we will run him, if we have a great tailback, we will design our offense around him, and if we have a good passing attack, we will throw the ball." Once again, Bruce's six years at Iowa State emphasize the fact that the offense varied from year to year, even from game to game. This willingness to change removes the predictable quality that opposing teams hope to find.

Defensively Ohio State will align in basically an odd-man front and will feature a rover back. Here again there will be some new defensive concepts.

About The Experienced Returnees

Coach Bruce and his staff have made it clear to the squad that *ALL* starting positions are open. Even the two-year starters must prove to the new coaching staff that they are the best qualified to start.

Keith Ferguson    Ken Fritz

Art Schlichter    Paul Campbell    Doug Donley

The Offense

Ohio State returns 23 lettermen from last year on offense, including five starters. In addition, there are three letter winners from the 1977 team who did not win awards last season.

The regulars include tackle Keith Ferguson, guard Ken Fritz, quarterback Art Schlichter, flanker Doug Donley and fullback Paul Campbell. Since the new Buckeye staff is giving serious thought to moving Ferguson from offensive tackle to defensive outside linebacker, Ohio State would then only have one returning regular from the seven line positions, guard Fritz. Obviously this is an area of major concern.

Offensive Line

At tight end, Ohio State has Ron Barwig, Jim Houston, Chuck Hunter and John Meade with experience plus Bill Jaco, a regular in 1977 who did not play last year because of illness. Since Ohio State used two tight ends most of the time last year, it will make for keen competition in 1979, when the offense will feature chiefly one tight end.

Help is needed at split end, where only Tyrone Hicks has any experience. Hunter will likely be moved from tight end along with Alvin Taylor, a reserve at flanker last season. The Buckeye staff is anxious to look at Gary Williams, who figured to play in the defensive backfield last year, but missed the entire year due to an injury.

The ranks are alarmingly thin at tackle, especially if Ferguson does move to defense. Only two lettermen are available, Tim Brown and Tim Burke, and Burke has only limited experience. Fortunately Doug Mackie, a reserve in 1976 and '77, has recovered from a knee injury that kept him out of competition last season. A trio of sophomores, Tom Levenick, Mike Palahnuk and Kevin Akins saw no game action as freshmen, but should be able to bolster the tackle positions. Brown and Mackie have exceptional skills. Brown started several games last year and played well until a ligament tear in his knee kayoed him for the remainder of the season.

There is quality if not quantity at the guard positions. Ken Fritz, a first team all-Big Ten player last year is back along with Ernie Andria, who split the playing time at right guard in 1978, plus Scott Burris, a much improved reserve. Fritz is perhaps the strongest man on the Buckeye football team and may well be one of the top guards in college football. Andria has impressive size and Burris is a converted tackle. Ernie Epitropoulos and Russ Gatewood will be tried at the guard positions. Gatewood, a sophomore, was a linebacker last season, but did not see any game action.

A new center must be found. Tom Waugh, who divided his time between guard and center last season, will concentrate on the center position this year. Waugh played a total of 118 minutes in 1978. Joe Smith, a sophomore who did not have any playing time last year as a defensive tackle, has moved to center, where he is expected to add strength and depth. Dave Medich did not play last year at guard and has been moved to center this season. Specialist John Hutchins, who unerringly made the long snaps last season on punts, field goals and extra points, returns for 1979.

The Buckeye coaches believe there is talent available for a formidable line, but proven personnel is scarce and depth is thin.

Offensive Backfield

Ohio State has three athletes who have won letters at quarterback, Art Schlichter, Greg Castignola and Mike Strahine. Strahine lettered in 1977.

In Schlichter the Buckeyes have a rare talent. He started all 12 games last season as a freshman and played extremely well. He passed for 1,250 yards on 87 completions in 175 attempts. He was just as effective as a runner, netting 590 yards in 157 carries, an impressive 3.7 yards per carry that includes pass losses. Schlichter ran for 13 touchdowns, tops on the team, and threw four scoring passes. He proved to be remarkably durable, for Ohio State's pass protection suffered occasional breakdowns.

Castignola is a fine backup. He is a sound technician, an effective passer and a good runner. Castignola averaged 4.3 yards per try in rushing.

Strahine played more as a sophomore in 1977 than last year. He was a fine running back in high school and has done a good job learning the rudiments of quarterback play at Ohio State.

There is good depth at the tailback position with Calvin Murray and Ricky Johnson. In addition Ty Hicks has moved from wide receiver to tailback. Murray came into his own last year averaging 6.4 yards per try in 64 attempts. Although not big in size, he was equally dangerous running inside the tackles as on sweeps. An ankle injury to Murray in the Illinois game had a telling effect on the Buckeye running attack the final two regular season games last year.

Johnson played well with limited game experience. He carried 63 times and averaged five yards per try, including three touchdowns.

Hicks played several roles last season. He was the team's leading kickoff return specialist averaging 21 yards per return. He played both wide receiver and tailback on a limited basis. Hicks was the 1978 Big Ten 100-meter champion and is the team's fastest player.

Ohio State is eager to test two sophomores, Jim Gayle and Tim O'Cain, neither of whom played last year. With such unusual depth at tailback, one or more may be moved to another position.

Doug Donley may become Ohio State's best pass receiver ever. He started all 12 games at flanker last year and caught 24 passes for 510 yards and three touchdowns. He has excellent speed (he is a sprinter on the Ohio State indoor track team) and great hands. He and Schlichter form a dangerous passing combination that is capable of scoring from anywhere on the field.

There is virtually no experience behind Donley at the flanker spot. Doug Pauley played briefly in three games but did not catch a pass. Steve Lamb, a sophomore, saw no game action last year and has been moved to the flanker position. He was a state finalist in both the 100 and 220-yard events in track, so there is no question about his speed.

Last year's fullbacks, Paul Campbell, Ric Volley, Joel Payton and Cliff Belmer return intact along with Felix Lee, who missed the entire season because of knee surgery. Campbell edged out teammate Art Schlichter to lead the Buckeyes in rushing yardage, 591 to 590. Campbell scored nine touchdowns and caught five passes. He is the fastest of the fullbacks. Volley is an all-out athlete who plays

Calvin Murray *Tom Orosz*

with unusual emotion. He averaged 5.4 yards per try, especially high for short-yardage situations. Payton had an exceptional year in 1977, when he led the Big Ten in scoring. Last year, his effectiveness dropped off and so did his playing time. If Payton can put his game back together as it was in 1977, Ohio State will have a powerful offensive weapon.

Belmer missed the 1977 season due to a serious motorcycle accident and was slow to regain his sharpness last year. Buckeye coaches consider Belmer to be a fine athlete, who will get better and better during his college career.

As with the tailbacks, Ohio State has a wealth of fullbacks. The staff may decide to move one or two to another position where there is a need for additional manpower.

The Specialists

Last season's three kicking specialists all return. Tom Orosz was brilliant as a punter, averaging 43.7 yards per kick over the total season. Orosz led the Big Ten punters with a 44.4 average Kickoffs are handled by both Orosz and by Bob Atha. Both athletes consistently kick into the end zone.

Vlade Janakievski is back for extra points. He made 44 of 44 in 1977 and 40 of 43 last year. Atha is a dependable field goal kicker with six of eight last season, while Janakievski was one of two. Atha has better range and is likely to take over when field goals are needed. Atha also could be used for punting were Orosz unavailable.

About The Defense

Ohio State's defense had a dubious distinction last year; it gave up the fifth greatest number of points per game, 18, of any Buckeye

Vincent Skillings   *Al Washington*

defense in 89 years of football at Ohio State. Only the Ohio State teams of 1953, 1943, 1897 and 1893 yielded more points per game. Exactly why the 1978 defense broke down is difficult to explain, but you can bet Coach Bruce and his staff are determined to find the reasons and to make the necessary adjustments.

There are six starters back from the 1978 team; tackle Gary Dulin, linebacker Al Washington, cornerback Todd Bell, and the entire secondary, Mike Guess, Ray Ellis and Vince Skillings.

In all, there are 16 defensive award winners from last year plus linebacker Tom Blinco, who lettered in 1976 and '77, and middle guard Tim Sawicki, who lettered in 1976. Depth is needed in certain areas. This suggests two things: some position changes to take better advantage of the available talent, and the use of freshmen on defense.

Coach Bruce used basically odd-man defenses at Iowa State, so presumably, this will be his preference at Ohio State.

Jim Laughlin is the only outside linebacker with any appreciable game experience. He is one of those versatile, enthusiastic athletes who is dependable and is always ready when called upon. Ben Lee had brief experience but is considered a fine athlete. Leon Ellison is a rangy player who may come into his own this year. Buckeye coaches have strengthened this area by moving Keith Ferguson, last year's starting offensive tackle, to outside linebacker.

Dulin and Luther Henson divided the playing time at one tackle position last year. Each is back in 1979. Dulin has unusual strength and impressive size. Henson is only slightly smaller and is more active. A pair of tackles, Ron Miller and Nick Miller who are not related, and a second pair Dave Phillips and Larry Phillips who are brothers, round out the tackle hopefuls.

Neither of the Millers nor the Phillips has lettered, but the opportunity to play is there.

Tim Sawicki is the only middle guard with any experience. He won a letter as a freshman in 1976, but has not had sufficient playing time to pick up a second award. A series of injuries, not all football-related, have been his downfall. Sawicki is quick and extremely hard to block. All he needs is to stay healthy.

Jerome Foster is a sophomore who saw no game action last year. He is a striking contrast to Sawicki, in that he stands 6-4 and weighs 246. He is a punishing, physical type of middle guard.

Al Washington is a solid linebacker who is expected to be even better in 1979. He started all 12 games and was second on the squad in tackles with 146. Rugged Tony Megaro, a reserve last year, and Tom Blinco, a two letter winner who missed last year because of knee surgery, are leading candidates for the position vacated by two-time All-American Tom Cousineau. Megaro and Blinco have different specialties, so it becomes a choice by the coaching staff of selecting the type of athlete that is most needed.

Untried but promising interior linebackers include John Epitropoulos, Ted Hall, Craig Pack and Joe Berner. The last three are sophomores and were not used in varsity competition last season.

Coach Bruce will use a rover back on defense. This is a complicated demanding position that is assigned only to a top athlete. It demands speed, versatility and strength. Ohio State has such an athlete in Todd Bell. Brian Schwartz and Otha Watson also incorporate the required ingredients for playing this position, but Bell is the likely choice.

Vince Skillings, Mike Guess and Ray Ellis are all returning starters from last year's secondary. Bob Murphy played fine football when pressed into service and Norm Burrows and Mark Eberts are good athletes.

About The Freshmen

Ohio State coaches are pleased with the incoming freshmen. The coaching change came at a critical time in recruiting. Coach Bruce and his six new assistants were unfamiliar with Ohio high school talent, nor did they know the high school coaches or the Ohio State alumni. Recruiting for the new staff was made even more difficult because the late start prevented a carefully planned program and rival schools were invading Ohio in large numbers. There wasn't time to study movies, talk to coaches, quiz alumni, check into grades and take all the other precautions that go into the intricate, highly involved recruiting process.

In view of this, Coach Bruce and his staff have done a remarkable job in recruiting the 1979 freshman class. Some general observations can be made.

There are 24 in the freshmen football class. There are 11 on offense and 13 on defense. A further breakdown shows there are six offensive interior linemen, one tight end, one quarterback, two tailbacks and one fullback. On defense there are three interior linemen, seven linebackers, and three halfbacks. All but three are from Ohio. As a group the team is neither extremely heavy nor tall, but Buckeye coaches believe there is good individual quickness. The emphasis was on interior linemen and on linebackers.

1979 Ohio State Football Recruits

Name	Pos.	Hgt.	Wgt.	Home Town (High School)
Barton, Avery	DE	6-3	202	Detroit, Mich. (Northern)
Barnard, Eric	MG	6-1	235	Massillon, O. (Washington)
Brown, Bernie	C	6-1	215	Marietta, O. (Marietta)
Burrows, Scott	LB	6-2	200	Portsmouth, O. (Portsmouth)
Cobb, Glen	LB	6-3	212	Washington C.H., O. (Miami Trace)
Corbin, Steve	OL	6-5	230	Lima, O. (Central Catholic)
DeCamp, Steve	OL	6-3	240	Gahanna, O. (Lincoln)
Dwelle, Brad	TE	6-4	210	Sandusky, O. (Perkins)
Galloway, Tim	DB	6-2	185	Columbus, O. (Eastmoor)
Gorley, Rod	DB	6-0	180	Cincinnati, O. (Princeton)
Lewis, Doyle	DB	6-1	180	Canton, O. (McKinley)
Lindsey, Kelvin	TB	6-0	180	Sandusky, O. (Sandusky)
Lukens, Joe	OL	6-3	230	Cincinnati, O. (Moeller)
Marshall, Linwood	OLB	6-2	220	Cincinnati, O. (Western Hills)
Marek, Marcus	LB	6-2	208	Masury, O. (Brookfield)
McTier, Dave	QB	6-2	195	Eustis, Fla.,
Moran, Dave	DT	6-3	230	Columbus, O. (West)
Myers, Ray	FB	6-3	220	Toledo, O. (Bowsher)
Olman, Kevin	LB	6-3	225	Toledo, O. (Maumee)
Riehm, Chris	DT	6-6	230	Wadsworth, O. (Wadsworth)
Simpson, Steve	OL	6-5	225	Temperance, Mich. (Bedford)
Spencer, Tim	TB	6-0	200	St. Clairsville, O. (St. Clairsville)
Thomas, Bill	OL	6-5	250	Cincinnati, O. (Aiken)
Wilson, Bill	OLB	6-2	220	Columbus, O. (Massanutten Acad.)

About The Schedule

The 1979 schedule is demanding but not as rigorous as last year when Ohio State's first opponent was Penn State, who had played two earlier games. This year's three non-conference opponents, Syracuse, Washington State and U.C.L.A. replace Penn State, Baylor and Southern Methodist. There is one change in the eight Big Ten opponents: Michigan State replaces Purdue on the schedule.

Conclusion

Ohio State figures to have another good football team in 1979. It is vital that the new coaching staff and the players adapt to each other readily and that the transition is smooth. Some players will make the change easier than others. The starters in the offensive and defensive lines must come through and depth needs to be developed. The defense must be shored up and the number of points given up drastically reduced. The offensive backfield is talented and deep. There is speed and power to make the ground game go as well as a fine passer and a gifted receiver. The punting is topflight. Ohio State does not have as many great football players as in recent years but there are an unusual number who are promising but untried.

Look for Ohio State to be a contender once again.

PURDUE *Boilermakers*

Just about 15 years ago Purdue University added 11,000 new permanent seats to Ross-Ade Stadium on its West Lafayette, Indiana campus. At approximately the same time a crew-cut sophomore quarterback was gaining his varsity eligibility. His name was Bob Griese.

It was a few months before Boilermaker football fans began to fill up those shiny new seats, but fill them up they did and Purdue achieved a new height in its proud football history. Under head coach Jack (The Ripper) Mollenkopf, the Boilers posted 40 wins against 10 losses and a tie in his last five seasons (1965-69). His teams fought for the Big Ten Conference title and in '67 tied for the championship with Minnesota and Indiana, the last time schools other than Ohio State and Michigan have topped the league.

Bob Griese threw 609 times for 4,402 yards and 28 touchdowns, much to the delight of the record crowds that flocked to Ross-Ade. Boiler faithfuls considered themselves "quarterback experts". After all, they had seen Len Dawson, Dale Samuels, and Bob DeMoss before Griese and grew to expect wide-open, passing football from Purdue teams.

Griese gave way to another passing whiz in Mike Phipps, who erased nearly every record he had established. And it wasn't long until another NFL draftee, Gary Danielson (Detriot Lions), stepped in to satisfy Boiler fans' passing fever.

Then came a dry spell in Purdue passing quarterbacks and the losses surpassed the wins. Boiler football remained competitive, but like seven other Big Ten universities, it could not break the stronghold Michigan and Ohio State had on the number 1-2 spot in the premier football league in the country.

Then, like a breath of fresh air, two seasons ago in Spartan Stadium on the campus of Michigan State University, a tall, lanky freshman quarterback for Purdue trotted onto the field with 10:40 to play in the first half. His name was Mark Herrmann.

Herrmann threw 32 times that afternoon and completed 20 passes for a total of 282 yards and two touchdowns—the first a 53-yard strike *that marked the first Boilermaker scoring pass in a season and a half!*

The Boilermakers lost that game, 19-14, by virtue of four field goals by MSU's Hans Nielson. But the heartbreaking loss was quickly forgotten as Herrmann's performance brought back memories of seasons past for Purdue partisans. The forward pass was back, and no place more appropriately than at the Big Ten school synonymous with astronauts and throwing quarterbacks.

Mark Herrmann's record-breaking accomplishments are documented in the Big Ten record books. But, for the time being, they are only temporary because "On The Mark" has two seasons of Big Ten football ahead of him, and with him ride the fortunes of Purdue football.

Ironically, it may turn out to be the forward pass that ultimately threatens the Michigan-Ohio State dominance. Last season, four Big Ten quarterbacks threw over 150 passes in conference action—surely a record. Michigan State tied for the regular-season title and Purdue was just a half game back in undisputed third place.

With Herrmann came a success-proven and innovative head coach in Jim Young (Or was it the other way around?) who refused to be classified as a disciple of Michigan's Bo Schembechler, but nevertheless, spent nine years as his assistant. Young and his youthful (no pun intended) staff (that boasted an average age of 30) brought to Purdue a new style that not only included the forward passing of Mark Herrmann, but a wide-open offensive philosophy and a daring defensive approach that finished fourth in the nation in scoring defense a year ago by yielding just 9.9 points per game.

For the second consecutive season under Young, Purdue football entertained its fans to the tune of 22.4 points per game—including 32 TD passes! Ross-Ade Stadium was rockin' and rollin' again—drawing nearly three-quarters of a million fans and setting all-time attendance records.

The Boilermakers' storybook season of 1978 ended with a magnificent 41-21 victory over Georgia Tech in the Peach Bowl, finishing with an overall 9-2-1 mark. Young was named Big Ten Coach-of-the-Year and six of his Boilers were named to various all-Big Ten teams.

To say that this is only the beginning might have to be considered a gross understatement. On paper, as the cliche goes, Purdue should be even stronger in 1979. But even "the paper" won't hide the fact that the Boilers non-conference schedule replaced Ohio University and Wake Forest with UCLA and Oregon to join rival Notre Dame. Neither will it hide the three starting members of Purdue's secondary that completed their eligibility and the starting punter and record-setting place kicker who graduated.

However, it's true that all eleven starters who lined up on offense in the Peach Bowl victory return for the '79 season. The Boilermaker offense ranked second in conference passing, seventh in rushing, fifth in total offense, and fifth in scoring.

Quite obviously the offensive potential centers around Herrmann—already the Big Ten's number four all-time career passer with 4,357 yards just 23 games into his college career. There is little

Mark Herrmann   Dave Young   Mike Harris

question that he will enter the '79 campaign as one of the nation's "name" quarterbacks.

Evaluated individually, Herrmann's passing totals as a freshman and sophomore are the third and fifth-highest single-season totals in Big Ten history!!! He needs just 45 yards to move into second place among Purdue's all-time passing record holders and 1,066 to become the leading passer in Boilermaker history.

"Mark's passing ability speaks for itself," Young says, "but last year as a sophomore he improved greatly in the other areas of his game, especially his leadership. He matured as a quarterback and we're really looking forward to his leadership over the next two seasons."

The search has been on for a new back-up to Herrmann because last year's number two signal caller, Chuck Oliver, has given up football to devote full time to his studies. Oliver saw considerable action a year ago spelling Herrmann and operating the second unit. He played three quarters of the Michigan game after Herrmann was felled with a neck injury.

Joe Linville, who right now figures as Purdue's number one punter and spent time at both quarterback and wide receiver last fall (and who, like Herrmann, hails from Carmel, Indiana) is the number two quarterback this spring. However, it is not unlikely that a freshman could take over back-up quarterback duties next fall and find Linville moved back to split end and concentrating on his punting.

Herrmann completed 166 passes in 1978. One hundred and twenty-six of those receptions were caught by Boilermakers who return in '79, giving "Herm" a veteran receiving corps. The headliners will be tight end Dave Young, and wide receivers Bart Burrell, Mike Harris, and Raymond Smith.

Dave Young is a formidable target for Herrmann at 6-6 and has added considerably to his 220-pound playing weight of last season. He snagged 27 aerials last year including Herrmann's longest scoring pass of his career—a 75-yard pass and run at Wisconsin. The former all-stater from Akron (East) split time last season with graduated senior Tim Eubank, who might have been considered a "designated blocker". Eubank caught just two passes.

Harris was a transfer two years ago from California/Fullerton Junior College and openly admits he came to Purdue to "catch for Herrmann". He is the leading receiver among the returnees (34 for 495 yards and four TDs) and might be considered the Boilermakers' "smartest" pass catcher. Although not possessed with lightning speed, Harris runs excellent pass routes and is a clutch, sure-handed receiver. He is the one Herrmann will usually look for in crucial situations.

"Mike is a good receiver," says Coach J. Young. "He is experienced and has grown accustomed to Mark's timing. We expect a lot from our wide receivers and we can count on him getting the job done for us."

Senior wide receiver Raymond Smith possesses probably the most speed of any offensive starter. Smith had an "off" year in '78 after leading the Boilermakers in '77 with 38 catches. Suffering a knee injury just prior to the season opener, Smith was held out until the Notre Dame game. Against the Irish, Smith made a diving catch for a first down at the ND 13-yard line, but separated his shoulder later in the game and sat out the next four outings.

Smith will be the Boilermakers' "deep threat" and has the ability to break a game open with circus-like catches and long runs after he catches the football. A healthy Smith would add a key weapon to Herrmann's already explosive arsenal.

Junior Bart Burrell saw plenty of action at wide receiver a year ago and gathered 31 of his roommate's (Herrmann) passes. He's compared often to the former Colt great Raymond Berry, in the fact that he doesn't possess super speed or size (6-2 and 180) but has the ability to get open and catch anything within reach.

"Bart works the sidelines as well as anybody," explains perimeter coach Ed Zaunbrecher, "and he consistently grades out high. He's an extremely hard worker, always trying to improve himself."

Purdue's starting offensive line, remaining intact from last season, is a veteran unit with three members having played side-by-side for two consecutive years. Dale Schwan (6-4, 230), Pete Quinn (6-2, 245), and Steve McKenzie (6-5, 260) are the senior starters who have logged 17 straight regular assignments. Schwan and McKenzie were all-Big Ten a year ago and will anchor the line from the left guard and right tackle spots, respectively. Both are expected to go high in the 1980 NFL draft.

Quinn, at the pivot, is like most centers who receive little recognition but consistently turn in solid performances. The 245-pound senior was credited with throwing the key block in last year's come-from-behind win over Michigan State, downing two defenders, and springing Russell Pope for a 62-yard romp into the end zone. Quinn is the key to Young's frequently used "shot gun" formation that enables Herrmann to receive the snap from eight yards deep on passing situations.

Quinn missed spring drills this season due to knee surgery involving minor calcium deposits and is expected to be at full speed this summer. Fortunately, his injury was not related to the dreaded cartilage damage that hampers so many top athletes.

Junior left tackle Henry Feil (6-4, 255), who might have been one of the most consistent offensive linemen last season, returns to his spot and has added considerable weight and muscle since the Peach Bowl game.

"Our line did a good job for us last year," offers Coach Young, "but we were able to generate a running attack that helped take some pressure off, especially in pass protection. Nevertheless, the offensive linemen are experienced and barring injury we should be in pretty good shape."

Young's stable of running backs should complement his veteran line, despite the graduation loss of tailback Russell Pope (673 yards on 164 carries). The Boilermakers' leading ground gainer John Macon narrowly missed a 1,000-yard season, rushing for a net 913 yards—an average of 4.1 per carry.

The solid junior tipped the scales at 210 pounds this spring and has worked hard to solidify his fullback spot despite stiff competition. Macon rushed the football a record 33 times against Illinois a year ago for 132 yards earning himself the Chevrolet TV Offensive Player-of-the-Game award.

Macon, last season, saw duty at both running back spots and Young explained that he "would give him the ball 40 times a game if he could." Only a nagging ankle injury kept Macon from eclipsing the 1,000-yard plateau.

During spring drills, it appeared that Macon was slated for full-time duty at the fullback slot. However, he received a battle from senior Mike Augustyniak, who might have won offensive MVP honors last year against arch-rival Indiana while filling in for Macon.

The rugged "Augie" battered Hoosier defenders for 135 yards on 23 carries. He finished the season a distant third on the Boilers' rushing stats with 308 yards. However, he carried just 52 times which computes to just under six yards per carry! Augustyniak is probably Young's best blocking back and is expected to see plenty of duty during the season.

Hard-running sophomore tailback Wally Jones, who like Augustyniak ran rampant against IU by picking up 104 yards overland, operated most of the spring at the tailback position. Jones was an all-stater at Detroit (Mich.) Central High School, and

Dale Schwan Steve Mckenzie John Macon

has his sights set on a starting berth for '79.

A slashing-type runner who runs the ball with reckless abandon, Jones is well aware of a highly-recruited running back with a big reputation expected to join Purdue in the fall. "If he's going to take the starting job," says Jones, "he'll have to earn it."

There is yet another trio of quality backs waiting in Young's paddock. Bobby Williams earned the starting tailback spot last summer and carried 16 times in the season opener against Michigan State before a knee injury forced him to accept 1978 as a red shirt year.

Ben McCall, a hard-working junior, and Dwight Robinson, a senior speedster, join with Williams in trying to impress the staff and earn their spot among the so-called "regulars". McCall and Robinson saw specialty-team duty last year while carrying the ball 35 times.

Defensively, the Boilermakers show vacancies. However, spring drills produced some very pleasant surprises and showed signs that the '79 unit may be even better than the one that just one year previously finished fourth nationally in scoring defense.

Last season's defenders were coined the "Junk Defense" because of their many complicated-looking formations. Young this past spring went so far as to call it "the defense of the future, at least for colleges."

Big Ten statistics a year ago showed that the Boiler "D" ranked just about in the middle of rushing defense, passing defense, and, consequently, total defense. Even the scoring defense (permitting 9.9 points per game for the entire schedule) showed Purdue ranked a close third.

"They may get that two or three yards," explains the brain trust of the "Junk," assistant head coach and defensive coordinator Leon Burtnett, "but that's not going to beat us. The thing that helped us (last season) more than anything else is that our op-

Keena Turner   Ken Loushin

ponents were only successful 19% of the time on third-down situations."

Burtnett and his innovative staff picked and sorted what they liked of defenses from Arkansas, Florida State, and the Dallas Cowboys. Defenses that "give a little, but take a lot."

In 1978, for example, the Junk Defense tackled enemy ball carriers and passers 79 times for a total of 465 yards lost, recovered 18 fumbles, broke up 47 passes, and intercepted 15 more.

"The idea is to cover the linebackers from being blocked out of the play," explains Burtnett, "and to do that you have to take advantage of quickness and strength up front."

Quickness and strength up front is exactly what the Boilermakers have returning for the '79 season. All-Big Ten selections Keena Turner (defensive end) and Ken Loushin (middle guard) will be back along with tackles Marcus Jackson and Calvin Clark, the latter voted the most valuable defender in the Peach Bowl, and veteran linebacker Kevin Motts, Purdue's all-time leading tackler.

Turner's cat-quick speed earned him Purdue's MVP nod last fall along with honorable mention all-America recognition. He and Loushin, the strongest of the strong with a bench press of over 400 pounds, join Jackson and Clark, who may be the best of them all in '79, in forming as formidable a defensive front as there will be in the Big Ten.

Purdue's primary losses this coming season have been in the secondary where three (Willie Harris, Rock Supan, and Rick Moss) regulars completed their collegiate careers in the Peach Bowl. To fill the gap, Young and his staff lured four junior-college transfers from California—a move uncharacteristic of Young but necessary to help complement a very talented and experienced football team.

The *jucos,* however, did not arrive as instant starters. The lone returning regular, Wayne Smith, may be the fastest Boilermaker and should reclaim his cornerback spot. Smith earned the right to be called one of the "most improved" Boilers a year ago and has his sights set on some post-season honors. Numerous times last season, Smith was assigned the opponent's quickest receiver and films showed that nearly as many times, that receiver was switched "away" from the Purdue speedster in the foe's offensive alignment.

A pair of hard-hitting underclassmen will be very difficult to "beat out" for the two safety positions. In fact, Burtnett (who spends the majority of his time with the secondary) offers that "(Bill) Kay and (Tim) Seneff played together the entire season last year and know each other well. We won't be nearly as bad off there as many people think."

Kevin Motts *Calvin Clark* *Marcus Jackson*

Seneff, a sophomore who came to Purdue last season from Merrillville touted as the finest all-round football player in the state of Indiana, is a ferocious tackler and assumed the number one strong safety spot during the spring. Kay, a junior who saw a good deal of action in '78 as the fifth back in a "nickle defense" look, has laid claim to free safety.

The other corner is the one all the transfers have their sights set on. Through the spring workouts, it appeared that Glen Fletcher, a 6-0, 175-pounder from Pasadena (Calif.) City College had the inside track. Just who will open there on September 8th against Wisconsin is anybody's guess. But it's hardly a guess at all that whatever combination does start against the Badgers, it will be a formidable one—regardless of what appears "on paper."

Purdue's kicking game is unquestionably the area hardest hit by graduation. Record-setting Scott Sovereen capably handled the Boilermakers' place and field goal kicking and scoring records going to Atlanta last year for the Peach Bowl game. His absence will be sorely felt.

Although a kicking specialist ranked high on Young's list of recruiting priorities, there are few freshmen who can be expected to step in and perform under the pressures of Big Ten football. Senior John Seibel raised some eyebrows during the spring season with consistency and adequate range. His experience, however, is varsity reserve and only time will tell about his abilities under game conditions.

Punter Dave Eagin, who averaged just over 37 yards a boot last season, has departed, but not before he nearly lost his starting role to freshman Joe Linville. Eagin suffered from inconsistency despite his regular status for two consecutive seasons. Linville punted seven times against Indiana in the regular-season finale, averaging 36.1. His three punts in the Peach Bowl likewise hit for 36 yards each.

Linville has the ability to get his boot off quickly and his hang-time is above average, but he did not have a good spring punting the football because his primary concern was learning quarterback back-up to Mark Herrmann.

Another hazard in the Boilermakers' attempt at an encore of their 9-2-1 season of a year ago is the schedule. Gone are Mid-American foe Ohio University (a team outscored by Purdue 68-7 in the last two campaigns) and Atlantic Coast Conference visitor Wake Forest. Replacing them on the Boiler card will be Oregon and a trip to the West Coast against perennial power and regular bowl participant UCLA. Remaining on the non-conference schedule will be Cotton Bowl champion Notre Dame, which returns 12 starters and is reputed to have recruited one of the top freshmen classes in the nation.

Minnesota will replace Ohio State in '79 for Purdue's always-tough league slate. Defending champion Michigan will be a visitor in Ross-Ade stadium—called a "sand box" by Schembechler—while the Boilermakers must play at Michigan State, a team many feel destined to crack the Ohio State-Michigan dominance.

"We do have a few things going for us this coming year," admits Young, "but our schedule definitely is not one of them. It may be one of the toughest schedules a Purdue team has faced in many, many years."

The prospectus of any college football team is considered incomplete without some mention of the incoming freshmen class. However, football on the level of the Big Ten rarely has a place for the "rookie" to step right in and make immediate contributions. Only too often the so-called "blue chip" athlete has a difficult time making the varsity in his initial season. Similarly, players carrying lesser reputations from prep competition come on to surprise everyone and help fill the void that can make a team a contender.

Again, the term "on paper" must be used in describing a team's freshman group. The Boilermakers are as optimistic about their recruits as any team. In fact, Young calls his incoming class "the finest since I've been a head coach."

The single prepster drawing the most attention has been running back Jimmy Smith (6-2, 190) from Kankakee, Illinois. Reportedly courted by such universities as Oklahoma, Michigan, Alabama, and Southern California, Smith amassed high school statistics that included 25 touchdowns rushing, 2500 yards rushing, 95-yard kick returns, etc. Whether or not he can, in fact, live up to his reputation remains to be seen.

Smith notwithstanding, the best of Young's prize list might be the linemen. It's no secret that the Boilers appear to lack depth along the offensive and defensive lines. Of his 26 signees, 14 are linemen. If size means anything, they average 6-4 and 244 pounds. Heading the list might be Tom Jelesky, from Merrillville, Indiana Jelesky's signing marks the third straight time Young has nabbed the Hoosier state's top prospect. (Seneff and Herrmann are the other two.)

A trio of linemen may deserve special mention based on their high school careers and what college recruiters evaluated. Claybon Fields (6-7, 270) played at Woodson High School in Washington D.C., Mark Rawls (6-5, 230) from General Braddock High School in Pittsburgh, and Leonard Scott (6-4, 235) who started at Dunbar H.S. in Chicago all are expected to provide immediate depth in Purdue's defensive line.

Thanks to the 9-2-1 Peach Bowl champion Boilermakers of last fall and the Big Ten tri-champion (and National Invitation Tournament finalist) basketball Boilermakers of last winter, interest in athletics at Purdue never has been higher!!!

The feverish interest and anticipation for the proverbial "next year," which for Purdue means the return of most of the starters from both teams, has moved Boilermaker athletics close to the top of the mountain that success in major-college athletics has become.

More people saw Purdue play football in Ross-Ade Stadium in 1978 than ever had before; more people saw Purdue play basketball in Mackey Arena in 1978-79 than ever had before. It should be more of the same in 1979-80!!

And why not? With last year's Big Ten Coach-of-the-Year (Young) coaching and a bonafide all-America quarterback (Herrmann) throwing, the football potential at Purdue for the near future is as high as the sky.

A 9-2-1 season and a convincing bowl victory is hard to better ...but it can be done. At Purdue, it just might be done this fall.

Head Coach Jim Young

Jim Young—two words now synonymous with winning football teams and soaring attendance throughout the college football world.

No longer a rookie Big Ten head coach, the 42-year-old Young completed his second tour of duty in the nation's premier football conference last fall.

What a year it was! After taking over a program in December of 1976 that had enjoyed but one winning season since 1969, Young was certain he'd have the Boilermakers back to winning ways before long! Fans, alumni, and media alike sat back to give him the time to get the job done. He gave himself no time.

The result was a glittering 9-2-1 record in 1978 in his second season, including a 41-21 thrashing of Georgia Tech in the Peach Bowl last Christmas Day, Purdue's first bowl appearance since 1967 and only the school's second in 92 years of football. And for the second consecutive year, more fans (373,504) came to see the Jim Young-coached Boilermakers play in Purdue's Ross-Ade Stadium than ever had before.

No one should have been too surprised at the almost instant success. Young has the winning football bloodline to prove there is wisdom in his ways!

Six seasons ago, Young undertook a similar undertaking at the University of Arizona. Bound and determined to turn the Wildcats' football fortunes around, Young did just that in his first season, the first of four he spent at the Tucson school.

Picked to finish fourth in the Western Athletic Conference (WAC) that year in pre-season polls, Arizona tied Arizona State for the conference championship. It was Arizona's best performance ever in the WAC, and the 8-3 overall record tied the school record for victories in a season.

As if to prove the first-year accomplishment was no fluke, Young's teams produced back-to-back 9-2 seasons the next two years and reset the school record for victories in a season. Arizona was ranked in the nation's Top 20 for each of those first three years and Young was the only coach in the last decade to beat arch rival Arizona State.

As a result of Young's success (31-13 in four seasons), attendance soared at Arizona and a 17,000-seat stadium addition was built, bringing the capacity in Arizona Stadium to 57,000, the largest in the WAC.

His record as a winner goes back to his high school days. After earning all-state honors as a fullback at Van Wert (Ohio) High, he attended Ohio State University and played on the 1954 national championship team. The following year he transferred to Bowling Green University with his backfield coach Doyt Perry. It was during his career at Bowling Green that Young met Bo Schembechler, then line coach for the Falcons.

Young's first job was a wrestling, track and assistant football coach at Findlay (Ohio) College. Even though he had no experience in wrestling, his team was 11-0. His track team was 8-2 and won the conference championship.

He returned to Bowling Green as wrestling coach and freshman football coach. His football team had a winning season and his wrestling team won the Mid-American Conference championship.

Young then became football coach at Lima (Ohio) Shawnee High School, where his teams posted a 28-10-2 composite record and won two league titles in four years. At one point, his teams won 23 straight games. His 1963 team averaged 44.3 points per game.

Schembechler, who in the meantime had become head coach at Miami of Ohio, asked Young to join him as an assistant. The two were associated in coaching for the next nine years.

During that time, Schembechler-Young coached teams were 73-19-1 for a .784 winning percentage. Young served in almost every assistant coach capacity—freshman, defensive secondary, offensive line, offensive backfield, offensive coordinator and defensive coordinator.

When the two moved on to the University of Michigan, Young was defensive coordinator for five years and his defenders were second nationally in total defense in 1971, first in the nation against the score in both '71 and '72, fifth nationally in pass defense and second nationally overall in 1972.

When Schembechler was hospitalized with a mild heart attack in Pasadena, California, Young assumed head coaching responsibilities for the Wolverines in the 1970 Rose Bowl game.

His coaching philosophy is based on execution of basic fundamentals, a sound defense, a diversified offense, and a good kicking game.

For example, his 1975 offense at Arizona averaged 30 points per game, was ranked fifth nationally in total offense, yet had the fewest turnovers in the nation (nine).

Young and his wife Jane have five children: Laura, 20; Elaine, 17; Joan, 16; Colleen, 12; and James Jr., 4.

1979 Purdue Freshman and Transfer Students

Name	Pos.	Ht.	Wt.	Hometown	High School, Coach
Scott Craig	WR	6-1	185	Palos Heights, Ill.	St. Rita, Pat Cronin
Jim Detmer	DL	6-5	240	Chicago, Illinois	Prosser, Pete Ebner
Walt Drapeza	PK	6-1	205	Goshen, Indiana	Goshen, Ken Mirer
Claybon Fileds	OL/DL	6-7	270	Washington, D.C.	Woodson, Bob Headen
*Glen Fletcher	DB	6-0	173	Pasadena, California	Pasadena, Tom Hamilton
Larry Gates	QB	6-4	180	Cincinnati, Ohio	Moeller, Gerry Faust
Andy Gladstone	TE	6-3	215	St. Louis, Missouri	Lindberg, Stan Mach
Matt Hernandez	OL	6-6	255	East Detroit, Mich.	East Detroit, Al Torp
‡‡David Hill	DB	6-0	180	San Francisco, Ca.	Balboa, Archie Chagonjian
Tom Jelesky	TE	6-6	260	Merrillville, Indiana	Merrillville, Ken Haupt
Eric Jordan	RB	6-1	185	Las Vegas, Nevada	Chapperal, John Chura
Bob Lashley	DB	6-3	195	Mt. Clemens, Mich.	Mt. Clemens, Richard Chapman
Brian Liston	DL	6-4	235	Palos Heights, Ill.	Marist, Tony Pietrzak
**James Looney	LB	5-11	230	Los Angeles, Ca.	Crenshaw, Jim Brown
Casey Moore	DL	6-1	240	Youngstown, Ohio	Ursuline, Jim Maughn
Bob Nommensen	RB	6-3	225	Palos Hills, Illinois	Stagg, Henry Meier
Jim Owen	RB	6-2	195	Olmsted Falls, Ohio	Olmstead Falls, Dick Cromwell
†Larry Perry	DB	6-0	170	Tustin, California	Bay Shore (N.Y.), Joe Erickson
Bob Pickering	LB	6-2	215	Broadview Hgts., Oh	Brecksville, Joe Vadini
Chris Prince	DL	6-3	265	Upper Marlboro, Md	Roosevelt, James Tillerson
Mark Rawls	DL	6-5	230	Braddock, Pa.	General Braddock, Charles Thomas
David Retherford	WR	6-0	170	Tampa, Florida	Jesuit, Bill Minahan
Paul Royer	OL	6-2	222	Euclid, Ohio	St. Joseph, Bill Gutbrod
‡Don Schwer	OL	6-2	247	Beecher, Illinois	Sandburg, Cliff Eade
Leonard Scott	DL	6-4	235	Chicago, Illinois	Dunbar, Bob Hunter
Vic Senk	DL	6-4	225	Girard, Ohio	Girard, Charles Jamieson
Ron Serluco	OL	6-5	245	Miami, Florida	Columbus, Dave Riley
Jimmy Smith	RB	6-0	190	Kankakee, Illinois	Westview, Bill Wendling
Keith Spaeth	OL	6-3	240	Hamilton, Ohio	Badin, Terry Malone
Don Stockton	QB	6-3	190	West Chicago, Ill.	West Chicago, Larry Parker
**Robert Thomas	DB	6-1	188	Los Angeles, Ca.	Washington, Ron Fowlkes

* Pasadena City College transfer.
** Los Angeles Southwest Junior College transfer.
† Santa Ana Junior College transfer.
‡ Joliet Junior College transfer.
‡‡ San Francisco Junior College transfer.

WISCONSIN *Badgers*

Coach Dave McClain's first Wisconsin football team in 1978 produced a winning season — 5-4-2 — the Badgers first since 1974, and only the second since 1963.

A total of 32 lettermen return to form the nucleus of Wisconsin's 1979 football squad and the Badger mentor will be looking for some surprises to fill the void left by graduation, injuries and ineligibility.

McClain contends, "You can't win football games unless you can play defense."

He points out, "I don't care what sport it is — football, hockey, baseball, whatever. When you keep the opponent out of the end zone or off the bases or out of the net, then you've got a chance to win."

As he looks forward to 1979, McClain notes, "I'm concerned about our defense. We're thin in a lot of places."

Wisconsin's secondary is depleted. Gone are starters like All-American Lawrence Johnson, Greg Gordon, Scott Erdmann (lost by injury in the fourth game of 1978), and Dan Schieble.

Dan Relich, a second time All-Big Ten choice at middle guard, has completed his eligibility.

Outstanding linebackers Dave Crossen and Kurt Holm are also gone.

A total of fifteen lettermen from last year's team return to man the defensive platoon.

They include outside linebackers Dave Ahrens, Guy Boliaux, Don Lorenz, and Jeff Vine; inside linebackers Dennis Christenson and Dave Levenick; tackles Curt Blaskowski, Thomas Houston, Tom Schremp and Bruce Woodford; and defensive backs Ross Anderson, Mickey Casey, Terry Stroede and George Welch.

Ahrens played superbly for the Badgers during his freshman and sophomore seasons until sidelined by injury in the second to last game of 1978 at Iowa. He was named to the Freshman All-American team as picked by FOOTBALL NEWS in 1977. Playing in ten games he was credited with 50 solo tackles and 36 assists in 1978 to go along with 28 solo tackles and 40 assisted stops as a 1977 freshman.

Christenson, at inside linebacker, ranked fifth in tackles last year with 38 solo and 35 assisted tackles.

Schremp performed steadily at left tackle with 37 solo and 20 assisted stops, while Cabral and Blaskowski shared starting

Dave Ahrens    *Tom Shremp*    *Mike Kalasmiki*

assignments on the right side of the defensive line. Cabral turned in 25 solo and 17 assisted tackles and had a single game high for the Badgers last year with three tackles for loss (14 yards total) at Northwestern.

Both Ross Anderson and George Welch were starters in the secondary in 1978. Welch had 49 tackles — 26 of them solo — while Anderson's 41 tackles numbered 25 solo.

Help will be available from a group of redshirts — 1978 freshmen with potential who sat out last year gaining maturity — with defensive possibilities being Mark Shumate at tackle; Willie Collins at middle guard; and Vaughn Thomas, Nick Savage, Richard Wray, and Dan Messenger in the secondary.

Offensively, there are holes to fill, too.

The Badgers lost their top rusher — Ira Matthews — and their top pass receiver — David Charles — plus the heart of the offensive line in center Jim Moore, guards Brad Jackomino and Pat Kelly and left tackle Dave Krall.

The most valuable player of the 1978 season — quarterback Mike Kalasmiki — couldn't practice with the Badgers in their spring drills because he had to make up scholastic deficiencies at Madison Area Technical College.

Injuries to tackle Jerry Doerger and quarterback Jeff Buss force them to miss the spring drills, too.

Matthews paced the Badgers in rushing in 1978 — 654 yards on 130 carries — and was first in the nation in punt returns (he had led the nation in kickoff returns in 1976) — and accounted for 1,185 all-purpose yards last season and 3,700 during his career to rank second on Wisconsin's all-time list in that category. He'll be sorely missed.

David Charles caught 38 passes for 573 yards and five scores in 1978 and completed his career as a Badger third on the all-time pass catching list with 101 receptions for 1,459 yards and 11 touchdowns.

Kalasmiki came off the bench in the third game of the season — Oregon — to pass the Badgers to an exciting 22-19 come-from-behind victory over the Ducks and went on to start seven of the final eight games finishing as Wisconsin's most valuable player and among the nation's leading passers — 11.9 completions per game.

A total of 17 lettermen, including kicking specialists John Kiltz and Steve Veith, form the offensive nucleus.

Receivers returning include tight end Ray Sydnor and flanker

Ray Sydnor  *Ray Snell*

Tom Stauss   *John Josten*  *Wayne Souza*

Wayne Souza who caught 27 and 24 passes, respectively in 1978. Sydnor had 392 yards on his receptions and a pair of touchdowns, while Souza's catches totalled 323 yards and three scores.

Others include Tim Stracka, who caught four passes for 68 yards and touchdowns on his first two collegiate catches; Tom Braker, Mike Krepfle, and Joe Ruetz.

Interior linemen returning include Ray Snell, Steve Namnick, and Jerry Doerger (out of spring drills with injury) at tackles; Jim Martine at guard, and Joe Rothbuaer at center.

McClain points out, "Up front, we're thin again." He's hoping some of the incoming freshmen will come in and push real hard for starting assignments.

John Josten returns at quarterback for his sophomore season after four starts as a freshman — he was hurt early in the Oregon game — while fullback Tom Stauss and Tailback Dave Mohapp also return.

Stauss was Wisconsin's second leading rusher last year with 485 yards on 82 carries, including two games — Northwestern and Minnesota — of over 100 yards gained.

Mohapp gained 158 yards on 34 carries playing behind Ira Matthews at tailback.

One position switch to be made in spring drills finds Stauss moving to tailback and Mohapp to fullback — both as regulars. Curtis Richardson, who saw some action as a freshman, is also in the picture. McClain points out that the three will interchange, each learning both positions.

Redshirts from 1978 who should help offensively are Jeff Luko at guard; Ron Versnik at center, and Scott Moeschl at quarterback.

The Wisconsin coach also looks for help from two junior college transfers, both of whom participated in spring drills. They are Tom Reber at offensive tackle, and Tom Dalgleish at tight end.

McClain commented, "Another big problem is Kalasmiki (Mike) not being in spring practice. But it will give us a good chance to look at Josten, Moeschl (Scott), and Parish (Steve)."

The latter (Parish) is a transfer from Kansas State — he prepped at Evansville, Wisconsin — who is reputed to be a fine passer. He sat out last year after transferring and picked up much experience directing the Badgers' scout team.

The kicking game returns John Kiltz, a junior, who averaged 37.6 yards punting and Steve Veith, a placekicking specialist who was 2-for-8 in field goal tries last year after going 9 of 17 as a 1977 sophomore.

Help from both Wisconsin's offensive and defensive units could be coming from among the freshmen recruited by McClain and his staff during the winter.

"I think a lot of those freshmen will come in and push real hard. Hopefully, by the middle of the season some will mature and be able to play quite a bit of football for us. I think a lot of these freshmen can play. But you're not going to win in the Big Ten with freshmen."

McClain's recruiting efforts centered around big, rangy offensive linemen, a solid crops of linebackers, and some elusive, hard-running backs.

Among the offensive linemen recruited are Dan Berriman 6-3, 240; Robert Budde, 6-5, 255; Doug Fouty, 6-3, 255; Mark Orszula, 6-4, 240; Pete Severson, 6-3, 220; Jim Straka, 6-7, 235; Mark Subach 6-3,

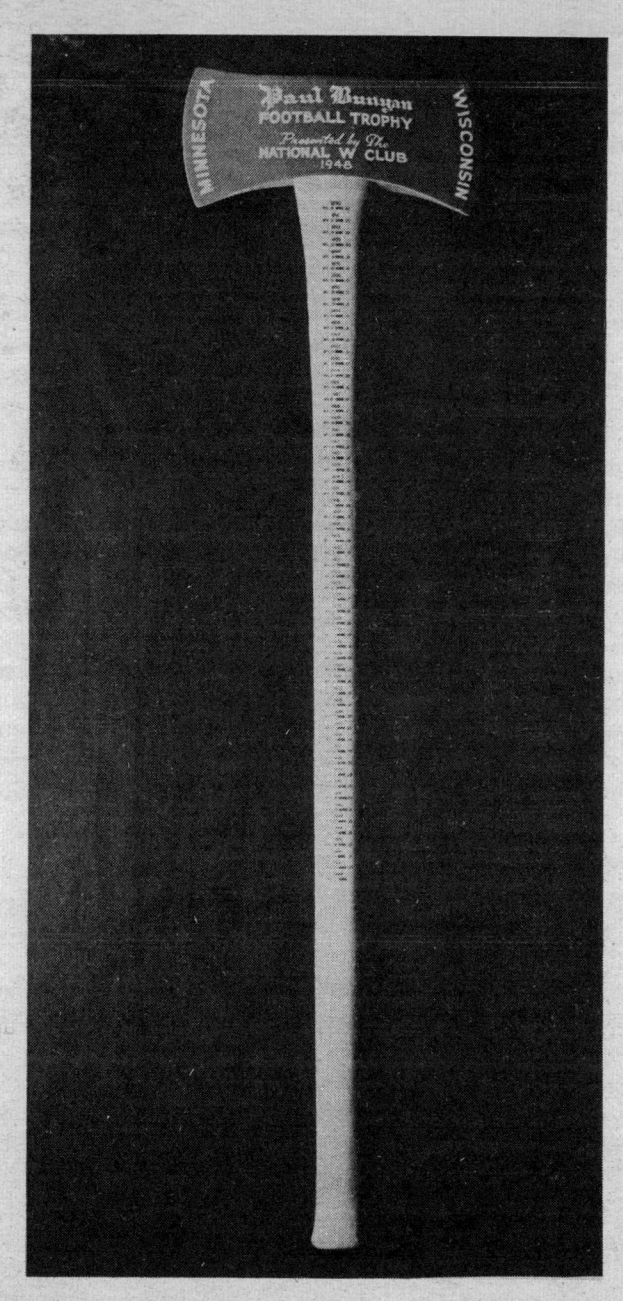

Paul Bunyan Axe, Trophy for which Wisconsin and Minnesota compete each year.

230; and Bob Winckler, 6-4, 255.

The linebackers include four Wisconsin all-staters — Kyle Borland, 6-3, 205; Mike Herrington, 6-4, 220; Tim Krumrie, 6-2, 230; and Ed Senn, 6-4, 221. From out-of-state comes Frank Fulco, 6-3, 220, the Maryland High School "Player of the Year", and Jody O'Donnell, 6-3, 215, from Lockport, Il.

The running backs include Chucky Davis, 6-2, 210; Troy King, 5-10, 175; Marvin Neal, 5-10, 170; Clint Sims, 5-11, 185; Mike Stassi, 5-11, 188; and John Williams, 6-1, 185, along with fullback Gerald Green, 6-2, 230.

Receivers recruited include tight ends Wally Malone, 6-5, 219; and Bob Gallmeier, 6-3, 220; and wide receiver Sankar Montoute, 6-5, 205, while defensive linemen include Tom Baldwin, 6-4, 220, Tom Booker, 6-4, 230; Gerald Queener, 6-2, 230, and Mark Tryon, 6-5, 200.

David Greenwood, 6-3, 195 from Park Falls, WI., was the lone defensive back recruited.

McClain notes, "We think we've had a good recruiting year. I wouldn't say great, but a good year. We should have a competitive football team.

"We've got some skill but it's all going to depend a lot on how some of these young people are going to come in and help us because injuries always take their toll. You lose an Ahrens, or a Schremp, and somebody has to step in there. That's the whole problem we had last year. Depth again is going to be a problem."

1979
ILLINOIS ALPHABETICAL TEAM ROSTER

NO.	NAME	POS.	HT.	WT.	'79 CLASS	HOMETOWN
37	Adams, Earnest	OLB	6-3	205	Jr.	Ft. Lauderdale, Fla.
61	Antonacci, Rich	OG	6-3	246	Jr.	Chicago
84	Atkins, Kelvin	OLB	6-4	220	So.	Orlando, FL.
51	Barry, Joe	LB	6-1	200	So.	Chicago
71	Belmont, Lou	OT	6-4	255	So.	Northfield
83	Blalock, Harold	OLB	6-3	205	So.	Chicago
63	Boeke, Greg	C	6-4	230	Jr.	Winnebago
80	Boeke, Leroy	TE	6-4	225	Jr.	Winnebago
15	Bonner, Bonji	DHB	6-3	210	So.	St. Louis, MO.
73	Brown, Reggie	OG	6-3½	220	Jr.	Maywood
31	Burgard, Pete	MG	6-4	220	So.	Ypsilanti, Mich.
50	Byrne, John	LB	5-11	190	Jr.	Wilmette, IL.
58	Carmien, Tab	OLB	6-2	200	Jr.	St. Joseph
90	Carr, Chris	TE	6-4	226	Sr.	Kettering, OH
60	Carrington, Mike	OG	6-2	236	So.	Chicago
74	Coady, Tom	OT	6-2	260	Jr.	Greendale, WI.
98	Cozen, Doug	TE	6-3	215	Sr.	Oaklawn, IL.
25	Curtis, Joe	TB	6-0	175	So.	Chicago
28	Dismuke, Mark	TB	5-8	173	So.	Peoria
95	Doney, Scott	MG	5-11	205	Sr.	Mt. Prospect, IL.
66	Durrell, Kenny	MG	6-4	230	So.	Chicago
49	Dwyer, Dave	LB	6-2	230	Jr.	Hillside
1	Finzer, David	P	6-0	188	Jr.	Chicago
52	Flynn, Dennis	DT	6-3	235	Jr.	Munster, Ind.
36	Foster, Greg	FL	6-2	205	Jr.	St. Louis, MO.
6	George, Rick	DHB	6-1	180	So.	Collinsville
38	Gillen, John	LB	6-3	215	Jr.	Arlington Hts.
87	Gillen, Ken	DT	6-4	220	So.	Arlington Hts.
45	Hauser, Bob	LB	6-3	210	Sr.	La Crosse, WI.
54	Helle, Mark	C	6-2	230	So.	Edwardsville
48	Holm, Tim	DHB	6-2	190	Sr.	Ellsworth, KS.
5	Holmes, Mike	TB	6-3	210	Jr.	Chicago
35	Janus, Shawn	WR	6-2	185	Jr.	Chicago Hts., IL.
3	Jones, Cliff	K	5-11	185	Jr.	Tuscola
27	Kelly, Dave	DHB	6-0	194	Sr.	LaGrange
68	Kolloff, Tom	OT	6-4	249	Sr.	Chicago
21	Levitt, Lloyd	DHB	6-2	185	Sr.	Chicago
13	Lopez, John	WR	6-3	180	So.	Elk Grove
99	MacLean, Dan	LB	6-2	205	Sr.	Southfield, Mich
9	McAvoy, Tim	OB	6-4	201	Jr.	Chicago
53	McBeth, Mike	OG	6-2	227	Sr.	Dayton, OH.
76	McClure, Bob	OG	6-1	223	Sr.	Ladue, MO.
11	McCullough, Lawr.	OB	6-2	190	Sr.	Jacksonville, Fla.
62	McMillin, Troy	OG	6-3	230	Jr.	DeKalb
30	Moton, Jay	DB	6-0	186	So.	Peoria
79	Moton, Joe	DT	6-4	225	So.	Peoria
69	Mulchrone, John	LB	6-2	220	Jr.	Chicago

#	Name	Pos	Ht	Wt	Yr	Hometown
57	Mulchrone, Pete	LB	6-2	217	So.	Chicago
46	Murphy, Mike	FB	5-9	195	So.	Chicago
29	Mitchell, Eldridge	DHB	6-3	200	So.	Memphis, Tenn.
56	Noelke, Bob	OG	6-3	235	Sr.	Glen Ellyn
72	Norman, Tim	OT	6-6	265	Jr.	Winfield
78	Pavesic, Ray	DT	6-2	220	Sr.	Harvey
20	Perez, Dave	TB	5-8	190	So.	Carol Stream
26	Powell, Larry	TB	5-11	176	Sr.	Newport News, VA.
59	Priebe, Mike	OT	6-4	243	Sr.	Normal (Community)
86	Ralph, Stanley	MG	6-3	235	Sr.	Hempstead, N.Y.
94	Ramshaw, Jerry	OLB	6-4	217	Sr.	Champaign (Centennial)
40	Risley, John	QB	6-1	197	Jr.	St. Joseph, IL.
39	Scholz, Scott	LB	6-2	210	Sr.	Schaumburg, IL.
92	Scott, John	OLB	6-3	215	Jr.	Lockport
12	Shaw, Kenny	QB	6-1	175	So.	Orlando, Fla.
81	Sherrod, Mike	TE	6-6	225	Sr.	Robbins
19	Shea, Dan	MG	5-10	205	So.	Chicago
70	Smith, Bobby	LB	6-2	227	Sr.	Toledo, OH.
10	Sowa, Nick	QB	6-1	191	Sr.	Chicago
34	Squirek, Jack	OLB	6-4	220	So.	Cuyahoga Hts., OH
23	Strader, Wayne	FB	6-3	215	Jr.	Geneseo
42	Thomas, Calvin	FB	6-0	220	So.	St. Louis
7	Venegoni, John	W	6-1	200	Jr.	Peoria
43	Walsh, Mark	LB	5-10	195	So.	Tupelo, Miss.
14	Weiss, Rich	QB	6-1	205	Jr.	Winnetka
93	Wilson, Darryl	OLB	6-4	235	So.	University City, MO.
16	Worthy, Tyrone	DHB	6-0	190	So.	Detroit, Mich.

ILLINOIS FRESHMAN TEAM ROSTER

NAME	POS.	HT.	WT.	HOMETOWN (High School)
Boettle, Troy	OT	6-5"	220	Gurnee (Warren)
Brookins, Mitchell	TB	6-0"	175	Chicago (Phillips)
Brooks, Terry	TB	6-0"	185	Rock Island (Rock Island)
Clear, Samuel	DB	6-2"	185	Chicago (Martin Luther King)
Daniel, Cullen	WR	6-2"	185	Lima, OH (Lima)
Daugherty, Tory	DT	6-4"	240	Washington (Washington)
Finis, Marty	OG	6-2"	240	Palatine (Fremd)
Gregus, Dan	DT	6-5"	235	Burbank (St. Laurence)
Griffin, John	W	6-2"	205	Rockford (East)
Hahn, Rick	OT	6-7"	260	Lombard (Glenbard East)
Hallberg, Tom	OLB	6-3"	200	Rockford (Jefferson)
Hofer, Lance	QB	6-2"	185	Geneseo (Geneseo)
Larsen, Randy	TB	6-1"	195	Detroit, Mich. (Catholic Central)
Lingner, Adam	C	6-5"	210	Rock Island (Aleman)
Martin, Mike	WR	5-10"	165	Washington, D.C. (Eastern)
McDonald, Ken	DB	6-3"	190	Schiller Park (East Leyden)
Moraska, Tom	DT	6-5"	220	Rockford (Jefferson)
Navarro, Armando	K	5-8"	160	Aurora (West)
Reed, James	WR	6-3"	195	Detroit, Mich. (Rockford Auburn)
Scarcelli, Tony	OLB	6-4"	215	Detroit, Mich. (Warren Woods)
Singbush, Norm	WR	6-2"	180	Geneseo (Geneseo)

Slipetz, Carl	DT	6-10"	280	Toronto, Ontario (York Memorial)
Thomas, W.J.	TB	6-2"	190	St. Louis, MO (Hazelwood)
Zirbel, Craig	DB	6-0"	185	Burbank (St. Laurence)

JUNIOR COLLEGE TRANSFER

Dentino, Greg	WR	6-1"	195	Peoria (Independence J.C. - Independence, KS)

1979
INDIANA ALPHABETICAL TEAM ROSTER

(* Denotes letters won)

	Player	Pos.	Ht.	Wt.	Age	Class	Hometown-High School
	Adams, Duff	T	6-3	220	17	Fr.	Dayton, O. (Meadowdale)
	Ahrens, Tony	RB	5-9	175	20	So.	Jasper (Garden City Kan. JC)
*	Ahting, Gerhard	T	6-5	256	21	Jr.	Cincinnati, O. (Sycamore)
*	Alexander, Chuck	FB	5-10	188	21	Sr.	Mishawaka
	Angelo, Michael	DT	6-3	245	18	Fr.	Pittsburgh, PA. (Peabody)
**	Arbuckle, Aaron	LB	6-3	220	21	Sr.	Greenwood (Center Grove)
	Ball, Kenneth	DT	6-2	245	19	So.	Cincinnati, O. (Purcell) (Garden City, Kan. JC)
*	Bowers, Jerry	RB	6-0	199	21	Jr.	Chapin, S.C.
	Boyd, John	WR	6-3	190	18	Fr.	New Castle
	Brooks, Glenn	RB	5-9	176	19	So.	Louisville, Ky. (Valley)
	Brown, Greg	T	6-4	220	20	Sr.	Dayton, O.
	Burke, Kevin	RB	6-0	205	19	So.	Silver Springs, Md. (Northwood)
	Burtis, Christ	DE	6-2	229	19	So.	Hamilton, O. (Taft)
	Cameron, Cam	QB	6-3	180	18	Fr.	Terre Haute (South)
	Christy, Al	RB	5-11	195	18	Fr.	Westerville, O. (North)
	Claussen, Chris	DB	5-8	182	21	Sr.	Hinsdale, Ill.
*	Clifford, Tim	QB	6-1	200	20	Jr.	Cincinnati, O. (Colerain)
	Corso, Steve	WR	5-11	162	20	Sr.	Bloomington (North)
	Cross, Mike	G	6-0	220	21	Sr.	Cincinnati, O. (LaSalle)
	Darring, Al	DB	6-0	196	21	Jr.	Indianapolis (North Central)
	Davis, Ralph	DB	5-11	165	20	Jr.	Northbrook, Ill. (Glenbrook North)
*	DeBord, Eric	DE	5-11	208	20	Jr.	Gaston (Wes Del)
	DeVault, Brett	QB	6-2	198	21	Sr.	Evansville (Mater Dei)
**	D'Orazio, Tony	FB	6-0	210	22	Sr.	Chicago Hts., Ill. (Homewood-Flossmoor)
	Dugan, Tim	G	6-2	230	18	Sr.	Cincinnati, O. (Moeller)
	Evans, Greg	K	5-8	151	21	Jr.	Bloomington (South)
	Evans, Marlin	LB	6-2	209	19	So.	Cincinnati, O. (Aiken)
***	Fishel, Mark	WR	6-0	179	22	Sr.	Martinsville
**	Flemming, Marlon	T	6-2	310	22	Jr.	Evansville (Reitz)
*	Friede, Mike	WR	6-4	192	22	Sr.	Goodland, Kan. (Garden City, Kan., JC)
	Frye, Kevin	DE	6-1	210	21	Jr.	Elwood
	Galloway, Terry	RB	5-9	182	20	Jr.	Columbus, O.

	Name	Pos	Ht	Wt	Age	Yr	Hometown
	Gannon, Charles	T	6-6	255	18	Fr.	Ypsilanti, Mich.
	Gedman, Jeff	DB	5-11	178	19	Fr.	Duquesne, Pa.
	Gianakopoulos, George	T	6-3	235	18	Fr.	Park Ridge, Ill. (Maine South)
	Goldin, Jeff	G	6-2	233	21	Sr.	Los Angeles, CA (Eagle rock)
	Gray, Stoner	DB	6-2	170	19	So.	Evansville (North)
*	Harangody, Dave	TE	6-4	245	21	Jr.	Whiting
**	Harkrader, Mike	RB	5-7	180	21	Jr.	Middletown, O. (Fenwick)
	Harkrader, Robert	RB	5-9	182	18	Fr.	Middletown, O. (Fenwick)
	Huck, Chad	FL	6-1	189	20	Jr.	Indianapolis (Roncalli)
	Hueser, Steve	T	6-3	262	18	Fr.	Chicago, Ill.
*	Iatarola, Bob	T	6-2	245	22	Sr.	Gary (Andrean)
	Johnson, Lonnie	FB	6-1	204	20	Jr.	Akron, O. (North)
*	Johnson, Mark	G	6-3	258	21	Sr.	Cincinnati, O. (Anderson)
	Kalil, Fred	LB	5-9	190	20	Jr.	Mishawaka
	Kazanowski, Mike	FB	6-2	210	18	Fr.	Dearborn, Mich.
	Kellogg, Kevin	K	6-0	193	21	Jr.	Attica, N.Y.
	Kenley, Kevin	LB	6-2	218	20	So.	Columbus, O. (Mifflin) (Garden City, Kan., JC)
	King, Kevin	DE	6-1	220	18	Fr.	Bloomington (South)
	Lawson, Randy	DT	6-3	235	19	So.	Union Mills (Garden City, Kan. JC)
	Longshore, Marc	DB	6-0	185	19	So.	Massillon, O.
*	Lovett, Larry	P	6-2	169	22	Sr.	Pointblank, Tex. (Coldpsring)
*	Lundy, Nate	WR	6-0	160	20	Jr.	Chicago, Ill. (Community)
	Madlung, Jerry	DT	6-0	235	22	Sr.	Lafayette (Garden City, Kan., JC)
	Marchewka, Mike	TE	6-5	220	18	Fr.	Palatine, Ill. (Frend)
	Michalek, Tony	DE	6-1	217	19	So.	Midlothian, Ill. (Brother Rice)
*	Michko, Gerald	T	6-3	257	20	Sr.	Chicago, Ill. (DeSales)
	Mills, Dennis	C	6-1	225	18	Fr.	Martinsville
	Mineo, John	RB	6-1	215	18	Fr.	Chesterfield, Mo.
	Mitchell, Steve	DB	6-0	177	19	So.	Washington, D.C. (Dunbar)
	Moorman, Steve	MG	6-3	235	18	Fr.	Owensboro, Ky. (Catholic)
*	Oakley, Darrell	DE	6-3	208	21	Sr.	Wichita, Kan. (Garden City, Kan., JC)
	Otto, Mike	T	6-4	261	21	Jr.	Indianapolis (Franklin Central)
**	Patton, Mel	G	5-9	216	22	Sr.	Milwaukee, Wis. (Tech)
	Pennick, Ron	DB	5-9	165	20	Jr.	Chicago, Ill. (Vocational)
***	Phipps, Jeff	G	6-2	225	21	Sr.	Evansville (Central)
*	Ramsey, Dart	DB	6-2	191	19	So.	Dayton, O. (Alter)
*	Ramsey, Mark	LB	6-3	222	20	Jr.	Dayton, O. (Alter)
	Rodriguez, Mark	OT	6-0	265	19	So.	Indianapolis (Lawrence North)
	Rohan, Matt	TE	6-4	232	21	Sr.	Chicago, Ill. (Leo)
	Rohe, Steve	TE	6-2	218	18	Fr.	Cincinnati, O. (Elder)
	Roggeman, John	RB	5-10	180	18	Fr.	Mishawaka
	Sakanich, James	G-T	6-2	230	18	Fr.	West Homestead, Pa. (Steel Valley)
	Sizemore, Duane	G	6-4	230	18	Fr.	Osceola (Penn)
	Smith, Denver	MG	6-0	242	20	So.	Dayton, O. (Meadowdale)
	Smith, Steve	RB	6-1	200	18	Fr.	Englewood, O.
	Smythe, Mark	DT	6-3	242	18	Fr.	Bloomington (North)
	Sparks, Ozie	LB	6-0	195	20	So.	Duquesne, Pa.
	Speer, Kevin	C-T	6-4	240	20	Jr.	Evansville (Harrison)
*	Stephenson, Robert	TE	6-3	229	20	So.	Evansville (Reitz)
**	Stewart, Dave	DE	5-10	222	21	Sr.	Terre haute (North)
*	Straub, Steve	K	5-10	182	21	Sr.	Indianapolis (North Central)

	Player	Pos	Ht.	Wt.	Year	Hometown (High School)
	Sutor, Mark	QB	6-3	195	18 Fr.	Hickory Hills, Ill.
*	Tallen, Terry	MG-DT	6-0	227	20 Jr.	Hamilton, O. (Badin)
	Taylor, John	MG	6-1	233	20 Jr.	Fort Wayne (Homestead)
	Taylor, Robert	RB	6-0	205	19 Fr.	Beaver Falls, Pa. (Riverside)
	Tillery, Bob	DT	6-2	252	22 Sr.	Indianapolis (Ben Davis)
	Tillery, Steve	LB	6-1	222	21 Jr.	Indianapolis (Ben Davis)
**	Tisdale, Brent	DE	6-4	238	20 Jr.	Cleveland, O. (Shaw)
	Walden, Rodney	T	6-6	265	25 So.	Indianapolis (Arlington) (Garden City, Kan., JC)
*	Wallace, Lucky	C	6-2	238	20 Jr.	Cincinnati, O. (Glen Este)
	Walls, Craig	LB	6-1	210	19 So.	Pittsburgh, Pa. (Peabody)
	Wiebell, Jeff	C	6-3	205	18 Fr.	Cincinnati, O. (Moeller)
	Weinberg, James	WR-DB	5-11	175	18 Fr.	Palatine, Ill. (Frend)
	Weir, Dave	DB	6-0	183	19 So.	West Homestead, Pa. (Steel Valley)
*	Weissert, Steve	MG	6-0	243	22 Sr.	Fort Wayne (Dwenger)
*	Wilbur, Tim	DB	6-0	182	19 So.	Indianapolis (Ben Davis)
*	Willhite, Randy	LB	6-1	227	21 Sr.	Lebanon (Iowa Lakes JC)
	Young, Marty	DT	6-2	245	20 Jr.	Oscaloosa, La. (Tyler, Tex. JC)
	Zeolli, Dave	DB	6-2	180	19 So.	Jeannette, Pa. (Penn-Trafford)

1979
IOWA ALPHABETICAL TEAM ROSTER

(* Denotes letters won)

	Player	Pos	Ht.	Wt.	Year	Hometown (High School)
	Brad Ahearn	OG	6-1	211	Soph.	Cedar Rapids, IA (Regis)
	Steve Allison	QB	6-3	199	Jun.	Fairfield, IA (Pekin-Packwood)
	Joe Aulisi	DB	6-0	179	Soph.	South Orange, NJ (Seton Hall)
	Marty Ball	FB	6-1	197	Soph.	Dubuque, IA (Hempstead)
*	Phil Blatcher	RB	5-9	179	Soph.	New Orleans, LA (St. Augustine)
	Jeff Bobek	LB	6-1	216	Sen.	Clinton, IA (Clinton)
	Bill Bradley	DE	6-2	219	Soph.	Cedar Falls, IA (Cedar Falls)
***	Mike Brady	SE	5-10	174	Sen.	Canoga Park, CA (Carmelite)
	Jeff Brown	WB	5-11	150	Soph.	Fremont, O (Fremont)
*	Ken Burke	RB	6-1	201	Soph.	Chicago, IL (Morgan Park)
	Louis Burke	FB	6-0	180	Jun.	Chicago, IL (Morgan Park)
	Keith Chappelle	SE	6-0	175	Jun.	Inglewood, CA (Inglewood)
	Mel Cole	LB	6-3	228	Soph.	Elgin, IL (Elgin)
*	Tracy Crocker	DB	5-11	176	Soph.	Cedar Rapids, IA (Kennedy)
	Mike Dalton	TE	6-2	213	Soph.	Dubuque, IA (Wahlert)
	Jeff Davis	TE	6-4	228	Soph.	Riverside, IA (Highland)
*	Pat Dean	NG	6-2	230	Jun.	W. Islip, N.Y. (W. Islip)
**	Doug Dunham	WB	6-2	197	Jun.	Iowa City, IA (City)
**	Kent Ellis	DB	6-1	186	Jun.	DeWitt, IA (DeWitt-Clinton)
**	Kevin Ellis	DB	6-3	188	Jun.	DeWitt, IA (DeWitt-Clinton)
	Darin Erickson	QB	6-5	194	Soph.	Northridge, CA (Cleveland)
	Steve Flood	OG	5-11	213	Soph.	Des Moines, IA (Valley)
	Tom Frantz	TE	6-3	187	Sen.	Iowa City, IA (City)
**	Jim Frazier	DB	5-10	175	Jun.	Waterloo, IA (West)
	Keith Frisk	OT	6-5	248	Jun.	Ackley, IA (Ackley-Geneva)
*	Peter Gales	QB	6-3	166	Jun.	Paterson, N.J. (Kennedy)

	Name	Pos	Ht	Wt	Yr	Hometown
**	Greg Gilbaugh	OG	6-4	236	Jun.	Rockford, IL (Harlem)
	Brian Grace	C	6-1	230	Jun.	Des Moines, IA (Dowling)
**	Lemuel Grayson	OG	6-3	231	Sen.	Detroit, MI (Cass Tech.)
*	Jeff Green	QB	6-0	183	Jun.	Newhall, CA (Hart)
	John Hager	DT	6-5	272	Sen.	Sioux City, IA (Heelan)
	Ron Hallstrom	DT	6-6	276	Jun.	Moline, IL (Moline)
	Herlyn Harrington	OG	6-3	222	Sen.	Kansas City, MO (Central)
	Frank Harty	LB	6-3	225	Soph.	Des Moines, IA (Dowling)
**	Jay Hilgenberg	C	6-2	240	Jun.	Iowa City, IA (City)
**	Bobby Hill	LB	6-1	214	Sen.	Mt. Clemens, MI (Mt. Clemens)
	John Hogarty	OT	6-0	257	Sen.	Staten Island, N.Y. (Tottenville)
**	Dave Holsclaw	K	6-2	194	Sen.	Clinton, IA (Clinton)
*	Gene Holtorf	LB	6-3	222	Sen.	Ft. Dodge, IA (Ft. Dodge)
	Anthony Hyde	SE	6-0	191	Jun.	Markham, IL (Thornwood)
**	Mike Jackson	DB	6-0	189	Sen.	Harvey, IL (Thornton)
	Jeff Jansen	RB	5-11	186	Soph.	Davenport, IA (Assumption)
	Straun Joseph	DE	6-2	196	Soph.	Newton, IA (Newton)
*	Lou King	DB	6-1	175	Soph.	Jersey City, N.J. (Snyder)
**	Bruce Kittle	OG	6-6	221	Jun.	Cedar Falls, IA (Cedar Falls)
	Kip Kula	FB	6-0	190	Soph.	Cedar Rapids, IA (Regis)
	Mike Lamson	DB	6-2	198	Soph.	Evergreen, CO (Evergreen)
	Jim Langland	DT	6-2	234	Jun.	Ottumwa, IA (Ottumwa)
**	Mark Mahmens	DT	6-1	262	Sen.	Clinton, IA (NE Gooselake)
	Glen Manning	NG	6-2	268	Jun.	Waterloo, IA (East)
	Dennis Martin	RB	6-0	202	Jun.	Cedar Rapids, IA (Regis)
*	Dave Mayhan	OG	6-5	235	Soph.	Omaha, NE (Gross)
*	Dean McKillip	FB	6-2	206	Jun.	Galesburg, IL (Senior)
*	Phil Michel	NG	6-3	225	Sen.	Iowa City, IA (Regina)
***	Jim Molini	DE	6-4	226	Sen.	Norfolk, NE (Norfolk)
**	Rod Morton	WB	6-0	192	Sen.	Neptune, N.J. (Neptune)
***	Dennis Mosley	RB	5-11	179	Sen.	Youngstown, O. (Rayen)
*	Dave Oakes	C	6-2	224	Soph.	Mason City, IA (Mason City)
***	Mario Pace	DB	5-11	184	Sen.	Stow, O (Stow)
***	Sam Palladino	OT	6-3	247	Sen.	Lindenhurst, N.Y. (Lindenhurst)
*	George Person	DB	6-0	185	Jun.	Newark, N.J. (Barrington)
—	Nate Person	SE	6-0	181	Jun.	Camden, N.J. (Camden)
**	Matt Petrezelka	OT	6-7	241	Jun.	Cedar Rapids, IA (Regis)
*	Paul Postler	OT	6-4	227	Jun.	Madison, WI (West)
	John Prenner	DB	5-10	184	Jun.	Chicago, IL
**	Brad Reid	WB	6-0	174	Sen.	Marion, IA (Linn-Mar)
**	Tom Renn	RB	5-9	181	Sen.	Lowell, IN (Lowell)
	Tony Ricciardulli	QB	6-2	183	Jun.	Pittsburgh, PA (Jefferson)
	Tom Riley	FB	6-0	186	Jun.	Iowa City, IA (City)
*	Scott Schilling	K	6-1	217	Sen.	Wauwatosa, WI (Wauwatosa)
*	Greg Schlickman	DB	6-0	196	Soph.	Dubuque, IA (Wahlert)
	Tom Schroeder	DE	6-5	230	Soph.	Bloomington, IL (Bloomington)
***	Cedric Shaw	DB	6-0	193	Sen.	Newark, N.J. (Barrington)
*	Todd Simonsen	LB	6-2	220	Soph.	Racine, WI (Case)
	Ray Simpson	SE	6-1	184	Jun.	Milwaukee, WI (N. Division)
**	Brian Skradis	DE	6-1	211	Jun.	Omaha, NE (South)
	Bobby Stoops	DB	5-11	177	Soph.	Youngstown, O (Cardinal Mooney)
*	Phil Suess	QB	6-5	187	Sen.	Des Moines, IA (Dowling)
***	Jim Swift	TE	6-5	241	Sen.	Des Moines, IA (Dowling)
*	Milton Turner	FB	5-9	190	Jun.	Cedar Rapids, IA (Washington)
	Clay Uhlenhake	DT	6-3	257	Soph.	Moravia, IA (Moravia)
*	Brian Ward	OT	6-4	233	Jun.	Lindenhurst, N.Y. (Lindenhurst)

	Name	Pos.	Hgt.	Wgt.	Class	Hometown
*	Brad Webb	DE	6-1	204	Soph.	Glen Ellyn, IL (Beret)
***	Leven Weiss	LB	6-2	218	Sen.	Detroit, MI (Cass Tech)
**	Don Willey	DT	6-2	233	Sen.	St. Louis, MO (Bishop-Dubourg)
	Dwayne Williams	RB	5-11	183	Soph.	Bayonne, N.J. (Bayonne)
*	Ben Wozniak	TE	6-6	221	Sen.	Lombard, IL (Glenbard East)
	Gene Yambor	DB	5-11	175	Jun.	Council Bluffs, IA (Jefferson)

88-man squad (27 seniors, 33 juniors, 28 sophomores)

1979 MICHIGAN
ALPHABETICAL TEAM ROSTER

(* Denotes letters won)

No.	Name	Pos.	Hgt.	Wgt.	Class	Hometown
35	Agnew, Doug	OLB	6-2¼	195	So.	Plymouth
21	Allen, Jay	FB	6-0	212	Sr.	McDonald, PA
58	Angood, David	C	6-4½	232	Sr.	Battle Creek
64	**Arbeznik, John	OG	6-3½	240	Sr.	University Heights, OH
12	Bates, Brad	DB	6-1	193	Jr.	Port Huron
65	*Becker, Kurt	OG	6-6	243	Jr.	Aurora, IL
85	Betts, Norm	OLB	6-5	222	So.	Midland
3	Body, Marion	DB	5-10½	175	So.	Detroit
28	**Braman, Mark	DHB	6-1¼	197	Sr.	Midland
8	Breaugh, Jim	QB	6-2	189	Jr.	West Bloomfield
48	Brewster, David	FB	6-1	219	So.	Grafton, WI
25	Brockington, Fred	WR-DB	6-2	205	So.	Detroit
57	Butts, Mike	C	6-4½	227	So.	Fenton
41	*Cannavino, Andy	ILB	6-1	220	Jr.	Cleveland, OH
9	Carpenter, Brian	DB	5-11	163	So.	Flint
85	Christian, Chuck	TE	6-3	219	Jr.	Detroit
22	**Clayton, Ralph	WB	6-3½	210	Sr.	Detroit
79	Coles, Cedric	DT	6-2	238	So.	Detroit
37	Czarnata, Mike	ILB	6-2	220	So.	Detroit
35	Davis, Michael	FB	6-1½	230	Sr.	Woodbridge, VA
10	*Dickey, B.J.	QB	5-11½	188	Jr.	Ottawa, OH
29	*Diggs, Gerald	DB	6-0	190	Sr.	Chicago, IL
32	*Edwards, Stanley	TB	6-0	203	Jr.	Detroit
18	*Feaster, Rodney	WR	6-1	191	Jr.	Flint
51	Felten, Jeff	C	6-2	216	So.	Centerville, OH
20	Fisher, Brad	QB	6-0	190	So.	Ortonville
54	Garrity, Tom	C	6-4	234	So.	Grafton, WI
29	Gilligan, Kevin	QB	5-11½	160	So.	Ann Arbor
90	**Godfrey, Chris	DT	6-4	240	Sr.	Miami Lakes, FL
95	***Greer, Curtis	DT	6-5	236	Sr.	Detroit
4	**Harden, Michael	DB	6-0½	183	Sr.	Detroit
31	*Harris, Stuart	Wolf	6-3	196	Jr.	Chagrin Falls, OH
75	Hetts, Chuck	OG	6-4½	231	Sr.	Taylor
58	*Humphries, Jim	MG	5-10½	223	Sr.	Detroit
97	Jackson, Jeff	OLB	6-7¼	227	Jr.	Toledo, OH
21	*Jackson, Tony	WB	5-10½	170	So.	Cleveland, OH
13	Jelinek, Jerome	QB	6-0	179	So.	Ann Arbor

579

#	Name	Pos	Ht	Wt	Yr	Hometown
15	Johnson, Irvin	OLB	6-2¼	208	Sr.	Warren, OH
81	Johnson, Oliver	OLB	6-3¼	210	Jr.	Detroit
16	***Jolly, Michael	DB	6-3½	181	Sr.	Melvindale
44	Jones, Rick	ILB	6-3	199	Jr.	Detroit
55	**Keitz, Dale	DT	6-1¼	233	Sr.	Columbus, OH
99	Keller, Tom	OLB	6-2½	210	Sr.	Grand Rapids
13	Kelsie, Tony	DB	5-11¼	197	So.	Dover, DE
57	Keough, Kelly	DT	6-3	237	Jr.	Merrillville, IN
39	Kligis, Mike	Wolf	6-2	192	Jr.	Lombard, IL
69	Kwiatkowski, Dan	OT	6-5	246	Jr.	Detroit
17	Lee, Gary	QB	6-3	198	So.	Flint
93	Lemirande, Mike	OLB	6-4½	219	So.	Grafton, WI
76	*Leoni, Mike	OT	6-2½	246	Sr.	Flint
34	*Leoni, Tony	TB	5-11	192	Sr.	Flint
59	**Lilja, George	C	6-4½	247	Sr.	Palos Park, IL
20	Longe, Kevin	FB	5-10½	184	Jr.	Ferndale
80	**Marsh, Doug	TE	6-3	233	Sr.	Akron, OH
30	*Mitchell, Alan	WR	6-1½	185	Jr.	Detroit
54	Moss, Tom	MG	5-8¼	204	Sr.	Detroit
52	Motley, Fred	MG	6-2	234	Jr.	Dayton, OH
72	Muransky, Ed	OT	6-7	280	So.	Youngstown, OH
27	*Murray, Dan	Wolf	6-0½	198	Sr.	Ann Arbor
78	Neal, Tom	OG	6-5¼	245	So.	Edgewater, FL
83	*Needham, Ben	OLB	6-4	214	Jr.	Groveport, OH
96	Nicolau, Dave	DT	6-5	232	Jr.	Arlington Heights, IL
78	Osbun, Tony	DT	6-5	253	Jr.	Kenton, OH
53	*Owens, Mel	OLB	6-2	230	Sr.	DeKalb, IL
12	Paciorek, James	QB	6-3	208	So.	Orchard Lake
75	*Paris, Bubba	OT	6-6¼	280	So.	Louisville, KY
45	Parks, Marshall	DB	6-3	217	So.	Dayton, Oh
89	Payne, David	OLB	6-1¼	206	Sr.	Detroit
86	Petsch, Michael	TE	6-4¼	208	So.	Detroit
67	**Powers, John	OG	6-3	265	Sr.	Oak Park, IL
71	Prepolec, John	OG	6-4	249	Jr.	Bloomfield Hills
70	Quinn, Gary	OG	6-3	248	Sr.	Quincy, MA
38	Raiford, Frank	DB	5-11	175	Fr.	Detroit
43	Reeves, Jeff	DB	6-1	192	So.	Columbus, OH
23	*Reid, Lawrence	FB	6-1½	213	Sr.	Philadelphia, PA
65	Reilly, Steve	OT	6-5	238	So.	Boston, MA
74	Rowland, Charles	OT	6-4½	255	So.	Barberton, OH
94	Shaw, Vincent	TE	6-2	218	So.	Louisville, KY
40	***Simpkins, Ron	ILB	6-1½	220	Sr.	Detroit
6	Smith, Kevin	DB	6-2½	191	So.	Dallas, TX
84	Strenger, Richard	TE	6-7	233	So.	Grafton, WI
18	Tech, Karl	PK-DB	6-0	179	So.	Grosse Pointe Shores
99	Thompson, Robert	OLB	6-3½	220	So.	Blue Island, IL
77	**Trgovac, Mike	MG	6-2	227	Jr.	Austintown, OH
2	*Virgil, Bryan	PK	5-9½	185	Sr.	Buchanan
37	Wallace, Zeke	WR	6-4	194	So.	Pompano Beach, FL
66	Wandersleben, Tom	OG	6-2½	245	Jr.	Euclid, OH
5	Wangler, John	QB	6-2½	192	Sr.	Royal Oak
60	Warth, Mark	OG	6-5½	241	So.	Zanesville, OH
49	Washington, Sanford	ILB	6-2¼	214	So.	Youngstown, OH
62	*Weber, Gary	DT	6-2	239	Sr.	Matawan, NJ
49	Webster, Mike	TB	6-0½	194	Jr.	Dearborn
62	Welch, Bill	C	6-2½	231	So.	Winnetka, IL

| 24 | *Woolfolk, Butch | TB | 6-2 | 203 | So. | Westfield, NJ |
| 56 | Wunderli, Greg | OG | 6-6 | 227 | Jr. | St. Louis, MO |

1979 MICHIGAN STATE ALPHABETICAL TEAM ROSTER

(* Denotes letters won)

	Name	Pos.	Ht.	Wt.	Cl.	Home/School
*	Andersen, Morton	PK	6-1	180	So.	Struer, Denmark/Indianapolis, Ind./Davis
*	Anderson, Mark	DB	6-2	189	Sr.	Akron, Ohio/Springfield
*	Audas, Sedric	C	6-3	231	Jr.	Saginaw/Arthur Hill
	Baca, Ben	DT	6-3	239	Fr.	Montebello, Calif./Los Ang. Loyola
	Bailey, Terry +	ILB	6-4	230	Jr.	San Francisco, Calif./City College
*	Bass, Dan	ILB	6-1	221	Sr.	Bath/Same
	Blank, Steven	ILB	6-2	214	Fr.	Grand Rapids/Northview
	Boak, Bryan	OG	6-3	234	Fr.	New Castle, Pa./Same
*	Brammer, Mark	TE	6-4	233	Sr.	Traverse City/Same
	Brown, Darryl	OLB	6-4	215	Fr.	Jacksonville, Fla./Wolfson
*	Burroughs, James	DB	6-1	183	Jr.	Pahokee, Fla./Same
*	Byrd, Eugene	SE	6-0	178	Sr.	East St. Louis, Ill./Same
*	Clark, Bryan	QB	6-2	178	So.	Los Altos, Calif./Bloomfield Hills
*	Converse, Craig	MG	5-11	207	Jr.	Utica/Eisenhower
*	Cooper, George	OLB	6-2	207	So.	Detroit/Northern
*	Davis, Alan	DB	6-1	179	Sr.	Huntington Woods/Berkley
*	Decker, Michael	ILB	6-2	224	Sr.	Roseville/Detroit DeLaSalle
*	Densmore, Michael	OG	6-3	257	Sr.	Lapeer/West
	Ellis, Anthony +	TB	6-1	200	Fr.	Coolidge, Ariz./Same
	English, Jon +	QB	6-3	190	Fr.	Birmingham/Brother Rice
	Fehlan, Jeffrey	OT	6-5	239	Fr.	Wellington, Ohio/Same
*	Fields, Angelo	OT	6-6	284	Sr.	Washington, D.C./Wilson
*	Foster, Matthew	C	6-3	228	Sr.	Livonia/Churchill
*	Grabenhorst, Ted	OT	6-6	270	Sr.	Mt. Morris/Johnson
	Grant, Otis +	QB	6-3	195	Fr.	Atlanta, Ga./Carver
	Greene, Rickey	DB	6-0	181	Fr.	Miami, Fla./Carol City
*	Griffin, Curtis	OLB	6-3	217	Sr.	Southfield/Birmingham Brother Rice
*	Griffin, Isaac	DT	6-5	230	So.	Gary, Ind./Lew Wallace
	Harewicz, Joseph	OG	6-3	230	Fr.	Pittsburgh, Pa./Upper St. Clair
	Harris, Tony	DB	6-2	197	Fr.	Niles/Brandywine
*	Hay, Bernard	MG	6-3	235	Jr.	Riviera Beach, Fla./Palm B. Gardens
*	Haynes, Johnny Lee	OLB	6-2	225	Jr.	Delray Beach, Fla./Boca Raton
	Hodo, James +	TB	5-9	180	Fr.	Flint/Southwestern
*	Howard, Samson	FL	5-8	165	So.	Miami, Fla./Northwestern
*	Hughes, Derek	TB	6-2	194	So.	Charleston, S.C./Bishop England
	Jacquemain, Joe	C	6-5	228	So.	Mt. Clemens/L'Anse Creuse
*	Jones, Eric	DT	5-11	238	Sr.	Grosse Pointe/South
*	Jones, Mark	SE	5-8	167	Jr.	Ypsilanti/Same
	Jones, Ted +	FL	6-1	180	Fr.	Akron, Ohio/East
	Jones, Mike	FL	6-3	180	Fr.	South Haven/Same
	Kaiser, James	OT	6-3	232	So.	Alpena/Same
	Kimichik, Alan	TE	6-2	195	So.	Norway/Same
	Kirkling, Jack	MG	6-1	240	Fr.	Greensburg, Pa./Hemfield Area
*	Kolodziej, Joseph	ILB	6-2	202	So.	Nashville, Tenn./Overton
	Langerveld, Todd +	DB	6-4	200	Fr.	Portage/Central

581

	Name	Pos	Ht	Wt	Cl	Hometown/High School
	Lark, Randy +	DT	6-1	236	Fr.	Wyoming/Lee
	Lauble, Greg +	LB	6-0	205	Fr.	Pittsburgh, Pa./Central Catholic
	Lavelle, Denis +	QB	6-1	190	Fr.	Rocky River, Ohio/Lakewood St. Edward
	Leister, John +	QB	6-1	185	Fr.	Great Falls, Mon./Russell
	Maidlow, Steven	ILB	6-2	223	Fr.	East Lansing/Same
	Mantos, Marvin	OG	6-4	222	Fr.	Bloomingdale, Ohio/Wintersville
*	Marshall, Michael	DB	6-3	190	Jr.	Detroit/Southwestern
	Mazur, Scot	OT	6-4	248	Fr.	Bowling Green, Ohio/Same
	McAdoo, Howard +	LB	6-2	250	Fr.	Rancho Palos Verdes, Calif./Rolling Hill
	McClelland, Darrin	FB	6-0	216	Fr.	Detroit/Central
*	McCormick, John	OLB	6-2	211	Jr.	Marquette/Same
	McDowell, Terry	ILB	6-2	180	Jr.	Flint/Ainsworth
*	McQuaide, Regis	OT	6-6	251	Sr.	Pittsburgh, Pa./Brentwood
*	Middleton, Lonnie	FB	6-1	217	Sr.	Orangeburg, S.C./Orang./Wilkinson
	Mitchem, Ronald	DT	6-4	247	Fr.	South Bend, Ind./Adams
	Mitten, Patrick	DT	6-5	221	Fr.	Naperville, Ill./Central
	Mouch, Bob +	OT	6-5	237	Fr.	Redford/Union
	Muster, Michael	ILB	6-2	214	So.	Utica/Eisenhower
	Neely, James +	LB	6-3	220	Fr.	South Bend, Ind./Adams
*	Otis, Steven	ILB	6-3	210	Jr.	Chicago, Ill./Gordon Tech
	Perkins, Calvin	MG	6-4	275	Fr.	Atlanta, Ga./Harper
*	Piette, Thomas	C	6-4	221	So.	Redford Township/Det. Red. Union
*	Reeves, Bruce	TB	5-11	177	Jr.	Irmo, S.C./Same
*	Robinson, Kenneth	DB	6-1	191	Sr.	Ypsilanti/Same
	Saunders, Craig	TE	6-4	220	Fr.	Huron, Ohio/Same
*	Savage, Larry	OLB	6-3	213	Sr.	Warren, Ohio/Howland
	Scarlett, Todd	DB	5-11	175	Fr.	Okemos/Same
*	Schario, Richard	PK	6-0	181	So.	Lyndhurst, Ohio/Brush
*	Schramm, Andrew	FB	6-2	226	Jr.	Findlay, Ohio/Same
	Schramm, Walter +	OT	6-4	235	Fr.	Findlay, Ohio/Same
*	Sciarini, Michael	OG	6-2	225	So.	Fort Wayne, Ind. Bishop Dwenger
	Sheeran, Brett	DT	6-3	240	So.	W. Bloomfield/Birmingham Groves
	Smith, Steve	TB	5-8	175	Jr.	Louisville, Ky./DuPont Manual
*	Stachowicz, Raymond	P	6-1	190	Jr.	Broadview Hts., Ohio/Brecksville
	Stachowicz, Robert	QB	6-2	193	Jr.	Broadview Hts., Ohio/Brecksville
*	Stanton, Edmund	OT	6-3	239	Sr.	Battle Creek/Lakeview
	Stevens, Joe +	TE	6-5	218	Fr.	Mentor, Ohio/Same
*	Strata, Rodney	OG	6-2	240	Jr.	Canton, Ohio/Massillon Perry
	Tanker, Terry +	TE	6-3	205	Fr.	Westlake, Ohio/Lakewood St. Edward
	Toney, Marcus +	DB	6-2	185	Fr.	Muskegon/Catholic Central
	Townsend, Tony	DB	5-11	163	So.	Grand Rapids/Union
	VanPelt, Chris +	DB	6-4	190	Fr.	Fort Wayne, Ind./Elmhurst
*	Vaughn, Bert	QB	6-4	215	Jr.	Mogadore, Ohio/Same
	Vielhaber, John	FL	5-11	178	Sr.	Findlay, Ohio/Same
*	Webb, Tanya	DT	6-7	254	Sr.	Augusta, Ark./Same
	Whittle, David	OT	6-5	244	Jr.	Seattle, Wash./Shoreline
	Williams, Bruce	MG	6-3	220	Fr.	Wheaton, Ill./North
	Williams, Carl +	DB	6-3	202	Fr.	Detroit/Royal Oak Shrine
*	Williams, James	SE	5-11	160	Jr.	San Diego, Calif./Madison
	Williams, Van	DB	5-9	175	Jr.	Delray Beach, Fla./Boca Raton
	Wiska, Jeffrey	OG	6-3	238	So.	Farmington Hills/Detroit Catholic Central
	Woods, Tony +	SE	6-4	185	Fr.	Chicago, Ill./Sullivan

+ Denotes new Signee
\# Class by Eligibility

1979 MINNESOTA ALPHABETICAL TEAM ROSTER

(* Denotes letters won)

	Name	Pos.	Hgt.	Wgt.	Age	Class	Hometown (High School)
*	Anderson, Jim	OG	6-1½	233	20	So.	Fairbault, MN
**	Anhorn, Jeff	FL	6-2½	186	22	Sr.	Blue Island, IL (Eisenhower)
**	Artis, Roy	TB	6-1½	179	20	Jr.	Lawnside, N.J. (Hadden Heights)
**	Avery, Wendell	Q3	6-0	182	22	Sr.	Corpus Christi, TX (Moody)
	Bach, Curt	LB	6-3	211	20	So.	Wheaton, MN
**	Bailey, Elmer	SE	6-0½	193	21	Sr.	St. Paul, MN (Mechanic Arts)
	Bankson, Kurt	NG	5-10	241	19	Fr.	Franklin Park, IL (E. Leyden)
**	Barber, Marion	TB	6-2½	204	19	Jr.	Detroit, MI (Chadsey)
	Bennett, Chris	C	6-3	220	18	Fr.	Stillwater, MN
	Bifulk, Ed	WR	6-1	196	19	Fr.	St. Paul, MN (St. Thomas)
	Bish, Steve	DT	6-4½	234	19	Fr.	LeSeur, MN
**	Blanshan, Alan	DT	6-5½	251	21	Sr.	Mankato, MN (East)
***	Bourquin, Glenn	TE	6-3½	231	22	Sr.	Cottage Grove, MN (St. Paul Park)
	Burditte, Elwin	WR	5-11	187	21	Sr.	Minnetonka, MN
	Cardelli, Glenn	CB	5-10	171	19	Fr.	Elmwood Park, IL (Holy Cross)
**	Carlson, Mark	QB	5-11	186	21	Sr.	Deerfield, IL
*	Cooper, Chester	WR	6-2	183	20	So.	*Paulsboro, N.J.
***	Cunningham, Steve	DE	6-6	241	22	Sr.	Waseca, MN
	Curtis, Mike	TE	6-3	202	18	Fr.	Eau Claire, WI
	Dagner, Paul	DB	6-1	185	18	Fr.	Richfield, MN
	Dahlson, Rick	OG	6-2½	222	20	So.	St. Cloud, MN (Tech)
*	Dallafior, Ken	OT	6-4	251	20	So.	Madison Heights, MI
	Davidson, Nick	QB	5-10	170	18	Fr.	Miami, FL (Carol City)
	Davis, Anthony	DE	6-0	201	19	Fr.	Detroit, MI (Chadsey)
	Davis, Howard	DB	6-0	190	18	Fr.	Detroit, MI (Chadsey)
	Denney, Jeff	DL	6-2	220	18	Fr.	Washington, D.C. (Archbishop Carrol)
	Dilulo, Ray	WR	6-0	203	20	Jr.	Boise, ID
**	Edwards, Keith	FS	5-11	201	21	Sr.	Grand Rapids, MI (Creston)
*	Fahnhorst, Jim	LB	6-3½	218	20	Jr.	St. Cloud, MN (Tech)
	Farrow, Lonnie	WR	5-10	165	18	Fr.	Pompano, FL (Ely)
	Frazier, Roger	SE	5-11	175	21	Sr.	Richmond, IN
*	Gardner, Dave	DT	6-4	236	22	Sr.	Rochester, MN (Mayo)
	Gehrke, Keith	OL	6-5	225	18	Fr.	Prospect, IL (Prospect)
	Gregory, Duane	TB	5-10	194	20	So.	Chicago, Il (Proviso East)
	Hallstrom, Todd	TE	6-4½	221	19	Fr.	Brook Park, Mn (Mora)
	Harms, Brent	LB	6-2	212	20	So.	Rice Lake, WI
	Hesse, Scott	CB	5-10	173	20	So.	Stillwater, MN

	Name	Pos	Ht	Wt	Age	Yr	Hometown
*	Hoffman, John	SS	5-11	199	22	Sr.	Duluth, MN (Morgan Park)
	Houle, John	LB	6-2	210	18	Fr.	St. Paul, MN (Harding)
	Hoverman, Randy	QB	6-2½	186	19	Fr.	Osceola, WI
	Howard, Glenn	DE	6-1½	211	19	So.	Paulsboro, N.J.
	Humphries, Bill	OG	6-2	234	18	Fr.	Detroit, MI (chadsey)
	Izban, Paul	LB	6-2	206	20	Fr.	Mount Prospect, IL (Prospect)
#	Jenkins, Kelvin	WR	5-9	175	20	Jr.	Long beach, CA (Long Beach C.C)
	Johanson, Tom	LB	6-3	224	20	So.	Clouet, MN
	Jones, Walter	WR	6-3	178	21	Jr.	St. Louis, MO (Soldan)
	Jurgens, Duane	P	6-2	182	18	So.	Mundelein, IL
	Kellin, Kevin	DT	6-5½	229	19	Fr.	Grand Rapids, MN
***	Kitzman, Kent	FB	6-2½	204	22	Sr.	Rochester, MN (John Marshall)
*	Kuduck, John	NG	6-2	220	21	Sr.	Minneapolis, MN (Edison)
	Laliberte, Mike	LB	6-3	210	18	Fr.	Hibbing, MN
	Lewis, Glenn	TB	6-1	205	21	Jr.	Edina, MN (West)
	Lowell, Chuck	TB	6-0	181	18	Fr.	White Bear Lake, MN
	McNeely, Angus	SE	5-11	160	20	So.	Racine, WI
	Mangum, Kurt	DE	6-1½	208	20	So.	Evanston, IL
**	Meyer, Don	LB	6-2	219	21	Sr.	Arlington Hgts., MN (Prospect)
	Mia, Darryl	DE	6-1	209	19	Fr.	Detroit, MI (Highland Park)
	Miller, Van	TW	6-2	214	19	Fr.	Columbia Heights, MN
*	Murphy, Tom	DE	6-2½	218	22	Sr.	Watertown, S.D.
*	Murtha, Greg	OT	6-6½	251	22	Sr.	Minneapolis, MN (Southwest)
	Nash, McKinley	OG	6-3	244	19	So.	Evanston, IL
	Nielson, Mike	Dt	6-7	255	20	So.	Sturgeon Bay, WI
*	Noel, Dana	CB	5-10	178	21	Jr.	Wheaton, IL (Central)
	Odegard, Brad	C	6-5	227	20	So.	Agoura, CA
	Olson, Ed	C	6-3	219	19	Fr.	Crystal, MN (Armstrong)
	Orgas, Fred	DE	6-4	213	19	Fr.	Brooklyn Center, MN (Park Ctr)
	Orgas, Mike	OG	6-4	232	21	So.	Brooklyn, Center, MN (Park Ctr.)
	Owens, Mark	OT	6-4	244	21	Jr.	Rochester, MN (Mayo)
	Pence, Tom	QB	6-2	190	18	Fr.	Crystal Lake, IL
	Penovich, Kent	OT	6-6½	267	21	Jr.	Muskego, WI
*	Peppe, Mike	SS	5-11	182	20	So.	Brooklyn Park, MN (Cooper)
	Peters, Kevin	FB	5-11	199	20	So.	Cloquet, Mn
	Peterson, Todd	LB	6-1½	207	19	Fr.	Richfield, MN
	Prairie, Bill	FS	6-0	172	20	So.	Rosemont, MN
	Pylatiuk, Greg	QB	6-1	184	20	So.	Columbia Heights, MN
	Quam, Dan	TB	5-8½	166	21	Jr.	Minneapolis, MN (Cooper)
#	Reimer, Rick	QL	6-4	245	20	Jr.	Willmar, MN (Willmar J.C.)
	Renzi, Ronnie	LB	6-2	210	18	Fr.	Arlington, VA
	Robb, Mike	SS	6-2	192	19	Fr.	Cottage Grove, MN (Woodbury)
	Ross, Marvell	OB	5-9	170	18	Fr.	Detroit, MI (Osborn)

	Name	Pos.	Hgt.	Wgt.	Class	Hometown (High School)
***	Rogind, Paul	CB-K	5-10	176	21	Sr.	Farmington, MI (Harrison)
*	Sapp, Tom	DE	6-3	214	22	Sr.	Bloomington, MN (Jefferson)
	Schuh, Jeff	DE	6-2½	219	21	Jr.	Crystal, MN (Armstrong)
**	Schwen, Darell	QB	6-4	232	21	Sr.	Great Falls, MT
	Shareef, Ahmad	QB	5-10	169	20	Fr.	Pittsburgh, PA (Westinghouse)
*	Simmons, Terry	TE-P	6-1	161	21	Sr.	Birmingham, MI (Brother Rice)
	Smith, Tom	P	6-0½	186	21	Jr.	Edina, MN (East)
	Snodgrass, Jeff	NG	6-2	228	20	So.	Valparaiso, IN
*	Sonnenfeld, Randy	TE	6-5	226	21	Jr.	Robbinsdale, MN
**	Stein, Marty	OT	6-4	247	22	Sr.	Eau Claire, WI (Memorial)
	Stensrud, Mike	WR	6-4	220	18	Fr.	Apple Valley, MN
	Stroup, Bob	DB	6-1	190	18	Fr.	Fargo, ND (Fargo North)
	Thomas, Tracy	TE	6-4	220	18	Fr.	Detroit, MI (Osborn)
**	Thompson, Jeff	FS	6-2	216	21	Sr.	Bloomington, MN (Jefferson)
	Thompson, Terry	OL	6-3	240	18	Fr.	Fridley, MN (Grace)
***	Tobin, Steve	C	6-4½	247	22	Sr.	Moorhead, MN
	Tonn, Mark	QB	6-6	216	22	Sr.	Green Bay, WI (Preble)
	Veldman, Greg	TE	6-3½	211	19	Fr.	South St. Paul, MN
	Weinzierl, Mike	DT	6-5½	238	22	Sr.	Shakopee, MN
**	White, Garry	FB	5-11	197	20	Jr.	Rockdale, TX
	Wiecks, Reed	TE	6-3	230	18	Fr.	Walnut, Grove, MN
	Williams. DeWayne	OB	6-2	215	18	Fr.	Waukegan, IL (West)
	Witthus, Rick	FS	6-3	186	20	Fr.	Glencoe, MN
	Wozniak, Anthony	OT	6-4½	209	19	Fr.	Lombard, IL (Glengard)
***	Wypyszynski, Ken	OG	6-5½	243	21	Sr.	DePere, WI (West)

\# - transfer
\+ - year in school next fall

1979 NORTHWESTERN ALPHABETICAL TEAM ROSTER

(* Denotes letters won)

No.	Name	Pos.	Hgt.	Wgt.	Class	Hometown (High School)
20	**Adams, Mark	DB	6-0	188	Jr.	Detroit, MI (MacKenzie)
96	*Ahern, Tom	DT	6-3	225	Sr.	Warren, OH (Howland)
	Anderson, Bobby	QB/DB	5-11	187	Fr.	Rockford, IL (Auburn)
	Anderson, Jay	TE/PK	6-3	195	Fr.	Lutsen, MN (Grand Marie)
84	*Bahoric, Dave	WR	5-10	175	So.	Johnstown, PA (Bishop McCourt)
94	*Bambauer, Don	DT	6-4	240	So.	North Royalton, OH (North Royalton)
81	Bayer, David	DB	5-10	190	So.	Baraboo, WI (Baraboo)
98	**Berg, Kevin	OLB	6-2	211	Sr.	St. Paul, MN (St. Thomas Academy)
95	Biancamano, Bob	OLB	6-3	185	Jr.	Dover, OH (Central Catholic)
83	*Bogan, Steve	WR	6-1	185	So.	Weston, CT (Weston)
66	Brown, Kelby	OG/DT	6-4	220	So.	Mt. Pelier, OH (Mt. Pelier)
24	Burns, John	S	6-3	195	Jr.	Warren, OH (Howland)
37	*Butler, Ben	S	6-4	191	So.	Chicago, IL (Mt. Carmel)

	Callaway, Dave	FB	6-3	215	Fr.	Appleton, WI (East)
33	**Cammon, Mike	FB	5-11	190	Jr.	Detroit, MI (University)
11	Capstran, Chris	QB	6-4	212	So.	Menominee, WI (Menominee Falls)
50	*Carnicom, Todd	C	6-0	225	Sr.	Trenton, MI (Trenton)
1	*Carver, Brett	DB	5-7	140	Jr.	Northbrook, IL (Glenbrook North)
7	*Christensen, Jeff	K/QB	6-4	190	So.	Gibson City, IL (Gibson City)
	Cohn, Jeff	RB	5-10	185	Fr.	Chicago, IL (Mendel)
14	Coleman, Ron	OLB	6-1	205	Jr.	Evanston, IL (Evanston Township)
	Crist, Tom	OL	6-4	250	Fr.	Kenosha, WI (St. Joseph)
67	Crowder, Jim	OG	6-4	212	So.	Hinsdale, IL (Fenwick)
	Currie, Walt	OL	6-6	260	Fr.	Washington, MI (Eisenhower)
	Dennis, Keith	FB	6-2	210	Fr.	University City, MO (U-City)
17	*Dierberger, Bill	QB	6-0	185	Sr.	West St. Paul, MN (Bradley)
49	*Dorsey, Doug	LB	6-3	212	So.	Freeport, IL (Freeport)
65	**Draznik, Bill	OG	6-4	231	Jr.	Joliet, IL (Joliet Catholic)
38	*Duncan, Scott	LB	6-2	215	Sr.	Findlay, OH (Findlay)
	Edwards, Ricky	RB	5-10	170	Fr.	White Plains, NY (White Plains)
	Epich, Tom	OLB	6-1½	215	Fr.	Evergreen Park, IL (Marist)
	Erdman, Pat	DT	6-3	230	Fr.	Erie, PA (Tech Memorial)
57	**Fiedler, Mike	C	6-3	235	Sr.	Toledo, OH (Whitmer)
80	*Finn, John	LB/TE	6-6	215	So.	Wadsworth, OH (Wadsworth)
76	**Ford, Jim	OT	6-4	255	Sr.	Burbank, IL (St. Laurence)
88	*Gildner, Bill	DT	6-4	237	So.	Springfield, OH (Griffin)
70	**Greer, Bill	OT	6-4	240	Sr.	Athens, OH (Athens)
99	**Grelle, Curt	DT	6-2	215	Sr.	Indianapolis, IN (Warren Central)
	Groves, Roosevelt	WR/DB	6-5	185	Fr.	St. Louis, MO (Central)
	Harrell, Terry	DT	6-4	235	Fr.	Beloit, WI (Memorial)
86	**Hemphill, Dana	DB	6-0	170	Jr.	Gaithersburg, MD (Gaithersburg)
31	Hickey, Dave	DT	6-3	220	Jr.	Burbank, IL (St. Laurence)
23	*Hill, Tim	RB/WR	6-1	175	Jr.	Cincinnati, OH (St. Xavier)
	Hinton, Chris	OLB	6-4	218	Fr.	Chicago, IL (Phillips)
41	*Hoffman, David	DB	6-1	183	Jr.	Cincinnati, OH (LaSalle)
9	Humphreys, Charlie	QB	6-2	185	So.	Mt. Herman, MA (Mt. Herman)
69	*Hunter, Hal	LB	6-1	220	So.	Belle Vernon, PA (Belle Vernon)
36	**Johnson, Donald	LB	6-3	210	Jr.	Evanston, IL (Evanston Township)
	Kadlec, Tim	DT	6-4	215	Fr.	Robbins, IA (Cedar Rapids Kennedy)
	Kaiser, Steve	LB/CAT	6-6	205	Fr.	Bloomfield Hills, MI (Brother Rice)
77	Karstan, Adrian	DT	6-7	220	So.	Horicorn, WI (Horicorn)
	Karstens, Jim	DE	6-6	205	Fr.	Melrose Park, IL (Proviso East)
85	**Kasprycki, Wally	TE	6-4	225	Sr.	Hammond, IN (Bishop Noll)
59	**Kenyon, Kevin	OG	6-4	225	Sr.	Buffalo, NY (Nicholas)
21	**Kern, Chuck	LB	6-2	210	Jr.	New Castle, IN (Chrysler)
12	Kerrigan, Mike	QB	6-3	190	So.	Chicago, IL (Mt. Carmel)
	Kornegay, Bill	FB	6-3	200	Fr.	Grand Blanc, MI (Grand Blanc)
54	Kreider, Jack	OT	6-4	230	So.	Pittsburgh, PA (Jefferson)
35	**Lawrence, Tim	OLB	5-11	211	Sr.	Oak Lawn, IL (Brother Rice)
79	Lemaster, Brian	DT	6-3	225	Fr.	Chillicothe, IL (Chillicothe)
72	*Ley, Michael	C	6-3	210	So.	Hialeah, FL (Hialeah)
48	*Lizak, Matt	LB	6-1	218	So.	Oak Forest, IL (Oak Forest)
8	Lyons, Darryl	QB	6-2	185	So.	Chicago, IL (Corliss)

#	Name	Pos	Ht	Wt	Yr	Hometown (High School)
	Maher, Jeff	WR	5-11	175	Fr.	Highland Falls, NY (Highland Falls)
39	Maul, Tom	TE	6-1	212	So.	Belleville, IL (Althoff)
80	Maycan, Jim	TE	6-2	210	Sr.	Palatine, IL (Fremd)
43	**McGlade, Tom	CAT	6-1	182	Jr.	Park Ridge, IL (Maine South)
	Mead, Jack	DL	6-7	225	Fr.	Whitewater, WI (Whitewater)
62	**Miller, Jim	LB	6-2	225	Sr.	Kohler, WI (Kohler)
32	**Mishler, Dave	RB	6-0	215	Jr.	Metamora, IL (Spaulding Institute)
	Moore, Richard	DL	6-4	220	Fr.	Harvey, IL (Thornton)
82	*North, Tom	WR	6-3	185	Jr.	Arlington Heights, IL (Arlington)
91	*Pals, Steve	OLB	6-3	215	Jr.	Glen Ellyn, IL (Glenbard West)
97	**Payne, Dean	OLB	6-4	210	Jr.	Chester, PA (Chester)
27	Pearsall, Al	CAT	5-10	190	So.	Akron, OH (Phillips Academy)
	Potts, Mike	QB	5-10	185	Fr.	Peoria, IL (Central)
89	***Poulos, Sam	K/TE	6-2	201	Sr.	Northbrook, IL (Glenbrook North)
	Pratt, Bob	OL	6-5	255	Fr.	Sharon, PA (Kennedy Christian)
87	*Prichard, Clarke	TE	6-6	220	So.	Lima, OH (Bath)
	Raffin, Rich	WR/DHB	6-3	185	Fr.	Valparaiso, IN (Chesterton)
55	***Reitz, Phil	OT	6-2	235	Sr.	Brown Deer, WI (Brown Deer)
73	**Robinett, Bruce	DT	6-5	225	Sr.	Xenia, OH (Xenia)
16	Schanzer, Dave	OLB	6-3	200	So.	Williamsville, NY (East)
60	*Schmidt, Bill	OG	6-2	230	Sr.	Clintonville, WI (Clintonville)
28	**Schmitt, Bob	FB	6-2	205	Jr.	Sun Prairie, WI (Prairie)
71	**Schober, John	OT	6-5	250	Sr.	Findlay, OH (Findlay)
	Shaw, Dave	DB	6-0	180	Fr.	Peoria, IL (Woodruff)
26	**Sheets, Todd	WR	6-0	175	Jr.	Nappanee, IN (Northwood)
46	Sobeck, Fred	CAT	6-2	185	So.	Miami, FL (Columbus)
40	*Stasiewicz, Brian	DT	5-11	220	Jr.	Columbus, OH (Watterson)
13	*Strasser, Kevin	QB	6-3	190	Sr.	Elmhurst, IL (Immaculate Conception)
	Szpak, Bob	C	6-4	205	Fr.	Parma, OH (Padua)
5	Taylor, Matt	P/QB	6-2	190	So.	Pleasant Hill, CA (De LaSalle)
75	*Taylor, Rob	DT	6-6	240	So.	Kettering, OH (Fairmont East)
	Thornton, James	OL	6-5	265	Fr.	Atlanta, GA (Southwest)
42	*Tiberi, Lou	FB/DB	6-0	185	So.	Blue Island, IL (Eisenhower)
3	Vucovich, Dan	QB	6-0	185	So.	Mt. Prospect, IL (Hersey)
22	*Washington, Greg	RB/FB	6-0	185	So.	Miami, FL (Gulliver Academy)
29	*Webb, Jo Jo	TB	5-7	156	So.	Clairton, PA (Clairton)
25	Weir, Bill	WR	6-1	180	Jr.	Coshocton, OH (Coshocton)
74	**Wells, Norm	DT	6-4	236	Sr.	Warren, MI (Mott)
19	Westerhausen, Don	DB	6-0	200	Jr.	Apple Valley, MN (Rosemont)
	Woods, Jerome	RB/FB	6-2½	190	Fr.	St. Louis, MO (Hazelwood East)
44	Wuldner, Andy	DB	5-10	190	So.	Alton, IL (Alton)

1979 OHIO STATE ALPHABETICAL TEAM ROSTER

(* Denotes letters won)

	Name	Pos	Wgt.	Hgt.	Age	Class	Hometown
*	Andria, Ernest	OG	238	6-3	22	Sr.	Wintersville, O.
*	Atha, Bob	PK	182	6-0	20	So.	Worthington, O.
*	Bach, Terry	MG	210	5-10	21	Jr.	Centerville, O.
	Balen, Alan	DT	221	6-1	20	Jr.	Lackawanna, N.Y.
	Barnard, Eric	MG	235	6-1	18	Fr.	Massillon, O.
	Barton, Avery	OLB	202	6-3	18	Fr.	Detroit, Mich.
*	Barwig, Ron	TE	250	6-8	21	Sr.	Willoughby Hills, O.
*	Bell, Todd	DB	202	6-1	20	Jr.	Middletown, O.
*	Belmer, Cliff	FB	203	6-1	21	Jr.	Mansfield, O.
	Berner, Joe	LB	215	6-3	19	So.	Avon Lake, O.
*	Blinco, Tom	LB	221	6-2	21	Sr.	Lewiston, N.Y.
	Brown, Bernie	C	216	6-1	18	Fr.	Marietta, O.
*	Brown, Tim	OT	270	6-6	22	Sr.	Warren, O.
*	Burke, Tim	OT	252	6-5	22	Sr.	Wapakoneta, O.
*	Burris, Scott	OG	236	6-3	21	Sr.	Point Pleasant, W. Va.
*	Burrows, Norman	DB	182	5-11	20	Jr.	Portsmouth, O.
	Burrows, Scott	LB	200	6-2	18	Fr.	Portsmouth, O.
*	Campbell, Paul	FB	217	6-1	22	Sr.	Ravenna, O.
*	Castignola, Greg	QB	180	6-2	21	Sr.	Trenton, Mich.
	Cobb, Glen	LB	212	6-3	18	Fr.	Washington C.H., O.
	Corbin, Steve	OT	232	6-5	18	Fr.	Lima, O.
	D'Andrea, Mike	OLB	218	6-4	19	So.	Akron, O.
	DeCamp, Steve	OT	240	6-3	18	Fr.	Gahanna, O.
	DeLeone, Jim	C	217	5-11	21	Jr.	Kent, O.
*	Donley, Doug	FL	180	6-1	20	Jr.	Cambridge, O.
*	Dulin, Gary	DT	258	6-4	22	Sr.	Madisonville, Ky.
	Dwelle, Brad	TE	210	6-4	18	Fr.	Sandusky, O.
	Eberts, Mark	DB	187	5-11	20	So.	Canton, O.
	Echols, Reggie	DT	222	6-1	21	Sr.	Chardon, O.
*	Ellis, Ray	DB	194	6-2	20	Jr.	Canton, O.
	Ellison, Leon	OLB	211	6-2	21	Jr.	Washington, D.C.
	Epitropoulos, Ernest	OG	225	6-2	20	Jr.	Warren, O.
*	Epitropoulos, John	LB	225	6-2	20	Jr.	Warren, O.
*	Ferguson, Keith	OLB	232	6-5	20	Jr.	Miami, Fla.
	Foster, Jerome	MG	240	6-4	19	So.	Detroit, Mich.
*	Fritz, Ken	OG	238	6-3	21	Sr.	Ironton, O.
	Galloway, Tim	DB	186	6-2	18	Fr.	Columbus, O.
	Gatewood, Russell	OG	225	6-3	19	So.	Orlando, Fla.
	Gayle, Jim	TB	190	5-10	19	So.	Hampton, Va.
	Gorley, Rod	DB	182	6-0	19	Fr.	Cincinnati, O.
*	Guess, Mike	DB	176	5-11	21	Sr.	Columbus, O.
	Hafner, Steve	LB	228	6-0	20	So.	Sandusky, O.
	Hall, Ted	LB	212	6-2	19	So.	Gahanna, O.
	Harris, Dennis	SE	176	5-11	22	Sr.	Cleveland, O.
*	Henson, Luther	DT	241	6-2	20	Jr.	Sandusky, O.
*	Hicks, Tyrone	TB	180	5-11	22	Jr.	Warren, O.
*	Houston, Jim	TE	218	6-3	19	So.	Akron, O.
*	Hunter, Chuck	SE	203	6-2	22	Sr.	Newark, Del.

*	Hutchings, John	C	215	6-0	21	Jr.	Fremont, O.
*	Jaco, Bill	TE	248	6-5	22	Sr.	Toledo, O.
	James, Greg	LB	206	6-2	20	Jr.	Bloomfield, Conn.
*	Janakievski, Vlade	PK	158	5-8	22	Sr.	Columbus, O.
*	Johnson, Ricky	TB	192	6-0	20	Sr.	Santa Maria, Calif.
	Jusek, Jerry	DB	195	6-3	20	Jr.	Eastlake, O.
	Lamb, Steve	FL	190	6-0	19	So.	Findlay, O.
*	Laughlin, Jim	OLB	214	6-2	21	Sr.	Lyndhurst, O.
*	Lee, Ben	OLB	196	6-0	20	So.	Canton, O.
	Lee, Felix	FB	229	6-1	20	Jr.	Highland Park, N.J.
	Lewis, Doyle	DB	183	6-1	19	Fr.	Canton, O.
	Levenick, Tom	OT	244	6-4	19	So.	Washington, Ill.
	Lindsey, Kelvin	TB	180	6-0	18	Fr.	Sandusky, O.
	Lukens, Joe	OT	234	6-3	18	Fr.	Cincinnati, O.
*	Mackie, Doug	OT	250	6-4	22	Sr.	Saugus, Mass.
	Manning, Rob	OLB	210	6-1	20	Jr.	Columbus, O.
	Marek, Marcus	LB	214	6-2	18	Fr.	Masury, O.
	Marshall, Linwood	OLB	220	6-2	18	Fr.	Cincinnati, O.
	McEldowney, Doug	PK	186	5-11	20	Jr.	Centerville, O.
	McTier, Dave	QB	196	6-2	18	Fr.	Eustis, Fla.
	Medich, Dave	C	237	6-2	20	Jr.	Steubenville, O.
*	Megaro, Tony	LB	227	6-2	20	Jr.	Chicago, Ill.
	Miller, Nick	DT	226	6-3	19	Jr.	Upland, Pa.
	Miller, Ron	DT	226	6-3	20	Jr.	Auburn, N.Y.
	Moberger, Steve	OG	220	6-2	22	Sr.	Lima, O.
	Moran, Dave	DT	233	6-3	18	Fr.	Columbus, O.
*	Murphy, Bob	DB	193	6-1	21	Jr.	Santa Ynez, Calif.
*	Murray, Calvin	TB	185	5-11	20	Jr.	Woodbine, N.J.
	Myers, Ray	FB	220	6-3	18	Fr.	Toledo, O.
	O'Cain, Tim	TB	174	5-10	20	So.	Gahanna, O.
	Olman, Kevin	LB	225	6-3	18	Fr.	Toledo, O.
*	Orosz, Tom	P	207	6-1	20	Jr.	Fairport Harbor, O.
	Pack, Craig	LB	218	6-2	19	So	Orrville, O.
	Palahnuk, Mike	OT	235	6-2	19	So.	Hicksville, N.Y.
	Pauley, Doug	FL	180	6-1	20	Jr.	Carpinteria, Calif.
*	Payton, Joel	FB	221	6-2	20	Jr.	Mentor, O.
	Phillips, Dave	DT	221	6-5	21	Jr.	Vienna, W. Va.
	Phillips, Larry	DT	230	6-3	20	So.	Vienna, W. Va.
	Riehm, Chris	DT	240	6-6	18	Fr.	Wadsworth, O.
	Rolf, Rex	TE	213	6-2	22	Sr.	Gibsonburg, O.
*	Sawicki, Tim	MG	217	6-0	21	Sr.	Mayfield, O.
*	Schlichter, Art	QB	197	6-2	19	So.	Bloomingburg, O.
*	Schwartz, Brian	DB	190	6-1	21	Sr.	Simi Valley, Calif.
	Simpson, Steve	OT	228	6-5	18	Fr.	Temperance, Mich.
*	Skillings, Vince	DB	172	6-0	20	Jr.	Brenizer, Pa.
	Spencer, Tim	TB	200	6-0	18	Fr.	St. Clairsville, O.
	Smith, Joe	C	242	6-3	19	So.	Cincinnati, O.
*	Strahine, Mike	QB	194	6-0	21	Sr.	Lakewood, O.
	Sullivan, Mark	MG	205	5-9	20	So.	Cleveland, O.
*	Taylor, Alvin	SE	182	6-0	21	Sr.	Newport News, Va.
	Thomas, Bill	OT	255	6-5	18	Fr.	Cincinnati, O.
*	Volley, Ricardo	FB	208	6-0	21	Sr.	Lynchburg, Va.
*	Washington, Al	LB	222	6-3	20	Jr.	Cleveland, O.
	Watson, Otha	DB	200	6-0	20	So.	Dayton, O.
*	Waugh, Tom	C	242	6-1	22	Sr.	Norwalk, O.
	Williams, Gary	SE	197	6-2	19	So.	Wilmington, O.

Player	Pos.	Ht./Wt.	Class	Exp. L-Min.	Hometown (High School)
Willis, Ken	DB	181	6-0	20 Jr.	Columbus, O.
Wilson, Bill	OLB	220	6-2	18 Fr.	Columbus, O.
* Meade, John	TE	237	6-5	19 So.	Mokena, Ill.

1979
PURDUE ALPHABETICAL TEAM ROSTER

(* Denotes letters won)   Seniors: 2   Juniors: 30   Sophmores: 35

Player	Pos.	Ht./Wt.	Class	Exp. L-Min.	Hometown (High School)
Mark Adamle	DE	6-0/197	Sr.	2-92	Kent, OH (Roosevelt)
Jay Allison	OL	6-7/285	So.	0-10	Gahanna, OH (Westerville)
Mike Augustyniak	FB	6-1/217	Sr.	1-130	Leo, IN (Leo)
Joe Barioli	PK	5-9/190	So.	0-0	Ft. Lauderdale, Fl (St. Thomas Aquinas)
Jim Barr	MG	5-10/230	Sr.	1-33	Greensburg, IN (New Castle Chrysler)
Tom Barr	TE	6-3/223	So.	0-15	Greensburg, IN (Greensburg)
Joe Battaglia	C	6-2/242	Sr.	0-0	Chicago, IL (Loyola Academy)
Joe Betulius	QB	6-2/200	Jr.	0-2	Evansville, IN (Reitz)
David Booker	RB	6-0/190	So.	0-0	Plymouth, MI (Plymouth Salem)
Dean Bordigioni	LB	6-2/220	Jr.	1-78	Las Vegas, NV (Clark)
Mike Brown	OL	6-0/214	So.	0-0	West Palm Beach, FL (Twin Lakes)
Matt Bunchek	OL	6-0/202	So.	0-0	Chesterton, IN (Chesterton)
Bart Burrell	WR	6-2/180	Jr.	2-249	Carmel, IN (Carmel)
Kelly Cheesewright	OL	6-3/210	So.	0-0	Dana, IN (South Vermillion)
Calvin Clark	DT	6-5/234	Jr.	2-420	Atlanta, GA (Brown)
Dennis Dodge	OL	6-5/238	Jr.	0-6	Port Clinton, OH (Port Clinton)
Frank Doria	FB	5-11/210	Jr.	0-3	Flushing, NY (St. Francis)
Guy East	OL	6-5/222	So.	0-0	Indianapolis, IN (North Central)
John Ernst	DE	6-4/218	Jr.	1-30	Cincinnati, OH (St. Xavier)
Mike Farris	LB	6-3/233	Sr.	0-0	Cleveland, OH (Benedictine)
Henry Feil	OT	6-4/255	Jr.	2-313	Long Island, NY (Berner)
Jim Fritzsche	OL	6-8/245	So.	0-1	Parma, OH (Valley Forge)
Mike Fuetterer	WR	6-3/191	So.	0-2	Columbus, IN (Columbus East)
Issaac Gooden	DE	6-3/202	So.	0-0	Detroit, MI (Cass Tech)
Keevan Grimmett	DE	6-4/226	Jr.	2-110	Harvey, IL (Thornton Township)
Ray Gunner	OL	6-2/225	So.	0-10	Toledo, OH (Woodward)
Don Guyton	RB	5-11/178	So.	0-1	Memphis, TN (Northside)
Don Hall	OL	6-4/224	Sr.	2-87	Glen Ellyn, IL (Glenbard West)
Terry Hanley	MG	5-11/220	So.	0-0	Oak Park, IL (Fenwick)
Paul Hanna	DL	6-4/230	So.	0-12	Westlake, OH (Westlake)
Labraunt Harris	WR	5-10/187	So.	0-5	Miami, FL (Carol City)
Mike Harris	WR	6-0/182	Sr.	1-223	Los Angeles, CA (Cerritos)
Mark Herrmann	QB	6-5/194	Jr.	2-506	Carmel, IN (Carmel)
Tim Hull	OL	6-3/227	Jr.	1-45	Indianapolis, IN (North Central)
Marcus Jackson	DT	6-4/260	Sr.	3-667	Lima, OH (Lima)
Mark Johanson	LB	6-2/211	Sr.	2-210	Indianapolis, IN (Lawrence Central)
Jerome Johnson	WR	6-0/183	Jr.	0-0	Harvey, IL (Bremen)
Robert Jones	DL	6-3/211	Jr.	0-4	McKenney, VA (Dinwiddie)
Wally Jones	RB	6-1/192	So.	1-29	Detroit, MI (Central)
Mark Josten	DE	6-3/214	Sr.	2-65	Indianapolis, IN (Warren Central)
Bill Kay	DB	6-2/183	Jr.	2-205	Chicago, IL (Proviso East)
Ron Keith	RB	6-1/185	So.	0-4	St. Marys, OH (Memorial)
Tom Kingsbury	DE	5-11/198	Jr.	2-70	Chicago, IL (St. Rita)
Terry Kingseed	P	5-11/196	Sr.	0-0	Greentown, IN (Eastern)
Steve Krol	OL	6-5/238	Jr.	2-137	Chicago, IL (De La Salle)

Player	Pos.	Ht./Wt.	Class	Exp. L-Min.	Hometown (High School)
Greg Lehman	OL	6-2/216	Sr.	0-0	Lima, OH (Bath)
Mark Leveritt	DL	6-3/222	So.	0-0	Valparaiso, IN (Valparaiso)
Joe Linville	P-QB	6-1/161	So.	1-16	Carmel, IN (Carmel)
Ken Loushin	MG	6-2/248	Sr.	2-565	Richmond Hts., OH (Richmond)
Moe Lovely	DB	6-3/194	So.	0-0	Chicago, IL (Mendel)
John Macon	FB	6-1/205	Jr.	2-233	Marion, IN (Marion)
Bryan Maher	WR	6-1/195	So.	0-1	Highland Falls, NY (Choate)
Mike Marks	LB	6-3/229	Jr.	1-123	Chicago, IL (Leo)
Desi Martello	LB	6-1/205	So.	0-0	Chicago, IL (Leo)
Don McAfee	RB	5-9/175	Sr.	0-3	Eau Claire, MI (Eau Claire)
Ben McCall	RB	6-0/193	Jr.	1-56	Chicago, IL (Mendel)
Steve McKenzie	OT	6-5/260	Sr.	3-610	Chicago, IL (De La Salle)
Marcus McKinnie	DB	6-2/178	So.	0-18	Barberton, OH (Barberton)
Jim Meyer	FB	5-11/202	So.	0-7	Elk Grove, IL (Elk Grove)
Tom Mihal	WR	6-0/184	Sr.	0-5	Muncie, IN (Northside)
Kevin Motts	LB	6-2/230	Sr.	3-776	South Bend, IN (Mishawaka Marian)
Tom Munro	DE	6-6/212	So.	0-14	Elk Grove, IL (Elk Grove)
Don Myers	OL	6-4/240	So.	0-6	Greenfield, IN (Central)
Elwood Nolen	DB	5-10/190	Jr.	0-0	Newark, NJ (Eastside)
Mark Osman	LB	6-1/212	Sr.	0-12	Wilmette, IL (Loyola Academy)
Greg Palumbo	OL	6-3/226	Sr.	2-45	Cleveland, OH (Cathedral Latin)
Cleo Peete	WR	6-3/182	So.	0-2	Memphis, TN (Northside)
Bob Pruitt	RB	6-0/193	Jr.	0-3	Chicago, IL (Phillips)
Pete Quinn	C	6-2/243	Sr.	2-472	Indianapolis, IN (Scecina)
Dave Rastovski	TE	6-5/212	Sr.	0-2	Merrillville, IN (Merrillville)
Tim Rastovski	DE	6-3/213	Sr.	0-0	Merrillville, IN (Merrillville)
Dwight Robinson	RB	5-11/184	Sr.	2-42	Ft. Wayne, IN (Snider)
Steve Schlundt	OL	6-5/230	Sr.	2-177	Mishawaka, IN (Mishawaka)
Dale Schwan	OL	6-4/228	Sr.	2-416	Westlake, OH (Westlake)
John Seibel	PK	5-11/176	Sr.	0-1	Cincinnati, OH (Princeton)
Tim Seneff	DB	6-2/200	So.	1-80	Merrillville, IN (Merrillville)
Ray Smith	WR	6-2/197	Sr.	2-560	Paris, KY (Paris)
Wayne Smith	DB	6-0/180	Sr.	1-282	Chicago, IL (Harper)
Jeff Speedy	WR	6-3/186	So.	1-30	Louisville, KY (Fairdale)
Jeff Thorson	OL	6-5/214	Sr.	1-6	Pittsburgh, PA (Upper St. Clair)
Steve Townsend	DL	6-2/228	So.	0-1	Hartford City, IN (Blackford County)
Keena Turner	DE	6-3/212	Sr.	3-610	Chicago, IL (Vocational)
Gary Vargyas	DB	5-9/187	Sr.	0-9	South Bend, IN (Mishawaka Marian)
Eddie Webber	DE	6-4/210	So.	0-4	Hazelwood, MO (Hazelwood)
Mike Weissert	OL	5-11/236	Jr.	1-40	Ft. Wayne, IN (Bishop Dwenger)
Jim Wilkinson	OL	6-3/227	So.	0-0	Munster, IN (Munster)
Robert Williams	TB	5-10/180	Jr.	1-93	St. Louis, MO (Sumner)
Jeff Williamson	QB	6-2/190	So.	0-0	Morocco, IN (North Newton)
Ammon Wynn	LB	6-2/196	So.	0-0	Chicago, IL (Vocational)
Dave Young	TE	6-6/222	Jr.	2-310	Akron, OH (East)
John Zordani	DE	6-3/209	Jr.	0-0	Chicago, IL (Brother Rice)

1979 WISCONSIN ALPHABETICAL TEAM ROSTER

(* Denotes letters won)

No.	Name of Player	Pos	HGT	WGT	AGE	Class	Home Town and School
41	**Ahrens, Dave	OLB	6-3	216	20	Jr	Oregon, WI
69	Aldrich, Mark	LOT	6-5½	251	19	So	Angola, IN
29	*Anderson, Ross	WSC	5-10	175	20	Jr	Madison (LaFollette)
85	*Blaskowski, Curt	LDT	6-3	220	20	Jr	Schofield (D.C. Everest)
95	*Boliaux, Guy	OLB	6-½	203	19	So	DesPlaines,IL(Maine East)
19	**Braker, Tom	X	6-5	205	21	Sr	Beaver Dam, WI
65	Burney, Richard	ILB	6-1	201	21	Sr	Norfolk,VA(Lake Taylor)
3	Buss, Jeff	QB	6-1½	211	20	Sr	Wisconsin Dells, WI
67	**Cabral, Kasey	N	6-3½	244	20	Sr	New Bedford, MA
30	*Casey, Mickey	CSC	5-11	180	20	Sr	Eau Claire (Regis)
	Chapman, William	RDT	6-1	220	19	So	West Bend, WI
48	*Christenson, Dennis	ILB	6-1	222	22	Sr	Oregon, WI
74	Coleman, Tim	RDT	6-5	269	22	Sr	Baltimore, MD(Douglas) (Iowa Lakes JC)
60	Collins, Willie	N	6-3	218	19	So	Detroit, MI(McKenzie)
	Dalgleish, Tom	Y	6-4	240	20	Jr	Grand Rapids, MI (Grand Rapids JC)
16	Delaney, Patrick	CSC	5-9½	178	19	Jr	Stratford, WI
61	Dixon, John	ROG	5-10	215	20	Jr	Wisconsin Dells, WI
70	*Doerger, Jerry	ROT	6-5	238	18	So	Cincinnati, OH(LaSalle)
44	Fixmer, Mike	Y	6-2	196	20	Jr	Rhinelander
32	Goff, Mark	FB	6-1	194	18	So	Monona (Monona Grove)
	Grimes, Darryl	TB	6-1	185	19	So	Racine (St. Catherine)
35	Griffith, Gene	FB	6-0	205	20	Jr	Stow, OH
22	Hable, Ben	OLB	6-4	200	20	Sr	Madison (Memorial)
90	*Houston, Thomas	LDT	6-3	238	21	Sr	Washington,DC(Woodson)
	Hughes, Paul	B	6-2	200	19	Jr	Detroit, MI(Cooley)
13	*Josten, John	QB	6-1	187	18	So	Palatine, IL (St. Viator)
	Johnson, Brian	QB	6-3	190	21	Jr	Cambridge, WI
71	Joyce, Leo	LOG	5-11	243	19	Jr	Wisconsin Dells, WI
	Kalasmiki, Mike	QB	6-4	210	21	Sr	Addison, IL
31	*Kiltz, John	KS	6-4	215	19	Jr	Hartland, WI(Arrowhead)
91	Krein, Joel	LDT	6-3	238	20	Sr	Racine (Park)
88	*Krepfle, Mike	Y	6-2	198	19	Jr	Potosi, WI
	Larkin, Tim	TB	5-11	180	19	So	Wisconsin Dells, WI
	Lawrence, Timothy	B	6-1	195	19	So	Cuba City, WI
47	**Levenick, Dave	ILB	6-2	204	19	Jr	Grafton, WI
57	Lewis, Richard	ILB	6-2	209	20	Jr	Akron, OH(Springfield)
43	*Lorenz, Don	OLB	6-4	215	20	Sr	Marshfield, WI
62	Luko, Jeff	LOG	6-3	215	19	So	Oconomowoc, WI
	Mansfield, Edward von	WSC	5-10	180	18	So	Milwaukee (University School)
63	*Martine, Jim	ROG	6-1	231	20	Sr	Neenah, WI
92	Mathews, Ed	OLB	6-1	185	20	So	Verona, WI
	Mathews, Terry	KS	5-11	180	20	Jr	Ft. Wayne, IN
	McDonald, Sean	RDT	6-4	260	19	So	Menomonee Falls,WI (North)

#	Name	Pos	Ht	Wt	Age	Yr	Hometown
40	McKinnon, Kyle	Z	5-10	180	18	So	Verona, WI
1	Messenger, Dan	WSC	6-1	177	19	So	Marinette, WI
78	Miskinis, Greg	ROT	6-5½	262	19	Jr	Racine, WI(Horlick)
17	Moeschl, Scott	QB	6-3	204	19	So	Cincinnati, OH(Elder)
28	*Mohapp, Dave	FB	5-11	202	18	So	Woodstock, IL
16	Moyl, Kevin	QB	6-2	185	19	Jr	Sun Prairie, WI
73	Namnick, Steve	LOT	6-5	230	18	So	Morton Growe, IL (Gordon Tech)
	Parish, Steve	QB	6-1	190	21	So	Evansville, WI
	Reber, Tom	LOT	6-3½	235	19	Jr	Grand Rapids, MI (Grand Rapids JC)
33	Richardson, Curtis	TB	6-1	182	19	So	Youngstown, OH(North)
	Roberstad, David	QB	6-0	185	19	So	Madison, WI(East)
9	Rogness, Mark	TB	6-0	175	20	So	Osseo, WI(Osseo-Fairchild)
59	*Rothbauer, Joe	C	6-0	226	21	Sr	Oshkosh, WI(Lourdes)
81	*Ruetz, Joe	Y	6-1½	215	20	Jr	Racine, WI(St. Catherine)
64	Rutenberg, Bill	ROG	5-10	208	19	Jr	Waunakee, WI
24	Savage, Nick	S	6-0	170	18	So	Baltimore, MD (Northwestern)
76	**Schremp, Tom	RDT	6-3½	251	21	Sr	Antigo, WI
97	Seamonson, Al	Z	6-0	178	19	So	Stoughton, WI
81	Seis, Dean	ROT	6-4	221	21	Jr	Antigo, WI
46	Shumate, Mark	LDT	6-3	205	19	So	Poynette, WI
55	Skoglund, Dan	N	6-1	212	18	So	LaGrange Park, IL (Fenwick)
75	**Snell, Ray	ROT	6-3	251	21	Sr	Baltimore, MD (Northwestern)
6	**Souza, Wayne	Z	6-2	187	20	Sr	New Bedford, MA
	Sprinkel, Greg	WSC	5-10	180	19	So	Montfort, WI
49	Spurklin, Larry	ILB	6-0	217	19	So	Albany, GA(Dougherty)
26	**Stauss, Tom	TB	5-11	194	21	Sr	Jefferson, WI
42	*Stracka, Tim	X	6-4	195	19	So	Madison, WI(West)
5	Stroede, Terry	B	6-0	188	20	Sr	Baraboo, WI
87	*Sydnor, Ray	Y	6-8	225	20	Sr	Baltimore, MD (Northwestern)
27	Thomas, Vaughn	CSC	6-0	175	18	So	Columbus, OH(Eastmoor)
	Thurston, Griff	FB	6-1	195	19	So	Neenah, WI
94	Timmer, Jeff	CSC	6-2	177	19	So	Oconomowoc, WI
	Vanden Boom, Mathew	X	6-3	180	18	So	Kimberly, WI
7	**Veith, Steve	KS	6-1	196	21	Sr	Sun Prairie, WI
58	Versnik, Ron	C	6-4	228	18	So	West Allis (Hale)
89	**Vine, Jeff	OLB	6-3	202	20	Sr	Granton, WI(Neillsville)
51	Walter, Ted	C	6-1½	203	20	Jr	Akron, OH(St. V-St.Mary)
12	**Welch, George	S	6-1	195	20	Sr	Benton Harbor, MI(St.Jose)
	Westphal, John	B	5-11	191	19	So	Janesville, WI(Craig)
54	Wicks, Doug	ILB	6-2	219	19	Jr	Blue Island, IL(Eisenhower)
70	*Woodford, Bruce	LDT	6-3	240	20	Sr	South Bend, IN(Adams)
96	Wray, Richard	CSC	6-1	176	18	So	Toledo, OH(Whitmer)
61	Yourg, Dan	N	6-1	213	20	Sr	Arlington Hgts., IL (St. Viator)

MODERN ERA (Since 1939) RECORDS
(Based on Conference Games Only)
INDIVIDUAL SINGLE GAME RECORDS
(Home Team in Caps)

SCORING
Most Points: 30, HB Ron Johnson (5 TD), MICHIGAN vs. Wisconsin, 11-16-68
30, HB Mike Northington (5 TD), PURDUE vs. Iowa, 11-3-73
30, HB Billy Marek (5 TD), WISCONSIN vs. Minnesota, 11-23-74
Most Touchdowns: 5, HB Ron Johnson, MICHIGAN vs. Wisconsin, 11-16-68
5, HB Billy Marek, WISCONSIN vs. Minnesota, 11-23-74
5, HB Mike Northington, PURDUE vs. Iowa, 11-3-73
Most PAT Attempts: 11, HB Vic Janowicz (10 made), OHIO STATE vs. Iowa 10-28-50
Most PAT Made: 10, Vic Janowicz (11 att.), OHIO STATE vs. Iowa 10-28-50
Most Field Goals: 5, Dan Beaver, ILLINOIS vs. Purdue (52, 44, 35, 34, 32), 10-13-73
4, Five players have accomplished this, last of whom was Hans Nielsen, MICHIGAN STATE vs. Purdue, 9-10-77

LONGEST SCORING PLAYS
Run from Scrimmage: 96 yds., HB Eddie Vincent, IOWA vs. Purdue, 11-6-54
94 yds., FB Mike Pruitt, Purdue vs. IOWA, 11-2-74
Pass: 95 yds., QB Len Dawson to HB Erich Barnes, PURDUE vs. Northwestern, 11-12-55
Field goal: 59 yds., PK Tom Skladany, Ohio State vs. ILLINOIS, 11-8-75
Pass Interception: 99 yds., LB Dan Bass, MSU vs. Wisconsin, 10-28-78
KO Return: 100 yds., HB George Rice, Iowa vs. PURDUE, 10-6-51; HB Bill Wentz, Ohio State vs. ILLINOIS, 10-8-60; Rick Upchurch, Minnesota vs. WISCONSIN, 11-23-74; Ira Matthews, WISCONSIN vs. Indiana, 11-6-76 & Bobby Weber, Minnesota vs. OHIO STATE, 9-17-77
Punt Return: 95 yds., E Al Brenner, MSU vs. ILLINOIS, 10-1-66
Recovered Fumble: 92 yds., Dale Keneipp, Indiana vs. MINNESOTA, 11-4-78
Blocked Kick Return: 92 yds., Earl Faison, Indiana vs. MSU, 11-8-58 (FG att.)

RUSHING
Most Rushes: 57, FB Kent Kitzmann (266 yds.), Minnesota vs. ILLINOIS, 11-12-77
Most Yds. Gained: 350 yds., TB Eric Allen (29 rushes), MSU vs. PURDUE, 10-30-71
347 yds., HB Ron Johnson (31 rushes), MICHIGAN vs. Wisconsin, 11-16-68
316 yds., HB Mike Adamle (40 rushes), NORTHWESTERN vs. Wisconsin, 10-18-69
306 yds., HB Billy Marek (43 rushes), WISCONSIN vs. Minnesota, 11-23-74
Most Yds. Per Play: 18.0, FB Rob Lytle (10-180), MICHIGAN vs. Michigan St., 10-9-76
17.9, FB Mike Pruitt (10-179), PURDUE vs. Iowa, 11-2-74

PASSING
Most Attempts: 49, QB Gary Snook (26 compl., 310 yds.), IOWA vs. Purdue, 10-24-64
Most Completed: 28, QB Craig Curry (47 att., 297 yds.), Minnesota vs. OHIO STATE, 10-17-70
Most Yds. Gained: 369 yds., QB Ed Smith (20 of 30 att.), MSU vs. Indiana, 10-21-78
351 yds., QB Mitch Anderson (20 of 34 att.), NU vs. MSU, 11-25-72
320 yds., QB Ed Smith (19 of 29 att.), MSU vs. Wisconsin, 10-28-78
Best Completion Pct.: (10 or more att.): .857, QB Dale Samuels, Purdue vs. ILLINOIS (12 of 14), 10-25-52
Most Consec. Compl.: 12, QB Bill Mrukowski, OHIO STATE vs. Illinois, 10-14-61
Most Had Interc.: 6, Tom O'Connell (34 att., 22 comp.), Illinois vs. IOWA, 11-8-52; Don Swanson (17 att., 6 comp.), Minnesota vs. WISCONSIN, 11-20-54
Most TD Passes: 5, QB Fred Riddle (16 att., 10 comp., 155 yds.), IOWA vs. Indiana, 10-12-63 (TD Passes of 5, 5, 3, 76 & 4 yds.)
5, QB Mitch Anderson (41 att., 22 comp. 315 yds.), NORTHWESTERN vs. Minnesota, 11-3-73 (TD Passes of 18, 19, 21, 13 and 20 yds.)

TOTAL OFFENSE
Most Plays: 61, QB Dennis Brown (30 rush, 31 pass), MICHIGAN vs. Indiana, 10-21-67
Most Yds. Gained: 369 yds., QB Ed Smith (4-0 rush, 30-20-369 pass) MSU vs. Indiana, 10-21-78
353 yds., Art Schlichter (16-64 rush, 34-20-289 pass) Ohio State vs. PURDUE, 10-14-78
350 yds., TB Eric Allen (29-350 rush), MSU vs. Purdue, 10-30-71
347 yds., HB Ron Johnson (31-347 rush) MICHIGAN vs. Wisconsin, 11-16-68
Yds. Per Play: 17.9, FB Mike Pruitt (10-179 rush), PURDUE vs. Iowa, 11-2-74
17.3, HB Bobby Mitchell (10-173 rush), Illinois vs. MICHIGAN, 11-5-55

RECEIVING
Most Caught: 13, E Don Stonesifer (140 yds., 2 TD), NORTHWESTERN vs. Minnesota, 10-14-50
Most Yds. Gained: 226, Jim Lash (9 catches), NU vs. MSU, 11-25-72
Most Passes Interc.: 4, Clarence Bratt, WISCONSIN vs. Minnesota, 11-20-54
4, Paul Beery, Purdue vs. WISCONSIN, 10-9-76
Most Yds. Interc. Ret.: 140, DB Walt Bowser (3 interc.), Minnesota vs. MSU, 11-14-70
Most TD Passes: 4, Reggie Arnold, PURDUE vs. Iowa, 10-22-77

PUNTING
Most Kicked: 24, HB Chuck Ortmann (723 yds.), Michigan vs. OHIO STATE, 11-25-50
Most Yds. Kicked: 723 yds., HB Chuck Ortmann (24 punts), Michigan vs. OHIO STATE, 11-25-50
685 yds., FB Vic Janowicz (21 punts), OHIO STATE vs. Michigan, 11-25-50
Best Average: 57.3, FB Fred Morrison (4 punts, 229 yds.), OSU vs. WISCONSIN, 10-22-49
Longest Punt: 96 yds., G George O'Brien, Wisconsin vs. IOWA, 10-18-52
Most Punts Returned: 10, William Lane (83 yds.), WISCONSIN vs. Indiana, 11-3-51
Most Yards Returned: 201, Nile Kinnick, IOWA vs. Indiana, 10-7-39
Most Blocked: 2, T Mike Enich, Iowa vs. PURDUE, 11-4-39

KICKOFFS
Most Returned: 8, Craig Clemons (165 yds.), Iowa vs. MICHIGAN, 11-6-71
Most Yds. Returned: 203, Ron Engel (7 ret.), Minnesota vs. MICHIGAN, 10-27-51

INDIVIDUAL SEASON RECORDS

(Figures in parentheses denote number of
Conference games played in season.)

SCORING
Most Points: 110, TB Eric Allen, Michigan State (8), 1971 (18 TD, 2-pt. conv.)
96, FB Harold Henson, Ohio State (8), 1972 (16 TD)
96, FB Pete Johnson, Ohio State (8), 1975 (16 TD)
92, HB Ron Johnson, Michigan (7), 1968 (15 TD, 2-pt. conv.)
90, HB Leroy Keyes, Purdue (7), 1967 (15 TD)
90, HB Billy Marek, Wisconsin (8), 1974 (15 TD)
Most Touchdowns: 18, TB Eric Allen, Michigan State (8), 1971
16, FB Harold Henson, Ohio State (8), 1972
16, FB Pete Johnson, Ohio State (8), 1975
15, HB Leroy Keyes, Purdue (7), 1967
15, HB Ron Johnson, Michigan (7), 1968
15, HB Billy Marek, Wisconsin (8), 1974
Most PAT: 44, PK Morten Anderson, Michigan State (8), 1978 (45 att.)
38, PK Tom Klaban, Ohio State (8), 1975 (39 att.)
36, PK Dana Coin, Michigan (8), 1971 (36 att.)
36, PK Blair Conway, Ohio State (8), 1973 (42 att.)
36, PK Bob Wood, Michigan (8), 1976 (36 att.)
Most Field Goals: 13, PK Hans Nielsen, Michigan State (8), 1977 (18 att.)
11, PK Chris Gartner, Indiana (8), 1972 (18 att.)
11, PK Dan Beaver, Illinois (8), 1973 (17 att.)
11, PK Vince Lamia, Wisconsin (8), 1976 (18 att.)
11, PK Paul Rogind, Minnesota (8), 1977 (17 att.)

RUSHING
Most Rushes: 250, FB Mike Adamle, Northwestern (7), 1970
Highest Avg. Rushes
 Per Game: 35.7, FB Mike Adamle, Northwestern (7), 1970
Most Yards Gained (Net): 1,283, TB Eric Allen, Michigan State (8), 1971 (209 rushes)
1,181, HB Archie Griffin, Ohio State (8), 1973 (196 rushes)
1,176, HB Otis Armstrong, Purdue (8), 1972 (201 rushes)
1,139, TB Rob Lytle, Michigan (8), 1976 (160 rushes)
1,134, HB Archie Griffin, Ohio State (8), 1974 (175 rushes)
1,063, TB Gordon Bell, Michigan (8), 1975 (182 rushes)
1,053, FB Mike Adamle, NU (7), 1970 (250 rushes)
1,037, HB Courtney Snyder, Indiana (8), 1974 (232 rushes)
1,017, HB Ron Johnson, Michigan (7), 1968 (181 rushes)
Highest Avg. Per Game: 167.3, FB Bill Daley, Michigan (3), 1943
160.4, TB Eric Allen, Michigan State (8), 1978
Highest Avg. Gain 20 to 40 Attempts: 11.85, HB Tom James, Ohio State, 1942 (20 att.)
 Per Rush: 40 to 50 Attempts: 8.8, HB Willie Fleming, Iowa, 1958 (41 att.)
50 to 75 Attempts: 8.8, HB Bob Mitchell, Illinois, 1955 (53 att.)
Over 75 Attempts: 7.3, TB Steve Smith, Michigan State

PASSING
Most Attempted: 270, Kevin Strasser, Northwestern (9), 1978
238, Mike Phipps, Purdue (7), 1969
224, Ed Smith, Michigan State (8), 1978
Most Passes Completed: 132, Kevin Strasser, Northwestern (9), 1978
130, Ed Smith, Michigan State (8), 1978
118, Mike Phipps, Purdue (7), 1969
Best Completion Pct.: .645, Rod Gerald, Ohio State (8), 1977 (49 comp., 76 att.)
.642, John Coatta, Wisconsin (7), 1950 (52 comp., 81 att.)
Most Yards Gained: 1,779, Ed Smith, Michigan State (8), 1978
1,599, Mike Phipps, Purdue (7), 1969
Most TD passes: 16, Ed Smith, Michigan State (8), 1978

TOTAL OFFENSE
Most Plays: 316, QB Kevin Strasser, Northwestern (46 rush, 270 pass) (8), 1978
302, QB Mike Phipps, Purdue (64 rush, 238 pass) (7), 1969
Most Yards Gained
 Rushing & Passing: 1,808, Ed Smith, Michigan State (29 rush, 1,779 pass) (8), 1978
1,699, QB Mike Phipps, Purdue (100 rush, 1,599 pass) (7), 1969

PASS RECEIVING
Most Caught: 50, Jack Clancy, Michigan (7), 1966
Most Yards Gained: 698, Jack Clancy, Michigan (7), 1966 (50 catches)
TD Passes Caught: 8, Ashley Bell, Purdue (7), 1969

PASS INTERCEPTIONS
Most: 9, DB Tom Curtis, Michigan (7), 1968 (182 ret. yds.)
Most Yds. Returned: 203, DB Walt Bowser, Minnesota (7), 1970 (5 int.)

PUNTING
Most Kicked: 64, QB Frank Sunderman, Iowa (8), 1971 (37.7 avg.)
Best Avg.: 47.2, P Tom Skladany, Ohio State (8), 1975 (26 punts, 1226 yds.)
46.1, P Tom Skladany, Ohio State (8), 1974 (19 punts, 876 yds.)

PUNT RETURNS
Most: 33, DB Tom Campana, Ohio State (8), 1971 (404 yds.)
Best Avg.: 32.5 yds., HB Dean Look, Michigan State (6), 1958 (6 ret.)
Most Touchdowns: 3, TB Ira Matthews, Wisconsin (8)

KICKOFF RETURNS
Most: 26, HB Jim Pooler, Northwestern (8), 1974 (550 yds.)
Best Avg.: 41.1, HB Stan Brown, Purdue (6), 1970 (12 ret. 493 yds.)
Most Touchdowns: 3, HB Stan Brown, Purdue (6), 1970 (ret. of 100, 96 & 93 yds.)

TEAM SINGLE GAME RECORDS

(Home Team in Caps)

SCORING
Most Points: 85, Michigan vs. CHICAGO, 10-21-39
83, OHIO STATE vs. Iowa, 10-28-50
Most Touchdowns: 12, Michigan vs. CHICAGO, 10-21-39
12, OHIO STATE vs. Iowa, 10-28-50
Most Safeties: 2, Iowa vs. PURDUE, 11-4-39; Purdue vs. INDIANA, 11-19-55; Wisconsin vs. PURDUE, 10-20-51
Most PAT made: 11, OHIO STATE vs. Iowa (12 att.), 10-28-50
10, Michigan vs. CHICAGO (12 att.), 10-21-39
Most Field Goals: 5, ILLINOIS vs. Purdue, 10-13-73
4, INDIANA vs. Wisconsin, 10-14-72
4, MICHIGAN STATE vs. Ohio State, 11-11-72
4, OHIO STATE vs. Michigan, 11-23-74

RUSHING
Most Rushes: 92, PURDUE vs. Iowa (483 yds.), 10-26-68
Fewest Rushes: 21, Indiana vs. PURDUE (47 yds.), 11-20-48
Most Yards Gained: 573, Michigan State vs. PURDUE (70 rushes), 10-30-71
573, MICHIGAN vs. Northwestern (69 rushes), 10-8-75
551, Wisconsin vs. NORTHWESTERN (79 rushes), 11-16-74
524, MICHIGAN vs. Iowa (77 rushes), 11-15-69
Fewest Yards Gained: (-87), Iowa vs. WISCONSIN (29 rushes), 10-18-41
Best Avg. Per Rush: 10.33 yds., PURDUE vs. Illinois (39 rushes, 403 yds.), 10-2-43

PASSING
Most Attempts: 52, Northwestern vs. PURDUE (19 compl., 286 yds.), 10-25-69
50, IOWA vs. Purdue (26 compl., 310 yds.), 10-24-64
Fewest Attempts: 0, Minnesota vs. OHIO STATE, 10-19-40
Most Completed: 29, MINNESOTA vs. Ohio State (49 att.), 10-17-70
Fewest Completed: 0, by numerous teams
Most Yards Gained: 369, MSU vs. Indiana (30 att., 20 comp.), 10-21-78
Best Completion Avg.: 1.000, OHIO STATE vs. Iowa (8-8, 117 yds.), 10-11-75
(More than 8 attempts): .889, MICHIGAN vs. Minnesota (8-9, 203 yds.), 10-27-51
.883, Michigan State vs. INDIANA (10-12, 204 yds.), 10-13-56
Most TD passes: 5, OHIO STATE vs. Iowa, 10-28-50; IOWA vs. Indiana, 10-12-63 and NORTHWESTERN vs. Minnesota, 11-3-73
Most Had Interc.: 7, Minnesota vs. WISCONSIN, 11-20-54

TOTAL OFFENSE
Most Plays: 107, MICHIGAN vs. Minnesota (77 rushes, 30 passes; 453 yds.), 10-26-68
101, Iowa vs. MINNESOTA, 11-2-68
101, OHIO STATE vs. Illinois, 10-25-69
100, Illinois vs. INDIANA 10-5-68
Fewest Plays: 34, Iowa vs. INDIANA (31 rush, 3 pass), 10-28-44
35, ILLINOIS vs. Ohio State (28 rush, 7 pass), 11-16-46
Most Yards Gained: 698, Michigan State vs. PURDUE (573 rush, 125 pass), 10-30-71
673, Michigan vs. IOWA (524 rush, 149 pass), 11-15-69
660, MICHIGAN STATE vs. Iowa (489 rush, 171 pass), 11-23-74
655, OHIO STATE vs. Illinois (517 rush, 127 pass), 11-2-75
645, MSU vs. Wisconsin (295 rush, 350 pass), 10-28-78
Fewest Yards Gained: -19, Iowa vs. WISCONSIN (-87 rush, 68 pass), 10-18-41

PUNTING

Most Punts: 24, Michigan vs. OHIO STATE (723 yds.), 11-25-50
Fewest Punts: 0, ILLINOIS vs. Purdue 10-7-44; MICHIGAN STATE vs. Michigan, 10-13-62; Indiana vs. MINNESOTA, 10-5-46; WISCONSIN, vs. Iowa, 10-17-64; NORTHWESTERN vs. Illinois, 10-6-62; MINNESOTA vs. Indiana, 10-9-65 and MICHIGAN STATE vs. Purdue, 10-30-76
Most Yards Kicked: 723 yds., Michigan vs. OHIO STATE (24 punts), 11-25-50
685 yds., OHIO STATE vs. Michigan (21 punts), 11-25-50
531 yds., ILLINOIS vs. Northwestern (14 punts), 10-28-39
Best Average: 56.5 yds. Ohio State vs. Illinois (226 yds.), 11-8-75

FIRST DOWNS

Most by Rushing: 32, Wisconsin vs. NORTHWESTERN, 11-16-74
31, PURDUE vs. Iowa, 10-26-68
Fewest by Rushing: 0, Indiana vs. MICHIGAN, 11-12-49
0, Michigan vs. OHIO STATE, 11-25-50
0, Ohio State vs. MICHIGAN STATE, 10-16-65
Most by Passing: 19, MSU vs. Minnesota, 11-11-78
Fewest by Passing: 0, by numerous teams
Most Total First Downs: 37, Wisconsin vs. NORTHWESTERN, 11-16-74
34, Ohio State vs. NORTHWESTERN, 11-1-69
34, Michigan vs. IOWA, 11-15-69
34, Michigan State vs. NORTHWESTERN, 11-18-78
Fewest Total First Downs: 0, Michigan vs. OHIO STATE, 11-25-50
1, Purdue vs. OHIO STATE (1 rush), 10-17-42

FUMBLES

Most: 14, MICHIGAN STATE vs. Iowa (3 lost), 10-23-71
12, Wisconsin vs. MICHIGAN (5 lost), 11-8-44
11, Illinois vs. WISCONSIN (8 lost), 10-20-45
Fewest: 0, by numerous teams
Most Lost: 8, Illinois vs. WISCONSIN (11 fumbles), 10-20-48

PENALTIES

Most: 17, Michigan State vs. INDIANA, 9-28-57
Most Yards: 171, PURDUE vs. Northwestern, 10-25-69
Fewest Penalties: 0, by numerous teams, last of which was Illinois vs. MINNESOTA, 11-18-78

TEAM SEASON RECORDS

(Because of the varying number of Conference games played from year to year, the statistical marks are per game averages rather than totals. Figures in parentheses denote number of Conference games played in season.)

SCORING

Most Points: 41.0, Michigan State (328 points in 8), 1978
40.0, Ohio State (280 points in 7), 1969
Fewest Points: 0, Chicago (3), 1939
2.6, Illinois (5), 1941
Most Points by Opponents: 64.0, Chicago (192 in 3), 1939
41.9, Illinois (293 in 7), 1969
Fewest Points by Opponents: 3.8, Illinois (6), 1951

RUSHING

Most Rushes: 69.5, Ohio State (8), 1973;
65.7, Ohio State (7), 1969
Fewest Rushes: 26.7, Iowa (6), 1964
Most Yards Gained: 365.1, Ohio State (8), 1973;
364.1, Ohio State (8), 1974
Fewest Yards Gained: 59.0, Indiana (6), 1948
Most Yards Gained by Opponents: 374.5, Iowa (8), 1973;
363.3, Chicago (3), 1939
Fewest Yards Gained by Opponents: 34.6, Michigan State (7), 1965

PASSING

Most Attempted: 39.8, Iowa (6), 1964
Most Completed: 18.7, Iowa (6), 1964
18.1, Michigan State (8), 1978
Fewest Attempted: 4.0, Minnesota (5), 1943
Fewest Completed: 1.0, Minnesota (6), 1940
1.0, Minnesota (5), 1943
Most Yards Gained: 266.8, Iowa (6), 1964
Fewest Yards Gained: 12.8, Ohio State (6), 1955
Most Yards Gained by Opponents: 216.3, Michigan State (7), 1969
216.3, Purdue (7), 1969
Fewest Yards Gained by Opponents: 26.0, Michigan (6), 1943

597

Highest Average Completed:	.662, Ohio State (8), 1977 (53 of 80)
	.616, Ohio State (8), 1974 (67 of 143)
Lowest Average Completed:	.193, Minnesota (6), 1940
Highest Average Opponents' Passes Completed:	.587, Iowa (6), 1951
	.582, Minnesota (8), 1974 (71 of 122)
Lowest Average Opponents' Passes Completed:	.237, Illinois (6), 1945

TOTAL OFFENSE

Most Plays:	91.7, Ohio State (7), 1969
Most Yards Gained:	523.1, Michigan State (8), 1978
	481.9, Iowa (7), 1968
Fewest Yards Gained:	118.6, Purdue (5), 1942
Most Yards Gained by Opponents:	468.4, Illinois (7), 1969
Fewest Yards Gained by Opponents:	131.0, Michigan (6), 1943

PUNTING

Most Punts:	10.8, Northwestern (6), 1939
Fewest Punts:	2.25, Ohio State (8), 1977
Highest Average:	47.2, Ohio State (8), 1975
Lowest Average:	27.8, Minnesota (7), 1953

FIRST DOWNS

Most:	28.3, Ohio State (7), 1969
Fewest:	6.5, Iowa (6), 1944
Most Opponents' First Downs:	25.1, Northwestern (9), 1978
Fewest Opponents' First Downs:	6.0, Michigan (4), 1940

FUMBLES

Most:	5.5, Indiana (6), 1946 and Michigan State (6), 1962; (8), 1971
Fewest:	1.0, Purdue (8), 1975 and Minnesota (8), 1976
Most Fumbles Lost:	3.7, Michigan State (6), 1962
Fewest Fumbles Lost:	.25, Purdue (8), 1975
Most Opponents' Fumbles Recovered:	3.0, Purdue (6), 1943; Illinois (6), 1943; Minnesota (6), 1952
Fewest Opponents' Fumbles Recovered:	.25, Indiana (4), 1942

PENALTIES

Most:	8.5, Michigan State (6), 1964
Fewest:	2.0, Indiana (6), 1946; Northwestern (6), 1960
Most Yards Penalized:	82.8, Michigan State (6), 1956
Fewest Yards Penalized:	15.2, Wisconsin (6), 1948

ALL-TIME ALL BIG TEN FOOTBALL TEAM

The Big Ten celebrated its 75th anniversary in 1970 by naming an All Time Big Ten Football Team. The squad was selected by the Big Ten Skywriters from a list of 121 former greats who were selected to their schools' All Time Squads.

DIAMOND ANNIVERSARY TEAM ROSTER

ENDS	Wes Fesler	Ohio State	1928-30
	Ron Kramer	Michigan	1954-56
	Bennie Oosterbaan	Michigan	1925-27
	Pete Pihos	Indiana	1943-45
	Gene Washington	Michigan State	1964-66
TACKLES	Carl Eller	Minnesota	1961-63
	Alex Karras	Iowa	1955-57
	Bronko Nagurski	Minnesota	1927-29
	Leo Nomelini	Minnesota	1947-49
	Fred "Duke" Slater	Iowa	1919-21
GUARDS	Alex Agase	Illinois & Purdue	1942-43 & 1946
	Calvin Jones	Iowa	1953-55
	Jim Parker	Ohio State	1954-56
CENTER	Dick Butkus	Illinois	1962-64
QUARTERBACKS	Bob Griese	Purdue	1964-66
	Jay Berwanger	Chicago	1934-36

HALFBACKS	Harold "Red" Grange	Illinois	1923-25
	Tom Harmon	Michigan	1938-40
	Leroy Keyes	Purdue	1966-68
	Nile Kinnick	Iowa	1937-39
FULLBACKS	Alan "The Horse" Ameche	Wisconsin	1951-54
	George Webster	Michigan State	1964-66

1978 ALL-BIG TEN FOOTBALL PICKS

(Consensus of Associated Press and United Press International Teams)

* — AP Selection   ** — UPI Selection   No Marks — AP & UPI Selection

NOTE: Players' names in ALL CAPS were seniors in 1978

OFFENSE

FIRST TEAM	POS.	SECOND TEAM
Eugene Byrd, Michigan St.	Wide Receiver	*Brad Reid, Iowa
	Wide Receiver	DAVID CHARLES, Wisconsin
Mark Brammer, Michigan St.	Tight End	*Doug Marsh, Michigan
	Tight End	**JIMMY MOORE, Ohio State
JIM HINESLY, Michigan St.	Tackle	Steve McKenzie, Purdue
*JOE ROBINSON, Ohio State	Tackle	**Keith Ferguson, Ohio State
JON GIESLER, Michigan	Tackle	
Ken Fritz, Ohio State	Guard	**JOHN LEFEBER, Purdue
**John Arbeznik, Michigan	Guard	GREG BARTNICK, Michigan
	Guard	*Dale Schwan, Purdue
MARK HEIDEL, Indiana	Center	STEVE NAUTA, Michigan
KIRK GIBSON, Michigan St.	Flanker	**Ralph Clayton, Michigan
RICK LEACH, Michigan	Quarterback	ED SMITH, Michigan St.
RUSSELL DAVIS, Michigan	Running Back	Mike Harkrader, Indiana
Marion Barber, Minnesota	Running Back	John Macon, Purdue
Paul Rogind, Minnesota	Place Kicker	*SCOTT SOVEREEN, Purdue
	Place Kicker	**GREGG WILLNER, Michigan
**Ray Stachowicz, Michigan St.	Punter	
*Tom Orosz, Ohio State	Punter	

DEFENSE

FIRST TEAM	POS.	SECOND TEAM
**STAN SYTSMA, Minnesota	End	JERRY METER, Michigan
Keena Turner, Purdue	End	
*KELTON DANSLER, Ohio State	End	
Curtis Greer, Michigan	Tackle	Marcus Jackson, Purdue
MELVIN LAND, Michigan St.	Tackle	**BYRON CATO, Ohio State
	Tackle	*JIM RONAN, Minnesota
Ken Loushin, Purdue	Middle Guard	**DOUG FRIBERG, Minnesota
	Middle Guard	*DAN RELICH, Wisconsin
TOM COUSINEAU, Ohio State	Linebacker	TOM RUSK, Iowa
JOE NORMAN, Indiana	Linebacker	*JOHN SULLIVAN, Illinois
*Ron Simpkins, Michigan	Linebacker	*Dan Bass, Michigan St.
**Mike Guess, Ohio State	Defensive Back	**LAWRENCE JOHNSON, Wisconsin
Mike Jolly, Michigan	Defensive Back	Mark Anderson, Michigan St.
**KEITH BROWN, Minnesota	Defensive Back	*PAT GEEGAN, Northwestern
**Mike Harden, Michigan	Defensive Back	*DAVE ABRAMS, Indiana
*Vince Skillings, Ohio State	Defensive Back	
*TOM GRAVES, Michigan St.	Defensive Back	

ALL-TIME STANDINGS

Beginning of the Modern Era

	Conference Standing						Full Season					
1939	W.	L.	T.	Pct.	Pts.	O.Pts.	W.	L.	T.	Pct.	Pts.	O.Pts.
Ohio State	5	1	0	.833	156	51	6	2	0	.750	189	54
Iowa	4	1	1	.800	82	85	6	1	1	.857	130	91
Purdue	2	1	2	.667	30	30	3	3	2	.500	56	53
Northwestern	3	2	1	.600	47	37	3	4	1	.429	47	67
Michigan	3	2	0	.600	147	57	6	2	0	.750	219	94
Illinois	3	3	0	.500	75	48	3	4	1	.429	75	74
Minnesota	2	3	1	.400	92	76	3	4	1	.429	154	82
Indiana	2	3	0	.400	56	69	2	4	2	.333	70	96
Chicago	0	3	0	.000	0	192	2	6	0	.250	37	308
Wisconsin	0	5	1	.000	33	83	1	6	1	.143	54	113
1940												
Minnesota	6	0	0	1.000	122	50	8	0	0	1.000	154	71
Michigan	3	1	0	.750	94	20	7	1	0	.875	196	34
Northwestern	4	2	0	.667	110	64	6	2	0	.750	170	64
Wisconsin	3	3	0	.500	86	108	4	4	0	.500	125	134
Ohio State	3	3	0	.500	62	85	4	4	0	.500	99	113
Iowa	2	3	0	.400	66	84	4	4	0	.500	125	98
Indiana	2	3	0	.400	36	74	3	5	0	.375	69	100
Purdue	1	4	0	.200	54	73	2	6	0	.250	96	106
Illinois	0	5	0	.000	33	105	1	7	0	.125	71	144
1941												
Minnesota	5	0	0	1.000	124	32	8	0	0	1.000	186	38
Michigan	3	1	1	.750	60	34	6	1	1	.857	147	41
Ohio State	3	1	1	.750	101	89	6	1	1	.857	167	110
Northwestern	4	2	0	.667	116	57	5	3	0	.625	173	67
Wisconsin	3	3	0	.500	117	153	3	5	0	.375	144	208
Iowa	2	4	0	.333	53	77	3	5	0	.375	91	99
Purdue	1	3	0	.250	21	42	2	5	1	.286	27	62
Indiana	1	3	0	.250	53	60	2	6	0	.250	101	126
Illinois	0	5	0	.000	13	114	2	6	0	.250	112	163
1942												
Ohio State	5	1	0	.833	150	71	9	1	0	.900	337	114
Wisconsin	4	1	0	.800	70	38	8	1	1	.889	149	68
Illinois	3	2	0	.600	80	99	6	4	0	.600	227	126
Michigan	3	2	0	.600	111	81	7	3	0	.700	221	134
Indiana	2	2	0	.500	61	46	7	3	0	.700	256	79
Iowa	3	3	0	.500	61	87	6	4	0	.600	148	135
Minnesota	3	3	0	.500	81	75	5	4	0	.556	152	91
Purdue	1	4	0	.200	14	78	1	8	0	.111	27	179
Northwestern	0	6	0	.000	61	114	1	9	0	.100	96	209
1943												
Michigan	6	0	0	1.000	207	32	8	1	0	.889	302	73
Purdue	6	0	0	1.000	151	42	9	0	0	1.000	214	55
Northwestern	5	1	0	.883	170	39	6	2	0	.750	189	64
Indiana	2	3	1	.400	73	65	4	4	2	.500	193	106
Minnesota	2	3	0	.400	77	132	5	4	0	.556	170	184
Illinois	2	4	0	.333	103	181	3	7	0	.300	154	308
Ohio State	1	4	0	.200	57	134	3	5	0	.375	136	159
Wisconsin	1	6	0	.143	27	189	1	9	0	.100	41	282
Iowa	0	4	1	.000	43	94	1	6	1	.143	83	153
1944												
Ohio State	6	0	0	1.000	153	54	9	0	0	1.000	287	79
Michigan	5	2	0	.714	137	65	8	2	0	.800	204	91
Purdue	4	2	0	.667	143	87	5	5	0	.500	207	166
Minnesota	3	2	1	.600	134	116	5	3	1	.625	225	162
Indiana	4	3	0	.571	119	79	7	3	0	.700	292	79

600

	Conference Standing						Full Season					
	W.	L.	T.	Pct.	Pts.	O.Pts.	W.	L.	T.	Pct.	Pts.	O.Pts.
Illinois	3	3	0	.500	122	105	5	4	1	.556	273	149
Wisconsin	2	4	0	.333	66	110	3	6	0	.333	112	180
Northwestern	0	5	1	.000	40	114	1	7	1	.125	102	160
Iowa	0	6	0	.000	20	204	1	7	0	.125	53	240

1945

	W.	L.	T.	Pct.	Pts.	O.Pts.	W.	L.	T.	Pct.	Pts.	O.Pts.
Indiana	5	0	1	1.000	153	34	9	0	1	1.000	279	56
Michigan	5	1	0	.833	106	36	7	3	0	.700	186	99
Ohio State	5	2	0	.714	133	65	7	2	0	.778	194	71
Northwestern	3	3	1	.500	102	108	4	4	1	.500	127	148
Purdue	3	3	0	.500	115	99	7	3	0	.700	198	125
Wisconsin	2	3	1	.400	81	79	3	4	2	.429	128	128
Illinois	1	4	1	.250	64	79	2	6	1	.250	93	104
Minnesota	1	5	0	.167	68	148	4	5	0	.444	177	155
Iowa	1	5	0	.167	54	228	2	7	0	.222	74	310

1946*

	W.	L.	T.	Pct.	Pts.	O.Pts.	W.	L.	T.	Pct.	Pts.	O.Pts.
Illinois	6	1	0	.857	133	58	**8	2	0	.800	172	91
Michigan	5	1	1	.785	165	46	6	2	1	.722	233	73
Indiana	4	2	0	.667	76	67	6	3	0	.667	129	95
Iowa	3	3	0	.500	63	44	5	4	0	.556	129	92
Minnesota	3	4	0	.429	51	108	5	4	0	.556	130	114
Northwestern	2	3	1	.416	89	87	4	4	1	.500	156	136
Ohio State	2	3	1	.416	112	144	4	3	2	.555	166	170
Wisconsin	2	5	0	.286	78	137	4	5	0	.444	140	144
Purdue	0	5	1	.083	68	144	2	6	1	.277	97	207

* — Starting with this season in conjunction with determining official champions, ties are counted as a half-game won and a half-game lost in computing percentage standings.

** — Includes Illinois' victory over UCLA, 45-14, in Rose Bowl game at Pasadena, Calif., Jan. 1, 1947.

1947

	W.	L.	T.	Pct.	Pts.	O.Pts.	W.	L.	T.	Pct.	Pts.	O.Pts.
Michigan	6	0	0	1.000	172	40	*10	0	0	1.000	394	53
Wisconsin	3	2	1	.583	120	69	5	3	1	.611	171	156
Illinois	3	3	0	.500	130	88	5	3	1	.611	204	107
Minnesota	3	3	0	.500	110	108	6	3	0	.667	174	127
Purdue	3	3	0	.500	108	101	5	4	0	.556	205	130
Iowa	2	3	1	.417	79	136	3	5	1	.367	145	179
Indiana	2	3	1	.417	50	90	5	3	1	.611	156	102
Northwestern	2	4	0	.333	83	141	3	6	0	.333	128	196
Ohio State	1	4	1	.250	47	99	2	6	1	.278	60	150

* — Includes Michigan's victory over Southern California, 49-0, in Rose Bowl game at Pasadena, Calif., Jan. 1, 1948.

1948

	W.	L.	T.	Pct.	Pts.	O.Pts.	W.	L.	T.	Pct.	Pts.	O.Pts.
Michigan	6	0	0	1.000	190	37	9	0	0	1.000	252	44
Northwestern	5	1	0	.833	97	65	*8	2	0	.800	191	91
Minnesota	5	2	0	.714	144	81	7	2	0	.778	203	94
Ohio State	3	3	0	.500	102	87	6	3	0	.667	184	82
Indiana	2	4	0	.333	49	147	2	7	0	.222	75	217
Iowa	2	4	0	.333	67	89	4	5	0	.444	127	142
Purdue	2	4	0	.333	72	118	3	6	0	.333	126	175
Illinois	2	5	0	.286	74	114	2	6	0	.333	135	140
Wisconsin	1	5	0	.167	79	136	2	7	0	.222	119	193

* — Includes Northwestern's victory over California, 20-14, in Rose Bowl game at Pasadena, Calif., Jan. 1, 1949.

1949

	W.	L.	T.	Pct.	Pts.	O.Pts.	W.	L.	T.	Pct.	Pts.	O.Pts.
Ohio State	4	1	1	.750	128	65	*7	1	2	.800	207	136
Michigan	4	1	1	.750	94	54	6	2	1	.722	135	85
Minnesota	4	2	0	.667	131	47	7	2	0	.778	231	80
Wisconsin	3	2	1	.583	98	81	5	3	1	.611	207	129

601

Beginning of Modern Era (Continued)

	Conference Standing					Full Season				
	W.	L.	T.	Pct.	Pts.	O.Pts.	W.	L.	T.	Pct.	Pts.	O.Pts.
Illinois	3	3	1	.500	109	93	3	4	2	.444	149	140
Iowa	3	3	0	.500	118	147	4	5	0	.444	184	247
Northwestern	3	4	0	.429	91	120	4	5	0	.444	137	156
Purdue	2	4	0	.333	52	93	4	5	0	.444	119	135
Indiana	0	6	0	.000	57	178	1	8	0	.111	117	254

* — Includes Ohio State's victory over California, 17-14, in Rose Bowl game at Pasadena, Calif., Jan. 2, 1950.

1950

Team	W.	L.	T.	Pct.	Pts.	O.Pts.	W.	L.	T.	Pct.	Pts.	O.Pts.
Michigan	4	1	1	.750	96	60	*6	3	1	.650	150	114
Ohio State	5	2	0	.714	218	72	6	3	0	.667	286	111
Wisconsin	5	2	0	.714	109	71	6	3	0	.667	137	97
Illinois	4	2	0	.667	75	35	7	2	0	.778	137	56
Northwestern	3	3	0	.500	82	107	6	3	0	.667	155	143
Iowa	2	4	0	.333	81	159	3	5	1	.389	121	201
Minnesota	1	4	1	.250	40	109	1	7	1	.167	79	196
Purdue	1	4	0	.200	69	112	2	7	0	.222	143	200
Indiana	1	4	0	.200	41	86	3	5	1	.389	99	155
Michigan State	—	—	—	—	—	—	8	1	0	.889	196	53

* — Includes Michigan's victory over California, 14-6, in Rose Bowl game, Jan. 1, 1951.

1951

Team	W.	L.	T.	Pct.	Pts.	O.Pts.	W.	L.	T.	Pct.	Pts.	O.Pts.
Illinois	5	0	1	.917	85	23	*9	0	1	.950	220	83
Purdue	4	1	0	.800	116	101	5	4	0	.554	153	152
Wisconsin	5	1	1	.786	158	40	7	1	1	.833	196	53
Michigan	4	2	0	.667	115	54	4	5	0	.444	135	122
Ohio State	2	2	2	.500	66	66	4	3	2	.554	109	104
Northwestern	2	4	0	.333	41	89	5	4	0	.554	112	124
Minnesota	1	4	1	.250	89	158	2	6	1	.278	162	258
Indiana	1	5	0	.167	73	107	2	7	0	.222	118	191
Iowa	0	5	1	.083	91	196	2	5	2	.333	161	233
Michigan State	—	—	—	—	—	—	9	0	0	1.000	270	114

* — Includes Illinois' victory over Stanford, 40-7, in Rose Bowl game, Jan. 1, 1952.

1952

Team	W.	L.	T.	Pct.	Pts.	O.Pts.	W.	L.	T.	Pct.	Pts.	O.Pts.
Wisconsin	4	1	1	.750	158	97	6	*3	1	.650	228	150
Purdue	4	1	1	.750	147	91	4	3	2	.555	188	151
Ohio State	5	2	0	.714	148	91	6	3	0	.667	187	114
Michigan	4	2	0	.667	138	86	5	4	0	.555	207	134
Minnesota	3	1	2	.667	92	96	4	3	2	.555	131	171
Illinois	2	5	0	.286	113	154	4	5	0	.444	194	175
Northwestern	2	5	0	.286	146	201	2	6	1	.278	166	252
Iowa	2	5	0	.286	107	167	2	7	0	.222	121	220
Indiana	1	5	0	.167	89	155	2	7	0	.222	143	224
Michigan State	—	—	—	—	—	—	9	0	0	1.000	312	84

* — Includes Wisconsin's loss to USC, 7-0, in Rose Bowl game, Jan. 1, 1953.

1953

Team	W.	L.	T.	Pct.	Pts.	O.Pts.	W.	L.	T.	Pct.	Pts.	O.Pts.
Illinois	5	1	0	.833	154	78	7	1	1	.833	228	133
Michigan State	5	1	0	.833	131	50	*9	1	0	.900	240	110
Wisconsin	4	1	1	.750	146	86	6	2	1	.722	179	110
Ohio State	4	3	0	.571	137	139	6	3	0	.667	182	164
Minnesota	3	3	1	.500	108	129	4	4	1	.500	150	160
Iowa	3	3	0	.500	98	58	5	3	1	.611	187	91
Michigan	3	3	0	.500	63	80	6	3	0	.667	163	101
Purdue	2	4	0	.333	61	96	2	7	0	.222	89	167
Indiana	1	5	0	.167	77	166	2	7	0	.222	119	227
Northwestern	0	6	0	.000	71	164	3	6	0	.333	166	205

* — Includes MSC's victory over UCLA, 28-20, in Rose Bowl game, Jan. 1, 1954.

Beginning of Modern Era (Continued)

1954

	W.	L.	T.	Pct.	Pts.	O.Pts.	W.	L.	T.	Pct.	Pts.	O.Pts.
Ohio State	7	0	0	1.000	184	55	*10	0	0	1.000	249	75
Wisconsin	5	2	0	.714	133	77	7	2	0	.778	200	98
Michigan	5	2	0	.714	118	61	6	3	0	.667	139	87
Minnesota	4	2	0	.667	86	107	7	2	0	.778	195	127
Iowa	4	3	0	.571	126	101	5	4	0	.555	192	141
Purdue	3	3	0	.500	94	107	5	3	1	.611	165	134
Indiana	2	4	0	.333	62	111	3	6	0	.333	110	143
Michigan State	1	5	0	.167	64	113	3	6	0	.333	177	149
Northwestern	1	5	0	.167	60	102	2	7	0	.222	101	243
Illinois	0	6	0	.000	55	148	1	8	0	.111	103	180

* — Includes Ohio State's victory over USC, 20-7, in Rose Bowl game, Jan. 1, 1955.

1955

	W.	L.	T.	Pct.	Pts.	O.Pts.	W.	L.	T.	Pct.	Pts.	O.Pts.
Ohio State	6	0	0	1.000	159	51	7	2	0	.778	201	97
Michigan State	5	1	0	.833	144	48	*9	1	0	.900	253	83
Michigan	5	2	0	.714	111	85	7	2	0	.778	179	94
Purdue	4	2	1	.643	92	74	5	3	1	.611	113	103
Illinois	3	3	1	.500	89	101	5	3	1	.611	149	114
Wisconsin	3	4	0	.429	123	119	4	5	0	.444	172	166
Iowa	2	3	1	.417	111	116	3	5	1	.389	166	173
Minnesota	2	5	0	.286	85	123	3	6	0	.333	110	172
Indiana	1	5	0	.167	56	110	3	6	0	.333	91	150
Northwestern	0	6	1	.071	52	195	0	8	1	.056	66	241

* — Includes Michigan State's victory over UCLA, 17-14, in Rose Bowl game, Jan. 2, 1956.

1956

	W.	L.	T.	Pct.	Pts.	O.Pts.	W.	L.	T.	Pct.	Pts.	O.Pts.
Iowa	5	1	0	.833	88	44	*9	1	0	.900	219	84
Michigan	5	2	0	.714	143	96	7	2	0	.778	233	123
Minnesota	4	1	2	.714	84	67	6	1	2	.778	127	87
Michigan State	4	2	0	.667	133	49	7	2	0	.778	238	87
Ohio State	4	2	0	.667	88	47	6	3	0	.667	160	81
Northwestern	3	3	1	.500	80	79	4	4	1	.500	107	112
Purdue	1	4	2	.286	95	101	3	4	2	.444	139	122
Illinois	1	4	2	.286	79	106	2	5	2	.333	124	154
Wisconsin	0	4	3	.214	46	116	1	5	3	.278	93	129
Indiana	1	5	0	.167	85	216	3	6	0	.333	129	263

* — Includes Iowa's victory over Oregon State, 35-19, in Rose Bowl game, Jan. 1, 1957.

1957

	W.	L.	T.	Pct.	Pts.	O.Pts.	W.	L.	T.	Pct.	Pts.	O.Pts.
Ohio State	7	0	0	1.000	208	60	*9	1	0	.900	257	85
Michigan State	5	1	0	.833	184	60	8	1	0	.889	264	75
Iowa	4	1	1	.750	152	72	7	1	1	.833	263	112
Purdue	4	3	0	.571	141	96	5	4	0	.556	178	114
Wisconsin	4	3	0	.571	129	103	6	3	0	.667	234	122
Michigan	3	3	1	.500	145	141	5	3	1	.611	187	147
Illinois	3	4	0	.427	121	117	4	5	0	.444	167	133
Minnesota	3	5	0	.375	155	181	4	5	0	.444	201	188
Indiana	0	6	0	.000	33	253	1	8	0	.111	47	307
Northwestern	0	7	0	.000	38	223	0	9	0	.000	57	271

* — Includes Ohio State's victory over Oregon, 10-7, in Rose Bowl game, Jan. 1, 1958.

1958

	W.	L.	T.	Pct.	Pts.	O.Pts.	W.	L.	T.	Pct.	Pts.	O.Pts.
Iowa	5	1	0	.833	173	100	*8	1	1	.859	272	146
Wisconsin	5	1	1	.786	131	77	7	1	1	.833	201	77
Ohio State	4	1	2	.714	147	105	6	1	2	.778	182	132
Purdue	3	1	2	.667	103	80	6	1	2	.778	184	102
Indiana	3	2	1	.583	56	104	5	3	1	.611	81	141
Illinois	4	3	0	.571	117	117	4	5	0	.444	144	150
Northwestern	3	4	0	.429	142	120	5	4	0	.556	199	148
Michigan	1	5	1	.214	98	172	2	6	1	.278	132	211
Minnesota	1	6	0	.142	87	120	1	8	0	.111	115	157
Michigan State	0	5	1	.083	37	96	3	5	1	.389	117	123

* — Includes Iowa's victory over California, 38-12, in Rose Bowl game, Jan. 1, 1959.

Beginning of Modern Era (Continued)

	\multicolumn{5}{c}{Conference Standing}	\multicolumn{5}{c}{Full Season}
	W.	L.	T.	Pct.	Pts.	O.Pts.	W.	L.	T.	Pct.	Pts.	O.Pts.

1959
Team	W.	L.	T.	Pct.	Pts.	O.Pts.	W.	L.	T.	Pct.	Pts.	O.Pts.
Wisconsin	5	2	0	.714	97	85	7	*3	0	.700	165	149
Michigan State	4	2	0	.667	110	91	5	4	0	.556	149	118
Illinois	4	2	1	.643	82	59	5	3	1	.611	111	93
Purdue	4	2	1	.643	81	74	5	2	2	.667	109	81
Northwestern	4	3	0	.571	99	97	6	3	0	.667	174	134
Iowa	3	3	0	.500	119	68	5	4	0	.556	233	100
Michigan	3	4	0	.429	89	134	4	5	0	.444	122	161
Indiana	2	4	1	.357	86	85	4	4	1	.500	142	105
Ohio State	2	4	1	.357	69	84	3	5	1	.389	83	114
Minnesota	1	6	0	.143	66	121	2	7	0	.222	98	159

* — Includes Wisconsin's loss to Washington, 44-8, in Rose Bowl game, Jan. 1, 1960.

1960
Team	W.	L.	T.	Pct.	Pts.	O.Pts.	W.	L.	T.	Pct.	Pts.	O.Pts.
Iowa	5	1	0	.833	163	89	8	1	0	.889	234	108
Minnesota	5	1	0	.833	105	50	8	*2	0	.800	221	71
Ohio State	4	2	0	.667	129	83	7	2	0	.778	209	90
Michigan State	3	2	0	.600	87	96	6	2	1	.722	193	118
Illinois	2	4	0	.333	80	103	5	4	0	.556	140	117
Michigan	2	4	0	.333	52	71	5	4	0	.556	133	84
Northwestern	2	4	0	.333	60	91	5	4	0	.556	107	103
Purdue	2	4	0	.333	99	111	4	4	1	.500	212	163
Wisconsin	2	5	0	.286	89	170	4	5	0	.444	148	183
Indiana	—	—	—	—	—	—	1	8	0	.111	69	243

* — Includes Minnesota's loss to Washington, 17-7, in Rose Bowl game, Jan. 2, 1961.

1961
Team	W.	L.	T.	Pct.	Pts.	O.Pts.	W.	L.	T.	Pct.	Pts.	O.Pts.
Ohio State	6	0	0	1.000	179	61	8	0	1	.944	221	83
Minnesota	6	1	0	.875	126	62	*8	2	0	.800	161	78
Michigan State	5	2	0	.714	144	40	7	2	0	.778	192	50
Purdue	4	2	0	.667	94	53	6	3	0	.667	146	87
Wisconsin	4	3	0	.571	149	138	6	3	0	.667	179	158
Michigan	3	3	0	.500	117	135	6	3	0	.667	212	163
Iowa	2	4	0	.333	110	100	5	4	0	.556	215	162
Northwestern	2	4	0	.333	68	85	4	5	0	.444	131	105
Indiana	0	6	0	.000	38	132	2	7	0	.222	96	162
Illinois	0	7	0	.000	36	255	0	9	0	.000	53	289

* — Includes Minnesota's victory over UCLA, 21-3, in Rose Bowl game, Jan. 1, 1962.

1962
Team	W.	L.	T.	Pct.	Pts.	O.Pts.	W.	L.	T.	Pct.	Pts.	O.Pts.
Wisconsin	6	1	0	.857	199	67	8	*2	0	.800	322	130
Minnesota	5	2	0	.714	110	61	6	2	1	.722	131	61
Northwestern	4	2	0	.667	136	125	7	2	0	.778	237	158
Ohio State	4	2	0	.667	131	75	6	3	0	.667	205	98
Purdue	3	3	0	.500	103	45	4	4	1	.500	141	68
Michigan State	3	3	0	.500	107	67	5	4	0	.556	189	96
Iowa	3	3	0	.500	87	116	4	5	0	.444	127	166
Illinois	2	5	0	.286	52	178	2	7	0	.222	75	234
Indiana	1	5	0	.167	64	113	3	6	0	.333	126	140
Michigan	1	6	0	.143	40	182	2	7	0	.222	70	214

* — Includes Wisconsin's loss to So. California, 42-37, in Rose Bowl game, Jan. 1, 1963.

1963
Team	W.	L.	T.	Pct.	Pts.	O.Pts.	W.	L.	T.	Pct.	Pts.	O.Pts.
Illinois	5	1	1	.786	125	77	*8	1	1	.850	170	96
Michigan State	4	1	1	.750	95	43	6	2	1	.722	148	63
Ohio State	4	1	1	.750	83	60	5	*3	1	.611	110	102
Purdue	4	3	0	.571	112	140	5	4	0	.536	119	149
Michigan	2	3	2	.429	91	85	3	4	2	.444	131	127
Northwestern	3	4	0	.429	102	106	5	4	0	.556	162	124
Wisconsin	3	4	0	.429	95	115	5	4	0	.556	150	124
Iowa	2	3	1	.417	95	91	3	3	2	.500	126	112
Minnesota	2	5	0	.286	64	95	3	6	0	.333	95	117
Indiana	1	5	0	.167	89	139	3	6	0	.333	151	188

* — Includes Illinois' victory over Washington, 17-7, in Rose Bowl game, Jan. 1, 1964.

Beginning of Modern Era (Continued)

	Conference Standing						Full Season					
	W.	L.	T.	Pct.	Pts	O.Pts.		W.	L.	T.	Pct.	Pts	O.Pts.

1964

Michigan	6	1	0	.857	156	69	*9	1	0	.900	235	83
Ohio State	5	1	0	.833	102	41	7	2	0	.778	146	76
Purdue	5	2	0	.714	136	112	6	3	0	.667	168	146
Illinois	4	3	0	.571	96	79	6	3	0	.667	142	100
Minnesota	4	3	0	.571	89	85	5	4	0	.556	136	131
Michigan State	3	3	0	.500	97	79	4	5	0	.444	136	141
Northwestern	2	5	0	.286	61	133	3	6	0	.333	95	164
Wisconsin	2	5	0	.286	74	152	3	6	0	.333	98	190
Iowa	1	5	0	.167	108	139	3	6	0	.333	170	209
Indiana	1	5	0	.167	91	121	2	7	0	.222	154	188

* — Includes Michigan's victory over Oregon State, 34-7, in Rose Bowl game, Jan. 1, 1965.

1965

Michigan State	7	0	0	1.000	203	56	10	*1	0	.909	263	76
Ohio State	6	1	0	.857	130	83	7	2	0	.778	156	118
Minnesota	5	2	0	.714	149	109	5	4	1	.550	188	160
Purdue	5	2	0	.714	150	92	7	2	1	.750	227	127
Illinois	4	3	0	.571	155	92	6	4	0	.600	235	118
Northwestern	3	4	0	.429	105	139	4	6	0	.400	141	208
Michigan	2	5	0	.286	137	115	4	6	0	.400	185	161
Wisconsin	2	5	0	.286	75	228	2	7	1	.250	81	291
Indiana	1	6	0	.143	96	183	2	8	0	.200	134	225
Iowa	0	7	0	.000	47	150	1	9	0	.100	94	192

* — Includes Michigan State's loss to UCLA, 14-12, in Rose Bowl game, Jan. 1, 1966.

1966

Michigan State	7	0	0	1.000	213	71	9	0	1	.950	293	99
Purdue	6	1	0	.857	192	89	*9	2	0	.818	297	154
Illinois	4	3	0	.571	149	140	4	6	0	.400	173	193
Michigan	4	3	0	.571	171	110	6	4	0	.600	236	138
Minnesota	3	3	1	.500	75	99	4	5	1	.450	124	160
Ohio State	3	4	0	.429	72	78	4	5	0	.444	108	123
Northwestern	2	4	1	.357	109	129	3	6	1	.350	137	213
Wisconsin	2	4	1	.357	61	133	3	6	1	.350	87	212
Indiana	1	5	1	.214	87	160	1	8	1	.150	104	229
Iowa	1	6	0	.143	52	172	2	8	0	.200	86	253

* — Includes Purdue's victory over Southern California, 14-13, in Rose Bowl game, Jan. 2, 1967.

1967

Indiana	6	1	0	.857	122	113	9	*2	0	.818	197	159
Minnesota	6	1	0	.857	127	84	8	2	0	.800	163	106
Purdue	6	1	0	.857	225	91	8	2	0	.800	291	154
Ohio State	5	2	0	.714	108	106	6	3	0	.667	145	120
Illinois	3	4	0	.429	102	146	4	6	0	.400	143	213
Michigan	3	4	0	.429	104	136	4	6	0	.400	144	179
Michigan State	3	4	0	.429	137	111	3	7	0	.300	173	193
Northwestern	2	5	0	.286	125	143	3	7	0	.300	149	213
Iowa	0	6	1	.071	113	174	1	8	1	.150	161	277
Wisconsin	0	6	1	.071	93	152	0	9	1	.050	120	224

* — Includes Indiana's loss to Southern California, 14-3, in Rose Bowl game, Jan. 1, 1968.

1968

Ohio State	7	0	0	1.000	240	114	*10	0	0	1.000	323	150
Michigan	6	1	0	.857	207	115	8	2	0	.800	277	155
Purdue	5	2	0	.714	182	112	8	2	0	.800	291	167
Minnesota	5	2	0	.714	149	125	6	4	0	.600	207	190
Indiana	4	3	0	.571	174	175	6	4	0	.600	250	262
Iowa	4	3	0	.571	256	190	5	5	0	.500	322	289
Michigan State	2	5	0	.286	139	114	5	5	0	.500	202	151
Illinois	1	6	0	.143	92	184	1	9	0	.100	107	333
Northwestern	1	6	0	.143	88	245	1	9	0	.100	109	325
Wisconsin	0	7	0	.000	62	214	0	10	0	.000	86	310

* — Includes Ohio State's win over Southern California, 27-16, in Rose Bowl game, Jan. 1, 1969.

Beginning of Modern Era (Continued)

	Conference Standing						Full Season					
	W.	L.	T.	Pct.	Pts.	O.Pts.	W.	L.	T.	Pct.	Pts.	O.Pts.
1969												
Michigan	6	1	0	.857	245	77	8	*3	0	.727	352	148
Ohio State	6	1	0	.857	280	79	8	1	0	.889	383	93
Purdue	5	2	0	.714	248	180	8	2	0	.800	354	264
Minnesota	4	3	0	.571	135	135	4	5	1	.450	210	260
Indiana	3	4	0	.429	173	165	4	6	0	.400	252	242
Iowa	3	4	0	.429	149	179	5	5	0	.500	255	275
Northwestern	3	4	0	.429	121	187	3	7	0	.300	137	306
Wisconsin	3	4	0	.429	145	224	3	7	0	.300	196	349
Michigan State	2	5	0	.286	124	163	4	6	0	.400	202	231
Illinois	0	7	0	.000	62	293	0	10	0	.000	106	397

* — Includes Michigan's loss to Southern California, 10-3, in Rose Bowl game, Jan. 1, 1970.

1970

Ohio State	7	0	0	1.000	183	70	9	*1	0	.900	290	115
Michigan	6	1	0	.857	237	68	9	1	0	.900	288	75
Northwestern	6	1	0	.857	192	93	6	4	0	.600	233	161
Iowa	3	3	1	.500	105	173	3	6	1	.350	129	259
Michigan State	3	4	0	.429	146	130	4	6	0	.400	190	215
Wisconsin	3	4	0	.429	148	144	4	5	1	.450	198	195
Minnesota	2	4	1	.357	109	161	3	6	1	.350	180	237
Purdue	2	5	0	.286	120	127	4	6	0	.400	161	189
Illinois	1	6	0	.143	109	240	3	7	0	.300	165	279
Indiana	1	6	0	.143	69	212	1	9	0	.100	102	300

* — Includes Ohio State's loss to Stanford, 27-17, in Rose Bowl game, Jan. 1, 1971.

1971

Michigan	8	0	0	1.000	269	70	11	*1	0	.917	421	83
Northwestern	6	3	0	.667	192	127	7	4	0	.636	211	183
Illinois	5	3	0	.625	149	131	5	6	0	.455	163	238
Michigan State	5	3	0	.625	190	131	6	5	0	.545	225	169
Ohio State	5	3	0	.625	123	99	6	4	0	.600	224	120
Minnesota	3	5	0	.375	147	192	4	7	0	.364	212	278
Purdue	3	5	0	.375	168	182	3	7	0	.300	210	228
Wisconsin	3	5	0	.375	161	200	4	6	1	.405	240	258
Indiana	2	6	0	.250	138	235	3	8	0	.273	152	260
Iowa	1	8	0	.111	74	228	1	10	0	.100	121	379

* — Includes Michigan's loss to Stanford, 13-12, in Rose Bowl game, Jan. 1, 1972.

1972

Michigan	7	1	0	.875	162	34	10	1	0	.909	264	57
Ohio State	7	1	0	.875	199	97	9	*2	0	.818	280	171
Purdue	6	2	0	.750	196	61	6	5	0	.545	245	135
Michigan State	5	2	1	.688	136	68	5	5	1	.500	158	156
Minnesota	4	4	0	.500	151	183	4	7	0	.364	185	304
Illinois	3	5	0	.375	149	156	3	8	0	.273	197	277
Indiana	3	5	0	.375	131	205	5	6	0	.455	204	272
Iowa	2	6	1	.278	80	183	3	7	1	.318	109	208
Wisconsin	2	6	0	.250	83	188	4	7	0	.364	152	229
Northwestern	1	8	0	.111	119	231	2	9	0	.182	146	290

* — Includes Ohio State's loss to Southern California, 42-17, in Rose Bowl game, Jan. 1, 1973.

1973

Ohio State	7	0	1	.938	307	37	*10	0	1	.954	413	64
Michigan	7	0	1	.938	245	58	10	0	1	.954	330	68
Minnesota	6	2	0	.750	193	198	7	4	0	.636	260	294
Illinois	4	4	0	.500	127	109	5	6	0	.454	164	157
Michigan State	4	4	0	.500	69	108	5	6	0	.454	114	164
Northwestern	4	4	0	.500	162	220	4	7	0	.363	188	299
Purdue	4	4	0	.500	147	162	5	6	0	.454	200	213
Wisconsin	3	5	0	.375	137	161	4	7	0	.363	216	237
Indiana	0	8	0	.000	96	228	2	9	0	.182	151	271
Iowa	0	8	0	.000	94	296	0	11	0	.000	140	401

* — Includes Ohio State's 42-21 win over Southern California in Rose Bowl game, Jan. 1, 1974.

1974

Team	W	L	T	Pct								
Ohio State	7	1	0	.875	299	85	10	*2	0	.833	437	129
Michigan	7	1	0	.875	214	59	10	1	0	.909	324	75
Michigan State	6	1	1	.813	223	121	7	3	1	.682	270	196
Wisconsin	5	3	0	.625	240	179	7	4	0	.636	341	243
Illinois	4	3	1	.563	134	149	6	4	1	.590	210	206
Purdue	3	5	0	.375	171	218	4	6	1	.410	223	261
Minnesota	2	6	0	.250	110	241	4	7	0	.364	161	332
Iowa	2	6	0	.250	133	230	3	8	0	.273	157	308
Northwestern	2	6	0	.250	116	277	3	8	0	.273	140	385
Indiana	1	7	0	.125	124	205	1	10	0	.091	166	292

* — Includes Ohio State's 18-17 loss to Southern California in Rose Bowl game, Jan. 1, 1975.

1975

Team	W	L	T	Pct								
Ohio State	8	0	0	1.000	284	43	11	*1	0	.917	384	102
Michigan	7	1	0	.875	254	76	8	**2	2	.750	324	130
Michigan State	4	4	0	.500	161	136	7	4	0	.636	222	167
Illinois	4	4	0	.500	169	166	5	6	0	.455	229	260
Purdue	4	4	0	.500	119	170	4	7	0	.363	128	220
Wisconsin	3	4	1	.438	98	194	4	6	1	.409	174	269
Minnesota	3	5	0	.375	167	185	6	5	0	.545	236	192
Iowa	3	5	0	.375	149	212	3	8	0	.273	182	279
Northwestern	2	6	0	.250	126	243	3	8	0	.273	149	318
Indiana	1	6	1	.188	73	175	2	8	1	.227	104	254

* — Includes Ohio State's 23-10 loss to UCLA in Rose Bowl, Jan. 1, 1976.
** — Includes Michigan's 14-6 loss to Oklahoma in Orange Bowl, Jan. 1, 1976.

1976

Team	W	L	T	Pct								
Michigan	7	1	0	.875	274	67	10	*2	0	.833	432	95
Ohio State	7	1	0	.875	235	100	**9	2	1	.792	305	149
Minnesota	4	4	0	.500	145	149	6	5	0	.445	201	211
Purdue	4	4	0	.500	133	159	5	6	0	.455	188	233
Illinois	4	4	0	.500	178	194	5	6	0	.455	235	248
Indiana	4	4	0	.500	76	172	5	6	0	.455	130	254
Iowa	3	5	0	.375	113	170	5	6	0	.455	161	234
Wisconsin	3	5	0	.375	194	197	5	6	0	.455	298	266
Michigan State	3	5	0	.375	178	213	4	6	1	.409	236	278
Northwestern	1	7	0	.125	119	224	1	10	0	.091	134	311

* — Includes Michigan's 14-6 loss to Southern California in Rose Bowl, Jan. 1, 1977.
** — Includes Ohio State's 27-10 victory over Colorado in Orange Bowl, Jan. 1, 1977.

1977

Team	W	L	T	Pct								
Michigan	7	1	0	.875	257	78	10	*2	0	.833	353	124
Ohio State	7	1	0	.875	264	49	9	**3	0	.750	343	120
Michigan State	6	1	1	.813	199	107	7	3	1	.682	260	162
Indiana	4	3	1	.563	148	155	5	5	1	.500	205	228
Minnesota	4	4	0	.500	108	133	7	***5	0	.583	171	187
Purdue	3	5	0	.375	137	192	5	6	0	.456	231	247
Iowa	3	5	0	.375	136	144	4	7	0	.364	171	229
Wisconsin	3	6	0	.333	97	187	5	6	0	.456	133	200
Illinois	2	6	0	.250	86	218	3	8	0	.273	141	292
Northwestern	1	8	0	.111	92	262	1	10	0	.091	103	337

* — Includes Michigan's 27-20 loss to Washington in Rose Bowl, Jan. 2, 1978.
** — Includes Ohio State's 35-6 loss to Alabama in Sugar Bowl, Jan. 2, 1978.
*** — Includes Minnesota's 17-7 loss to Maryland in Hall of Fame Bowl, Dec. 22, 1977.

1978

Team	W	L	T	Pct								
Michigan	7	1	0	.875	261	57	10	*2	0	.833	372	105
Michigan State	7	1	0	.875	328	90	8	3	0	.727	411	170
Purdue	6	1	1	.813	176	92	**9	2	1	.792	261	130
Ohio State	6	2	0	.750	155	117	7	***4	1	.625	339	216
Minnesota	4	4	0	.500	155	221	5	6	0	.455	210	267
Wisconsin	3	4	2	.444	194	252	5	4	2	.545	223	277
Indiana	3	5	0	.375	180	190	4	7	0	.364	228	290
Iowa	2	6	0	.250	113	224	2	9	0	.182	125	291
Illinois	0	6	2	.125	62	223	1	8	2	.182	103	317
Northwestern	0	8	1	.056	71	329	0	10	1	.046	92	440

* — Includes Michigan's 17-10 loss to Southern California in Rose Bowl, Jan. 1, 1979.
** — Includes Purdue's 42-21 victory over Georgia Tech in Peach Bowl, Dec. 25, 1978.
*** — Includes Ohio State's 17-15 loss to Clemson in Gator Bowl, Dec. 28, 1978.

607

COMPOSITE 1979 BIG TEN FOOTBALL SCHEDULE

SEPTEMBER 8
WISCONSIN AT PURDUE
ILLINOIS AT MICHIGAN STATE
INDIANA AT IOWA
MICHIGAN AT NORTHWESTERN
OHIO UNIVERSITY AT MINNESOTA
SYRACUSE AT OHIO STATE

SEPTEMBER 15
AIR FORCE AT WISCONSIN
MISSOURI AT ILLINOIS
VANDERBILT AT INDIANA
IOWA AT OKLAHOMA
NOTRE DAME AT MICHIGAN
OREGON AT MICHIGAN STATE
WYOMING AT NORTHWESTERN
OHIO STATE AT MINNESOTA
PURDUE AT UCLA

SEPTEMBER 22
UCLA AT WISCONSIN
ILLINOIS AT AIR FORCE
KENTUCKY AT INDIANA
NEBRASKA AT IOWA
KANSAS AT MICHIGAN
MIAMI (OH) AT MICHIGAN STATE
MINNESOTA AT SOUTHERN CALIFORNIA
NORTHWESTERN AT SYRACUSE
WASHINGTON STATE AT OHIO STATE
NOTRE DAME AT PURDUE

SEPTEMBER 29
WISCONSIN AT SAN DIEGO STATE
NAVY AT ILLINOIS
COLORADO AT INDIANA
IOWA STATE AT IOWA
MICHIGAN AT CALIFORNIA
MICHIGAN STATE AT NOTRE DAME
MINNESOTA AT NORTHWESTERN
OHIO STATE AT UCLA
OREGON AT PURDUE

OCTOBER 6
INDIANA AT WISCONSIN
IOWA AT ILLINOIS
MICHIGAN AT MICHIGAN STATE
NORTHWESTERN AT OHIO STATE
PURDUE AT MINNESOTA

OCTOBER 13
MICHIGAN STATE AT WISCONSIN
ILLINOIS AT PURDUE
INDIANA AT OHIO STATE
IOWA AT NORTHWESTERN
MINNESOTA AT MICHIGAN

OCTOBER 20
WISCONSIN AT OHIO STATE
MICHIGAN AT ILLINOIS
MINNESOTA AT IOWA
NORTHWESTERN AT INDIANA
PURDUE AT MICHIGAN STATE

OCTOBER 27
IOWA AT WISCONSIN
ILLINOIS AT MINNESOTA
INDIANA AT MICHIGAN
MICHIGAN STATE AT OHIO STATE
NORTHWESTERN AT PURDUE

NOVEMBER 3
WISCONSIN AT MICHIGAN
MINNESOTA AT INDIANA
MICHIGAN STATE AT NORTHWESTERN
OHIO STATE AT ILLINOIS
PURDUE AT IOWA

NOVEMBER 10
NORTHWESTERN AT WISCONSIN
INDIANA AT ILLINOIS
IOWA AT OHIO STATE
MICHIGAN AT PURDUE
MINNESOTA AT MICHIGAN STATE

NOVEMBER 17
WISCONSIN AT MINNESOTA
ILLINOIS AT NORTHWESTERN
MICHIGAN STATE AT IOWA
OHIO STATE AT MICHIGAN
PURDUE AT INDIANA